Sentencing Law and Policy

Sentencing Law and Policy

Cases, Statutes, and Guidelines

Nora V. Demleitner

Hofstra University School of Law

Douglas A. Berman

*The Ohio State University
Moritz College of Law*

Marc L. Miller

Emory University School of Law

Ronald F. Wright

Wake Forest University School of Law

ASPEN
PUBLISHERS

1185 Avenue of the Americas, New York, NY 10036
www.aspenpublishers.com

© 2004 Aspen Publishers, Inc.
A Wolters Kluwer Company
www.aspenpublishers.com

> Permissions
> Aspen Publishers
> 1185 Avenue of the Americas
> New York, NY 10036

Printed in the United States of America

1 2 3 4 5 6 7 8 9 0

ISBN 0-7355-3658-9

Library of Congress Cataloging-in-Publication Data

Sentencing law and policy: cases, statutes, and guidelines/Nora V. Demleitner . . . [et al.].
    p.   cm.
    Includes index.
    ISBN 0-7355-3658-9
    1. Sentences (Criminal procedure) — United States — Cases.   I. Demleitner,
Nora V., 1966-
    KF9685.A7S46   2004
    345.73'0772'0264 — dc22   2003052384

About Aspen Publishers

Aspen Publishers, headquartered in New York City, is a leading information provider for attorneys, business professionals, and law students. Written by preeminent authorities, our products consist of analytical and practical information covering both U.S. and international topics. We publish in the full range of formats, including updated manuals, books, periodicals, CDs, and online products.

Our proprietary content is complemented by 2,500 legal databases, containing over 11 million documents, available through our Loislaw division. Aspen Publishers also offers a wide range of topical legal and business databases linked to Loislaw's primary material. Our mission is to provide accurate, timely, and authoritative content in easily accessible formats, supported by unmatched customer care.

To order any Aspen Publishers title, go to *www.aspenpublishers.com* or call 1-800-638-8437.

To reinstate your manual update service, call 1-800-638-8437.

For more information on Loislaw products, go to *www.loislaw.com* or call 1-800-364-2512.

For Customer Care issues, e-mail *CustomerCare@aspenpublishers.com;* call 1-800-234-1660; or fax 1-800-901-9075.

Aspen Publishers
A Wolters Kluwer Company

To my parents, Alfred and
Walburga Demleitner.

NVD

To my grandfather and mother,
Seymour Kleinman and Dale Berman.

DAB

To Daniel J. Freed.

MLM

To my mother, Marian Stallings Wright.

RFW

Summary of Contents

Contents

— 2 —
‖ *Who Sentences?* ‖

— 3 —

‖ *Regulating Discretion* ‖   *117*

— 4 —

Sentencing Inputs: The Crime and Its Effects 221

— **5** —

Sentencing Inputs: The Offender's Record and Background 283

— 6 —

Procedure and Proof at Sentencing

— 7 —

‖ *Sentencing Outcomes: The Scale of Imprisonment* ‖   457

— 8 —

‖ *Sentencing Outcomes: Nonprison Punishments* ‖   507

— **9** —

‖ *Race, Class, and Gender* ‖   *587*

— 10 —

Alternatives to Criminal Sentences

— 11 —

|| *Sentences Reconsidered* || *695*

Preface

What claim does sentencing have in the modern law school curriculum, which already seems filled to capacity? We believe that the law of sentencing has plenty to offer all law students, even those not inclined toward a career in criminal law. This field provides an insightful case study in the dynamics of law reform; requires synthesis of theoretical and practical issues of doctrine, procedure, and policy; and touches deep and abiding issues about the nature and structure of law in society. Sentencing, in our view, illustrates superbly what advanced courses should offer, with its virtues extending to all law students by building effectively on the themes and goals pursued in an introductory criminal law and procedure class.

Of course, for students interested in a career in criminal law, the law of sentencing will serve as the central legal framework defining their day-to-day practice. Sentencing outcomes are the true bottom line of criminal law practice, and thoughtful defense attorneys and candid prosecutors regularly state that sentencing rules should be a lawyer's very first consideration in a criminal case. Moreover, because sentencing issues are frequently the focal point of criminal justice policy debates, many lawyers working for the government or for public interest groups are regularly engaged with sentencing controversies and concerns. Since criminal cases occupy such a large part of the courts' dockets, all judges (and their law clerks) spend a considerable portion of their working days on issues of sentencing law and policy.

A Law Reform Experiment

Criminal sentences involve some of the most severe actions that governments take against their own citizens and residents. Because every criminal conviction results in some kind of sentence, sentencing occurs all the time and involves a huge number of people. In an average year, federal, state, and local governments make more than 15 million arrests and obtain around 1 million felony convictions and several million additional misdemeanor convictions. Right now, more than 1.5 million people are serving time in U.S. prisons. Another 600,000 are held in jail, and another 4.6 million are on probation or parole.

Sentences are essential (though often hidden) elements of every substantive crime and every criminal process. Teachers in the first-year criminal law course point again and again to issues that will be resolved at sentencing; they explain that finer gradations or more subtle principles are possible at sentencing than in the rough-cut efforts to define crimes. Teachers of criminal procedure often note that defendants and their lawyers, as well as prosecutors, care most about the sentence because it represents the bottom line of all their procedural transactions.

Given the elemental role of sentencing in criminal law and procedure and the large social costs and benefits of criminal sentences, one might expect the law in this area to be highly evolved. In fact, for much of our history there has been very little law of sentencing. While some sentencing principles and punishments are ancient, the body of law that regulates sentences remained undeveloped and unexamined until recently.

Rules prescribing the punishment for wrongdoers are found in the Bible and in the Koran. The earliest recorded legal codes, such as the Babylonian Code of Hammurabi (c. 1780 B.C.E.), spell out sanctions for various harms. Yet by the late twentieth century, 4,000 years of world civilization produced sentencing systems in the United States (and in many other countries) that reflected only the most rudimentary qualities of law — for most offenses, only broad legislative specification of sentencing ranges, no rules to guide judges in sentencing within those ranges, and actual determination of sentences not by judges but by executive release authorities.

Social and legal evolution can occur in the blink of an eye, and that has been the case for the law of sentencing. Starting in the 1970s, sentencing has undergone a political and legal revolution; it has become an area replete with law. Various kinds of "structured" or "guideline" systems now govern felony sentencing in many states and in the federal system; another intricate body of law now applies to capital sentencing, driven by an ongoing constitutional and policy dialogue between courts and legislatures. The emergence of sentencing law is one of the most dramatic and interesting law reform experiments in American legal history.

Sentencing, Law School, and the Nature of Law

Though young in its details, the law of sentencing wrestles with profound and ancient themes of justice and the nature of law. These themes echo throughout the law: what makes rules and procedures wise, which institutions should design and implement these rules, how much discretion should (or must) be allowed in each case, and what impact the law will have on human lives. This combination of new laws and long-standing problems, of the familiar and the unfamiliar, gives students an opportunity to synthesize many aspects of the lawyer's art.

Some law students end their first year of studies (or their second) and yearn for more opportunities to confront questions of justice, fairness, politics, and efficiency. Even the most cursory reading of daily newspapers will confirm that sentencing is an area in which all these concepts remain openly in play. Indeed, media coverage of current sentencing debates enriches students' appreciation of the importance of this field and enables teachers to place current controversies within the enduring theoretical and doctrinal issues of sentencing law and policy.

Advanced courses should move beyond the mastery of doctrines and the already honed skill of reading appellate decisions. Sentencing integrates substantive criminal law with criminal procedure, and it often does so through institutions other than appellate courts. Sentencing law adds a strong dose of a subject not taught in most law schools — criminal justice policy (or criminology). The emergence of a language and grammar for sentencing has made it possible to explore the substantive, procedural, and policy aspects of criminal justice together in one place in the law school curriculum.

The Approach of This Book

Two particular areas of sentencing law have received the most attention in law schools. The promulgation of the federal sentencing guidelines has interested many scholars, and courses and seminars on federal sentencing have been developed at a number of schools. The persistence of capital sentencing on the American agenda has also sparked substantial scholarly and classroom interest in the death penalty.

But these dramatic areas of sentencing turn out to be only two slices of a much larger pie. The rapid emergence of sentencing as an area of law has created legal flux and remarkable variety. Drawing from a rich background, the book presents the common themes and trends in this emerging field of law, looking to its practical, political, social, and historical roots. We do not focus on a single system or jurisdiction, but rather try to capture the central issues and elements for all systems in all places.

This book has no separate sections for guideline versus indeterminate sentencing, state versus federal systems, or domestic versus foreign systems. Constitutional issues also are not segregated into a separate unit, because lawyers do not think about all the constitutional doctrine together. Instead, they think about stages of the process, and how various sources of law — constitutional and otherwise — have some bearing on that stage.

Throughout the book, we draw on the most relevant examples from three distinct sentencing worlds: guideline-determinate, indeterminate, and capital. The examples from structured guideline jurisdictions — the dominant modern sentencing reform — occupy the center of attention. There is simply more "law" in a determinate system than an indeterminate one, and more explicit discussion of what remains implicit in the older discretionary systems. Because the federal system is so well funded and closely critiqued, the book devotes steady attention to that system, but it features several key state systems as well.

We also examine capital punishment materials from time to time. Although detailed coverage of capital sentencing merits a full course and a full book in its own right, we focus here on the revealing comparisons between capital and noncapital sentencing practices.

Organization and Selection of Materials

An introductory unit surveys the social purposes (Chapter 1) and social institutions at work (Chapter 2) in the sentencing area, and then presents two case studies—guideline and capital regimes—showing how the legal system regulates the exercise of sentencing discretion (Chapter 3).

After this introduction, the volume follows an intuitive organization that tracks the basic sequence of decisions made in criminal sentencing. The book first reviews the basic "inputs" that go into the sentencing decision: Chapter 4 weighs the importance of the crime and its effects, and Chapter 5 considers the background of the offender. Chapter 6 reviews the distinctive procedures that shape how judges and others evaluate these sentencing inputs, both before and during the sentencing hearing.

The next three chapters explore the "outputs" of sentencing: prison (Chapter 7), nonprison punishments (Chapter 8), and the patterns of race, gender, and class that appear in sentencing outcomes (Chapter 9).

The book closes by discussing punishment choices that arise in institutional settings other than the criminal trial court. Chapter 10 looks at alternatives to criminal sentences, and Chapter 11 flags the important judicial and executive review that can occur after sentences are imposed.

Our principal materials come from many sources, reflecting the many institutions that shape and apply sentencing law. The U.S. Supreme Court makes occasional forays into the noncapital sentencing realm, but it leaves the great majority of the legal questions here for others. We blend decisions from the U.S. Supreme Court, state high courts, and the federal appellate courts, along with a sprinkling of cases from foreign jurisdictions and supranational tribunals.

State cases carry substantial weight in this book, since well over 95 percent of all criminal defendants are sentenced in state court and many of the most interesting modern sentencing reforms have occurred in the states. The amazing variety among state systems also offers instructive class discussions about the sentencing choices available.

We do not reprint only appellate judicial opinions as principal materials. We often use statutes or guideline provisions to lay out the common choices made by those who try to change sentencing practices. Reports and data from sentencing commissions and other agencies also help set the scene.

To keep track of the options and to prevent our celebration of variety from obscuring core concepts, we strive in the notes to tell readers directly what the most common practices are in various U.S. jurisdictions. The principal materials usually explain (and often embody) this majority position, but we also underscore this fact in the notes. To the extent possible in an emerging field of law such as sentencing, we estimate in the notes how often a lawyer is likely to encounter a given practice in American jurisdictions.

Central Themes in this Book

A small number of themes are central to the study of sentencing; these themes are present throughout the study of the law, even in areas completely unrelated to the criminal process. The book returns regularly to five major themes:

1. *Variety and change.* There is no single law of sentencing but rather many laws of sentencing, providing varied answers to a range of similar problems. This variation is apparent both across jurisdictions and

within jurisdictions over time. Why are there different answers to similar questions?

2. *Multiple institutions.* One of the most striking aspects of sentencing is the variety of participants, both in lawmaking and in application. These participants include not only the top officials within the legislative, executive, and judicial branches but also various lower-level actors and institutions. Thus, we highlight distinctions between the roles of sentencing judges and appellate judges, spotlight the role of prosecutors, and consider the special role of sentencing commissions, parole boards, and probation officers. We continually ask students to compare decision makers both descriptively and normatively—when does it (and when should it) matter whether judges or legislators make a certain type of decision?

3. *Purposes and politics.* Sentencing and punishment serve many different purposes: some explicit and others implicit, some philosophical and others practical and perhaps base. We repeatedly ask students to consider the connections between specific sentencing rules and the purposes, politics, and practicalities of criminal justice.

4. *Impact and knowledge.* Modern sentencing law sometimes invokes an optimistic belief that knowledge and research can form a sound basis for creating and improving legal systems. Most research considers the visible impact of different sentencing rules on crime and on actual sentencing patterns. Experience, however, tempers the perhaps naïve hope of empirically grounded reform. Still, the materials in this book try to flag the effects of sentencing practices on the work of judges and attorneys and on defendants of different social groups.

5. *Discretion and equality.* A major theme of sentencing across systems has been the need to individualize sentences to account for relevant variations among convicted offenders. At the same time, one of the major goals of modern sentencing reform has been to regulate the discretion of those who sentence and punish individuals, with the aim of reducing or eliminating unjust disparity. Of particular concern here are sentencing disparities based on race, class, or gender. We believe it is impossible to assess properly any aspect of criminal justice in the United States, including sentencing, without explicit and steady attention to issues of race. One chapter in the book specifically addresses issues of race, class, and gender, but the themes are raised throughout the volume.

Each of these larger lessons attends to the nature of law. The dramatic construction of a new field over a relatively short time—yet a field replete with links to ancient puzzles and problems—provides a special kind of clarity into these deeper themes.

Our Hopes

We believe that sentencing has blossomed into one of the most provocative and revealing areas of the law. It has become a powerful entry point into the workings of the law itself and into the nature of our social order. We wrote this book in the belief that the study of sentencing will be valuable to all lawyers and law students.

Sentencing law itself is still in its infancy. For sentencing law to become not only an illustration but a model of legal reform and justice, the sentencing arena badly needs excellent lawyers, well-informed legislators, and knowledgeable commissioners. We hope that some of those who study sentencing will be ready and willing to join the fray and work to produce better systems and greater justice.

Nora V. Demleitner
Douglas A. Berman
Marc L. Miller
Ronald F. Wright

December 2003

Acknowledgments

Modern sentencing law, with structured sentencing at its core, has emerged over the past 30 years, and a community of sentencing scholars, judges, and practitioners has emerged along with it. We have all spent part of our scholarly careers nurturing and critiquing the work that happens in this field; it is terrifically gratifying for us to see criminal sentencing treated, at long last, as a "field" for study.

Course books reflect not only the immediate work of the editors but also the influence of colleagues and friends. Among the most important influences on this book came from our close collaborators on other sentencing projects, most notably our fellow editors of the *Federal Sentencing Reporter* over the years: Dan Freed, Frank Bowman, Steve Chanenson, Mark Harris, and Aaron Rappaport.

A special word is in order about Dan Freed: there is a part of Dan in everything we see or do about sentencing. His farsighted and impassioned work for sentencing justice draws others, including us, to this corner of the world. We hope this book reflects Dan's joyful engagement with the ideas and realities of criminal sentencing.

Colleagues in this field around the country have been generous with their observations and encouragement during this project. Steve Chanenson and Michael E. Smith gave us crucial feedback on this book by teaching from the manuscripts and offering us wise suggestions along the way. There are a number of scholars whose work in sentencing and related areas have influenced this volume. On this score, we thank Albert Alschuler, Sara Sun Beale, Stephanos Bibas, David Boerner, Dennis Curtis, George Fisher, George Fletcher, Richard Frase, Jim Jacobs, Eric Janus, Pam Karlan, Joe Kennedy, Nancy King, Susan Klein, Tracy Meares, Michael O'Hear, Kevin Reitz, Michael Simons, Kate Stith, Sandra Guerra Thompson, Michael Tonry, Robert Weisberg, Bert Westbrook, James Q. Whitman, and Deborah Young.

Advice and support also came from our home institutions, and we want to thank Sharon Davies, Terry Gordon, Kay Levine, Alan Michaels, Nancy Rogers, Robert Schapiro, Charlie Shanor, and David Yellen. We received timely and thorough research assistance from several students, including Kris Armstrong, Leslie Cory, Jon Cowley, Jeffrey Davis, Amy DeWitt, Rudolph Fusco, Andrew Harris, Christine Robek, Daniel Smith, Jennifer Wiggins, and Robert Zayac. And of course, the long-suffering students in our courses and seminars tolerated many drafts and many false starts to help us bring the book to its current form.

It is encouraging to meet so many judges around the country who give us important insights about the work of sentencing that commands so much of their time and energy. We particularly want to thank Samuel Alito Jr., Myron Bright, Guido Calabresi, Paul Cassell, Avern Cohen, Nancy Gertner, John Godbold, Frank Johnson, Gerard Lynch, John Martin, Michael Mihm, Jon O. Newman, Jim Rosenbaum, and Jack Weinstein. Prosecutors and defense attorneys such as Stephen Bright, Judy Clarke, Roger Haines, Tom Hillier, Margy Love, Jon Sands, and Benson Weintraub prevented us from losing sight of the realities on the ground as we observe from our academic vantage points. In addition, probation officers, including Maggie Jensen and Matt Rowland, have provided us with useful glimpses into the difficulties of their work. Finally, our gratitude extends to scholars and researchers outside the United States. Their contributions to sentencing have informed our thinking about reforms and changes. Among them are Hans-Jörg Albrecht, Andrew Ashworth, Albin Eser, Andrew von Hirsch, Stephan Terblanche, Dirk van Zyl Smit, Susanne Walther, and Emily Zimmerman.

Sentencing law and policy benefit from the vision and tireless work of reformers, based at institutions such as the Vera Institute, the Sentencing Project, the Urban Institute, the U.S. Sentencing Commission, and many state sentencing commissions. We are grateful for insights from Paul Hofer, Susan Katzenelson, Robin Lubitz, Marc Mauer, Linda Drazga Maxfield, Tom Ross, Julie Stewart, Chris Stone, Jeremy Travis, Nick Turner, Ronald Weich, and Dan Wilhelm.

All writers of texts for students come to appreciate their own teachers even more. We are grateful, more than ever, to Steven Duke, Dan Freed, Owen Fiss, Edward Levi, Norval Morris, and Frank Zimring.

The editors at Aspen remained supportive throughout. Richard Mixter first got the ball rolling and shared with us his wisdom about the nature of learning and the direction of legal education. We deeply value the encouragement and advice we receive from Carol McGeehan, whose work with us — including discussions about when it would be appropriate to produce a volume on sentencing law — now stretches back over a decade. The book also profited from the great talents of Curt Berkowitz, Melody Davies, Michael Gregory, Leslie Keros, and Barbara Roth.

Books do not take shape only in professional surroundings; this book followed the authors home and lived among our families. We are grateful to our families for playing host to this book in their lives, even though the guest may have overstayed its welcome. Our thanks and our love go to Michael D. Smith, Cordell Demleitner Smith, Walburga Demleitner, Christine Anne Berman, Charlotte Lindsay Berman, Rebecca Elise Berman, Chris Cutshaw, Owen Miller, Amy Wright, Andrew Wright, and Joanna Wright. This book, like everything else we do, would be unthinkable for us without them.

The authors acknowledge the following authors and copyright holders for permission to use material reprinted in this book.

American Bar Association, Standards for Criminal Justice Sentencing (3d ed. 1994). Copyright © 1994 by the American Bar Association. Reprinted with permission.

Americans for Gun Safety Foundation, The Enforcement Gap: Federal Gun Laws Ignored (2003). Copyright © 2003 by the Americans for Gun Safety Foundation. Reprinted by permission.

Hugo Adam Bedau, The Death Penalty in America (3d ed. 1982). Copyright © 1982 by Oxford University Press, Inc. Used by permission of Oxford University Press, Inc.

Walter Berns, For Capital Punishment: The Morality of Anger, Harpers, Apr. 1979, at 15-20. Copyright © 1979 by Harpers. Reprinted with permission.

Alfred Blumstein, Jacqueline Cohen, Susan E. Martin, and Michael H. Tonry, Research on Sentencing: The Search for Reform (1983). Copyright © 1983 by National Academy Press. Reprinted with permission.

William J. Bowers, The Capital Jury Project: Rationale, Design, and Preview of Early Findings, 70 Ind. L.J. 1043 (1995). Copyright © 1995 by the Indiana Law Journal. Reprinted with permission.

Francesca D. Bowman, The Greening of Probation Officers in Their New Role, 4 Fed. Sentencing Rep. 99 (1991). Copyright © 1991 The Vera Institute of Justice. Reprinted with permission from the author and the Federal Sentencing Reporter.

Stephen Breyer, Speech to the University of Nebraska College of Law (Nov. 18, 1998), in 11 Fed. Sentencing Rep. 180 (1999). Copyright © 1999 The Vera Institute of Justice. Reprinted with permission.

Teresa Carns, Michael Hotchkin, and Elaine Andrews, Therapeutic Justice in Alaska's Courts, 19 Alaska L. Rev. 1 (2002). Copyright © 2002 by the Alaska Law Review. Reprinted with permission.

Leslie A. Cory, Looking at the Federal Sentencing Process One Judge at a Time, One Probation Officer at a Time, 51 Emory L.J. 379 (2002). Copyright © 2002 Emory Law Journal. Reprinted with permission.

Michel Foucault, Discipline and Punish: The Birth of the Prison (1977). Copyright © 1977 by Pantheon Books. Reprinted with permission.

Marvin E. Frankel, Criminal Sentencing: Law Without Order (1973). Copyright © 1973 by Hill and Wang Publishers. Reprinted with permission.

Richard S. Frase, Sentencing Guidelines in Minnesota, Other States, and the Federal Courts: A Twenty-Year Retrospective, 12 Fed. Sentencing Rep. 69 (1999). Copyright © 1999 by the University of California Press. Reprinted with permission.

Frank S. Gilbert, A Probation Officer's Perception of the Allocation of Discretion, 4 Fed. Sentencing Rep. 109 (1991). Copyright © 1991 The Vera Institute of Justice. Reprinted with permission from the author and the Federal Sentencing Reporter.

Catharine M. Goodwin, The Independent Role of the Probation Officer at Sentencing and in Applying Koon v. United States, 60 Fed. Probation 71 (1996). Copyright © 1996. Reprinted with permission.

David Greenberg and Valerie West, State Prison Populations and Their Growth, 1971-1991, 39 Criminology 615 (2001). Copyright © 2001 by the American Society of Criminology. Reprinted with permission.

Sally T. Hillsman, Day Fines, in Intermediate Sanctions in Overcrowded Times (Michael Tonry and Kate Hamilton eds., 1995). Copyright © 1995 by Northeastern University Press, Inc. Reprinted with permission.

Magdeline E. Jensen, Has the Role of the U.S. Probation Officer Really

Sentencing Law and Policy

=1=

The Purposes of Punishment and Sentencing

The simplest question about sentencing is also one of the hardest: what purposes does society achieve, or hope to achieve, when it sentences people convicted of crimes? One dominant and long-standing view is that society wishes to punish individuals who violate social norms and that sentencing systems are the means to impose punishments. But this simple observation raises myriad problems: governments sometimes punish individuals outside the criminal justice system, and if criminal sentencing is about imposing punishment, then the question becomes what is the purpose for the imposition of punishment.

Such fundamental issues of purpose confront all organized societies, but they are especially important in the United States, which is now a world leader in punishing its citizens. As of 2002, more than two million persons are incarcerated in prisons and jails in the United States, and nearly five million others are subject to criminal justice supervision through probation or parole. (For point of reference, this is a group larger than the entire population of the state of Indiana.) These basic numbers, however, mask enormous variation in how offenders are sentenced and punished.

Though sentencing is an important and dynamic field, sentencing discussions and decision making often take place without any explicit reference to underlying purposes. It is possible to study the law of sentencing without considering fundamental purposes, but doing so would produce at best expertise in technical rules and procedures without a deep understanding of the reasons (or lack of reasons) for those rules and procedures. Though such crabbed discussions are found in many legal, political, and administrative settings, it is important to recognize that sentencing decisions reflect implicit or unconscious choices about sentencing purposes even when such purposes are not considered explicitly. Consequently, to acquire knowledge and make sound policy about sentencing, and more generally about law and society, requires addressing the purposes of sentencing up front and maintaining an awareness of purposes throughout the book.

The first part of this chapter considers the various stated or implicit purposes that society tries to achieve through the sentencing process. This part reveals that none of the "traditional" justifications for punishment — retribution, deterrence, incapacitation, and rehabilitation — is self-defining, and that each is contested, both conceptually and practically. This part also examines other social purposes that have been suggested formally by philosophers and informally by observers of actual punishment and sentencing systems.

The second part of this chapter illuminates two fundamental points that demonstrate why it is unrealistic and probably inappropriate to imagine a single purpose for sentencing and punishment. First, several different purposes may operate together to justify or limit punishment structures or sentencing systems in various ways. Second, the purposes that may justify certain systemwide sentencing rules or procedures may differ from those that justify case-specific sentencing outcomes.

A.   SOCIAL PURPOSES OF SENTENCING

Organized societies devise many ways to sanction individuals who violate social norms. But formal and substantial punishments are delivered through the criminal justice system, where governments consciously and intentionally seek to condemn individuals. All aspects of criminal law — substantive, procedural, and political — must grapple with the core question of purpose and justification: Why should governments condemn and harm their own citizens?

In answering this question, philosophers have traditionally fallen into two camps. *Consequentialist philosophers,* who judge actions based on their consequences, justify state punishment as a means of reducing the overall harms created by criminal behavior. *Deontological philosophers,* who judge actions based on notions of moral duty, justify state punishment as a means of righting the moral wrongs of criminal behavior. Consequentialist philosophers generally endorse forward-looking utilitarian theories of punishment, believing that punishment can benefit society through *deterrence* of potential offenders from committing future crimes or through *incapacitation* to render the current offender unable to commit future crimes or through *rehabilitation* of the offender to prevent any further wrongdoing. Deontological philosophers generally endorse backward-looking theories of punishment, described in terms of *retribution* or *just deserts* and based on the notion that punishment is just when it restores the moral balance that criminal behavior upsets.

The materials in this section raise a number of questions: What purposes should a sentencing system seek? Is it possible or helpful to state those purposes explicitly? Can any unstated purposes be discovered? Can a system pursue multiple purposes, and if so, can it produce reasonably coherent and consistent outcomes across cases? We also consider whether the philosophical justifications for punishment are necessary for a principled system, and whether it is possible to describe and implement a decent system without any guiding purpose or purposes.

It is useful to stop at this point and articulate an initial reason or set of reasons why you think a government is justified to condemn and harm its own citizens through criminal punishments. You should attempt to rank the importance of these reasons if you list more than one. The coherence and relevance of various purposes will become clearer if you compare the purposes as described in this chapter with your own initial beliefs.

1. Stated Purposes

How can we tell what purposes a system serves? Some systems in statutes, and some sentencers in opinions, articulate one or more purposes to justify a sentence. What is the impact and relevance of expressed and intentional assertions of purposes by the legislator or sentencer?

This section begins with an effort by model law reformers (in this case the American Bar Association (ABA)) to state explicitly which purposes legislatures should consider when designing a sentencing system. Is this statement of purposes complete? If not, what is missing? Is it too sweeping? Is it helpful?

In the second reading, we see how Montana's legislature has specified sentencing purposes for that state. The third major reading offers a radically different approach to sentencing dynamics than presented by traditional court systems. It highlights a different perspective on the purposes that punishment and sentencing systems can (and should?) serve.

|| *ABA Standards for Criminal Justice,*
Sentencing 18-2.1
(3d ed. 1994) ||

MULTIPLE PURPOSES; CONSEQUENTIAL AND RETRIBUTIVE APPROACHES

(a) The legislature should consider at least five different societal purposes in designing a sentencing system:
(i) To foster respect for the law and to deter criminal conduct.
(ii) To incapacitate offenders.
(iii) To punish offenders.
(iv) To provide restitution or reparation to victims of crimes.
(v) To rehabilitate offenders.
(b) Determination of the societal purposes for sentencing is a primary element of the legislative function. . . .

COMMENTARY

Every aspect of a criminal justice system, including sentencing, derives legitimacy from the advancement of social ends.[2] Current criminal codes are

---

2. This statement is meant to encompass both consequentialist and retributive views of criminal justice policy. Consequentialists seek to promote the prospective social good of reducing future crime. Retributivists find a different social end in the punishment of past criminal acts, even where no forward-looking benefits result.

generally lacking in useful articulation of the policy objectives sought in the sentencing of offenders. This Standard calls attention to the vital need for a policy foundation upon which the sentencing system can be built. Without reasonably clear identification of goals and purposes, the administration of criminal justice will be inconsistent, incoherent, and ineffectual.

THE CHOICE OF SOCIETAL PURPOSES

The Standards' drafters recognized that there is no national consensus regarding the operative purposes of criminal sentencing. Indeed, even among philosophers there has been unceasing disagreement over the goals of sanctions. Some current systems have been characterized as predominately retributive in nature. Other observers have claimed that the prevailing penology of the 1980s and early 1990s has been that of incapacitation. One need not go far back in time to find periods in which theories of rehabilitation and deterrence were of high prominence. Indeed, the resurgence of interest in community-based sanctions signals that, at least for the sentencing of some offenders, rehabilitative theory is alive and flourishing.

Paragraph (a) catalogs five different societal purposes a legislature should consider when designing a sentencing system. No hierarchy of importance is intended in the ordering of the five subsections, nor is it contemplated that every jurisdiction must implement all five purposes. Rather, the Standard is drafted in recognition of the wide diversity of viewpoints that exist concerning ultimate goals, and is meant to express a conclusion that different schemas can be imagined consistent with rational and desirable public policy.

Subparagraph (a)(i) recognizes that criminal sanctions may be used in an attempt to foster respect for the law and deter criminal conduct. This goal might be understood as "general deterrence," which operates through the exemplary and educative force of criminal law.[7] If the public is made to believe that criminal behavior will be answered by painful consequences, it is hoped that some individuals will be discouraged from risking such consequences. On a more abstract plane, the imposition of punishment may disseminate a generalized message that criminal transgressions are treated seriously by society. Thus, information about criminal sentences may encourage people to respect the law as a whole and increase the numbers of law-abiding citizens.

Subparagraph (a)(ii) states that a jurisdiction may legitimately consider the goal of incapacitating offenders in designing a sentencing system. There is no question that some degree of disablement occurs whenever groups of offenders are incarcerated or are subjected to the restraint and surveillance of nonprison sanctions. To this extent, all sentencing systems are incapacitative, intentionally or not. A jurisdiction may further choose to pursue incapacitation in deliberate and targeted ways, however, and such choices are matters of fair policy debate.

---

7. Some theorists have spoken in terms of "general deterrence" and "specific deterrence." The latter term refers to the tendency of painful punishments to deter the offender, who experiences them directly, from future criminal conduct. Under this Standard, such offender-specific effects are classified as "rehabilitation."

Subparagraph (a)(iii) acknowledges that the punishment of offenders is a reasonable objective that legislatures may incorporate into a sentencing system. While retributivism had fallen from favor in the middle of this century, at least in the academic community, the theory has enjoyed both a scholarly and political rejuvenation since the 1970s. Today, a number of states have identified punishment or the meting out of "just deserts" as the central objective of their sentencing laws.

Subparagraph (a)(iv) identifies victim restitution and reparation as an eligible goal of sentencing. This consequentialist purpose aims toward the restoration of losses suffered by crime victims, when possible. Obviously, restitution cannot adequately be achieved in all criminal cases. Some injuries defy compensation and most offenders lack the resources to make adequate payments. Where restitution can be made, however, it is hard to posit a reason not to provide for it in the criminal justice system. Accordingly, the Standards elsewhere take the position that victim restitution should be given priority over the assessment and collection of other economic sanctions.

Last, subparagraph (a)(v) states that the legislature should consider the goal of rehabilitation of offenders when designing a sentencing system. As recently as the 1960s and early 1970s, rehabilitation was the prevailing theory of sentencing and corrections, and was the principal justification for the traditional structure of indeterminate sentences and parole. In the intervening years rehabilitation has lost its position of preeminence almost everywhere, but has hardly disappeared from view. Many incarcerative and nonincarcerative programs continue to attempt to reform offenders while at the same time serving other goals, such as punishment, deterrence, and incapacitation. The Standards endorse this as a worthy aim. It should be noted, in this regard, that the Standards take the view that rehabilitation, standing alone, is never an adequate basis for criminal punishment. In effect, reform should be attempted only in connection with sentences that are independently justified on some other ground.

The preceding description of eligible purposes is only a starting point in the development of a meaningful statement of societal goals for a working sentencing system. To be useful, such a statement must identify which purpose or purposes the legislature wishes to pursue. If multiple goals are selected, a system of priorities is needed so that when two purposes conflict, decision makers have a guidepost for choosing between competing objectives. As suggested below, the legislature may even wish the hierarchy of relevant goals to change for crimes of lesser and greater severity.

NOTES

1. *Historical trends in punishment theory.*   Adoption of particular theories of sentencing and punishment has varied greatly by jurisdiction and especially by era. Retribution is perhaps the oldest theory of punishment, with clear biblical roots and a beautiful illustration in the Code of Hammurabi, a set of laws created by a ruler of Babylon in the eighteenth century B.C. (excerpts reprinted in Chapter 2). More modern history marks a turn in punishment theory in the late 1700s and early 1800s due to the influential writings of Jeremy Bentham, an English philosopher and social scientist, who argued against natural law theories

and urged an approach to law and punishment grounded in principles of utility. Writing around this same period, the equally influential German philosopher Immanuel Kant provided a more contemporary argument that retribution is the proper moral justification for punishment.

As a result of a variety of social forces, including the development of prison systems and modern American optimism in the ability of humans to improve other humans, during the nineteenth and early twentieth centuries rehabilitation took center stage as the dominant (though not the only) theory justifying punishment. See Williams v. New York, 337 U.S. 241 (1949). But rehabilitation as a general justifying theory came under a sustained attack in the 1960s and 1970s, illustrated by Professor Francis Allen's famous book, *The Decline of the Rehabilitative Ideal: Penal Policy and Social Purpose* (1981). These attacks were capped by Robert Martinson's widely discussed short paper, What Works?— Questions and Answers About Prison Reform, 25 The Public Interest 25 (1974), which reviewed numerous studies evaluating efforts at penal rehabilitation. Martinson's conclusions, which were generally discouraging, became quickly oversimplified into the assertion that "nothing works." Commentators and others have tended to overstate the prior dominance of rehabilitation, as well as the modern failings of rehabilitative efforts and the general decline of the role of rehabilitation in sentencing. Indeed, though different theories of punishment have been expressly favored or disfavored in different eras, a thoughtful observer can probably identify the impact of each classic theory in nearly every punishment or sentencing system throughout history.

2. *Modern views of punishment theory.*   As the ABA excerpt highlights, the academic debates and practical realities surrounding punishment theories remain dynamic and contested today. It is probably fair to say that most systems now recognize, either expressly or implicitly, some combination of retribution, deterrence, incapacitation, and a sprinkling of other rationales. One of the most interesting developments in modern thinking about punishment is the decline of the once-dominant theory of rehabilitation: note that the ABA states expressly that "rehabilitation, standing alone, is never an adequate basis for criminal punishment [and] reform should be attempted only in connection with sentences that are independently justified on some other ground." Why do you think the ABA declared rehabilitation to be the one traditional theory that cannot alone provide an adequate justification for punishment?

Some scholars assert that a dominant modern rationale has emerged through the idea of "limiting retributivism," an idea often attributed to Professors H. L. A. Hart and Norval Morris (writing separately). This theory suggests that retribution sets the upper and lower boundaries of just punishment, within which other purposes can hold sway, including utilitarian theories of deterrence, incapacitation, and rehabilitation. See Richard Frase, Limiting Retributivism: the Consensus Model of Criminal Punishment, in Michael Tonry, ed., The Future of Imprisonment in the 21st Century (forthcoming 2004). This theory has recently been endorsed by the American Law Institute during its ongoing effort to revise the Model Penal Code's sentencing provisions, although the exact meaning and the appropriateness of this decision is already being debated in academic circles. See Paul H. Robinson, The A.L.I.'s Proposed Distributive Principle of "Limiting Retributivism": Does It Mean in Practice Anything Other Than Pure Desert?

(manuscript on Social Science Research Network, April 29, 2003) available at www.ssrn.com/abstract=397540; Edward L. Rubin, Just Say No to Retribution (manuscript on Social Science Research Network, June 11, 2003) available at www.ssrn.com/abstract=413666.

3. *Single or multiple theories?* Some philosophers have contended that utilitarian and retributive theories of punishment are incommensurable and that an initial choice must be made between them to develop a truly principled sentencing system. Others, however, perhaps because of the strong intuitive appeal of both approaches, have endeavored to develop hybrid theories of punishment that are compatible with both theoretical perspectives. The theory of limiting retributivism may be popular in large part because it seems to be one of the more satisfying hybrid theories. The ABA sentencing standards suggest that a legislature may legitimately select multiple purposes for its sentencing system, but "[i]f multiple goals are selected, a system of priorities is needed so that when two purposes conflict, decision makers have a guidepost for choosing between competing objectives."

Punishment and sentencing choices frequently reflect a variety of purposes, as Professor Norval Morris astutely observed more than 50 years ago:

> No one theory explains the different punitive measures to be found in our criminal law. . . . *All too often the purposes of punishment are discussed as if they could be treated as a single problem. . . . Surely the truth is that we have a series of related problems rather than a single problem. . . .* Surely, at the present level of our knowledge, we aim at a whole congeries of various purposes in respect not only of various types of crime but various types of criminals. . . . [B]ecause we do not seek any single purpose or set of purposes through our penal sanctions, we must not suppose we are facing an academic and impractical problem. . . . Prevention, reformation, deterrence, retribution, expiation, vindication of the law, and the Kantian argument that punishment is an end in itself all mingle in the wild dialectic confusion which constitutes most discussions of the purposes of punishment. . . .

Norval Morris, Sentencing Convicted Criminals, 27 The Australian L. J. 186, 188-189 (1953) (emphasis added).

4. *Inherent conundrums in applying punishment theory.* Though selection of multiple purposes creates the added challenge of establishing priorities, even a jurisdiction's decision to pursue only one theory of punishment does not magically simplify the conundrums inherent in developing a sound sentencing system. For one thing, each theory of punishment has conceptual variations. Retributive principles of just deserts can focus on the subjective culpability of an offender or the objective harms created by the offense; rehabilitation can be understood simply in terms of offenders no longer committing crimes or more dynamically in terms of offenders becoming productive contributors to the community. In addition, each goal raises challenging (and perhaps unanswerable) empirical and factual questions. Rarely do we have unassailable evidence about what punishments will deter (or rehabilitate) which offenders, and rarely can we establish indisputably what an offender thought (or did) to assess just deserts. Further, punishment goals must be reconciled with a jurisdiction's various other commitments and limitations; a commitment to the right of due process, for example, may make a particular theory of punishment more difficult to

pursue, as can limitations on the resources that a jurisdiction is able to devote to these matters.

In the following statute, the Montana legislature specifies the sentencing and correctional purposes for that state. A minority of states have statutes explicitly stating the purposes of sentencing. Does the Montana legislature make more concrete and specific the abstract memorandum of purposes offered by the ABA? Which purposes does Montana accept and reject? How does Montana prioritize or resolve disputes among the stated purposes? Following this statute, we set forth a problem based on the facts of a real case from Montana. Is this statute helpful in assessing an appropriate sentence in Problem 1-1?

‖ *Montana Code Annotated §46-18-101* ‖

CORRECTIONAL AND SENTENCING POLICY

(1) It is the purpose of this section to establish the correctional and sentencing policy of the state of Montana. Laws for the punishment of crime are drawn to implement the policy established by this section.

(2) The correctional and sentencing policy of the state of Montana is to:

(a) punish each offender commensurate with the nature and degree of harm caused by the offense and to hold an offender accountable;

(b) protect the public, reduce crime, and increase the public sense of safety by incarcerating violent offenders and serious repeat offenders;

(c) provide restitution, reparation, and restoration to the victim of the offense; and

(d) encourage and provide opportunities for the offender's self-improvement to provide rehabilitation and reintegration of offenders back into the community.

(3) To achieve the policy outlined in subsection (2), the state of Montana adopts the following principles:

(a) Sentencing and punishment must be certain, timely, consistent, and understandable.

(b) Sentences should be commensurate with the punishment imposed on other persons committing the same offenses.

(c) Sentencing practices must be neutral with respect to the offender's race, gender, religion, national origin, or social or economic status.

(d) Sentencing practices must permit judicial discretion to consider aggravating and mitigating circumstances.

(e) Sentencing practices must include punishing violent and serious repeat felony offenders with incarceration.

(f) Sentencing practices must provide alternatives to imprisonment for the punishment of those nonviolent felony offenders who do not have serious criminal records.

(g) Sentencing and correctional practices must emphasize that the offender is responsible for obeying the law and must hold the offender accountable for the offender's actions. . . .

(h) Sentencing practices must emphasize restitution to the victim by the offender. . . .

(i) Sentencing practices should promote and support practices, policies, and programs that focus on restorative justice principles.

PROBLEM 1-1.   RICHARD GRAVES

One summer evening, Betsy Baker and her boyfriend ate dinner and had several beers at a local bar. As they drove home, Betsy's boyfriend was arrested for driving while under the influence (DUI). Richard Graves, a stranger, approached Betsy and offered to drive her truck home. Betsy agreed. After Richard returned with Betsy to her trailer, he then followed Betsy inside. Betsy allowed Richard to stay, but told him he could sleep either on the bed or on the couch and she would stay on the other because they were not sleeping together.

Betsy awakened when she felt someone penetrating her vagina from behind her. She dove off of the bed and yelled at Richard to leave. Richard told Betsy to "hold on" and calm down, but she kept yelling for him to get out. Before he left, Betsy asked Richard, "Did we make love?" Richard replied, "I didn't mean to hurt you," then ran out the door. Betsy's loud crying brought a neighbor to her door, and she asked the neighbor to call the police. An officer arrived who recognized Betsy from the earlier DUI stop and arrest. After Betsy calmed down, she told the officer that a man offered to drive her home after the arrest and that she had been raped.

The officer located Richard Graves based on Betsy's description. When the officer asked what had happened that night, Richard said, "What, nothing happened." When the officer said he knew something happened, Richard told him that Betsy offered to let him sleep in the bed, but that he declined, telling Betsy, "No, that's your bed. I'll sleep on the couch." Richard then said Betsy was with him on the bed and began touching him, but then they fell asleep and that "nothing really happened after that." After Richard became evasive answering follow-up questions, the officer advised him of his rights.

After Richard was booked, he and Betsy were both taken for a rape examination, which revealed sperm, biologically consistent with Richard, in Betsy. Richard was charged with the offense of sexual intercourse without consent. He was tried before a jury and testified on his own behalf. Richard claimed that, as he drove Betsy home, she flirted with him and gave him a hug and kissed him affectionately. Richard also testified that after he had fallen asleep in her trailer, he awoke to find Betsy fondling his groin area. He testified that after brief foreplay, intercourse took place.

Based on Betsy's testimony and other corroborating evidence, the jury found Richard Graves guilty of sexual intercourse without consent. Montana law provides that "A person convicted of sexual intercourse without consent shall be punished by life imprisonment or by imprisonment in the state prison for a term of not less than 2 years or more than 100 years and may be fined not more than $50,000."

At a hearing before the judge at sentencing, Richard again admitted to having sexual intercourse with Betsy, and he suggested that any mistake as to consent might have resulted from the fact that he had a lot to drink that night. Richard said he was sorry for any harm he caused, and also indicated that he had enrolled in a treatment program to deal with his alcohol problems. Richard also noted that despite a disadvantaged upbringing, which included a brief stint in a juvenile corrections facility following an assault conviction, he had had only minor contacts with the criminal justice system since becoming an adult.

If you were the prosecutor in Richard Graves's case, what sentence would you recommend? If you were a defense attorney assigned to represent Richard Graves, what sentence would you recommend? How would the provisions of Mont. Code Ann. §46-18-101 influence your recommendation? Would you seek additional information before making a specific recommendation to the judge? Would you emphasize a particular theory or theories of punishment in your recommendation?

If you were the sentencing judge in Richard Graves's case, what sentence would you impose? How would the provisions of Mont. Code Ann. §46-18-101 influence your decision? Would you want additional information before making your decision? Would you emphasize a particular theory or theories of punishment in your decision?

Cf. State v. Graves, 901 P.2d 549 (Mont. 1995).

NOTES

1. *Deterrence.* Deterrence is not only a plausible concept but one that most people rely on in their everyday activities. Indeed, no one seriously disputes that creating a criminal justice system that punishes wrongdoing has some deterrent impact. But far more debatable — indeed, hotly debated — is the concept of marginal deterrence, which postulates that an additional quantum of punishment can lead to a measurable decrease in a particular crime (or all crimes). Complicating this issue is the likelihood, according to many researchers, that extralegal factors such as moral views, family, and community structures and other social dynamics have more of a deterrent impact than specific legal sanctions. Consequently, a growing body of social science research suggests that we should not expect to decrease crime rates significantly through changes in criminal law rules or through the specific distribution of criminal punishments. See Paul H. Robinson and John M. Darley, Does Criminal Law Deter? A Social Science Investigation,— Oxford J. Legal Stud.— (forthcoming 2004).

Moreover, defenders of deterrence as a justification for punishment must confront the argument that it is immoral to punish one person to deter others. Because of his eloquence and stature, philosopher Immanuel Kant's arguments classically set out the terms of this debate:

> [P]unishment [by government for crime] can never be administered merely as a means for promoting another good either with regard to the criminal himself or to civil society, but must in all cases be imposed only because the individual on whom it is inflicted has committed a crime. For one man ought never to be dealt with merely as a means subservient to the purpose of another, nor be mixed up with the subjects of real right. . . . He must first be found guilty and punishable, before there can be any thought of drawing from his punishment any benefit for himself or his fellow-citizens. The penal law is a categorical imperative; and woe to him who creeps through the serpent-windings of utilitarianism to discover some advantage that may discharge him from the justice of punishment, or even from the due measure of it. . . .

Immanuel Kant, The Science of Right 195 (W. Hastie trans., 1790). This statement is often read solely as a justification for retribution or just deserts. But notice that Kant argues that it is immoral to punish an individual "merely" to promote another good. Kant recognizes that if a person is guilty of crime, then utilitarian reasons might come into play.

2. *Incapacitation.* Because of the indisputable efficacy of some punishments to incapacitate offenders, one could reasonably view incapacitation as the most tangible and certain goal for punishment. (In addition, one could, after examining the history of punishment laws and the realities of punishment practices, reasonably conclude that incapacitation has been the goal most regularly and consistently pursued.) But because of the almost limitless reach of a theory of incapacitation and the obvious costs of its blind pursuit — to achieve "perfect" incapacitation, every offender would be executed — deciding how to pursue the theory poses a very serious challenge.

In the mid-twentieth century, a somewhat refined approach to incapacitation — operating under the label "selective incapacitation"— gained adherents based on the contention that judges and parole officials could accurately determine which offenders were especially dangerous to society and thus should serve longer prison terms than typical offenders. But much research conducted over the past four decades has shown that it is exceedingly difficult to predict future serious criminal behavior. Researchers generally concluded that even with the best information, predictions of future dangerousness would be wrong more often than right, and the challenge of obtaining all needed information for these assessments only increased the risk of "false positives." See Norval Morris and Marc Miller, Predictions of Dangerousness, 6 Crime & Justice 1 (1985).

3. *Retribution.* Though having intuitive appeal, the seemingly simple retributivist notion that offenders deserve to be, and thus should be, punished proves to be a difficult concept to pin down. As Professor Richard Frase explains, the theory of retribution can have many facets:

> The theory of retribution (or "just deserts") views punishment as being proper for its own sake, or for the sake of fairness to the victims of crime; to law-abiding offenders; to other offenders who have been punished for the same offense; and to this offender (who deserves to be punished no more severely than other, similar offenders were punished). There are several versions of retributive theory. What some have called "defining" retributivism seeks to impose penalties which are directly proportional to the seriousness of the offense and the offender's blameworthiness. A more modest version of desert theory, "limiting" retributivism, merely sets upper and lower bounds — sentences must not be excessively severe or unduly lenient; within these outer limits, punishment is scaled according to what is needed to achieve other purposes . . . and should be the least severe sanction necessary to achieve all of these other punishment goals (a concept sometimes referred to as sentencing parsimony).

Richard S. Frase, Criminal Punishment, in Encyclopedia of Crime and Justice 197 (2003). Though the concept of just deserts has broad appeal in the abstract, the difficulty of deciding exactly what punishment and how much punishment is "deserved" has proven to be the greatest enduring challenge in turning retributive theory into sentencing practice. Indeed, the hybrid theory of limiting retributivism may garner many adherents because it does not actually try to ascribe specific punishments based on notions of desert.

4. *Rehabilitation.*   As a theory of punishment, rehabilitation is at once inevitable and oxymoronic. Interest in rehabilitation is inevitable because, unless every offender is to be executed or locked away for life, jurisdictions will want their punishment systems to reduce the likelihood that past offenders will reoffend when returned to the community. Yet a commitment to rehabilitation is oxymoronic because efforts by the state to improve the life and behavior of criminal offenders — through counseling, treatment, education, or training — does not seem like a form of punishment at all. These practical tensions have persistently burdened the concept of rehabilitation as a theory of punishment: Jurisdictions have always recognized the importance of rehabilitating criminals, but they have rarely devoted sufficient money and energy to the programs most likely to succeed.

The conclusion drawn from Robert Martinson's famous article that "nothing works" to rehabilitate criminals is now well known to be a gross overstatement. Martinson himself came to recognize this, and within several years he published partial retractions of his position, noting that many rehabilitation programs had some modest impacts on individual behavior. See Robert Martinson, New Findings, New Views: A Note of Caution Regarding Sentencing Reform, 7 Hofstra L. Rev. 243 (1979). But continued research on rehabilitative efforts has tended to support a pessimistic view of the criminal justice system's ability to effectively reform offenders, although a few programs do have a track record of success. See Gerald G. Gaes et al., Adult Correction Treatment, 26 Crime & Justice 361 (1999); see also Rick Sarre, Beyond "What Works?" A 25-Year Jubilee Retrospective of Robert Martinson's Famous Article, 34 Australian and New Zealand J. of Criminology 1 (April 2001).

5. *Other theories and considerations.*   Though debate over the traditional theories of punishment has raged for centuries and continues to be quite lively, a number of philosophers and policy makers who have found the traditional debate unsatisfying or unhelpful have explored other approaches to punishment and sentencing. Notice that the ABA sentencing standards, for example, endorse sentencing systems that "foster respect for the law" and "provide restitution or reparation to victims of crimes."

Stressing the role and importance of the criminal law in establishing norms of behavior in society, modern philosophers have often spoken of the "educative" or "expressive" value of punishment and have stressed the ways in which criminal justice systems can and should communicate societal condemnation of crime and criminals. See Joel Feinberg, The Expressive Function of Punishment, in Doing and Deserving 98 (1970); Dan M. Kahan, What Do Alternative Sanctions Mean?, 63 U. Chi. L. Rev. 591 (1996). Though some suggest that the educative and expressive approaches to punishment are simply intriguing hybrid theories melding aspects of retributivist and utilitarian philosophy, they define sufficiently distinct perspectives that their proponents often argue for different sorts of punishment schemes.

Highlighting harms suffered by both offenders and their victims in traditional sentencing and punishment schemes, many modern advocates of reform have urged the application of "restorative justice" principles throughout the criminal justice system. In its broadest terms, restorative justice is fundamentally concerned with restoring social relationships; in the context of crime and punishment, restorative justice has been described as a process through which all the parties with a stake in a particular offense come together to resolve collectively how to deal with the aftermath of the offense and its implications for the future. The growing interest in restorative justice ideas can be seen through Montana's 2001 amendment to the statute reprinted above, which added subsection (i) stating that "[s]entencing practices should promote and support practices, policies, and programs that focus on restorative justice principles."

One of the most tangible expressions of restorative justice concepts comes through the use of sentencing circles in some criminal justice systems. Sentencing circles are based on sentencing practices typical of native communities in Canada, the United States, and Australia. Their value is being increasingly emphasized by those interested in developing the broader applicability and usefulness of restorative justice ideas for all members of society.

A sentencing circle is typically a community-directed process, conducted in partnership with the criminal justice system, to develop consensus on an appropriate sentencing plan that addresses the concerns of all interested parties. Sentencing circles are traditional peacemaking rituals and are structured to involve the victim, victim supporters, the offender, offender supporters, traditional criminal justice personnel, and other community members. Within the circle, people are asked to speak from the heart in a shared search for understanding of the event, and together try to identify the steps necessary to assist in healing all affected parties and prevent future crimes.

Modern sentencing circles have been developed most extensively in Saskatchewan, Manitoba, and the Yukon and have been used occasionally in several other communities. Their use spread to the United States in 1996, when a pilot project was initiated in Minnesota. As you review the following discussion of one sentencing circle experience, consider what values and goals find expression in this sort of response to criminal wrongdoing. Also consider whether sentencing circles, and the ideas of restorative justice more generally, have potential to transform traditional perspectives on theories of punishment.

A Healing Circle in the Innu Community of Sheshashit
Justice as Healing (Native Law Centre of Canada), Summer 1997

[During the fall of 1994 Gavin Sellon, while attending a clinic for alcohol and substance abuse, disclosed to counsellors that he had committed a sexual assault the year before. On his return to Sheshashit, Labrador, Mr. Sellon went to the Royal Canadian Mounted Police detachment and gave a cautioned statement admitting to having intercourse with L. without her consent. The police then began to investigate the incident.

The accused first appeared in provincial court on June 12, 1995, where he elected to be tried in the Newfoundland Supreme Court, Trial Division, waiving the preliminary inquiry. On August 9, 1995, in the supreme court, the accused indicated that he wished to plead guilty and to make an application for a sentencing circle. The Crown opposed the motion and the matter was set over to December 18, 1995, for argument, at which time the application for a sentencing circle was withdrawn. Counsel for the accused indicated that he intended to pursue an informal healing circle outside the courtroom setting and in the community of Sheshashit, and asked Judge O'Regan to give strong consideration to viewing the sentencing of Sellon with a restorative approach rather than a punitive approach. Counsel for the Crown argued that the accused, being a non-native, should be treated using the traditional methods of sentencing. Judge O'Regan indicated to both counsel that if they wished to attend the healing circle they could do so and he would place what he deemed to be appropriate weight on the results of the healing circle.]

On Sunday January 21, 1996 a circle was held in the Alcohol Centre in Sheshashit. This circle was unique because unlike previous circles that have been held, the participants of this circle were aware in advance of the circle that a written report about the circle would be completed to share with the court. The following is a report of that circle.

Much thought and discussion went into the planning and preparation for this circle. Initially Innu Nation workers in health and justice were involved in this planning. Workers all began by referring to this circle as a "sentencing" circle. Workers discussed what needs and whose needs were to be met with this circle and how best to try and meet these varied needs. There was a great deal of concern expressed that the circle needed to be witnessed by members of the justice system so that Innu would not be open to seemingly inevitable criticism that we had something to hide or fear in the circle process. The same concern was raised should we not have witnesses from the Innu public.

Those involved in planning the circle were all able to agree that as the service provider, Innu Nation has a real need to demonstrate, both to Innu and the non Innu public and justice system, that Innu can develop and deliver services best suited to meet the needs of Innu. . . . We knew that this particular circle, with its direct connection to the court, would have a bearing on any future circles, court related or not. . . .

Therefore a conscious decision was made to be clear and specific about what needs and whose needs we were trying to meet through this process. We could then evaluate the effectiveness of the circle based clearly on what we set out to do. It was decided to tailor the circle to meet L.'s need for an opportunity to be heard within a supportive circle of those most directly affected by and involved with what happened between Gavin and her.

We also made a deliberate decision that it was not suitable or accurate to call this planned circle a "sentencing" circle. Sentencing is a justice system process to be done in court by court participants and the Judge. This circle would be held as a circle of concern and support for L. and Gavin. Included in the circle as part of the process would be recommendations made by the participants which would be shared with the court to be used by the Judge as he saw fit. . . .

We are able to determine the purpose of this circle as twofold:

1. to provide Gavin an opportunity to acknowledge responsibility for his actions and

2.   to provide L. an opportunity to say what needed to happen for her to feel that the situation was being made more right.

Several weeks prior to the circle Jack Penashue met with L. to ask if she would be willing and able to participate in a circle with Gavin and others to deal with the incident which had resulted in a charge of sexual assault against Gavin. L. said she was willing and able to participate. After this, separate meetings were held with her father and then her mother to determine their support for their daughter's decision to participate as well as their own willingness to participate. They said they supported their daughter in her decision and were themselves willing to participate if asked by L.

Another meeting was then held with L. and Lyla Andrew [the facilitator]. Again she was asked if she felt comfortable about participating and was asked who she wanted to have participate in the circle. She said she wanted to have her sisters and parents be present. The names of other possible participants, Innu and non Innu . . . were given to L. and she indicated that "it was fine" if they wanted to attend. More information was shared with L. about the purpose of the circle and about the way it was thought the circle would happen. L. again indicated her willingness to participate. Her only request was that the circle take place soon. When she was told that her Dad would be working in Davis Inlet and not able to attend anytime soon, L. asked that the circle go ahead anyway and so the January 21 date was set.

Once this date was set Lyla met with Gavin Sellon to invite his participation in the circle. He was told who L. had invited and was asked if there were people he wanted to invite. He requested his mother, stepfather and his spouse. L. had already agreed to their participation and Gavin was told this. He also asked if Jack Penashue could attend and was informed that Jack would be a facilitator of the circle. . . .

Sunday there were 10 participants: L., G. (L.'s mom), R.N. (L.'s sister), Gavin Sellon, Patricia Nuna (Gavin's spouse), Lynne Gregory (Gavin's mom), Apenam Pone (Gavin's stepfather), Germaine Benuen [Labrador Legal Services court liaison in Sheshashit], Jack Penashue (facilitator) and Lyla Andrew (facilitator).

The participants had coffee and tea prior to the circle starting. Then all participants moved into the large meeting room and sat in a circle on the floor. With joined hands a prayer was shared. Jack then explained to the participants the symbolism of burning sweetgrass and smudging. If participants found it meaningful, they were invited to smudge and Jack went around the circle. He spoke Innuaimen first and then in English. When this was completed, Jack asked Lyla to explain the process.

It was explained to participants that what happened in the circle should be guided by the participants' acceptance and use of four principles: honesty, kindness, sharing and respect. Each person in turn would have the chance to speak uninterrupted. If they chose not to speak, they would pass the small "talking stone" on to the next person because no one would be forced to speak. There were four rounds of the circle so there were four opportunities for speaking.

The first round of the circle was for each participant to explain why they were present in the circle. The second round was a chance for each participant to speak directly to L., to share concern, support and encouragement. The third round was for each participant to speak directly to Gavin, to share with him directly feelings about him. The fourth round was the chance for each participant to make recommendations to those in the circle, and especially to Gavin, about what could or should be done at this point in time to help bring about resolution to this situation.

Before the facilitators began the rounds, the possible need for interpretation between Innuaimum and English was discussed. It was agreed that participants would speak the language of their choice and anyone could request interpretation. Jack Penashue agreed to provide the interpretation. . . .

When the fourth and final round was completed . . . participants joined hands and closed the circle with a shared prayer.

It is very difficult to put into words an assessment of the effectiveness and power of this circle. Participants in circles learn the power of the circle through their active participation and learn that equally important to what is said by the participants is the atmosphere or feeling created within the circle by the participants. The comments which follow are those of the facilitators and Germaine Benuen in relation to their impressions about the intangibles of the circle process, about why it was effective and powerful.

As the participants began arriving at the building there was a noticeable tension among some. L. arrived with her mom and was quiet, almost sad, speaking little, standing off to the side while others chatted in twos or threes. All the participants seemed to be nervous. The facilitators had to be very direct to get participants into the room to start the circle. L.'s mother (G.) was the third participant to speak and she said directly that she was scared. The tension noticeably lessened and participants explained why they were present. It seemed to help that all participants had equal opportunity to say something. Even when L. did not speak in the first round, she began to appear less tense and less pressured, perhaps because she was not put on the spot to speak. We felt that in a way the process, and the participants in the process, showed respect to L. by not forcing her to speak. . . . When the circle started L. was seated in between her mom and Gavin's mom. She sat herself in such a way that she could look at her mom and at her cousin, but she had her back to almost everyone else in the circle. By the fourth round she had shifted around so that she could see and be seen by all the participants. She was smiling sometimes and by the end of the circle was laughing when appropriate with the other participants.

Another important aspect of the circle process was the expression of emotion by participants. Facilitators had no way to know what emotions, whether anger, sadness or frustration, might be voiced and or displayed by the participants. Facilitators knew from previous experiences that the process of the circle was powerful because honesty and emotion are an integral part of the process. How people spoke would in many ways be just as important to the impact of the circle as what people had to say.

There were two occasions when participants broke down weeping. Both L. and Gavin's mom wept. The other circle participants remained seated without speaking and waited for the person to compose themselves and then proceed when they were able. . . . G. commented that if she had been crying and someone had asked that there be a break to give her time to stop crying that it would feel like a rejection of her and her genuine feelings. She felt it was respectful of people to let them show emotion in a setting that was safe. If participants had taken a break, it would have been more because of participants' discomfort than anything else. Participants had been asked to try and be honest and respectful, and accepting the expression of emotion seemed very much a part of that honesty and respect. . . .

An assumption is made that the recommendations of the circle participants in the final round are of most importance to the court. Prior to the circle meeting, participants had been asked in preparation for the circle to think about recommendations they would want to make to be shared with the court. However, it is important to stress that what was said in the earlier three rounds and how that was expressed, had great influence on, indeed shaped the recommendations which eventually were made.

Probably the single most important comments made by any participant affecting the recommendations finally offered, were the comments made by Gavin. In the first round Gavin spoke in a clear voice, in a direct way that he had come to the circle to apologize to everyone that he had hurt for what he had done. He said that he wanted to find out what people wanted from him, what they expected from him and he repeated that he had come to apologize and to say that he was sorry for his behaviour. In the round when everyone was invited to speak to L. Gavin spoke emphasizing that L. was in no way to blame for what had happened, that he took full responsibility for his actions. He explained that when he had gone to the Brentwood Treatment Centre that he had shared a lot of things that had happened in his life and that one of those things was what had happened between him and L. He said the reason he shared that at treatment was because of his shame. He told us that he knew that what he had done was wrong and he thought that if he shared how he felt about what he had done that it might help him to get better. He also thanked people for coming to the circle.

Because of the seating, L. had the opportunity in each round to speak before Gavin. She didn't speak in the first or second rounds but she spoke in the third round to Gavin and said that she was happy that he had opened up about what had happened between them. She said she would not have been strong enough to open up to others about what happened but she was glad he had. She also told participants she was happy to be a part of the circle. After this when Gavin spoke he said he wanted L. to know that what had happened was his fault. He also wanted his family to know that he was not blaming them in any way, that his actions were his own and he was responsible for his behaviour. . . .

Jack began the final round by saying that he felt what needed to be said had been said. He said he saw what had happened in the circle and he felt what had happened and he felt honoured to have been a part of the process where participants who cared about each other were able to say the things they needed to say. Jack spoke about his hesitation to say anything more but on a very personal note he said that he wanted to say what he felt should now happen, what could now happen. He said he thought that L. and Gavin should start talking to one another if they were not already doing so, that they both needed to accept what had happened because it was his experience that people sometimes "over say things and over think things." He said maybe it wouldn't happen right now but what needed to happen was for L. and Gavin to start having contact again maybe to try and hug each other. . . .

Lyla then began speaking and said she too found the last round the most difficult even though she knew that the earlier rounds had been difficult because what was said and expressed was more painful. The difficulty with making recommendations came with a sense of having to satisfy someone or [some] group outside the circle, someone who hadn't experienced what had happened in the circle.

She then shared the same concern as Jack that where there had been friendships and family ties connecting Gavin and L. and Gavin's spouse and children, and where those connections had been broken or damaged, that through Gavin's actions, with the permission and agreement of others, that he needed to try and mend those connections. . . .

One recommendation was shared with L. This was that she accept and use . . . the caring that her family clearly has for her . . . to grow into being her own person. As a young mother L. was encouraged to remember the people who care for her deeply and to go to them for support and help when needed. . . .

Another specific recommendation was made about Gavin. If he were to be placed on probation, and obviously we couldn't know this, but if he was, it was recommended that rather than being supervised directly by the adult probation office, that he be made accountable through a period of probation to people in the community to whom he is connected and who know why he would be on probation and who would have real concern about how he was going to do while on probation. Both Jack and Germaine were suggested as a team who might be able to take on this responsibility. If the "system" is going to be keeping an eye on Gavin it should be done through people who can offer support and guidance based on a real knowledge of Gavin and the circumstances and who would be able to challenge Gavin to do the things which he himself acknowledges he needs to do in order to be healthier. . . .

Through interpretation L.'s mom G. said that she was really happy that Gavin had come to the circle and shared what he had with the participants. It was her opinion that Gavin was a strong young man because he had shared so much and taken responsibility. . . .

Apenam [Gavin's stepfather] recommended to Gavin that he continue to work at what Apenam knew Gavin had learned from going to the Brentwood treatment program. Apenam recommended this because he himself had gone to Brentwood many years before Gavin to change his own behaviour. . . .

Apenam said he wanted to say openly that he loves Gavin. Apenam said he doesn't always know how to show his love and that this is one of the biggest problems in his own life. He said he knows Gavin has a birth father but that he still wants to continue to be a father to Gavin as he has tried to be for many years, and if Gavin needs his help, Apenam offers it to him. . . .

In Innuaimun, L. was asked by Jack if she understood and she made a reply right away. . . . Jack . . . interpreted that L. had made a very broad statement and what she meant was that she had no problems or difficulties talking with Gavin or sharing with Gavin or anything like that. She would like to do that in fact and she had no worries or difficulties about doing that. Jack checked with L. if this was accurate and she replied it was. . . . Everyone agreed to close the circle and stood up with hands joined and together repeated the "serenity prayer."

At this point the tape was turned off and participants embraced one another at their own choosing. It is noted that L.'s mom went over to Gavin and embraced him and most significantly that L. and Gavin embraced one another. . . .

[A report of the circle was prepared and attached . . . to the decision of Judge O'Regan of the Newfoundland Supreme Court, Trial Division. In considering sentencing, Judge O'Regan found that "the concern of the Crown" that Gavin was non Inuit was "a non-issue," especially since Gavin "did grow up in the community of Sheshashit and was exposed to the Innu Culture and thus can benefit from the community's involvement in such things as a 'healing circle' which he attended." Judge O'Regan accepted the recommendations of the healing circle and imposed a noncustodial sentence.]

NOTES

1. *Sentencing circles, restorative justice, and traditional purposes.*   Do sentencing circles serve any, or even all, of the traditional purposes of punishment? Which traditional purpose or purposes were served or not served by the healing circle involving Gavin, L., and their families? See Julian V. Roberts and Carol LaPrairie, Sentencing Circles: Some Unanswered Questions, 39 Crim. L.Q. 69 (1997) (exploring the relationship of sentencing circles to traditional purposes of punishment).

What non-traditional purposes were served in the sentencing of Gavin? Proponents of sentencing circles say the goals of the process are to promote healing for all affected parties; provide an opportunity for the offender to make amends; empower victims, community members, families, and offenders by giving them a voice and a shared responsibility in finding constructive resolutions; address the underlying causes of criminal behavior; build a sense of community and its capacity for resolving conflict; and promote and share community values. Do you think sentencing circles represent a radically distinct substantive approach to crime and punishment? Or do they simply represent a more meaningful and effective means to achieve traditional goals?

2. *Use of sentencing circles.*   Should sentencing circles be an option in all criminal justice settings — that is, should jurisdictions explore the possibility of using sentencing circles for all sorts of crimes and all sorts of offenders? Proponents of sentencing circles readily concede that the process is not appropriate for all offenders. They stress the importance of several factors in determining whether a case is appropriate for a sentencing circle, including the strength of the offender's connection to the community, the sincerity and nature of the offender's efforts to be healed, the input of victims, and the dedication of the offender's support group. What about the nature of the offense itself? Would a sentencing circle be useful for an offender convicted of murder? For an offender convicted of stock fraud? For an offender convicted of trafficking cocaine? For an offender convicted of domestic violence? Cf. Rashmi Goel, No Women at the Center: The Use of the Canadian Sentencing Circle in Domestic Violence Cases, 15 Wis. Women's L.J. 293 (2000).

3. *Assessing the efficacy of sentencing circles.*   Very little research has been conducted to date on the effectiveness of sentencing circles, in part because most punishment systems are judged in terms of crime rates while sentencing circles are clearly concerned with a range of other interests. There have been a number of positive anecdotal reports about sentencing circles, but they have not

been seriously examined empirically. See Roberts and LaPrairie, Sentencing Circles at 82-83 (arguing that before sentencing circles are used broadly, "it is incumbent upon advocates to produce the kind of rigorous scientific evidence that sentencing circles are more effective than the current system").

4. *Other approaches to restorative justice.*   The movement toward restorative justice finds many manifestations besides sentencing circles. Especially for less serious offenses, a number of jurisdictions have developed various novel criminal justice forums and procedures that emphasize repairing harm, healing, and rebuilding relations among victims, offenders, and communities. In addition to sentencing circles, popular restorative justice practices include victim-offender mediation, family group conferencing, citizen panels, and various restitution initiatives. See generally Leena Kurki, Restorative and Community Justice in The United States, 27 Crime & Justice 235 (2000); Frederick W. Gay, Restorative Justice and The Prosecutor, 27 Fordham Urb. L.J. 1651 (2000).

2.   Implicit Purposes

In the excerpt earlier in this chapter, the American Bar Association states in its model sentencing standards that "[w]ithout reasonably clear identification of goals and purposes, the administration of criminal justice will be inconsistent, incoherent, and ineffectual." Yet most criminal justice systems operate without reasonably clear identification of goals and purposes. But just because goals and purposes have not been articulated does not mean that they do not operate. And even in systems with explicit purposes, truer, deeper purposes (acknowledged or unacknowledged) may operate.

Consider the implicit purpose or purposes of punishment suggested in the following materials.

> ### Discipline and Punish: The Birth of the Prison,
> ### Michel Foucault
> #### Pages 3-8, 16-30, 200-221 (1977)

On 1 March 1757 Damiens the regicide was condemned "to make the *amende honorable* before the main door of the Church of Paris," where he was to be "taken and conveyed in a cart, wearing nothing but a shirt, holding a torch of burning wax weighing two pounds"; then, "in the said cart, to the Place de Grève, where, on a scaffold that will be erected there, the flesh will be torn from his breasts, arms, thighs and claves with red-hot pincers, his right hand, holding the knife with which he committed the said parricide, burnt with sulphur, and, on those places where the flesh will be torn away, poured molten lead, boiling oil, burning resin, wax and sulphur melted together and then his body drawn and quartered by four horses and his limbs and body consumed by fire, reduced to ashes and his ashes thrown to the winds" (*Pièces originales*, 372-4).

"Finally, he was quartered," recounts the *Gazette d'Amsterdam* of 1 April 1757. "This last operation was very long, because the horses used were not accustomed to drawing; consequently, instead of four, six were needed; and when that did not suffice, they were forced, in order to cut off the wretch's thighs, to sever the sinews and hack at the joints. . . . It is said that, though he was always a great swearer, no blashemy escaped his lips; but the excessive pain made him utter horrible cries, and he often repeated: 'My God, have pity on me! Jesus, help me!' The spectators were all edified by the solicitude of the parish priest of St Paul's who despite his great age did not spare himself in offering consolation to the patient." . . .

Eighty years later, Léon Faucher drew up his rules "for the House of young prisoners in Paris":

"Art. 17. The prisoners' day will begin at six in the morning in winter and at five in summer. They will work for nine hours a day throughout the year. Two hours a day will be devoted to instruction. Work and the day will end at nine o'clock in winter and at eight in summer.

Art. 18. *Rising.* At the first drum-roll, the prisoners must rise and dress in silence, as the supervisor opens the cell doors. At the second drum-roll, they must be dressed and make their beds. At the third, they must line up and proceed to the chapel for morning prayer. There is a five-minute interval between each drum-roll.

Art. 19. The prayers are conducted by the chaplain and followed by a moral or religious reading. This exercise must not last more than half an hour.

Art. 20. *Work.* At a quarter to six in the summer, a quarter to seven in winter, the prisoners go down into the courtyard where they must wash their hands and faces, and receive their first ration of bread. Immediately afterwards, they form into work-teams and go off to work, which must begin at six in summer and seven in winter.

Art. 21. *Meal.* At ten o'clock the prisoners leave their work and go to the refectory; they wash their hands in their courtyards and assemble in divisions. After the dinner, there is recreation until twenty minutes to eleven.

Art. 22. *School.* At twenty minutes to eleven, at the drum-roll, the prisoners form into ranks, and proceed in divisions to the school. The class lasts two hours and consists alternately of reading, writing, drawing and arithmetic.

Art. 23. At twenty minutes to one, the prisoners leave the school, in divisions, and return to their courtyards for recreation. At five minutes to one, at the drum-roll, they form into workteams.

Art. 24. At one o'clock they must be back in the workshops: they work until four o'clock.

Art. 25. At four o'clock the prisoners leave their workshops and go into the courtyards where they wash their hands and form into divisions for the refectory.

Art. 26. Supper and the recreation that follows it last until five o'clock: the prisoners then return to the workshops.

Art. 27. At seven o'clock in the summer, at eight in winter, work stops; bread is distributed for the last time in the workshops. For a quarter of an hour one of the prisoners or supervisors reads a passage from some instructive or uplifting work. This is followed by evening prayer.

Art. 28. At half-past seven in summer, half-past eight in winter, the prisoners must be back in their cells after the washing of hands and the inspection of clothes in the courtyard; at the first drum-roll, they must undress, and at the second get into bed. The cell doors are closed and the supervisors go the rounds in the corridors, to ensure order and silence" (Faucher, 274, 82).

We have, then, [from the two distinct examples] a public execution and a timetable. They do not punish the same crimes or the same type of delinquent. But they each define a certain penal style. Less than a century separates them. [Between 1760 and 1840] in Europe and in the United States, the entire economy of punishment was redistributed. It was a time of great "scandals" for traditional justice, a time of innumerable projects for reform. It saw a new theory of law and crime, a new moral or political justification of the right to punish; old laws were abolished, old customs died out. "Modern" codes were planned or drawn up: Russia, 1769; Prussia, 1780; Pennsylvania and Tuscany, 1786; Austria, 1788; France, 1791, Year IV, 1808 and 1810. It was a new age for penal justice.

Among so many changes, I shall consider one: the disappearance of torture as a public spectacle. Today we are rather inclined to ignore it; perhaps, in its time, it gave rise to too much inflated rhetoric; perhaps it has been attributed too readily and too emphatically to a process of "humanization," thus dispensing with the need for further analysis. And, in any case, how important is such a change, when compared with the great institutional transformations, the formulation of explicit, general codes and unified rules of procedure; with the almost universal adoption of the jury system, the definition of the essentially corrective character of the penalty and the tendency, which has become increasingly marked since the nineteenth century, to adapt punishment to the individual offender? Punishment of a less immediately physical kind, a certain discretion in the art of inflicting pain, a combination of more subtle, more subdued sufferings, deprived of their visible display, should not all this be treated as a special case, an incidental effect of deeper changes? And yet the fact remains that a few decades saw the disappearance of the tortured, dismembered, amputated body, symbolically branded on face or shoulder, exposed alive or dead to public view. The body as the major target of penal repression disappeared.

If the penalty in its most severe forms no longer addresses itself to the body, on what does it lay hold? The answer of the theoreticians — those who, about 1760, opened up a new period that is not yet at an end — is simple, almost obvious. It seems to be contained in the question itself: since it is no longer the body, it must be the soul. The expiation that once rained down upon the body must be replaced by a punishment that acts in depth on the heart, the thoughts, the will, the inclinations. Mably formulated the principle once and for all: "Punishment, if I may so put it, should strike the soul rather than the body." . . .

Bentham's Panopticon is the architectural figure of this composition. We know the principle on which it was based: at the periphery, an annular building; at the centre, a tower; this tower is pierced with wide windows that open onto the inner side of the ring; the peripheric building is divided into cells, each of which extends the whole width of the building; they have two windows, one on the inside, corresponding to the windows of the tower; the other, on the outside, allows the light to cross the cell from one end to the other. All that is needed, then, is to place a supervisor in a central tower and to shut up in each cell a madman, a patient, a condemned man, a worker or a schoolboy. By the effect of backlighting, one can observe from the tower, standing out precisely against the light, the small captive shadows in the cells of the periphery. They are like so many cages, so many small theaters, in which each actor is alone, perfectly individualized and constantly visible.

. . . Each individual, in his place, is securely confined to a cell from which he is seen from the front by the supervisor; but the side walls prevent him from coming into contact with his companions. He is seen, but he does not see; he is the object of information, never a subject in communication. The arrangement of his room, opposite the central tower, imposes on him an axial visibility. And this invisibility is a guarantee of order. If the inmates are convicts, there is no danger of a plot, an attempt at collective escape, the planning of new crimes for the future, bad reciprocal influences; if they are patients, there is no danger of contagion; if they are madmen there is no risk of their committing violence upon one another; if they are schoolchildren, there is no copying, no noise, no chatter, no waste of time; if they are workers, there are no disorders, no theft, no coalitions, none of those distractions that slow down the rate of work, make it less perfect or cause accidents. The crowd, a compact mass, a locus of multiple exchanges, individualities merging together, a collective effect, is abolished and replaced by a collection of separated individualities. . . . (Bentham, 60-64).

Hence the major effect of the Panopticon: to induce in the inmate a state of conscious and permanent visibility that assures the automatic functioning of power. So to arrange things that the surveillance is permanent in its effects, even if it is discontinuous in its action; that the perfection of power should tend to render its actual exercise unnecessary; that this architectural apparatus should be a machine for creating and sustaining a power relation independent of the person who exercises it; in short, that the inmates should be caught up in a power situation of which they are themselves the bearers. . . .

So much for the question of observation. But the Panopticon was also a laboratory; it could be used as a machine to carry out experiments, to alter behaviour, to train or correct individuals. To experiment with medicines and monitor their effects. To try out different punishments on prisoners, according to their crimes and character, and to seek the most effective ones. To teach different techniques simultaneously to the workers, to decide which is the best. To try out pedagogical experiments. . . . The Panopticon is a privileged place for experiment on men, and for analysing with complete certainty the transformations that may be obtained from them. The Panopticon may even provide an apparatus for supervising its own mechanisms. In this central tower, the director may spy on all the employees that he has under his orders: nurses, doctors, foremen, teachers, warders; he will be able to judge them continuously, alter their behaviour, impose upon them the methods he thinks best; and it will even be possible to observe the director himself. . . .

. . . The Panopticon . . . is polyvalent in its applications; it serves to reform prisoners, but also to treat patients, to instruct schoolchildren, to confine the insane, to supervise workers, to put beggars and idlers to work. It is a type of location of bodies in space, of distribution of individuals in relation to one another, of hierarchical organization, of disposition of centres and channels of power, of definition of the instruments and modes of intervention of power, which can be implemented in hospitals, workshops, schools, prisons. . . .

[I]t is not that the beautiful totality of the individual is amputate, repressed, altered by our social order, it is rather that the individual is carefully fabricated in it, according to a whole technique of forces and bodies. . . . The panoptic modality of power . . . is not under the immediate dependence or a direct extension of the great juridical-political structures of a society; it is nonetheless not absolutely independent. Historically, the process by which the bourgeoisie became in the course of the eighteenth century the politically dominant class was masked by the establishment of an explicit, coded and formally egalitarian juridical framework, made possible by the organization of a parliamentary, representative regime. But the development and generalization of disciplinary mechanisms constituted the other, dark side of these processes. The general juridical form that guaranteed a system of rights that were egalitarian in principle was supported by these tiny, everyday, physical mechanisms, by all those systems of micro-power that are essentially non-egalitarian and asymmetrical that we call the disciplines. And although, in a formal way, the representative regime makes it possible . . . for the will of all to form the fundamental authority of sovereignty, the disciplines provide, at the base, a guarantee of the submission of forces and bodies. The real, corporal disciplines constituted the foundation of the formal, juridical liberties. The contract may have been regarded as the ideal foundation of law and political power; panopticism constituted the technique, universally widespread, of coercion. It continued to work in depth on the juridical structures of society, in order to make the effective mechanisms of power function in opposition to the formal framework that it had acquired. The "Enlightenment," which discovered the liberties, also invented the disciplines.

How can we determine any implicit purposes of sentencing in the United States at the start of the twenty-first century? Perhaps one way is to offer a snapshot of current punishment—what sanctions are used, for how many, and for whom.* Imagine this is not a country you know, but a foreign country. If you look only at this picture of punishment described below, what possible theories of implicit purpose does the picture suggest (whatever explicit claims might be made)?

- The total number of prisoners under the jurisdiction of federal or state adult correctional authorities was 1,440,655 at year-end 2002. With more than 660,000 people held in local jails, the total number of people incarcerated at year-end 2002 was greater than two million.
- About 1 of every 110 men and 1 of every 1,656 women were sentenced prisoners under the jurisdiction of state or federal authorities. The rate of incarceration in prison and jail was 701 inmates per 100,000 residents in 2002, up from 601 in 1995. At year-end 2002, 1 of every 143 U.S. residents was incarcerated in state or federal prison or a local jail.
- At year-end 2002, state prisons were operating between 1 percent and 16 percent above capacity, while federal prisons were operating at 33 percent above capacity. At year-end 2002, privately operated facilities housed 93,771 inmates (5.8 percent of state and 12.4 percent of federal inmates).
- Among the more than 1,380,000 sentenced inmates at year-end 2002, an estimated 442,300 were black men between the ages of 20 and 39. At year-end 2002, 10.4 percent of black men ages 25 to 29 were in

---

* *Sources:* U.S. Dept. of Justice, Bureau of Justice Statistics, Prisoners in 2002 (NCJ 200248, July 2003); U.S. Dept. of Justice, Bureau of Justice Statistics, Probation and Parole in the United States, 2002 (NCJ 201135, August 2003).

ADULT CORRECTIONAL POPULATIONS, 1980-2002

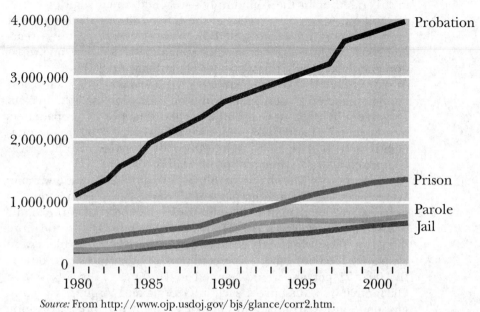

Source: From http://www.ojp.usdoj.gov/bjs/glance/corr2.htm.

prison, compared to 2.4 percent of Hispanic men and 1.2 percent of white men in the same age group.

- At year-end 2002, 97,491 women were in state or federal prisons — 6.8 percent of all prison inmates. Since 1995 the number of male prisoners has grown 24 percent, while the number of female prisoners has increased 42 percent. Relative to their number in the U.S. resident population, men were about 15 times more likely than women to be incarcerated in a state or federal prison. Black non-Hispanic women were more than three times as likely as Hispanic women and five times more likely than white non-Hispanic women to be in prison at year-end 2002.

- The five states with the highest incarceration rates at year-end 2002 were all in the South. Louisiana had the highest prison incarceration rate (794 sentenced inmates per 100,000 residents), followed by Mississippi (743), Texas (692), Oklahoma (667), and Alabama (612). The five states with the lowest incarceration rates at year-end 2002 were all in the North: Maine (141), Minnesota (141), North Dakota (161), Rhode Island (191), and New Hampshire (192).

- An estimated 596,100 inmates in state prison at year-end 2001 were held for violent offenses: 159,200 for murder, 155,300 for robbery, 118,800 for assault, and 118,500 for rape and other sexual assaults. In addition, 233,000 inmates were held for property offenses, 246,100 for drug offenses, and 129,900 for public order offenses.

- Prisoners sentenced for drug offenses constituted the largest group of federal inmates (55 percent) in 2000. Between 1995 and 2000, the number of federal inmates held for immigration offenses increased 339 percent, and the number held for weapons offenses increased 68 percent.

- The total federal, state, and local adult correctional population — incarcerated or in the community — reached a new high of nearly 6.7 million. About 3.1 percent of the U.S. adult population, or 1 of every 32 adults, was incarcerated or on probation or parole at year-end 2002. A total of 3,995,165 adult men and women were on probation and 753,141 adults were on parole at year-end 2002.

- At year-end 2002, 1 of 5 probationers was a woman, 1 of 3 was black. Women made up 23 percent of adults on probation in 2002, up from 18 percent in 1990. At year-end 2002 about half of all probationers were white (2,212,700), one-third were black (1,228,300), and one-eighth were of Hispanic origin (485,600). Persons of other races comprised about 2 percent of probationers (68,700).

- About 1 of every 7 adults on parole in 2002 (108,200) was a woman. Women represented a larger percentage of the parole population (14 percent) in 2002 than in 1990 when they were 8 percent. More than 2 of 5 adults on parole at year-end 2002 were black (313,800), and more than 1 of 3 was white (292,400). Nineteen percent of parolees were Hispanic (136,600). About 1 percent were of other races (10,400).

- In 2002, 71 persons were executed in 13 states: 33 in Texas; 7 in Oklahoma; 6 in Missouri; 4 each in Georgia and Virginia; 3 each in Florida, South Carolina, and Ohio; 2 each in Alabama, Mississippi, and North Carolina; and 1 each in Louisiana and California. Of persons executed in 2002, 53 were white, 8 were black, 69 were men, and 2 were women. In 2002, 38 states and the federal government had capital statutes.

PRISONERS ON DEATH ROW, 1953-2001

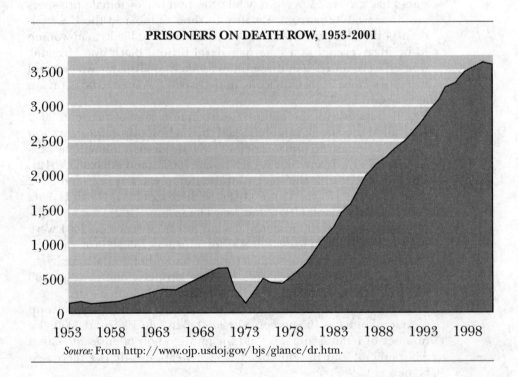

Source: From http://www.ojp.usdoj.gov/bjs/glance/dr.htm.

- At year-end 2001, 37 states and the federal prison system held 3,581 prisoners under sentence of death, 20 fewer than at year-end 2000. All had committed murder.
- Of persons under sentence of death in 2001, 1,969 were white, 1,538 were black, 28 were American Indian, 33 were Asian, and 13 were of unknown race.
- At year-end 2001, 51 women were under a sentence of death. The 358 Hispanic inmates under sentence of death accounted for 11 percent of inmates with a known ethnicity. Among inmates under sentence of death and with available criminal histories: nearly 2 of 3 had a prior felony conviction — about 1 of 12 had a prior homicide conviction.

NOTES

1. *Inferring purposes from historical trends in punishment.*   What purpose or purposes can be inferred from many societies' reliance on brutal physical punishments throughout history and up to the eighteenth century? What purpose or purposes can be inferred from the United States' modern reliance on (mass) incarceration?

As Foucault suggests, there have been significant shifts in the overall approach to, and fundamental types of, punishment throughout Western history. While modern sentencing systems usually consider imprisonment as the primary mode of punishment, the very concept of incarceration was largely unknown before the nineteenth century. Physical and financial punishments were the norm in medieval times, and the sanctions imposed by the state (typically in the form of the Crown) could be quite harsh and brutal for even minor offenses. Serious crimes were punished with death or banishment, and nearly all punishments were carried out in public for members of the community to witness. See Arthur W. Campbell, Law of Sentencing, §1 (1978).

Influenced in part by the development and ascendancy of imprisonment as a principal mode of punishment, nearly all Western societies have abandoned the official use of brutal physical punishments, and rarely are any punishments ever carried out in public settings. Though these "modernizing" trends seem to make our systems of punishment more "civilized," the Foucault reading should lead you to consider whether torturing the human soul may be even worse than torturing the human body. Another question to consider is whether the "civilization" of our methods of punishment may be making them less effective when judged against our theories of punishment. Might certain theories of punishment be better served by forms of physical torture imposed in public than by terms of imprisonment served in private?

2. *Modern variations in types of punishment.*   The cumulative statistics presented above do not reveal the significant variations in how individuals are incarcerated and how terms of probation and parole are structured and controlled. The experience of incarceration for offenders can and does vary greatly depending in part on whether the time served is in halfway houses, local jails, minimum-security prisons, general state or federal prisons, or high-security (supermax) prisons. See generally Norval Morris, The Contemporary Prison: 1965-Present, in

The Oxford History of the Prison 227 (1995). The experience of probation or parole likewise can and does vary considerably depending on the nature and type of conditions placed on probationers or parolees and on other forms of sanctions (both official and unofficial) that can accompany community supervision. See generally Andrew Horwitz, Coercion, Pop-Psychology, and Judicial Moralizing: Some Proposals for Curbing Judicial Abuse of Probation Conditions, 57 Wash. & Lee L. Rev. 75 (2000); Nora V. Demleitner, Preventing Internal Exile: The Need for Restrictions on Collateral Sentencing Consequences, 11 Stan. L. & Poly. Rev. 153 (1999).

3. *Questions.*   Which of the statistics reflecting modern sentencing and punishment dynamics in the United States surprises you the most? Which of the statistics disturbs you the most?

B.   PURPOSES IN PRACTICAL CONTEXT

For several millennia philosophers have discussed the ins and outs, the pros and cons, of different theories of punishment. English philosopher H. L. A. Hart advanced the theoretical debate when he observed that these discussions involve three conceptually distinct issues:

(1)   the "general justifying aim"—the general goal of the social institution of punishment
(2)   the question of liability—who specifically should be punished for certain behavior
(3)   the question of amount—exactly how much punishment should be administered

See H. L. A. Hart, Prolegomenon to the Principles of Punishment, in Punishment and Responsibility 1-28 (1968).

Hart's insight reinforces the fact that while philosophers have the luxury of discussing theoretical issues in the abstract, societies must confront the complicated practical realities of constructing and operating a workable criminal justice system and then distributing specific punishments to offenders. The materials in this section demonstrate that the actual practice of administering and enforcing punishments through a sentencing and corrections system implicates many levels of complexity beyond the basic questions of punishment theory. Rather than working through these issues by starting with general questions and then moving to specific cases, we will begin with a specific case and then telescope out to broader systemwide questions.

1.   Use of Purposes in Sentencing an Individual Offender

Though the purposes of punishment are often debated at a high level of abstraction, individual decision makers (usually judges) necessarily confront them when deciding what sentence to impose in a particular case. Norval Morris, writing in 1953, noted not only the inevitability of considering purposes when sentencing individual offenders but also the importance of blending purposes on a case-by-case basis:

> When a court decides what sentence to impose on a criminal . . . , it must do so with reference to some purpose or purposes, conscious or unconscious, articulate or inarticulate. [A] compass is desirable . . . , even if only for a short distance and over a particular part of the journey. [F]or certain types of criminals reformation is one important aim. None will dispute that our hope of deterring the criminal from repeating his crime by the punishment we inflict and by that same punishment deterring others who are like-minded also plays a considerable part. Few will deny that there is in the community a deep-rooted hatred of the criminal . . . and that in our penal sanctions we must take into account these emotional demands of the community. The extent to which these aims of reformation, deterrence and community satisfaction blend in relation to any particular offender will vary considerably.

Norval Morris, Sentencing Convicted Criminals, 27 The Australian L. J. 186, 192-198 (1953).

Many modern sentencing systems that structure how judges can exercise their sentencing power often prescribe certain sentencing ranges for particular offenders committing particular offenses, but then allow the sentencing judge to sentence outside these ranges in "extraordinary" circumstances or for "substantial and compelling" reasons. Judges in these systems thus have an opportunity to consider the purposes of sentencing in the selection of specific sentences both within and outside of the prescribed ranges.

The Washington State Sentencing Reform Act of 1981 provides that the purposes of sentencing are to: (1) ensure that the punishment for a criminal offense is proportionate to the seriousness of the offense and the offender's criminal history; (2) promote respect for the law by providing punishment that is just; (3) impose punishment that is commensurate with the punishment imposed on others committing similar offenses; (4) protect the public; (5) offer offenders an opportunity to improve themselves; and (6) make frugal use of the state's resources. See Wash. Rev. Code §9.94A.010. In the following case, consider the role of purposes and the kinds of purposes the court uses to decide whether an exceptional sentence was appropriate.

State v. Michael Deshon Gaines
859 P.2d 36 (Wash. 1993)

GUY, J.

On February 12, 1990, Seattle Police Department Officer M. Alphin made contact with Gaines while working undercover narcotics detail. Alphin asked Gaines if he had a "twenty," a street term for a $20 piece of rock cocaine. Gaines got in Alphin's car, said that he could get some cocaine, and called to a juvenile female who was on the street. The young woman walked over to the car and got into the back seat. Alphin gave Gaines a $20 bill, which Gaines handed to the juvenile female. The juvenile female then handed some cocaine to Gaines, and he gave it to Alphin. Gaines later explained that his reason for assisting in this transaction was that he hoped to obtain a small amount of cocaine for his own use from either the buyer or the seller. Shortly thereafter, Gaines and the juvenile female were arrested.

At the time of his arrest, Gaines was 19 years old. He had one prior adult felony conviction for a violation of the Uniform Controlled Substances Act, and two juvenile felony-level convictions, one for taking a motor vehicle without permission and the other for promoting prostitution. He also had misdemeanor convictions for hit and run, alcohol offense, menacing (two convictions), simple assault, theft (two convictions), trespass (three convictions), false reporting, and prostitution.

Gaines pled guilty to the charge of delivery of cocaine and was convicted. The standard sentence range for his offense was 31 to 41 months. The presentence investigator recommended a 36-month term. The prosecutor recommended 41 months. Defense counsel urged the court to impose an exceptional sentence consisting of 12 months in custody followed by release into the Seadrunar inpatient treatment program for a period of 9 to 12 months. In support of this request, the defense submitted a diagnostic substance abuse evaluation prepared by TASC (Treatment Alternatives to Street Crime). The TASC report details Gaines's substance abuse problems, which apparently began when he was 14 years old. The report states that Gaines dropped out of school at the age of 16, and that he worked briefly as a janitor and an actor. The report further states that Gaines "presented a history which is consistent with a diagnosis of middle stage alcoholism, and cocaine and marijuana addiction," and concludes that his prognosis is poor. The report recommends drug treatment and states that if Gaines were to complete a residential treatment program and all recommendations of aftercare, "it is unlikely he would be as high of risk to re-offend."

The trial court gave Gaines an exceptional sentence of 12 months' confinement and 12 months of community supervision. To support the exceptional sentence, the trial court entered the following findings of fact:

> 1.3 — The defendant is addicted and/or abused a number of substances, including alcohol, marijuana, heroin, amphetamines and cocaine. Defendant's prior and current criminal activity is directly related to his addiction and substance abuse dependency.
>
> 1.4 — That a standard sentencing range of total confinement would not promote the State's interest in both punishing the defendant for his criminal offenses and rehabilitating the defendant so that future criminal offenses do not occur. Treatment professionals indicate that the defendant requires intensive inpatient treatment, beyond that which is available in the Department of Corrections facilities.
>
> 1.5 — That defendant is amenable to a long term residential drug treatment program. . . .
>
> 1.6 — Without treatment for drug dependency, defendant is very likely to reoffend. Society would be better protected by placing defendant, at his own request, in a treatment program. . . .

THE TRIAL COURT'S FINDINGS

The State [first] argues that the trial court's findings of fact in support of the exceptional sentence were not adequately supported by the record. We agree with the Court of Appeals that the record adequately supported the findings.

Finding 1.3 provides that Gaines's drug addiction has been a cause of all his criminal activity, and the unchallenged first sentence of finding 1.6 states that without treatment for drug dependency Gaines is likely to reoffend. These findings adequately support the conclusion of law contained in the second sentence of finding 1.6 that society would be better protected if Gaines is given treatment for his addiction.

Finally, the State challenges the first sentence in finding 1.4, which provides:

> That a standard sentencing range of total confinement would not promote the State's interest in both punishing the defendant for his criminal offenses and rehabilitating the defendant so that future criminal offenses do not occur . . .

The trial court found that "[t]reatment professionals indicate that the defendant requires intensive inpatient treatment, beyond that which is available in the Department of Corrections facilities." If Gaines needs drug treatment beyond what is available in Department of Corrections (DOC) facilities, and if Gaines's criminal activity is related to his drug addiction, then confinement in a DOC facility would not serve the State's interest in rehabilitation. See RCW 9.94A.010(5) (identifying rehabilitation as one of the SRA's goals). This adequately supports the statement expressed by the first sentence of finding 1.4.

DRUG ADDICTION AS THE BASIS FOR AN EXCEPTIONAL SENTENCE

The State further contends that the trial court's reasons were not adequate as a matter of law to support an exceptional sentence below the standard range. Whether the reasons supplied by the trial court justify an exceptional sentence is a question of law. Those reasons must be "substantial and compelling," and must distinguish the defendant's crime from others in the same category.

In the present case, the trial court's grounds for departing from the standard sentence range focus on Gaines's drug addiction and the fact that it was directly related to his crime. This was error. Drug addiction and its causal role in an addict's offense may not serve to justify a durational departure from a standard range sentence. . . . This conclusion is required under [one of] our recent decisions [in which we held that] findings that the defendant suffered from . . . alcoholism [which] impaired the defendant's ability to appreciate the wrongfulness of his conduct . . . were inadequate to support use of the mitigating factor defined in RCW 9.94A.390(1)(e), which provides:

> The defendant's capacity to appreciate the wrongfulness of his conduct or to conform his conduct to the requirements of the law, was significantly impaired (voluntary use of drugs or alcohol is excluded).

[That decision] thus prohibits alcoholism to be relied upon as a causal factor under RCW 9.94A.390(1)(e). [And in another case in which] the trial court had imposed an exceptional sentence under RCW 9.94A.390(1)(e) based on the consideration that the defendant was an addict whose drug use diminished his ability to appreciate the wrongfulness of his actions, [w]e held that RCW 9.94A.390(1)(e) excludes consideration of the unforced, and not fraudulently induced, use of drugs or alcohol as a mitigating factor, regardless of whether the defendant suffers from drug addiction. In so holding, we limited consideration of drug use as a mitigating factor under RCW 9.94A.390(1)(e) to only those circumstances in which the use might have formed the basis for a defense, that is, to those circumstances when the defendant's intoxication at the time of the offense was induced by fraud or force.

Although [these cases] focus on alcoholism and drug addiction as mitigating factors under RCW 9.94A.390(1)(e), consistency with these decisions requires disallowing substance abuse as a nonstatutory mitigating factor as well. In other words, because substance abuse may not serve as a mitigating factor pursuant to the diminished capacity provision stated in RCW 9.94A.390(1)(e), neither may it serve as a nonstatutory mitigating factor. . . .

Gaines [argues based on a broad interpretation of another precedent] that a defendant's addiction may justify an exceptional sentence if there is evidence that the addiction was a "direct cause" of his criminal conduct. We reject such a broad interpretation. [The precedent relied upon by Gaines] stands only for the proposition that when a defendant's drug addiction is the direct cause of the offense, that fact may serve as justification not for a departure from the standard sentence range, but for imposing drug treatment as an exceptional condition of a community supervision sentence.

In summary, we hold that drug addiction and its causal role in an addict's criminal offense may not properly serve as justification for a durational departure from the standard range. Therefore, the fact that Gaines's drug addiction was directly related to his offense cannot be relied upon to justify a durational departure from the standard sentence range for his offense.

Finally, we comment upon the Court of Appeals' analysis of the question whether the trial court's reasons were legally sufficient to justify the exceptional sentence.

The trial court reasoned in part that because Gaines's drug addiction was directly related to his crime, the SRA's goals of rehabilitation of criminals and protecting the public would be better served by requiring Gaines to undergo drug treatment. See RCW 9.94A.010 (stating goals of the SRA). The Court of Appeals approved of this reasoning. We do not.

As we explained in State v. Allert, 815 P.2d 752, 759 (Wash. 1991), "[t]he SRA was designed to provide proportionate punishment, protect the public and provide rehabilitation, and the presumptive ranges established for each crime represent the *Legislature's judgment* as to how best to accommodate those interests." For this reason a sentencing court's determination that a standard range term would not advance rehabilitative goals or would not protect the public is not adequate to justify departure from the normal sentence range. Therefore, the trial court's determination here that a standard range sentence would not rehabilitate Gaines or adequately protect the public does not justify an exceptional sentence. . . .

In conclusion, the trial court's reasons for imposing an exceptional sentence were adequately supported by the record. However, the court erred in relying on the fact that Gaines's drug addiction was directly related to his offense as a basis for a durational departure from the standard sentence range. . . .

MADSEN, J., dissenting.

[In stating the purposes of sentencing listed in RCW 9.94A.010], [t]he Legislature has not indicated that any one of these objectives is any more significant than another. However, in construing the SRA, this court has determined that the primary objectives of the statute are to ensure punishment, protect the public, and offer rehabilitative opportunities:

> At times there is tension among these acknowledged purposes. The tension between utilitarian purposes, in which the goal is to accomplish some future objective, and principles of retribution and desert, which focus on what has occurred in the past, is deep and persistent. Historically, most theoreticians have denied the possibility that these purposes could be integrated. . . .
>   . . . The Sentencing Reform Act's statement of purposes is drawn from and based upon the thesis that this integration can be accomplished. . . . [I]t is clear that the Act does not accept the argument of those theoreticians who argue for just deserts as the sole purpose for which punishment should be imposed.

State v. Barnes, 818 P.2d 1088, 1095 (Wash. 1991) (Dolliver, J., dissenting).

As Justice Dolliver observed, "[w]hile arguably at odds with the ideal of just deserts, these utilitarian objectives are no less a part of the overall scheme of the SRA." The drafters of the SRA noted in the "Purpose" section that the statute "does not eliminate . . . discretionary decisions affecting sentences." This is in line with earlier decisions from this court. . . .

[T]he exceptional sentence given by the trial court is justified by "substantial and compelling" circumstances which distinguish it from other crimes or criminals in the same category. The defendant in this case was a young man who committed a minor drug offense for the purpose of acquiring a small quantity of drugs to support his own habit. Based on the record, the Court of Appeals correctly concluded that the factors relied on by the trial court to impose an exceptional sentence were supported by the evidence. Expert testimony was offered to support the court's findings that (1) the defendant was drug and/or alcohol addicted; (2) that the defendant's prior and current criminal activity was directly related to his addiction; (3) that intensive, inpatient treatment was required to rehabilitate the defendant so that future criminal offenses would not occur; (4) that such treatment was not available in the Department of Corrections; and (5) that the defendant was amenable to treatment and desired to have such treatment. . . . I find that the factors relied on here were substantial and compelling and would affirm the exceptional sentence in this case. . . .

Trial court judges are asking this court to allow them to impose sentences which they believe are appropriate under the totality of circumstances. . . . I see nothing which compels a reversal of that case, the result of which will be to further limit judges in the exercise of their discretion. We must take care when interpreting the SRA that we do not eliminate "justice" from the criminal justice system by so far limiting the trial court's discretion to impose an exceptional sentence where the facts and circumstances of a particular case justify the court's actions. Consideration of the human being in the context of the crime is at the heart of judging. We should recognize that judges are highly trained professionals who, having the parties before them, are in the best position to dispense justice.

NOTES

1. *Applying purposes in individual cases.*   Is the application of punishment purposes in individual sentencing decisions a factual issue or a legal issue? Is it a decision best made by legislatures, trial courts, appellate courts, or some other decision maker? Note that the Washington Supreme Court in *Gaines* did not dispute the trial court's factual conclusion that a standard sentencing term would not advance rehabilitative goals or would not protect the public; rather, it held as a matter of law that these factual conclusions were inadequate to justify a departure from the normal sentence range. More generally, the Washington Supreme Court appeared to conclude that the trial court was not entitled to make these legal judgments because the Washington legislature had already sought to accommodate the purposes of punishment through the establishment of the standard sentencing terms. Are you convinced by the majority's reasoning, or are you moved more by Justice Madsen's dissenting opinion?

2. *"Consistency" affecting the application of purposes.*   Critical to the holding in *Gaines* seems to be the Washington Supreme Court's interest in consistency. The majority held that despite the trial court's assessment and application of the purposes of punishment for defendant Gaines, "because substance abuse may not serve as a mitigating factor pursuant to the diminished capacity provision stated in RCW 9.94A.390(1)(e), neither may it serve as a nonstatutory mitigating factor." The court further said "consistency . . . requires" this decision. What purpose does consistency serve? Is furthering consistency across cases more important than furthering the purposes of punishment in individual cases?

2. Use of Purposes in System Components

Not only do judges and other decision makers face challenges in trying to integrate purposes into case-specific sentencing judgments, legislators and other rule makers also confront challenges when integrating purposes into structural aspects of a sentencing system. Institutions responsible for creating sentencing rules that apply to a range of cases must consider whether and to what extent particular purposes should be considered for certain types of crimes, certain types of offenders, and certain types of punishment.

As you review the materials in the following sections, consider how your initial beliefs about the purposes of punishment bear on questions such as the appropriate sentencing rules for repeat offenders or the appropriateness of the death penalty.

a. The Relevance of Prior Crimes to Current Punishment

The justifications for punishment may help to explain specific sentencing rules. Consider some of the most basic sentencing questions: Should an offender be punished more severely if she has a prior conviction? Multiple convictions? Does it matter if the prior offense is the same as the current offense? How old the prior offense is? How the offender was punished for the prior offense?

First write down your answers to these questions. Then, informed by your own instincts and insights, consider the following materials, which wrestle with these matters in two important and distinct contexts. In the *Ewing* case, the U.S. Supreme Court assesses whether the reliance on prior offenses to substantially aggravate later sentences raises federal constitutional concerns; in the policy paper, the U.S. Sentencing Commission explores the ways and means of developing concrete and comprehensive criminal history rules for the federal guideline sentencing system.

|| *John Albert Ewing v. California* ||
538 U.S. 11 (2003)

O'CONNOR, J.

In this case, we decide whether the Eighth Amendment prohibits the State of California from sentencing a repeat felon to a prison term of 25 years to life under the State's "Three Strikes and You're Out" law.

I

California's three strikes law reflects a shift in the State's sentencing policies toward incapacitating and deterring repeat offenders who threaten the public safety. The law was designed "to ensure longer prison sentences and greater punishment for those who commit a felony and have been previously convicted of serious and/or violent felony offenses." Cal. Penal Code §667(b). . . .

California's current three strikes law consists of two virtually identical statutory schemes designed to increase the prison terms of repeat felons. When a defendant is convicted of a felony, and he has previously been convicted of one or more prior felonies defined as "serious" or "violent" in Cal. Penal Code Ann. §§667.5 and 1192.7, sentencing is conducted pursuant to the three strikes law. . . . If the defendant has one prior "serious" or "violent" felony conviction, he must be sentenced to twice the term otherwise provided as punishment for the current felony conviction. If the defendant has two or more prior "serious" or "violent" felony convictions, he must receive an indeterminate term of life imprisonment. Defendants sentenced to life under the three strikes law become eligible for parole on a date calculated by reference to a "minimum term," which is the greater of (a) three times the term otherwise provided for the current conviction, (b) 25 years, or (c) the term determined by the court pursuant to §1170 for the underlying conviction, including any enhancements. . . .

On parole from a 9-year prison term, petitioner Gary Ewing walked into the pro shop of the El Segundo Golf Course in Los Angeles County on March 12, 2000. He walked out with three golf clubs, priced at $399 apiece, concealed in his pants leg. A shop employee, whose suspicions were aroused when he observed Ewing limp out of the pro shop, telephoned the police. The police apprehended Ewing in the parking lot.

Ewing is no stranger to the criminal justice system. In 1984, at the age of 22, he pleaded guilty to theft. The court sentenced him to six months in jail (suspended), three years' probation, and a $300 fine. In 1988, he was convicted of felony grand theft auto and sentenced to one year in jail and three years' probation. After Ewing completed probation, however, the sentencing court reduced the crime to a misdemeanor, permitted Ewing to withdraw his guilty plea, and dismissed the case. In 1990, he was convicted of petty theft with a prior and sentenced to 60 days in the county jail and three years' probation. In 1992, Ewing was convicted of battery and sentenced to 30 days in the county jail and two years' summary probation. One month later, he was convicted of theft and sentenced to 10 days in the county jail and 12 months' probation. In January 1993, Ewing was convicted of burglary and sentenced to 60 days in the county jail and one year's summary probation. In February 1993, he was convicted of possessing drug paraphernalia and sentenced to six months in the county jail and three years' probation. In July 1993, he was convicted of appropriating lost property and sentenced to 10 days in the county jail and two years' summary probation. In September 1993, he was convicted of unlawfully possessing a firearm and trespassing and sentenced to 30 days in the county jail and one year's probation.

In October and November 1993, Ewing committed three burglaries and one robbery at a Long Beach, California, apartment complex over a 5-week period. [During the robbery], Ewing accosted a victim in the mailroom of the apartment complex. Ewing claimed to have a gun and ordered the victim to hand over his wallet. When the victim resisted, Ewing produced a knife and forced the victim back to the apartment itself. While Ewing rifled through the bedroom, the victim fled the apartment screaming for help. Ewing absconded with the victim's money and credit cards. . . . A jury convicted Ewing of first-degree robbery and three counts of residential burglary. Sentenced to nine years and eight months in prison, Ewing was paroled in 1999.

Only 10 months later, Ewing stole the golf clubs at issue in this case. He was charged with, and ultimately convicted of, one count of felony grand theft of personal property in excess of $400. As required by the three strikes law, the prosecutor formally alleged, and the trial court later found, that Ewing had been convicted previously of four serious or violent felonies for the three burglaries and the robbery in the Long Beach apartment complex. . . .

Before sentencing Ewing, the trial court took note of his entire criminal history, including the fact that he was on parole when he committed his latest offense. . . . As a newly convicted felon with two or more "serious" or "violent" felony convictions in his past, Ewing was sentenced under the three strikes law to 25 years to life. . . .

II

[Our precedents have explained that] the Eighth Amendment's ban on cruel and unusual punishments prohibits sentences that are disproportionate to the crime committed, and that the constitutional principle of proportionality has been recognized explicitly in this Court for almost a century. [These precedents] have identified four principles of proportionality review — the primacy of the legislature, the variety of legitimate penological schemes, the nature of our federal system, and the requirement that proportionality review be guided by objective factors — that inform the final one: The Eighth Amendment does not require strict proportionality between crime and sentence. Rather, it forbids only extreme sentences that are grossly disproportionate to the crime. . . . The proportionality principles in our cases . . . guide our application of the Eighth Amendment in the new context [of California's three strikes law] that we are called upon to consider.

For many years, most States have had laws providing for enhanced sentencing of repeat offenders. Yet between 1993 and 1995, three strikes laws effected a sea change in criminal sentencing throughout the Nation. These laws responded to widespread public concerns about crime by targeting the class of offenders who pose the greatest threat to public safety: career criminals. . . .

Throughout the States, legislatures enacting three strikes laws made a deliberate policy choice that individuals who have repeatedly engaged in serious or violent criminal behavior, and whose conduct has not been deterred by more conventional approaches to punishment, must be isolated from society in order to protect the public safety. Though three strikes laws may be relatively new, our tradition of deferring to state legislatures in making and implementing such important policy decisions is longstanding.

Our traditional deference to legislative policy choices finds a corollary in the principle that the Constitution does not mandate adoption of any one penological theory. A sentence can have a variety of justifications, such as incapacitation, deterrence, retribution, or rehabilitation. Some or all of these justifications may play a role in a State's sentencing scheme. Selecting the sentencing rationales is generally a policy choice to be made by state legislatures, not federal courts.

When the California Legislature enacted the three strikes law, it made a judgment that protecting the public safety requires incapacitating criminals who have already been convicted of at least one serious or violent crime. Nothing in the Eighth Amendment prohibits California from making that choice. To the contrary, our cases establish that States have a valid interest in deterring and segregating habitual criminals. Recidivism has long been recognized as a legitimate basis for increased punishment.

California's justification is no pretext. Recidivism is a serious public safety concern in California and throughout the Nation. According to a recent report, approximately 67 percent of former inmates released from state prisons were charged with at least one "serious" new crime within three years of their release. See U.S. Dept. of Justice, Bureau of Justice Statistics, Special Report: Recidivism of Prisoners Released in 1994, p. 1 (June 2002). In particular, released property offenders like Ewing had higher recidivism rates than those released after committing violent, drug, or public-order offenses. . . .

In 1996, when the *Sacramento Bee* studied 233 three strikes offenders in California, it found that they had an aggregate of 1,165 prior felony convictions, an average of 5 apiece. The prior convictions included 322 robberies and 262 burglaries. About 84 percent of the 233 three strikes offenders had been convicted of at least one violent crime. In all, they were responsible for 17 homicides, 7 attempted slayings, and 91 sexual assaults and child molestations. . . .

The State's interest in deterring crime also lends some support to the three strikes law. . . . Four years after the passage of California's three strikes law, the recidivism rate of parolees returned to prison for the commission of a new crime dropped by nearly 25 percent. California Dept. of Justice, Office of the Attorney

General, "Three Strikes and You're Out"—Its Impact on the California Criminal Justice System After Four Years 10 (1998). Even more dramatically:

> an unintended but positive consequence of "Three Strikes" has been the impact on parolees leaving the state. More California parolees are now leaving the state than parolees from other jurisdictions entering California. This striking turnaround started in 1994. It was the first time more parolees left the state than entered since 1976. This trend has continued and in 1997 more than 1,000 net parolees left California.

To be sure, California's three strikes law has sparked controversy. Critics have doubted the law's wisdom, cost-efficiency, and effectiveness in reaching its goals. This criticism is appropriately directed at the legislature, which has primary responsibility for making the difficult policy choices that underlie any criminal sentencing scheme. We do not sit as a "superlegislature" to second-guess these policy choices. It is enough that the State of California has a reasonable basis for believing that dramatically enhanced sentences for habitual felons advances the goals of its criminal justice system in any substantial way.

III

. . . Against this backdrop, we consider Ewing's claim that his three strikes sentence of 25 years to life is unconstitutionally disproportionate to his offense of "shoplifting three golf clubs." We first address the gravity of the offense compared to the harshness of the penalty. At the threshold, we note that Ewing incorrectly frames the issue. The gravity of his offense was not merely "shoplifting three golf clubs." Rather, Ewing was convicted of felony grand theft for stealing nearly $1,200 worth of merchandise after previously having been convicted of at least two "violent" or "serious" felonies. Even standing alone, Ewing's theft should not be taken lightly. . . . Theft of $1,200 in property is a felony under federal law, 18 U.S.C. §641, and in the vast majority of States. . . .

In weighing the gravity of Ewing's offense, we must place on the scales not only his current felony, but also his long history of felony recidivism. Any other approach would fail to accord proper deference to the policy judgments that find expression in the legislature's choice of sanctions. . . . To give full effect to the State's choice of this legitimate penological goal, our proportionality review of Ewing's sentence must take that goal into account.

. . . To be sure, Ewing's sentence is a long one. But it reflects a rational legislative judgment, entitled to deference, that offenders who have committed serious or violent felonies and who continue to commit felonies must be incapacitated. . . . Ewing's is not the rare case in which a threshold comparison of the crime committed and the sentence imposed leads to an inference of gross disproportionality. We hold that Ewing's sentence of 25 years to life in prison, imposed for the offense of felony grand theft under the three strikes law, is not grossly disproportionate and therefore does not violate the Eighth Amendment's prohibition on cruel and unusual punishments. . . .

SCALIA, J., concurring.

[The] Eighth Amendment's prohibition of "cruel and unusual punishments" was aimed at excluding only certain *modes* of punishment, and was not a guarantee against disproportionate sentences. . . . Proportionality — the notion that the punishment should fit the crime — is inherently a concept tied to the penological goal of retribution. It becomes difficult even to speak intelligently of "proportionality," once deterrence and rehabilitation are given significant weight — not to mention giving weight to the purpose of California's three strikes law: incapacitation. In the present case, the game is up once the plurality has acknowledged that "the Constitution does not mandate adoption of any one penological theory.". . . That acknowledgment having been made, it no longer suffices merely to assess the gravity of the offense compared to the harshness of the penalty . . . ; that classic description of the proportionality principle (alone and in itself quite resistant to policy-free, legal analysis) now becomes merely the "first" step of the inquiry. . . . Having completed that step (by a discussion which, in all fairness, does not convincingly establish that 25-years-to-life is a "proportionate" punishment for stealing three golf clubs), the plurality must then *add* an analysis to show that "Ewing's sentence is justified by the State's public-safety interest in incapacitating and deterring recidivist felons." . . .

Which indeed it is — though why that has anything to do with the principle of proportionality is a mystery. Perhaps the plurality should revise its terminology, so that what it reads into the Eighth Amendment is not the unstated proposition that all punishment should be reasonably proportionate to the gravity of the offense, but rather the unstated proposition that all punishment should reasonably pursue the multiple purposes of the criminal law. That formulation would make it clearer than ever, of course, that the plurality is not applying law but evaluating policy. . . .

NOTES

1. *Constitutional limits and punishment theory.*   The Eighth Amendment of the U.S. Constitution states that "[e]xcessive bail shall not be required, nor excessive fines imposed, nor cruel and unusual punishments inflicted." In your view, does the Amendment expressly embrace a particular theory of punishment? Does it prevent a legislature or other sentencing decision maker from embracing a particular theory of punishment or set of theories?

2. *Proportionality and punishment theory.*   As discussed in *Ewing,* the Supreme Court has generally interpreted the Eighth Amendment's prohibition of cruel and unusual punishments to incorporate a "narrow proportionality principle that applies to noncapital sentences." (The application of the Eighth Amendment to capital sentencing is a more intricate story and is discussed more fully in Chapter 3.) Yet while reaffirming a proportionality limit on punishments based on the Constitution, Justice O'Connor asserted in the excerpt above that "the Constitution does not mandate adoption of any one penological theory. A sentence can have a variety of justifications, such as incapacitation, deterrence, retribution, or rehabilitation. Some or all of these justifications may play a role in a State's sentencing scheme." Are these positions reconcilable, or is Justice Scalia correct when he asserts that proportionality "is inherently a concept tied to the penological goal of retribution" and that one can hardly "speak

intelligently of 'proportionality' once deterrence and rehabilitation are given significant weight"?

Though Justice Scalia is not alone in linking proportionality concepts to theories of retribution, philosophers who favor other theories of punishment have also embraced proportionality. Eighteenth-century English philosopher Jeremy Bentham, a chief proponent of utilitarian justifications for punishment, argued at some length "that a punishment [should] adapt itself to rules of proportionality," and he warned that "if the evil of the punishment exceeds the evil of the offense, the legislator will produce more suffering than he prevents." Jeremy Bentham, The Theory of Legislation 322-338 (C. K. Ogden ed., Harcourt, Brace and Co. 1931) (1802).

Though five Justices voted to uphold Ewing's sentence, four others asserted that his sentence violated the Constitution's proportionality requirement. In his dissenting opinion (a portion of which is reprinted in Chapter 7), Justice Breyer stated he could not accept the assertion that Ewing's sentence " would further a significant criminal justice objective":

> One might argue that those who commit several *property* crimes should receive long terms of imprisonment in order to "incapacitate" them, i.e., to prevent them committing further crimes in the future. But that is not the object of this particular three strikes statute. Rather, as the plurality says, California seeks "to reduce *serious* and *violent* crime." The statute's definitions of both kinds of crime include crimes against the person, crimes that create danger of physical harm, and drug crimes. They do not include even serious crimes against property, such as obtaining large amounts of money, say, through theft, embezzlement, or fraud. Given the omission of vast categories of property crimes . . . from the "strike" definition, one cannot argue, on *property-crime-related incapacitation grounds,* for inclusion of Ewing's crime among the triggers.
>
> Nor do the remaining criminal law objectives seem relevant. No one argues for Ewing's inclusion within the ambit of the three strikes statute on grounds of "retribution." [I]n terms of "deterrence," Ewing's 25-year term amounts to overkill. And "rehabilitation" is obviously beside the point. The upshot is that, in my view, the State cannot find in its three strikes law a special criminal justice need sufficient to rescue a sentence that other relevant considerations indicate is unconstitutional.

3. *Recidivism and punishment theory.*   The Supreme Court's decision in *Ewing* establishes that states are not constitutionally precluded from harshly punishing repeat offenders, but it does not embrace such harsh punishment as a matter of theory or policy. If you had been the prosecutor or the judge involved in the conviction and sentencing of John Albert Ewing, and you realized that California's law gave you some discretion in the application of the three-strikes statute, would you want to "throw the book" at Ewing and seek to impose the longest possible sentence because of his significant criminal record? Consider whether your answer to this question should be influenced not only by constitutional concerns but also by your own sense of the intended application of California's three-strikes law. Put another way, do you think those who voted for the passage of California's three-strikes law thought a life sentence for stealing a few golf clubs was a sound and appropriate sentence for John Albert Ewing in light of his criminal history? If you are not convinced of the soundness of this sentence, is your position based on one or more of the classic theories of punishment or on some other grounds?

California embraced, through its three-strikes law, incapacitation as its principal theory of punishment for sentencing repeat offenders. Do you think incapacitation should be a central theory of punishment for any and every offender with any criminal record, or only for offenders with extensive criminal histories? If the adoption of incapacitation theory is sound for repeat offenders, should it also be adopted for first offenders? Does the nature of an offender's crimes and prior sentences influence your answers to these questions? For example, should the role of incapacitative theory vary depending on whether an offender has committed violent offenses like assault, property offenses like theft, sex offenses like rape, or other offenses like drug trafficking? Should the role of incapacitative theory vary depending on whether an offender was given a fine or sentenced to probation or incarcerated in prison for a prior offense?

The following policy paper drafted by the U.S. Sentencing Commission reveals some of the complications that arise when devising structured and comprehensive rules for considering criminal history at sentencing.

Simplification Paper: Criminal History
U.S. Sentencing Commission, reprinted in 9 Fed. Sentencing Rep. 216 (1997)

Criminal history [is incorporated in the federal sentencing guidelines through a series of rules that], in conjunction with [rules for defining the seriousness of the current offense], determines the guideline range. This paper discusses Chapter Four [which establishes the rules for sentencing consideration of criminal history].

There are both philosophical and practical reasons for including criminal history as a major component of the federal sentencing guidelines. Criminal history can serve several important functions in setting sentencing recommendations. It can be used to measure increased culpability, predict future criminality, and selectively target dangerous offenders. . . .

There have been various debates as to propriety and purpose of using criminal history to determine a defendant's sentence. Retributionists or those who believe in the "just deserts" philosophy argue that punishment should be proportionate to the defendant's culpability for his/her current offense of conviction. Those who argue that retribution is a key principle in sentencing argue for a significantly reduced role for criminal history. For example, Richard Singer (1978) argues that criminal history is inappropriate to consider at sentencing because the defendant has already been punished for the previous offense. He contends that a defendant has no greater culpability (blameworthiness) because of having committed the prior offense; nor is victimization greater in the current offense as a result of the prior offense.

Andrew Von Hirsch, a noted retributionist, argues that criminal history should play only a minor role at sentencing, impacting sentence only to the extent that the defendant's culpability is enhanced due to his/her prior offenses. Von Hirsch argues that offenders who are being sentenced for their first offense have less culpability due to their not having been punished previously. According to Von Hirsch, the first sentence communicates that the behavior is wrong and will not be tolerated. A sentence for a second violation can reflect the "full" weight of the law because the offender has been alerted previously to the unacceptability of the behavior.[2]

A contrary theory of the role of criminal justice is incapacitation. This approach advocates the expanded use of imprisonment to incapacitate offenders. Incapacitation takes two forms: collective and selective. Both forms assume that while offenders are incarcerated they will not be able to engage in additional criminal behavior. Collective incapacitation seeks to prevent crime by increasing the rate and duration of imprisonment for a broad range of offenders, without specific prediction of future criminality. In contrast, selective incapacitation seeks to prevent crime by using certain criteria to identify for restraint a smaller number of offenders who are predicted to commit more crime and/or serious crime. Selective incapacitation also can reduce punishment for persons who are predicted to be less likely to commit additional crimes or to commit serious crimes.

Society and its elected representatives have reached a level of frustration with crime so that current policies more frequently tend to reflect the selective incapacitation philosophy in sentencing practices in general and criminal history in particular. Advocates of selective incapacitation argue that some offenders have shown themselves to be too dangerous (given the frequency or severity of their criminal conduct) to be permitted to remain in society. These advocates have successfully swayed Congress and state legislators that, for the safety of society, presence of an extensive or violent prior record warrants severe sanction for the current offense (e.g., habitual offender provisions in the states and career offender provision in the federal system).[3] Consequently, in many criminal justice systems, criminal history is seen as a crucial component of the determination of an offender's sentence because of its use as a predictor of future criminality.

The Commission determined that criminal history was a major factor in past sentencing practices and should be a major component in the sentencing guidelines. In addition, the Commission believed that with its congressional mandate to consider the breadth of sentencing purposes (rehabilitation, deterrence, incapacitation, and just punishment), it had to consider criminal history as a major component of the guideline sentence. In designing Chapter Four, the Commission considered various philosophical arguments regarding the

---

2. Currently, no guideline system completely disregards the defendant's prior record in the determination of sentence. However, some states do consider aspects of retributionist theory. Minnesota, for example, used this theory in a modified format by adjusting the slope of its imprisonment/non-imprisonment line to focus more on the current offense.

3. States vary in their use of selective incapacitation. For example, in the Pennsylvania guidelines, all prior convictions are included in the computation of the criminal history score, although some offenses are weighed more heavily than others. Because the focus is on the number of prior offenses, little distinction is made between types of offender. In contrast, Oregon uses a typography classification of offenders that focuses not on the number of prior convictions, but, instead, the type of prior offenses committed with violent offenders and repeat non-violent felony offenders targeted for longer sentences. Each prior conviction does not necessarily contribute to the criminal history score.

appropriate use of prior record in determining a defendant's sentence, including arguments regarding "just deserts" and selective incapacitation. The Commission hoped to diminish the conflict between the two ideologies by incorporating elements from both in assessing criminal history.

A defendant with a record of prior criminal behavior is more culpable than a first offender and thus deserving of a greater punishment. General deterrence of criminal conduct dictates that a clear message be sent to society that repeated criminal behavior will aggravate the need for punishment with each recurrence. To protect the public from further crimes of the particular defendant, the likelihood of recidivism and future criminal behavior must be considered. Repeated criminal behavior is an indicator of a limited likelihood of successful rehabilitation.

In the end, Chapter Four was designed to address the frequency, seriousness, and recency of the defendant's prior record. The Commission believed these items were reliable predictors of future criminal conduct. . . .

[T]he federal sentencing guidelines are unique in their approach to criminal history. It is the only system that measures the severity of the prior offense by the length of the sentence imposed for the previous conviction. Specifically, the guidelines give three points for each sentence greater than one year and one month, two points for each sentence of 60 days but not more than one year and one month, and one point for any other sentence. Up to three points also can be assigned if the defendant was under a criminal justice sentence at the time the instant offense was committed, and he/she had been released from a sentence of imprisonment within two years of the commencement of the instant offense. This criminal history score is translated into one of six criminal history categories in the Sentencing Table. The higher the category, the higher the guideline sentence for any given offense level. . . .

While there is some variation in approach, almost every sentencing guideline system considers a defendant's prior record in the determination of the sentence. Most states measure both the number and seriousness of prior convictions. Some states weigh prior convictions depending on their severity. Minnesota, for example, assigns prior felony offenses from one-half to two points depending upon the offense's "severity level." [I]n the Pennsylvania Sentencing Guidelines, the most serious category of prior convictions includes murder, voluntary manslaughter, kidnapping, rape, involuntary deviate intercourse, arson, and robbery. Convictions for these offenses receive four points, the maximum amount assessable for a prior conviction. Similarly, in Oregon, criminal history is categorized by prior offense type specifically violent versus nonviolent offenses. . . .

[One] criticism of the federal guidelines' present scheme is its lack of precision in measuring the severity of prior record. For example, because three points are given for each sentence of more than one year and one month, the guidelines make no distinction between a 14-month sentence and a 15-year sentence. Arguably, these two sentences may reflect the seriousness of substantially different prior offenses. Under the current system, there is no differentiation between a fraud and a rape if they both receive sentences of imprisonment of more than one year and one month.

Another area in which the current criminal history score treats seemingly different offenders the same is in Criminal History Category I. . . . Currently,

Criminal History Category I treats a wide range of defendants similarly despite the fact that they have dissimilar levels of previous contact with the criminal justice system. For example, defendants who have no prior record (no prior arrests, no pending charges, no dismissed charges, no prior convictions) are in Category I along with defendants who have at least one prior conviction that received a sentence of imprisonment of at least 60 days.[13] Title 28, section 994(j) requires the Commission to "insure that the guidelines reflect the general appropriateness of imposing a sentence other than imprisonment in cases in which the defendant is a first offender who has not been convicted of a crime of violence or an otherwise serious offense. . . ." By not incorporating a "first offender category" in the guidelines, critics argue that the Commission did not adequately address the statutory directive at Title 28, section 994(j) related to first offenders. However, the Commission's compliance with this directive has been challenged in a number of cases and uniformly rejected. . . .

There is general agreement among sentencing theorists that the importance of a previous conviction diminishes over time. In keeping with this theory, the Commission chose to limit the impact of "decaying" prior convictions by requiring that they fall within various time periods. It is not the limitation of old prior convictions that adds complexity. The complexity results because the guidelines have five different applicable time periods for the assessment of criminal history points. These time periods depend upon both the length of the sentence imposed and the age of the defendant when the prior offense was committed, and in one instance, whether the prior was imposed as an adult or juvenile sentence.

State guideline systems vary in their use of applicable time periods. States that limit consideration of offenses generally use one applicable time period for all offenses. . . . Some states that do not restrict the time period in which prior offenses can be counted instead have "crime-free" periods from which the defendant benefits. In these states, if the defendant remains "conviction free" for a period of time (usually 10 or 15 years not including periods of imprisonment or release on probation or parole) prior to the instant offense, any convictions prior to that period are not counted. Others leave this item as a departure consideration.

One of the frequently debated issues regarding the prior record measurement is whether to include juvenile adjudications, and if so, to what extent. Currently, the federal guidelines consider offenses that occurred prior to the defendant's eighteenth birthday, except under certain circumstances. Some would argue that juvenile adjudications should not contribute to the criminal history score because juvenile courts typically focus on the juvenile's welfare and treatment, and generally have a more informal process. Moreover, the juvenile courts' standard of proof may be somewhat lower than adult courts. More importantly, juvenile records are less reliable than adult records because

---

13. This category includes the following defendants: (1) a person with no contact with any criminal justice system of any kind, (2) a person who may have had contact with the criminal justice system, such as arrests or dismissed charges and, (3) a person with convictions not countable under the guidelines for a variety of reasons, such as the "age" of the conviction, the locality where the conviction occurred, and the minor nature of the offense.

of different jurisdictional policies on recording and disclosing juvenile offenses. This inconsistency can result in great disparity in the criminal history score computation.

Nonetheless, most states include juvenile adjudications in the computation of criminal history score because many argue that juvenile record, in particular violent behavior, is a strong predictor of future criminal conduct. In fact, some restrict the use of juvenile offenses to include only convictions for violent offenses. Others restrict the use of juvenile offenses if the defendant is an older offender. For example, in Maryland, juvenile convictions are not included in the sentence determination if the defendant is 26 years of age or older at the time of commission of the instant offense; the argument being that as the offender gets older, the use of a juvenile record as predictor of criminality diminishes. . . .

NOTES

1. *Recidivism and punishment theory in practice.* The above discussion of criminal history rules in the federal sentencing guidelines begins by highlighting the linkage between considerations of prior criminal history and sentencing theories, as well as the robust debate among theorists about these matters. But note the conclusion of this theoretical discussion:

> In designing Chapter Four, the Commission considered various philosophical arguments regarding the appropriate use of prior record in determining a defendant's sentence, including arguments regarding "just deserts" and selective incapacitation. The Commission hoped to diminish the conflict between the two ideologies by incorporating elements from both in assessing criminal history.

Is it possible to design sentencing rules to "diminish the conflict" between the just-desert and incapacitation theories? Do the rules for considering criminal history under the federal sentencing guidelines as described in this excerpt succeed in diminishing the conflict? Consider the following assessment of the actual rules developed for the federal sentencing guidelines:

> [T]he arguments for viewing the criminal history guidelines as utilitarian in orientation are powerful. Utilitarianism offers a coherent justification for taking prior criminal records into account generally. It helps to explain specific structural features of the Commission's rules. It is consistent with the considerations the Commission actually took into account when developing these guidelines. In its Supplementary Report on the original guidelines, the Commission virtually acknowledged that utilitarianism was the dominant justification for the criminal history rules [by stating the rules were] "included primarily for crime-control considerations."

Aaron J. Rappaport, Rationalizing the Commission: The Philosophical Premises of the U.S. Sentencing Guidelines, 52 Emory L. J. 558, 594-595 (2003).

2. *Detailed sentencing rules and punishment theory in practice.* As the excerpt above highlights, numerous complications and many intricate details arise in the development of structured sentencing rules; this is true not only for criminal history issues but for all areas of sentencing decision making, as we shall see

throughout the book. Can the resolution of these complications and details turn on matters of punishment theory? Should they?

b. Justifying Particular Forms of Punishment Such as the Death Penalty

Should the consideration and application of theories of punishment change when particular forms of punishment are being considered? Historically, there has often been a direct connection between the forms of punishment employed and the theories of punishment being pursued.

For example, one of the most important (and ironic) modern sentencing developments concerns the evolution of imprisonment as a form of punishment and of prisons as an institution for punishment. The penitentiary was developed and structured as a form of punishment with the express goal of "curing" offenders of their criminal tendencies. The belief in the nineteenth century was that imprisonment, by removing an offender from certain corrupting influences in his community while also providing an offender with the time and opportunity to reflect on his misdeeds, would reform and rehabilitate criminals in ways that physical punishment could not. See generally David J. Rothman, Perfecting the Prison: United States, 1789-1865, in The Oxford History of the Prison 111 (1995). For more than a century, many proponents of imprisonment continued to argue that rehabilitation could be furthered through incarceration.

But, by the mid-1980s, many observers had come to recognize that most prison environments, in which prisoners were more often warehoused than treated, were more likely to provide criminal training than to rehabilitate effectively. Consequently, in the Sentencing Reform Act of 1984, Congress expressly instructed the U.S. Sentencing Commission that its development of federal sentencing rules should "reflect the inappropriateness of imposing a sentence to a term of imprisonment for the purpose of rehabilitating the defendant or providing the defendant with needed educational or vocational training, medical care, or other correctional treatment." 28 U.S.C. §994(k). But even today, despite the widespread belief that prison is not an effective environment for rehabilitation, many state sentencing systems (and even aspects of the federal system) continue to pursue rehabilitative goals through incarceration. Indeed, at least one scholar has recently asserted that the "only rationale for the design of prison programs that is possible and acceptable in this society is rehabilitation." Edward Rubin, The Inevitability of Rehabilitation, 19 Law & Ineq. 343 (2001).

Perhaps even more than imprisonment, the use of the death penalty has generated considerable debate and commentary about the connection between certain forms of punishment and the purposes of punishment. In fact, though most public debates over sentencing issues are rarely cast in theoretical terms, modern public debates over the death penalty frequently explore whether it is an effective deterrent to murder, whether a life sentence without the possibility of parole can incapacitate as well as an execution, and whether concepts of retribution justify use of this ultimate punishment for the most heinous of crimes. The unique severity and finality of the death penalty always brings added attention and a heightened dynamic to traditional debates over the theories of punishment.

Many insights can be drawn from a close examination of the classic theoretical debates surrounding the death penalty. Perhaps an even deeper insight might be drawn from the fact that capital punishment's severity prompts us to explore these theoretical issues more frequently and explicitly. Part of what makes the death penalty so worthy of study is that the unique mental impact of life-and-death decision making helps ensure that we do not become complacent in our consideration of the issues that surround sentencing and punishment choices. To seize on a well-worn phrase in these debates, "death is different," and that difference informs our thinking about sentencing theory in ways that few other punishments can.

Rather than provide a standard review of the ways in which classic theories of punishment have been analyzed and discussed in the context of the death penalty, the next reading is designed to reorient your perspective on the death penalty in particular and on sentencing and punishment more generally. As the reading suggests, it can be argued that the unique drama of the death penalty may itself justify the use of this ultimate punishment; this insight should in turn prompt reconsideration of the importance of the "expressive" function of sentencing and punishment.

For Capital Punishment: The Morality of Anger, Walter Berns
Harpers, Apr. 1979, at 15-20

Until recently, my business did not require me to think about the punishment of criminals in general or the legitimacy and efficacy of capital punishment in particular. In a vague way, I was aware of the disagreement among professionals concerning the purpose of punishment — whether it was intended to deter others, to rehabilitate the criminal, or to pay him back — but like most laymen I had no particular reason to decide which purpose was right or to what extent they may all have been right. I did know that retribution was held in ill repute among criminologists and jurists — to them, retribution was a fancy name for revenge, and revenge was barbaric — and, of course, I knew that capital punishment had the support only of policemen, prison guards, and some local politicians. . . . The intellectual community denounced it as both unnecessary and immoral. It was the phenomenon of Simon Wiesenthal that allowed me to understand why the intellectuals were wrong and why the police, politicians, and the majority of the voters were right: We punish criminals principally in order to pay them back, and we execute the worst of them out of moral necessity. Anyone who respects Wiesenthal's mission will be driven to the same conclusion.

Of course, not everyone will respect that mission. It will strike the busy man — I mean the sort of man who sees things only in the light cast by a concern for his own interests — as somewhat bizarre. Why should anyone devote his life — more than thirty years of it! — exclusively to the task of hunting down the Nazi war criminals who survived World War II and escaped punishment? Wiesenthal says his conscience forces him "to bring the guilty ones to trial." But why punish them? What do we hope to accomplish now by punishing SS Obersturmbannführer Adolf Eichmann or SS Obersturmbannführer Franz Stangl or someday — who knows? — Reichsleiter Martin Bormann? We surely don't expect to rehabilitate them, and it would be foolish to think that by punishing them we might thereby deter others. The answer, I think, is clear: We want to punish them in order *to pay them back*. We think they must be made to pay for their crimes with their lives, and we think that we, the survivors of the world they violated, may legitimately exact that payment because we, too, are their victims. By punishing them, we demonstrate that there are laws that bind men across generations as well as across (and within) nations, that we are not simply isolated individuals, each pursuing his selfish interests and connected with others by a mere contract to live and let live. To state it simply, Wiesenthal allows us to see that it is right, morally right, to be angry with criminals and to express that anger publicly, officially, and in an appropriate manner, which may require the worst of them to be executed.

Modern civil-libertarian opponents of capital punishment do not understand this. They say that to execute a criminal is to deny his human dignity; they also say that the death penalty is not useful, that nothing useful is accomplished by executing anyone. Being utilitarians, they are essentially selfish men, distrustful of passion, who do not understand the connection between anger and justice, and between anger and human dignity.

Anger is expressed or manifested on those occasions when someone has acted in a manner that is thought to be unjust, and one of its origins is the opinion that men are responsible, and should be held responsible, for what they do. Thus, as Aristotle teaches us, anger is accompanied not only by the pain caused by the one who is the object of anger, but by the pleasure arising from the expectation of inflicting revenge on someone who is thought to deserve it. We can become angry with an inanimate object (the door we run into and then kick in return) only by foolishly attributing responsibility to it, and we cannot do that for long, which is why we do not think of returning later to revenge ourselves on the door. For the same reason, we cannot be more than momentarily angry with any one creature other than man; only a fool and worse would dream of taking revenge on a dog. And, finally, we tend to pity rather than to be angry with men who — because they are insane, for example — are not responsible for their acts. Anger, then, is a very human passion not only because only a human being can be angry, but also because anger acknowledges the humanity of its objects: it holds them accountable for what they do. And in holding particular men responsible, it pays them the respect that is due them as men. Anger recognizes that only men have the capacity to be moral beings and, in so doing, acknowledges the dignity of human beings. Anger is somehow connected with justice, and it is this that modern penology has not understood; it tends, on the whole, to regard anger as a selfish indulgence.

Anger can, of course, be that; and if someone does not become angry with an insult or an injury suffered unjustly, we tend to think he does not think much of himself. But it need not be selfish, not in the sense of being provoked only by an injury suffered by oneself. There were many angry men in America when President Kennedy was killed; one of them — Jack Ruby — took it upon himself to exact the punishment that, if indeed deserved, ought to have been exacted by the law. There were perhaps even angrier men when Martin Luther King, Jr. was killed, for King, more than anyone else at the time, embodied a people's quest for justice; the anger — more, the "black rage" — expressed on that occasion was simply a manifestation of the great change that had occurred among black men in America, a change wrought in large part by King and his associates in the civil-rights movement; the servility and fear of the past had been replaced by pride and anger, and the treatment that had formerly been accepted as a matter of course or as if it were deserved was now seen for what it was, unjust and unacceptable. King preached love, but the movement he led depended on anger as well as love, and that anger was not despicable, being neither selfish nor unjustified. On the contrary, it was a reflection of what was called solidarity and may more accurately be called a profound caring for others, black for other blacks, white for blacks, and, in the world King was trying to build, American for other Americans. If men are not saddened when someone else suffers, or angry when someone else suffers unjustly, the implication is that they do not care for anyone other than themselves or that they lack some quality that befits a man. When we criticize them for this, we acknowledge that they ought to care for others. If men are not angry when a neighbor suffers at the hands of a criminal, the implication is that their moral faculties have been corrupted, that they are not good citizens.

Criminals are properly the objects of anger, and the perpetrators of terrible crimes — for example, Lee Harvey Oswald and James Earl Ray — are properly the objects of great anger. They have done more than inflict an injury on an isolated individual; they have violated the foundations of trust and friendship, the necessary elements of a moral community, the only community worth living in. A moral community, unlike a hive of bees or a hill of ants, is one whose members are expected freely to obey the laws, and unlike those in a tyranny, are trusted to obey the laws. The criminal has violated that trust, and in so doing has injured not merely his immediate victim but the community as such. He has called into question the very possibility of that community by suggesting that men cannot be trusted to respect freely the property, the person, and the dignity of those with whom they are associated. If, then, men are not angry when someone else is robbed, raped, or murdered, the implication is that no moral community exists, because those men do not care for anyone other than themselves. Anger is an expression of that caring, and society needs men who care for one another, who share their pleasures and their pains, and do so for the sake of the others. It is the passion that can cause us to act for reasons having nothing to do with selfish or mean calculation; indeed, when educated, it can become a generous passion, the passion that protects the community or country by demanding punishment for its enemies. It is the stuff from which heroes are made.

A moral community is not possible without anger and the moral indignation that accompanies it. Thus the most powerful attack on capital punishment was written by a man, Albert Camus, who denied the legitimacy of anger and moral indignation by denying the very possibility of a moral community in our time. The anger expressed in our world, he said, is nothing but hypocrisy. His novel *L'Etranger* (variously translated as *The Stranger* or *The Outsider*) is a brilliant portrayal of what Camus insisted is our world, a world deprived of God, as he put it. It is a world we would not choose to live in and one that Camus, the hero of the French Resistance, disdained. Nevertheless, the novel is a modern masterpiece, and Meursault, its antihero (for a world without anger can have no heroes), is a murderer.

[Other people] pretend not to know what Camus the opponent of capital punishment tells: namely, that "our civilization has lost the only values that, in a certain way, can justify that penalty . . . [the existence of] a truth or a principle that is superior to man." There is no basis for friendship and no moral law; therefore, no one, not even a murderer, can violate the terms of friendship or break that law; and there is no basis for the anger that we express when someone breaks that law. The only thing we share as men, the only thing that connects us one to another, is a "solidarity against death," and a judgment of capital punishment "upsets" that solidarity. The purpose of human life is to stay alive. . . .

. . . In *Macbeth,* Shakespeare shows us murders committed in a political world by a man so driven by ambition to rule that world that he becomes a tyrant. He shows us also the consequences, which were terrible, worse even than Macbeth feared. The cosmos rebelled, turned into chaos by his deeds. He shows a world that was not "benignly indifferent" to what we call crimes and especially to murder, a world constituted by laws divine as well as human, and Macbeth violated the most awful of those laws. Because the world was so constituted, Macbeth suffered the torments of the great and the damned, torments far beyond the "practice" of any physician. He had known glory and had deserved the respect and affection of king, countrymen, army, friends, and wife; and he lost it all. At the end he was reduced to saying that life "is a tale told by an idiot, full of sound and fury, signifying nothing"; yet, in spite of the horrors provoked in us by his acts, he excites no anger in us. We pity him; even so, we understand the anger of his countrymen and the dramatic necessity of his death. *Macbeth* is a play about ambition, murder, tyranny; about horror, anger, vengeance, and, perhaps more than any other of Shakespeare's plays, justice. Because of justice, Macbeth has to die, not by his own hand — he will not "play the Roman fool, and die on [his] sword"— but at the hand of the avenging Macduff. The dramatic necessity of his death would appear to rest on its *moral* necessity. Is that right? Does this play conform to our sense of what a murder means? Lincoln thought it was "wonderful."

Surely Shakespeare's is a truer account of murder than the one provided by Camus, and by truer I mean truer to our moral sense of what a murder is and what the consequences that attend it must be. Shakespeare shows us vengeful men because there is something in the souls of men — then and now — that requires such crimes to be revenged. Can we imagine a world that does not take its revenge on the man who kills Macduff's wife and children? (Can we imagine the play in which Macbeth does not die?) Can we imagine a people that does not hate murderers? (Can we imagine a world where Meursault is an outsider only because he does not *pretend* to be outraged by murder?) Shakespeare's poetry could not have been written out of the moral sense that the death penalty's opponents insist we ought to have. Indeed, the issue of capital punishment can be said to turn on whether Shakespeare's or Camus' is the more telling account of murder.

. . . In *Macbeth* the majesty of the moral law is demonstrated to us; . . . it teaches us the awesomeness of the commandment Thou shalt not kill. In a similar fashion, the punishments imposed by the legal order remind us of the reign of the moral order; not only do they remind us of it, but by enforcing its prescriptions, they enhance the dignity of the legal order in the eyes of moral men, in the eyes of those decent citizens who cry out "for gods who will avenge injustice." That is especially important in a self-governing community, a community that gives laws to itself. . . .

Supreme Court Justices have occasionally complained of our habit of making "constitutionality synonymous with wisdom." But the extent to which the Constitution is venerated and its authority accepted depends on the compatibility of its rules with our moral sensibilities; despite its venerable character, the Constitution is not the only source of these moral sensibilities. There was even a period, before slavery was abolished by the Thirteenth Amendment, when the Constitution was regarded by some very moral men as an abomination: Garrison called it "a covenant with death and an agreement with Hell," and there were honorable men holding important political offices and judicial appointments who refused to enforce the Fugitive Slave Law even though its constitutionality had been affirmed. In time this opinion spread far beyond the ranks of the original abolitionists until those who held it composed a constitutional majority of the people, and slavery was abolished.

But Lincoln knew that more than amendments were required to make the Constitution once more worthy of the veneration of moral men. That is why, in the Gettysburg Address, he made the principle of the Constitution an inheritance from "our fathers." That it should be so esteemed is especially important in a self-governing nation that gives laws to itself, because it is only a short step from the principle that the laws are merely a product of one's own will to the opinion that the only consideration that informs the law is self-interest; and this opinion is only one remove from lawlessness. A nation of simple self-interested men will soon enough perish from the earth.

[Lincoln's] words at Gettysburg serve to remind Americans in particular of what Hegel said people in general needed to know, and could be made to know by means of war and the sacrifices demanded of them in wars; namely, that their country is something more than a "civil society" the purpose of which is simply the protection of individual and selfish interests.

Capital punishment, like Shakespeare's dramatic and Lincoln's political poetry (and it is surely that, and was understood by him to be that), serves to remind us of the majesty of the moral order that is embodied in our law, and of the terrible consequences of its breach. The law must not be understood to be merely a statute that we enact or repeal at our will, and obey or disobey at our convenience — especially not the criminal law. Wherever law is regarded as merely statutory, men will soon enough disobey it, and will learn how to do so without any inconvenience to themselves. The criminal law must possess a dignity far beyond that possessed by mere statutory enactment or utilitarian and self-interested calculations. The most powerful means we have to give it that dignity is to authorize it to impose the ultimate penalty. The criminal law must be made awful, by which I mean inspiring, or commanding "profound respect or reverential fear." It must remind us of the moral order by which alone we can live as *human* beings, and in America, now that the Supreme Court has outlawed banishment, the only punishment that can do this is capital punishment.

The founder of modern criminology, the eighteenth-century Italian Cesare Beccaria, opposed both banishment and capital punishment because he understood that both were inconsistent with the principle of self-interest, and self-interest was the basis of the political order he favored. If a man's first and only duty is to himself, of course he will prefer his money to his country; he will also prefer his money to his brother. In fact, he will prefer his brother's money to his brother, and a people of this description, or a country that understands itself in this Beccarian manner, can put the mark of Cain on no one. For the same reason, such a country can have no legitimate reason to execute its criminals, or, indeed, to punish them in any manner. What would be accomplished by punishment in such a place? Punishment arises out of the demand for justice, and justice is demanded by angry, morally indignant men; its purpose is to satisfy that moral indignation and thereby promote the law-abidingness that, it is assumed, accompanies it. But the principle of self-interest denies the moral basis of that indignation.

Not only will a country based solely on self-interest have no legitimate reason to punish; it may have no need to punish. It may be able to solve what we call the crime problem by substituting a law of contracts for a law of crimes. According to Beccaria's social contract, men agree to yield their natural freedom to the "sovereign" in exchange for his promise to keep the peace. As it becomes more difficult for the sovereign to fulfill his part of the contract, there is a demand that he be made to pay for his nonperformance. From this comes compensation or insurance schemes embodied in statutes whereby the sovereign (or state), being unable to keep the peace by punishing criminals, agrees to compensate its contractual partners for injuries suffered at the hands of criminals, injuries the police are unable to prevent. The insurance policy takes the place of law enforcement and the *posse comitatus,* and John Wayne and Gary Cooper give way to Mutual of Omaha. There is no anger in this kind of law, and none (or no reason for any) in the society. The principle can be carried further still. If we ignore the victim (and nothing we do can restore his life anyway), there would appear to be no reason why — the worth of a man being his price, as Beccaria's teacher, Thomas Hobbes, put it — coverage should not be extended to the losses incurred in a murder. If we ignore the victim's sensibilities (and what are they but absurd vanities?), there would appear to be no reason why — the worth of a woman being *her* price — coverage should not be extended to the losses incurred in a rape. Other examples will no doubt suggest themselves.

This might appear to be an almost perfect solution to what we persist in calling the crime problem, achieved without risking the terrible things sometimes done by an angry people. A people that is not angry with criminals will not be able to deter crime, but a people fully covered by insurance has no need to deter crime: they will be insured against all the losses they can, in principle, suffer. What is now called crime can be expected to increase in volume, of course, and this will cause an increase in the premiums paid, directly or in the form of taxes. But it will no longer be necessary to apprehend, try, and punish criminals, which now costs Americans more than $1.5 billion a month (and is increasing at an annual rate of about 15 percent), and one can buy a lot of insurance for $1.5 billion. There is this difficulty, as Rousseau put it: To exclude anger from the human community is to concentrate all the passions in a "self-interest of the meanest sort," and such a place would not be fit for human habitation.

When, in 1976, the Supreme Court declared death to be a constitutional penalty, it decided that the United States was not that sort of country; most of us, I think, can appreciate that judgment. We want to live among people who do not value their possessions more than their citizenship, who do not think exclusively or even primarily of their own rights, people whom we can depend on even as they exercise their rights, and whom we can trust, which is to say, people who, even in the absence of a policeman, will not assault our bodies or steal our possessions, and might even come to our assistance when we need it, and who stand ready, when the occasion demands it, to risk their lives in defense of their country. If we are of the opinion that the United States may rightly ask of its citizens this awful sacrifice, then we are also of the opinion that it may rightly impose the most awful penalty; if it may rightly honor its heroes, it may rightly execute the worst of its criminals. By doing so, it will remind its citizens that it is a country worthy of heroes.

NOTES

1. *Arguments for and against the death penalty.*   For many observers, the fundamental question about the legitimacy of the death penalty turns on moral arguments. In response to arguments such as that made by Berns, critics argue that the taking of life is immoral, even when done by the state. Other critics attack the barbarity of the sanction itself. Yet others question whether any government can be trusted with such an awesome power, even if the morality of retribution itself is recognized. The literature is vast and impassioned, and includes striking historical, geographical, social, and comparative arguments. See, e.g., Encyclopedia of Capital Punishment (1998); Franklin Zimring, The Contradictions of American Capital Punishment (2003).

2. *New deterrence literature.*   Though long debated and frequently studied, the fundamentally important empirical question of whether the death penalty deters remains unresolved. In 1975 Professor Isaac Ehrlich influenced the course of this debate when he concluded, based on a sophisticated study on data from 1933 to 1969 in the United States, that "an additional execution per year . . . may have resulted (on the average) in 7 or 8 fewer murders." Isaac Ehrlich, The Deterrent Effect of Capital Punishment: A Question of Life and Death, 65 Am. Econ. Rev. 414 (June 1975). Though Ehrlich's data analysis and conclusions have been widely and powerfully assailed, his work succeeded at the time in convincing at least some persons of the potential deterrent impact of capital punishment. See Ernest Van Den Haag, In Defense of the Death Penalty: A Practical and Moral Analysis, 14 Crim. L. Bull. 51 (1978).

Because of significant changes in the modern administration of capital punishment (as explored in Chapter 3), it would be inappropriate to draw a conclusion from Ehrlich's data about the deterrent effect of capital punishment in the United States in the twenty-first century. A number of new studies, however, have purported to establish that the death penalty has a deterrent impact in modern times. See Dale O. Cloninger and Roberto Marchesini, Execution and Deterrence: A Quasi-Controlled Group Experiment, 33 Applied Econ. 569 (2001); Hashem Dezhbakhsh, Paul H. Rubin, and Joanna M. Shepherd, Does Capital Punishment Have a Deterrent Effect? New Evidence from Post-moratorium Panel Data, 5 Amer. L. & Econ. Rev. 344 (2003); H. Naci Mocan and R. Kaj Gittings, Pardons, Executions, and Homicide, NBER Working Paper 8639 (Dec. 2001). As with prior studies making such claims, the data and conclusions in these papers are hotly disputed, and it still is (and likely will always be) difficult to make conclusive statements about the deterrent effect of capital punishment.

Though firm deterrence data may always be elusive, would a truly conclusive and indisputable study resolve the debate over the death penalty? Suppose, based on new research evidence, we could be absolutely positive that each execution of a convicted murderer would deter ten murders and thus save ten innocent lives. In light of such data, could there be any conclusive argument against the death penalty? Imagine the empirical evidence running the other way. Suppose we could be absolutely positive that each execution of a convicted murderer would cause ten additional murders (because of the brutalization impact of having society in the business of state killing) and thus cost ten innocent lives. In light of such data, could there be any conclusive argument for the death penalty?

3. *At what price?*   One fairly isolated argument concerning the death penalty involves the financial cost of operating a functional capital punishment system. Death penalty cases are enormously expensive. See The Costs of the Death Penalty, testimony of Richard C. Deiter, executive director of the Death Penalty Information Center, before the Massachusetts Legislature, Joint Committee on Criminal Justice (available at http://www.deathpenaltyinfo.org/MassCostTestimony.pdf) (reporting various calculations and estimates of the cost of capital cases in different jurisdictions). Indeed, many prosecutors with capital charging authority use it rarely or not at all in part to shepherd resources for the full range of cases, apart from moral, philosophical, or political concerns. See E. Michael McCann, Opposing Capital Punishment: A Prosecutor's Perspective, 79 Marq. L. Rev. 649 (1996) (noting prosecutors' concerns about the costs of the death penalty). Death penalty proponents respond that the costs are high in part because of excessive relitigation of capital claims, and that even at a high cost, a capital sentence may be justified. Other observers find the entire conversation about the cost of the capital system distasteful, holding that moral arguments should be determinative. Some people consider the idea of assessing economic costs in the absence of measures of human cost stilted.

4. *Death as the appropriate penalty for what types of crimes?*   Walter Berns points to the atrocities of the Nazi regime, including genocide and crimes against humanity, as offenses meriting death. Compared to the magnitude of those crimes, what other crimes, if any, deserve the death penalty? Does it not denigrate the enormity and brutality of those offenses if death becomes the punishment for any murder? Consider also that the judges of the recently instituted International Criminal Court cannot impose death sentences even though they try cases of genocide, crimes against humanity, war crimes, and the crime of aggression.

3.   Use of Purposes for Entire Systems

a.   Statutory Direction: Multiple Purposes

When legislators think about the purposes of criminal sentences and punishment, they often articulate goals that do not fit neatly into the traditional philosophical categories. They also likely do not think about individual offenders, but rather imagine more broadly the values and interests that they hope their jurisdiction's entire criminal justice system will pursue. An ever present challenge in modern sentencing systems is to connect legislative statements of purpose with the traditional purposes discussed by philosophers and with actual offenders who confront judges. Consider first in the abstract the various kinds of purposes and goals identified in the following state statutes, and then try to effectuate those purposes and goals in the context of the case study presented in Problem 1-2. Ask yourself whether legislators in the following materials provide useful guidance to prosecutors or sentencing judges, and why legislators may highlight purposes different in some important ways from the classic philosophical justifications explored earlier in this chapter.

‖ *18 United States Code §3553* ‖

IMPOSITION OF A SENTENCE

(a) Factors to be considered in imposing a sentence.— The court shall impose a sentence sufficient, but not greater than necessary, to comply with the purposes set forth in paragraph (2) of this subsection. The court, in determining the particular sentence to be imposed, shall consider—

(1) the nature and circumstances of the offense and the history and characteristics of the defendant;

(2) the need for the sentence imposed—

(A) to reflect the seriousness of the offense, to promote respect for the law, and to provide just punishment for the offense;

(B) to afford adequate deterrence to criminal conduct;

(C) to protect the public from further crimes of the defendant; and

(D) to provide the defendant with needed educational or vocational training, medical care, or other correctional treatment in the most effective manner;

(3) the kinds of sentences available;

(4) the kinds of sentence and the sentencing range established [in the federal sentencing guidelines]; . . .

(6) the need to avoid unwarranted sentence disparities among defendants with similar records who have been found guilty of similar conduct; and

(7) the need to provide restitution to any victims of the offense.

‖ *Ohio Revised Code §2929.11* ‖

PURPOSES OF FELONY SENTENCING

(A) A court that sentences an offender for a felony shall be guided by the overriding purposes of felony sentencing. The overriding purposes of felony sentencing are to protect the public from future crime by the offender and others and to punish the offender. To achieve those purposes, the sentencing court shall consider the need for incapacitating the offender, deterring the offender and others from future crime, rehabilitating the offender, and making restitution to the victim of the offense, the public, or both.

(B) A sentence imposed for a felony shall be reasonably calculated to achieve the two overriding purposes of felony sentencing set forth in division (A) of this section, commensurate with and not demeaning to the seriousness of the offender's conduct and its impact upon the victim, and consistent with sentences imposed for similar crimes committed by similar offenders.

(C) A court that imposes a sentence upon an offender for a felony shall not base the sentence upon the race, ethnic background, gender, or religion of the offender.

‖ *Tennessee Code §40-35-102* ‖

PURPOSE AND INTENT

The foremost purpose of this chapter [on criminal sentencing] is to promote justice [and] in so doing, the following principles are hereby adopted:

(1) Every defendant shall be punished by the imposition of a sentence justly deserved in relation to the seriousness of the offense;

(2) This chapter is to assure fair and consistent treatment of all defendants by eliminating unjustified disparity in sentencing and providing a fair sense of predictability of the criminal law and its sanctions;

(3) Punishment shall be imposed to prevent crime and promote respect for the law by:

(A) Providing an effective general deterrent to those likely to violate the criminal laws of this state;

(B) Restraining defendants with a lengthy history of criminal conduct;

(C) Encouraging effective rehabilitation of those defendants, where reasonably feasible, by promoting the use of alternative sentencing and correctional programs that elicit voluntary cooperation of defendants; and

(D) Encouraging restitution to victims where appropriate;

(4) Sentencing should exclude all considerations respecting race, gender, creed, religion, national origin and social status of the individual;

(5) In recognition that state prison capacities and the funds to build and maintain them are limited, convicted felons committing the most severe offenses, possessing criminal histories evincing a clear disregard for the laws and morals of society, and evincing failure of past efforts at rehabilitation shall be given first priority regarding sentencing involving incarceration; and

(6) A defendant who does not fall within the parameters of subdivision (5) and who is an especially mitigated or standard offender convicted of a Class C, D or E felony is presumed to be a favorable candidate for alternative sentencing options in the absence of evidence to the contrary.

PROBLEM 1-2.   BROMLEY HEATH

A federal grand jury indicted John Thompson, a 24-year-old African American man, on narcotics violations stemming from an investigation of crack cocaine trafficking at the Bromley Heath Housing Development in Jamaica Plain, Massachusetts. The charges grew out of a joint federal-state investigation of crack cocaine trafficking at Bromley Heath. Pursuant to a plea agreement, the defendant pled guilty to one count of distributing cocaine base in violation of 21 U.S.C. §841(a)(1).

Thompson has one prior conviction but has never been incarcerated. His criminal record includes possession of a controlled substance at age 17, a charge that was dismissed; assault and battery at age 19, which resulted in a guilty finding and a six-month probation term; drinking alcohol in public at age 20, a charge that was dismissed; and another recent charge of possession with intent to distribute a controlled substance (a charge brought shortly after the events that form the basis of the current charge, to which he pled guilty).

Thompson lived his entire life in Bromley Heath. He describes his childhood as rough; the majority of it was spent without his father, who was incarcerated much of the time. Thompson dropped out of high school in the eleventh grade when he learned that his girlfriend, Breii Murray, was pregnant with their first child. Thompson was determined to provide for her and their daughter, Jabria, despite his youth and lack of education.

Thompson became a member of Union Local 223 and maintained steady employment until his arrest on these charges. At the time of his arrest, he was employed by M. Solberg Enterprises Corp. and earned about $2,000 per month setting planks, drilling cords, and cutting concrete. His employer has provided a letter saying that Thompson was wanted back at his job.

Murray and Thompson have been in a steady relationship for seven years and are engaged to be married. They now have two daughters together. Thompson is a good father who spends a lot of time with his daughters and enjoys a solid relationship with both of them, particularly Jabria, the elder daughter. He supports his fiancée, their children, and his fiancée's family both economically and emotionally. Murray, along with Murray's mother, aunt, and grandmother, are all supportive of Thompson. They describe him as a wonderful person who has substantially assisted in the upkeep of their home by running errands, doing chores, and contributing $100 per week. All of the women stressed that Thompson's incarceration would make a detrimental impact on their lives, and particularly on the lives of his daughters.

What should Thompson's sentence be? What purposes should guide that sentence? See United States v. Thompson, 190 F. Supp. 2d 138 (D. Mass. 2002).

NOTES

1. *Structure, content, and meaning.*   The structure and language of the three "purposes" statutes reprinted above vary considerably. Consider also the Montana provision that appears at the beginning of this chapter. Do the content and meaning of these statutes vary along with their structure? Do your answers to Problem 1-2 vary depending on which jurisdiction's statute is being applied? Which theory or theories of punishment are adopted in Ohio, Tennessee, and the federal system? Which theory or theories of punishment do these jurisdictions reject?

2. *Parsimony.*   Note that the opening line in the federal statute provides what has been called a "parsimony" requirement by stating that the court "shall impose a sentence sufficient, but not greater than necessary, to comply with the purposes" of punishment. Why do you think Congress included this provision, and what do you think it means? Does it reflect one of the traditional theories of punishment or a different set of values? Notice that neither Ohio nor Montana seems to have a comparable provision, although one might view subdivisions (5) and (6) of Tennessee's statute to pursue related interests. If you were a member of the legislature in Ohio or Montana, would you propose the addition of a parsimony provision?

In the federal system, the parsimony provision has been ignored by the courts and by commentators. How could such strong language have so little impact?

b.   Equality/Disparity Concerns

Because of justifiable concerns about equality (not to mention constitutional requirements), the Ohio statute reprinted above provides that a court shall not base a sentence "upon the race, ethnic background, gender, or religion of the offender." Tennessee similarly provides that sentencing "should exclude all considerations respecting race, gender, creed, religion, national origin and social status of the individual," and Montana states that sentencing practices "must be neutral with respect to the offender's race, gender, religion, national origin, or social or economic status." Federal law has a similar provision, 28 U.S.C. §994(d), which instructs the U.S. Sentencing Commission to "assure that the [sentencing] guidelines and policy statements are entirely neutral as to the race, sex, national origin, creed, and socioeconomic status of offenders." Do you think these requirements of equality are readily integrated with traditional purposes of punishment, or can you envision some tensions between traditional notions of equality and traditional theories of punishment? Consider the following recommendation from the ABA, which focuses on the importance of ensuring principles of equality are safeguarded in sentencing systems.

|| *ABA Standards for Criminal Justice,* ||
Sentencing 18-2.5
(3d ed. 1994)

(a) The legislature should create a sentencing structure that enables the agency performing the intermediate function to make reasonably accurate forecasts of the aggregate of sentencing decisions, including forecasts of the types of sanctions and severity of sentences imposed, so that the legislature can make informed changes in sentence patterns through amendment of the criminal code, or the agency can do so through revised guidance to sentencing courts.

(b) The legislature should create a sentencing structure that sufficiently guides the exercise of sentencing courts' discretion to the end that unwarranted and inequitable disparities in sentences are avoided. . . .

COMMENTARY

Systems of "indeterminate" sentencing, which invest sentencing judges and parole boards with broad discretion in making sentencing decisions, have resulted in unwarranted disparity in individual sentences. . . .[1] Prior editions of these Standards have noted the prevalence of unwarranted sentencing disparities in specific cases, demonstrated in analyses of sentence patterns for similar offenses and in studies of sentence choices by different judges considering identical cases. Some observers have condemned the arbitrary and random nature of indeterminate sentences; others have claimed that such a sentencing structure allows racial and class biases to infect sentencing decisions.

At every level of the drafting process (in the Task Force, the Standards Committee, and the Criminal Justice Section Council), the ABA consistently decided that the traditional practices of indeterminate sentencing, still followed in most states, should be rejected. It is a telling point that through four years of ABA debate, no defense was raised of the old practices of indeterminacy. . . .

The third edition adds an important new component of the requirement of determinacy: Standard 18-2.5(a) states that the sentencing structure should be sufficiently determinate to allow for reasonably accurate forecasts of aggregate sentencing decisions so that the legislature can make informed changes in sentence patterns through amendment of the criminal code, or the agency can do so through revised guidance to sentencing courts. Thus, the Standard contemplates a system in which policy decisions can be made to have predictable impacts on the system as a whole. Also, with adequate determinacy the legislature and agency can address discrete problems in targeted ways. For example, a jurisdiction that wants to heighten the severity of sentences for violent crimes can do so with some precision. If the resulting changes will overload the prison system, the agency can propose offsetting amendments, such as fractional reductions in sentences for nonviolent crimes. Substantial state experience through the 1980s has shown that the related goals of predictability and manageability can be realized in determinate sentencing structures.

This Standard must be read in conjunction with Standard 18-2.6 regarding the "individualization of sentences." Determinacy, as a systemic and case-specific value, is not an absolute good that must be pursued to the exclusion of other concerns. As argued by Kenneth Culp Davis, predictable and uniform rules must always coexist with a degree of flexibility and discretion. The problem is finding the optimum balance between rule and discretion. In the realm of sentencing, this tension is vividly pronounced. . . .

NOTES

1. *The goal of reducing sentencing disparity.*   As discussed more fully in Chapter 3, one of the most prominent goals of modern sentencing reform has been to

---

1. As to the injustices of individualized disparities, the classic work is Marvin E. Frankel, Criminal Sentences: Law Without Order (1973). A valuable study of the unplanned expansion of American prison systems since the 1970s is Franklin E. Zimring & Gordon Hawkins, The Scale of Imprisonment (1991).

reduce unwarranted sentencing disparity. The problems of defining, measuring, and finding solutions to disparity arise throughout sentencing systems. Some of these problems are endemic to discussions of equality and disparity in all contexts. When, for example, are two individuals similar and when are they different? Other problems are especially acute in sentencing; these include the difficulty of describing each offense and offender (for example, is similarity based on offenders' "actual" behavior or the charges for which offenders are convicted?) and the difficulty of measuring and assessing actual sentences (are we concerned with sentences imposed or sentences served? Should fines of fixed dollar amounts be the same if offenders have vastly different resources?).

In practice, among the greatest areas of concern in modern reforms for both apparent and actual inequalities are disparities in treatment by race and, to a lesser extent, gender. Yet there have also been, both historically and throughout modern systems, wide sentencing disparities based on socioeconomic class, geography, and other "status" characteristics. Given the wide range of potential sentencing disparities (and the challenges in defining, measuring, and remedying such disparities), are there certain types of disparity that call for extra attention? In considering this question, examine again the somewhat different groups and commands articulated in the equality provisions of the state statutes reprinted above.

2. *Surface equality and a deep understanding of disparity.*   Concepts of disparity and equality in sentencing can be baffling in part because of three additional puzzles that are worth noting as an introduction to this topic. First, what might be seen as apparent equality — such as giving every offender a five-year sentence — can in fact represent great inequality if offenders or their offenses or both are different in pertinent ways. Because equality means not only treating like cases alike, but also treating different cases differently, an example of two cases sentenced in the same way could actually be evidence of *inequality* if these cases were different in ways that should have led to different sentences. Second, even when two convicted offenders who are similar are sentenced in the same way, inequality can exist if a third similar offender either escapes without being charged or is prosecuted in a different jurisdiction or is charged with a different offense. The different treatment of the third similar offender who "escapes" the standard punishment creates a form of disparity that, though very difficult to measure, undermines efforts to achieve true sentencing equality. Finally, the very ability to assess what factors can and should matter in judging equality and disparity depends in large part on initially selecting an underlying theory of punishment. Two offenders committing similar crimes might deserve similar punishments if sentenced according to retributivist theory, but their personal backgrounds might call for quite different punishments if sentenced with the goal of rehabilitation. If we cannot or do not adopt defined theories of punishment, it becomes very hard to distinguish *warranted* from *unwarranted* sentencing disparity. See Kevin Cole, The Empty Idea of Sentencing Disparity, 91 Nw. U. L. Rev. 1336 (1997).

c.   Cents and Sentencing Ability

A central aspect of most legislative sentencing discussions does not concern traditional justifications for punishment at all. Consider the following document developed by criminal justice policy experts in Ohio to explain to the public what factors influenced criminal punishments and sentencing outcomes in that state. What non-philosophical justifications are offered to define, justify, or limit sentences? How might you characterize these additional kinds of justifications?

> ## The State of Crime and Criminal Justice
> ## in Ohio
> ### The Office of Criminal Justice Services (Jan. 1995)

REASONS FOR CRIMINAL SANCTIONS IN OHIO

How Should Crime Be Punished?

The question, itself, testifies to the complexity of the issue in that it wrongly assumes that punishment (e.g., imprisonment, death) is the only legitimate function of justice at the sentencing level. Incapacitation, deterrence, rehabilitation, restitution and, more recently, forfeiture, are other goals which can and do drive the decisions of legislators, judges, parole officials, corrections authorities, and others who administer criminal sanctions — the carrying out of court sentences — in this State.

For these reasons and others (e.g., legal issues, humane and equitable treatment of offenders) prisons and jails are not necessarily the best sanctions for all felony offenders, as is often assumed. "Alternatives to incarceration," rather than suggesting a second or third preferred choice in the sanctioning process, may in fact provide the best means at a government's disposal for dealing with certain kinds of offenders. . . .

Resources can also dictate choice of sanctions, where judges are given such sentencing discretion. Sometimes judges, faced with severely crowded local jails and little in the way of intermediate options, must choose between the polar extremes of prison and probation in felony sentencing. The problem has grown more extreme in recent years in the face of a dramatic increase in drug-related prison sentences which could be diminished, in number and perhaps severity, by sufficient resources devoted to treatment programs.

Ohioans' attitudes and opinions about sanctions reflect uncertainty about appropriate responses to criminal offenders. There appears to be a general presumption that citizens are frustrated by the leniency and inefficiency of the Criminal Justice System, that they are continually seeking harsher felony punishments than those being handed down in Ohio's criminal courts. Research in Ohio and at the national level suggests that key decision makers, such as legislators, rather consistently assume that the public will not support sanctions which propose something in lieu of prison/jail sentences. However, citizen attitude surveys in Ohio and elsewhere have found that these assumptions overestimate public inflexibility, and that given sufficient information regarding the circumstances of the criminal behavior citizens will support a wide range of other sanction options.

Less than one-third of the citizen respondents in a statewide Office of Criminal Justice Services (OCJS) survey readied for release in 1993 stated a preference for building our way out of the prison/jail crowding crisis in Ohio, while more than half opted for community treatment centers (35%), emergency releases (18%), and more use of probation (7%).

When presented a list of six specific options which could be used to replace or ease incarceration for non-violent offenders the same respondents found five of the six options agreeable by margins ranging from 68% to 76%. Only "fines" fell below the level of public acceptability (48%). "Victim compensation" (68%), "community supervision" (69%), "work release" (73%), "education release" (76%), and "early release" (78%) all found solid support. These results were virtually unchanged from those obtained in a 1984 survey which examined the same question.

Five critical issues largely determine Ohio's capacity to administer effective criminal justice sanctions.

Institutional crowding: Both the Departments of Youth Services (DYS) and Rehabilitation and Correction (DRC) have experienced unprecedented increases in institutional populations during the past decade. DYS populations have risen by half, while DRC's numbers have doubled. Virtually all of the 24 DRC institutions are operating above capacity — 180% statewide. The tremendous growth in numbers appears largely unrelated to broader crime trends, instead being driven by decision choices within the criminal justice system (i.e., legislative, prosecutorial/judicial, parole). Every aspect of Ohio's sanctioning procedures is negatively affected by the institutional crowding crisis.

Impact of substance abuse: This nationwide problem has created special stress for the sanctioning function in criminal justice. Tougher laws and sentencing relative to drunk driving and drug abuse, combined with the usage explosion of crack-cocaine in the latter 1980s have proven especially burdensome for already crowded prisons, jails, youth detention facilities, and treatment programs.

Escalating costs: Funding for new institutional construction is not the major economic cost concern relative to sanctions; the cost of running those institutions is. The average per-year, per-prisoner operational cost to DRC exceeds $12,000, ballooning that agency's annual budget to the three quarters of a billion dollar range. Meeting the basic needs of county jail inmates and juvenile offenders adds more hundreds of millions of dollars each year. In the aftermath of the Lucasville uprising it appears that security costs will dramatically increase in at least some state facilities. While technology promises hope for minimizing the costs of some sanctions (e.g., ankle bracelets for electronic monitoring of house arrestees, hair testing for drug usage supervision of parolees, etc.), the fact remains that Ohio's expenditures on criminal sanctions are increasing dramatically at a time when most items in government budgets are holding level or being reduced.

Effectiveness of treatment: Sentenced criminal offenders bring a wide range of social disorders relating to sexual problems, gambling, child abuse, substance addiction, learning disabilities, and others. Frequently, criminal sanctions include treatment provisions for these disorders, but it is difficult to determine how effective these treatment programs are, especially in light of very limited treatment resources. Much of the future of criminal sanctions may ride on treatment programs with a proven capacity to interrupt criminal careers.

Availability of sanctioning options: Ohio's institutional crowding crisis alone, with its enormous implications for state and local budgets, strongly suggests the development of non-incarceration options for at least some types of offenders. Other issues of justice are also linked to this development, such as sentencing equity, long-term crime costs to society, and the potential tapping of resources outside of the traditional criminal justice arena (e.g., public health).

NOTES

1. *Functional purposes: politics.* Why does this excerpt discuss at some length the results of a survey of Ohio citizens about their attitudes concerning punishment and sentencing? Why should decision makers, who presumably have more knowledge about and time to consider the reasons for and consequences of particular punishment and sentencing issues, be concerned with the opinions of average citizens? Do any of the traditional purposes of punishment depend on or incorporate the perspectives of a majority of average citizens?

Though one can debate whether the views of the general public should matter in determining sentencing and punishment decision making, there is little question that they do have a profound influence on sentencing systems in the United States. Every legislature making sentencing rules in the United States is elected by popular vote, and most judges and prosecutors in state systems are also elected officials. Even sentencing decision makers who are appointed, including some judges and prosecutors and most members of sentencing commissions, typically can attribute their position to being well regarded by an elected official who is in turn well regarded by a majority of the electorate. A profound and enduring issue in modern sentencing systems, in many specific sentencing decisions, is the role of politics in the development of sentencing rules. See generally Carol A. Bergman, The Politics of Federal Sentencing on Cocaine, 10 Fed. Sentencing Rep. 196 (1998); Peter J. Benekos and Alida V. Merlo, Three Strikes and You're Out! The Political Sentencing Game, 59 Fed. Probation, Mar. 1995, at 3; Stephen B. Bright and Patrick J. Keenen, Judges and the Politics of Death: Deciding Between the Bill of Rights and the Next Election in Capital Cases, 75 B.U. L. Rev. 760 (1995).

2. *Functional purposes: costs.* An obvious theme running through the "five critical issues" influencing Ohio's capacity to administer effective criminal justice sanctions is money (or the lack thereof). In other words, limited resources are another powerful purpose guiding sentencing decision making, especially in states where punishment resources (prisons, jails, probation officers) and prosecutorial and judicial resources are always scarce. Sometimes resource constraints provide the superstructure within which policy makers must allocate sentences. An illustration of this approach is the "capacity constraint" provision in some states, which directs sentencing commissions to design sentencing rules that do not exceed available prison space. Some states explain punishment priorities in light of limited resources. For example, Florida's legislature has decided that punishment is the primary purpose of sentencing. Along with other limitations, the Florida legislature prioritizes the incarceration of serious offenders and recidivists "in order to maximize the finite capacities of state and local correctional facilities." Fla. Stat. §921.002.

Resources can constrain sentencing and punishment systems driven initially by philosophical, political, or more random considerations. Consider the developments in state sentencing described by Daniel Wilhelm and Nicholas Turner in late 2002:

> Corrections budgets have been especially hard hit by the current [fiscal] crisis. In FY 2002, 25 states were forced to reduce their corrections budgets. Higher education was the only government sector affected more often, in 29 states. As budget cuts have been imposed or threatened, corrections

departments have responded in three predominant ways: closing prisons, re-ducing staff, and curtailing programs. . . .

Concern about the spiraling cost of incarcerating offenders has created pressure on corrections administrators to do more than cut costs quickly. In a number of states, lawmakers have used the moment to re-examine sentencing schemes and to engage in targeted mitigation of certain punishments. In some cases, this has resulted in the repeal of mandatory minimum sentences now per-ceived as too harsh and too financially onerous. In others, it has led to the reclassification of certain offenses so that they no longer automatically result in prison sentences.

In 2001 and 2002, 13 states took legislative action to ameliorate the effects of stringent sentencing laws. Of these, Connecticut, Indiana, and North Dakota repealed mandatory minimum sentences relating to some nonviolent offenses. (Legislation has also been introduced in three other jurisdictions — Colorado, Delaware, and Michigan — tempering mandatory minimum sentences.) Missis-sippi pared back truth-in-sentencing requirements. Louisiana, Virginia, and Texas expanded the number of inmates eligible for early release. Iowa granted judges greater discretion in sentencing certain felony offenders. Alabama and New Mexico eased habitual offender laws. And Idaho, Oregon, and Washington enhanced treatment options for nonviolent drug offenders. In many of these states, rising prison populations and incarceration costs were factors for win-ning passage of legislation.

Daniel Wilhelm and Nicholas Turner, Is the Budget Crisis Changing the Way We Look at Sentencing and Incarceration?, 15 Fed. Sentencing Rep. 41, 41-44 (2002).

PROBLEM 1-3.   SENTENCING WITHOUT PRISON OR DEATH

If prisons and the death penalty were declared unconstitutional or became wildly unpopular politically (perhaps on moral or economic grounds), would the only option be anarchy? How might policy makers respond to a world with crime but without prisons or capital punishment as sentencing options?

PROBLEM 1-4.   SENTENCING BUDGETS

Given the profound difficulty of specifying, finding political agreement on, and applying purposes of punishment, do functional justifications or other practical resource limits offer the best hope for "forcing" relatively principled sentencing and use of punishment?

Should a legislature decide how many prison beds it wants, and then tell an executive agency to allocate those beds to best achieve one or more stated pur-poses or whatever mix of purposes the executive agency decides? Are there more profound kinds of budgets that might produce a fairer or more decent so-ciety? What if legislatures specified a particular number of prosecutions, convic-tions, or prison cells for a specific crime — say, 300 person-years for persons convicted of possession of narcotics with intent to sell?

=2=

‖ *Who Sentences?* ‖

In most criminal justice systems, several institutions share the decision about the proper sentence to impose: Legislatures and judges always have a say in the sentence, and juries, parole commissions, and sentencing commissions may participate. But the precise division of labor in setting sentencing policy and sentences in particular cases varies a great deal from place to place. We begin with a survey of the actors, and then we take a closer look at the distinctive capabilities of each.

‖ *Research on Sentencing: The Search for Reform,*
Alfred Blumstein, Jacqueline Cohen, Susan
Martin, and Michael Tonry
Vol. 1, pp. 41-47 (1983) ‖

Any effort . . . to understand sentencing must take into account the existence of the many participants and decisions that together constitute "sentencing" and the conflicting values, perspectives, and interests among them. This very complexity, however, frustrates efforts to change the criminal justice process in America.

Victims and Witnesses.   Victims initiate criminal justice action when they decide to complain to the police. They also, subsequently, affect the likelihood of conviction and punishment through their ability and willingness to cooperate with the prosecution. Victim and witness noncooperation is a major cause of charge dismissal in the United States. According to the National Crime Survey, 56 percent of violent crimes went unreported in 1978 (including 35 percent of robberies with injury), as did 75 percent of personal crimes of theft and 64 percent of household crimes. . . .

Police.   Police decide whom to notice, to stop, to arrest, to book, and (in some jurisdictions) to charge. Police officers have the primary authority to decide who will *not* be pursued by the criminal justice system. . . . The exercise of discretion in the police decision to arrest largely dictates the outcome in [misdemeanor cases involving public disorder, family violence, and small-scale drug trafficking]. The police also possess substantial autonomy in handling serious crimes of violence and investigating organized illegal activities and large property loss or damage. Police are relatively free to decide which complaints to follow up, with what diligence and resources, and to select their means of investigation. . . .

Prosecutors.   Prosecutors establish priorities and determine the vigor with which various kinds of cases will be pursued. In the 1970s, for example, many prosecutors ceased prosecuting marijuana possession cases; in effect, those prosecutors decriminalized marijuana use in their jurisdictions.

Prosecutors also exercise substantial discretion over individual cases. Prosecutors decide what charges to file or, if the police file charges, what to dismiss. Like the decisions of police officers, prosecutors' decisions to [dismiss or reduce charges] are not subject to independent review. . . .

Plea bargaining takes diverse forms. In *horizontal charge bargains,* a prosecutor agrees to drop several charges for an offense type if the defendant pleads guilty to the remaining charges (e.g., three burglary charges are dropped when the defendant pleads guilty to a fourth). In *vertical charge bargains,* a prosecutor agrees to drop the highest charge if the defendant pleads guilty to a less serious charge (e.g., a narcotics trafficking charge is dropped if the defendant pleads guilty to a narcotics possession charge, or a charge of armed robbery is dropped if the defendant pleads guilty to a charge of robbery). In sentence bargains, a prosecutor agrees that the defendant will receive a specific sentence in return for a guilty plea. In fact bargains, a prosecutor agrees not to introduce evidence of specific aggravating circumstances. Other plea bargaining variants involve prosecutorial agreements to recommend or not to oppose particular sentences or to dismiss charges in consideration of the defendant's cooperation in other prosecutions or investigations. Whatever form plea bargaining takes, the prosecutor and to a lesser extent the defense counsel often stand supreme. The judge sometimes has little choice but to ratify their decisions. . . .

Judges.   Judges impose sentences. They decide who goes to prison and who does not; they set the terms of nonincarcerative sentences; and (depending on whether there is a parole board and on the rules governing parole eligibility) they set minimum, maximum, or actual lengths of jail and prison terms. . . .

Judges' powers [are also] informally but importantly affected by the work of other court personnel. First, in jurisdictions in which sentence bargaining is common, often a judge's choice is whether to ratify the negotiated sentence. Second, where charge bargaining is prevalent, a judge usually accedes to proposed charge dismissals and may impose a sentence only within the constraints set by any statutory sentence provisions. Third, probation officers devote more time to investigation of the offender's circumstances and to consideration of the case than judges possibly can, and so they control the flow of information to judges. Probation officers are attached to most modern felony courts; presentence reports containing their recommendations are commonly provided to judges, and these recommendations are usually followed.

Parole Boards.   Although parole boards have been abolished in some jurisdictions — and in others they have lost their authority to determine release dates — in the majority of states they retain control over parole release. Judges often set maximum sentences (and in some states minimums as well), but the maximum is often very long; parole boards decide who and when to release prior to sentence expiration; the conditions to which a parolee will be subject while on parole; when and why parole can be revoked; and when after revocation, if at all, an offender can be re-released prior to the end of the maximum sentence. . . .

Parole boards traditionally make individualized release decisions, taking account of a wide variety of offender characteristics. In establishing uniform criteria for releasing offenders, they, too, face the basic dilemma in criminal justice: How much emphasis should be placed on the seriousness of the conviction offense in attempting to follow the injunction to "treat like cases alike" and how much on the characteristics of the defendant, including prior record and employment status, in predicting whether the release constitutes a danger to the community?

Corrections Administrators.   Corrections administrators affect the duration of imprisonment by the award, withdrawal, or denial of time off for good behavior and by their recommendations and reports to parole boards when a prisoner is being considered for early release. Corrections administrators also influence the quality of a prisoner's confinement through decisions about institutional assignments and participation in various kinds of furlough programs. Whether an inmate spends time in a maximum security prison, in a less restrictive minimum security facility, or in a group home in his or her hometown is almost entirely in the hands of corrections authorities. . . .

Executive Clemency: Commutations and Pardons.   Although pardons and similar executive release mechanisms once played a major part in prison releases, these ad hoc powers are no longer extensively used in most states.

Legislatures.   Legislative influence in sentencing is first and last: it is first because a legislature constructs and can always alter the basic statutory framework that other officials are charged to carry out; it is last because most punishments prescribed by law are not self-executing but can be realized only through other officials. If those officials behave inconsistently with the law, there is little a legislature can do. Even such seemingly authoritative laws as those calling for mandatory minimum sentences can be effected only through others; if prosecutors and judges choose to circumvent the law, mandatory terms will not be imposed. . . . Sometimes statutes are drafted so broadly that they provide little guidance in individual cases. For example, the maximum prison terms authorized for most offenses — 5 or 10 or 25 years — are so much longer than the sentences typically imposed or served that the legislative decision has little significance for the operation of the system.

The System as a Whole.   The operations of this complex system of criminal justice, with its network of multiple, overlapping, and interconnecting discretions and conflicting goals, are not easily altered; like the operation of any complex system, they are influenced by powerful forces of tradition, institutional convenience, scarcity of resources, and self-interest. Officials who wish to circumvent or undermine a new law can usually find ways to do so; legislative changes are impositions from outside and are often resisted. . . .

Such reactions are foreseeable. The staffs of prosecutors' offices and the courts have institutional goals and personal interests to serve and limited resources to expend. Sometimes their personal views of justice and injustice may not easily accept legislative solutions to the crime problem. Since new laws are seldom accompanied by appropriation of funds sufficient to permit literal and wholehearted compliance with them, something must give, and that something is often compliance. The complexity of the system also often confounds reform initiatives by merely shifting the locus of decision-making power from one agency to another. . . .

NOTES

1. *Victim participation in sentencing.*   Victim participation in criminal justice has grown more important since the original publication of the passage reprinted above. Legislation in all 50 states now formalizes victim participation at various stages in the criminal process. For instance, laws in many states require the prosecutor to notify the victim before dismissing any serious charges, and the law often gives the victim the opportunity to speak at the offender's sentencing hearing and sometimes to recommend a sentence. Victims also figure prominently in some parole hearings. Do these contacts between the victim and various government officials amount to a grant of "sentencing" power to the victim?

2. *Pardon and clemency boards.*   The passage above mentions that executive clemency is "no longer extensively used in most states," and it is true that governors today grant pardons and commute sentences far less often than they once did. Governors do still grant pardons, however, and there are now active and elaborate bureaucracies at work in many states to assist the governor in deciding when to grant pardons and when to commute sentences. About two-thirds of the states leave the pardon decision entirely to the discretion of the governor. In about ten states, the governor can only consider clemency recommendations issued by a clemency board. We discuss the pardon and clemency power in Chapter 11.

A.   SENTENCING IN THE COURTROOM

The immediate answer to the question "who sentences" may be the sentencing judge who announces a sentence in the courtroom. But the legal framework for sentencing is always more complex. In the United States, the closest approximation to the pure, unadulterated image of the judge as law giver and law applier is found in "indeterminate" sentencing systems, which traditionally vest enormous discretion in the sentencing judge and provide little review of the sentence imposed. But even in indeterminate systems, the seemingly vast power of the judge is circumscribed by modest guidance from legislatures and, more important, by postsentence executive branch review by parole boards.

The materials that follow illuminate the nature of sentencing by judges and parole boards in indeterminate systems. If one of the purposes of criminal sentences is to reflect the community's response to the violation of social norms, should a group of representative community members, in the familiar form of a jury, decide the sentence? While conceptually intriguing, jury sentencing has played a major role in the United States only in capital cases. The second section below examines one special noncapital setting and the handful of states that grant juries the authority to sentence.

1. Judges and Parole Boards During Indeterminate Sentencing

Until recently, sentencing in the United States was characterized more by discretion than law. In 1950 every state and the federal system used indeterminate sentencing. Under this type of system, the legislature prescribed broad potential sentencing ranges and the trial judge sentenced without meaningful legal guidance and typically without offering detailed explanation for the sentence. An executive branch agency (usually a parole board) ultimately determined the actual sentence each defendant would serve. There were virtually no judicial opinions explaining or reviewing a sentence, and legal counsel ordinarily made oral arguments at sentencing hearings without any written submissions to the court. The unwritten nature of the arguments and the decisions made it difficult for anyone to get a handle on sentencing law and practice. Perhaps that reality demonstrates the most important point about such a system: Sentencing happened without much law.

The following materials offer a glimpse of indeterminate sentencing systems at work. The U.S. Supreme Court's 1949 decision in Williams v. New York, which came at the high water mark for indeterminate sentencing, reveals not only the huge discretion given to trial judges but also some of the principles underlying that discretion. The documents related to the 1989 sentencing of Col. Oliver North were filed after his conviction for obstruction of a congressional investigation into a secret (and illegal) use of funds, derived from a sale of weapons to Iran, to support insurgents in Nicaragua known as Contras (hence the name "Iran-Contra affair"). The specific charges involved in North's case are less important for our purposes than the style of argument at work. The documents present, in an unusually visible and systematic form, the types of arguments and reasoning that operate in the many cases still sentenced today in indeterminate sentencing systems.

|| **Samuel Williams v. New York** ||
337 U.S. 241 (1949)

BLACK, J.

A jury in a New York state court found appellant guilty of murder in the first degree. The jury recommended life imprisonment, but the trial judge imposed a sentence of death. In giving his reasons for imposing the death sentence the judge discussed in open court the evidence upon which the jury had convicted stating that this evidence had been considered in the light of additional information obtained through the court's "Probation Department, and through other sources." [A New York statute authorized the court to consider "any information that will aid the court in determining the proper treatment of such defendant." Williams claimed that the sentence, which was based on information supplied by witnesses, violated his due process rights because he had no chance to confront or cross-examine the witnesses or to rebut the evidence.]

The record shows a carefully conducted trial lasting more than two weeks in which appellant was represented by three appointed lawyers who conducted his defense with fidelity and zeal. The evidence proved a wholly indefensible murder committed by a person engaged in a burglary. . . .

About five weeks after the verdict of guilty with recommendation of life imprisonment, and after a statutory pre-sentence investigation report to the judge, the defendant was brought to court to be sentenced. [T]he judge gave reasons why he felt that the death sentence should be imposed. . . . He stated that the pre-sentence investigation revealed many material facts concerning appellant's background which though relevant to the question of punishment could not properly have been brought to the attention of the jury in its consideration of the question of guilt. He referred to the experience appellant "had had on 30 other burglaries in and about the same vicinity" where the murder had been committed. The appellant had not been convicted of these burglaries although the judge had information that he had confessed to some and had been identified as the perpetrator of some of the others. The judge also referred to certain activities of appellant as shown by the probation report that indicated appellant possessed "a morbid sexuality" and classified him as a "menace to society." The accuracy of the statements made by the judge as to appellant's background and past practices [was] not challenged by appellant or his counsel, nor was the judge asked to disregard any of them or to afford appellant a chance to refute or discredit any of them by cross-examination or otherwise.

The case presents a serious and difficult question. The question relates to the rules of evidence applicable to the manner in which a judge may obtain information to guide him in the imposition of sentence upon an already convicted defendant. . . . To aid a judge in exercising this discretion intelligently the New York procedural policy encourages him to consider information about the convicted person's past life, health, habits, conduct, and mental and moral propensities. The sentencing judge may consider such information even though obtained outside the courtroom from persons whom a defendant has not been permitted to confront or cross-examine. . . .

Tribunals passing on the guilt of a defendant always have been hedged in by strict evidentiary procedural limitations. But both before and since the American colonies became a nation, courts in this country and in England practiced a policy under which a sentencing judge could exercise a wide discretion in the sources and types of evidence used to assist him in determining the kind and the extent of punishment to be imposed within limits fixed by law. Out-of-court affidavits have been used frequently, and of course in the smaller communities sentencing judges naturally have in mind their knowledge of the personalities and backgrounds of convicted offenders. . . .

In addition to the historical basis for different evidentiary rules governing trial and sentencing procedures there are sound practical reasons for the distinction. In a trial before verdict the issue is whether a defendant is guilty of having engaged in certain criminal conduct of which he has been specifically accused. Rules of evidence have been fashioned for criminal trials which narrowly confine the trial contest to evidence that is strictly relevant to the particular offense charged. These rules rest in part on a necessity to prevent a time consuming and confusing trial of collateral issues. They were also designed to prevent tribunals concerned solely with the issue of guilt of a particular offense from being influenced to convict for that offense by evidence that the defendant had habitually engaged in other misconduct. A sentencing judge, however, is not confined to the narrow issue of guilt. His task within fixed statutory or constitutional limits is to determine the type and extent of punishment after the issue of guilt has been determined. Highly relevant — if not essential — to his selection of an appropriate sentence is the possession of the fullest information possible concerning the defendant's life and characteristics. And modern concepts individualizing punishment have made it all the more necessary that a sentencing judge not be denied an opportunity to obtain pertinent information by a requirement of rigid adherence to restrictive rules of evidence properly applicable to the trial.

Undoubtedly the New York statutes emphasize a prevalent modern philosophy of penology that the punishment should fit the offender and not merely the crime. The belief no longer prevails that every offense in a like legal category calls for an identical punishment without regard to the past life and habits of a particular offender. This whole country has traveled far from the period in which the death sentence was an automatic and commonplace result of convictions — even for offenses today deemed trivial. . . . Indeterminate sentences, the ultimate termination of which are sometimes decided by nonjudicial agencies, have to a large extent taken the place of the old rigidly fixed punishments. . . . Retribution is no longer the dominant objective of the criminal law. Reformation and rehabilitation of offenders have become important goals of criminal jurisprudence. . . .

Under the practice of individualizing punishments, investigation techniques have been given an important role. Probation workers making reports of their investigations have not been trained to prosecute but to aid offenders. Their reports have been given a high value by conscientious judges who want to sentence persons on the best available information rather than on guesswork and inadequate information. To deprive sentencing judges of this kind of information would undermine modern penological procedural policies that have been cautiously adopted throughout the nation after careful consideration and experimentation. We must recognize that most of the information now relied upon by judges to guide them in the intelligent imposition of sentences would be unavailable if information were restricted to that given in open court by witnesses subject to cross-examination. And the modern probation report draws on information concerning every aspect of a defendant's life. The type and extent of this information make totally impractical if not impossible open court testimony with cross-examination. Such a procedure could endlessly delay criminal administration in a retrial of collateral issues.

The considerations we have set out admonish us against treating the due-process clause as a uniform command that courts throughout the nation abandon their age-old practice of seeking information from out-of-court sources to guide their judgment toward a more enlightened and just sentence. . . . So to treat the due-process clause would hinder if not preclude all courts — state and federal — from making progressive efforts to improve the administration of criminal justice. We hold that appellant was not denied due process of law. . . .

United States v. Oliver North
Government's Sentencing Memorandum
(June 19, 1989)

The Government respectfully submits this memorandum in connection with the sentencing of Oliver L. North, scheduled for June 23, 1989. [We] focus on those matters we believe are appropriate for the Court to consider in imposing sentence.

The most striking thing about North's posture on the eve of sentencing is his insistence that he has done nothing wrong. Instead, on the day of the verdict, he declared that his "vindication" was not "complete," and promised to "continue the fight" until it is. At the same time, he continues to profit from his notoriety, even while he decries the wastefulness and injustice of his prosecution.

[North] apparently sees nothing wrong with alteration and destruction of official national security records. His participation in the preparation of a false and misleading chronology [to present during a congressional hearing on the Iran-Contra affair] has not led to any acknowledgment of wrongdoing. Certainly, he sees nothing wrong with lying to Congress, when in the view of himself and his superiors lying is necessary. . . .

In fashioning a just sentence in this case, we urge the Court to consider the seriousness of North's abuse of the public trust, the need for deterrence, North's failure to accept personal responsibility for his actions, his lack of remorse and his perjury on the witness stand. Taking all of these factors into account . . . the Government submits that a term of incarceration is appropriate and necessary.

[The] Court, in its sentence, should [demonstrate] that if officials engaging in such conduct are caught and convicted, the punishment will be severe. Further, the private citizens of this country, who continue to follow this case closely, are entitled to the reassurance only this Court can give that these are serious crimes and that powerful government officials are not accorded special treatment. . . .

A sentence in this case that included no period of incarceration would send exactly the wrong message to government officials and to the public. It would be a statement that 15 years after Watergate, government officials can participate in a brazen cover-up, lie to Congress and collect a substantial gratuity and still receive only a slap on the wrist.

[A]cting in his position at the National Security Council, North wielded enormous power in the government. By his own description, he met with presidents and kings. He was the primary official responsible for the coordination of counterterrorism, the release of American hostages and relations with the

Contras. . . . Thus, North held a position of substantial public trust that far exceeded his military rank. . . .

Although he calls himself a "scapegoat," he invited this role. He joked about the danger that he would be jailed and bragged that he would be protected because "the old man love[s] my ass." Similarly, his decision to stand trial and gamble on acquittal, a right granted by the Constitution, was also undertaken as a challenge to the capability of our system of justice to respond to crimes with political overtones, given the expressed sympathy and support of this country's then President and Vice President. . . .

North was not content merely to exercise his constitutional right to put the Government to its proof at trial. Instead, he sought to pervert the processes of justice much as he had corrupted the processes of government. With supreme faith in his ability to deceive, North took the stand and perjured himself. For example, his unsupported claim that he had a $15,000 fund in a steel box in his closet echoed the flimsy lies offered by corrupt municipal officials in the days of Tammany Hall. . . .

North's lack of remorse is particularly troubling in view of the fact that he continues to travel throughout the country, like a politician on the stump, giving speeches and discoursing on his defiance of Congress. Apparently, North has become a wealthy man in the process. The fact that this defendant is cultivating a popular following, which reinforces his lack of remorse, makes it all the more important for the Court to underscore the gravity of North's offenses by imposing a term of incarceration.

Oliver North's sentence will be known to, and closely evaluated by, all who view the perversion of government as a permissible means to the attainment of their goals. The sentence will also be carefully considered by those officials who may now be weighing the advantages of deception, obstruction and personal greed against the risks of punishment. It will also be noted by those serving substantial prison sentences for more personal crimes far less damaging to the nation. Most importantly, the sentence will be closely scrutinized by a citizenry whose confidence in government and the political system has been seriously undermined by the activities of this defendant. . . . Under all these circumstances, we respectfully submit that a term of incarceration is appropriate and necessary.

Sentencing Memorandum on Behalf of Oliver North

Lt. Col. Oliver L. North is before the court for sentencing upon being found guilty of 3 of the 16 charges brought against him by the IC.* . . . The IC's memorandum demonstrates that it will stop at nothing in its effort to crush Oliver North. The Supreme Court declared more than 50 years ago that the prosecutor "may strike hard blows, but he is not at liberty to strike foul ones." Berger v. United States, 295 U.S. 78 (1935). The IC has ignored the court's command; the blows

---

* North was prosecuted by a special prosecutor, known at that time in the federal system as an "independent counsel," or IC. — EDS.

that it strikes in its memorandum are as foul as any we have seen. It attacks Lt. Col. North for asserting his constitutional right to assert his innocence and stand trial; it ignores his 20 years of loyal and courageous service to this country; it takes him to task for asserting a simple truth — that most of the conduct with which he was charged was authorized by his superiors; and it blasts him for failing to show remorse, when his trial testimony makes clear that he deeply regrets many of his actions. [Furthermore, the IC] actually levels new charges, accusing Oliver North of having "supreme faith in his ability to deceive" and claiming without a shred of support that Lt. Col. North committed perjury at trial. . . .

We submit that Lt. Col. North has already been punished sufficiently for the three offenses of which he was found guilty. He was fired from his job at the NSC. He has lost his career as a Marine Corps officer. He may lose his Marine Corps pension after 20 years of service. He remains under threat of assassination by a dangerous terrorist organization as a direct result of his service to this country. He has been subjected to unrelenting and often hostile press scrutiny for the past two-and-a-half years. Every detail of his life has been probed, first in nationally televised hearings conducted by the joint Iran/Contra committee and then by the IC. He has heard himself likened to Hitler by a prosecutor who appears to lack any sense of fairness and [has heard] rumors in the press, before Congress, in court, in a nationally televised "docudrama," and now in the IC's memorandum. His children have been tormented. By any standard, the toll that this ordeal has already taken on Lt. Col. North and his family fulfills every legitimate purpose of punishment. If the Court accepts the IC's view that this punishment is not enough — that Oliver North must be punished further for the three offenses of which he was found guilty — then that punishment should take the form of probation conditioned on community service. . . .

In determining the proper sentence for Oliver North, the Court should consider the man as an individual, not — as the IC would have it — merely as a vehicle through which to send a "public message." The Court should weigh carefully Lt. Col. North's service to this country and to society, the devastating impact that imprisonment would have on his family, and the unique confluence of circumstances that gave rise to his conduct. This careful, individualized sentencing is essential to ensure that "the punishment should fit the offender and not merely the crime." Williams v. New York, 337 U.S. 241 (1949).

Oliver North devoted 20 years to the service of this country, from Vietnam to Tehran to Beirut. He has risked his own life and saved the lives of others. We submit that the Court should weigh this service in Lt. Col. North's favor at sentencing.

Upon graduation from the Naval Academy in 1968, Oliver North was commissioned in the United States Marine Corps and served as a platoon commander in Vietnam. His courage protected the lives of many young Marines, including Bill Haskell. In his letter to the Court, Mr. Haskell describes how Oliver North rescued him in the face of hostile fire as he lay wounded:

> . . . Ollie came to the rescue. In the face of an almost unbelievable barrage of enemy fire, he led a counterattack with his platoon driving the enemy back so that the Marines could medivac their wounded. I think I know Ollie well enough to say that his primary motivation for such heroic action was the desire to save his fellow Marines rather than just to achieve victory over the enemy. Ollie saved my life that day.

Oliver North received the Silver Star Medal for his heroism in saving Bill Haskell and his platoon. He received other medals as well for his service in Vietnam, including two Purple Hearts; a Bronze Star Medal with Combat "V"; and a Navy Commendation Medal with Combat "V." . . .

In 1981, Oliver North was assigned to the National Security Council staff. At the NSC, he quickly established himself as a dedicated and hard-working staff officer. . . . By 1984, Oliver North was responsible for two principal areas: counterterrorism and Central America. He worked tirelessly to fulfill these responsibilities. . . .

A further example demonstrates Lt. Col. North's courageous service to this country. In May 1986, at the President's direction, he and a handful of others undertook a dangerous mission to Tehran in an effort to achieve an opening to Iran and free the American hostages held in Lebanon. This trip entailed great personal danger to Lt. Col. North and his companions; they were the first American officials to travel to Iran since the revolution, and radical Iranians posed a significant threat of death or torture. The danger was particularly great because the trip was absolutely secret. But Lt. Col. North left his family behind — unable even to tell them where he was going — and risked his life for his country and for those held hostage. We ask that the Court give this record of service great weight in choosing the appropriate sentence for Oliver North.

Oliver North . . . has worked to improve society in other ways as well. Since the Congressional hearings of 1987, he has put his unsought and unwanted notoriety to use in service of his fellow citizens, particularly America's youth. Two examples illustrate Lt. Col. North's compassion and concern — and put the lie to the IC's claim that Lt. Col. North displays "contempt for the public."

First, shortly after his Congressional testimony, Lt. Col. North learned that it was the dream of a terminally ill boy to see him before the boy died. Lt. Col. North agreed to meet the boy to give him courage in his final days. The woman who arranged the meeting describes what happened in her letter to the Court:

> [The boy] told me he wanted to meet Lt. Col. North because this was the strongest person that he could ever know. [The boy] said that he needed this man to teach him how to become stronger mentally so that he could deal with his fast-approaching death. . . .
>
> To my amazement and delight, Lt. Col. North brought with him a large Bible with certain scriptures marked throughout the Bible that he said he lives by, that his strength comes from his faith in God. He sat down and read with the child from the Bible and they prayed together that [the boy] would find his answers. Lt. Col. North spent one and a half hours alone with [the boy] helping him to find the strength that the child was very much in need of. . . .

Lt. Col. North placed the following inscription on a photograph for the dying boy: "Courageous Hero, Inspiration, Fighter — Semper Fidelis. 18 September '87, Oliver L. North."

Second, Lt. Col. North has spoken out throughout America against drug use and in favor of improved drug prevention and rehabilitation. As but one example, he delivered a speech on behalf of the drug-prevention organization Reach Out America. . . .

Oliver and Betsy North have been married for almost 21 years. They have three daughters and one son. In sentencing Oliver North, the Court should consider both the devastation that this matter has already inflicted on the North family, and the further damage that any term of imprisonment would cause. . . . Two of Oliver North's daughters have been cruelly mocked at school. The family has been portrayed in grossly unfair ways in a nationally televised "docudrama." And the press has forced Oliver North and his family into an inescapable limelight — sometimes cruel, sometimes favorable, but always present. . . .

Criminal punishment serves four legitimate purposes: it incapacitates the offender, to prevent him from harming society; it rehabilitates him; it deters him and others from committing further offenses; and it reflects the seriousness of the offenses. The punishment that Oliver North and his family have suffered to date more than adequately fulfills each of these purposes.

1. *Incapacitation.*   There is no need to incapacitate Oliver North. Far from representing a threat to society, Lt. Col. North devoted his professional life to ensuring the safety of Americans at home and abroad. . . .

2. *Rehabilitation.*   No one can seriously contend that Oliver North needs rehabilitation, and it would be preposterous to suggest that, if rehabilitation *were* necessary, it would occur in prison. . . .

3. *Deterrence.*   The punishment that Oliver North has suffered to date fully satisfied any need for deterrence; no additional sentence is necessary. First, there is no need for a harsh punishment to achieve *specific* deterrence — deterrence of Lt. Col. North from future unlawful acts. In light of his record of service to this country and the excruciating ordeal that he and his family have endured, there is no chance that he will commit offenses in the future. Second, *general* deterrence — deterrence of those other than Lt. Col. North — provides no basis for harsh punishment. The punishment that Lt. Col. North has suffered to date — including the loss of his position at the NSC, the loss of his career in the Marine Corps, and the minute and public scrutiny of his most private affairs by Congress, the IC, and frequently the media — should amply deter others. . . .

4. *The Seriousness of the Offense.*   The punishment that Lt. Col. North has suffered to date more than adequately reflects the gravity of the offenses of which he was found guilty. The three offenses — aiding and abetting an obstruction of Congress, destroying, altering, and/or removing official NSC documents, and accepting an unlawful gratuity — are serious. Each is a felony; each has a maximum prison term of between two and five years; and each carries a maximum fine of $250,000. But the seriousness of these offenses is significantly reduced by the unique circumstances of this case. . . .

|| *United States v. Oliver North* ||
Transcript (D.D.C. July 5, 1989)

GESELL, J.

I can assure you, Colonel North, that I'm going to take into full consideration the important fact that before you came to the White House you had served your country with distinction in the highest traditions of the Marine Corps. And the court is not going to overlook that there were major matters of military and quasi-military nature which you performed, again with the highest distinction at great personal risk to yourself after you came to the White House. But I'm sure you realize that this case has little to do with your military behavior, commitment or expertise.

The indictment involves your participation in particular covert events. I do not think that in this area you were a leader at all, but really a low ranking subordinate working to carry out initiatives of a few cynical superiors. [However,] you're not the fall guy for this tragic breach of the public trust. . . . You're here now because of your own conduct when the truth was coming out. Apparently you could not face disclosure and decided to protect yourself and others. You destroyed evidence, altered and removed official documents, created false papers after the events to keep Congress and others from finding out what was happening.

Now, I believe that you knew this was morally wrong. It was against your bringing up. It was against your faith. It was against all of your training. Under the stress of the moment it was easier to choose the role of a martyr but that wasn't a heroic, patriotic act nor was it in the public interest.

You have had great remorse for your family and understandably so. It is often the tragic part of what happens when mistakes are made. I believe you still lack full understanding, however, of how the public service has been tarnished. Nonetheless, what you believe is your own business and jail would only harden your misconceptions. Given the many highly commendable aspects of your life your punishment will not include jail. Indeed, community service may in the end make you more conscious of certain values which at times you and your associates appear to have overlooked in the elite isolation of the White House. . . .

I fashioned a sentence that punishes you. It is my duty to do that. But it leaves the future up to you. This is the sentence of the court. On count six where you are found guilty of aiding and abetting [an] obstruction of Congress, I'm going to impose a sentence of three years and suspend the execution of the sentence, place you on probation for two years, fine you $100,000 and I have to impose a special assessment of $50. Under count nine, altering, removing and destroying the permanent historical records of the National Security Council, I impose a sentence of two years, suspend the execution of sentence, place you on probation for two years, fine you $35,000 and impose a special assessment of $50 and I am required by the statute to impose another mandatory penalty. You are hereby disqualified from holding any office under the United States. Under count ten, receiving an illegal gratuity, I'll impose a sentence of one year, suspend the execution of that sentence, place you on probation for two years, fine you $15,000 and impose a special assessment again of $50. These sentences and the probation are to run concurrently. The fines are to run consecutively. Your probation shall consist . . . of community service in a total amount of 1200, 800 the first year, and 400 the second year and you will remain under the supervision of the District of Columbia probation officer who is familiar with your situation and who has prepared the pre-sentence report. . . .

NOTES

1. *Informal procedure at sentencing: majority position.*   The New York statute discussed in *Williams,* which allowed the sentencing judge to consider evidence inadmissible at trial under the rules of evidence, typifies sentencing practices in most states. See Tex. Crim. Proc. Code Ann. §37.07(3). The informal presentation of evidence supposedly supports an effort to obtain the most information

possible about the offender and the offense and to make an individualized (perhaps even clinical) decision. Over time, many different actors participate in the decision about how best to respond to an individual offender. Thus, the indeterminate sentencing system is one of "multiple discretions." More than half the states use this system for large groups of cases, although many of these states use more narrowly circumscribed sentencing rules for some crimes.

2. Williams *revisited.*   Samuel Titto Williams, a black man, was 18 years old at the time he killed 15-year-old Selma Graff, who surprised him during a burglary. Williams had no record of prior convictions, but he had been accused of burglary at age 11. The judgment in juvenile court was suspended. The probation report — a report prepared by probation officers prior to sentencing, also called a presentence investigation report — informed the judge that Williams was suspected of (but not charged with) committing 30 burglaries during the two months before the murder. A seven-year-old girl who was present during one of those burglaries told the probation officer that Williams had sexually molested her. She identified Williams as the perpetrator two weeks after the incident. The probation report also stated that Williams was living with two women, and brought different men into the apartment for the purpose of having sexual relations with the women. It alleged that Williams had once gone to a local school to photograph "private parts of young children." Finally, the sentencing judge relied on injuries inflicted on the murder victim's brother during the burglary. The prosecutor did not bring any charges based on the assault. See Kevin Reitz, Sentencing Facts: Travesties of Real-Offense Sentencing, 45 Stan. L. Rev. 523 (1993). Is the problem in *Williams* the presentation of new offender information at sentencing or the fact that Williams did not know the judge would hear these allegations?

3. *Capital punishment and informal procedure.*   Although the *Williams* Court emphasized that rehabilitative purposes of sentencing required far-reaching information about an offender, the proposed "treatment" for Williams was execution. It brings to mind the statement attributed to the comedian W. C. Fields, who quoted a condemned prisoner on his way to the electric chair, saying, "This will certainly be a lesson to me." *Williams* is still cited with approval in support of informal sentencing procedures generally, but it has been partially overruled in the context of capital sentencing. In Gardner v. Florida, 430 U.S. 349 (1977), the trial judge sentenced a defendant to death after consulting confidential and unrebutted information in the presentence investigation report. A plurality of the Supreme Court found that due process required, at least in capital cases, that the defendant have access to information that will influence the sentencing judge and have an opportunity to test its reliability.

4. *Styles of argument in indeterminate sentencing.*   When judges describe the factors they consider in sentencing under an indeterminate system, they often list the types of considerations that the lawyers and the judge discussed in the Oliver North case. One study of sentences in federal white-collar crime cases concluded that judges considered three common principles during sentencing: (1) the harm the offense produced; (2) the blameworthiness of the defendant, judged from the defendant's criminal intent, from other details of the crime, and from the defendant's earlier life; and (3) the consequences of the punishment,

both for deterring future wrongdoing and for the well-being of the defendant's family and community. Despite the presence of these common principles for sentencing, judges selected very different sentences because they did not agree on how to measure each of the principles or the relative weight to place on each. See Stanton Wheeler, Kenneth Mann, and Austin Sarat, Sitting in Judgment: The Sentencing of White-Collar Criminals (1988).

Observers in higher-volume courts, such as state misdemeanor courts, describe a very different reality. During plea bargaining the parties settle quickly on a proper sentence, hinging largely on the charges filed and the parties' interpretation of the facts as reflected in the police reports. These negotiations do not often involve individualized haggling; rather, they are "more akin to modern supermarkets in which prices for various commodities have been clearly established and labeled." Malcolm Feeley, The Process Is the Punishment: Handling Cases in a Lower Criminal Court 187 (1979). What determines whether a given case will receive the "supermarket" form of sentencing or a more individualized assessment?

5. *Probation officers.* Judges who sentence a defendant after a guilty plea have not heard an extensive presentation of the evidence at trial and thus depend heavily on the presentence investigation that probation officers perform to provide information about the offender and the offense. How might a prosecutor or a defense attorney influence the recommendations of the probation officer? What institutional or individual biases might the probation officer bring to her assessment (and recommendation) of proper sentences? We consider further the work of probation officers and their interaction with attorneys and judges in Chapter 6.

Parole Consideration and Eligibility, Georgia Board of Pardons and Paroles
http://www.pap.state.ga.us/parole_consideration. htm (2003)

. . . Before the Board considers an inmate for parole, it conducts investigations, detailed reports of which become a part of the Board's case file. . . . First, a parole officer studies arrest and court records and may talk with arresting officers, court officials, victims, and witnesses in order to write a Legal Investigation report on the details of the inmate's current offense and a summary of any prior offenses in the same county. Next, a parole officer interviews the inmate and completes a Personal History Statement questionnaire. The inmate is asked, among other things, where he has resided and worked; who his family members are and where they live; where he plans to live and work; and what his own account is of his crime. Finally, a parole officer conducts a Social Investigation, which includes interviews with persons mentioned in the Personal History Statement as well as others. The written report presents a revealing picture of the inmate's life from birth to current imprisonment and may also indicate the degree of his truthfulness.

Before the inmate is paroled, the Board receives a Parole Review Summary from the Department of Corrections. This discusses the inmate's behavior, attitude, physical status, mental and emotional condition, participation in activities, and performance in work and training. The Board may, at its discretion, request detailed psychological or psychiatric opinions. Other documents in the case file usually include a Federal Bureau of Investigation or Georgia Crime Information Center record of arrests and convictions. . . .

For inmates serving non-life sentences, the Board generally establishes a Tentative Parole Month within eight to ten months after the inmate enters state prison. . . . The Parole Board requires all violent offenders as well as residential burglars to serve a minimum of 90 percent of their court-imposed terms of incarceration. The policy affects offenders convicted . . . for twenty crimes not covered under two strikes legislation. That legislation, passed in 1994, already requires offenders convicted of murder, rape, aggravated sodomy, armed robbery, kidnapping, aggravated child molestation, and aggravated sexual battery to serve 100 percent of their prison sentence.

Crimes covered under the Board's 90-percent policy are: attempted rape, voluntary manslaughter, aggravated battery on a police officer, aggravated battery, child molestation, hijacking a motor vehicle, robbery, aggravated assault on a police officer, aggravated assault (with injury or weapon), enticing a child for indecent purposes, cruelty to children, feticide, incest, statutory rape, criminal attempt to murder, bus hijacking, vehicular homicide (while DUI or habitual violator), involuntary manslaughter, aggravated stalking, and residential burglary. Offenders released under the 90-percent policy will serve the remainder of their sentence under parole supervision so they can be reintegrated into the community with structure and surveillance. . . .

Parole Decision Guidelines assist the State Board of Pardons and Paroles in making consistent, soundly based, and understandable parole decisions on inmates serving non-life sentences. Guidelines help the Board decide on a Tentative Parole Month (TPM) for the inmate or that he will complete his sentence without parole.

A Board hearing examiner identifies an inmate's Crime Severity Level from a table of offenses ranked in seven levels. The higher the severity, the longer the inmate is recommended to serve. Then the hearing examiner calculates the inmate's Parole Success Likelihood Score by adding weighted factors with proven predictive value from the inmate's criminal and social history, . . . such as a juvenile record, prior imprisonment, parole or probation failure, heroin or cocaine use or possession, and joblessness. . . . The hearing examiner cross-refers the inmate's Crime Severity Level and Parole Success Likelihood Factor Score on the Guidelines Grid [to obtain] a months-to-serve recommendation for the Board's discretionary consideration.

The Board votes to accept or reject the months-to-serve recommendation. If the Board votes to reject the recommendation, the Board then makes a fully discretionary clemency determination which may or may not permit parole for the inmate. [Any] TPM is conditioned on good conduct in prison and sometimes also on successful completion of a drug, alcohol, sex-offender counseling program, or other pre-condition. . . . Parole Guidelines help keep the Board on track toward its goal of seeing that inmates serving for similar offenses with similar histories are treated the same. . . .

Board members select the lowest-risk offenders for parole, acknowledging that a certain number of inmates must be paroled to allow room for newly

Georgia's Correctional Population — FY 2001

Crime type	Probation		Inmate		Parole		Total
Violent Personal	17,960	44%	19,813	48%	3,321	8%	41,094
Sex Offense	5,189	47%	5,730	52%	207	2%	11,126
Property	46,587	74%	10,058	16%	6,694	11%	63,330
Drug Sales	8,525	50%	4,198	25%	4,260	25%	16,983
Drug Possession	34,448	82%	3,454	8%	4,084	10%	41,986
Habitual Violator, DUI	5,684	81%	588	8%	787	11%	7,059
Other	8,556	76%	1,662	15%	972	9%	11,190
TOTAL	126,940	66%	45,503	24%	20,325	10%	192,768

sentenced, incoming prisoners. The "least risky" offender is therefore correlated to the characteristics of an ever-changing prison population, with its steady influx of both violent and non-violent, first-time and serial felons. One of Georgia Parole's strengths, in addition to its careful parole-selection process, is its ability to tailor parole community supervision strategies to the risk and needs presented by each offender.*

PROBLEM 2-1.   SAVINGS PLAN

The state of Georgia is experiencing a budget crisis, and the governor's office has instructed various state agencies to trim their budgets. The Department of Corrections and the Board of Pardons and Paroles have been told that the state needs to reduce the number of corrections officers on staff and therefore needs to reduce the prison population by a significant amount.

You are a staff member working for the Board of Pardons and Paroles. What strategies would you recommend for increasing the number of prison inmates released on parole? Would you ask the board to restrict its "90 percent policy" to a shorter list of crimes? Perhaps you would recommend abandoning the 90 percent policy altogether. Alternatively, you might concentrate on the method used to select prisoners to parole from among the groups that are currently eligible. Should the board amend its Parole Decision Guidelines or abandon those guidelines in favor of a case-by-case approach? Should the board lobby the legislature to change the two-strikes law that makes offenders convicted of some specified crimes ineligible for parole? Cf. Daniel F. Wilhelm and Nicholas R. Turner, Is the Budget Crisis Changing the Way We Look at Sentencing and Incarceration?, 15 Fed. Sentencing Rep. 41 (2002).

NOTES

1. *Parole and sentencing purposes.* When parole first appeared in this country, it embodied the rehabilitative ideal. Prisoners received longer prison terms to allow the criminal sanctions plenty of time to do their rehabilitative work, and parole marked the successful completion of the process. Parole also served an incapacitation purpose, because it was unfair to society to release prisoners

---

* This paragraph, along with the chart for 2001, derive from the board's 2001 Annual Report. — EDS.

before they were rehabilitated. In theory, the parole board assessed whether rehabilitation had taken place, but in practice this determination was never very
precise. A staff member for the Pennsylvania parole commission described in
1927 the process of selecting prisoners for parole release:

> [Parole boards] must attempt to separate the sheep from the goats; to liberate
> certain prisoners and hold others. There are certain factors which generally
> influence this decision. Of these, prison conduct is usually given the greatest
> weight. . . . Another factor generally considered is the nature of the crime for
> which the prisoner was committed. . . . A third item which generally has weight
> with paroling authorities is the prior criminal record of the applicant for pa-
> role. . . . The only other factor generally entering into parole decisions is the ap-
> pearance, personality, or general demeanor of the applicant. Truthfulness,
> square shoulders, a good voice, or a steady eye may go far toward winning a
> scoundrel his freedom in more than one State. Members of parole boards are
> human, like the rest of us, and are often inclined to congratulate themselves on
> their ability to read character at a glance. And so, shrewd but experimental
> guesswork, prejudices, and hunches many times decide whether a boy is to
> spend another two or three years behind prison walls or to be allowed to circu-
> late among us.

National Commission on Law Observance and Enforcement (Wickersham
Commission), Report on Penal Institutions, Probation and Parole (Report No. 9)
at 133 (1931). Does the Georgia Board of Pardons and Paroles still purport to
serve both rehabilitation and incapacitation purposes?

    2. *Parole and parole guidelines.*   Even after rehabilitation becomes less im-
portant and convincing as a purpose of criminal sentences, states find it necessary
to give parole or corrections authorities the power to review sentences. This later
review imposes a centralized perspective on the decisions of judges or juries from
all over the state, and it coordinates the sentences with the amount of correctional resources available. Parole boards decide on the actual time an offender
will serve *after* the judge has announced a sentence. Some parole boards decide
cases according to formal parole guidelines, while others make more ad hoc decisions, depending on prison capacity and other factors. What are the advantages
and disadvantages of setting the release date later in the process through a parole
board rather than through a judge applying up-front sentencing rules? We examine parole boards and parole guidelines in more detail in Chapter 11.

    Parole today is less central to sentencing in the United States than it was in
the middle of the twentieth century. More than a dozen states have abolished
parole, and the law in other states restricts parole to certain classes of cases or
gives judges more power to set the minimum prison term to be served, leaving
the parole authority with less to decide. The movement to restrict parole authority is part of the broader shift to more determinate sentencing laws, a topic
we consider more fully in Chapter 3.

    3. *Parole and the Constitution.*   Several procedural due process rulings affect
the way that parole boards decide whether to grant parole to inmates and whether
to revoke the parole granted at some earlier time. In Morrissey v. Brewer, 408 U.S.
471 (1972), the Court held that due process requires an informal hearing before
a parole board can revoke an earlier grant of parole. The hearing must be
conducted by an impartial hearing officer, and the parolee must receive written

notice of the claimed violations and an opportunity to respond to the evidence. A discretionary decision to *grant or deny* parole requires a less formal hearing. Under Greenholtz v. Inmates of Nebraska Penal and Correctional Complex, 442 U.S. 1 (1979), the parole authority must simply review the prisoner's file, give the prisoner an opportunity to be heard, and inform the inmate who is denied parole the reasons that he or she falls short.

4. *Good-time reductions to prison terms.* Prison officials also have some influence over the length of a prison sentence served. In most states, corrections officials have the power to reduce the sentence by up to one-third the maximum set by the judge or the parole authority. Prison authorities use this discretion to reward good behavior by inmates: The reductions are known as "good time." In the federal system, the maximum amount of these reductions is 15 percent. The federal government encourages states to keep their good time discounts below 15 percent by offering prison funding to states that comply with federal "truth in sentencing" guidelines. Jim Jacobs has pointed out the anomaly of placing legal controls on other sentencing decisions while leaving good-time decisions unregulated. Jacobs, Sentencing by Prison Personnel: Good Time, 30 UCLA L. Rev. 217 (1982). Which institutions would be best suited to create legal constraints on good-time decisions?

2. Sentencing Juries

Juries play a central role in most capital sentencing systems. In a half-dozen states — Arkansas, Kentucky, Missouri, Oklahoma, Texas, and Virginia — juries in some noncapital cases not only rule on guilt or innocence but also decide the sentence to impose. If sentencing is a community judgment, should the community's representatives decide the sentence? Is a judge or legislature or sentencing commission as much of a representative as a sentencing jury? Consider these questions in light of the following Arkansas statutes and the special and intriguing jury sentencing provisions for courts-martial under the Code of Military Justice.

‖ Arkansas Code §16-97-101 ‖
Bifurcated Sentencing Procedures

The following procedure shall govern jury trials which include any felony charges:

(1) The jury shall first hear all evidence relevant to every charge on which a defendant is being tried and shall retire to reach a verdict on each charge.

(2) If the defendant is found guilty of one (1) or more charges, the jury shall then hear additional evidence relevant to sentencing on those charges. Evidence introduced in the guilt phase may be considered, but need not be reintroduced at the sentencing phase.

(3) Following the introduction of additional evidence relevant to sentencing, if any, instruction on the law, and argument, the jury shall again retire and determine a sentence within the statutory range.

(4) The court, in its discretion, may also instruct the jury that counsel may argue as to alternative sentences for which the defendant may qualify. The jury, in its discretion, may make a recommendation as to an alternative sentence. However, this recommendation shall not be binding on the court.

(5) After a jury finds guilt, the defendant, with the agreement of the prosecution and the consent of the court, may waive jury sentencing, in which case the court shall impose sentence.

(6) After a plea of guilty, the defendant, with the agreement of the prosecution and the consent of the court, may be sentenced by a jury impaneled for purposes of sentencing only.

|| *Arkansas Code §16-97-103* ||
Evidence

Evidence relevant to sentencing by either the court or a jury may include, but is not limited to, the following, provided no evidence shall be construed under this section as overriding the rape shield statute . . . :

(1) The law applicable to parole, meritorious good time, or transfer;

(2) Prior convictions of the defendant, both felony and misdemeanor. The jury may be advised as to the nature of the previous convictions, the date and place thereof, the sentence received, and the date of release from confinement or supervision from all prior offenses;

(3) Prior judicial determinations of delinquency in juvenile court, subject to the following limitations:

(i) That prior delinquency adjudications be subject to a judicial determination that the relevant value of the prior juvenile adjudication outweigh its prejudicial value;

(ii) That consideration only be given to juvenile delinquency adjudications for crimes for which the juvenile could have been tried as an adult; and

(iii) That in no event shall delinquency adjudications for acts occurring more than ten (10) years prior to the commission of the offense charged be considered;

(4) Victim impact evidence or statements;

(5) Relevant character evidence;

(6) Evidence of aggravating and mitigating circumstances. The criteria for departure from the sentencing standards may serve as examples of this type of evidence;

(7) Evidence relevant to guilt presented in the first stage;

(8) Evidence held inadmissible in the first stage may be resubmitted for consideration in the second stage if the basis for exclusion did not apply to sentencing; and

(9) Rebuttal evidence.

|| *Arkansas Code §16-90-107* ||
Fixing of Punishment Generally

(a) When a jury finds a verdict of guilty and fails to agree on the punishment to be inflicted, or does not declare the punishment in its verdict, or if it assesses a punishment not authorized by law, and in all cases of a judgment on confession, the court shall assess and declare the punishment and render judgment accordingly.

(b)(1) Juries and courts shall have the power to assess the punishment of one convicted of a felony at a general sentence to the penitentiary. The sentence shall not be less than the minimum nor greater than the maximum time provided by law.

(2) At any time after the expiration of the minimum time, upon the recommendation of the superintendent and it appearing that a prisoner has a good record as a convict, his sentence may be terminated by the [parole] board.

(c) If the jury in any case assesses a greater punishment, whether of fine or imprisonment, than the highest limit declared by law for the offense for which they convict the defendant, the court shall disregard the excess and enter judgment and pronounce sentence according to the highest limit prescribed by law in the particular case.

(d) If the jury in any case assesses a punishment, whether of fine or imprisonment, below the limit prescribed by law for offenses of which the defendant is convicted, the court shall render judgment and pronounce sentence according to the lowest limit prescribed by law in such cases.

(e) The court shall have power, in all cases of conviction, to reduce the extent or duration of the punishment assessed by a jury if, in the opinion of the court, the conviction is proper and the punishment assessed is greater than, under the circumstances of the case, ought to be inflicted, so that the punishment is not, in any case, reduced below the limit prescribed by law in such cases.

	Manual for Courts-Martial, United States	
	Exec. Order No. 12,473, 49 Fed. Reg. 17,152	
	(Apr. 13, 1984)	

RULE 1002.   SENTENCE DETERMINATION

Subject to limitations in this Manual, the sentence to be adjudged is a matter within the discretion of the court-martial; except when a mandatory minimum sentence is prescribed by the code, a court-martial may adjudge any punishment authorized in this Manual, including the maximum punishment or any lesser punishment, or may adjudge a sentence of no punishment. . . .

RULE 1006.   DELIBERATIONS AND VOTING ON SENTENCE

(a) In general. The members shall deliberate and vote after the military judge instructs the members on sentence. Only the members shall be present during deliberations and voting. Superiority in rank shall not be used in any manner to control the independence of members in the exercise of their judgment.

(b) Deliberations. Deliberations may properly include full and free discussion of the sentence to be imposed in the case. Unless otherwise directed by the military judge, members may take with them in deliberations their notes, if any, any exhibits admitted in evidence, and any written instructions. Members may request that the court-martial be reopened and that portions of the record be read to them or additional evidence introduced. The military judge may, in the exercise of discretion, grant such requests.

(c) Proposal of sentences. Any member may propose a sentence. Each proposal shall be in writing and shall contain the complete sentence proposed. The junior member shall collect the proposed sentences and submit them to the president.

(d) Voting.

(1) Duty of members. Each member has the duty to vote for a proper sentence for the offenses of which the court-martial found the accused guilty, regardless of the member's vote or opinion as to the guilt of the accused.

(2) Secret ballot. Proposed sentences shall be voted on by secret written ballot.

(3) Procedure.

(A) Order. All members shall vote on each proposed sentence in its entirety beginning with the least severe and continuing, as necessary, with the next least severe, until a sentence is adopted by the concurrence of the number of members required under subsection (d)(4) of this rule. The process of proposing sentences and voting on them may be repeated as necessary until a sentence is adopted.

(B) Counting votes. The junior member shall collect the ballots and count the votes. The president shall check the count and inform the other members of the result.

(4) Number of votes required.

(A) Death. A sentence which includes death may be adjudged only if all members present vote for that sentence.

(B) Confinement for life or more than 10 years. A sentence which includes confinement for life or more than 10 years may be adjudged only if at least three-fourths of the members present vote for that sentence.

(C) Other. A sentence other than those described in subsection (d)(4)(A) or (B) of this rule may be adjudged only if at least two-thirds of the members present vote for that sentence.

(5) Mandatory sentence. When a mandatory minimum is prescribed under Article 118 the members shall vote on a sentence in accordance with this rule.

(6) Effect of failure to agree. If the required number of members do not agree on a sentence after a reasonable effort to do so, a mistrial may be declared as to the sentence and the case shall be returned to the convening authority, who may order a rehearing on sentence only or order that a sentence of no punishment be imposed. . . .

NOTES

1. *Sentencing juries.* As mentioned above, in a half-dozen states juries not only rule on guilt or innocence but can also decide the sentence to impose, even

in noncapital cases. In some of these states, the jury's choice is binding. Va. Code Ann. §29.2-295.1 (jury sentences unless "jury cannot agree on a punishment" and defendant, prosecutor, and court agree that the court should determine punishment). In other states, such as Kentucky, "the judge can modify a jury sentence if the jury penalty is unduly harsh." Ky. Rev. Stat. §532.070. In Missouri, the sentencing jury recommends a range for sentencing. Mo. Rev. Stat. §557.036. See also Tex. Crim. Proc. Code Ann. §37.07 (judge can assess punishment if defendant does not request probation or jury sentence; jury must be instructed about parole and other devices for reducing actual amount of prison time offender must serve).

The ABA Standards for Criminal Justice, Sentencing 18-1.4 (3d ed. 1994), calls for the abolition of jury sentencing in noncapital cases. Earlier versions of the ABA standards took the same position, leading to the abolition of jury sentencing in Alabama (in 1977), Indiana (1976), and Montana (1967). Why do the ABA standards, along with the strong majority of the states, give sentencing responsibilities to the judge and not the jury, the representatives of the community? For a proposal to expand the use of jury sentencing, see Jenia Iontcheva, Jury Sentencing as Democratic Practice, 88 Va. L. Rev. 311 (2003).

Even in a system that gives no formal sentencing power to juries, the jury might consider likely punishments as it deliberates on the verdict in the case, and jurors might acquit if they believe the sanction is too severe. See Paul Butler, Racially Based Jury Nullification: Black Power in the Criminal Justice System, 105 Yale L.J. 677 (1995). As defense counsel, would you recommend that your client choose jury sentencing? If so, for what types of cases?

2. *Jury sentencing and disparity.*   One of the most significant concerns about jury sentencing in noncapital cases (and in capital cases as well) is that different juries might impose significantly different sentences in similar cases. Another source of disparity might come from the difference in judge and jury sentencing choices in states that give the defendant the option of jury or judge sentencing, such as Arkansas (above) or Missouri (defendant must request in writing before voir dire that the judge assess the punishment in the case of a finding of guilt). Very little is known about whether jury sentencing in fact produces greater disparity. See Adriaan Lanni, Jury Sentencing in Non-Capital Cases: An Idea Whose Time Has Come (Again)?, 108 Yale L.J. 1775 (1999). Another systematic concern of modern reformers, allocating scarce punishment resources, may also be difficult for juries to assess. Perhaps the several states that allow judges to reduce (but not increase) jury sentences, or that allow juries to recommend sentencing ranges, accommodate both the virtues of a jury's sentencing judgment and more systematic concerns.

Is sentencing an "expert" function? Is the expertise the product of sentencing experience, or life experience, or something else? If sentencing is appropriately a judicial function, does that function have constitutional foundations? See Mistretta v. United States, 488 U.S. 361 (1989). Can — and should — legislatures (or commissions) remove most, or all, sentencing discretion?

3. *Code of Military Justice and nonunanimous sentences.*   Should the sentencing jury be required to vote unanimously for a particular sentence? Should its voting rules be the same as the rules for its vote on guilt and innocence?

Recall that in the Manual for Courts-Martial, Rule 1006(c) and (d), members of the court-martial panel propose sentences, and the panel must consider each proposed sentence from least severe to most severe, with the necessary voting requirements turning on the nature of the sentence. How much less protection is provided to defendants by allowing for confinement for more than ten years by three-fourths of the jury members? What aspects of the military, if any, might justify the use of sentencing juries in courts-martial as distinguished from regular state felony juries?

B.   LEGISLATURES AND COMMISSIONS

Although indeterminate sentencing was the norm in this country for most of the twentieth century, new arrangements have emerged over the past generation. Some of those alternative approaches put the legislature more firmly in control of sentencing. Legislators have decided for themselves the precise sentence that will attach to various types of offenses; other sentencing institutions such as courts are supposed to carry out the instructions of the legislature without adding any meaningful choices of their own. For instance, under 18 U.S.C. §924(c), any person who "uses or carries" a firearm during any federal drug trafficking crime "shall, in addition to the punishment provided for [the] drug trafficking crime . . . be sentenced to a term of imprisonment of not less than 5 years [and] if the firearm is brandished, be sentenced to a term of imprisonment of not less than 7 years; and . . . if the firearm is discharged, be sentenced to a term of imprisonment of not less than 10 years."

Sentences dominated by legislative choices go back to some of the earliest recorded sources of law, including the Code of Hammurabi, excerpted below. This code reflects a society very different from our own; would a review of our current statutes on criminal punishments create a fairly accurate portrait of our own times?

‖ *Code of Hammurabi* ‖
(C. H. W. Johns trans., 1911)

§1: If a man weave a spell and put a ban upon a man, and has not justified himself, he that wove the spell upon him shall be put to death.

§8: If a man has stolen ox or sheep or ass, or pig, or ship, whether from the temple or the palace, he shall pay thirtyfold. If he be a poor man, he shall render tenfold. If the thief has naught to pay, he shall be put to death.

§195: If a man has struck his father, his hands one shall cut off.

§196: If a man has caused the loss of a gentleman's eye, his eye one shall cause to be lost.

§197: If he has shattered a gentleman's limb, one shall shatter his limb.

§198: If he has caused a poor man to lose his eye or shattered a poor man's limb, he shall pay one mina of silver.

§209: If a man has struck a gentleman's daughter and caused her to drop what is in her womb, he shall pay ten shekels of silver for what was in her womb.

§210: If that woman has died, one shall put to death his daughter.

§211: If the daughter of a poor man through his blows he has caused to drop that which is in her womb, he shall pay five shekels of silver.

§212: If that woman has died, he shall pay half a mina of silver.

> ## *Mandatory Minimum Penalties in the Federal Criminal Justice System*
> ### U.S. Sentencing Commission, Pages 5-15, 27-32
> ### (1991)

Mandatory minimum sentences are not new to the federal criminal justice system. As early as 1790, mandatory penalties had been established for capital offenses. In addition, at subsequent intervals throughout the 19th Century, Congress enacted provisions that required definite prison terms, typically quite short, for a variety of other crimes. Until recently, however, the enactment of mandatory minimum provisions was generally an occasional phenomenon that was not comprehensively aimed at whole classes of offenses.

A change in practice occurred with the passage of the Narcotic Control Act of 1956, which mandated minimum sentences of considerable length for most drug importation and distribution offenses. . . . In 1970, Congress drew back from the comprehensive application of mandatory minimum provisions to drug crimes enacted 14 years earlier. Finding that increases in sentence length "had not shown the expected overall reduction in drug law violations," Congress passed [legislation] that repealed virtually all mandatory penalties for drug violations.

[Growing criticism of efforts to rehabilitate inmates led lawmakers] to renew support for mandatory minimum penalties. On the state level this trend began in New York in 1973, with California and Massachusetts following soon thereafter. While the trend toward mandatory minimums in the states was gradual, by 1983, 49 of the 50 states had passed such provisions. . . . On the federal level, a comparable but more comprehensive trend was underway. Beginning in 1984, and every two years thereafter, Congress enacted an array of mandatory minimum penalties specifically targeted at drugs and violent crime. . . . Today there are approximately 100 separate federal mandatory minimum penalty provisions located in 60 different criminal statutes. . . . Of the 59,780 cases sentenced under mandatory minimum statutes [between 1984 and 1990], four statutes account for approximately 94 percent of the cases. These four statutes . . . all involve drugs and weapons violations. . . .

REASONS CITED IN SUPPORT OF MANDATORY MINIMUMS

[Field interviews with] judges, assistant United States attorneys, defense attorneys, and probation officers . . . identified six commonly-offered rationales for mandatory minimum sentencing provisions.

Retribution or "Just Deserts." Perhaps the most commonly-voiced goal of mandatory minimum penalties is the "justness" of long prison terms for particularly serious offenses. Proponents generally agree that longer sentences are deserved and that, absent mandatory penalties, judges would impose sentences more lenient than would be appropriate.

Deterrence.   . . . Those supporting mandatory minimums on deterrence grounds point not only to the strong deterrent value of the *certainty* of substantial punishment these penalties are intended to provide, but also to the deterrent value of sentence *severity* that these penalties are intended to ensure in the war against crime.

Incapacitation, Especially of the Serious Offender.   Mandating increased sentence severity aims to protect the public by incapacitating offenders convicted of serious crimes for definite, and generally substantial, periods of time. Proponents argue that one way to increase public safety, particularly with respect to guns and drugs, is to remove drug dealers and violent offenders from the streets for extended periods of time.

Disparity.   Indeterminate sentencing systems permit substantial latitude in setting the sentence, which in turn can mean that defendants convicted of the same offense are sentenced to widely disparate sentences. Supporters of mandatory minimum penalties contend that they greatly reduce judicial discretion and are therefore more fair. Mandatory minimums are meant to ensure that defendants convicted of similar offenses receive penalties that at least begin at the same minimal point.

Inducement of Cooperation.   Because they provide specific lengthy sentences, mandatory minimums encourage offenders to assist in the investigation of criminal conduct by others. This is because cooperation — that is, supplying information concerning the activities of other criminally involved individuals — is the only statutorily-recognized way to permit the court to impose a sentence below the length of imprisonment required by the mandatory minimum sentence.

Inducement of Pleas.   Although infrequently cited by policymakers, prosecutors express the view that mandatory minimum sentences can be valuable tools in obtaining guilty pleas, saving scarce enforcement resources and increasing the certainty of at least some measure of punishment. In this context, the value of a mandatory minimum sentence lies not in its imposition, but in its value as a bargaining chip to be given away in return for the resource-saving plea from the defendant to a more leniently sanctioned charge.

[Now we turn to some of the criticisms of mandatory minimum sentences.]

THE "TARIFF" EFFECT OF MANDATORY MINIMUM

Years ago, Congress used tariff sentences in sanctioning broad categories of offenses, ranging from quite serious crimes (e.g., homicide) to fairly minor property theft. This tariff approach has been rejected historically primarily because there were too many defendants whose important distinctions were obscured by this single, flat approach to sentencing. A more sophisticated, calibrated approach that takes into account gradations of offense seriousness, criminal record, and level of culpability has long since been recognized as a more appropriate and equitable method of sentencing. . . .

The mandatory minimums set forth in 21 U.S.C. §841(b), applicable to defendants convicted of trafficking in the more common street drugs, are illustrative. For those convicted of drug trafficking under this section, one offense-related factor, and only one, is determinative of whether the mandatory minimum applies: the weight of the drug or drug mixture. Any other sentence-individualizing factors that might pertain in a case are irrelevant as far as the statute is concerned. Thus, for example, whether the defendant was a peripheral participant or the drug ring's kingpin, whether the defendant used a weapon, whether the defendant accepted responsibility or, on the other hand, obstructed justice, have no bearing on the mandatory minimum to which each defendant is exposed. . . .

The "Cliff" Effect of Mandatory Minimums

Related to the proportionality problems posed in mandatory minimums already described are the sharp differences in sentence between defendants who fall just below the threshold of a mandatory minimum compared with those whose criminal conduct just meets the criteria of the mandatory minimum penalty. Just as mandatory minimums fail to distinguish among defendants whose conduct and prior records in fact differ markedly, they distinguish far too greatly among defendants who have committed offense conduct of highly comparable seriousness.

[A] lack of coordination between statutory maximum and mandatory minimum penalties for the same or similar offenses can create dramatic sentencing cliffs among similarly-situated defendants. For example, 21 U.S.C. §884 mandates a minimum five-year term of imprisonment for a defendant convicted of first-offense, simple possession of 5.01 or more grams of "crack." . . . However, a first-offender convicted of simple possession of 5.0 grams of crack is subjected to a *maximum* statutory penalty of one year imprisonment. . . .

The "Charge-Specific" Nature of Mandatory Minimums

. . . In general, a mandatory minimum becomes applicable only when the prosecutor elects to *charge* and the defendant is *convicted* of the specific offense carrying the mandatory sentence. . . . Mandatory minimums employ a structure that allows a shifting of discretion and control over the implementation of sentencing policies from courts to prosecutors. [There] is substantial reason to believe that mandatory minimums are not in fact pursued by prosecutors in all instances that the underlying statutes otherwise would require. . . .

NOTES

1. *Judicial discretion and mandatory penalties.*   Many criticisms of mandatory minimum statutes focus on the loss of judicial discretion in sentencing.

Consider, for example, the 1970 statement of then Representative George H.W. Bush:

> Federal judges are almost unanimously opposed to mandatory minimums, because they remove a great deal of the court's discretion. In the vast majority of cases which reach the sanctioning stage today, the bare minimum sentence is levied — and in some cases, less than the minimum mandatory is given. . . . Probations and outright dismissals often result. Philosophical differences aside, practicality requires a sentence structure which is generally acceptable to the courts, to prosecutors, and to the general public.

116 Cong. Rec. H33314, Sept. 23, 1970. Many state and federal judges share these views and believe that mandatory minimum statutes too often force them to impose a fundamentally unjust sentence. In a 2003 survey of federal judges, most of the judges believed that mandatory minimum punishments had a negative effect on their ability to "impose sentences that reflect the statutory purposes of sentencing." See Survey of Article III Judges on the Federal Sentencing Guidelines, http://www.ussc.gov/judsurv/judsurv.htm. Are all mandatory minimums subject to the criticisms about uneven enforcement and loss of judicial discretion? Could a legislature address these problems by narrowly defining the offenses and offenders eligible for a mandatory sentence?

Can any decision maker other than a judge — who decides many individual cases — appreciate the facts about an offender's past that should lead to a lighter sentence? Why might judges impose sentences lighter than those set by the legislature? Do judges generally share a different political view on crime control? Do they see too many individual cases?

2. *Mandatory mandatories.*   Most mandatory minimum statutes instruct the judge to impose a particular sentence for a particular charge, but they do not require the prosecutor to file a given charge when adequate facts are present. Thus, typical mandatory sentencing statutes give prosecutors considerable bargaining power during plea negotiations; they also offer prosecutors opportunities to avoid mandatory minimum sentences when they believe that such sentences would be unjust or a poor use of resources. Stephen Schulhofer and Ilene Nagel surveyed charging practices and concluded that prosecutors' concerns about mandatory minimum sentences led them in a substantial number of cases to charge some lesser crime even though the evidence was available to charge for the mandatory minimum crime. Schulhofer and Nagel, A Tale of Three Cities: An Empirical Study of Charging and Bargaining Practices Under the Federal Sentencing Guidelines, 66 S. Cal. L. Rev. 501 (1992).

Legislatures sometimes constrain this prosecutorial power by passing statutes that prevent plea bargaining and require the prosecutor to file charges whenever adequate evidence is available. For instance, in 1973 New York passed a "Rockefeller drug law" imposing severe mandatory minimums and restricting plea bargaining. After passage of this law, there were fewer arrests, indictments, and convictions for drug offenses, but those convicted served longer terms. Jacqueline Cohen and Michael Tonry, Sentencing Reforms and the Impacts, in Research on Sentencing: The Search for Reform 348-349 (Alfred Blumstein et al. eds., 1983). This sort of "mandatory mandatory" statute is rare. Why do legislators hesitate to pass statutes that remove the prosecutor's discretion to decline charges or to select a charge not subject to the minimum penalty?

3. *Net effects of mandatory minimum penalties on sentencing patterns.*   Studies of mandatory minimum penalties have reached different conclusions about the effect of these laws on the crime rates for the targeted offenses. Some studies have found a deterrent effect for gun crimes and homicides, but other studies have found no effect on the commission of drug crimes or violent crimes generally. The effects of mandatory minimum penalties on the criminal justice system are clearer. These laws consistently lead to fewer arrests for the designated crimes, fewer charges filed, more dismissals of charges, more trials rather than guilty pleas, and longer sentences imposed and served. See Dale Parent, Terence Dunworth, Douglas McDonald, and William Rhodes, Key Legislative Issues in Criminal Justice: Mandatory Sentencing (National Institute of Justice, Research in Action, NCJ 161839, Jan. 1997).

4. *Self-correcting democratic process.*   If mandatory minimum sentences truly produced the ill effects described by critics, wouldn't the democratically elected legislature recognize these flaws after a time and abandon the experiment? This has happened in a few states. In 2001 the Connecticut legislature granted judges authority to depart from mandatory minimum sentences for certain drug crimes, such as first-time sales or possession within 1,500 feet of a school. Also that year, Indiana eliminated mandatory 20-year sentences for cocaine dealers (anyone caught with more than three grams of powder cocaine), and Louisiana repealed mandatory sentences for some simple possession and other nonviolent drug offenses. Meanwhile, other jurisdictions, such as New York, have debated for years about changing mandatory minimum drug sentences, without ever taking action. See Ronald F. Wright, Are the Drug Wars De-escalating? Where to Look for Evidence, 14 Fed. Sentencing Rep. 141 (2002). What might prevent the legislature from rethinking self-destructive legislation? Who brings information to the legislators' attention as they debate proposals or create an agenda? Is the problem a lack of information, a lack of time, or something else?

Legislatures in just under half the states have empowered permanent "sentencing commissions" to create rules to guide judges as they select sentences within the statutory range. These guidelines (some embodied in statutes and others in administrative rules) are different from statutory maximum and minimum punishments because they allow judges, under some circumstances, to go above or below the recommended range so long as the final sentence remains within the statutorily authorized range.

Legislatures typically create sentencing commissions after other institutions fail. Judges, executive branch officials, and legislators have failed in predictable patterns over the years when they have tried to change or administer sentencing policy. You might think of these patterns of institutional failure as "pathologies," or deviations from the more ordinary and effective functions of these governmental institutions.

Judicial Pathologies.   Judges create two sorts of difficulties in the sentencing system, both arising because the judges sentence individually rather than as a coordinated group. First, different judges sometimes give disparate sentences to offenders who, in every relevant way, seem to be alike. Second, sentencing judges do not conserve corrections resources. There is a fixed number of prison beds and slots in corrections programs, yet each judge has little incentive to use only her proportional share of this "public good."

A sentencing commission is one potential solution to both problems. A commission could reduce disparity by designating, within narrow boundaries, the "ordinary" sentences for particular types of offenses and offenders. A commission could also designate ordinary sentences at a level not likely to overburden the corrections system.

Executive Pathologies.   Some executive branch pathologies in sentencing are possible because parole release decisions are not easily visible to the public. The parole decision receives less attention than the sentence itself, and it is made by an executive official who, unlike many state court judges, is not directly accountable to the voters.

The difficulties with low-visibility release decisions are the classic objections to all low-visibility discretionary decisions: they may not be based on consistent or proper reasons. The release date may depend on no articulable principles at all, or it may depend on the personal views of the executive officer involved rather than principles endorsed by the public. Sentencing commissions offer one way to make release decisions more visible and consistent. Under a guideline system, the release date turns on principles adopted through a public process, as applied and announced by a publicly accountable government official, the judge.

Legislative Pathologies.   Legislators make their own pathological contributions to sentencing policy. But the accounts of exactly how the legislature does so are not altogether consistent. According to some accounts, legislatures need to delegate sentencing authority to a permanent commission because they do not have enough time or expertise to make proper changes in sentencing laws. The complexity of sentencing issues makes it difficult, during the limited time available, for the legislators and their staffs to acquire the necessary information to make wise choices.

Other critics of the legislative role in sentencing argue that the legislature spends far too *much* time dealing with sentencing. Legislators, according to this view, pander to the perceived passions and frustrations of their constituents about crime; they pass laws that prove later to be expensive, ineffectual, and cruel. Periodic tinkering by the legislature creates an inconsistent sentencing scheme, riddled with exceptions. According to these critics, the legislature has more difficulty dealing rationally with crime than with most other subjects.

Just as the descriptions of legislative pathologies are not entirely consistent, the prescriptions for a commission's proper response to the legislative pathologies are in some tension with each other. Under one model, the ideal commission strategy is to minimize legislative involvement in criminal punishment issues. A successful system, in this view, will reduce the legislators' opportunities to interfere with the judgment of the expert members and staff of the commission. The commission will anticipate and deal with any criminal justice crises that could provoke the legislature to take action. Under a second model, the sentencing commission merely attempts to improve legislative deliberation about criminal legislation. The commission can inform the legislators about the consequences (especially the fiscal consequences) of different bills, and it can advocate consistency and rationality in sentencing.

The following materials highlight the different roles that sentencing commissions and sentencing guidelines play in a jurisdiction. They also point out how commissions, when they arrive on the scene, can change the established roles among the existing sentencing institutions in the jurisdiction.

ABA Standards for Criminal Justice, Sentencing 18-4.1
(3d ed. 1994)

(a) Implementation of legislative policy determinations within the statutory framework of the criminal code requires a state-wide agency to develop a more specific set of provisions that guide sentencing courts to presumptive sentences and in the appropriate use of aggravating and mitigating factors, offenders' criminal history, and offenders' personal characteristics. . . .

(b) The agency performing the intermediate function should be the information center for all elements of the criminal justice system. The agency should collect, analyze and disseminate information on the nature and effects of sentences imposed and carried out. The agency should develop means to monitor, evaluate, and predict patterns of sentencing, including levels of severity of sentences imposed and relative use of each type of sanction. . . .

Commentary. This standard gives definition to the concept of the "intermediate function" in sentencing systems. This term [describes] the work done "in between" the legislature's statutory commands and the case-by-case decisions of sentencing judges. Every jurisdiction should create a permanently chartered agency to perform the intermediate function, either in the form of a sentencing commission or an equivalent body in the legislative or judicial branch. . . .

Typically, statutory maxima are set at high levels so that the range of statutorily authorized penalties is wide indeed. One critical function of the sentencing agency, as intermediary between legislature and the courts, is to give structure to the decision-making process for selecting particular sentences within the expansive range allowed by the code.

The agency performs this role through the creation of presumptive sentences and other provisions for the guidance of sentencing judges, including provisions relating to aggravating and mitigating circumstances, and the effect of offenders' prior criminal histories and personal characteristics. Through such measures, courts across the jurisdiction can approach sentencing decisions from a common baseline and can employ similar steps of logic and analysis in adjusting sentences away from the presumptive baseline when required. . . .

Modeling Discretion in American Sentencing Systems, Kevin Reitz
20 Law & Pol. 389 (1998)

. . . I have found it helpful to think in pictorial terms about an array of actors in sentencing systems who potentially have sentencing discretion. A generic

FIGURE 1
A Discretion Diagram for Sentencing Systems

Systemic Level

Case-Specific Level

"discretion diagram," such as that reproduced in Figure 1, can be used to visualize many of the important relationships in existing punishment systems.

[One] function of Figure 1 is to recognize that some discretionary actors operate primarily on the "systemic level" while others discharge their authorities primarily on the "case-specific level." . . . Systemic actors make discretionary decisions intended to influence whole categories of cases; case-specific actors make discretionary judgments that, for the most part, operate on the individual cases before them. . . .

Indeterminate Sentencing Systems

. . . Indeterminate schemes, still in effect in roughly half of the American states, are represented below in Figure 3. . . .

A number of the distinctive features of indeterminacy jump out from Figure 3. . . . First, the shrunken compartment for the legislature in Figure 3 indicates the very loose statutory boundaries upon punishment outcomes that generally exist in the traditional systems. It would not be unusual in an indeterminate jurisdiction, for example, to find that the legislatively authorized sanction for a crime such as aggravated assault reaches as low as a suspended sentence without conditions, up to a term of incarceration in the ballpark of thirty-two years. . . .

The second defining characteristic of indeterminate structures is their diffusion of meaningful sentencing discretion across numerous actors at the case-specific level. Prosecutors most of the time enjoy unregulated charging discretion; plea bargains between the parties (sometimes including sentence bargains) can have sizable impact on punishment; probation officers, at least in some jurisdictions, make sentence recommendations that are highly influential

FIGURE 3
A Discretion Diagram of Indeterminate Sentencing

Systemic Level

Case-Specific Level

with judges; the judges themselves usually have a boggling array of choices remaining open to them on the day of sentencing; and following a judicially pronounced prison sentence, correctional officials and parole boards hold impressive powers to fix actual release dates — which can sometimes be set after only a small fraction of the court's sentence has been served.

The only case-specific actor without meaningful sentencing discretion in traditional indeterminate systems, as it turns out, is the appellate judiciary. For reasons of historical practice, deference to trial courts, and caseload pressures, appellate courts almost universally have resisted responsibility to participate in sentencing outcomes. . . .

THE FEDERAL SYSTEM

The most salient discretionary feature of the U.S. sentencing system, especially in comparison with its state counterparts, is the federal system's attempt to concentrate discretionary authority at the systemic level and to constrain such authority at the case-specific level. . . . In comparison with the weak legislative presence in indeterminate sentencing structures, Congress made itself an important discretionary actor in the new federal scheme. Through its many mandatory sentencing laws, and through oversight of the U.S. Sentencing Commission, Congress has assumed and held a major role in the ongoing determination of sentencing outcomes.

More distinctive than the enlargement of the legislative role, however, has been the great measure of authority granted to or assumed by the U.S. Sentencing Commission vis-à-vis downstream players in the sentencing system. [The] federal commission was introduced as a new and authoritative actor, absorbing important discretions that formerly were exercised by other decision makers. . . .

The systemic power wielded by the U.S. commission was compounded by the fact that, when creating the federal guidelines system, Congress abolished parole release and imposed sharp limits on the amount of good-time credit that may be awarded federal prisoners. . . . Thus, the commission's discretion to say what a sentence should be in a particular case could be overruled infrequently by a trial judge, and was subject only to minor adjustment at the "back door" of the incarceration process. . . .

PENNSYLVANIA

While the federal sentencing system may be seen primarily as an attempt to concentrate authority at the systemic level, the Pennsylvania guidelines structure is distinguished by its very weak exertions of systemwide control over punishment decisions. . . . In comparison with the detailed legislative mandate enacted by Congress for the new federal structure, the Pennsylvania legislature authored a cryptic and open-ended scheme. Notably, the state legislature described the guidelines to be created by the commission as one factor among many, or as merely "considerations," for trial courts to weigh when imposing sentences. . . .

In Pennsylvania, as it turned out, the most important structural decisions about the apportionment of sentencing discretion were made by the state's appellate courts. . . . By the late 1980s, the state supreme court ruled that the new guidelines were only "advisory," that the legislature had required no more than that trial courts "take notice of" the commission's work before choosing a sentence, and that reviewing courts had no power to hear appeals based on the claim that the guidelines had not been followed, except in "exceptional cases." The discretionary implications of these decisions are pictured in Figure 5 below. . . .

FIGURE 5
A Discretion Diagram of the Pennsylvania System

Systemic Level

(Legislature)   (Pa. Comm.)

Case-Specific Level

The Parties   Probation Officer   Trial Court   Appellate Courts   Corrections Officials   Parole Board

The result, in Pennsylvania, has been to privilege trial court discretion while leaving the parties' plea negotiation powers unregulated. In these terms, Figure 5 still resembles the traditional indeterminate sentencing structure that preceded the Pennsylvania guidelines. No one is in charge at the systemic level; nearly all meaningful sentencing authority has settled down to the case-specific level. [The] discretionary patterns of the Pennsylvania system [reminds us that] not all guideline structures are created equal. With respect to one critical variable — the degree of systemwide control attempted in each structure — the [federal and Pennsylvania guidelines] could hardly be more different. . . .

NOTES

1. *Reasons to create sentencing commissions and guidelines.* Almost half the states use sentencing guidelines created by sentencing commissions. The federal system also operates under sentencing guidelines, created in 1987 by the U.S. Sentencing Commission. A state sentencing commission typically drafts the initial set of guidelines on behalf of the legislature, which then enacts an integrated package of sentencing reforms. In states without a commission, the state judiciary adopts a package of guidelines as procedural rules or as informal guidance to judges.

Why would a legislature ask a commission to create a set of sentencing guidelines? Does a commission have any advantages over a legislature in setting specific sentencing ranges for particular types of offenses and offenders? Legislatures turn to commissions when the legislators recognize that they do not have enough time or expertise themselves to do the job well. Political theory also suggests some less noble motives that might lead legislators to deal with criminal sentencing through a commission. When it comes to statutes involving criminal punishments, legislators often have political incentives to advocate severe punishment so that they can be seen as tough on crime. Stiff penalties may be appropriate for the extreme cases that dominate legislative debates; a wide definition of the crime will include both the imagined and the as-yet unimagined evils.

At the same time, legislators want to avoid blame for the costs of criminal punishments. They would rather leave it to prosecutors to weigh the human costs of unnecessarily strong punishments, since prosecutors can decline prosecution when justice requires it. And they might prefer some other institution, such as a sentencing commission, to make the hard decisions about how to economize on the limited prison and corrections resources available.

Very few jurisdictions outside the United States have created bodies such as sentencing commissions to serve an intermediate function between the legislature and the judges. If sentencing commissions are a good idea, why do we not see them in other places in the world?

2. *Research instead of rules.* Most guidelines created by commissions are, to some degree or another, presumptive. That is, a judge who sentences outside the presumed range for sentences risks reversal. Are presumptive sentencing rules, created by commissions and approved by legislatures, subject to the same criticisms leveled against legislatively determined sentences? Would sentencing

commissions be more valuable if they limited their recommendations to the most commonly encountered "paradigm" cases for sentencing and conducted research into the effects of various types of sanctions? Is lack of knowledge a more pressing concern than lack of uniformity among sentencing judges? See Albert Alschuler, The Failure of Sentencing Guidelines: A Plea for Less Aggregation, 58 U. Chi. L. Rev. 901 (1991).

C.   PROSECUTORS

Just as they are central to most other aspects of criminal justice, prosecutors are central to sentencing. Prosecutors select the charges that define the outer statutory boundaries for the sentence. Because criminal codes in the United States are typically stuffed with different crimes covering similar conduct, and specific crimes are often defined with broad terms that could cover a wide range of behavior, the prosecutor normally has a number of legal options that could plausibly fit the facts as alleged. Some crimes include mandatory sentences, and in some systems prosecutors can specify particular aggravating factors with dramatic sentencing implications.

The prosecutor also can negotiate a plea agreement with the defendant. Defendants pleading guilty tend to receive substantially lower sentences than defendants who go to trial (in some studies the "plea discount" has been one-third or more off post-trial sentences), but judges tend to sentence based on the original charges filed rather than the charges forming the basis of the guilty plea. And the prosecutor often recommends a particular sentence to the judge, a recommendation that carries great weight, especially in high-volume courtrooms where the judges and probation officers must depend heavily on the parties to inform them about each case.

Under these conditions, prosecutors have substantial and often determinative sentencing power. Do effective controls exist to prevent an individual prosecutor from misusing this power? As the materials below indicate, such controls are not likely to come from the judiciary, because judges are extremely reluctant to review the merits of prosecutorial charging decisions. The study of the prosecutor's office in New Orleans excerpted below raises the possibility of effective controls over individual prosecutors originating internally, from the prosecutor's office itself.

|| ***People v. Wayne Robert Stewart*** ||
|| **55 P.3d 107 (Colo. 2002)** ||

MULLARKEY, C.J.
. . . The crimes occurred on a Sunday evening in March 1997 when Wayne Stewart left the bar of a restaurant located in a suburban shopping center. As Stewart began to drive his sports utility vehicle out of the shopping center parking lot, he encountered three pedestrians — Richard Ehrmann, Christine Castro, and Jeffrey Pippenger, in that order — walking abreast in the middle of

the driving lane. The pedestrians had just left a video rental store and, as they walked to their vehicle, they were looking up at the Hale Bopp comet streaking across the sky. The testimony of disinterested bystanders established that Stewart veered toward the pedestrians at an angle; Ehrmann, who was closest to the traffic lane, was brushed by Stewart's vehicle. A verbal altercation ensued, after which Stewart began driving back and forth at an angle and in an aggressive manner. [Stewart's car hit Ehrmann, and when the car abruptly stopped, Ehrmann rolled off the hood and landed hard on the ground next to the driver's side. The SUV continued to roll forward, and the rear wheel on the driver's side ran over Ehrmann's head.] Stewart left the scene without stopping. As a result of the incident, Ehrmann suffered massive brain injury and lay comatose for approximately two and one-half years. Ultimately, the victim died.

The state charged Stewart with one count of first degree assault against Ehrmann, a class 3 felony in violation of section 18-3-202(1)(a); one count of reckless second degree assault against Ehrmann, a class 4 felony, in violation of §18-3-203(1)(d); four counts of violent crime, pursuant to §16-11-309; one count of vehicular assault against Ehrmann, a class 5 felony, in violation of §18-3-205(1)(a); and four counts of reckless endangerment against the other two pedestrians and two bystanders, a class 3 misdemeanor, in violation of §18-3-208. Stewart pleaded not guilty to the charges.

At trial, the People contended that Stewart intentionally hit Ehrmann or, in the alternative, that Stewart used his vehicle to scare and intimidate Ehrmann. Stewart took the position . . . that Ehrmann jumped onto [the hood of] Stewart's vehicle and that he was unaware that he ran over Ehrmann. . . .

A jury convicted Stewart of reckless second degree assault of Ehrmann and two counts of reckless endangerment against the other two pedestrians. At the sentencing hearing, the trial court found that Stewart "did drive his car at Mr. Ehrmann in an act of anger," and sentenced Stewart to five years in the Department of Corrections for the second degree assault conviction. . . .

Stewart argues that his conviction for reckless second degree assault with a deadly weapon violates his right to equal protection because the statutes governing vehicular assault and reckless second degree assault with a deadly weapon proscribe the same conduct but mete out disparate punishments. He asserts that there is no rational distinction between second degree reckless assault, a class 4 felony requiring mandatory sentencing for a term of five to sixteen years, and vehicular assault, a class 5 felony that is punishable by one to three years of imprisonment in the presumptive range and two to six years in the aggravated range, and which neither requires a mandatory sentence nor precludes probation. The lack of any rational basis for distinguishing the two offenses, he maintains, coupled with the significant difference in penalty, renders his conviction of second degree assault violative of equal protection by penalizing him more severely for the identical criminal conduct proscribed by the lesser offense of vehicular assault. We disagree.

The Fourteenth Amendment to the United States Constitution provides in part that no state "shall deny to any person within its jurisdiction the equal protection of the laws." A similar guarantee is implicit in the due process clause of the Colorado Constitution. Colo. Const., art. II, §25. Colorado, however, has taken a stricter view of the protections afforded by our equal protection guarantee than has the United States Supreme Court in interpreting the federal

Constitution. The Supreme Court has held that equal protection is not offended when statutes proscribe identical conduct but authorize different penalties. United States v. Batchelder, 442 U.S. 114 (1979).

By contrast, we have consistently held that if a criminal statute proscribes different penalties for identical conduct, a person convicted under the harsher penalty is denied equal protection unless there are reasonable differences or distinctions between the proscribed behavior. The statutory classification of crimes must be based on differences that are both real in fact and also reasonably related to the general purposes of the criminal legislation.

Equally well established is the principle that a single act may violate more than one criminal statute. We have emphasized that equal protection is offended only when two statutes forbid *identical* conduct. . . . To determine whether two statutes proscribe identical conduct, we analyze the elements of each. We emphasize that this task requires a facial examination of the elements comprising each crime. . . . The crime of reckless second degree assault with a deadly weapon is defined in §18-3-203(1)(d), as follows: "(1) A person commits the crime of assault in the second degree if . . . (d) He recklessly causes serious bodily injury to another person by means of a deadly weapon." . . . Vehicular assault is defined in §18-3-205(1)(a), as follows: "If a person operates or drives a motor vehicle in a reckless manner, and this conduct is the proximate cause of serious bodily injury to another, such person commits vehicular assault." . . .

The language of the statutes differs in [several] ways. First, second degree assault applies to a range of unspecified conduct; the defendant can "recklessly cause" injury in a multitude of ways. The conduct specified in the vehicular assault statute, on the other hand, is strictly limited to "driving or operating" a motor vehicle. . . . An elemental comparison thus illustrates that the two statutes, by their terms, target different conduct. To achieve a conviction under the vehicular assault statute, the prosecution must demonstrate that the defendant drove or operated a motor vehicle. Accordingly, one who causes serious bodily injury by dint of a motor vehicle that is used as a weapon, but that is not driven or operated, could be convicted of reckless second degree assault with a deadly weapon but not vehicular assault. For example, if an adult locks a child in a car on a sweltering summer day to punish or intimidate the child, the adult obviously is not driving or operating the car. Assuming that the other elements of the crime are met, however, the adult could be charged with reckless second degree assault but not vehicular assault. . . .

[Another] difference between second degree assault and vehicular assault lies in the means by which the defendant allegedly caused serious bodily injury. The vehicular assault statute provides that, to be convicted, the defendant's reckless driving or operation of a "motor vehicle" must have proximately caused serious bodily injury. The second degree assault statute requires that the defendant use a "deadly weapon." . . . Section 18-1-901(3)(e), provides the statutory definition of deadly weapon:

> "Deadly weapon" means any of the following which in the manner it is used or intended to be used is capable of producing death or serious bodily injury: (I) A firearm, whether loaded or unloaded; (II) A knife; (III) A bludgeon; or (IV) Any other weapon, device, instrument, material, or substance, whether animate or inanimate. . . .

We have consistently held that whether an object is a deadly weapon for the purposes of section 18-1-903(e)(IV) depends on the manner in which the object is used. People v. Ross, 831 P.2d 1310 (Colo. 1992) (holding that a fist can be a deadly weapon).... Any object can be a deadly weapon if it is used in a manner capable of producing death or serious bodily injury.... The same is true of a motor vehicle. It is not always a deadly weapon under the statutory definition. A motor vehicle may be a deadly weapon, however, depending on how it is used in a particular situation.

The difference between the "deadly weapon" requirement of the second degree assault statute and the "motor vehicle" element of vehicular assault justifies the disparate penalties established by the General Assembly. The legislature could rationally decide that "road rage" or the use of a car as a deadly weapon justifies an increased penalty. At the same time, it could rationally determine that it is less reprehensible for one to cause serious bodily injury by mere reckless driving of a vehicle as a vehicle. This court cannot hold that the General Assembly has constitutionally erred in providing a more severe penalty for an act which it believes to be of greater social consequence....

Stewart argues that even if the statutes are not identical, he can be convicted only of the more specific crime, motor vehicle assault, and not of the more general crime, second degree assault. Generally, the prosecution has discretion to determine what charges to file when a defendant's conduct violates more than one statute. See §18-1-408(7) ["If the same conduct is defined as criminal in different enactments or in different sections of this code, the offender may be prosecuted under any one or all of the sections or enactments"]. There are certain circumstances in which this general rule does not apply. See, e.g., People v. Smith, 938 P.2d 111, 115-116 (Colo. 1997) [General Assembly can supplant the more general offense by creating a specific offense supported by clear legislative intent to limit prosecution to that statute; in adopting the comprehensive Liquor Code, the General Assembly intended to require the offense of falsely filling out a liquor application to be prosecuted under the Liquor Code and not under the general felony offense of offering a false instrument for recording].

Stewart has failed to show that his crimes fall into this category. He simply asserts that the General Assembly intended to punish motor vehicle offenses pursuant to the motor vehicle statutes. He cites no authority such as statutory language or legislative history to support his theory and we reject it. The prosecution had discretion to charge second degree assault in this case and the jury verdict convicting Stewart on that charge stands....

The Screening/Bargaining Tradeoff,
Ronald Wright and Marc Miller
55 Stan. L. Rev. 29 (2002)

[All] prosecutors "screen" when they make any charging decision. By prosecutorial screening we mean a far more structured and reasoned charge selection process than is typical in most prosecutors' offices in this country. The prosecutorial screening system we describe has four interrelated features, all internal to the prosecutor's office: early assessment, reasoned selection, barriers to bargains, and enforcement.

First, the prosecutor's office must make an early and careful assessment of each case, and demand that police and investigators provide sufficient information before the initial charge is filed. Second, the prosecutor's office must file only appropriate charges. Which charges are "appropriate" is determined by several factors. A prosecutor should only file charges that the office would generally want to result in a criminal conviction and sanction. In addition, appropriate charges must reflect reasonably accurately what actually occurred. They are charges that the prosecutor can very likely prove in court. Third, and critically, the office must severely restrict all plea bargaining, and most especially charge bargains. Prosecutors should also recognize explicitly that the screening process is the mechanism that makes such restrictions possible. Fourth, the kind of prosecutorial screening we advocate must include sufficient training, oversight, and other internal enforcement mechanisms to ensure reasonable uniformity in charging and relatively few changes to charges after they have been filed. If prosecutors treat hard screening decisions as the primary alternative to plea bargaining, they can produce changes in current criminal practice that would be fundamental, attractive, and viable. . . .

THE SCREENING/BARGAINING TRADEOFF IN PRACTICE: NODA DATA

. . . Harry Connick was elected as the District Attorney for Orleans Parish in 1974. He has remained in that office for the past twenty-eight years. Connick first ran for office in 1969 against incumbent Jim Garrison, the flamboyant District Attorney made famous in the film *JFK*. His first unsuccessful campaign did not focus on plea bargaining. He promised faster prosecution and better tracking of defendants who failed to appear for trial. His 1973 campaign began with a similar emphasis on swift prosecution. As the campaign wore on, however, Connick's speeches began to feature attacks on plea bargaining. . . .

Connick told voters that widespread plea bargaining was wrong; years later, he explained that victims were right to resent it when cases were bargained away simply because of a "lazy" prosecutor. He promised to eliminate "baseless" plea bargaining and to hire full-time prosecutors who would not use plea bargains just to move cases from the docket.

As in other American cities, the criminal courts in New Orleans deal with enormous volume. In the face of this large urban caseload, Connick needed a strategy to carry out his campaign statements about plea bargaining. During the weeks between his election victory and taking office, he started speaking publicly about a plan with two central components. First, Connick planned to devote expertise and resources to screening. He proposed a screening procedure that "would weed out those cases really not worthy of being on the criminal docket, so more courtroom emphasis can be devoted to the violent offender." Second, he instructed his prosecutors not to engage in plea bargaining — particularly charge bargaining — except under very limited circumstances. . . .

The distinctiveness of the screening process in the NODA office is apparent from a closer examination of the path each new case takes through the system. Police officers develop a case folder after they complete an investigation and file charges with the magistrate. The first stop for the case folder in the NODA office is the Magistrate Section, where the least experienced assistants work. They typically have logged six months or fewer on the job. The ADA from the Magistrate Section appears for the state at the first appearance and bail hearing before the magistrate. A public defender is also present for the first appearance, but the case is reassigned immediately after the hearing and there is typically no further defense presence or participation in the case until after the DA files an information or obtains an indictment.

After any proceedings in the Magistrate Division, the folder moves to the Screening Section of the NODA office. Connick devotes extraordinary resources to this operation. For instance, in the late 1990s, about fifteen of the eighty-five attorneys in the office worked in Screening. . . . All attorneys in the Screening Section served previously (usually a couple of years) in the Trial Section. This level of experience comes at a premium in New Orleans, where the turnover among prosecuting attorneys is quite high. The average tenure of an ADA in the NODA office is around two years. . . .

The screener reviews the investigation file, speaks to all the key witnesses and the victims (often by telephone, but sometimes in person), and generally gauges the strength of the case. If the police report neglects to mention a factual issue that is likely to arise at trial, the screening attorney will speak directly with the police officer to resolve it. There is a powerful office expectation that the Screening Attorney will make a decision within ten days of receiving the folder.

NODA instituted a variety of measures to ensure reasonable uniformity in screening decisions. Connick committed his screening principles to writing in an office policy manual. The general office policy is to charge the most serious crime the facts will support at trial. The policy does not, on its face, allow individual prosecutors to consider for themselves the equities in the case when selecting the charge. By the same token, however, Connick insists that overcharging is unacceptable, because the charges chosen for the information will stay in place through the trial. If screening prosecutors overcharge cases too often, the Chief of the Trial Section might send the screening attorney back into the courtroom on at least one of those overcharged matters to "get his teeth kicked in." Supervisors review all refusals to charge. . . .

Neither Connick nor any attorneys in his office claim to have abolished plea bargaining entirely from the New Orleans system. Prosecutors in the office acknowledge that sometimes new information appears and changes the value of a case. Witnesses leave town, victims decide not to testify, new witnesses appear, and investigators find new evidence. On occasion, the screening attorney makes a bad judgment and overcharges, and a plea could save the case.

Nevertheless, office policy tries to keep these changes in charges to a minimum. A supervisor must approve any decision to drop or change charges after the information is filed. The attorney requesting the change must complete a special form naming the screening and trial attorneys, and explaining the reason for the decision, drawing from a list of acceptable reasons. The ADAs believe there is a "stigma" involved in reducing charges, however strong the reasons for a reduction might be.

Attorneys from the NODA office believe that they decline to prosecute an exceptional number of cases. They view this as a necessary part of training police officers to investigate more thoroughly. The relatively high rate of declination also created a political challenge for Connick over the years. During each of his reelection campaigns — in 1978, 1984, 1990, and 1996 — Connick's challengers criticized the number of cases that the NODA office declined to prosecute. As his opponent Morris Reed put it in many public debates, "the PD arrests them and the DA turns them loose." Connick had several replies. Poor police work made declinations necessary. Further, he pointed to specific examples of how his office dealt severely with defendants once they were charged. Connick also explicitly linked his screening policies to his plea bargaining policies: Tough screening, he said, made it possible to keep plea bargaining at low levels.

Connick drew on case data to make specific claims about low rates of plea bargaining in the office: He asserted that plea bargaining in Jim Garrison's day reached 60 to 70%, but fell to 7 or 8% of all cases filed under his office policy. He also routinely mentioned the high number of trials in New Orleans compared to other Louisiana jurisdictions. In addition, Connick pointed to his routine use of the habitual felon law to enhance sentences. By the end of each of the four reelection campaigns, Connick convinced the voters that it was possible both to decline many cases and to run a tough prosecutor's office at the same time. . . .

NOTES

1. *Prosecutorial "sentencing" through selection of charges.*   Prosecutorial selection of charges can have an immense impact on sentencing decisions. Scholars concerned about the exercise of prosecutorial discretion often call for judicial regulation of prosecutors, but as the decision in People v. Stewart illustrates, courts have yet to hear their call, refusing to review prosecutorial decisions except in extraordinarily limited circumstances. See, e.g., James Vorenberg, Decent Restraint of Prosecutorial Power, 94 Harv. L. Rev. 1521 (1981). The experience described above in the New Orleans District Attorney's office under Harry Connick raises the question whether "decent restraint" might come from within prosecutor's offices rather than from external sources. See Michael Simons, Prosecutorial Discretion and Prosecution Guidelines: A Case Study in Controlling Federalization, 75 N.Y.U. L. Rev. 893 (2000). Prosecutorial control of sentences raises particular issues for guideline sentencing systems that claim to provide legislative or administrative guidance to sentencing judges but not to prosecutors. See David Boerner, Sentencing Guidelines and Prosecutorial Discretion, 78 Judicature 196 (1995). Guidelines or highly structured criminal codes may provide prosecutors with even greater authority to "specify" the effect at sentencing of the concessions offered in a plea bargain. When the price of a trial becomes this clear, few defendants will ever risk going to trial. In such systems, for all the apparent involvement of multiple actors and rule-based equality, to a considerable extent the true sentencer becomes the prosecutor. See George Fisher, Plea Bargaining's Triumph 205-230 (2003).

2. *Prosecutorial accountability to community priorities.*   Should prosecutors also be able to make charging decisions on the basis of local needs? Should prosecutorial needs and resources then be allowed to affect sentences? An important illustration of these questions arises in the courts in southern California. The

U.S. Attorney's office in San Diego receives far more immigration cases than it can prosecute. Of the 565,581 illegal aliens apprehended in fiscal year 1992, the U.S. Attorney prosecuted 245 felony immigration cases and another 5,000 misdemeanors. Because the San Diego district attorney, as a matter of policy, will not prosecute any cases related to the border, these cases must be prosecuted in federal court or not at all. William Braniff, Local Discretion, Prosecutorial Choices and the Sentencing Guidelines, 5 Fed. Sentencing Rep. 309 (1993). If every alien apprehended at the border were prosecuted for felony reentry (most are reentering), the size of the entire federal prison system would need to quadruple in a single year based on cases in this one district alone. Of course, the local U.S. Attorney's office has the resources to prosecute only a fraction of these cases — as the numbers indicate. How should a sentencing judge respond to the limited prosecutorial resources that sometimes force unpleasant choices on prosecutors? Should the judge enhance a sentence when she knows that an unusually large number of offenders are going unpunished? Should the judge reduce the sentence out of concern for selective and discriminatory treatment or ignore prosecutorial priorities entirely? How should a judge in a neighboring district react to the nonprosecution or lesser sentencing in the adjacent area? See United States v. Banuelos-Rodriguez, 215 F.3d 969 (9th Cir. 2000) (rejecting sentencing disparities arising from different charging and plea bargaining policies of different U.S. Attorneys as a basis for departure from presumptive sentencing range); Linda Drazga Maxfield and Keri Burchfield, Immigration Offenses Involving Unlawful Entry: Is Federal Practice Comparable Across Districts?, 15 Fed. Sentencing Rep. 260 (2002).

3. *Prosecutorial punishment: critical yet hidden.* The regulation (or lack thereof) of prosecutorial discretion is one of the great puzzles of the criminal justice system. The puzzle is hidden beneath the surface whenever analysts study whether offenders *convicted* of the same offense are treated similarly: These analyses ignore whether similar offenders were not charged at all or were charged or convicted of a different offense. The impact of a prosecutor's sorting decisions may also be felt when prosecutorial office policy assigns a case to one of two or more possible screening or trial attorneys. Although these kinds of decisions are hard to study, any full assessment of sentencing or the equal treatment of individuals must address these preconviction sorting decisions.

PROBLEM 2-2. LOW-HANGING FRUIT

The purposes of prosecution take on additional levels of complexity when multiple jurisdictions might prosecute for the offense, whether those jurisdictions are the federal and one state government, or multiple state governments. In a speech to law enforcement officers on May 13, 2003, U.S. Attorney General John Ashcroft asserted that the Department of Justice was "taking gun-toting thugs off the streets." The next day, the Justice Department echoed his assertion with the following statement:

> This Justice Department has made the aggressive prosecution of those who violate our nation's gun laws a priority, and the 38% increase in prosecutions demonstrates we have been very busy taking criminals who misuse guns off

the streets. Last year, the Department had the largest recorded increase in prosecuting and convicting defendants for violating our nation's gun laws. [We have] seen increases in prosecutions of many firearms crimes over the last year, including a 100% increase in gun trafficking prosecutions, [and] a 25% increase in obliterated serial number cases. . . .

There should be no doubt: the Justice Department is working hard to enforce all federal firearms laws and lock up those who criminally misuse guns. We are also working in very close coordination with our state and local partners, who are also prosecuting gun crimes at higher rates. Our message is clear: gun crime means hard time. . . .

In the same week, a policy group seeking more federal prosecutions, Americans for Gun Safety, released a study with more mixed findings:

Conclusion #1 — There is a vast enforcement gap between the level of federal gun crimes and the number of federal prosecutions.

Over the past three fiscal years, prosecutors have filed 25,002 federal gun crime cases. During the same period:

- More than 330,000 guns used in violent gun crimes showed telltale signs of black market trafficking;
- 420,000 firearms were stolen;
- 450,000 individuals lied on the federal background check form used to determine eligibility for a gun;
- 93,000 gun crimes were committed by those under the age of 18; and
- Thousands of guns with obliterated serial numbers were recovered by law enforcement.

It is a violation of federal law to traffic in firearms, steal guns, lie on the background check form, sell to minors, and obliterate serial numbers. This translates into well over a million crimes where it is likely or certain that a federal law was broken. The 25,002 prosecutions represent a ratio of about 2 federal prosecutions for every 100 federal gun crimes.

Conclusion #2 — Twenty of twenty-two of the major federal gun statutes are rarely enforced.

Of the 25,002 federal firearms cases over the past three years, 85% of the prosecutions were for violations of just two federal statutes: the illegal possession of a firearm by a felon or other prohibited buyer, and the possession of a firearm while in the commission of a violent or drug-related federal crime. During both the Clinton and Bush Administrations, the other twenty statutes went virtually unenforced. For example, only 2% of prosecutions were for crimes associated with illegal gun trafficking and less than 1% for illegally selling a gun to a minor. . . . [T]he paucity of prosecutions under the other twenty statutes mean that the federal government is doing little or nothing to break up the vast black market in illegal guns.

The Enforcement Gap: Federal Gun Laws Ignored (May 2003). Can you determine whether the federal government is prosecuting too much gun crime, too little gun crime, or the wrong gun crimes? Criminologist Alfred Blumstein described current gun prosecutions as aimed at the "low-hanging fruit." See Eric Lichtblau, Justice Dept. Plans to Step Up Gun-Crime Prosecutions, New York Times, May 14, 2003. Given the very large number of crimes that might be prosecuted under firearms statutes and that typically can be prosecuted by federal or state authorities, how can the federal government or a state government decide how best to allocate prosecutorial gun-crime resources? What priority should gun crimes take compared to violent offenses against the person, drug crimes, stock fraud, environmental crimes, or immigration offenses? Should Congress authorize and fund new prosecutorial lines solely to prosecute gun crimes? In general, who should make the policy judgments about which crimes to prosecute, how should those policies be articulated, and what institution should see that the policies are consistently applied?

D. APPELLATE COURT GUIDANCE

In indeterminate sentencing systems, appellate courts play almost no role, and appellate sentencing law before 1980 is almost impossible to find. Appellate courts typically have the simple task of determining whether the sentence of the trial court falls within the statutory minimum and maximum for the charged crimes — a very limited notion of legality. In some states, statutes affirmatively limit appellate courts to this measly role. In states that do not explicitly constrain appellate sentencing authority, appellate judges avoid developing sentencing rules, perhaps because they believe that there is little "law" for them to apply. But this explanation is inadequate: In other areas with little law to apply, courts have exercised either interpretive or common law powers and developed rules to guide important discretionary decisions. Why have appellate courts shied away from developing a common law of sentencing?

In a more modern trend in the United States, especially in structured sentencing systems, legislatures provide for more searching appellate review of sentences. In such a system, the appellate court confirms both the legality and the "reasonableness" or "proportionality" of the sentence. An illustration comes from section 244.11 of the Minnesota statutes:

> An appeal to the court of appeals may be taken by the defendant or the state from any sentence imposed or stayed by the district court. . . . On an appeal pursuant to this section, the court may review the sentence imposed or stayed to determine whether the sentence is inconsistent with statutory requirements, unreasonable, inappropriate, excessive, unjustifiably disparate, or not warranted by the findings of fact issued by the district court. . . .

When appellate courts have broader authority to review sentences, they are more likely to come up with sentencing guidance as part of statutory interpretation (an entire legal regime can be created by allowing review for "reasonableness" of sentences) or as part of a common law of sentencing.

In addition to sentencing individuals, there are other ways that judges in general, and appellate judges in particular, might help set the sentencing rules. Judges might be called to testify before a legislature or sentencing commission, or a judge might serve on a sentencing commission. Judges might gather together formally (in a judicial conference) or informally (say, over lunch) and issue nonbinding sentencing recommendations.

Another approach, with its strongest illustration in England, finds appellate courts issuing "guideline judgments" that are announced in specific cases.

English appellate courts have become one of the main institutions for developing sentencing policy, because those courts establish benchmark sentences and sentencing principles to operate within broad statutory ranges.

In R. v. Aramah, 76 Crim. App. R. 190 (1983), the Court of Appeal, Criminal Division, first set out a framework for sentencing in drug cases. Aramah was convicted of importing 59 kilograms of cannabis valued between £100,000 and £135,000. The defendant was a 50-year-old man of Nigerian origin who had two previous convictions for drug offenses, one involving the importation of 88 kilograms of cannabis in 1972 for which he had been sentenced to three years' imprisonment. He was sentenced in this most recent case to six years' imprisonment. After stating the facts, the court began its decision by making "some general observations about the level of sentences for drug offences, since our list, as will have been observed, is entirely composed of such crimes." The court then gave the following guidelines:

Class "A" Drugs and Particularly Heroin and Morphine

It is common knowledge that these are the most dangerous of all the addictive drugs for a number of reasons: first of all, they are easy to handle. Small parcels can be made up into huge numbers of doses. Secondly, the profits are so enormous that they attract the worst type of criminal. Many of such criminals may think, and indeed do think, that it is less dangerous and more profitable to traffic in heroin or morphine than it is to rob a bank. [The] heroin taker, once addicted [may require] anything up to hundreds of pounds a week to buy enough heroin to satisfy the craving, depending upon the degree of addiction of the person involved. The [person might obtain these sums by] trafficking in the drug itself and disseminating accordingly its use still further.

[Lastly], and we have purposely left it for the last, because it is the most horrifying aspect, comes the degradation and suffering and not infrequently the death which the drug brings to the addict. It is not difficult to understand why in some parts of the world traffickers in heroin in any substantial quantity are sentenced to death and executed. Consequently anything which the courts of this country can do by way of deterrent sentences on those found guilty of crimes involving these class "A" drugs should be done.

[With large scale importation of heroin, morphine, and so on], where the street value of the consignment is in the order of £100,000 or more, sentences of seven years and upwards are appropriate. There will be cases where the values are of the order of £1 million or more, in which case the offence should be visited by sentences of 12 to 14 years. It will seldom be that an importer of any appreciable amount of the drug will deserve less than four years.

This, however, is one area in which it is particularly important that offenders should be encouraged to give information to the police, and a confession of guilt, coupled with considerable assistance to the police, can properly be marked by a substantial reduction in what would otherwise be the proper sentence.

Next, supplying heroin, morphine, etc.: it goes without saying that the sentence will largely depend on the degree of involvement, the amount of trafficking and the value of the drug being handled. It is seldom that a sentence of less than three years will be justified and the nearer the source of supply the defendant is shown to be, the heavier will be the sentence. There may well be cases where sentences similar to those appropriate to large scale importers may be necessary. It is, however, unhappily all too seldom that those big fish amongst the suppliers get caught.

Possession of heroin, morphine, etc. (simple possession): it is at this level that the circumstances of the individual offender become of much greater importance. Indeed the possible variety of considerations is so wide, including often those of a medical nature, that we feel it impossible to lay down any practical guidelines. On the other hand the maximum penalty for simple possession of class "A" drugs is seven years' imprisonment and/or a fine, and there will be very many cases where deprivation of liberty is both proper and expedient.

Class "B" Drugs, Particularly Cannabis

[Importation] of very small amounts [of cannabis] for personal use can be dealt with as if it were simple possession, with which we will deal later. Otherwise importation of amounts up to about 20 kilograms of herbal cannabis, or the equivalent in cannabis resin or cannabis oil, will, save in the most exceptional cases, attract sentences of between 18 months and three years, with the lowest ranges reserved for pleas of guilty in cases where there has been small profit to the offender. The good character of the courier (as he usually is) is of less importance than the good character of the defendant in other cases. The reason for this is, it is well known that the large scale operator looks for couriers of good character and for people of a sort which is likely to exercise the sympathy of the court if they are detected and arrested. . . . There are few, if any, occasions when anything other than an immediate custodial sentence is proper in this type of importation.

Medium quantities over 20 kilograms will attract sentences of three to six years' imprisonment, depending upon the amount involved, and all the other circumstances of the case. Large scale or wholesale importation of massive quantities will justify sentences in the region of 10 years' imprisonment for those playing other than a subordinate role.

Supply of cannabis: here again the supply of massive quantities will justify sentences in the region of 10 years for those playing anything more than a subordinate role. Otherwise the bracket should be between one to four years' imprisonment, depending upon the scale of the operation. Supplying a number of small sellers — wholesaling if you like — comes at the top of the bracket. At the lower end will be the retailer of a small amount to a consumer. Where there is no commercial motive (for example, where cannabis is supplied at a party), the offence may well be serious enough to justify a custodial sentence.

Possession of cannabis: when only small amounts are involved being for personal use, the offence can often be met by a fine. If the history shows, however, a persisting flouting of the law, imprisonment may become necessary.

The court then applied its own guidelines to the case before it and upheld the six-year sentence, finding that there was "very large quantity of cannabis" and no "mitigating feature," including the absence of a plea of guilty, and prior convictions for drug offenses.

Four years later, the same court reconsidered its *Aramah* guidelines in light of subsequent developments.

R. v. Edward Bilinski
86 Crim. App. R. 146 (1987)

THE LORD CHIEF JUSTICE

On February 20, 1987 in the Crown Court at Chelmsford the appellant pleaded guilty to importing 3.036 kilograms of heroin into the United Kingdom. He was sentenced to 12 years' imprisonment. Against that sentence he now appeals by leave of the single judge.

The material facts are as follows. On November 7, 1986 the M.V. *Gdansk II* was searched at Tilbury by Customs Officers. They discovered three packages containing white powder subsequently found to be heroin hidden behind a wiring duct 30 feet above the deck. Suspicion fell on the appellant who was a senior member of the crew. He was questioned in Polish through an interpreter. He denied all knowledge of the packages. However, his fingerprints were found on the sticky side of adhesive tape binding the packages. At first he said that he did not know "by what miracle" his prints had been placed there. The following day on further questioning, however, he admitted that he was responsible for the packages being on board. He had been approached by two Polish men at a time when his finances were at a low ebb. They had suggested he should assist them in transporting drugs from Hamburg to Sydney via Tilbury. He was to be paid the equivalent of some £3,500 in U.S. dollars. The size of the reward, he said, clouded his judgment. He was given the packages in Hamburg. According to his story, he was told that the drugs were cannabis. When they were handed to him the packages were malleable and wrapped in transparent plastic. He could see a white powder inside. He had later wrapped and secured them in further plastic material (hence the fingerprints) in order to protect the contents from the damp, because he had been told to be careful to prevent them from coming to any harm. He said he did not recognize the powder as heroin; he had never seen heroin before; the two men had told him the drug had come from the Far East, but even then he did not realize it might be heroin. Amongst other items found in the appellant's cabin was a book entitled "Heroina," which we are told is the Polish for heroin. Surprisingly this volume had come from the ship's library.

The heroin was of very high purity — 90 per cent. Its street value in this country was in the region of £600,000. The mitigation was in essence based on four matters:

(1)   The appellant thought he was smuggling cannabis not heroin.

(2)   He had pleaded guilty and given what assistance he could to the authorities in the shape of the names of his suppliers.

(3)   He was only a courier whose reward as it transpires was to be a minute fraction of the value of the drugs.

(4)   He was of hitherto good character.

Steyn J., in the course of passing sentence, said this: . . . "It is said that you did not know that it was heroin. I regard that (and I make that clear) as irrelevant. . . . If it had been relevant, I would have directed an issue to be tried on it, but I find that it is irrelevant." [Defense counsel] makes two submissions to this Court: (1) That the judge was in error in regarding the appellant's belief as to the nature of the drug as irrelevant so far as sentence was concerned. (2) That the sentence of 12 years was in any event too long. . . .

Is it relevant? On the one hand is the argument that anyone who chooses to engage in smuggling prohibited drugs must accept the risk that the drug is of a kind different from that which he believes or has been told it is. . . . On the other hand, submits [defense counsel], if a defendant genuinely has been misled as to the type of drug, then in light of the fact that the maximum sentence for importing heroin is imprisonment for life as against the 12 years maximum for importation of cannabis, it would be unjust not to allow some mitigation at least of the punishment. . . .

We are of the view that the defendant's belief in these circumstances is relevant to punishment and that the man who believes he is importing cannabis is indeed less culpable than he who knows it to be heroin. . . . To what extent the punishment should be mitigated by this factor will obviously depend upon all the circumstances, amongst them being the degree of care exercised by the defendant.

How should the issue be determined? In some cases no doubt it will be necessary for the judge to hear evidence. . . . If that procedure had been adopted in the present case . . . the appellant would probably have been the only witness, apart perhaps from someone to speak as to the street value of these packages had they contained cannabis rather than heroin. It is difficult to see what the appellant could have said other than that which he had already stated in his interviews with the Customs officers. If so, it is scarcely likely that the judge would have been in any doubt but that the appellant must have known that the substance was heroin. . . . Where the defendant's story is manifestly false the judge is entitled to reject it out of hand without hearing evidence. Whether that is so or not, we take the view that the exercise of only a small degree of curiosity, enquiry or care would have revealed the true nature of the drug in this case and that accordingly the mitigating effect of the belief, if held, was small.

The next question is what the proper sentence should be for the carrier/importer of this quantity of 90 per cent pure heroin. The guidelines in *Aramah* . . . must be updated to take account of the fact that the maximum sentence for the importation of Class A drugs has now been increased by the Controlled Drugs (Penalties) Act 1985, from 14 years to life imprisonment. It was suggested in *Aramah* that where the street value of the consignment is in the order of £100,000 or more, sentences of seven years and upwards are appropriate, and that 12 to 14 years' imprisonment is appropriate where the value of the drugs involved is £1 million or more. The former figure should now be increased to 10 years and upwards and the latter to 14 years and upwards.

Thus a term of 12 years or thereabouts would have been appropriate for this level of importation in the absence of any mitigating features. There are, however, these matters to be taken into account in mitigation of the penalty. First, the plea of guilty. Secondly, the fact that the appellant gave all the help which he could to the authorities by naming his suppliers and, thirdly, for what it is worth, the possibility (in the absence of a finding to the contrary by the judge) that the appellant may have believed the drugs to be cannabis. We think that in the light of those factors, and taking into account all the circumstances of the case a term of 8 years' imprisonment would have been appropriate. . . .

NOTES

1. *Appellate court guideline sentencing rules.* The English experiment with appellate guideline judgments has been under way for about 25 years. The guideline judgments have not kept Parliament from enacting additional sentencing legislation, including harsher punishments for drug offenses. See Aaron Rappaport, Sentencing in England: The Rise of Populist Punishment, 10 Fed. Sentencing Rep. 247 (1998). What sorts of reasons might persuade an appellate court to change its own sentencing guidelines? Based on the drug guidelines in *Aramah* as modified by *Bilinski,* what advantages do you think appellate judges have over legislators in developing sentencing rules? Over sentencing experts such as sentencing commission members? Over trial judges?

In R. v. Barrick, 81 Crim. App. R. 78 (1985), the English Court of Appeal set out guidelines for fraud cases. The defendant in *Barrick* was convicted on four counts of false accounting, four counts of obtaining by deception, and two counts of theft. He was sentenced to two years' imprisonment on each count to run concurrently. The defendant handled the accounting for a small finance company, and in that capacity he created imaginary borrowers and stole around £9,000. The court used the case as "an opportunity to make some observations upon the proper sentence to be passed in respect of certain types of theft and fraud":

> The type of case with which we are concerned is where a person in a position of trust, for example, an accountant, solicitor, bank employee or postman, has used that privileged and trusted position to defraud his partners or clients or employers or the general public of sizeable sums of money. He will usually, as in this case, be a person of hitherto impeccable character. It is practically certain, again as in this case, that he will never offend again. . . . It was not long ago that this type of offender might expect to receive a term of imprisonment of three or four years, and indeed a great deal more if the sums involved were substantial. More recently, however, the sentencing climate in this area has changed. . . .
>
> In *Jacob* (1981), . . . a solicitor who had over a period of some three years stolen money from clients and his partners to the tune of between £40,000 and £57,000 had his sentence of four years' imprisonment reduced by this Court to eighteen months. . . . On the other hand postmen do not seem to have fared quite so well. In *Eagleton* (1982), a postman had been sentenced to five years' imprisonment for three offences of theft of packets in transit by mail with 80 offences taken into consideration. A sentence of thirty months' imprisonment was substituted. *Briggs* (1982), was another postman case. The defendant had stolen from the mail goods worth about £1,300, most of which were recovered. On appeal a term of two years' imprisonment was substituted for the three years which had been imposed by the trial judge. We can see no proper basis for distinguishing between cases of this kind simply on the basis of the defendant's occupation. . . .
>
> It is, we appreciate, dangerous to generalize where the circumstances of the offender and the offence may vary so widely from case to case. In the hope that they may be helpful to sentencers generally, and may lead to a little more uniformity, we make the following suggestions.
>
> In general a term of immediate imprisonment is inevitable, save in very exceptional circumstances or where the amount of money obtained is small. Despite the great punishment that offenders of this sort bring upon themselves, the Court should nevertheless pass a sufficiently substantial term of imprisonment to mark publicly the gravity of the offence. The sum involved is obviously not the only factor to be considered, but it may in many cases provide a useful guide. Where the amounts involved cannot be described as small but are less than £10,000 or thereabouts, terms of imprisonment ranging from the very short up to about eighteen months are appropriate. Cases involving sums of between about £10,000 and £50,000 will merit a term of about two to three years' imprisonment. Where greater sums are involved, for example those over £100,000, then a term of three and a half years to four and a half years would be justified. . . .
>
> The following are some of the matters to which the Court will no doubt wish to pay regard in determining what the proper level of sentence should be: (i) the quality and degree of trust reposed in the offender including his rank; (ii) the period over which the fraud or the thefts have been perpetrated; (iii) the use to which the money or property dishonestly taken was put; (iv) the effect upon the victim; (v) the impact of the offences on the public and public confidence; (vi) the effect on fellow-employees or partners; (vii) the effect on the offender himself; (viii) his own history; (ix) those matters of mitigation special to himself such as illness; being placed under great strain by excessive responsibility or the like; where, as sometimes happens, there has been a long delay, say over two years, between his being confronted with his dishonesty by his

professional body or the police and the start of his trial; finally, any help given by him to the police.

The court found that Barrick had committed "mean offences" from people of modest means and had given "no help to the police," so the court upheld the two-year sentence. See also R. v. Billam, 8 Crim. App. R. (S.) 48 (1986) (guidelines for sexual assault); D. A. Thomas, Sentencing Sex Offenders — English Law, 10 Fed. Sentencing Rep. 74 (1997) (reviewing interaction of legislation and English guideline decisions); Andrew Ashworth, Three Techniques for Reducing Sentencing Disparity, in Principled Sentencing 282 (Andrew von Hirsch and Andrew Ashworth eds., 1992).

2. *Judges and rule making in the United States.*   Could appellate courts make rules for sentencing in the United States? Or would this violate the separation of powers, because rule making would be either a legislative or executive function? See State v. Wentz, 805 P.2d 962 (Alaska 1991) (limiting use of judicially created "benchmark" sentence for assault). Appellate courts now play a more substantial role in modern U.S. structured sentencing systems, such as the federal and many state guideline systems. Sentencing issues generate lots of work for appellate courts. In the federal system in 2001, 51 percent of the appeals in criminal cases raised sentencing issues alone, and another 22 percent challenged the sentence along with the conviction.

Given that judges see so many individual cases and develop such expertise in sentencing, shouldn't judges develop sentencing rules rather than just apply rules that others create? Statutes establishing sentencing commissions often reserve some commission posts for judges. Are there other ways to involve judges in the creation of general sentencing rules? Under the federal guidelines and in many structured state systems, courts that sentence outside the recommended range must explain the decision. The sentencing commission collects data on these sentences and in theory uses the feedback to amend the sentencing rules. We consider the judicial power to depart from sentencing guidelines more closely in Chapter 3.

3. *Regional appellate tribunals.* National criminal courts traditionally handle criminal trials and sentencing, even if the offenses involve foreign nationals who committed crimes on their territory. While criminal jurisdiction is primarily territorial (the territoriality principle), countries also have the right to try their nationals who commit crimes abroad (the nationality principle), to try offenders who commit crimes against their territory or political and judicial structure (the protective principle), and offenders who run afoul of universal prohibitions (the universality principle). Some courts have also exercised jurisdiction if the victim was one of its nationals (the passive personality principle). As regional human rights organizations evolved in Europe and the Americas, regional tribunals, such as the European Court of Human Rights (ECHR) and the Inter-American Court of Human Rights, acquired limited appellate jurisdiction over criminal cases tried in the courts of the member nations.

Sentencing appeals have come to the ECHR under Article 3 of the European Convention on Human Rights, which protects individuals against inhuman or degrading treatment or punishment, and Article 5, which guarantees the right to liberty and security of persons. The ECHR has decided what practices constitute torture and whether discretionary decisions as to the release of life prisoners must be subject to judicial control.

4. *The ICTR and the ICTY.*   In the wake of the conflicts in Yugoslavia and Rwanda, the U.N. Security Council established two ad hoc tribunals in 1993 and 1994, respectively: the International Criminal Tribunal for Yugoslavia (ICTY), with its seat in The Hague, Netherlands, and the International Criminal Tribunal for Rwanda (ICTR), located in Arusha, Tanzania. Both courts have jurisdiction over genocide, crimes against humanity, war crimes, and select breaches of the Geneva Conventions. Their jurisdiction is complementary to that of national courts, but they have the primary right to prosecute and try war criminals. As of February 2002 the ICTY has filed charges in more than 70 cases. As of early 2003, the ICTR had tried nine individuals, resulting in eight convictions and one acquittal. Those convicted in the ICTR include Jean Kambanda, the prime minister of Rwanda during the genocide, who was the first head of government to be indicted and subsequently convicted for genocide. See www.un.org/icty or www.ictr.org.

The maximum sentence either tribunal can hand down is life imprisonment, with the sentence to be served in countries that have entered into agreements with the ad hoc tribunals. The jurisprudence developed by the two tribunals will shape the definition and prosecution of international crimes and has already affected the decision making of national courts. See Mark Drumbl and Kenneth S. Gallant, Sentencing Policies and Practices in the International Criminal Tribunals, 15 Fed. Sentencing Rep. 140 (2002).

5. *Sentencing in the International Criminal Court.*   Even though attempts were made immediately after World War II to establish an international criminal tribunal, it took more than 50 years to become reality. The International Criminal Court (ICC) came into existence in 2002 and opened for business in 2003. By February 2003, 89 countries had ratified the Statute of Rome, which sets up the ICC, and 139 countries had signed the treaty. The United States withdrew its signature in May 2002, because of concerns about the treaty's applicability to its military personnel, and has since negotiated a number of bilateral treaties intended to shield U.S. nationals from prosecution by the ICC.

The ICC has jurisdiction over genocide, crimes against humanity, war crimes, and the yet undefined crime of aggression. The ICC's jurisdiction complements that of national courts, with trials occurring only if national courts are unwilling or unable to prosecute suspects. The maximum sentence is a life term "when justified by the extreme gravity of the crime and the individual circumstances of the convicted person," with a 30-year maximum for all other offenders (Art. 77, Statute of Rome). A list of aggravating and mitigating circumstances is set out in the Rules of Procedure and Evidence. In addition to imprisonment, the ICC may order a fine, restitution, and forfeiture of property and proceeds received from the crime committed. See www.un.org/law/icc.

=3=

‖ *Regulating Discretion* ‖

Before a defendant is convicted of a crime, discretion plays a key role in the criminal justice system. Victims exercise discretion in reporting crimes, police exercise discretion in investigations, and prosecutors exercise discretion in charging, plea bargaining, and trial decisions. The exercise of sentencing discretion following a defendant's conviction is also common, and it is also sometimes controversial. Indeed, many modern sentencing reforms have been prompted by concern over the discretion that judges and juries possess in their sentencing.

Sentencing discretion has both positive and negative aspects. Because, in the words of the Supreme Court, "every convicted person [is] an individual and every case [is] a unique study in human failings," Koon v. United States, 518 U.S. 81, 113 (1996), it has long been thought essential that sentencers possess some discretion to fine-tune punishments to fit specific circumstances of particular cases. Yet, discretion exercised across a set of cases can result in sentencing disparity: different judges and juries, even when exercising their discretion soundly, may reach different sentencing judgments in seemingly similar cases. And some sentencing disparity may reflect a form of discrimination if irrelevant or illegitimate factors influence the outcomes.

This chapter presents two case studies in efforts to regulate sentencing discretion. First is the emergence of guideline systems to structure the exercise of noncapital sentencing discretion. Second is the development of constitutional rules to structure the exercise of capital sentencing discretion.

A. SENTENCING GUIDELINE STRUCTURES: REGULATING DISCRETION THROUGH ADMINISTRATIVE RULES

1. *Origins and Foundation*

Beginning in the late nineteenth and continuing through most of the twentieth century, a highly discretionary, rehabilitative "medical" model dominated criminal sentencing. Trial judges in federal and state systems had nearly unfettered discretion to impose on defendants any sentence selected from within wide statutory ranges. Such broad judicial discretion — complemented by parole officials exercising similar discretion concerning prison release dates — was viewed as necessary to achieve sentences that were tailored to the rehabilitative prospects and progress of each offender.

But by the 1970s, criminal justice researchers and scholars became concerned about the unpredictable and widely disparate sentences that indeterminate sentencing systems produced. Empirical and anecdotal evidence revealed that sentencing judges' discretionary choices created substantial and undue differences in both the lengths and types of sentences meted out to similar defendants. Even more worrisome, some studies found that purportedly irrelevant personal factors such as an offender's race, gender, and socioeconomic status were affecting sentencing outcomes.

Troubled by the disparity and discrimination resulting from highly discretionary sentencing practices — and fueled by concerns over increasing crime rates and powerful criticisms of the entire rehabilitative model of punishment and corrections — many criminal justice experts proposed reforms to bring greater consistency and certainty to the sentencing enterprise. Perhaps the most powerful and influential criticism of then prevailing sentencing practices was delivered by Judge Marvin Frankel, who drew on his personal experiences as a federal district judge to author one of the most influential books in American criminal justice.

Criminal Sentences: Law Without Order, Marvin E. Frankel
Pages 3-10, 16-19, 39-41, 47, 89-123 (1973)

We boast that ours is a "government of laws, not of men." We do not mean . . . that men make no difference in the administration of law. Among the basic things we do mean is that all of us, governors and governed alike, are or ought to be bound by laws of general and equal application. We mean, too, that in a just legal order, the laws should be knowable and intelligible so that, to the fullest extent possible, a person meaning to obey the law may know his obligations and predict within decent limits the legal consequences of his conduct. . . .

As to the penalty that may be imposed, our laws characteristically leave to the sentencing judge a range of choice that should be unthinkable in a "government of laws, not of men." . . . The almost wholly unchecked and sweeping powers we give to judges in the fashioning of sentences are terrifying and intolerable for a society that professes devotion to the rule of law.

For examples of such unbounded "discretion" [consider that] the federal kidnapping law authorizes "imprisonment for any term of years or for life." To take some of our most common federal crimes — driving a stolen car across state lines may result in a term of "not more than five years," robbing a federally insured bank "not more than twenty-five years." [F]ederal trial judges, answerable only to their varieties of consciences, may and do send people to prison for terms that may vary in any given case from none at all up to five, ten, thirty, or more years. . . .

The result . . . is a wild array of sentencing judgments without any semblance of the consistency demanded by the ideal of equal justice. . . . The broad statutory ranges might approach a degree of ordered rationality if there were prescribed any standards for locating a particular case within any range. But neither our federal law nor that of any state I know contains meaningful criteria for this purpose. [O]ur legislators have not done the most rudimentary job of enacting meaningful sentencing "laws" when they have neglected even to sketch democratically determined statements of basic purpose. Left at large, wandering in deserts of uncharted discretion, the judges suit their own value systems insofar as they think about the problem at all. . . .

The prevalent thesis of the last hundred years or so has been that the treatment of criminals must be "individualized." [But] we ought to recall that individualized justice is prima facie at war with such concepts, at least as fundamental, as equality, objectivity, and consistency in the law. It is not self-evident that the flesh-and-blood judge coming (say) from among the white middle classes will inevitably achieve admirable results when he individualizes the narcotics sentences of the suburban college youth and the street-wise ghetto hustler.

[Judges] have expressed misgivings — about their own and (perhaps more strongly) about their colleagues' handling of [sentencing] powers so huge and so undefined over the lives of their fellow men. . . . Everyone connected with this grim business has his own favorite atrocity stories. . . . One story concerns a casual anecdote over cocktails in a rare conversation among judges touching the subject of sentencing. Judge X, to designate him in a lawyerlike way, told of a defendant for whom the judge, after reading the presentence report, had decided tentatively upon a sentence of four years' imprisonment. At the sentencing hearing in the courtroom, after hearing counsel, Judge X invited the defendant to exercise his right to address the court in his own behalf. The defendant [read] from a sheaf of papers . . . excoriating the judge, the "kangaroo court" in which he'd been tried, and the legal establishment in general. Completing the story, Judge X said, "I listened without interrupting. Finally, when he said he was through, I simply gave the son of a bitch five years instead of the four." None of the three judges listening to that (including me) tendered a whisper of dissent, let alone a scream of outrage. But think about it. . . . A year in prison for speaking disrespectfully to a judge. . . . Would we tolerate an act of Congress penalizing such an outburst by a year in prison? The question, however rhetorical, misses one truly exquisite note of agony: that the wretch sentenced by Judge X never knew, because he was never told, how the fifth year of his sentence came to be added. . . .

WALLS OF SILENCE

[The] swift ukase, without explanation, is the tyrant's way. The despot is not bound by rules. He need not justify or account for what he does. Criminal sentences, as our judges commonly pronounce them, are in these vital respects tyrannical. Largely unfettered by limiting standards, and thus having neither occasion nor meaningful terms for explaining, the judge usually supplies nothing in the way of a coherent and rational judgment when he informs the defendant of his fate.

[The] parties (especially the loser) are, on deep principles, not merely entitled to a decision; they are entitled to an explanation. . . . The duty to give an account of the decision is to promote thought by the decider, to compel him to cover the relevant points, to help him eschew irrelevancies — and, finally, to make him show that these necessities have been served. The requirement of reasons expressly stated is not a guarantee of fairness. The judge or other official may give good reasons while he acts upon outrageous ones. However, given decision-makers who are both tolerably honest and normally fallible, the requirement of stated reasons is a powerful safeguard against rash and arbitrary decisions. Knowing this to be so, we apply it to affairs of lesser consequence, yet we place no burden of explanation upon the judge who decides that the defendant before him must be locked up for ten years rather than five or one or none. . . .

Improvements in communications are less perceptible — they are practically nonexistent — when we move on to the parole stage. [P]arole boards, like judges and prison officials, for the most part neglect altogether to supply information or explanations. . . . Parole boards don't explain. They confer miracles or they refuse. . . . The general fact [is] that most parole boards, subject to no precise rules of any kind, decree secretly and silently how tens and hundreds of thousands of convict-years shall be passed.

INDETERMINATE SENTENCES

The case for the indeterminate sentence rests, initially, upon a laudable concern for each unique individual, coupled with a frequently baseless assumption that we are able effectively to understand and uniquely to "treat" the individual. The offender is "sick," runs the humane thought, and/or dangerous. He needs to be helped and "cured." Nobody, certainly not the sentencing judge, can know when he will be well and no more dangerous than the masses of us who are lucky enough not to have been convicted. Hence, those charged with "treatment" must be left to decide the time for release.

This "rehabilitative ideal" [is based on] the fallacious — or, at least, far too broad — assumption that criminals are "sick" in some way that calls for "treatment." . . . We sentence many people every day who are not "sick" in any identifiable respect and are certainly not candidates for any form of therapy or "rehabilitation" known thus far. Many convicted criminals. . . are not driven by, or "acting out," neurotic or psychotic impulses. Instead, they have coldly and deliberately figured the odds, risked punishment for rewards large enough (in their view) to justify the risk, but then had the misfortune to be caught. It seems likely that many of those in organized crime fall within this category. The same is true for large numbers (though by no means all) of those who scheme to defraud, to evade taxes, to counterfeit the currency, or to commit other varieties of acquisitive crime. . . .

The apostles of rehabilitation and indeterminate sentences posit "sickness" without identifying its character and then urge "treatment" no better defined or specified. The absence of treatment or facilities is by itself a fatal defect [as] there is no justification for a regime of rehabilitation through indeterminate sentences unless we have some substantial hope or prospect of rehabilitating. Our subject is, after all, the confinement of people for long and uncertain periods of time. It is an evil to lock people up. There may be compensating goods that warrant it. But a mythical goal of rehabilitation is no good at all. . . .

Believing, then, that there is need for broad and drastic reform of the law, I [offer these] legislative proposals. . . . To begin at the elementary beginning, we have an almost entire absence in the United States of legislative determinations — of "law" — governing the basic questions as to the purposes and justifications of criminal sanctions. Without binding guides on such questions, it is inevitable that individual sentencers will strike out on a multiplicity of courses chosen by each decision-maker for himself. The result is chaos. . . .

Along with the declaration of sentencing purposes, the legislature would — certainly it should — provide that the judge (or sentencing tribunal) must state which among the allowable purposes were the supposed bases for each particular sentence. The simple requirement would compel the judge to think connectedly about his reasons and to justify explicitly decisions now taken on unarticulated hunches. . . . And it would open the way for intelligent scrutiny on appeal since an appellate court can function usefully only when it knows the grounds of the decision brought to it for review. . . .

TOWARD CODIFIED WEIGHTS AND MEASURES

[We allow the sentencing judge] not merely to "weigh" the various elements that go into a sentence [but also] leave to his unfettered (and usually unspoken) preferences the determination as to what factors ought to be considered at all, and in what direction. . . . We do not allow each judge to make up the law for himself on other questions. We should not allow it with respect to sentencing. . . .

Beyond codifying the numerous factors affecting the length or severity of sentences, an acceptable code of penal law should, in my judgment, prescribe guidelines for the application and assessment of these factors. While it may seem dry, technical, unromantic, and "mechanical," I have in mind the creation eventually of a detailed chart or calculus — to be used (1) by the sentencing judge in weighing the many elements that go into the sentence; (2) by lawyers, probation officers, and others undertaking to persuade or enlighten the judge; and (3) by appellate courts in reviewing what the judge has done.

[The sentencing judge] will presumably consider a host of factors in the case: the relative seriousness of the particular offense — the degree of danger threatened, cruelty, premeditation; the prior record of the defendant; situational factors — health, family disturbance, drug use; the defendant's work history, skills, potential; etc. In the existing mode of handling the sentence, the judge is under no pressure — and is without guidelines — toward systematic, exhaustive, detailed appraisal of such things one by one. He probably does not list them even for himself. He certainly does not record or announce the analysis. Probably, in most cases, he broods in a diffuse way toward a hunch that becomes a sentence. . . .

The partial remedy I propose is a kind of detailed profile or checklist of factors that would include, wherever possible, some form of numerical or other objective grading. Still being crude and cursory, I suggest that "gravity of offense" could be graded along a scale from, perhaps, 1 to 5. Other factors could be handled in the same way. The overall result might be a score — or, possibly, an individual profile of sentencing elements — that would make it feasible to follow the sentencer's estimates, criticize them, and compare the sentence in the given case with others.

The justification for such a technique does not require that we accept delusions of precision. Admittedly, "gravity of offense" does not lend itself to weighing with the mechanical simplicity of grocery or jewelers' scales. But we know from sufficiently analogous fields that numerical statements may serve, for obviously non-quantifiable subjects, as useful implements for clarification of thought, comparisons, and criticism. . . . The physician who speaks of a grade-three heart murmur may not be reporting a measurement as precise as the number of feet in a yard. But he says a meaningful thing that informs and guides others professionally trained. . . . It is not necessary, or desirable, to imagine that sentencing can be completely computerized. . . .

A COMMISSION ON SENTENCING

Using the jargon of our time, entirely apt in this instance, there are huge needs for organized research and development in the field of sentencing. . . . There must be a commitment to change, to application of the learning as it is acquired. . . . Since we deal with the law, the normal agency of change is, increasingly, the legislature. But the subject of sentencing is not steadily exhilarating to elected officials. There are no powerful lobbies of prisoners, jailers, or, indeed, judges, to goad and reward. Thus, accounting in good part for our plight, legislative action tends to be sporadic and impassioned, responding in haste to momentary crises, lapsing then into the accustomed state of inattention. . . .

These thoughts . . . lead to my proposed "Commission on Sentencing" [which] would be a permanent agency responsible for (1) the study of sentencing, corrections, and parole; (2) the formulation of laws and rules to which the studies pointed; and (3) *the actual enactment of rules,* subject to traditional checks by Congress and the courts. . . . The commission would require prestige and credibility. It would be necessary to find for it people of stature, competence, devotion, and eloquence. The kinds of people . . . could include lawyers, judges, penologists, and criminologists. They should also include sociologists, psychologists, business people, artists, and, lastly for emphasis, former or present prison inmates. . . .

[T]he commission would have the function of actually enacting rules — i.e., making law. This suggestion would presumably generate controversy; legislators do not (and should not) lightly delegate their authority. Nevertheless, there is both precedent and good reason for delegating in this instance. As I have said, the subjects of sentencing, corrections, and parole are going to need ongoing study and an indefinite course of revision. Sweeping changes of policy, touching basic principles and institutions, will naturally remain for the legislature to determine from time to time. But relative details, numerous and cumulatively important, neither require nor are likely to receive from the legislature the necessary measure of steady attention. Thinking along such lines, Congress has delegated in a variety of fields — e.g., securities, transportation, communications — rulemaking powers with substantial day-to-day impact upon the affected areas. The suggestion here contemplates an analogous arrangement. . . .

The uses of a commission, if one is created, will warrant volumes of debate and analysis. For this moment and this writer, the main thing is to plead for an instrumentality, whatever its name or detailed form, to marshal full-time wisdom and power against the ignorance and the barbarities that characterize sentencing for crimes today. . . .

NOTES

1. *Rise and fall of the rehabilitative ideal.*   As highlighted by Judge Frankel, the grant of broad discretion to sentencing judges and parole officials was linked to a rehabilitative "medical" model of sentencing and corrections in which authority to individualize punishments seemed essential. This model of punishment emerged in the United States from the early development of the modern penitentiary in the late 1800s. See David Rothman, Perfecting the Prison, in The Oxford History of the Prison 111-129 (Norval Morris and David Rothman eds. 1995). The rehabilitative model grew in prominence throughout the 1900s, finding expression in state statutes and model codes, Supreme Court opinions, and major governmental reports. See, e.g., Model Penal Code §6.10 ("An offender sentenced to an indefinite term of imprisonment in excess of one year . . . shall be released conditionally on parole at or before the expiration of the maximum of such term"); §7.04 ("The Court may sentence a person who has been convicted of a misdemeanor or petty misdemeanor to an extended term of imprisonment if it finds [that the defendant] is a chronic alcoholic, narcotic addict, prostitute or person of abnormal mental condition who requires rehabilitative treatment for a substantial period of time"); Williams v. New York, 337 U.S. 241 (1949) (explaining that "reformation and rehabilitation of offenders have become important goals of criminal jurisprudence" and noting the "prevalent modern philosophy that the punishment should fit the offender and not merely the crime"); President's Commission on Law Enforcement and Administration of Justice, The Challenge of Crime in a Free Society 159-166, 171-177 (1967) (discussing the new "reform model" in which an offender is a "patient" and the system follows "a new maxim — 'Let the treatment fit the needs of the individual offender'").

As the excerpt above highlights, Judge Frankel questioned both the effectiveness and appropriateness of a purely rehabilitative model of corrections within his broader criticisms of discretionary sentencing practices. Writing around the same time, many other commentators from across the political spectrum — liberals stressing concerns about inequitable and uncertain treatment of offenders, and conservatives highlighting increased crime rates and the apparent ineffectiveness of rehabilitative efforts — developed similar criticisms about indeterminate sentencing and the "rehabilitative ideal." See American Friends Service Committee, Struggle for Justice (1971); James Q. Wilson, Thinking About Crime (1975); Francis A. Allen, The Decline of the Rehabilitative Ideal 3-20 (1981) (discussing the "dominance" of the rehabilitative ideal through the late 1960s and the subsequent "wide and precipitous decline of penal rehabilitationism" as a foundational theory for the criminal justice system).

2. *Evidence of disparity and other calls for reform.*   Judge Frankel was not alone in identifying the problem of sentencing disparity and the consequent

need for sentencing reform. An influential 1976 report of the Twentieth Century Fund Task Force on Criminal Sentencing lamented that discretionary sentencing schemes were creating "unexplained and seemingly inexplicable sentencing disparity," and it marshaled some of the evidence of this disparity:

> One recent study . . . of felony sentences imposed by judges in one Ohio county [showed that] one judge granted probation to 26% of convicted offenders; another judge imposed probationary terms upon 51% of convicted offenders. . . . One judge imprisoned 56% of black defendants but only 35% of white defendants. . . . A South Carolina sample of sentencing [showed] in two marijuana cases, the same judge sentenced a white youth to one year's probation and a $400 fine; a black male received a two year sentence. . . . A recent study commissioned by the judges of the U.S. Court of Appeals for the Second Circuit involved 50 federal judges who were given 20 identical files drawn from actual cases and asked what sentence they would impose on each defendant. In [an extortion case], one judge proposed a sentence of 20 years' imprisonment plus a $65,000 fine [while] another judge proposed a 3-year sentence with no fine.

Fair and Certain Punishment: Report of the Twentieth Century Fund Task Force on Criminal Sentencing 3-29 (1976). For similar expressions of concern about sentencing disparity and uncertainty in discretionary sentencing systems, see National Conference of Comm'rs on Unif. State Laws, Model Sentencing and Corrections Act (1979); David Fogel, "We Are the Living Proof": The Justice Model for Corrections (1976).

   3. *Frankel's impact on federal and state reforms.*   Because Judge Frankel provided a provocative blueprint for change, his book served as a major catalyst for modern sentencing reforms. Most tangibly, Judge Frankel's work became the centerpiece of a series of policy workshops at Yale Law School, which culminated in a book proposing federal legislation for sentencing reform. See Pierce O'Donnell et al., Toward a Just and Effective Sentencing System (1977). The findings of the Yale workshops and accompanying book in turn provided the foundation for a federal sentencing reform bill first introduced by Senator Edward Kennedy of Massachusetts. In addition, many states looked directly to Judge Frankel's suggestions when embarking on their own sentencing reform efforts. Professor Kevin Reitz has effectively summarized the importance and impact of Judge Frankel's work:

> Judge Frankel's *Criminal Sentences* may be the single most influential work of criminal justice scholarship in the last 20 years. It stands as the best indictment of traditional, indeterminate sentencing practices in the literature. Its proposals have charted the general outline of sentencing reform through the 1980s and into the 1990s [and] the ABA adopted a new edition of its Sentencing Standards modeled largely on Judge Frankel's early plan for commission-based regulation of sentencing discretion.

Kevin R. Reitz, Sentencing Reform in the States: An Overview of the Colorado Law Review Symposium, 64 U. Colo. L. Rev. 645, 650 n.21 (1993). Current drafts of the American Law Institute's project to revise the sentencing provisions of the Model Penal Code also endorse the use of a sentencing commission to develop coherent sentencing policy.

2. *Development and Structure of State Guideline Systems*

Through the late 1970s and early 1980s, legislatures in a few states — most notably California and North Carolina — passed determinate sentencing statutes that abolished parole and created presumptive sentencing ranges for various classes of offenses. Minnesota became the first state to turn Judge Frankel's ideas into a full-fledged reality when in 1978 the state legislature established the Minnesota Sentencing Guidelines Commission to develop comprehensive sentencing guidelines. Pennsylvania and Washington soon thereafter created their own distinctive forms of sentencing commissions and sentencing guidelines, and the federal government followed suit through the passage of the Sentencing Reform Act of 1984, which created the U.S. Sentencing Commission to develop guidelines for federal sentencing. By the year 2000, nearly every state in the country had adopted some form of structured sentencing; though a number of states did so only through a few mandatory sentencing statutes, many states created sentencing commissions to develop comprehensive guideline schemes.

   Because so many states have now adopted some form of sentencing guidelines and because each state's system has some unique features, it is difficult to summarize the development and fundamental characteristics of all state guideline systems. One state worth examining closely is Minnesota, the first to create comprehensive sentencing guidelines through the work of a sentencing commission. Minnesota has enjoyed a quarter-century of success with its reforms and stands as a trailblazer for state guideline systems.

|| *Structuring Criminal Sentencing, Dale Parent* ||
Pages 51-53, 57-60 (1988)

   In at least three major respects, Minnesota's venture altered traditional institutions and concepts in the realm of criminal sentencing:

- It substituted a new system — guided discretion — for the more extreme methods of dividing authority over the punishment process between legislatures and courts.
- It inserted a new governmental entity — the sentencing commission — between the legislature and the judiciary, and authorized the commission to monitor and continuously adjust criminal sentences.
- And it established an unprecedented conceptual connection — known as capacity constraint — between the degree of severity with which guidelines could specify prison sentences and the extent to which state prison resources were available to carry such sentences into effect. . . .

   Minnesota's innovation [conferred] on guidelines the force of law. The former system of indeterminate prison sentences set by a judge, subject to the possibility of early release in the discretion of a parole board, was abolished. In its place came a system of determinate sentences, set by the judge under guidance from the sentencing commission, with review by an appellate court. Five key elements were incorporated into this plan:

- First, sentences would be scaled to take account of differences both in the gravity of crimes and the prior records of offenders. Guidance would be specified in the form of sentencing ranges, rather than precise sentences.
- Second, factors relevant to the individualization process would be standardized and weighted in advance. Clear rules would encourage similar outcomes in similar cases. Proportionality among different cases would be facilitated by a carefully constructed hierarchy of offense seriousness.
- Third, a set of departure principles would define the circumstances under which judges could deviate from the guideline sentencing range with good reasons. Judges would thus retain discretion to set the actual sentence, to do justice on a case-by-case basis.
- Fourth, sentencing judges would be required to state reasons for each sentence that differed from the applicable guideline, to assure accountability and reviewability.
- Fifth, all sentences would be subject to review by an appellate court whose written opinions could, over time, evolve finely tuned principles to guide future sentencers. . . .

The [1978 Minnesota] law created a nine-member Sentencing Guidelines Commission, consisting of the chief justice or his designee, two district court judges appointed by the chief justice, the Commission of Corrections, the chairman of the Minnesota Corrections Board, and four gubernatorial appointees — a prosecutor, a public defender, and two citizens. . . . The [Commission's] guidelines . . . were to recommend when state imprisonment was appropriate and to recommend presumptive sentencing durations. . . . Judges had to give written reasons for sentences that departed from the guidelines recommendation. The state or the defense could appeal any sentence. . . .

The Commission sought to assure that guideline punishments would be proportional to the seriousness of offenders' crimes. To achieve that proportionality, it was necessary for the Commission to rank crimes in the order of their seriousness. The seriousness of a crime varies according to the gravity of the offense and the blameworthiness of the offender. Gravity is determined by the harm caused, directly or as a consequence of the crime. Blameworthiness is determined by the offender's motivation, intent, and behavior in the crime and is enhanced if the offender previously has been convicted of and sentenced for criminal acts. . . .

Although most of us have an intuitive sense of offense seriousness, the concept is highly complex. [Judgments] about the seriousness of criminal events may involve facts about offenders, victims, and criminal acts. Some factors can be dismissed because all would agree they are irrelevant to assessing gravity or ascribing blame — for example, that the victim was a Mason or the offender was a Methodist. Some facts are both irrelevant and invidious — such as that the offender and the victim were of the same or different races. But there is a long list of factors that some would consider relevant to assessing harm or ascribing blame.

TABLE 4.1
Most Frequent Offenses in Seriousness Scale

Seriousness Level	Most Frequent Offenses
1.	Aggravated forgery, less than $100
	Possession of marijuana (more than 1.5 ounces)
	Unauthorized use of a motor vehicle
2.	Aggravated forgery, $150 to $2,500
	Sale of marijuana . . .
3.	Aggravated forgery, over $2,500
	Arson, third degree . . .
	Theft crimes, $150 to $2,500
	Sale of cocaine
	Possession of LSD, PCP
4.	Burglary, nondwellings and unoccupied dwellings
	Theft crimes, over $2,500
	Receiving stolen goods, $150 to $2,500
	Criminal sexual assault, fourth-degree
	Assault, third-degree (injury)
5.	Criminal negligence (resulting in death)
	Criminal sexual conduct, third-degree
	Manslaughter, second-degree . . .
	Witness tampering
	Simple (unarmed) robbery . . .
6.	Assault, second-degree (weapon)
	Burglary (occupied dwelling)
	Criminal sexual conduct, second-degree . . .
	Kidnapping (released in a safe place)
	Sale, LSD or PCP
	Sale, heroin and remaining hard narcotics
	Receiving stolen goods, over $2,500
7.	Aggravated (armed) robbery
	Arson, first-degree
	Burglary (victim injured) . . .
	Kidnapping (not released in a safe place)
	Manslaughter, first-degree . . .
8.	Assault, first-degree (great bodily harm)
	Kidnapping (great bodily harm)
	Criminal sexual conduct, first-degree
9.	Murder, third-degree
10.	Murder, second-degree

The victim may be a normal healthy adult or a person who may be especially vulnerable due to age or infirmity. In violent crimes the extent of physical injury may vary from a scratch to death. Some victims may recover fully from physical injuries, while others suffer permanent damage or impairment. In property crimes, the victim's loss could range from a small amount to a fortune. The consequences of property loss may vary greatly with the economic status of the victim. The crime may involve one victim or many. A crime might involve an offender acting alone or in concert with others. . . .

Given events as complex and diverse as criminal acts, how was the Commission to go about judging their seriousness? In the initial unsatisfactory effort [to rank offenses,] each member received a randomly arranged deck of sixty offense cards. Each card listed one offense [and] its statutory maximum sentence. . . . Each member arranged his or her deck in decreasing order of seriousness. [For] the most serious person offenses — homicides — the members' individual ranks clustered together, reflecting a high level of consensus. For less serious person offenses — robberies, sexual assaults, and so forth — consensus declined.

[The] Commission expressed concern about the initial ranking exercise [because it] had overloaded members with information. [The Commission created a subcommittee to divide the task into more manageable components. The subcommittee grouped] crimes into 6 categories — violent, arson, sex, drug, property, and miscellaneous — 5 of which contained 20 or fewer crimes. . . . The subcommittee instructed the Commission to focus on the usual or typical case in [a] ranking exercise. . . . In phase one, individual Commission members ranked crimes within each of the six categories. . . . Phases two, three, and four relied on identification of differences among members, on the articulation of reasons for those differences, and on debate about those reasons. . . . When differences existed it assured that the basis of the differences would be discovered and scrutinized and that the final rankings would reflect a majority opinion. [T]he Commission divided the overall ranking into ten seriousness levels. . . . Table 4.1 shows the most common types of offenses within each of the ten seriousness levels.

NOTES

1. *Voluntary and presumptive sentencing guidelines in the states.*   Though the federal sentencing guidelines garner the most attention from courts and commentators, nearly half the states regulate their sentencing judges' discretion through their own guidelines. In most states, a sentencing commission drafts an initial set of guidelines on behalf of the state legislature, which then enacts it as an integrated package of sentencing reforms. But in a few states, the judiciary adopts a package of guidelines as procedural rules or as informal guidance to judges. Some guidelines are only voluntary: there is no review of a judge's application of the guidelines or decision to sentence outside the range recommended in the guidelines so long as the judge remains within the statutory maximum and minimum for the crime. Other guidelines are presumptive: a judge who misapplies the guidelines or sentences outside the presumed range for sentences without an adequate justification can be overturned on appeal.

If you were a legislator in a state considering the adoption of sentencing guidelines, would you create a sentencing commission or instead look for mechanisms through which the judiciary might develop sentencing structures on its own? Regardless of the institution used to develop guidelines, would you prefer a voluntary or a presumptive approach? What do you see as the potential benefits and drawbacks of each approach to the development of sentencing guidelines?

2. *Policy authority given to sentencing commissions.*   As highlighted above, the Minnesota Sentencing Commission was given broad authority to assess the

seriousness of various offenses when developing sentencing guidelines. Indeed, as Professor Michael Tonry has noted, the Minnesota Sentencing Commission initially made many "bold policy decisions":

> First, it decided to be "prescriptive" and to establish its own explicit sentencing priorities [rather than] to be "descriptive," to attempt to replicate existing sentencing patterns. Second, the commission decided to de-emphasize imprisonment as a punishment for property offenders and to emphasize imprisonment for violent offenders. . . . Third, in order to attack sentencing disparities, the commission decided to establish narrow sentencing ranges (for example, 30 to 34 months, or 50 to 58 months) and to authorize departures from guideline ranges only when "substantial and compelling" reasons were present. Fourth, the commission elected to adopt "just deserts" as the governing premise of its policies concerning who receives prison sentences. Fifth, the commission chose to interpret an ambiguous statutory injunction that it take correctional resources into "substantial consideration" as a mandate that its guidelines not increase prison populations beyond existing capacity constraints. . . . Sixth, the commission forbade consideration at sentencing of many personal factors — such as education, employment, marital status, living arrangements — that many judges believed to be legitimate. This decision resulted from a policy that sentencing decisions not be based on factors that might directly or indirectly discriminate against minorities, women, or low-income groups. . . .

Michael Tonry, Sentencing Guidelines and Their Effects 16-20 (1987). If you had been a legislator who had voted in favor of (or against) establishing the Minnesota Sentencing Commission, would you override any of the commission's important policy decisions? How and to what extent should legislatures and sentencing commissions interact when making key policy decisions about the structure and content of guideline systems? Are there certain policy decisions that ought to be made only by elected legislatures and not by appointed commissions?

   3. *Discretion within ranges and departure authority.*   Even in guideline systems that are presumptive, judges typically retain a measure of sentencing discretion through their power to select a specific sentence from within the sentencing ranges set forth in the guidelines as well as through their more limited authority to depart from those ranges. In a few states, guidelines provide fairly broad ranges from which judges make their sentencing decisions, although these states tend to be more restrictive concerning departures from the ranges. Representing the most extreme example, North Carolina's guidelines establish ranges in which the longest available sentence is often twice the duration of the shortest available sentence, but they do not permit departures from these ranges for any reason. See http://www.nccourts.org/Courts/CRS/Councils/spac/Documents/felonypunishmentchart.pdf. In most states, the ranges provided in the guidelines are fairly narrow, but authority to depart is given to sentencing judges. In Kansas, for example, the longest sentence within a prescribed range is usually no more than 20 percent higher than the shortest sentence, but judges can depart from these ranges on numerous grounds.

   Departures may affect either the disposition of the sentence (active prison term or nonprison sanctions) or the duration of the sentence (the number of months to serve), and departure statutes generally require the judge to explain in writing any departure. In most jurisdictions, the selection of a particular sentence from within the applicable guidelines sentencing range is not subject to appeal, but departure decisions are appealable and reliance on improper grounds or inadequate explanations for a departure can lead to reversal. Although appellate courts in many jurisdictions have developed extensive case law approving or disapproving of various grounds for departure, rarely do they examine a sentencing judge's decision not to depart. Should defendants and prosecutors have equal opportunities to appeal a decision *not* to depart as a decision to depart from the guidelines?

4. *Amending the rules.* States with sentencing guidelines sometimes need to amend those guidelines over time, whether in response to the passage of new criminal prohibitions or to problematic judicial interpretations of certain guidelines, or when particular guidelines provisions do not work well. States typically give the leading role in the amendment process to a permanent sentencing commission, although the extent of the commission's power to amend the guidelines varies. In the largest group of states, the commission only recommends changes to the guidelines, and the legislature (and sometimes the state supreme court) must approve the changes before they become law. See Kan. Stat. Ann. §74-9101(b)(2), (6), (7); N.C. Gen. Stat. §§164-36, 164-43. Elsewhere, amendments to the guidelines take effect at the end of the commission's administrative rule-making process or after a waiting period that allows the legislature a chance to pass a statute disapproving of the changes. See Minn. Stat. Ann. §244.09(11); 42 Pa. Cons. Stat. §2153(a)(1). Would you expect these procedural variations to make any difference in the content of sentencing guidelines?

PROBLEM 3-1. THE MINNESOTA MACHINE

Clayton James Hanks broke into a home outside Minneapolis one night and stole some stereo equipment, worth about $1,000. He also went into the backyard of the home and took some tools. The prosecutor charged Hanks with residential burglary and theft; Hanks pled guilty to both charges. Hanks has no prior arrests or convictions on his record.

At sentencing, the trial court calculated the outcome prescribed under the Minnesota sentencing guidelines. The presumptive sentence for any felon is determined by locating the appropriate cell of the Sentencing Guidelines Grid, reprinted below. The vertical axis of the grid represents the severity of the offense, and the severity level is determined by the offense of conviction. When an offender is convicted of two or more felonies, the severity level is determined by the most severe offense of conviction. The most frequently occurring offenses within each severity level are listed on the vertical axis of the grid.

The horizontal axis of the grid looks to the offender's criminal history. The offender is assigned a particular score for every prior criminal or juvenile sentence, with the more severe prior crimes receiving a larger number of points.

The guidelines remind judges that "the capacities of state and local correctional facilities are finite" and that "incarcerative sanctions should be limited to those convicted of more serious offenses or those who have longer criminal histories." In general, the "sanctions used in sentencing convicted felons should be the least restrictive necessary to achieve the purposes of the sentence."

SENTENCING GUIDELINES GRID
Presumptive Sentence Lengths in Months

Italicized numbers within the grid denote the range within which a judge may sentence without the sentence being deemed a departure. Offenders with nonimprisonment felony sentences are subject to jail time according to law.

SEVERITY LEVEL OF CONVICTION OFFENSE (Common offenses listed in italics)		CRIMINAL HISTORY SCORE						
		0	1	2	3	4	5	6 or more
Murder, 2nd Degree (intentional murder; drive-by-shootings)	XI	306 *299-313*	326 *319-333*	346 *339-353*	366 *359-373*	386 *379-393*	406 *399-413*	426 *419-433*
Murder, 3rd Degree Murder, 2nd Degree (unintentional murder)	X	150 *144-156*	165 *159-171*	180 *174-186*	195 *189-201*	210 *204-216*	225 *219-231*	240 *234-246*
Criminal Sexual Conduct, 1st Degree[2] Assault, 1st Degree	IX	86 *81-91*	98 *93-103*	110 *105-115*	122 *117-127*	134 *129-139*	146 *141-151*	158 *153-163*
Aggravated Robbery 1st Degree	VIII	48 *44-52*	58 *54-62*	68 *64-72*	78 *74-82*	88 *84-92*	98 *94-102*	108 *104-112*
Felony DWI	VII	36	42	48	54 *51-57*	60 *57-63*	66 *63-69*	72 *69-75*
Criminal Sexual Conduct, 2nd Degree (a) & (b)	VI	21	27	33	39 *37-41*	45 *43-47*	51 *49-53*	57 *55-59*
Residential Burglary Simple Robbery	V	18	23	28	33 *31-35*	38 *36-40*	43 *41-45*	48 *46-50*
Nonresidential Burglary	IV	12[1]	15	18	21	24 *23-25*	27 *26-28*	30 *29-31*
Theft Crimes (Over $2,500)	III	12[1]	13	15	17	19 *18-20*	21 *20-22*	23 *22-24*
Theft Crimes ($2,500 or less) Check Forgery ($200-$2,500)	II	12[1]	12[1]	13	15	17	19	21 *20-22*
Sale of Simulated Controlled Substance	I	12[1]	12[1]	12[1]	13	15	17	19 *18-20*

Presumptive commitment to state imprisonment. First Degree Murder is excluded from the guidelines by law and continues to have a mandatory life sentence. See section II.E. **Mandatory Sentences** for policy regarding those sentences controlled by law, including minimum periods of supervision for sex offenders released from prison.

Presumptive stayed sentence; at the discretion of the judge, up to a year in jail and/or other non-jail sanctions can be imposed as conditions of probation. However, certain offenses in this section of the grid always carry a presumptive commitment to state prison. These offenses include Third Degree Controlled Substance Crimes when the offender has a prior felony drug conviction, Burglary of an Occupied Dwelling when the offender has a prior felony burglary conviction, second and subsequent Criminal Sexual Conduct offenses and offenses carrying a mandatory minimum prison term due to the use of a dangerous weapon (e.g., Second Degree Assault). See sections II.C. **Presumptive Sentence** and II.E. **Mandatory Sentences.**

The Minnesota guidelines are presumptive, meaning that any sentence selected from outside the designated range is subject to appeal. The guidelines say that departures from the presumptive sentences established in the guidelines "should be made only when substantial and compelling circumstances exist."

As a judge, what arguments from the prosecution or the defense might be persuasive as you decide whether to depart from the presumptive outcome under the guidelines? What facts would be important to you?

> *Sentencing Guidelines in Minnesota, Other*
> *States, and the Federal Courts: A Twenty-Year*
> *Retrospective, Richard S. Frase*
> 12 Fed. Sentencing Rep. 69 (1999)

As of 1999, about one-third of the states had sentencing guidelines in effect, and guidelines reforms were being considered in a number of other states. But guidelines systems are not all alike. . . . Although state guidelines systems are very diverse, they have a couple of things in common which distinguish them from the federal guidelines. Without exception, state systems are more flexible than the federal guidelines. There is a range; some state systems are so flexible that they are hardly "guidelines" at all, others are much more restrictive. . . .

Another thing that distinguishes state guidelines is that they are relatively simple to apply. The federal guidelines are quite ambitious; they try to regulate every decision. This is related to the flexibility point, but it goes beyond that. State guidelines are generally relatively short documents; sometimes very short. [It] is important to keep guidelines relatively easy to apply and easy for courts, defendants, and the public to understand. That is an important point which was lost in the federal system.

[There are some] important structural differences among guidelines systems. . . . For instance, Delaware, Florida, and Ohio don't use a grid (although their "narrative" or "point-system" guidelines could be translated into a grid). State and federal grids vary considerably in such things as: whether certain offenses have a separate grid; the number of grid cells; the breadth of cell ranges; and whether the ranges of adjoining cells overlap. Guidelines systems also differ in the number of disposition options permitted for a given case (e.g., prison, jail, restrictive intermediate sanctions, etc.); whether any guidance is offered as to the choice among sentencing purposes; how criminal history is defined; how multiple offenses are sentenced; and the extent to which the sentencing commission has made independent judgments about appropriate sentences (socalled "prescriptive" rules), rather than simply compiling guidelines which are descriptive of past judicial and paroling practices. . . .

THE CHANGING PURPOSES OF SENTENCING GUIDELINES

The original goals of sentencing guidelines reforms were two-fold. First, to reduce sentencing discretion and its resulting disparities; and second, to promote more rational sentencing policy developed and monitored by a specialized sentencing commission. . . . Since Minnesota's Guidelines first became effective, sentencing goals and values in Minnesota and other guidelines jurisdictions have evolved considerably. [I]t appears that the goal of disparity reduction has become somewhat less important, while other goals have become more important. . . . Almost every guidelines system which was adopted or revised since the mid-1980s has included resource-impact assessments, in an attempt to avoid prison overcrowding and control the growth of prison populations. More recent guideline reforms are also more likely to regulate and attempt to encourage the use of intermediate sanctions. Broader use of such sanctions is intended to

reduce unnecessary prison use — thus avoiding prison over-crowding and reducing prison costs — and also to better promote public safety. . . .

WHAT HAVE GUIDELINES ACCOMPLISHED?

How well have state guidelines [worked]? Any such assessment must begin
with a frank admission: no "expert" on sentencing guidelines can say very much
about how most state guidelines systems have worked in practice. In some cases,
this is because a state's system is too new to have generated enough data for evaluation. In other cases, the guidelines commission has not published or commissioned any evaluations, nor is there some professor or other outside re-
searcher who takes a special interest in that state's guidelines. So much of what
follows is based on a few, well-documented systems, and some "educated guesswork" about the rest.

Disparity Reduction.   Since most guidelines systems have abolished parole,
they have eliminated that form of disparity. Judicial sentencing disparities have
also been reduced, at least in the states which have been evaluated. Minnesota
is the only system to have been subjected to extensive outside evaluation, but
data reported by sentencing commissions or their staff suggest that disparity has
also been reduced in Delaware, Oregon, Pennsylvania and Washington. Two of
these five jurisdictions do not have legally-binding guidelines (Delaware's are
formally voluntary, and Pennsylvania's lack effective appellate review). . . .

More Rational Sentencing Policy.   [Most] guidelines systems include a permanent sentencing commission. Although some are more active than others, all
of these commissions have begun to develop useful sentencing policy expertise,
a comprehensive state-wide view of punishment priorities, better management
of resources, and a long-term perspective. Even in states with fairly weak guidelines, sentencing commissions can play an important role, not just in drafting
guidelines but also by advising the legislature as to various sentencing policy
matters of current concern.

As for the increasingly important goal of resource-impact assessment,
there is considerable evidence that sentencing guidelines can help to avoid
prison overcrowding and the kinds of dramatic (and very expensive) escalation
in prison populations which has occurred in many non-guidelines states in the
past 20 years. Minnesota pioneered this concept, and has successfully avoided
major prison overcrowding problems for almost two decades — a period in
which most non-guidelines states experienced both overcrowding and court intervention. Although Minnesota's prison population has increased substantially
since 1979, the average annual rate of growth (about 5 percent per year) has
only been about two-thirds the rate for the nation as a whole (8 percent per
year). Other guidelines jurisdictions which emphasized resource-management
goals have also had low average annual growth rates. . . .

Truth in Sentencing.   Any system which has abolished parole release discretion — as the majority of guidelines systems have done — has achieved a
greater degree of "truth in sentencing." Of course, this goal has also been
achieved in a number of states which abolished parole without adopting judicial

sentencing guidelines. However, there is reason to believe that the abolition of parole works much better in a system with such guidelines. [Systems] with judicial guidelines have less need to rely on state-wide parole standards as a means of reducing disparity in the sentences imposed by local judges. [Further,] systems with guidelines and a permanent sentencing commission are in a better position to predict the effects abolition of parole will have on prison populations; such systems can then either build more prisons, modify the guidelines to lower prison commitment or duration rates, or pursue a combination of these strategies. In contrast, the abolition of parole, in a system without judicial guidelines, eliminates a means of counteracting judicial disparity and prison overcrowding at the "back end" of the sentencing process, without providing any means of controlling these problems from the "front end."

Public Safety. States with sentencing guidelines have generally had stable or falling crime rates since their guidelines became effective. However, crime rates have recently been stable or falling in most states, with or without guidelines. And, of course, crime rates depend on many social and economic factors in addition to sentencing policy; a thorough examination of the relationship between guidelines and public safety would thus be very complex (and has not been attempted by quantitative criminologists). But the stable or falling pattern of crime rates, noted above, at least suggests that sentencing guidelines do not threaten public safety. . . .

TWO PERSISTENT CHALLENGES

Despite the accomplishments of many state guidelines, there are a number of legitimate criticisms which can be leveled at even the best of these systems. Two of the most important problems are the failure to effectively regulate prosecutorial discretion and plea bargaining; and the limited efforts to regulate and encourage the use of non-custodial ("intermediate") sanctions. Although each of these "gaps" in guidelines coverage is a problem, neither is a major problem in well-designed systems; indeed they may even be strengths, helping these systems accommodate important contemporary sentencing goals and values.

Prosecutorial Discretion and Plea Bargaining. . . . Since guidelines limit the range of sentences available for a given offense, the power to drop or not drop charges is the power to select the sentence range available to the court (that is, what "box" on the grid the case ends up in). Thus, any disparity in charging translates into disparity in sentencing. Unregulated charging and plea bargaining also make it more difficult for the sentencing commission to predict future resource needs. Yet no guidelines system has come up with an effective way of structuring prosecutorial sentencing power, and its potential for disparity and unpredictability. Washington has state-wide charging guidelines, but they are not legally enforceable. The federal Guidelines tried to mitigate this problem by requiring trial courts to consider certain alleged criminal acts ("relevant conduct") whether or not such acts were included in any conviction offense. But this essentially lawless approach goes too far in the opposite direction — allowing sentences to be based on weak charges which were properly dismissed, resulted in acquittal, or were never even filed.

What should be done? Clearly efforts to structure prosecutorial discretion and plea bargaining should continue, especially by means of internal, administrative measures within prosecutor's offices, such as written policies and review of decisions by supervising staff. [But it will be very difficult to enforce controls,] especially to impose lower limits on charge and recommended-sentence severity (since, in most cases, neither prosecutors nor defendants will appeal cases of prosecution leniency).

However, I believe that most state guidelines systems are valuable reforms even if prosecutorial decisions remain substantially unregulated. I have two reasons for this belief. First, the absence of widespread complaints about prosecutorial dominance in state guidelines systems is an important sign, suggesting that closer regulation may not be needed. Specifically, I am suggesting that, in a properly balanced guidelines system — that is, one with reasonable sentence severity levels and few mandatory minimum statutes, in which courts retain substantial sentencing discretion for any given offense (due to broad guidelines ranges, limited appellate scrutiny, and/or flexible departure powers) — it is rare that prosecutorial decisions will produce sentences which judges strongly disapprove, yet are powerless to prevent (as often seems to occur in federal courts). Second, prosecutorial charging and plea bargaining are valuable sources of flexibility and moderation in sentencing. These discretionary powers permit systems to consider individual offense and offender factors which may not fit squarely within formal statutory and guidelines rules. And of course, prosecutorial discretion also allows systems to tailor sentencing severity to the available resources and evidence.

Intermediate Sanctions. Only a few guidelines jurisdictions have attempted to regulate the conditions of non-custodial sanctions, or even to encourage broader use of such sanctions. Even the few jurisdictions which have attempted to address these issues have not gone very far. Several systems authorize judges, in certain cases, to substitute specified amounts of certain intermediate sanctions for custody; for example, sixteen hours of community service, or a day of home detention, might be substituted for a day of custody. Two states, Pennsylvania and North Carolina, have attempted to define large groups of offenders for whom various kinds of intermediate sanctions are appropriate. These guidelines first classify penalties into three types: incarceration (prison or jail), severe intermediate sanctions (such as residential treatment), and mild intermediate sanctions (such as community service). . . . But the Pennsylvania and North Carolina Guidelines provide no guidance as to the choice to be made, when more than one sanction type is allowed in a given cell, or (when a non-custodial option is chosen), how much of that option to impose (for instance, what length of home detention or community service). . . .

CONCLUSION

After two decades of guidelines reforms, what have we learned? Here is a short list of the most important lessons which a review of this experience teaches:

First: guidelines in a number of states have succeeded in improving sentencing policy and practice — reducing bias and disparity in sentencing; avoiding serious prison over-crowding; and ensuring that adequate prison space is available for the most serious offenders. State guidelines regulate but do not eliminate discretion. . . . Most state guidelines systems have abolished parole release discretion, which serves to achieve Truth in Sentencing; offenders serve most of the sentence imposed by the trial court, and there is no pretense that sentences are longer than they really are. State guidelines have achieved more rational sentencing policy because they are developed and monitored by an independent, non-partisan agency charged with the responsibility of collecting detailed data on sentencing practices and resources, evaluating sentencing policy from a long-term perspective, setting priorities for use of limited resources, and developing a comprehensive approach to the sentencing of all crimes, thereby avoiding the problems of piecemeal reforms. [Yet] other major public and private stakeholders . . . have significant input into the development and implementation of state sentencing policy. The Legislature maintains oversight and ultimate control over major policy issues, and important roles are also played by trial and appellate judges, the defense and prosecution, victims, community representatives, and correctional officials. And yet — most state guidelines systems remain relatively simple to understand and apply.

Second: the best state guidelines work better, in all of the ways described above, than any other sentencing system which has yet been tried or even proposed. Quite simply, there is no realistic alternative as a means of accommodating all of the many important values and principles which we want sentences to serve. The prior indeterminate sentencing system permitted intolerable extremes of disparity; the unpredictable nature of indeterminate sentencing also prevented effective resource-management, and violated the public's desire for Truth in Sentencing. . . .

Third: state sentencing guidelines are politically viable. They have been successfully implemented in many states, and have survived — in some cases for almost 20 years, which is a very long time, given the extreme political salience and volatility of sentencing issues in recent years. These systems have survived because they work. . . .

Fourth: state guidelines continue to evolve and improve. Newer systems are more likely to take advantage of the potential which guidelines provide for resource-management and the promotion and structuring of intermediate sanctions. Most older systems are better today than when they began, not only because they have added desirable features (a permanent commission; resource-management; intermediate sanctions) which they originally lacked, but also because these system[s] now openly recognize and incorporate a wide variety of sentencing goals and values. . . .

Fifth: the development of sentencing guidelines remains an area of state, not federal leadership. This reform began in the states; state guidelines have improved over time more than the federal version. [The] great diversity of guidelines systems provides a rich menu of reform options and experience to guide sentencing reformers in other states — and in the federal system — in their efforts to design, implement, improve, and preserve guidelines systems.

NOTES

1. *Evolving goals for state guideline system.* The principal goal of early sentencing reforms was to regulate sentencing discretion and thereby to limit

sentencing disparities. As Professor Frase explains, however, the goals of sentencing reform in many states transformed over time to emphasize controlling the growth of prison populations and encouraging the use of intermediate sanctions. What forces do you think prompted this evolution in the goals of modern sentencing reform? Do you think a sentencing guideline system managed by a sentencing commission is better suited to effectuate these changed goals than the legislature?

2. *Developing guidelines in the shadow of the federal system.* Though Minnesota and a few other states adopted guideline systems before the creation of the federal sentencing guidelines, most states with guidelines began their reform efforts afterward. Many states have expressly rejected the federal sentencing guidelines as a model for their own reforms. Professor Michael Tonry has noted that in numerous states considering sentencing reforms, "commissions at early meetings adopted resolutions expressly repudiating the federal guidelines as a model for anything they might develop." Michael Tonry, Sentencing Matters 134 (1996); see Kevin R. Reitz and Curtis R. Reitz, Building a Sentencing Reform Agenda: The ABA's New Sentencing Standards, 78 Judicature 189, 189-192 (1995) (explaining that during the American Bar Association's drafting of model standards, "the federal system was held out repeatedly as a bad example," requiring the proposed standards "to be defended as very different than the federal guidelines").

3. Development and Structure of the Federal Sentencing Guidelines

a. Statutory Foundations

Though Judge Marvin Frankel's ideas were the catalyst for many reforms, Senator Edward Kennedy was the central political figure in turning Judge Frankel's ideas into a specific proposal for federal sentencing reform. Throughout the 1970s, Senator Kennedy championed Judge Frankel's ideas, as shown in the following excerpt:

> The absence in the federal criminal code of any articulated purposes or goals of sentencing has led to a situation where different judges often mete out different sentences to similar defendants convicted of similar crimes, depending on the sentencing attitudes of the particular judge. [Some] convicted offenders (including repeat offenders) escape jail altogether while others — convicted of the same crime — go to jail for excessively long periods. . . .
> An important prerequisite of any effective crime-fighting program — certainty of punishment — is absent. In addition, the criminal justice system appears arbitrary and unjust, a game of chance in which the offender may "gamble" on receiving not just a lenient term of imprisonment but no jail sentence at all. . . . Sentencing disparity also strikingly demonstrates the fallacy of fighting crime by increasing maximum sentences which can be imposed. Counterfeiting carries a maximum penalty of fifteen years imprisonment; not only is the average sentence actually imposed less than five years, but almost 50% of convicted counterfeiters receive no imprisonment at all. Simply increasing maximum penalties is an exercise in futility. . . .
> What can be done? I have introduced legislation in the U.S. Senate, [entitled] the Sentencing Guidelines bill, [which] would bring welcome uniformity

to the sentencing process by articulating for the first time the general purposes and goals of sentencing that a judge should consider before imposing a sentence of imprisonment. The bill also provides for appellate review of sentences and creates a United States Commission on Sentencing to establish specific, fixed sentencing ranges for similar defendants who commit similar crimes. . . .

Edward M. Kennedy, Criminal Sentencing: A Game of Chance, 60 Judicature 208, 210-212 (1976).

Despite the force of Senator Kennedy's advocacy, it took nearly a decade before a version of his reform bill was passed into law as the Sentencing Reform Act of 1984 (SRA). In an account of the SRA's legislative history, Kate Stith and Steve Koh observed that the "legislative history of federal sentencing reform [reveals a] subtle transformation of sentencing reform legislation: conceived by liberal reformers as an anti-imprisonment and antidiscrimination measure, but finally born as part of a more conservative law-and-order crime control measure." Kate Stith and Steve Koh, The Politics of Sentencing Reform: The Legislative History of the Federal Sentencing Guidelines, 28 Wake Forest L. Rev. 223, 226 (1993). Cf. Marc L. Miller and Ronald F. Wright, Your Cheatin' Heart(land): The Long Search for Administrative Sentencing Justice, 2 Buff. Crim. L. Rev. 723 (1999) (providing a somewhat different account of the SRA's legislative history). What might appeal to a political conservative, such as Senator Orrin Hatch, about presumptive sentencing guidelines?

Though the passage of the SRA in 1984 created the U.S. Sentencing Commission and provided the statutory foundation for federal sentencing guidelines, the commission struggled to fulfill the SRA's mandates, and its initial set of guidelines did not become effective until November 1987. Moreover, the guidelines did not become fully operational until 1989 because many of the first guideline cases focused primarily on constitutional challenges to the SRA's entire approach to sentencing reform. The *Mistretta* decision excerpted below provides background on the statutory framework created by the SRA for regulating federal sentencing discretion; it also details the Supreme Court's affirmation of the constitutionality of this framework.

‖ *John Mistretta v. United States* ‖
488 U.S. 361 (1989)

BLACKMUN, J.

For almost a century, the Federal Government employed in criminal cases a system of indeterminate sentencing. . . . Serious disparities in sentences, however, were common. Rehabilitation as a sound penological theory came to be questioned and, in any event, was regarded by some as an unattainable goal for most cases. In 1958, Congress authorized the creation of judicial sentencing institutes and joint councils, to formulate standards and criteria for sentencing. In 1973, the United States Parole Board adopted guidelines that established a "customary range" of confinement. Congress in 1976 endorsed this initiative through the Parole Commission and Reorganization Act, an attempt to envision for the Parole Commission a role, at least in part, to moderate the disparities in the sentencing practices of individual judges. . . . This proved to be no more than a way station. Fundamental and widespread dissatisfaction with the uncertainties and the disparities continued to be expressed. Congress had wrestled with the problem for more than a decade when, in 1984, it enacted the sweeping reforms that are at issue here. . . .

Before settling on a mandatory-guideline system, Congress considered other competing proposals for sentencing reform. It rejected strict determinate sentencing because it concluded that a guideline system would be successful in reducing sentence disparities while retaining the flexibility needed to adjust for unanticipated factors arising in a particular case. The Judiciary Committee rejected a proposal that would have made the sentencing guidelines only advisory.

THE ACT

The Act, as adopted, revises the old sentencing process in several ways:

1. It rejects imprisonment as a means of promoting rehabilitation, and it states that punishment should serve retributive, educational, deterrent, and incapacitative goals.
2. It consolidates the power that had been exercised by the sentencing judge and the Parole Commission to decide what punishment an offender should suffer. This is done by creating the United States Sentencing Commission, directing that Commission to devise guidelines to be used for sentencing, and prospectively abolishing the Parole Commission.
3. It makes all sentences basically determinate. A prisoner is to be released at the completion of his sentence reduced only by any credit earned by good behavior while in custody.
4. It makes the Sentencing Commission's guidelines binding on the courts, although it preserves for the judge the discretion to depart from the guideline applicable to a particular case if the judge finds an aggravating or mitigating factor present that the Commission did not adequately consider when formulating guidelines. The Act also requires the court to state its reasons for the sentence imposed and to give "the specific reason" for imposing a sentence different from that described in the guideline.
5. It authorizes limited appellate review of the sentence. It permits a defendant to appeal a sentence that is above the defined range, and it permits the Government to appeal a sentence that is below that range. It also permits either side to appeal an incorrect application of the guideline. . . .

The [U.S. Sentencing] Commission is established "as an independent commission in the judicial branch of the United States." It has seven voting members (one of whom is the Chairman) appointed by the President "by and with the advice and consent of the Senate." At least three of the members [must] be Federal judges selected after considering a list of six judges recommended to the President by the Judicial Conference of the United States. No more than four members of the Commission shall be members of the same political party. The Attorney General, or his designee, is an ex officio non-voting member.

The Chairman and other members of the Commission are subject to removal by the President "only for neglect of duty or malfeasance in office or for other good cause shown." [A] voting member serves for six years and may not serve more than two full terms.

In addition to the duty the Commission has to promulgate determinative-sentence guidelines, it is under an obligation periodically to "review and revise" the guidelines. . . . It must report to Congress any amendments of the guidelines [and submit] annually an analysis of the operation of the guidelines [and] issue "general policy statements" regarding their application. . . .

DELEGATION OF POWER

Petitioner argues that in delegating the power to promulgate sentencing guidelines for every federal criminal offense to an independent Sentencing Commission, Congress has granted the Commission excessive legislative discretion in violation of the . . . nondelegation doctrine. . . .

In light of our [prior] approval of broad delegations, we harbor no doubt that Congress' delegation of authority to the Sentencing Commission is sufficiently specific and detailed to meet constitutional requirements. Congress charged the Commission with three goals: to "assure the meeting of the purposes of sentencing as set forth" in the Act; to "provide certainty and fairness in meeting the purposes of sentencing, avoiding unwarranted sentencing disparities among defendants with similar records . . . while maintaining sufficient flexibility to permit individualized sentences," where appropriate; and to "reflect, to the extent practicable, advancement in knowledge of human behavior as it relates to the criminal justice process." Congress further specified four "purposes" of sentencing that the Commission must pursue in carrying out its mandate: "to reflect the seriousness of the offense, to promote respect for the law, and to provide just punishment for the offense"; "to afford adequate deterrence to criminal conduct"; "to protect the public from further crimes of the defendant"; and "to provide the defendant with needed . . . correctional treatment."

In addition, Congress prescribed the specific tool — the guidelines system — for the Commission to use in regulating sentencing. More particularly, Congress directed the Commission to develop a system of "sentencing ranges" applicable "for each category of offense involving each category of defendant." . . . Congress also required that for sentences of imprisonment, "the maximum of the range established for such a term shall not exceed the minimum of that range by more than the greater of 25 percent or 6 months. . . ." Moreover, Congress directed the Commission to use current average sentences "as a starting point" for its structuring of the sentencing ranges.

To guide the Commission in its formulation of offense categories, Congress directed it to consider seven factors: the grade of the offense; the aggravating and mitigating circumstances of the crime; the nature and degree of the harm caused by the crime; the community view of the gravity of the offense; the public concern generated by the crime; the deterrent effect that a particular sentence may have on others; and the current incidence of the offense. Congress set forth 11 factors for the Commission to consider in establishing categories of defendants. These include the offender's age, education, vocational skills, mental and emotional condition, physical condition (including drug dependence), previous employment record, family ties and responsibilities, community ties, role in the offense, criminal history, and degree of dependence upon crime for a livelihood. Congress also prohibited the Commission from considering the "race, sex, national origin, creed, and socioeconomic status of offenders," and instructed that the guidelines should reflect the "general inappropriateness" of considering certain other factors, such as current unemployment, that might serve as proxies for forbidden factors.

In addition to these overarching constraints, Congress provided even more detailed guidance to the Commission about categories of offenses and offender characteristics. Congress directed that guidelines require a term of confinement at or near the statutory maximum for certain crimes [and] assure a substantial term of imprisonment for [various other offenses]. . . . On the other hand, Congress directed that guidelines reflect the general inappropriateness of imposing a sentence of imprisonment [for certain first offenders]. Congress also enumerated various aggravating and mitigating circumstances . . . to be reflected in the guidelines. In other words, although Congress granted the Commission substantial discretion in formulating guidelines, in actuality it legislated a full hierarchy of punishment . . . and stipulated the most important offense and offender characteristics to place defendants within these categories.

We cannot dispute petitioner's contention that the Commission enjoys significant discretion in formulating guidelines. The Commission does have discretionary authority to determine the relative severity of federal crimes and to assess the relative weight of the offender characteristics that Congress listed for the Commission to consider. The Commission also has significant discretion to determine which crimes have been punished too leniently, and which too severely. [But] developing proportionate penalties for hundreds of different crimes by a virtually limitless array of offenders is precisely the sort of intricate, labor-intensive task for which delegation to an expert body is especially appropriate. . . . We have no doubt that in the hands of the Commission the criteria which Congress has supplied are wholly adequate for carrying out the general policy and purpose of the Act.

SEPARATION OF POWERS

Mistretta argues that Congress, in constituting the Commission as it did, effected an unconstitutional accumulation of power within the Judicial Branch while at the same time undermining the Judiciary's independence and integrity. . . .

The Sentencing Commission unquestionably is a peculiar institution within the framework of our Government. Although placed by the Act in the Judicial Branch, it is not a court and does not exercise judicial power. Rather, the Commission is an "independent" body comprised of seven voting members including at least three federal judges, entrusted by Congress with the primary task of promulgating sentencing guidelines. Our constitutional principles of separated powers are not violated, however, by mere anomaly or innovation. . . .

Given the consistent responsibility of federal judges to pronounce sentence within the statutory range established by Congress, we find that the role of the Commission in promulgating guidelines for the exercise of that judicial function bears considerable similarity to the role of this Court in establishing rules of procedure under the various enabling Acts. . . . Just as the rules of procedure bind judges and courts in the proper management of the cases before them, so the Guidelines bind judges and courts in the exercise of their uncontested responsibility to pass sentence in criminal cases. In other words, the Commission's functions, like this Court's function in promulgating procedural rules, are clearly attendant to a central element of the historically acknowledged mission of the Judicial Branch. . . .

We recognize that the task of promulgating rules regulating practice and pleading before federal courts does not involve the degree of political judgment integral to the Commission's formulation of sentencing guidelines. . . . We do not believe, however, that the significantly political nature of the Commission's work renders unconstitutional its placement within the Judicial Branch. Our separation-of-powers analysis does not turn on the labeling of an activity as "substantive" as opposed to "procedural," or "political" as opposed to "judicial." . . . In this case, the "practical consequences" of locating the Commission within the Judicial Branch pose no threat of undermining the integrity of the Judicial Branch or of expanding the powers of the Judiciary beyond constitutional bounds. . . .

SCALIA, J., dissenting.

. . . I dissent from today's decision because I can find no place within our constitutional system for an agency created by Congress to exercise no governmental power other than the making of laws. . . .

Statutorily permissible sentences for particular crimes cover as broad a range as zero years to life, and within those ranges the Commission was given broad discretion to prescribe the "correct" sentence. Average prior sentences were to be a starting point for the Commission's inquiry, but it could and regularly did deviate from those averages as it thought appropriate. It chose, for example, to prescribe substantial increases over average prior sentences for white-collar crimes such as public corruption, antitrust violations, and tax evasion. . . . The Commission also determined when probation was permissible, imposing a strict system of controls because of its judgment that probation had been used for an "inappropriately high percentage of offenders guilty of certain economic crimes." . . . Congress also gave the Commission discretion to determine whether 7 specified characteristics of offenses, and 11 specified characteristics of offenders, "have any relevance," and should be included among the factors varying the sentence. Of the latter, it included only three among the factors required to be considered, and declared the remainder not ordinarily relevant. It should be apparent from the above that the decisions made by the Commission are far from technical, but are heavily laden (or ought to be) with value judgments and policy assessments. . . .

If rulemaking can be entirely unrelated to the exercise of judicial or executive powers, I foresee all manner of "expert" bodies, insulated from the political process, to which Congress will delegate various portions of its lawmaking responsibility. How tempting to create an expert Medical Commission (mostly M.D.'s, with perhaps a few Ph.D.'s in moral philosophy) to dispose of such thorny, "no-win" political issues as the withholding of life-support systems in federally funded hospitals, or the use of fetal tissue for research. This is an undemocratic precedent that we set — not because of the scope of the delegated power, but because its recipient is not one of the three Branches of Government. The only governmental power the Commission possesses is the power to make law; and it is not the Congress. . . .

I think the Court errs . . . because it fails to recognize that this case is . . . about the creation of a new Branch altogether, a sort of junior-varsity Congress. It may well be that in some circumstances such a Branch would be desirable; perhaps the agency before us here will prove to be so. But there are many desirable dispositions that do not accord with the constitutional structure we live under. And in the long run the improvisation of a constitutional structure on the basis of currently perceived utility will be disastrous.

NOTES

1. *Judicial resistance to federal sentencing reform.* Though *Mistretta* ultimately found the constitutional challenges to be unavailing, more than 200 district judges and one circuit court had ruled that the SRA was unconstitutional on various grounds. Commentators have suggested that federal judges' apparent eagerness to strike down the SRA regime revealed their distaste for the entire project of guideline sentencing. See Michael Tonry, Sentencing Matters 73-74 (1996). Revealing their views more directly, federal judges were among the most vocal critics of the federal sentencing guidelines following their enactment. See, e.g., Jose A. Cabranes, Sentencing Guidelines: A Dismal Failure, N.Y.L.J., Feb. 11, 1992, at 2; Marc Miller, Rehabilitating the Federal Sentencing Guidelines, 78 Judicature 180, 180-183 (1995) (detailing widespread judicial hostility to the federal guidelines). Some commentators and some members of the commission suggested that these complaints simply represented judges' displeasure about losing some of their broad sentencing powers. Others, however, believed these judicial criticisms were sound indicators of serious problems with the SRA's entire approach to sentencing reform. See Kate Stith and Jose A. Cabranes, Fear of Judging: Sentencing Guidelines in the Federal Courts (1998).

2. *Congress's mandatory sentencing provisions and their impact on the guidelines.* In the very same legislative session in which it enacted the SRA, Congress also began relying on mandatory sentencing laws to restrict judicial sentencing discretion. In 1984 Congress created a set of general minimum sentences for certain felonies and enacted a mandatory five-year sentence increase for crimes of violence involving a gun. Additional sentencing mandates followed nearly every two years — synchronized, not coincidentally, with federal election cycles. Of most consequence, in 1986 Congress enacted a five-year mandatory enhancement for use of a firearm in a drug crime and created a broad set of mandatory minimum penalties for drug trafficking that linked the minimum sentence to the amount of drugs involved in the offense.

Though mandatory sentencing statutes have proved consistently popular with Congress, they have been assailed by judges, researchers, and commentators. In a speech about federal sentencing reform, Justice Stephen Breyer, a member of the original U.S. Sentencing Commission, effectively summarized the many criticisms of mandatory sentencing provisions:

> [Statutory] mandatory sentences prevent the Commission from carrying out its basic, congressionally mandated task: the development, in part through research, of a rational, coherent set of punishments. Mandatory minimums will sometimes make it impossible for the Commission to adjust sentences in light of factors that its research shows to be directly relevant. . . . They will sometimes prevent the application of Guidelines that would reduce a sentence in light of, for example, a minimal role in a drug offense, thereby sentencing similarly offenders who are very different, perhaps like a drug lord and a mule. Most seriously, they skew the entire set of criminal punishments, for Congress rarely considers more than the criminal behavior directly at issue when it writes these provisions. . . .
>
> Moreover, mandatory minimums . . . may permit the prosecutor, not the judge, to select the sentence by choosing . . . to charge, or not to charge, a violation of a statute that carries a mandatory prison term. [A] 1991 Commission study indicates that in nearly 40% of the cases involving conduct to which a mandatory minimum attached, the offender received a sentence lower than the minimum, perhaps because the prosecutor charged a different crime. . . . In sum, Congress, in simultaneously requiring Guideline sentencing and mandatory minimum sentencing, is riding two different horses. And those horses, in terms of coherence, fairness, and effectiveness, are traveling in opposite directions.

Speech of Associate Justice Stephen Breyer, University of Nebraska College of Law (Nov. 18, 1998), in 11 Fed. Sentencing Rep. 180, 184-185 (1999).

In addition to their direct consequences, the mandatory sentencing laws enacted in 1984 and 1986 skewed the initial development of the federal sentencing guidelines. Especially in the creation of the guidelines' drug sentencing provisions, the U.S. Sentencing Commission felt it had to alter its standard approach to guideline development in order to harmonize its provisions with Congress's sentencing mandates, which focused almost exclusively on drug quantities. See William W. Wilkins Jr. et al., Competing Sentencing Policies in a "War on Drugs" Era, 28 Wake Forest L. Rev. 305, 319-321 (1993).

3. *Composition of a sentencing commission.* Recall that Judge Frankel encouraged broad-based membership in a sentencing commission to ensure a well-rounded and knowledgeable group that could insulate sentencing rules from political pressures. In many states, the creation of sentencing commissions lived up to Frankel's ideals. In the words of Professor Michael Tonry, "sentencing commissions in [many states] have operated much as Judge Frankel hoped they would [and they] have achieved and sustained specialized institutional competence, insulated sentencing policy from short-term 'crime of the week' political pressures, and maintained a focus on comprehensive system-wide policymaking." Michael Tonry, The Success of Judge Frankel's Sentencing Commission, 64 U. Colo. L. Rev. 713, 713 (1993).

In the federal system, however, the U.S. Sentencing Commission has, more often than not, reflected the "tough on crime" philosophy of appointing presidents and confirming Congresses, and commentators have noticed that commission deliberations generally reflect a prosecutorial orientation. See Douglas A. Berman, Common Law for This Age of Federal Sentencing: The Opportunity and Need for Judicial Lawmaking, 11 Stan. L. & Poly. Rev. 93, 108-109 (1999).

The statutory structure might explain this turn of events: the SRA provides for a designee of the attorney general to be an ex officio member of the commission, but provides no equivalent representation to a member of the defense bar. See 28 U.S.C. §991(a). And in 2003, apparently as a result of concerns that the U.S. Sentencing Commission was not controlling judicial sentences tightly enough, Congress altered the judicial representation on the commission. The SRA's initial mandate that "at least three" of the commission's seven voting members had to be federal judges was changed to provide that the commission is to be composed of "not more than three" federal judges. P. L. 108-21, 117 Stat. 650, §401(n). It is now possible for the commission to have no judicial representation at all.

b. Basic Guideline Structure

Though the SRA in 1984 created a basic statutory framework as well as a general direction for the development of federal sentencing guidelines, it still left the U.S. Sentencing Commission with enormous authority and many difficult decisions about how best to regulate judicial discretion through sentencing guidelines. After three years of deliberation and drafting in which the U.S. Sentencing Commission considered a range of approaches to reform, in 1987 the commission finally produced the initial sentencing guidelines. The excerpt below, taken from the introduction to the *Guidelines Manual*, gives important background on many structural and policy choices the commission made in its first guidelines.

> ## U.S. Sentencing Guidelines Manual, Chapter One — Introduction and General Application Principles
> ### U.S. Sentencing Commission (1987)

... The initial sentencing guidelines and policy statements were developed after extensive hearings, deliberation, and consideration of substantial public comment. The Commission emphasizes, however, that it views the guideline-writing process as evolutionary. It expects, and the governing statute anticipates, that continuing research, experience, and analysis will result in modifications and revisions to the guidelines through submission of amendments to Congress. To this end, the Commission is established as a permanent agency to monitor sentencing practices in the federal courts. . . .

THE BASIC APPROACH (POLICY STATEMENT)

The [Sentencing Reform Act's] basic objective was to enhance the ability of the criminal justice system to combat crime through an effective, fair sentencing system. To achieve this end, Congress first sought honesty in sentencing. It sought to avoid the confusion and implicit deception that arose out of the pre-guidelines sentencing system which required the court to impose an indeterminate sentence of imprisonment and empowered the parole commission to determine how much of the sentence an offender actually would serve in prison. . . . Second, Congress sought reasonable uniformity in sentencing by narrowing the wide disparity in sentences imposed for similar criminal offenses committed by similar offenders. Third, Congress sought proportionality in sentencing through a system that imposes appropriately different sentences for criminal conduct of differing severity.

Honesty is easy to achieve: the abolition of parole makes the sentence imposed by the court the sentence the offender will serve, less approximately fifteen percent for good behavior. There is a tension, however, between the mandate of uniformity and the mandate of proportionality. Simple uniformity — sentencing every offender to five years — destroys proportionality. Having only a few simple categories of crimes would make the guidelines uniform and easy to administer, but might lump together offenses that are different in important respects. [But] a sentencing system tailored to fit every conceivable wrinkle of each case would quickly become unworkable and seriously compromise the certainty of punishment and its deterrent effect. For example: a bank robber with (or without) a gun, which the robber kept hidden (or brandished), might have frightened (or merely warned), injured seriously (or less seriously), tied up (or simply pushed) a guard, teller, or customer, at night (or at noon), in an effort to obtain money for other crimes (or for other purposes), in the company of a few (or many) other robbers, for the first (or fourth) time. . . .

The larger the number of subcategories of offense and offender characteristics included in the guidelines, the greater the complexity and the less workable the system. [Probation] officers and courts, in applying a complex system having numerous subcategories, would be required to make a host of decisions regarding whether the underlying facts were sufficient to bring the case within a particular subcategory. The greater the number of decisions required and the greater their complexity, the greater the risk that different courts would apply the guidelines differently to situations that, in fact, are similar, thereby reintroducing the very disparity that the guidelines were designed to reduce. . . .

In the end, there was no completely satisfying solution to this problem. The Commission had to balance the comparative virtues and vices of broad, simple categorization and detailed, complex subcategorization, and within the constraints established by that balance, minimize the discretionary powers of the sentencing court. Any system will, to a degree, enjoy the benefits and suffer from the drawbacks of each approach.

A philosophical problem arose when the Commission attempted to reconcile the differing perceptions of the purposes of criminal punishment. . . . Some argue that appropriate punishment should be defined primarily on the basis of the principle of "just deserts." Under this principle, punishment should be scaled to the offender's culpability and the resulting harms. Others argue that punishment should be imposed primarily on the basis of practical "crime control" considerations. This theory calls for sentences that most effectively lessen the likelihood of future crime, either by deterring others or incapacitating the defendant.

Adherents of each of these points of view urged the Commission to choose between them and accord one primacy over the other. As a practical matter, however, this choice was unnecessary because in most sentencing decisions the application of either philosophy will produce the same or similar results.

In its initial set of guidelines, the Commission sought to solve both the practical and philosophical problems of developing a coherent sentencing system by taking an empirical approach that used as a starting point data estimating pre-guidelines sentencing practice. It analyzed data drawn from 10,000 presentence investigations, the differing elements of various crimes as distinguished in substantive criminal statutes, the United States Parole Commission's guidelines and statistics, and data from other relevant sources in order to determine which distinctions were important in pre-guidelines practice. After consideration, the Commission accepted, modified, or rationalized these distinctions. . . .

The Commission did not simply copy estimates of pre-guidelines practice as revealed by the data. . . . Rather, it departed from the data at different points for various important reasons. Congressional statutes, for example, suggested or required departure, as in the case of the Anti-Drug Abuse Act of 1986 that imposed increased and mandatory minimum sentences. In addition, the data revealed inconsistencies in treatment, such as punishing economic crime less severely than other apparently equivalent behavior.

Despite these policy-oriented departures from pre-guidelines practice, the guidelines represent an approach that begins with, and builds upon, empirical data. The guidelines will not please those who wish the Commission to adopt a single philosophical theory and then work deductively to establish a simple and perfect set of categorizations and distinctions. The guidelines may prove acceptable, however, to those who seek more modest, incremental improvements in the status quo, who believe the best is often the enemy of the good, and who recognize that these guidelines are, as the Act contemplates, but the first step in an evolutionary process. . . .

DEPARTURES

The sentencing statute permits a court to depart from a guideline-specified sentence only when it finds "an aggravating or mitigating circumstance of a kind, or to a degree, not adequately taken into consideration by the Sentencing Commission in formulating the guidelines that should result in a sentence different from that described." 18 U.S.C. §3553(b). The Commission intends the sentencing courts to treat each guideline as carving out a "heartland," a set of typical cases embodying the conduct that each guideline describes. When a court finds an atypical case, one to which a particular guideline linguistically applies but where conduct significantly differs from the norm, the court may consider whether a departure is warranted. Section 5H1.10 (Race, Sex, National Origin, Creed, Religion, and Socio-Economic Status), §5H1.12 (Lack of Guidance as a Youth and Similar Circumstances), the third sentence of §5H1.4 (Physical Condition, Including Drug or Alcohol Dependence or Abuse), and the last sentence of §5K2.12 (Coercion and Duress) list several factors that the court cannot take into account as grounds for departure. With those specific exceptions, however, the Commission does not intend to limit the kinds of factors, whether or not mentioned anywhere else in the guidelines, that could constitute grounds for departure in an unusual case.

The Commission has adopted this departure policy for two reasons. First, it is difficult to prescribe a single set of guidelines that encompasses the vast range of human conduct potentially relevant to a sentencing decision. The Commission also recognizes that the initial set of guidelines need not do so. The Commission is a permanent body, empowered by law to write and rewrite guidelines, with progressive changes, over many years. By monitoring when courts depart from the guidelines and by analyzing their stated reasons for doing so and court decisions with references thereto, the Commission, over time, will be able to refine the guidelines to specify more precisely when departures should and should not be permitted.

Second, the Commission believes that despite the courts' legal freedom to depart from the guidelines, they will not do so very often. This is because the guidelines, offense by offense, seek to take account of those factors that the Commission's data indicate made a significant difference in pre-guidelines sentencing practice. Thus, for example, where the presence of physical injury made an important difference in pre-guidelines sentencing practice (as in the case of robbery or assault), the guidelines specifically include this factor to enhance the sentence. . . .

SENTENCING RANGES

. . . While the Commission has not considered itself bound by pre-guidelines sentencing practice, it has not attempted to develop an entirely new system of sentencing on the basis of theory alone. Guideline sentences, in many instances, will approximate average pre-guidelines practice and adherence to the guidelines will help to eliminate wide disparity. . . . In some instances, short sentences of incarceration for all offenders in a category have been substituted for a pre-guidelines sentencing practice of very wide variability in which some defendants received probation while others received several years in prison for the same offense. Moreover, inasmuch as those who pleaded guilty under pre-guidelines practice often received lesser sentences, the guidelines permit the court to impose lesser sentences on those defendants who accept responsibility for their misconduct. For defendants who provide substantial assistance to the government in the investigation or prosecution of others, a downward departure may be warranted. . . .

The Commission has also examined its sentencing ranges in light of their likely impact upon prison population. Specific legislation, such as the Anti-Drug Abuse Act of 1986 and the career offender provisions of the Sentencing Reform Act of 1984, required the Commission to promulgate guidelines that will lead to substantial prison population increases. These increases will occur irrespective of the guidelines. The guidelines themselves, insofar as they reflect policy decisions made by the Commission (rather than legislated mandatory minimum or career offender sentences), are projected to lead to an increase in prison population . . . estimated at approximately 10 percent over a period of ten years. . . .

THE SENTENCING TABLE

The Commission has established a sentencing table that for technical and practical reasons contains 43 levels. Each level in the table prescribes ranges that overlap with the ranges in the preceding and succeeding levels. By overlapping the ranges, the table should discourage unnecessary litigation. Both prosecution and defense will realize that the difference between one level and another will not necessarily make a difference in the sentence that the court imposes. Thus, little purpose will be served in protracted litigation trying to determine, for example, whether $10,000 or $11,000 was obtained as a result of a fraud. At the same time, the levels work to increase a sentence proportionately. A change of six levels roughly doubles the sentence irrespective of the level at which one starts. The guidelines, in keeping with the statutory requirement that the maximum of any range cannot exceed the minimum by more than the greater of 25 percent or six months (28 U.S.C. §994(b)(2)), permit courts to exercise the greatest permissible range of sentencing discretion. . . .

A CONCLUDING NOTE

The Commission emphasizes that it drafted the initial guidelines with considerable caution [by relying] upon pre-guidelines sentencing practice as revealed by its own statistical analyses based on summary reports of some 40,000 convictions, a sample of 10,000 augmented presentence reports, the parole guidelines, and policy judgments. The Commission recognizes that some will criticize this approach as overly cautious, as representing too little a departure from pre-guidelines sentencing practice. Yet, it will cure wide disparity. The Commission is a permanent body that can amend the guidelines each year. Although the data available to it, like all data, are imperfect, experience with the guidelines will lead to additional information and provide a firm empirical basis for consideration of revisions.

NOTES

1. *Theoretical choices (or lack thereof).*   Many of the early calls for sentencing reform urged that reforms be driven by a specific theoretical commitment to a just deserts or "limiting retributivism" philosophy. See Andrew von Hirsch, Doing Justice: The Choice of Punishments (1976); Norval Morris, The Future of Imprisonment (1974). As noted before, Minnesota's sentencing commission heeded this recommendation when it adopted just deserts as the governing premise of its policies concerning who receives prison sentences. As explained in the introduction to the federal sentencing guidelines, however, the U.S. Sentencing Commission concluded that "[a]s a practical matter" any choice between crime control and retributivist philosophies of punishment in the construction of the guidelines "was unnecessary because in most sentencing decisions the application of either philosophy will produce the same or similar results." Do you agree with this assertion?

2. *Training exercises.*   One of the functions of the U.S. Sentencing Commission is to train the judges, probation officers, and attorneys who work with the guidelines daily. The extensive Web site for the commission, at http:// www.ussc.gov, includes training exercises and detailed study papers on how to apply the guidelines in various situations. It is easier to appreciate the design choices the commission made in constructing the guidelines machine if you

have at least glimpsed that machine in operation. Now, or after reviewing the following overview of the federal guidelines in operation, would be a good time to use the worksheets on the commission's Web site to step through one or more of the training exercises (perhaps the Robbery Exercise, available at http://www.ussc.gov/training/ws_ex_rob.pdf (hypothetical facts) and http://www.ussc.gov/training/sent_ex_rob.pdf (completed worksheet)). The worksheets helpfully point the way through the tangled wiring of the guidelines.

‖ *Overview of the Federal Sentencing Guidelines* ‖
U.S. Sentencing Commission (2001)

How the Sentencing Guidelines Work

The sentencing guidelines take into account both the seriousness of the offense and the offender's criminal history.

Offense Seriousness.   The sentencing guidelines provide 43 levels of offense seriousness — the more serious the crime, the higher the offense level. . . . Each type of crime is assigned a base offense level, which is the starting point for determining the seriousness of a particular offense. More serious types of crimes have higher base offense levels (for example, a trespass has a base offense level of 4, while kidnapping has a base offense level of 24).

In addition to base offense levels, each offense type typically carries with it a number of specific offense characteristics. These are factors that vary from offense to offense, but that can increase or decrease the base offense level and, ultimately, the sentence an offender receives. Some examples:

- One of the specific base offense characteristics for theft (which has a base offense level of 6) increases the offense level based on the amount of loss involved in the offense. If a theft involved a $6,000 loss, there is to be a 2-level increase to the base offense level, bringing the level up to 8. If a theft involved a $50,000 loss, there is to be a 6-level increase, bringing the total to 12.
- One of the specific offense characteristics for robbery (which has a base offense level of 20) involves the use of a firearm. If a firearm was displayed during the robbery, there is to be a 5-level increase, bringing the level to 25; if a firearm was actually discharged during the robbery, there is to be a 7-level increase, bringing the level to 27.

Adjustments.   Adjustments are factors that can apply to any offense. Like specific offense characteristics, they increase or decrease the offense level. Categories of adjustments include: victim-related adjustments, the offender's role in the crime, and obstruction of justice. Examples of adjustments are as follows:

- If the offender was a minimal participant in the offense, the offense level is decreased by 4 levels.
- If the offender knew that the victim was unusually vulnerable due to age or physical or mental condition, the offense level is increased by 2 levels.

- If the offender obstructed justice, the offense level is increased by 2 levels. . . .
- [The judge may decrease the offense level by two levels if, in the judge's opinion, the offender accepted responsibility for his offense.]

When there are multiple counts of conviction, the sentencing guidelines provide instructions on how to achieve a "combined offense level." These rules provide incremental punishment for significant additional criminal conduct. The most serious offense is used as a starting point. The other counts determine whether to and how much to increase the offense level. . . .

Criminal History.   The guidelines assign each offender to one of six criminal history categories based upon the extent of an offender's past misconduct and how recently these crimes took place. Criminal History Category I is assigned to the least serious criminal record and includes many first-time offenders. Criminal History Category VI is the most serious category and includes offenders with lengthy criminal records.

Determining the Guideline Range.   The final offense level is determined by taking the base offense level and then adding or subtracting from it any specific offense characteristics and adjustments that apply. The point at which the final offense level and the criminal history category intersect on the Commission's sentencing table determines the defendant's sentencing guideline range. [An] offender with a Criminal History Category of I and a final offense level of 20 would have a guideline range of 33 to 41 months. . . .

Sentencing Options.   In addition to providing a guideline range, there are a series of rules that determine the availability of non-imprisonment sentencing options for offenders. For example, if the applicable guideline range is 0-6 months, the judge has a number of options, including a guideline sentence of probation only, or a sentence of up to six months' imprisonment.

Departures.   After the guideline range is determined, if the court determines that there is a factor that the guidelines did not adequately consider, it may "depart" from the guideline range. That is, the judge may sentence the offender above or below the range. When departing, the judge must state the reason for the departure. If the sentence is an upward departure, the offender may appeal the sentence; if it is a downward departure, the government may appeal. One special kind of departure is the "substantial assistance" departure. This downward departure may be granted if the offender has provided substantial assistance in the investigation or prosecution of another offender. A motion to depart for substantial assistance must be made by the prosecution, but it is the judge who decides whether to grant it and, if so, to what extent.

Commentary to Sentencing Table

The Offense Level (1-43) forms the vertical axis of the Sentencing Table. The Criminal History Category (I-VI) forms the horizontal axis of the Table. The intersection of the Offense Level and Criminal History Category displays the Guideline Range in months of imprisonment. "Life" means life imprisonment.

SENTENCING TABLE
(in months of imprisonment)

	Offense Level	Criminal History Category (Criminal History Points)					
		I (0 or 1)	II (2 or 3)	III (4, 5, 6)	IV (7, 8, 9)	V (10, 11, 12)	VI (13 or more)
	1	0-6	0-6	0-6	0-6	0-6	0-6
	2	0-6	0-6	0-6	0-6	0-6	1-7
	3	0-6	0-6	0-6	0-6	2-8	3-9
	4	0-6	0-6	0-6	2-8	4-10	6-12
Zone A	5	0-6	0-6	1-7	4-10	6-12	9-15
	6	0-6	1-7	2-8	6-12	9-15	12-18
	7	0-6	2-8	4-10	8-14	12-18	15-21
	8	0-6	4-10	6-12	10-16	15-21	18-24
	9	4-10	6-12	8-14	12-18	18-24	21-27
Zone B							
	10	6-12	8-14	10-16	15-21	21-27	24-30
Zone C	11	8-14	10-16	12-18	18-24	24-30	27-33
	12	10-16	12-18	15-21	21-27	27-33	30-37
	13	12-18	15-21	18-24	24-30	30-37	33-41
	14	15-21	18-24	21-27	27-33	33-41	37-46
	15	18-24	21-27	24-30	30-37	37-46	41-51
	16	21-27	24-30	27-33	33-41	41-51	46-57
	17	24-30	27-33	30-37	37-46	46-57	51-63
	18	27-33	30-37	33-41	41-51	51-63	57-71
	19	30-37	33-41	37-46	46-57	57-71	63-78
	20	33-41	37-46	41-51	51-63	63-78	70-87
	21	37-46	41-51	46-57	57-71	70-87	77-96
	22	41-51	46-57	51-63	63-78	77-96	84-105
	23	46-57	51-63	57-71	70-87	84-105	92-115
	24	51-63	57-71	63-78	77-96	92-115	100-125
	25	57-71	63-78	70-87	84-105	100-125	110-137
	26	63-78	70-87	78-97	92-115	110-137	120-150
	27	70-87	78-97	87-108	100-125	120-150	130-162
Zone D	28	78-97	87-108	97-121	110-137	130-162	140-175
	29	87-108	97-121	108-135	121-151	140-175	151-188
	30	97-121	108-135	121-151	135-168	151-188	168-210
	31	108-135	121-151	135-168	151-188	168-210	188-235
	32	121-151	135-168	151-188	168-210	188-235	210-262
	33	135-168	151-188	168-210	188-235	210-262	235-293
	34	151-188	168-210	188-235	210-262	235-293	262-327
	35	168-210	188-235	210-262	235-293	262-327	292-365
	36	188-235	210-262	235-293	262-327	292-365	324-405
	37	210-262	235-293	262-327	292-365	324-405	360-life
	38	235-293	262-327	292-365	324-405	360-life	360-life
	39	262-327	292-365	324-405	360-life	360-life	360-life
	40	292-365	324-405	360-life	360-life	360-life	360-life
	41	324-405	360-life	360-life	360-life	360-life	360-life
	42	360-life	360-life	360-life	360-life	360-life	360-life
	43	life	life	life	life	life	life

For example, the guideline range applicable to a defendant with an Offense Level of 15 and a Criminal History Category of III is 24-30 months of imprisonment.

NOTES

1. *Guideline commentary.* In addition to the detailed instructions set forth in guideline provisions, most guidelines are accompanied by official commentary from the U.S. Sentencing Commission in the form of "application notes" and

"background." This commentary is designed to aid courts when applying specific provisions by defining key terms or providing insights into the development and purpose of the provision. In Stinson v. United States, 508 U.S. 36 (1993), the Supreme Court unanimously ruled that "commentary in the *Guidelines Manual* that interprets or explains a guideline is authoritative unless it violates the Constitution or a federal statute, or is inconsistent with, or a plainly erroneous reading of, that guideline." In other words, courts and others interpreting and applying the guidelines must generally treat the commentary as binding and having the same force as the actual guideline provisions.

2. *Conflicting judicial interpretations of guideline provisions.* As with any other intricate set of legal rules, the federal sentencing guidelines are often interpreted in conflicting ways by different judges. In Braxton v. United States, 500 U.S. 344 (1991), the Supreme Court unanimously ruled that the U.S. Sentencing Commission is to have the initial and primary responsibility of responding to circuit conflicts over guideline interpretations. According to the Court in *Braxton*, "in charging the Commission 'periodically [to] review and revise' the guidelines, Congress necessarily contemplated that the Commission would periodically review the work of the courts, and would make whatever clarifying revisions to the guidelines conflicting judicial decisions might suggest." Though the Supreme Court in *Braxton* said that it should be more "restrained and circumspect" in using its certiorari power to resolve circuit conflicts for guidelines issues, the Court has still played a role in the development of federal sentencing law by deciding more than two dozen significant sentencing cases in the past decade.

3. *Guideline complexity.* Though simplified in the summary above, the federal sentencing guidelines are quite complex. The complexity of the federal guideline system has been a concern since the U.S. Sentencing Commission promulgated its initial guidelines in 1987: There were more than 100 multisection guidelines filling more than 200 pages in the first *Guidelines Manual,* and they included an intricate nine-step process for determining a defendant's applicable sentencing range from within a 258-box grid known as the "sentencing table." Judicial decisions have since increased the corpus of federal sentencing law and thus complicated an already intricate sentencing process: confronted with numerous interpretive questions in applying the guidelines, district and circuit courts issue hundreds of guideline sentencing opinions each year. Meanwhile, the U.S. Sentencing Commission, honoring its statutory obligation to review and revise the guidelines, has passed more than 600 amendments to the guidelines over the past 15 years. The *U.S. Sentencing Guidelines Manual* now runs more than 400 pages and has an even lengthier, separate appendix that chronicles the amendments. Tens of thousands of federal court opinions have interpreted these guidelines.

Many judges, practitioners, and commentators have lamented the system's complexity, in part because complex guidelines increase the risk that the sentencing rules will be misunderstood or misapplied. Thus, complexity undercuts the goals of sentencing predictability and certainty. Justice Stephen Breyer, a member of the original Sentencing Commission, notes that there is also a link between complexity and judicial discretion:

> The original 1987 Guidelines draft was just over 200 pages long, and many criticized that draft as too lengthy and too complex. The Guidelines are now twice

as long [and] the greatest obstacle to [simplification] is, I believe, the legal mind itself. We judges and lawyers love to make distinctions. For sentencing purposes, distinctions about how a crime was carried out are important in order to assure sentencing proportionality. . . . But it is important to know when to stop. [The] Commission should review the present Guidelines, acting forcefully to diminish significantly the number of offense characteristics attached to individual crimes. The characteristics that remain should be justified for the most part by data that shows their use by practicing judges to change sentences. . . . The Commission originally stated that each Guideline was to cover only the "heartland" of the offense at issue. That concept — the "heartland" — should remain our guiding principle. Less typical cases may be left to departures imposed by the sentencing judge, and perhaps guided, though not directly mandated, by the Commission. . . . The result would be an increase in the discretionary authority of the sentencing judge.

Speech of Associate Justice Stephen Breyer, in 11 Fed. Sentencing Rep. at 185-186. The U.S. Sentencing Commission has often indicated that simplifying the guidelines is an institutional goal, but it has failed so far to engineer such changes. In addition to other impacts, the guidelines' complexity also creates serious problems for the defense bar in providing effective representation for federal defendants. See Alan J. Chaset, A Teacher at the Top: Another Reason to Have a Representative of the Criminal Defense Bar on the Sentencing Commission, 11 Fed. Sentencing Rep. 309, 309-310 (1999) (suggesting guidelines may "involve too much law for the average practitioner to keep current with"); Douglas A. Berman, From Lawlessness to Too Much Law? Exploring the Risk of Disparity from Differences in Defense Counsel Under Guidelines Sentencing, 87 Iowa L. Rev. 435 (2002).

4. *Offender characteristics.*   Though the characteristics of an *offense* play a central role in establishing applicable sentencing ranges under the federal sentencing guidelines, characteristics of an offender (other than past criminal history) play almost no role in the determination of applicable guideline ranges. Such matters are addressed in the federal guidelines only through policy statements that seek to regulate departures, and these provisions state that many such offender characteristics are "not relevant" or "not ordinarily relevant" to a departure decision. See, e.g., U.S. Sentencing Guidelines Manual §5H1.12 ("Lack of guidance as a youth and similar circumstances indicating a disadvantaged upbringing are not relevant grounds for imposing a sentence outside the applicable guideline range"); §5H1.2 ("Education and vocational skills are not ordinarily relevant in determining whether a sentence should be outside the applicable guideline range"); §5H1.4 ("Drug or alcohol dependence or abuse is not a reason for imposing a sentence below the guidelines"); §5H1.6 ("Family ties and responsibilities and community ties are not ordinarily relevant in determining whether a sentence should be outside the applicable guideline range").

Many judges and commentators have been especially critical of the guidelines' failure to account for offender characteristics such as disadvantaged background or family circumstances that judges often used as mitigating considerations in preguidelines sentencing practice. See, e.g., Kate Stith and Jose A. Cabranes, Judging Under the Federal Sentencing Guidelines, 91 Nw. U. L. Rev. 1247 (1997); Daniel J. Freed, Federal Sentencing in the Wake of Guidelines: Unacceptable Limits on the Discretion of Sentencers, 101 Yale L.J. 1681 (1992);

Charles J. Ogletree, The Death of Discretion? Reflections on the Federal Sentencing Guidelines, 101 Harv. L. Rev. 1938 (1988). Congress and the U.S. Sentencing Commission have not generally heeded these criticisms. In fact, Congress in 2003 passed legislation that further curtailed the ability of sentencing judges in certain cases to depart from the guidelines based on offender characteristics, and it also directed the commission to review critically how judges were using their departure authority to take into account offender characteristics.

c. Departures and Discretion

Though the Sentencing Reform Act significantly altered the judicial role in sentencing, the judge's discretion has not been removed from the federal sentencing process entirely. Despite the strictures of mandatory sentencing laws and complex guidelines, the SRA and the guidelines preserve an important role for the sentencing judge.

First and foremost, the guidelines preserve a judicial role simply through the adoption of sentencing ranges. Like most state guideline systems, the federal guidelines do not specify an exact sentence for each offense and offender; they establish a sentencing range from which sentencing judges select a specific sentence. Notably, Congress specifically mandated in the SRA that sentencing ranges in the federal guidelines be fairly narrow by providing that "the maximum of the range established for [any imprisonment] term shall not exceed the minimum of that range by more than the greater of 25 percent or 6 months." 28 U.S.C. §994(b)(2). Because district judges have complete discretion to select a sentence from within this range and this decision is not subject to appeal, the independent determination and judgment of district judges still in effect controls at least one-quarter of every federal guideline sentence.

The SRA also gives judges express authority to depart from the guidelines whenever there is a "circumstance of a kind, or to a degree, not adequately taken into consideration by the Sentencing Commission in formulating the guidelines that should result in a sentence different from that described." 18 U.S.C. §3553(b). How the U.S. Sentencing Commission and courts should understand this provision has been intensely debated since the guidelines' inception, and for good reason. The rules governing departures are the focal point of the guideline system's efforts to achieve greater sentencing consistency without sacrificing necessary flexibility. If departure authority too readily allows judges to deviate from the guidelines' presumptive sentences, then the system will be too pliant and unwarranted sentencing disparity may persist. Yet if departure authority too rarely allows judges to depart from the guidelines' presumptive sentences, then the system will be too rigid, judicial discretion will be overly limited, and unwarranted sentencing uniformity may occur.

Departure authority technically takes two different basic forms in the federal guideline system. The commission used the departure mechanism in U.S.S.G. §5K1.1 to implement Congress's directive that judges generally impose lower sentences "to take into account a defendant's substantial assistance in the investigation and prosecution" of others. 28 U.S.C. §994(n). This provision for departures based on a prosecutor's motion plays a critical role not only in the sentence imposed but also in plea negotiations, in which prosecutors use their

authority to recommend departures as a way to persuade defendants to cooperate in further criminal investigations. Commentators have noted that section
5K1.1 and other guideline provisions enhance the sentencing discretion of
prosecutors; the uneven application of section 5K1.1 and prosecutorial discretion more generally is discussed below.

Even more fundamental to the operation of the guidelines and the preservation of judicial discretion is the district judge's distinct power to depart without a motion from the prosecutor. This statutory authority to deviate from the
guidelines is potentially applicable in every case, and the scope of departure authority — and more particularly, the potential for appellate review to encourage
or discourage its use — came before the Supreme Court in one of the most controversial of possible settings. The police beating of motorist Rodney King in Los
Angeles made an impact on federal sentencing law that almost rivals the impact
this event made on race relations in the United States.

|| *Stacey Koon v. United States* ||
|| 518 U.S. 81 (1993) ||

KENNEDY, J.

I.

On the evening of March 2, 1991, Rodney King [drove with] two of his
friends [while] intoxicated. California Highway Patrol officers observed King's
car traveling at a [very high] speed . . . and ordered him by loudspeaker to pull
over, but he continued to drive. [When King stopped after a chase of eight
miles, the] officers ordered King and his two passengers to exit the car and to
assume a felony prone position — that is, to lie on their stomachs with legs
spread and arms behind their backs. . . . King got on his hands and knees but
did not lie down. Officers Powell, Wind, Briseno and Solano tried to force King
down, but King resisted and became combative, so the officers retreated. Koon
then fired taser darts (designed to stun a combative suspect) into King.

The events that occurred next were captured on videotape by a bystander.
As the videotape begins, it shows that King rose from the ground and charged
toward Officer Powell. Powell took a step and used his baton to strike King on
the side of his head. King fell to the ground. From the eighteenth to the 30th
second on the videotape, King attempted to rise, but Powell and Wind each
struck him with their batons to prevent him from doing so. From the 35th to the
51st second, Powell administered repeated blows to King's lower extremities;
one of the blows fractured King's leg. . . . At 1:05 on the videotape, Briseno, in
the District Court's words, "stomped" on King's upper back or neck. King's body
writhed in response. At 1:07, Powell and Wind again began to strike King with a
series of baton blows, and Wind kicked him in the upper thoracic or cervical
area six times until 1:26. At about 1:29, King put his hands behind his back and
was handcuffed. . . . Powell radioed for an ambulance. He sent two messages
over a communications network to the other officers that said "ooops" and

"I haven't beaten anyone this bad in a long time." Koon sent a message to the police station that said: "Unit just had a big time use of force. . . . Tased and beat the suspect of CHP pursuit big time."

King was taken to a hospital where he was treated for a fractured leg, multiple facial fractures, and numerous bruises and contusions. Learning that King worked at Dodger Stadium, Powell said to King: "We played a little ball tonight, didn't we Rodney? . . . You know, we played a little ball, we played a little hardball tonight, we hit quite a few home runs. . . . Yes, we played a little ball and you lost and we won."

Koon, Powell, Briseno, and Wind were tried in state court on charges of assault with a deadly weapon and excessive use of force by a police officer. The officers were acquitted of all charges, with the exception of one assault charge against Powell that resulted in a hung jury. The verdicts touched off widespread rioting in Los Angeles. More than 40 people were killed in the riots, more than 2,000 were injured, and nearly $1 billion in property was destroyed.

On August 4, 1992, a federal grand jury indicted the four officers under 18 U.S.C. §242, charging them with violating King's constitutional rights under color of law. . . . After a trial in United States District Court for the Central District of California, the jury convicted Koon and Powell but acquitted Wind and Briseno. . . .

The District Court sentenced petitioners pursuant to USSG §2H1.4, which applies to violations of 18 U.S.C. §242. Section 2H1.4 prescribes a base offense level [of 21 when the underlying offense is assault. Adjustments for use of a dangerous weapon and for bodily injury brought the offense level to 27], and because neither petitioner had a criminal record, each fell within criminal history category I. The sentencing range for an offense level of 27 and a criminal history category I was . . . 70-to-87 months' imprisonment. Rather than sentencing petitioners to a term within the Guideline range, however, the District Court departed downward eight levels. The departure determinations are the subject of this controversy.

The court granted a five-level departure because "the victim's wrongful conduct contributed significantly to provoking the offense behavior," §5K2.10, [policy statement]. The court also granted a three-level departure, based on a combination of four factors. First, as a result of the "widespread publicity and emotional outrage which have surrounded this case," petitioners were "particularly likely to be targets of abuse" in prison. Second, petitioners would face job-termination proceedings, after which they would lose their positions as police officers, be disqualified from prospective employment in the field of law enforcement, and suffer the "anguish and disgrace these deprivations entail." Third, petitioners had been "significantly burdened" by having been subjected to successive state and federal prosecutions. Fourth, petitioners were not "violent, dangerous, or likely to engage in future criminal conduct," so there was "no reason to impose a sentence that reflects a need to protect the public from [them]." The court concluded these factors justified a departure when taken together, although none would have been sufficient standing alone.

The departures yielded an offense level of 19 and a sentencing range of 30-to-37 months' imprisonment. The court sentenced each petitioner to 30 months' imprisonment. . . . The Court of Appeals reviewed de novo whether the district court had authority to depart. The court reversed the five-level departure for victim misconduct [and also] rejected each factor cited [for the three-level departure].

II.

. . . Congress allows district courts to depart from the applicable Guideline range if "the court finds that there exists an aggravating or mitigating circumstance of a kind, or to a degree, not adequately taken into consideration by the Sentencing Commission in formulating the guidelines that should result in a sentence different from that described."

Turning our attention . . . to the *Guidelines Manual,* we learn that the Commission did not adequately take into account cases that are, for one reason or another, "unusual." USSG ch. 1, pt. A, intro. comment. 4(b). The Introduction to the Guidelines explains:

> The Commission intends the sentencing courts to treat each guideline as carving out a "heartland," a set of typical cases embodying the conduct that each guideline describes. When a court finds an atypical case, one to which a particular guideline linguistically applies but where conduct significantly differs from the norm, the court may consider whether a departure is warranted.

The Commission lists certain factors that never can be bases for departure (race, sex, national origin, creed, religion, socioeconomic status, lack of guidance as a youth, drug or alcohol dependence, and economic hardship), but then states that with the exception of those listed factors, it "does not intend to limit the kinds of factors, whether or not mentioned anywhere else in the guidelines, that could constitute grounds for departure in an unusual case." [The Commission explains that] atypical cases were not "adequately taken into consideration," and factors that may make a case atypical provide potential bases for departure. Potential departure factors "cannot, by their very nature, be comprehensively listed and analyzed in advance," USSG §5K2.0, of course. Faced with this reality, the Commission chose to prohibit consideration of only a few factors, and not otherwise to limit, as a categorical matter, the considerations that might bear upon the decision to depart.

Sentencing courts are not left adrift, however. The Commission provides considerable guidance as to the factors that are apt or not apt to make a case atypical, by listing certain factors as either encouraged or discouraged bases for departure. . . . Victim provocation, a factor relied upon by the District Court in this suit, is an example of an encouraged downward departure factor. . . . Discouraged factors, by contrast, are those "not ordinarily relevant to the determination of whether a sentence should be outside the applicable guideline range." ch. 5, pt. H, intro. comment. Examples include the defendant's family ties and responsibilities, his or her education and vocational skills, and his or her military, civic, charitable, or public service record. The Commission does not view discouraged factors "as necessarily inappropriate" bases for departure but says they should be relied upon only "in exceptional cases." . . .

If a factor is unmentioned in the Guidelines, the court must, after considering the structure and theory of both relevant individual guidelines and the Guidelines taken as a whole, decide whether it is sufficient to take the case out of the Guideline's heartland. The court must bear in mind the Commission's expectation that departures based on grounds not mentioned in the Guidelines will be "highly infrequent." ch. 1, pt. A, p. 6. Against this background, we consider the standard of review.

III.

Before the Guidelines system, a federal criminal sentence within statutory limits was, for all practical purposes, not reviewable on appeal. The Act altered this scheme in favor of a limited appellate jurisdiction to review federal sentences. Among other things, it allows a defendant to appeal an upward departure and the Government to appeal a downward one. That much is clear. Less clear is the standard of review on appeal. The Government advocates de novo review, saying that, like the Guidelines themselves, appellate review of sentencing, and in particular of departure decisions, was intended to reduce unjustified disparities in sentencing. . . .

We agree that Congress was concerned about sentencing disparities, but we are just as convinced that Congress did not intend, by establishing limited appellate review, to vest in appellate courts wide-ranging authority over district court sentencing decisions. Indeed, the text of §3742 manifests an intent that district courts retain much of their traditional sentencing discretion [by providing] that courts of appeals "give due deference to the district court's application of the guidelines to the facts." . . . The deference that is due depends on the nature of the question presented. The district court may be owed no deference, for instance, when the claim on appeal is that it made some sort of mathematical error in applying the Guidelines; under these circumstances, the appellate court will be in as good a position to consider the question as the district court was in the first instance.

A district court's decision to depart from the Guidelines, by contrast, will in most cases be due substantial deference, for it embodies the traditional exercise of discretion by a sentencing court. . . . Whether a given factor is present to a degree not adequately considered by the Commission, or whether a discouraged factor nonetheless justifies departure because it is present in some unusual or exceptional way, are matters determined in large part by comparison with the facts of other Guidelines cases. District courts have an institutional advantage over appellate courts in making these sorts of determinations, especially as they see so many more Guidelines cases than appellate courts do. In 1994, for example, 93.9% of Guidelines cases were not appealed. . . .

This does not mean that district courts do not confront questions of law in deciding whether to depart. . . . The Government is quite correct that whether a factor is a permissible basis for departure under any circumstances is a question of law, and the court of appeals need not defer to the district court's resolution of the point. . . .

IV.

The principles we have explained require us to reverse the rulings of the Court of Appeals in significant part.

A.

The District Court departed downward five levels because King's "wrongful conduct contributed significantly to provoking the offense behavior." Victim misconduct was an encouraged basis for departure under the 1992 Guidelines and is so now. . . .

The District Court's analysis . . . showed a correct understanding in applying §2H1.4 as a mechanical matter and in interpreting its heartland. After summarizing King's misconduct — his driving while intoxicated, fleeing from the police, refusing to obey the officers' commands, attempting to escape from police custody, etc. — the District Court concluded that a downward departure pursuant to §5K2.10 was justified:

> Koon and Powell were convicted of conduct which began as a legal use of force against a resistant suspect and subsequently crossed the line to unlawfulness, all in a matter of seconds, during the course of a dynamic arrest situation. However, the convicted offenses fall under the same Guideline Sections that would apply to a jailor, correctional officer, police officer or other state agent who intentionally used a dangerous weapon to assault an inmate, without legitimate cause to initiate a use of force. . . .

The District Court did not abuse its discretion in differentiating between the classes of cases [or] in concluding that unprovoked assaults constitute the relevant heartland. . . .

B.

We turn now to the three-level departure. As an initial matter, the Government urges us to hold each of the factors relied upon by the District Court to be impermissible departure factors under all circumstances. [However], for the courts to conclude a factor must not be considered under any circumstances would be to transgress the policy-making authority vested in the Commission.

[Turning] to the four factors underlying the District Court's three-level departure, [the] first question is whether the District Court abused its discretion in relying on the collateral employment consequences petitioners would face as a result of their convictions. The District Court stated:

> . . . In combination, the additional proceedings, the loss of employment and tenure, prospective disqualification from the field of law enforcement, and the anguish and disgrace these deprivations entail, will constitute substantial punishment in addition to any court-imposed sentence. In short, because Koon and Powell are police officers, certain unique burdens flow from their convictions.

[The] District Court abused its discretion by considering petitioners' career loss because the factor, as it exists in these circumstances, cannot take the suit out of the heartland of §2H1.4. [Section] 242 offenses may take a variety of forms, but they must involve willful violations of rights under color of law[, and] it is not unusual for a public official who is convicted of using his governmental authority to violate a person's rights to lose his or her job and to be barred from future work in that field.

[Similarly], the low likelihood of petitioners' recidivism was not an appropriate basis for departure. Petitioners were first-time offenders and so were classified in criminal history category I. The District Court found that "within Criminal History Category I, the Guidelines do not adequately distinguish defendants who, for a variety of reasons, are particularly unlikely to commit crimes in the future." [However, the Commission stated that] "the lower limit of the range for Criminal History Category I is set for a first offender with the lowest risk of recidivism. Therefore, a departure below the lower limit of the guideline range for Criminal History Category I on the basis of the adequacy of criminal history cannot be appropriate." USSG §4A1.3. The District Court abused its discretion by considering appellants' low likelihood of recidivism. The Commission took that factor into account in formulating the criminal history category.

The two remaining factors are susceptibility to abuse in prison and successive prosecutions. The District Court did not abuse its discretion in considering these factors. [We do not dispute] the District Court's finding that "the extraordinary notoriety and national media coverage of this case, coupled with the defendants' status as police officers, make Koon and Powell unusually susceptible to prison abuse." . . . The District Court's conclusion that this factor made the case unusual is just the sort of determination that must be accorded deference by the appellate courts. As for petitioners' successive prosecutions, . . . the District Court did not abuse its discretion in determining that a "federal conviction following a state acquittal based on the same underlying conduct . . . significantly burdened the defendants." The state trial was lengthy, and the toll it took is not beyond the cognizance of the District Court.

V.

The goal of the Sentencing Guidelines is, of course, to reduce unjustified disparities and so reach toward the evenhandedness and neutrality that are the distinguishing marks of any principled system of justice. In this respect, the Guidelines provide uniformity, predictability, and a degree of detachment lacking in our earlier system. This, too, must be remembered, however. It has been uniform and constant in the federal judicial tradition for the sentencing judge to consider every convicted person as an individual and every case as a unique study in the human failings that sometimes mitigate, sometimes magnify, the crime and the punishment to ensue. We do not understand it to have been the congressional purpose to withdraw all sentencing discretion from the United States District Judge. Discretion is reserved within the Sentencing Guidelines, and reflected by the standard of appellate review we adopt. . . .

SOUTER, J., concurring in part and dissenting in part.

[Both] Congress and the Commission envisioned that departures would require some unusual factual circumstance, but would be justified only if the factual difference "should" result in a different sentence. Departures, in other words, must be consistent with rational normative order.

[The] District Court concluded that petitioners would be subject to abuse [in prison] not simply because they were former police officers, but in large part because of the degree of publicity and condemnation surrounding their crime.

But that reasoning overlooks the fact that the publicity stemmed from the remarkable brutality of petitioners' proven behavior, which it was their misfortune to have precisely documented on film. To allow a departure on this basis is to reason, in effect, that the more serious the crime, and the more widespread its consequent publicity and condemnation, the less one should be punished; the more egregious the act, the less culpable the offender. . . . This moral irrationality cannot be attributed to the heartland scheme, however, and rewarding the relatively severe offender could hardly have been in the contemplation of [the] Commission. . . .

I [also] believe that it was also an abuse of discretion for the District Court to depart downward because of the successive prosecutions. In these cases, there were facial showings that the state court system had malfunctioned when the petitioners were acquitted. [It] would be a normatively obtuse sentencing scheme that would reward a defendant whose federal prosecution is justified solely because he has obtained the advantage of injustice produced by the failure of the state system. . . .

BREYER, J., concurring in part and dissenting in part.

In my view, the relevant Guideline, USSG §2H1.4, encompasses the possibility of a double prosecution. That Guideline applies to various civil rights statutes, which Congress enacted, in part, to provide a federal forum for the protection of constitutional rights where state law enforcement efforts had proved inadequate. Before promulgating the Guidelines, the Commission "examined the many hundreds of criminal statutes in the United States Code," USSG ch.1, pt. A, intro. comment. 5, and it would likely have been aware of this well-known legislative purpose. [The] Commission would have considered a "double prosecution" case as one ordinarily within, not outside, the "civil rights" Guideline's "heartland." . . .

The departure on the basis of potential mistreatment in prison presents a closer question. Nonetheless, differences in prison treatment are fairly common — to the point where too frequent use of this factor as a basis for departure could undermine the uniformity that the Guidelines seek. [T]he Guidelines themselves embody an awareness of potentially harsh (or lenient) treatment in prison, thereby permitting departure on that basis only in a truly unusual case[, and] I cannot find in this record anything sufficiently unusual, compared, say, with other policemen imprisoned for civil rights violations, as to justify departure.

NOTES

1. *Departure patterns before and after* Koon.   Prior to the Supreme Court's decision in *Koon*, federal district judges used their departure authority rather sparingly, perhaps in part because many circuit courts reviewed decisions to depart de novo while refusing to review any discretionary decision *not* to depart from the guidelines. Before *Koon*, district judges exercised their independent authority to depart from the guidelines in only about 10 percent of cases (although, during the same period, prosecutors requested and judges granted departures based on defendants' substantial assistance in about twice as many

cases). The *Koon* decision, perhaps responding to judicial and academic complaints about guideline rigidity, seemed designed through its emphasis on sentencing discretion and its adoption of an "abuse of discretion" review standard to enhance sentencing courts' departure authority. If this was indeed the Supreme Court's goal, *Koon* proved to be a very effective ruling. The total number of departures increased by nearly 20 percent every year following the *Koon* decision, and in 2001 there were roughly twice as many departures as there were in 1995.

Notably, almost all departures involve decisions by sentencing judges to impose a sentence *below* the applicable guideline range. Since the start of guideline sentencing, upward departures have never comprised much more than 1 percent of all sentenced cases, and in 2001 there were 30 times more downward departures than upward departures. Did these trends occur because federal sentencing judges generally disapprove of the severity of sentences under the guidelines, or is some other dynamic at work?

Though consistent in direction, judicial departure rates have not been consistent across federal districts and circuits. The U.S. Sentencing Commission reported in 2001 that among districts with more than 100 cases, the percentage of downward departures ranged from a low of 1.4 percent in the Eastern District of Kentucky to a high of 62.8 percent in the District of Arizona; among the circuits that same year, the Ninth Circuit had the highest downward departure rate at 38.7 percent, while the Fourth Circuit had the lowest at 5.2 percent. See United States Sentencing Commission, 2001 Annual Report. (A high departure rate in certain southwestern border districts such as Arizona could be traced in part to "fast track" departures programs adopted in districts with a high volume of immigration cases; this program was designed to encourage prompt disposition of cases in which a defendant would ultimately be deported following any term of imprisonment.) Should statistics revealing significant regional variations in the use of departure authority be a source of particular concern?

2. *Congressional reaction to* Koon *through the Feeney Amendment.* Though on occasion the Department of Justice and a few commentators expressed some concerns about increased use of downward departure authority after *Koon,* many judges and most commentators welcomed the increased sentencing flexibility that *Koon* seemed to endorse through its expanded view of departure authority. In 2003, however, Congress decreed through a provision known as the Feeney Amendment that the use of departure authority needed to be reined in. As originally proposed, the Feeney Amendment called for a return to de novo appellate review of departures (effectively overruling the *Koon* decision) and also eliminated all grounds for downward departure except for those based on a factor that was affirmatively and specifically identified as a permissible ground for downward departure by the U.S. Sentencing Commission. Objections from many quarters led to the narrowing of the scope of the Feeney Amendment, but the provisions ultimately signed into law still required circuit courts to apply de novo review of departures and directed the commission to amend the guidelines to "substantially reduce" the number of downward departures. P.L. 108-21, 117 Stat. 650, §401(m). Congress provided no specific guidance to the commission on how to interpret or effectuate this directive.

3. *Extent of departures.* Though the SRA defines a standard for the decision to depart and the commission and courts have expounded upon this

standard at length, neither the SRA nor the commission specifies the "extent" of departures. The SRA simply states in 18 U.S.C. §3742 that the extent of any departure must be "reasonable," and the commission has not elaborated on what might qualify as "reasonable." Given the emphasis on the decision to depart, the failure to be concerned with the extent of departures is somewhat curious in the federal system; because the commission constructed its sentencing table with overlapping sentencing ranges, departures of one or two levels are of limited consequence, and it is really only *large* departures that pose a significant threat of serious sentencing disparities under the guidelines. Notably, the Minnesota Supreme Court early in the history of the Minnesota sentencing guidelines held that upward durational departures should not generally exceed twice the presumptive duration. See State v. Evans, 311 N.W.2d 481 (Minn. 1981).

4. *State approaches to departure authority.* As in the federal system, most state guidelines allow the judge to depart from the sentence range designated in the guidelines. In some states, the departures are categorized according to whether they affect either the disposition of the sentence or the duration of the sentence. Departure standards in most states are generally not as detailed or restrictive as in the federal system: state systems providing for departures typically permit the sentencing court to depart for any "substantial" or "compelling" reasons or they set forth nonexclusive lists of reasons for departures. The departure statutes generally require the judge to explain any departure, and an inadequate explanation can lead to reversal on appeal. Appellate courts in these jurisdictions have developed extensive case law approving or disapproving various grounds for departure. The case law in some states, such as Pennsylvania, gives the trial judge much wider latitude than the case law in other states, such as Minnesota.

Despite more permissive departure standards, the number of departures in state systems have still remained well below the number of cases sentenced within the state guidelines. For instance, in Minnesota dispositional departures have occurred in around 10 percent of the total cases sentenced, while durational departures have occurred in about 25 percent of the cases involving an active prison term. See Richard Frase, Implementing Commission-Based Sentencing Guidelines: The Lessons of the First Ten Years in Minnesota, 2 Cornell J.L. & Pub. Poly. 279 (1993). By what criteria could a sentencing commission decide how many departures are too many?

> ## *Substantial Assistance: An Empirical Yardstick Gauging Equity in Current Federal Policy and Practice, Linda Drazga Maxfield and John H. Kramer*
> **Pages 2-4, 19-21 (1999)**

THE UNDEFINED SUBSTANCE OF SUBSTANTIAL ASSISTANCE

Congress directed the Commission to create [a method to] decrease sentences below the guideline range for offenders who assist in the investigation or prosecution of another person committing a criminal offense. The Sentencing

Commission's response to this congressional mandate took the form of guideline policy statement 5K1.1 — Substantial Assistance to Authorities:

> Upon motion of the government stating that the defendant has provided substantial assistance in the investigation or prosecution of another person who has committed an offense, the court may depart from the guidelines. . . .

Issues raised in the substantial assistance policy statement, but left unanswered elsewhere . . . include [several] that are cited below.

First, the factors to be used by the prosecutor prior to sentencing to determine whether the cooperation of a given defendant is "substantial" — and therefore warrants a substantial assistance departure motion — are unaddressed. . . . What objective and equitable parameters distinguish between "substantial" assistance and "non-substantial" assistance?

Second, the authority to move for a §5K1.1 departure is limited to the prosecution. This exclusivity has resulted in spirited debate in the criminal justice community. Government prosecutors defend the appropriateness of their substantial assistance monopoly by citing the government's unique capability to judge accurately the benefit obtained from the type and extent of assistance provided. The critical response is that predicating a substantial assistance departure on a government motion is a potential source of disparity because the unilateral government decision whether to make the substantial assistance motion is not subject to challenge by the defense and is not reviewable by the court (unless constitutional grounds are cited). . . .

Finally, apparently not all substantial assistance is equal. The policy statement places no conditions on the magnitude of the sentence reduction to be given. Consequently, extensive cooperation theoretically would deserve a larger sentence reduction than less extensive (but still substantial) cooperation. What is the link between assessing the value of a defendant's substantial assistance and deciding on the magnitude of the sentence reduction? . . . Achieving equity in the substantial assistance process has major ramifications for the overall equity of the guidelines system; 19 percent of federal criminal convictions — roughly 7,500 cases per year — were granted downward departures under §5K1.1 over the past three fiscal years (1994 through 1996). . . .

SUMMARY AND IMPLICATIONS

[A] working group was established to explore the policies and procedures across the judicial districts, and to study the factors associated with §5K1.1 sentence reductions and the magnitudes of the departures [through] a diversity of research methodologies. . . . The data reported were not able to find direct correlations between type of cooperation provided, type of benefit or result received by the government, the making of a §5K1.1 motion, and the extent of the substantial assistance departure received. [The] consistency of the findings across methodologies reveals . . . an equity problem requiring subsequent research.

First, this analysis uncovered that the definition of "substantial assistance" was not being consistently applied across the federal districts. Not only were some districts considering cooperation that was not being considered by other districts, but the components of a given behavior that classified it as "substantial" were unclear.

Second, while the U.S. attorney offices are required to record the reason for making a substantial assistance motion, there is no provision that this information be made available for review. It is exactly such a lack of review, inherent in preguideline judicial discretion, that led to charges of unwarranted sentencing disparity and passage of the SRA. Under the SRA, the court is now compelled to report a reason for the sentence imposed and a reason for a departure. . . . A comparable §5K1.1 "statement of reasons" appears appropriate for a guideline process affecting nearly one in every five federal defendants. DOJ information on district charging practices, plea bargaining practices, degree and type of co-operation, and usefulness of information to the prosecution is crucial in an assessment of §5K1.1. . . .

Third, the evidence consistently indicated that factors that were associated with either the making of a §5K1.1 motion and/or the magnitude of the departure were not consistent with principles of equity. Expected factors (e.g., type of cooperation, benefit of cooperation, defendant culpability or function, relevant conduct, offense type) generally were found to be inadequate in explaining §5K1.1 departures. Even more worrisome, legally irrelevant factors (e.g., gender, race, ethnicity, citizenship) were found to be statistically significant in explaining §5K1.1 departures. . . .

Data indicate that currently judges relate the magnitude of departure to the length of the predeparture sentence: higher predeparture guideline ranges bring more absolute months of departure. However, no evidence supports the conclusion that defendants facing higher sentences, in fact, provide absolutely more cooperation, or absolutely more beneficial cooperation, to warrant a larger relative departure. The issue is whether the magnitude of a substantial assistance departure should be an absolute amount (all defendants who cooperate at a given substantial assistance level receive a set and absolute number of months reduction in sentence) or a relative amount (all defendants who cooperate at a given substantial assistance level receive a proportional . . . reduction in sentence). The philosophical debate that addresses the assumptions and ramifications of the absolute versus proportional approach is long overdue.

NOTES

1. *Prosecutorial discretion under the guidelines.*   In part because §5K1.1 of the federal guidelines requires a government motion before the court can reduce the sentence based on the defendant's cooperation (and because 18 U.S.C. §3553(e) requires the same before a court can reduce a sentence below a statutory mandatory minimum), many commentators lament that prosecutors ultimately possess more sentencing discretion than judges within the federal sentencing system. For instance, Professor Kate Stith and Judge Jose Cabranes contend that mandatory sentencing schemes "inevitably shift power toward prosecutors":

Because the sentencing rules are known in advance, prosecutors may greatly influence the ultimate sentence through their decisions on charges, plea agreements, and motions to depart for substantial assistance to law enforcement authorities. Although prosecutors have always had significant discretion in charging and plea bargaining, the prosecutor's decisions on these matters have far greater significance for sentencing in the Guidelines regime; they determine not only the maximum term of a sentence (as provided in the statute prohibiting the conduct), but, in many cases, the precise sentence range that a sentencing court may consider. . . .

Kate Stith and Jose A. Cabranes, To Fear Judging No More: Recommendations for the Federal Sentencing Guidelines, 11 Fed. Sentencing Rep. 187-188 (1999). Though few dispute that prosecutors possess considerable power and discretion with the federal system, some question whether the guidelines themselves are responsible for shifting power to the prosecutors. For example, Justice Stephen Breyer has argued that the guidelines have actually "shifted the power to determine sentences away from prosecutors in at least some ways":

> Prosecutors should find it more difficult than under pre-Guideline practice to control the sentence by manipulating the charge. For, within broad limits, the offender's actual conduct, not the charge, will determine the sentence. For this same reason plea bargaining over charges should have diminished, because again within broad limits, a defendant's promise to plead guilty to a particular, perhaps less serious, charge likely will not affect the sentence. . . . This is not to deny the prosecutor's considerable bargaining power. The prosecutor still may choose to charge an offense that carries a lower statutory maximum penalty (and statutory maximum penalties trump the Guidelines). He may enter into a plea agreement for a fixed sentence, an agreement that will carry significant weight with the judge. He can simply ignore certain conduct, believing that the probation officer will not discover it. And he can ask the judge to depart from a Guideline sentence. But the prosecutor possessed all these powers before the Guidelines as well — and to a greater extent. . . .
>
> I recognize, however, other sources of special prosecutor power. Upon recommendation of the prosecutor, a court may depart downward from a Guideline sentence, and below even a statutory mandatory minimum, where there is "substantial assistance in the investigation or prosecution of another person who has committed an offense." U.S.S.G. §5K1.1. Moreover, statutory mandatory minimum sentences and Guideline sentences written to reflect those mandatory minimums — particularly in respect to drug crimes — may increase the pressure upon a defendant to provide "substantial assistance" in order to obtain a downward departure, or to plead guilty to an offense with a low statutory maximum (e.g., simple possession).
>
> Both factors — "substantial assistance" and "mandatory minimum"— rest upon special provisions in the Guideline statute. Moreover, those two factors play a particularly important role in federal drug prosecutions, which account for about 40% of all federal sentencing. Viewed in light of Guideline history, however, these two special "power-shifting" factors are nonessential, peripheral features of the Guidelines. And, for that reason, I believe it promotes accuracy in analysis, and leads to more constructive recommendations, to point to these two special statutory provisions, rather than the Guidelines themselves, as having increased prosecutorial power. . . .

Speech of Associate Justice Stephen Breyer, in 11 Fed. Sentencing Rep. at 182-183.

2. *Departures, disparity, and discrimination.*   Though departure authority provides judges with an opportunity to adjust sentences in light of unique circumstances in particular cases, it also provides a means for disparity and even

discrimination to work their way back into a guideline system. Consider again the U.S. Sentencing Commission report on substantial assistance departures, which stated that "legally irrelevant factors (e.g., gender, race, ethnicity, citizenship) were found to be statistically significant in explaining §5K1.1 departures." Does this conclusion, and data that show significant circuit-by-circuit discrepancies in the use of departure authority, suggest that guideline systems must more carefully circumscribe and more closely monitor any retained areas of discretion? What role should Congress, the U.S. Sentencing Commission, and appellate courts play in response to such evidence of disparity in the application of departure authority?

3. *Unavoidable tensions between equal justice and individual justice?* One could summarize the entire guideline sentencing movement, as well as the support and criticisms of structured sentencing reforms, as just another chapter in an endless struggle to calibrate effectively the unavoidable tension between efforts to achieve equal justice across cases and to achieve individual justice in specific cases. Kate Stith and Jose Cabranes, leading critics of the federal sentencing guidelines, argue that in the federal system this effort has inappropriately prioritized equal justice over individual justice:

> Grounded in a fear of judging, the Guidelines seek not to channel the exercise of informed judicial discretion, but to repress judgment and replace it with a calculus of justice.... This structure ignores the most important capacity that judges bring to criminal sentencing: the ability to pronounce moral judgment that takes into account all aspects of the crime and the offender.... It is not that the idea of equal treatment is unworthy; rather, this ideal cannot be, and should not be, pursued through complex, mandatory guidelines.... Uniform treatment ought to be one objective of sentencing, to be sure, but not the sole or overriding objective. A just sentence must also be a reasoned sentence and a proportional sentence, imposed through procedures that comport with our basic understandings of due process of law in a constitutional system of checks and balances.
>
> In its quest for sentencing free of "unwarranted disparity," the Commission found it necessary to pigeon-hole crimes and offenders along complex gradients of severity and to greatly confine judicial discretion in all but "atypical" or "extraordinary" cases. Yet every case that comes before a judge for sentencing is different and special. The attempt by the Sentencing Commission to develop a system of rules that would both ensure uniformity and recognize the variability of crimes and offenders has generated inordinate complexity and confusion in Guidelines definition and application, imposed burdens on both trial and appellate courts, generated case law jurisprudence that is at once trivial and voluminous, dehumanized the sentencing process, and undermined the moral dimension of sentencing and punishment.
>
> In the traditional ritual of sentencing, the judge pronounced not only a sentence but society's condemnation as well.... The sentencing ritual was predicated on the fundamental understanding that only a person can pass moral judgment, and only a person can be morally judged. In emphasizing the human face of justice, we are not blind to the limitations of the traditional sentencing hearing. Human judgment is fallible. Unfortunately, this is a fact of our existence for which there can be no easy technological solution. By replacing the case-by-case exercise of human judgment with a mechanical calculus, we do not judge better or more objectively, nor do we judge worse. Instead, we cease to judge at all. We process individuals according to a variety of purportedly objective criteria. But genuine judgment, in the sense of moral reckoning, cannot be inscribed in a table of offense levels and criminal history categories. . . .

Stith and Cabranes, 11 Fed. Sentencing Rep. at 187-188.

B.   CAPITAL PUNISHMENT: REGULATING DISCRETION THROUGH CONSTITUTIONAL RULES

Though many view capital punishment as markedly distinct from other types of sentencing, the regulation of sentencing *discretion* in the modern death penalty closely parallels its regulation in modern noncapital sentencing. As detailed throughout this section, the modern administration of the death penalty has been centrally concerned with the limitation of sentencing discretion. Two features differentiate the death penalty from other sentencing: the actors targeted for regulation are usually jurors, and the catalyst of reform has been the U.S. Supreme Court. In nondeath sentencing it has been sentencing commissions that have operated as the main innovators in structuring the exercise of judges' discretion.

1.   Origins and Foundations

The death penalty once occupied the center of attention in criminal justice; it was the penalty most commonly authorized and imposed under English law before the American colonial period. In part because prison systems did not develop fully until the end of the nineteenth century, the death penalty was a central component of the American criminal justice system during the colonial period and through the eighteenth and early nineteenth centuries. By some counts, there may have been 15,000 authorized executions (and perhaps as many lynchings) during this period, many of which took place in southern states and disproportionately involved African Americans. An abolitionist movement took root soon after the nation's founding and gained force through the nineteenth century. This movement combined with the creation of penitentiaries to diminish the reliance on capital punishment, although 100 to 150 executions still happened each year between the Civil War and World War II.

As explained in the following excerpt, discretion claimed a central role long ago in the American story of the death penalty. The late nineteenth and early twentieth centuries saw most states move away from statutes mandating death as the punishment for certain crimes toward new laws that gave juries discretion to choose which defendants would be sentenced to die.

> ## The Death Penalty in America,
> ### Hugo Adam Bedau
> **Pages 9-12 (3d ed. 1982)**

Traditionally, under English law, death penalties were mandatory; once the defendant was found guilty of a capital offense, the court had no alternative but a death sentence. Thus the jury could avoid a death penalty in a capital case only by acquitting the defendant or by a finding of guilt on a lesser offense (e.g., manslaughter rather than murder). Remission of the death sentence in favor of transportation to the colonies, or some lesser punishment . . . remained a prerogative of the Crown. But as long as the death penalty was a mandatory punishment, there was always the possibility of acquitting a clearly guilty defendant in order to avoid a death sentence, especially in rare cases where the defendant was unusually pitiable or his conduct was thought to be morally excusable. This threat of "jury nullification," as it has come to be called, on the one side, and the undemocratic character of unbridled executive power to pardon, on the other, encouraged the American colonies to reject the traditional mandatory death penalty in favor of some alternative. What eventually developed was the characteristically American practice that divided murder into degrees and gave the court some sentencing discretion in capital cases. . . .

The first of the [Massachusetts] Bay Colony's capital statutes to authorize an alternative penalty to the death sentence was for the crime of rape. Under a law enacted in 1642, rape was punishable by death or by some "other grievous punishment," at the discretion of the court. A severe whipping and the humiliation of standing on the gallows with a rope around one's neck quickly became the most common punishment for the convicted rapist (unless he was a Negro or an Indian, in which case his punishment was likely to be sale into slavery). The heritage of sentencing discretion did not carry over into the post-Revolutionary period, however. [By] 1780 Massachusetts's seven capital felonies (including rape) were subject to a mandatory death penalty. . . .

Elsewhere in the nation, discretionary capital laws slowly replaced mandatory death penalties. . . . In Maryland, where the jury already had the power to fix degrees of murder, the death penalty became optional in 1809 for treason, rape, and arson, but not for homicide. Tennessee (1838) and Alabama (1841) were the first to authorize a discretionary death sentence for murder, and Louisiana (1846) appears to have been the first jurisdiction to make all its capital crimes optionally punishable by life imprisonment. Between 1886 and 1900, twenty states and the federal government followed suit; by 1926, the practice had been adopted in 33 jurisdictions [and] seven more . . . introduced this procedure for the punishment of murder [by 1963].

No doubt the development of jury sentencing-discretion in capital cases was seen in part in some jurisdictions as an effective compromise with forces that might otherwise continue to press for complete abolition. . . . In other jurisdictions, however, a very different motivation prevailed. In the postbellum South, research has shown that where the number of capital statutes increased dramatically, as they did in Virginia, they tended to be enacted in a discretionary rather than a mandatory form. With black Americans newly freed from slavery, but disqualified from testifying against whites, excluded by law from serving on juries, and lacking in trained counsel of their own race, the dominant white class could comfortably place their trust in the judgment of white judges and white juries to administer these discretionary death penalty statutes in the desired manner.

NOTES

1. *Legislative control of the death penalty.*   Before the U.S. Supreme Court's significant involvement in capital punishment administration starting in the 1970s, America's history with the death penalty had been a story primarily about statutes and legislative debate. State legislatures were responsible for the evolution (and even sometimes the abandonment) of capital punishment in the

American criminal justice system from the colonial era through the twentieth century. A number of colonial legislative enactments, though influenced by England's embrace of the death penalty, defined for themselves a subset of crimes that were to be subject to capital punishment. State legislatures further narrowed the reach of the death penalty through the early nineteenth century as states, led by developments in Pennsylvania, divided the offense of murder into degrees and provided that only the most aggravated murderers would be subject to punishment of death. And, as highlighted above, this period also saw a slow but steady evolution in the death penalty from a mandatory punishment to a discretionary one. As Hugo Adam Bedau further explained, these legislative developments reflect "the struggle between abolitionists and retentionists, as well as larger social forces shaping the pattern and institutions of criminal justice." Hugo Adam Bedau, The Death Penalty in America 4 (3d ed. 1982).

2. *Parallel paths in Europe and the United States.* The path followed by the death penalty in Europe paralleled that in the United States. While a few countries abolished it during the nineteenth and early twentieth century, capital punishment saw a resurgence during and after World War I. With the end of World War II, however, a number of European countries abolished the death penalty in their constitutions, largely as a reaction to the abuse of capital punishment during the war. Others accomplished the same feat judicially or through legislation. Most countries gradually used the death penalty less often, and by the late 1960s it was virtually no longer employed. In England, for example, though all first-degree murder remained subject to the death penalty until the 1960s, executive clemency commuted most death sentences to life imprisonment until Parliament changed the law.

3. *Constitutional text and capital punishment.* Capital punishment was a well-established and well-accepted practice during the nation's founding, and the drafters of the Constitution apparently contemplated that it would be a lawful practice in the United States. For instance, the Fifth Amendment says that "[n]o person shall be held to answer for a capital, or otherwise infamous crime, unless on a presentment or indictment of a Grand Jury. . . ." The Amendment's Double Jeopardy Clause provides that no person shall "be twice put in jeopardy of life or limb," and its Due Process Clause declares that no person shall be "deprived of life . . . without due process of law." Do you think this text conclusively establishes the constitutionality of capital punishment so long as appropriate procedural rules are followed? Does the Eighth Amendment's prohibition of "cruel and unusual punishments" change the textual analysis in any way?

Despite the U.S. Constitution's apparent acceptance of capital punishment, the seemingly arbitrary use of discretion in capital cases led lawyers in the 1950s to start questioning the constitutionality of the penalty. Legal challenges to the death penalty took many forms in lower courts through the 1960s, and this litigation helped produce a de facto moratorium on the death penalty as courts stayed executions while they considered various constitutional objections. Broad constitutional challenges to the death penalty first came before the Supreme Court in cases from California and Ohio in which defendants challenged as a violation of due process the discretionary systems under which they were sentenced to death.

|| **Dennis McGautha v. California** ||
|| 402 U.S. 183 (1971) ||

HARLAN, J.

... McGautha and his codefendant Wilkinson were charged with committing two armed robberies and a murder. ... In accordance with California procedure in capital cases, the trial was in two stages, a guilt stage and a punishment stage. [Based on testimonial and physical evidence, the jury found both defendants guilty at the guilt stage.] At the penalty trial, which took place on the following day but before the same jury, the State . . . presented evidence of McGautha's prior felony convictions and sentences, and then rested. [Wilkinson and McGautha thereafter both testified, each claiming that his accomplice fired the fatal shot. Wilkinson also called character witnesses who testified that he had] a good reputation and was honest and peaceable. The jury was instructed in the following language:

> In this part of the trial the law does not forbid you from being influenced by pity for the defendants and you may be governed by mere sentiment and sympathy for the defendants in arriving at a proper penalty in this case; however, the law does forbid you from being governed by mere conjecture, prejudice, public opinion or public feeling.
>
> [You] should consider all of the evidence received here in court presented by the People and defendants throughout the trial before this jury. You may also consider all of the evidence of the circumstances surrounding the crime, of each defendant's background and history, and of the facts in aggravation or mitigation of the penalty which have been received here in court. However, it is not essential to your decision that you find mitigating circumstances on the one hand or evidence in aggravation of the offense on the other hand. . . . Notwithstanding facts, if any, proved in mitigation or aggravation, in determining which punishment shall be inflicted, you are entirely free to act according to your own judgment, conscience, and absolute discretion. . . .
>
> Now, beyond prescribing the two alternative penalties [of death or life imprisonment], the law itself provides no standard for the guidance of the jury in the selection of the penalty, but, rather, commits the whole matter of determining which of the two penalties shall be fixed to the judgment, conscience, and absolute discretion of the jury. In the determination of that matter, if the jury does agree, it must be unanimous as to which of the two penalties is imposed.

The jury returned verdicts fixing Wilkinson's punishment at life imprisonment and McGautha's punishment at death.

[In a companion case on this appeal, John] Crampton was indicted for the murder of his wife. . . . He pleaded not guilty and not guilty by reason of insanity. [Physical evidence linked Crampton to his wife's killing, although his attorney submitted evidence suggesting her shooting was accidental.] In accordance with the Ohio practice which Crampton challenges, his guilt and punishment were determined in a single unitary proceeding. The jury was instructed that: "If you find the defendant guilty of murder in the first degree, the punishment is death, unless you recommend mercy, in which event the punishment is imprisonment in the penitentiary during life." The jury was given no other instructions specifically addressed to the decision whether to recommend mercy, but was told in connection with its verdict generally:

> You must not be influenced by any consideration of sympathy or prejudice. It is your duty to carefully weigh the evidence, to decide all disputed questions of fact, to apply the instructions of the court to your findings and to render your verdict accordingly. In fulfilling your duty, your efforts must be to arrive at a just verdict.
>
> Consider all the evidence and make your finding with intelligence and impartiality, and without bias, sympathy, or prejudice, so that the State of Ohio and the defendant will feel that their case was fairly and impartially tried.

The jury deliberated for over four hours and returned a verdict of guilty, with no recommendation for mercy.

[McGautha and Crampton both] claim that the absence of standards to guide the jury's discretion on the punishment issue is constitutionally intolerable. [They] contend that to leave the jury completely at large to impose or withhold the death penalty as it sees fit is fundamentally lawless and therefore violates the basic command of the Fourteenth Amendment that no State shall deprive a person of his life without due process of law. Despite the undeniable surface appeal of the proposition, we conclude that the courts below correctly rejected it. . . .

The history of capital punishment . . . reveals continual efforts, uniformly unsuccessful, to identify before the fact those homicides for which the slayer should die. [Jurors on occasion took the law into their own hands when facing cases that seemed] clearly inappropriate for the death penalty. In such cases they simply refused to convict of the capital offense. [To] meet the problem of jury nullification, legislatures . . . adopted the method of forthrightly granting juries the discretion which they had been exercising in fact. [Our precedents have consistently suggested the lawfulness of] standardless jury sentencing in capital cases, [stressing that juries] express the conscience of the community on the ultimate question of life or death. . . .

In recent years academic and professional sources have suggested that jury sentencing discretion should be controlled by standards of some sort. The American Law Institute first published such a recommendation in 1959. Several States have enacted new criminal codes in the intervening 12 years, some adopting features of the Model Penal Code. Other States have modified their laws with respect to murder and the death penalty in other ways. None of these States have followed the Model Penal Code and adopted statutory criteria for imposition of the death penalty. In recent years, challenges to standardless jury sentencing have been presented to many state and federal appellate courts. No court has held the challenge good. . . .

Those who have come to grips with the hard task of actually attempting to draft means of channeling capital sentencing discretion have confirmed the lesson taught by the history recounted above. To identify before the fact those characteristics of criminal homicides and their perpetrators which call for the death penalty, and to express these characteristics in language which can be fairly understood and applied by the sentencing authority, appear to be tasks which are beyond present human ability.

Thus the British Home Office, which [selected] the cases from England and Wales which should receive the benefit of the Royal Prerogative of Mercy, observed: "No simple formula can take account of the innumerable degrees of culpability, and no formula which fails to do so can claim to be just or satisfy public opinion. . . . Discretionary judgment on the facts of each case is the only way in which they can be equitably distinguished." . . .

The draftsmen of the Model Penal Code [declared] "that it is within the realm of possibility to point to the main circumstances of aggravation and of mitigation that should be weighed and weighed against each other when they are presented in a concrete case." The circumstances the draftsmen selected . . . were not intended to be exclusive. The Code provides simply that the sentencing authority should "take into account the aggravating and mitigating circumstances enumerated . . . and any other facts that it deems relevant," and that the court should so instruct when the issue was submitted to the jury.

It is apparent that such criteria do not purport to provide more than the most minimal control over the sentencing authority's exercise of discretion. They do not purport to give an exhaustive list of the relevant considerations or the way in which they may be affected by the presence or absence of other circumstances. They do not even undertake to exclude constitutionally impermissible considerations. And, of course, they provide no protection against the jury determined to decide on whimsy or caprice. In short, they do no more than suggest some subjects for the jury to consider during its deliberations, and they bear witness to the intractable nature of the problem of "standards" which the history of capital punishment has from the beginning reflected. Thus, they indeed caution against this Court's undertaking to establish such standards itself, or to pronounce at large that standards in this realm are constitutionally required.

In light of history, experience, and the present limitations of human knowledge, we find it quite impossible to say that committing to the untrammeled discretion of the jury the power to pronounce life or death in a capital case is offensive to anything in the Constitution. The States are entitled to assume that jurors confronted with the truly awesome responsibility of decreeing death for a fellow human will act with due regard for the consequences of their decision and will consider a variety of factors, many of which will have been suggested by the evidence or by the arguments of defense counsel. For a court to attempt to catalog the appropriate factors in this elusive area could inhibit rather than expand the scope of consideration, for no list of circumstances would ever be really complete. The infinite variety of cases and facets to each case would make general standards either meaningless "boiler-plate" or a statement of the obvious that no jury would need. . . .

It may well be, as the American Law Institute and the National Commission on Reform of Federal Criminal Laws have concluded, that bifurcated trials and criteria for jury sentencing discretion are superior means of dealing with capital cases if the death penalty is to be retained at all. But the Federal Constitution, which marks the limits of our authority in these cases, does not guarantee trial procedures that are the best of all worlds, or that accord with the most enlightened ideas of students of the infant science of criminology, or even those that measure up to the individual predilections of members of this Court. The Constitution requires no more than that trials be fairly conducted and that guaranteed rights of defendants be scrupulously respected. . . .

NOTES

1. *Meaning of due process.* Dennis McGautha and John Crampton based their constitutional objection to standardless jury sentencing in capital cases on the Fourteenth Amendment's guarantee that no State shall "deprive any person of life . . . without due process of law." Do you agree with Justice Harlan's core conclusion that the jury instructions used in the trials of McGautha and Crampton provided due process? Do you think the requirements concerning what process is "due" should be heightened in death penalty cases?

2. *Establishing jury standards and the institutions for reform.* Do you concur with Justice Harlan's assertion in *McGautha* that to "identify before the fact those characteristics of criminal homicides and their perpetrators which call for the death penalty, and to express these characteristics in language which can be fairly understood and applied by the sentencing authority, appear to be tasks which are beyond present human ability"? Notably, the drafters of the Model Penal Code, though they took "no position on the desirability of the death penalty," developed a detailed set of possible aggravating and mitigating circumstances that could be used by states adopting the death penalty to guide juries when deciding whether to sentence a particular offender to death. See Model Penal Code §210.6(3) and (4). Justice Harlan's opinion does seem on firmer ground when stating that the history of capital reforms "caution against this Court's undertaking to establish [death penalty] standards itself, or to pronounce at large that standards in this realm are constitutionally required." In other words, though Justice Harlan's assertion about the impossibility of developing jury standards seems questionable, his apparent unwillingness for the Supreme Court to constitutionally mandate such standards seems much more sound.

2. Constitutional Regulation of Capital Sentencing Systems

Right after its decision in *McGautha,* the Supreme Court revisited the constitutionality of the death penalty through three cases posing challenges based on the Eighth Amendment's prohibition of "cruel and unusual punishments." This strategy seemed unlikely to succeed since, in Trop v. Dulles, 356 U.S. 86 (1958), a noncapital case in which the defendant raised an Eighth Amendment claim, Chief Justice Warren suggested in dicta that the death penalty, by dint of tradition, must be a constitutionally permissible punishment:

> Whatever the arguments may be against capital punishment, both on moral grounds and in terms of accomplishing the purposes of punishment — and they are forceful — the death penalty has been employed throughout our history, and, in a day when it is still widely accepted, it cannot be said to violate the constitutional concept of cruelty.

In the same opinion, however, Chief Justice Warren further elaborated on how courts should interpret the Eighth Amendment's vague restriction on government power, suggesting that even historically accepted punishments could still be subjected to renewed constitutional scrutiny. In an oft-quoted passage, Chief Justice Warren stressed: "The basic concept underlying the Eighth Amendment is nothing less than the dignity of man. [T]he words of the Amendment are not precise, and their scope is not static. The Amendment must draw its meaning from the evolving standards of decency that mark the progress of a maturing society."

In Furman v. Georgia and companion cases, Justices Potter Stewart and Byron White joined three of the dissenters in *McGautha* to hold that existing capital punishment statutes were applied in a manner that violated the Eighth Amendment's prohibition on "cruel and unusual punishments." There was no majority opinion in *Furman,* just the per curiam order set forth below, and each Justice authored a separate — and lengthy — opinion. (*Furman* still ranks among the longest decisions in U.S. Supreme Court history, occupying 233 pages in the official Supreme Court reporter.)

How can the outcome in *Furman* be explained in light of *McGautha*? Did McGautha and Crampton merely stake their claims on the wrong amendment?

William Henry Furman v. Georgia
408 U.S. 238 (1972)

PER CURIAM

[Appeals were consolidated here from convictions in three cases. Furman was convicted of murder in Georgia; Jackson was convicted of rape in Georgia; Branch was convicted of rape in Texas. All three were sentenced to death.] Certiorari was granted limited to the following question: "Does the imposition and carrying out of the death penalty in [these cases] constitute cruel and unusual punishment in violation of the Eighth and Fourteenth Amendments?" The Court holds that the imposition and carrying out of the death penalty in these cases constitute cruel and unusual punishment in violation of the Eighth and Fourteenth Amendments. The judgment in each case is therefore reversed insofar as it leaves undisturbed the death sentence imposed, and the cases are remanded for further proceedings. So ordered. . . .

STEWART, J., concurring.

The constitutionality of capital punishment in the abstract is not . . . before us in these cases. . . . Instead, the death sentences now before us are the product of a legal system that brings them, I believe, within the very core of the Eighth Amendment's guarantee against cruel and unusual punishments, a guarantee applicable against the States through the Fourteenth Amendment. In the first place, it is clear that these sentences are "cruel" in the sense that they excessively go beyond, not in degree but in kind, the punishments that the state legislatures have determined to be necessary. In the second place, it is equally clear that these sentences are "unusual" in the sense that the penalty of death is infrequently imposed for murder, and that its imposition for rape is extraordinarily rare. But I do not rest my conclusion upon these two propositions alone.

These death sentences are cruel and unusual in the same way that being struck by lightning is cruel and unusual. For, of all the people convicted of rapes and murders in 1967 and 1968, many just as reprehensible as these, the petitioners are among a capriciously selected random handful upon whom the sentence of death has in fact been imposed. My concurring Brothers have demonstrated that, if any basis can be discerned for the selection of these few to be sentenced to die, it is the constitutionally impermissible basis of race. But racial discrimination has not been proved, and I put it to one side. I simply conclude that the Eighth and Fourteenth Amendments cannot tolerate the infliction of a sentence of death under legal systems that permit this unique penalty to be so wantonly and so freakishly imposed. . . .

WHITE, J., concurring.

The narrower question to which I address myself concerns the constitutionality of capital punishment statutes under which (1) the legislature authorizes the imposition of the death penalty for murder or rape; (2) the legislature does not itself mandate the penalty in any particular class or kind of case (that is, legislative will is not frustrated if the penalty is never imposed), but delegates to judges or juries the decisions as to those cases, if any, in which the penalty will be utilized; and (3) judges and juries have ordered the death penalty with such infrequency that the odds are now very much against imposition and execution of the penalty with respect to any convicted murderer or rapist. . . .

The [death] penalty has not been considered cruel and unusual punishment in the constitutional sense because it was thought justified by the social ends it was deemed to serve. At the moment that it ceases realistically to further these purposes, [it] would violate the Eighth Amendment . . . for its imposition would then be the pointless and needless extinction of life with only marginal contributions to any discernible social or public purposes. A penalty with such negligible returns to the State would be patently excessive and cruel and unusual punishment violative of the Eighth Amendment.

It is also my judgment that this point has been reached with respect to capital punishment as it is presently administered under the statutes involved in these cases. . . . I cannot avoid the conclusion that as the statutes before us are now administered, the penalty is so infrequently imposed that the threat of execution is too attenuated to be of substantial service to criminal justice. [It is clear that] the death penalty is exacted with great infrequency even for the most atrocious crimes and that there is no meaningful basis for distinguishing the few cases in which it is imposed from the many cases in which it is not. . . .

DOUGLAS, J., concurring.

. . . Juries (or judges, as the case may be) have practically untrammeled discretion to let an accused live or insist that he die. . . . Former Attorney General Ramsey Clark has said, "It is the poor, the sick, the ignorant, the powerless and the hated who are executed." One searches our chronicles in vain for the execution of any member of the affluent strata of this society. . . .

Jackson, a black, convicted of the rape of a white woman, was 21 years old. . . . Furman, a black, killed a householder while seeking to enter the home at night. . . . Branch, a black, entered the rural home of a 65-year-old widow, a white, while she slept and raped her, holding his arm against her throat. . . . We cannot say from facts disclosed in these records that these defendants were sentenced to death because they were black. Yet our task is not restricted to an effort to divine what motives impelled these death penalties. Rather, we deal with a system of law and of justice that leaves to the uncontrolled discretion of judges or juries the determination whether defendants committing these crimes should die or be imprisoned. Under these laws no standards govern the selection of the penalty. People live or die, dependent on the whim of one man or of 12. . . .

The high service rendered by the "cruel and unusual" punishment clause of the Eighth Amendment is to require legislatures to write penal laws that are evenhanded, nonselective, and nonarbitrary, and to require judges to see to it that general laws are not applied sparsely, selectively, and spottily to unpopular groups. A law that stated that anyone making more than $50,000 would be exempt from the death penalty would plainly fall, as would a law that in terms said that blacks, those who never went beyond the fifth grade in school, those who made less than $3,000 a year, or those who were unpopular or unstable should be the only people executed. A law which in the overall view reaches that result in practice has no more sanctity than a law which in terms provides the same. . . .

Thus, these discretionary statutes are unconstitutional in their operation. They are pregnant with discrimination and discrimination is an ingredient not compatible with the idea of equal protection of the laws that is implicit in the ban on "cruel and unusual" punishments. . . .

BRENNAN, J., concurring.

[The] Cruel and Unusual Punishments Clause prohibits the infliction of uncivilized and inhuman punishments. The State, even as it punishes, must treat its members with respect for their intrinsic worth as human beings. A punishment is "cruel and unusual," therefore, if it does not comport with human dignity. . . .

The primary principle is that a punishment must not be so severe as to be degrading to the dignity of human beings. Pain, certainly, may be a factor in the judgment. . . . More than the presence of pain, however, is comprehended in the judgment that the extreme severity of a punishment makes it degrading to the dignity of human beings. The barbaric punishments condemned by history, "punishments which inflict torture, such as the rack, the thumbscrew, the iron boot, the stretching of limbs and the like," . . . have been condemned [because] they treat members of the human race as nonhumans, as objects to be toyed with and discarded. They are thus inconsistent with the fundamental premise of the Clause that even the vilest criminal remains a human being possessed of common human dignity.

[A] second principle inherent in the Clause [is] that the State must not arbitrarily inflict a severe punishment [because] the State does not respect human dignity when, without reason, it inflicts upon some people a severe punishment that it does not inflict upon others. Indeed, the very words "cruel and unusual punishments" imply condemnation of the arbitrary infliction of severe punishments. [W]hen a severe punishment is inflicted in the great majority of cases in which it is legally available, there is little likelihood that the State is inflicting it arbitrarily. If, however, the infliction of a severe punishment is something different from that which is generally done in such cases, there is a substantial likelihood that the State, contrary to the requirements of regularity and fairness embodied in the Clause, is inflicting the punishment arbitrarily. This principle is especially important today. There is scant danger, given the political processes in an enlightened democracy such as ours, that extremely severe punishments will be widely applied. The more significant function of the Clause, therefore, is to protect against the danger of their arbitrary infliction.

A third principle inherent in the Clause is that a severe punishment must not be unacceptable to contemporary society. Rejection by society, of course, is a strong indication that a severe punishment does not comport with human dignity. In applying this principle, however, we must make certain that the judicial determination is as objective as possible. Thus, for example, . . . one factor that may be considered is the existence of the punishment in jurisdictions other than those before the Court. [Another] factor to be considered is the historic usage of the punishment. . . . Accordingly, the judicial task is to review the history of a challenged punishment and to examine society's present practices with respect to its use. Legislative authorization, of course, does not establish acceptance. The acceptability of a severe punishment is measured, not by its availability, for it might become so offensive to society as never to be inflicted, but by its use.

The final principle inherent in the Clause is that a severe punishment must not be excessive. A punishment is excessive under this principle if it is unnecessary: The infliction of a severe punishment by the State cannot comport with human dignity when it is nothing more than the pointless infliction of suffering. If there is a significantly less severe punishment adequate to achieve the purposes for which the punishment is inflicted, the punishment inflicted is unnecessary and therefore excessive. . . .

The outstanding characteristic of our present practice of punishing criminals by death is the infrequency with which we resort to it. . . . There has been a steady decline in the infliction of this punishment in every decade since the 1930's, the earliest period for which accurate statistics are available. In the 1930's, executions averaged 167 per year; in the 1940's, the average was 128; in the 1950's, it was 72; and in the years 1960-1962, it was 48. There have been a total of 46 executions since then, 36 of them in 1963-1964. Yet our population and the number of capital crimes committed have increased greatly over the past four decades. The contemporary rarity of the infliction of this punishment is thus the end result of a long-continued decline. . . . When the punishment of death is inflicted in a trivial number of the cases in which it is legally available, the conclusion is virtually inescapable that it is being inflicted arbitrarily. Indeed, it smacks of little more than a lottery system.

[The] punishment of death is inconsistent with all four principles: Death is an unusually severe and degrading punishment; there is a strong probability that it is inflicted arbitrarily; its rejection by contemporary society is virtually total; and there is no reason to believe it serves any penal purpose more effectively than the less severe punishment of imprisonment. The function of these principles is to enable a court to determine whether a punishment comports with human dignity. Death, quite simply, does not. . . .

MARSHALL, J., concurring.

[A] penalty may be cruel and unusual because it is excessive and serves no valid legislative purpose. [There are several] purposes conceivably served by capital punishment: retribution, deterrence, prevention of repetitive criminal acts . . . and economy. . . .

The fact that the State may seek retribution against those who have broken its laws does not mean that retribution may then become the State's sole end in punishing. . . . If retribution alone could serve as a justification for any particular penalty, then all penalties selected by the legislature would by definition be acceptable means for designating society's moral approbation of a particular act. . . .

The most hotly contested issue regarding capital punishment is whether it is better than life imprisonment as a deterrent to crime. [Thorsten Sellin, one of the leading authorities on capital punishment, compiled statistics to] demonstrate that there is no correlation between the murder rate and the presence or absence of the capital sanction. He compares States that have similar characteristics and finds that irrespective of their position on capital punishment, they have similar murder rates. . . . Sellin also concludes that abolition and/or reintroduction of the death penalty had no effect on the homicide rates of the various States involved. This conclusion is borne out by others who have made similar inquiries and by the experience of other countries. . . .

Much of what must be said about the death penalty as a device to prevent recidivism is obvious — if a murderer is executed, he cannot possibly commit another offense. The fact is, however, that murderers are extremely unlikely to commit other crimes either in prison or upon their release. For the most part, they are first offenders, and when released from prison they are known to become model citizens. Furthermore, most persons who commit capital crimes are not executed. With respect to those who are sentenced to die, it is critical to note that the jury is never asked to determine whether they are likely to be recidivists. In light of these facts, if capital punishment were justified purely on the basis of preventing recidivism, it would have to be considered to be excessive; no general need to obliterate all capital offenders could have been demonstrated, nor any specific need in individual cases. . . .

As for the argument that it is cheaper to execute a capital offender than to imprison him for life, even assuming that such an argument, if true, would support a capital sanction, it is simply incorrect. A disproportionate amount of money spent on prisons is attributable to death row. Condemned men are not productive members of the prison community, although they could be, and executions are expensive. Appeals are often automatic, and courts admittedly spend more time with death cases. . . . When all is said and done, there can be no doubt that it costs more to execute a man than to keep him in prison for life.

[E]ven if capital punishment is not excessive, it nonetheless violates the Eighth Amendment because it is morally unacceptable to the people of the United States at this time in their history. In judging whether or not a given penalty is morally acceptable, most courts have said that the punishment is valid unless "it shocks the conscience and sense of justice of the people." [But] whether or not a punishment is cruel and unusual depends, not on whether its mere mention shocks the conscience and sense of justice of the people, but on whether people who were fully informed as to the purposes of the penalty and its liabilities would find the penalty shocking, unjust, and unacceptable. . . . In other words, the question with which we must deal is not whether a substantial proportion of American citizens would today, if polled, opine that capital punishment is barbarously cruel, but whether they would find it to be so in the light of all information presently available. . . .

It has often been noted that American citizens know almost nothing about capital punishment [and much that I have propounded in this opinion is] critical to an informed judgment on the morality of the death penalty: e.g., that the death penalty is no more effective a deterrent than life imprisonment, that convicted murderers are rarely executed, but are usually sentenced to a term in prison; that convicted murderers usually are model prisoners, and that they almost always become law-abiding citizens upon their release from prison; that the costs of executing a capital offender exceed the costs of imprisoning him for life; that while in prison, a convict under sentence of death performs none of the useful functions that life prisoners perform; that no attempt is made in the sentencing process to ferret out likely recidivists for execution; and that the death penalty may actually stimulate criminal activity.

This information would almost surely convince the average citizen that the death penalty was unwise, but [the] desire for retribution . . . might influence the citizenry's view of the morality of capital punishment. [Yet] no one has ever seriously advanced retribution as a legitimate goal of our society. Defenses of capital punishment are always mounted on deterrent or other similar theories. This should not be surprising. It is the people of this country who have urged in the past that prisons rehabilitate as well as isolate offenders, and it is the people who have injected a sense of purpose into our penology. I cannot believe that at this stage in our history, the American people would ever knowingly support purposeless vengeance. Thus, I believe that the great mass of citizens would conclude on the basis of the material already considered that the death penalty is immoral and therefore unconstitutional.

But, if this information needs supplementing, I believe that the following facts would serve to convince even the most hesitant of citizens to condemn death as a sanction: capital punishment is imposed discriminatorily against certain identifiable classes of people; there is evidence that innocent people have been executed before their innocence can be proved; and the death penalty wreaks havoc with our entire criminal justice system. . . .

Regarding discrimination, it . . . is usually the poor, the illiterate, the underprivileged, the member of the minority group — the man who, because he is without means, and is defended by a court-appointed attorney — who becomes society's sacrificial lamb. . . . Indeed, a look at the bare statistics regarding executions is enough to betray much of the discrimination. A total of 3,859 persons have been executed since 1930, of whom 1,751 were white and 2,066 were Negro. . . .

Assuming knowledge of all the facts presently available regarding capital punishment, the average citizen would, in my opinion, find it shocking to his conscience and sense of justice. For this reason alone capital punishment cannot stand.

BURGER, C.J., dissenting.

. . . Counsel for petitioners properly concede that capital punishment was not impermissibly cruel at the time of the adoption of the Eighth Amendment. Not only do the records of the debates indicate that the Founding Fathers were limited in their concern to the prevention of torture, but it is also clear from the language of the Constitution itself that there was no thought whatever of the elimination of capital punishment. . . .

In the 181 years since the enactment of the Eighth Amendment, not a single decision of this Court has cast the slightest shadow of a doubt on the constitutionality of capital punishment. . . . Today the Court has not ruled that capital punishment is per se violative of the Eighth Amendment; nor has it ruled that the punishment is barred for any particular class or classes of crimes. The substantially similar concurring opinions of Mr. Justice Stewart and Mr. Justice White, which are necessary to support the judgment setting aside petitioners' sentences, stop short of reaching the ultimate question. The actual scope of the Court's ruling, which I take to be embodied in these concurring opinions, is not entirely clear. This much, however, seems apparent: if the legislatures are to continue to authorize capital punishment for some crimes, juries and judges can no longer be permitted to make the sentencing determination in the same manner they have in the past. . . .

Real change could clearly be brought about if legislatures provided mandatory death sentences in such a way as to deny juries the opportunity to bring in a verdict on a lesser charge; under such a system, the death sentence could only be avoided by a verdict of acquittal. If this is the only alternative that the legislatures can safely pursue under today's ruling, I would have preferred that the Court opt for total abolition.

It seems remarkable to me that with our basic trust in lay jurors as the keystone in our system of criminal justice, it should now be suggested that we take the most sensitive and important of all decisions away from them. I could more easily be persuaded that mandatory sentences of death, without the intervening and ameliorating impact of lay jurors, are so arbitrary and doctrinaire that they violate the Constitution. The very infrequency of death penalties imposed by jurors attests their cautious and discriminating reservation of that penalty for the most extreme cases. I had thought that nothing was clearer in history, as we noted in *McGautha* one year ago, than the American abhorrence of "the common-law rule imposing a mandatory death sentence on all convicted murderers." 402 U.S. at 198. [The] nineteenth century movement away from mandatory death sentences marked an enlightened introduction of flexibility into the sentencing process. It recognized that individual culpability is not always measured by the category of the crime committed. I do not see how this history can be ignored and how it can be suggested that the Eighth Amendment demands the elimination of the most sensitive feature of the sentencing system. . . .

BLACKMUN, J., dissenting.
. . . Cases such as these provide for me an excruciating agony of the spirit. I yield to no one in the depth of my distaste, antipathy, and, indeed, abhorrence, for the death penalty, with all its aspects of physical distress and fear and of moral judgment exercised by finite minds. . . . Were I a legislator, I would do all I could to sponsor and to vote for legislation abolishing the death penalty. [However, as judges we] should not allow our personal preferences as to the wisdom of legislative and congressional action, or our distaste for such action, to guide our judicial decision in cases such as these. . . . Although personally I may rejoice at the Court's result, I find it difficult to accept or to justify as a matter of history, of law, or of constitutional pronouncement. I fear the Court has overstepped. It has sought and has achieved an end.

POWELL, J., dissenting.
[A] comment on the racial discrimination problem seems appropriate. The possibility of racial bias in the trial and sentencing process has diminished in recent years. The segregation of our society in decades past, which contributed

substantially to the severity of punishment for interracial crimes, is now no longer prevalent in this country. Likewise, the day is past when juries do not represent the minority group elements of the community. The assurance of fair trials for all citizens is greater today than at any previous time in our history. Because standards of criminal justice have "evolved" in a manner favorable to the accused, discriminatory imposition of capital punishment is far less likely today than in the past.

. . . It is important to keep in focus the enormity of the step undertaken by the Court today. Not only does it invalidate hundreds of state and federal laws, it deprives those jurisdictions of the power to legislate with respect to capital punishment in the future, except in a manner consistent with the cloudily outlined views of those Justices who do not purport to undertake total abolition. Nothing short of an amendment to the United States Constitution can reverse the Court's judgments. Meanwhile, all flexibility is foreclosed. The normal democratic process, as well as the opportunities for the several States to respond to the will of their people expressed through ballot referenda . . . is now shut off. . . .

REHNQUIST, J., dissenting.

The Court's judgments today strike down a penalty that our Nation's legislators have thought necessary since our country was founded. My Brothers Douglas, Brennan, and Marshall would at one fell swoop invalidate laws enacted by Congress and 40 of the 50 state legislatures, and would consign to the limbo of unconstitutionality under a single rubric penalties for offenses as varied and unique as murder, piracy, mutiny, highjacking, and desertion in the face of the enemy. My Brothers Stewart and White, asserting reliance on a more limited rationale — the reluctance of judges and juries actually to impose the death penalty in the majority of capital cases, join in the judgments in these cases. Whatever its precise rationale, today's holding necessarily brings into sharp relief the fundamental question of the role of judicial review in a democratic society. . . .

The task of judging constitutional cases [cannot] be avoided, but it must surely be approached with the deepest humility and genuine deference to legislative judgment. Today's decision to invalidate capital punishment is, I respectfully submit, significantly lacking in those attributes. . . . I conclude that this decision holding unconstitutional capital punishment is not an act of judgment, but rather an act of will.

NOTES

1. *Meaning of "cruel and unusual."*   Do you agree with the *Furman* majority's core holding that William Furman's punishment was cruel and unusual? Does your answer hinge, as it did for the Court, on the fact that Furman was sentenced through a system of standardless jury discretion that allowed, in the words of Justice Stewart, "this unique penalty to be so wantonly and so freakishly imposed"?

Considering these issues more generally, by what standards should a judge or other official assess whether a punishment inflicted is cruel and unusual? Or, drawing on Chief Justice Warren's famous discussion of the Eighth Amendment in Trop v. Dulles quoted earlier, how should judges or other officials assess "the evolving standards of decency that mark the progress of a maturing society"?

What impact, if any, should international developments — such as the abolition of capital punishment in Great Britain or the European Union — have on the interpretation of the Eighth Amendment's prohibition of cruel and unusual punishments? Notably, when the European Convention for the Protection of Human Rights and Fundamental Freedoms was adopted in the early 1950s, the death penalty was still widely in use. Therefore, its prohibition on "torture or . . . inhuman or degrading treatment or punishment" in Article 3 did not apply to capital punishment. Protocol 6, in force since 1988, however, explicitly abolishes the death penalty in peace time. Signature of this protocol has become a virtual prerequisite for membership in the European human rights regime. Consequently, when considered against the backdrop of the near universal abolition of the death penalty in other Western nations, the use of capital punishment in the United States is now unusual. When and how should international human rights norms influence interpretations of U.S. constitutional provisions that implicate human rights concerns?

2. *Discretion, disparity, and discrimination.*   What seemed to be the central concern of the Justices voting in the majority in *Furman*? Was it the fact that the juries exercised discretion without having any standards to guide life-and-death decisions? Was it the disparity in outcomes (that is, who was sentenced to die) that resulted from the exercise of standardless jury discretion? Was it the likelihood that the results of standardless jury discretion in capital cases seemed to reflect discriminatory judgments? Justice Douglas's opinion makes clear that the potentially discriminatory application of standardless jury discretion was his chief concern, suggesting that the constitutional provision transgressed was actually the Fourteenth Amendment's Equal Protection Clause rather than the Eighth Amendment: "The [discretionary statutes] are pregnant with discrimination and discrimination is an ingredient not compatible with the idea of equal protection of the laws."

3. *The Marshall hypothesis.*   In one of the more famous passages from the *Furman* opinions, Justice Marshall argues that the more fully informed people become about the operation of the death penalty, the less likely they are to support its use. (Indeed, Justice Marshall justified his vote in *Furman* by contending that the average citizen, with "knowledge of all the facts presently available regarding capital punishment, would . . . find it shocking to his conscience and sense of justice.") This argument has come to be known as "the Marshall hypothesis." Is it appropriate (and even sensible) for legislators or executive branch officials to defer especially to the judgment of those with the most knowledge or expertise in an area? Is there anything in the role of a judge that should prevent reliance on such arguments? As you work through the remainder of the materials in this chapter and throughout this book, watch for other examples of this argument at work and try to gauge whether your own (or others') opinions about the death penalty change as you become more informed about its application.

4. *State responses to* Furman.   The Supreme Court's holding in *Furman* effectively declared unconstitutional the death penalty statutes then in place in 40 states and commuted the sentences of 629 death row inmates around the country.

Because only Justices Brennan and Marshall asserted the death penalty was per se unconstitutional, the opinions of Justices Stewart, White, and Douglas suggested that states could rewrite their death penalty statutes to remedy the constitutional problems. Led by Florida, which enacted a new death penalty statute five months after *Furman*, 35 states reacted to the decision by passing new death penalty statutes: Ten states addressed the unconstitutionality of standard-less jury discretion by making the death penalty mandatory for all offenders convicted of certain capital crimes; 25 other states sought to limit discretion by setting forth aggravating and mitigating factors for judge and jury to consider.

5. *The tide turns in 1976.*   The nationwide ban on capital punishment that the Court created in 1972 with its opinion in *Furman* did not last long. In 1976, the Court decided a set of five cases testing the constitutionality of various state death penalty statutes passed in reaction to *Furman*. In the lead case, Gregg v. Georgia, 428 U.S. 153 (1976), Justice Stewart authored the opinion of the court, which held that "the punishment of death does not invariably violate the Constitution." First the Court took note of the widespread debate about capital punishment in state legislatures:

> Despite the continuing debate, dating back to the nineteenth century, over the morality and utility of capital punishment, it is now evident that a large proportion of American society continues to regard it as an appropriate and necessary criminal sanction.
>
> The most marked indication of society's endorsement of the death penalty for murder is the legislative response to *Furman*. The legislatures of at least 35 States have enacted new statutes that provide for the death penalty for at least some crimes that result in the death of another person. And the Congress of the United States, in 1974, enacted a statute providing the death penalty for aircraft piracy that results in death. [The] post-*Furman* statutes make clear that capital punishment itself has not been rejected by the elected representatives of the people.
>
> [The] actions of juries in many States since *Furman* are fully compatible with the legislative judgments, reflected in the new statutes, as to the continued utility and necessity of capital punishment in appropriate cases. At the close of 1974 at least 254 persons had been sentenced to death since *Furman*, and by the end of March 1976, more than 460 persons were subject to death sentences.

428 U.S. at 179-182.

The Court also accepted both deterrence and retribution as appropriate social purposes justifying the use of the death penalty:

> In part, capital punishment is an expression of society's moral outrage at particularly offensive conduct. This function may be unappealing to many, but it is essential in an ordered society that asks its citizens to rely on legal processes rather than self-help to vindicate their wrongs. . . . Retribution is no longer the dominant objective of the criminal law, but neither is it a forbidden objective nor one inconsistent with our respect for the dignity of men. . . . Indeed, the decision that capital punishment may be the appropriate sanction in extreme cases is an expression of the community's belief that certain crimes are themselves so grievous an affront to humanity that the only adequate response may be the penalty of death.
>
> Statistical attempts to evaluate the worth of the death penalty as a deterrent to crimes by potential offenders have occasioned a great deal of debate. The results simply have been inconclusive. Although some of the studies

suggest that the death penalty may not function as a significantly greater deterrent than lesser penalties, there is no convincing empirical evidence either supporting or refuting this view. We may nevertheless assume safely that there are murderers, such as those who act in passion, for whom the threat of death has little or no deterrent effect. But for many others, the death penalty undoubtedly is a significant deterrent. There are carefully contemplated murders, such as murder for hire, where the possible penalty of death may well enter into the cold calculus that precedes the decision to act. . . . The value of capital punishment as a deterrent of crime is a complex factual issue the resolution of which properly rests with the legislatures, which can evaluate the results of statistical studies in terms of their own local conditions and with a flexibility of approach that is not available to the courts.

Id. at 183-186.

Finally, the Court considered the procedural devices that the Georgia statute used to guide the discretion of the sentencing jury:

Jury sentencing has been considered desirable in capital cases in order "to maintain a link between contemporary community values and the penal system. . . ." But it creates special problems. Much of the information that is relevant to the sentencing decision may have no relevance to the question of guilt, or may even be extremely prejudicial to a fair determination of that question. This problem, however, is scarcely insurmountable. Those who have studied the question suggest that a bifurcated procedure, one in which the question of sentence is not considered until the determination of guilt has been made, is the best answer. [And though] members of a jury will have had little, if any, previous experience in sentencing, [this] problem will be alleviated if the jury is given guidance regarding the factors about the crime and the defendant that the State, representing organized society, deems particularly relevant to the sentencing decision. . . .

While some have suggested that standards to guide a capital jury's sentencing deliberations are impossible to formulate, the fact is that such standards have been developed. When the drafters of the Model Penal Code faced this problem, they concluded "that it is within the realm of possibility to point to the main circumstances of aggravation and of mitigation that should be weighed and *weighed against each other* when they are presented in a concrete case." While such standards are by necessity somewhat general, they do provide guidance to sentencing authority and thereby reduce the likelihood that it will impose a sentence that fairly can be called capricious or arbitrary. Where the sentencing authority is required to specify the factors it relied upon in reaching its decision, the further safeguard of meaningful appellate review is available to ensure that death sentences are not imposed capriciously or in a freakish manner.

[To] guard further against a situation comparable to that presented in *Furman,* the Supreme Court of Georgia compares each death sentence with the sentences imposed on similarly situated defendants to ensure that the sentence of death in a particular case is not disproportionate. On their face these procedures seem to satisfy the concerns of *Furman.* No longer should there be "no meaningful basis for distinguishing the few cases in which [the death penalty] is imposed from the many cases in which it is not."

The basic concern of *Furman* centered on those defendants who were being condemned to death capriciously and arbitrarily. Under the procedures before the Court in that case, sentencing authorities were not directed to give attention to the nature or circumstances of the crime committed or to the character or record of the defendant. Left unguided, juries imposed the death sentence in a way that could only be called freakish. The new Georgia sentencing procedures, by contrast, focus the jury's attention on the particularized nature of the crime and the particularized characteristics of the individual defendant. While the jury is permitted to consider any aggravating or mitigating circumstances, it must find and identify at least one statutory aggravating factor before it may impose a penalty of death. In this way the jury's discretion is channeled. No longer can a jury wantonly and freakishly impose the death sentence; it is always circumscribed by the legislative guidelines. In addition, the review function of the Supreme Court of Georgia affords additional assurance that the concerns that prompted our decision in *Furman* are not present to any significant degree in the Georgia procedure applied here. [The] statutory system under which Gregg was sentenced to death does not violate the Constitution.

Id. at 190-198, 206-207.

6. *Key features of approved death penalty schemes.* Two of the other cases decided the same day as *Gregg* also upheld newly revised statutory schemes to impose the death penalty for some murders. See Jurek v. Texas, 428 U.S. 262 (1976); Proffitt v. Florida, 428 U.S. 242 (1976). The statutes involved in these three cases shared some important features. Each called for bifurcated proceedings, with a jury hearing the evidence relevant to the choice of punishment only after deliberating and delivering a guilty verdict after trial. The statutes also specified aggravating factors for the jury to find as a prerequisite to the death penalty and provided for automatic review of the case in the state's appellate courts. While the Court stopped short of saying that any of these features was absolutely essential to the judgment that they satisfied the Eighth Amendment, each feature drew positive comment in the opinions. Ultimately, the Court's language in *Gregg* about the importance of "a carefully drafted statute that ensures that the sentencing authority is given adequate information and guidance," combined with the Court's rejection of a mandatory death sentencing scheme (detailed below), made it clear that a state's development of a system of "guided discretion" was central to the constitutionality of its use of the death penalty.

7. *Strategic litigation.* Numerous commentators expected *Furman* to end the death penalty in the United States. Instead, the opposite occurred: The Court's decision reinvigorated capital punishment. To what extent is this a cautionary tale about using the Court to bring about social change? Compare Brown v. Board of Education, 349 U.S. 294 (1954) (striking down the existence of segregated elementary schools); Roe v. Wade, 410 U.S. 113 (1973) (striking down Texas's absolute prohibition of abortions unless the mother's life was at stake).

‖ *James Tyrone Woodson v. North Carolina* ‖
428 U.S. 280 (1976)

STEWART, J.

The question in this case is whether the imposition of a death sentence for the crime of first-degree murder under the law of North Carolina violates the Eighth and Fourteenth Amendments.

The petitioners, James Tyrone Woodson and Luby Waxton, were convicted of first-degree murder as the result of their participation in an armed robbery of a convenience food store, in the course of which the cashier was killed and a customer was seriously wounded. There were four participants in the robbery: the petitioners Woodson and Waxton and two others, Leonard Tucker and

Johnnie Lee Carroll. At the petitioners' trial Tucker and Carroll testified for the prosecution after having been permitted to plead guilty to lesser offenses. . . . The petitioners were found guilty on all charges, and, as was required by statute, sentenced to death.

The North Carolina General Assembly in 1974 [after the invalidation of its death penalty statute in the wake of *Furman*] enacted a new statute that was essentially unchanged from the old one except that it made the death penalty mandatory. . . . It was under this statute that the petitioners were tried, convicted, and sentenced to death.

North Carolina, unlike Florida, Georgia, and Texas, has thus responded to the *Furman* decision by making death the mandatory sentence for all persons convicted of first-degree murder. . . . Although it seems beyond dispute that, at the time of the *Furman* decision in 1972, mandatory death penalty statutes had been renounced by American juries and legislatures, there remains the question whether the mandatory statutes adopted by North Carolina and a number of other States following *Furman* evince a sudden reversal of societal values regarding the imposition of capital punishment. In view of the persistent and unswerving legislative rejection of mandatory death penalty statutes beginning in 1838 and continuing for more than 130 years until *Furman,* it seems evident that the post-*Furman* enactments reflect attempts by the States to retain the death penalty in a form consistent with the Constitution, rather than a renewed societal acceptance of mandatory death sentencing. The fact that some States have adopted mandatory measures following *Furman* while others have legislated standards to guide jury discretion appears attributable to diverse readings of this Court's multi-opinioned decision in that case. . . .

It is now well established that the Eighth Amendment draws much of its meaning from "the evolving standards of decency that mark the progress of a maturing society." [One] of the most significant developments in our society's treatment of capital punishment has been the rejection of the common-law practice of inexorably imposing a death sentence upon every person convicted of a specified offense. North Carolina's mandatory death penalty statute for first-degree murder departs markedly from contemporary standards respecting the imposition of the punishment of death and thus cannot be applied consistently with the Eighth and Fourteenth Amendments' requirement that the State's power to punish "be exercised within the limits of civilized standards."

A separate deficiency of North Carolina's mandatory death sentence statute is its failure to provide a constitutionally tolerable response to *Furman*'s rejection of unbridled jury discretion in the imposition of capital sentences. Central to the limited holding in *Furman* was the conviction that the vesting of standardless sentencing power in the jury violated the Eighth and Fourteenth Amendments.

It is argued that North Carolina has remedied the inadequacies of the death penalty statutes held unconstitutional in *Furman* by withdrawing all sentencing discretion from juries in capital cases. But when one considers the long and consistent American experience with the death penalty in first-degree murder cases, it becomes evident that mandatory statutes enacted in response to *Furman* have simply papered over the problem of unguided and unchecked jury discretion. . . .

Instead of rationalizing the sentencing process, a mandatory scheme may well exacerbate the problem identified in *Furman* by resting the penalty determination on the particular jury's willingness to act lawlessly. While a mandatory death penalty statute may reasonably be expected to increase the number of persons sentenced to death, it does not fulfill *Furman*'s basic requirement by replacing arbitrary and wanton jury discretion with objective standards to guide, regularize, and make rationally reviewable the process for imposing a sentence of death.

A third constitutional shortcoming of the North Carolina statute is its failure to allow the particularized consideration of relevant aspects of the character and record of each convicted defendant before the imposition upon him of a sentence of death. In *Furman,* members of the Court acknowledged what cannot fairly be denied — that death is a punishment different from all other sanctions in kind rather than degree. A process that accords no significance to relevant facets of the character and record of the individual offender or the circumstances of the particular offense excludes from consideration in fixing the ultimate punishment of death the possibility of compassionate or mitigating factors stemming from the diverse frailties of humankind. It treats all persons convicted of a designated offense not as uniquely individual human beings, but as members of a faceless, undifferentiated mass to be subjected to the blind infliction of the penalty of death. . . .

Consideration of both the offender and the offense in order to arrive at a just and appropriate sentence has been viewed as a progressive and humanizing development. While the prevailing practice of individualizing sentencing determinations generally reflects simply enlightened policy rather than a constitutional imperative, we believe that in capital cases the fundamental respect for humanity underlying the Eighth Amendment requires consideration of the character and record of the individual offender and the circumstances of the particular offense as a constitutionally indispensable part of the process of inflicting the penalty of death.

This conclusion rests squarely on the predicate that the penalty of death is qualitatively different from a sentence of imprisonment, however long. Death, in its finality, differs more from life imprisonment than a 100-year prison term differs from one of only a year or two. Because of that qualitative difference, there is a corresponding difference in the need for reliability in the determination that death is the appropriate punishment in a specific case.

For the reasons stated, we conclude that the death sentences imposed upon the petitioners under North Carolina's mandatory death sentence statute violated the Eighth and Fourteenth Amendments and therefore must be set aside. . . .

REHNQUIST, J., dissenting.

[The plurality's holding] will result in the invalidation of a death sentence imposed upon a defendant convicted of first-degree murder under the North Carolina system, and the upholding of the same sentence imposed on an identical defendant convicted on identical evidence of first-degree murder under the Florida, Georgia, or Texas systems, a result surely as "freakish" as that condemned in the separate opinions in *Furman*. . . .

In any event, while the imposition of such unlimited consideration of mitigating factors may conform to the plurality's novel constitutional doctrine that a "jury must be allowed to consider on the basis of all relevant evidence not only why a death sentence should be imposed, but also why it should not be imposed," the resulting system seems as likely as any to produce the unbridled discretion which was condemned by the separate opinions in *Furman*. The plurality seems to believe that provision for appellate review will afford a check upon the instances of juror arbitrariness in a discretionary system. But it is not at all apparent that appellate review of death sentences, through a process of comparing the facts of one case in which a death sentence was imposed with the facts of another in which such a sentence was not imposed, will afford any meaningful protection against whatever arbitrariness results from jury discretion. . . .

The plurality's insistence on "standards" to "guide the jury in its inevitable exercise of the power to determine which . . . murderers shall live and which shall die" is squarely contrary to the Court's opinion in *McGautha*. . . . So is the plurality's latter-day recognition . . . that *Furman* requires "objective standards to guide, regularize, and make rationally reviewable the process for imposing a sentence of death." . . . The plurality's insistence on individualized consideration of the sentencing . . . does not depend upon any traditional application of the prohibition against cruel and unusual punishment contained in the Eighth Amendment. . . . What the plurality opinion has actually done is to import into the Due Process Clause of the Fourteenth Amendment what it conceives to be desirable procedural guarantees where the punishment of death, concededly not cruel and unusual for the crime of which the defendant was convicted, is to be imposed. . . .

NOTES

1. *Mandatory death penalty.* In Louisiana v. Roberts, 428 U.S. 325 (1976), a companion case decided the same day as *Woodson* and *Gregg,* the Court struck down another capital sentencing statute that made the death penalty mandatory for five narrowly defined categories of first-degree murder (and also required juries to be instructed on manslaughter and second-degree murder even if there was no evidence to support such a verdict). Together, *Woodson* and *Roberts* established that the Supreme Court would not let states respond to *Furman*'s concerns about standardless jury discretion by creating mandatory death penalty systems that simply eliminated jury discretion. In subsequent cases, the Supreme Court ultimately ruled that no form of mandatory death penalty could be constitutional. See Sumner v. Shuman, 483 U.S. 66 (1987) (invalidating a mandatory death penalty statute for life-term inmates convicted of murder).

Isn't a mandatory sentencing system the best way to deal with *Furman*'s concerns about arbitrary and potentially discriminatory exercise of juries' capital sentencing discretion? Is the requirement of individualization propounded in *Woodson* and *Roberts* really a constitutional necessity, or just a good idea? Compare the decision of the English Privy Council upholding Singapore's mandatory death penalty statute for certain drug offenses, in which it distinguished legal guilt and moral guilt. The Privy Council did not find Singapore in violation of its equality and due process provisions because "the Constitution is not concerned with equal punitive treatment for equal moral blameworthiness; it is concerned with equal punitive treatment for similar legal guilt." Ong Ah Chuan v. Public Prosecutor, [1981] A.C. 648, 674 (P.C.).

2. *Categorical exclusion of certain offenses.* In Coker v. Georgia, 433 U.S. 584 (1977), the Supreme Court struck down the death penalty as a sentencing

option in the rape of an adult woman; as in *Furman,* the constitutional basis for the decision was the Eighth Amendment's prohibition of cruel and unusual punishments. Since then only murder convictions have led to death sentences. In addition, through a series of cases culminating in Tison v. Arizona, 481 U.S. 137 (1987), the Supreme Court held that only killers with a mens rea of reckless indifference to human life or worse are sufficiently culpable to be constitutionally subject to the death penalty.

If no crime can trigger a mandatory death sentence, on what basis should a court hold that certain crimes categorically can never be eligible for the death penalty? By what yardstick can and should the Supreme Court determine whether a particularly heinous crime, such as the rape of a young child or attempted murder of a police officer, can justify the death penalty? Some states believe there are offenses other than murder for which death might be the appropriate sanction; Louisiana, for example, has made death an eligible punishment for the rape of a minor child. See La. Rev. Stat. §14:42(D)(2)(a). (This statute has been upheld by the Louisiana Supreme Court in State v. Wilson, 685 So. 2d 1063 (La. 1996), but not yet considered by the U.S. Supreme Court.) Should such proportionality determinations be the province of the legislature? Do you see any link between the concerns expressed in *Furman* about the arbitrary imposition of the death penalty and the categorical exclusion of certain offenses from capital punishment?

The federal system allows for the death penalty in cases of treason and terrorism, as do some of the states. During wartime the death penalty may be imposed in cases of desertion. Many European states that have otherwise abolished capital punishment have retained the death penalty during times of war. More than ten countries, however, have signed on to Protocol 11 of the European Convention of Human Rights (effective in 1998), which outlaws capital punishment even during wartime. Why should more offenses be punishable by death during wartime?

3. *Categorical exclusion of certain offenders.*   In 2002 the Supreme Court outlawed execution of the mentally retarded because it violates the Eight Amendment's prohibition of cruel and unusual punishments. The decision in Atkins v. Virginia, 536 U.S. 304 (2002), reversed the Court's prior decision Penry v. Lynaugh, 492 U.S. 302 (1989), which had held that the Constitution did allow the execution of mentally retarded individuals. The Court's reversal in *Atkins* reflected the shift in legislative thinking since the *Penry* decision in 1989: during those years, nearly half the states that authorize capital punishment had removed offenders with mental retardation from the reach of the death penalty. Researchers estimate that since the death penalty was reinstated in 1976, at least 35 people with mental retardation were executed in the United States before the Supreme Court declared this punishment unconstitutional in *Atkins.*

Through another pair of cases in the late 1980s, the Supreme Court held that the Constitution does not permit the execution of an offender who was 15 or younger at the time of his or her crime but that it does allow the execution of an offender who was 16 or older at the time of the crime. See Stanford v. Kentucky, 492 U.S. 362 (1989) (allowing execution of 16- and 17-year-old killers); Thompson v. Oklahoma, 487 U.S. 815 (1988) (prohibiting execution of killers age 15 or younger). Between 1976 and the beginning of 2003, 22 men were executed for crimes committed as juveniles; currently, there are 80 inmates on death row (all male) who were sentenced as juveniles, constituting about 2 percent of the total death row population. The United States is one of the few countries is the world that still executes juvenile offenders. Since 1990, juvenile offenders are known to have been executed in only six other countries: Democratic Republic of Congo, Iran, Pakistan, Yemen, Nigeria, and Saudi Arabia. Article 6(5) of the International Covenant on Civil and Political Rights — which the United States ratified with a reservation to Article 6(5) — requires that a sentence of death "not be imposed for crimes committed by persons below eighteen years of age."

Do you see any link between the concerns expressed in *Furman* about the arbitrary imposition of the death penalty and the categorical exclusion of certain offenders from capital punishment? Is there any risk that the definition of "mental retardation" could lead to further inequities in the application of capital punishment? The Supreme Court in *Atkins* left it to states to define which individuals are mentally retarded and thus exempt from capital punishment. As a legislator, how might you draft a definition of mental retardation to minimize disparate application of the death penalty?

|| *Sandra Lockett v. Ohio* ||
438 U.S. 586 (1978)

BURGER, C.J.

We granted certiorari in this case to consider, among other questions, whether Ohio violated the Eighth and Fourteenth Amendments by sentencing Sandra Lockett to death pursuant to a statute that narrowly limits the sentencer's discretion to consider the circumstances of the crime and the record and character of the offender as mitigating factors. . . .

Lockett [suggested to acquaintances Al Parker and Nathan Earl Dew] that they could get some money by robbing a grocery store and a furniture store in the area[, and she] also volunteered to get a gun from her father's basement to aid in carrying out the robberies. . . . Lockett's brother [later] suggested a plan for robbing a pawnshop. . . . No one planned to kill the pawnshop operator in the course of the robbery. Because she knew the owner, Lockett was not . . . among those entering the pawnshop, though she did guide the others to the shop that night. The robbery proceeded according to plan until the pawnbroker grabbed the gun when Parker announced the "stickup." The gun went off . . . firing a fatal shot into the pawnbroker, and Parker went back to the car where Lockett waited with the engine running. . . .

Parker was subsequently apprehended and charged with aggravated murder with specifications, an offense punishable by death, and aggravated robbery. Prior to trial, he pleaded guilty to the murder charge and agreed to testify against Lockett, her brother, and Dew. In return, the prosecutor dropped the aggravated robbery charge and the specifications to the murder charge, thereby eliminating the possibility that Parker could receive the death penalty. . . . Two weeks before Lockett's separate trial, the prosecutor offered to permit her to plead guilty to voluntary manslaughter and aggravated robbery (offenses which each carried a maximum penalty of 25 years' imprisonment and a maximum fine of $10,000) if she would cooperate with the State, but she rejected the offer. . . .

Once a verdict of aggravated murder with specifications had been returned, the Ohio death penalty statute required the trial judge to impose a death sentence unless, after "considering the nature and circumstances of the offense" and Lockett's "history, character, and condition," he found by a preponderance of the evidence that (1) the victim had induced or facilitated the offense, (2) it was unlikely that Lockett would have committed the offense but for the fact that she "was under duress, coercion, or strong provocation," or (3) the offense was "primarily the product of [Lockett's] psychosis or mental deficiency." . . . After considering the reports and hearing argument on the penalty issue, the trial judge concluded that the offense had not been primarily the product of psychosis or mental deficiency. Without specifically addressing the other two statutory mitigating factors, the judge said that he had "no alternative, whether [he liked] the law or not" but to impose the death penalty. He then sentenced Lockett to death. . . .

Lockett challenges the constitutionality of Ohio's death penalty statute [based on the fact that it] did not permit the sentencing judge to consider, as mitigating factors, her character, prior record, age, lack of specific intent to cause death, and her relatively minor part in the crime. . . .

Prior to Furman v. Georgia, 408 U.S. 238 (1972), every State that authorized capital punishment had abandoned mandatory death penalties, and instead permitted the jury unguided and unrestrained discretion regarding the imposition of the death penalty in a particular capital case. . . . The constitutional status of discretionary sentencing in capital cases changed abruptly, however, as a result of the separate opinions supporting the judgment in *Furman*. . . . In the last decade, many of the States have been obliged to revise their death penalty statutes in response to the various opinions supporting the judgments in *Furman* and *Gregg* and its companion cases. The signals from this Court have not, however, always been easy to decipher. The States now deserve the clearest guidance that the Court can provide; we have an obligation to reconcile previously differing views in order to provide that guidance. With that obligation in mind we turn to Lockett's attack on the Ohio statute. Essentially she contends that the Eighth and Fourteenth Amendments require that the sentencer be given a full opportunity to consider mitigating circumstances in capital cases and that the Ohio statute does not comply with that requirement. She relies, in large part, on the plurality opinions in *Woodson*. . . .

Although legislatures remain free to decide how much discretion in sentencing should be reposed in the judge or jury in noncapital cases, the plurality opinion in *Woodson*, after reviewing the historical repudiation of mandatory sentencing in capital cases, concluded that "in capital cases the fundamental respect for humanity underlying the Eighth Amendment . . . requires consideration of the character and record of the individual offender and the circumstances of the particular offense as a constitutionally indispensable part of the process of inflicting the penalty of death." That declaration rested "on the predicate that the penalty of death is qualitatively different" from any other sentence. We are satisfied that this qualitative difference between death and other penalties calls for a greater degree of reliability when the death sentence is imposed. The mandatory death penalty statute in *Woodson* was held invalid because it permitted *no* consideration of "relevant facets of the character and record of the individual offender or the circumstances of the particular offense." The plurality did not attempt to indicate, however, which facets of an offender or his offense it deemed "relevant" in capital sentencing or what degree of consideration of "relevant facets" it would require.

We are now faced with those questions and we conclude that the Eighth and Fourteenth Amendments require that the sentencer, in all but the rarest kind of capital case, not be precluded from considering, *as a mitigating factor,* any aspect of a defendant's character or record and any of the circumstances of the offense that the defendant proffers as a basis for a sentence less than death. We recognize that, in noncapital cases, the established practice of individualized sentences rests not on constitutional commands, but on public policy enacted into statutes. The considerations that account for the wide acceptance of individualization of sentences in noncapital cases surely cannot be thought less important in capital cases. Given that the imposition of death by public authority is so profoundly different from all other penalties, we cannot avoid the conclusion that an individualized decision is essential in capital cases. The need for treating each defendant in a capital case with that degree of respect due the uniqueness of the individual is far more important than in noncapital cases. A variety of flexible techniques — probation, parole, work furloughs, to name a few — and various postconviction remedies may be available to modify an initial sentence of confinement in noncapital cases. The nonavailability of corrective or modifying mechanisms with respect to an executed capital sentence underscores the need for individualized consideration as a constitutional requirement in imposing the death sentence.

There is no perfect procedure for deciding in which cases governmental authority should be used to impose death. But a statute that prevents the sentencer in all capital cases from giving independent mitigating weight to aspects of the defendant's character and record and to circumstances of the offense proffered in mitigation creates the risk that the death penalty will be imposed in spite of factors which may call for a less severe penalty. When the choice is between life and death, that risk is unacceptable and incompatible with the commands of the Eighth and Fourteenth Amendments. . . .

NOTES

1. *Access to mitigating evidence.*   In a series of cases, the Court elaborated on the basic holding of *Lockett,* that a capital jury must have access to a wide range of information about the crime and the offender's character and background. Just as the statutory language at issue in *Lockett* unduly limited access, jury instructions or evidentiary rulings could create the same problem. See Eddings v. Oklahoma, 455 U.S. 104 (1982) (court's instructions wrongly told jury to ignore nonstatutory mitigating evidence); Skipper v. South Carolina, 476 U.S. 1 (1986) (defendant can put in evidence of good behavior in prison to demonstrate nondangerousness). Defense counsel must also have access to the aggravating evidence that the prosecutor plans to present, to prepare for cross-examination or other testing of its accuracy. See Gardner v. Florida, 430 U.S. 349 (1977) (defense counsel must have access to all information in the presentence investigation report provided to the sentencer, based on right to confrontation).

2. *Instructions to underscore mitigating evidence.*   Some Supreme Court rulings have required the trial judge not only to give the jury access to mitigating evidence but also to instruct the jury to take special care in considering certain kinds of mitigating evidence, such as the youth of the offender. See Penry v. Lynaugh, 492 U.S. 302 (1989) (stressing the necessity of instructions that inform the jury how to "consider and give effect" to mitigating evidence so that the jury is "provided with a vehicle for expressing its reasoned moral response to that evidence"). Another series of cases provides that trial judges in capital cases have a special obligation to instruct the jury on lesser included offenses. See Beck v. Alabama, 447 U.S. 625 (1980) (court must instruct on lesser included offense whenever a jury issue as to that offense is present); Schad v. Arizona, 501 U.S. 624 (1991) (enough to instruct on second-degree murder but not theft; jury not faced with all-or-nothing choice).

3. *Access to aggravating evidence.*   After having established that defendants have a broad right to present all sorts of mitigating evidence to the capital sentencing decision maker, the Supreme Court faced cases in which prosecutors argued that they should have similarly broad rights to present all sorts of aggravating evidence. These dynamics had perhaps their greatest impact in Payne v. Tennessee, 501 U.S. 808 (1991), in which the Supreme Court overruled two prior holdings that had limited victim impact evidence in capital cases. After *Payne,* capital sentencing juries are allowed to receive victim impact evidence relating to the personal characteristics of the murder victim and the emotional impact of the death on the victim's family, and prosecutors are allowed to make statements about the personal qualities of the victim.

4. *Impact of individualization on women.*   Capital prosecutions involving women are extremely rare, and the execution of women rarer still. Though women account for about one in ten murder arrests, they account for only one in 52 death sentences imposed at the trial level; of more than 850 persons executed since *Furman,* only ten have been women. See Victor L. Streib, Gendering the Death Penalty: Countering Sex Bias in a Masculine Sanctuary, 63 Ohio St. L.J. 433 (2002). Usually capital cases involve women who killed their children or who are serial killers. The execution in Texas in 1999 of Karla Faye Tucker — who was involved in a brutal double-murder when under the influence of a drug addiction, but then became a model prisoner during more than a decade on death row — led to widespread national and international protests. Though the United States usually does not join international agreements that restrict the use of the death penalty, the United States has signed on to the global ban on executing pregnant women.

What factors may account for the apparent gender disparity in executions? Do female offenders appear less threatening? Does the execution of a woman seem particularly repulsive? Or does the execution of women perhaps pose different issues than the execution of men, differences that might come to light when we consider the battered spouse syndrome or the existence of young children?

5. *Inevitability of failure?*   Many observers have noted a tension in the Supreme Court's capital punishment cases under the Eighth Amendment. On one hand, cases like *Furman* and *Gregg* emphasize the importance of guiding or

structuring the sentencing jury's discretion through the use of statutory aggravating factors, bifurcated proceedings, appellate review, and other legal controls. On the other hand, cases such as *Woodson* and *Lockett* insist that the decision to impose the death penalty must be individualized, and legal rules must
not unduly restrict the information the jury receives about the case or the ability of individual jurors to act on that information. Does the current Eighth
Amendment jurisprudence reconcile these competing ambitions? If such a goal
is beyond reach, how should judges and other decision makers in the legal system respond? Justices Blackmun and Scalia debated this question in Callins v.
Collins, 510 U.S. 1141 (1994). Although the Court denied the petition for writ
of certiorari in the case, Justice Blackmun dissented and explained the dilemma
he faced in death cases:

> [The] problems that were pursued down one hole with procedural rules and
> verbal formulas have come to the surface somewhere else, just as virulent and
> pernicious as they were in their original form. Experience has taught us that the
> constitutional goal of eliminating arbitrariness and discrimination from the ad-
> ministration of death can never be achieved without compromising an equally
> essential component of fundamental fairness — individualized sentencing.

Blackmun returned to themes explored in the "partly prophetic" opinion
of Justice Harlan in *McGautha,* agreeing that to "identify before the fact those
characteristics of criminal homicides and their perpetrators which call for the
death penalty" appears to be a task "beyond human ability." Blackmun noted the
varying efforts states made to address *Furman*'s constitutional barrier by guiding
jury discretion but found that none could balance "fairness to the individual . . .
without sacrificing the consistency and rationality promised in *Furman*." Although *Furman, Gregg,* and *Lockett* attempted to strike a balance between consistent sentencing and individualized sentencing in the capital context, Blackmun
declared that effort a failure:

> In the first stage of capital sentencing, the demands of *Furman* are met by "nar-
> rowing" the class of death-eligible offenders according to objective, fact-bound
> characteristics of the defendant or the circumstances of the offense. Once the
> pool of death-eligible defendants has been reduced, the sentencer retains the
> discretion to consider whatever relevant mitigating evidence the defendant
> chooses to offer.
>   Over time, I have come to conclude that even this approach is unaccept-
> able: It simply reduces, rather than eliminates, the number of people subject to
> arbitrary sentencing. It is the decision to sentence a defendant to death — not
> merely the decision to make a defendant eligible for death — that may not be
> arbitrary. While one might hope that providing the sentencer with as much rel-
> evant mitigating evidence as possible will lead to more rational and consistent
> sentences, experience has taught otherwise. It seems that the decision whether
> a human being should live or die is so inherently subjective — rife with all of
> life's understandings, experiences, prejudices, and passions — that it inevitably
> defies the rationality and consistency required by the Constitution.

Summarizing his views, Blackmun explained that "[e]xperience has shown
that the consistency and rationality promised in *Furman* are inversely related to
the fairness owed the individual when considering a sentence of death. A step
toward consistency is a step away from fairness." And this failure to reconcile the

requirements of consistency and individualized fairness, in Blackmun's view, caused the Court to "retreat" from its earlier ambitious efforts to regulate discretion, "allowing relevant mitigating evidence to be discarded, vague aggravating circumstances to be employed, and providing no indication that the problem of race in the administration of death will ever be addressed." Blackmun declared himself unwilling any longer to play a part in this enterprise:

> From this day forward, I no longer shall tinker with the machinery of death. For more than 20 years I have endeavored — indeed, I have struggled — along with a majority of this Court, to develop procedural and substantive rules that would lend more than the mere appearance of fairness to the death penalty endeavor. Rather than continue to coddle the Court's delusion that the desired level of fairness has been achieved and the need for regulation eviscerated, I feel morally and intellectually obligated simply to concede that the death penalty experiment has failed. . . .

Justice Scalia agreed with Justice Blackmun that the competing aspirations of the Court's Eighth Amendment jurisprudence could not be reconciled, but he argued for a different response to this dilemma. Because the text of the Constitution, in the Fifth and Eighth Amendments, indicates that the use of the death penalty is a legitimate criminal punishment, he argued that the Court had no business blocking the government from using this sanction. Instead of declaring that the death penalty cannot be administered in accord with the Constitution, Scalia urged the Court to reach a different conclusion:

> Though Justice Blackmun joins those of us who have acknowledged the incompatibility of the Court's *Furman* and *Lockett* lines of jurisprudence, he unfortunately draws the wrong conclusion for the acknowledgment. [At] least one of these judicially announced irreconcilable commands which cause the Constitution to prohibit what its text explicitly permits must be wrong. Convictions in opposition to the death penalty are often passionate and deeply held. That would be no excuse for reading them into a Constitution that does not contain them, even if they represented the convictions of a majority of Americans. . . . If the people conclude that . . . brutal deaths may be deterred by capital punishment — indeed, if they merely conclude that justice requires such brutal deaths to be avenged by capital punishment — the creation of false, untexual, and unhistorical contradictions within "the Court's Eighth Amendment jurisprudence" should not prevent them.

Do you agree with Justice Blackmun's reasoning, or is Justice Scalia's resolution of this conundrum more satisfactory? Or are both Justices wrong to conclude that the competing aspirations of consistency and individualized sentencing cannot be balanced in an acceptable way? Doesn't much, if not all, of what Justice Blackmun says about the tensions between consistency and individualized fairness in the application of the death penalty also apply to other sanctions?

3. Capital Discretion in Operation

There is often a profound gap between the law on paper and the law in practice. The same is true of capital punishment, and for two important reasons: (1) the constitutional rules established by the Supreme Court provide only broad parameters for the structure of capital sentencing, so particular capital statutes in individual states determine the rules under which death penalty systems actually operate; and (2) though statutory provisions structure how states apply the death penalty, the way these provisions are understood and applied by prosecutors, defense counsel, juries, and judges determine the day-to-day operation of the death penalty.

Both legal and social factors have significantly affected the operation of the death penalty since the Supreme Court's 1976 decision in *Gregg*. Most tangibly, 12 states (nearly all in the northern parts of the United States) and the District of Columbia do not authorize capital punishment, and thus the law precludes the operation of the death penalty in these jurisdictions. In the 38 other states (and in the federal system), the use of capital punishment varies dramatically in terms of both the number of persons sentenced to death and the number of executions carried out. Applying either metric, southern states — particularly Texas and Florida — have been national leaders. Between 1976 and mid-2003, Texas executed more than 300 persons, three times more than any other state, and had another 450 defendants on death row. Some states, particularly California, Pennsylvania, and Ohio, have sentenced many offenders to death but have carried out relatively few executions. Other states, such as Virginia and Missouri, have carried out a large number of executions but have relatively small death row populations.

The impact of appellate review in capital cases can explain some of the differences among states in the number of death sentences imposed and the number of executions carried out. As detailed more fully in Chapter 11, typically both state and federal courts review every death sentence imposed, although the rigor of this review varies greatly by court and region. In total, since *Gregg*, nearly 10,000 death sentences have been imposed, and more than half of these sentences have been reversed on appeal. As of mid-2003, roughly 3,500 defendants were on death row and more than 850 persons executed since 1976.

When state legislatures during the years after 1976 created acceptable systems of capital punishment, they based their decisions on some speculation about how prosecutors, jurors, defense lawyers, defendants, judges, and the public would respond. In other words, efforts by courts and legislatures to regulate capital sentencing discretion often relied on a variety of assumptions about how this discretion is exercised. As you review the material in the rest of this chapter, consider whether the capital sentencing structures that emerged as a result of the Supreme Court's regulatory efforts have effectively addressed the problems of arbitrariness that the Court identified in *Furman*.

a.   Statutory Schemes

State legislatures responded to the various opinions in *Furman* with different strategies for limiting the sentencer's discretion to choose a lengthy prison term or death. As detailed above, the Supreme Court ultimately ruled unconstitutional the efforts by some states to make the death penalty mandatory for certain crimes, and it also required states to allow the consideration of nearly all mitigating circumstances. Other than these basic requirements, however, states have fairly broad latitude to decide exactly how to structure death penalty decisions. Some states give the decision exclusively to a jury, while others allow the judge to make the choice after the jury renders an advisory verdict. Some statutes provide lengthy lists of aggravating and mitigating factors, while others set forth much shorter lists or none at all.

The statutes in operation throughout the various states generally adopt two or three distinct strategies to guide sentencing discretion. Some states, including Georgia, are known as "threshold" states. Their statutes require jurors to find beyond a reasonable doubt at least one aggravating factor from the list included in the statute; after crossing that threshold, the jurors are free to impose life or death without further instructions. The largest group of states, including Florida, use "balancing" statutes. These laws require jurors to determine the presence or absence of aggravating and mitigating factors specified in the statute, and then to balance the aggravating factors against the mitigating factors. In some of these states, the jury is instructed to impose a death penalty if the aggravating factors outweigh the mitigating factors; in others, the jury remains free to impose a life term even if the aggravating factors weigh more heavily than the mitigating factors. Finally, a third group of "directive" or "limiting" states, including Texas, give further structure to the jury's decision by presenting a sequence of special questions to the jury (often related to the future dangerousness of the offender) that supposedly determine the jury's decision on death or life.

The problem below provides an opportunity to see how different capital sentencing statutes operate in the context of a specific case. As you work through the problem, consider whether these death penalty statutes sufficiently address the problems and other issues that lay behind the Supreme Court's decisions and reasoning in *Furman, Gregg,* and the other early constitutional cases.

PROBLEM 3-2. CHOOSE YOUR POISON

During the 1980s and 1990s, Theodore Kaczynski sent a series of bombs through the mail, and a number of them exploded and killed the recipients of the packages. Kaczynski selected as his victims key figures in universities and in transportation, advertising, and high-technology firms because he believed that resort to computers and other technological devices was a disastrous trend for modern society, a trend he hoped his bombs would reverse. Kaczynski became known as the "Unabomber." Using this name, he wrote lengthy letters to major newspapers from time to time, explaining his views on the evils of technology and modern life and his reasons for sending the bombs. After years of investigation, authorities found the Unabomber in a small cabin in Montana, and the federal government charged him with several counts of murder. As the proceedings moved along, it became clear that there was some question about Kaczynski's sanity, and prosecutors decided to accept a guilty plea in exchange for a sentence of life in prison without possibility of parole.

This outcome does not satisfy some prosecutors in states where victims were killed; they still want a piece of the action. Imagine now that prosecutors from Texas and Florida can establish jurisdiction in their states and have contacted the U.S. Attorney General, asking for custody of Kaczynski to try him for murder in their states. (The law of double jeopardy allows states to prosecute a person for a crime even after the federal government has obtained a conviction for that same crime, but the state authorities must have physical custody of Kaczynski before proceeding with a murder trial.)

Lawyers serving on Kaczynski's appointed defense team have asked for your advice about which jurisdiction they should want to assume custody. (The team has explained to you that the Attorney General feels obliged to allow one state to try Kaczynski but is eager to minimize legal battles over this case now that the federal charges have been resolved. Consequently, the Attorney General wants a transfer decision to have defense counsel's acquiescence to avoid any legal challenges.) Read the two statutes below, then give the defense lawyers your best advice about the prospects for the government to obtain a death sentence under each statute. Do the different statutes change the aggravating and mitigating evidence that will be considered or emphasized at trial?

Texas Code of Criminal Procedure, Art. 37.071

Section 1. If a defendant is found guilty in a capital felony case in which the state does not seek the death penalty, the judge shall sentence the defendant to life imprisonment.

Section 2(a)(1) If a defendant is tried for a capital offense in which the state seeks the death penalty, on a finding that the defendant is guilty of a capital offense, the court shall conduct a separate sentencing proceeding to determine whether the defendant shall be sentenced to death or life imprisonment. The proceeding shall be conducted in the trial court and . . . before the trial jury as soon as practicable. In the proceeding, evidence may be presented by the state and the defendant or the defendant's counsel as to any matter that the court deems relevant to sentence, including evidence of the defendant's background or character or the circumstances of the offense that mitigates against the imposition of the death penalty. This subsection shall not be construed to authorize the introduction of any evidence secured in violation of the Constitution of the United States or of the State of Texas. The state and the defendant or the defendant's counsel shall be permitted to present argument for or against sentence of death. The court, the attorney representing the state, the defendant, or the defendant's counsel may not inform a juror or a prospective juror of the effect of a failure of a jury to agree on issues submitted under Subsection (c) or (e) of this article. . . .

(b) On conclusion of the presentation of evidence, the court shall submit the following issues to the jury:

(1) whether there is a probability that the defendant would commit criminal acts of violence that would constitute a continuing threat to society; and

(2) in cases in which the jury charge at the guilt or innocence stage permitted the jury to find the defendant guilty as [an accomplice], whether the defendant actually caused the death of the deceased or did not actually cause the death of the deceased but intended to kill the deceased or another or anticipated that a human life would be taken.

(c) The state must prove each issue submitted under Subsection (b) of this article beyond a reasonable doubt, and the jury shall return a special verdict of "yes" or "no" on each issue submitted under Subsection (b) of this Article.

(d) The court shall charge the jury that:

(1) in deliberating on the issues submitted under Subsection (b) of this article, it shall consider all evidence admitted at the guilt or innocence stage and the punishment stage, including evidence of the defendant's background or character or the circumstances of the offense that militates for or mitigates against the imposition of the death penalty;

(2) it may not answer any issue submitted under Subsection (b) of this article "yes" unless it agrees unanimously and it may not answer any issue "no" unless 10 or more jurors agree; and

(3) members of the jury need not agree on what particular evidence supports a negative answer to any issue submitted under Subsection (b) of this article.

(e)(1) The court shall instruct the jury that if the jury returns an affirmative finding to each issue submitted under Subsection (b) of this article, it shall answer the following issue: Whether, taking into consideration all of the evidence, including the circumstances of the offense, the defendant's character and background, and the personal moral culpability of the defendant, there is a sufficient mitigating circumstance or circumstances to warrant that a sentence of life imprisonment rather than a death sentence be imposed. . . .

(f) The court shall charge the jury that in answering the issue submitted under Subsection (e) of this article, the jury:

(1) shall answer the issue "yes" or "no";

(2) may not answer the issue "no" unless it agrees unanimously and may not answer the issue "yes" unless 10 or more jurors agree;

(3) need not agree on what particular evidence supports an affirmative finding on the issue; and

(4) shall consider mitigating evidence to be evidence that a juror might regard as reducing the defendant's moral blameworthiness.

(g) If the jury returns an affirmative finding on each issue submitted under Subsection (b) of this article and a negative finding on an issue submitted under Subsection (e) of this article, the court shall sentence the defendant to death. If the jury returns a negative finding on any issue submitted under Subsection (b) of this article or an affirmative finding on an issue submitted under Subsection (e) of this article or is unable to answer any issue submitted under Subsection (b) or (e) of this article, the court shall sentence the defendant to confinement in the institutional division of the Texas Department of Criminal Justice for life.

(h) The judgment of conviction and sentence of death shall be subject to automatic review by the Court of Criminal Appeals.

Florida Statutes Annotated §921.141

(1) *Separate proceedings on issue of penalty.* Upon conviction or adjudication of guilt of a defendant of a capital felony, the court shall conduct a separate sentencing proceeding to determine whether the defendant should be sentenced to death or life imprisonment. . . . The proceeding shall be conducted by the trial judge before the trial jury as soon as practicable. . . . If the

trial jury has been waived, or if the defendant pleaded guilty, the sentencing proceeding shall be conducted before a jury impaneled for that purpose, unless waived by the defendant. In the proceeding, evidence may be presented as to any matter that the court deems relevant to the nature of the crime and the character of the defendant and shall include matters relating to any of the aggravating or mitigating circumstances enumerated in subsections (5) and (6). Any such evidence which the court deems to have probative value may be received, regardless of its admissibility under the exclusionary rules of evidence, provided the defendant is accorded a fair opportunity to rebut any hearsay statements. However, this subsection shall not be construed to authorize the introduction of any evidence secured in violation of the Constitution of the United States or the Constitution of the State of Florida. The state and the defendant or the defendant's counsel shall be permitted to present argument for or against sentence of death.

(2) *Advisory sentence by the jury.* After hearing all the evidence, the jury shall deliberate and render an advisory sentence to the court, based upon the following matters:

(a) Whether sufficient aggravating circumstances exist as enumerated in subsection (5);

(b) Whether sufficient mitigating circumstances exist which outweigh the aggravating circumstances found to exist; and

(c) Based on these considerations, whether the defendant should be sentenced to life imprisonment or death.

(3) *Findings in support of sentence of death.* Notwithstanding the recommendation of a majority of the jury, the court, after weighing the aggravating and mitigating circumstances, shall enter a sentence of life imprisonment or death, but if the court imposes a sentence of death, it shall set forth in writing its findings upon which the sentence of death is based as to the facts:

(a) That sufficient aggravating circumstances exist as enumerated in subsection (5), and

(b) That there are insufficient mitigating circumstances to outweigh the aggravating circumstances.

In each case in which the court imposes the death sentence, the determination of the court shall be supported by specific written findings of fact based upon the circumstances in subsections (5) and (6) and upon the records of the trial and the sentencing proceedings. If the court does not make the findings requiring the death sentence within 30 days after the rendition of the judgment and sentence, the court shall impose sentence of life imprisonment. . . .

(4) *Review of judgment and sentence.* The judgment of conviction and sentence of death shall be subject to automatic review by the Supreme Court of Florida and disposition rendered within 2 years after the filing of a notice of appeal. Such review by the Supreme Court shall have priority over all other cases and shall be heard in accordance with rules promulgated by the Supreme Court.

(5) *Aggravating circumstances.* Aggravating circumstances shall be limited to the following:

(a) The capital felony was committed by a person previously convicted of a felony and under sentence of imprisonment or placed on community control or on felony probation.

(b) The defendant was previously convicted of another capital felony or of a felony involving the use or threat of violence to the person.

(c) The defendant knowingly created a great risk of death to many persons.

(d) The capital felony was committed while the defendant was engaged, or was an accomplice, in the commission of, or an attempt to commit, or flight after committing or attempting to commit, any: robbery; sexual battery; aggravated child abuse; abuse of an elderly person or disabled adult resulting in great bodily harm, permanent disability, or permanent disfigurement; arson; burglary; kidnapping; aircraft piracy; or unlawful throwing, placing, or discharging of a destructive device or bomb.

(e) The capital felony was committed for the purpose of avoiding or preventing a lawful arrest or effecting an escape from custody.

(f) The capital felony was committed for pecuniary gain.

(g) The capital felony was committed to disrupt or hinder the lawful exercise of any governmental function or the enforcement of laws.

(h) The capital felony was especially heinous, atrocious, or cruel.

(i) The capital felony was a homicide and was committed in a cold, calculated, and premeditated manner without any pretense of moral or legal justification.

(j) The victim of the capital felony was a law enforcement officer engaged in the performance of his or her official duties.

(k) The victim of the capital felony was an elected or appointed public official engaged in the performance of his or her official duties if the motive for the capital felony was related, in whole or in part, to the victim's official capacity.

(l) The victim of the capital felony was a person less than 12 years of age.

(m) The victim of the capital felony was particularly vulnerable due to advanced age or disability, or because the defendant stood in a position of familial or custodial authority over the victim.

(n) The capital felony was committed by a criminal street gang member, . . .

(6) *Mitigating circumstances.* Mitigating circumstances shall be the following:

(a) The defendant has no significant history of prior criminal activity.

(b) The capital felony was committed while the defendant was under the influence of extreme mental or emotional disturbance.

(c) The victim was a participant in the defendant's conduct or consented to the act.

(d) The defendant was an accomplice in the capital felony committed by another person and his or her participation was relatively minor.

(e) The defendant acted under extreme duress or under the substantial domination of another person.

(f) The capacity of the defendant to appreciate the criminality of his or her conduct or to conform his or her conduct to the requirements of law was substantially impaired.

(g) The age of the defendant at the time of the crime.

(h) The existence of any other factors in the defendant's background that would mitigate against imposition of the death penalty.

NOTES

1. *Impact of legal standards.* In terms of the decision whether to sentence a defendant to death, do the standards that the sentencing jury employs make a difference? Consider the likely outcome for two infamous defendants. Would Timothy McVeigh, the Oklahoma City bomber who killed 168 people in 1995, have received a death sentence under either or both of these statutes? How about John Allen Mohammad, one of the two Washington-area sniper suspects apprehended in 2002?

2. *Impact of procedural rules.* Can and should the procedures used at a standard criminal trial apply during a capital sentencing hearing? Consider, for example, the traditional rules of evidence, and the possibility that strict adherence to them might significantly limit the ability of prosecutors and defense counsel to present all the evidence they might consider important at a sentencing hearing. How, if at all, might these rules or other traditional trial procedures influence the outcome of a capital sentencing hearing?

b.   Jury Selection and Decision Making

Though very few states rely on juries for noncapital sentencing decisions, nearly all states that authorize the death penalty give juries a central role in capital sentencing. This reality raises a number of important and interesting questions: why do states believe juries are the appropriate decision makers in capital cases when life and death are at stake, but do not include juries in other sentencing decisions? Should the jury that decides a defendant's guilt also decide whether a defendant receives the death penalty, or should two different juries make these decisions? Can we be confident that any system of jury decision making in capital cases will be free of the problems that prompted the Supreme Court's decision in *Furman*?

Beyond these broad questions, the reliance on juries to make capital punishment decisions raises a host of more intricate legal and practical issues that can greatly influence the operation of death penalty systems — for example, should a jury have to render a unanimous verdict to impose a death sentence? What standard of proof should a jury apply when making a death penalty decision? Should a defendant have a right to request that a judge instead of a jury make the death sentencing decision? Can we be confident that jurors will understand and follow the detailed instructions in most death penalty statutes?

As we have seen, the thrust of the constitutional rules that regulate capital punishment is to channel and preserve the discretion of the sentencing authority, usually the jury. Whenever the law assigns discretion to someone, it becomes critical to know *who* will exercise that discretion. Thus, the method of selecting the jury members in a capital case becomes a crucial piece of this system that depends so much on guided discretion. When life is at stake, both prosecutors and defense counsel are very interested in the jury's composition, especially since determining whether to sentence a person to death is fundamentally a moral decision rather than a factual one. As the following case highlights, there is good reason to fear that in the operation of capital sentencing systems, the very processes used in jury selection may prompt some of the same concerns that troubled the Supreme Court in *Furman*.

Thomas Joe Miller-El v. Janie Cockrell
537 U.S. 322 (2003)

KENNEDY, J.

In 1986 two Dallas County assistant district attorneys used peremptory strikes to exclude 10 of the 11 African-Americans eligible to serve on the jury which tried Thomas Joe Miller-El. During the ensuing 17 years, petitioner has been unsuccessful in establishing, in either state or federal court, that his conviction and death sentence must be vacated because the jury selection procedures violated the Equal Protection Clause and our holding in Batson v. Kentucky, 476 U.S. 79 (1986). The claim now arises in a federal petition for writ of habeas corpus [and we consider whether the federal habeas corpus statute precludes further consideration of Miller-El's claim].

Petitioner, his wife Dorothy Miller-El, and one Kenneth Flowers robbed a Holiday Inn in Dallas, Texas. They emptied the cash drawers and ordered two employees, Doug Walker and Donald Hall, to lie on the floor. Walker and Hall were gagged with strips of fabric, and their hands and feet were bound. Petitioner asked Flowers if he was going to kill Walker and Hall. When Flowers hesitated or refused, petitioner shot Walker twice in the back and shot Hall in the side. Walker died from his wounds.

The State indicted petitioner for capital murder. He pleaded not guilty, and jury selection took place during five weeks in February and March 1986. When voir dire had been concluded, petitioner moved to strike the jury on the grounds that the prosecution had violated the Equal Protection Clause of the Fourteenth Amendment by excluding African-Americans through the use of peremptory challenges. . . .

A comparative analysis of the venire members demonstrates that African-Americans were excluded from petitioner's jury in a ratio significantly higher than Caucasians were. Of the 108 possible jurors reviewed by the prosecution and defense, 20 were African-American. Nine of them were excused for cause or by agreement of the parties. Of the 11 African-American jurors remaining, however, all but 1 were excluded by peremptory strikes exercised by the prosecutors. On this basis 91% of the eligible black jurors were removed by peremptory strikes. In contrast the prosecutors used their peremptory strikes against just 13% (4 out of 31) of the eligible nonblack prospective jurors qualified to serve on petitioner's jury.

These numbers, while relevant, are not petitioner's whole case. During voir dire, the prosecution questioned venire members as to their views concerning the death penalty and their willingness to serve on a capital case. Responses that disclosed reluctance or hesitation to impose capital punishment were cited as a justification for striking a potential juror for cause or by peremptory challenge [based upon this Court's decision in] Wainwright v. Witt, 469 U.S. 412 (1985). The evidence suggests, however, that the manner in which members of the venire were questioned varied by race. . . .

Most African-Americans (53%, or 8 out of 15) were first given a detailed description of the mechanics of an execution in Texas:

> If those three [sentencing] questions are answered yes, at some point Thomas Joe Miller-El will be taken to Huntsville, Texas. He will be placed on death row and at some time will be taken to the death house where he will be strapped on

a gurney, an IV put into his arm and he will be injected with a substance that will cause his death . . . as the result of the verdict in this case if those three questions are answered yes.

Only then were these African-American venire members asked whether they could render a decision leading to a sentence of death. Very few prospective white jurors (6%, or 3 out of 49) were given this preface prior to being asked for their views on capital punishment. Rather, all but three were questioned in vague terms: "Would you share with us . . . your personal feelings, if you could, in your own words how you do feel about the death penalty and capital punishment and secondly, do you feel you could serve on this type of a jury and actually render a decision that would result in the death of the Defendant in this case based on the evidence?"

There was an even more pronounced difference, on the apparent basis of race, in the manner the prosecutors questioned members of the venire about their willingness to impose the minimum sentence for murder. Under Texas law at the time of petitioner's trial, an unwillingness to do so warranted removal for cause. This strategy normally is used by the defense to weed out pro-state members of the venire, but, ironically, the prosecution employed it here. The prosecutors first identified the statutory minimum sentence of five years' imprisonment to 34 out of 36 (94%) white venire members, and only then asked: "If you hear a case, to your way of thinking [that] calls for and warrants and justifies five years, you'll give it?" In contrast, only 1 out of 8 (12.5%) African-American prospective jurors were informed of the statutory minimum before being asked what minimum sentence they would impose. The typical questioning of the other seven black jurors was as follows:

> [Prosecutor]: Now, the maximum sentence for [murder] . . . is life under the law. Can you give me an idea of just your personal feelings what you feel a minimum sentence should be for the offense of murder the way I've set it out for you?
> [Juror]: Well, to me that's almost like it's premeditated. But you said they don't have a premeditated statute here in Texas. . . .
> [Prosecutor]: Again, we're not talking about self-defense or accident or insanity or killing in the heat of passion or anything like that. We're talking about the knowing—
> [Juror]: I know you said the minimum. The minimum amount that I would say would be at least twenty years.

Furthermore, petitioner points to the prosecution's use of a Texas criminal procedure practice known as jury shuffling. This practice permits parties to rearrange the order in which members of the venire are examined so as to increase the likelihood that visually preferable venire members will be moved forward and empaneled. With no information about the prospective jurors other than their appearance, the party requesting the procedure literally shuffles the juror cards, and the venire members are then reseated in the new order. Tex. Code Crim. Proc. Ann., Art. 35.11. Shuffling affects jury composition because any prospective jurors not questioned during voir dire are dismissed at the end of the week, and a new panel of jurors appears the following week. So jurors who are shuffled to the back of the panel are less likely to be questioned or to serve.

On at least two occasions the prosecution requested shuffles when there were a predominate number of African-Americans in the front of the panel. On yet another occasion the prosecutors complained about the purported inadequacy of the card shuffle by a defense lawyer but lodged a formal objection only after the postshuffle panel composition revealed that African-American prospective jurors had been moved forward.

[As additional evidence to support his claims,] petitioner subpoenaed a number of current and former Dallas County assistant district attorneys, judges, and others who had observed firsthand the prosecution's conduct during jury selection over a number of years. Although most of the witnesses denied the existence of a systematic policy to exclude African-Americans, others disagreed. A Dallas County district judge testified that, when he had served in the District Attorney's Office from the late 1950s to early 1960s, his superior warned him that he would be fired if he permitted any African-Americans to serve on a jury. Similarly, another Dallas County district judge and former assistant district attorney from 1976 to 1978 testified that he believed the office had a systematic policy of excluding African-Americans from juries.

Of more importance, the defense presented evidence that the District Attorney's Office had adopted a formal policy to exclude minorities from jury service. A 1963 circular by the District Attorney's Office instructed its prosecutors to exercise peremptory strikes against minorities: "Do not take Jews, Negroes, Dagos, Mexicans or a member of any minority race on a jury, no matter how rich or how well educated." A manual entitled "Jury Selection in a Criminal Case" was distributed to prosecutors. It contained an article authored by a former prosecutor (and later a judge) under the direction of his superiors in the District Attorney's Office, outlining the reasoning for excluding minorities from jury service. Although the manual was written in 1968, it remained in circulation until 1976, if not later, and was available at least to one of the prosecutors in Miller-El's trial.

Some testimony casts doubt on the State's claim that these practices had been discontinued before petitioner's trial. For example, a judge testified that, in 1985, he had to exclude a prosecutor from trying cases in his courtroom for race-based discrimination in jury selection. Other testimony indicated that the State, by its own admission, once requested a jury shuffle in order to reduce the number of African-Americans in the venire. Concerns over the exclusion of African-Americans by the District Attorney's Office were echoed by Dallas County's Chief Public Defender.

[The] State now concedes that petitioner satisfied step one [under the standards established in Batson v. Kentucky, 476 U.S. 79 (1986)]: "There is no dispute that Miller-El presented a prima facie claim" that prosecutors used their peremptory challenges to exclude venire members on the basis of race. Petitioner, for his part, acknowledges that the State proceeded through step two [of the *Batson* analysis] by proffering facially race-neutral explanations for these strikes. Under *Batson*, then, the question remaining is step three: whether Miller-El "has carried his burden of proving purposeful discrimination." . . .

In this case, the statistical evidence alone raises some debate as to whether the prosecution acted with a race-based reason when striking prospective jurors. The prosecutors used their peremptory strikes to exclude 91% of the eligible African-American venire members, and only one served on petitioner's jury.

In total, 10 of the prosecutors' 14 peremptory strikes were used against African-Americans. Happenstance is unlikely to produce this disparity. . . .

In this case, three of the State's proffered race-neutral rationales for striking African-American jurors pertained just as well to some white jurors who were not challenged and who did serve on the jury. The prosecutors explained that their peremptory challenges against six African-American potential jurors were based on ambivalence about the death penalty; hesitancy to vote to execute defendants capable of being rehabilitated; and the jurors' own family history of criminality. In rebuttal of the prosecution's explanation, petitioner identified two empaneled white jurors who expressed ambivalence about the death penalty in a manner similar to their African-American counterparts who were the subject of prosecutorial peremptory challenges. One indicated that capital punishment was not appropriate for a first offense, and another stated that it would be "difficult" to impose a death sentence. Similarly, two white jurors expressed hesitation in sentencing to death a defendant who might be rehabilitated; and four white jurors had family members with criminal histories. As a consequence, even though the prosecution's reasons for striking African-American members of the venire appear race neutral, the application of these rationales to the venire might have been selective and based on racial considerations. Whether a comparative juror analysis would demonstrate the prosecutors' rationales to have been pretexts for discrimination is an unnecessary determination at this stage, but the evidence does make debatable the District Court's conclusion that no purposeful discrimination occurred.

We question the Court of Appeals' and state trial court's dismissive and strained interpretation of petitioner's evidence of disparate questioning. . . . Disparate questioning did occur. Petitioner submits that disparate questioning created the appearance of divergent opinions even though the venire members' views on the relevant subject might have been the same. It follows that, if the use of disparate questioning is determined by race at the outset, it is likely a justification for a strike based on the resulting divergent views would be pretextual. In this context the differences in the questions posed by the prosecutors are some evidence of purposeful discrimination. . . .

We agree with petitioner that the prosecution's decision to seek a jury shuffle when a predominate number of African-Americans were seated in the front of the panel, along with its decision to delay a formal objection to the defense's shuffle until after the new racial composition was revealed, raise a suspicion that the State sought to exclude African-Americans from the jury. Our concerns are amplified by the fact that the state court also had before it, and apparently ignored, testimony demonstrating that the Dallas County District Attorney's Office had, by its own admission, used this process to manipulate the racial composition of the jury in the past. Even though the practice of jury shuffling might not be denominated as a *Batson* claim because it does not involve a peremptory challenge, the use of the practice here tends to erode the credibility of the prosecution's assertion that race was not a motivating factor in the jury selection. . . .

Finally, in our threshold examination, we accord some weight to petitioner's historical evidence of racial discrimination by the District Attorney's Office. . . . Irrespective of whether the evidence could prove sufficient to support a charge of systematic exclusion of African-Americans, it reveals that the culture of the District Attorney's Office in the past was suffused with bias against

African-Americans in jury selection. Both prosecutors [in Miller-El's case] joined the District Attorney's Office when assistant district attorneys received formal training in excluding minorities from juries. The supposition that race was a factor could be reinforced by the fact that the prosecutors marked the race of each prospective juror on their juror cards. . . .

To secure habeas relief, petitioner must demonstrate that a state court's finding of the absence of purposeful discrimination was incorrect by clear and convincing evidence, 28 U.S.C. §2254(e)(1), and that the corresponding factual determination was "objectively unreasonable" in light of the record before the court. The State represents to us that petitioner will not be able to satisfy his burden. That may or may not be the case. It is not, however, the question before us [as we are considering only whether his claim may proceed under the federal habeas statute, and that] inquiry asks only if the District Court's decision was debatable. Our threshold examination convinces us that it was.

NOTES

1. *Death-qualification and life-qualification of jurors.* As briefly mentioned in the *Miller-El* decision, the Supreme Court developed special rules to govern the selection and exclusion of jurors in death penalty cases. Through its decisions in Witherspoon v. Illinois, 391 U.S. 510 (1968), and Wainwright v. Witt, 469 U.S. 412 (1985), the Supreme Court established that jurors may be excused for cause when they indicate they are so opposed to capital punishment that they would not find the defendant guilty regardless of the evidence, or would not consider death as a possible sentence regardless of the circumstances of the crime. Many commentators have assailed the practice of excluding jurors who express sincere misgivings about capital punishment — a process known as "death qualifying" a juror — arguing that it biases the decision making of capital juries and denies capital defendants their constitutional rights to an impartial jury and to a jury drawn from a fair cross-section of the community. See Craig Haney, Aida Hurtado, and Luis Vega, Modern Death Qualification: New Data on Its Biasing Effects, 18 Law & Hum. Behav. 619, 624-631 (1994); Stephen Gillers, Deciding Who Dies, 129 U. Pa. L. Rev. 1 (1980).

Following the same principles it applied in *Witt*, the Supreme Court subsequently held in Morgan v. Illinois, 504 U.S. 719 (1992), that a defendant could seek to "life qualify" a capital jury by excluding for cause any juror who indicates he or she will automatically vote for the death penalty regardless of any presented mitigating circumstances. The efficacy of the Supreme Court's rules regulating the selection of capital jurors has been repeatedly questioned, with a number of commentators raising serious concerns based on data collected by the Capital Jury Project (see below) about the decisions of actual capital jurors. See John H. Blume et al., Probing "Life Qualification" Through Expanded Voir Dire, 29 Hofstra L. Rev. 1209 (2001); William J. Bowers et al., Foreclosed Impartiality in Capital Sentencing: Jurors' Predispositions, Guilt-Trial Experience, and Premature Decision Making, 83 Cornell L. Rev. 1476 (1998).

2. *Review of death sentencing procedures.* The Supreme Court in *Miller-El* was not asked to resolve the merits of the defendant's constitutional claim because the case was enmeshed in the complicated procedural issues that

surround federal habeas review of state death sentences. Because state courts rejected Miller-El's claims on their merits, and because the federal district court
denied relief, the specific question before the Supreme Court was whether
Miller-El's claim was sufficiently "debatable" to permit further appellate review
in the federal courts. Given the force of the factual evidence presented by
Miller-El, why do you think the state courts rejected his claims of an equal protection violation? Given the concerns expressed by the Supreme Court in *Furman*, do you think capital cases warrant a higher standard of appellate review?

3. *Potential sources of racial bias.*   As highlighted earlier, a clear concern for
certain justices who voted in the majority in *Furman* was not just the possibility
of arbitrary death sentencing but the real potential for discriminatory decisions
in capital cases. Do the racial realities revealed in the *Miller-El* case suggest that
unique safeguards against racial bias are needed in capital cases? The Supreme
Court's struggles with racial discrimination in the administration of the death
penalty are covered more fully in Chapter 9.

> ## The Capital Jury Project: Rationale, Design,
> ## and Preview of Early Findings,
> ## William J. Bowers
> ### 70 Ind. L.J. 1043 (1995)

Now underway in fourteen states, the Capital Jury Project ("CJP") is a mul-
tidisciplinary study of how jurors make their life or death sentencing decisions.
Drawing upon three-to-four-hour interviews with 80 to 120 capital jurors in
each of the participating states, the CJP is examining the extent to which jurors'
exercise of capital sentencing discretion is still infected with, or now cured of,
the arbitrariness which the United States Supreme Court condemned in
Furman v. Georgia, and the extent to which the principal kinds of post-*Furman*
guided discretion statutes are curbing arbitrary decision-making — as the Court
said they would in Gregg v. Georgia and its companion cases. . . .

THE GUILT PHASE

Jurors' responses to questions about the guilt phase of the trial suggest that
many of them began considering aggravation and punishment while they were
still deciding on the defendant's guilt, and indeed, that many began to take a
stand on what the defendant's punishment should be well before being exposed
to the statutory guidelines for this decision. We see these indications in their responses to questions about topics they discussed during the jury's guilt deliberations and in their answers to a question about what they thought the punishment should be prior to the punishment phase of the trial.

Considerations of Aggravation and Punishment

When the questioning turned to the jury's deliberations at the guilt phase
of the trial, we asked jurors about a number of specific topics they might have

discussed, including some that are legally irrelevant or impermissible in determining guilt, such as the defendant's likely future dangerousness and jurors' feelings about the appropriate punishment — considerations explicitly reserved for the later punishment phase of the trial. . . .

Jurors were evidently concerned with the defendant's future dangerousness and the punishment to be imposed during their deliberation on the defendant's guilt. More than six out of ten said the jury's guilt deliberations focused on each of these topics a "great deal" or a "fair amount." One-half of the jurors said that there was a great deal of discussion about the "right punishment."

Conscious that jurors might not clearly distinguish between the guilt and punishment deliberations in response to this question, and that some topics discussed during guilt deliberations might not have actually figured in the decision-making about guilt, we asked a further question explicitly worded to focus the juror's attention exclusively on the defendant's punishment as a relevant consideration in the jury's decision about the defendant's guilt. [We asked]: In deciding guilt, did jurors talk about whether or not the defendant would, or should, get the death penalty? Here, too, a sizable number (over 30%) of jurors recall that in deciding guilt, there was explicit discussion of what the defendant's punishment would or should be.

Timing of the Punishment Decision

In addition to these questions about what the jury did as a group, CJP investigators also asked the individual jurors about their own personal thinking and decision-making with respect to the defendant's punishment prior to the sentencing phase of the trial. In particular, we asked whether they had come to a decision on punishment, what they thought the punishment should be, and how convinced they were of their decision. . . .

One-half of the jurors were undecided, but the other one-half said that they had chosen (more or less firmly) between a life or death sentence at the guilt stage of the trial. A second follow-up question, addressed only to those who, at this stage, thought that the defendant should be given a life or death sentence, asked: How strongly did you think so? [M]ost of the jurors who had decided what the punishment should be before the sentencing phase of the trial were "absolutely convinced" of their punishment decision, and nearly all the rest were at least "pretty sure." In effect, it appears that three out of ten jurors had essentially made up their minds, and another two in ten were leaning one way or the other, before hearing from the judge about the standards that should guide their sentencing decisions.

THE PUNISHMENT PHASE

Guidelines and Instructions

If statutory standards are to guide the exercise of sentencing discretion, they must, of course, be understood and applied in the course of actually making the sentencing decision. Among the various questions we asked to tap jurors' understanding of sentencing guidelines, the responses to the question regarding the substance of the statutory standards were unsettling. . . .

Contrary to the laws of their states, four out of ten capital jurors believed that they were required to impose the death penalty if they found that the crime was heinous, vile, or depraved, and three out of ten thought that the death penalty was required if they found that the defendant would be dangerous in the future. . . .

Three out of four participating jurors said that the evidence proved that the crime was heinous, vile, or depraved, and that the defendant would be dangerous in the future. In combination with the percentages of those who believed that the death penalty was required if these factors were proved, it appears that between 21% and 33% of the jurors mistakenly believed that the state's proof of heinousness required them to vote for the death penalty. In addition, between 8% and 24% of jurors wrongly believed that evidence of the defendant's dangerousness required them to vote in favor of death. . . .

Responsibility for the Punishment

One criticism of guided discretion capital statutes is that they tend to allay jurors' sense of responsibility for their life or death sentencing decisions by appearing to provide them with an authoritative formula that yields the "correct" or "required" punishment. . . . To see where capital jurors located responsibility for punishment, we asked them to: *Rank the following from "most" through "least" responsible for [the defendant's] punishment.*

Unmistakably, jurors placed responsibility for the defendant's punishment elsewhere. Eight out of ten jurors feel that the defendant or the law is the most responsible for the defendant's punishment. More jurors believe that the greatest responsibility lies with the defendant rather than with the law. . . .

CONCLUSION

The early indications in our research . . . sketch out a picture of the exercise of capital sentencing discretion that differs from that found in current Supreme Court precedent. [T]he emerging picture is noteworthy for the questions it raises concerning the Supreme Court's presumptions about the exercise of capital sentencing discretion. . . .

[We] find that many jurors appear to make their decisions apart from, and indeed prior to, sentencing instructions on the bases of their unguided feelings or reactions to the crime. The findings also show that sentencing guidelines provide "legal cover" to many who have already made up their minds, and "legal leverage" for persuading the undecided. In either case, the guidelines appear to lessen the sense of responsibility for imposing an awful punishment. Yet, these are still early soundings of what the jurors have to tell us about how they think about the crimes, the defendants, the victims, and how they decide what the defendant's punishment should be. The yet unanswered critical questions, of course, are how standardless is this decision-making process; how widespread is such standardless decision-making; and — for the Court to answer — does it represent a constitutionally unacceptable level or risk of arbitrariness?

NOTES

1. *Challenges to jurors' life-or-death decision.*   Is it surprising that jurors typi-cally do not fully understand or adhere to the instructions that are designed to guide their decisions? After comparing the modern capital sentencing statutes used in Texas and Florida (reprinted above) with the instructions used in pre-*Furman* cases in California and Ohio (discussed in *McGautha* above), it is easy to appreciate how the detailed instructions to jurors in capital cases today recast capital sentencing as a legal issue rather than a moral issue for the jury to de-cide. Should a death sentencing decision be recast in these terms? Whether it is a legal or a moral decision, are you confident that juries are the best sentencers in capital cases? For a dynamic discussion of the psychology surrounding capital jury decision making, see Craig Haney, Violence and the Capital Jury: Mecha-nisms of Moral Disengagement and the Impulse to Condemn to Death, 49 Stan. L. Rev. 1447 (1997).

2. *Judicial decisions to impose death sentences.*   A few jurisdictions have given some sentencing discretion to judges in capital cases. In some states, this dis-cretion is secondary to the discretion exercised by a capital jury; in Ohio, for ex-ample, the trial judge may decide a defendant does not deserve to die even if the jury recommends death, but the judge may not impose a death sentence if a jury does not so recommend. See Ohio Rev. Code §2929.03. In other states (such as Florida, whose statute is reprinted above), judges can "override" a jury decision of either death or life.

The constitutionality of capital sentencing systems that invest much sen-tencing authority in judges was recently thrown into question by the Supreme Court's decision in Ring v. Arizona, 536 U.S. 584 (2002), which overruled the Court's prior decision in Walton v. Arizona, 497 U.S. 639 (1990). In *Ring* the Court held that the Sixth Amendment's right to trial by jury in criminal prose-cutions requires a jury to determine the presence of those aggravating factors necessary for a sentence of death. Though *Ring* still allows judges to be the final decision maker concerning whether to impose a death sentence, it precludes judges from finding those facts that can form a basis for a death sentence under a state's statutory scheme.

c.   Executive Discretion

Though the discretion exercised by a jury when deciding whether to sen-tence a defendant to death is the most tangible and visible discretionary deci-sion in capital cases, many other actors make discretionary judgments about the availability and imposition of a death sentence. Prosecutors possess wide (and essentially unreviewable) discretion when initially deciding whether to charge certain murders as capital crimes and whether to reduce capital charges as part of a plea agreement. In addition, nearly every state grants its governor or board of pardons, or both, the authority to commute death sentences. As you review the following materials, think about whether these sorts of discretionary de-cisions are likely to aggravate or ameliorate the concerns expressed by the Su-preme Court in *Furman*.

Speech at Northwestern University College of Law, Illinois Governor George Ryan
Jan. 11, 2003

Four years ago I was sworn in as the 39th Governor of Illinois. That was just four short years ago; that's when I was a firm believer in the American System of Justice and the death penalty. I believed that the ultimate penalty for the taking of a life was administrated in a just and fair manner. Today, three days before I end my term as Governor, I stand before you to explain my frustrations and deep concerns about both the administration and the penalty of death. . . .

During my time in public office I have always reserved my right to change my mind if I believed it to be in the best public interest, whether it be about taxes, abortions or the death penalty. But I must confess that the debate with my-self has been the toughest concerning the death penalty. I suppose the reason the death penalty has been the toughest is because it is so final — the only pub-lic policy that determines who lives and who dies. In addition it is the only issue that attracts most of the legal minds across the country. I have received more ad-vice on this issue than any other policy issue I have dealt with in my 35 years of public service. I have kept an open mind on both sides of the issues of commu-tation for life or death. . . .

The other day, I received a call from former South African President Nelson Mandela who reminded me that the United States sets the example for justice and fairness for the rest of the world. Today the United States is not in league with most of our major allies: Europe, Canada, Mexico, most of South and Central America. These countries rejected the death penalty. We are partners in death with several third world countries. Even Russia has called a moratorium. . . .

I never intended to be an activist on this issue. I watched in surprise as freed death row inmate Anthony Porter was released from jail. A free man, he ran into the arms of Northwestern University Professor Dave Protess who poured his heart and soul into proving Porter's innocence with his journalism students. He was 48 hours away from being wheeled into the execution cham-ber where the state would kill him. It would all be so antiseptic and most of us would not have even paused, except that Anthony Porter was innocent of the double murder for which he had been condemned to die.

After Mr. Porter's case there was the report by *Chicago Tribune* reporters Steve Mills and Ken Armstrong documenting the systemic failures of our capital punishment system. Half of the nearly 300 capital cases in Illinois had been re-versed for a new trial or resentencing. Nearly Half! 33 of the death row inmates were represented at trial by an attorney who had later been disbarred or at some point suspended from practicing law.

Of the more than 160 death row inmates, 35 were African American de-fendants who had been convicted or condemned to die by all-white juries. More than two-thirds of the inmates on death row were African American. 46 inmates were convicted on the basis of testimony from jailhouse informants. . . .

Then over the next few months, there were three more exonerated men, freed because their sentence hinged on a jailhouse informant or new DNA tech-nology proved beyond a shadow of doubt their innocence. We then had the du-bious distinction of exonerating more men than we had executed. 13 men found innocent, 12 executed. As I reported yesterday, there is not a doubt in my mind that the number of innocent men freed from our Death Row stands at 17, with the pardons of Aaron Patterson, Madison Hobley, Stanley Howard and Leroy Orange. That is an absolute embarrassment. 17 exonerated death row inmates is nothing short of a catastrophic failure. But the 13, now 17 men, is just the beginning of our sad arithmetic in prosecuting murder cases. During the time we have had capital punishment in Illinois, there were at least 33 other people wrongly convicted on murder charges and exonerated. Since we reinstated the death penalty there are also 93 people — 93 — where our criminal justice system imposed the most severe sanction and later rescinded the sentence or even released them from custody because they were innocent. How many more cases of wrongful conviction have to occur before we can all agree that the system is broken?

In the United States the overwhelming majority of those executed are psychotic, alcoholic, drug addicted or mentally unstable. They frequently are raised in an impoverished and abusive environment. Seldom are people with money or prestige convicted of capital offenses, even more seldom are they executed. . . .

At stake throughout the clemency process was whether some, all or none of these inmates on death row would have their sentences commuted from death to life without the possibility of parole. One of the things discussed with family members was [that] life without parole was seen as a life filled with perks and benefits. Some inmates on death row don't want a sentence of life without parole. Danny Edwards wrote me and told me not to do him any favors because he didn't want to face a prospect of a life in prison without parole. They will be confined in a cell that is about 5-feet-by-12 feet, usually double-bunked. Our prisons have no air conditioning, except at our supermax facility where inmates are kept in their cell 23 hours a day. In summer months, temperatures in these prisons exceed one hundred degrees. It is a stark and dreary existence. They can think about their crimes. Life without parole has even, at times, been described by prosecutors as a fate worse than death. . . .

I started with this issue concerned about innocence. But once I studied, once I pondered what had become of our justice system, I came to care above all about fairness. Fairness is fundamental to the American system of justice and our way of life. The facts I have seen in reviewing each and every one of these cases raised questions not only about the innocence of people on death row, but about the fairness of the death penalty system as a whole. If the system was making so many errors in determining whether someone was guilty in the first place, how fairly and accurately was it determining which guilty defendants deserved to live and which deserved to die? What effect was race having? What effect was poverty having?

And in almost every one of the exonerated 17, we not only have breakdowns in the system with police, prosecutors and judges, we have terrible cases of shabby defense lawyers. There is just no way to sugar coat it. There are defense attorneys that did not consult with their clients, did not investigate the case and were completely unqualified to handle complex death penalty cases. They often didn't put much effort into fighting a death sentence. If your life is on the line, your lawyer ought to be fighting for you. As I have said before, there is more than enough blame to go around.

In Illinois, I have learned, we have 102 decision makers. Each of them are politically elected, each beholden to the demands of their community and, in some cases, to the media or especially vocal victims' families. In cases that have the attention of the media and the public, are decisions to seek the death penalty more likely to occur? What standards are these prosecutors using?

Some people have assailed my power to commute sentences. . . . But prosecutors in Illinois have the ultimate commutation power, a power that is exercised every day. They decide who will be subject to the death penalty, who will get a plea deal or even who may get a complete pass on prosecution. By what objective standards do they make these decisions? We do not know, they are not public. There were more than 1000 murders last year in Illinois. There is no doubt that all murders are horrific and cruel. Yet, less than 2 percent of those murder defendants will receive the death penalty. . . . Moreover, if you look at the cases, as I have done — both individually and collectively — a killing with the same circumstances might get 40 years in one county and death in another county. [You are five times more likely to get a death sentence for first-degree murder in the rural area of Illinois than you are in Cook County.] I have also seen where co-defendants who are equally or even more culpable get sentenced to a term of years, while another less culpable defendant ends up on death row.

In my case-by-case review, I found three people that fell into this category: Mario Flores, Montel Johnson and William Franklin. Today I have commuted their sentences to a term of 40 years to bring their sentences into line with their co-defendants and to reflect the other extraordinary circumstances of these cases.

Supreme Court Justice Potter Stewart has said that the imposition of the death penalty on defendants in this country is as freakish and arbitrary as who gets hit by a bolt of lightning. . . . What are we to make of the studies that showed that more than 50% of Illinois jurors could not understand the confusing and obscure sentencing instructions that were being used? What effect did that problem have on the trustworthiness of death sentences? A review of the cases shows that often even the lawyers and judges are confused about the instructions — let alone the jurors sitting in judgment. Cases still come before the Supreme Court with arguments about whether the jury instructions were proper. . . .

As I prepare to leave office, I had to ask myself whether I could really live with the prospect of knowing that I had the opportunity to act, but that I failed to do so because I might be criticized. Could I take the chance that our capital punishment system might be reformed, that wrongful convictions might not occur, that enterprising journalism students might free more men from death row? . . . Our own study showed that juries were more likely to sentence to death if the victim were white than if the victim were black — three-and-a-half times more likely to be exact. . . . Is our system fair to all? Is justice blind? These are important human rights issues. . . .

In 1994, near the end of his distinguished career on the Supreme Court of the United States, Justice Harry Blackmun wrote an influential dissent in the body of law on capital punishment. 20 years earlier he was part of the court that issued the landmark *Furman* decision. . . . But 20 years later, after affirming hundreds of death penalty decisions, Justice Blackmun came to the realization, in the twilight of his distinguished career, that the death penalty remains "fraught with arbitrariness, discrimination, caprice and mistake." He expressed frustration with a 20-year struggle to develop procedural and substantive safeguards.

In a now famous dissent he wrote in 1994, "From this day forward, I no longer shall tinker with the machinery of death.". . . The Governor has the constitutional role in our state of acting in the interest of justice and fairness. Our state constitution provides broad power to the Governor to issue reprieves, pardons and commutations. Our Supreme Court has reminded inmates petitioning them that the last resort for relief is the governor.

At times the executive clemency power has perhaps been a crutch for courts to avoid making the kind of major change that I believe our system needs. Our systemic case-by-case review has found more cases of innocent men wrongfully sentenced to death row. Because our three year study has found only more questions about the fairness of the sentencing; because of the spectacular failure to reform the system; because we have seen justice delayed for countless death row inmates with potentially meritorious claims; because the Illinois death penalty system is arbitrary and capricious — and therefore immoral — I no longer shall tinker with the machinery of death. I cannot say it more eloquently than Justice Blackmun.

The legislature couldn't reform it. Lawmakers won't repeal it. But I will not stand for it. I must act. Our capital system is haunted by the demon of error, error in determining guilt, and error in determining who among the guilty deserves to die. Because of all of these reasons today I am commuting the sentences of all death row inmates. . . .

NOTES

1. *Executive clemency.* Although it was common early in the twentieth century for governors to pardon offenders and to commute many death sentences to life terms, most governors have not used this discretionary power extensively since the courts became actively involved in constitutional regulation and review of capital sentencing. From 1955 to 1965, more than 200 death sentences were commuted and roughly the same number of executions were carried out; from 1985 to 1995, about 20 death sentences were commuted and roughly *ten times* as many executions were carried out. As detailed in the excerpt above, in January 2003 Governor George Ryan of Illinois followed up his 2000 decision to impose a moratorium on executions in his state with the decision, as one of his last acts in office, to empty death row by pardoning four persons and commuting the sentences of the remaining 156 to life imprisonment.

2. *European involvement in capital sanctions.* Increasingly, European countries have fought a multifront battle against capital punishment in the United States and Japan. They have particularly attacked the execution of those who committed capital offenses while under the age of 18 and those who suffer from a mental disability. Because of Europe's opposition to the death penalty, its use has caused serious problems for U.S. diplomats in conducting foreign policy. See Nora V. Demleitner, The Death Penalty in the United States: Following the European Lead?, 81 Or. L. Rev. 131 (2002). To what extent should the determination of common standards of decency depend on international developments? Why should a traditionally domestic issue, such as criminal sanctions, be dictated by international bodies or concerns?

3. *The death row phenomenon.*   Many death row inmates spend a decade or more awaiting their execution. While the inmate's appeals frequently cause this delay, a number of foreign countries have declared this so-called death row phenomenon — years on death row under the restrictive conditions imposed by that type of confinement — an unjust punishment in its own right. See, e.g., Soering v. United Kingdom, 11 Eur. H.R. Rep. 439 (Eur. Ct. H.R. 1989). Therefore, countries within the European human rights system as well as Canada no longer extradite individuals to the United States unless they are given explicit guarantees that the prosecution will not request a death sentence at trial. Any defendant successful enough to escape into one of these countries effectively insulates herself from the death penalty. Should a prosecutor consent not to seek a death sentence so that the defendant can be tried in the United States? Or is it preferable not to enter into such agreements?

4. *Consular notification.*   Foreign nationals in the United States have the right to have their consulate notified of their arrest. Many foreign countries provide counsel free of charge to their nationals. Since foreign countries are often willing and able to pay for excellent capital counsel, foreign-national defendants whose home country is not being notified of their need for trial counsel are at a severe disadvantage. Because U.S. law enforcement officials frequently do not notify the representatives of foreign governments, a number of such countries, including Paraguay, Germany, and Mexico, filed suit before the International Court of Justice against the United States for its violation of the consular convention.

In the case of the LaGrand brothers, two German nationals, the ICJ found that by not informing them of their convention rights and subsequently by not permitting review and reconsideration of their convictions and sentences, the United States violated their rights as well as Germany's rights. It also held the United States in breach for failing to take all measures to prevent Walter LaGrand's execution after the ICJ issued a stay order. The court accepted the United States' assurance that it would implement specific measures to comply with its obligations under the convention. Nevertheless, the ICJ required that should German nationals be sentenced to "severe penalties, without their rights under Article 36, paragraph 1(b), of the Convention having been respected, the United States, by means of its own choosing, shall allow the review and reconsideration of the conviction and sentence by taking account of the violation of the rights set forth in that Convention." LaGrand Case (Germany v. United States of America), 40 I.L.M. 1069 (I.C.J. 2001).

PROBLEM 3-3.   MORATORIUM

You are the state governor's chief advisor on criminal justice issues. She has asked for your opinion about whether she should declare a moratorium on the use of capital punishment in the state. She raised the question with you after hearing about the actions of Illinois Governor George Ryan and then receiving a copy of a report from the American Bar Association about the administration of capital punishment. In 1997 the ABA recommended that states not carry out the death penalty "until the jurisdiction implements policies and procedures that are consistent with . . . longstanding American Bar Association policies intended to (1) ensure that death penalty cases are administered fairly and impartially, in accordance with due process, and (2) minimize the risk that innocent persons may be executed. . . ."

The ABA pointed to inadequate defense counsel (and insufficient funding for those lawyers) as one of the central flaws in the system:

> Jurisdictions that employ the death penalty have proven unwilling to establish the kind of legal services system that is necessary to ensure that defendants charged with capital offenses receive the defense they require. Many death penalty states have no working public defender programs, relying instead upon scattershot methods for selecting and supporting defense counsel in capital cases. For example, some states simply assign lawyers at random from a general list — a scheme destined to identify attorneys who lack the necessary qualifications and, worse still, regard their assignments as a burden. Other jurisdictions employ "contract" systems, which typically channel indigent defense business to attorneys who offer the lowest bids. Other states use public defender schemes that appear on the surface to be more promising, but prove in practice to be just as ineffective.
>
> It is scarcely surprising that the results of poor lawyering are often literally fatal for capital defendants. Systematic studies reveal . . . the inexperience of lawyers appointed to represent capital clients. In [many instances, state trial courts have] assigned capital cases to young lawyers who had passed the bar only a few months earlier; [to] a lawyer who had never finished a criminal trial of any kind; and [even] allowed a third-year law student to handle most of a capital trial. . . . Even when experienced and competent counsel are available in capital cases, they often are unable to render adequate service for want of essential funding to pay the costs of investigations and expert witnesses. In some rural counties in Texas, an appointed attorney receives no more than $800 to represent a capital defendant. Similar limits are in place in other states. In Virginia, the hourly rate for capital defense services works out to about $13. In an Alabama case, the lawyer appointed to represent a capital defendant in a widely publicized case was allowed a total of $500 to finance his work, including any investigations and expert services needed. With that budget, it is hardly surprising that the attorney conducted no investigation at all. . . .

Another systematic problem cited by the ABA was more recent: restrictions on the procedures available for capital defendants to get judicial review of legal and factual errors in their trials. The report noted that in 1996, Congress amended the federal habeas corpus statutes to make it "even more difficult for the federal courts to adjudicate federal claims in capital cases."

Finally, the ABA report pointed to race discrimination in the administration of capital punishment:

> Numerous studies have demonstrated that defendants are more likely to be sentenced to death if their victims were white rather than black. Other studies have shown that in some jurisdictions African Americans tend to receive the death penalty more often than do white defendants. And in countless cases, the poor legal services that capital clients receive are rendered worse still by racist attitudes of defense counsel. . . .

As you formulate your advice to the governor, what sources will you consult? What sorts of arguments or evidence will be relevant to her decision?

=4=

Sentencing Inputs: The Crime and Its Effects

Chapter 1 introduced the social purposes of punishment, Chapter 2 surveyed the groups and individuals who create sentencing rules and impose sentences, and Chapter 3 offered two case studies of sentencing systems designed to control discretion. Along the way, you became familiar with the basic contours of sentencing guidelines and the capital punishment system. Building on this foundation, we now turn to the substantive components of sentencing decisions, starting in this chapter with the relevance of the crime and its effects. In Chapter 5 we consider the background and characteristics of the criminal offender. Together, these two chapters address the raw materials of the sentencing decision, what we call "sentencing inputs."

Sentencing practice always informs sentencing theory. Hence, our discussion of the crime and its effects begins with an introductory sentencing exercise. The exercise calls on you to sentence a mythical criminal offender, Rob Anon, and introduces you to the difficulties of selecting a criminal punishment, even in this seemingly simple case. Throughout the next two chapters, we return to Rob's case periodically to see whether our detailed study of sentencing systems changes your initial perspective on Rob's status.

PROBLEM 4-1. ROB ANON

A jury found Rob Anon guilty of one count of armed bank robbery. The evidence at trial proved that Rob planned the robbery and then recruited his two co-defendants to participate. According to the testimony of co-defendant Zweite (who pled guilty to the charge pursuant to a plea agreement with the government), Rob gave each participant in the robbery a firearm and a ski mask. Rob also provided a getaway car, although the origins and current location of the car remain unknown.

According to the testimony at trial, the activities of the three defendants inside the bank were as follows: Rob disabled the surveillance cameras and alarms; co-defendant Tercero kept his firearm pointed at the teller while Zweite vaulted the counter and collected more than $200,000 in cash. As the threesome hurried out of the bank, Tercero pushed to the ground an elderly man who walked into the bank during the robbery. The man broke his hip when he fell. In dividing the loot, Rob gave Zweite and Tercero one-fourth of the proceeds each, keeping half for himself.

The government's evidence at Rob's trial included surveillance photos, eyewitnesses, physical evidence, and testimony by Zweite and Tercero. From the moment of his indictment and throughout his prosecution, Rob denied responsibility for the robbery and claimed he was "set up."

Rob is 22 years old, and has produced a spotty employment record since dropping out of high school at age 16. Rob was last employed in a series of construction projects with a local landscaping company; he previously worked for a shoe store as a salesman on a part-time basis. Reared by a single mother in an economically depressed urban area and the second youngest of five children, Rob seems to have few friends and mostly keeps to himself. Rob's mother recalls that Rob's siblings taunted and teased him because of his small stature. She believes that Rob became addicted to cocaine in the past year.

Rob's criminal record includes two prior offenses. Six years ago, a juvenile court convicted Rob for shoplifting and sentenced him to 100 hours of community service. Two years ago, Rob was convicted of receipt of stolen goods and sentenced to three years' probation. Rob was still serving that term of probation at the time of the bank robbery. Armed bank robbery carries a maximum penalty of 25 years in prison or a fine of $250,000 or both. Compare http://www.ussc.gov/training/ws_ex_rob.pdf.

1. Assume you are the sentencing judge for Rob in a jurisdiction that places no limits on your discretion to choose a sentence ranging anywhere from probation to the statutory maximum. What sentence would you impose? If you feel you need more information before choosing a sentence, what additional information would you seek?
2. If the robbers had taken less money (say, only $500), would your sentencing decision change?
3. If the elderly man had not been injured, would your sentencing decision change?
4. If you knew that Zweite received a sentence of five years' probation as a result of a plea agreement, would your sentencing decision change?

A. WHICH CRIME?

It is often said that the punishment must fit the crime. This is true, but radically incomplete. Sentencing judges consider more than the crime — they also consider other wrongdoing by the offender, some of it proven during the criminal trial and some of it not mentioned until the presentence investigation or the sentencing hearing. Some conduct constitutes a separate crime, while some of the wrongdoing is not criminal at all. What guidance does the law give to the sentencing judge, who must sort out the defendant's various forms of wrongdoing?

1. Real Offense Versus Conviction Offense

It might seem obvious (to lawyers, at any rate) that defendants can be punished only for the crimes of which they have been *convicted*. Obvious, perhaps, but that is not the law in most jurisdictions. To varying degrees, sentencing laws allow judges to impose punishments based on the "real offense" and not just for the offense of conviction.

Uses for Uncharged Conduct

How can defendants be punished for acts that are not the basis for a conviction? Under an indeterminate sentencing system, the sentencing judge can consider any evidence of the offender's wrongdoing, regardless of whether the conduct formed the basis of the criminal charges. The statutory floor and ceiling for punishing the crime of conviction leave the judge with plenty of latitude to set a punishment, even if it is based in part on uncharged conduct. It is difficult to define offenses in sufficient detail to capture the facts that intuition suggests should affect the sentence. According to the Supreme Court in Williams v. New York, 337 U.S. 241 (1949) (reprinted in Chapter 2), the importance of "individualizing punishments" supports the "age-old practice of seeking information from out-of-court sources" and means that sentencing judges should "not be denied an opportunity to obtain pertinent information by a requirement of rigid adherence to restrictive rules of evidence properly applicable to the trial."

Even structured sentencing systems tend to allow a *range* of presumptive sentences, and when choosing a sentence within that range, a judge may account for circumstances that the elements of the crime cannot cover. Structured systems also usually allow judges to depart up or down from the range of preferred sentences, based on specified details of the crime such as the use of a weapon or the amount of loss or harm inflicted. In death penalty cases, facts about the "real offense" can determine life or death, as capital statutes make murderers eligible for the death penalty only if the killing involved specific "aggravating circumstances."

Types of Uncharged Conduct

Judges receive information about conduct beyond the offense itself from several sources: in plea agreements or during trial, in presentence investigation reports, and from prosecutors during the sentencing hearing. Even if a prosecutor ignores or is unaware of some wrongdoing, a probation officer or other presentence investigator may discover this conduct and the judge may still take it into account.

The defendant's uncharged conduct might be an *element* of an offense other than the one charged. For instance, the defendant may have used a gun during the robbery, even though the charge was robbery and not armed robbery. Other facts about the offense, such as the defendant's role in a multiparty offense, may receive no mention in the statutory framework. The extra information could involve criminal conduct that is *conceptually connected* to the charged crime, such as uncharged criminal conduct that happened during the same time period as the charged crime, or uncharged conduct that was part of the same overarching criminal scheme. Finally, the court might rely on the defendant's past *noncriminal* conduct that is nevertheless blameworthy.

When a judge looks at the defendant's behavior beyond the facts necessary to prove the offense of conviction, the judge is said to be considering (to use the vernacular of the federal sentencing guidelines) "relevant conduct." Under indeterminate sentencing, it was possible for a judge to consider all this information, though judges could reject some of it as irrelevant or unreliable. Structured sentencing brought the issue of relevant conduct to a more formal and visible level. Legislatures, sentencing commissions, and judges must now decide explicitly which additional facts a sentencing judge may or may not consider and how much impact the uncharged relevant conduct should have. The sentencing laws that allow the judge to consider uncharged conduct are sometimes called "real offense" systems (as opposed to "charge offense" systems) because the judge sentences based on the "real" criminal behavior, independent of the prosecutor's charging decisions.

Practical Impact of Limiting Use of Uncharged Conduct

The key fact to remember about relevant conduct is the difference in methods of proof at trial and at sentencing. At trial, the prosecution must prove all elements of the crime to a jury, beyond a reasonable doubt. At a noncapital sentencing hearing, the prosecution proves any additional relevant facts to the sentencing judge by a preponderance of the evidence. Thus, any decision to restrict the judge's consideration of relevant conduct for sentencing also makes it harder for the prosecutor to use facts proven by a preponderance of evidence at the sentencing hearing. At the same time, rules that limit the use of uncharged conduct make the charges that the prosecutor selects all the more important; such rules make it more difficult for the judge to "correct" any perceived problems with the prosecutor's selection of charges. As you consider the material below sketching various approaches to the problem of uncharged conduct, keep in mind the effects of the rules on prosecutors, in a world where the law places few limits on the prosecutor's choice among potential criminal charges.

|| *U.S. Sentencing Guidelines Manual* ||

§1B1.3(a) Relevant Conduct (Factors that Determine the Guideline Range)

[The seriousness of the offense] shall be determined on the basis of the following:

    (1)(A) all acts and omissions committed, aided, abetted, counseled, commanded, induced, procured, or willfully caused by the defendant; and

(B) in the case of a jointly undertaken criminal activity (a criminal plan . . . undertaken by the defendant in concert with others, whether or not charged as a conspiracy), all reasonably foreseeable acts and omissions of others in furtherance of the jointly undertaken criminal activity,

that occurred during the commission of the offense of conviction, in preparation for that offense, or in the course of attempting to avoid detection or responsibility for that offense. . . .

(3) all harm that resulted from the acts and omissions specified in [subsection (a)(1)], and all harm that was the object of such acts and omissions. . . .

|| ***United States v. Vernon Watts*** ||
519 U.S. 148 (1997)

PER CURIAM

[The] Court of Appeals for the Ninth Circuit held that sentencing courts could not consider conduct of the defendants underlying charges of which they had been acquitted. Every other Court of Appeals has held that a sentencing court may do so, if the Government establishes that conduct by a preponderance of the evidence. [Because the Ninth Circuit's holding conflicts with] the clear implications of 18 U.S.C. §3661, the Sentencing Guidelines, and this Court's decisions, particularly Witte v. United States, 515 U.S. 389 (1995), we grant the petition and reverse.

[Police] discovered cocaine base in a kitchen cabinet and two loaded guns and ammunition hidden in a bedroom closet of Watts' house. A jury convicted Watts of possessing cocaine base with intent to distribute, in violation of 21 U.S.C. §841(a)(1), but acquitted him of using a firearm in relation to a drug offense, in violation of 18 U.S.C. §924(c). Despite Watts' acquittal on the firearms count, the District Court found by a preponderance of the evidence that Watts had possessed the guns in connection with the drug offense. In calculating Watts' sentence, the court therefore added two points to his base offense level under [the federal sentencing guidelines. The court of appeals held that a sentencing judge may not, under any standard of proof, rely on facts of which the defendant was acquitted].

We begin our analysis with 18 U.S.C. §3661, which codifies the longstanding principle that sentencing courts have broad discretion to consider various kinds of information. The statute states: "No limitation shall be placed on the information concerning the background, character, and conduct of a person convicted of an offense which a court of the United States may receive and consider for the purpose of imposing an appropriate sentence."

We reiterated this principle in Williams v. New York, 337 U.S. 241 (1949), in which a defendant convicted of murder and sentenced to death challenged the sentencing court's reliance on information that the defendant had been involved in 30 burglaries of which he had not been convicted. We contrasted the different limitations on presentation of evidence at trial and at sentencing: "Highly relevant — if not essential — to [the judge's] selection of an appropriate sentence is the possession of the fullest information possible concerning the defendant's life and characteristics." Neither the broad language of §3661 nor our holding in *Williams* suggests any basis for the courts to invent a blanket prohibition against considering certain types of evidence at sentencing. Indeed, under the pre-Guidelines sentencing regime, it was well established that a sentencing judge may take into account facts introduced at trial relating to other charges, even ones of which the defendant has been acquitted.

The Guidelines did not alter this aspect of the sentencing court's discretion. Very roughly speaking, relevant conduct corresponds to those actions and circumstances that courts typically took into account when sentencing prior to the Guidelines' enactment. Section 1B1.4 of the Guidelines reflects the policy set forth in 18 U.S.C. §3661: "In determining the sentence to impose within the guideline range, or whether a departure from the guidelines is warranted, the court may consider, without limitation, any information concerning the background, character and conduct of the defendant, unless otherwise prohibited by law."

Section 1B1.3, in turn, describes in sweeping language the conduct that a sentencing court may consider in determining the applicable guideline range. The commentary to that section states: "Conduct that is not formally charged or is not an element of the offense of conviction may enter into the determination of the applicable guideline sentencing range." With respect to certain offenses, . . . USSG §1B1.3(a)(2) requires the sentencing court to consider "all acts and omissions . . . that were part of the same course of conduct or common scheme or plan as the offense of conviction." Application Note 3 . . . gives the following example: "Where the defendant engaged in three drug sales of 10, 15, and 20 grams of cocaine, as part of the same course of conduct or common scheme or plan, subsection (a)(2) provides that the total quantity of cocaine involved (45 grams) is to be used to determine the offense level even if the defendant is convicted of a single count charging only one of the sales." Accordingly, the Guidelines conclude that "relying on the entire range of conduct, regardless of the number of counts that are alleged *or on which a conviction is obtained,* appears to be the most reasonable approach to writing workable guidelines for these offenses."

Although the dissent concedes that a district court may properly consider "evidence adduced in a trial that resulted in an acquittal" when choosing a particular sentence within a guideline range, it argues that the court must close its eyes to acquitted conduct at earlier stages of the sentencing process because the "broadly inclusive language of §3661" is incorporated only into §1B1.4 of the Guidelines. This argument ignores §1B1.3 which, as we have noted, directs sentencing courts to consider all other related conduct, whether or not it resulted in a conviction. The dissent also contends that because Congress instructed the Sentencing Commission, in 28 U.S.C. §994(*l*), to ensure that the Guidelines provide incremental punishment for a defendant who is convicted of multiple offenses, it could not have meant for the Guidelines to increase a sentence based on offenses of which a defendant has been acquitted. The statute is not, however, cast in restrictive or exclusive terms. Far from limiting a sentencing court's power to consider uncharged or acquitted conduct, §994(*l*) simply ensures that, at a minimum, the Guidelines provide additional penalties when defendants are convicted of multiple offenses. . . . In short, we are convinced that a sentencing court may consider conduct of which a defendant has been acquitted.

As we explained in Witte v. United States, 515 U.S. 389 (1995), . . . sentencing enhancements do not punish a defendant for crimes of which he was not convicted, but rather increase his sentence because of the manner in which he committed the crime of conviction. In *Witte,* we held that a sentencing court could, consistent with the Double Jeopardy Clause, consider uncharged cocaine importation in imposing a sentence on marijuana charges that was within the statutory range, without precluding the defendant's subsequent prosecution for the cocaine offense. We concluded that "consideration of information about the defendant's character and conduct at sentencing does not result in 'punishment' for any offense other than the one of which the defendant was convicted." Rather, the defendant is "punished only for the fact that the *present* offense was carried out in a manner that warrants increased punishment."

The Court of Appeals failed to appreciate the significance of the different standards of proof that govern at trial and sentencing. [Acquittal] on criminal charges does not prove that the defendant is innocent; it merely proves the existence of a reasonable doubt as to his guilt. [It] is impossible to know exactly why a jury found a defendant not guilty on a certain charge. Thus, contrary to the Court of Appeals' assertion . . . , the jury cannot be said to have "necessarily rejected" any facts when it returns a general verdict of not guilty.

For these reasons, an acquittal in a criminal case does not preclude the Government from relitigating an issue when it is presented in a subsequent action governed by a lower standard of proof. The Guidelines state that it is "appropriate" that facts relevant to sentencing be proved by a preponderance of the evidence, USSG §6A1.3 commentary, and we have held that application of the preponderance standard at sentencing generally satisfies due process. McMillan v. Pennsylvania, 477 U.S. 79, 91-92 (1986). . . . We therefore hold that a jury's verdict of acquittal does not prevent the sentencing court from considering conduct underlying the acquitted charge, so long as that conduct has been proved by a preponderance of the evidence.

[In this case], the jury acquitted the defendant of using or carrying a firearm during or in relation to the drug offense. That verdict does not preclude a finding by a preponderance of the evidence that the defendant did, in fact, use or carry such a weapon, much less that he simply *possessed* the weapon in connection with a drug offense.

STEVENS, J., dissenting.

The Sentencing Reform Act of 1984 revolutionized the manner in which district courts sentence persons convicted of federal crimes. . . . Strict mandatory rules have dramatically confined the exercise of judgment based on a totality of the circumstances. . . .

In 1970, during the era of individualized sentencing, Congress enacted the statute now codified as 18 U.S.C. §3661 to make it clear that otherwise inadmissible evidence could be considered by judges in the exercise of their sentencing discretion. The statute, however, did not tell the judge how to weigh the significance of any of that evidence. The judge was free to rely on any information that might shed light on a decision to grant probation, to impose the statutory maximum, or to determine the precise sentence within those extremes. Wisdom and experience enabled the judge to give appropriate weight to uncorroborated hearsay or to evidence of criminal conduct that had not resulted in a conviction. . . . Like a jury in a capital case, the judge could exercise discretion to dispense mercy on the basis of factors too intangible to write into a statute.

Although the Sentencing Reform Act of 1984 has cabined the discretion of sentencing judges, the 1970 statute remains on the books. As was true when it was enacted, §3661 does not speak to questions concerning the relevance or the weight of any item of evidence. That statute is not offended by provisions in the Guidelines that proscribe reliance on evidence of economic hardship, drug or alcohol dependence, or lack of guidance as a youth, in making certain sentencing decisions. Conversely, that statute does not command that any particular weight—or indeed that any weight at all—be given to evidence that a defendant may have committed an offense that the prosecutor failed to prove beyond a reasonable doubt. . . .

A closer examination of the interaction among §3661, the other provisions of the Sentencing Reform Act, and the Guidelines demonstrates that the role played by §3661 is of a narrower scope than the Court's opinion suggests. The Sentencing Reform Act was enacted primarily to address Congress' concern that similar offenders convicted of similar offenses were receiving an unjustifiably wide range of sentences. . . . The [statute requires] that for any sentence of imprisonment in the Guidelines, "the maximum of the range established for such a term shall not exceed the minimum of that range by more than the greater of 25 percent or 6 months," 28 U.S.C. §994(b)(2). The determination of which of these narrow ranges a particular sentence should fall into is made by operation of mandatory rules, but within the particular range, the judge retains broad discretion to set a particular sentence.

By their own terms, the Guidelines incorporate the broadly inclusive language of §3661 only into those portions of the sentencing decision in which the judge retains discretion. [The] Guidelines Manual §1B1.4 provides: "In determining the sentence to impose within the guideline range, or whether a departure from the guidelines is warranted, the court may consider, without limitation, any information concerning the background, character and conduct of the defendant, unless otherwise prohibited by law. See 18 U.S.C. §3661."

Thus, as in the pre-Guidelines sentencing regime, it is in the area in which the judge exercises discretion that §3661 authorizes unlimited access to information concerning the background, character, and conduct of the defendant. When the judge is exercising such discretion, I agree that he may consider otherwise inadmissible evidence, including evidence adduced in a trial that resulted in an acquittal. But that practice, enshrined in §3661 and USSG §1B1.4, sheds little, if any, light on the appropriateness of the District Courts' application of USSG §1B1.3, which defines relevant conduct for the purposes of determining the Guidelines range within which a sentence can be imposed. . . .

In 28 U.S.C. §994(*l*) Congress specifically directed the Commission to ensure that the Guidelines included incremental sentences for multiple offenses. That subsection provides: "The Commission shall insure that the Guidelines promulgated [reflect] the appropriateness of imposing an incremental penalty for each offense in a case in which a defendant is convicted of (A) multiple offenses committed in the same course of conduct . . . and (B) multiple offenses committed at different times. . . ." It is difficult to square this explicit statutory command to impose incremental punishment for each of the "multiple offenses" of which a defendant "is convicted" with the conclusion that Congress intended incremental punishment for each offense of which the defendant has been acquitted. . . .

In my opinion the statute should be construed in the light of the traditional requirement that criminal charges must be sustained by proof beyond a reasonable doubt. That requirement has always applied to charges involving multiple offenses as well as a single offense. Whether an allegation of criminal conduct is the sole basis for punishment or merely one of several bases for punishment, we should presume that Congress intended the new sentencing Guidelines that it authorized in 1984 to adhere to longstanding procedural requirements enshrined in our constitutional jurisprudence. The notion that a charge that cannot be sustained by proof beyond a reasonable doubt may give rise to the same punishment as if it had been so proved is repugnant to that jurisprudence. I respectfully dissent.

|| **Charles Frederick Barr v. State** ||
674 So. 2d 628 (Fla. 1996)

HARDING, J.

. . . Charles Frederick Barr stole a car at gunpoint. Thereafter, when a police officer spotted the stolen car and attempted to pull the car over, Barr fled. A high speed chase followed in heavy traffic, nearly causing several accidents. Barr was charged with armed robbery and possession of a firearm by a convicted felon.

A jury convicted Barr of armed robbery. He was sentenced to twenty-five years in prison, which was an upward departure from Barr's recommended guideline sentence of seven to nine years, with a permitted range of five and one-half to twelve years. The trial court entered a written departure order, reasoning that Barr displayed a flagrant disregard for the safety of others by recklessly driving during the chase with the police and endangering the lives of numerous innocent citizens. . . .

Barr argues that Florida Rule of Criminal Procedure 3.701(d)(11) . . . prohibits upward departure sentences when the conduct can be separately charged as another crime. Barr further argues that a contrary holding would eliminate a defendant's constitutional right to a trial as it would permit sentencing for a crime for which the defendant has not been convicted. Thus, he contends, a defendant must be charged and convicted for each instance of criminal conduct.

The State argues, however, that Florida Statutes §921.0016, which includes endangering the lives of many persons as a valid reason for upward departure sentences, controls the instant case instead of Rule 3.701(d)(11). Section 921.0016 addresses recommended sentences and departure sentences. [The statute lists a number of aggravating circumstances that reasonably justify departure from the sentencing guidelines, such as the creation of a "substantial risk of death or great bodily harm to many persons."]

We find that §921.0016 is not applicable to the instant case as it only applies to offenses committed on or after January 1, 1994. Barr was arrested and charged on November 24, 1993. Instead, we look to the language of Rule 3.701(d)(11) to determine whether departure was proper in this case. Rule 3.701(d)(11) provides that "[r]easons for deviating from the guidelines shall not include factors relating to . . . the instant offenses for which convictions have not been obtained."

As this Court explained in State v. Tyner, 506 So. 2d 405 (Fla. 1987), the language of Rule 3.701(d)(11) is "plain" and specifically provides that judges "may consider only that conduct of the defendant relating to an element of the offense for which he has been convicted." *Tyner* involved a defendant originally charged with two counts of first-degree murder and one count of armed burglary. After the murder counts were dismissed, the defendant was convicted of armed burglary. The defendant's departure sentence was invalidated because it was based upon the murders for which Tyner had not yet been found guilty. We concluded that "[to] hold otherwise would effectively circumvent the basic requirement of obtaining a conviction before meting out punishment."

We adhered to this position in State v. Varner, 616 So. 2d 988 (Fla. 1993), and specifically held that "departure may not be based on conduct that could have, but has not yet, resulted in criminal conviction." Varner was convicted of shooting into a building, shooting into a vehicle, and aggravated assault. Prior to his trial, Varner allegedly threatened a witness and the trial court entered a departure sentence based in part upon that threat. On appeal, the district court found this to be an invalid reason for departure. In our review of the case, we approved the district court's decision and explained that "[if] the State wishes to punish such collateral misconduct, the proper method is to separately charge and convict." . . .

Relying upon the reasoning in . . . *Tyner* and *Varner*, a departure sentence based on flagrant disregard for the safety of others is not valid where the conduct at issue could be separately charged and convicted. See, e.g., Felts v. State, 537 So. 2d 995 (Fla. App. 1988) (finding that high speed chase and resulting fatal accident were not valid basis for departure because they involved circumstances surrounding the offense for which convictions were not obtained). However, where the conduct evincing such disregard involves a situation where the conduct could not be separately charged as another crime it can be a valid reason for departure. See, e.g., *Felts* (finding that gun battle with Georgia police officers which posed unnecessary risk of harm was valid basis for departure where the subsequent Georgia convictions for aggravated assault could not be factored into scoresheet); Burgess v. State, 524 So. 2d 1132 (Fla. App. 1988) (upholding departure based on flagrant disregard for safety of others where defendant shot two victims who were standing in an alley while three bystanders stood nearby).

In the instant case, the auto chase that ensued after the officer attempted to stop Barr constituted criminal conduct. Barr could have been charged either with fleeing or attempting to elude a law enforcement officer pursuant to Florida Statutes §316.1935(1), or with reckless driving pursuant to Florida Statutes §316.192(1). Thus, this criminal conduct for which Barr was neither charged nor convicted cannot be a valid reason for a departure sentence. Moreover, while it is not determinative of our conclusion here, we note that Barr's departure sentence far exceeds any sentence that could have been imposed if he had been convicted of the uncharged offenses of eluding a police officer or reckless driving. [At the time of Barr's arrest, fleeing or attempting to elude an officer was punishable by imprisonment for a period not to exceed one year. Reckless driving is punishable for up to 90 days' imprisonment for a first offense and up to six months imprisonment for a second offense.] Accordingly, we quash the decision below and remand for imposition of an appropriate guideline sentence. . . . It is so ordered.

NOTES

1. *Relevant conduct in state sentencing: majority position.*   Sentencing judges in indeterminate sentencing systems have the power (but not the obligation) to consider any conduct of the defendant, whether charged or uncharged. This conduct might influence the judge's choice of a maximum or minimum sentence from within the broad statutory range. See State v. O'Donnell, 495 A.2d 798, 803 (Me. 1985) ("we find nothing objectionable in treating trial evidence of a defendant's uncharged conduct regarding other victims as relevant information for sentencing purposes on the ground that it indicates a continuing course of conduct over a substantial period of time"); Anderson v. People, 337 P.2d 10 (Colo. 1959) (conviction for forgery; evidence at sentencing of forgeries submitted to six additional victims); see also Williams v. New York, 337 U.S. 961 (1949) (death sentence imposed by judge based on presentence report suggesting defendant had been involved in "30 other burglaries" in area of murder).

States with more structured sentencing systems place more restrictions on the use of the defendant's uncharged conduct. Formally, the structured state systems adopt charge offense rather than real offense sentencing. The charged offense determines a fairly small range of options available to the judge in the normal case. But real and charge offense concepts define the ends of a spectrum, and all systems allow some amount of real offense conduct to affect the sentencing determination. At a minimum, the uncharged conduct is available to influence the judge's selection of a sentence *within* the narrow range that the guidelines designate for typical cases. Some states go further and allow judges to use uncharged conduct as a basis for a departure from the designated normal range of sentences. Other structured sentencing states (such as Florida) prevent the judge from using some types of uncharged conduct to depart from the guideline sentence. Commentary to the Minnesota sentencing guidelines states that "departures from the guidelines should not be permitted for elements of alleged offender behavior not within the definition of the offense of conviction." Minn. Stat. Ann. §244 cmt. II.D.103. The ABA Standards for Criminal Justice, Sentencing 18-3.6 (3d ed. 1994), also opts for an offense-of-conviction model.

2. *Relevant conduct in federal sentencing.*   In contrast to the states, the federal guidelines create a modified real offense system. In a 1995 self-study report, the U.S. Sentencing Commission described the tradeoffs at stake in framing a relevant conduct provision:

> If uncharged misconduct is considered, punishment is based on facts proven outside procedural protections constitutionally defined for proving criminal charges, introducing an argument of unfairness. . . . The scope of conduct considered at sentencing will also affect, at least to some extent, the complexity of a sentencing system. The scope can be as limited as the conduct defined by the elements of the offense or as broad as any wrongdoing ever committed by the defendant or the defendant's partners in crime. All things being equal, a large scope of considered conduct will require more fact-finding than a more limited scope. . . . Besides fairness and complexity, the scope of conduct considered at sentencing may have serious implications for the balance between prosecutorial and judicial power in sentencing. For example, if the scope of considered conduct is confined to the offense of conviction, many argue that the sentencing system will provide relatively more power to prosecutors to

control sentences. . . . Finding the right balance among fairness, complexity, and the role of the prosecutor has been a struggle for sentencing commissions generally. . . .

Discussion Paper, Relevant Conduct and Real Offense Sentencing (1995) (available at http://www.ussc.gov/simple/relevant.htm). The federal system uses the offense of conviction as a starting point for guideline calculations but then requires many adjustments (and permits a few discretionary adjustments) to the offense level based on other relevant conduct.

The commission explained its support for real offense factors on several grounds. First, such a system mirrored prior practices in the indeterminate system. It also gave judges a means to refine and rationalize the chaotic federal criminal code. Finally, the real offense features of the system gave judges a way to check the prosecutor's power to dictate a sentence based on the selection of charges. When the rules allow the trial judge to look behind the charged offense to select a sentence based on the real offense conduct, the judge serves as a counterweight to the prosecutor. See Julie R. O'Sullivan, In Defense of the U.S. Sentencing Guidelines' Modified Real-Offense System, 91 Nw. U. L. Rev. 1342 (1997).

The use of relevant conduct to enhance sentences in the federal system has come under sharp attack from scholars. See Kate Stith and Jose A. Cabranes, Fear of Judging: Sentencing Guidelines in the Federal Courts 66-77 (1998); Elizabeth Lear, Is Conviction Irrelevant?, 40 UCLA L. Rev. 1179 (1993); David Yellen, Illusion, Illogic and Injustice: Real-Offense Sentencing and the Federal Sentencing Guidelines, 78 Minn. L. Rev. 403 (1993). Critics have attacked the uses of uncharged or dismissed conduct as bad policy because of the uncertain proof of the uncharged conduct during the sentencing hearing. They also point out the difficulty of remaining consistent from case to case in deciding how much uncharged conduct is relevant. They also have raised constitutional questions about whether reliance on such information violates due process (by punishing a person for conduct that is not proven beyond a reasonable doubt) or undermines the investigative and charging functions of the grand jury.

3. *Acquitted conduct versus uncharged conduct.* Although indeterminate sentencing systems typically allow judges to consider prior misconduct when setting a sentence, many states make an exception for acquitted conduct — conduct that formed the basis for a charge resulting in an acquittal at trial. Judges in many states have developed common law rules preventing the use of acquitted conduct at sentencing. See State v. Cobb, 732 A.2d 425 (N.H. 1999); Bishop v. State, 486 S.E.2d 887 (Ga. 1997); Anderson v. State, 448 N.E.2d 1180 (Ind. 1983). On the other hand, a roughly equal number of states approve the use of acquitted conduct. State v. Huey, 505 A.2d 1242 (Conn. 1986); State v. Woodlief, 90 S.E. 137 (N.C. 1916); State v. Leiter, 646 N.W.2d 341 (Wis. 2002). Why do so many states limit the use of acquitted conduct but permit sentencing judges to consider prior convictions and prior uncharged conduct more generally?

The Supreme Court in *Watts* confirmed that neither the Constitution nor the federal sentencing statutes or guidelines bar a judge from using acquitted conduct. See also Edwards v. United States, 523 U.S. 511 (1998) (sentencing judge can determine that defendants were trafficking in both crack and powder, even if jury believed defendants were trafficking only in powder). But the Court did not resolve the policy issue of whether the guidelines *should* limit the use of acquitted conduct. Justices Breyer and Scalia, in separate opinions in *Watts* not reprinted above, disagreed about whether 18 U.S.C. §3661 blocks the U.S. Commission from creating such a rule. The statute says that "no limitation shall be placed on the information concerning the background, character, and conduct of a person convicted" that the sentencing judge may "receive and consider." Can the commission limit the use of acquitted conduct, consistent with this statute?

Just before the Court decided *Watts,* the commission did in fact consider several options for limiting the use of acquitted conduct. One option would have excluded "the use of acquitted conduct as a basis for determining the guideline range" but would have allowed upward departures based on acquitted conduct. Another option would have allowed acquitted conduct only if it was proved at sentencing by clear and convincing evidence (rather than the usual preponderance standard). A third option would have allowed judges to use acquitted conduct in setting the guideline range but also would have authorized downward departures from the range to avoid fundamental unfairness. 62 Fed. Reg. 151, 161 (Jan. 2, 1997). In the end, the commission did not adopt any of these options. Why do you suppose the commission kept the status quo? Are sentencing commissions better situated than judges to create limits on the use of acquitted conduct?

4. *Criminal elements versus noncriminal wrongdoing.* As *Barr* shows, some states prevent sentencing judges from considering the defendant's wrongdoing if that conduct could form the basis for additional criminal charges or more serious criminal charges. Other conduct, while blameworthy, does not affect the charging options available to the prosecutor. For example, under the federal criminal code, a mail fraud that nets $10,000 is eligible for the same punishment as a mail fraud that nets $100,000. Should it matter to a sentencing judge (or to a sentencing commission creating sentencing guidelines) whether the conduct in question is an element of some crime for which the defendant was not charged? Consider this approach to the problem in Kan. Stat. §21-4716(b)(3): "If a factual aspect of a crime is a statutory element of the crime . . . that aspect of the current crime of conviction may be used as an aggravating or mitigating factor only if [it] is significantly different from the usual criminal conduct captured by the aspect of the crime."

Review again the provisions of Fla. R. Crim. Proc. 3.701(d)(11) and Fla. Stat. §921.0016, discussed in the *Barr* case. Why did Florida lawmakers generally prohibit sentencing judges from increasing the sentence above the normal guideline range based on "factors relating to . . . the instant offenses for which convictions have not been obtained"? Did the Florida legislature meaningfully change the system when it passed §921.0016(3)(i), which authorizes a departure to a more serious sentence when the offense of conviction "created a substantial risk of death or great bodily harm to many persons"? Should it matter to a sentencing judge whether the defendant's relevant (but uncharged) conduct is recent? What should Florida judges do in cases involving uncharged criminal conduct that is not part of the same transaction or series of events as the crime of conviction?

5. *Conduct after charging.*   Sometimes the defendant's relevant conduct occurs after the government files charges, perhaps during or after the trial. For instance, the law in about 30 states authorizes the sentencing judge to select a higher sentence from within the authorized range if the judge believes the defendant committed perjury at trial. See People v. Redmond, 633 P.2d 976 (Cal. 1981); see also People v. Stewart, 473 N.E.2d 840 (Ill. 1984) (allowing consideration of conduct in jail awaiting trial); Alabama v. Smith, 490 U.S. 794 (1989) (allowing judge who imposes sentence after guilty plea to impose higher sentence on same defendant after appeal and retrial based on information about crime and postconviction conduct). In the federal system, U.S. Sentencing Guidelines Manual §3C1.1 increases the offense level when a defendant obstructs the administration of justice during the prosecution of the offense; this rule can be applied whenever a court finds that the defendant committed perjury at trial. The Supreme Court in United States v. Dunnigan, 507 U.S. 87 (1993), upheld the constitutionality of this provision against a claim that it undermines a defendant's right to testify on his own behalf. But compare Mitchell v. United States, 526 U.S. 314 (1999) (Fifth Amendment privilege against self-incrimination bars judge from drawing inferences about details of crime from defendant's silence at sentencing).

6. *Double jeopardy for enhancing sentences based on prior crimes.*   When criminal conduct gives a sentencing judge the basis for increasing a sentence against a defendant charged with some separate crime, would a later sentence for the original crime constitute multiple punishment for double jeopardy purposes? In Witte v. United States, 515 U.S. 389 (1995), the defendant raised such a claim. Witte was involved in two illegal drug transactions, one in 1990 and the other in 1991. The judge sentencing Witte for the 1991 sale increased the sentence based on the amount of drugs involved in the 1990 sale, because the judge considered the two sales to be part of a single continuing conspiracy. Later, a grand jury indicted Witte for the 1990 sale, and Witte raised a double jeopardy objection because the judge in the earlier proceeding had already punished him for that conduct. The Supreme Court rejected the challenge, noting that sentencing courts have traditionally "considered a defendant's past criminal behavior, even if no conviction resulted from that behavior." The opinion also concluded that the same practice is acceptable under the federal sentencing guidelines: "Regardless of whether particular conduct is taken into account by rule or as an act of discretion, the defendant is still being punished only for the offense of conviction." The state high courts that have addressed a double jeopardy challenge on similar facts have reached the same result. See, e.g., Traylor v. State, 801 S.W.2d 267 (Ark. 1990).

In capital punishment cases, extensive appeals and habeas corpus proceedings lead to the reversal of many convictions. A retrial on the charges can raise some double jeopardy issues. If the jury in the first capital trial imposes a life sentence rather than the death penalty, double jeopardy prevents the prosecutor from seeking a death penalty in the later retrial. But if the jury in the first trial deadlocks on the question of the proper penalty and the judge imposes a life term, the prosecutor remains free to seek the death penalty during a later retrial after the conviction is reversed on appeal. See Sattazahn v. Pennsylvania, 537 U.S. 101 (2003).

7. *Checks on prosecutorial power at sentencing.* Criminal codes typically give prosecutors several options when deciding which (if any) charges to file based on a given set of acts. As the Supreme Court explained in Bordenkircher v. Hayes, 434 U.S. 357, 364 (1978), other institutions generally do not review the prosecutor's choices: "In our system, so long as the prosecutor has probable cause to believe that the accused committed an offense defined by statute, the decision whether or not to prosecute, and what charge to file or bring before a grand jury, generally rests entirely in his discretion." While courts might overturn charging decisions based on racial or other invidious discrimination, the decision in United States v. Armstrong, 517 U.S. 456 (1996), established that defendants face a heavy burden in obtaining pretrial discovery to prove that their prosecutions were racially motivated.

Sentencing rules, at least in theory, can expand the effects of the prosecutor's charging decisions. Guidelines that instruct judges to set the sentence based largely on charge of conviction give the prosecutor more power to influence the sentence, especially since the vast majority of convictions are secured through plea bargains. Do real offense elements in a sentencing system offer sentencing judges a realistic method of reviewing the prosecutor's charging and plea bargaining decisions after conviction? Can a real offense system constrain prosecutorial discretion if it authorizes the prosecutor to prove some conduct at the sentencing hearing under a lower standard of proof? The workloads of prosecutors may affect their willingness to manipulate charges to obtain different sentencing results, since prosecutors with heavy dockets might simply carry forward traditional charging patterns.

8. *The importance of presentence investigations.* Judges often rely heavily on the investigatory work of probation officers or other court personnel, embodied in a presentence report. Historically, in indeterminate sentencing systems that expressly pursued rehabilitative goals, such presentence investigations and reports focused on defendants' character and background to assess their amenability to various rehabilitative possibilities. With structured sentencing systems now considering real offense conduct more formally, these presentence investigations sometimes have been transformed into initial evaluations of defendants' relevant conduct. Especially in the federal system, commentators have expressed concerns about the role of probation officers' efforts on guidelines calculations. See, e.g., Kate Stith and Jose A. Cabranes, Fear of Judging: Sentencing Guidelines in the Federal Courts 87-91 (1998). Some defense attorneys have complained that probation officers often act as a sort of "second prosecutor" by uncovering aggravating facts or additional wrongdoing by defendants that did not come to light at trial or in plea negotiations. See, e.g., Felicia Sarner, "Fact Bargaining" Under the Sentencing Guidelines: The Role of the Probation Department, 8 Fed. Sentencing Rep. 328 (1996).

PROBLEM 4-2. ROB ANON REVISITED

Recall the case of Rob Anon, described in Problem 4-1. As a probation officer assigned to prepare a presentence report before Rob's sentencing, would you spend any time investigating the background and status of the getaway car used in the robbery? As a sentencing judge in an indeterminate sentencing jurisdiction, would evidence that the getaway car had been reported stolen influence the sentence you select? Suppose this evidence comes to light right before sentencing when the prosecutor reports that the car had just been recovered. Should a sentencing judge in such a situation hold an evidentiary hearing to give Rob and his lawyer a chance to respond to the car theft allegation? As a member of a state sentencing commission, would you want to draft guidelines that instruct judges to consider (or not to consider) facts such as these? Should such a commission also draft procedural rules to govern this sort of factfinding?

2.   *Multiple Convictions*

Many defendants are convicted of more than one crime at trial, and the judge imposes sentences for the multiple convictions during a single sentencing hearing. The judge might impose sentences on the different convictions to run concurrently (all the terms begin at the same time) or consecutively (a second sentence starts after the first one ends). Even if the judge imposes concurrent sentences, he might increase the sentence for the most serious charge to reflect the fact that the defendant committed multiple crimes. States have created a variety of rules to guide sentencing judges as they account for multiple convictions.

Justice (then Judge) Stephen Breyer used the following example to illustrate traditional practices involving multiple convictions:

Column A	Column B
1. *D*, in a brawl, injures one person seriously.	1. *D*, in a brawl, injures six persons seriously.
2. *D* sells 100 grams of cocaine.	2. *D* sells 600 grams of cocaine.
3. *D* robs one bank.	3. *D* robs six banks.

Most persons react to these examples in accordance with two principles: [First, the] behavior in Column B warrants more severe punishment with respect to each example than the behavior in the Column A. [Second, the] punishment for behavior in Column B . . . should not be six times as severe as that in Column A. . . . These two widely held principles, or perceptions, make it difficult to write rules that properly treat "multiple counts."

Some state commissions have dealt with this problem by giving the trial judge considerable discretion as to whether to sentence defendants convicted of several counts consecutively or concurrently. A moment's thought suggests, however, that this approach leaves the prosecutor and the judge free to construct almost any sentence whatsoever. . . .

Other guidelines have distinguished among types of crimes, requiring, for example, concurrent sentences for multiple counts charging property crimes but consecutive sentences for crimes against the person. This approach, however, violates both principles. It violates the first principle with respect to property crimes, since it would treat the Column B defendants no more severely than the Column A defendants; it violates the second principle with respect to crimes against the person, because it is too severe. The federal Commission has tried to satisfy both principles through a system that treats additional counts as warranting additional punishment but in progressively diminishing amounts. . . . The upshot is that a bank robber who robs six banks will receive roughly twice as much (not six times as much punishment) as the robber who robs one bank.

The Federal Sentencing Guidelines and the Key Compromises upon Which They Rest, 17 Hofstra L. Rev. 1, 25-28 (1988). Read the statutes below carefully, and consider how they would guide a sentencing judge in Problem 4-3. Each statute offers judges distinctive guidance in choosing between consecutive and concurrent sentences. The North Carolina statute leaves the decision entirely in the judge's hands. The Indiana statute directs the judge's attention to particular considerations that are relevant to this choice, while the Kansas statute offers no substantive guidance but caps the possible impact of consecutive sentences.

PROBLEM 4-3. TAKE TWO

Review the facts of Problem 4-1. In addition to the bank robbery (which occurred in early December), Rob Anon and his co-defendants pleaded guilty to two other armed robberies. The first, committed on November 12, involved an evening holdup of Joru's Tavern. When Anon, Zweite, and Tercero entered the tavern about 9:00 P.M., Anon acted as lookout while the others took $240 from the tavern cash register. Tercero was armed with a shotgun, and the robbers took wallets and jewelry from three tavern patrons. The proceeds totaled $600.

The second robbery occurred on November 26. It involved the late evening holdup of Mike and Ginny's Tap. Anon, Zweite, and Tercero entered the tavern at 11:20 P.M. Anon was armed with a long-bladed knife, which he held to the throat of tavern owner Virginia Brown, stating, "Where's the money? Give me all of it or I'll slit your throat." Brown sustained a small cut on her right hand when she tried to push the knife away from her throat. One of the other robbers pointed a handgun at tavern patrons. The proceeds this time totaled $225.

Recall that armed robbery is punishable by a prison term of up to 25 years or a fine of up to $250,000 or both. The judge will impose sentences for the bank robbery and the two other robberies at the same time. What sentences are available to a judge applying each of the statutes below?

‖ *North Carolina General Statutes §15A-1340.15* ‖

(a) *Consecutive Sentences.* This Article [setting penalty ranges for particular crimes] does not prohibit the imposition of consecutive sentences. Unless otherwise specified by the court, all sentences of imprisonment run concurrently with any other sentences of imprisonment.

(b) *Consolidation of Sentences.* If an offender is convicted of more than one offense at the same time, the court may consolidate the offenses for judgment and impose a single judgment for the consolidated offenses. The judgment shall contain a sentence disposition specified for the class of offense and prior record level of the most serious offense, and its minimum sentence of imprisonment shall be within the ranges specified for that class of offense and prior record level, unless applicable statutes require or authorize another minimum sentence of imprisonment.

‖ *Indiana Code §35-38-1-7.1(b)* ‖

The court may consider the following factors as aggravating circumstances or as favoring imposing consecutive terms of imprisonment:

(1) The person has recently violated the conditions of any probation, parole, or pardon granted to the person.

(2) The person has a history of criminal or delinquent activity.

(3) The person is in need of correctional or rehabilitative treatment that can best be provided by commitment of the person to a penal facility.

(4) Imposition of a reduced sentence or suspension of the sentence and imposition of probation would depreciate the seriousness of the crime.

(5) The victim of the crime was less than twelve years of age or at least sixty-five years of age.

(6) The victim of the crime was mentally or physically infirm. . . .

(14) The person committed the offense in the presence or within hearing of a person who is less than eighteen years of age who was not the victim of the offense.

‖ *Kansas Statutes §21-4720* ‖

(b) The sentencing judge shall . . . have discretion to impose concurrent or consecutive sentences in multiple conviction cases. . . . In cases where consecutive sentences may be imposed by the sentencing judge, the following shall apply: . . .

(2) The sentencing judge must establish a base sentence for the primary crime. The primary crime is the crime with the highest crime severity ranking. . . .

(4) The total prison sentence imposed in a case involving multiple convictions arising from multiple counts within an information, complaint or indictment cannot exceed twice the base sentence. . . .

(c) The following shall apply for a departure from the presumptive sentence based on aggravating factors within the context of consecutive sentences:

(1) The court may depart from the presumptive limits for consecutive sentences only if the judge finds substantial and compelling reasons to impose a departure sentence for any of the individual crimes being sentenced consecutively.

(2) When a departure sentence is imposed for any of the individual crimes sentenced consecutively, the imprisonment term of that departure sentence shall not exceed twice the maximum presumptive imprisonment term that may be imposed for that crime.

(3) The total imprisonment term of the consecutive sentences, including the imprisonment term for the departure crime, shall not exceed twice the maximum presumptive imprisonment term of the departure sentence following aggravation.

PROBLEM 4-4.   PREDISPOSED TO PRISON

Anthony Soto met an informant and a police officer who was working undercover. The informant asked Soto about drugs, but Soto replied that he was not involved in the sale of drugs at that time. After this conversation, the informant called Soto three times to discuss a purchase of cocaine. Soto finally agreed to locate some cocaine for the informant because Soto was in bad financial shape.

Soto later agreed to meet the informant and the undercover police officer in a parking lot on February 8, where the undercover officer informed Soto that he had $1,300 for an ounce of cocaine. Soto left the area for five minutes and returned with a bag containing 27 grams of cocaine, which he exchanged with the officer for the money. At that meeting, the officer asked Soto if he could buy two or three more ounces of cocaine from him at a later time. Soto responded that it would be no problem. On February 11 Soto again met with the informant and the undercover police officer in the same parking lot to sell two ounces of cocaine for $2,600. Once again, the officer asked Soto at this meeting if he could buy a larger amount later, and Soto again replied that it was no problem.

After the February 11 sale, the informant and the undercover police officer called Soto at least three times a week to arrange a larger sale of cocaine. On March 11 the officer met Soto and asked to buy eight ounces of cocaine. The officer agreed to buy ten ounces for $1,150 per ounce and they arranged a time to meet later in the day. When the officer arrived at a shopping center to meet with Soto, he was wired with a body microphone and had several officers in the area monitoring him. Soto arrived and gave the officer ten ounces of cocaine in exchange for $11,500. After the exchange was completed, Soto was arrested by the backup officers.

Soto was charged with one count of sale of cocaine in the first degree, and the state offered not to charge him with two additional counts if he would testify against two of his accomplices. Soto declined the offer, and the prosecutors amended their complaint by adding two counts. At trial, Soto asserted the defense of entrapment, but the jury found him guilty of three counts of sale of cocaine in the first degree. The sentencing judge imposed concurrent sentences on the three convictions, with the most serious sentence attached to the March 11 sale, count 3, because of the large amount of drugs involved. The judge also increased the sentence for count 3 based on the fact that Soto engaged in multiple sales.

Soto argues on appeal that the sentencing court should not use the fact that the government charged multiple counts of drug violations as a reason to enhance the guideline sentence for some of the counts. He says that such a sentencing rule would permit police officers and prosecutors to manipulate investigative or charging procedures to achieve a specific sentence. For instance, Soto argues that police officers could manipulate the amount of drugs or the number of sales involved, while prosecutors could separate the drug sales into multiple charges to ensure that a higher sentence would be imposed. Soto further argues that permitting police officers and prosecutors to have such discretion creates the potential for racially biased decisions and perpetuates racial disparities in the prosecution of drug crimes. How would you rule? Compare State v. Soto, 562 N.W.2d 299 (Minn. 1997).

NOTES

1. *Multiple counts, indeterminate systems.*   Defendants are often convicted of multiple offenses arising from the same transaction or course of conduct. The sentencing judge in an indeterminate system typically has the discretion to impose separate sentences for the multiple convictions and to decide whether those sentences will be served concurrently or consecutively. The sentencing judge faces such a choice if the defendant was convicted of multiple crimes at one trial, or if the defendant is serving some other criminal sentence at the time of sentencing for the current conviction. As the Indiana Supreme Court put it in Williams v. State, 690 N.E.2d 162, 172 (Ind. 1997), "[i]t is within the trial court's discretion to determine . . . whether multiple sentences are to be concurrent or consecutive. The trial court will be reversed only upon a showing of a manifest abuse of discretion." Judges with complete power over the concurrent or consecutive nature of sentences have tended to give what might be termed a "volume discount." Additional convictions will increase the total sentence served, but in decreasing amounts for each extra conviction. Is there any reason to favor either consecutive or concurrent sentences as the presumptive or normal outcome? Cf. ABA Standards Relating to Sentencing Alternatives and Procedures 18-6.5 (3d ed. 1994) (sentencing court "ordinarily should designate" sentences to be served concurrently).

2. *Multiple counts, structured systems.*   Some state systems limit the judge's ability to adjust a sentence based on multiple convictions. The Kansas statute above offers one example. The grouping rules of the federal sentencing guidelines, designed to address this issue, are particularly complex. The basic strategy of the grouping rules of Chapter 3D of the federal guidelines is to increase the sentence for the most serious crime by diminishing amounts for each extra conviction. You might want to practice using the federal grouping rules; try completing Worksheet B at http://www.ussc.gov/training/worksheets01.pdf and the online exercise at http://www.ussc.gov/training/quizmc.pdf.

But controls over sentences for multiple counts are not a necessary part of sentencing guidelines. Some states start with a presumption of concurrent sentences but direct the sentencing judge to consider specific factors that might lead to a consecutive sentence instead. See Utah Code §76-3-401(1). North Carolina has adopted a highly structured sentencing system, yet judges retain all of their traditional authority to choose between consecutive and concurrent sentences. Does a rule such as North Carolina's undermine the predictability and uniformity of sentences that are the underlying purposes of many guideline sentencing systems?

3. *Special rules for special crimes.*   From time to time, a legislature specifies in a criminal statute that any sentence imposed under the statute must be consecutive rather than concurrent. For instance, under Idaho Code §18-2502(1), a sentence for escape by a prisoner "shall commence at the time [the prisoner] would otherwise have been discharged." Similarly, the Supreme Court in United States v. Gonzales, 520 U.S. 1 (1997), interpreted 18 U.S.C. §924(c) to prevent the federal firearm enhancement from being imposed concurrently with an existing state or federal sentence. Are there general criteria that legislatures might follow in selecting crimes to receive consecutive sentences automatically? See

also 11 Del. C. §1447(c). Should sentencing courts set consecutive or concurrent sentences based on what they believe was the legislative intent of the criminal statute violated by the defendant?

4. *Multiplicity and sentencing.* The rules growing out of the constitutional bar on double jeopardy for the same offense help determine whether the prosecutor can charge multiple crimes based on a single set of related acts. In most states, so long as two crimes each require proof of an element that the other does not require, the prosecutor can file distinct charges, even if they are based on essentially the same conduct. Blockburger v. United States, 284 U.S. 299 (1932). Indeed, so long as the legislature intended to create separate criminal statutes punishing the same conduct, multiple convictions and punishments do not create double jeopardy problems. Missouri v. Hunter, 459 U.S. 359 (1983). Does the law guiding the sentencing judge's choice of consecutive or concurrent sentences supplement these minimal double jeopardy rules aiming to prevent multiple punishments?

The International Criminal Tribunal for Yugoslavia (ICTY) and the International Criminal Tribunal for Rwanda (ICTR) have both addressed the double jeopardy question in connection with multiple charges. The ICTR held that under national and international law "it is acceptable to convict the accused of two offences in relation to the same set of facts in the following circumstances: (1) where the offences have different elements; or (2) where the provisions creating the offences protect different interests; or (3) where it is necessary to record a conviction for both offences in order fully to describe what the accused did." The Prosecutor v. Akayesu, Case No. ICTR-96-4-T, Judgement of Sept. 2, 1998, at para. 468. The court found genocide, crimes against humanity, and war crimes to have different elements and to protect different interests so as to justify multiple convictions arising from the same underlying conduct.

5. *Sentence entrapment and manipulation: majority position.* Entrapment, like other complete criminal defenses, is an all-or-nothing doctrine, allowing no subtlety or gradation in the analysis of government behavior or its effect. Sentencing, defendants claim, is a proper time to make more carefully graded judgments about both the offender's relative culpability (compared to offenders not subject to government encouragement) and the harms more properly attributed to government actions. Claims of sentencing entrapment or sentencing manipulation often arise in drug cases in which the amount of drugs in a transaction can have a major impact on the likely sentence.

Indeterminate sentencing statutes do not tell a judge whether to take corrective action if she believes that government agents attempted to manipulate a sentence. Likewise, most sentencing guidelines do not address the issue of sentencing entrapment or manipulation. A few courts have refused to recognize government behavior as a potential factor at sentencing. See Commonwealth v. Garcia, 659 N.E.2d 741 (Mass. 1996).

More courts have recognized the possibility of accounting for government behavior but have not found facts that support a departure in a particular case. See United States v. Barth, 990 F.2d 422 (8th Cir. 1993); Leech v. State, 66 P.3d 987 (Okla. Crim. App. 2003). A few lower state courts in structured sentencing systems have altered sentences because of investigators' choices. For instance, in State v. Sanchez, 848 P.2d 208 (Wash. Ct. App. 1993), the government arranged a series of three small drug transactions between the defendant and one confidential informant, and the trial court departed downward to a sentence greater than the norm for one buy but less than the norm for three independent buys. Compare Graham v. State, 608 So. 2d 123 (Fla. Dist. Ct. App. 1992) (undercover officer selects location for drug sale at night within 650 feet of school, increasing penalties).

6. *Developing rules for sentence manipulation.*   "Reverse buys"— in which the government agent sells to the target of the investigation and can choose the amount and price to offer — highlight claims about sentencing manipulation, especially in the federal system, where the type and amount of drugs involved in the offense have significant and specified impact on final sentencing ranges. The federal sentencing guidelines instruct judges facing this situation: "If, in a reverse sting operation . . . , the court finds that the government agent set a price for the controlled substance that was substantially below the market value of the controlled substance, thereby leading to the defendant's purchase of a significantly greater quantity of the controlled substance than his available resources would have allowed him to purchase . . . a downward departure may be warranted." U.S. Sentencing Guidelines Manual §2D1.1, cmt. n.17. Is this policy an adequate response to potential government manipulation of the sentence? Perhaps government agents could be required to arrest a suspect whenever they have enough proof to make conviction at trial likely. A court might require the government to state its reasons for continuing its investigation after obtaining enough evidence for a conviction. What reasons might the government give?

7. *Inadequate self-defense and other "partial" substantive criminal law defenses.* Should courts develop refined or modified versions of substantive criminal law defenses other than entrapment, such as self-defense or duress? For instance, a defendant's self-defense argument may not result in an acquittal, but the court may nevertheless rely on the argument to reduce a sentence. Some state sentencing statutes explicitly recognize "partial" or "near-miss" defenses at sentencing: In Tennessee, the court may reduce a sentence if "substantial grounds exist tending to excuse or justify the defendant's criminal conduct, though failing to establish a defense." Tenn. Code §40-35-113(3); see also United States v. Whitetail, 956 F.2d 857 (8th Cir. 1992) (battered woman defense); United States v. Cheape, 889 F.2d 477 (3d Cir. 1989) (duress; defendant participated in robbery at gunpoint). Does the lack of a more refined set of "partial" defenses undermine the purposes of punishment?

8. *Pro-defendant sentencing manipulation and plea bargaining.*   How should a sentencing judge respond if the terms of a plea agreement suggest that the prosecution and defense have not fully disclosed to the court all of the defendant's relevant conduct? See U.S. Sentencing Guidelines Manual §5K2.21 (court may increase sentence above the guideline range to reflect "actual seriousness of the offense" based on conduct underlying a dismissed charge or a charge not pursued, if that conduct did not enter into the selection of the applicable guideline range). Especially in the federal system, there is evidence to suggest that, in perhaps as many as one-third of all cases, prosecutors underreport offense facts that could aggravate a defendant's guidelines sentence in order to secure

a guilty plea. See Stephen J. Schulhofer and Ilene H. Nagel, Plea Negotiations Under the Federal Sentencing Guidelines: Guidelines Circumvention and Its Dynamics in the Post-*Mistretta* Period, 91 Nw. U. L. Rev. 1284 (1997). Should such pro-defendant manipulation of sentencing outcomes concern us as much as (or perhaps even more than) manipulation of offense facts that potentially harm defendants?

3. Role in a Group Offense

The language of crime recognizes that the pecking order in a group crime matters. We often speak of kingpins and bosses, henchmen and mules. To what extent should a sentencing judge consider the relative blameworthiness of defendants who have different roles in the same offense?

‖ U.S. Sentencing Guidelines Manual ‖

§3B1.1 AGGRAVATING ROLE

Based on the defendant's role in the offense, increase the offense level as follows:

(a) If the defendant was an organizer or leader of a criminal activity that involved five or more participants or was otherwise extensive, increase by 4 levels.

(b) If the defendant was a manager or supervisor (but not an organizer or leader) and the criminal activity involved five or more participants or was otherwise extensive, increase by 3 levels.

(c) If the defendant was an organizer, leader, manager, or supervisor in any criminal activity other than described in (a) or (b), increase by 2 levels.

§3B1.2 MITIGATING ROLE

Based on the defendant's role in the offense, decrease the offense level as follows:

(a) If the defendant was a minimal participant in any criminal activity, decrease by 4 levels.

(b) If the defendant was a minor participant in any criminal activity, decrease by 2 levels.

In cases falling between (a) and (b), decrease by 3 levels.

‖ United States v. Donald Carpenter ‖
252 F.3d 230 (2d Cir. 2001)

MESKILL, J.

This appeal arises out of defendant-appellee Donald Carpenter's plea of guilty to conspiring to steal firearms from two Dick's Clothing and Sporting Goods (Dick's) stores located near Syracuse, New York. . . . The mechanics of the conspiracy's firearm theft and resale scheme are not complicated. [Marty Wise, a sales associate at Dick's,] initially approached Carpenter with the plan to steal firearms from Dick's. As part of their scheme, Wise would contact Carpenter and inform him when a specific theft should occur. When Carpenter arrived at Dick's, Wise handed Carpenter a pre-selected firearm. Carpenter then completed the Alcohol, Tobacco and Firearms (ATF) Form 4473 transferring the firearm from Dick's to himself, and Wise signaled to the cashier that Carpenter "was all set" and could leave without paying for the firearm. . . . Carpenter was in charge of disposing of the firearms stolen from Dick's. As a partner in a business named "The Gun Room," which possessed a federal firearms license, Carpenter was able regularly to acquire firearms and subsequently resell them to Dick's and other businesses. . . .

The thefts were discovered by David Murano, the store manager at Dick's, after Carpenter was unable to produce the sales receipt for one of the firearms he allegedly purchased from Dick's. After being confronted by Murano, Carpenter confessed to his and Wise's involvement in numerous firearm thefts from Dick's. A few months later, Carpenter and Wise made a similar confession to ATF agents. [An] ATF audit revealed that between October 1993 and March 1997, the period the conspiracy was active, Carpenter and Wise engaged in fifty separate firearm thefts from Dick's. . . . Wise kept the proceeds from nineteen guns; Carpenter kept the proceeds from nineteen guns; Wise and Carpenter split the proceeds from three guns; and one firearm actually was purchased by Carpenter.

On July 2, 1998, Carpenter pleaded guilty to an information charging him with one count of conspiring to steal firearms from a licensed firearms dealer. . . . At sentencing, the district court heard extensive argument from both parties on the issue of whether Carpenter was entitled to a mitigating role adjustment. The district court then reduced Carpenter's base offense level by three levels pursuant to U.S.S.G. §3B1.2 for his role in the firearm theft conspiracy. . . .

The base offense level for Carpenter's offense was twelve. Because the offense involved 25-49 firearms, the offense level was increased by five levels. The district court then departed downward three levels for a mitigating role adjustment, and two levels for acceptance of responsibility. This resulted in a total offense level of twelve. This offense level, combined with a criminal history category of I, resulted in a guideline imprisonment range of 10 to 16 months. [T]he district court sentenced Carpenter at the lowest end of that range, and ordered him to serve a term of imprisonment of five months, followed by five months in home detention. The district court also ordered Carpenter to pay restitution in the amount of $17,975.04. . . . Wise, who also pleaded guilty to one count of conspiracy to steal firearms from a licensed firearms dealer, was sentenced to a term of imprisonment of fifteen months and ordered to pay restitution in the amount of $18,975.04. . . .

On appeal, the government argues that the district court misapplied U.S.S.G. §3B1.2 as a matter of law when it held that Carpenter was entitled to a mitigating role adjustment on the ground that his conduct was less culpable than that of Wise, his co-conspirator. We agree that the district court erred. . . . We review factual findings underlying the district court's application of the Sentencing Guidelines for clear error, giving due deference to the district court's application of the guidelines to the facts. In applying [this standard], we are mindful that a sentencing court's assessment of the defendant's role in criminal activity is highly fact-specific and depends upon the nature of the defendant's relationship to other participants, the importance of the defendant's actions to the success of the venture, and the defendant's awareness of the nature and scope of the criminal enterprise. . . .

Section 3B1.2 of the Sentencing Guidelines provides for a four-level downward adjustment if the defendant was a "minimal participant" in criminal activity, and a two-level downward adjustment where the defendant was a "minor participant." The commentary to the Guidelines provides that a "minimal role" adjustment applies to a defendant who is "plainly among the least culpable of those involved in the conduct of a group." U.S.S.G. §3B1.2, commentary (n.1). "Under this provision, the defendant's lack of knowledge or understanding of the scope and structure of the enterprise and of the activities of others is indicative of a role as minimal participant." The Guidelines make clear that the "minimal role" adjustment should be used "infrequently." In comparison, a "minor role" adjustment applies to "any participant who is less culpable than most other participants, but whose role could not be described as minimal." U.S.S.G. §3B1.2, commentary (n.3). The Guidelines further provide that a mitigating role adjustment is appropriate if the defendant is "substantially less culpable than the *average participant*." . . .

On numerous occasions we have reiterated that a reduction pursuant to U.S.S.G. §3B1.2 will not be available simply because the defendant played a lesser role than his co-conspirators; to be eligible for a reduction, the defendant's conduct must be "minor" or "minimal" as compared to the average participant in such a crime. Accordingly, the fact that a defendant played a minimal or minor role in his offense vis-à-vis the role of his co-conspirators is insufficient, in and of itself, to justify a mitigating role reduction.

The rationale for such a rule is self-evident. [If] participation in the offense were measured solely in relation to the co-defendants, the anomaly would arise that a deeply involved participant would be rewarded with a downward adjustment, just because his co-defendants were even more culpable. Further, such a result runs contrary to the statutory purposes of sentencing, which are aimed at reducing unwarranted sentencing disparities among defendants with similar records who have been found guilty of similar criminal conduct. . . .

In ruling that Carpenter's base offense level should be reduced by three levels pursuant to §3B1.2 for his role in the conspiracy, the district court found that

> Carpenter's role in the offense is much less culpable than that of Marty Wise, the co-defendant. It's clear from the record that Wise initiated the offense and recruited Carpenter to take part in the thefts and that [Wise] was the one that had unlimited access to the guns, decided which guns would be stolen, when the thefts would take place, et cetera. Wise used Carpenter and four other individuals to accomplish these thefts and reaped the most from the crimes. . . .

Because the district court compared Carpenter's role to that of Wise, rather than to the *average* participant in a similar firearm theft conspiracy, the sentence imposed by the district court must be vacated.

The government next argues that Carpenter's role in the conspiracy and his knowledge of the scope and structure of the conspiracy render him ineligible as a matter of law for a mitigating role adjustment under U.S.S.G. §3B1.2. . . . Because the relevant facts on this issue are clear from the record, we choose to decide the question of Carpenter's entitlement to a mitigating role adjustment in the first instance, rather than remand that determination to the district court for additional factfinding.

Carpenter's active involvement in stealing the firearms from Dick's and re-selling them to various third parties confirms that he played an important and significant part in the conspiracy to violate federal firearms laws to which he pleaded guilty. . . . As a partner in a business that was a federally licensed dealer, Carpenter was able to regularly purchase and transfer firearms without drawing suspicion. This fact was critical to the success of the conspiracy. Further, Carpenter falsely executed the ATF forms that were designed to conceal the thefts of the firearms. Given these facts, we conclude that Carpenter possessed an intimate "knowledge or understanding of the scope and structure of the enterprise" for which he pleaded guilty. U.S.S.G. §3B1.2, commentary (n.1).

The fact that Wise recruited Carpenter for the *first* of fifty firearm thefts does not render Carpenter an unwitting participant in the two and one-half year conspiracy during which he actively and systematically stole firearms and illegally resold them for personal profit. This is not a situation involving the isolated theft of a single firearm; instead, this case involved a scheme designed to deal in stolen firearms. The continuing nature of the conspiracy, coupled with Carpenter's repeated involvement in the firearm thefts and resales, further render Carpenter ineligible for a mitigating role adjustment. . . .

Finally, Carpenter argues . . . that he is entitled to a mitigating role adjustment because the firearms were not used for unlawful purposes. Specifically, Carpenter contends that "the firearms Carpenter obtained were used primarily by him for hunting and target shooting. . . . Unlike many, if not most people involved in gun thefts, Carpenter did not knowingly act as a conduit for supplying weapons in reckless disregard of whether they were to be used in the commission of other illegal acts." Even accepting Carpenter's facts as true, they are irrelevant to our determination of whether Carpenter is entitled to a mitigating role adjustment and, specifically, to the issue of Carpenter's knowledge of the scope and structure of the conspiracy and the scope of his role within that conspiracy. . . .

The judgment imposed by the district court is vacated as to the sentence only and the matter is remanded to the district court with instructions to resentence Carpenter at a base offense level of 15 and a criminal history category of I, which carries a sentencing range of 18-24 months. . . .

NOTES

1. *Impact of role in offense.*   As we saw in the *Carpenter* case, the federal sentencing guidelines decrease the sentence by specific amounts for those who take relatively small roles in an offense carried out by a group. In an indeterminate sentencing system, the judge also traditionally considers the defendant's relative culpability in the group offense. The extent of any decrease or increase based on this factor is impossible to judge. More structured guideline systems in some states may mention the offender's relative culpability in a group offense as one

possible reason to depart from the ordinary sentence range. See Md. Sentencing Guidelines §9.2 (departure below guideline range allowed based on "offender's minor role in the offense"); N.C. Gen. Stat. §15A-1340.16(d)(1), (e)(2) (listing as an aggravating factor the fact that defendant "occupied a position of leadership or dominance over other participants" and listing as a mitigating factor the fact that defendant "was a passive participant or played a minor role in the commission of the offense"). Under the capital punishment statutes in some states, the defendant's role in the offense can mean the difference between life and death. Ohio and Florida, among others, include the defendant's relatively minor role as a mitigating factor that could lead a jury to recommend a life sentence rather than capital punishment. See Ohio Rev. Code §2929.04(B)(6); Fla. Stat. Ann. §921.141(6)(d).

The federal provision flushes out several questions that are not explicitly addressed in the typical state system (either indeterminate or guideline). What is the proper amount to decrease or increase a sentence based on this factor? In judging the relative culpability of a defendant, what is the proper comparison point: others involved in the current crime, or those involved in similar crimes around the country? Note that your answer to these questions might change depending on the size of the group involved or the seriousness of the crime committed. See United States v. Almanza, 225 F.3d 845 (7th Cir. 2000) (Posner, J.) ("The 'mule' who transports one kilogram of cocaine is a more minor participant in a conspiracy to distribute 1,000 kilograms of cocaine than in a conspiracy to distribute 10 kilograms of cocaine, because the potential punishment of a member of the first conspiracy is so much greater, even though his conduct is identical").

2. *Co-defendant's sentence as a basis for departure.*   How should a judge respond when the sentencing rules indicate a sentence for one defendant that is higher than the sentence already imposed on a more culpable co-defendant? In the federal system, courts have usually refused to depart from the sentencing guidelines in an effort to give comparable sentences to co-defendants in the same crime. See United States v. Joyner, 924 F.2d 454, 460-461 (2d Cir. 1991) (consideration of the sentences given to co-defendants "creates a new and entirely unwarranted disparity between the defendant's sentence and that of all similarly situated defendants throughout the country"). The sentencing judge could impose a sentence out of line with the sentence already received by other participants in the present crime, or a sentence out of line with the lesser participants in similar crimes from other districts. Which is the greater (and more visible) threat to the principle of equal treatment at sentencing?

3. *Relative culpability and cooperation with the government.*   Conspirators who plead guilty and cooperate with the government in prosecutions against other members of the conspiracy often receive sentence discounts, both in federal and state systems. Recall U.S. Sentencing Guidelines Manual §5K1.1 (allowing departure for substantial assistance). This often means that some higher-ranking conspiracy members — those who know the most about the operation — receive lesser sentences than some lower-ranking conspiracy members who have less to offer the government. Especially in the federal system, in which a substantial assistance departure is authorized only upon a motion by the prosecutor, defendants who cooperate on a similar basis could receive different sentences because

of different practices of prosecutors in different districts. Can a sentencing judge counteract these sources of unequal sentences? If a judge learns that prosecutors in the local district deal with some co-conspirators differently from prosecutors in other districts (for instance, by offering immunity under U.S. Sentencing Guidelines Manual §1B1.8 in exchange for information about the conspiracy), should the judge adjust the sentence to equalize outcomes in different districts? See United States v. Buckendahl, 251 F.3d 753 (8th Cir. 2001).

PROBLEM 4-5.   ROB ANON REVISITED

Look again at §3B1.1 of the federal guidelines, reprinted above. The application notes to this guideline do not define the key terms such as "leader" or "manager." How would these provisions apply to the sentence of Rob Anon, based on the facts described in Problem 4-1? Was this enterprise "otherwise extensive" within the meaning of §3B1.1(a)? The commentary offers some hope for the prosecution here: "In assessing whether an organization is 'otherwise extensive,' all persons involved during the course of the entire offense are to be considered. Thus, a fraud that involved only three participants but used the unknowing services of many outsiders could be considered extensive." Where might the prosecutor find evidence about other "persons involved"?

B.   ASSESSING OFFENSE SERIOUSNESS

Deciding the scope of behavior that will form the basis for a sentence is only one step in choosing an appropriate sentence. Sentencing authorities must also judge the *seriousness* of the defendant's offense.

In all sentencing systems, legislatures make initial judgments about offense seriousness through the grading of offenses. They decide which crimes to label as felonies or misdemeanors and further subdivide these broad categories by using degrees or classes to specify appropriate punishment ranges. These decisions can sometimes raise constitutional concerns, because the Supreme Court has interpreted the Eighth Amendment's prohibition of cruel and unusual punishments to preclude grossly disproportionate punishments (see Chapter 7). More fundamentally, these legislative decisions always implicate policy choices, because legislatures must decide which aspects of an offense should be categorized as more or less serious.

Basic legislative grading choices are only one component of the many judgments made about the seriousness of offense behavior in the sentencing process. Legislatures also authorize or require specific sentencing enhancements based on particular aspects of offense behavior, such as gun possession. And other sentencing decision makers — including sentencing commissions, prosecutors, judges, and parole officials — measure the seriousness of offense behavior in ways that change final sentencing outcomes.

The following excerpt from the Senate report supporting the Sentencing Reform Act of 1984 instructs the U.S. Sentencing Commission how to establish sentencing rules for different categories of offenses. The report mentions the numerous offense-related elements that become relevant when passing judgment on the overall seriousness of criminal behaviors.

U.S. Senate Report No. 98-225
Pages 169-171 (1984)

[Title 28 U.S.C. §994(c) of the Sentencing Reform Act] lists a number of offense characteristics that the sentencing commission is required to examine [in the establishment of sentencing guidelines. This provision] specifies that the commission consider the degree of relevance of the grade of the offense to the sentencing decision. [All] offenses are graded according to their relative seriousness. [The grading provides] some guide as to the congressional view of the relative seriousness of similar offenses. The rough approximations practical for statutory purposes are expected . . . to be refined considerably by the sentencing guidelines.

[This provision further] specifies that the commission consider the relevance to the sentencing decision of the circumstances under which the offense was committed that might aggravate or mitigate the seriousness of the offense. Among the considerations the commission might examine under this factor are whether the offense was particularly heinous; whether the offense was committed on the spur of the moment or after substantial planning; whether the offense was committed in reckless disregard of the safety of others; whether the offense involved a threat with a weapon or use of a weapon; whether the offense was committed in a manner plainly designed to limit the danger to the victims; whether the defendant was acting under a form of duress not rising to the level of a defense; etc.

[This provision further] specifies that the commission consider the relevance to the sentencing decision of the nature and degree of the harm caused by the offense, including whether it involved property, irreplaceable property, a person, a number of persons, or a breach of public trust. The commission might include in this consideration, or in policy statements, an evaluation of the role that unusual vulnerability of the victim that is known to the defendant should play in the sentencing decision.

[This provision further] specifies that the commission consider the relevance of the community view of the gravity of the offense to the sentencing decision, . . . public concern generated by an offense, . . . the deterrent effect a particular sentence may have on the commission of the offense by others[, and] the current incidence of the offense in the community and in the nation as a whole.

NOTES

1. *The centrality of harm and culpability on legislative grading of offenses.* Most criminal codes state that the fundamental requirements for criminal liability are a voluntary act (the objective component) and a mens rea, or culpable mental state (the subjective component). See, e.g., N.Y. Penal Code §15.10; Ohio Rev.

Code §2901.21; Tex. Penal Code §§6.01-6.04. Similarly, the initial grading of a criminal offense by the legislature typically depends on the objective seriousness of the harm or threat of harm resulting from the defendant's behavior and on the defendant's subjective culpability. Certain classes of crimes share a common objective harm, leading to offense grades that turn entirely on the defendant's subjective mental state. For instance, homicides are usually defined in terms of causing another person's death; the grade of offense depends on whether the killing was intentional, provoked, unintentional, or accidental. See, e.g., Cal. Penal Code §§187-192; Kan. Stat. Ann. §§21-3401B to 21-3404. Other crimes share a common subjective mental state, leading to offense grades that depend on the objective harm inflicted. For example, most forms of theft require the intent to deprive others of property; the grade principally depends on the value of the property stolen.

2. *Institutional roles in judging offense seriousness.*   Historically, legislatures made only general assessments of offense seriousness through grading choices, juries applied offense grades to the facts of specific cases, and sentencing judges made more particularized judgments about the seriousness of the defendant's crime when ascribing specific sentences. Professor Paul Robinson has suggested that this traditional allocation of responsibility is fundamentally sound:

> The amount of punishment to be imposed is in large measure a function of the value of the interest injured or threatened and the culpability of the act. In a democracy, . . . the relative value of the interest is a judgment uniquely within the authority of a legislative body[, and] the actor's culpability, which necessarily requires an inferential judgment, is a judgment within the expertise of a jury of peers. [Because] a criminal code cannot take account of every factor that contributes to the amount of punishment a defendant deserves . . . codes generally give only an approximation of the amount of punishment that should be imposed. The judge must determine the exact amount on the facts of the particular case, which requires exercise of judicial discretion to refine the code's "first cut," or to account for relevant factors not taken into account by the code.

Paul H. Robinson, Are Criminal Codes Irrelevant?, 68 S. Cal. L. Rev. 159, 183 (1994). How should a sentencing commission fit into Professor Robinson's taxonomy of institutional roles? Should the work of sentencing commissions be conceived primarily in traditional legislative terms, focusing on developing sentencing rules which provide only a "first cut" as to the amount of punishment a court ought to impose? Or should the work of sentencing commissions be conceived instead in traditional judicial terms, focusing on developing sentencing rules to account for factors appearing less often in individual cases?

1.   Qualitative Assessments of Harm

The harm or threat of harm that arises from a defendant's behavior profoundly influences final sentencing choices, perhaps even more than it affects legislative grading of criminal offenses. Various legal structures and rules translate judgments about the seriousness of harm into final sentencing outcomes.

When legislatures, sentencing commissions, and judges think about the seriousness of offenses, they sometimes consider the *type* of harm the crime causes or threatens rather than the *amount* of harm. Which types of harm deserve the most serious punishments? As you read the following cases and materials, think about the inherent challenge of making qualitative judgments about the relative seriousness of violent crimes versus drug crimes versus sex crimes versus economic crimes. Consider also how judges, legislatures, and commissions make these rankings.

‖ *Ehrlich Anthony Coker v. Georgia* ‖
433 U.S. 584 (1977)

WHITE, J.
Georgia Code §26-2001 provides that "(a) person convicted of rape shall be punished by death or by imprisonment for life, or by imprisonment for not less than one nor more than 20 years." Petitioner Coker was convicted of rape and sentenced to death. Coker [contends] that the punishment of death for rape violates the Eighth Amendment.

While serving various sentences for murder, rape, kidnaping, and aggravated assault, petitioner escaped from [prison. Petitioner] entered the house of Allen and Elnita Carver through an unlocked kitchen door. Threatening the couple with a "board," he tied up Mr. Carver in the bathroom, obtained a knife from the kitchen, and took Mr. Carver's money and the keys to the family car. Brandishing the knife and saying "you know what's going to happen to you if you try anything, don't you," Coker then raped Mrs. Carver. Soon thereafter, petitioner drove away in the Carver car, taking Mrs. Carver with him. Mr. Carver, freeing himself, notified the police; and not long thereafter petitioner was apprehended. Mrs. Carver was unharmed.

Petitioner was charged with [various offenses, including] rape. . . . The jury returned a verdict of guilty, rejecting his general plea of insanity. A sentencing hearing was then conducted in accordance with [our decision in] Gregg v. Georgia, 428 U.S. 153 (1976), where this Court sustained the death penalty for murder when imposed pursuant to [certain] procedures. . . . The jury's verdict on the rape count was death by electrocution.

Furman v. Georgia, 408 U.S. 238 (1972), and the Court's decisions last Term in Gregg v. Georgia, 428 U.S. 153 (1976) [and companion cases] settled that the death penalty is not invariably cruel and unusual punishment within the meaning of the Eighth Amendment; it is not inherently barbaric or an unacceptable mode of punishment for crime; neither is it always disproportionate to the crime for which it is imposed. In sustaining the imposition of the death penalty in *Gregg*, however, the Court firmly embraced the holdings and dicta from prior cases to the effect that the Eighth Amendment bars not only those punishments that are "barbaric" but also those that are "excessive" in relation to the crime committed. Under *Gregg*, a punishment is "excessive" and unconstitutional if it (1) makes no measurable contribution to acceptable goals of punishment and hence is nothing more than the purposeless and needless imposition of pain and suffering; or (2) is grossly out of proportion to the severity of the crime. . . . We have concluded that a sentence of death is grossly disproportionate and excessive punishment for the crime of rape and is therefore forbidden by the Eighth Amendment as cruel and unusual punishment.

[We] seek guidance in history and from the objective evidence of the country's present judgment concerning the acceptability of death as a penalty for rape of an adult woman. At no time in the last 50 years have a majority of the States authorized death as a punishment for rape. In 1925, 18 States, the District of Columbia, and the Federal Government authorized capital punishment for the rape of an adult female. By 1971 just prior to the decision in *Furman,* that number had declined, but not substantially, to 16 States plus the Federal Government. *Furman* then invalidated most of the capital punishment statutes in this country, including the rape statutes. . . .

In reviving death penalty laws to satisfy *Furman*'s mandate, none of the States that had not previously authorized death for rape chose to include rape among capital felonies. Of the 16 States in which rape had been a capital offense, only three provided the death penalty for rape of an adult woman in their revised statutes, Georgia, North Carolina, and Louisiana. . . . It should be noted that Florida, Mississippi, and Tennessee also authorized the death penalty in some rape cases, but only where the victim was a child and the rapist an adult. . . . The current judgment with respect to the death penalty for rape is not wholly unanimous among state legislatures, but it obviously weighs very heavily on the side of rejecting capital punishment as a suitable penalty for raping an adult woman.

It was also observed in *Gregg* that "the jury . . . is a significant and reliable objective index of contemporary values because it is so directly involved," and that it is thus important to look to the sentencing decisions that juries have made in the course of assessing whether capital punishment is an appropriate penalty for the crime being tried. [Out] of all rape convictions in Georgia since 1973, . . . 63 cases had been reviewed by the Georgia Supreme Court as of the time of oral argument; and of these, 6 involved a death sentence. [Recent] experience surely does not prove that jurors consider the death penalty to be a disproportionate punishment for every conceivable instance of rape, no matter how aggravated. Nevertheless, it is true that in the vast majority of cases, at least 9 out of 10, juries have not imposed the death sentence.

These recent events evidencing the attitude of state legislatures and sentencing juries do not wholly determine this controversy, for the Constitution contemplates that in the end our own judgment will be brought to bear on the question of the acceptability of the death penalty under the Eighth Amendment. . . .

We do not discount the seriousness of rape as a crime. It is highly reprehensible, both in a moral sense and in its almost total contempt for the personal integrity and autonomy of the female victim and for the latter's privilege of choosing those with whom intimate relationships are to be established. Short of homicide, it is the "ultimate violation of self." It is also a violent crime because it normally involves force, or the threat of force or intimidation, to overcome the will and the capacity of the victim to resist. Rape is very often accompanied by physical injury to the female and can also inflict psychological damage. Because it undermines the community's sense of security, there is public injury as well.

Rape is without doubt deserving of serious punishment; but in terms of moral depravity and of the injury to the person and to the public, it does not compare with murder, which does involve the unjustified taking of human life. Although it may be accompanied by another crime, rape by definition does not include the death of or even the serious injury to another person. The murderer kills; the rapist, if no more than that, does not. Life is over for the victim of the murderer; for the rape victim, life may not be nearly so happy as it was, but it is not over and normally is not beyond repair. We have the abiding conviction that the death penalty, which is unique in its severity and irrevocability, is an excessive penalty for the rapist who, as such, does not take human life. . . .

POWELL, J., concurring in the judgment in part and dissenting in part.

I concur in the judgment of the Court on the facts of this case, and also in the plurality's reasoning supporting the view that ordinarily death is disproportionate punishment for the crime of raping an adult woman. Although rape invariably is a reprehensible crime, there is no indication that petitioner's offense was committed with excessive brutality or that the victim sustained serious or lasting injury.

[However], the plurality draws a bright line between murder and all rapes regardless of the degree of brutality of the rape or the effect upon the victim. I dissent because I am not persuaded that such a bright line is appropriate. [T]here is extreme variation in the degree of culpability of rapists. The deliberate viciousness of the rapist may be greater than that of the murderer. Rape is never an act committed accidentally. Rarely can it be said to be unpremeditated. There also is wide variation in the effect on the victim. . . . Some victims are so grievously injured physically or psychologically that life is beyond repair. . . .

BURGER, C.J., dissenting.

. . . On December 5, 1971 Ehrlich Anthony Coker raped and then stabbed to death a young woman. Less than eight months later Coker kidnaped and raped a second young woman. After twice raping this 16-year-old victim, he stripped her, severely beat her with a club, and dragged her into a wooded area where he left her for dead. He was apprehended and pleaded guilty to offenses stemming from these incidents. He was sentenced by three separate courts to three life terms, two 20-year terms, and one 8-year term of imprisonment. Each judgment specified that the sentences it imposed were to run consecutively rather than concurrently. Approximately one and a half years later, on September 2, 1974, petitioner escaped from the state prison where he was serving these sentences. He promptly raped another 16-year-old woman in the presence of her husband, abducted her from her home, and threatened her with death and serious bodily harm. It is this crime for which the sentence now under review was imposed.

The Court today holds that Georgia may not impose the death penalty on Coker. In so doing, it prevents the State from imposing any effective punishment upon Coker for his latest rape. The Court's holding, moreover, bars Georgia from guaranteeing its citizens that they will suffer no further attacks by this habitual rapist . . . who has shown total and repeated disregard for the welfare, safety, personal integrity, and human worth of others, and who seemingly cannot be deterred from continuing such conduct. . . .

A rapist not only violates a victim's privacy and personal integrity, but inevitably causes serious psychological as well as physical harm in the process. The long-range effect upon the victim's life and health is likely to be irreparable; it is impossible to measure the harm which results. Volumes have been written by victims, physicians, and psychiatric specialists on the lasting injury suffered by rape victims. Rape is not a mere physical attack, it is destructive of the human personality. The remainder of the victim's life may be gravely affected, and this in turn may have a serious detrimental effect upon her husband and any children she may have. . . . Victims may recover from the physical damage of knife or bullet wounds, or a beating with fists or a club, but recovery from such a gross assault on the human personality is not healed by medicine or surgery. To speak blandly . . . of rape victims who are "unharmed," or to classify the human outrage of rape . . . in terms of "excessively brutal," versus "moderately brutal," takes too little account of the profound suffering the crime imposes upon the victims and their loved ones.

The question of whether the death penalty is an appropriate punishment for rape is surely an open one. It is arguable that many prospective rapists would be deterred by the possibility that they could suffer death for their offense; it is also arguable that the death penalty would have only minimal deterrent effect. It may well be that rape victims would become more willing to report the crime and aid in the apprehension of the criminals if they knew that community disapproval of rapists was sufficiently strong to inflict the extreme penalty; or perhaps they would be reluctant to cooperate in the prosecution of rapists if they knew that a conviction might result in the imposition of the death penalty. Quite possibly, the occasional, well-publicized execution of egregious rapists may cause citizens to feel greater security in their daily lives; or, on the contrary, it may be that members of a civilized community will suffer the pangs of a heavy conscience because such punishment will be perceived as excessive. We cannot know which among this range of possibilities is correct, but today's holding forecloses the very exploration we have said federalism was intended to foster.

[Rape] is not a crime "light years" removed from murder in the degree of its heinousness; it certainly poses a serious potential danger to the life and safety of innocent victims apart from the devastating psychic consequences. . . . Whatever our individual views as to the wisdom of capital punishment, I cannot agree that it is constitutionally impermissible for a state legislature to make the "solemn judgment" to impose such penalty for the crime of rape. Accordingly, I would leave to the States the task of legislating in this area of the law.

NOTES

1. *Constitutional proportionality between harm and severity of punishment.* As *Coker* reveals, the Supreme Court has placed some substantive constitutional limitations on the use of capital punishment for certain crimes. In addition to *Coker*'s preclusion of capital punishment for the crime of adult rape, the Supreme Court has held through a line of decisions culminating in Tison v. Arizona, 481 U.S. 137 (1987), that the death penalty is permissible in homicide cases only for offenders who acted at least with the culpable mental state of reckless indifference to human life. As detailed in Chapter 7, the Supreme Court has also held that noncapital sentences can be unconstitutional if they are "grossly disproportionate" to the offender's crime.

Coker precluded the use of capital punishment only in cases of adult rape. At least a few states have legislation allowing for the death penalty for rape of a child. In Louisiana, for example, defendants convicted of "aggravated rape" can be subject to the death penalty if "the victim was under the age of twelve years." La. Rev. Stat. §14:42. Both the constitutionality and appropriateness of imposing the death penalty on child rapists has generated significant academic commentary. See, e.g., J. Richard Broughton, "On Horror's Head Horrors Accumulate": A Reflective Comment on Capital Child Rape Legislation, 39 Duq. L. Rev. 1 (2000); Annaliese Flynn Fleming, Louisiana's Newest Capital Crime: The Death Penalty for Child Rape, 89 J. Crim. L. & Criminology 717 (1999). Does rape of a child create a different *type* of harm than rape of an adult?

Consider all the people who had to agree that Ehrlich Anthony Coker should die for his crime: the Georgia legislature had to authorize the death penalty for certain rapes; the local prosecutor (influenced perhaps by the victim's input) had to charge and pursue Coker's case as a capital crime; the sentencing jury had to conclude not only that Coker was guilty but also that he deserved to die for his crime; the Georgia state courts had to decide, pursuant to their own state laws, that Coker's sentence was proportionate to the crime. Does the U.S. Supreme Court bring something to the job of measuring the seriousness of Coker's crime that the other actors were missing?

2. *Nonjudicial assessments of harm and severity of punishment.*   Distinct from any constitutional questions about permissible punishments are the policy questions concerning appropriate punishments. As to the death penalty, 38 states along with the federal government permit the imposition of capital punishment for certain aggravated homicides, although there is some notable variation in these jurisdictions as to exactly which sorts of aggravating factors make a particular killer eligible for capital punishment. See the Death Penalty Information Center web site at http://www.deathpenaltyinfo.org/capitaloffenses.html; Va. Code §18.2-31(12) ("killing of a person under the age of fourteen by a person age twenty-one or older"); Ala. Code §13A-5-40(a)(11) ("when the victim is a state or federal public official or former public official and the murder stems from or is caused by or is related to his official position"); Ind. Code §35-50-2-9(b) ("killing the victim while committing or attempting to commit any of the following [crimes]: arson, burglary, child molesting, criminal deviate conduct, kidnapping, rape, robbery, carjacking, criminal gang activity, dealing in cocaine or a narcotic drug"). Do these aggravating factors speak to the same basic types of harm?

While varying in their use and application of the death penalty, nearly all jurisdictions deem aggravated forms of homicide to be the most serious of crimes. In states without the death penalty, this means the crime is punished by life imprisonment without the possibility of parole. Similarly, though *Coker* makes the death penalty unavailable for the crime of adult rape, most jurisdictions still provide severe sanctions for serious sexual offenses, especially when these crimes include additional physical harm to the victim or when the victim is young or especially vulnerable. See Ohio Rev. Code §2907.02.

How do legislatures and commissions make judgments about the relative seriousness of offenses less obvious than murder or rape? Consider again Dale Parent's description, reprinted in Chapter 3, of the efforts of the Minnesota Sentencing Commission to rank different offenses. What other methods might you recommend?

_____

Though legislatures and commissions must grade offenses in comparison to other offenses, they also guide sentencing judges in how to distinguish among offenders convicted of the same crime. The following materials highlight two ways that sentencing rules can specifically respond to various harms and threats of harms.

State v. Stanley Royster
590 N.W.2d 82 (Minn. 1999)

STRINGER, J.

On February 12, 1997, the Minneapolis Police executed a search warrant at Royster's residence [searching for illegal drugs]. Police found Royster and another man inside. Items recovered in Royster's search included cash in his pocket and some pre-recorded buy money from the Minneapolis Narcotics Unit. In the premises search, specifically of Royster's bedroom, the police recovered additional pre-recorded buy money, a bag of crack-cocaine in a boot, and a fully-loaded .22 revolver from underneath his mattress located approximately three feet from the boot containing the crack-cocaine. After his arrest Royster admitted to the police that he was selling cocaine out of his home and claimed that his father had given him the revolver for protection because he lived in a dangerous neighborhood. . . .

When Minnesota Statute §609.11, subdivision 5, was enacted in 1981, it originally provided in relevant part [that any defendant convicted of specified offenses] in which "the defendant or an accomplice, at the time of the offense, used, whether by brandishing, displaying, threatening with, or otherwise employing, a firearm" [must receive a minimum prison term of at least three years.] Another subdivision pertaining to commission of a predicate offense while "in possession of a firearm," mandated a minimum sentence of one year. . . . In 1994 the Minnesota Legislature [consolidated these subdivisions to provide that] both *possession* and *use* while committing a predicate felony offense triggered the three-year mandatory minimum sentence.

Royster argues that [the "possession" term in the 1994 amendment] must be read in conjunction with "brandishing, displaying, threatening with, or otherwise employing" [the firearm] to trigger the mandatory minimum sentence and because his firearm was not so employed but rather lay dormant under his mattress, he did not have the "possession" contemplated by the legislature. Clearly the statute cannot be read to reach such a conclusion however, for it is obvious that in 1994 the legislature intended to increase the sentence for those who possess a firearm while committing a crime even though they do not actually use a firearm. To conclude that "possession" must be accompanied by some kind of "brandishing" would render the 1994 amendment meaningless. . . . We hold that "brandishing" is not required as an element of proof of possession to trigger the [three-year] mandatory minimum sentence. . . .

Finally, we consider what should be the test for determining when constructive possession while committing the predicate offense should trigger the mandatory minimum sentence. The sentence enhancement amendment reflects the obvious reality that possession of a firearm while committing a predicate felony offense substantially increases the risk of violence, whether or not the offender actually uses the firearm. The firearm in possession was recognized by the legislature as an "insurance policy . . . to be used to further the crime if need be" and clearly raises the stakes of severe injury or death as a result of the commission of the predicate offenses. It seems reasonable then to examine all aspects of the firearm in possession to determine whether it was reasonable to assume that its presence increased the risk of violence and to what degree the risk is increased: the nature, type and condition of the firearm, its ownership, whether it was loaded, its ease of accessibility, its proximity to the drugs, why the firearm was present and whether the nature of the predicate offense is frequently or typically accompanied by use of a firearm, to name a few of the considerations.

Applying these standards to the present case, we hold that the state presented sufficient evidence to prove beyond a reasonable doubt that Royster's possession of a firearm while committing the predicate felony offense met the requisites of section 609.11, subdivision 5. Because Royster's .22 caliber pistol, fully loaded, was found under Royster's mattress within 3 feet of 2.9 grams of crack-cocaine, the trial court could reasonably infer that possession of the firearm substantially increased the risk of violence related to his drug trafficking.

‖ *U.S. Sentencing Guidelines Manual* ‖

§2B3.1 ROBBERY

(a) Base Offense Level: 20
(b) Specific Offense Characteristics
(1) If the property of a financial institution or post office was taken, or if the taking of such property was an object of the offense, increase by 2 levels.
(2) (A) If a firearm was discharged, increase by 7 levels; (B) if a firearm was otherwise used, increase by 6 levels; (C) if a firearm was brandished or possessed, increase by 5 levels; (D) if a dangerous weapon was otherwise used, increase by 4 levels; (E) if a dangerous weapon was brandished or possessed, increase by 3 levels; or (F) if a threat of death was made, increase by 2 levels.
(3) If any victim sustained bodily injury, increase the offense level according to the seriousness of the injury:

Degree of Bodily Injury	*Increase in Level*
(A) Bodily Injury	add 2
(B) Serious Bodily Injury	add 4
(C) Permanent or Life-Threatening Bodily Injury	add 6
(D) If the degree of injury is between that specified in subdivisions (A) and (B), add 3 levels; or	
(E) If the degree of injury is between that specified in subdivisions (B) and (C), add 5 levels.	

Provided, however, that the cumulative adjustments from (2) and (3) shall not exceed 11 levels.

NOTES

1. *Legislative and commission roles in defining offense seriousness.* Sometimes legislative bodies decide for themselves the specific increases in sentences that must occur when particular harms or threats are present. The *Royster* case gives one example of legislatively enacted mandatory sentencing laws that have proven popular at both the federal and state levels, especially in the context of narcotics and weapons offenses. In the federal system, more than 75 statutes now establish fixed prison terms or minimum sentences that judges must impose based on certain offense factors. Over the past two decades, nearly every state has also adopted some form of mandatory sentencing provisions. See, e.g., Dale Parent et al., National Institute of Justice, Mandatory Sentencing (January 1997). As we saw in Chapter 2, legislators often embrace mandatory sentencing laws primarily for immediate political benefits, even though studies have generally shown that these laws are not applied uniformly and thus have limited deterrent impact and produce sentencing disparities. Indeed, the consensus within the criminal justice community is that, in practice, mandatory sentencing laws are ineffectual and often produce unjust outcomes. See, e.g., Jonathan P. Caulkins et al., Rand Corporation, Mandatory Minimum Drug Sentences: Throwing Away the Key or the Taxpayer's Money (1997); Barbara S. Vincent and Paul J. Hofer, Federal Judicial Center, The Consequences of Mandatory Minimum Prison Terms: A Summary of Recent Findings (1994); Gary T. Lowenthal, Mandatory Sentencing Laws: Undermining the Effectiveness of Determinate Sentencing Reform, 81 Cal. L. Rev. 61 (1993).

Judges also tend to have a low regard for mandatory minimum sentences set by legislatures. In August 2003, Justice Anthony Kennedy delivered a speech to the American Bar Association that was frankly critical of mandatory sentencing laws in the federal system: "Our resources are being misspent. Our punishments are too severe. Our sentences are too long." He urged the ABA to tell Congress, "Don't take discretion away from the courts. . . . Let judges be judges." Although he agreed with the need for federal sentencing guidelines to set uniform sentences, he contrasted guidelines with mandatory minimum sentences: "I can accept neither the wisdom, the justice nor the necessity of mandatory minimums. . . . In all too many cases, they are unjust. . . . A country which is secure in its institutions and confident in its laws should not be ashamed of the concept of mercy."

Section 2B3.1 of the federal sentencing guidelines illustrates an important alternative to mandatory minimum sentences. Structured sentencing jurisdictions can employ a more refined approach to assessing offense seriousness. In the federal system, determinations of an offense's overall seriousness can be highly detailed; for example, in addition to the portion reprinted above, §2B3.1 has four additional subsections and incorporates three pages of application notes. In state guideline systems, the computation is less complex but the idea is similar. The guidelines list particularly serious harms or threats as grounds for increasing the presumptive sentence. See N.C. Gen. Stat. §15A-1340.16(d)(8), (13) (aggravating factor if the defendant "knowingly created a great risk of death to more than one person" or "involved a person under the age of 16 in the commission of the crime").

2. *Sentencing enhancements based on "use" of firearm or weapon.*   Federal criminal law and the laws of many states increase criminal penalties and sometimes mandate certain minimum sentences when the offense behavior involves use of a firearm or other weapon. See, e.g., 18 U.S.C. §924(c) (mandating five years' imprisonment consecutive to the sentence for the underlying offense whenever a defendant "uses or carries" a firearm "during and in relation to" any crime of violence or drug trafficking offense); 42 Pa. Cons. Stat. Ann. §9712 (mandating five-year minimum sentence for "visibly possessing a firearm or a replica of a firearm during the commission of a crime of violence").

As *Royster* highlights, statutes that include such weapons enhancements often raise legal questions about the "use" or "possession" that is sufficient to trigger the special sanctions. For example, in Bailey v. United States, 516 U.S. 137 (1995), the Supreme Court narrowed application of the "uses" provision in the federal firearms enhancement, overturning a conviction of a defendant who possessed a loaded pistol that police found inside a bag in his locked car trunk after they arrested him for possession of cocaine that they found in the passenger compartment. Congress soon amended the statute to cover all forms of possession of a firearm "in furtherance of" the crime and also introduced even higher mandatory penalties for brandishing or discharging a weapon, for repeat offenders, and for using certain types of dangerous guns. As a legislator, would you attach use of a weapon to particular crimes, or would you use it as a sentence enhancement for any crime? Are certain crimes made more harmful by the presence or use of a gun?

3. *Bodily harm and other aggravating factors.*   Federal criminal law and the laws of many states increase criminal penalties or mandate certain minimum sentences, or both, when offenses result in bodily harm. Sometimes these enhancements are codified as elements of other crimes. For example, many kidnapping statutes increase the penalty when the offender harms the seized victims. See, e.g., 18 U.S.C. §1201; Cal. Penal Code §209. Especially in states with guidelines, it is common to place such enhancements in general sentencing instructions. See, e.g., Fla. Stat. Ann. §921.0016(3)(*l*) (allowing departure from guideline sentence if the victim "suffered extraordinary physical or emotional trauma or permanent physical injury"). Courts have addressed many issues under these statutes, including whether certain injuries are severe enough to constitute harm within the statutory meaning and whether harm inflicted by an accomplice or accessory can be attributed to the defendant for sentencing purposes.

Many other indicators of serious harms or threats can operate just like use of a firearm or bodily injury. Legislatures or sentencing commissions designate these factors as a basis for increased sentences. Sometimes the increase is defined, and in other instances the judge is allowed to increase the sentence in her discretion. See, e.g., U.S. Sentencing Guidelines Manual §3B1.4 (increasing offense level by two if defendant used a minor to commit crime); Utah Sentencing Guidelines Form 4 (listing as an aggravating sentencing factor the fact that the "offense was characterized by extreme cruelty or depravity").

PROBLEM 4-6.   ROB ANON REVISITED

Recall again Rob Anon, described above in Problem 4-1, and then reexamine the specifics of §2B3.1 of the federal guidelines. Based on that provision, how many offense levels should be added to the base offense level of 20? Though it appears that at least nine levels must be added, interpretation of the provision's key terms might suggest that as many as 13 levels should be added; the difference between adding nine or adding 13 levels could mean a sentencing range for Rob as low as eight to ten years or as high as 12 to 15 years.

2. *Quantitative Assessments of Harm*

Certain types of offenses — particularly drug crimes and economic crimes — lend themselves to quantitative measures of offense seriousness. For drug crimes, offense harms are defined in terms of the type and quantity of the drugs involved. For economic crimes, offense harms are defined in terms of the quantity of money taken. Larger quantities of drugs or a larger amount of money mean a more severe sentence.

As the following case highlights, the amount of "quantified harm," especially in drug cases under federal law, can have a dramatic impact on sentence length, eclipsing the impact of all other sentencing factors. For example, even for a first-time offender, the amount of drugs involved in a drug distribution offense could mean the difference between a sentence of life imprisonment (for very large quantities) or a sentence of probation (for very small quantities). See U.S. Sentencing Guidelines Manual §2D1.1(c). As you read the following case, consider why jurisdictions rely so heavily on quantifiable measures of offense seriousness in drug crimes and financial crimes, and also consider whether there can and should be other ways to judge offense seriousness in these settings.

‖ *Richard Chapman v. United States* ‖
500 U.S. 453 (1991)

REHNQUIST, C.J.

Section 841(b)(1)(B)(v) of Title 21 of the United States Code calls for a mandatory minimum sentence of five years for the offense of distributing more than one gram of a "mixture or substance containing a detectable amount of lysergic acid diethylamide (LSD)." We hold that it is the weight of the blotter paper containing LSD, and not the weight of the pure LSD, which determines eligibility for the minimum sentence.

Petitioner Richard L. Chapman [was] convicted of selling 10 sheets (1,000 doses) of blotter paper containing LSD. The District Court included the total weight of the paper and LSD in determining the weight of the drug to be used in calculating petitioners' sentences. . . . [Chapman and his copetitioner claim] that the blotter paper is only a carrier medium, and that its weight should not be included in the weight of the drug for sentencing purposes. Alternatively, [they argue] that, if the statute and Sentencing Guidelines were construed so as to require inclusion of the blotter paper or other carrier medium when calculating the weight of the drug, this would violate the right to equal protection incorporated in the Due Process Clause of the Fifth Amendment. . . .

Title 21 U.S.C. §841(b)(1)(B) provides that [a person who distributes one gram or more of a "mixture or substance containing a detectable amount" of

LSD must be sentenced to a prison term of at least five years; §841(b)(1)(A)(v) calls for a mandatory minimum of ten years' imprisonment for a violation involving ten grams or more]. Section 2D1.1(c) of the Sentencing Guidelines parallels the statutory language and requires the base offense level to be determined based upon the weight of a "mixture or substance containing a detectable amount of" LSD.

According to the Sentencing Commission, the LSD in an average dose weighs 0.05 milligrams; there are therefore 20,000 pure doses in a gram. The pure dose is such an infinitesimal amount that it must be sold to retail customers in a "carrier" [such as] paper or gel . . . cut into "one-dose" squares and sold by the dose. . . . Although gelatin and paper are light, they weigh much more than the LSD. The ten sheets of blotter paper carrying the 1,000 doses sold by petitioners weighed 5.7 grams; the LSD by itself weighed only about 50 milligrams, not even close to the one gram necessary to trigger the 5-year mandatory minimum.

Petitioners argue that §841(b) should not require that the weight of the carrier be included when computing the appropriate sentence for LSD distribution, for the words "mixture or substance" are ambiguous, and should not be construed to reach an illogical result. Because LSD is sold by dose, rather than by weight, the weight of the LSD carrier should not be included when determining a defendant's sentence, because it is irrelevant to culpability. They argue that including the weight of the carrier leads to anomalous results, viz: a major wholesaler caught with 19,999 doses of pure LSD would not be subject to the five-year mandatory minimum sentence, while a minor pusher with 200 doses on blotter paper, or even one dose on a sugar cube, would be subject to the mandatory minimum sentence. Thus, they contend, the weight of the carrier should be excluded, the weight of the pure LSD should be determined, and that weight should be used to set the appropriate sentence.

We think that petitioners' reading of the statute — a reading that makes the penalty turn on the net weight of the drug, rather than the gross weight of the carrier and drug together — is not a plausible one. The statute refers to a "mixture or substance containing a detectable amount." So long as it contains a detectable amount, the entire mixture or substance is to be weighed when calculating the sentence.

This reading is confirmed by the structure of the statute. With respect to various drugs, including heroin, cocaine, and LSD, it provides for mandatory minimum sentences for crimes involving certain weights of a "mixture or substance containing a detectable amount" of the drugs. With respect to other drugs, however, namely phencyclidine (PCP) or methamphetamine, it provides for a mandatory minimum sentence based either on the weight of a mixture or substance containing a detectable amount of the drug, or on lower weights of pure PCP or methamphetamine. . . . Thus, with respect to these two drugs, Congress clearly distinguished between the pure drug and a "mixture or substance containing a detectable amount of" the pure drug. But with respect to drugs such as LSD, which petitioners distributed, Congress declared that sentences should be based exclusively on the weight of the "mixture or substance." Congress knew how to indicate that the weight of the pure drug was to be used to determine the sentence, and did not make that distinction with respect to LSD. . . .

The history of Congress's attempts to control illegal drug distribution shows why Congress chose the course that it did with respect to sentencing.

The Comprehensive Drug Abuse Prevention and Control Act of 1970 . . . did not link penalties to the quantity of the drug possessed; penalties instead depended upon whether the drug was classified as a narcotic or not. The Controlled Substances Penalties Amendments Act of 1984 . . . first made punishment dependent upon the quantity of the controlled substance involved [and was] intended "to provide a more rational penalty structure for the major drug trafficking offenses," by eliminating sentencing disparities caused by classifying drugs as narcotic and non-narcotic. Penalties were based instead upon the weight of the pure drug involved.

The current penalties for LSD distribution originated in the Anti-Drug Abuse Act of 1986. Congress adopted a "market-oriented" approach to punishing drug trafficking, under which the total quantity of what is distributed, rather than the amount of pure drug involved, is used to determine the length of the sentence. To implement that principle, Congress set mandatory minimum sentences corresponding to the weight of a "mixture or substance containing a detectable amount of" the various controlled substances, including LSD. It intended the penalties for drug trafficking to be graduated according to the weight of the drugs in whatever form they were found — cut or uncut, pure or impure, ready for wholesale or ready for distribution at the retail level. Congress did not want to punish retail traffickers less severely, even though they deal in smaller quantities of the pure drug, because such traffickers keep the street markets going. . . .

Petitioners argue that the due process of law guaranteed them by the Fifth Amendment is violated by determining the lengths of their sentences in accordance with the weight of the LSD "carrier," a factor which they insist is arbitrary. . . . We find that Congress had a rational basis for its choice of penalties for LSD distribution. The penalty scheme set out in the Anti-Drug Abuse Act of 1986 is intended to punish severely large-volume drug traffickers at any level. . . . That is a rational sentencing scheme.

This is as true with respect to LSD as it is with respect to other drugs. Although LSD is not sold by weight, but by dose, and a carrier medium is not, strictly speaking, used to "dilute" the drug, that medium is used to facilitate the distribution of the drug. Blotter paper makes LSD easier to transport, store, conceal, and sell. It is a tool of the trade for those who traffic in the drug, and therefore it was rational for Congress to set penalties based on this chosen tool. Congress was also justified in seeking to avoid arguments about the accurate weight of pure drugs which might have been extracted from blotter paper had it chosen to calibrate sentences according to that weight. . . .

Petitioners argue that those selling different numbers of doses, and, therefore, with different degrees of culpability, will be subject to the same minimum sentence because of choosing different carriers. The same objection could be made to a statute that imposed a fixed sentence for distributing any quantity of LSD, in any form, with any carrier. Such a sentencing scheme — not considering individual degrees of culpability — would clearly be constitutional. Congress has the power to define criminal punishments without giving the courts any sentencing discretion. Determinate sentences were found in this country's penal codes from its inception, and some have remained until the present. . . . That distributors of varying degrees of culpability might be subject to the same sentence does not mean that the penalty system for LSD distribution is unconstitutional. . . .

STEVENS, J., dissenting.

The consequences of the majority's construction of 21 U.S.C. §841 are so bizarre that I cannot believe they were intended by Congress. [There] is no evidence that Congress intended the weight of the carrier to be considered in the sentence determination in LSD cases, and that there is good reason to believe Congress was unaware of the inequitable consequences of the Court's interpretation of the statute. . . .

In light of the ambiguity of the phrase "mixture or substance" and the lack of legislative history to guide us, it is necessary to examine the congressional purpose behind the statute. [The] majority's construction will lead to anomalous sentences that are contrary to one of the central purposes of the Sentencing Guidelines, which was to eliminate disparity in sentencing. [Widely] divergent sentences may be imposed for the sale of identical amounts of a controlled substance simply because of the nature of the carrier. If 100 doses of LSD were sold on sugar cubes, the sentence would range from 188-235 months, whereas if the same dosage were sold in its pure liquid form, the sentence would range only from 10-16 months. The absurdity and inequity of this result is emphasized in Judge Posner's dissent:

> . . . A person who sells five doses of LSD on sugar cubes is not a worse person than a manufacturer of LSD who is caught with 19,999 doses in pure form, but the former is subject to a ten-year mandatory minimum no-parole sentence, while the latter is not even subject to the five-year minimum. If defendant Chapman, who received five years for selling a thousand doses of LSD on blotter paper, had sold the same number of doses in pure form, his Guidelines sentence would have been fourteen months. . . . In none of these computations, by the way, does the weight of the LSD itself make a difference — so slight is its weight relative to that of the carrier — except of course when it is sold in pure form. Congress might as well have said: if there is a carrier, weigh the carrier and forget the LSD. . . .

Sentencing disparities that have been described as "crazy" and "loony" could well be avoided if the majority did not insist upon stretching the definition of "mixture" to include the carrier along with the LSD. It does not make sense to include a carrier in calculating the weight of the LSD because LSD, unlike drugs such as cocaine or marijuana, is sold by dosage, rather than by weight. Thus, whether one dose of LSD is added to a glass of orange juice or to a pitcher of orange juice, it is still only one dose that has been added. But if the weight of the orange juice is to be added to the calculation, then the person who sells the single dose of LSD in a pitcher, rather than in a glass, will receive a substantially higher sentence. If the weight of the carrier is included in the calculation, not only does it lead to huge disparities in sentences among LSD offenders, but also it leads to disparities when LSD sentences are compared to sentences for other drugs. [The severity of the sentences in LSD cases would be comparable to those in other drug cases only if the weight of the LSD carrier were disregarded. Congress] did not express any intention to treat those who sell LSD differently from those who sell other dangerous drugs. . . .

NOTES

1. *Quantity-based measures of harm in drug offenses.* Federal statutes and guidelines make sentences for most drug convictions depend primarily on the

type and amount of drugs involved in the offense. Section 2D1.1(c) of the federal guidelines provides that the base offense level for most drug convictions depends on the type and amount of drugs involved. Much of the wrangling at sentencing hearings in drug cases (the largest single category of crimes now charged in the federal system) revolves around the amount of drugs actually involved in the sale or the amount "reasonably foreseeable" to the defendant. Courts must determine how to calculate specific drug quantities and the requisite mens rea for attributing drug amounts to particular offenders so as to quantify the harm created by a particular offender.

As intimated in *Chapman,* federal drug sentencing has not always relied on drug quantities. In 1956 Congress mandated minimum sentences for drug importation and distribution offenses through the Narcotic Control Act, but in the Comprehensive Drug Abuse Prevention and Control Act of 1970 Congress repealed these mandates and returned significant discretion to judges in setting drug sentences. Through a series of statutory enactments in the mid-1980s, however, Congress directly linked mandatory minimum penalties and sentencing ranges to the type and quantity of drugs involved in the offense. When it first created the federal sentencing guidelines, the U.S. Sentencing Commission also adopted a quantity-based scheme for drug sentencing in an effort to harmonize its guidelines with Congress's sentencing mandates. See William W. Wilkins Jr. et al., Competing Sentencing Policies in a "War on Drugs" Era, 28 Wake Forest L. Rev. 305 (1993).

Many state jurisdictions in the 1970s and 1980s also joined the trend of using quantity-based measures of culpability and mandatory sentencing terms for drug crimes. New York began this trend in 1973 with the passage of the "Rockefeller drug laws" (named for Governor Nelson Rockefeller) requiring mandatory 15-year prison sentences for possession or sales of relatively small amounts of narcotics. The New York Court of Appeals interpreted the statute to require proof that a defendant knew about the amount of drugs involved, but the state legislature later eliminated this requirement. See People v. Ryan, 626 N.E.2d 51 (N.Y. 1993). In 1978 Michigan enacted the so-called 650 lifer law, which required mandatory life imprisonment for possession or sale of 650 grams of cocaine or heroin. See Harmelin v. Michigan, 501 U.S. 957 (1991) (upholding this sanction against a constitutional challenge). A number of states that have adopted guideline systems (including Virginia and Kansas) have separate sentencing grids for drug offenses, and these systems also rely heavily on drug types and quantities.

2. *Quantification of crack versus powder cocaine.* The use of quantity measures for assessing the seriousness of drug offenses has proved most controversial in the context of cocaine, especially in the federal system. Federal statutes and guidelines incorporate a "100-to-1 ratio" between powder cocaine and crack — that is, an offense must involve 500 grams of powder cocaine, but only 5 grams of crack, to trigger a five-year minimum penalty. As discussed more fully in Chapter 9, this 100-to-1 ratio has been the subject of heated debate for a number of years, primarily because of its disparate impact on minority defendants.

3. *Quantity-based measures of harm for economic offenses.* Under the federal sentencing guidelines, sentence severity for economic offenses such as fraud increases with the value of the property involved. For losses greater than $5,000,

§2B1.1 calls for incremental increases in the offense level as the amount of loss rises. The sentencing judge adds two levels for losses over $5,000, four levels for losses over $10,000, and so on, to the top of the scale: add 26 levels for losses of more than $100 million. Because the U.S. Sentencing Commission made the concept of "loss" the centerpiece for setting sentence length in fraud and theft cases, loss calculations have generated lots of litigation and numerous doctrinal splits within the federal circuits. As a result, the commission in 2001 made a considered effort to reform the guidelines' "loss table" to created a doctrinally coherent, easy-to-apply set of rules. The old rules defined "loss" to mean "the value of the property taken, damaged or destroyed." The current amended rules give more specific guidance on the question of causation. The sentence turns on the actual or intended loss, whichever is greater, and actual loss is defined as "the reasonably foreseeable pecuniary harm that resulted from the offense." This definition requires, at a minimum, that the defendant's offense be a cause-in-fact of the economic harm. But it also limits losses to those foreseeable to a reasonable person. See Frank O. Bowman III, The 2001 Economic Crime Sentencing Reform: An Analysis and Legislative History, 35 Ind. L. Rev. 5 (2001).

In the federal system, all fraud and theft offenses use the same loss table, and the amount of loss determines the bulk of the punishment (for fraud, the base offense is six and the loss could add up to 26 levels to that base). Robbery, under §2B3.1, uses a separate loss table and the loss determines a smaller proportion of the sentence: the base offense is 20, and the amount of loss could add only seven further levels. Why does loss account for relatively more of the sentence in fraud or theft than in robbery cases? Are there recurring features of frauds or thefts that should figure more heavily in the sentence? Think again about the robberies described in Problems 4-1 and 4-3. To what extent does the amount of money lost in each robbery determine in your mind the seriousness of the crime?

4. *Statutory interpretation absurd results.*   As the dissenting opinion in *Chapman* argues, the LSD punishment scheme based on weight of the carrier can produce absurd results. How can judges best respond to such a statute? Two distinguished federal judges, Frank Easterbrook and Richard Posner, debated this question in the lower court opinions in this case. Judge Easterbrook suggested that judges ordinarily must enforce what they believe to be an unwise sentencing scheme:

> A preference for giving statutes a constitutional meaning is a reason to construe, not to rewrite or "improve." Canons are doubt-resolvers, useful when the language is ambiguous and a construction of the statute is fairly possible by which the question may be avoided. "Substance or mixture containing a detectable quantity" is not ambiguous. . . . The canon about avoiding constitutional decisions, in particular, must be used with care, for it is a closer cousin to invalidation than to interpretation. It is a way to enforce the constitutional penumbra, and therefore an aspect of constitutional law proper. Constitutional decisions breed penumbras, which multiply questions. Treating each as justification to construe laws out of existence too greatly enlarges the judicial power.

United States v. Marshall, 908 F.2d 1312, 1318 (7th Cir. 1990). Judge Posner's dissent described a more active form of statutory interpretation for judges:

> Well, what if anything can we judges do about this mess? The answer lies in the shadow of a jurisprudential disagreement . . . between the severely positivistic

view that the content of law is exhausted in clear, explicit, and definite enactments . . . from legislatures, and the natural lawyer's or legal pragmatist's view
that the practice of interpretation and the general terms of the Constitution
(such as "equal protection of the laws") authorize judges to enrich positive law
with the moral values and practical concerns of civilized society. Judges who in
other respects have seemed quite similar, such as Holmes and Cardozo, have
taken opposite sides of this issue. Neither approach is entirely satisfactory. The
first buys political neutrality and a type of objectivity at the price of substantive
injustice, while the second buys justice in the individual case at the price of considerable uncertainty and, not infrequently, judicial willfulness. It is no wonder
that our legal system oscillates between the approaches. The positivist view, applied unflinchingly to this case, commands the affirmance of prison sentences
that are exceptionally harsh by the standards of the modern Western world, dictated by an accidental, unintended scheme of punishment nevertheless implied
by the words (taken one by one) of the relevant enactments. The natural law or
pragmatist view leads to a freer interpretation, one influenced by norms of
equal treatment.

908 F.2d at 1334-1335. Is it possible to generalize about when judges should use
each of these approaches to statutory interpretation?

PROBLEM 4-7.   GETTING TOUGH ON DRUNK DRIVERS

The National Commission Against Drunk Driving reports that state laws
"frequently fail to reflect the seriousness" of driving while intoxicated. "Courts
frequently impose lenient sentences without regard for the offender's driving
and criminal record, alcohol problems, or the damage caused to the victims.
This undercuts any general deterrent effect of the laws regulating the drinking
driver."

You are a senator in a state where a number of serious, well-publicized accidents have occurred recently involving intoxicated drivers with a history of
drinking and driving. Your state law currently provides for a maximum sentence
of six months' imprisonment for a first drunk-driving offense and a three-year
maximum for a repeat offender. Bills are circulating to increase the statutory
penalties for driving while intoxicated.

One bill—entitled Responding to Inebriated Drivers (RID)—increases
the range of available punishment for driving under the influence. The RID bill
proposes to raise the maximum sentence for a first offense to five years and the
maximum sentence for repeat offenders to 20 years. The bill gives sentencing
judges broad discretion to individualize punishments while suggesting that
higher sentences would be more fitting for offenders with high blood-alcohol
content at the time of arrest.

Another bill—entitled Taking on Utterly Grotesque Harmers
(TOUGH)—mandates minimum sentences for those who cause property or
bodily harm while drinking and driving. Specifically, the TOUGH bill requires
at least a one-year imprisonment term for anyone who causes more than $500
of property damage, at least five years' imprisonment for anyone who causes serious physical harm, and 20 years' imprisonment for anyone who causes a death
while driving under the influence.

Which bill would you support? Why?

3.   The Role of Mens Rea and Motive

a.   Strict Liability Sentencing Factors

Legal philosopher H. L. A. Hart, in his renowned text on criminal law and punishment theory entitled *Punishment and Responsibility,* referred to this fundamental principle of just punishment: "causing harm intentionally must be punished more severely than causing the same harm unintentionally." Though legislatures have usually taken this advice to heart when grading offenses, they do not give mens rea concepts so much weight at sentencing.

‖ *United States v. Ana Marin de Velasquez* ‖
28 F.3d 2 (2d Cir. 1994)

McLaughlin, J.

Ana Marin de Velasquez arrived at New York's John F. Kennedy International Airport from Colombia. During a customs inspection, she appeared to be extremely nervous and was sweating profusely. A search of the soles of the shoes she was wearing revealed that the shoes contained 167.8 grams of heroin. Customs agents also determined that she was transporting 636.3 grams of heroin internally, for a total of 804.1 grams.

After her arrest, the defendant admitted to agents that she was transporting drugs internally, but disclaimed all knowledge of the drugs found in the soles of her shoes. She claimed that Colombian drug traffickers gave her a pair of shoes that would identify her to her New York contact but she never knew the shoes contained heroin. Eventually, defendant pled guilty to importing heroin. During the plea allocution, defendant stated that she knew she was importing narcotics, although she did not know what kind. . . . In calculating the total quantity of heroin defendant possessed for sentencing purposes, the court included the heroin in defendant's shoes.

Defendant argues that the mens rea doctrine and considerations of due process required the district court to exclude the heroin in her shoes when calculating the total amount of drugs she possessed for sentencing purposes. In the alternative, she argues that the heroin in her shoes should have been included only if it was reasonably foreseeable that her shoes contained heroin.

[We have previously] held that neither due process nor the doctrine of mens rea requires that a defendant actually know the total quantity of drugs in his possession to be sentenced for the full amount under the Sentencing Guidelines. We reaffirm that holding here. We now [also] hold that in a possession case the sentence should be based on the total amount of drugs in the defendant's possession, without regard to foreseeability.

[Federal law] makes it a crime to "knowingly" import certain illicit drugs into the United States [and] makes it a crime to "knowingly" manufacture, distribute, or otherwise possess illicit drugs. Quantity is not part of the corpus delicti, i.e., forms no part of the substantive offense under any of these statutes. Conviction rests solely on the knowing possession of some quantity, however large or small, of illicit drugs.

Quantity comes into play only at the sentencing stage, where it determines the minimum or maximum penalty the defendant may receive. It is settled that the minimum and maximum sentences are to be strictly imposed, regardless of the defendant's state of mind concerning the total quantity of drugs in his possession. Mens rea and due process concerns are fully satisfied at the conviction stage, where the defendant must be found guilty of, or plead to, "knowingly" possessing some amount of drugs. . . .

Particularly in drug offense cases, it is by no means unusual to peg the sentence to factors that were not known — or even foreseeable — to the defendant at the time the crime was committed. For example, a defendant who distributes drugs within 1000 feet of a school is subject to twice the maximum penalties for drug distribution. This is true, regardless of whether he knew or could foresee that he was within the proscribed distance. Similarly, a defendant who distributes drugs to a minor is subject to twice the maximum penalty, regardless of whether he knew or could foresee that the buyer was a minor. Thus, there is nothing startling, or even notable, in the conclusion that a defendant who knows she is carrying some quantity of illicit drugs should be sentenced for the full amount on her person. This remains true even where, as here, defendant claims she did not know she was carrying an additional quantity of drugs — additional to the packet she agreed to carry.

A fertile imagination can conjure bizarre situations where the defendant's possession is tenuous and fleeting. The statute has yet to be drafted that could not be unconstitutionally applied in some extraordinary case, and these cases will have to be dealt with if they arise. Here, however, the defendant was wearing the very shoes that contained the heroin. Clearly, her possession was not ephemeral, and the statute properly applied to her. . . .

There is no requirement under the Guidelines that the defendant know or foresee the total quantity of drugs in his possession to be sentenced for the full amount — just as there is no such requirement under the statutes. [The] Guidelines provide that defendants are accountable for "all quantities" of drugs with which they are "directly involved."

The Guidelines contain two enlightening illustrations. In the first, a hypothetical defendant is arrested while assisting in offloading a ship containing a large amount of marijuana. In the second, a defendant transports a suitcase knowing that it contains some quantity of drugs. In both cases, the Guidelines conclude, the defendant's sentence should be based on the full amount of drugs involved, "without regard to the issue of reasonable foreseeability" and "regardless of his knowledge or lack of knowledge." Thus, the Guidelines make clear that a defendant who knowingly possesses some quantity of illicit drugs cannot disclaim "direct involvement" with the full amount on the ground that the full amount was not foreseeable. . . .

In a possession case, . . . we see no reason why a defendant who knowingly traffics in drugs should not bear the risk that his conduct may be more harmful to society than he intends or foresees. We decline to fashion a rule that would permit a defendant to avoid the consequences of that risk because of a fortuitous lack of knowledge or foreseeability — fortuities which apparently occur with some frequency. See United States v. Ekwunoh, 12 F.3d 368, 369 (2d Cir. 1993) (defendant thought she possessed 400 grams of heroin instead of one kilogram); United States v. Obi, 947 F.2d 1031, 1032 (2d Cir. 1991) (defendant thought he was importing cocaine rather than heroin). In the drug trade, there is always the chance, as is alleged in most of these cases, that the supplier will not recognize "the punctilio of an honor the most sensitive." Meinhard v. Salmon, 164 N.E. 545, 546 (N.Y. 1928) (Cardozo, J.). . . .

It is certainly possible, of course, to imagine a situation where the gap between belief and actuality was so great as to make the Guideline grossly unfair in application. In such cases, a downward departure may be appropriate. The Guidelines, however, were designed to apply to the ordinary mine-run case. This is such a case. Applying the foregoing principles, we believe Ana Marin de Velasquez was properly sentenced for the total amount of heroin in her possession, without regard to whether she knew or could foresee the heroin concealed in her shoes.

NOTES

1. *The role (or lack thereof) of mens rea at sentencing.*   Though mens rea concepts are usually integral to legislative grading of offenses, mens rea issues are secondary or altogether ignored at sentencing. In the federal system, drug type and quantity (along with a number of other increases to the offense level) apply as a matter of strict liability. See United States v. Litchfield, 986 F.2d 21 (2d Cir. 1993) (guideline increasing sentence for possession of stolen firearm did not require knowledge that firearm was stolen); United States v. Lewin, 900 F.2d 145 (8th Cir. 1990) (upholding penalty enhancement for distribution of drugs when sale occurs within 1,000 feet of school, regardless of defendant's knowledge of proximity); United States v. Schnell, 982 F.2d 216 (7th Cir. 1992) (upholding enhancement for possession of firearm with an altered or obliterated serial number regardless of knowledge about obliteration). Jack B. Weinstein, a federal district court judge, laments the lowly place of mens rea in federal sentencing:

> Mens rea, a principle central to our criminal law, is crucial in linking punishment to individual culpability. It is the bridge between morality and law. Yet, in the guidelines era, mens rea has been all but eliminated from the sentencing of drug offenders. This development is a disastrous departure from the great traditions of Anglo-American law. . . .
> Courts have defended the absence of mens rea protections in sentencing as not "in any way criminaliz[ing] otherwise innocent activity." Is this really so? In *de Velasquez*, the defendant effectively committed a second crime of which she had no knowledge. Had the drugs in her shoes been the only contraband on her, mens rea principles dictate that she could not have been convicted.

Jack B. Weinstein and Fred A. Bernstein, The Denigration of Mens Rea in Drug Sentencing, 7 Fed. Sentencing Rep. 121, 121-122 (1994). The authors illustrate their point with a "simple hypothetical":

> Your daughter is packing up her car to return home after her first year of college. A friend who is helping her pack asks her to carry a parcel home to a mutual friend, Steven. To your daughter's query, "What's in it?" her friend answers, "Some Stephen King novels and a couple of joints." In fact, there is more than a kilogram of cocaine in the box, which is discovered when your daughter is pulled over for a traffic violation. Your daughter is properly charged with

possession with intent to distribute (to Steven). Her intent related to two marijuana cigarettes, yet the government contends that she should be punished for
transporting a kilogram of cocaine. The sentence? Years in prison. Despite this
frightening prospect, the government insists that your daughter's contention —
that she was unaware that she was carrying cocaine — is irrelevant "at the sentencing stage."

Weinstein and Bernstein, 7 Fed. Sentencing Rep. at 123. Is the government's argument in this hypothetical case a necessary logical consequence of the holding
in *de Velasquez*?

2. *Reasonable foreseeability in conspiracy cases.* Though mens rea does not
have a guaranteed place in sentencing determinations, the federal sentencing
guidelines do provide in commentary to the relevant conduct rules that a defendant charged with conspiracy will be sentenced only for conduct that was
reasonably foreseeable by the individual defendant. See U.S. Sentencing Guidelines Manual §1B1.3, cmt. n.1 ("In the case of criminal activity undertaken in
concert with others . . . the conduct for which the defendant 'would be otherwise accountable' also includes conduct of others in furtherance of the execution of the jointly-undertaken criminal activity that was reasonably foreseeable
by the defendant"). Though it is akin to a test of a defendant's subjective mens
rea, federal courts in sentencing cases have stressed that the "test as to whether
conduct is reasonably foreseeable is an objective one." United States v. Cochran,
14 F.3d 1128, 1133 (6th Cir. 1994).

b.   Hate Crimes and the Relevance of Motive

While mens rea matters *less* at sentencing than for the substantive crime, a
defendant's motives (that is, her reasons for committing the crime) tend to matter *more* at sentencing. Sentencing statutes and rules allow judges to consider
motives. Indeed, for some particular motives, the rules call for mandatory increases in the sentence.

|| *Wisconsin v. Todd Mitchell* ||
508 U.S. 476 (1993)

REHNQUIST, C.J.
Respondent Todd Mitchell's sentence for aggravated battery was enhanced
because he intentionally selected his victim on account of the victim's race. The
question presented in this case is whether this penalty enhancement is prohibited by the First and Fourteenth Amendments. We hold that it is not.

On the evening of October 7, 1989, a group of young black men and boys,
including Mitchell, gathered at an apartment complex in Kenosha, Wisconsin.
Several members of the group discussed a scene from the motion picture
"Mississippi Burning," in which a white man beat a young black boy who was pray-
ing. The group moved outside and Mitchell asked them: "Do you all feel hyped
up to move on some white people?" Shortly thereafter, a young white boy approached the group on the opposite side of the street where they were standing.
As the boy walked by, Mitchell said: "You all want to fuck somebody up? There

goes a white boy; go get him." Mitchell counted to three and pointed in the boy's direction. The group ran toward the boy, beat him severely, and stole his tennis shoes. The boy was rendered unconscious and remained in a coma for four days.

After a jury trial in the Circuit Court for Kenosha County, Mitchell was convicted of aggravated battery. That offense ordinarily carries a maximum sentence of two years' imprisonment. But because the jury found that Mitchell had intentionally selected his victim because of the boy's race, the maximum sentence for Mitchell's offense was increased to seven years under [a Wisconsin statutory provision that] enhances the maximum penalty for an offense whenever the defendant "[i]ntentionally selects the person against whom the crime . . . is committed . . . because of the race, religion, color, disability, sexual orientation, national origin or ancestry of that person. . . ." The Circuit Court sentenced Mitchell to four years' imprisonment for the aggravated battery. Mitchell . . . appealed his conviction and sentence, challenging the constitutionality of Wisconsin's penalty-enhancement provision on First Amendment grounds. The Wisconsin . . . Supreme Court held that the statute "violates the First Amendment directly by punishing what the legislature has deemed to be offensive thought." . . .

The State argues that the statute does not punish bigoted thought, as the Supreme Court of Wisconsin said, but instead punishes only [the conduct of intentional selection of a victim]. While this argument is literally correct, it does not dispose of Mitchell's First Amendment challenge. To be sure, . . . a physical assault is not by any stretch of the imagination expressive conduct protected by the First Amendment. But the fact remains that under the Wisconsin statute the same criminal conduct may be more heavily punished if the victim is selected because of his race or other protected status than if no such motive obtained. . . . Because the only reason for the enhancement is the defendant's discriminatory motive for selecting his victim, Mitchell argues (and the Wisconsin Supreme Court held) that the statute violates the First Amendment by punishing offenders' bigoted beliefs.

Traditionally, sentencing judges have considered a wide variety of factors in addition to evidence bearing on guilt in determining what sentence to impose on a convicted defendant. The defendant's motive for committing the offense is one important factor. See 1 W. LaFave & A. Scott, Substantive Criminal Law §3.6(b) (1986) ("Motives are most relevant when the trial judge sets the defendant's sentence, and it is not uncommon for a defendant to receive a minimum sentence because he was acting with good motives, or a rather high sentence because of his bad motives"). Thus, in many States the commission of a murder, or other capital offense, for pecuniary gain is a separate aggravating circumstance under the capital sentencing statute.

[M]otive plays the same role under the Wisconsin statute as it does under federal and state antidiscrimination laws, which we have previously upheld against constitutional challenge. Title VII of the Civil Rights Act of 1964, for example, makes it unlawful for an employer to discriminate against an employee "*because of* such individual's race, color, religion, sex, or national origin." 42 U.S.C. §2000e-2(a)(1) (emphasis added). [We have] rejected the argument that Title VII infringed employers' First Amendment rights. . . .

Nothing in our decision last Term in R.A.V. v. St. Paul, 505 U.S. 377 (1992), compels a different result here. That case involved a First Amendment challenge to a municipal ordinance prohibiting the use of "fighting words" that insult, or provoke violence, "on the basis of race, color, creed, religion or gender." Because the ordinance only proscribed a class of "fighting words" deemed particularly offensive by the city — i.e., those "that contain . . . messages of bias-motivated hatred," we held that it violated the rule against content-based discrimination. But whereas the ordinance struck down in *R.A.V.* was explicitly directed at expression (i.e., "speech" or "messages"), the statute in this case is aimed at conduct unprotected by the First Amendment.

Moreover, the Wisconsin statute singles out for enhancement bias-inspired conduct because this conduct is thought to inflict greater individual and societal harm. For example, according to the State and its amici, bias-motivated crimes are more likely to provoke retaliatory crimes, inflict distinct emotional harms on their victims, and incite community unrest. The State's desire to redress these perceived harms provides an adequate explanation for its penalty-enhancement provision over and above mere disagreement with offenders' beliefs or biases. As Blackstone said long ago, "it is but reasonable that among crimes of different natures those should be most severely punished, which are the most destructive of the public safety and happiness." 4 W. Blackstone, Commentaries.

Finally, there remains to be considered Mitchell's argument that the Wisconsin statute is unconstitutionally overbroad because of its "chilling effect" on free speech. Mitchell argues (and the Wisconsin Supreme Court agreed) that the statute is "overbroad" because evidence of the defendant's prior speech or associations may be used to prove that the defendant intentionally selected his victim on account of the victim's protected status. . . .

The sort of chill envisioned here is far more attenuated and unlikely than that contemplated in traditional "overbreadth" cases. [T]he prospect of a citizen suppressing his bigoted beliefs for fear that evidence of such beliefs will be introduced against him at trial if he commits a more serious offense against person or property . . . is simply too speculative a hypothesis to support Mitchell's overbreadth claim. . . .

NOTES

1. *Hate crimes legislation.*   States have passed an array of hate crimes laws that either create new crimes based on the offender's motives or enhance penalties for existing crimes if the government proves that the offender committed the crime because of characteristics of the victim. See, e.g., Fla. Stat. Ann. §921.0016(3); Haw. Rev. Stat. §706-662(6). In addition to statutes prohibiting violence or intimidation toward persons based on certain characteristics, some state laws prohibit vandalism of religious sites, the wearing of masks, and the burning of crosses. States still differ as to the size of the penalty enhancement, the types of biases that trigger these sentence enhancements, and the predicate offenses that may qualify as hate crimes. Congress has often debated but never passed federal hate crimes legislation. It did in 1994 enact the Hate Crime Statistics Act, 28 U.S.C. §534, which requires the federal government to collect and publish information concerning crimes that "manifest evidence of prejudice based on race, religion, disability, sexual orientation, or ethnicity."

Following the lead of Wisconsin v. Mitchell, most state courts hold that sentencing enhancements for hate crimes are consistent with their state constitutions. See, e.g., In re M.S., 896 P.2d 1365 (Cal. 1995); State v. McKnight,

511 N.W.2d 389 (Iowa 1994); State v. Wyant, 624 N.E.2d 722 (Ohio 1994). Though broad consensus exists concerning the constitutionality of most hate crimes legislation, considerable dispute remains over the soundness of these politically popular provisions. Scholarly commentary on the functioning of hate crimes has been dynamic and varied. See James B. Jacobs and Kimberly Potter, Hate Crimes: Criminal Law and Identity Politics 4 (1998). Apart from worries about the free speech and association rights of a defendant, can you think of any potential negative effects of a sentencing enhancement for offenders who select their victims based on race? On religion? On sex? On sexual orientation?

2. *Economic motives as an aggravating factor.*   As the *Mitchell* Court notes, sentencing judges and juries have a long tradition of considering various motives at sentencing. In capital cases in particular, many jurisdictions have statutes that call for the judge or jury to consider whether a murder was committed for "pecuniary gain." See, e.g., 18 U.S.C. §3952(c)(8); Ariz. Rev. Stat. Ann. §13-703(F)(5). In addition, a number of sentencing guideline states provide that an economic motivation aggravates the offense in ways calling for an enhanced sentence. See N.C. Gen. Stat. §15A-1340.16(d)(4) (aggravating factor present when "defendant was hired or paid to commit the offense").

PROBLEM 4-8.   ROB ANON (a.k.a. JEAN VALJEAN?) REVISITED

Though it is common for statutes or guidelines to provide expressly that certain "bad" motives will increase a sentence, rarely are there provisions expressly stating that "good" motives can reduce a sentence. An exception might be provisions that encourage a mitigated sentence when a defendant commits an offense because of serious coercion, blackmail, or duress. These rules might well be understood as reducing the defendant's sentence because his reason for doing wrong is not so bad. The provision of the federal sentencing guidelines that encourages a reduced sentence based on coercion or duress, U.S. Sentencing Guidelines Manual §5K2.12, goes on to state that "personal financial difficulties and economic pressures upon a trade or business do not warrant a decrease in sentence."

Do you agree with the U.S. Sentencing Commission that personal financial pressures should not warrant a decrease in sentence? Consider again the case of Rob Anon, described above in Problem 4-1, and now imagine that he had a profound personal motivation for his crime: his fiancée was in a car accident and lacked medical insurance or the personal funds needed to pay for a life-saving operation. In light of this "personal financial difficulty," would you be willing to decrease his sentence? Cf. *John Q.* (New Line Cinema 2002).

C.   THE ROLE OF VICTIMS AND THE COMMUNITY

One key source of information about the harm that a crime causes is the victim of the crime. In a traditional indeterminate sentencing system, victims do not formally address the sentencing court. Of course, the prosecutor attempts in many cases to bring the victim's concerns or information to the court's attention, and the judge may account for this in imposing a sentence. But until recently, the victim had little opportunity to speak directly to the sentencing court.

In recent decades, most jurisdictions have created a formal role for victims at sentencing. But what impact should victims have on individual sentences? Should the victim's personal or family circumstances matter? Will these factors, if considered, become a cover for invidious factors such as wealth and race?

State v. Rasheed Muhammad
678 A.2d 164 (N.J. 1996)

GARIBALDI, J.

Defendant is charged with the kidnapping, rape, and murder of an eight-year-old child, Jakiyah McClain. On the afternoon of April 1, 1995, Jakiyah received permission from her mother to visit a friend, Ah-Tavia Maxey, who lived only a few blocks away. Jakiyah arrived at her friend's apartment between 4:00 P.M. and 5:00 P.M. . . .

While Jakiyah and Ah-Tavia were talking, defendant entered the apartment building. He volunteered to walk Jakiyah upstairs. He knew Jakiyah's mother. Ah-Tavia watched defendant take Jakiyah's hand and lead her upstairs. Ah-Tavia apparently remained on the ground floor. Shortly after, Ah-Tavia heard kicking, banging, and the sound of Jakiyah's screams. [The next day, the] police found Jakiyah's body, curled in a fetal position with her underpants around one ankle, under a pile of clothes in the bedroom closet [of Muhammad's apartment]. Ah-Tavia Maxey identified defendant as the man she saw the day before with Jakiyah.

Defendant was taken into custody. He gave a statement to the police in which he admitted to kidnapping, sexually assaulting, and murdering Jakiyah. An autopsy of the victim indicated that the cause of death was asphyxiation and that the victim was sexually assaulted. On June 27, 1995, an Essex County Grand Jury indicted defendant for the capital murder of Jakiyah McClain. . . . Defendant brought a pretrial motion, challenging the constitutionality of the victim impact statute under both the New Jersey and United States Constitutions. The trial court granted defendant's motion and declared the statute unconstitutional under both Constitutions. . . .

In 1985, the Legislature enacted the Crime Victim's Bill of Rights, which granted crime victims and witnesses certain rights, including the right to be treated with dignity, the right to be informed about the criminal justice process, and the right to be told about available remedies and social services. The following year, the Legislature [allowed] family members of murder victims to include a written statement in the defendant's presentence report. In 1991, the Legislature amended the Crime Victim's Bill of Rights to provide victims with the opportunity to submit to a representative of the county prosecutor's office a written statement about the impact of the crime on the family and to allow victims to make in-person victim impact statements in non-capital cases directly to the sentencing court.

Finally, on November 5, 1991, the New Jersey electorate overwhelmingly approved Article I, paragraph 22 of the New Jersey Constitution, which is better known as the Victim's Rights Amendment. . . . The Victim's Rights Amendment explicitly authorizes the Legislature to provide victims with "those rights and remedies" that are deemed appropriate to effectuate the purpose of that amendment. On the basis of that constitutional authority . . . the New Jersey Legislature enacted the victim impact statute [in 1995].

The various victims' statutory rights enacted in this State are the product of a "victims' rights" movement that has swept through this nation over the last two decades. Historically, the legal system did not view crime victims as having any rights. Because criminal attacks were viewed as attacks and threats on the entire community, and were prosecuted by the state on behalf of "the people," the actual victim was treated as merely another piece of evidence. Although victims were expected to cooperate with authorities and to testify as part of the state's case-in-chief, little attention was paid to the financial, physical, and emotional needs of victims. [Crime] victims are largely excluded from the criminal justice system, and . . . those who are able to participate suffer a "second victimization" at the hands of the system. That feeling of isolation from the system causes many victims and their families to report widespread dissatisfaction with the criminal system. . . .

The victim impact statute provides that if the defendant presents evidence of his character or record pursuant to [a "catch-all" statutory provision allowing introduction of any mitigating evidence during his capital sentencing trial], the State may present evidence of the murder victim's character and background and of the impact of the murder on the victim's survivors. . . . Defendant alleges that the admission of victim impact statements in a capital case is likely to confuse and impassion the jury, and thus creates an impermissible risk that the penalty decision will be made in an arbitrary and capricious manner rather than on the basis of the relevant evidence. . . . The State contends that victim impact evidence is relevant to the sentencing decision because it illustrates each victim's uniqueness as a human being and the nature of the harm caused by the defendant's criminal conduct. . . .

The victim impact statute does not violate the United States Constitution. [In Payne v. Tennessee, 501 U.S. 808 (1991), the] Supreme Court overruled the prior holdings of Booth v. Maryland, 482 U.S. 496 (1987), in which the Court held that the Eighth Amendment prohibits a capital sentencing jury from receiving victim impact evidence relating to the personal characteristics of the murder victim and the emotional impact of the death on the victim's family, and South Carolina v. Gathers, 490 U.S. 805 (1989), in which the Supreme Court extended the rule adopted in *Booth* to statements made by the prosecutor about the personal qualities of the victim.

In reevaluating the exclusion of victim impact evidence, the Court [in *Payne*] rejected two of the premises underlying *Booth* and *Gathers:* first, that evidence of the personal characteristics of the victim and of the emotional impact of the crimes on the family does not in general reflect on the defendant's blameworthiness, and second, that only evidence of moral culpability is relevant to a capital sentencing decision. . . . The Court opined that . . . *Booth* had "unfairly weighted the scales in a capital trial" because it allowed the defendant to introduce virtually all mitigating evidence concerning his own circumstance, but barred the State from offering any victim impact evidence. . . .

The *Payne* Court thus held that if a "State chooses to permit the admission of victim impact evidence and prosecutorial argument on that subject, the

Eighth Amendment erects no per se bar." The majority opined that "[v]ictim impact evidence is simply another form or method of informing the sentencing authority about the specific harm caused by the crime in question, evidence of a general type long considered by sentencing authorities." *Payne* left undisturbed the holding in *Booth* that the admission of a victim's family members' characterizations and opinions about the crime, the defendant, and the appropriate sentence violates the Eighth Amendment.

[Our] State Constitution explicitly provides victims of crimes with more rights than the Federal Constitution. The Victim's Rights Amendment expressly authorizes the Legislature to provide crime victims with "those rights and remedies" as it determines are necessary. Even if we were inclined to diverge from the holding in *Payne* and interpret the Cruel and Unusual Punishment Clause of our State Constitution as providing greater protections against the arbitrary imposition of the death penalty, the text of the New Jersey Constitution demands that we not pursue such an independent course. . . . To hold the victim impact statute unconstitutional would require us to ignore the Victim's Rights Amendment and the will of the electorate that overwhelmingly approved the constitutional amendment. . . .

Defendant asserts that, to the extent that a victim impact statement presents evidence about conditions that the defendant was unaware [of] when he committed the criminal act, such as the victim's occupation and marital status, the statement is irrelevant and impermissibly diverts the jury from making its sentencing decision on the character of the defendant and the circumstances of the crime. However, [while] it is clear that a defendant's foreknowledge of the specific consequences that his acts are likely to have is relevant to sentencing, the foreseeable consequences of a defendant's actions are equally relevant. Murder has foreseeable consequences. . . . Defendants who intentionally choose to kill know that their actions will destroy a unique individual who is likely to be a parent, child, spouse, brother, or sister.

While a defendant might be unaware of the specific characteristics of his victim or of the particular survivors that the victim will leave behind, it is completely foreseeable that the killing will eliminate a unique person and destroy a web of familial relationships. That conclusion is buttressed by the facts of this case. When the killer brutally attacked eight-year-old Jakiyah, it was completely foreseeable that the homicidal behavior would eliminate a uniquely individual human being and cause great harm to the survivors of the little girl. Although the killer might have been ignorant of the details about Jakiyah and her family, it does not violate the Constitution if the jury is permitted to take into account such obviously foreseeable consequences.

Although victim impact evidence when offered to rebut a defendant's presentation of catch-all mitigation evidence is not prohibited by the New Jersey Constitution, it must nevertheless be relevant and reliable. The admission of evidence relating to the victim's character or the impact of the murder on the victim's family requires a balancing of the probative value of the proffered evidence against the risk that its admission may pose the danger of undue prejudice or confusion to the jury. . . .

Although the decision to admit specific victim impact statements will typically be in the discretion of the trial court, certain statements are clearly impermissible. For example, the State will not be permitted to elicit testimony concerning the victim's family members' characterizations and opinions about the defendant, the crime, or the appropriate sentence. . . . Victim impact evidence should be limited to statements designed to show the impact of the crime on the victim's family and to statements that demonstrate that the victim was not a faceless stranger, but was a unique individual human being. There is no place in a capital case for unduly inflammatory commentary. . . .

The Legislature has taken appropriate steps to reduce the possibility that jurors will misuse victim impact evidence. Under the victim impact statute, the admission of victim impact evidence is limited to a clearly delineated course. Only if the jury finds that the State has proven at least one aggravating factor beyond a reasonable doubt and the jury finds the existence of a [catch-all] mitigating factor may the jury consider victim impact evidence. Even if these requirements are met, the victim impact statements can be used solely for the purpose of determining how much weight to attach to the catch-all mitigating factor. Victim impact testimony may not be used as a general aggravating factor or as a means of weighing the worth of the defendant against the worth of the victim. Our law does not regard a crime committed against a particularly virtuous person as more heinous than one committed against a victim whose moral qualities are perhaps less noteworthy or apparent. . . . While legislatures in other states have enacted statutes that allow victim impact evidence to be admitted for any purpose, . . . the New Jersey Legislature was very careful not to allow victim impact evidence to be used as a general aggravating factor. . . .

To harmonize the victim impact statute with the due process clauses of the Federal and State Constitutions, the Attorney General and County Prosecutors Association have both urged us to devise additional procedural safeguards to reduce the possibility that victim impact evidence is admitted for improper purposes or is used inappropriately. As a matter of fairness, we hold that certain additional procedures must be followed before victim impact statements can be entered into evidence. The defendant should be notified prior to the commencement of the penalty phase that the State plans to introduce victim impact evidence if the defendant asserts the catch-all factor. The State shall also provide the defendant with the names of the victim impact witnesses that it plans to call so that defense counsel will have an opportunity to interview the witnesses prior to their testimony. The greater the number of survivors who are permitted to present victim impact evidence, the greater the potential for the victim impact evidence to unduly prejudice the jury against the defendant. Thus, absent special circumstances, we expect that the victim impact testimony of one survivor will be adequate to provide the jury with a glimpse of each victim's uniqueness as a human being and to help the jurors make an informed assessment of the defendant's moral culpability and blameworthiness. Further, minors should not be permitted to present victim impact evidence except under circumstances where there are no suitable adult survivors and thus the child is the closest living relative.

Before a family member is allowed to make a victim impact statement, the trial court should ordinarily conduct a hearing, outside the presence of the jury, to make a preliminary determination as to the admissibility of the State's proffered victim impact evidence. The witness's testimony should be reduced to writing to enable the trial court to review the proposed statement to avoid any prejudicial content. The testimony can provide a general factual profile of the victim, including information about the victim's family, employment, education, and interests. The testimony can describe generally the impact of the victim's death on his or her immediate family. The testimony should be factual, not emotional, and should be free of inflammatory comments or references.

The trial court should weigh each specific point of the proffered testimony to ensure that its probative value is not substantially outweighed by the risk of undue prejudice or misleading the jury. N.J.R.E. 403. Determining the relevance of the proffered testimony is particularly important because of the potential for prejudice and improper influence that is inherent in the presentation of victim impact evidence. However, in making that determination, there is a strong presumption that victim impact evidence that demonstrates that the victim was a unique human being is admissible. During the preliminary hearing, the trial court should inform the victim's family that the court will not allow a witness to testify if the person is unable to control his or her emotions. That concern should be alleviated by our requirement that the witness be permitted only to read his or her previously approved testimony. . . . Finally, the trial court should inform the prosecutor that any comments about victim impact evidence in his or her summation should be strictly limited to the previously approved testimony of the witness. . . .

Even though we hold that the introduction of victim impact statements during the sentencing phase of a capital case does not violate the New Jersey Constitution, we recognize that under certain circumstances victim impact statements could render a defendant's sentencing fundamentally unfair and could lead to the arbitrary imposition of the death penalty. . . . We have confidence in the ability of the courts to determine whether a defendant has been impermissibly prejudiced by the admission of unduly inflammatory victim impact evidence. . . .

HANDLER, J., dissenting.

[Expanding] "relevant evidence" to include victim-impact evidence will effectively prevent a jury from rendering a death penalty verdict based on the defendant's character and the circumstances of the crime. Evidence about the crime victim has always been admissible in a capital prosecution when it is relevant to guilt or innocence. Victim-impact evidence, as now authorized, however, is not relevant to criminal guilt or innocence. A death sentence must be based on a determination of the defendant's deathworthiness in terms of his or her character and the circumstances of the case. The constitutionality of the death penalty based on that determination hinges on the requirement that clear standards guide jury discretion. A jury's consideration of victim-impact evidence, as now authorized by the Court, cannot be controlled by any standards. Jurors will not be capable of disregarding victim-impact evidence's extreme prejudicial effects or avoiding its distorting and devastating impact. Thus, victim-impact evidence will inevitably derail the jury's function and purpose, resulting in the unconstitutional imposition of the death penalty. . . .

The introduction of victim-impact evidence unacceptably exacerbates the racial disparities evident in capital sentencing. Victim-impact evidence encourages jurors to examine and use, both consciously and unconsciously, the comparative worth of the defendant and the victim. Race unquestionably influences our perceptions. . . . Jurors will utilize their unconscious impressions of the victim's worth when considering whether the credibility of the victim-impact evidence and the degree to which the survivors' suffering will counter the weight of the [general mitigating] evidence. First, jurors will consider whether the victim-impact evidence correlates to what the jurors believe is the appropriate impact for the victim's death. Second, jurors will make a moral determination of the gravity of the victim's death. Such steps accentuate disparate capital sentencing on the basis of the victim's race. For these reasons, victim-impact evidence raises the foreboding possibility that death-penalty sentencing decisions influenced by victim-impact evidence will be based on the same invidious motives as race-based discrimination. . . .

NOTES

1. *Victim input at sentencing.*   Over the past 20 years, nearly every state has increased victim involvement at sentencing. See generally National Victim Center, The 1996 Victims' Rights Sourcebook: A Compilation and Comparison of Victims' Rights Laws (1996). Almost all states now permit victim input through the presentence report. Many state laws allow victims a separate opportunity to make a written or oral statement regarding sentencing, often detailing the kinds of information victims may offer. A few states have retained sharper limits, such as those allowing judges to choose whether to admit or refuse victim impact information; Texas allows a victim to make a personal statement in court only *after* sentencing, Tex. Code Crim. Proc. art. 42.03. The Victim and Witness Protection Act of 1982 amended the Federal Rules of Criminal Procedure to require the inclusion of a victim impact statement as a part of the presentence investigation report in federal court. See Fed. R. Crim. P. 32 (presentence report must contain "verified information, stated in a nonargumentative style, containing an assessment of the financial, social, psychological, and medical impact on any individual against whom the offense has been committed"). Why do some jurisdictions (such as New Jersey) accept the victim's statements about the impact of the crime but not the victim's opinion about an appropriate sentence? Cf. Fryer v. State, 68 S.W.2d 628 (Tex. 2002) (law allows sentencing court to consider victim's opinion about proper punishment, as recorded in presentence report; here, victim recommends that defendant in sexual assault case not receive probation).

Victim impact information is supposed to influence the judge; indeed, many statutes require the judge to take account of victim information. The rich variety of statutes has not produced detailed case law regarding victim impact statements outside the capital sentencing context. Is victim impact evidence a less difficult issue in the noncapital setting because a judge rather than a jury selects the sentence? Is a judge more likely to ignore any "emotional" aspects of the victim's testimony? Is it even *possible* to distinguish, as the *Muhammad* court attempted to do, between emotional and informational statements from victims?

2. *Support services for victims.*   Although the law in many jurisdictions now allows a victim to provide formal input to the sentencer (whether jury or judge), most victims in noncapital cases do not take advantage of the opportunity. What practical hurdles might block the routine participation of victims at sentencing?

What support services might a prosecutor's office (or some other government agency) offer to victims that could increase the number of victims who take an active role at sentencing? Do prosecutors have incentives to provide such services?

3. *Vulnerable victims.*   Structured sentencing rules often instruct a judge to enhance a sentence if the victim of the crime was vulnerable or otherwise worthy of exceptional protection. The Minnesota sentencing guidelines authorize the judge to decrease a sentence if "the victim was an aggressor in the incident" and to increase the sentence if the "victim was particularly vulnerable due to age, infirmity, or reduced physical or mental capacity, which was known or should have been known to the offender" or if the "victim was treated with particular cruelty for which the individual offender should be held responsible." Minn. Sentencing Guidelines II.D.2.a.1, II.D.2.b.1 to II.D.2.b.2. The federal guidelines contain a similar provision for enhancement of the sentence by a designated amount if "the defendant knew or should have known that a victim of the offense was unusually vulnerable due to age, physical or mental condition, or that a victim was otherwise particularly susceptible to criminal conduct." U.S. Sentencing Guidelines Manual §3A1.1. A specified increase is also required when the victim is "a government officer or employee" or a law enforcement officer.

4. *Community perspectives at sentencing.*   Crimes rarely have only one victim. Indeed, many crimes affect an entire community. How can the sentencing judge learn about such wide-ranging effects? The Sentencing Reform Act requires the U.S. Sentencing Commission to consider, when creating the federal sentencing guidelines, "the community view of the gravity of the offense." 28 U.S.C. §944(c)(4). Should the commission interpret that instruction to require polls on the views of the national "community" to create one set of guidelines, or does it instead call for the creation of guideline provisions that are uniquely attentive to the various communities that make up the United States? Since the commission chose to create uniform federal guidelines, would it be appropriate for judges in different federal jurisdictions to weigh community impact differently? Federal judge Reena Raggi argues that federal guidelines should allow local variation among federal districts because particular crimes may create special harms in some localities and because the judges in that area develop special expertise on certain topics:

> I first began to question [the nationally uniform approach of the sentencing guidelines] when I had to impose sentences on a number of defendants who had unlawfully transported firearms into New York from other states. Almost daily my fellow New Yorkers and I would read in the press of the senseless shooting of young children, on the streets, even in their own homes, all victims of random gun fire. . . . Almost invariably the guns used in these crimes, as well as most others unlawfully possessed in this area, had come from out of state.
>
> This sort of interstate transportation of guns into the New York area is big business. In the two years between 1990 and 1992, a joint federal-state task force operating in New York arrested 260 people for such trafficking. And yet, when it came time for me to impose sentences in my cases that summer of 1990, I was confronted by a guideline range that rarely exceeded six months' incarceration. When I voiced my concern to the Sentencing Commission about these guidelines for gun trafficking as they applied in New York, I was told that other parts of the country viewed gun crimes differently and that the guidelines were meant to reflect an average. . . .

The insight judges have about crimes in their particular districts goes beyond simply recognizing which conduct is more destructive to a community. It also reaches the question of how different levels of conduct contribute to an area's crime problems. For example, . . . few judges have as broad an experience dealing with drug importation and large-scale distribution as my colleagues in the Eastern District of New York. The piers and airports of the district make it . . . the entry point for a large percentage of the contraband entering this country. . . . The fact that a sentencing factor . . . does not pertain nationwide, indeed, the fact that it may be unique to the case at hand, does not make the factor irrelevant to the imposition of a just sentence. District judges should enjoy more discretion — indeed they should be encouraged — to depart from the guidelines to reflect specific local concerns.

Reena Raggi, Local Concerns, Local Insights, 5 Fed. Sentencing Rep. 306-308 (1993). As a member of the U.S. Sentencing Commission, how might you respond?

=5=

Sentencing Inputs: The Offender's Record and Background

In Chapter 4, we reviewed how various features of the crime can affect sentencing outcomes. But that review covered only one side of the substantive components of sentencing decisions — the offense. In this chapter, we turn to another major sentencing input, the background and characteristics of the criminal offender. A prior criminal record, cooperation with the government in other investigations, and other aspects of the offender's personal history and prospects can all play a role in the sentencing decision. The foundational question to consider throughout this chapter is just why sentence determinations should turn on *who* the offender is in addition to *what* the offender did.

As we stressed at the outset of Chapter 4, sentencing practice always informs sentencing theory, and thus it is again appropriate to begin our discussion of offender characteristics with an introductory sentencing exercise — indeed, the same basic exercise that started Chapter 4. Below we supplement the facts relating to the fictitious offender Rob Anon. The questions following the facts highlight the relevance of Rob's personal characteristics rather than his crime. As before, you should be prepared to return to Rob's case periodically to see whether our detailed study of sentencing systems changes your initial perspective on Rob's status.

PROBLEM 5-1.   ROB ANON

A jury found Rob Anon guilty of one count of armed bank robbery. The evidence at trial proved that Rob planned the robbery and then recruited his two co-defendants to participate. According to the testimony of co-defendant Zweite (who pled guilty to the charge pursuant to a plea agreement with the government), Rob gave each participant in the robbery a firearm and a ski mask. Rob also provided a getaway car, although the origins and current location of the car remain unknown.

According to the testimony at trial, the activities of the three defendants inside the bank were as follows: Rob disabled the surveillance cameras and alarms;

co-defendant Tercero kept his firearm pointed at the teller while Zweite vaulted the counter and collected more than $200,000 in cash. As the threesome hurried out of the bank, Tercero pushed to the ground an elderly man who walked into the bank during the robbery. The man broke his hip when he fell. In dividing the loot, Rob gave Zweite and Tercero one-fourth of the proceeds each, keeping half for himself.

The government's evidence at Rob's trial included surveillance photos, eyewitnesses, physical evidence, and testimony by Zweite and Tercero. From the moment of his indictment and throughout his prosecution, Rob denied responsibility for the robbery and claimed he was "set up."

Rob is 22 years old and has produced a spotty employment record since dropping out of high school at age 16. Rob was last employed in a series of construction projects with a local landscaping company; he previously worked for a shoe store as a salesman on a part-time basis. Reared by a single mother in an economically depressed urban area and the second youngest of five children, Rob seems to have few friends and mostly keeps to himself. Rob's mother recalls that Rob's siblings taunted and teased him because of his small stature. She believes that Rob became addicted to cocaine in the past year.

Rob's criminal record includes two prior offenses. Six years ago, a juvenile court convicted Rob of one count of shoplifting and sentenced him to 100 hours of community service. Two years ago, Rob was convicted of receipt of stolen goods and sentenced to three years' probation. Rob was still serving that term of probation at the time of the bank robbery. In the federal system, armed bank robbery carries a maximum penalty of 25 years in prison or a fine of $250,000 or both. Compare http://www.ussc.gov/training/ws_ex_rob.pdf.

1. You are the sentencing judge for Rob in a jurisdiction that places no limits on your discretion to choose a sentence from probation to the statutory maximum of 25 years. What sentence would you impose? If you need more information before choosing a sentence, what additional information would you seek?
2. If this had been Rob's first offense rather than his third, would your sentencing decision change?
3. If Rob accepted responsibility for his action, pleaded guilty to the charged offense, and agreed to testify against his co-conspirators, would your sentencing decision change?
4. If Rob was 45 years old with a Ph.D. and had been raised in an affluent home, would your sentencing decision change?
5. If Rob (and an expert testifying on his behalf) claimed that his criminal behavior was the product of his cocaine addiction and Rob had now voluntarily enrolled in an intensive drug treatment program, would your sentencing decision change?

A.   PRIOR CRIMINAL RECORD

At sentencing, the court learns about the defendant's life before the crime of conviction took place. Probation officers collect some of this information;

attorneys for either the prosecution or the defense present facts about the offender's personal background and history as well. Often the offender's past includes prior convictions or other encounters with the criminal justice system. In an unstructured sentencing system, the judge gives the prior criminal record whatever weight she thinks appropriate. Sentencing statutes and guidelines, however, instruct judges in some systems more precisely about the effect that a prior criminal record must have on a sentence.

1. "Strikes" Laws and Other Mandatory Rules

|| *People v. Jerry Garcia* ||
976 P.2d 831 (Cal. 1999)

CHIN, J.

In this case, we consider whether a trial court, when applying the "Three Strikes" law, Penal Code §§667(b)-(i), 1170.12(a)-(d), may exercise its discretion under Penal Code §1385(a), so as to dismiss a prior conviction allegation with respect to one count but not another. We conclude that a court may exercise its discretion in this way and that the trial court did not abuse its discretion in doing so here. . . .

On June 19, 1996, Barbara Gantt left her home suddenly to go to the hospital and inadvertently left a window open. She returned home less than two hours later and found the place ransacked. Various items were missing, including a translating machine, jewelry, and a videocassette recorder. As she was cleaning up, she found a wallet with defendant's driver's license on the floor among some of her papers.

On September 4, 1996, Grace Kobel returned home to find defendant bicycling out of her driveway. A window was broken, the screen was lying on the ground, and her front door was open. Kobel called the police, who arrived a few minutes later. She entered the house with the police and found various items missing, including a telephone, jewelry, and a toy airplane. About the same time, police officers spotted defendant riding a bicycle several blocks away and stopped him. Defendant was holding two plastic bags that contained many of the items missing from Kobel's home. He also had jewelry in his pockets. . . .

The court found defendant guilty on [two counts of burglary]. The court also found true an allegation that defendant had five prior serious felony convictions qualifying as "strikes" for purposes of the Three Strikes law.* These

---

* Penal Code §667(e)(2) provides:

    (A) If a defendant has two or more prior felony convictions [qualifying as serious or violent felonies under this law], the term for the current felony conviction shall be an indeterminate term of life imprisonment with a minimum term of the indeterminate sentence calculated as the greater of [three] times the term otherwise provided as punishment for each current felony conviction subsequent to the two or more prior felony convictions [or] imprisonment in the state prison for 25 years. . . .

    (B) The indeterminate term described in subparagraph (A) shall be served consecutive to any other term of imprisonment for which a convictions, all on July 17, 1991, were for five burglaries that took place on separate occasions during a short crime spree. The court also found that the same five burglary convictions qualified as one prior serious felony conviction for purposes of the five-year enhancement set forth in §667(a)(1).** Finally, for purposes of the one-year enhancement set forth in §667.5(b),+ the court found true an allegation that defendant had served three prior prison terms. The first of these terms was for a January 10, 1985, conviction for receiving stolen property, the second for a February 19, 1987, conviction for possession of heroin, and the third for the five 1991 burglary convictions already mentioned.

At the sentencing hearing, the court considered a probation report indicating defendant had a history of burglarizing homes and then trading stolen property for drugs. Barbara Gantt and Grace Kobel then described the impact defendant's crimes had on them and asked the court to give defendant the maximum sentence. Next, defendant's girlfriend described defendant's difficult life, saying he grew up in foster homes and was addicted to heroin by age 12. Finally, defendant expressed remorse about the burglaries and asked for forgiveness.

Defense counsel then asked the court to exercise its discretion under §1385(a),++ and dismiss, or "strike," four of the five prior conviction allegations as to both counts, thereby making the case a "second strike" case and reducing defendant's sentence to a term of twenty-two years and eight months. The court responded that "the interests of justice would not be served by striking four strikes in this case," and to do so "would be for the sole purpose of avoiding the sentence I'm required to hand down by law." The court noted that defendant committed five separate residential burglaries, went to state prison, and then, shortly after his release and while still on parole, committed two more residential burglaries. "[I]f the Three Strikes law was meant for anyone it was meant for Mr. Garcia," the court said. [The] court agreed that defendant's drug addiction

---

consecutive term may be imposed by law. Any other term imposed subsequent to any indeterminate term described in subparagraph (A) shall not be merged therein but shall commence at the time the person would otherwise have been released from prison.— EDS.

** Penal Code §667(a)(1) provides as follows: "[Any] person convicted of a serious felony who previously has been convicted of a serious felony in this state or of any offense committed in another jurisdiction which includes all of the elements of any serious felony, shall receive, in addition to the sentence imposed by the court for the present offense, a five-year enhancement for each such prior conviction on charges brought and tried separately. The terms of the present offense and each enhancement shall run consecutively."— EDS.

+ Penal Code §667.5(b) provides: "[Where] the new offense is any felony for which a prison sentence is imposed, in addition and consecutive to any other prison terms therefor, the court shall impose a one-year term for each prior separate prison term served for any felony; provided that no additional term shall be imposed under this subdivision for any prison term served prior to a period of five years in which the defendant remained free of both prison custody and the commission of an offense which results in a felony conviction."— EDS.

++ Penal Code §1385(a) provides: "The judge or magistrate may, either of his or her own motion or upon the application of the prosecuting attorney, and in furtherance of justice, order an action to be dismissed. The reasons for the dismissal must be set forth in an order entered upon the minutes. . . ."— EDS.

was "a factor in mitigation." The court also noted that all defendant's prior serious felony convictions arose from a single period of aberrant behavior for which he served a single prison term. The court commented that defendant had cooperated with police both in 1991 and when they arrested him for the current offenses. Finally, the court stated that defendant had no record of violence.

As to the Kobel burglary, the court sentenced defendant to a term of 30 years to life in state prison. This sentence included 25 years to life under the Three Strikes law plus the mandatory 5-year enhancement under §667(a)(1). The court initially imposed three 1-year enhancements under §667.5(b), for the prior prison terms, but then exercised its discretion under §1385(a), and struck these enhancements. As to the Gantt burglary, the court exercised its discretion under §1385(a), and struck all the prior conviction allegations. In a minute order, the court stated it was striking the prior conviction allegations because they "all refer [to] one case, defendant has cooperated with police in both cases, is addicted to drugs and has not suffered any violent priors." The court calculated a sentence of 16 months, which was one-third the middle term of 4 years. The court ordered that this sentence be served consecutive to the sentence on the Kobel burglary, because the two counts reflected "two separate incidents on two separate dates." Nevertheless, the court stated that a sentence of 30 years to life was "appropriate" and that, but for the constraints of the Three Strikes law, it would have ordered that the 16-month sentence on the Gantt burglary be served concurrently. Defendant's total sentence on both counts was 31 years and 4 months to life. The court imposed a $200 restitution fine, and also ordered $400 restitution to Grace Kobel and $20,000 restitution to Barbara Gantt, less the value of any property returned.

[On appeal, the Attorney General] asserted that the trial court lacked authority under §1385(a) to strike the prior conviction allegations as to the Gantt burglary while not striking them as to the Kobel burglary, claiming that therefore defendant's sentence was unauthorized. [He argued] that striking prior conviction allegations as to some, but not all, current counts was inconsistent with the requirement in the Three Strikes law that sentences be consecutive for current felonies relating to separate criminal episodes. . . .

Section 1385(a) authorizes a trial court to act on its own motion to dismiss a criminal action "in furtherance of justice." We have long held that this power includes the ability to strike prior conviction allegations that would otherwise increase a defendant's sentence. People v. Burke, 301 P.2d 241 (Cal. 1956). Our reasoning in *Burke* is particularly relevant to the issue in this case. In *Burke,* the defendant had been convicted of possession of marijuana . . . , and he admitted a prior conviction for the same offense. At that time, Health and Safety Code former §11712 provided: "Any person convicted . . . for having in possession any narcotic [if] such a person has been previously convicted [of the same offense] shall be imprisoned in the state prison for not less than two years. . . ." Nevertheless, the trial court struck the prior conviction allegation and sentenced the defendant to county jail. . . . We concluded that this power to strike a sentencing allegation fell within the broader power to dismiss an entire action under section 1385. More importantly, however, we also concluded that "[the] striking or dismissal of a charge of prior conviction . . . is not the equivalent of a determination that defendant did not in fact suffer the conviction [citations]; such judicial action is taken . . . for the purpose of sentencing only and any dismissal of charges of prior convictions . . .

does not wipe out such prior convictions or prevent them from being considered in connection with later convictions." Thus, we acknowledged that a court might strike a prior conviction allegation in one context, but use it in another.

In People v. Superior Court (Romero), 928 P.2d 1171 (Cal. 1996), we held that the Three Strikes law did not remove or limit this §1385 power to strike sentencing allegations. The defendant in *Romero* pleaded guilty to possession of 0.13 grams of cocaine base. . . . The information also alleged five prior felony convictions, two of which — attempted burglary and first degree burglary of an inhabited dwelling — qualified as strikes for purposes of the Three Strikes law. The trial court struck the prior conviction allegations and imposed a sentence of six years in state prison. This sentence represented three years (the upper term) for possession of a controlled substance plus three consecutive one-year enhancements for prior prison terms. [We] concluded that, in a Three Strikes case, the trial court can, on its own motion and over the prosecutor's objection, strike a prior conviction allegation in furtherance of justice.

Our holding in *Romero* flowed directly from the plain language of the Three Strikes law, which expressly authorizes prosecutors to move to strike prior conviction allegations "pursuant to" §1385(a). We reasoned that, because the Three Strikes law makes express reference to §1385 and does not anywhere bar courts from acting pursuant to that section, the drafters of the law must have intended that section to apply without limitation in Three Strikes cases. . . .

Nevertheless, we stressed that "[a] court's discretion to strike prior felony conviction allegations in furtherance of justice is limited." [A] court may not strike a sentencing allegation solely "to accommodate judicial convenience or because of court congestion." Nor may a court strike a sentencing allegation "simply because a defendant pleads guilty." Finally, we stated that a court may not strike a sentencing allegation "guided solely by a personal antipathy for the effect that the three strikes law would have on [a] defendant," while ignoring defendant's background, the nature of his present offenses, and other individualized considerations.

In People v. Williams, 948 P.2d 429 (Cal. 1998), we further delineated the parameters that govern a trial court's discretion under §1385(a), to strike prior conviction allegations in a Three Strikes case. *Williams* involved a defendant who pleaded guilty to driving a vehicle under the influence of phencyclidine (PCP). . . . The defendant had a 19-year criminal history, including convictions for attempted robbery, rape, and spousal battery, and a series of convictions for firearm possession and driving under the influence. The attempted robbery and rape convictions, which the defendant admitted, qualified as strikes for purposes of the Three Strikes law. However, because those convictions were about 13 years old and because of "the lack of any kind of violence related crimes from then until now," the trial court vacated its finding with respect to the prior attempted robbery conviction, leaving only the prior rape conviction. [We] concluded that the trial court had abused its discretion by vacating one of its prior conviction findings [and] discussed the factors a trial court may legitimately consider when exercising its §1385 discretion in a Three Strikes case. We said that the trial court could give "no weight whatsoever . . . to factors extrinsic to the [Three Strikes] scheme." On the other hand, the court must accord "preponderant weight . . . to factors intrinsic to the scheme, such as the nature and circumstances of the defendant's present felonies and prior serious and/or violent felony convictions, and the particulars of his background, character, and prospects." Ultimately, a court must determine whether "the defendant may be deemed outside the scheme's spirit, in whole or in part."

The reasoning of *Romero* and the standards we enunciated in *Williams* logically support the trial court's action in this case. In *Romero*, we concluded that, by referencing §1385, the Three Strikes law incorporated that section without limitation. [The] standards we enunciated in *Williams* indicate that a trial court has discretion in a Three Strikes case to strike prior conviction allegations on a count-by-count basis. In *Williams*, we instructed trial courts to consider among other things, "individualized considerations" such as the nature and circumstances of the defendant's present felonies and his "prospects." In many cases, "the nature and circumstances" of the various felonies described in different counts will differ considerably. A court might therefore be justified in striking prior conviction allegations with respect to a relatively minor current felony, while considering those prior convictions with respect to a serious or violent current felony.

The Attorney General argues, however, that in a case such as this one, where both current felonies are for the same or similar crimes, the "individualized considerations" we enumerated in *Williams* do not provide a "principled basis" for treating the felonies differently. We disagree. Even if the current offenses are virtually identical, a defendant's "prospects" will differ greatly from one count to another because a Three Strikes sentence on one count will itself radically alter those prospects. Here, for example, once the trial court had sentenced defendant to a term of 30 years to life for the Kobel burglary, his "prospects" for committing future burglaries diminished significantly. [A] defendant's sentence is . . . a relevant consideration when deciding whether to strike a prior conviction allegation; in fact, it is the overarching consideration because the underlying purpose of striking prior conviction allegations is the avoidance of unjust sentences. . . .

The Attorney General, however, points to the requirement in the Three Strikes law that sentencing on distinct current offenses be consecutive, §§667(c)(6)-(8), 1170.12(a)(6)-(8), and without any aggregate term limitation, §§667(c)(1), 1170.12(a)(1). The Attorney General argues that striking prior conviction allegations with respect to one count, but not with respect to another, undermines this principle of consecutive Three Strikes sentences. Again, we disagree. A requirement that a defendant serve the individual sentences for different current felonies consecutively does not indicate how the trial court should determine the lengths of those individual sentences. Here, for example, the trial court conformed to the consecutive sentencing requirement by ordering that the 16-month sentence for the Gantt burglary be served consecutively to the 30-year-to-life sentence for the Kobel burglary. . . .

The Attorney General also argues that the trial court here "eviscerated" the Three Strikes law, the purpose of which was to restrict the discretion of "soft-on-crime judges" and "ensure longer prison sentences." We agree with the Attorney General that a primary purpose of the Three Strikes law was to restrict judicial discretion, but the Attorney General's argument merely begs the question of *how* judicial discretion was to be restricted. The answer to that question can be found only by examining the language of the act. The Three Strikes law expressly incorporates the power to strike prior conviction allegations under §1385(a).

Therefore, rather than eviscerating the Three Strikes law, the trial court in this case *applied* that law, which expressly contemplates the trial court's action.

[Appellate] review of a trial court's §1385 decision is not de novo. [The abuse of discretion] standard is deferential. But it is not empty. Although variously phrased in various decisions, it asks in substance whether the ruling in question falls outside the bounds of reason under the applicable law and the relevant facts. Here, we cannot say that the trial court's decision to strike the prior conviction allegations as to count 3 "falls outside the bounds of reason." The court sentenced defendant to 31 years and 4 months to life in state prison. This sentence is not lenient. . . . Moreover, as the trial court noted, defendant's prior convictions all arose from a single period of aberrant behavior for which he served a single prison term. Defendant cooperated with police, his crimes were related to drug addiction, and his criminal history does not include any actual violence. Cumulatively, all these circumstances indicate that "defendant may be deemed outside the [Three Strikes] scheme's spirit," at least in part, and that the trial court acted within the limits of its §1385 discretion. . . .

BROWN, J., dissenting.

I respectfully dissent. This case asks the age-old question: does judicial commitment to principle matter? The majority gives the modern answer. Not if it gets in the way of expediency.

The "Three Strikes" law reflects the public's long-simmering frustration with perceived laxity in a criminal justice system that allowed repeatedly convicted felons to be released after serving modest sentences with time off for good behavior. All too often, this revolving door led to more crimes, new victims, and greater tragedies. The public saw "soft on crime" judges who were more solicitous of criminal defendants than public safety as the problem; they viewed Three Strikes as the solution. . . .

Under our precedents, the trial court retains discretion under Penal Code §1385 or §17(b), to remove a case from the reach of the law. But, until today, in choosing to rely upon these latter statutes, a trial court had to make a principled determination that the defendant did not come within the spirit of the Three Strikes law and therefore should not be subject to its letter. Thus, I disagree that a court can dismiss prior convictions on a count-by-count basis. Moreover, even if in rare cases a court has that power, the principles we articulated in our recent precedents bar the trial court from doing so here.

[Unless] carefully circumscribed, the power to strike prior felony conviction allegations "in furtherance of justice" . . . carries with it the real potential for undermining the intent of the Three Strikes law itself — namely, to restrict courts' discretion in sentencing repeat offenders. In *Williams*, we . . . undertook to "render §1385(a)'s concept of 'furtherance of justice' somewhat more determinate." We concluded that "in ruling whether to strike or vacate a prior serious and/or violent felony conviction allegation or finding under the Three Strikes law, on its own motion, 'in furtherance of justice' pursuant to §1385(a), or in reviewing such a ruling, the court in question must consider whether, in light of the nature and circumstances of his present felonies and prior serious and/or violent felony convictions, and the particulars of his background, character, and prospects, the defendant may be deemed outside the scheme's spirit, in whole or in part, and hence should be treated as though he had not previously been convicted of one or more serious and/or violent felonies. If it is striking or vacating an allegation or finding, it must set forth its reasons in an order entered on the minutes, and if it is reviewing the striking or vacating of such allegation or finding, it must pass on the reasons so set forth." We emphasized that "no weight whatsoever may be given to factors extrinsic to the [Three Strikes] scheme, such as the mere desire to ease court congestion or, a fortiori, bare antipathy to the consequences for any given defendant."

While professing to follow *Williams,* in reality, the majority tosses aside its carefully crafted limits on judicial discretion. [Notwithstanding] *Williams*'s unequivocal holding that "bare antipathy to the consequences for any given defendant" should be given "no weight whatsoever," the majority now concludes that the "overarching consideration" in determining whether to strike prior felony conviction allegations with respect to some, but not all, counts is the total length of a defendant's sentence "because the underlying purpose of striking prior conviction allegations is the avoidance of unjust sentences." In other words, the "overarching consideration" in determining whether to strike prior felony conviction allegations "in furtherance of justice" under §1385(a) is the trial court's antipathy to the sentence the law would otherwise require. . . .

One need only compare the facts of this case to the facts of *Williams* to see how standardless things have become. In *Williams,* in concluding that the trial court had abused its discretion in striking one of Williams's prior felony convictions, we pointed to his failure to "follow through in efforts to bring his substance abuse problem under control." Here, in upholding the trial court's decision to strike, the majority points to the fact defendant's crimes were related to drug addiction. In *Williams,* in concluding that the trial court had abused its discretion in striking one of Williams's prior felony convictions, we noted that "as to his present felony: It is a conviction of driving under the influence that followed three other convictions of driving under the influence; the existence of such convictions reveals that he had been taught, through the application of formal sanction, that such criminal conduct was unacceptable — but had failed or refused to learn his lesson." Here, in upholding the trial court's decision to strike, the majority glosses over the fact defendant's two present convictions for burglary followed quickly on the heels of five previous convictions for exactly the same offense. . . .

The real effect of today's decision is to make the defendant's eligibility for punishment under Three Strikes a factor in mitigation. When a defendant receives a lengthy Three Strikes term on the first of multiple counts, the trial court may disregard the law as to all other counts. . . . *Romero* is no longer reserved for the rare case involving a particularly harsh sentence for a relatively minor offense. Courts may now routinely apply *Romero* to the benefit of recidivists for whom such solicitude is not appropriate. That is not what I heard the voters demand when they enacted the Three Strikes law. Three Strikes was not about judicial discretion; it was about accountability. It was not about "just" sentences; it was about swift, certain, and harsh retribution. Moreover, by encouraging courts to impose only a single Three Strikes sentence regardless of the circumstances, the majority's decision rewards the industrious career criminal — after the first count, the rest are virtually free. . . .

The sentence imposed here was lengthy. But that is beside the point. It was still less than the law required. When the Legislature enacted, and the voters passed, the Three Strikes law, they intended to restrict trial courts' discretion in sentencing. The trial court here had it right when it initially observed that striking defendant's prior felony convictions "would be for the sole purpose of avoiding the sentence I'm required to hand down by law" and that "if the Three Strikes law was meant for anyone it was meant for Mr. Garcia." Today's holding eviscerates the intent of the Three Strikes law. . . .

NOTES

1. *Habitual offender statutes, the "three-strikes" variety.*   The provision under which Garcia was sentenced, California Penal Code §667, is an example of a habitual offender law popularly known as "three strikes and you're out." Almost all states have habitual felon statutes, which increase sentences by designated amounts for offenders with a particular prior felony record. The three-strikes variety is distinctive for the type of prior record necessary and the amount of increase in the sentence. California's three-strikes law is the most severe in the nation for several reasons: many types of prior convictions qualify as "serious" or "violent" and thus count as a strike, a third felony results in a minimum sentence of 25 years to life even if the third felony is neither violent nor serious, and sentences are doubled even for offenders with only one strike. As detailed more fully in Chapter 7, the U.S. Supreme Court in 2003 upheld the application of California's three-strikes law to two shoplifters with extended criminal histories who claimed that their lengthy imprisonment terms violated the Eighth Amendment's prohibition of cruel and unusual punishments. See Ewing v. California, 538 U.S. 11 (2003) (reprinted in Chapter 7); Lockyer v. Andrade, 538 U.S. 63 (2003).

About half the states have enacted three-strikes laws, but they vary considerably in reach and impact. A few states have two-strikes provisions for particularly serious felonies, while others have adopted four-strikes provisions. See, e.g., Ga. Code Ann. §17-10-7 (providing a sentence of life without parole for two serious violent felonies); Fla. Stat. Ann. §775.084 (requiring three prior felonies to trigger sentence of life imprisonment). See generally Michael Vitiello, Three Strikes: Can We Return to Rationality?, 87 J. Crim. L. & Criminology 395 tbls. 1-2 (1997) (reviewing key features of three-strikes laws enacted in various states). The federal three-strikes law imposes a mandatory sentence of life imprisonment on defendants convicted of a serious federal violent felony if they have been previously convicted in state or federal court of two or more serious violent felonies or one serious violent felony and one serious drug offense. See 18 U.S.C. §3559.

2. *Impact of three strikes in California and elsewhere.*   Because of its broad reach, California's three-strikes law has had the biggest impact of any jurisdiction's, although that impact is certain only with respect to increased prison rolls. There is a robust debate over whether decreases in crime rates in California through the 1990s could be attributed to the deterrent or incapacitation effects of California's three-strikes law. Critics of the law noted that some states with no comparable three-strikes law had crime drops equal to or greater than California's. Compare Bill Jones, Why the Three Strikes Law Is Working in

California, 11 Stan. L. & Poly. Rev. 23 (1999) (arguing that significant decreases in California's crime rates could be attributed to three-strikes law), with Mike Males and Dan Macallair, Striking Out: The Failure of California's "Three Strikes Law and You're Out" Law, 11 Stan. L. & Poly. Rev. 65 (1999) (arguing based on statistical analysis that California's three-strikes law had no measurable deterrent or incapacitation impact). The studies offer vastly different assessments of how potential offenders might respond to the three-strikes law's harsh sanctions. Compare Thomas B. Marvell and Carlisle E. Moody, The Lethal Effects of Three-Strikes Laws, 30 J. Legal Stud. 89 (2001) (contending that three-strikes laws actually increase homicides because a few criminals, fearing the enhanced penalties, will murder victims and witnesses to limit resistance and identification), with Joanna Shepherd, Fear of the First Strike: the Full Deterrent Effect of California's Two- and Three-Strikes Legislation, 31 J. Legal Stud. 159 (2002) (suggesting pronounced deterrent impact from three-strikes laws as potential criminals diligently endeavor to avoid a *first* strike).

A recent work by Frank Zimring, Gordon Hawkins, and Sam Kamin, Punishment and Democracy: Three Strikes and You're Out in California (2001), suggests that while the three-strikes law probably provides some deterrent effect, it will have its most significant and tangible long-term impact on California's future prison population. Indeed, researchers at the Sentencing Project, a public advocacy group, report that as of May 31, 2001, more than 50,000 prisoners were serving additional time because of California's three-strikes law — nearly 7,000 were serving 25 years to life in prison on three-strikes convictions and more than 43,000 were serving double time under the law's two-strike provisions. See Ryan S. King and Marc Mauer, Aging Behind Bars: "Three Strikes" Seven Years Later (Aug. 2001). California's prisons now house more than 160,000 offenders, and its rate of imprisonment (471 per 100,000 residents) ranks in the top third of the states. See Chapter 7.

While California's three-strikes law is having a significant impact on that state's criminal justice system, this is not true in other states with similarly named but less far-reaching habitual offender provisions. As a National Institute of Justice paper explains, these states have experienced no major repercussions from enacting such laws:

> With the noted exception of California, there has been virtually no impact on the courts, local jails, or State prisons; nor does there appear to have been an impact on crime rates. [The] projected effects of the law have not been realized as . . . local criminal justice system[s] (the courts in particular) have found ways to circumvent the law. [It seems that in most instances] this form of legislation was carefully crafted to be largely symbolic.

James Austin, John Clark, Patricia Hardyman, and D. Alan Henry, Three Strikes and You're Out: The Implementation and Impact of Strike Laws Abstract (National Institute of Justice, NCJ 181297, 1999).

3. *Prosecutors and habitual felons.* Although habitual felon laws in California and elsewhere empower the prosecutor to file additional charges that result automatically in increased sentences, the laws usually do not *require* the prosecutor to file the habitual felon charge for every qualifying defendant. Not many

California citizens appreciate how much prosecutorial discretion remains in this law and how much its use varies around the state. Steve Cooley won election in 2000 as the new district attorney in Los Angeles on a platform of more screening of three-strikes cases. Cooley appealed both to the public's perception that the law was creating unjust outcomes and to the need to concentrate resources on more truly serious offenses. See Twila Decker, Lawyers Say D.A. Breaking Three-Strikes Pledge, L.A. Times, Jan. 22, 2001, at B1 (policy described as means of reserving mandatory sentences for most serious felonies). Since Los Angeles is the largest source of three-strikes cases in California, Cooley's policy makes an enormous difference in the state's crime budget.

Habitual felon laws in other states (not just the three-strikes variety) also give prosecutors the critical power to choose which among the eligible defendants will be charged as habitual felons. See North Carolina Sentencing and Policy Advisory Commission, Sentencing Practices Under North Carolina's Structured Sentencing Laws 38-40 (March 2002), available at http://www.nccourts. org/Courts/CRS/Councils/spac/Publications/Practices.asp. (One practical concern that traditionally limited how often prosecutors invoked habitual felon laws — the need to collect formal documentation establishing the prior convictions — is fast disappearing in a world of electronic records.) If you were the chief prosecutor for a county, what instructions would you give your trial attorneys about which defendants to charge under the habitual felon law?

4. *Politics surrounding passage of three-strikes laws.* A high-profile crime by a repeat offender often serves as the catalyst for the enactment of three-strikes laws. In California, the drive for a three-strikes ballot initiative was instigated by Mike Reynolds, a Fresno photographer whose 18-year-old daughter was murdered in 1992 by a parolee. The three-strikes movement became a national phenomenon the following year after 12-year-old Polly Klaas was kidnapped and murdered by Richard Allen Davis, a repeat violent criminal. Though headline-making crimes gave the public the impression that tougher criminal sanctions were needed for repeat offenders, most jurisdictions already had laws in place that provided lengthy terms of imprisonment for serious recidivists.

Of course, the distorting influences of politics and symbolism in the criminal justice system are not new. As discussed in Chapter 2, the development of sentencing commissions was driven in large part by the hope that this sort of institution — consisting of knowledgeable experts, insulated from short-term political pressures, who would have the time and opportunity to study sentencing — would avoid these influences while developing sound criminal justice laws and policies. But in the face of politicians and the public clamoring for tough habitual offender laws, most sentencing commissions have not successfully limited the impact of this legislation. See Ronald F. Wright, Three Strikes Legislation and Sentencing Commission Objectives, 20 Law & Poly. 429, 437 (1998). What features of a three-strikes law might create special problems for a sentencing commission advocating cautious changes in sentencing laws?

2. Long Records

An offender's criminal past played a central role in sentencing well before the enactment of modern three-strikes laws. The law rarely mandated a particular sentence based on an offender's criminal history in the era of indeterminate sentencing, but judges still used their discretion to impose longer sentences on defendants who had a lengthy criminal record. Modern sentencing reforms have focused on systematizing the effect that a criminal record has on the sentence imposed.

United States v. Anthony Croom
50 F.3d 433 (7th Cir. 1995)

EASTERBROOK, J.

Anthony Croom is a punk who grew up to be a thug. His first juvenile conviction was for battery. Next came a conviction for child molestation: when 13 years old, Croom had sexual intercourse with an 11 year old girl. Later Croom was convicted of burglary and other offenses. The burglary conviction disqualified Croom from possessing guns, but he thumbed his nose at the law. One day, while attired like a refugee from a gangster movie, with gloves and a hat pulled down to cover his face, Croom bolted from a meal into the arms of police, who recovered a semi-automatic weapon. He was charged with violating 18 U.S.C. §922(g)(1) and released pending trial. Ten days later Croom invaded a fast food restaurant, drew a gun, ordered the staff into the meat locker (threatening them with death if they did not cooperate), and emptied the till. He did not get far, and his capture led to another federal weapons charge. Croom pleaded guilty to both; another similar charge was dismissed as part of a plea bargain. His sentence of 160 months' imprisonment exceeds the guideline range of 110-137 months for a level 28 offense by someone with a criminal history category of IV, and he appeals from the upward departure.

A district judge may give a sentence exceeding the range specified by the Sentencing Guidelines only on account of circumstances "not adequately taken into consideration" by the Sentencing Commission. 18 U.S.C. §3553(b). The district judge gave this explanation of his decision:

> [C]onsidering the offenses which did not count for criminal history score points . . . as well as the . . . short period of time which elapsed between the defendant's last incarceration and the first of these offenses and [the fast food robbery committed after the initial gun arrest], and considering the nature of the offenses reflected in [the presentence investigation report plus the charges to which Croom pleaded guilty], I find . . . that the criminal history category IV does not adequately reflect the seriousness of the defendant's past criminal conduct, and perhaps more so the likelihood that the defendant will commit other crimes. I think there is a clearly ascertainable and projectable pattern here by this defendant of ever increasing in ever more dangerous offenses as he proceeds through life. . . . So I will depart upward to a criminal history category of VI. . . .

The judge did not reveal which of these factors he believed the Sentencing Commission has "not adequately taken into consideration" or why he increased the criminal history category from IV to VI rather than V. Croom has earned a substantial sentence, but 137 months' imprisonment — more than 11 years without possibility of parole — is stern punishment. The stated rationale for tacking on two years is problematic under §3553(b).

The judge's explanation starts with the observation that the Guidelines did not count two of Croom's juvenile convictions. Under U.S.S.G. §4A1.2(d)(2) juvenile convictions the sentences for which ended more than five years before the commission of the latest offense do not contribute any criminal history points. Far from representing an aspect of criminal history that the Sentencing Commission overlooked or did not consider adequately, this exclusion is a conscious decision, one a district judge may not override by the mechanism of an upward departure. The Sentencing Commission believed that old juvenile convictions should be "forgiven" in assigning criminal history points; that the district judge is less forgiving than the Commission does not authorize him to strike out on a different path. To forgive is not necessarily to forget, however; as we explain below the judge may consider the juvenile convictions as part of the larger picture when deciding whether to depart under the criteria of U.S.S.G. §4A1.3.

After remarking on the juvenile convictions, the judge observed that Croom committed the first federal gun offense shortly after release from his most recent state imprisonment, then committed the second gun offense while on pretrial release from the first. These are surely grounds for increasing a sentence — but the Sentencing Commission took them into consideration. Croom received two criminal history points under §4A1.1(d) for committing the first gun offense while on parole from a state sentence, and one point under §4A1.1(e) for committing that offense within two years after leaving prison. He paid for the close relation between the first and second gun offenses by forfeiting the three-level reduction for acceptance of responsibility that otherwise would have been available to one who entered a prompt plea of guilty. The judge did not explain why these adjustments are an insufficient recognition of the circumstances.

The district court's final observation — that Croom has led a life of essentially continual crime, of increasing violence — is a sound reason for a departure. Croom not only has a long record but also admitted that he possessed guns all the time between 1991 and 1993. That amounts to many additional offenses under §922(g). He scarcely gets out of the jail's shadow before committing another crime. The Guidelines are designed for normal cases; a defendant who has demonstrated criminal propensities that make him more dangerous than the ordinary person with the same criminal history score may receive a higher sentence. So the Commission said in §4A1.3, describing some situations that it has not fully considered and that therefore authorize departures. Thus, for example, the fact that Croom committed his second gun offense while on release from the first led to the denial of a reduction for acceptance of responsibility; but the fact that he committed the second, more serious, gun offense swiftly after release on the first also shows that he is incorrigible — an armed career criminal in fact if not technically one under 18 U.S.C. §924(e)(1). His juvenile convictions may not be counted directly, but they may be considered as part of the pattern of recidivism. U.S.S.G. §4A1.2 Application Note 8. Meeting most of the criteria for designation as an armed career criminal (or "career offender" under the Guidelines) does not permit the judge to impose the penalties designed for those who meet all of the criteria, but it does permit a departure in the *direction* of those penalties.

What we have, then, is a good reason for departure coupled with two bad ones. The district court must reconsider Croom's sentence but need not necessarily lower it. On remand the court should hew to the considerations approved in §4A1.3 and choose the offense level that best approximates the seriousness of Croom's record and the threat of future crimes it portends. How much to increase the sentence is a judgment call, which if thoughtfully explained will not be disturbed on any later appeal. . . .

ROVNER, J., concurring.

Although I concur in the result and rationale of the majority, I believe that the appropriate exercise of our judicial function requires restraint in the language we use to describe the people who come before us, regardless of how dreadful their transgressions.

NOTES

1. *Considering prior convictions at sentencing.*   In all U.S. sentencing systems, the offender's prior convictions are among the most important determinants of the sentence imposed. As *Croom* highlights, most sentencing guideline systems place onto a severity scale the number and seriousness of prior convictions. The federal sentencing guidelines, for example, convert prior offenses into criminal history points, which are then grouped into criminal history categories ranging from I (for first offenders) to VI (for offenders with lengthy records); these categories are then used to determine the offender's applicable sentencing range. In most sentencing guideline systems, more serious prior offenses increase the sentence more than less serious prior offenses; prior convictions for the same type of crime as the current offense often increase a sentence more than prior convictions for unrelated wrongdoing. Minnesota, for example, assigns prior felony offenses from one-half to two points depending on the offense's "severity level." Similarly, Pennsylvania assigns four criminal history points, the maximum amount available, for the most serious prior convictions such as murder, voluntary manslaughter, kidnapping, rape, involuntary deviate intercourse, arson, and robbery.

2. *Theoretical foundations for considering criminal history.*   Why increase a defendant's sentence for the current offense based on *past* criminal behavior? Are such enhanced sentences designed to deter the offender, or other offenders, from committing future crimes? Are they designed to select a sentence proportionate to the crime committed (that is, to give the offender her just deserts)? Consider this excerpt from a U.S. Sentencing Commission report discussing the philosophy behind using criminal history to help determine sentencing outcomes:

> Those who argue that retribution is a key principle in sentencing [contend] that criminal history is inappropriate to consider at sentencing because the defendant has already been punished for the previous offense [and] that a defendant has no greater culpability (blameworthiness) because of having committed the prior offense; nor is victimization greater in the current offense as a result of the prior offense. . . . A contrary theory of the role of criminal justice is incapacitation. This approach advocates the expanded use of imprisonment to incapacitate offenders[, assuming] that while offenders are incarcerated they will not be able to engage in additional criminal behavior. [S]elective incapacitation seeks to prevent crime by using certain criteria to identify for restraint

a smaller number of offenders who are predicted to commit more crime and/or serious crime. . . . Society and its elected representatives have reached a level of frustration with crime so that current policies more frequently tend to reflect the selective incapacitation philosophy in sentencing practices in general and criminal history in particular.

U.S. Sentencing Commission, Simplification Draft Paper (1995) (see http://www.ussc.gov/simple/crimhist.htm). What role would criminal records play for those who emphasize the rehabilitative power of criminal sentences?

3. *Intricacies and complexities in assessing criminal history.* As the decision in *Croom* suggests, the federal guidelines that quantify a defendant's criminal history are complex, in large part because the U.S. Sentencing Commission decided to base its criminal history points on the *length* of prior sentences imposed. Consequently, the federal guidelines include intricate application notes and commentary that address the myriad of possible state court dispositions and instruct judges how to assess each prior sentence, including the custodial component, sentence type, and length. State sentencing rules typically group prior convictions into only a few categories (such as felonies and misdemeanors), which simplifies the criminal history calculation. Nevertheless, quantifying the variations in offenders' criminal records is always intricate. In Maryland, for example, calculation of the offender score has four primary components (relationship to criminal justice system when instant offense occurred, juvenile delinquency, prior adult criminal record, and prior adult criminal justice violation), each of which has multiple subparts with detailed application instructions. See Md. Sentencing Guidelines §5.2.

4. *Stale offenses.* Older convictions tell us less about an offender than more recent ones. Should older convictions have less of an impact (or no impact at all) on the sentence for the current crime? Guideline systems often consider the time period of a prior conviction when assessing criminal history. The federal guidelines use five different time periods for calculating criminal history points, based on the length of the sentence imposed and the age of the defendant when the prior offense was committed. State rules that discount or ignore older convictions generally set one applicable expiration date for all offenses (say, all convictions more than ten years old). Instead of setting an expiration date for older crimes, some states allow defendants to benefit from "crime free" periods. In these states, if the defendant was conviction free for a certain length of time (usually ten or 15 years not including periods of imprisonment, probation, or parole) prior to the instant offense, the sentencing judge does not count any convictions prior to that period. Other states leave this item as a departure consideration.

5. *Unreliable prior convictions.* The use of prior convictions to enhance the sentence for the current offense becomes more controversial when there are reasons to question the accuracy of the earlier conviction. This is true especially when the earlier conviction occurred without the involvement of defense counsel. The Constitution bars the use at sentencing of some uncounseled prior convictions, but only if the government obtained the prior conviction by violating the defendant's constitutional right to counsel. See Nichols v. United States, 511 U.S. 738 (1994) (sentencing court may consider defendant's previous

uncounseled misdemeanor conviction in sentencing him for subsequent offense); United States v. Tucker, 404 U.S. 443 (1972) (conviction obtained in violation of Sixth Amendment rights cannot enhance later sentence). These questions often arise when the prior conviction took place in the juvenile system or when the earlier case dealt with charges of driving while intoxicated. See State v. LaMunyon, 911 P.2d 151 (Kan. 1996) (finding no constitutional or statutory bar to using juvenile adjudication when calculating criminal history status); State v. Brown, 676 A.2d 350 (Vt. 1996) (explaining that certain prior uncounseled DUI convictions should not be used to enhance a sentence for a later offense).

6. *Foreign convictions.* While the federal guidelines do not factor foreign convictions in the calculation of a defendant's prior criminal record, such convictions may be considered for departure purposes. Federal courts have used foreign convictions to enhance the sentence for drug convictions under 21 U.S.C. §851(a). See United States v. Kole, 164 F.3d 164 (3d Cir. 1998) (sentence enhancement granted based on prior drug trafficking conviction in the Philippines that did not violate due process requirements). Courts can consider only foreign convictions that were not obtained in violation of the Constitution. What types of violations should lead a court not to consider a foreign conviction? Violations of the right to jury trial? Violations of the right to counsel?

Not considering foreign convictions in sentencing may lead to inappropriately low sentences for foreign nationals or immigrants. A study by the U.S. Sentencing Commission found that noncitizens have disproportionately fewer criminal history points, possibly because their foreign convictions do not count. Yet the process of ascertaining foreign convictions may create logistical problems for probation offices and lead the court into difficult considerations concerning the fairness of convictions in foreign systems. See Michael Edmund O'Neill, Abraham's Legacy: An Empirical Assessment of (Nearly) First-Time Offenders in the Federal System, 42 B.C. L. Rev. 291 (2001) (discussing consideration of foreign convictions).

3. The First-Time Offender

Since all sentencing systems increase punishment levels for repeat offenders, they conversely and necessarily provide lesser sentences for first-time offenders. But is there something special about first-time offenders compared to those with a limited previous criminal record? Should special rules be in place that further mitigate the sentence of first-time offenders?

‖ Washington Revised Code §9.94A.650 ‖

FIRST-TIME OFFENDER WAIVER

(1) This section applies to offenders who have never been previously convicted of a felony in this state, federal court, or another state, and who have never participated in a program of deferred prosecution for a felony, and who are convicted of a felony that is not:

(a) Classified as a violent offense or a sex offense under this chapter;

(b) Manufacture, delivery, [sale] or possession with intent to manufacture or deliver [various] controlled substances. . . .

(2) In sentencing a first-time offender the court may waive the imposition of a sentence within the standard sentence range and impose a sentence
which may include up to ninety days of confinement in a [local jail] facility. . . . The sentence may also include a term of community supervision or
community custody [and] may include requirements that the offender perform any one or more of the following:

(a) Devote time to a specific employment or occupation;

(b) Undergo available outpatient treatment . . . , or inpatient treatment not to exceed the standard range of confinement for that offense;

(c) Pursue a prescribed, secular course of study or vocational training;

(d) Remain within prescribed geographical boundaries and notify
the community corrections officer prior to any change in the offender's
address or employment;

(e) Report as directed to a community corrections officer; or

(f) Pay all court-ordered legal financial obligations . . . and/or perform community service work.

|| *State v. Joshua Fowler* ||
38 P.3d 335 (Wash. 2002)

ALEXANDER, C.J.

On October 30, 1997, Joshua Fowler joined friends . . . at "Fast Freddy's
Tavern" in Kent. Fowler, who had gone without sleep for three days while drinking alcohol and using methamphetamine, ingested additional alcohol and
methamphetamine at the tavern. Fowler [later] departed the tavern [with com-
panions] to collect a debt he believed [Ken] Carroll owed to him, . . . armed with
a handgun and knife. Once inside [Carroll's] apartment, an argument ensued
between Fowler and Carroll. This led to Fowler hitting Carroll in the head with
the gun that Fowler was carrying. Carroll was then taken to a back bedroom
where . . . he was threatened and beaten by Fowler. As Fowler administered the
beating, he told Carroll that he would "cut him" in order to "teach him a lesson."
Carroll's roommate, Thomas Gochanour . . . was struck in the face by Fowler
with the flat side of the knife that Fowler was carrying. Fowler also threatened to
cut Gochanour's throat with the knife. After engaging in this activity, Fowler and
his accomplices fled taking some videotapes, a cellular phone, a wallet, and
some money from the apartment.

Eighteen months after the above-described incident, Fowler turned himself in to the police. He was thereafter charged with and pleaded guilty to first
degree robbery. At sentencing, the trial court determined that because Fowler
had no prior criminal history, the standard sentencing range for the offense was
31 to 41 months, plus a mandatory 60 month firearm enhancement penalty.
Fowler sought an exceptional sentence of six months, exclusive of the firearm
enhancement, basing his request on what he claimed was the presence of
three statutory mitigating factors. Although the trial court did not find any of
those factors present, it nevertheless imposed a 15 month exceptional sentence
based on its determination that Fowler: (1) had no history of violent behavior

and no pertinent criminal history; (2) was experiencing symptoms of extreme sleep deprivation at the time of the offense; (3) exhibited behavior at the time of the offense that was aberrational and represented an isolated incident of violence; (4) had strong family support; and (5) was a low to moderate risk to reoffend. . . .

A court must generally impose a sentence within the standard sentence range. It may, however, impose a sentence above or below the standard range for reasons that are "substantial and compelling." [Washington's Sentencing Reform Act] contains a list of aggravating and mitigating factors "which the court may consider in the exercise of its discretion to impose an exceptional sentence." Although this list is not exclusive, any such reasons must relate to the crime and make it more, or less, egregious. . . . A sentencing court may not, in imposing an exceptional sentence, take into account the defendant's criminal history and the seriousness level of the offense because those are considered in computing the presumptive range for the offense. . . .

The first factor the sentencing court relied on in imposing an exceptional sentence was that the "defendant [had] no history of violent behavior and no pertinent criminal history." Although Fowler concedes that a defendant's lack of criminal history alone is an insufficient ground for a sentence below the standard range, he asserts that a clean record combined with a complete absence of police contacts may be a substantial and compelling reason for imposing an exceptional sentence.

This argument is without merit. Saying that the defendant had no history of violent behavior and no pertinent criminal history is essentially equivalent to saying that he has no criminal record. [A] lack of a criminal history is not a mitigating factor because criminal history is already encompassed in the sentencing guidelines. The only exception to this general rule is that a lack of criminal history may be considered "in combination with the finding that the defendant was 'induced' to commit the crime" or lacked a predisposition to commit the crime. State v. Ha'mim, 132 Wash. 2d 834, 842-843 (1997). Here, the trial court rejected a finding that Fowler was either induced by others to commit the crime or that he lacked a predisposition to commit the crime. . . .

The trial court also found that a downward exceptional sentence was justified on the basis that Fowler's behavior during the commission of the crime was aberrational and represented an isolated incident of violence. Specifically the trial court stated:

> I have absolutely no trouble believing the defendant when he said and his family said that the behavior that occurred on the night of this incident was an aberration. It was unusual. It was out of character for him. . . . I believe the defendant when he says that his behavior was fueled by some form of chemical imbalance, whether it was chronic depression I can't say. I certainly think there is every indication that it was fueled by sleep deprivation, ingestion of methamphetamines, ingestion of alcohol.

. . . Fowler argues here that federal case law supports the proposition that aberrant behavior is a valid mitigating factor. [However, the] fact that a defendant's criminal conduct is exceptional or aberrant does not distinguish the defendant's crime from others in the same category. Furthermore, to say that conduct is an aberration is tantamount to saying that the defendant "has not done anything like this before." That, in our view, is yet another way of saying that the defendant has little or no history of criminal behavior. . . .

Even if we were inclined to follow the lead of the federal circuit courts that have recognized that aberrational behavior may justify a departure from the standard range, Fowler's conduct does not resemble the type of conduct that those courts have found to be aberrational. The act Fowler committed was not committed without forethought and planning, and thus fails the spontaneity test enunciated in [federal cases on this subject]. Indeed, the record shows that Fowler's motivation in going to Ken Carroll's house was to collect a debt. To aid himself in that endeavor he armed himself with a handgun and knife, items that he subsequently used in the commission of the robbery. This was hardly a spontaneous act. Neither can it be said that any of the factors [are present] evidencing aberrational behavior under the "totality of the circumstance test," . . . i.e., that the defendant suffered from a psychological disorder, that he was under external pressure, that his motivation was other than pecuniary gain, or that he took steps to mitigate the effects of his acts. In short, Fowler's conduct was not aberrational, even under the case law or federal guidelines. . . .

Fowler also contends that . . . what the trial court described as his low to moderate risk to reoffend is . . . a substantial and compelling reason for imposing an exceptional sentence. Specifically, he argues that a low risk of reoffense is a valid factor when a court finds by clear and convincing evidence that a standard range disposition would be detrimental to the goal of rehabilitating the offender. . . . The sentencing court's finding that Fowler was a low to moderate risk to reoffend was based upon an evaluation and report of the Washington State Department of Corrections. [However, our prior cases establish] that the risk of reoffense is not a substantial and compelling reason for an exceptional sentence. State v. Estrella, 798 P.2d 289 (Wash. 1990). [Protection] of the public has already been considered by the legislature in computing the presumptive sentencing range.

MADSEN, J., dissenting.

. . . The defendant, Joshua Fowler, urges the court to follow federal cases recognizing aberrant behavior as a mitigating factor in sentencing. The majority summarily concludes that calling a defendant's criminal conduct aberrational is simply another way of saying that the defendant has little or no history of criminal behavior. . . . Federal courts agree that a lack of criminal history is not a basis for a downward sentence under the federal scheme. They conclude, however, that "aberrational behavior" is not equivalent to a lack of criminal history. . . . All of the federal circuits have recognized aberrational behavior as a factor that may, in the appropriate case, justify an exceptional sentence downward. A split developed in the circuits, however, as to what constitutes aberrational behavior. Some courts concluded that "a spontaneous and seemingly thoughtless act, rather than one which was the result of substantial planning" was a single act of aberrant behavior. Others applied a totality of circumstances approach, considering a number of factors. . . . In November 2000, the federal sentencing commission added §5K2.20 to the guidelines, defining "aberrant behavior" as "a single criminal occurrence or single criminal transaction that (A) was committed without significant planning; (B) was of limited duration; and (C) represents a marked deviation by the defendant from an otherwise law-abiding life." The commission directed that in deciding whether to depart from the guideline sentences on the basis of aberrant behavior, a court could consider the defendant's "(A) mental and emotional conditions; (B) employment record; (C) record of prior good works; (D) motivation for committing the offense; and (E) efforts to mitigate the effects of the offense."

[Some] crimes represent the truly unusual behavior of individuals who are generally nonviolent, law-abiding citizens [and were committed] under unusual circumstances. Similar to the federal approach, this court should hold that a trial court may, in its discretion, impose an exceptional sentence downward based upon aberrant behavior. . . .

The majority also rejects the trial court's reliance on a low to moderate risk of reoffending as supporting a downward sentence. [The sentencing statutes do not currently account for this factor.] A presumptive sentencing range is based upon the seriousness level of the current offense and the defendant's offender score. Whether the individual defendant has a low, moderate, or high risk of reoffending is not part of the calculation. . . . Further, this court has in the past accepted the premise that future dangerousness is an appropriate nonstatutory aggravating factor under certain circumstances involving offenders convicted of sex offenses. If future dangerousness can justify an upward sentence, albeit in limited cases, why should a low risk of reoffending be rejected as a mitigating factor? At least two of the goals of the SRA favor allowing sentencing discretion to impose a downward sentence where there is a low risk of reoffending: the promotion of respect for the law by provision of just punishment, and making frugal use of the state's resources. . . .

NOTES

1. *Treatment of first-time offenders at sentencing.*   In indeterminate sentencing systems, sentencing informally reflects the maxim that everyone deserves a second chance. With the exception of the most serious and violent offenses, most first-time offenders can expect a sentencing judge to impose a relatively brief sentence of imprisonment or suspend any incarceration and place the offender on probation. As the statute from Washington highlights, this tendency to cut first-time offenders a break has been codified in many structured sentencing systems. The Sentencing Reform Act requires the U.S. Sentencing Commission to "insure that the [federal] guidelines reflect the general appropriateness of imposing a sentence other than imprisonment in cases in which the defendant is a first offender who has not been convicted of a crime of violence or an otherwise serious offense." 28 U.S.C. §994(j).

More generally, all structured sentencing systems provide for first-time offenders to receive no criminal history points or the lowest possible offender score, which in turn limits the upper level of the sentencing range designated for the offense. Many of these systems, however, group the true first-time offender with other offenders who have some minor criminal history. In the federal system, for example, Criminal History Category I treats a wide range of defendants the same; defendants who have no prior record (no prior arrests, no pending charges, no dismissed charges, no prior convictions) fall into Category I, along with defendants who have one prior conviction and received a sentence of imprisonment of as long as 60 days. This category also includes defendants who may have had contact with the criminal justice system, such as arrests or dismissed charges, and defendants with convictions not counted under the guidelines for a variety of reasons, such as the "age" of the conviction, the locality where the conviction occurred, or the minor nature of the offense. What reasons might support such a structure for considering criminal history, which seems to allow defendants "one free bite at the apple"?

2. *Departures for first-time offenders and "aberrant behavior."*   In part because many guideline systems group true first-time offenders with other offenders who have some minor criminal history, cases like *Fowler* arise in many jurisdictions in which a sentencing judge departs below the applicable guideline sentence because the offender's wrongdoing seems truly exceptional and the judge believes the offender is unlikely to engage in criminal activity again. Most appellate courts rule that first-offender status and related concerns have already been considered in the guideline scheme and thus cannot serve as the basis for a departure. See, e.g., Koon v. United States, 518 U.S. 81, 110-112 (1996) (holding that district court could not depart based on defendants' "low likelihood of recidivism" because the U.S. Sentencing Commission took that factor into account in formulating the lowest criminal history category); cf. State v. Grady, 258 Kan. 72, 87-88 (1995) ("While generally criminal history is an improper departure factor because criminal history has already been used to set the presumptive sentence, we believe the legislature intended in the interest of justice that a trial court have discretion to impose a downward dispositional departure where a defendant has no prior criminal history and has a failed common-law or statutory defense that is not meritless.").

As noted in *Fowler*, the federal system developed a way to reduce sentences in exceptional cases based on the concept of "aberrational behavior." A federal sentencing judge may depart downward when the defendant's background and the nature of the offense show that the offense grew out of peculiar circumstances not likely to be repeated. The rationale has been among the most common for downward departures, with more than 800 offenders receiving a reduced sentence on this basis in 2001. As noted in the *Fowler* dissent, the federal courts of appeals were initially divided over when to allow an aberrant behavior departure. Some required the offense to be a single "spontaneous and seemingly thoughtless act"; others allowed sentencing judges more latitude under a "totality of the circumstances" approach. The U.S. Sentencing Commission's policy statement in §5K2.20 adopted a compromise view of what constitutes aberrant behavior, going beyond a "single act" to include "a single criminal *occurrence* or single criminal *transaction* that (A) was committed without significant planning; (B) was of limited duration; and (C) represents a marked deviation by the defendant from an otherwise law-abiding life" (emphasis added). The policy statement also barred departures on this basis for certain crimes, including serious drug trafficking offenses, those that cause "serious bodily injury or death," and crimes in which the defendant uses a dangerous weapon. Does the fact that a defendant used a gun make a crime any less aberrational?

3. *Safety valve to ameliorate mandatory sentences.*   One common complaint lodged against mandatory sentencing statutes is that by requiring a particular sentence based only on the offense, the provisions fail to allow for mitigated sentences for first-time offenders. Congress responded to these concerns in the

context of federal mandatory minimum drug sentences by enacting a "safety valve" provision as part of the Violent Crime Control and Law Enforcement Act of 1994. This provision instructs judges to apply the federal guidelines, rather than the often harsher mandatory minimum drug sentencing statutes, when five criteria are satisfied: (1) the defendant does not have more than one criminal history point, as determined under the federal sentencing guidelines; (2) the defendant did not use violence or possess a dangerous weapon in connection with the offense; (3) the offense did not result in death or serious bodily injury; (4) the defendant was not an organizer, leader, manager, or supervisor of others in the offense; and (5) the defendant provided the government with complete information about the crime and related offenses. 18 U.S.C. §3553(f). For a detailed empirical analysis of the impact of this safety valve provision, see Celesta A. Albonetti, The Effects of the "Safety Valve" Amendment on Length of Imprisonment for Cocaine Trafficking/Manufacturing Offenders: Mitigating the Effects of Mandatory Minimum Penalties and Offender's Ethnicity, 87 Iowa L. Rev. 401 (2002).

B. THE COOPERATIVE DEFENDANT

By the time a convicted defendant faces a sentencing judge, several months or even years may have passed since the crime occurred. During that time, the defendant performs many acts that can have some bearing on the sentence. For a sentencing judge who emphasizes retributive purposes of a criminal sentence, with a focus on the harm created by the crime, this postcrime behavior might have little effect. But for a sentencing judge (or a sentencing system) placing more weight on utilitarian goals such as incapacitation or rehabilitation, postcrime behavior plays a significant role. This recent conduct offers important clues about how the defendant will act in the near future. In this section, we explore postcrime conduct that signals the defendant's willingness to cooperate with the authorities, both in her own case and in other cases.

1. Acceptance of Responsibility and Plea Bargains

Most courtroom veterans believe that a guilty plea produces big advantages at sentencing, and empirical research confirms this belief. Defendants pleading guilty tend to receive substantially lower sentences than defendants who go to trial (in some studies the "plea discount" has been more than one-third off post-trial sentences).

In structured sentencing systems, the rules give sentencing judges different instructions about the impact of a plea agreement. Some rules say that plea agreements should not change the sentence at all; other rules allow the judge to accept the parties' recommendations within certain broad limits. For instance, under the Minnesota sentencing guidelines, judges must impose the sentence indicated in the guideline grid unless there is a valid ground for departure.

A plea agreement, standing alone, is not a sufficient reason to depart from the guidelines. In Washington state, statutory guidelines tell the judge to "determine if the agreement is consistent with the interests of justice and with the [statutory] prosecuting standards" and to reject the agreement if it is not. Wash. Rev. Code §9.94A.090(1). The federal sentencing guidelines also advise judges to limit the impact of a guilty plea at sentencing. The court may accept sentencing recommendations offered in a plea agreement "if the court is satisfied either that (1) the recommended sentence is within the applicable guideline range; or (2) the recommended sentence departs from the applicable guideline range for justifiable reasons." U.S. Sentencing Guidelines Manual §6B1.2(b).

If it is true that sentencing judges in most systems reward defendants who plead guilty, does that mean that sentencing judges punish a defendant for exercising the right to a trial? Do sentencing rules discourage judges from honestly explaining what they are doing?

State v. David Tiernan
645 A.2d 482 (R.I. 1994)

WEISBERGER, Acting C.J.

. . . The precise issue we confront in this appeal is the question of whether the trial justice improperly considered either defendant's exercise of his privilege against self-incrimination under the Fifth Amendment to the United States Constitution or his exercise of his right to a public trial guaranteed by the Sixth Amendment to the United States Constitution and article 1, section 10, of the Rhode Island Constitution. We answer this question in the negative. . . .

In November 1990 defendant was convicted of two counts of second-degree child molestation after a trial by jury in Superior Court. At the sentencing hearing defendant argued that in light of his background, the absence of any prior record, and the nature of the crime involved, he should be given a sentence involving only treatment and counseling rather than imprisonment. The prosecutor disagreed, arguing that such treatment would not be effective unless defendant acknowledged his wrongdoing, which defendant refused to do. As a matter of deterrence and punishment, the prosecutor urged the court to impose a lengthy jail sentence.

The trial justice agreed with the prosecutor, citing five factors that were considered in formulating his decision — "the nature of the offense and the offender, punishment, rehabilitation and deterrence." The trial justice explained that "some program of counseling could be effective if culpability is accepted, but the problem is defendant's continued protestations of innocence." The trial justice explained this comment, stating that "it is my understanding from everybody knowledgeable in this area that treatment is not effective unless and until the person being treated, the defendant, acknowledges guilt, and the defendant still protests his innocence, and has done so here in court." Therefore, the trial justice reasoned that since rehabilitation was improbable, . . . "punishment and deterrence are most important to the Court in this case when determining an appropriate sentence." In light of the aforementioned factors, the trial justice sentenced defendant to two terms of twenty years, eight years to serve and twelve years suspended on each count, to be served concurrently.

[The] defendant filed a timely Rule 35 motion to reduce sentence. At the hearing on the motion, defendant presented the court with an admission of guilt and a profession of remorse — the key ingredients that the trial justice had found lacking at the time of the original sentencing with respect to defendant's potential for rehabilitation. The defendant attempted to justify his delayed acknowledgment of his crime by explaining that at the time of the sentencing hearing he had not yet come to terms with the sexual molestation that, he revealed to the court, he himself had endured in his own childhood. After hearing from defendant, the trial justice was presented with testimony from the victim's mother who painfully recounted the traumatic effect that the molestation and the trial had had upon her daughter.

After considering the testimony presented, the trial justice denied defendant's motion to reduce sentence and made the following observations:

> [I observed] that little girl testify. The defendant sat there and required her to testify. She did, and although she was a little girl, she was believed by the jury and by me; and yet he stood up and indicated to me that he intended to pursue all of his rights of appeal, again, which I believe he had his right to do, everybody does. He did that knowing full well that what that little girl said from the stand was absolutely true and he let her go through it. While I am somewhat moved by defense counsel's argument and even the defendant's own statements, I am not persuaded by them, not in the least. . . .

On appeal defendant challenges his sentence on the grounds that at both the sentencing hearing and the Rule 35 hearing the trial justice violated defendant's constitutional rights by considering improper factors. First, defendant claims that at the sentencing hearing the trial justice's decision was tainted by his consideration of the fact that defendant invoked his Fifth Amendment privilege against self-incrimination and he used that fact to justify the imposition of a lengthy sentence upon defendant. Then at the Rule 35 hearing, when defendant waived his Fifth Amendment right and admitted his guilt, defendant claims that the trial justice justified defendant's lengthy sentence with an alternative, but equally objectionable, fact — that defendant had exercised his right to stand trial and thereby forced his child victim to endure a painful court experience. The defendant cites to us in support of his assertions a plethora of cases from other jurisdictions. . . .

A motion to reduce sentence under Rule 35 is basically a plea by a defendant for leniency and, as such, is addressed to the sound discretion of the trial justice. Because of our strong policy against interfering with a trial justice's exercise of discretion with respect to such motions, we shall interfere with the lower court's decision only in the rarest of cases. With this deferential standard of review in mind, we now turn to the applicable substantive law.

A judge has no more difficult duty nor awesome responsibility than the pronouncement of sentence in a criminal case. To guide trial justices in carrying out this responsibility, we have identified the following factors as falling within the scope of constitutionally permissible sentencing considerations: (1) the severity of the crime, (2) the defendant's personal, educational, and employment background, (3) the potential for rehabilitation, (4) the element of societal deterrence, and (5) the appropriateness of the punishment. State v. Bertoldi, 495 A.2d 247 (R.I. 1985); State v. Upham, 439 A.2d 912 (R.I. 1982).

Most of these factors are multidimensional and require a trial justice to reflect upon a variety of subsidiary factors. For example, with respect to the element of rehabilitation, a trial justice may consider a defendant's attitude toward society, his sense of remorse, as well as his inclination and capacity to take his place as an honest and useful member of society. Likewise, a defendant's giving of false testimony may be probative of his attitude toward society and consequently his prospects for rehabilitation.

In addition to the above five factors, a trial justice may also take into consideration a corollary factor to justify reducing a sentence — that a defendant exhibited contrition and consideration for the victims of his or her criminal activity and pled guilty to the crime charged. See Brady v. United States, 397 U.S. 742 (1970) ("encouraging a guilty plea by opportunity or promise of leniency" does not violate Fifth Amendment). We are mindful that a defendant, by pleading guilty, waives a broad array of rights, including the right to trial by jury, the presumption of innocence, the state's burden to prove one guilty beyond a reasonable doubt, the privilege against self-incrimination, the right to confront and cross-examine one's accusers, the right to testify and call witnesses in one's defense, and the right to appeal one's conviction to this court. By waiving these rights, a defendant, first, has spared the state from expending considerable time, money and other precious judicial and law enforcement resources and, second, has prevented the public scrutiny of and embarrassment to the victim that derives from recounting his or her victimization in a public forum. In exchange therefor a defendant may properly be extended a certain amount of leniency in sentencing.

Although we have recognized the propriety of extending leniency when a defendant pleads guilty, we have specifically prohibited the lengthening of a sentence on the basis of a defendant's refusal to plead guilty or his or her insistence on holding the state to its burden of proving guilt beyond a reasonable doubt at trial. State v. Rollins, 359 A.2d 315, 320 (R.I. 1976). [The] rights implicated when a defendant chooses to stand trial . . . are some of the most jealously guarded and deeply embedded rights of our criminal justice jurisprudence, rights that both the Federal and our State Constitutions unconditionally extend to criminal defendants. To exact a price or impose a penalty upon a defendant in the form of an enhanced sentence for invoking such rights would amount to a deprivation of due process of law, and that we shall not condone. . . .

FIFTH AMENDMENT PRIVILEGE AGAINST SELF-INCRIMINATION CLAIM

Reviewing the transcript of the original sentencing hearing, we cannot say that the trial justice improperly considered in his sentencing decision defendant's exercise of his Fifth Amendment privilege against self-incrimination. In making the sentencing determination, the trial justice articulated and applied the very five factors we condoned in *Upham* and *Bertoldi:* the nature of the offense and of the offender, punishment, rehabilitation, and deterrence. [The trial justice] considered defendant's refusal to acknowledge guilt for the limited purpose of assessing defendant's potential for rehabilitation. Underlying rehabilitation is the thesis that the offender needs assistance in making behavioral and/or psychological changes. In order for that assistance to be effective, a defendant must be open and receptive to the proffered treatment. A defendant's adamant denial of engaging in any wrongful conduct—the very conduct that necessitates the treatment—cannot be said to be indicative of any receptiveness to rehabilitation. Accordingly we hold that the trial justice properly considered defendant's refusal to admit perpetrating the molestation in his assessment of defendant's rehabilitative potential. Other courts have similarly recognized the probative value of a defendant's refusal to acknowledge wrongdoing with respect to assessing the element of rehabilitative capacity. See Gallucci v. State, 371 So. 2d 148, 150 (Fla. App. 1979). . . .

After evaluating defendant's questionable potential for rehabilitation, the trial justice properly determined that "example type" sentencing was demanded. [Defendant] was not penalized for refusing to waive his Fifth Amendment right; rather he was simply not extended a benefit which he might have enjoyed had he waived his rights and pled either guilty or nolo to the charges.

THE RIGHT TO STAND TRIAL

. . . In considering defendant's motion to reduce his sentence, the trial justice remarked that defendant had "required" the child to testify by exercising his right to stand trial, after which defendant indicated his intention to appeal while "knowing full well that what that little girl said from the stand was absolutely true." The defendant claims that these remarks evidence an intent to penalize him for standing trial. We cannot agree.

At the outset we are compelled to point out that the right guaranteed to defendant by the Sixth Amendment to the United States Constitution and article 1, section 10, of the Rhode Island Constitution is the right to stand trial and *truthfully* testify in his own behalf. This defendant did not do. Rather defendant exercised his right and took the opportunity to present false testimony to the court in the hopes of escaping conviction and punishment.

The trial justice's remarks clearly related to the fact that defendant had, while under a solemn oath and in a court of law, knowingly and intentionally perpetrated a falsehood. The trial justice proceeded to identify the impact upon the victim of defendant's decision to stand trial and tell a falsehood—namely, that she was forced to endure the trauma of testifying about embarrassing and intimate sexual details and to undergo an intense cross-examination.

[T]he trial justice's consideration of defendant's false testimony and the impact of the trial upon the victim was proper as these factors related to his prospects for rehabilitation. With respect to defendant's falsehood, we stated in *Bertoldi* that a defendant's willingness to take the stand and lie "not only demonstrates a disrespect for the law and the judicial system, but also evidences an important character trait. It reveals that the defendant is perfectly willing to commit a crime in an attempt to conceal an earlier crime. . . ." The fact that defendant claimed to have lied because of an event he endured in his childhood does not cast a different light onto his falsehood or justify in any way, shape, or form his decision to give false testimony while under a solemn judicial oath to tell the truth.

Likewise, consideration of the impact of the trial upon the child victim, especially in the face of a posttrial confession, is proper as it reflects a defendant's attitude toward his victim and society. In State v. Farnham, 479 A.2d 887 (Me. 1984), the Supreme Judicial Court of Maine upheld consideration of this factor in circumstances very similar to those in the case at hand. [As the court noted, although the defendant] "had an absolute right to a trial and to conduct vigorous cross-examination in connection with a crime for which he soon after admitted his guilt, he cannot escape the fact that his exercise of those rights are probative of his attitude towards the victim and society." . . .

We note that this was not a case in which the trial justice threatened pretrial to impose a harsher sentence if defendant opted to stand trial, see United States v. Stockwell, 472 F.2d 1186 (9th Cir. 1973), or one in which the trial justice stated posttrial that a more severe sentence was warranted because defendant wasted time, public funds, and resources by insisting on a trial, see United States v. Hutchings, 757 F.2d 11 (2d Cir. 1985). . . .

The length of the sentence imposed was well within the parameters set forth by the Legislature in G.L. 1956 (1981 Reenactment) §11-37-8.4 ("every person who shall commit second degree child molestation sexual assault shall be imprisoned for not less than six years nor more than thirty years"). Given our limited scope of review, we hold that the trial justice remained soundly within the bounds of his discretion. . . .

Charles Hynes v. Albert Tomei
706 N.E.2d 1201 (N.Y. 1998)

KAYE, C.J.

Thirty years ago, the United States Supreme Court struck down the death penalty provision of the Federal Kidnaping Act, which allowed a defendant to be sentenced to death only after a jury trial. The Supreme Court invalidated the provision because, by needlessly encouraging guilty pleas and jury waivers to avoid death sentences, it impermissibly burdened defendants' Fifth Amendment right against self-incrimination and Sixth Amendment right to a jury trial. United States v. Jackson, 390 U.S. 570 (1968). Despite the passage of three decades, a plethora of decisions involving the death penalty and a sea change in plea bargaining, the Supreme Court has never overruled *Jackson*, which binds this Court. Indeed, every other death penalty State has fit its capital murder plea-bargaining procedures within the rationale of *Jackson*.

Three years ago, the New York State Legislature enacted a capital punishment statute that — like the Federal Kidnaping Act — allows a defendant to be sentenced to death only after a jury trial. Bench trials are not permitted in capital cases, N.Y. Const., art. I, §2, and the statute bars imposition of a death sentence upon a guilty plea. The New York law thus explicitly provides two levels of penalty for the same offense, imposing death only on those who assert innocence and proceed to trial. . . . We are convinced that *Jackson* compels [us to] declare CPL §§220.10(5)(e) and 220.30(3)(b)(vii) unconstitutional. . . .

The Federal Kidnaping Act considered in *Jackson* provided [that whoever knowingly transports in interstate commerce a kidnaped person] "shall be punished (1) by death if the kidnaped person has not been liberated unharmed, and if the verdict of the jury shall so recommend, or (2) by imprisonment for any term of years or for life, if the death penalty is not imposed." Because the

Act authorized the death penalty only on the recommendation of a jury, while a defendant convicted of the same offense on a guilty plea or by a Judge escaped the threat of capital punishment, the Supreme Court concluded that the Act "needlessly" encouraged guilty pleas and jury waivers. The Court acknowledged that restricting the death penalty to cases in which a jury recommends it is a legitimate goal, and that such a restriction would likely decrease the frequency of capital punishment. However, the Court concluded these considerations did not save the Act from constitutional infirmity. While the Act's chilling effect on a defendant's exercise of the Fifth Amendment right against self-incrimination and Sixth Amendment right to a jury trial may have been incidental, the effect was also "unnecessary and therefore excessive," since Congress could have achieved its goals by allowing juries to sentence defendants to the full range of punishments regardless of how guilt was determined.

Shortly after *Jackson*, this Court invalidated two provisions of the former Code of Criminal Procedure that required waiver of a jury trial in order to receive the benefit of youthful offender treatment. See People v. Michael A.C., 261 N.E.2d 620 (N.Y. 1970). Although respondents who refused to waive a jury trial were not subject to the death penalty, they were exposed to longer prison sentences than those prosecuted as youthful offenders. Drawing a parallel to *Jackson*, this Court held that "a procedure which offers an individual a reward for waiving a fundamental constitutional right, or imposes a harsher penalty for asserting it, may not be sustained."

New York's death penalty statute authorizes a District Attorney to file a notice of intent to seek the death penalty against a defendant charged with murder in the first degree. Upon conviction by a jury, a capital defendant faces a separate sentencing proceeding before a jury to determine whether the penalty imposed will be death or life imprisonment without parole. The statute affords a defendant the opportunity to ensure a maximum sentence of life without parole by pleading guilty pursuant to the following provisions:

> A defendant may not enter a plea of guilty to the crime of murder in the first degree . . . ; provided, however, that a defendant may enter such a plea with both the permission of the court and the consent of the people when the agreed upon sentence is either life imprisonment without parole or a term of imprisonment for . . . murder in the first degree other than a sentence of life imprisonment without parole. CPL §§220.10(5)(e); 220.30(3)(b)(vii).

> A defendant who has entered a plea of not guilty to an indictment may, with both the permission of the court and the consent of the people, withdraw such plea at any time before the rendition of a verdict and enter . . . a plea of guilty to part of the indictment . . . but subject to the limitation in subdivision five of section 220.10. CPL §220.60(2)(a). . . .

Thus, like the invalidated Federal Kidnaping Act provision, New York's death penalty statute explicitly provides for the imposition of the death penalty only upon a jury verdict. As a result, under the New York statute, only those defendants who exercise the Fifth Amendment right against self-incrimination and Sixth Amendment right to a jury trial put themselves at risk of death.

[Respondents] argue that the challenged New York provisions are distinguishable from the Federal Kidnaping Act because they merely codify permissible plea bargaining, which was not at issue in *Jackson*. Subsequent to *Jackson*, both the Supreme Court and this Court have acknowledged the legitimacy and desirability — indeed, the necessity — of plea bargaining. See Santobello v. New York, 404 U.S. 257 (1971); People v. Selikoff, 318 N.E.2d 784 (N.Y. 1974). Plea bargaining serves important functions for both prosecutors and defendants, such as individualized justice, leniency and economy. A State clearly may encourage guilty pleas by offering benefits to defendants in return for a guilty plea. Furthermore, plea bargaining becomes no less lawful or desirable when it is codified in statutory form.

While plea bargaining is permissible, the Supreme Court in *Jackson* prohibited statutes that "needlessly" encourage guilty pleas, which are not constitutionally protected, by impermissibly burdening constitutional rights. Given the availability of alternatives that do not impermissibly burden defendants' constitutional rights, the plea provisions of the statute before us cannot be justified by an ostensible purpose such as the facilitation of plea bargaining.

Respondents rely heavily on Corbitt v. New Jersey, 439 U.S. 212 (1978), in which the Supreme Court held that it is constitutionally permissible to offer a defendant the possibility of escaping the most severe penalty by pleading guilty. The New Jersey statute at issue in *Corbitt,* however, provided for the same maximum sentence — life imprisonment — regardless of a defendant's plea. While a lesser sentence was permitted for those defendants who pleaded guilty, it was not guaranteed. Thus, the statute survived constitutional scrutiny because it did "not reserve the maximum punishment for murder for those who insist on a jury trial." This situation is readily distinguishable from the challenged New York provisions, which indeed prescribe a lesser agreed-upon sentence for those who plead guilty. . . .

In sum, respondents' attempts to distinguish New York's death penalty statute from the death penalty invalidated by the Supreme Court in *Jackson* fail. [By] statutory mandate, the death penalty hangs over only those who exercise their constitutional rights to maintain innocence and demand a jury trial. Thus, *Jackson* compels us to invalidate these provisions, just as it has compelled other State high courts to invalidate their capital plea provisions with the same constitutional infirmity. See State v. Johnson, 595 A.2d 498 (N.H. 1991); Commonwealth v. Colon-Cruz, 470 N.E.2d 116 (Mass. 1984); State v. Frampton, 627 P.2d 922 (Wash. 1981); State v. Funicello, 286 A.2d 55 (N.J. 1972). By contrast, the death penalty statutes of States that have rejected a *Jackson* challenge, with one exception, provide for the possibility of a death sentence upon a guilty plea. See State v. Mann, 959 S.W.2d 503 (Tenn. 1996); Conger v. Warden, 510 P.2d 1359 (Nev. 1973). The exception, Arkansas, avoided a *Jackson* problem because the Trial Judge, not the jury, made the final determination of whether the death penalty would be imposed, and because guilty pleas were permitted only after the prosecutor waived the death penalty. See Ruiz v. State, 630 S.W.2d 44 (Ark. 1982).

[Invalidation of the death penalty is not] necessary to obviate the *Jackson* problem: excision of the capital pleading provisions eliminates the burden on constitutional rights prohibited by *Jackson,* since without those provisions there is only one maximum penalty for first degree murder. [While] CPL §§221.10(5)(e) and 220.30(3)(b)(vii) relate exclusively to pleas in first degree murder cases and "needlessly" encourage guilty pleas in violation of *Jackson,* CPL §220.60(2)(a) is not limited to first degree murder cases, nor does it, in the absence of CPL §220.10(5)(e), violate *Jackson.* Therefore, only CPL §§220.10(5)(e) and

220.30(3)(b)(vii) must be stricken. Under the resulting statute, a defendant may not plead guilty to first degree murder while a notice of intent to seek the death penalty is pending.

We realize this result will reduce the flexibility of both prosecutors and defendants who wish to plea bargain in capital cases. Indeed, our reversal in these cases may well have an ironic twist in that capital defendants will have fewer opportunities to avoid the possibility of the death penalty. . . . While reducing the flexibility of plea bargaining in capital cases, excision of the unconstitutional provisions does not prevent pleas of guilty to first degree murder when no notice of intent to seek the death penalty is pending, since defendants in that situation face the same maximum sentence regardless of how they are convicted. Nor does the resulting statute prevent a defendant from pleading guilty to another offense not punishable by death, even when a notice of intent to seek the death penalty is pending, since nothing in *Jackson* prohibits imposing different penalties for different crimes. . . . Thus, while a defendant may not plead guilty to first degree murder while a notice of intent to seek the death penalty is pending, plea bargaining to lesser offenses even when a notice of intent is pending, or to first degree murder in the absence of a notice of intent, remains unaffected. . . .

‖ *U.S. Sentencing Guidelines Manual* ‖

§3E1.1 ACCEPTANCE OF RESPONSIBILITY

(a) If the defendant clearly demonstrates acceptance of responsibility for his offense, decrease the offense level by 2 levels.

(b) If the defendant qualifies for a decrease under subsection (a), the offense level determined prior to the operation of subsection (a) is level 16 or greater, and upon motion of the government stating that the defendant has assisted authorities in the investigation or prosecution of his own misconduct by timely notifying authorities of his intention to enter a plea of guilty, thereby permitting the government to avoid preparing for trial and permitting the government and the court to allocate their resources efficiently, decrease the offense level by 1 additional level.

‖ *United Kingdom Statute 2000, Ch. 6, Pt. VIII, §152* ‖

(1) In determining what sentence to pass on an offender who has pleaded guilty to an offence in proceedings before that or another court, a court shall take into account —

(a) the stage in the proceedings for the offence at which the offender indicated his intention to plead guilty; and

(b) the circumstances in which this indication was given.

(2) If, as a result of taking into account any matter referred to in subsection (1) above, the court imposes a punishment on the offender which is less severe than the punishment it would otherwise have imposed, it shall state in open court that it has done so.

(3) In the case of an offence the sentence for which falls to be imposed under subsection (2) of section 110 or 111 above [dealing with minimum sentences for drug and burglary crimes], nothing in that subsection shall prevent the court, after taking into account any matter referred to in subsection (1) above, from imposing any sentence which is not less than 80 per cent of that specified in that subsection.

NOTES

1. *The guilty plea discount and the trial penalty at sentencing.* Courts walk a fine line when talking about the effect of a guilty plea on a sentence. On the one hand, they routinely say that a sentencing court may not penalize a defendant for exercising the constitutional rights that go along with a criminal trial. On the other hand, courts declare that a sentencing judge may reward a defendant for pleading guilty. State v. Balfour, 637 A.2d 1249 (N.J. 1994) (defendant's agreement to plead guilty can appropriately be weighed in the decision to downgrade an offense to a lower degree at sentencing). The defendant who pleads guilty saves the resources of the system for other cases; the administrative reasons for rewarding this choice are obvious. Is there a meaningful difference between penalizing a defendant and refusing to reward a defendant who insists on a trial? Do these rules encourage judges to do anything more than choose their words carefully?

The sentencing judge often reasons that a defendant's decision to go to trial reveals a lack of remorse or a refusal to accept responsibility for the crime. These facts have some bearing on the defendant's prospects for rehabilitation, or perhaps on the chances that he will commit crimes in the future. Cf. Ohio Rev. Code §2929.12 (D)(5) (providing that judges should consider the fact that "offender shows no genuine remorse for the offense" as a factor indicating a greater likelihood of recidivism). Thus, the judges say, an enhanced penalty after trial merely responds to this relevant information and does not directly punish the exercise of rights. Jennings v. State, 664 A.2d 903 (Md. 1995). Similarly, the judge might believe that the impact of a trial on a victim (particularly a vulnerable victim who must testify at trial) justifies a more severe sentence. Does this reasoning apply to most (or all) defendants who go to trial? See Michael O'Hear, Remorse, Cooperation and "Acceptance of Responsibility": The Structure, Implementation and Reform of Section 3E1.1 of the Federal Sentencing Guidelines, 91 Nw. U. L. Rev. 1507 (1997).

2. *Legislative and commission rules on the guilty plea discount.* The New York court in the *Tomei* case discussed the constitutional limits on the use of incentives to plead guilty in death penalty cases. The court looked for guidance in United States v. Jackson, 312 U.S. 275 (1968), but distinguished another case, Corbitt v. New Jersey, 439 U.S. 212 (1978). In *Corbitt* a statute required the sentencing judge in first-degree murder cases to impose a life sentence when the defendant was convicted after trial. If the defendant pleaded guilty, however, the judge could choose either a life term or a 30-year term (the punishment for second-degree murder). How do you explain the difference in the outcomes in *Jackson* and *Corbitt*? See Joseph L. Hoffmann, Marcy L. Kahn, and Steven W. Fisher, Plea Bargaining in the Shadow of Death, 63 Fordham L. Rev. 2313 (2001).

Are plea negotiations conducted differently when legislatures or sentencing commissions set the possible bargaining terms for all cases rather than when the prosecutor sets possible terms for a particular case? Many jurisdictions with structured sentencing rules provide for some form of guilty plea discount, either directly or indirectly. The Massachusetts sentencing guidelines list the plea agreement as a mitigating factor for a court to consider at sentencing. North Carolina law lists two mitigating factors: that the defendant accepted responsibility for the crime or that "prior to arrest or at an early stage of the criminal process, the defendant voluntarily acknowledged wrongdoing in connection with the offense to a law enforcement officer." N.C. Gen. Stat. §15A-1340.16 (e)(11), (15).

Section 3E1.1 of the federal sentencing guidelines (reprinted above) allows courts to reduce a sentence for a defendant who accepts responsibility. The application notes indicate that pleading guilty operates as a close proxy for accepting responsibility:

> This adjustment is not intended to apply to a defendant who puts the government to its burden of proof at trial by denying the essential factual elements of guilt, is convicted, and only then admits guilt and expresses remorse. Conviction by trial, however, does not automatically preclude a defendant from consideration for such a reduction. In rare situations a defendant may clearly demonstrate an acceptance of responsibility for his criminal conduct even though he exercises his constitutional right to a trial. This may occur, for example, where a defendant goes to trial to assert and preserve issues that do not relate to factual guilt . . . .

The commentary goes on to remind courts that pleading guilty will not necessarily lead to a lower sentence: "A defendant who enters a guilty plea is not entitled to an adjustment under this section as a matter of right." Yet historically well over 90 percent of offenders who plead guilty get this reduction. Is section 3E1.1 significantly different from a sentencing guideline provision that sets a uniform discount for the sentences of all defendants who plead guilty? Does it reward cooperation that produces administrative savings or remorse for the crime or both?

The international tribunals for criminal matters in Rwanda and Yugoslavia have given sentence discounts for defendants who showed sincere remorse, but they have not done so in all cases. According to the rules of procedure for those tribunals, counseling in favor of a sentence decrease are the enormous costs of these trials and the ability of guilty pleas to add to national reconciliation and truth-finding. Still, in some cases the gravity of the offense has caused the courts to discount the value of the guilty plea.

3. *Prevalence and size of the discount.* In discretionary sentencing systems, judges give different discounts to defendants for pleading guilty (or for accepting responsibility or expressing remorse, if you prefer). Those studying sentences in the aggregate have estimated that a guilty plea can reduce a sentence by 15 to 40 percent.

Under the federal guidelines section 3E1.1, if a defendant "clearly demonstrates acceptance of responsibility," her "offense level" can be reduced by two or three levels. The three-level discount was once available to any defendant charged with the most serious crimes who pled guilty early or who cooperated in the investigation of her own crimes. But Congress amended the guidelines in 2003 to condition this greater discount on a motion by the prosecution stating that the defendant's early plea or cooperation was beneficial to the government. What was Congress's goal in specifying a motion by the government as a pre-requisite to an increased reduction for acceptance of responsibility? A three-level discount could mean a reduction of as much as 50 percent of the sentence for lesser crimes or as little as 20 percent for more serious offenses.

The structured sentencing rules in most states do not specify how much the judge should discount the sentence of a defendant who pleads guilty. Compare this to the cap contained in the legislation from the United Kingdom, reprinted above. It does appear that early guilty pleas in the Crown Court lead to more nonprison sentences and to shorter prison terms. See Ralph J. Henham, Sentence Discounts and the Criminal Process (2001). If a state were to pass a statute identical to the U.K. legislation, would it survive constitutional challenge? Some state statutes in the United States do specify the maximum size of the discount that a court may grant for pleading guilty. See Iowa Code §901.10(3) (in sentencing certain drug defendants otherwise subject to a mandatory minimum sentence, "the court may, at its discretion, reduce the maximum sentence by up to one-third" for a defendant who pleads guilty).

In a world where more than 90 percent of all felony defendants plead guilty, how many defendants fail to receive a discount? In the federal system in 2001, only 9 percent of offenders failed to receive a some discount for acceptance of responsibility (with 63 percent receiving three-level discounts and 28 percent receiving two-level discounts). Only 3.4 percent of the defendants convicted in federal court in 2001 actually went to trial. Does this pattern undermine the claim that courts are not punishing defendants who exercise their trial rights?

4. *Silence, perjury, and sentencing.* As the Rhode Island court in *Tiernan* mentioned, defendants have a right to trial, but they have no right to perjury. A defendant who testifies at trial might receive a stiffer punishment if the judge believes that the testimony was not truthful. See United States v. Dunnigan, 507 U.S. 87, 97 (1993) (sentencing court can enhance defendant's sentence by designated amount under federal guidelines if the court finds that the defendant committed perjury at trial; court must make "findings to support all the elements of a perjury violation in the specific case").

But the trial is not the only setting in which it is dangerous for the defendant to speak. The probation officer who prepares a presentence investigation report might ask to interview the defendant. If the officer believes that the defendant lied during the interview, he might recommend against any discount for acceptance of responsibility. Cf. People v. Hicks, N.E.2d 205 (N.Y. 2002) (approving imposition of an enhanced sentence after defender lied about crime to probation officer). At the same time, the Fifth Amendment's privilege against self-incrimination limits the consequences of a defendant's decision to remain silent. In Mitchell v. United States, 526 U.S. 314 (1999), the defendant faced a sentence anywhere from one year to life depending on the quantity of drugs involved in her offense. Mitchell did not testify at the sentencing hearing, but contended that the evidence established only a small amount of cocaine. The Supreme Court held that the trial court could not consider Mitchell's silence as a basis for a factual finding that higher amounts of drugs were involved in the case. Drawing such inferences from her silence impermissibly burdened her exercise of the constitutional right against compelled self-incrimination. Would the same reasoning apply to a defendant who declines a probation officer's invitation to discuss the case? Consider this application note to section 3E1.1: "[A] defendant is not required to volunteer, or affirmatively admit, relevant conduct beyond the offense of conviction in order to obtain a reduction."

5. *"Vindictive" sentencing after retrial.*   Just as courts insist that a sentence may not be increased to punish a defendant for exercising the right to trial, federal and state courts say that a trial judge may not punish a defendant for exercising the statutory right to appeal. If a defendant successfully appeals a conviction and is convicted again after retrial, a sentence higher than the original sentence imposed is presumed to be a product of vindictiveness by the sentencing judge. A sentence motivated by such vindictiveness violates federal due process. The judge must rebut this presumption by placing on the record her reasons for increasing the sentence after the second conviction. See North Carolina v. Pearce, 395 U.S. 711, 726 (1969). The Court in *Pearce* stated that those reasons could be based on "objective information concerning identifiable conduct on the part of the defendant occurring after the time of the original sentence proceeding." In a latter case, the Court held that a trial judge could rebut the presumption of vindictiveness by pointing to any "objective information" that the judge did not consider during the first sentencing proceeding. See Texas v. McCullough, 475 U.S. 134 (1986).

6. *Plea bargaining and structured sentencing rules.*   When sentencing rules place a specified weight on the charges, offense facts, and criminal history, the prosecutor has greater influence over the sentence to be imposed. Through investigations, indictments, and plea bargains, the prosecutor can often specify exactly what charges, facts, and history get admitted by the defendant and become known to the sentencing court. Interestingly, early research has suggested that prosecutors do not tend to change their customary charging or plea bargaining practices to exploit their power to influence sentences in structured sentencing states. Specifically, this research shows that structured systems have not produced dramatically longer sentences or changed rates of guilty pleas. See Terance Miethe, Charging and Plea Bargaining Practices Under Determinate Sentencing: An Investigation of the Hydraulic Displacement of Discretion, 78 J. Crim. L. & Criminology 155 (1987). Why do you suppose that structured sentencing rules have affected guilty plea rates so little?

This is not to say that plea bargains have no effect on either the plea process or the uniformity of individual sentences in structured systems. Available evidence suggests that in a significant number of cases (perhaps as many as one-third), prosecutors and defendants use plea bargains to circumvent the strictures of the guidelines by agreeing to charges and to factual and guideline stipulations that place the sentence outside the range that would ordinarily be prescribed — without asking the judge to depart from the guidelines. See Ilene Nagel and Stephen Schulhofer, A Tale of Three Cities: An Empirical Study of Charging and Bargaining Practice Under the Federal Sentencing Guidelines, 66 S. Cal. L. Rev. 501 (1992); Frank O. Bowman, To Tell the Truth: The Problem of Prosecutorial "Manipulation" of Sentencing Facts, 8 Fed. Sentencing Rep. 324

(1996); Linda Drazgo Maxfield and Keri Burchfield, Immigration Offenses Involving Unlawful Entry: Is Federal Practice Comparable Across Districts?, 14 Fed. Sentencing Rep. 260 (2002).

2.   Substantial Assistance

Sometimes it takes a crook to catch a crook. A defendant can tell investigators about crimes that others committed in the past or can agree to take part in future sting operations. In the federal system, substantial assistance to the government is by far the most common single reason judges give for departing downward to give a sentence lower than the range specified in the guidelines. Judges relied on substantial assistance departures in more than 17 percent of all federal cases in 2001.

It is clear that all sentencing systems allow trial judges to reduce a defendant's sentence based on cooperation. What is less clear is exactly *who* can determine whether the defendant should benefit from an effort to cooperate, and how much the benefit should be.

‖ *Harold Ray Wade v. United States* ‖
504 U.S. 181 (1992)

SOUTER, J.

Section 3553(e) of Title 18 of the United States Code empowers district courts, "[u]pon motion of the Government," to impose a sentence below the statutory minimum to reflect a defendant's "substantial assistance in the investigation or prosecution of another person who has committed an offense." Similarly, §5K1.1 of the United States Sentencing Commission, Guidelines Manual permits district courts to go below the minimum required under the Guidelines if the Government files a "substantial assistance" motion. This case presents the question whether district courts may subject the Government's refusal to file such a motion to review for constitutional violations. We hold that they may, but that the petitioner has raised no claim to such review.

On October 30, 1989, police searched the house of the petitioner, Harold Ray Wade, Jr., discovered 978 grams of cocaine, two handguns, and more than $22,000 in cash, and arrested Wade. In the aftermath of the search, Wade gave law enforcement officials information that led them to arrest another drug dealer. In due course, a federal grand jury indicted Wade for distributing cocaine and possessing cocaine with intent to distribute it . . . , for conspiring to do these things . . . , and for using or carrying a firearm during, and in relation to, a drug crime. . . . Wade pleaded guilty to all four counts.

The presentence report put the sentencing range under the Guidelines for the drug offenses at 97 to 121 months, but added that Wade was subject to a 10-year mandatory minimum sentence, 21 U.S.C. §841(b)(1)(B), narrowing the actual range to 120 to 121 months, see USSG §5G1.1(c)(2). The report also stated that both USSG §2K2.4(a) and 18 U.S.C. §924(c) required a 5-year sentence on the gun count. At the sentencing hearing in the District Court, Wade's lawyer urged the court to impose a sentence below the 10-year minimum for the drug counts to reward Wade for his assistance to the Government. The court responded that the Government had filed no motion as contemplated in 18 U.S.C. §3553(e) and USSG §5K1.1 for sentencing below the minimum, and ruled that, without such a motion, a court had no power to go beneath the minimum. Wade got a sentence of 180 months in prison.

In the United States Court of Appeals for the Fourth Circuit, Wade argued the District Court was in error to say that the absence of a Government motion deprived it of authority to impose a sentence below 10 years for the drug convictions. Wade lost this argument, and failed as well on his back-up claim that the District Court was at least authorized to enquire into the Government's motives for filing no motion, the court saying that any such enquiry would intrude unduly upon a prosecutor's discretion. . . .

The full text of 18 U.S.C. §3553(e) is this: "Upon motion of the Government, the court shall have the authority to impose a sentence below a level established by statute as minimum sentence so as to reflect a defendant's substantial assistance in the investigation or prosecution of another person who has committed an offense. . . ." And this is the relevant portion of USSG §5K1.1: "Upon motion of the government stating that the defendant has provided substantial assistance in the investigation or prosecution of another person who has committed an offense, the court may depart from the guidelines." . . .

Wade concedes, as a matter of statutory interpretation, that §3553(e) imposes the condition of a Government motion upon the district court's authority to depart, and he does not argue otherwise with respect to §5K1.1. He does not claim that the Government-motion requirement is itself unconstitutional, or that the condition is superseded in this case by any agreement on the Government's behalf to file a substantial assistance motion. Wade's position is consistent with the view, which we think is clearly correct, that in both §3553(e) and §5K1.1 the condition limiting the court's authority gives the Government a power, not a duty, to file a motion when a defendant has substantially assisted.

Wade nonetheless argues, and again we agree, that a prosecutor's discretion when exercising that power is subject to constitutional limitations that district courts can enforce. Because we see no reason why courts should treat a prosecutor's refusal to file a substantial-assistance motion differently from a prosecutor's other decisions, see, e.g., Wayte v. United States, 470 U.S. 598, 608-609 (1985) [courts may remedy prosecutor's selection among potential criminal defendants based on invidious discrimination], we hold that federal district courts have authority to review a prosecutor's refusal to file a substantial-assistance motion and to grant a remedy if they find that the refusal was based on an unconstitutional motive. Thus, a defendant would be entitled to relief if a prosecutor refused to file a substantial-assistance motion, say, because of the defendant's race or religion.

It follows that a claim that a defendant merely provided substantial assistance will not entitle a defendant to a remedy or even to discovery or an evidentiary hearing. Nor would additional but generalized allegations of improper motive. [A] defendant has no right to discovery or an evidentiary hearing unless he makes a substantial threshold showing.

Wade has failed to make one. He has never alleged, much less claimed to have evidence tending to show, that the Government refused to file a motion for suspect reasons such as his race or his religion. Instead, Wade argues now that the District Court thwarted his attempt to make quite different allegations on the record because it erroneously believed that no charge of impermissible motive could state a claim for relief. Hence, he now seeks an order of remand to allow him to develop a claim that the Government violated his constitutional rights by withholding a substantial-assistance motion "arbitrarily" or "in bad faith." . . .

As the Government concedes, Wade would be entitled to relief if the prosecutor's refusal to move was not rationally related to any legitimate Government end, cf. Chapman v. United States, 500 U.S. 453, 464-465 (1991), but his argument is still of no avail. [H]is claim as presented to the District Court failed to rise to the level warranting judicial enquiry. The District Court expressly invited Wade's lawyer to state for the record what evidence he would introduce to support his position if the court were to conduct a hearing on the issue. In response, his counsel merely explained the extent of Wade's assistance to the Government. This, of course, was not enough, for although a showing of assistance is a necessary condition for relief, it is not a sufficient one. The Government's decision not to move may have been based not on a failure to acknowledge or appreciate Wade's help, but simply on its rational assessment of the cost and benefit that would flow from moving. It is clear, then, that, on the present record, Wade is entitled to no relief, and that the judgment of the Court of Appeals must be affirmed.

|| *Nevada Revised Statutes §453.3405(2)* ||

The judge, upon an appropriate motion, may reduce or suspend the sentence of any person convicted of violating any of the [code provisions dealing with trafficking in controlled substances] if he finds that the convicted person rendered substantial assistance in the identification, arrest or conviction of any of his accomplices, accessories, coconspirators or principals or of any other person involved in trafficking in a controlled substance. . . . The arresting agency must be given an opportunity to be heard before the motion is granted. Upon good cause shown, the motion may be heard in camera.

PROBLEM 5-2. HELPING OTHERS

The County Police Department of Nassau, New York, and the U.S. Bureau of Alcohol, Tobacco and Firearms (BATF) conducted a joint investigation of Lancelotte Kaye's illegal trafficking in narcotics and firearms. During this investigation, Kaye sold both marijuana and illegal firearms to an undercover Nassau County detective. The state authorities arrested Kaye for selling marijuana; the federal authorities arrested him for illegal possession of firearms. Soon after his indictments on these charges, Kaye agreed to cooperate with both state and federal authorities in the identification and conviction of other wrongdoers.

His efforts for the state investigators proved fruitful. Kaye covertly recorded conversations with various individuals, at some personal risk. As a result of these recordings, the Nassau P.D. arrested two individuals, one of whom pleaded guilty to a misdemeanor. In Nassau County Court, Kaye pleaded guilty to a lesser drug felony and was sentenced to time served. Unfortunately, Kaye's efforts on behalf of the federal authorities were unproductive. Kaye recorded phone conversations with the individual who sold him weapons. He also met with that individual and provided the BATF with his first name, telephone number, and home address. Nevertheless, the BATF made no arrests.

In federal district court, Kaye pleaded guilty to possession of firearms with obliterated serial numbers. The prosecutor declined to move for a downward departure pursuant to section 5K1.1. In a letter to the court, the prosecutor acknowledged that Kaye had cooperated in Nassau County but noted that he had received the benefit of a light sentence in return. The letter went on: "The federal effort was ultimately unsuccessful. As such, the government cannot certify that the defendant has provided substantial assistance."

As defense counsel for Kaye in federal court, how might you construct arguments for a downward departure based on Kaye's cooperation in the state and federal investigations? How is Kaye's case different from the typical refusal by federal prosecutors to request a departure under section 5K1.1? How might you use section 5K2.0, which empowers a sentencing judge to depart downward from a sentence designated under the guidelines if the case presents a factor that the U.S. Sentencing Commission did not "adequately consider" as it formulated the guidelines? Compare United States v. Kaye, 140 F.3d 86 (2d Cir. 1998).

PROBLEM 5-3. EARNED TIME

Return your attention to the robbery case involving Rob Anon and his accomplices. Suppose that during pretrial negotiations, the prosecutor made the same plea offer to Anon, Zweite, and Tercero: The government would move for a downward departure from the presumptive sentence under the sentencing guidelines, based on substantial assistance to the government, if one of the defendants would plead guilty and testify against the other defendants. The prosecutor told all three defendants that he did not care which of them received the downward departure motion but that the government would make the motion for only one defendant.

Several weeks passed. Tercero finally accepted the offer and entered a plea agreement. He pled guilty and testified at the trial of Anon and Zweite; the jury convicted the two defendants on all charges. At the sentencing hearing, the prosecutor recommended a sentence of 12 months for Tercero, which was a downward departure from the presumptive sentence under the guidelines. The government recommended sentences within the relevant guideline range for Anon and Zweite, 108-135 months. The sentencing guidelines in the jurisdiction would make it difficult for the sentencing judge to depart downward (below 108 months) for Anon or Zweite.

As a law clerk to the sentencing judge, what sentence would you recommend for the three defendants? As a member of a sentencing commission, would you draft rules placing any limits on the use of substantial assistance as a basis for a departure? Any limits on the size of such a departure? Compare United States v. Maddox, 48 F.3d 791 (4th Cir. 1995).

NOTES

1. *Assisting in other investigations.*   In the unstructured sentencing states, cooperation with the government in investigating and trying other criminal cases is generally believed to have some positive effect both on the sentencing court's disposition of the case and on the duration of the sentence imposed. See State v. Johnson, 630 N.W.2d 583 (Iowa 2001). Even in highly discretionary sentencing systems, statutes commonly address the sentencing discount a court must give to a defendant who provides assistance to the government. See Brugman v. State, 339 S.E.2d 244 (Ga. 1986) (discussing statute). The more structured sentencing states have followed the same route, instructing the judge that cooperation with the government can serve as a basis for departing from the guideline sentence and imposing some lesser sentence. See Or. Admin. R. 253-08-002(1)(F).

Is this reduction of the sentence a necessary evil, the price that prosecutors pay for creating additional criminal cases? Or would courts adjust a sentence in light of a defendant's cooperation even in an ideal world? Michael Simons argues that "cooperating" defendants are ostracized from their communities, so they have already been punished to some extent, and the criminal sanction should be reduced accordingly. He also suggests that cooperation encourages the defendant's atonement, increasing the odds that she will eventually reintegrate into the community. See Michael Simons, Retribution for Rats: Cooperation, Punishment, and Atonement, 56 Vand. L. Rev. 1 (2003). Should prosecutors consider the defendant's prospects for atonement through cooperation when recommending a reduced sentence for that defendant, or should the recommendation simply turn on the value of the help the defendant provided? If the latter, consider this irony: the "biggest fish" in any criminal organization is likely to know the most and to offer the most value to the government's investigators. Thus, the largest sentence reductions might go to the most important (and most culpable) defendants.

2. *Substantial in whose eyes?*   There is some variation in the amount of control the prosecution has over the use of the "substantial assistance" sentencing factor. If the prosecution refuses to accept a defendant's offer of cooperation, then the sentence usually will not be affected. See Matos v. State, 878 P.2d 288 (Nev. 1994). But what happens if the government accepts the cooperation and later determines that it was not valuable or complete? As we have seen, section 5K1.1 of the federal guidelines requires a government motion before the court can reduce the sentence based on the defendant's cooperation. 18 U.S.C. §3553(e) requires the same before a court can reduce a sentence below a statutory mandatory minimum. Should the court have an independent power to reduce a sentence on these grounds, even in the absence of a government motion? State legislatures and courts have been debating this issue for years, although the state debate has not figured at all in the later federal discussions of this question. See State v. Sarabia, 875 P.2d 227 (Idaho 1994) (declaring unconstitutional on state grounds a statute allowing sentence below mandatory minimum only when prosecutor moves for reduction based on substantial assistance).

3. *Arbitrary and inconsistent prosecutor decisions.*   According to the U.S. Supreme Court in *Wade*, the Constitution places some outer boundaries on the prosecutor's power to refuse to request a reduced sentence based on a

defendant's substantial assistance. But only when the defendant makes a "substantial threshold showing" of a prosecutor's unconstitutional motive can the trial judge adjust the sentence without a government motion. Besides a refusal based on race or religion, what else might qualify as a constitutionally improper reason for a prosecutor to withhold a motion? How can a defendant gather evidence that an unconstitutional motive influenced the prosecutor's decision?

The real debate over limiting prosecutorial power in this sphere takes place at the nonconstitutional level. Legislatures and sentencing commissions must decide whether to make a prosecutor's motion a necessary precondition to this sort of sentence reduction. The concern, of course, is that an unsupervised prosecutor will make or refuse to make the recommendations on arbitrary or inconsistent grounds. The D.C. Circuit debated this question when it decided whether the sentencing judge retained authority under section 5K1.1 to depart down despite the government's refusal to move for a substantial assistance departure. Although *Wade* answered no to this question, the increased departure authority described in Koon v. United States, 518 U.S. 81 (1996) (reprinted in Chapter 3) reopened the question. A panel of the D.C. Circuit originally held that district courts could depart without a government motion, but the en banc court decided that a government motion remained necessary. See In re Sealed Case, 149 F.3d 1198 (D.C. Cir. 1998), *rev'd en banc,* 181 F.3d 128 (D.C. Cir. 1999). Are other institutions, such as sentencing courts, able to evaluate the prosecutor's decisions about which defendants provided substantial assistance? What advantages does a prosecutor have in making this choice? See Daniel Richman, The Challenge of Investigating Section 5K1.1 In Practice, 11 Fed. Sentencing Rep. 75 (1998).

In the federal system, prosecutors have attempted to regulate themselves by creating written policies about which defendants should receive a reduced sentence for substantial assistance. About 80 percent of the federal districts have adopted written guidelines on the subject, and their content is fairly consistent. A study sponsored by the U.S. Sentencing Commission (known as the Maxfield-Kramer Study), however, found great variety among the 94 federal districts in their granting of substantial assistance motions. See Linda Drazga Maxfield and John Kramer, Substantial Assistance: Empirical Yardstick Gauging Equity in Federal Policy and Practice (1998). Nationwide, less than 40 percent of defendants who provided assistance to the government received a substantial assistance motion. Defendants who testified at trial, participated in undercover investigations, or provided tangible evidence such as documents received the motions most often. Defendants at various levels in drug conspiracies (high-level traffickers, street-level dealers, or lower-level support functionaries) all received the motions at comparable rates. The study found that the demographic characteristics of defendants had some influence on whether they received a motion:

Holding constant important variables such as offense type, guideline range, mitigating and/or aggravating factors, weapon involvement, and a host of other possible explanatory concepts, [we] found that personal characteristics remained significant predictors of who received substantial assistance departures. [Defendants who were male, black, Hispanic, non-citizens, and older were all less likely to receive a motion. Controlling] for all other personal, judicial, and guideline factors in the model, a Hispanic defendant was seven percentage points less likely than a non-Hispanic defendant to receive a substantial assistance departure.

As a chief prosecutor, how would you react to this news? Could you create guidelines within your office that would promote more consistent decisions about sentence discounts for cooperating defendants? See Frank Bowman, Substantial Assistance: An Old Prosecutor's Meditation on *Singleton, Sealed Case*, and the Maxfield-Kramer Report, 12 Fed. Sentencing Rep. 45 (1999). Would this report be sufficient for a threshold showing under *Wade*?

4. *Magnitude and type of discount.*   The federal guidelines do not instruct the sentencing judge on how much of a departure to grant to a cooperating defendant, but section 5K1.1 does list a few factors to consider: the "usefulness of the defendant's assistance," the "truthfulness, completeness, and reliability of any information or testimony provided," and "any injury suffered, or any danger or risk of injury to the defendant or his family resulting from his assistance." The Maxfield-Kramer Study found that judges gave larger departures for the cases involving the highest sentences, not necessarily for the defendants who provided the most valuable cooperation or who cooperated under the most dangerous circumstances. It also found that demographic features of defendants affected the size of the discount awarded. After controlling for various features of the crime and the type of cooperation, "female defendants received departures that were nine percentage points higher than did similar male defendants. Smaller, but still significant, differences were measured for ethnicity and citizenship (five percentage points), age (four percentage points), and race and education (two percentage points)." As a U.S. Sentencing Commission member, would you favor limits on the magnitude of a departure expressed in absolute terms (say, two years or two offense levels) or in relative terms (say, 20 percent of the sentence)?

Defendants can receive not just different amounts of discounts but different *types* of benefits than sentence adjustments for their cooperation with government investigations. These include a reduction of charges during plea negotiations or favorable treatment for immigration purposes. See Nora V. Demleitner, Immigration Threats and Rewards: Effective Law Enforcement Tools in the War on Terrorism?, 51 Emory L. J. 1059 (2002).

C.   THE OFFENDER'S CHARACTER AND CIRCUMSTANCES

A criminal defendant is not merely the sum of his or her contacts with the criminal justice system; there is, of course, much more to every offender than simply a criminal record and some postoffense behavior. Indeed, many people think that personal characteristics — ethnicity, gender, age, family context, educational background, and social and economic history — define not only who we are but also how we ought to be judged by others. Sentencing judges usually learn facts about an offender's personal background and circumstances, and historically they have adjusted sentences in light of the offender's overall character, often giving particular attention to facts relating to the offender's family, physical or mental health, and prospects for rehabilitation. A persistent challenge in modern sentencing reform efforts has been to identify and regulate the appropriate role for so-called offender characteristics.

PROBLEM 5-4.   TURNING GUIDANCE INTO GUIDELINES

It is spring 1985 and you have been appointed as one of the U.S. Sentencing Commission's first seven commissioners. Your institution has the enormous task of turning all the mandates of the recently passed Sentencing Reform Act (SRA) into sentencing guidelines for use by federal courts. The commissioners agreed to subdivide the work ahead, with each taking responsibility for drafting one part of the guidelines. You are assigned the section dealing with offender characteristics, and your work is guided by the following provisions of 28 U.S.C. §994, part of the SRA:

> (d) The U.S. Sentencing Commission in establishing [sentencing guidelines for federal offenses] shall consider whether the following matters, among others with respect to a defendant, have any relevance to the nature, extent, place of service, or other incidents of an appropriate sentence . . . : (1) age; (2) education; (3) vocational skills; (4) mental and emotional condition . . . ; (5) physical condition, including drug dependence; (6) previous employment record; (7) family ties and responsibilities; (8) community ties; . . .
> The Commission shall assure that the guidelines and policy statements are entirely neutral as to the race, sex, national origin, creed, and socioeconomic status of offenders.
> (e) The Commission shall assure that the guidelines and policy statements, in recommending a term of imprisonment or length of a term of imprisonment, reflect the general inappropriateness of considering the education, vocational skills, employment record, family ties and responsibilities, and community ties of the defendant.

How will you turn the SRA's guidance into specific guidelines for courts to follow when sentencing individual offenders? Will you leave all these questions to the sentencing judge, or will you instead try to encourage or require judges to adjust a sentence up or down in light of some of these factors? Is it a good idea to specify the amount of adjustment that the judge should use in a normal case? Should you instruct judges only to move sentences *down* based on these personal characteristics of the offender? Cf. U.S. Sentencing Guidelines Manual §5H1.1 (age); §5H1.2 (education and vocational skills); §5H1.3 (mental and emotional conditions); §5H1.4 (physical condition, including drug or alcohol dependence or abuse); §5H1.5 (employment record); §5H1.6 (family ties and responsibilities and community ties).

NOTES

1. *Offender characteristics at sentencing: majority rule.*   Every U.S. jurisdiction allows judges at sentencing to consider various aspects of the defendant's life, including events occurring far before the offense, matters that do not bear directly on guilt or innocence, and postoffense activities. In unstructured sentencing systems, it is difficult to establish or measure just how much an

offender's personal background and characteristics tend to influence the sentence, although anecdotal reports suggest that the influence can be large. Most structured systems do not directly integrate personal characteristics into the calculation of offenders' presumptive guideline sentences; instead, they often allow (and even encourage in some instances) sentencing judges to depart from the guidelines to impose a higher or lower sentence than otherwise prescribed based on these factors. In addition, legislatures as well as sentencing commissions sometimes instruct judges *not* to consider certain offender characteristics. The Minnesota sentencing guidelines, for example, state that the following factors "should not be used as reasons for departing from the presumptive sentences" provided in their sentencing guidelines:

(a) Race
(b) Sex
(c) Employment factors, including: (1) occupation or impact of sentence on profession or occupation; (2) employment history; (3) employment at time of offense; (4) employment at time of sentencing, [and]
(d) Social factors, including: (1) educational attainment; (2) living arrangements at time of offense or sentencing; (3) length of residence; (4) marital status.

Minn. Sentencing Guidelines II.D.1.

2. *Theory and concerns behind considering offender characteristics.*   What is the theoretical justification for altering a defendant's sentence based on certain personal characteristics? Could one argue from a retributivist perspective that certain personal characteristics, such as mental condition, education, and drug dependence, are not only relevant but fundamental to determining what sentence is needed to give an offender his just deserts? Could one argue from a utilitarian perspective that certain other personal characteristics, such as age, employment circumstances, and family background, are not only relevant but fundamental to determining what sentence is needed to effectively incapacitate, deter, or rehabilitate an offender?

Many modern structured sentencing reforms were prompted by concerns that personal factors such as an offender's ethnicity, gender, and socioeconomic status were influencing judges' exercise of their broad sentencing discretion resulting in unwarranted sentencing disparities. As detailed in Problem 5-4 above, Congress addressed this concern in federal sentencing reform by mandating that the federal sentencing guidelines be "entirely neutral as to the race, sex, national origin, creed, and socioeconomic status of offenders." Do you think this mandate is realistic or merely aspirational — that is, is it truly possible for a sentencing system to be "entirely neutral" with respect to all these factors? Can a principled argument be made that at least some of these listed factors ought to be considered at sentencing?

A number of other personal factors are closely associated with these forbidden factors. Employment and education, for example, are highly correlated with socioeconomic class; pregnancy is associated with gender, as can be some child-rearing realities. To the extent that gender and socioeconomic status are deemed per se illegitimate as sentencing considerations, should rules also bar any consideration of these related factors at sentencing? Consider the commentary to the Minnesota guidelines provision discussed above in note 1:

> The [Minnesota Sentencing] Commission believes that sentencing should
> be neutral with respect to offenders' race, sex, and income levels. Accordingly,
> the Commission has listed several factors which should not be used as reasons
> for departure from the presumptive sentence, because these factors are highly
> correlated with sex, race, or income levels. Employment is excluded as a reason
> for departure not only because of its correlation with race and income levels, but
> also because this factor is manipulable — offenders could lessen the severity of
> the sentence by obtaining employment between arrest and sentencing.

Minn. Sentencing Guidelines II.D.101, cmt. Do you agree that consideration of
employment history and status should be prohibited at sentencing? Is such a
prohibition the best way to address the concerns raised by the Minnesota Sentencing Commission?

1.   Immutable Characteristics

Should the treatment of certain personal characteristics at sentencing depend
on whether they are within the offender's control? The immutability of certain
factors that seem irrelevant to an offender's culpability and future prospects —
factors such as race or creed — might suggest firm rules forbidding their consideration at sentencing. However, the immutability of other factors that seem
quite relevant to an offender's culpability and future prospects — factors such as
mental or physical condition — might suggest the need for rules requiring
judges to consider them at sentencing.

ABA Standards for Criminal Justice, Sentencing 18-3.4(d)
(3d ed. 1994)

The legislature should specify that the following personal characteristics shall
not, in and of themselves, be used for . . . any purpose with regard to sentencing: (i) Race, (ii) Gender or sexual orientation, (iii) National origin, (iv) Religion or creed, (v) Marital status, (vi) Political affiliation or belief.

Daryl Atkins v. Virginia
536 U.S. 304 (2002)

STEVENS, J.

I

. . . Petitioner, Daryl Renard Atkins . . . and William Jones, armed with a
semiautomatic handgun, abducted Eric Nesbitt [in August 1996], robbed him
of the money on his person, drove him to an automated teller machine in his

pickup truck where cameras recorded their withdrawal of additional cash, then took him to an isolated location where he was shot eight times and killed.

Jones and Atkins both testified in the guilt phase of Atkins' trial. [In exchange for testifying against Atkins, Jones pleaded guilty to first-degree murder and became ineligible to receive the death penalty.] Each confirmed most of the details in the other's account of the incident, with the important exception that each stated that the other had actually shot and killed Nesbitt. Jones' testimony, which was both more coherent and credible than Atkins', was obviously credited by the jury and was sufficient to establish Atkins' guilt. At the penalty phase of the trial, the State introduced victim impact evidence and proved two aggravating circumstances: future dangerousness and vileness of the offense. . . .

In the penalty phase, the defense relied on . . . Dr. Evan Nelson, a forensic psychologist who had evaluated Atkins before trial and concluded that he was mildly mentally retarded.[3] His conclusion was based on interviews with people who knew Atkins, a review of school and court records, and the administration of a standard intelligence test which indicated that Atkins had a full scale IQ of 59. . . . The State presented an expert rebuttal witness, Dr. Stanton Samenow, who expressed the opinion that Atkins was not mentally retarded, but rather was of average intelligence, at least, and diagnosable as having antisocial personality disorder. The jury . . . sentenced Atkins to death. The Supreme Court of Virginia affirmed the imposition of the death penalty, [rejecting the contention] that the imposition of the sentence of death upon a criminal defendant who has the mental age of a child between the ages of 9 and 12 is excessive.

II

The Eighth Amendment succinctly prohibits excessive sanctions. It provides: "Excessive bail shall not be required, nor excessive fines imposed, nor cruel and unusual punishments inflicted." [It] is a precept of justice that punishment for crime should be graduated and proportioned to the offense. . . . As Chief Justice Warren explained in Trop v. Dulles, 356 U.S. 86 (1958): "The basic concept underlying the Eighth Amendment is nothing less than the dignity of man. The Amendment must draw its meaning from the evolving standards of decency that mark the progress of a maturing society." Id. at 100-101.

Proportionality review under those evolving standards should be informed by objective factors to the maximum possible extent. We have pinpointed that the clearest and most reliable objective evidence of contemporary values is the legislation enacted by the country's legislatures. Relying in part on such legislative evidence, we have held that death is an impermissibly excessive punishment for the rape of an adult woman, Coker v. Georgia, 433 U.S. 584 (1977), or for a

---

[3] The American Association of Mental Retardation (AAMR) defines mental retardation as follows: *Mental retardation* refers to substantial limitations in present functioning. It is characterized by significantly subaverage intellectual functioning, existing concurrently with related limitations in two or more of the following applicable adaptive skill areas: communication, self-care, home living, social skills, community use, self-direction, health and safety, functional academics, leisure, and work. Mental retardation manifests before age 18. . . .

defendant who neither took life, attempted to take life, nor intended to take life, Enmund v. Florida, 458 U.S. 782 (1982). [But this] objective evidence, though of great importance, [does] not wholly determine the controversy, for the Constitution contemplates that in the end our own judgment will be brought to bear on the question of the acceptability of the death penalty under the Eighth Amendment. . . .

III

The parties have not called our attention to any state legislative consideration of the suitability of imposing the death penalty on mentally retarded offenders prior to 1986. In that year, the public reaction to the execution of a mentally retarded murderer in Georgia apparently led to the enactment of the first state statute prohibiting such executions. In 1988, when Congress enacted legislation reinstating the federal death penalty, it expressly provided that a sentence of death shall not be carried out upon a person who is mentally retarded. In 1989, Maryland enacted a similar prohibition. It was in that year that we decided Penry v. Lynaugh, 492 U.S. 302 (1989), and concluded that those two state enactments, even when added to the 14 States that have rejected capital punishment completely, do not provide sufficient evidence at present of a national consensus [against the execution of the mentally retarded].

Much has changed since then. Responding to the national attention received by [an] execution [of a mentally retarded defendant in Georgia] and our decision in *Penry*, state legislatures across the country began to address the issue. In 1990 Kentucky and Tennessee enacted statutes similar to those in Georgia and Maryland, as did New Mexico in 1991, and Arkansas, Colorado, Washington, Indiana, and Kansas in 1993 and 1994. In 1995, when New York reinstated its death penalty, it emulated the Federal Government by expressly exempting the mentally retarded. Nebraska followed suit in 1998. There appear to have been no similar enactments during the next two years, but in 2000 and 2001 six more States — South Dakota, Arizona, Connecticut, Florida, Missouri, and North Carolina — joined the procession. The Texas Legislature unanimously adopted a similar bill, and bills have passed at least one house in other States, including Virginia and Nevada.

It is not so much the number of these States that is significant, but the consistency of the direction of change. Given the well-known fact that anti-crime legislation is far more popular than legislation providing protections for persons guilty of violent crime, the large number of States prohibiting the execution of mentally retarded persons (and the complete absence of States passing legislation reinstating the power to conduct such executions) provides powerful evidence that today our society views mentally retarded offenders as categorically less culpable than the average criminal. The evidence carries even greater force when it is noted that the legislatures that have addressed the issue have voted overwhelmingly in favor of the prohibition. Moreover, even in those States that allow the execution of mentally retarded offenders, the practice is uncommon. [E]ven among those States that regularly execute offenders and that have no prohibition with regard to the mentally retarded, only five have executed offenders possessing a known IQ less than 70 since we decided *Penry*. The practice, therefore, has become truly unusual, and it is fair to say that a national consensus has developed against it.[21]

To the extent there is serious disagreement about the execution of mentally retarded offenders, it is in determining which offenders are in fact retarded. In this case, for instance, the Commonwealth of Virginia disputes that Atkins suffers from mental retardation. Not all people who claim to be mentally retarded will be so impaired as to fall within the range of mentally retarded offenders about whom there is a national consensus. As was our approach in Ford v. Wainwright, with regard to insanity [at the time of execution], we "leave to the State[s] the task of developing appropriate ways to enforce the constitutional restriction upon its execution of sentences." 477 U.S. 399, 405, 416-417 (1986).

IV

. . . Mentally retarded persons frequently know the difference between right and wrong and are competent to stand trial. Because of their impairments, however, by definition they have diminished capacities to understand and process information, to communicate, to abstract from mistakes and learn from experience, to engage in logical reasoning, to control impulses, and to understand the reactions of others. There is no evidence that they are more likely to engage in criminal conduct than others, but there is abundant evidence that they often act on impulse rather than pursuant to a premeditated plan, and that in group settings they are followers rather than leaders. Their deficiencies do not warrant an exemption from criminal sanctions, but they do diminish their personal culpability.

In light of these deficiencies, our death penalty jurisprudence provides two reasons consistent with the legislative consensus that the mentally retarded should be categorically excluded from execution. First, there is a serious question as to whether either justification that we have recognized as a basis for the death penalty applies to mentally retarded offenders. Gregg v. Georgia, 428 U.S. 153, 183 (1976), identified retribution and deterrence of capital crimes by prospective offenders as the social purposes served by the death penalty. Unless the imposition of the death penalty on a mentally retarded person measurably

---

[21]Additional evidence makes it clear that this legislative judgment reflects a much broader social and professional consensus. For example, several organizations with germane expertise have adopted official positions opposing the imposition of the death penalty upon a mentally retarded offender. See Brief for American Psychological Association et al. as *Amici Curiae*. In addition, representatives of widely diverse religious communities in the United States, reflecting Christian, Jewish, Muslim, and Buddhist traditions, have filed an *amicus curiae* brief explaining that even though their views about the death penalty differ, they all share a conviction that the execution of persons with mental retardation cannot be morally justified. Moreover, within the world community, the imposition of the death penalty for crimes committed by mentally retarded offenders is overwhelmingly disapproved. Finally, polling data shows a widespread consensus among Americans, even those who support the death penalty, that executing the mentally retarded is wrong. Although these factors are by no means dispositive, their consistency with the legislative evidence lends further support to our conclusion that there is a consensus among those who have addressed the issue.

contributes to one or both of these goals, it is nothing more than the purposeless and needless imposition of pain and suffering, and hence an unconstitutional punishment.

With respect to retribution — the interest in seeing that the offender gets his just deserts — the severity of the appropriate punishment necessarily depends on the culpability of the offender. Since *Gregg,* our jurisprudence has consistently confined the imposition of the death penalty to a narrow category of the most serious crimes. . . . If the culpability of the average murderer is insufficient to justify the most extreme sanction available to the State, the lesser culpability of the mentally retarded offender surely does not merit that form of retribution. . . .

With respect to deterrence — the interest in preventing capital crimes by prospective offenders — it seems likely that capital punishment can serve as a deterrent only when murder is the result of premeditation and deliberation. [The] same cognitive and behavioral impairments that make [the mentally retarded] less morally culpable — for example, the diminished ability to understand and process information, to learn from experience, to engage in logical reasoning, or to control impulses —. . . also make it less likely that they can process the information of the possibility of execution as a penalty and, as a result, control their conduct based upon that information. Nor will exempting the mentally retarded from execution lessen the deterrent effect of the death penalty with respect to offenders who are not mentally retarded. Such individuals are unprotected by the exemption and will continue to face the threat of execution. . . .

The risk that the death penalty will be imposed in spite of factors which may call for a less severe penalty is enhanced, not only by the possibility of false confessions, but also by the lesser ability of mentally retarded defendants to make a persuasive showing of mitigation in the face of prosecutorial evidence of one or more aggravating factors. Mentally retarded defendants may be less able to give meaningful assistance to their counsel and are typically poor witnesses, and their demeanor may create an unwarranted impression of lack of remorse for their crimes. [Moreover], reliance on mental retardation as a mitigating factor can be a two-edged sword that may enhance the likelihood that the aggravating factor of future dangerousness will be found by the jury. Mentally retarded defendants in the aggregate face a special risk of wrongful execution.

Our independent evaluation of the issue reveals no reason to disagree with the judgment of the legislatures that have recently addressed the matter and concluded that death is not a suitable punishment for a mentally retarded criminal. We are not persuaded that the execution of mentally retarded criminals will measurably advance the deterrent or the retributive purpose of the death penalty. Construing and applying the Eighth Amendment in the light of our evolving standards of decency, we therefore conclude that such punishment is excessive. . . .

REHNQUIST, C.J., dissenting.

[I write separately] to call attention to the defects in the Court's decision to place weight on foreign laws, the views of professional and religious organizations, and opinion polls in reaching its conclusion. The Court's suggestion that these sources are relevant to the constitutional question finds little support in our precedents and, in my view, is antithetical to considerations of federalism, which instruct that any permanent prohibition upon all units of democratic government must [be apparent] in the operative acts (laws and the application of laws) that the people have approved. . . .

SCALIA, J., dissenting.

. . . After spending the day drinking alcohol and smoking marijuana, petitioner Daryl Renard Atkins and a partner in crime drove to a convenience store, intending to rob a customer. Their victim was Eric Nesbitt, an airman from Langley Air Force Base, whom they abducted, drove to a nearby automated teller machine, and forced to withdraw $200. They then drove him to a deserted area, ignoring his pleas to leave him unharmed. According to the co-conspirator, whose testimony the jury evidently credited, Atkins ordered Nesbitt out of the vehicle and, after he had taken only a few steps, shot him one, two, three, four, five, six, seven, eight times in the thorax, chest, abdomen, arms, and legs.

The jury convicted Atkins of capital murder [and] heard extensive evidence of petitioner's alleged mental retardation. A psychologist testified that petitioner was mildly mentally retarded with an IQ of 59, that he was a slow [learner], who showed a lack of success in pretty much every domain of his life, and that he had an impaired capacity to appreciate the criminality of his conduct and to conform his conduct to the law. Petitioner's family members offered additional evidence in support of his mental retardation claim (e.g., that petitioner is a follower). The State contested the evidence of retardation and presented testimony of a psychologist who found absolutely no evidence other than the IQ score indicating that [petitioner] was in the least bit mentally retarded and concluded that petitioner was of average intelligence, at least.

The jury also heard testimony about petitioner's 16 prior felony convictions for robbery, attempted robbery, abduction, use of a firearm, and maiming. The victims of these offenses provided graphic depictions of petitioner's violent tendencies: He hit one over the head with a beer bottle; he slapped a gun across another victim's face, clubbed her in the head with it, knocked her to the ground, and then helped her up, only to shoot her in the stomach. . . .

As the foregoing history demonstrates, petitioner's mental retardation was a *central issue* at sentencing. The jury concluded, however, that his alleged retardation was not a compelling reason to exempt him from the death penalty in light of the brutality of his crime and his long demonstrated propensity for violence. In upsetting this particularized judgment on the basis of a constitutional absolute, the Court concludes that no one who is even slightly mentally retarded can have sufficient moral responsibility to be subjected to capital punishment for any crime. As a sociological and moral conclusion that is implausible; and it is doubly implausible as an interpretation of the United States Constitution. . . .

The Court makes no pretense that execution of the mildly mentally retarded would have been considered cruel and unusual in 1791. Only the *severely* or *profoundly* mentally retarded, commonly known as idiots, enjoyed any special status under the law at that time. . . . Due to their incompetence, idiots were [excused] from the guilt, and of course from the punishment, of any criminal action committed. . . . Instead, they were often committed to civil confinement or made wards of the State, thereby preventing them from [going] loose, to the terror of the king's subjects. Mentally retarded offenders with less severe impairments — those who were not idiots — suffered criminal prosecution and punishment, including capital punishment.

The Court is left to argue, therefore, that execution of the mildly retarded is inconsistent with the evolving standards of decency that mark the progress of a maturing society. [The Court] miraculously extracts a national consensus forbidding execution of the mentally retarded from the fact that 18 States — less than *half* (47%) of the 38 States that permit capital punishment (for whom the issue exists) — have very recently enacted legislation barring execution of the mentally retarded. Even that 47% figure is a distorted one. [Only] seven — 18% of death penalty jurisdictions — have legislation [that precludes the execution of all mentally retarded defendants]. Eleven of those that the Court counts enacted statutes prohibiting execution of mentally retarded defendants [only prospectively and not retroactively]. That is not a statement of absolute moral repugnance, but one of current preference between two tolerable approaches. . . .

Even less compelling (if possible) is the Court's argument that evidence of national consensus is to be found in the infrequency with which retarded persons are executed in States that do not bar their execution. . . . It is not at all clear that execution of the mentally retarded is uncommon, as even the sources cited by the Court suggest, see D. Keyes, W. Edwards, & R. Perske, People with Mental Retardation are Dying Legally, 35 Mental Retardation (Feb. 1997) (updated by Death Penalty Information Center) (June 12, 2002) (showing that 12 States executed 35 allegedly mentally retarded offenders during the period 1984-2000); R. Bonner & S. Rimer, Executing the Mentally Retarded Even as Laws Begin to Shift, N.Y. Times, Aug. 7, 2000, p.A1 (reporting that 10% of death row inmates are retarded). . . .

The genuinely operative portion of the opinion, then, is the Court's statement of the reasons why it agrees with the contrived consensus it has found, that the diminished capacities of the mentally retarded render the death penalty excessive. . . . First, the diminished capacities of the mentally retarded raise a serious question whether their execution contributes to the social purposes of the death penalty, viz., retribution and deterrence. . . . Retribution is not advanced, the argument goes, because the mentally retarded are *no more culpable* than the average murderer, whom we have already held lacks sufficient culpability to warrant the death penalty. Who says so? Is there an established correlation between mental acuity and the ability to conform one's conduct to the law in such a rudimentary matter as murder? [And] what scientific analysis can possibly show that a mildly retarded individual who commits an exquisite torture-killing is no more culpable than the average murderer in a holdup-gone-wrong or a domestic dispute? Or a moderately retarded individual who commits a series of 20 exquisite torture-killings? Surely culpability, and deservedness of the most severe retribution, depends not merely (if at all) upon the mental capacity of the criminal (above the level where he is able to distinguish right from wrong) but also upon the depravity of the crime — which is precisely why this sort of question has traditionally been thought answerable not by a categorical rule of the sort the Court today imposes upon all trials, but rather by the sentencers weighing of the circumstances (both degree of retardation and depravity of crime) in the particular case. . . .

As for the other social purpose of the death penalty that the Court discusses, deterrence: [the] Court does not say that *all* mentally retarded individuals cannot process the information of the possibility of execution as a penalty and . . . control their conduct based upon that information; it merely asserts that they are less likely to be able to do so. But surely the deterrent effect of a penalty is adequately vindicated if it successfully deters many, but not all, of the target class. . . .

The Court throws one last factor into its grab bag of reasons why execution of the retarded is excessive in all cases: Mentally retarded offenders face a special risk of wrongful execution because they are less able to make a persuasive showing of mitigation, to give meaningful assistance to their counsel, and to be effective witnesses. "Special risk" is pretty flabby language (even flabbier than "less likely") and I suppose a similar special risk could be said to exist for just plain stupid people, inarticulate people, even ugly people. If this unsupported claim has any substance to it (which I doubt) it might support a due process claim in all criminal prosecutions of the mentally retarded; but it is hard to see how it has anything to do with an *Eighth Amendment* claim that execution of the mentally retarded is cruel and unusual. . . .

NOTES

1. *Treatment of immutable characteristics: majority position.*   Driven by constitutional concerns and also policy considerations, every jurisdiction has either expressly or implicitly adopted the ABA's recommendation to bar the consideration at sentencing of factors such as race, gender, religion, and national origin. But, as Chapter 9 details, many sentencing practices still have a disproportionate impact on these groups despite the formal legal rules.

Statutory and guideline provisions take different approaches when it comes to certain other immutable personal factors such as mental condition, physical disability, and age. See, e.g., U.S. Sentencing Guidelines Manual §§5H1.1, 5H1.3, 5H1.4 (deeming age, mental condition, and physical condition "not ordinarily relevant" at federal sentencing); N.C. Gen. Stat. §15A-1340.16(e)(3), (4) (providing that defendant's "mental or physical condition" and defendant's "age, immaturity, or limited mental capacity" can serve as the basis for a mitigated sentence).

2. *Procedures to determine mental retardation in capital cases.*   The unique severity of capital punishment explains in large part why many jurisdictions have statutes prohibiting the execution of the mentally retarded, and it also explains why *Atkins* drew from these legislative decisions to find in the Eighth Amendment a constitutional ban against applying the death penalty to the mentally retarded. Notice, however, that the Supreme Court did not suggest specific procedures for determining which offenders are mentally retarded and thus exempt from the death penalty; Justice Stevens's opinion for the Court left to individual states "the task of developing appropriate ways to enforce" the rule announced in *Atkins.* If you were a legislator or a sentencing commissioner or a judge in a state that had not previously addressed this issue, what sorts of procedures would you propose? Should it be for a judge or for a jury to decide whether an offender is mentally retarded? Should an offender have the burden of proving mental retardation by a preponderance of the evidence to avoid

execution, or should a prosecutor have to disprove any claim of retardation beyond a reasonable doubt? Should an inquiry about an offender's mental status occur before any indictment on a capital charge, or only after an offender has been convicted of a crime that qualifies for the death penalty? See State v. Lott, 779 N.E.2d 1011 (Ohio 2002) (adopting procedure for capital defendants to follow in raising mental retardation claims); James W. Ellis, Mental Retardation and the Death Penalty: A Guide to State Legislative Issues (2002) (providing suggestions to legislatures for implementing *Atkins*).

3. *Mental impairments in noncapital sentencing.*   If reduced mental capacity in the form of mental retardation justifies a categorical reduction in the available sentence in capital cases, does it likewise justify an automatic sentence reduction in noncapital cases? Recall that the Supreme Court's opinion in *Atkins* viewed the decision by many states to exempt mentally retarded persons from the death penalty as "powerful evidence that today our society views mentally retarded offenders as categorically less culpable than the average criminal." Does this suggest that mentally retarded offenders also ought to be exempt from the strictures of mandatory sentencing provisions or guideline sentencing systems altogether? Cf. People v. Watters, 595 N.E.2d 1369 (Ill. App. Ct. 1992) (finding that Illinois law authorized sentencing below an applicable mandatory minimum imprisonment term based on a defendant's mental retardation).

As Justice Scalia mentions in his *Atkins* dissent, at common law those with severe mental impairments could be excused from guilt altogether, but offenders with lesser impairments would usually be subject to the same punishments as mentally sound offenders. In more recent times, judges in unstructured sentencing jurisdictions have had discretion to consider the defendant's mental condition in setting the sentence, while judges in structured sentencing systems face varying instructions concerning the way mental retardation or mental condition ought to be considered at sentencing. See, e.g., N.C. Gen. Stat. §15A-1340.16(e)(3), (4) (authorizing a mitigated sentence when the defendant "was suffering from a mental . . . condition" or had "limited mental capacity" that "significantly reduced the defendant's culpability for the offense"); Or. Sentencing Guidelines §213-008-0002(C) (providing that a mitigating departure factor can be that the "defendant's mental capacity was diminished").

In the federal system, section 5H1.3 of the federal sentencing guidelines provides that mental and emotional conditions "are not ordinarily relevant in determining whether a sentence should be outside the applicable guideline range [but] may be relevant in determining the conditions of probation or supervised release; e.g., participation in a mental health program." But another federal guidelines provision, section 5K2.13, states that a "sentence below the applicable guideline range may be warranted if the defendant committed the offense while suffering from a significantly reduced mental capacity." While making diminished capacity an "encouraged" basis for a departure, the federal guidelines further state that a court may not depart if "(1) the significantly reduced mental capacity was caused by the voluntary use of drugs or other intoxicants; (2) the facts and circumstances of the defendant's offense indicate a need to protect the public because the offense involved actual violence or a serious threat of violence; or (3) the defendant's criminal history indicates a need to incarcerate the defendant to protect the public." Similarly, the Oregon sentencing guidelines provide that a mitigating departure factor can be that the "defendant's mental capacity was diminished," but this provision expressly excludes "diminished capacity due to voluntary drug or alcohol abuse." Or. Sentencing Guidelines §213-008-0002(C).

4. *Age as mitigating (or aggravating?) factor.*   Under common-law rules and through modern times, very young children are generally exempted from all criminal responsibility. And because of the view that even older children are less responsible for their actions and have more potential to be redeemed even after doing wrong, every jurisdiction has special courts and legal rules for juvenile offenders. Because the punishments imposed under these special rules tend to be less severe than those imposed under the rules for adults, age serves as a mitigating factor at sentencing for young offenders who are eligible for the specialized juvenile systems. Jurisdictions vary considerably in defining the exact age and circumstances when an offender will be handled as a juvenile rather than as an adult.

The age of a defendant at the time of a crime also affects capital punishment. In a set of decisions that parallel the *Atkins* ruling, the Supreme Court has held that the Eighth Amendment prohibits the execution of offenders who were 15 or younger at the time of their offense, see Thompson v. Oklahoma, 487 U.S. 815 (1988), but that it is constitutionally permissible to seek to execute offenders who are 16 or older. See Stanford v. Kentucky, 492 U.S. 361 (1989). Nevertheless, a majority of capital jurisdictions, including the federal system, statutorily require an offender to be at least 18 at the time of the offense for the death penalty to be available as a punishment. State laws vary concerning the age at which offenders are eligible to be sentenced to life without parole.

Once an offender comes within the jurisdiction of the adult criminal justice system, her age rarely serves as a definite or formal criterion for a reduced sentence. Social science data reveal, however, that recidivism rates for older offenders are much lower than for offenders in their teens and twenties. See, e.g., U.S. Dept. of Justice, Probation and Parole Violators in State Prison, 1991 (Aug. 1995) (detailing a much lower rate of reincarceration for older parolees and probationers). Consequently, a sentencing system or sentencing judge concerned particularly with incapacitation goals might reasonably assign longer sentences to younger offenders and shorter sentences to older offenders. Indeed, anecdotal evidence suggests that in unstructured systems, judges and parole officials do grant a "senior sentencing discount." Structured sentencing systems, however, have not consistently codified such sentencing discounts based on the offender's age. Compare U.S. Sentencing Guidelines Manual §5H1.1 ("Age (including youth) is not ordinarily relevant in determining whether a sentence should be outside the applicable guideline range [but] may be a reason to impose a sentence below the applicable guideline range when the defendant is elderly and infirm and where a form of punishment such as home confinement might be equally efficient as and less costly than incarceration") with N.C. Gen. Stat. §15A-1340.16(e)(4) (authorizing a mitigated sentence if the "defendant's age [or] immaturity . . . at the time of commission of the offense significantly reduced the defendant's culpability for the offense") and Utah Sentencing Guidelines Form 4 (providing that a mitigating factor to be considered at sentencing is that "offender is young").

5. *Does immutability matter?* Is the immutability of certain personal characteristics a significant consideration in deciding whether that characteristic should play a role at sentencing, or is the only relevant question whether the factor is related to the offender's culpability and future prospects? If immutability is an important and influential consideration, should certain conditions like drug dependency, treatable mental illness, or socioeconomic class be deemed immutable?

2. Circumstances Within the Defendant's Control

A criminal conviction holds a defendant responsible for the criminal act; the criminal sentence carries the ideal of responsibility one step further. Sentencing allows the judge to fine-tune the clumsy notions of responsibility, such as those embodied in the insanity defense. A defendant who is guilty, but who is less clearly responsible than some other defendants convicted of similar crimes, will often receive a lesser sentence.

Moreover, the concept of responsibility at sentencing extends to events that happen after the crime. Some defendants take actions after their crime or even after their arrest — such as enrolling in treatment programs or making restitution to victims — to show they are amenable to rehabilitation and will not present a danger in the future. Do sentencing rules and sentencing judges treat these notions of responsibility during the crime and after the crime similarly? Do they react consistently to the various ways that defendants signal their prospects for rehabilitation?

|| *State v. Vickie Keith* ||
|| 995 P.2d 966 (Mont. 2000) ||

NELSON, J.

. . . On the evening of May 7, 1998, [Vickie] Keith, her boyfriend Dean Yates, and a mutual friend, Richard Wolde, went out to a local tavern to drink and dance. They returned to Keith's apartment around midnight. Keith lay down on a mattress on the living room floor and took a short nap. According to Yates, Keith was very inebriated. When Keith awoke from her nap, she was angry and hostile towards Yates and started saying "crazy sounding things." . . . Keith told Yates that she wanted him out of her life and she ordered him to leave. Yates agreed and began gathering his things while Keith went into her bedroom and locked the door.

As Yates and Wolde were leaving the apartment, they heard a gun shot from Keith's bedroom. Yates was attempting to break the lock on the door when they heard a second shot. When they entered the room, they found Keith sitting in a corner holding a .357 caliber handgun. Before they could reach her, Keith fired the gun a third time in the direction of the window. Yates grabbed the gun in an attempt to disarm Keith, but before he could get it away from her, a fourth shot was fired. This shot went through a desk and into a wall that separated Keith's apartment from the apartment next door. In the next apartment, Keith's neighbor, Mary Snyder, awoke to the sounds of gun fire and muffled screams.

Snyder called 911 and, while talking to the dispatcher, she heard the fourth shot hit her bedroom wall. When the officers arrived at the scene, they arrested Keith who proceeded to scream obscenities at the officers.

On May 19, 1998, the State charged Keith by Information with criminal endangerment, a felony. . . . The Information also contained notice that Keith could receive an additional sentence for the use of a weapon pursuant to [Mont. Code Ann.] §46-18-221. On August 27, 1998, Keith filed a motion to add her psychiatrist, Dr. Noel Hoell, as a witness. Keith had been undergoing treatment with Dr. Hoell since 1990. . . . In an affidavit in support of the motion, Keith's counsel stated that the combination of stress, a change in Keith's medication, and the consumption of alcohol may have precluded Keith from knowingly committing the crime. Counsel stated that while he did not believe that Keith had a mental disease or defect, "her mental thoughts and processes were impaired." The District Court granted Keith's motion. . . .

At trial, Dr. Hoell testified that Keith had been under a great deal of stress the past year because her daughter had been molested and because of the molestation trial that followed. He explained that Keith was suffering from anxiety and depression and "general emotional turmoil" during this time. Dr. Hoell also testified that Keith was suffering considerable pain and discomfort because, a few months before the shooting incident, Keith had an altercation with someone in which her neck and shoulder were injured.

Dr. Hoell further testified that he had prescribed three medications for Keith; Prozac, Doxepin, and Valium. He stated that on the day of the shooting, Keith had contacted him regarding her Valium prescription. She told him that the generic Valium she was taking was not as effective as the brand name and she requested a different medication. Dr. Hoell gave Keith a new prescription. According to Wolde, although he was unsure whether Keith took any of this new medication, he was with Keith when she filled the prescription later that day.

As to the physiological effects of these drugs when taken in conjunction with alcoholic beverages, Dr. Hoell testified that while Prozac does not have any specific interaction with alcohol, alcohol mixed with Doxepin could cause sleepiness and confusion, and the combination of Valium and alcohol could cause sedation, confusion and agitation. Dr. Hoell also testified that he prescribed the Valium for Keith with the understanding that she would refrain from using alcohol. [The] jury found Keith guilty of criminal endangerment. The District Court ordered a presentence investigation report.

[Prior to the sentencing hearing itself, the court declared that it would entertain argument on exceptions to the mandatory minimum sentence. During the hearing, the court heard Keith's claim that her mental capacity was impaired at the time of the offense. In support of this argument, Keith pointed to portions of Dr. Hoell's trial testimony regarding the stress she was under at the time of the crime and that she had taken drugs and alcohol before to the offense. The court also questioned Keith regarding her claim. Defense counsel argued that the mandatory minimum sentence under the weapon enhancement statute] did not apply here because Keith was under a great deal of stress and she had ingested drugs and alcohol prior to the offense. The court responded that in order to waive the mandatory minimum sentence, there would have to be some evidence that Keith's mental capacity was significantly impaired. The court explained that under §46-18-222(2), it could not give Keith the benefit of any type of voluntarily induced intoxicated or drugged state. The court concluded that there was no evidence of mental impairment in this case sufficient to require waiving the mandatory minimum sentence. The District Court sentenced Keith to 10 years in the Women's State Prison in Billings for the offense of criminal endangerment plus an additional 10 years for the use of a weapon in connection with that offense. The court subsequently suspended 15 years of Keith's sentence. . . .

This Court reviews a criminal sentence only for legality (i.e., whether the sentence is within the parameters provided by the statute). Section 46-18-221 [of the Montana Code Annotated], the weapon enhancement statute, provides that a person who uses a weapon in the commission of an offense "shall, in addition to the punishment provided for the commission of such offense, be sentenced to a term of imprisonment in the state prison of not less than 2 years or more than 10 years, except as provided in 46-18-222." Section 46-18-222(2) provides, in pertinent part,

> Mandatory minimum sentences prescribed by the laws of this state [do not apply if] the offender's mental capacity, at the time of the commission of the offense for which the offender is to be sentenced, was significantly impaired, although not so impaired as to constitute a defense to the prosecution. However, a voluntarily induced intoxicated or drugged condition may not be considered an impairment for the purposes of this subsection.

Keith contends that, at the time of the crime, her mental capacity was impaired due to physical pain, mental anguish, high levels of stress, and the taking of prescription drugs and alcohol. She argues that although her mental state was not so diminished as to support a claim for mental disease or defect under §46-14-312,* her mental condition was "significantly impaired," thus she falls within the exceptions to mandatory minimum sentences as provided for in §46-18-222(2).

While §46-18-222(2) does permit the sentencing court to reject the mandatory minimum sentence if it determines that the defendant's mental capacity was significantly impaired during the commission of the offense, this Court has repeatedly held that this statute does not apply in cases where the maximum sentence or any sentence greater than the mandatory minimum is imposed. State v. Zabawa 928 P.2d 151, 157 (Mont. 1996).

As the State points out, Keith's argument would only have merit if the District Court had intended to sentence Keith to less than the two-year mandatory minimum sentence and was prevented from doing so because it found that the exceptions under §46-18-222 did not apply. In this case, there is no indication that the District Court ever intended to sentence Keith to either the two-year

---

* Section 46-14-312(2) provides: "If the court finds that the defendant at the time of the commission of the offense suffered from a mental disease or defect . . . any mandatory minimum sentence prescribed by law for the offense need not apply and the court shall sentence the defendant to be committed to . . . an appropriate correctional or mental health facility for custody, care, and treatment for a definite period of time not to exceed the maximum term of imprisonment that could be imposed [in the absence of the mental disease or defect]."—EDS.

mandatory minimum or to a period of time less than the two-year mandatory minimum, therefore, the exceptions are not applicable in this case.

[Keith's mental] impairment was based in part on the alcohol and drugs she voluntarily consumed. Moreover, as the District Court noted, being under stress is not the same as having your mental capacity significantly impaired. Accordingly, we hold that the District Court did not err in failing to apply the exceptions to mandatory minimum sentences, as set forth in §46-18-222, in this case. . . .

PROBLEM 5-5.   TREATMENT AND TIMING

Review again the facts from State v. Joshua Fowler, reprinted earlier in this chapter. Suppose that Fowler's abuse of alcohol and methamphetamines during the three days before the crime was typical. The day after he committed the crime, Fowler realized that his addictions had become a major problem, and he sought help by enrolling in a treatment program. During the 18 months between the crime and the time he turned himself in to authorities, Fowler made real progress in the program.

You are the judge who must sentence Fowler for first-degree armed robbery. In Washington, the standard sentencing range for the offense is 31 to 41 months, plus a mandatory 60-month firearm enhancement penalty. Fowler asks for an exceptional sentence of six months, given that he voluntarily enrolled in a treatment program before his arrest and has nearly completed the program. If the relevant law leaves you with discretion on this question, would you impose a sentence below the standard range based on this factor?

Now suppose that federal authorities charged Fowler with illegal possession of a weapon, and the guidelines produce an adjusted offense level of 9, resulting in a presumptive prison term of four to ten months for somebody with no prior criminal history. As a federal judge, would you depart below the guideline range and grant a probationary sentence based on Fowler's enrollment in the treatment program?

Finally, let us consider the timing of Fowler's decision to undertake treatment. As a sentencing judge, would you still consider Fowler's treatment in setting the criminal sentence if he began his treatment after arrest but before prosecution? After conviction but before sentencing? Would you grant a motion to reconsider the sentence if he began treatment after you imposed the original sentence?

A policy statement in the federal guidelines addresses the last question. Section 5K2.19 provides that "post-sentencing rehabilitative efforts, even if exceptional" are not an appropriate basis for a downward departure when resentencing the defendant for the original offense. But postsentencing rehabilitation can give corrections authorities reason to shorten the defendant's period of "supervised release" to be served at the end of a prison term. Note also that the federal policy statement does not restrict departures based on extraordinary postoffense rehabilitation that occurs *before* the original sentencing, even if it begins after arrest or after conviction. See United States v. Brock, 108 F.3d 31 (4th Cir. 1997). Should the federal guidelines discourage or prohibit judges from reducing sentences based on any postarrest rehabilitation efforts?

PROBLEM 5-6.   RESTITUTION AND REHABILITATION

Cattle rancher William Oligmueller misrepresented the number of cattle he owned when applying for a loan from First State Bank. The bank discovered the fraud when bank officers arrived at the ranch to inspect the collateral. At the time the officers discovered the fraud, Oligmueller owed the bank approximately $894,000 on the loan, which was secured by livestock, feed, and machinery.

Oligmueller began liquidating his assets in September 1997 to begin repaying the bank. He tended the crops until harvest, and the livestock until sale, increasing the price that the bank ultimately received through the sales. He often worked 16-hour days. He loaded the hay trucks for the bank. Oligmueller pledged assets not previously pledged to the bank, including his ranch. He turned over to the bank his life insurance policy and his wife's certificate of deposit, and he and his wife sold their home and moved in with their daughter. Oligmueller also took a job with a farm supply company and set up a lawn mower repair business. In addition, he sent to the bank approximately half of his Social Security check each month to pay his debts.

By October 1998, through asset liquidation, Oligmueller had repaid the bank approximately $808,000. The bank also received $28,000 in cash payments directly from Oligmueller. This brought the bank's loss down to approximately $58,000.

A federal grand jury indicted Oligmueller in August 1998 for making false statements to the bank. He pleaded guilty; you are the district court judge who will preside at the upcoming sentencing hearing.

Under section 2F1.1 of the U.S. Sentencing Guidelines, the amount of loss used to determine a sentence for a fraudulent loan application is the greater of the actual loss to the victim or the intended loss. In determining the amount of actual loss, the application notes to the guidelines say that a sentencing court cannot consider payments made to the bank after the fraud is discovered unless the payments are the result of the sale of pledged assets. Of the $808,000 paid to the bank from the sale of assets, only $65,000 resulted from the sale of pledged assets. The sentencing guidelines also allow either a downward or an upward departure if the amount of loss significantly overstates or understates the risk to the lending institution. See U.S. Sentencing Guidelines Manual §2F1.1, cmt. n.8(b).

Oligmueller argues that his offense level should be reduced based on his "acceptance of responsibility." Commentary to the sentencing guidelines lists "post-offense efforts to rehabilitate" and "voluntary payment of restitution before adjudication of guilt" as two factors that tend to show when a defendant qualifies for a two-level reduction for "acceptance of responsibility." U.S. Sentencing Guidelines Manual §3E1.1, cmt. n.1. Oligmueller also requests a downward departure from the guideline sentence based on his extraordinary efforts at rehabilitation.

As a sentencing judge, how will you calculate the amount of loss (and thus the initial offense level) involved in this fraud? Will you reduce the offense level based on Oligmueller's acceptance of responsibility? Will you grant any further downward departure? How much restitution will you order him to pay? Cf. United States v. Oligmueller, 198 F.3d 669 (8th Cir. 1999).

NOTES

1. *Addiction at sentencing.*   The fact that a defendant was extremely intoxicated at the time of the crime can, in some states and for some crimes, lead to an acquittal because the intoxication prevents the defendant from forming a criminal intent. But this argument rarely succeeds as a complete defense to criminal charges. Cf. Montana v. Egelhoff, 518 U.S. 37 (1996) (finding constitutionally permissible Montana's statute barring consideration of intoxication as a defense). Intoxication or addiction at the time of an offense matters more often at the sentencing stage. In unstructured sentencing jurisdictions, the judge usually has discretion (and little direction) concerning how to consider the defendant's addiction in setting the sentence. Does substance abuse share any features with mental impairments such as those considered in the previous section? Should the law insist on the same sentence for two defendants, one whose addiction contributed to the crime and another who faced no substance abuse problems?

In most jurisdictions with more structured sentencing rules, the law instructs a sentencing judge to give limited or no consideration to substance abuse. Under the federal guidelines, section 5H1.4 states that drug or alcohol dependence or abuse "is not a reason for imposing a sentence below the guidelines. Substance abuse is highly correlated to an increased propensity to commit crime." Substance abuse can lead a judge to order treatment during a prison term or a period of supervised release. See U.S. Sentencing Guidelines Manual §5D1.3(d)(4). While the law in Florida at one time provided that addiction was a valid ground for a downward departure, the legislature amended the law in 1997 to remove this basis for a reduced sentence. See 1997 Fla. Laws ch. 97-194, §41, at 3728 (codified at Fla. Stat. Ann. §921.0026(3)); State v. Lazo, 761 So. 2d 1244, 1245 (Fla. Dist. Ct. App. 2000) ("A defendant's drug addiction and amenability to rehabilitation are no longer valid reasons for a downward departure from sentencing guidelines."). In other jurisdictions, this result has been reached through case law. See, e.g., State v. Gaines, 859 P.2d 36, 42 (Wash. 1993) (holding that "drug addiction and its casual role in an addict's criminal offense may not properly serve as justification for a durational departure from the standard range").

Can an argument be made that sentencing rules should authorize (or even require) judges to treat addiction as an aggravating factor that can (or must) increase a sentence? See Ariz. Stat. §41-1604.15 ("Notwithstanding any law to the contrary, any person who is convicted of a violent crime . . . that is committed while the person is under the influence of marijuana, a dangerous drug or a narcotic drug . . . is not eligible for probation or release on any basis until the entire sentence has been served"; statute passed by voter initiative also providing for nonprison treatment sanctions for drug possession offenses). Alaska law provides that "voluntary alcohol or other drug intoxication or chronic alcoholism or other drug addiction may not be considered an aggravating or mitigating factor." Alaska Stat. §12.55.155(g).

2. *Postarrest efforts at rehabilitation.*   Defendants with substance abuse problems sometimes enroll themselves in treatment programs before the time of conviction or sentencing. Does this action suggest an effort to manipulate the sentence or a genuine willingness to fix the root problem behind the crime? In

the federal courts, it is clear that truly "extraordinary" rehabilitation efforts can create a basis for a downward departure. See United States v. Newlon, 212 F.3d 423 (8th Cir. 2000) (departure for drug addiction treatment); United States v. Whitaker, 152 F.3d 1238 (10th Cir. 1998). A number of state systems also allow drug treatment or even amenability to treatment to serve as a basis for a mitigated sentence. See Md. Sentencing Guidelines §9.2(7) (providing as a reason for a departure an "offender's commitment to substance abuse treatment or other therapeutic program"); Or. Sentencing Guidelines §213-008-0002(I) (providing for a mitigated sentence when "offender is amenable to treatment and an appropriate treatment program is available to which the offender can be admitted within a reasonable period of time; the treatment program is likely to be more effective than the presumptive prison term in reducing the risk of offender recidivism; and the probation sentence will serve community safety interests by promoting offender reformation").

3. *Education and employment.*   There is an obvious correlation between employment and crime. A person with a steady job is less likely to commit a crime. Further, education can create skills that make a person easier to employ. Should a sentencing judge consider the defendant's education, vocational skills, and employment record as a basis for choosing a lower sentence? As a sentencing judge, would you find postarrest *changes* in education or employment status to be more significant than education or employment at the time of the crime?

In the federal system, sections 5H1.2 and 5H1.5 of the sentencing guidelines provide that education, vocational skills, and employment record are "not ordinarily relevant in determining whether a sentence should be outside the applicable guideline range," but they can be relevant in selecting appropriate conditions for probation or community service activities. What reasons could explain the reluctance to consider education, vocational skills, and employment record in the federal system? The consideration of these factors in state systems varies considerably. Compare Minn. Sentencing Guidelines II.D.1 (precluding departures based on "employment factors" or "educational attainment") with Delaware Sentencing Accountability Commission, Sentencing Policies and Standards M9 (providing for an exceptional sentence below the presumptive range if the "offender is gainfully employed and will more than likely lose his/her job if the sentencing standard is imposed") and State v. Crawford, 908 P.2d 638 (Kan. Ct. App. 1995) (asserting that "impressive employment record" alone would not justify a departure but could be a factor combined with others that would allow departure).

4. *Voluntary restitution before sentencing.*   Most state systems allow the judge to consider voluntary restitution as a basis for reducing a sentence. See Wash. Code §9.94A.390(1)(b) (mitigating circumstance present if "[b]efore detection, the defendant compensated, or made a good faith effort to compensate, the victim of the criminal conduct for any damage or injury sustained"); Fla. Stat. Ann. §921.0016(4)(h) (authorizing a departure if "[b]efore the identity of the defendant was determined, the victim was substantially compensated"). Is it realistic, as many of these statutes require, to expect an offender to make restitution before his crime is detected? As Problem 5-6 indicated, the federal system allows a judge to consider voluntary restitution in several contexts. What features does voluntary restitution share with postoffense addiction treatment as a

mitigating factor? Does voluntary restitution give more affluent defendants a chance to "buy" a lower sentence?

3. Social Context of the Offender

Even offenders who might be described as loners have a lifetime of social history and interpersonal connections. Should such social contexts play any role in sentencing decision making? Consider what theoretical grounds might support consideration or exclusion of such factors at sentencing.

|| **United States v. Marver Lin Carter**
122 F.3d 469 (7th Cir. 1997) ||

CUDAHY, J.

On August 23, 1995, on their way from Tucson, Arizona to Fort Wayne, Indiana, Marver Carter and his passenger were stopped by Sergeant Ed Delmore . . . for having no license plates. Sergeant Delmore . . . asked for and received permission to search the car. In a suitcase, Sergeant Delmore found what, from his experience, appeared to be a kilogram package of cocaine. He arrested Carter and his passenger. Continuing his search, Sergeant Delmore found what appeared to be four more kilograms of cocaine in the suitcase. A field test of one of the packages proved Sergeant Delmore correct. Both suspects were read their *Miranda* rights and they agreed to cooperate.

Carter placed a taped call to his buyer in Fort Wayne, Indiana. Drug Enforcement Agency agents then escorted Carter to Fort Wayne to meet his buyer at a motel. After the drug transaction took place, police arrested the buyer, Jiermal Walker, who also agreed to cooperate. This led to the arrest of another buyer, Shaft Jones. All four men were indicted[, and] Carter pleaded guilty without a plea agreement.

The probation office prepared its presentence investigation report (PSI), which noted a substantial number of Carter's virtues. According to the PSI, Carter is a married father of three young children. While on bail, Carter worked at the Sunnyside School District as a teacher's aide and specialized in working with disabled children. Carter did not blame others for his predicament and held no grudges toward those who arrested and prosecuted him. These circumstances led the probation officer to consider Carter to be somewhat unique and unlike most defendants. Under the Sentencing Guidelines, Carter's base offense level was calculated as 34, to which four points were added under U.S.S.G. §3B1.1 because of his role as a leader or organizer. Then three points were subtracted under U.S.S.G. §3E1.1 for Carter's acceptance of responsibility. This led to an adjusted offense level of 35. Carter had no prior criminal history, placing him in Category I, and resulting in a sentence range of 168 to 210 months.

Carter requested a downward departure, citing his family and community ties, work history and unique level of remorse. He requested that the district court examine the four purposes of sentencing (deterrence, incapacitation, retribution and correction) in considering a departure, arguing that these purposes would be fully served by a more lenient sentence. He also cited his immediate acceptance of responsibility for his crime and his cooperation with prosecutors. The district court denied Carter's requests and sentenced him to 168 months in prison (the guideline minimum). . . .

We review for abuse of discretion. See Koon v. United States, 518 U.S. 81 (1996). A district court abuses its discretion when it makes an error of law. A district court's decision to depart (or not) from the guidelines is due substantial deference, for it embodies the traditional exercise of discretion by a sentencing court. District courts have an institutional advantage over appellate courts in making sentencing determinations, and we accept the district court's findings of fact supporting a refusal to depart unless clearly erroneous.

STATUTORY GOALS OF SENTENCING

Carter argues that the Sentencing Guidelines procedure was adopted to ensure that the four goals of sentencing (deterrence, incapacitation, retribution and correction) would be applied in sentencing determinations. See 18 U.S.C. §3553(a)(2)(A)-(D) (1994). He further argues that the district court refused to consider the purposes of sentencing when calculating his sentence. Carter argues that these sentencing goals compel a more lenient sentence in the instant case. Carter argues that his 14-year prison sentence cannot be described as "sufficient, but not greater than necessary" to serve the purposes of sentencing. Carter interprets 18 U.S.C. §3553(a)(2) as directing the courts to test potential departure factors against the sentencing goals and to reject factors that are inconsistent with them. Carter points to the Supreme Court's opinion in Koon. . . . to highlight his argument that the guidelines should be interpreted to serve the purposes of sentencing given all the facts of each case.

Carter misunderstands [the holding in Koon]. What the Supreme Court actually held in Koon was that courts are not limited to the goals of sentencing, not that the courts must abide by them, as Carter contends. The Koon Court actually *rejected* a limitation on sentencing discretion by holding that a departure from the guidelines does not always have to be consistent with the four goals. . . . The statute requires a court to consider the listed goals. . . . The statute says nothing about requiring each potential departure factor to advance one of the specified goals. Carter's argument therefore fails.

CARTER'S SPECIAL CIRCUMSTANCES

Carter next argues that the district court erred in failing to consider the exceptional nature of his circumstances which, he says, favor a downward departure, instead of the formalistic application of the guidelines. [A] factor supporting departure from the guidelines must be sufficiently unusual either in type or degree to take the case out of the Guidelines' heartland. The Supreme Court in Koon set out a test for a sentencing court considering a departure:

(1)   What features of this case, potentially, take it outside the Guidelines' "heartland" and make of it a special, or unusual case?

(2)   Has the Commission forbidden departures based on those features?[3]
(3)   If not, has the Commission encouraged departures based on those features?
(4)   If not, has the Commission discouraged departures based on those features?[5]

The Supreme Court then held:

> If the special factor is a forbidden factor, the sentencing court cannot use it as a basis of departure. If the special factor is an encouraged factor, the court is authorized to depart if the applicable Guideline does not already take it into account. If the special factor is a discouraged factor, or an encouraged factor already taken into account by the applicable Guideline, the court should depart only if the factor is present to an exceptional degree or in some other way makes the case different from the ordinary case where the factor is present.

Following *Koon,* the district court considered the special "discouraged" factors presented by Carter, such as his family and community ties and work record, and determined that his circumstances did not make his case a sufficiently exceptional one. . . .

Family Considerations

As the district court noted, family considerations are "discouraged" and warrant a departure only in the extraordinary and unusual case. See, e.g., United States v. Gaskill, 991 F.2d 82 (3d Cir. 1993) (allowing departure when defendant solely responsible for care of his mentally ill wife); United States v. Johnson, 964 F.2d 124 (2d Cir. 1992) (allowing departure when defendant, single mother, served as sole support for three small children under age six, institutionalized daughter's six-year-old child and seventeen-year-old son). More common are the cases which have denied a downward departure for family responsibilities, even in compelling situations. See, e.g., United States v. Bieri, 21 F.3d 811 (8th Cir. 1994) (departure rejected where both parents of small children were incarcerated); United States v. Mogel, 956 F.2d 1555 (11th Cir. 1992) (departure rejected though defendant supported two minor children and her mother and was first-time offender).

Carter's family circumstances, when compared to the foregoing cases, do not remove him from the heartland. [It] is not unusual to find that a convicted drug offender is a parent with family responsibilities. [Only] the nature and magnitude of family responsibilities (many children? with handicaps? no money? no place for children to go?) may transform the "ordinary" case . . . into a case that is not at all ordinary. While Carter's wife and three children will suffer during his incarceration, his children do have a mother to look after them, and, as Carter has repeatedly pointed out, loving grandparents (his parents), who will help her. The disintegration of existing family life or relationships is insufficient to warrant a departure, as that is to be expected when a family

---

[3] "Forbidden" factors include race, sex, national origin, creed, religion and socio-economic status. U.S.S.G. §5H1.10.

[5] "Discouraged" factors are ones "not ordinarily relevant to the determination of whether a sentence should be outside the applicable guideline range" and include family ties and responsibilities, U.S.S.G. §5H1.6, education or vocational skills, U.S.S.G. §5H1.2, and any military, civic, charitable or public service record. U.S.S.G. §5H1.11.

member engages in criminal activity. Disruption of the defendant's life, and the concomitant difficulties for those who depend on the defendant, are inherent in the punishment of incarceration.

Further, the goal of the guidelines is to place federal sentencing on an objective, uniform, and rational (or at least articulable, nonintuitive) basis. [If] family history were in an average case a permissible basis for leniency, this would resurrect the pre-guidelines regime of discretionary sentencing. . . . Carter wants us to use his solid family history as a "permissible basis for leniency" under the guise of fulfilling statutory sentencing purposes. By this means the guidelines [would] be unraveled before the eyes of the judge.

Employment Considerations

Carter argues that his post-arrest employment and "unusually firm dedication to reversing the course of his life" also merit a downward departure. The district court did not find Carter's employment extraordinary. In the lower court, Carter analogized his situation to that found in United States v. Big Crow, 898 F.2d 1326 (8th Cir. 1990). The district court, however, found *Big Crow* to be "a bird of a different feather altogether." In *Big Crow,* the Eighth Circuit affirmed a downward departure based on the defendant's steady, pre-arrest employment over six years. He had earned enough to "more than adequately" care for his wife and two children on an Indian reservation with an unemployment rate of 72% and an average annual income of only $1042. The defendant had also made consistent efforts to overcome the difficult environment of the reservation. In contrast, Carter stresses that he has two caring parents as well as a supportive wife. In that environment, it is not necessarily exceptional that Carter would hold a job or improve his life. Rather, this conduct might be expected of him.

Further, employment is a "discouraged" factor and warrants consideration only in exceptional cases. While the district court found Carter's employment "laudable," the court did not find it to be "so extraordinary as to suggest its presence to a degree not adequately taken into consideration by the acceptance of responsibility reduction." In fact, the district court noted that included in the terms of Carter's release in lieu of detention before trial was a requirement that he seek and maintain employment. Here, of course, the nature of the employment was strikingly meritorious. However, the district court's decision not to depart, since based on the correct standards, is not reviewable. . . .

This is a difficult case because we cannot gainsay the defendant's virtues and the sympathetic considerations that he presents. But, as our discussion indicates, they do not require of the district court a different exercise of discretion. We conclude that the district court understood the parameters of its discretion and made its decision within them. We therefore cannot review the decision nor disturb the sentence. . . .

NOTES

1. *Consideration of social context factors: majority position.* Historically, in indeterminate sentencing systems, social context factors such as family history and situation, educational background, and employment record were of great importance to sentencing judges (and parole officials) when exercising their

discretion to individualize sentences with the offender's rehabilitation in mind. Presentence reports often provided considerable detail on each offender's social history, education, and employment, and they suggested how these background factors might affect the offender's rehabilitative prospects and progress.

Anecdotal and empirical research suggests that undue sentencing disparity, and the apparent disfavoring of certain minority offenders, can be traced back to the emphasis on these sorts of social context factors. As a result, many modern sentencing reforms have precluded or greatly restricted the consideration of these factors. As the *Carter* case highlights, the U.S. Sentencing Commission has mostly excluded these social context factors from sentencing calculations and has further declared most social context matters "not ordinarily relevant" to a departure determination. See, e.g., U.S. Sentencing Guidelines Manual §§5H1.2 (education and vocational skills), 5H1.5 (employment record), 5H1.6 (family ties and responsibilities and community ties), and 5H1.11 (military, civic, charitable, or public service). As *Carter* also details, however, federal case law has interpreted these instructions to mean that social context factors can be the basis for a departure in "extraordinary" cases. Likewise, in many state structured sentencing systems, social context factors are not directly incorporated into most sentencing determinations, but they can on occasion serve as a basis for a departure. See, e.g., Utah Guidelines Form 4 (providing that a mitigating factor to be considered at sentencing is that "offender has exceptionally good employment and/or family relationships").

2. *Relevance (or irrelevance) of offenders' social context.*   In some cases, certain social context factors might directly bear on the offender's culpability; an offender with many children who steals in order to feed his family, for example, seems less culpable than a thief who lacks any such family needs. Such factors might seem important considerations in light of the traditional purposes of sentencing. But should consideration of such social context factors be permitted at sentencing when they do not directly bear on an offender's culpability or future prospects? Consider ABA Standard for Criminal Justice, Sentencing 18-3.4 (3d ed. 1994), which suggests the following approach for allowing limited consideration of the offender's personal characteristics at sentencing:

> (a) The legislature and [sentencing commission] should authorize sentencing courts, sentencing individual offenders, to consider their physical, mental, social and economic characteristics, even though not material to their culpability for the offense, only as provided in this Standard.
> (b) The legislature and [sentencing commission] should permit sentencing courts to use information about offenders' financial circumstances for the purpose of determination of the amount or terms of fines or other economic sanctions.
> (c) Except as provided in (b), the legislature and the agency should provide that sentencing courts may take into account personal characteristics of offenders not material to their culpability to determine the appropriate types of sanctions to impose or, if the characteristics are indicative of circumstances of hardship, deprivation, or handicap, to lessen the severity of sentences that would have been imposed.

What uses of personal history are permitted and not permitted under this standard? Why, if an offender's "physical, mental, social and economic characteristics" are "not material to [his or her] culpability for the offense," should these characteristics be considered at all at sentencing? The commentary to the standards explains its compromise position:

> Many determinate jurisdictions have sought to restrict or prohibit the sentenc-
> ing consideration of personal characteristics unrelated to culpability on the the-
> ory that such consideration can act to preserve or exacerbate preexisting class
> and race disparities in sentencing patterns. At least in the federal system such
> restrictions have prompted criticism that the sentencing process has been de-
> humanized, that the life history of defendants can no longer be argued to show
> extenuating circumstances, and that desirable individualization of sentences
> cannot occur. The Standards attempt to find a balance between the need to
> avoid class and race disparities and the need to preserve a meaningful level of
> individualization in sentences.

3. *Family circumstances.*   Especially because offenders at sentencing will often highlight family situations when pleading for leniency, sentencing judges
are frequently asked to consider the impact of a proposed sentence on the defendant's family. As detailed in *Carter,* the federal sentencing guidelines attempt
to limit this practice by declaring that "family ties and responsibilities" are "not
ordinarily relevant" to a sentence, and appellate courts have upheld departure
sentences based on such circumstances only when they are present to an "extraordinary" degree. The federal circuits have been less than perfectly consistent in assessing what sorts of family situations qualify as extraordinary. Compare
United States v. Johnson, 964 F.2d 124 (2d Cir. 1992) (departure allowed for female offender who was sole support for three children under seven years, institutionalized adult daughter, 17-year-old son, and six-year-old granddaughter),
with United States v. Sweeting, 213 F.3d 95 (3d Cir. 2000) (departure reversed
for mother of six children, including one suffering from Tourette's Syndrome),
and compare United States v. Haverstat, 22 F.3d 790 (8th Cir. 1994) (upholding
departure on grounds that caring for ill family member was "extraordinary"
family circumstance), with United States v. Allen, 87 F.3d 1224 (11th Cir. 1996)
(disallowing departure on similar grounds).

Because of the number of cases and families affected, this is a high-stakes
decision for every sentencing system. Consider the following excerpt from an
opinion by Judge Patricia Wald, dissenting from the denial of a motion for rehearing in United States v. Dyce, 91 F.3d 1462, 1472-1478 (D.C. Cir. 1996), a case
in which a panel of the U.S. Court of Appeals for the D.C. Circuit decided that
the mother of three young children, including a three-month-old still being
breastfed, did not warrant a downward departure based on family circumstances:

> The question of when family obligations rise to [the level of a departure
> ground] is an issue affecting tens of thousands of federal offenders and their
> families. More than half of all female prisoners and more than one-quarter of all
> male prisoners are caring for minor children at the time they enter prison. Other
> prisoners have primary responsibility for the care of parents, siblings, spouses, or
> grandchildren. In these cases, the impact of imprisonment on a defendant's fam-
> ily is profound; it imposes not just financial and emotional hardship, but in some
> cases, loss of children to foster care or even complete severance of parental
> rights. [In] light of the significant detriment experienced by children as a result
> of a parent's incarceration, the Commission's initial presumption against con-
> sidering family ties is unwarranted, short-sighted, and unwise. . . .
> In reviewing §5H1.6 departures, courts are asked (mistakenly, I believe)
> to undertake a "mission impossible" of identifying where the ephemeral line be-
> tween "ordinary" and "extraordinary" lies in the tragic realm of family breakup
> and disruption of children's lives. Obviously no bright-line rule is reasonable, or

even feasible — for example, "single parent with two or more children and dependent parent," or "single parent with young child and infant"; the variety of family structures, attachments, personalities, and track records in fulfilling responsibilities defies any such easy categorization. . . .

I believe rehearing en banc is [needed] to define for the district court some comprehensible parameters for departure under §5H1.6. The cumulation of rulings by our sister circuits provides only suggestions, not a great deal of firm guidance. . . . Several circuits have refused to sanction departures simply because incarceration will jeopardize the parental ties of a young child, where a relative is available to care for the children during the parent's incarceration. But other circuits have affirmed departures in circumstances markedly less compelling than this defendant's. The First Circuit — though denying departures in several earlier cases . . . involving dependent minor children — did permit a departure based on a showing of a strong relationship between a defendant and his lover's son, even though the child's mother had custody of her son. In other cases, departures have been authorized on the grounds that the defendant has several young children, in many cases without discussion of whether other relatives can or will care for the children. One circuit left open the possibility that a departure would be permissible based solely on defendant's role as a "good father" to "three exemplary children." . . .

The precedent is admittedly conflicting, perhaps because the task assigned by the Guidelines is so frustrating and counterintuitive — that is, where on the spectrum we should draw the line between "ordinary" and "extraordinary" family tragedies? But the fact remains that our trial judges must wrestle with the problem every day. . . .

In your view, what are extraordinary family circumstances? According to a 1991 survey, 61.6 percent of all federal prisoners and 56.7 percent of all state prisoners had children under age 18. Among female prisoners, the comparable numbers are 61.4 percent and 66.6 percent. In the state systems, 42.9 percent of the prisoners with children under 18 had only one child below that age; 28.9 percent had two; 15.4 percent had three; and 12.8 percent had four or more. Bureau of Justice Statistics, Comparing Federal and State Prison Inmates (National Institute of Justice, NCJ 145864, 1994). In light of Judge Wald's criticisms of the existing approach, if you were a staff attorney for the U.S. Sentencing Commission, would you propose developing different standards for sentencing courts in identifying the sorts of family circumstances that should lead to a departure up or down from the ordinary sentence? Do you think a more structured approach to this issue — for example, one that depends on the number of children affected or the likely home for children if the parent is incarcerated — would provide for more sensible and consistent results? Do you think the ABA approach would be an improvement?

PROBLEM 5-7.   PILLAR OF THE COMMUNITY

John Morken owned and operated a cattle brokerage business based in a small town in Minnesota. When the company's cash flow began to suffer, Morken began "kiting" checks (shifting funds among several bank accounts to create the illusion of larger bank accounts), thus inflating his purchasing power in the cattle market. He used the nonexistent funds to buy more cattle, and then cattle prices fell. Ultimately, Morken put the business into bankruptcy. A federal grand jury indicted Morken for bank fraud and making false statements to a financial institution. He pleaded guilty to one count of bank fraud, and the Government dropped the remaining charges. The applicable provisions of the U.S. Sentencing Guidelines call for a prison term between 63 and 78 months.

Many citizens of Morken's hometown (with a population just over 1,000) wrote to the sentencing judge, asking him to impose a lenient sentence. The letters portrayed Morken as a hard-working and honest businessman, the owner of a once-thriving operation. Morken's father started the business in the 1930s. Morken joined it in 1964 and took over leadership of the company in 1992. The letters to the judge also praised Morken for his community service. They spoke of him as an accommodating neighbor and a good friend. He advised local business owners, hired young people, served on his church council, and raised money for charity.

In addition to the family cattle brokerage business, Morken owned and operated the All Phase Arena, which hosted horse shows, farm and home shows, and the like. This operation provided dozens of jobs for local workers and generated revenue for local businesses. The All Phase Arena was unaffected by the bankruptcy of Morken's cattle operation, but it would likely not survive if Morken were to serve a lengthy prison term.

The federal sentencing guidelines advise judges that "community ties are not ordinarily relevant in determining whether a sentence should be outside the applicable guideline range." U.S. Sentencing Guidelines Manual §5H1.6. They also say that "[m]ilitary, charitable, or public service; employment-related contributions; and similar prior good works are not ordinarily relevant in determining whether a sentence should be outside the applicable guideline range." U.S. Sentencing Guidelines Manual §5H1.11. As the district court judge in this case, what sentence would you impose? How would you explain your decision? Cf. United States v. Morken, 133 F.3d 628 (8th Cir. 1998).

NOTES

1. *The significance of prior good works.* As noted earlier in this chapter, every jurisdiction views an offender's criminal history as an aggravating factor justifying an enhanced sentence for the current offense. Because these criminal history rules essentially mandate an increased sentence based on the defendant's past *bad* acts, logic would seem to dictate that jurisdictions should also have sentencing rules which mandate a reduced sentence based on the defendant's past *good* works. In other words, if defendants are to be penalized for prior bad behavior, shouldn't they also be rewarded for prior good behavior? A few jurisdictions follow this logic. North Carolina, for example, provides that a mitigated sentence could be appropriate when the defendant "has been a person of good character or has had a good reputation in the community" or when the defendant "has been honorably discharged from the United States armed services." N.C. Gen. Stat. §15A-1340.16(e)(12), (14). As noted in Problem 5-7, however, the federal sentencing guidelines provide that "[m]ilitary, charitable, or public service; employment-related contributions; and similar prior good works are not ordinarily relevant in determining whether a sentence should be outside the applicable guideline range." U.S. Sentencing Guidelines Manual §5H1.11. Why do you think the U.S. Sentencing Commission deemed these

factors discouraged as the basis for a departure? Should service to the country through the military merit some consideration in sentencing?

2. *The significance of third-party impact.*   The criminal conviction and potential incarceration of an offender almost always affect various third parties — most commonly the offender's immediate family and dependents, but often also the offender's employer or employees. As part of a plea for leniency, sentencing judges will almost invariably hear from the defendant or defense counsel about the hardships that third parties may suffer if the defendant is incarcerated. Should sentencing judges reduce sentences to try to minimize the harm to third parties, or does that unfairly reward defendants who are fortunate enough to have others depend on them? Professor Darryl Brown has recently noted that both prosecutors and judges have historically considered third-party interests in their charging and sentencing decisions, even though traditional criminal law theories do not suggest the consideration of such interests. See Darryl K. Brown, Third-Party Interests in Criminal Law, 80 Tex. L. Rev. 1383 (2002).

At least a few states have codified in their structured sentencing reforms the idea that judges should consider third-party concerns at sentencing. See Utah Guidelines Form 4 (providing that a mitigating factor to be considered at sentencing is that "imprisonment would entail excessive hardship on offender or dependents"). In the federal system, the appropriateness and place for considering third-party interests are less defined and less clear, although a number of commentators urge federal judges to incorporate these interests in their departure decision making. See Douglas A. Berman, Addressing Why: Developing Principled Rationales for Family-Based Departures, 13 Fed. Sentencing Rep. 274 (2001) (suggesting that third-party harms are primarily motivating federal departures based on family circumstances).

3. *The significance of upbringing and social environment.*   Criminologists, psychologists, and other social scientists trace the roots of much crime to deep social causes relating to the offenders' childhood social environment and upbringing. Recognizing that a poor childhood environment is not the offender's fault, should sentencing judges consider reducing an offender's sentence when her wrongdoing can be linked to childhood abuse or an otherwise unfortunate early social history? Not long after the federal sentencing guidelines were enacted, one federal circuit held that a downward departure was permissible based on the defendant's "youthful lack of guidance." United States v. Floyd, 945 F.2d 1096 (9th Cir. 1991). Fearing the potentially expansive reach of this ground for departing from the guidelines, the U.S. Sentencing Commission amended the sentencing guidelines to provide that "lack of guidance as a youth and similar circumstances indicating a disadvantaged upbringing are not relevant grounds for imposing a sentence outside the applicable guideline range." U.S. Sentencing Guidelines Manual §5H1.12. If you were a commissioner during this period, would you have favored or opposed this amendment? For a more general discussion of social environment theories and criminal law, see Patricia J. Falk, Novel Theories of Criminal Defense Based upon the Toxicity of the Social Environment: Urban Psychosis, Television Intoxication, and Black Rage, 74 N.C. L. Rev. 731 (1996). The defendant's unsupportive or abusive family of origin often figures into capital murder trials as defendants attempt to establish mitigating circumstances for the crime.

=6=

Procedure and Proof at Sentencing

Chapter 1 explored why society punishes, Chapter 2 focused on who sentences, Chapter 3 examined the discretion of sentencers, and Chapters 4 and 5 together examined what elements are factored into sentencing and punishment decisions. This chapter looks at how sentencing and punishment decisions are made.

Sentencing procedures involve two critical and related issues, one doctrinal, the other functional. The doctrinal issue concerns the applicability of established criminal trial rights to sentencing procedures. The Fifth and Sixth Amendments set forth some foundational rules for the prosecution and trial of criminal offenses. These provisions include both specific commands (for example, requiring "presentment or indictment" for "capital, or otherwise infamous" crimes) and notoriously abstract provisions (no person shall be "deprived of life, liberty, or property, without due process of law"). They are conspicuously silent, however, on the subject of sentencing. Determining whether and when certain trial rights apply at sentencing is discussed in the first half of this chapter.

The functional issue revolves around the reality that, even in the criminal justice system, justice is far more commonly negotiated than adjudicated. Though judges ultimately impose sentences in court, what happens before offenders appear in court to be sentenced — that is, the procedures that attend the charging and plea bargaining practices of prosecutors and the presentence investigations of probation officers — functions as the most critical determinant of the sentence for most offenders. These procedures are explored in the second part of this chapter.

A. CONSTITUTIONAL SENTENCING PROCEDURES: TRIAL VERSUS SENTENCING

The distinction between criminal trials and criminal sentencing is fairly obvious: trials determine a defendant's legal guilt; sentencing determines how a guilty defendant will be treated. Far less obvious is what this substantive distinction means for purposes of criminal procedures. Should the rights typically afforded to criminal defendants at trial also apply at sentencing? Should the same basic adjudicative procedures be utilized at both trial and sentencing or do the distinct concerns of each call for distinct sets of procedures? Should your answers to these questions be influenced by the reality that very few criminal defendants ever experience trial procedures because, in many jurisdictions, nine of every ten defendants waive their right to a trial by pleading guilty?

If you believe that different criminal procedures are appropriate (or inevitable) for trial and sentencing, who defines and decides which issues and facts are resolved at trial and which issues and facts will be considered only at sentencing? Should legislatures, which are usually responsible for defining crimes and also for authorizing punishments, have sole and unfettered authority to define what "elements" are subject to resolution at trial and what "sentencing factors" are subject to consideration only at sentencing after a guilty verdict has been secured? Or should courts have a role in defining what can be an element and what can be a sentencing factor?

1. Foundations

The Fifth and Sixth Amendments to the Constitution provide rules for the prosecution and trial of criminal offenses. Read the text of the Amendments closely: Do you find these commands specific or abstract compared to other rights specified in the Bill of Rights?

U.S. Const. Amend. V

No person shall be held to answer for a capital, or otherwise infamous crime, unless on a presentment or indictment of a grand jury . . . ; nor shall any person be subject for the same offense to be twice put in jeopardy of life or limb; nor shall be compelled in any criminal case to be a witness against himself, nor be deprived of life, liberty, or property, without due process of law. . . .

U.S. Const. Amend. VI

In all criminal prosecutions, the accused shall enjoy the right to a speedy and public trial, by an impartial jury . . . , and to be informed of the nature and cause of the accusation; to be confronted with the witnesses against him; to have compulsory process for obtaining witnesses in his favor, and to have the assistance of counsel for his defense.

Noticeably absent from the Amendments and indeed from most of the Constitution are explicit procedural rights at sentencing. When the Constitution speaks to punishment, it speaks to the legislative obligation to specify crimes and punishments before the crime and to give them general application (the Ex Post Facto and Bill of Attainder Clauses), or it limits the kinds of appropriate sanctions (the prohibition of "cruel and unusual punishments"), or it recognizes that convicted criminals have qualified civil rights (the Thirteenth Amendment's decree that "Neither slavery nor involuntary servitude, except as a punishment for crime whereof the party shall have been duly convicted, shall exist within the United States").

The silence on sentencing process is perhaps not surprising given the sentencing dynamics at the time of the founding: Following English traditions, during the founding era each particular criminal offense had a distinct and specific sentencing consequence, and thus the procedures and results of a criminal trial directly and conclusively determined an offender's sentence. See Report of the Twentieth Century Fund Task Force on Criminal Sentencing, Fair and Certain Punishment 83-85 (1976). In other words, the Constitution's failure to prescribe or mention specific regulations for the procedures at sentencing likely just reflects the fact that at the time of the founding there were no distinct sentencing procedures to be regulated.

But with the emergence of the penitentiary and a shift in punishment theory toward a rehabilitative model in the late nineteenth century, the direct connection between criminal verdict and the imposed sentence was severed and distinct sentencing proceedings emerged. Trial judges were given nearly unfettered discretion to impose on defendants any sentence from within the broad statutory ranges provided for criminal offenses and were permitted to consider any and all evidence when crafting a sentence. Over the first half of the twentieth century, such broad judicial discretion in the consideration of information and the imposition of sentencing terms came to be viewed as necessary to ensure that sentences could be tailored to the rehabilitative prospects of each offender. Judge and commentator Nancy Gertner has succinctly summarized this evolution:

> [I]n colonial times verdict and sentencing were closely linked. Felony conviction led to a definite punishment, often death, unless the defendant could offer a legal reason to excuse it. The jury's verdict was the pivotal event. Pronouncement of the sentence by the judge was an essentially ministerial task.
>
> By the nineteenth century, tradition and changes in penology dramatically altered the function of sentencing, while the jury's functions changed little. The sentencing model was now a therapeutic one, seeking to rehabilitate the offender. Each offense carried a very broad range of potential sentences; the judge had the discretion to pick any sentence within the range.

Nancy Gertner, *Apprendi* and the Return of the Criminal Code, 37 Crim. L. Bull. 553, 557 (2001).

The emergence of a distinct sentencing proceeding raised questions about whether traditional trial rights ought to apply at sentencing. These questions came before the Supreme Court most dramatically in Williams v. New York, 337 U.S. 241 (1949), after the progressive rehabilitative model of sentencing had already been dominant for nearly half a century. The trial judge in *Williams* sentenced to death a defendant convicted of first-degree murder, despite a jury recommendation of life imprisonment, relying on information of illegal and unsavory activities by the defendant that was not presented at trial but was alleged in a presentence report. Williams appealed and claimed that he had a right at sentencing — as he would at trial on the question of guilt or innocence — to confront and cross-examine the witnesses against him.

The Supreme Court in *Williams* approved the reliance on informal procedures at sentencing. The Court stressed that "[r]eformation and rehabilitation of offenders have become important goals of criminal jurisprudence" and spoke approvingly of the "prevalent modern philosophy of penology that the punishment should fit the offender and not merely the crime." Thus the Constitution should not be read to require courts to abandon the "practice of seeking information from out-of-court sources," because "[t]o deprive sentencing judges of this kind of information would undermine modern penological procedural policies," which rely on judges' access to "the fullest information possible concerning the defendant's life and characteristics."

According to the *Williams* Court, the value of "modern concepts individualizing punishments" meant that sentencing judges should "not be denied an opportunity to obtain pertinent information by a requirement of rigid adherence to restrictive rules of evidence properly applicable to the trial." In other words, the rehabilitative ideal not only justified entrusting judges with enormous sentencing discretion, it also called for sentencing judges to be freed from any procedural trial rules that might work to limit the sound exercise of their discretion.

Williams was decided before the Supreme Court began "revolutionizing" criminal procedure by expansively interpreting the Constitution to provide criminal defendants with an array of procedural rights. Nevertheless, throughout the 1960s and 1970s, as numerous pretrial and trial rights were being established for defendants, the Supreme Court continued to cite *Williams* favorably and continued to suggest that sentencing was to be treated differently — and should be far less procedurally regulated — than a traditional criminal trial. See Chaffin v. Stynchcombe, 412 U.S. 17, 21-25 (1973) (reviewing *Williams* while stressing "the need for flexibility and discretion in the sentencing process"); North Carolina v. Pearce, 395 U.S. 711, 723 (1969) (favorably citing *Williams* while stressing "the freedom of a sentencing judge" to consider a defendant's postconviction conduct in imposing a sentence).

Though the Supreme Court did hold that defendants had a right to an attorney at sentencing hearings in Mempa v. Rhay, 389 U.S. 128 (1967), and suggested defendants also had a right to discovery of evidence that could affect a sentence in Brady v. Maryland, 373 U.S. 83 (1963), the Court did not formally extend other Bill of Rights protections to the sentencing process. Indeed, the Supreme Court throughout this period repeatedly stated that at sentencing "a judge may appropriately conduct an inquiry broad in scope, largely unlimited either as to the kind of information he may consider, or the source from which it may come." United States v. Grayson, 438 U.S. 41, 52 (1978).

As the Supreme Court continued to cite *Williams* favorably and to sanction informal sentencing procedures, the theory supporting the rehabilitative model of sentencing itself came under attack. Through the 1960s and 1970s, criminal justice researchers and scholars grew increasingly concerned about the unpredictable and disparate sentences produced by highly discretionary sentencing systems, and such concerns dovetailed with broader complaints about increasing crime rates and with potent theoretical and practical criticisms of the rehabilitative model of punishment and corrections.

Reform proposals eventually began to surface, and before long jurisdictions started to adopt structured sentencing laws in the form of determinate sentencing statutes, which abolished parole and created presumptive sentencing ranges, or in the form of full-fledged sentencing guideline systems. During the last quarter of the twentieth century, legislatures and sentencing commissions continued to adopt structured sentencing reforms, and these legal changes created a considerable amount of sentencing law by defining an array of issues and facts that judges must or should address at sentencing.

But conspicuously absent from modern sentencing reform has been an express concern for sentencing procedures. Despite creating a significant body of substantive sentencing law, lawmakers and commissions have largely ignored fundamental issues such as notice to parties, burdens of proof, appropriate factfinders, evidentiary rules, and hearing processes, even though these procedural matters play a central role in the application of general sentencing rules to specific cases.

Some critics of lax sentencing procedures blame this neglect on the Supreme Court's decision in McMillan v. Pennsylvania, 477 U.S. 79 (1986). Litigated during the early development of structured sentencing reforms, *McMillan* involved a constitutional challenge to a Pennsylvania statute passed in 1982 requiring that a five-year minimum sentence be imposed if the judge finds, by a preponderance of evidence, that an offender visibly possessed a firearm during the commission of certain offenses. The defendant in *McMillan* argued that the Constitution required treating the fact of firearm possession as an offense element with the traditional trial procedures of proof beyond a reasonable doubt and the right to a jury. Consider the Supreme Court's response to this claim.

Dynel McMillan v. Pennsylvania
477 U.S. 79 (1986)

Rehnquist, J.

Pennsylvania's Mandatory Minimum Sentencing Act, 42 Pa. Cons. Stat. 9712 (1982) (the Act) . . . was adopted in 1982. It provides that anyone convicted of certain enumerated felonies is subject to a mandatory minimum sentence of five years' imprisonment if the sentencing judge finds, by a preponderance of the evidence, that the person "visibly possessed a firearm" during the commission of the offense. At the sentencing hearing, the judge is directed to consider the evidence introduced at trial and any additional evidence offered by either the defendant or the Commonwealth. The Act operates to divest the judge of discretion to impose any sentence of less than five years for the underlying felony; it does not authorize a sentence in excess of that otherwise allowed for that offense. . . .

McMillan, who shot his victim in the right buttock after an argument over a debt, was convicted by a jury of aggravated assault. [T]he Commonwealth gave notice that at sentencing it would seek to proceed under the Act, [but] the sentencing judge . . . found the Act unconstitutional. . . . Petitioners' principal argument was that visible possession of a firearm is an element of the crimes for which they were being sentenced and thus must be proved beyond a reasonable doubt under In re Winship, 397 U.S. 358 (1970). . . . Petitioners also contended that even if visible possession is not an element of the offense, due process requires more than proof by a preponderance of the evidence. The Supreme Court of Pennsylvania rejected [these claims, unanimously concluding that the Act is consistent with due process].

Petitioners argue that under the Due Process Clause . . . , if a State wants to punish visible possession of a firearm it must undertake the burden of proving that fact beyond a reasonable doubt. We disagree. *Winship* held that "the Due Process Clause protects the accused against conviction except upon proof beyond a reasonable doubt of every fact necessary to constitute the crime with which he is charged." In Mullaney v. Wilbur, 421 U.S. 684 (1975), we held that the Due Process Clause "requires the prosecution to prove beyond a reasonable doubt the absence of the heat of passion on sudden provocation when the issue is properly presented in a homicide case." But in Patterson [v. New York, 432 U.S. 197 (1977)], we rejected the claim that whenever a State links the "severity of punishment" to "the presence or absence of an identified fact" the State must prove that fact beyond a reasonable doubt. In particular, we upheld against a due process challenge New York's law placing on defendants charged with murder the burden of proving the affirmative defense of extreme emotional disturbance.

Patterson stressed that in determining what facts must be proved beyond a reasonable doubt the state legislature's definition of the elements of the offense is usually dispositive: "[T]he Due Process Clause requires the prosecution to prove beyond a reasonable doubt all of the elements included in the definition of the offense of which the defendant is charged." While "there are obviously constitutional limits beyond which the States may not go in this regard," "[t]he applicability of the reasonable-doubt standard . . . has always been dependent on how a State defines the offense that is charged in any given case."

As the Supreme Court of Pennsylvania observed, the Pennsylvania Legislature has expressly provided that visible possession of a firearm is not an element of the crimes enumerated in the mandatory sentencing statute, but instead is a sentencing factor that comes into play only after the defendant has been found guilty of one of those crimes beyond a reasonable doubt. . . . While visible possession might well have included as an element of the enumerated offenses, Pennsylvania chose not to redefine those offenses in order to so include it, and *Patterson* teaches that we should hesitate to conclude that due process bars the State from pursuing its chosen course in the area of defining crimes and prescribing penalties.

As *Patterson* recognized, of course, there are constitutional limits to the State's power in this regard; in certain limited circumstances *Winship*'s reasonable-doubt requirement applies to facts not formally identified as elements of the offense charged. Petitioners argue that Pennsylvania has gone beyond those limits and that its formal provision that visible possession is not an element of the crime is therefore of no effect. We do not think so. While we have never attempted to define precisely the constitutional limits [on] the extent to which due process forbids the reallocation or reduction of burdens of proof in criminal cases, and do not do so today, we are persuaded by several factors that Pennsylvania's Mandatory Minimum Sentencing Act does not exceed those limits.

We note first that the Act plainly does not . . . discard the presumption of innocence [nor] relieve the prosecution of its burden of proving guilt; §9712 only becomes applicable after a defendant has been duly convicted of the crime for which he is to be punished. [Further] §9712 neither alters the maximum penalty for the crime committed nor creates a separate offense calling for a separate penalty; it operates solely to limit the sentencing court's discretion in selecting a penalty within the range already available to it without the special finding of visible possession of a firearm. Section 9712 "ups the ante" for the defendant only by raising to five years the minimum sentence which may be imposed within the statutory plan. The statute gives no impression of having been tailored to permit the visible possession finding to be a tail which wags the dog of the substantive offense. Petitioners' claim that visible possession under the

Pennsylvania statute is "really" an element of the offenses for which they are being punished — that Pennsylvania has in effect defined a new set of upgraded felonies — would have at least more superficial appeal if a finding of visible possession exposed them to greater or additional punishment, but it does not. . . .

Finally, we note that the specter raised by petitioners of States restructuring existing crimes in order to "evade" the commands of *Winship* just does not appear in this case. As noted above, §9712's enumerated felonies retain the same elements they had before the Mandatory Minimum Sentencing Act was passed. The Pennsylvania Legislature did not change the definition of any existing offense. It simply took one factor that has always been considered by sentencing courts to bear on punishment — the instrumentality used in committing a violent felony — and dictated the precise weight to be given that factor if the instrumentality is a firearm. Pennsylvania's decision to do so has not transformed against its will a sentencing factor into an "element" of some hypothetical "offense."

Petitioners seek support for their due process claim by observing that many legislatures have made possession of a weapon an element of various aggravated offenses. But the fact that the States have formulated different statutory schemes to punish armed felons is merely a reflection of our federal system, which demands tolerance for a spectrum of state procedures dealing with a common problem of law enforcement. That Pennsylvania's particular approach has been adopted in few other States does not render Pennsylvania's choice unconstitutional. . . .

Our inability to lay down any "bright line" test may leave the constitutionality of statutes . . . to depend on differences of degree, but the law is full of situations in which differences of degree produce different results. We have no doubt that Pennsylvania's Mandatory Minimum Sentencing Act falls on the permissible side of the constitutional line.

Having concluded that States may treat "visible possession of a firearm" as a sentencing consideration rather than an element of a particular offense, we now turn to petitioners' subsidiary claim that due process nonetheless requires that visible possession be proved by at least clear and convincing evidence. Like the court below, we have little difficulty concluding that in this case the preponderance standard satisfies due process. [P]etitioners do not and could not claim that a sentencing court may never rely on a particular fact in passing sentence without finding that fact by "clear and convincing evidence." Sentencing courts have traditionally heard evidence and found facts without any prescribed burden of proof at all. See Williams v. New York, 337 U.S. 241 (1949). Pennsylvania has deemed a particular fact relevant and prescribed a particular burden of proof. We see nothing in Pennsylvania's scheme that would warrant constitutionalizing burdens of proof at sentencing.

Petitioners apparently concede that Pennsylvania's scheme would pass constitutional muster if only it did not remove the sentencing court's discretion, i.e., if the legislature had simply directed the court to consider visible possession in passing sentence. We have some difficulty fathoming why the due process calculus would change simply because the legislature has seen fit to provide sentencing courts with additional guidance. Nor is there merit to the claim that a heightened burden of proof is required because visible possession is a fact concerning the crime committed rather than the background or character of the defendant. Sentencing courts necessarily consider the circumstances of an offense in selecting the appropriate punishment, and we have consistently approved sentencing schemes that mandate consideration of facts related to the crime, without suggesting that those facts must be proved beyond a reasonable doubt.

In light of the foregoing, petitioners' final claim — that the Act denies them their Sixth Amendment right to a trial by jury — merits little discussion. Petitioners again argue that the jury must determine all ultimate facts concerning the offense committed. Having concluded that Pennsylvania may properly treat visible possession as a sentencing consideration and not an element of any offense, we need only note that there is no Sixth Amendment right to jury sentencing, even where the sentence turns on specific findings of fact.

STEVENS, J., dissenting.

. . . It is common ground that "the Due Process Clause requires the prosecution to prove beyond a reasonable doubt all of the elements included in the definition of the offense of which the defendant is charged." Patterson v. New York, 432 U.S. 197 (1977). Today the Court holds that state legislatures may not only define the offense with which a criminal defendant is charged, but may also authoritatively determine that the conduct so described — i.e., the prohibited activity which subjects the defendant to criminal sanctions — is not an element of the crime which the Due Process Clause requires to be proved by the prosecution beyond a reasonable doubt. In my view, a state legislature may not dispense with the requirement of proof beyond a reasonable doubt for conduct that it targets for severe criminal penalties. Because the Pennsylvania statute challenged in this case describes conduct that the Pennsylvania Legislature obviously intended to prohibit, and because it mandates lengthy incarceration for the same, I believe that the conduct so described is an element of the criminal offense to which the proof beyond a reasonable doubt requirement applies.

Once a State defines a criminal offense, the Due Process Clause requires it to prove any component of the prohibited transaction that gives rise to both a special stigma and a special punishment beyond a reasonable doubt. This much has been evident at least since In re Winship, 397 U.S. 358 (1970)[, which] "explicitly" held that "the Due Process Clause protects the accused against conviction except upon proof beyond a reasonable doubt of every fact necessary to constitute the crime with which he is charged." . . . In re Winship thus took a purposive approach to the constitutional standard of proof: when the State threatens to stigmatize or incarcerate an individual for engaging in prohibited conduct, it may do so only if it proves the elements of the prohibited transaction beyond a reasonable doubt.

It is true, as the Court points out, that the applicability of the reasonable-doubt standard has always been dependent on how a State defines the offense that is charged in any given case. A State's freedom in this regard, however, has always been understood to reflect the uncontroversial proposition that a State has power, subject of course to constitutional limits, to attach criminal penalties to a wide variety of objectionable transactions; when it does so, the prosecution need establish beyond a reasonable doubt only the constituent elements of the specified criminal transaction. Nothing in Patterson or any of its predecessors authorizes a State to decide for itself which of the ingredients of the prohibited transaction are "elements" that it must prove beyond a reasonable doubt at trial.

Indeed, contrary to the supposition of the majority, Patterson v. New York is entirely in keeping with the limit on state definitional power implied in *Winship*. *Patterson* . . . clarified that the Due Process Clause requires proof beyond a reasonable doubt of conduct which exposes a criminal defendant to greater stigma or punishment, but does not likewise constrain state reductions of criminal penalties — even if such reductions are conditioned on a prosecutor's failure to prove a fact by a preponderance of the evidence or on proof supplied by the criminal defendant. . . . In re Winship and *Patterson* teach that a State may not advance the objectives of its criminal laws at the expense of the accurate factfinding owed to the criminally accused who suffer the risk of nonpersuasion.

It would demean the importance of the reasonable-doubt standard — indeed, it would demean the Constitution itself — if the substance of the standard could be avoided by nothing more than a legislative declaration that prohibited conduct is not an "element" of a crime. A legislative definition of an offense named "assault" could be broad enough to encompass every intentional infliction of harm by one person upon another, but surely the legislature could not provide that only that fact must be proved beyond a reasonable doubt and then specify a range of increased punishments if the prosecution could show by a preponderance of the evidence that the defendant robbed, raped, or killed his victim "during the commission of the offense."

Appropriate respect for the rule of In re Winship requires that there be some constitutional limits on the power of a State to define the elements of criminal offenses. The high standard of proof is required because of the immense importance of the individual interest in avoiding both the loss of liberty and the stigma that results from a criminal conviction. It follows, I submit, that if a State provides that a specific component of a prohibited transaction shall give rise both to a special stigma and to a special punishment, that component must be treated as a "fact necessary to constitute the crime" within the meaning of our holding in In re Winship.

Pennsylvania's Mandatory Minimum Sentencing Act reflects a legislative determination that a defendant who "visibly possessed a firearm" during the commission of an aggravated assault is more blameworthy than a defendant who did not. A judicial finding that the defendant used a firearm in an aggravated assault places a greater stigma on the defendant's name than a simple finding that he committed an aggravated assault. . . .

It is true, as the Court points out, that the enhanced punishment is within the range that was authorized for any aggravated assault. That fact does not, however, minimize the significance of a finding of visible possession of a firearm whether attention is focused on the stigmatizing or punitive consequences of that finding. The finding identifies conduct that the legislature specifically intended to prohibit and to punish by a special sanction. In my opinion the constitutional significance of the special sanction cannot be avoided by the cavalier observation that it merely "ups the ante" for the defendant. . . .

NOTES

1. *Standard of proof at sentencing.* In *McMillan*, the Court noted that "[s]entencing courts have traditionally heard evidence and found facts without

any prescribed burden of proof at all." What does it mean to have no prescribed burden of proof? Can sentencing judges rely on whatever facts tickle their fancy? A more plausible reading of the *McMillan* holding is that the Constitution's Due Process Clause allows states to treat some facts relevant to the sentence as "sentencing factors" subject only to proof by a preponderance of the evidence at sentencing. Legislatures, the Court said, ordinarily have the authority to decide which facts are "elements" of a crime, to be proven to a jury at trial beyond a reasonable doubt, and which are "sentencing factors," to be proven after conviction to a sentencing judge by a preponderance. Only when an extreme increase in punishment attaches to a sentencing factor — or, to use the Court's terms, when the "tail" of the sentencing factor "wags the dog" of the substantive offense — will a federal court overturn the legislature's choices.

Virtually all states use the preponderance standard for facts to be proven at sentencing, although this seemingly critical issue of sentencing procedure has not been litigated (or even expressly considered) as often as one might expect. When the issue does arise, most state courts have held that their state constitutions allow the prosecution to prove certain facts to increase a sentence using the lower standard of proof at sentencing. See, e.g., People v. Williams, 599 N.E.2d 913 (Ill. 1992). Does the issue of allocating facts between the offense and sentencing arise in an indeterminate sentencing system? In such a system, in which sentencing judges typically pronounce sentences from the bench without any written opinion, how can a defendant know what standard of proof was applied? Are the judges making factual determinations that can be regulated through standards of proof or are they making legal judgments for which standards of proof seem less applicable?

Structured sentencing systems, which distinctly define the factual issues and determinations that can have an impact on sentencing outcomes, often expressly establish preponderance of the evidence as the standard of proof at sentencing. In the federal system, the U.S. Sentencing Commission, in commentary to a policy statement on resolution of disputed factors, stated that "use of a preponderance of the evidence standard is appropriate to meet due process requirements and policy concerns in resolving disputes regarding application of the guidelines to the facts of a case." U.S. Sentencing Guidelines Manual §6A1.3. Do you agree with this conclusion? Why shouldn't the traditional standard of proof beyond a reasonable doubt apply at sentencing? Might one argue that some other standard (such as clear and convincing evidence) would be more sensible as a standard of proof at sentencing?

As previously noted in Chapter 3, most state sentencing guideline systems look to the offense of conviction when determining a presumptive guideline sentencing range. Thus, structured sentencing decisions in most states begin with factual determinations relating to the offense of conviction that are either proven beyond a reasonable doubt at trial or admitted by the defendant in a guilty plea. Yet state guideline systems typically allow judges to select a specific sentence from within sometimes broad sentencing ranges, and also, to varying degrees, allow departures from the sentencing ranges provided in the guidelines. Judges' selection of a specific sentence and consideration of possible departures might be based on facts developed only at a sentencing hearing, and on these matters judges seem content to rely on facts established only by a preponderance of the evidence (to the extent they consider the standard of proof issues at all).

In guideline systems, not only can certain aggravating factors lead to an increase in the applicable sentence, but certain mitigating factors can lead to a decrease in the applicable sentence. For example, in the federal system, the sentencing guidelines provide that a defendant's sentence will be more severe if the prosecution establishes that the defendant led a large criminal enterprise but significantly less severe if the defendant establishes that her role was minor or minimal. Should the Constitution be interpreted to require different standards of proof depending on whether a fact is raised by prosecutors seeking an increase in the applicable sentence or by defendants seeking a decrease in the applicable sentence? Whether or not the Constitution might recognize such a distinction, should legislatures and sentencing commissions develop different procedural rules and evidence standards for aggravating and mitigating facts?

2. *Consequences of* McMillan. It is important to remember that in 1986, when *McMillan* was decided, only a few states had guideline systems in place, and the federal guideline system was in development stages. Since then, as many more jurisdictions have adopted forms of structured sentencing, two contrasting developments have emerged. State courts and lower federal courts, citing *McMillan* and *Williams* as controlling authority, have consistently rejected constitutional challenges to structured sentencing systems that imposed punishment without affording defendants at sentencing the procedural protections of a criminal trial. See, e.g., State v. Rettinghaus, 591 N.W.2d 15 (Iowa 1999); Farris v. McKune, 911 P.2d 177 (Kan. 1996); State v. Christie, 506 N.W.2d 293 (Minn. 1993); United States v. Mergerson, 995 F.2d 1285 (5th Cir. 1993); United States v. Restrepo, 946 F.2d 654 (9th Cir. 1991) (en banc). At the same time, individual judges and academic commentators have regularly lamented the continued adherence to *McMillan* and *Williams* as controlling authority, citing the unfairness of subjecting defendants to fact-driven guideline sentencing determinations without significant procedural rights. See, e.g., United States v. Concepcion, 983 F.2d 369, 389, 396 (2d Cir. 1992) (Newman, C.J., concurring); Mark D. Knoll and Richard G. Singer, Searching for the "Tail of the Dog": Finding "Elements" of Crimes in the Wake of McMillan v. Pennsylvania, 22 Seattle U. L. Rev. 1057 (1999); Deborah Young, Fact-Finding at Federal Sentencing: Why the Guidelines Should Meet the Rules, 79 Cornell L. Rev. 299 (1994); Sara Sun Beale, Procedural Issues Raised by Guidelines Sentencing: The Constitutional Significance of the "Elements of the Sentence," 35 Wm. & Mary L. Rev. 147 (1993); Kevin R. Reitz, Sentencing Facts: Travesties of Real-Offense Sentencing, 45 Stan. L. Rev. 523 (1993).

3. *Tails wagging dogs.* The opinion in McMillan v. Pennsylvania noted the concern that prosecutors might manipulate charges so that the most questionable evidence would be heard for the first time after conviction at a sentencing hearing involving a lower standard of proof. Obviously, the success of such efforts will depend on how the legislature defines the elements of the crime. Most state courts have upheld legislative decisions that allow the government to prove some facts as "sentencing enhancements" at the sentencing hearing. See Vega v. People, 893 P.2d 107 (Colo. 1995). Only rarely have courts found that a fact introduced at sentencing was so important that it required proof by some standard higher than a preponderance. In United States v. Kikumura, 918 F.2d 1084 (3d Cir. 1990), the federal sentencing guidelines prescribed a sentence of between 27 and 33 months for explosives and passport violations. The sentencing

court, however, departed from this range to impose a 30-year sentence based on evidence that the defendant was engaged in terrorist activities for the Japanese Red Army. Although the appeals court acknowledged that most sentencing facts could be proven under a preponderance standard, it held that a clear and convincing standard should apply to this case: "[Here] we are dealing with findings that would increase Kikumura's sentence from about 30 months to 30 years. . . . This is perhaps the most dramatic example imaginable of a sentencing hearing that functions as 'a tail which wags the dog of the substantive offense.'"

4. *Informal procedures and rules of evidence at sentencing.*   Most states allow sentencing judges to consider evidence inadmissible under the rules of evidence. See Tex. Crim. Proc. Code Ann. §37.07(3). Particularly in states with an indeterminate sentencing system, the informal presentation of evidence supposedly supports an effort to obtain the most information possible about the offender and the offense and to make an individualized (perhaps even clinical) decision about the best response to the case and the offender at hand. More than half of the states use such an indeterminate sentencing system for large groups of cases, although many of these same states use more narrowly circumscribed sentencing rules for some crimes.

Most states indicate that evidence presented at sentencing must be relevant and reliable with the terms defined broadly to ensure that sentencing is governed by individualized considerations based on information from a wide variety of sources. As in *Williams*, reliable hearsay is often allowed, and many sentencings are based mostly or entirely on hearsay. According to one court, the Constitution prohibits sentencing only on "materially untrue information." State v. Ramsay, 499 A.2d 15, 20 (Vt. 1985).

Williams further established that, as a matter of federal constitutional law, the rules of evidence that apply in criminal trials need not apply in sentencing hearings. The federal rules of evidence adopt this position explicitly: "the rules (other than with respect to privileges) do not apply in . . . sentencing." Fed. R. Evid. 1101(d)(3). The federal sentencing guidelines adopt the following standard: "any information may be considered, so long as it has sufficient indicia of reliability to support its probable accuracy." U.S. Sentencing Guidelines Manual §6A1.3(a). Is the federal guideline standard higher or lower than *Williams*?

Those who argue in favor of the current federal position (and a similar position in many states) explain that rules of evidence do not apply because of the burden they would place on sentencing judges, converting the sentencing hearing into a second trial. Should Congress or the U.S. Sentencing Commission change positions and apply the rules of evidence to sentencing hearings? Professor Deborah Young favors use of the rules of evidence over other methods of increasing the reliability of factfinding at sentencing because it corrects both potential errors that benefit the prosecution along with those that benefit the defense. She argues that evenhanded factfinding rules make sense at sentencing since an offender has already been convicted and should no longer be given the benefit of the presumption of innocence. Deborah Young, Fact-Finding at Federal Sentencing: Why the Guidelines Should Meet the Rules, 79 Cornell L. Rev. 299 (1994).

5. *Confrontation of witnesses.*   Although the evidentiary rules governing hearsay do not apply to sentencing hearings in federal or state courts, the

overlapping protections of the Sixth Amendment's Confrontation Clause (and the equivalent provisions of a state constitution) still might require that a defendant be allowed to cross-examine witnesses at the sentencing hearing. The small group of courts addressing this question have mostly concluded that the Confrontation Clause does not apply to the evidence presented during a sentencing hearing. For example, in United States v. Wise, 976 F.2d 393 (8th Cir. 1992), the sentencing court relied on hearsay testimony by a probation officer regarding facts contained in the presentence investigation report. The judge allowed the defendant to cross-examine the probation officer and to introduce witnesses of his own, but did not prevent the probation officer from introducing hearsay statements into evidence. The appellate court upheld the sentence and concluded that confrontation of witnesses at sentencing was not necessary. See also State v. DeSalvo, 903 P.2d 202 (Mont. 1995).

In capital sentencing proceedings, however, different rules apply, since the imposition of a death sentence based on information that a defendant does not have the opportunity to deny or explain may run afoul of the Confrontation Clause. See Gardner v. Florida, 430 U.S. 349 (1977); Grandison v. State, 670 A.2d 398 (Md. 1995). The Supreme Court has held that the sentencing hearing is part of the "criminal proceedings" and that the right to counsel applies at that stage of the proceedings. Mempa v. Rhay, 389 U.S. 128 (1967) (establishing right to counsel at sentencing). If the Sixth Amendment's right to counsel (granted to "the accused") applies at sentencing, why doesn't the same conclusion apply to the Sixth Amendment's right to confront witnesses?

6. *Right to remain silent.*   In Mitchell v. United States, 526 U.S. 314 (1999), the Supreme Court held that a defendant, after pleading guilty to a specific offense, can assert her Fifth Amendment privilege against self-incrimination at the sentencing hearing and not have a judge draw an adverse inference from the defendant's sentence. Mitchell had refused to testify at a sentencing hearing about her involvement in a cocaine conspiracy. The sentencing judge drew a negative inference from the defendant's refusal to discuss the amount of drugs involved in the offense and sentenced the defendant to ten years' imprisonment. The Supreme Court reversed, holding that neither the defendant's guilty plea nor her statements at a plea colloquy functioned as a waiver of her right to remain silent at sentencing. Furthermore, relying on Griffin v. California, 380 U.S. 609 (1995), which held that it was constitutionally impermissible for the prosecutor or judge to comment on a criminal defendant's refusal to testify, the Court concluded that the defendant should have been allowed to remain silent without its being held against her.

7. *Other rights at sentencing.*   Although many academic commentators focus on (and lament) the courts' refusal to extend to sentencing traditional trial rights and procedures relating to proof and evidence standards, Professor Alan Michaels has pointed out that many more trial rights apply at sentencing than one might be led to believe. In a recent article, Michaels systematically examined judicial decisions regarding the applicability of constitutional trial rights to sentencing proceedings and produced a comprehensive taxonomy of sentencing rights. Summarizing his work, Michaels explained that

> examin[ing] twenty-five rights — from employing an attorney to not having inferences drawn from one's silence, from bail and Brady to presence and

proceeding pro se — [reveals] that the Supreme Court has found roughly one quarter apply at sentencing and one quarter do not. The rights in the remaining half, still undecided at the Supreme Court level, have been resolved with similar percentages by lower courts — some apply, some do not, and about half remain unresolved.

Alan C. Michaels, Trial Rights at Sentencing, 81 N.C. L. Rev. 1771, 1775 (2003). According to Michaels, the Court's decisions tend to follow what he calls a "best estimate" principle: "[trial] rights that are directed primarily at determining the correct result apply at sentencing, whereas those rights designed to offer special protection to a defendant's liberty or autonomy interests do not." *Id.* at 1771. The chart below shows Michaels' findings with regard to U.S. Supreme Court and lower court rulings on whether a particular right applies at sentencing (**YES** or **NO** for a definitive decision that the right does or does not apply at sentencing; **yes** or **no** for a strong indication that the right does or does not apply at sentencing) or is still unresolved (**?**).

| | At Sentencing | | |
Right	U.S. Supreme Court	Lower Courts	Source
Counsel			
to use an attorney	YES	—	6th
for indigents	YES	—	6th
effective assistance	yes	YES	6th
counsel of choice	?	yes/split	6th
proceed pro se	?	split	6th
Bail			
nonexcessive bail	yes	?	8th
bail at all	no	no	5th
Notice of charges	?	yes	5th/6th
Trial by jury	NO	—	6th
Discovery (*Brady*)	yes	YES	5th
Double jeopardy			
no postverdict adverse change	NO	—	5th
collateral estoppel	?	?	5th
Speedy trial	?	split	6th
Public trial	?	yes	6th
Proof beyond a reasonable doubt	NO	—	
Confrontation			
use of hearsay	no	NO	6th
in court procedures	?	no	6th
right of presence	?	YES	6th
To present evidence			
to speak	?	split	5th/6th
to rebut state's evidence	?	yes	5th
to call witnesses	?	no	6th
To remain silent			
not to testify	YES	—	5th
no use of compelled testimony	?	split	5th
no inference regarding facts	YES	—	5th
no inference regarding other	?	?	5th

2. Modern Understanding

As detailed above, the absence of express constitutional provisions regulating sentencing proceedings explains in part the Supreme Court's decisions in Williams v. New York and McMillan v. Pennsylvania to uphold sentencing schemes that afforded defendants only limited procedural rights. Yet, also of considerable significance was the Court's ability to recognize and rely on a considered philosophical justification for such sentencing schemes. Particularly in *Williams,* the Court permitted the informal presentation of evidence within an indeterminate sentencing system to foster obtaining broad information about the offender and the offense that would facilitate an individualized, rehabilitation-oriented sentencing decision.

But as faith in the rehabilitative ideal began to decline, and many jurisdictions developed structured sentencing reforms in which sentencing determinations turned on predetermined and particularized facts, sentencing began to resemble a more trial-like enterprise and the justification for having limited procedural rights at sentencing lost a key foundation. Yet legislators and sentencing commissions enacting structured sentencing reforms paid little attention to procedural rules and generally failed to set forth express justifications for continuing to rely on lax procedures even as sentencing proceedings became more trial-like. As a result, the soundness and stability of *Williams* and *McMillan* became progressively more questionable.

Nevertheless, throughout the 1990s, a series of procedural rulings by the Supreme Court still seemed to sanction limited procedural rights at sentencing. In Nichols v. United States, 511 U.S. 738 (1994), the Court held that a sentencing court may consider a defendant's previous uncounseled misdemeanor conviction when sentencing him for a subsequent offense, and it cited both *Williams* and *McMillan* when stressing that the "traditional understanding of the sentencing process [is] . . . less exacting than the process of establishing guilt." In Witte v. United States, 515 U.S. 389 (1995), the Court, relying heavily on *Williams* and *McMillan* and on sentencing courts' tradition of considering a wide range of information without the procedural protections of a criminal trial, held that there was no double jeopardy violation when a prior conviction increased punishment through sentence calculations under the federal sentencing guidelines. In United States v. Watts, 519 U.S. 148 (1997), the Court stressed the "significance of the different standards of proof that govern at trial and sentencing" in holding that courts sentencing under the federal guidelines could consider conduct relating to charges of which defendants had been acquitted.

Although Justice Stevens was alone in expressing dissatisfaction with these holdings, they ultimately preceded the watershed change in the modern understanding of required sentencing procedures established in the *Apprendi* decision reprinted below. Throughout the 1990s, defendants' repeated claims for greater procedural rights at sentencing served to highlight the impact of limited procedural guarantees at sentencing. The claims also underscored the conceptual difficulties of preserving a uniquely limited procedural regime for sentencing when sentencing decision making, because of structured sentencing reforms, was becoming more of a trial-like enterprise. Indeed, though now overshadowed by the *Apprendi* decision, the Supreme Court's decisions in Almendarez-Torres v. United States, 523 U.S. 224 (1998), and Jones v. United States, 526 U.S.

227 (1999), showed that the traditional approach to sentencing procedures was being strained to the breaking point.

In *Almendarez-Torres,* the Supreme Court interpreted the federal alien reentry statute, which imposed punishment of up to two years in prison if a deported alien reentered the United States without permission but provided for an enhanced maximum sentence of 20 years if the alien had been convicted of an aggravated felony before deportation. Although the United States sought the enhanced sentence for defendant Almendarez-Torres, the government had not alleged his prior felony in the indictment or proven it at trial but rather submitted proof of it only at sentencing. On appeal, Almendarez-Torres claimed that he could not be given a sentence longer than two years, arguing that the recidivism issue could not be treated as a mere sentencing enhancement but rather constituted an element of the separate aggravated felony authorizing the 20-year sentence. In a 5-4 decision, the Supreme Court interpreted the reentry statute as providing that the recidivism enhancement was only a sentencing factor, and thus not subject to the procedural rules and limitations that surround the consideration of elements of crimes at trial. The majority opinion, authored by Justice Breyer, emphasized that recidivism long has been a sentencing factor not needing to be proven to the jury. The dissent, authored by Justice Scalia, urged interpreting the recidivism sentence enhancement as an element of the offense so as to avoid constitutional questions over whether the prior felony conviction had to be proved as an element before the maximum sentence could be increased beyond two years.

When a similar issue arose the following term in Jones v. United States, there were five votes to recast what looked like a sentencing factor as a traditional element of an offense. Reinterpreting *Almendarez-Torres* as creating a recidivism "exception" to a rule that provisions establishing higher penalties must be considered elements of the offense, the 5-4 majority in *Jones* thought that the federal carjacking statute created distinct crimes with distinct elements when successive subsections defined increasing maximum penalty levels if the offense resulted in serious bodily injury or death. In a revealing footnote, the *Jones* Court asserted that "a set of constitutional concerns that have emerged through a series of our decisions over the past quarter century" suggested the principle that "under the Due Process Clause of the Fifth Amendment and the notice and jury trial guarantees of the Sixth Amendment, any fact (other than prior conviction) that increases the maximum penalty for a crime must be charged in an indictment, submitted to a jury, and proven beyond a reasonable doubt."

With that foundation laid, the Supreme Court heard a case from New Jersey that squarely presented the constitutional question whether states could continue to deem as sentencing factors those facts that operated to increase the maximum sentence that the defendant could face.

Charles Apprendi v. New Jersey
530 U.S. 466 (2000)

STEVENS, J.

The question presented is whether the Due Process Clause of the Fourteenth Amendment requires that a factual determination authorizing an increase in the maximum prison sentence for an offense . . . be made by a jury on the basis of proof beyond a reasonable doubt.

At 2:04 A.M. on December 22, 1994, Charles C. Apprendi, Jr., fired several .22-caliber bullets into the home of an African-American family that had recently moved into a previously all-white neighborhood in Vineland, New Jersey. Apprendi was promptly arrested and admitted that he was the shooter. After further questioning, he made a statement — which he later retracted — that even though he did not know the occupants of the house personally, "because they are black in color he does not want them in the neighborhood."

A grand jury returned a 23-count indictment charging Apprendi with [crimes arising from] shootings on four different dates, as well as the unlawful possession of various weapons. [Pursuant to a plea agreement] Apprendi pleaded guilty to two counts of 2d-degree possession of a firearm for an unlawful purpose, and one count of the 3d-degree offense of unlawful possession of an antipersonnel bomb; the prosecutor dismissed the other 20 counts. Under state law, a 2d-degree offense carries a penalty range of 5-10 years; a 3d-degree offense carries a penalty range of between 3-5 years. As part of the plea agreement, however, the State reserved the right to request the court to impose a higher "enhanced" sentence on [the December 22 shooting possession count] on the ground that that offense was committed with a biased purpose. . . .

At the plea hearing, the trial judge heard sufficient evidence to establish Apprendi's guilt. . . . Because the plea agreement provided that the sentence on the sole 3d-degree offense would run concurrently with the other sentences, the potential sentences on the two 2d-degree counts were critical. If the judge found no basis for the biased purpose enhancement, the maximum consecutive sentences on those counts would amount to 20 years in aggregate; if, however, the judge enhanced the sentence on [the December 22 count], the maximum on that count alone would be 20 years and the maximum for the two counts in aggregate would be 30 years, with a 15-year period of parole ineligibility.

After the trial judge accepted the three guilty pleas, the prosecutor filed a formal motion for an extended term. The trial judge thereafter held an evidentiary hearing on the issue of Apprendi's "purpose" for the shooting on December 22. Apprendi adduced evidence from a psychologist and from seven character witnesses who testified that he did not have a reputation for racial bias. He also took the stand himself, explaining that the incident was an unintended consequence of overindulgence in alcohol, denying that he was in any way biased against African-Americans, and denying that his statement to the police had been accurately described. The judge, however, found the police officer's testimony credible, and concluded that the evidence supported a finding that the crime was motivated by racial bias. Having found by a preponderance of the evidence that Apprendi's actions were taken "with a purpose to intimidate" as provided by the statute, the trial judge held that the hate crime enhancement applied [and] sentenced him to a 12-year term of imprisonment on [the December 22 count], and to shorter concurrent sentences on the other counts. [New Jersey appellate courts upheld the sentence.]

In his 1881 lecture on the criminal law, Oliver Wendell Holmes, Jr., observed: "The law threatens certain pains if you do certain things, intending thereby to give you a new motive for not doing them. If you persist in doing them, it has to inflict the pains in order that its threats may continue to be believed." New Jersey threatened Apprendi with certain pains if he unlawfully possessed a weapon and with additional pains if he selected his victims with a purpose to intimidate them because of their race. As a matter of simple justice, it seems obvious that the procedural safeguards designed to protect Apprendi from unwarranted pains should apply equally to the two acts that New Jersey has singled out for punishment. Merely using the label "sentence enhancement" to describe the latter surely does not provide a principled basis for treating them differently.

At stake in this case are constitutional protections of surpassing importance: the proscription of any deprivation of liberty without "due process of law," and the [Sixth Amendment] guarantee that "[i]n all criminal prosecutions, the accused shall enjoy the right to a speedy and public trial, by an impartial jury." Taken together, these rights indisputably entitle a criminal defendant to a jury determination that he is guilty of every element of the crime with which he is charged, beyond a reasonable doubt. [T]he historical foundation for our recognition of these principles extends down centuries into the common law. . . . Equally well founded is the companion right to have the jury verdict based on proof beyond a reasonable doubt. . . .

Any possible distinction between an "element" of a felony offense and a "sentencing factor" was unknown to the practice of criminal indictment, trial by jury, and judgment by court as it existed during the years surrounding our Nation's founding. As a general rule, criminal proceedings were submitted to a jury after being initiated by an indictment containing "all the facts and circumstances which constitute the offence, stated with such certainty and precision, that the defendant may be enabled to determine the species of offence they constitute, in order that he may prepare his defence accordingly and that there may be no doubt as to the judgment which should be given, if the defendant be convicted." J. Archbold, Pleading and Evidence in Criminal Cases 44 (15th ed. 1862). . . .

Thus, with respect to the criminal law of felonious conduct, the English trial judge of the later eighteenth century had very little explicit discretion in sentencing. The substantive criminal law prescribed a particular sentence for each offense. This practice at common law held true when indictments were issued pursuant to statute. Just as the circumstances of the crime and the intent of the defendant at the time of commission were often essential elements to be alleged in the indictment, so too were the circumstances mandating a particular punishment. . . .

We should be clear that nothing in this history suggests that it is impermissible for judges to exercise discretion — taking into consideration various factors relating both to offense and offender — in imposing a judgment within the range prescribed by statute. We have often noted that judges in this country have long exercised discretion of this nature in imposing sentence within statutory limits in the individual case. [O]ur periodic recognition of judges' broad discretion in sentencing — since the nineteenth-century shift in this country from statutes providing fixed-term sentences to those providing judges discretion within a permissible range — has been regularly accompanied by the qualification that that discretion was bound by the range of sentencing options prescribed by the legislature. . . .

We do not suggest that trial practices cannot change in the course of centuries and still remain true to the principles that emerged from the Framers' fears "that the jury right could be lost not only by gross denial, but by erosion." Jones v. United States, 526 U.S. 227 (1999). But practice must at least adhere to the basic principles undergirding the requirements of trying to a jury all facts necessary to constitute a statutory offense, and proving those facts beyond reasonable doubt. As we made clear in In re Winship, 397 U.S. 358 (1970), the "reasonable doubt" requirement has a vital role in our criminal procedure for cogent reasons. Prosecution subjects the criminal defendant both to the possibility that he may lose his liberty upon conviction and the certainty that he would be stigmatized by the conviction. We thus require this, among other, procedural protections in order to "provide concrete substance for the presumption of innocence," and to reduce the risk of imposing such deprivations erroneously. If a defendant faces punishment beyond that provided by statute when an offense is committed under certain circumstances but not others, it is obvious that both the loss of liberty and the stigma attaching to the offense are heightened; it necessarily follows that the defendant should not — at the moment the State is put to proof of those circumstances — be deprived of protections that have, until that point, unquestionably attached. . . .

It was in McMillan v. Pennsylvania, 477 U.S. 79 (1986), that this Court, for the first time, coined the term "sentencing factor" to refer to a fact that was not found by a jury but that could affect the sentence imposed by the judge. That case involved a challenge to the State's Mandatory Minimum Sentencing Act. According to its provisions, anyone convicted of certain felonies would be subject to a mandatory minimum penalty of five years imprisonment if the judge found, by a preponderance of the evidence, that the person "visibly possessed a firearm" in the course of committing one of the specified felonies. Articulating for the first time, and then applying, a multifactor set of criteria for determining whether the *Winship* protections applied to bar such a system, we concluded that the Pennsylvania statute did not run afoul of our previous admonitions against relieving the State of its burden of proving guilt, or tailoring the mere form of a criminal statute solely to avoid *Winship*'s strictures.

We did not, however, there budge from the position that (1) constitutional limits exist to States' authority to define away facts necessary to constitute a criminal offense, and (2) that a state scheme that keeps from the jury facts that expose defendants to greater or additional punishment may raise serious constitutional concern. . . .

Finally, . . . Almendarez-Torres v. United States, 523 U.S. 224 (1998), represents at best an exceptional departure from the historic practice that we have described. In that case, we considered a federal grand jury indictment, which charged the petitioner with "having been found in the United States after being deported," in violation of 8 U.S.C. §1326(a) — an offense carrying a maximum sentence of two years. Almendarez-Torres pleaded guilty to the indictment, admitting at the plea hearing that he had been deported, that he had unlawfully reentered this country, and that the earlier deportation had taken place "pursuant to" three earlier convictions for aggravated felonies. The Government then filed a presentence report indicating that Almendarez-Torres' offense fell within the bounds of §1326(b) because, as specified in that provision, his original deportation had been subsequent to an aggravated felony conviction; accordingly, Almendarez-Torres could be subject to a sentence of up to 20 years. Almendarez-Torres objected, contending that because the indictment "had not mentioned his earlier aggravated felony convictions," he could be sentenced to no more than two years in prison.

Rejecting Almendarez-Torres' objection, we concluded that sentencing him to a term higher than that attached to the offense alleged in the indictment did not violate the strictures of *Winship* in that case. Because Almendarez-Torres had admitted the three earlier convictions for aggravated felonies — all of which had been entered pursuant to proceedings with substantial procedural safeguards of their own — no question concerning the right to a jury trial or the standard of proof that would apply to a contested issue of fact was before the Court. [O]ur conclusion in *Almendarez-Torres* turned heavily upon the fact that the additional sentence to which the defendant was subject was the prior commission of a serious crime. Both the certainty that procedural safeguards attached to any "fact" of prior conviction, and the reality that Almendarez-Torres did not challenge the accuracy of that fact in his case, mitigated the due process and Sixth Amendment concerns otherwise implicated in allowing a judge to determine a fact increasing punishment beyond the maximum of the statutory range....

In sum, our reexamination of our cases in this area, and of the history upon which they rely, confirms [that] any fact that increases the penalty for a crime beyond the prescribed statutory maximum [except for the fact of a prior conviction] must be submitted to a jury, and proved beyond a reasonable doubt.

The New Jersey statutory scheme that *Apprendi* asks us to invalidate allows a jury to convict a defendant of a second-degree offense based on its finding beyond a reasonable doubt that he unlawfully possessed a prohibited weapon; after a subsequent and separate proceeding, it then allows a judge to impose punishment identical to that New Jersey provides for crimes of the first degree, based upon the judge's finding, by a preponderance of the evidence, that the defendant's "purpose" for unlawfully possessing the weapon was to intimidate his victim on the basis of a particular characteristic the victim possessed. In light of the constitutional rule explained above, and all of the cases supporting it, this practice cannot stand.

[New Jersey argues that] the required finding of biased purpose is not an "element" of a distinct hate crime offense, but rather the traditional "sentencing factor" of motive.... The text of the statute requires the factfinder to determine whether the defendant possessed, at the time he committed the subject act, a "purpose to intimidate" on account of, inter alia, race. By its very terms, this statute mandates an examination of the defendant's state of mind — a concept known well to the criminal law as the defendant's mens rea.

[Furthermore,] it does not matter whether the required finding is characterized as one of intent or of motive, because labels do not afford an acceptable answer. That point applies as well to the constitutionally novel and elusive distinction between "elements" and "sentencing factors." Despite what appears to us the clear "elemental" nature of the factor here, the relevant inquiry is one not of form, but of effect — does the required finding expose the defendant to a greater punishment than that authorized by the jury's guilty verdict? [T]he effect of New Jersey's sentencing "enhancement" here is unquestionably to turn a second-degree offense into a first-degree offense, under the State's own criminal code....

The New Jersey procedure challenged in this case is an unacceptable departure from the jury tradition that is an indispensable part of our criminal justice system. Accordingly, the judgment of the Supreme Court of New Jersey is reversed, and the case is remanded for further proceedings not inconsistent with this opinion.

SCALIA, J., concurring.

. . . I think it not unfair to tell a prospective felon that if he commits his contemplated crime he is exposing himself to a jail sentence of 30 years — and that if, upon conviction, he gets anything less than that he may thank the mercy of a tenderhearted judge (just as he may thank the mercy of a tenderhearted parole commission if he is let out inordinately early, or the mercy of a tender-hearted governor if his sentence is commuted). Will there be disparities? Of course. But the criminal will never get more punishment than he bargained for when he did the crime, and his guilt of the crime (and hence the length of the sentence to which he is exposed) will be determined beyond a reasonable doubt by the unanimous vote of 12 of his fellow citizens. In Justice Breyer's bureau-cratic realm of perfect equity, by contrast, the facts that determine the length of sentence to which the defendant is exposed will be determined to exist (on a more-likely-than-not basis) by a single employee of the State. . . .

What ultimately demolishes the case for the dissenters is that they are un-able to say what the right to trial by jury does guarantee if, as they assert, it does not guarantee — what it has been assumed to guarantee throughout our his-tory — the right to have a jury determine those facts that determine the maxi-mum sentence the law allows. They provide no coherent alternative. . . .

THOMAS, J., concurring.

I join the opinion of the Court in full. I write separately to explain my view that the Constitution requires a broader rule than the Court adopts. . . . Sen-tencing enhancements may be new creatures, but the question that they create for courts is not. Courts have long had to consider which facts are elements in order to determine the sufficiency of an accusation (usually an indictment). The answer that courts have provided regarding the accusation tells us what an ele-ment is, and it is then a simple matter to apply that answer to whatever consti-tutional right may be at issue in a case — here, *Winship* and the right to trial by jury. A long line of essentially uniform authority addressing accusations, and stretching from the earliest reported cases after the founding until well into the 20th century, establishes that the original understanding of which facts are ele-ments was even broader than the rule that the Court adopts today.

This authority establishes that a "crime" includes every fact that is by law a basis for imposing or increasing punishment (in contrast with a fact that miti-gates punishment). Thus, if the legislature defines some core crime and then provides for increasing the punishment of that crime upon a finding of some ag-gravating fact — of whatever sort, including the fact of a prior conviction — the core crime and the aggravating fact together constitute an aggravated crime, just as much as grand larceny is an aggravated form of petit larceny. The aggra-vating fact is an element of the aggravated crime. Similarly, if the legislature, rather than creating grades of crimes, has provided for setting the punishment of a crime based on some fact — such as a fine that is proportional to the value of stolen goods — that fact is also an element. No multi-factor parsing of statutes, of the sort that we have attempted since *McMillan*, is necessary. One need only look to the kind, degree, or range of punishment to which the prosecution is by law entitled for a given set of facts. Each fact necessary for that entitlement is an element.

[I]t is fair to say that *McMillan* began a revolution in the law regarding the definition of "crime." Today's decision, far from being a sharp break with the past, marks nothing more than a return to the status quo ante — the status quo that reflected the original meaning of the Fifth and Sixth Amendments. . . .

O'CONNOR, J., dissenting.

Our Court has long recognized that not every fact that bears on a defendant's punishment need be charged in an indictment, submitted to a jury, and proved by the government beyond a reasonable doubt. Rather, we have held that the legislature's definition of the elements of the offense is usually dispositive. Although we have recognized that there are obviously constitutional limits beyond which the States may not go, . . . we have proceeded with caution before deciding that a certain fact must be treated as an offense element despite the legislature's choice not to characterize it as such. We have therefore declined to establish any bright-line rule for making such judgments and have instead approached each case individually, sifting through the considerations most relevant to determining whether the legislature has acted properly within its broad power to define crimes and their punishments or instead has sought to evade the constitutional requirements associated with the characterization of a fact as an offense element. In one bold stroke the Court today casts aside our traditional cautious approach and instead embraces a universal and seemingly bright-line rule limiting the power of Congress and state legislatures to define criminal offenses and the sentences that follow from convictions thereunder. . . .

[I]t is possible that the Court's "increase in the maximum penalty" rule rests on a meaningless formalism that accords, at best, marginal protection for the constitutional rights that it seeks to effectuate. [One reading of the Court's holding] requires that a fact be submitted to a jury and proved beyond a reasonable doubt only if that fact, as a formal matter, extends the range of punishment beyond the prescribed statutory maximum. A State could, however, remove from the jury (and subject to a standard of proof below "beyond a reasonable doubt") the assessment of those facts that define narrower ranges of punishment, within the overall statutory range, to which the defendant may be sentenced. Thus, apparently New Jersey could cure its sentencing scheme, and achieve virtually the same results, by drafting its weapons possession statute in the following manner: First, New Jersey could prescribe, in the weapons possession statute itself, a range of 5 to 20 years' imprisonment for one who commits that criminal offense. Second, New Jersey could provide that only those defendants convicted under the statute who are found by a judge, by a preponderance of the evidence, to have acted with a purpose to intimidate an individual on the basis of race may receive a sentence greater than 10 years' imprisonment.

Under another reading of the Court's decision, it may mean only that the Constitution requires that a fact be submitted to a jury and proved beyond a reasonable doubt if it, as a formal matter, increases the range of punishment beyond that which could legally be imposed absent that fact. A State could, however, remove from the jury (and subject to a standard of proof below 'beyond a reasonable doubt') the assessment of those facts that, as a formal matter, decrease the range of punishment below that which could legally be imposed absent that fact. Thus, . . . New Jersey could cure its sentencing scheme, and achieve virtually the same results, by drafting its weapons possession statute in the following manner: First, New Jersey could prescribe, in the weapons possession statute itself, a range of 5 to 20 years' imprisonment for one who commits that criminal offense. Second, New Jersey could provide that a defendant convicted under the statute whom a judge finds, by a preponderance of the evidence, not to have acted with a purpose to intimidate an individual on the basis of race may receive a sentence no greater than 10 years' imprisonment. . . .

If New Jersey can, consistent with the Constitution, make precisely the same differences in punishment turn on precisely the same facts, and can remove the assessment of those facts from the jury and subject them to a standard of proof below beyond a reasonable doubt, it is impossible to say that the Fifth, Sixth, and Fourteenth Amendments require the Court's rule. For the same reason, the "structural democratic constraints" that might discourage a legislature from enacting either of the above hypothetical statutes would be no more significant than those that would discourage the enactment of New Jersey's present sentence-enhancement statute. . . .

Given the pure formalism of the above readings of the Court's opinion, one suspects that the constitutional principle underlying its decision is more far reaching. The actual principle underlying the Court's decision may be that any fact (other than prior conviction) that has the effect, in real terms, of increasing the maximum punishment beyond an otherwise applicable range must be submitted to a jury and proved beyond a reasonable doubt. . . . The principle thus would apply not only to schemes like New Jersey's, under which a factual determination exposes the defendant to a sentence beyond the prescribed statutory maximum, but also to all determinate sentencing schemes in which the length of a defendant's sentence within the statutory range turns on specific factual determinations (e.g., the federal Sentencing Guidelines).

[T]he apparent effect of the Court's opinion today is to halt the current debate on sentencing reform in its tracks and to invalidate with the stroke of a pen three decades' worth of nationwide reform, all in the name of a principle with a questionable constitutional pedigree. [Perhaps] the most significant impact of the Court's decision will be a practical one — its unsettling effect on sentencing conducted under current federal and state determinate-sentencing schemes. [W]ith respect to past sentences handed down by judges under determinate sentencing schemes, the Court's decision threatens to unleash a flood of petitions by convicted defendants seeking to invalidate their sentences in whole or in part on the authority of the Court's decision today. . . . Because many States, like New Jersey, have determinate-sentencing schemes, the number of individual sentences drawn into question by the Court's decision could be colossal. . . .

BREYER, J., dissenting.

[The majority's] rule would seem to promote a procedural ideal — that of juries, not judges, determining the existence of those facts upon which increased punishment turns. But the real world of criminal justice cannot hope to meet any such ideal. It can function only with the help of procedural compromises, particularly in respect to sentencing. . . .

In modern times the law has left it to the sentencing judge to find those facts which (within broad sentencing limits set by the legislature) determine the sentence of a convicted offender. The judge's factfinding role is not inevitable.

One could imagine, for example, a pure "charge offense" sentencing system in which the degree of punishment depended only upon the crime charged (e.g., eight mandatory years for robbery, six for arson, three for assault). But such a system would ignore many harms and risks of harm that the offender caused or created, and it would ignore many relevant offender characteristics. Hence, that imaginary charge offense system would not be a fair system, for it would lack proportionality, i.e., it would treat different offenders similarly despite major differences in the manner in which each committed the same crime.

[It] is important for present purposes to understand why judges, rather than juries, traditionally have determined the presence or absence of such sentence-affecting facts in any given case. And it is important to realize that the reason is not a theoretical one, but a practical one. . . . There are, to put it simply, far too many potentially relevant sentencing factors to permit submission of all (or even many) of them to a jury. . . .

At the same time, to require jury consideration of all such factors — say, during trial where the issue is guilt or innocence — could easily place the defendant in the awkward (and conceivably unfair) position of having to deny he committed the crime yet offer proof about how he committed it, e.g., "I did not sell drugs, but I sold no more than 500 grams." And while special postverdict sentencing juries could cure this problem, they have seemed (but for capital cases) not worth their administrative costs. Hence, before the Guidelines, federal sentencing judges typically would obtain relevant factual sentencing information from probation officers' presentence reports, while permitting a convicted offender to challenge the information's accuracy at a hearing before the judge without benefit of trial-type evidentiary rules. . . .

The majority raises no objection to traditional pre-Guidelines sentencing procedures under which judges, not juries, made the factual findings that would lead to an increase in an individual offender's sentence. How does a legislative determination differ in any significant way? For example, if a judge may on his or her own decide that victim injury or bad motive should increase a bank robber's sentence from 5 years to 10, why does it matter that a legislature instead enacts a statute that increases a bank robber's sentence from 5 years to 10 based on this same judicial finding?

[T]he majority also makes no constitutional objection to a legislative delegation to a commission of the authority to create guidelines that determine how a judge is to exercise sentencing discretion. But if the Constitution permits Guidelines, why does it not permit Congress similarly to guide the exercise of a judge's sentencing discretion?

[The majority] argues for a limiting principle that would prevent a legislature with broad authority from transforming (jury-determined) facts that constitute elements of a crime into (judge-determined) sentencing factors, thereby removing procedural protections that the Constitution would otherwise require. The majority's cure, however, is not aimed at the disease.

The same "transformational" problem exists under traditional sentencing law, where legislation, silent as to sentencing factors, grants the judge virtually unchecked discretion to sentence within a broad range. Under such a system, judges or prosecutors can similarly transform crimes, punishing an offender convicted of one crime as if he had committed another. A prosecutor, for example, might charge an offender with five counts of embezzlement (each subject to a 10-year maximum penalty), while asking the judge to impose maximum and consecutive sentences because the embezzler murdered his employer. And, as part of the traditional sentencing discretion that the majority concedes judges retain, the judge, not a jury, would determine the last-mentioned relevant fact, i.e., that the murder actually occurred.

This egregious example shows the problem's complexity. The source of the problem lies not in a legislature's power to enact sentencing factors, but in the traditional legislative power to select elements defining a crime, the traditional legislative power to set broad sentencing ranges, and the traditional judicial power to choose a sentence within that range on the basis of relevant offender conduct. Conversely, the solution to the problem lies, not in prohibiting legislatures from enacting sentencing factors, but in sentencing rules that determine punishments on the basis of properly defined relevant conduct, with sensitivity to the need for procedural protections where sentencing factors are determined by a judge (for example, use of a reasonable doubt standard), and invocation of the Due Process Clause where the history of the crime at issue, together with the nature of the facts to be proved, reveals unusual and serious procedural unfairness.

[T]he majority's rule would provide a degree of increased procedural protection in respect to those particular sentencing factors currently embodied in statutes. I nonetheless believe that any such increased protection provides little practical help and comes at too high a price. For one thing, by leaving mandatory minimum sentences untouched, the majority's rule simply encourages any legislature interested in asserting control over the sentencing process to do so by creating those minimums. That result would mean significantly less procedural fairness, not more. . . .

NOTES

1. *The meaning of* Apprendi. Is *Apprendi* a sentencing and criminal justice watershed, or a blip in the modern sentencing road? Put another way, is there a reading of *Apprendi* that would have a relatively modest impact on sentencing and criminal justice systems? Is there a reading that would be the revolution that Justice O'Connor predicted when she states that "the apparent effect of the Court's opinion today is to halt the current debate on sentencing reform in its tracks and to invalidate with the stroke of a pen three decades' worth of nationwide reform"? Compare Alan C. Michaels, Truth in Convicting: Understanding and Evaluating *Apprendi,* 12 Fed. Sentencing Rep. 320 (2000) (contending that *Apprendi* is a modest and limited restriction on how legislatures can define crimes and sentencing structures), with Jeffrey Standen, The End of the Era of Sentencing Guidelines: Apprendi v. New Jersey, 87 Iowa L. Rev. 775 (2002) (contending that the *Apprendi* decision means the demise of all structured sentencing reforms that relied on judicial findings for sentencing determinations).

Is the *Apprendi* opinion addressed primarily to legislators, prosecutors, or sentencers? Whose sentencing decisions and practices need to be adjusted the most in light of *Apprendi*'s watershed rule that "[o]ther than the fact of a prior conviction, any fact that increases the penalty for a crime beyond the prescribed statutory maximum must be submitted to a jury, and proved beyond a reasonable doubt"?

At the time it was decided, all observers realized that by establishing a constitutional limitation on the procedures attending a legislative sentencing scheme, *Apprendi* was a landmark decision for modern sentencing reform. The split 5-4 vote and the five separate opinions delivered by the Justices, however, raised questions about the scope and import of the Court's ruling. Indeed, lower courts and legislatures were left without a clear direction as to how to make sense of *Apprendi*'s "watershed" rule. See Nancy J. King and Susan R. Klein, *Apres Apprendi*, 12 Fed. Sentencing Rep. 331 (2000) (noting many major legal questions left in the immediate wake of the *Apprendi* decision). Although, as developed in the materials below, a number of the most pressing follow-up questions to *Apprendi* have been answered by the Supreme Court and other courts, the full array of implications from the *Apprendi* decision will likely take many years (and many appellate court decisions) to completely sort out.

2. *The value of* Apprendi.   Because the *Apprendi* decision reversed the defendant's sentence and more generally established that defendants are entitled to the full panoply of trial rights and procedures for facts that raise the applicable maximum sentence, the decision appears to be a considerable victory for defendants. Professor Stephanos Bibas has suggested, however, that in the "real world" of guilty pleas, the *Apprendi* rule might actually operate to "hurt many of the defendants it purports to help by undermining the procedural values it purports to safeguard." See Stephanos Bibas, Judicial Fact-Finding and Sentence Enhancements in a World of Guilty Pleas, 110 Yale L.J. 1097, 1100 (2001). Professor Bibas argues that in the end, the "trial right" protected by *Apprendi* "does little good [and] much harm" for the vast majority of defendants who opt to plead guilty instead of going to trial, primarily because the *Apprendi* rule gives prosecutors an incentive, and greater leverage, to pressure defendants into admitting as part of a plea agreement those facts that would support a higher sentence. Id. at 1151-1174.

Professors Nancy King and Susan Klein have contested Professor Bibas's claims and suggested that his analysis is "based on a faulty premise about bargaining behavior." Nancy J. King and Susan R. Klein, *Apprendi* and Plea Bargaining, 54 Stan. L. Rev. 295, 297 (2001). They argue that prosecutors have no more leverage over defendants after *Apprendi* than they did before, while defendants now have the additional bargaining chip of being able to force a prosecutor to prove certain facts to a jury beyond a reasonable doubt.

3. *A "meaningless formalism"?*   Perhaps as debatable as the value of *Apprendi* for defendants is the value of *Apprendi* for the development of crimes and sentencing laws. As the *Apprendi* dissenters and a number of commentators have noted, there seems to be a formalism to the constitutional rule of *Apprendi*. If only the facts that increase the penalty for a crime beyond the prescribed statutory maximum must be submitted to a jury and proved beyond a reasonable doubt, then legislatures seemingly can avoid procedural safeguards by raising the statutory maximum sentences for all crimes and then instructing judges as to what facts should lead to *reduced* sentences. Justice O'Connor's dissent in *Apprendi* assailed this apparent formalism and suggested that it rendered the *Apprendi* ruling "meaningless." Yet at least a few academic commentators have suggested that there is both meaning and value in even such a formalistic reading of *Apprendi*. See Benjamin J. Priester, Constitutional Formalism and the

Meaning of Apprendi v. New Jersey, 38 Am. Crim. L. Rev. 281 (2001); Alan C. Michaels, Truth in Convicting: Understanding and Evaluating *Apprendi*, 12 Fed. Sentencing Rep. 320 (2000).

In footnote 16 of his opinion for the Court, Justice Stevens provided this extended and interesting response to the formalism charge:

> The principal dissent would reject the Court's rule as a "meaningless formalism," because it can conceive of hypothetical statutes that would comply with the rule and achieve the same result as the New Jersey statute. While a State could, hypothetically, undertake to revise its entire criminal code in the manner the dissent suggests — extending all statutory maximum sentences to, for example, 50 years and giving judges guided discretion as to a few specially selected factors within that range — this possibility seems remote. Among other reasons, structural democratic constraints exist to discourage legislatures from enacting penal statutes that expose *every* defendant convicted of, for example, weapons possession, to a maximum sentence exceeding that which is, in the legislature's judgment, generally proportional to the crime. This is as it should be. Our rule ensures that a State is obliged to make its choices concerning the substantive content of its criminal laws with full awareness of the consequence, unable to mask substantive policy choices of exposing all who are convicted to the maximum sentence it provides. So exposed, the political check on potentially harsh legislative action is then more likely to operate.
>
> In all events, if such an extensive revision of the State's entire criminal code were enacted for the purpose the dissent suggests, or if New Jersey simply reversed the burden of the hate crime finding (effectively assuming a crime was performed with a purpose to intimidate and then requiring a defendant to prove that it was not), we would be required to question whether the revision was constitutional under this Court's prior decisions.
>
> Finally, the principal dissent ignores the distinction the Court has often recognized between facts in aggravation of punishment and facts in mitigation. If facts found by a jury support a guilty verdict of murder, the judge is authorized by that jury verdict to sentence the defendant to the maximum sentence provided by the murder statute. If the defendant can escape the statutory maximum by showing, for example, that he is a war veteran, then a judge that finds the fact of veteran status is neither exposing the defendant to a deprivation of liberty greater than that authorized by the verdict according to statute, nor is the Judge imposing upon the defendant a greater stigma than that accompanying the jury verdict alone. Core concerns animating the jury and burden-of-proof requirements are thus absent from such a scheme.

530 U.S. at 490 n.16.

4. *The logical reach of* Apprendi.   As the Court repeatedly states, the *Apprendi* rule that "any fact that increases the penalty for a crime beyond the prescribed statutory maximum must be submitted to a jury, and proved beyond a reasonable doubt" does not apply to "the fact of a prior conviction." Does this exception make any sense logically or was it created by the *Apprendi* majority simply to avoid having to overrule Almendarez-Torres v. United States, 523 U.S. 224 (1998), which held that prior convictions did not have to be established at trial to enhance an applicable maximum sentence? See Kyron Huigens and Danielle Chinea, "Three Strikes" Laws and *Apprendi*'s Irrational, Inequitable Exception for Recidivism, 37 Crim. L. Bull. 575 (2001).

Is Justice Thomas arguing in his concurrence that the logical reach of the *Apprendi* decision extends to every possible fact relied upon at sentencing? Recall his statement that "a 'crime' includes every fact that is by law a basis for imposing or increasing punishment (in contrast with a fact that mitigates punishment)."

Do you think the Constitution demands this "broader rule"? Can a distinction between facts that increase punishment and those that mitigate punishment, a distinction noted both by Justice Thomas and by Justice Stevens writing for the Court, be maintained? Justice Thomas in *Apprendi* stated that he "need not in this case address the implications of the rule" for capital sentencing or for guidelines sentencing, although he finished with a footnote hinting that his "rule regarding elements" might apply to the federal sentencing guidelines because the guidelines "have the force and effect of laws."

State and federal courts have confronted many claims about *Apprendi*'s reach sinced it was decided in June 2000. Consider the following case. Should the Supreme Court have given better guidance in *Apprendi*?

Kansas v. Crystal Gould
23 P.3d 801 (Kan. 2001)

SIX, J.

Defendant Crystal Gould appeals her convictions on three counts of child abuse [and] claims for the first time on appeal that Apprendi v. New Jersey, 530 U.S. 466 (2000), renders her enhanced sentence void and the Kansas upward departure sentencing scheme, part of the Kansas Sentencing Guidelines Act, unconstitutional. . . .

D.G. was born to Crystal and Leland Gould on September 20, 1996. Her brother, L.G., and sister, S.G., twins, were born on January 4, 1998. [A few weeks after the twins were born] Leland's parents noticed that D.G., 16 months old, was bruised and had a black eye. S.G. had bruises on her head, forehead, and knees. L.G. also had bruises on his forehead. When asked how the children got hurt, Gould said she did not know. She thought maybe D.G. hit her head on her baby bed. . . .

On Sunday, January 25, Gould and Leland took the children to a park and to the zoo. L.G. became fussy at home around 9 P.M. His parents could not soothe him. Between 10 and 10:30 P.M., Gould laid L.G. on her bed and turned on a radio. She was alone in the room with L.G., off and on, until around 11 P.M. Then, Gould came out to tell Leland that L.G. was not breathing. L.G.'s "color was kind of bad," and his arms and legs were limp. . . . Gould and Leland took L.G. to the emergency room.

When they arrived at the emergency room, L.G. was experiencing activity suggestive of seizures. He did not breathe for prolonged periods of time. The next day [a] CAT scan showed that L.G.'s brain was swollen. He suffered an acute bleed or epidural hematoma on the left posterior part of the brain and multiple areas of bleeding into the upper part of his brain. Further examination revealed two small circular bruises above his right hip and a hemorrhage in his left eye. The medical evidence showed that L.G. had suffered a stroke.

A physician specializing in pediatric critical care testified to the following at trial:

> This type of injury would have to have been the result of a very forceful blunt injury, either where a flat surface was brought against the fixed head, say a fist

hitting the skull, or shoe hitting the skull, something like that. Or where the child's head, itself, was being accelerated and ran into a fixed object of say a wall or a door.

The physician said that, based on the analysis of an MRI scan, the epidural hematoma could not have occurred before January 25, 1998. The multiple areas of subdural bleeds were consistent with forceful and repetitive shaking. According to the physician, L.G. will likely require total care for the rest of his life. L.G. "will probably suffer from spastic quadriplegia, which means his muscles will constantly be stiff and difficult for him to coordinate or move. He will probably not be able to talk."

S.G. and D.G. were examined on January 29. S.G. had three fractured ribs, a contusion on a rib, and a fractured thigh bone. A nuclear medicine physician testified that these injuries were consistent with a squeezing injury. S.G. also had a skull fracture and evidence of bleeding in her brain consistent with the type of injury an infant might sustain in an automobile accident. D.G. had a bruise on her right cheek, a smaller bruise on her left cheek, and some bruising on her forehead. She also had a broken rib consistent with a squeezing injury.

Gould denied harming her children. Two witnesses testified that Gould had abused her children. In November 1997, they saw Gould with D.G. at a laundromat. She jerked D.G. around by the arm, pulling her from washer to washer, and was "flicking" the child in the mouth. Another bystander confronted Gould, and one of the witnesses called the police.

In January 1998, one of the neighbors was in the laundry room next to Gould's apartment and heard a woman yelling inside the apartment. The neighbor heard a loud slapping sound, followed by a baby's scream. Another neighbor saw Gould, while she was still pregnant with the twins, pick D.G. up by the arm, kick her in the head and call her a "little f—— ng bitch."

[A] babysitter also testified regarding Gould's abusive activities. He said Gould was physically violent with the children when they cried. She would often place the children alone in her bedroom and turn on a radio. [The babysitter] described a closet/make-shift bedroom where D.G. was placed, with the louvered doors shut, for hours at a time [and he] had seen Gould slap the children. He saw her pick up S.G. by the ribs and shake her. He also saw Gould pick up L.G. by one arm, scream at him, slap his face, and drop him in a violent manner. This drop caused L.G. to tremble and his eyes to roll back into his head.

Gould was charged with three counts of child abuse under K.S.A. 21-3609. The jury convicted her on each count. [At sentencing] the district court imposed a controlling sentence of 136 months, with a post-release supervision period of 36 months. Under K.S.A. 21-3609, a defendant guilty of abuse of a child has committed a severity level 5 person felony. Gould had no criminal record and her criminal history score was I. The authorized sentencing range was 31-32-34 months. The State moved for an upward departure sentence citing as reasons: (1) the victims were Gould's children; (2) the abuse of L.G. was so bad that he will never walk, talk, or care for himself; (3) the abuse of S.G. was severe; and (4) Gould showed no emotion or remorse until she was found guilty.

The district court granted the motion and departed to 68 months each for Counts I and II (involving the twins), to run consecutively. Gould was sentenced to 34 months for Count III (involving D.G.), to run concurrent with Counts I and II. The three aggravating factors the judge found to be substantial and compelling reasons for imposing the departure sentences were: (1) the victims "were particularly vulnerable due to age, infirmity, or at least reduced physical capacity which was known or should have been known to the offender"; (2) "the defendant's conduct during the commission of the current offenses manifested excessive brutality to the victims in a manner not normally present in that offense"; and (3) "the offense involved a fiduciary relationship which existed between the victims and the defendant." Because K.S.A. 2000 Supp. 21-4720(c)(3) prohibits the "total imprisonment term of the consecutive sentences, including the imprisonment term for the departure crime" to "exceed twice the maximum presumptive imprisonment term of the departure sentence following aggravation" (the double-double rule), Gould's maximum total sentence was limited to 136 months. . . .

We [now] turn to consideration of Gould's attack on her sentence. She argues first that the statute which authorizes imposition of her upward departure sentence is unconstitutional and her sentence void. . . .

We first examine the holding in *Apprendi*. Apprendi pled guilty to [offenses that] carried a range of 5 to 10 years [imprisonment]. The State reserved the right to request imposition of an enhanced sentence . . . based on a New Jersey hate crime statute [which] provided for a sentence enhancement if the court found, by a preponderance of the evidence, that the defendant acted to intimidate on the basis of race, color, gender, handicap, religion, sexual orientation, or ethnicity. The court found, by a preponderance of the evidence, that Apprendi's purpose for unlawfully possessing the weapon was to intimidate his victim on the basis of race and sentenced Apprendi to 12 years.

The United States Supreme Court . . . observed as a threshold matter that "constitutional protections of surpassing importance" were at stake [and ruled that the collective rights mentioned in the Sixth and Fourteenth Amendment] formed the following guarantee: "Other than the fact of a prior conviction, any fact that increases the penalty for a crime beyond the prescribed statutory maximum must be submitted to a jury, and proved beyond a reasonable doubt." 530 U.S. at 490. The Court concluded that the New Jersey hate crime statute violated this principle because it allowed imposition of a sentence beyond the statutory maximum based upon a court's finding of a certain fact by a preponderance of the evidence.

Since the Supreme Court's June 26, 2000, ruling in *Apprendi*, "hundreds of appeals have been filed and scores of decisions handed down interpreting the ruling." David Rovella, A Looming *'Apprendi'* Tsunami?, The National Law Journal, Jan. 8, 2001, at A1. There is little dispute that *Apprendi* has had an immediate and dramatic impact on criminal law. Indeed, Justice O'Connor presaged the *Apprendi* phenomenon by warning in her dissent that the decision represented "a watershed change in constitutional law" whose effect on state and federal determinate sentencing schemes would likely be "severe." 530 U.S. at 524, 544 (O'Connor, J. dissenting).

Federal courts have applied *Apprendi* to sentences involving drug convictions under 21 U.S.C. §841(b) (1994), an enhancement statute. These courts have found that a quantity of drugs that increases the maximum sentence to which a defendant would otherwise be exposed for a conviction under 21 U.S.C.

§841(a) is a fact that must be found by a jury beyond a reasonable doubt [and concluded] that *Apprendi* undermined circuit precedent allowing a judge to determine drug quantity at sentencing by a preponderance of the evidence.

Apprendi is likewise affecting sentencing decisions on the state level. The State citations are for informational rather than precedential purposes. In State v. Guice, 141 N.C. App. 177, 541 S.E.2d 474 (2000), the North Carolina Court of Appeals vacated an enhanced sentence imposed under the state's firearm enhancement statute after applying *Apprendi* to hold the statute facially unconstitutional. The firearm enhancement statute said that "the court shall increase the minimum term of imprisonment to which the [defendant] is sentenced by 60 months" if the court "finds that the [defendant] used, displayed, or threatened to use or display a firearm at the time of the felony." The requisite factual determination was explicitly removed from the jury. The statute exposed Guice to a greater punishment than that authorized by the jury's verdict. The *Guice* court concluded that *Apprendi* "commands that we find the firearm enhancement statute unconstitutional." . . .

In State v. Grossman, 622 N.W.2d 394 (Minn. App. 2001), Grossman was convicted of attempted second-degree murder, first-degree assault, third-degree assault and three counts of first-degree criminal sexual conduct. A pretrial evaluation concluded that Grossman was "a dangerous sexual predator." The *Grossman* court considered a Minnesota statute which required imposition of an enhanced sentence upon certain court findings regarding whether the defendant is a patterned sex offender. Grossman relied on *Apprendi* in contending that his enhanced sentence violated due process because the court, not the jury, made the requisite findings. The Minnesota court agreed and invalidated the statute.

With this survey of the law in mind, we turn to the Kansas statute at issue. K.S.A. 2000 Supp. 21-4716, which provides a mechanism for imposing departure sentences, is part and parcel of the [Kansas Sentencing Guidelines Act] KSGA. The KSGA was enacted to reduce prison overcrowding by making a distinction between more serious and less serious offenders. The guidelines were also enacted to promote uniformity and standardize sentences so that similarly situated offenders would be treated in the same way.

Two grids, which contain the sentencing range for drug crimes and non-drug crimes, were developed for use as tools in sentencing. The KSGA grids provide an overview of presumptive felony sentences. The determination of a felony sentence is based on two factors: the current crime of conviction and the offender's prior criminal history. The sentence contained in the grid box at the juncture of the severity level of the crime of conviction and the offender's criminal history category is the presumed sentence.

Departure sentences by definition challenge the notion of uniformity. Therefore, it is only in exceptional circumstances that the district court may exercise its discretion and impose a sentence not based exclusively on offense severity and criminal history.

K.S.A. 2000 Supp. 21-4716(a) provides:

> The sentencing judge shall impose the presumptive sentence provided by the sentencing guidelines for crimes committed on or after July 1, 1993, unless the judge finds substantial and compelling reasons to impose a departure. If the sentencing judge departs from the presumptive sentence, the judge shall state

on the record at the time of sentencing the substantial and compelling reasons for the departure.

K.S.A. 2000 Supp. 21-4716(b) provides in pertinent part:

> (2) [The] following nonexclusive list of aggravating factors may be considered in determining whether substantial and compelling reasons for the departure exist:
>   (A) The victim was particularly vulnerable due to age, infirmity, or reduced physical or mental capacity which was known or should have been known to the offender.
>   (B) The defendant's conduct during the commission of the current offense manifested excessive brutality to the victim in a manner not normally present in that offense.
>   (C) The offense was motivated entirely or in part by the race, color, religion, ethnicity, national origin or sexual orientation of the victim.
>   (D) The offense involved a fiduciary relationship which existed between the defendant and the victim. . . .

Greatly simplified, K.S.A. 2000 Supp. 21-4716 allows imposition of a term beyond the maximum specified in the appropriate sentencing grid box based upon a court finding the existence of one or more aggravating factors. The statute is silent on a burden of proof to be utilized by the district judge to establish a substantial and compelling reason to depart. Facts "established for use in sentencing require less evidentiary weight than facts asserted for conviction." State v. Spain, 953 P.2d 1004 (Kan. 1998). In *Spain*, we held that the implicit standard of proof for aggravating circumstances under K.S.A. 21-4635(c) is preponderance of the evidence. As we point out in the following analysis, *Apprendi* supplies the standard for an upward departure.

The State contends at the outset that *Apprendi* does not apply to this case because Gould's sentence is not greater than the statutory maximum. The State argues that under the KSGA, a presumed sentence is established based upon the defendant's criminal history and the severity level of the crimes of conviction. The State reasons that the presumed sentence is not the maximum sentence allowed by law. The State here asserts that the maximum sentence Gould could have received for the multiple convictions of abuse of a child, based on her criminal history classification and the limitations of the "double-double rule," was 136 months' imprisonment. Thus, the sentence imposed by the district court did not exceed the statutory maximum as contemplated by *Apprendi*. The State's argument is not persuasive.

Under *Apprendi*, it does not matter how the required finding is labeled, but whether it exposes the defendant to a greater punishment than that authorized by the jury's verdict. Gould's jury verdict "authorized" a sentence of 31 to 34 months for each child abuse conviction. By imposing two 68-month sentences, the district court went beyond the maximum sentence in the applicable grid box and exposed Gould to punishment greater than that authorized by the jury's verdict. . . . Gould's sentence of 68 months for two counts of child abuse exceeded the statutory maximum, and *Apprendi* applies.

Gould argues that the holding in *Apprendi* reveals a fundamental flaw in K.S.A. 2000 Supp. 21-4716: It allows a fact or facts, other than that of a prior conviction, not found by a jury beyond a reasonable doubt, to be used to justify imposing a sentence beyond the statutory maximum for the underlying crime. Gould's arguments parallel the reasoning set forth in *Apprendi*.

Gould correctly asserts that the Due Process Clause of the United States Constitution "protects the accused against conviction except upon proof beyond a reasonable doubt of every fact necessary to constitute the crime with which he is charged." In re Winship, 397 U.S. 358 (1970). In *Apprendi*, the State argued that the fact findings required by the hate crime statute were not elements of the underlying crime of firearm possession but were separate sentencing factors which did not require proof beyond a reasonable doubt under *Winship*. The Court rejected this notion, noting the "constitutionally novel and elusive distinction between 'elements' and 'sentencing factors,'" but reasoning that "the relevant inquiry is one not of form, but of effect — does the required finding expose the defendant to a greater punishment than that authorized by the jury's guilty verdict?" . . .

Our inquiry continues with Gould's insistence that the Sixth and Fourteenth Amendments to the United States Constitution require trying to a jury any facts which, if found, expose her to a penalty beyond the statutory maximum. The *Apprendi* Court agreed, emphasizing that the right to a jury determination is "'the great bulwark of [our] civil and political liberties,'" and has been interpreted to require [that] "'the truth of every accusation . . . be confirmed by the unanimous suffrage of twelve of [the defendant's] equals.' . . ."

The district court made findings as to certain aggravating factors which increased Gould's sentence beyond the statutory maximum. The district court, rather than the jury, made these findings as required by K.S.A. 21-4716(a). *Apprendi* requires that such findings be made by the jury beyond a reasonable doubt. Because Kansas law authorizing upward departure sentences directly contravenes this requirement, the law is unconstitutional.

The State urges that Gould's sentences may withstand the constitutional infirmities of the Kansas scheme for upward departures. The State points out that one of the aggravating factors supporting upward departure was the existence of a fiduciary relationship between Gould and the victims, her children, and one was the extreme vulnerability of two of the victims. Indeed, we have recognized the existence of a fiduciary relationship between parent and child. State v. Ippert, 995 P.2d 858 (Kan. 2000). Here, the State reasons, there was no dispute that Gould was the mother of her victims nor was there dispute that two of her victims were 21 days old. Thus, the State concludes that neither of these matters need be presented to a jury or found beyond a reasonable doubt because they were not at all in question.

The State, in essence, urges this court to apply principles of harmless error. This we cannot do. The Kansas scheme for imposing upward departure sentences, embodied in K.S.A. 2000 Supp. 21-4716, is unconstitutional on its face. Gould received a sentence beyond the statutory maximum based upon a court finding of certain aggravating factors found by a preponderance of the evidence. *Apprendi*, on the other hand, requires "any fact that increases the penalty for a crime beyond the prescribed statutory maximum must be submitted to a jury, and proved beyond a reasonable doubt." Any other procedure "is an unacceptable departure from the jury tradition that is an indispensable part of our criminal justice system." Gould's sentence was imposed pursuant to an unconstitutional sentencing scheme and cannot stand. . . .

Apprendi dictates our conclusion that Kansas' scheme for imposing upward departure sentences, embodied in K.S.A. 2000 Supp. 21-4716, violates the due process and jury trial rights contained in the Sixth and Fourteenth Amendments to the United States Constitution. Gould's sentence must be vacated and remanded for resentencing.

ABBOTT, J., dissenting.

I find the *Apprendi* decision disturbing. It appears it is going to have a considerable impact on the judicial system in many areas and particularly on sentencing guidelines. I recognize that the legislature can play games with sentencing guidelines and amend them so that *Apprendi* would not apply to most sentences.

I am troubled by other matters, although I recognize that they probably do not fall under *Apprendi*. For instance, cases frequently come before us where, if the defendant is tried as a juvenile, the most he or she will have to serve is a few years. If, on the other hand, the defendant is tried as an adult for the same offenses, he or she may face up to 100 years. We have other areas of the law in which similar results are reached, and although they do not fall under *Apprendi*, they seem fundamentally unfair in light of *Apprendi*.

I would affirm this decision under the harmless error rule. I would even consider affirming it on the basis that the sentencing guidelines maximum sentence was not exceeded in this case. An "upward departure" simply allows the trial court to use a statutory maximum that the defendant can receive. Here, the defendant did not receive more than the guidelines authorized. She merely received more than the standard sentence because certain sentencing factors were present. . . .

Here, a fiduciary relationship existed. Gould recognizes that facts that do not increase a defendant's punishment beyond that authorized by the underlying statute need not be proven to a jury beyond a reasonable doubt, citing McMillan v. Pennsylvania, 477 U.S. 79 (1986). . . . One of the factors relied upon by the sentencing court in granting the upward departure was the fact that the defendant had a fiduciary relationship with the victims. The jury was presented with overwhelming evidence that Gould, the mother of the victims, had a fiduciary relationship with S.G., D.G., and L.G. . . . Not only was Gould the victims' mother, but she was also a primary caregiver to the victims. Thus, any error was harmless because it is clear beyond a reasonable doubt that a rational jury would have found that a fiduciary relationship existed. . . .

NOTES

1. *Impact of* Apprendi *on guideline systems.* As the *Gould* case highlights, the *Apprendi* decision potentially affects the application of guideline sentencing rules as well as legislative sentencing enhancements. In Fall 2003, the U.S. Supreme Court granted certiorari in Blakely v. Washington, 47 P.3d 149 (Wash. App. 2002), cert. granted No. 02-1632 (Oct. 20, 2003), a case raising the same basic issue considered in *Gould:* whether facts relied upon as the basis for an upward departures from legislatively-prescribed sentencing guidelines must be submitted to a jury and found beyond a reasonable doubt.

The defendant in *Blakely* highlighted a distinction between legislatively-prescribed guideline systems and judicially-developed guideline systems, and suggested that only upward departures in legislatively-prescribed systems are covered by the *Apprendi* ruling. However, the reach of the *Apprendi* logic might not be so easily limited. Moreover, if *Apprendi* requires facts supporting an upward departure to be submitted to a jury and found beyond a reasonable doubt, doesn't the holding also extend to all facts that support an enhanced guideline sentence, whether the basis for a departure or simply the basis for an adjustment to the applicable offense level or criminal history category?

2. *The broader impact of* Apprendi. The *Gould* decision provides both a useful example and a brief account of *Apprendi*'s profound impact on the landscape of modern sentencing reform. Thousands of appeals have been filed, raising an array of claims that seemingly well-established sentencing practices run afoul of the *Apprendi* rule that any fact (other than the fact of a prior conviction) "that increases the penalty for a crime beyond the prescribed statutory maximum must be submitted to a jury, and proved beyond a reasonable doubt." See, e.g., State v. Lucas, 548 S.E.2d 712 (N.C. 2001) (addressing what *Apprendi* means for indictment practices); State v. Harvey, 647 N.W.2d 189 (Wis. 2002) (addressing whether *Apprendi* allows judges to instruct juries to take judicial notice of particular aggravating facts); People v. Harris, 784 N.E.2d 792 (Ill. 2003) (addressing whether *Apprendi* affects the decision to sentence offenders to consecutive rather than concurrent terms); State v. Gonzales, 24 P.3d 776 (N.M. Ct. App.), *cert. granted,* 23 P.3d 929 (N.M. 2001) (examining what *Apprendi* means for juvenile court practices).

In short, though much can be debated about the *Apprendi* ruling and the Justices' opinions, it is indisputable that *Apprendi* has had an immediate and dramatic impact on the landscape of criminal law and that Justice O'Connor was right when she predicted in her dissent that the decision represented "a watershed change" that would have a profound impact on state and federal determinate sentencing schemes. Interestingly, though *Apprendi* has generated an enormous amount of litigation and a seemingly continuous stream of appellate decisions, Professor Stephanos Bibas has recently noted that its true impact on established criminal law doctrines has been relatively limited because "[s]tate courts have by and large interpreted *Apprendi* very cautiously and narrowly [and only] in a few areas have a few courts interpreted their own constitutions more broadly than the federal constitution." See Stephanos Bibas, *Apprendi* in the States, 625 J. Crim. L. & Criminology 1 (2003).

3. *Limiting the impact of* Apprendi. Although the future of *Apprendi* and its long-term impact remain both uncertain and critical, the U.S. Supreme Court has already, through its decision in United States v. Cotton, 536 U.S. 625 (2002), effectively limited the retroactive impact of *Apprendi* by ruling that indictments rendered defective by the *Apprendi* rule should be reviewed only for plain error and do not require automatic reversal of a conviction or sentence.

In Harris v. United States, 536 U.S. 545 (2002), the Court significantly restricted the reach of *Apprendi* by holding that facts that increase mandatory minimum penalties can still be treated as sentencing factors and thus do not require submission to a jury or proof beyond a reasonable doubt.

William Joseph Harris v. United States
536 U.S. 545 (2002)

KENNEDY, J.

Once more we consider the distinction the law has drawn between the elements of a crime and factors that influence a criminal sentence. Legislatures define crimes in terms of the facts that are their essential elements, and constitutional guarantees attach to these facts. . . . Yet not all facts affecting the defendant's punishment are elements. After the accused is convicted, the judge may impose a sentence within a range provided by statute, basing it on various facts relating to the defendant and the manner in which the offense was committed. Though these facts may have a substantial impact on the sentence, they are not elements, and are thus not subject to the Constitution's indictment, jury, and proof requirements. Some statutes also direct judges to give specific weight to certain facts when choosing the sentence. The statutes do not require these facts, sometimes referred to as sentencing factors, to be alleged in the indictment, submitted to the jury, or established beyond a reasonable doubt.

The Constitution permits legislatures to make the distinction between elements and sentencing factors, but it imposes some limitations as well. For if it did not, legislatures could evade the indictment, jury, and proof requirements by labeling almost every relevant fact a sentencing factor. The Court described one limitation in this respect two Terms ago in Apprendi v. New Jersey, 530 U.S. 466, 490 (2000): "Other than the fact of a prior conviction, any fact that increases the penalty for a crime beyond the prescribed statutory maximum," whether the statute calls it an element or a sentencing factor, "must be submitted to a jury, and proved beyond a reasonable doubt." Fourteen years before, in McMillan v. Pennsylvania, 477 U.S. 79 (1986), the Court had declined to adopt a more restrictive constitutional rule. *McMillan* sustained a statute that increased the minimum penalty for a crime, though not beyond the statutory maximum, when the sentencing judge found, by a preponderance of the evidence, that the defendant had possessed a firearm. The principal question before us is whether *McMillan* stands after *Apprendi*.

William Joseph Harris sold illegal narcotics out of his pawnshop with an unconcealed semiautomatic pistol at his side. He was later arrested for violating federal drug and firearms laws, including 18 U.S.C. §924(c)(1)(A). That statute provides in relevant part:

> Any person who, during and in relation to any crime of violence or drug trafficking crime . . . uses or carries a firearm, or who, in furtherance of any such crime, possesses a firearm, shall, in addition to the punishment provided for such crime of violence or drug trafficking crime —
> > (i) be sentenced to a term of imprisonment of not less than 5 years;
> > (ii) if the firearm is brandished, be sentenced to a term of imprisonment of not less than 7 years; and

> (iii) if the firearm is discharged, be sentenced to a term of imprisonment of not less than 10 years.

The Government proceeded on the assumption that §924(c)(1)(A) defines a single crime and that brandishing is a sentencing factor to be considered by the judge after the trial. For this reason the indictment said nothing of brandishing and made no reference to subsection (ii). . . .

Following his conviction, the presentence report recommended that petitioner be given the 7-year minimum because he had brandished the gun. Petitioner objected, . . . arguing that, as a matter of statutory interpretation, brandishing is an element of a separate offense, an offense for which he had not been indicted or tried. At the sentencing hearing the District Court overruled the objection, found by a preponderance of the evidence that petitioner had brandished the gun, and sentenced him to seven years in prison.

In the Court of Appeals for the Fourth Circuit petitioner again pressed his statutory argument. He added that if brandishing is a sentencing factor as a statutory matter, the statute is unconstitutional in light of *Apprendi* — even though, as petitioner acknowledged, the judge's finding did not alter the maximum penalty to which he was exposed. Rejecting these arguments, the Court of Appeals affirmed. Like every other Court of Appeals to have addressed the question, it held that the statute makes brandishing a sentencing factor.

We must first answer a threshold question of statutory construction: Did Congress make brandishing an element or a sentencing factor in §924(c)(1)(A)? . . . The statute does not say in so many words whether brandishing is an element or a sentencing factor, but the structure of the prohibition suggests it is the latter. Federal laws usually list all offense elements in a single sentence and separate the sentencing factors into subsections. Here, §924(c)(1)(A) . . . has this sort of structure, [and thus] we can presume that its principal paragraph defines a single crime and its subsections identify sentencing factors. . . .

We might have had reason to question that inference if brandishing or discharging altered the defendant's punishment in a manner not usually associated with sentencing factors. . . . The provisions before us now, however, have an effect on the defendant's sentence that is . . . consistent with traditional understandings about how sentencing factors operate; the required findings constrain, rather than extend, the sentencing judge's discretion. Section 924(c)(1)(A) does not authorize the judge to impose . . . higher penalties . . . once the facts in question are found. Since the subsections alter only the minimum, the judge may impose a sentence well in excess of seven years, whether or not the defendant brandished the firearm. The incremental changes in the minimum — from 5 years, to 7, to 10 — are precisely what one would expect to see in provisions meant to identify matters for the sentencing judge's consideration. . . .

[W]e conclude that, as a matter of statutory interpretation, §924(c)(1)(A) defines a single offense. The statute regards brandishing and discharging as sentencing factors to be found by the judge, not offense elements to be found by the jury.

Confident that the statute does just what *McMillan* said it could, we consider petitioner's argument that §924(c)(1)(A)(ii) is unconstitutional because *McMillan* is no longer sound authority [after] *Apprendi*, which, he says, cannot be reconciled with *McMillan*. We do not find the argument convincing. As we shall explain, *McMillan* and *Apprendi* are consistent because there is a fundamental distinction between the factual findings that were at issue in those two cases. *Apprendi* said that any fact extending the defendant's sentence beyond the maximum authorized by the jury's verdict would have been considered an element of an aggravated crime — and thus the domain of the jury — by those who framed the Bill of Rights. The same cannot be said of a fact increasing the mandatory minimum (but not extending the sentence beyond the statutory maximum), for the jury's verdict has authorized the judge to impose the minimum with or without the finding. As *McMillan* recognized, a statute may reserve this type of factual finding for the judge without violating the Constitution.

Though defining criminal conduct is a task generally left to the legislative branch, Congress may not manipulate the definition of a crime in a way that relieves the Government of its constitutional obligations to charge each element in the indictment, submit each element to the jury, and prove each element beyond a reasonable doubt. *McMillan* and *Apprendi* asked whether certain types of facts, though labeled sentencing factors by the legislature, were nevertheless "traditional elements" to which these constitutional safeguards were intended to apply.

McMillan's answer stemmed from certain historical and doctrinal understandings about the role of the judge at sentencing. The mid-19th century produced a general shift in this country from criminal statutes providing fixed-term sentences to those providing judges discretion within a permissible range. Under these statutes, judges exercise their sentencing discretion through "an inquiry broad in scope, largely unlimited either as to the kind of information [they] may consider, or the source from which it may come." United States v. Tucker, 404 U.S. 443, 446 (1972). The Court has recognized that this process is constitutional — and that the facts taken into consideration need not be alleged in the indictment, submitted to the jury, or proved beyond a reasonable doubt. As the Court reiterated in *Jones:* "It is not, of course, that anyone today would claim that every fact with a bearing on sentencing must be found by a jury; we have resolved that general issue and have no intention of questioning its resolution." Judicial factfinding in the course of selecting a sentence within the authorized range does not implicate the indictment, jury-trial, and reasonable-doubt components of the Fifth and Sixth Amendments.

That proposition, coupled with another shift in prevailing sentencing practices, explains *McMillan*. In the latter part of the 20th century, many legislatures, dissatisfied with sentencing disparities among like offenders, implemented measures regulating judicial discretion. These systems maintained the statutory ranges and the judge's factfinding role but assigned a uniform weight to factors judges often relied upon when choosing a sentence. One example of reform, the kind addressed in *McMillan,* was mandatory minimum sentencing. The Pennsylvania Mandatory Minimum Sentencing Act, 42 Pa. Cons. Stat. §9712 (1982), imposed a minimum prison term of five years when the sentencing judge found, by a preponderance of the evidence, that the defendant had possessed a firearm while committing the crime of conviction.

In sustaining the statute the *McMillan* Court placed considerable reliance on the similarity between the sentencing factor at issue and the facts judges contemplate when exercising their discretion within the statutory range. Given that the latter are not elements of the crime, the Court explained, neither was the former:

> Section 9712 neither alters the maximum penalty for the crime committed nor creates a separate offense calling for a separate penalty; it operates solely to limit the sentencing court's discretion in selecting a penalty within the range already available to it without the special finding of visible possession of a firearm. Section 9712 'ups the ante' for the defendant only by raising to five years the minimum sentence which may be imposed within the statutory plan. . . . Petitioners' claim that visible possession under the Pennsylvania statute is 'really' an element of the offenses for which they are being punished . . . would have at least more superficial appeal if a finding of visible possession exposed them to greater or additional punishment, . . . but it does not.

In response to the argument that the Act evaded the Constitution's procedural guarantees, the Court noted that the statute "simply took one factor that has always been considered by sentencing courts to bear on punishment . . . and dictated the precise weight to be given that factor."

That reasoning still controls. If the facts judges consider when exercising their discretion within the statutory range are not elements, they do not become as much merely because legislatures require the judge to impose a minimum sentence when those facts are found — a sentence the judge could have imposed absent the finding. . . . These facts, though stigmatizing and punitive, have been the traditional domain of judges; they have not been alleged in the indictment or proved beyond a reasonable doubt. There is no reason to believe that those who framed the Fifth and Sixth Amendments would have thought of them as the elements of the crime.

This conclusion might be questioned if there were extensive historical evidence showing that facts increasing the defendant's minimum sentence (but not affecting the maximum) have, as a matter of course, been treated as elements. The evidence on this score, however, is lacking. Statutes like the Pennsylvania Act, which alter the minimum sentence without changing the maximum, were for the most part the product of the 20th century, when legislatures first asserted control over the sentencing judge's discretion. . . .

McMillan was on firm historical ground, then, when it held that a legislature may specify the condition for a mandatory minimum without making the condition an element of the crime. The fact of visible firearm possession was more like the facts considered by judges when selecting a sentence within the statutory range — facts that, as the authorities from the 19th century confirm, have never been charged in the indictment, submitted to the jury, or proved beyond a reasonable doubt. . . . Since sentencing ranges came into use, defendants have not been able to predict from the face of the indictment precisely what their sentence will be; the charged facts have simply made them aware of the heaviest punishment they face if convicted. Judges, in turn, have always considered uncharged aggravating circumstances that, while increasing the defendant's punishment, have not "swelled the penalty above what the law has provided for the acts charged." [1 J. Bishop, Law of Criminal Procedure §85, at 54 (2d ed. 1872).] Because facts supporting a mandatory minimum fit squarely within that description, the legislature's choice to entrust them to the judge does not implicate the "competition . . . between judge and jury over . . . their respective roles," *Jones,* 526 U.S. at 245, that is the central concern of the Fifth and Sixth Amendments.

At issue in *Apprendi,* by contrast, was a sentencing factor that did "swell the penalty above what the law has provided," Bishop, *supra,* §85, at 54, and thus functioned more like a traditional element. The defendant had been convicted of illegal possession of a firearm, an offense for which New Jersey law prescribed a maximum of 10 years in prison. He was sentenced to 12 years, however, because a separate statute permitted an enhancement when the judge found, by a preponderance of the evidence, that the defendant "acted with a purpose to intimidate an individual or group of individuals because of race."

The Court held that the enhancement was unconstitutional. "Our cases in this area, and the history upon which they rely," the Court observed, confirmed the constitutional principle first identified in *Jones:* "Other than the fact of a prior conviction, any fact that increases the penalty for a crime beyond the prescribed statutory maximum must be submitted to a jury, and proved beyond a reasonable doubt." Those facts, *Apprendi* held, were what the Framers had in mind when they spoke of "crimes" and "criminal prosecutions" in the Fifth and Sixth Amendments: A crime was not alleged, and a criminal prosecution not complete, unless the indictment and the jury verdict included all the facts to which the legislature had attached the maximum punishment. Any "fact that . . . exposes the criminal defendant to a penalty *exceeding* the maximum he would receive if punished according to the facts reflected in the jury verdict alone," the Court concluded, would have been, under the prevailing historical practice, an element of an aggravated offense.

Apprendi's conclusions do not undermine *McMillan*'s. There was no comparable historical practice of submitting facts increasing the mandatory minimum to the jury, so the *Apprendi* rule did not extend to those facts. Indeed, the Court made clear that its holding did not affect *McMillan* at all:

> We do not overrule *McMillan.* We limit its holding to cases that do not involve the imposition of a sentence more severe than the statutory maximum for the offense established by the jury's verdict — a limitation identified in the *McMillan* opinion itself. . . .

Yet once the jury finds all those facts [that determine the maximum sentence], *Apprendi* says that the defendant has been convicted of the crime; the Fifth and Sixth Amendments have been observed; and the Government has been authorized to impose any sentence below the maximum. That is why, as *Apprendi* noted, "nothing in this history suggests that it is impermissible for judges to exercise discretion — taking into consideration various factors relating both to offense and offender — in imposing a judgment *within the range.*" That is also why, as *McMillan* noted, nothing in this history suggests that it is impermissible for judges to find facts that give rise to a mandatory minimum sentence below "the maximum penalty for the crime committed." In both instances the judicial factfinding does not "expose a defendant to a punishment greater than that otherwise legally prescribed." *Apprendi.* Whether chosen by the judge or the legislature, the facts guiding judicial discretion below the statutory maximum need not be alleged in the indictment, submitted to the jury, or proved beyond a reasonable doubt. When a judge sentences the defendant to a mandatory minimum, no less than when the judge chooses a sentence within the range, the grand and petit juries already have found all the facts necessary to authorize the Government to impose the sentence. The judge may impose the minimum, the maximum, or any other sentence within the range without seeking further authorization from those juries — and without contradicting *Apprendi.*

Petitioner argues, however, that the concerns underlying *Apprendi* apply with equal or more force to facts increasing the defendant's minimum sentence. Those factual findings, he contends, often have a greater impact on the defendant than the findings at issue in *Apprendi.* This is so because when a fact increasing the statutory maximum is found, the judge may still impose a sentence far below that maximum; but when a fact increasing the minimum is found, the judge has no choice but to impose that minimum, even if he or she otherwise would have chosen a lower sentence. Why, petitioner asks, would fairness not also require the latter sort of fact to be alleged in the indictment and found by the jury under a reasonable-doubt standard? The answer is that because it is beyond dispute that the judge's choice of sentences within the authorized range may be influenced by facts not considered by the jury, a factual finding's practical effect cannot by itself control the constitutional analysis. The Fifth and Sixth Amendments ensure that the defendant "will never get *more* punishment than he bargained for when he did the crime," but they do not promise that he will receive "anything less" than that. *Apprendi,* 530 U.S. at 498 (Scalia, J., concurring). If the grand jury has alleged, and the trial jury has found, all the facts necessary to impose the maximum, the barriers between government and defendant fall. The judge may select any sentence within the range, based on facts not alleged in the indictment or proved to the jury — even if those facts are specified by the legislature, and even if they persuade the judge to choose a much higher sentence than he or she otherwise would have imposed. That a fact affects the defendant's sentence, even dramatically so, does not by itself make it an element. . . .

The factual finding in *Apprendi* extended the power of the judge, allowing him or her to impose a punishment exceeding what was authorized by the jury. The finding in *McMillan* restrained the judge's power, limiting his or her choices within the authorized range. It is quite consistent to maintain that the former type of fact must be submitted to the jury while the latter need not be. Read together, *McMillan* and *Apprendi* mean that those facts setting the outer limits of a sentence, and of the judicial power to impose it, are the elements of the crime for the purposes of the constitutional analysis. Within the range authorized by the jury's verdict, however, the political system may channel judicial discretion — and rely upon judicial expertise — by requiring defendants to serve minimum terms after judges make certain factual findings. It is critical not to abandon that understanding at this late date. Legislatures and their constituents have relied upon *McMillan* to exercise control over sentencing through dozens of statutes like the one the Court approved in that case. Congress and the States have conditioned mandatory minimum sentences upon judicial findings that, as here, a firearm was possessed, brandished, or discharged, or among other examples, that the victim was over 60 years of age; that the defendant possessed a certain quantity of drugs; that the victim was related to the defendant; and that the defendant was a repeat offender. We see no reason to overturn those statutes or cast uncertainty upon the sentences imposed under them. . . .

The Court is well aware that many question the wisdom of mandatory minimum sentencing. Mandatory minimums, it is often said, fail to account for the unique circumstances of offenders who warrant a lesser penalty. These criticisms may be sound, but they would persist whether the judge or the jury found the facts giving rise to the minimum. We hold only that the Constitution permits the judge to do so, and we leave the other questions to Congress, the States, and the democratic processes.

BREYER, J., concurring in part and concurring in the judgment.

I cannot easily distinguish Apprendi v. New Jersey, 530 U.S. 466 (2000), from this case in terms of logic. For that reason, I cannot agree with the plurality's opinion insofar as it finds such a distinction. At the same time, I continue to believe that the Sixth Amendment permits judges to apply sentencing factors — whether those factors lead to a sentence beyond the statutory maximum (as in *Apprendi*) or the application of a mandatory minimum (as here). And because I believe that extending *Apprendi* to mandatory minimums would have adverse practical, as well as legal, consequences, I cannot yet accept its rule. I therefore join the Court's judgment, and I join its opinion to the extent that it holds that *Apprendi* does not apply to mandatory minimums.

In saying this, I do not mean to suggest my approval of mandatory minimum sentences as a matter of policy. During the past two decades, as mandatory minimum sentencing statutes have proliferated in number and importance, judges, legislators, lawyers, and commentators have criticized those statutes, arguing that they negatively affect the fair administration of the criminal law, a matter of concern to judges and to legislators alike.

Mandatory minimum statutes are fundamentally inconsistent with Congress' simultaneous effort to create a fair, honest, and rational sentencing system through the use of Sentencing Guidelines. Unlike Guideline sentences, statutory mandatory minimums generally deny the judge the legal power to depart downward, no matter how unusual the special circumstances that call for leniency. They rarely reflect an effort to achieve sentencing proportionality — a key element of sentencing fairness that demands that the law punish a drug "kingpin" and a "mule" differently. They transfer sentencing power to prosecutors, who can determine sentences through the charges they decide to bring, and who thereby have reintroduced much of the sentencing disparity that Congress created Guidelines to eliminate. They rarely are based upon empirical study. And there is evidence that they encourage subterfuge, leading to more frequent downward departures (on a random basis), thereby making them a comparatively ineffective means of guaranteeing tough sentences.

Applying *Apprendi* in this case would not, however, lead Congress to abolish, or to modify, mandatory minimum sentencing statutes. Rather, it would simply require the prosecutor to charge, and the jury to find beyond a reasonable doubt, the existence of the "factor," say, the amount of unlawful drugs, that triggers the mandatory minimum. In many cases, a defendant, claiming innocence and arguing, say, mistaken identity, will find it impossible simultaneously to argue to the jury that the prosecutor has overstated the drug amount. How, the jury might ask, could this "innocent" defendant know anything about that matter? The upshot is that in many such cases defendant and prosecutor will enter into a stipulation before trial as to drug amounts to be used at sentencing (if the jury finds the defendant guilty). To that extent, application of *Apprendi* would take from the judge the power to make a factual determination, while giving that power not to juries, but to prosecutors. And such consequences, when viewed through the prism of an open, fair sentencing system, are seriously adverse.

The legal consequences of extending *Apprendi* to the mandatory minimum sentencing context are also seriously adverse. Doing so would diminish further Congress' otherwise broad constitutional authority to define crimes through the specification of elements, to shape criminal sentences through the specification of sentencing factors, and to limit judicial discretion in applying those factors in particular cases. . . .

THOMAS, J., dissenting.

The range of punishment to which William J. Harris was exposed turned on the fact that he brandished a firearm, a fact that was neither charged in his indictment nor proved at trial beyond a reasonable doubt. The United States Court of Appeals for the Fourth Circuit nonetheless held, in reliance on McMillan v. Pennsylvania, 477 U.S. 79 (1986), that the fact that Harris brandished a firearm was a mere sentencing factor to which no constitutional protections attach. *McMillan,* however, conflicts with the Court's later decision in Apprendi v. New Jersey, 530 U.S. 466 (2000), as the dissenting opinion in *Apprendi* recognized. The Court's holding today therefore rests on either a misunderstanding or a rejection of the very principles that animated *Apprendi* just two years ago. . . .

According to the plurality, the historical practices underlying the Court's decision in *Apprendi* with respect to penalties that exceed the statutory maximum do not support extension of *Apprendi*'s rule to facts that increase a defendant's mandatory minimum sentence. Such fine distinctions with regard to vital constitutional liberties cannot withstand close scrutiny. . . .

As I discussed at great length in *Apprendi,* the original understanding of what facts are elements of a crime was expansive. . . .

I agree with the Court that a legislature is free to decree, within constitutional limits, which facts are elements that constitute a crime. But when the legislature provides that a particular fact shall give rise both to a special stigma and to a special punishment, the constitutional consequences are clear. As the Court acknowledged in *Apprendi,* society has long recognized a necessary link between punishment and crime. This link makes a great deal of sense: Why, after all, would anyone care if they were convicted of murder, as opposed to manslaughter, but for the increased penalties for the former offense, which in turn reflect the greater moral opprobrium society attaches to the act? We made clear in *Apprendi* that if a statute "annexes a higher degree of punishment" based on certain circumstances, exposing a defendant to that higher degree of punishment requires that those circumstances be charged in the indictment and proved beyond a reasonable doubt.

This constitutional limitation neither interferes with the legislature's ability to define statutory ranges of punishment nor calls into question judicial discretion to impose "judgment within the range prescribed by statute." *Apprendi.* But it does protect the criminal defendant's constitutional right to know, ex ante, those circumstances that will determine the applicable range of punishment and to have those circumstances proved beyond a reasonable doubt. . . .

The Court truncates this protection and holds that "facts, sometimes referred to as sentencing factors," do not need to be "alleged in the indictment, submitted to the jury, or established beyond a reasonable doubt," so long as they do not increase the penalty for the crime beyond the statutory maximum. This is so even if the fact alters the statutorily mandated sentencing range, by increasing the mandatory minimum sentence. But to say that is in effect to claim that the imposition of a 7-year, rather than a 5-year, mandatory minimum does not change the constitutionally relevant sentence range because, regardless, either sentence falls between five years and the statutory maximum of life, the longest sentence range available under the statute. This analysis is flawed precisely because the statute provides incremental sentencing ranges, in which the mandatory minimum sentence varies upward if a defendant "brandished" or "discharged" a weapon. As a matter of common sense, an increased mandatory minimum heightens the loss of liberty and represents the increased stigma society attaches to the offense. Consequently, facts that trigger an increased mandatory minimum sentence warrant constitutional safeguards.

Actual sentencing practices appear to bolster this conclusion. The suggestion that a 7-year sentence could be imposed even without a finding that a defendant brandished a firearm ignores the fact that the sentence imposed when a defendant is found only to have "carried" a firearm "in relation to" a drug trafficking offense appears to be, almost uniformly, if not invariably, five years. Similarly, those found to have brandished a firearm typically, if not always, are sentenced only to 7 years in prison while those found to have discharged a firearm are sentenced only to 10 years. This is true even though anyone convicted of violating §924(c)(1)(A) is theoretically eligible to receive a sentence as severe as life imprisonment. Yet under the decision today, those key facts actually responsible for fixing a defendant's punishment need not be charged in an indictment or proved beyond a reasonable doubt. . . .

It is true that *Apprendi* concerned a fact that increased the penalty for a crime beyond the prescribed statutory maximum, but the principles upon which it relied apply with equal force to those facts that expose the defendant to a higher mandatory minimum: When a fact exposes a defendant to greater punishment than what is otherwise legally prescribed, that fact is "by definition [an] 'element' of a separate legal offense." Whether one raises the floor or raises the ceiling it is impossible to dispute that the defendant is exposed to greater punishment than is otherwise prescribed.

This is no less true because mandatory minimum sentences are a 20th-century phenomena. As the Government acknowledged at oral argument, this fact means only that historical practice is not directly dispositive of the question whether facts triggering mandatory minimums must be treated like elements. The Court has not previously suggested that constitutional protection ends where legislative innovation or ingenuity begins. Looking to the principles that animated the decision in *Apprendi* and the bases for the historical practice upon which *Apprendi* rested (rather than to the historical pedigree of mandatory minimums), there are no logical grounds for treating facts triggering mandatory minimums any differently than facts that increase the statutory maximum. In either case the defendant cannot predict the judgment from the face of the felony, and the absolute statutory limits of his punishment change, constituting an increased penalty. In either case the defendant must be afforded the procedural protections of notice, a jury trial, and a heightened standard of proof with respect to the facts warranting exposure to a greater penalty. . . .

NOTES

1. *The* Harris *retreat.*   Though the majority opinion in *Apprendi* expressly distinguished McMillan v. Pennsylvania, there was an obvious tension between *Apprendi*'s "elements" rule for facts that raise maximum sentences and *McMillan*'s holding that facts that trigger mandatory minimum sentences can be found by a judge based on a preponderance standard of proof. It thus came as no surprise when the Supreme Court granted review in *Harris* to address the tension between these holdings.

More than the requisite procedure for mandatory minimum sentencing was at stake in *Harris.* Professor Stephanos Bibas has written that "*Apprendi*'s jury-sentencing principle could extend well beyond its holding" and, if taken to its extreme, "could have upset all judicial sentencing, including sentencing guidelines, in favor of jury sentencing." Stephanos Bibas, Back from the Brink: The Supreme Court Balks at Extending *Apprendi* to Upset Most Sentencing, 15 Fed. Sentencing Rep. 79, 79 (2002). By holding in *Harris* that only facts that raise maximum sentences, and not those that establish minimums, must be treated procedurally as elements, the Supreme Court, in Professor Bibas's words, "caged the potentially ravenous, radical *Apprendi* tiger that threatened to devour modern sentencing law." *Id.* at 82.

Federal district court judge Nancy Gertner has expressed concerns about the way the *Harris* decision ensures that guideline sentencing will continue under existing sentencing procedures. In a recent article, Judge Gertner wrote that reliance on informal sentencing procedures makes sense only when judges have the specialized role of sentencing experts within an indeterminate, rehabilitation-oriented sentencing scheme. The judge imposing sentences within a modern, determinate guideline sentencing system "is 'just' another fact finder, doing precisely what the jury does: finding facts with specific and often harsh sentencing consequences." Nancy Gertner, What Has *Harris* Wrought, 15 Fed. Sentencing Rep. 83, 84 (2002). Judge Gertner believes the Supreme Court should have been attentive to this important shift in sentencing dynamics and used *Apprendi* and its progeny to develop a refined set of "heightened due process protections" at sentencing; instead, she notes, the Court's approach after *Apprendi* and *Harris* "is 'all-or-nothing': if there is no jury trial, the 'all' of our criminal justice system, there is next to 'nothing,' the comparative informality of sentencing." *Id.* at 83.

2. *The true meaning of* Harris?   Does *Harris* ensure that the impact of *Apprendi* will be relatively modest and that the potential "threat" of *Apprendi* to guideline sentencing systems has been eliminated? How should we understand Justice Breyer's vote in *Harris* in light of his statement that he "cannot easily distinguish Apprendi v. New Jersey, 530 U.S. 466 (2000), from this case [involving mandatory minimum sentencing] in terms of logic [and] cannot agree with the plurality's opinion insofar as it finds such a distinction." Doesn't this statement suggest that there are actually five Justices who believe the *Apprendi* rule extends to mandatory minimum sentencing?

Professor Kyron Huigens provided an interesting explanation and defense of Justice Breyer's opinion in a recent article, which criticized the *Harris* decision's preservation of the notion of a sentencing factor as a basis for determinate sentencing consequences without the traditional procedural protections available at trial. See Kyron Huigens, *Harris, Ring,* and the Future of Relevant Conduct Sentencing, 15 Fed. Sentencing Rep. 88 (2002). Building a refined argument based on traditional concepts of criminal fault, Huigens suggested a different understanding of the meaning and force of *Apprendi* than provided by the *Harris* majority, but in so doing he explained why Justice Breyer's seemingly mysterious vote in *Harris* was "not only logical but prudent, and not only prudent, but admirable." Huigens maintained that "the very idea of a positive, determinate sentencing factor is a contradiction," as all positively enacted fault considerations must be considered "offense elements by virtue of their being enacted by the legislature in any form." Huigens claimed that his view of *Apprendi* and *Harris* did not mean the demise of all determinate sentencing systems, just the use of sentencing factors (such as the federal sentencing guidelines' reliance on relevant conduct). Huigens asserted that if his understanding of *Apprendi* were to prevail, Justice Breyer ultimately could embrace both the holding and the logic of that decision without undermining the entire concept of guideline sentencing reform.

PROBLEM 6-1.   COMPREHENDING *APPRENDI*

Responding to concerns expressed by the National Commission Against Drunk Driving and to a recent rise in alcohol-related accidents, last fall the Oliwood legislature passed a bipartisan package of bills amending the Oliwood Penal Code. The Oliwood Senate Report stated that the package was intended "to increase penalties and offer law enforcement, prosecutors, and courts additional tools to combat the problems of drunk driving, particularly with respect to those offenders who repeatedly commit serious alcohol-related driving offenses." The new laws include the following provisions:

- Operating a motor vehicle with a Blood Alcohol Concentration (BAC) greater than .08% constitutes the offense of Driving Under the Influence (DUI) requiring, in addition to license revocation and other administrative sanctions, a mandatory minimum sentence of no less than 5 days' imprisonment and a maximum sentence of no more than 1 year's imprisonment.
- Operating a motor vehicle with a BAC greater than .15% constitutes the offense of Driving While Intoxicated (DWI) requiring, in addition to administrative sanctions, a mandatory minimum sentence of no less than 3 months and a maximum sentence of no more than 2 years.
- Operating a motor vehicle with a BAC greater than .25% constitutes the offense of Aggravated Driving While Intoxicated (ADWI) requiring, in addition to administrative sanctions, a mandatory minimum sentence of no less than 2 years and a maximum sentence of no more than 5 years.
- If a defendant has previously been convicted of one drunk-driving-related charge, the required minimum sentence and allowed maximum sentences for these crimes shall be doubled. If the defendant

has previously been convicted of two or more drunk-driving-related charges, the required minimum sentence and allowed maximum sentences shall be multiplied by a factor of 10.

- A sentencing judge may sentence a defendant below the applicable mandatory minimum sentence if the defendant shows, by clear and convincing evidence, that the incident of drunk driving involved a completely aberrant act or was the result of an unavoidable and compelling necessity.
- A sentencing judge may sentence a defendant above the otherwise applicable maximum if the prosecution shows, by clear and convincing evidence, that the incident of drunk driving resulted in serious physical harm or death to any innocent persons.

Oliwood State professor Dugh Irman, the first person prosecuted under Oliwood's new drunk-driving laws, comes to you for legal advice. Here is his story:

This past weekend he drove to a friend's house (which was only two miles from his home) to watch a big football game on television. To calm his nerves while he rooted for his favorite team, Dugh consumed a beer every time his team made a poor play, and Dugh managed to polish off two six-packs of beers before the game's exciting finish. Though exhilarated, Dugh realized he was not fit to drive home after the conclusion of the event.

Upon calling his wife to tell her he planned to stay at his friend's house until the morning, Dugh found out that his young daughter was ill and that he was needed at home as soon as possible. Unable to secure a ride from his buddies (who themselves were intoxicated), Dugh quickly downed a few cups of coffee and convinced himself that he would now be able to navigate the ride home.

Dugh managed to drive safely and without incident until he reached the traffic light at the entrance to his subdivision. Feeling sleepy from the alcohol in his system, Dugh momentarily dozed off while waiting for the light to turn from red to green. He awoke to the sound of car horns and breaking glass, and saw that in front of him two cars had collided in the intersection. (Dugh's car remained untouched, idling in front of the traffic light.) Before Dugh could take in what was going on, the police and an ambulance arrived at the scene. The ambulance quickly drove away with a passenger from one of the smashed cars, who appeared to have a broken leg.

Dugh and the other motorists on the scene were given Breathalyzer tests. To Dugh's surprise and dismay, he registered a BAC of .254%. The other drivers tested fully sober. The police interviewed the drivers involved in the collision, and one blamed the accident on Dugh's failure to proceed when the traffic light turned green. This driver, Ima C. Kinmunny, told the police that, after sitting a while behind Dugh's car at the green light, she tried to navigate her car around Dugh's vehicle but apparently did not get through the intersection before the light changed and a car coming the other way drove into hers. After hearing this story, the police arrested Dugh for Aggravated DWI; he was processed that night and released on bail.

The Oliwood district attorney has now informed Dugh that he plans to prosecute fully in order to send a message concerning how the new Oliwood drunk-driving laws will be enforced. This DA told Dugh that he was aware of, and planned to bring to court, evidence establishing that Dugh had pled guilty to two prior DUIs: one 15 years ago when Dugh was a high-school junior (on the way home from his prom), and another 10 years ago when Dugh was a college senior. The DA indicated that he believed Dugh would thus be subject to a 20-year minimum prison sentence and at least a 50-year potential maximum sentence under the new laws. The DA also stated that he was prepared to establish that Dugh's drunk driving resulted in serious physical harm, which would authorize a prison sentence above the 50-year maximum.

Dugh feels the DA's approach to this case is not only unfair but must in some way run afoul of the Constitution. Does he have any viable constitutional claims that might limit his ultimate sentence? What procedural rights might Dugh have if he wishes to plead guilty to DWI but wants to contest some of the facts that seem to be the basis for an enhanced sentence?

PROBLEM 6-2.   INDICTING *APPRENDI*

Kevin Badoni was initially charged in 1998 with one count of murder, two counts of attempted murder "by any of the means with which death may be caused," aggravated battery, and tampering with evidence for disposing of a .380 handgun. All the charges resulted from a confrontation between two groups of young men during which one man was killed and two men were seriously wounded by gunshots. Badoni was convicted of second-degree murder and aggravated battery.

Through a special verdict, the jury found that Badoni used a firearm in the commission of these offenses. Badoni's attorney had opposed the use of the special verdict because the use of a firearm was not pled in the murder and attempted murder charges. Badoni was sentenced to 15 years in prison for the murder conviction, three years for aggravated battery, and 18 months for tampering with evidence. The murder and aggravated battery sentences were each enhanced by one year because of the use of a firearm under section 31-18-16, the firearm enhancement statute.

Badoni argues that, under *Apprendi,* the state must give formal notice in the criminal information or indictment that Badoni used a firearm in the commission of the offense before the state may seek to enhance Badoni's sentence under section 31-18-16.

How would you rule? See State v. Badoni, 62 P.3d 348 (N.M. Ct. App. 2002).

NOTE: CAPITAL SENTENCING PROCEDURES AND RING v. ARIZONA

The constitutional and statutory sentencing procedures that apply in death penalty cases can (and have) filled numerous textbooks and treatises. Although capital sentencing, as Williams v. New York reveals, once relied on the informal procedures common to indeterminate noncapital sentencing systems, the Supreme Court's landmark decisions in Furman v. Georgia, 408 U.S. 238 (1972), and Gregg v. Georgia, 428 U.S. 153 (1976), initiated a series of reforms that transformed capital sentencing into perhaps the most procedurally intricate and complicated area of any legal field. The concerns that motivated modern procedural regulation of the death penalty, as well as the basic outlines of modern capital procedures, were developed at some length in Chapter 3. The chapter also described a number of Supreme Court decisions since *Gregg* that played a major role in shaping the contours of capital sentencing procedures. It is now appropriate to provide a more detailed account of the shock waves that the *Apprendi* decision sent through the capital sentencing system.

On the same day the U.S. Supreme Court significantly restricted through Harris v. United States, 536 U.S. 545 (2002), the reach of *Apprendi* by deciding its "elements" rule did not apply to mandatory minimum sentencing, the Court also significantly expanded through Ring v. Arizona, 536 U.S. 584 (2002), the reach of *Apprendi* by holding that facts that establish eligibility for the death penalty must be treated as "elements" and thus require submission to a jury and proof beyond a reasonable doubt.

Timothy Ring was convicted of felony murder in the course of an armed robbery but acquitted of premeditated murder. Under Arizona law, the trial judge then held "a separate sentencing hearing to determine the existence or nonexistence of [certain enumerated] circumstances . . . for the purpose of determining the sentence to be imposed." Arizona law stated that "[t]he hearing shall be conducted before the court alone. The court alone shall make all factual determinations required by this section or the constitution of the United States or this state." The state's law authorized the judge to sentence the defendant to death only if there is at least one aggravating circumstance and "there are no mitigating circumstances sufficiently substantial to call for leniency." The trial judge sentenced Ring to death.

Because Ring was convicted of felony murder, not premeditated murder, the judge recognized that Ring was eligible for the death penalty only if he was the victim's actual killer or if he was "a major participant in the armed robbery that led to the killing and exhibited a reckless disregard or indifference for human life." Based on evidence at the sentencing hearing, the judge concluded that Ring was the killer and then found two aggravating factors, first that Ring committed the offense in expectation of receiving something of "pecuniary value" and, second, that the offense was committed "in an especially heinous, cruel or depraved manner."

On appeal, Ring argued that Arizona's capital sentencing scheme violated the Sixth and Fourteenth Amendments to the U.S. Constitution because it entrusted to a judge the finding of a fact raising the defendant's maximum penalty. The State, in response, noted that the Court had upheld Arizona's system in Walton v. Arizona, 497 U.S. 639 (1990), and had stated in *Apprendi* that *Walton* remained good law. But the U.S. Supreme Court through its decision in *Ring* ultimately concluded that *Walton* and *Apprendi* could not be reconciled. Writing for the majority, Justice Ginsberg explained:

> [T]his is not the first time we have considered the constitutionality of Arizona's capital sentencing system. In Walton v. Arizona, 497 U.S. 639 (1990), we upheld Arizona's scheme against a charge that it violated the Sixth Amendment. The Court had previously denied a Sixth Amendment challenge to Florida's capital sentencing system, in which the jury recommends a sentence but makes no explicit findings on aggravating circumstances; we so ruled, *Walton* noted, on the ground that "the Sixth Amendment does not require that the specific findings authorizing the imposition of the sentence of death be made by the jury." *Walton* found unavailing the attempts by the defendant-petitioner

in that case to distinguish Florida's capital sentencing system from Arizona's. In neither State, according to *Walton*, were the aggravating factors "elements of the offense"; in both States, they ranked as "sentencing considerations" guiding the choice between life and death. . . .

Walton could be reconciled with *Apprendi*, the Court finally asserted [in *Apprendi*]. The key distinction, according to the *Apprendi* Court, was that a conviction of first-degree murder in Arizona carried a maximum sentence of death. "Once a jury has found the defendant guilty of all the elements of an offense which carries as its maximum penalty the sentence of death, it may be left to the judge to decide whether that maximum penalty, rather than a lesser one, ought to be imposed."

The *Apprendi* dissenters called the Court's distinction of *Walton* "baffling," 530 U.S., at 538 (opinion of O'Connor, J.), [because] a "defendant convicted of first-degree murder in Arizona cannot receive a death sentence unless a judge makes the factual determination that a statutory aggravating factor exists. Without that critical finding, the maximum sentence to which the defendant is exposed is life imprisonment, and not the death penalty". *Walton*, the *Apprendi* dissenters insisted, if properly followed, would have required the Court to uphold Apprendi's sentence. "If a State can remove from the jury a factual determination that makes the difference between life and death, as *Walton* holds that it can, it is inconceivable why a State cannot do the same with respect to a factual determination that results in only a 10-year increase in the maximum sentence to which a defendant is exposed." 530 U.S., at 537 (opinion of O'Connor, J.).

The Arizona Supreme Court . . . found the *Apprendi* majority's portrayal of Arizona's capital sentencing law incorrect, and the description in Justice O'Connor's dissent precisely right: "Defendant's death sentence required the judge's factual findings." Recognizing that the Arizona court's construction of the State's own law is authoritative, we are persuaded that *Walton*, in relevant part, cannot survive the reasoning of *Apprendi*.

In an effort to reconcile its capital sentencing system with the Sixth Amendment as interpreted by *Apprendi*, Arizona first restates the *Apprendi* majority's portrayal of Arizona's system: Ring was convicted of first-degree murder, for which Arizona law specifies "death or life imprisonment" as the only sentencing options; Ring was therefore sentenced within the range of punishment authorized by the jury verdict. This argument overlooks *Apprendi*'s instruction that "the relevant inquiry is one not of form, but of effect." In effect, "the required finding [of an aggravated circumstance] exposed [Ring] to a greater punishment than that authorized by the jury's guilty verdict." The Arizona first-degree murder statute authorizes a maximum penalty of death only in a formal sense, for it explicitly cross-references the statutory provision requiring the finding of an aggravating circumstance before imposition of the death penalty. If Arizona prevailed on its opening argument, *Apprendi* would be reduced to a "meaningless and formalistic" rule of statutory drafting. See 530 U.S., at 541 (O'Connor, J., dissenting). . . .

Even if facts increasing punishment beyond the maximum authorized by a guilty verdict standing alone ordinarily must be found by a jury, Arizona further urges, aggravating circumstances necessary to trigger a death sentence may nonetheless be reserved for judicial determination. As Arizona's counsel maintained at oral argument, there is no doubt that "death is different." States have constructed elaborate sentencing procedures in death cases, Arizona emphasizes, because of constraints we have said the Eighth Amendment places on capital sentencing. [But] apart from the Eighth Amendment provenance of aggravating factors, Arizona presents "no specific reason for excepting capital defendants from the constitutional protections . . . extended to defendants generally, and none is readily apparent." *Id.*, at 539 (O'Connor, J., dissenting). The notion "that the Eighth Amendment's restriction on a state legislature's ability to define capital crimes should be compensated for by permitting States more leeway under the Fifth and Sixth Amendments in proving an aggravating fact necessary to a capital sentence . . . is without precedent in our constitutional jurisprudence." *Ibid.* . . .

Arizona suggests that judicial authority over the finding of aggravating factors "may . . . be a better way to guarantee against the arbitrary imposition of the death penalty." The Sixth Amendment jury trial right, however, does not turn on the relative rationality, fairness, or efficiency of potential factfinders. Entrusting to a judge the finding of facts necessary to support a death sentence might be

> an admirably fair and efficient scheme of criminal justice designed for a society that is prepared to leave criminal justice to the State. . . . The founders of the American Republic were not prepared to leave it to the State, which is why the jury-trial guarantee was one of the least controversial provisions of the Bill of Rights. It has never been efficient; but it has always been free. *Apprendi,* 530 U.S., at 498 (Scalia, J., concurring).

In any event, the superiority of judicial factfinding in capital cases is far from evident. Unlike Arizona, the great majority of States responded to this Court's Eighth Amendment decisions requiring the presence of aggravating circumstances in capital cases by entrusting those determinations to the jury.[6]

Although the doctrine of stare decisis is of fundamental importance to the rule of law, our precedents are not sacrosanct. We have overruled prior decisions where the necessity and propriety of doing so has been established. We are satisfied that this is such a case.

[W]e hold that *Walton* and *Apprendi* are irreconcilable; our Sixth Amendment jurisprudence cannot be home to both. Accordingly, we overrule *Walton* to the extent that it allows a sentencing judge, sitting without a jury, to find an aggravating circumstance necessary for imposition of the death penalty. Because Arizona's enumerated aggravating factors operate as "the functional equivalent of an element of a greater offense," the Sixth Amendment requires that they be found by a jury. . . .

The right to trial by jury guaranteed by the Sixth Amendment would be senselessly diminished if it encompassed the factfinding necessary to increase a defendant's sentence by two years, but not the factfinding necessary to put him to death. We hold that the Sixth Amendment applies to both.

Justice Scalia (joined by Justice Thomas) concurred. While disagreeing with the capital jurisprudence that requires findings of aggravating factors to justify a capital sentence, "the fundamental meaning of the jury-trial guarantee of the Sixth Amendment is that all facts essential to imposition of the level of punishment that the defendant receives—whether the statute calls them elements of the offense, sentencing factors, or Mary Jane—must be found by the jury beyond a reasonable doubt." Justice Scalia expressed greater concern with "the accelerating propensity of both state and federal legislatures to adopt 'sentencing factors' determined by judges that increase punishment beyond what is

---

6. Of the 38 States with capital punishment, 29 generally commit sentencing decisions to juries. Other than Arizona, only four States commit both capital sentencing factfinding and the ultimate sentencing decision entirely to judges. See Colo. Rev. Stat. §16-11-103 (2001) (three-judge panel); Idaho Code §19-2515 (Supp. 2001); Mont. Code Ann. §46-18-301 (1997); Neb. Rev. Stat. §29-2520 (1995). Four States have hybrid systems, in which the jury renders an advisory verdict but the judge makes the ultimate sentencing determinations. See Ala. Code §§13A-5-46, 13A-5-47 (1994); Del. Code Ann., Tit. 11, §4209 (1995); Fla. Stat. Ann. §921.141 (West 2001); Ind. Code Ann. §35-50-2-9 (Supp. 2001).

authorized by the jury's verdict," than with the (in his view) misguided capital jurisprudence. He concluded that "[w]e cannot preserve our veneration for the protection of the jury in criminal cases if we render ourselves callous to the need for that protection by regularly imposing the death penalty without it," and thus "wherever [aggravating] factors exist they must be subject to the usual requirements of the common law, and to the requirement enshrined in our Constitution, in criminal cases: they must be found by the jury beyond a reasonable doubt."

Justices Kennedy and Breyer would prefer to reverse *Apprendi*, not *Walton*, but so long as *Apprendi* was good law, then *Walton* had to be reversed. Justice O'Connor and Chief Justice Rehnquist dissented, agreeing that *Apprendi* and *Walton* were inconsistent, but that the experience of two years argued that *Apprendi* should be reversed. Justice O'Connor wrote:

I continue to believe . . . that the decision in *Apprendi* was a serious mistake. . . . *Apprendi*'s rule that any fact that increases the maximum penalty must be treated as an element of the crime is not required by the Constitution, by history, or by our prior cases. Indeed, the rule directly contradicts several of our prior cases. And it ignores the "significant history in this country of . . . discretionary sentencing by judges." The Court has failed, both in *Apprendi* and in the decision announced today, to offer any meaningful justification for deviating from years of cases both suggesting and holding that application of the "increase in the maximum penalty" rule is not required by the Constitution.

Not only was the decision in *Apprendi* unjustified in my view, but it has also had a severely destabilizing effect on our criminal justice system. I predicted in my dissent that the decision would "unleash a flood of petitions by convicted defendants seeking to invalidate their sentences in whole or in part on the authority of [*Apprendi*]." As of May 31, 2002, less than two years after *Apprendi* was announced, the United States Courts of Appeals had decided approximately 1,802 criminal appeals in which defendants challenged their sentences, and in some cases even their convictions, under *Apprendi*. These federal appeals are likely only the tip of the iceberg, as federal criminal prosecutions represent a tiny fraction of the total number of criminal prosecutions nationwide. The number of second or successive habeas corpus petitions filed in the federal courts also increased by 77% in 2001, a phenomenon the Administrative Office of the United States Courts attributes to prisoners bringing *Apprendi* claims. This Court has been similarly overwhelmed by the aftershocks of *Apprendi*. A survey of the petitions for certiorari we received in the past year indicates that 18% raised *Apprendi*-related claims. It is simply beyond dispute that *Apprendi* threw countless criminal sentences into doubt and thereby caused an enormous increase in the workload of an already overburdened judiciary.

The decision today is only going to add to these already serious effects. The Court effectively declares five States' capital sentencing schemes unconstitutional [by] identifying Colorado, Idaho, Montana, and Nebraska as having sentencing schemes like Arizona's. There are 168 prisoners on death row in these States, each of whom is now likely to challenge his or her death sentence. . . . In addition, I fear that the prisoners on death row in Alabama, Delaware, Florida, and Indiana, which the Court identifies as having hybrid sentencing schemes in which the jury renders an advisory verdict but the judge makes the ultimate sentencing determination may also seize on today's decision to challenge their sentences. There are 529 prisoners on death row in these States.

By expanding on *Apprendi*, the Court today exacerbates the harm done in that case. Consistent with my dissent, I would overrule *Apprendi* rather than *Walton*.

B. PROCEDURAL REALITIES

Defendants' concerns about what sentence they may receive shape the entire criminal process. Sentencing "process" might be said to encompass each stage of criminal proceedings that has a distinct impact on the sentence determination, as opposed to the identification of suspects or defendants, or the determination of guilt and innocence. While in some situations, constitutional rights (including any developing rights under *Apprendi*) may be an essential part of sentencing process, in most cases the principal procedures will be nonconstitutional, guided by statute and, to an even greater extent, by rules of procedure, prosecutorial policies, and local judicial culture.

The dominant procedural reality for all defendants is that the overwhelming majority of cases in both state and federal systems are resolved by guilty pleas, and those pleas generally reflect bargaining between prosecution and defense. What defendants are willing to plead to will turn in some cases on what the government knows or might prove, and hence on the product of criminal discovery. The contents of guilty pleas, going well beyond simply the offense of conviction, are likely to have a significant effect on the sentence.

After an exploration of the connection between plea negotiations and sentencing, the latter part of this chapter considers two procedures unique to sentencing — sentencing hearings and the creation of presentence investigation reports — along with the special institutional role of probation officers.

1. Plea Practices and Sentencing

About 96 percent of all felonies in state and federal systems are resolved through guilty pleas rather than trials, and the vast majority of these appear to be the product of plea bargains between the prosecution and the defense. The effect that these bargains have on a sentence may be modest or quite determinative. Sentencing may occur at the plea hearing or at a separate proceeding after the plea hearing.

This section considers the procedures that govern the acceptance of guilty pleas, with an emphasis on aspects of plea procedure that relate to sentencing. The section focuses on rules in the federal system, because they serve as the model for many states and since they have repeatedly prompted questions about the relationship of plea bargains to sentencing. The first part looks at the relevant statutes, guidelines, and rules of procedure. The second part examines a series of extraordinary federal prosecutorial policies that have tried to shape the relationship between traditional prosecutorial charging and plea bargaining discretion and sentencing guideline policy goals.

a. Plea Statutes and Rules

Given the importance of guilty pleas and the underlying plea bargains, it might seem that there should be a constitutional jurisprudence to match. There is not; indeed, there is surprisingly little caselaw or doctrine governing guilty pleas or plea bargains. There is, however, quite a bit of relevant law governing plea bargains and guilty pleas in statutes and rules.

What principles govern guilty pleas and plea bargains? Should defendants know the sentence they will face if they go to trial? If they plead? What range of sentence possibilities in each case is acceptable? Can a plea be voluntary (one of the few clear legal requirements) if the impact of the plea is highly uncertain? If a defendant wants to withdraw from a prior plea bargain or guilty plea upon hearing the sentence, should she be allowed to do so? Finally, are there any subjects that should not be allowed to be a part of plea bargains?

Is a plea bargain a close analog to a contract between two free parties, or are there substantial public policy interests at stake in the crime and punishment context that are not present in the private civil context? If so, what are those interests?

Consider the procedures for guilty pleas in the federal system and the expectations about the relationship of guilty pleas to sentencing. The first document is the federal rule governing plea procedures. That is followed by the brief provision on guilty pleas from the Sentencing Reform Act of 1984.

Federal Rule of Criminal Procedure 11
Pleas

(a) Entering a Plea.

(1) *In General.* A defendant may plead guilty, not guilty, or (with the court's consent) nolo contendere. . . .

(b) Considering and Accepting a Guilty or Nolo Contendere Plea.

(1) *Advising and Questioning the Defendant.*

Before the court accepts a plea of guilty or nolo contendere, the defendant may be placed under oath, and the court must address the defendant personally in open court. During this address, the court must inform the defendant of, and determine that the defendant understands, the following:

(A) the government's right, in a prosecution for perjury or false statement, to use against the defendant any statement that the defendant gives under oath;

(B) the right to plead not guilty, or having already so pleaded, to persist in that plea;

(C) the right to a jury trial;

(D) the right to be represented by counsel — and if necessary have the court appoint counsel — at trial and at every other stage of the proceeding;

(E) the right at trial to confront and cross-examine adverse witnesses, to be protected from compelled self-incrimination, to testify and present evidence, and to compel the attendance of witnesses;

(F) the defendant's waiver of these trial rights if the court accepts a plea of guilty or nolo contendere;

(G) the nature of each charge to which the defendant is pleading;

(H) any maximum possible penalty, including imprisonment, fine, and term of supervised release;

(I) any mandatory minimum penalty;

(J) any applicable forfeiture;

(K) the court's authority to order restitution;

(L) the court's obligation to impose a special assessment;

(M) the court's obligation to apply the Sentencing Guidelines, and the court's discretion to depart from those guidelines under some circumstances; and

(N) the terms of any plea-agreement provision waiving the right to appeal or to collaterally attack the sentence.

(2) *Ensuring that a Plea Is Voluntary.* Before accepting a plea of guilty or nolo contendere, the court must address the defendant personally in open court and determine that the plea is voluntary and did not result from force, threats, or promises (other than promises in a plea agreement).

(3) *Determining the Factual Basis for a Plea.* Before entering judgment on a guilty plea, the court must determine that there is a factual basis for the plea.

(c) Plea Agreement Procedure.

(1) *In General.* An attorney for the government and the defendant's attorney, or the defendant when proceeding pro se, may discuss and reach a plea agreement. The court must not participate in these discussions. If the defendant pleads guilty or nolo contendere to either a charged offense or a lesser or related offense, the plea agreement may specify that an attorney for the government will:

(A) not bring, or will move to dismiss other charges;

(B) recommend, or agree not to oppose the defendant's request, that a particular sentence or sentencing range is appropriate or that a particular provision of the Sentencing Guidelines, or policy statement, or sentencing factor does or does not apply (such a recommendation or request does not bind the court); or

(C) agree that a specific sentence or sentencing range is the appropriate disposition of the case, or that a particular provision of the Sentencing Guidelines, or policy statement, or sentencing factor does or does not apply (such a recommendation or request binds the court once the court accepts the plea agreement).

(2) *Disclosing a Plea Agreement.* The parties must disclose the plea agreement in open court when the plea is offered, unless the court for good cause allows the parties to disclose the plea agreement in camera.

(3) *Judicial Consideration of a Plea Agreement.* (A) To the extent the plea agreement is of the type specified in Rule 11(c)(1)(A) or (C), the court may accept the agreement, reject it, or defer a decision until the court has reviewed the presentence report. (B) To the extent the plea agreement is of the type specified in Rule 11(c)(1)(B), the court must advise the defendant that the defendant has no right to withdraw the plea if the court does not follow the recommendation or request.

(4) *Accepting a Plea Agreement.* If the court accepts the plea agreement, it must inform the defendant that to the extent the plea agreement is of the type specified in Rule 11(c)(1)(A) or (C), the agreed disposition will be included in the judgment.

(5) *Rejecting a Plea Agreement.* If the court rejects a plea agreement containing provisions of the type specified in Rule 11(c)(1)(A) or (C), the court must do the following on the record and in open court (or, for good cause, in camera):

(A) inform the parties that the court rejects the plea agreement;

(B) advise the defendant personally that the court is not required to follow the plea agreement and give the defendant the opportunity to withdraw the plea; and

(C) advise the defendant personally that if the plea is not withdrawn, the court may dispose of the case less favorably toward the defendant than the plea agreement contemplated.

(d) Withdrawing a Guilty or Nolo Contendere Plea. A defendant may withdraw a plea of guilty or nolo contendere:

(1) before the court accepts the plea, for any reason or no reason; or

(2) after the court accepts the plea, but before it imposes sentence if:

(A) the court rejects a plea agreement under Rule 11(c)(5); or

(B) the defendant can show a fair and just reason for requesting the withdrawal.

(e) Finality of a Guilty or Nolo Contendere Plea. After the court imposes sentence, the defendant may not withdraw a plea of guilty or nolo contendere, and the plea may be set aside only on direct appeal or collateral attack.

Sentencing Reform Act of 1984
28 U.S.C. §994(a)(2)(E)

The Commission . . . shall promulgate . . . general policy statements regarding application of the guidelines or any other aspect of sentencing or sentence implementation . . . including the appropriate use of . . . the authority granted under Rule 11(e)(2) of the Federal Rules of Criminal Procedure to accept or reject a plea agreement. . . .

When the U.S. Sentencing Commission created its initial set of guidelines, it included a policy statement about plea agreements. At the time, it was generally assumed that policy statements had less binding effect than the guidelines themselves, although later events have all but erased this distinction. As you review these provisions below, consider what the commission was trying to accomplish with regard to plea agreements.

U.S. Sentencing Guidelines Manual
§§6B1.2, 6B1.4 (Policy Statements)

§6B1.2   STANDARDS FOR ACCEPTANCE OF PLEA AGREEMENTS

(a) In the case of a plea agreement that includes the dismissal of any charges or an agreement not to pursue potential charges [under Rule 11(e)(1)(A)], the court may accept the agreement if the court determines, for reasons stated on the record, that the remaining charges adequately reflect the seriousness of the actual offense behavior and that accepting the agreement will not undermine the statutory purposes of sentencing or the sentencing guidelines. Provided, that a plea agreement that includes the dismissal of a charge or a plea agreement not to pursue a potential charge shall not preclude the conduct underlying such charge from being considered under the provisions of §1B1.3 (Relevant Conduct) in connection with the count(s) of which the defendant is convicted.

(b) In the case of a plea agreement that includes a nonbinding recommendation [under Rule 11(e)(1)(B)], the court may accept the recommendation if the court is satisfied either that: (1) the recommended sentence is within the applicable guideline range; or (2) the recommended sentence departs from the applicable guideline range for justifiable reasons.

(c) In the case of a plea agreement that includes a specific sentence [under Rule 11(e)(1)(C)], the court may accept the agreement if the court is satisfied either that: (1) the agreed sentence is within the applicable guideline range; or (2) the agreed sentence departs from the applicable guideline range for justifiable reasons.

§6B1.4 STIPULATIONS

(a) A plea agreement may be accompanied by a written stipulation of facts relevant to sentencing. [S]tipulations shall: (1) set forth the relevant facts and circumstances of the actual offense conduct and offender characteristics; (2) not contain misleading facts; and (3) set forth with meaningful specificity the reasons why the sentencing range resulting from the proposed agreement is appropriate.

(b) To the extent that the parties disagree about any facts relevant to sentencing, the stipulation shall identify the facts that are in dispute. . . .

(d) The court is not bound by the stipulation, but may with the aid of the presentence report, determine the facts relevant to sentencing.

NOTE

Plea procedures and sentencing. Federal Rule of Criminal Procedure 11 has been a model for many states. The types of pleas in Rule 11 were identified before the implementation of the federal guideline system; one of those types allows for plea agreements to particular sentences. Such binding sentence pleas are quite rare — most prosecutors refuse to make such pleas and some courts refuse to accept them.

Rule 11 was amended and reorganized effective December 1, 2002. Most of the cases and literature before that date and some (by force of habit) afterward use a reference to the prior rule — with "(e)(1)(A)" pleas being the prior form of current "(c)(1)(A)" (charge bargains), "(e)(1)(B)" pleas the earlier form of "(c)(1)(B)" (sentence recommendation bargains), and "(e)(1)(C)" the earlier form of "(c)(1)(C)" (binding pleas to a specific sentence).

Did Congress in the Sentencing Reform Act address the relevance of the overwhelming reliance on guilty pleas and plea bargains to the new guideline system it proposed? Did the commission respond thoughtfully in its policy statements? What would you guess has been the significance of these policy statements? To answer that question, how might you begin your research?

b. Prosecutorial Plea Bargaining Guidelines

Decisions whether to offer or accept plea bargains are often governed by executive branch policies. These policies vary in their level of detail; in many smaller offices, prosecutors follow consistent plea practices that may reflect unwritten (but explicit) guidelines, or they may simply reflect shared office culture and experience. Sometimes prosecutors develop formal plea review standards, describing substantively the types of bargains that are acceptable. Other times they create procedural review mechanisms, such as supervisory review or committee review of possible plea bargains. These guidelines or procedures might apply only for identified types of cases, such as those involving drugs or those likely to be controversial.

Federal prosecutors, under the central control of the U.S. attorney general, have developed a detailed series of written plea bargaining policies. In addition to the nationwide guidelines set out below, many of the U.S. Attorney's offices in the 93 federal districts around the country have developed additional guidance to reflect the distinctive caseloads, resources, and other factors in each district.

The following policies reward slow and careful reading. Note that some policies reverse earlier policies, while others add new standards or procedures. The following questions applied to each policy may help to reveal the dynamics at work.

- What are the goals of the policy and are they explicitly stated? Do the goals relate to authorizing statutes, general principles of justice (such as sentencing purposes), or internal administrative aims?
- Is the link between plea bargains and sentencing explicitly stated?
- Does the policy use substantive limitations (rules about the content of acceptable agreements) or procedures (written decisions, internal review and approval) to achieve its goals?

As you read these policies, remember that the federal rules authorize three kinds of pleas: (1) agreements to enter a guilty plea to one or more charges in return for dismissal of other charges (a charge bargain under Rule 11(c)(1)(A)); (2) agreements to recommend a sentence in exchange for a guilty plea, subject to the judge's power to select the final sentence after accepting the guilty plea (a sentence bargain under Rule 11(c)(1)(B)); and (3) an agreement to a particular sentence in exchange for a guilty plea (a stipulated sentence plea under Rule 11(c)(1)(C)).

The first policy below was promulgated before the legislation that created the federal guidelines, when the federal system (and most state systems) still operated with an indeterminate sentencing model. The subsequent policies were promulgated in light of the federal sentencing guidelines. To what extent were these original principles (developed in 1980) concerned with sentencing?

|| *Principles of Federal Prosecution* ||
U.S. Department of Justice (1980)

ENTERING INTO PLEA AGREEMENTS

1. The attorney for the government may, in an appropriate case, enter into an agreement with a defendant that, upon the defendant's plea of guilty or nolo contendere to a charged offense or to a lesser or related offense, he will move for dismissal of other charges, take a certain position with respect to the sentence to be imposed, or take other action.

2. In determining whether it would be appropriate to enter into a plea agreement, the attorney for the government should weigh all relevant considerations, including:

   (a) the defendant's willingness to cooperate in the investigation or prosecution of others;

   (b) the defendant's history with respect to criminal activity;

   (c) the nature and seriousness of the offense or offenses charged;

   (d) the defendant's remorse or contrition and his willingness to assume responsibility for his conduct;

   (e) the desirability of prompt and certain disposition of the case;

   (f) the likelihood of obtaining a conviction at trial;

   (g) the probable effect on witnesses;

   (h) the probable sentence or other consequences if the defendant is convicted;

   (i) the public interest in having the case tried rather than disposed of by a guilty plea;

   (j) the expense of trial and appeal; and

   (k) the need to avoid delay in the disposition of other pending cases.

Comment: . . . The provision is not intended to suggest the desirability or lack of desirability of a plea agreement in any particular case or to be construed as a reflection on the merits of any plea agreement that actually may be reached; its purpose is solely to assist attorneys for the government in exercising their judgment as to whether some sort of plea agreement would be appropriate in a particular case. Government attorneys should consult the investigating agency involved in any case in which it would be helpful to have its views concerning the relevance of particular factors or the weight they deserve. . . .

A plea disposition in one case may facilitate the prompt disposition of other cases, including cases in which prosecution might otherwise be declined. This may occur simply because prosecutorial, judicial, or defense resources will become available for use in other cases, or because a plea by one of several defendants may have a "domino effect," leading to pleas by other defendants. In weighing the importance of these possible consequences, the attorney for the government should consider the state of the criminal docket and the speedy trial requirements in the district, the desirability of handling a larger volume of criminal cases, and the workloads of prosecutors, judges, and defense attorneys in the district.

3. If a prosecution is to be concluded pursuant to a plea agreement, the defendant should be required to plead to a charge or charges:

    (a) that bears a reasonable relationship to the nature and extent of his criminal conduct;

    (b) that has an adequate factual basis;

    (c) that makes likely the imposition of an appropriate sentence under all the circumstances of the case; and

    (d) that does not adversely affect the investigation or prosecution of others.

Comment: [T]he considerations that should be taken into account in selecting the charge or charges to which a defendant should be required to plead guilty . . . are essentially the same as those governing the selection of charges to be included in the original indictment or information.

    (a) Relationship to criminal conduct — The charge or charges to which a defendant pleads guilty should bear a reasonable relationship to the defendant's criminal conduct, both in nature and in scope. . . . In many cases, this will probably require that the defendant plead to the most serious offense charged. . . . The requirement that a defendant plead to a charge that bears a reasonable relationship to the nature and extent of his criminal conduct is not inflexible. There may be situations involving cooperating defendants in which [lesser charges may be appropriate].

    (b) Factual basis — The attorney for the government should also bear in mind the legal requirement that there be a factual basis for the charge or charges to which a guilty plea is entered. This requirement is intended to assure against conviction after a guilty plea of a person who is not in fact guilty. . . .

    (c) Basis for sentencing — [T]he prosecutor should take care to avoid a "charge agreement" that would unduly restrict the court's sentencing authority. [I]f restitution is appropriate under the circumstances of the case, a sufficient number of counts should be retained under the agreement to provide a basis for an adequate restitution order. . . .

    (d) Effect on other cases — . . . Among the possible adverse consequences to be avoided are the negative jury appeal that may result when relatively less culpable defendants are tried in the absence of a more culpable defendant or when a principal prosecution witness appears to be equally culpable as the defendants but has been permitted to plead to a significantly less serious offense. . . .

    5. If a prosecution is to be terminated pursuant to a plea agreement, the attorney for the government should ensure that the case file contains a record of the agreed disposition, signed or initialed by the defendant or his attorney. . . .

The U.S. Department of Justice realized that the new system of guideline sentencing was complicated. Thus, it issued special guidance to prosecutors that appeared simultaneously with the guidelines. Is this internal guidance to prosecutors consistent with the law and policy of federal sentencing reform? What changes does it make to the 1980 Principles of Federal Prosecution?

> ## *Prosecutors' Handbook on Sentencing Guidelines ("The Redbook")*
> ### William Weld, Assistant Attorney General (1987)

[T]he validity and use of the Commission's policy statements by prosecutors should depend upon whether the agreement reflects charge bargaining or sentence bargaining under Rule 11(e).

SENTENCE BARGAINING

A significant problem with the Commission's policy statements on plea bargains which include a specific sentence under Rule 11(e)(1)(B) and (C), §6B1.2(b) and (c), is that the standard they set forth for acceptance or rejection of a sentence that departs from the guidelines appears to be of doubtful validity under the Sentencing Reform Act (SRA). The standard for departure from the guidelines is set forth in the Act and requires a finding that an aggravating or mitigating circumstance exists that was not adequately taken into consideration by the Commission in formulating the guidelines. Yet the Commission's policy statements relating to sentence bargains authorize departure "for justifiable reasons." We do not believe it is possible to argue that the Commission has not adequately taken into consideration the value of a plea agreement as a mitigating factor so as to support a departure. . . . We recognize, nonetheless, that many judges might be tempted to take a realistic approach; a sentence outside the guidelines in the context of a plea agreement is unlikely to result in an appeal of the sentence. Therefore, if urged to accept a plea agreement that departs from the guidelines, they will follow the policy statements despite their questionable basis.

Nevertheless, the Criminal Division has concluded that the apparent authority for a judge to depart from the guidelines pursuant to the Commission's policy statements, §6B1.2(b) and (c), for plea agreements involving a particular sentence under Rule 11(e)(1)(B) and (C) is at variance with the more restrictive departure language of [the statute] and that, consequently, these policy statements should not be used as a basis for recommending a sentence that departs from the guidelines. [P]rosecutors should not recommend or agree to a lower-than-guideline sentence merely on the basis of a plea agreement. They may, however, recommend or agree to a sentence at the low end of an applicable sentencing range [within the guidelines].

In addition to the above-described legitimate guideline reductions that may be used in sentence-type negotiations, a departure from the guidelines may be warranted and may be included in the recommended or agreed-upon sentence if the [statutory] standard . . . is met. That is, a mitigating circumstance must exist (other than the reaching of a plea agreement) that was not adequately taken into consideration by the Commission in formulating the guidelines and that should result in a sentence different from that described. Moreover, a departure from the guidelines may also be reflected in a plea agreement if the defendant provided substantial assistance in the investigation or prosecution of another person who has committed an offense. . . . Therefore, even though plea-bargained sentences must accord with the law and the guidelines, there is considerable room for negotiating.

The basic reason for rejecting the Commission's policy statements on sentence bargains and treating sentences which are the subject of a sentence bargain in the same manner as sentences which result from conviction after trial is that any other result could seriously thwart the purpose of the SRA to reduce unwarranted disparity in sentencing [among defendants with similar records who have been found guilty of similar criminal conduct]. Congress could not have expressed the concerns reflected in the SRA and the legislative history with unwarranted disparity and uncertainty in sentencing but have intended the reforms enacted to be limited to the small percentage of cases that go to trial. The legislative history of the SRA indeed indicates that Congress was concerned with the potential shift of discretion in sentencing from the court to the prosecutor through plea agreements and the unwarranted disparity that could result. . . .

CHARGE BARGAINING

The policy statement on charge bargaining addresses agreements that include the dismissal of any charges under Rule 11(e)(1)(A) or an agreement not to pursue potential charges. It authorizes the court to accept such an agreement if it determines, "for reasons stated on the record, that the remaining charges adequately reflect the seriousness of the actual offense behavior and that accepting the agreement will not undermine the statutory purposes of sentencing." §6B1.2(a). The requirement that the "remaining charges adequately reflect the seriousness of the actual offense behavior" in charge bargaining is important since the charge of conviction itself is the most significant factor in establishing the guideline sentence. . . .

Although Congress intended that courts exercise "meaningful" review of charge reduction plea agreements, it is our view that moderately greater flexibility legally can and does attach to charge bargains than to sentence bargains. While, as indicated previously, the Commission's quite liberal policy statements on sentence bargaining appear to be inconsistent with the controlling (and stricter) statutory departure standard, the statutory departure standard is not applicable in the charge-bargain context. . . .

Nevertheless, in order to fulfill the objectives of the Sentencing Reform Act prosecutors should conduct charge bargaining in a manner consistent with the direction in the applicable policy statement, §6B1.2(a), i.e., subject to the policy statement's instruction that the "remaining charges [should] adequately reflect the seriousness of the actual offense behavior" and that the agreement not undermine the statutory purposes of sentencing. In our view, this translates into a requirement that readily provable serious charges should not be bargained away. The sole legitimate ground for agreeing not to pursue a charge that is relevant under the guidelines to assure that the sentence will reflect the seriousness of the defendant's "offense behavior" is the existence of real doubt as to the ultimate provability of the charge.

Concomitantly, however, the prosecutor is in the best position to assess the strength of the government's case and enjoys broad discretion in making judgments as to which charges are most likely to result in conviction on the basis of the available evidence. For this reason, the prosecutor entering into a charge bargain may enjoy a degree of latitude that is not present when the plea bargain addresses only sentencing aspects. . . .

It is appropriate that the sentence for an offender who agrees to plead guilty to relatively few charges should be different from the sentence for an offender convicted of many charges since guilt has not been determined as to the dismissed charges. At the same time, however, sentence bargaining should not result in a vastly different sentence as compared to a sentence following trial. . . .

The overriding principle governing the conduct of plea negotiations is that plea agreements should not be used to circumvent the guidelines. This principle is in accordance with the policies set forth in the Principles of Federal Prosecution. . . . For example, charges should not be filed simply to exert leverage to induce a plea. Rather, the prosecutor should charge the most serious offense consistent with the defendant's provable conduct. . . .

A subsidiary but nonetheless important issue concerns so-called "fact" bargaining or stipulations. [The policy statement §6B1.4] attaches certain conditions to such stipulations. The most important condition, with which the Department concurs, is that stipulations shall "not contain misleading facts." Otherwise, the basic purpose of the SRA to reduce unwarranted sentence disparity will be undermined. Thus, if the defendant can clearly be proved to have used a weapon or committed an assault in the course of the offense, the prosecutor may not stipulate, as part of a plea agreement designed to produce a lower sentence, that no weapon was used or assault committed. If, on the other hand, certain facts surrounding the offense are not clear, e.g., the extent of the loss or injury resulting from the defendant's fraud, the prosecutor is at liberty to stipulate that no loss or injury beyond that clearly provable existed. Prosecutors may not, however, instruct investigators not to pursue leads, or make less than ordinary efforts to ascertain facts, simply to be in a position to say that they are unable clearly to prove a sentencing fact and thereby increase the latitude for bargaining. . . . Subject to the above constraints, however, the Department encourages the use of stipulations accompanying plea agreements to the extent practicable. . . .

After the first few months of practice under the new sentencing and plea bargaining rules, officials in the Department of Justice believed that federal prosecutors in the field were not adhering closely enough to the department's plea bargaining policies. The following revision of the policy represents an effort to increase compliance with the plea practices that the leadership of the department wanted. What elements of the policy did the revisers focus on? What were the likely effects of the revisions?

Plea Policy for Federal Prosecutors ("Thornburgh Bluesheet")
Richard Thornburgh, Attorney General (1989)

Whether bargaining takes place before or after indictment, the Department policy is the same: any departure from the guidelines should be openly identified rather than hidden between the lines of a plea agreement. It is inevitable that in some cases it will be difficult for anyone other than the prosecutor and the defendant to know whether, prior to indictment, the prosecutor bargained in conformity with the Department's policy. The Department will monitor, together with the Sentencing Commission, plea bargaining, and the Department will expect plea bargains to support, not undermine, the guidelines. . . .

Should a prosecutor determine in good faith after indictment that, as a result of a change in the evidence or for another reason (e.g., a need has arisen to protect the identity of a particular witness until he testifies against a more significant defendant), a charge is not readily provable or that an indictment exaggerates the seriousness of an offense or offenses, a plea bargain may reflect the prosecutor's reassessment. There should be a record, however, in a case in which charges originally brought are dropped. . . .

Department policy requires honesty in sentencing; federal prosecutors are expected to identify for U.S. District Courts departures when they agree to support them. For example, it would be improper for a prosecutor to agree that a departure is in order, but to conceal the agreement in a charge bargain that is presented to a court as a fait accompli so that there is neither a record of nor judicial review of the departure. . . .

The basic policy is that charges are not to be bargained away or dropped, unless the prosecutor has a good faith doubt as to the government's ability readily to prove a charge for legal or evidentiary reasons. It would serve no purpose here to seek to further define "readily provable." The policy is to bring cases that the government should win if there were a trial. There are, however, two exceptions.

First, if the applicable guideline range from which a sentence may be imposed would be unaffected, readily provable charges may be dismissed or dropped as part of a plea bargain. . . . Second, federal prosecutors may drop readily provable charges with the specific approval of the United States Attorney or designated supervisory level official for reasons set forth in the file of the case. This exception recognizes that the aims of the Sentencing Reform Act must be sought without ignoring other, critical aspects of the federal criminal justice system. For example, approval to drop charges in a particular case might be given because the United States Attorney's office is particularly overburdened, the case would be time-consuming to try, and proceeding to trial would significantly reduce the total number of cases disposed of by the office. . . .

The Department's policy is only to stipulate to facts that accurately represent the defendant's conduct. If a prosecutor wishes to support a departure from the guidelines, he or she should candidly do so and not stipulate to facts that are untrue. Stipulations to untrue facts are unethical. If a prosecutor has insufficient facts to contest a defendant's effort to seek a downward departure or to claim an adjustment, the prosecutor can say so. If the presentence report states facts that are inconsistent with a stipulation in which a prosecutor has joined, it is desirable for the prosecutor to object to the report or to add a statement explaining the prosecutor's understanding of the facts or the reason for the stipulation. . . .

In most felony cases, plea agreements should be in writing. If they are not in writing, they always should be formally stated on the record. Written agreements will facilitate efforts by the Department and the Sentencing Commission to monitor compliance by federal prosecutors with Department policies and the guidelines. . . .

After almost three more years of experience with the new system, the Department of Justice remained unsatisfied with the plea bargaining practices of its attorneys in the field. In the following 1992 revision of the plea bargaining policy, the department moved away from an emphasis on describing the types of bargains that are acceptable, and instead strengthened the procedural review process for plea agreements. What are the likely effects of these changes?

Department of Justice Policies ("Terwilliger Bluesheet")
George Terwilliger, Assistant Attorney General (1992)

This bluesheet is a clarification of [the procedures for plea bargaining described in Attorney General Thornburgh's memorandum of March 13, 1989]. The following procedures shall be adopted as to all pleas of guilty:

All negotiated plea agreements to felonies or misdemeanors negotiated from felonies shall be in writing and filed with the court. Thus any time a defendant enters into a negotiated plea, that fact and the conditions thereof will be memorialized and a copy of the plea agreement maintained in the office case file or elsewhere.

There shall be within each office a formal system for approval of negotiated pleas. The approval authority shall be vested in at least a supervisory criminal Assistant United States Attorney, or a supervisory attorney of a litigating division in the Department of Justice, who will have the responsibility of assessing the appropriateness of the plea agreement under the policies of the Department of Justice pertaining to pleas, including those set forth in the Thornburgh Memo. Where certain predictable fact situations arise with great frequency and are given identical treatment, the approval requirement may be met by a written instruction from the appropriate supervisor which describes with particularity the standard plea procedure to be followed, so long as that procedure is otherwise within Departmental guidelines. An example would be a border district which routinely deals with a high volume of illegal alien cases daily.

The plea approval process will be part of the office evaluation procedure....

After the 1992 elections, the Clinton administration appointed new leadership to the Department of Justice. The following memorandum represented the first major pronouncement of that administration on plea bargaining policies. What prior statements does it hearken back to? What, if anything, is new in the policy?

Charging and Plea Decisions ("Reno Bluesheet")
Janet Reno, Attorney General (1993)

As first stated in the preface to the original 1980 edition of the Principles of Federal Prosecution, "they have been cast in general terms with a view to providing guidance rather than to mandating results. The intent is to assure regularity without regimentation, to prevent unwarranted disparity without sacrificing flexibility."

It should be emphasized that charging decisions and plea agreements should reflect adherence to the Sentencing Guidelines. However, a faithful and honest application of the Sentencing Guidelines is not incompatible with selecting charges or entering into plea agreements on the basis of an individualized assessment of the extent to which particular charges fit the specific circumstances of the case, are consistent with the purposes of the federal criminal code, and maximize the impact of federal resources on crime. Thus, for example, in determining "the most serious offense that is consistent with the nature of the defendant's conduct, that is likely to result in a sustainable conviction," it is appropriate that the attorney for the government consider, inter alia, such factors as the sentencing guideline range yielded by the charge, whether the penalty yielded by such sentencing range (or potential mandatory minimum charge, if applicable) is proportional to the seriousness of the defendant's conduct, and whether the charge achieves such purposes of the criminal law as punishment, protection of the public, specific and general deterrence, and rehabilitation. Note that these factors may also be considered by the attorney for the government when entering into the plea agreements.

To ensure consistency and accountability, charging and plea agreement decisions must be made at an appropriate level of responsibility and documented with an appropriate record of the factors applied.

Congress may, of course, reshape or abolish the guideline sentencing system whenever it wants. In 2003 Congress enacted the PROTECT Act, P.L. 108-21, 117 Stat. 650. The act revealed congressional hostility to the operation of the federal guidelines and, in particular, the frequency with which judges were departing downward from the guidelines' presumptive sentences. The act made changes to federal sentencing law and to the duties and makeup of the U.S. Sentencing Commission. Section 401(l) of the act also encouraged the Attorney General to submit a report to the House and Senate Judiciary Committees that states in detail the policies and procedures that the Department of Justice has adopted subsequent to the enactment of this Act:

> (A) to ensure that Department of Justice attorneys oppose sentencing adjustments, including downward departures, that are not supported by the facts and the law;
> (B) to ensure that Department of Justice attorneys in such cases make a sufficient record so as to permit the possibility of an appeal;
> (C) to delineate objective criteria, specified by the Attorney General, as to which such cases may warrant consideration of an appeal, either because of the nature or magnitude of the sentencing error, its prevalence in the district, or its prevalence with respect to a particular judge;
> (D) to ensure that Department of Justice attorneys promptly notify the designated Department of Justice component in Washington concerning such adverse sentencing decisions; and
> (E) to ensure the vigorous pursuit of appropriate and meritorious appeals of such adverse decisions.

The same section provided for more onerous reporting requirements to be placed on the Attorney General if this general report of policies and procedures was not submitted within 90 days of the PROTECT Act. The following two policies were promulated by Attorney General John Ashcroft in light of the PROTECT Act. Note that the act was signed into law on April 30, 2003, and the first policy, below, appeared on July 28, 2003.

> ## Department Policies and Procedures Concerning Sentencing Recommendations and Sentencing Appeals
> **John Ashcroft, Attorney General (July 28, 2003)**

I.   INTRODUCTION

Earlier this year, the President signed into law the PROTECT Act. . . . The PROTECT Act . . . contains an important amendment, sponsored by Representative Feeney and supported by the Department of Justice, that enacts several key reforms designed to ensure that the Sentencing Guidelines would be more faithfully and consistently enforced, thereby achieving the consistency and predictability that Congress sought in the Sentencing Reform Act (which established the Guidelines System). See §401. Specifically, the legislation includes a number of reforms designed to reduce the number of "downward departures" from the Sentencing Guidelines, and it further instructs the Sentencing Commission to adopt additional measures "to ensure that the incidence of downward departures [is] substantially reduced." In our constitutional democracy, these fundamental policy choices as to the range of permissible sentences are ultimately for the Congress to make. . . .

II.   DEPARTMENT POLICIES AND PROCEDURES CONCERNING SENTENCING RECOMMENDATIONS AND APPEALS

The Sentencing Reform Act's key purposes were to "provide certainty and fairness in meeting the purposes of sentencing," and to "avoid unwarranted sentencing disparities among defendants with similar records who have been found guilty of similar criminal conduct." 28 U.S.C. §991(b)(1)(B). The recent passage of the PROTECT Act strongly reaffirms Congress' commitment to these goals. In order to fulfill these purposes, all Department attorneys must adhere to the following policies and procedures with respect to sentencing recommendations, sentencing hearings, and sentencing appeals.

A.   The Department's actions with respect to sentencings must in all respects be supported by the facts and the law.

Department of Justice policy requires honesty in sentencing, both with respect to the facts and the law. Accordingly, prosecutors' actions and recommendations with respect to sentencings must in all respects be consistent with the relevant facts and the applicable law. Several requirements follow from this general principle.

1. The sentencing recommendations of the Department must be supported by the facts and the law.

Department attorneys must ensure that the Sentencing Guidelines are applied as Congress and the Sentencing Commission intended them to be applied, regardless of whether an individual prosecutor agrees with that policy decision. Any sentencing recommendation made by the United States in a particular case must honestly reflect the totality and seriousness of the defendant's conduct and must be fully consistent with the Guidelines and applicable statutes and with the readily provable facts about the defendant's history and conduct.

Accordingly, if readily provable facts are relevant to calculations under the Sentencing Guidelines, the prosecutor must disclose them to the court, including the Probation Office. Thus, for example, a prosecutor may not fail to bring readily provable facts about relevant conduct to the court's attention (e.g., additional drug amounts or fraud losses). Concealment of such facts from the court imperils a cardinal principle of the Guidelines: that sentences are in large measure based upon the "real offense" instead of the "charge offense." See U.S.S.G. Ch. 1, Pt. A, P4(a).

Similarly, in negotiating plea agreements that address sentencing issues, federal prosecutors may not "fact bargain," or be party to any plea agreement that results in the sentencing court having less than a full understanding of all readily provable facts relevant to sentencing. . . . Likewise, if the United States agrees to make a non-binding recommendation for a particular sentence under Rule 11(c)(1)(B), or if the agreement is for a specific sentence under Rule 11(c)(1)(C), the agreement must not vitiate relevant provisions of the Sentencing Guidelines.

[P]rosecutors must not recommend downward departures unless they are fully consistent with the Sentencing Reform Act, the PROTECT Act, and the applicable provisions of the Guidelines Manual. . . .

2. Department attorneys must oppose sentencing adjustments that are not supported by the facts and the law.

Department attorneys also have an affirmative obligation to oppose any sentencing adjustments, including downward departures, that are not supported by the facts and the law. . . .

[P]rosecutors must not enter into plea agreements that waive the Government's right to object to adjustments that are not supported by the facts and the law. For example, a prosecutor may not enter into a plea agreement that binds the Government to "stand silent" with respect to a defendant's request for a particular adjustment, unless the prosecutor determines in good faith that the adjustment is supported by the facts and the law. . . .

[The policy added a series of reporting requirements for cases involving departures, and for other "adverse sentencing decisions."]

> ## Department Policy Concerning Charging
> ## Criminal Offenses, Disposition of Charges,
> ## and Sentencing
> ### John Ashcroft, Attorney General (Sept. 22, 2003)

The passage of the Sentencing Reform Act of 1984 was a watershed event in the pursuit of fairness and consistency in the federal criminal justice system. . . . In contrast to the prior sentencing system — which was characterized by largely unfettered discretion, and by seemingly severe sentences that were often sharply reduced by parole — the Sentencing Reform Act and the Sentencing Guidelines sought to accomplish several important objectives: (1) to ensure honesty and transparency in federal sentencing; (2) to guide sentencing discretion, so as to narrow the disparity between sentences for similar offenses committed by similar offenders; and (3) to provide for the imposition of appropriately different punishments for offenses of differing severity.

With the passage of the PROTECT Act earlier this year, Congress has reaffirmed its commitment to the principles of consistency and effective deterrence that are embodied in the Sentencing Guidelines. . . .

One part of this comprehensive review of Department policy has already been completed: on July 28, 2003, in accordance with section 401(*l*)(1) of the PROTECT Act, I issued a Memorandum that specifically and clearly sets forth the Department's policies with respect to sentencing recommendations and sentencing appeals. The determination of an appropriate sentence for a convicted defendant is, however, only half of the equation. The fairness Congress sought to achieve by the Sentencing Reform Act and the PROTECT Act can be attained only if there are fair and reasonably consistent policies with respect to the Department's decisions concerning what charges to bring and how cases should be disposed. Just as the sentence a defendant receives should not depend upon which particular judge presides over the case, so too the charges a defendant faces should not depend upon the particular prosecutor assigned to handle the case.

. . . This memorandum supersedes all previous guidance on this subject.

I. DEPARTMENT POLICY CONCERNING CHARGING AND PROSECUTION OF CRIMINAL OFFENSES

A. General Duty to Charge and to Pursue the Most Serious, Readily Provable Offense in All Federal Prosecutions

It is the policy of the Department of Justice that, in all federal criminal cases, federal prosecutors must charge and pursue the most serious, readily provable offense or offenses that are supported by the facts of the case, except as authorized by an Assistant Attorney General, United States Attorney, or designated supervisory attorney in the limited circumstances described below. The most serious offense or offenses are those that generate the most substantial sentence under the Sentencing Guidelines, unless a mandatory minimum sentence or count requiring a consecutive sentence would generate a longer sentence. A charge is not "readily provable" if the prosecutor has a good faith doubt, for legal or evidentiary reasons, as to the Government's ability readily to prove a charge at trial. Thus, charges should not be filed simply to exert leverage to induce a plea. Once filed, the most serious readily provable charges may not be dismissed except to the extent permitted in Section B.

B.   Limited Exceptions

The basic policy set forth above requires federal prosecutors to charge and to pursue all charges that are determined to be readily provable and that, under the applicable statutes and Sentencing Guidelines, would yield the most substantial sentence. There are, however, certain limited exceptions to this requirement:

1. Sentence Would Not Be Affected.   First, if the applicable guideline range from which a sentence may be imposed would be unaffected, prosecutors may decline to charge or to pursue readily provable charges. However, if the most serious readily provable charge involves a mandatory minimum sentence that exceeds the applicable guideline range, counts essential to establish a mandatory minimum sentence must be charged and may not be dismissed, except to the extent provided elsewhere below.

2. "Fast-Track" Programs.   With the passage of the PROTECT Act, Congress recognized the importance of early disposition or "fast-track" programs. . . . [T]he Act instructs the Sentencing Commission to promulgate, by October 27, 2003, a policy statement authorizing a downward departure of not more than 4 levels "pursuant to an early disposition program *authorized by the Attorney General* and the United States Attorney." Although the PROTECT Act requirement of Attorney General authorization only applies by its terms to fast-track programs that rely on downward departures, the same requirement will also apply, as a matter of Department policy, to any fast-track program that relies on "charge bargaining"— i.e., an expedited disposition program whereby the Government agrees to charge less than the most serious, readily provable offense. Such programs are intended to be exceptional and will be authorized only when clearly warranted by local conditions within a district. . . .

3. Post-indictment Reassessment.   In cases where post-indictment circumstances cause a prosecutor to determine in good faith that the most serious offense is not readily provable, because of a change in the evidence or some other justifiable reason (e.g., the unavailability of a witness or the need to protect the identity of a witness until he testifies against a more significant defendant), the prosecutor may dismiss the charge(s) with the written or otherwise documented approval of an Assistant Attorney General, United States Attorney, or designated supervisory attorney.

4. Substantial Assistance.   The preferred means to recognize a defendant's substantial assistance in the investigation or prosecution of another person is to charge the most serious readily provable offense and then to file an appropriate motion or motions under U.S.S.G. §5K1.1, 18 U.S.C. §3553(e), or Federal Rule of Criminal Rule of Procedure 35(b). However, in rare circumstances, where necessary to obtain substantial assistance in an important investigation or prosecution, and with the written or otherwise documented approval of an Assistant Attorney General, United States Attorney, or designated supervisory attorney, a federal prosecutor may decline to charge or to pursue a readily provable charge as part of [a] plea agreement that properly reflects the substantial assistance provided by the defendant in the investigation or prosecution of another person.

5. Statutory Enhancements. The use of statutory enhancements is strongly encouraged, and federal prosecutors must therefore take affirmative steps to ensure that the increased penalties resulting from specific statutory enhancements, such as the filing of an information pursuant to 21 U.S.C. §851 or the filing of a charge under 18 U.S.C. §924(c), are sought in all appropriate cases. . . . In many cases, however, the filing of such enhancements will mean that the statutory sentence exceeds the applicable Sentencing Guidelines range, thereby ensuring that the defendant will not receive any credit for acceptance of responsibility and will have no incentive to plead guilty. Requiring the pursuit of such enhancements to trial in every case could therefore have a significant effect on the allocation of prosecutorial resources within a given district. Accordingly, an Assistant Attorney General, United States Attorney, or designated supervisory attorney may authorize a prosecutor to forego the filing of a statutory enhancement, but *only* in the context of a negotiated plea agreement. . . .

6. Other Exceptional Circumstances. Prosecutors may decline to pursue or may dismiss readily provable charges in other exceptional circumstances with the written or otherwise documented approval of an Assistant Attorney General, United States Attorney, or designated supervisory attorney. This exception recognizes that the aims of the Sentencing Reform Act must be sought without ignoring the practical limitations of the federal criminal justice system. For example, a case-specific approval to dismiss charges in a particular case might be given because the United States Attorney's Office is particularly over-burdened, the duration of the trial would be exceptionally long, and proceeding to trial would significantly reduce the total number of cases disposed of by the office. However, such case-by-case exceptions should be rare; otherwise the goals of fairness and equity will be jeopardized.

II. DEPARTMENT POLICY CONCERNING PLEA AGREEMENTS

A. *Written Plea Agreements*

In felony cases, plea agreements should be in writing. If the plea agreement is not in writing, the agreement should be formally stated on the record. . . . The PROTECT Act specifically requires the court, after sentencing, to provide a copy of the plea agreement to the Sentencing Commission. 28 U.S.C. §994(w). Written plea agreements also avoid misunderstandings with regard to the terms that the parties have accepted.

B.   Honesty in Sentencing

As set forth in my July 28, 2003 Memorandum on "Department Policies and Procedures Concerning Sentencing Recommendations and Sentencing Appeals," Department of Justice policy requires honesty in sentencing, both with respect to the facts and the law. . . .

This policy applies fully to sentencing recommendations that are contained in plea agreements. . . . [F]ederal prosecutors may not "fact bargain," or be party to any plea agreement that results in the sentencing court having less than a full understanding of all readily provable facts relevant to sentencing. . . .

[I]t remains Department policy that the sentencing court should be informed if a plea agreement involves a "charge bargain." Accordingly, a negotiated plea that uses any of the options described in Section I(B) (2), (4), (5), or (6) must be made known to the court at the time of the plea hearing and at the time of sentencing, i.e., the court must be informed that a more serious, readily provable offense was not charged or that an applicable statutory enhancement was not filed.

C.   Charge Bargaining

Charges may be declined or dismissed pursuant to a plea agreement only to the extent consistent with the principles set forth in Section I of this Memorandum.

D.   Sentence Bargaining

There are only two types of permissible sentence bargains.

1. Sentences Within the Sentencing Guidelines Range.   Federal prosecutors may enter into a plea agreement for a sentence that is within the specified guideline range. For example, when the Sentencing Guidelines range is 18-24 months, a prosecutor may agree to recommend a sentence of 18 or 20 months rather than to argue for a sentence at the top of the range. Similarly, a prosecutor may agree to recommend a downward adjustment for acceptance of responsibility under U.S.S.G. §3E1.1 if the prosecutor concludes in good faith that the defendant is entitled to the adjustment.

2. Departures.   In passing the PROTECT Act, Congress has made clear its view that there have been too many downward departures from the Sentencing Guidelines, and it has instructed the Commission to take measures "to ensure that the incidence of downward departures [is] substantially reduced." The Department has a duty to ensure that the circumstances in which it will request or accede to downward departures in the future are properly circumscribed.

Accordingly, federal prosecutors must not request or accede to a downward departure except in the limited circumstances specified in this memorandum and with authorization from an Assistant Attorney General, United States Attorney, or designated supervisory attorney. Likewise, except in such circumstances and with such authorization, prosecutors may not simply stand silent when a downward departure motion is made by the defendant. . . .

An Assistant Attorney General, United States Attorney, or designated supervisory attorney may authorize a prosecutor to request or accede to a downward departure at sentencing only in the following circumstances:

a. Substantial assistance.   Section 5K1.1 of the Sentencing Guidelines provides that, upon motion by the Government, a court may depart from the guideline range. A substantial assistance motion must be based on assistance that is *substantial* to the Government's case. It is not appropriate to utilize substantial assistance motions as a case management tool to secure plea agreements and avoid trials. . . .

In sum, plea bargaining must honestly reflect the totality and seriousness of the defendant's conduct, and any departure must be accomplished through the application of appropriate Sentencing Guideline provisions.

Federal criminal law and procedure apply equally throughout the United States. As the sole federal prosecuting entity, the Department of Justice has a unique obligation to ensure that all federal criminal cases are prosecuted according to the same standards. Fundamental fairness requires that all defendants prosecuted in the federal criminal justice system be subject to the same standards and treated in a consistent manner.

NOTES

1. *Prosecutorial discretion and control.*   How would you describe these policies in terms of the control they exert over federal prosecutorial plea practices? Do all of these policies move toward increasing control over individual prosecutorial decisions? For further background on the creation of the federal policies up to 1994, see David Robinson, The Decline and Potential Collapse of Federal Guideline Sentencing, 74 Wash. U. L.Q. 881 (1996). Are executive plea bargaining policies a good idea? What problems could they solve? What problems might they create?

2. *Policies and practice.*   Do "line" attorneys follow directives from their boss? The most complete studies of federal plea practices during the early implementation of the sentencing guidelines concluded that prosecutors manipulated the guidelines in 20-35 percent of all cases. Stephen Schulhofer and Ilene Nagel, A Tale of Three Cities: An Empirical Study of Charging and Bargaining Practice Under the Federal Sentencing Guidelines, 66 S. Cal. L. Rev. 501 (1992). The U.S. Sentencing Commission found charge manipulation in 17 percent of all cases and 26 percent of drug cases. See U.S. Sentencing Commission, The Federal Sentencing Guidelines: A Report on the Operation of the Guidelines System and Short-Term Impacts on Disparity in Sentencing, Use of Incarceration, and Prosecutorial Discretion and Plea Bargaining, Executive Summary 31-54 (Dec. 1991). Why might line attorneys not follow plea guidelines? Why might different U.S. Attorneys' offices develop different patterns of plea bargaining?

3. *Policies and principles.*   In response to the Reno Bluesheet, on January 13, 1994, Senator Orrin Hatch (R-Utah), the ranking minority member on the Judiciary Committee, sent Attorney General Janet Reno the following letter:

> I want to express my strong opposition to a recent directive you issued to United States Attorneys. This directive reverses the Department of Justice's policy that

prosecutors must charge the most serious, readily provable offense or offenses consistent with the defendant's conduct. The Department's new policy now permits prosecutors to make independent decisions about whether a prescribed guideline sentence or mandatory minimum charge is not "proportional to the seriousness of the defendant's conduct." In other words, this new policy increases the potential for the unwarranted softening of offenses for violent offenders. . . .

While I support a review of charging practices to insure that prosecutors are not engaging in inappropriate conduct, I do not support the Department's announcement to drug traffickers and violent criminals that certain illegal conduct may not be charged because a Department employee may find the prescribed punishment too severe. If the Administration believes that existing sentences for drug cases and violent criminals are too severe, then it should seek to change the law or the relevant sentencing guidelines — not ignore them. I strongly urge you to reconsider your action in this matter.

Reno responded on March 8, 1994:

I write in response to your recent letter regarding the charging policy of the Department of Justice and the directive which was issued to United States Attorneys. Let me reiterate, as set forth in the clarifying bluesheet to which you allude, that it remains the directive of the Department of Justice that prosecutors charge the most serious offense that is consistent with the nature of the defendant's conduct, that is likely to result in a sustainable conviction; that prosecutors adhere to the Sentencing Guidelines; and that charging and plea agreements be made at an appropriate level of responsibility with appropriate documentation. In short, contrary to what you suggest, individual prosecutors are not free to follow their own lights or to ignore legislative directives. . . . We are steadfast in our opposition to unwarranted softening of sentences for violent offenders or drug traffickers. . . . You note your support for such efforts, and we look forward to working with you.

What impact should this correspondence have on how assistant U.S. Attorneys apply the Reno Bluesheet? Can they now enter sentencing agreements that request a sentence outside the guideline range even when a departure might not be justified under the statute? What is likely to occur in such cases?

4. *Written and unwritten guidance.* A striking feature of the plea bargaining policies in the federal system is the fact that they are written. Many state prosecutors' offices have pursued goals similar to those of the Department of Justice in creating their plea policies. They hope to maintain adequate control over prosecutors in the field and to send appropriate public signals about sentencing and plea bargaining. See Richard Kuh, Plea Bargaining: Guidelines for the Manhattan District Attorney's Office, 11 Crim. L. Bull. 48 (1975) ("unless all of us here follow like principles in plea bargaining, the quality of justice administered by this office will vary from Assistant to Assistant"). Nonetheless, within the state systems, such policies are rarely written, even when they are explicit. Why might a supervising prosecutor choose to keep such a critical office policy unwritten? See William Pizzi, Understanding Prosecutorial Discretion in the United States: The Limits of Comparative Criminal Procedure as an Instrument of Reform, 54 Ohio St. L.J. 1325 (1993) (discussing reasons that offices keep their plea bargaining policies informal and unwritten, including ill effects on deterrent value of criminal law, unfavorable public impressions of perceived lenient policies,

need for flexibility in unusual cases, need to avoid judicial review of prosecutorial decisions); but compare Kim Banks Mayer, Applying Open Records Policy to Wisconsin District Attorneys: Can Charging Guidelines Promote Public Awareness?, 1996 Wis. L. Rev. 295 (giving examples of prosecutorial charging and plea bargaining guidelines made public with no apparent ill effects; arguing generally for public availability of policies). Is there any reason not to create a written office policy, given that all plea agreements in individual cases will become a matter of public record?

5. *Sentencing guidelines and the shift to charge bargains.* State structured sentencing systems overwhelmingly reject the decision in the federal system to include "relevant conduct" (uncharged conduct) in the calculation of harm for purposes of sentencing. These sentencing systems make the selection of the criminal charge more important than it was under more discretionary sentencing systems, and perhaps more important than in the federal system, where the offense of conviction will shape but typically not sharply restrict the sentence (other than for applicable mandatory minimum sentences).

As a result of such changes, prosecutors and defendants in these state jurisdictions have shifted away from sentence bargains toward charge bargains and fact bargains. In Minnesota, which adopted a more determinate sentencing guideline system in 1980, studies focusing on the first few years of practice under the new laws revealed an increase in charge negotiations and a decrease in sentence negotiations. Terance Miethe, Charging and Plea Bargaining Practices Under Determinate Sentencing: An Investigation of the Hydraulic Displacement of Discretion, 78 J. Crim. L. & Criminology 155 (1987) (describing earlier studies).

One question about potential limits on the substantive content of pleas is whether defendants may waive the right to appeal or collaterally attack their sentences. This is an especially significant issue because of the importance of appellate decisions in providing law and norms for some structured sentencing systems, including the federal system. At the same time, sentencing appeals have made up a very significant proportion of criminal appeals, and indeed of all appeals in the federal system.

The following memo was circulated by the Department of Justice to all U.S. Attorneys to provide guidance on the drafting and use of sentencing appeal waivers in plea agreements. Though each of the 93 U.S. Attorney's offices sets its own policies — with some refusing to make use of these waivers and others using them regularly — the memorandum makes a determined argument for waivers to help reduce the burden of appellate and collateral litigation involving sentencing issues.

Use of Sentencing Appeal Waivers to Reduce the Number of Sentencing Appeals
John C. Keeney, Acting Assistant Attorney General
(Oct. 4, 1995)

This memorandum provides guidance regarding the possible use of waivers of sentencing appeal rights and post-conviction rights in plea agreements. The

Department recognizes that many districts currently incorporate such waivers into plea agreements. We believe that the use of these waivers in appropriate cases can be helpful in reducing the burden of appellate and collateral litigation involving sentencing issues. United States Attorneys' offices should evaluate whether waivers of sentencing appeal rights and post-conviction rights would be a useful addition to plea agreements in their districts and, if so, the extent and scope of such waivers.

(1)   LEGALITY

At the outset, it is important to note that the Supreme Court has repeatedly held that a criminal defendant can elect to waive many important constitutional and statutory rights during the plea bargaining process. See United States v. Mezzanatto, 115 S. Ct. 797 (1995); Tollett v. Henderson, 411 U.S. 256 (1973); Blackledge v. Allison, 431 U.S. 63 (1977). Consistent with that principle, the courts of appeals have upheld the general validity of a sentencing appeal waiver in a plea agreement.

A sentencing appeal waiver provision does not waive all claims on appeal. The courts of appeals have held that certain constitutional and statutory claims survive a sentencing appeal that [defendant] was denied the effective assistance of counsel at sentencing, that he was sentenced on the basis of his race, or that his sentence exceeded the statutory maximum, will be reviewed on the merits by a court of appeals despite the existence of a sentencing appeal waiver in a plea agreement.

(2)   SCOPE OF SENTENCING APPEAL WAIVERS

A plea bargain is a contract between the prosecutor and the defendant. Thus, the scope of a sentencing appeal waiver in a plea bargain will depend upon the precise language used in the sentencing appeal waiver provision.

(A)   Broad Waivers

A broad sentencing appeal waiver requires the defendant to waive any and all sentencing issues on appeal and through collateral attack. The following waiver provision is an example of a broad approach that may be used in plea agreements:

> The defendant is aware that Title 18, United States Code, Section 3742 affords a defendant the right to appeal the sentence imposed. Acknowledging all this, the defendant knowingly waives the right to appeal any sentence within the maximum provided in the statute(s) of conviction (or the manner in which that sentence was determined) on the grounds set forth in Title 18, United States Code, Section 3742 or on any ground whatever, in exchange for the concessions made by the United States in this plea agreement. The defendant also waives his right to challenge his sentence or the manner in which it was determined in any collateral attack, including but not limited to a motion brought under Title 28, U.S.C. Section 2255.

The advantage of a broad sentencing appeal waiver is that it will bar the appeal of virtually any sentencing guideline issue. . . .

The disadvantage of the broad sentencing appeal waiver is that it could result in guideline-free sentencing of defendants in guilty plea cases, and it could encourage a lawless district court to impose sentences in violation of the guidelines. It is imperative to guard against the use of waivers of appeal to promote circumvention of the sentencing guidelines. [T]he Sentencing Commission's policy statements allow judges to accept plea agreements that do not undermine the statutory purposes of sentencing or the sentencing guidelines; the policy statements also admonish the parties when using stipulations to set forth the relevant facts and circumstances of the actual offense conduct and offender characteristics and not to include misleading facts.

Use of waiver of appeal rights in a manner resulting in sentences in violation of the sentencing guidelines could prompt a court of appeals to reconsider its decision to uphold the validity of a sentencing appeal waiver. Alternatively, the reviewing court could construe a sentencing appeal waiver narrowly in order to correct an obvious miscarriage of justice. To avoid these concerns, we recommend that, in a case involving an egregiously incorrect sentence, the prosecutor consider electing to disregard the waiver and to argue the merits of the appeal. That would avoid confronting the court of appeals with the difficult decision of enforcing a sentencing appeal waiver that might result in a miscarriage of justice.

(B) Limited Waivers

A second kind of sentencing appeal waiver is limited in some respect, most likely with regard to a particular sentence, sentencing range, or guideline application. For example, a sentencing appeal waiver could preclude appeal of sentences consistent with a recommended sentence, sentencing range, or particular guideline application agreed to by the parties. Thus, if the plea agreement provides that the prosecutor will recommend the lower half of the available sentences for a particular offense level applicable to the case (subject to a determination of the criminal history category), the plea agreement could also provide for a waiver of the defendant's right to appeal any sentence imposed within the agreed-upon lower half of the applicable range. Alternatively, the sentencing appeal waiver could be narrowed to apply to a particular guideline application. For example, if the parties agree that a two-level reduction for acceptance of responsibility applies, the plea agreement could provide for a waiver of the defendant's right to appeal any sentence on the basis of such a two-level reduction.

A variation of the above limited sentencing appeal waiver could be used where the parties do not agree to a particular sentencing or guideline application. The defendant can, nevertheless, agree not to appeal the court's determination of a particular factor. Thus a waiver of appeal rights could apply to any determination by the court regarding acceptance of responsibility. Or, in a fraud case, where the amount of loss is disputed, the defendant could waive the right to appeal any determination within a specified range. Finally, a waiver could provide that the defendant will not appeal his sentence unless the sentence constitutes an upward departure from the guidelines range deemed applicable by the sentencing court, in which case the defendant's appeal will be limited to contesting the upward departure. . . .

(3)   Government's Right to Appeal

The use of a sentencing appeal waiver in a plea agreement to bar an appeal by the defendant does not require the government to waive its right to appeal an adverse sentencing ruling. The government's retention of its right to appeal the sentence while requiring the defendant to waive his right to appeal does not violate any right of the defendant. . . . Of course, in the interest of striking a bargain, a United States Attorney's office may decide that it is necessary for the government to waive its appeal rights when the defendant takes such action. This may be especially appropriate when a negotiated plea reflects the parties' agreement in connection with a particular sentence, sentencing range, or guideline application.

(4)   Ensuring that the Waiver is Knowing and Voluntary

A waiver of an important constitutional or statutory right must be knowing and voluntary to be valid. See Boykin v. Alabama, 395 U.S. 238, 243 (1969). Therefore, prosecutors should ensure that the record reflects that the defendant knowingly and voluntarily waived his right to appeal his sentence.

It is recommended that both the plea agreement and the Rule 11 colloquy specifically spell out the sentencing appeal waiver. . . .

NOTES

1. *Waivers of the right to appeal.*   Prosecutors in many systems will try to include explicit waivers of the right to appeal a conviction or sentence as part of the plea agreement. Most state courts have concluded that a defendant may explicitly waive the right to appeal a conviction as part of a plea agreement. See State v. Hinners, 471 N.W.2d 841 (Iowa 1991); People v. Seaberg, 541 N.E.2d 1022 (N.Y. 1989). A few courts maintain that public policy forbids prosecutors from insulating themselves from review by bargaining away a defendant's appeal rights. Cf. State v. Ethington, 592 P.2d 768 (Ariz. 1979) (defendant can appeal conviction, notwithstanding agreement not to appeal).

Is it necessary for a defendant to waive the right to appeal explicitly, or does it go without saying that a defendant who pleads guilty will not attack the conviction on appeal? If a defendant wants to appeal some aspect of a conviction based on a guilty plea, should she explicitly condition the guilty plea on the outcome of the planned appeal? How might we decide what must be explicit in a plea agreement, and what will be implied? Does this depend on what the parties are likely to have contemplated, even if they did not address the issue specifically? See Peter Westen, Away from Waiver: A Rationale for the Forfeiture of Constitutional Rights in Criminal Procedure, 75 Mich. L. Rev. 1214 (1977).

Federal prosecutors have engaged in more systematic efforts to include appeal waivers in plea agreements. The Department of Justice represented in the Keeney memo that the use of appeal waivers is "helpful in reducing the burden of appellate and collateral litigation involving sentencing issues," though it also cautions that the use of broad sentencing appeal waivers "could result in guideline-free sentencing of defendants in guilty plea cases, and it could encourage a lawless district court to impose sentences in violation of the guidelines." Noting the increased use of appeal waivers in plea agreements, the Committee on Criminal Law of the Judicial Conference of the United States issued a memorandum in July 1996 to aid district judges and probation officers in their consideration of such provisions. This memo noted that "waivers have been consistently upheld as legal, primarily because it is well established that a defendant can waive any right, even a constitutional right, as long as the waiver is knowing and voluntary." The committee suggested that courts provide all defendants with a "qualified, yet informative, advisement of the right to appeal at sentencing," followed by a specific oral colloquy about the terms of any appeal waiver provision to which a defendant has agreed.

As the use of appeal waivers has become more common in the federal system, judges have expressed concerns that such waivers, especially in their broadest forms, can be unlawful, inappropriate, and dangerous. A number of circuit courts have expressed concerns about broad appeal waivers that eliminate all appellate rights concerning any guideline sentence that is imposed. These courts have indicated that they would look closely at the particular facts of each case in order to ensure that a defendant fully understood and voluntarily accepted such a waiver. See United States v. Rosa, 123 F.2d 94 (2d Cir. 1997) (affirming appeal waiver while observing that a broad waiver "presents grave dangers and implicates both constitutional questions and ordinary principles of fairness and justice"). More dramatically, a number of district judges have refused to accept pleas that include broad appeal waivers. Will such positions by district judges lead to different outcomes in their courts? Will it create disparities in substance and sentence, or only in process?

2. *Substantive limits on bargains.*   There are a few types of legal challenges to a conviction that some courts say a defendant may not waive, even if the waiver appears explicitly in a plea agreement. Courts have taken this position on constitutional speedy trial rights, see People v. Callahan, 604 N.E.2d 108 (N.Y. 1992), and for sentences more severe than the statutory maximum allowable sentence, see Lanier v. State, 635 So. 2d 813 (Miss. 1994). Courts are split on whether the parties can agree to a sentence outside the statutorily authorized range of punishments; often they enforce illegal sentences falling below the authorized range of punishments but not illegal sentences set above the authorized range. See Ex parte Johnson, 669 So. 2d 205 (Ala. 1995) (enforces prosecutor's agreement to two-year prison term, even though prosecutor failed to account for sentencing enhancements requiring additional minimum sentences); but see Patterson v. State, 660 So. 2d 966 (Miss. 1995) (holding plea bargain to life without possibility of parole invalid because no statute authorizes such a sentence for murder).

When defendants attempt to raise challenges that they waived in plea agreements, claiming that the agreement is unenforceable, it is far more common for courts to refuse to hear the challenge. Courts allow defendants to bargain away rights of all sorts. See United States v. Mezzanatto, 513 U.S. 196 (1995) (allowing defendant to waive protections of Rule 11(e)(6), which prevented later introduction into evidence of statements made during plea negotiations); People v. Stevens, 610 N.W.2d 881 (Mich. 2000) (statements made during plea negotiations are admissible in prosecution's case-in-chief); Cowan v. Superior Court, 926 P.2d 438 (Cal. 1996) (allowing waiver of statute of limitations); People v. Allen, 658 N.E.2d 1012 (N.Y. 1995) (allowing waiver of double jeopardy); Joseph A. Colquitt, Ad Hoc Plea Bargaining, 75 Tul. L. Rev. 695 (2001).

Is there a pattern that separates the waivable from the nonwaivable rights? Are the waivable rights the lesser ones? Professor Nancy King notes the increasing willingness of courts to allow waivers. She favors keeping as nonwaivable rights only constitutional claims that have an impact on third parties, since legislatures can decide whether to protect statutory rights from waiver. See Nancy J. King, Priceless Process, 47 UCLA L. Rev. 113 (1999). Should courts allow defendants to waive their right to effective assistance of counsel?

3. *Waiving discovery.*   If defendants must know about the nature of the charges and the direct consequences of a guilty plea, must they also know about the basic facts the prosecutor could present against them at trial? In United States v. Ruiz, 536 U.S. 622 (2002), the Court held that the Fifth and Sixth Amendments did not "require federal prosecutors, before entering into a binding plea agreement with a criminal defendant, to disclose 'impeachment information relating to any informants or other witnesses.'" The Supreme Court's decision in *Ruiz* is typical in its refusal to declare a per se rule against bargaining away discovery rights. A few courts, however, have concluded that in some cases, accepting a guilty plea based on a plea agreement that prevents the defendant from engaging in discovery violates due process. See State v. Draper, 784 P.2d 259 (Ariz. 1989) (due process and right to counsel sometimes may prohibit plea agreement conditioned on defendant not interviewing victim of alleged crime; remand to determine defendant's access to state's evidence through other witnesses). Can you identify circumstances in which a defendant could make a knowing waiver of the right to a jury trial without discovery? The *Ruiz* Court found it significant that the condition relating to discovery was nonmandatory — the defendant could choose to go forward with discovery and forgo the plea agreement. Are there any terms that prosecutors simply may not offer because they prevent the defendant from making a knowing waiver?

4. *Are plea bargains contracts?*   Some scholars have accepted the essentially contractual nature of plea bargaining — a position that largely supports the right of defendants to bargain for whatever they want. Critics of plea bargaining, such as Professor Stephen Schulhofer, have rejected the notion that plea bargains are fair simply because the defendant agreed to the terms and because the agreement puts the defendant in a better position than if the defendant went to trial. Stephen Schulhofer, Plea Bargaining as Disaster, 101 Yale L.J. 1979 (1992). Schulhofer and other critics focus on the public interest in criminal justice that the contract model obscures. Does plea bargaining undermine public confidence in the criminal justice system? See Stanley Cohen and Anthony Doob, Public Attitudes to Plea Bargaining, 32 Crim. L.Q. 85 (1989-1990) (1988 survey found that more than two-thirds of Canadians disapprove of plea bargaining). What other public interests are at stake in plea bargains? In sentences?

2.   Presentence Reports and the Role of Probation Officers

Sentencing systems for the most part welcome judges to consider some additional information that was not presented at trial. The defense might want to provide additional information about the defendant. The prosecution might want to illuminate aspects of the crime or criminal record. A victim might want to speak about the harm the crime inflicted. As noted in Chapters 4 and 5, the scope of information that might be considered at sentencing can be extremely wide, especially in the federal system, which constructed its guidelines in reliance on the availability of additional facts about the defendant's "real offense" and "relevant conduct" (uncharged acts). 18 U.S.C. §3661, promulgated before the guidelines, remains in effect:

> No limitation shall be placed on the information concerning the background, character, and conduct of a person convicted of an offense which a court of the United States may receive and consider for the purpose of imposing an appropriate sentence.

Where do judges get the additional information that might inform their sentencing judgments? Who gathers the information?

The short answer in most sentencing systems is twofold: First, the parties may present additional evidence, and second, the judge will receive a presentence investigation report, typically prepared by a probation officer who works for the court. In the federal system, the presentence investigation report includes the probation officer's assessment of the applicable guidelines and a sentence recommendation to the judge.

Many issues are generated by these odd procedures, documents, and actors — odd, at least, in comparison with the model of an adversarial system in which advocates present and challenge information and arguments to a neutral judge. The issues surrounding presentence reports include the following:

- What will be included in the report?
- Do the attorneys have access to the report?
- Is there an opportunity to challenge the report?
- What deference or independent assessment does the judge bring to the report?

The first part of this section considers rules on the content and access to presentence investigation reports. The second part considers the role of the probation officer with a focus on the federal system.

a. Presentence Investigation Reports

How are the purposes of presentence reports (or of the sentencing system as a whole) served by the procedures used to produce and contest those reports? Consider the following rules.

Federal Rules of Criminal Procedure 32(c)-(h) *Sentencing and Judgment*

(c) Presentence Investigation.

(1) *Required Investigation.*

(A) *In General.* The probation officer must conduct a presentence investigation and submit a report to the court before it imposes sentence unless: . . .

(ii) the court finds that the information in the record enables it to meaningfully exercise its sentencing authority under 18 U.S.C. §3553, and the court explains its finding on the record.

(B) *Restitution.* If the law requires restitution, the probation officer must conduct an investigation and submit a report that contains sufficient information for the court to order restitution.

(2) *Interviewing the Defendant.* The probation officer who interviews a defendant as part of a presentence investigation must, on request, give the defendant's attorney notice and a reasonable opportunity to attend the interview.

(d) Presentence Report.

(1) *Applying the Sentencing Guidelines.* The presentence report must:

(A) identify all applicable guidelines and policy statements of the Sentencing Commission;

(B) calculate the defendant's offense level and criminal history category;

(C) state the resulting sentencing range and kinds of sentences available;

(D) identify any factor relevant to:

(i) the appropriate kind of sentence, or

(ii) the appropriate sentence within the applicable sentencing range; and

(E) identify any basis for departing from the applicable sentencing range.

(2) *Additional Information.* The presentence report must also contain the following information:

(A) the defendant's history and characteristics, including:

(i) any prior criminal record;

(ii) the defendant's financial condition; and

(iii) any circumstances affecting the defendant's behavior that may be helpful in imposing sentence or in correctional treatment;

(B) verified information, stated in a nonargumentative style, that assesses the financial, social, psychological, and medical impact on any individual against whom the offense has been committed;

(C) when appropriate, the nature and extent of nonprison programs and resources available to the defendant;

(D) when the law provides for restitution, information sufficient for a restitution order; . . .

(F) any other information that the court requires.

(3) *Exclusions.* The presentence report must exclude the following:

(A) any diagnoses that, if disclosed, might seriously disrupt a rehabilitation program;

(B) any sources of information obtained upon a promise of confidentiality; and

(C) any other information that, if disclosed, might result in physical or other harm to the defendant or others.

(e) Disclosing the Report and Recommendation.

(1) *Time to Disclose.* Unless the defendant has consented in writing, the probation officer must not submit a presentence report to the court or

disclose its contents to anyone until the defendant has pleaded guilty or nolo contendere, or has been found guilty.

(2) *Minimum Required Notice.* The probation officer must give the presentence report to the defendant, the defendant's attorney, and an attorney for the government at least 35 days before sentencing unless the defendant waives this minimum period.

(3) *Sentence Recommendation.* By local rule or by order in a case, the court may direct the probation officer not to disclose to anyone other than the court the officer's recommendation on the sentence.

(f) **Objecting to the Report.**

(1) *Time to Object.* Within 14 days after receiving the presentence report, the parties must state in writing any objections, including objections to material information, sentencing guideline ranges, and policy statements contained in or omitted from the report.

(2) *Serving Objections.* An objecting party must provide a copy of its objections to the opposing party and to the probation officer.

(3) *Action on Objections.* After receiving objections, the probation officer may meet with the parties to discuss the objections. The probation officer may then investigate further and revise the presentence report as appropriate.

(g) **Submitting the Report.** At least 7 days before sentencing, the probation officer must submit to the court and to the parties the presentence report and an addendum containing any unresolved objections, the grounds for those objections, and the probation officer's comments on them.

(h) **Notice of Possible Departure from Sentencing Guidelines.** Before the court may depart from the applicable sentencing range on a ground not identified for departure either in the presentence report or in a party's prehearing submission, the court must give the parties reasonable notice that it is contemplating such a departure. The notice must specify any ground on which the court is contemplating a departure.

|| *U.S. Sentencing Guidelines Manual*
§§6A1.1, 6A1.2 (Policy Statements) ||

§6A1.1 PRESENTENCE REPORT

A probation officer shall conduct a presentence investigation and report to the court before the imposition of sentence unless the court finds that there is information in the record sufficient to enable the meaningful exercise of sentencing authority pursuant to 18 U.S.C. §3553, and the court explains this finding on the record. Rule 32(b)(1), Fed. R. Crim. P. The defendant may not waive preparation of the presentence report.

§6A1.2 DISCLOSURE OF PRESENTENCE REPORT; ISSUES IN DISPUTE

Courts should adopt procedures to provide for the timely disclosure of the presentence report; the narrowing and resolution, where feasible, of issues in dispute in advance of the sentencing hearing; and the identification for the court of issues remaining in dispute. Rule 32(b)(6), Fed. R. Crim. P.

|| *Pennsylvania Rules of Criminal* ||
|| *Procedure 702, 703* ||

RULE 702.   AIDS IN IMPOSING SENTENCE

(A) Pre-sentence investigation report.

1. The sentencing judge may, in the judge's discretion, order a presentence investigation report in any case.

2. The sentencing judge shall place on the record the reasons for dispensing with the pre-sentence investigation report if the judge fails to order a pre-sentence report in any of the following instances:

(a) where incarceration for one year or more is a possible disposition under the applicable sentencing statutes;

(b) where the defendant is less than twenty-one years old at the time of conviction or entry of a plea of guilty; or

(c) where a defendant is a first offender in that he or she has not heretofore been sentenced as an adult.

3. The pre-sentence investigation report shall include information regarding the circumstances of the offense and the character of the defendant sufficient to assist the judge in determining sentence.

4. The pre-sentence investigation report shall also include a victim impact statement as provided by law. . . .

RULE 703.   DISCLOSURE OF PRE-SENTENCE REPORTS

(A) All pre-sentence reports and related psychiatric and psychological reports shall be confidential, and not of public record. They shall be available to the sentencing judge, and to:

1. an examining professional or facility appointed to assist the court in sentencing . . . ;

2. the attorney for the Commonwealth and counsel for the defendant, for inspection and copying, unless the sentencing judge orders that they be available for inspection only.

(B) If the defendant or the Commonwealth alleges any factual inaccuracy in a report under this rule, the sentencing judge shall, as to each inaccuracy found, order that the record be corrected accordingly. . . .

NOTES

1. *Presentence investigation reports.*   Presentence investigation reports are the focal point of the many kinds of information that may be relevant to sentencing. Traditionally probation officers expended much effort on offender facts that had no bearing on the determination of the offender's guilt or innocence. Now in the federal system probation officers include in their reports a wide range

of offense information (beyond the offense of conviction), offender information, and information impacting sentencing guideline application.

2. *Presentence reports and secrecy.*   One of the critical issues involving presentence reports is who gets to see them and when. Confidentiality in presentence reports is generally considered important to allow for a full exploration of the defendant's situation. For many years, however, rules kept not only the public but also defense counsel and the defendant from seeing the report. Questions about the processes for challenging reports and the standards of proof at sentencing fade in importance when such critical information is hidden.

The modern view is that the presentence report should (indeed, must) be shared with the defendant and defense counsel. But not all information in presentence reports is shared as a matter of course. For example, Federal Rule 32(e)(3) leaves the decision whether to share the sentencing recommendation with local federal courts and individual judges. This extraordinary variation in practice (and the interesting question of why a probation officer's sentence recommendation ought or ought not to be shared) has gone largely without remark in the caselaw and literature.

3. *Presentence reports and plea bargains.*   Rule 32 prohibits the probation officer from submitting the presentence report to the judge before guilty pleas (or a finding of guilt by a jury), unless the defendant consents in writing. The idea behind this limitation is that the judge should not be biased in accepting or rejecting the plea based on what is in the report. But without first seeing the report, how can the judge know when accepting a plea that includes dismissal of charges whether "the remaining charges adequately reflect the seriousness of the actual offense behavior and that accepting the agreement will not undermine the statutory purposes of sentencing or the sentencing guidelines"? U.S. Sentencing Guidelines Manual §6B1.2 (policy statement). And if a judge accepts a plea but then relies (as instructed by the sentencing guidelines) on relevant conduct revealed in the presentence report, how can it be said that the defendant's plea was "knowing" and "voluntary"? It is not hard to argue around these questions: The defendant knows what the presentence report is likely to say, and therefore what the judge might rely on, so the defendant takes the risks of sentence calculations, departures, and possible ranges into account in deciding whether to plea. But this technical answer leaves the deeper issue unaddressed: Either pleas are made with a full understanding of the consequences, or they are not; either the pleas are accepted with a full picture of the offense and offender, or they are not.

4. *Challenging presentence reports.*   Notice the timing requirements in Rule 32. The probation officer must give the presentence report to the defendant and both attorneys at least 35 days before sentencing unless the defendant waives this minimum period. The defendant then has 14 days to assess and challenge the report in writing. Is 14 days enough time? Should the same strict time frame apply to objections by the government? Compare United States v. Young, 140 F.3d 453 (2d Cir. 1998) (allowing untimely objections to presentence report by the government if defendant is given the opportunity to respond), with United States v. Chung, 261 F.3d 536 (5th Cir. 2001) (upholding refusal to consider supplemental objections by defendant to presentence report filed after 14-day limit). Rule 32 suggests that defendants and their counsel may object to information relevant to sentencing guideline application. As noted above, how-

ever, courts are left with the decision whether to share the probation officer's sentencing recommendation with the defendant. Can defendants fully appreciate the calculus of federal sentencing and judgment that underlies guilty pleas when they do not know what recommendation the judge will receive?

Perhaps the most fundamental question about presentence reports is whether and how much they contribute to effective sentencing decision making. In considering this question, note the following brief report from the Maryland sentencing commission, which highlights the fact that such reports are not available in all cases. Should they be?

Use of Pre-sentence Investigations in Maryland Circuit Courts, January 1999-June 2002, Jill Farrell
Sentencing Fax (Maryland State Commission on Criminal Sentencing Policy), Mar. 28, 2003

In Maryland, pre-sentence investigation reports (PSI) are prepared by the Division of Parole and Probation in an effort to provide background information on defendant and case characteristics. The information contained within PSIs is designed to assist the courts in the sentencing process. According to the Maryland statute, a PSI may be requested in, but not limited to, cases in which the defendant is (1) convicted of a felony or misdemeanor that resulted in serious physical injury or death to the victim or (2) being referred to Patuxent Institution.*

Between January 1999 and June 2002, 26% of all valid cases sentenced in Maryland circuit courts indicated the existence of a PSI report. PSIs were nearly three times more likely to be completed for felony offenses (72%) than for misdemeanors (28%). With respect to offense types (Fig. 1), PSI reports were most likely completed for property offenses (68%), followed closely by person offenses (62%). Drug offenses were the least likely offense type (16%) to have a PSI report submitted.

As indicated in Figure 2, there was substantial variation between circuits. Eighty percent of cases in Circuit 2 had PSI reports submitted, while only 6% of cases submitted reports in Circuit 8. This may be due in part to a disproportionate number of drug cases in Circuit 8, thus minimizing the necessity for a PSI report. On average, 25% of circuit court cases in Maryland included PSI reports (75% did not).

With regard to victim injury, Figure 3 shows a gradual increase in the presence of PSI reports. In cases where there was a victim, a PSI was more likely to be completed when the offense resulted in serious injury or death (58%) than when the injury was non-permanent (41%) or when there was no injury (32%).

---

*The Patuxent Institution is a facility in the Maryland system that focuses on offender remediation and treatment and includes mental health and substantive abuse populations. — EDS.

FIGURE 1
Cases with PSIs by Offense Type

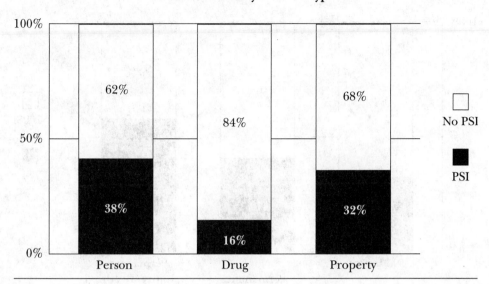

FIGURE 2
Cases with PSIs by Circuit 2

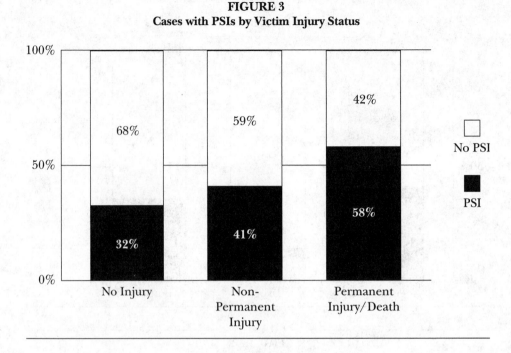

FIGURE 3
Cases with PSIs by Victim Injury Status

b. The Special Role of Probation Officers

In 1989 federal defender Judy Clarke foresaw the important role that probation officers would play in the federal guideline sentencing era:

> The federal probation officer has emerged as the guardian of the guidelines. The probation officer not only collects the factual data important to the sentencing decisions but also makes recommendations regarding application of the guidelines. The Sentencing Commission has one or more federal probation officers on assignment to provide training for probation officers. There is a Commission staffed hotline for probation officers to call for help with application problems. Federal probation officers send to the Commission copies of presentence reports which reflect the officer's application decisions as well as how the court imposed sentence. In a practical sense, federal probation officers have become guardians, a role which results from the probation officer being closely connected with the Commission's training efforts and becoming well versed in the Commission's view of the guidelines. Whether the prosecutor, defense attorney or sentencing court agree with the guardian's conclusion is insignificant — the guardian reports the result to the Commission and moves on to the next presentence report. All's well that ends.

Judy Clarke, Ruminations on Restrepo, 2 Fed. Sentencing Rep. 131 (1989). The phrase "guardians of the guidelines" and the ideas raised by Clarke caught on. Chief probation officer Charlie Varnon, however, begged to differ:

> I find it very interesting that some members of the defense bar are so hostile to the role of the probation officer in the guideline sentencing process. The pro-

bation officer's report to the court has no impact on the defendant whatsoever unless the judge adopts the recommended findings and guideline calculations. The defense and the prosecution have the opportunity to present their own recommended findings and calculations to the court. Under these circumstances, I might assume the real complaint is that the court too often adopts the recommendations of the probation officers and not those of the lawyers. It is more politic, I assume, to criticize the probation officer for making the recommendation than to criticize the court for adopting the recommendation.

Charlie E. Varnon, Response to Judy Clarke, 2 Fed. Sentencing Rep. 202, 202 (1990).

Probation officers may act below the radar of most scholars and many policymakers, but careful observers and participants agree that they are a central part of the guideline sentencing process. Consider the account of the probation officer's role — central or supportive, heroic or tragic — in the following report, written by a member of the U.S. Sentencing Commission, as well as in the subsequent brief commentaries, each written by people who have worked as chief or supervising probation officers.

> **The Independent Role of the Probation Officer
> at Sentencing and in Applying Koon v. United
> States, Catharine M. Goodwin**
> **60 Fed. Probation 71 (Sept. 1996)**

The question of the nature of the role of the probation officer in federal guidelines sentencing is a fundamental and recurring one. . . .

There are various ways the independent role of the probation officer at sentencing is challenged or impeded. The probation officer is sometimes impeded from doing a complete investigation by the parties' withholding information, and, for various reasons, plea agreements do not always accurately reflect the facts of the case. Critics of the guideline system have periodically complained about probation officer "advocacy" and called for restricting probation officers to computing the "matrix calculations" or restricting them from making recommendations on "discretionary decisions" such as departures. In addition, a court will sometimes ask the probation office to restrict its investigation to the parties' stipulations, and others may be tempted to do so, in order to avoid objections to the presentence report and disputed issues.

As an initial matter, it must be noted that the probation officer is an officer of the court. Ultimately, the court determines the scope of the probation officer's role in sentencing in any particular district or courtroom. . . .

I. THE ROLE OF THE PROBATION OFFICER IN GUIDELINE SENTENCING

The legal authorities which define the role of the probation officer in federal guideline sentencing consistently define it as an integral, independent function, apart from party stipulations.

A. Rule 32.   Rule 32, Federal Rules of Criminal Procedure (F.R.Cr.P.), indicates that the presentence report must contain:

> (B) the classification of the offense and of the defendant under the categories established by the Sentencing Commission under 28 U.S.C. §994(a), as the probation officer believes to be applicable to the defendant's case; the kinds of sentence and the sentencing range suggested for such a category of defendant as set forth in the guidelines issued by the Sentencing Commission under 28 U.S.C. §994(a)(1); and the probation officer's explanation of any factors that may suggest a different sentence — within or without the applicable guideline — that would be more appropriate, given all the circumstances.

Rule 32(b)(4)(B). Thus, the probation officer has a duty directed by the federal rules to compute and describe what the officer believes to be the appropriate sentence under the guidelines, as well as what, if any, departure the officer believes is appropriate. . . .

B. Sentencing Reform Act, Its Legislative History, and the Guidelines.   The Sentencing Reform Act provided that the probation officer would conduct an "investigation" of the defendant, pursuant to Rule 32 F.R.Cr.P. and report that investigation to the court. In addition, it is clear that Congress intended sentencing courts to actively exercise their discretion to accept or reject plea agreements to ensure that the resulting sentences meet the purposes of sentencing.

However, Congress recognized that the potential for prosecutorial charging and plea practices to effectively determine the sentence "could well reduce the benefits otherwise to be expected from the bill's guideline sentencing system." It directed the Sentencing Commission to promulgate policy statements for district courts to use in determining whether to accept plea agreements, in order "to provide an opportunity for meaningful judicial review of proposed charge-reduction plea agreements, as well as other forms of plea agreements, while at the same time to guard against improper judicial intrusion upon the responsibilities of the Executive Branch."

Accordingly, the Commission promulgated the Chapter Six Policy Statements to guide courts in accepting plea agreements. Those Policy Statements describe an active, independent role for the probation officer because, "[a] thorough presentence investigation is essential in determining the facts relevant to sentencing." . . . While the guidelines provide for "stipulations," which are points upon which the parties agree or disagree, "[t]he court is not bound by the stipulation, but may with the aid of the presentence report, determine the facts relevant to sentencing." Further:

> Even though stipulations are expected to be accurate and complete, the court cannot rely exclusively upon stipulations in ascertaining the factors relevant to the determination of the sentence. Rather, in determining the factual basis for the sentence, the court will consider the stipulation, together with the results of the presentence investigation, and any other relevant information. . . .

Clearly, the presentence report prepared by the probation officer is the only source of information outside the stipulations of the parties which the court can use to decide whether or not to accept those stipulations in fashioning the sentence. . . . This is also true regarding the court's determination whether to accept a plea agreement. For example, where the plea agreement includes a dismissal of charges or an agreement not to pursue potential charges, the court is asked to evaluate whether the remaining charges "adequately reflect the seriousness of the actual offense behavior," and whether the agreement will support the statutory purposes of sentencing or the sentencing guidelines. Therefore, it is easy to see that Congress intended that "The probation officers will be a crucial link in the effectiveness of both sentencing guidelines and policy statement."

C. Publication 107. There are numerous provisions to support the independent role of the probation officer in Publication 107. For example:

> A primary role of the probation officer is to prepare a presentence report of the highest quality for the court that will assist in sentencing a defendant. Under guideline sentencing, the probation officer's role as *the court's independent investigator* is critical, although the scope of the investigation may be determined by the court. . . . [In determining a tentative guideline range, the officer must] *thoroughly explore and analyze the circumstances of the offense and the offender.* (emphasis added)

The officer is to provide the court ". . . with relevant, objective, and verifiable information that will assist in the selection of a proper sentence"; and ". . . it is crucial that a probation officer exercise independence as an agent of the court by developing factual and rule-related assertions."

To underscore the fact that the monograph envisions the probation officer doing more than providing sentence calculations based on the parties' stipulations, it says that where the parties' stipulations differ from the results of the officer's investigation, the officer should "display the range that would have resulted if there had been no plea agreement" under the "Impact of the Plea Agreement" section of the PSR, to assist "the court in evaluating the impact of the plea agreement on the ultimate sentence." Finally, to further underscore the independent nature of the probation officer's investigation, the monograph also envisions that the probation officer will discuss any potential bases for departure, and possibly make a recommendation on departure in the "Factors That May Warrant Departure" section of the presentence report. . . .

D. Case Law. Not surprisingly, the courts have uniformly endorsed and upheld the independent role of the probation officer in federal guideline sentencing. . . .

E. The Officer's Investigation in the Presentence Report. The "Impact of the Plea Agreement" section of the presentence report should provide a comparison of the sentencing range which results from the independent investigation, where different, with that which results from the parties' stipulations. . . . The most important thing is that the court is provided with the maximum amount of information upon which to make the sentencing determination.

F. Practical and Logical Necessity for Independent Investigation. Realistically, the court has the ultimate authority to determine the "scope" of the probation officer's role at sentencing. And, to the extent that the officer's role is limited, the potential for objections to the presentence report is admittedly minimized. . . .

There are strong practical and logical needs for an independent probation officer at sentencing. The reason the court needs "objective" information, which may go beyond and differ from the stipulation of the parties, is that the court has the discretion, and, indeed, the responsibility, to determine whether to accept the plea agreement, pursuant to Rule 11(c)(1)(A) and (C), and whether to impose a sentence in accord with any non-binding recommendations ("stipulations") of the parties, pursuant to Rule 11(c)(1)(B). [T]he sentencing process must provide the court with the information necessary to perform its duty to supervise the plea process and to make a sentence determination.

To the extent that the court relies on stipulations and agreements, practical problems and concerns arise. The court is denied information on sentencing factors which the parties may not have anticipated or agreed upon. Stipulations sometimes omit, either intentionally or inadvertently, key facts necessary to apply the guidelines. Familiarity with the guidelines varies considerably among practitioners and prosecutors, and the parties cannot always identify and adequately address all pertinent sentencing factors or bases for departure at the plea stage. For example, if the parties do not stipulate to adequate facts to determine role, or do not anticipate what ultimately appears to be a meritorious basis for departure, a court that does not receive such information, or limits itself to the stipulations of the parties, loses the ability to employ its sentencing discretion in a fully knowledgeable manner.

Aside from such practical problems, larger, institutional concerns arise if the role of the probation officer in sentencing is limited. . . . Without the "check" on the system that the probation officer provides, we would still have a complicated, resource intensive guideline system, but without the measure of proportionality and uniformity in sentencing which the guidelines were created to achieve. This would primarily be because the court's ability to supervise the plea bargaining process and to sentence based on all the relevant information would be significantly diluted. . . .

G. Procedural Suggestions to Narrow the Gap and to Enhance Fact Finding and Dispute Resolution at Sentencing.   Critics periodically complain that the probation officer's independent investigation results in the probation officer recommending a sentence different than that recommended by the parties, thereby converting the officer into a "third advocate." There are many reasons that the officer may arrive at a different calculation than the parties, including the fact that the officer is not subject to the same negotiation pressures of the parties, and the fact that the officer does not always have the same perspective of the strength of some of the evidence as, for example, the government may have, given that the officer often receives merely a written summary of that evidence.

While some of these differences can be minimized with better communication . . . , wherever differences exist between the sentence calculations of the officer and the parties, the existence of an independent probation investigation does not eliminate nor diminish the opportunity for advocacy by the parties. On the contrary, it highlights and enhances the need for advocacy of the parties, and enriches the information given the court, thereby helping to ensure the best sentence determination possible by the court. Parties still have the opportunity to convince the court of the validity of their positions. The courts have denied any claim that the role of the probation officer improperly influences the court, finding that, in spite of recommendations made by probation officers on sentencing factors, the court is still required to resolve any and all disputes, and that the court has the ability to read a presentence report without being improperly influenced. . . .

1. Some districts have found it beneficial to require, or offer as a possibility, some form of pre-plea advisory conference with a probation officer for a non-binding computation of guidelines relevant to computing at least the offense level, or sometimes even an estimated range (with appropriate waivers that it is non-binding and subject to change upon preparation of a full presentence report). A few districts provide for a Magistrate, or non-sentencing district court judge, to conduct the conference, which becomes in essence a settlement conference. All pre-plea computations or conferences, if they are to be meaningful, depend on full discovery from the government, which is perhaps their primary value, which in turn assists plea negotiations and pre-sentencing disclosure.

2. Some districts require that the government (and defense, optionally) submit within so many days after a plea or trial, an early statement of the facts, disputed issues, and applicable sentencing and guideline factors, in order to focus attention early on sentencing factors and to assist the probation officer.

3. Rule 32(6)(B) F.R.Cr.P. suggests, after the parties submit objections to the presentence report, that the probation officer "may meet with the defendant, the defendant's counsel, and the attorney for the government to discuss those objections." While this is no doubt helpful, some districts find it useful, in addition to this requirement, to require or urge both counsel to meet with the probation officer earlier, during the preparation of the draft presentence report, in order to provide maximum assistance to the officer, to avoid misunderstandings regarding the evidence, and to focus the parties' attention on sentencing factors early in the process.

4. Rule 32 F.R.Cr.P. directs that objections, if any, be submitted to the draft presentence report be submitted to the probation officer. It does not specify what form the objection should take. . . .

5. [U.S. Court of Appeals Judge Edward R.] Becker suggests that courts provide an opportunity for a pre-sentence conference with the court (at least in more complicated cases) in order to narrow issues, plan evidence, minimize delay and avoid last-minute submissions.

· Obviously, most of these measures require court initiation, but probation officers can implement some on their own, such as requesting early conferences with the parties and asking parties to submit their sentencing positions (and legal authorities for those positions) prior to the issuance of the draft presentence report. Some probation offices may wish to . . . seek the court's endorsement of their requests for meetings and early submissions.

The Role of the Probation Officer in the Guideline System, Charlie E. Varnon
4 Fed. Sentencing Rep. 63 (1991)

The probation service has a long tradition of serving as the court's investigator. For almost fifty years, Rule 32 has directed the probation officer to provide the court with any information which may aid in sentencing. In 1984 Congress amended Rule 32(c)(2)(B) to require that the presentence report include a statement of the guidelines and policy statements the officer believes applicable in an individual case. The officer's relationship with the court and the purpose of the presentence report remain the same. The sentencing recommendation submitted prior to the guidelines was not binding on the court, and the guideline application recommendations now submitted are not binding.

The nature of the information in the presentence report has undergone drastic change. The probation officer no longer serves merely as a conduit for the prosecution's version and defendant's statement to the court. Judgments, though only preliminary and advisory, must be made by the probation officer to arrive at the statement of "the classification of the offense and of the defendant under the categories established by the Sentencing Commission," as required by Rule 32. The immediate impact of these judgments, if adopted by the court, is much more visible than were the officer's general conclusions and recommendations prior to the guidelines.

Criticism of the probation officer by counsel for candidly reporting the guideline he or she believes to apply is neither justified nor necessary. Both the government and the defense now have greater opportunity at the trial and appellate court levels to correct errors in the probation officer's judgment and analysis.

[P]robation officers are being characterized as "guardians of the guidelines," "plea busters," unlicensed practitioners of the law, and "more cutthroat than the government." The consistent theme is that it was a kinder and gentler system before the advent of guidelines. The primary source of contention . . . seems to be probation officers' reports to the court that do not endorse some elements of plea agreements. . . . Another factor which seems to influence the probation officer's relationships is the perception that officers are now making findings of fact and law which we are not trained or competent to make. . . .

> ## The Greening of Probation Officers in Their New Role, Francesca D. Bowman
> ### 4 Fed. Sentencing Rep. 99 (1991)

At [a] Chiefs and Deputies biennial meeting in Alexandria, an old colleague from another district queried me confidentially, "But isn't it fun to see how many points you can apply?" This unexpected interest in the guidelines for themselves is shared by many probation officers across the country. In fact, this aspect of guidelines application took most of us by surprise; thus when we admit to being smitten by the guidelines, it is with an apologetic, confessional tone.

For as a group we generally abhor being placed in an adversarial position. Probation officers traditionally were attracted to the job to have personal contact with the clients — to get into their lives. We are, by profession, nosey. We get into the client's home, figure out what went wrong and then are paid to fix it. The way it is fixed can vary from pure social work to investigation and surveillance. But it all amounts to the same thing — access to other people's lives. Our mindset, therefore, differs substantially from that of lawyers, who are always ready for a good fight, and from judges, who have left the good fight and now do referee work.

With the adoption of the guidelines, we found ourselves thrown into the fight with the professional heavyweights. At first we objected, but as we found ourselves sparring, the great American competitive spirit prevailed and it turned out to be not only interesting, but challenging — even fun. To the government, we have become a thorny contender; to the defense, we are accused of being more cutthroat than the government. For our part, it is all done in the name of being true to the guidelines. And we have been scrupulous.

This strict adherence to rules and laws established by Congress, however, may have somewhat numbed our senses to what is actually going on. . . .

Has the Role of the U.S. Probation Officer Really Changed?, Magdeline E. Jensen
4 Fed. Sentencing Rep. 94 (1991)

[T]he role of the probation officer has been variously criticized as an unwelcome third party in the adversary system, a guardian of the guidelines, and an interpreter of the law without a license to practice. . . .

The criticisms are misdirected in that they are attempting to "kill the messenger," rather than directing attention to a message which is not being well received. . . .

In analyzing the role of the probation officer, it is important to bear in mind who the probation officer works for — who hires and fires. The Probation Act of 1925 created the position of the U.S. probation officer and authorized district judges to appoint one salaried probation officer and other unsalaried probation officers, subject to civil service regulations. As a result of dissatisfaction among judges, the statute was amended in June 1930 to do away with the civil service provision of the Act, directing that the district court was responsible for appointment. This procedure continues today, and the district court is also responsible for removal of a probation officer. 18 U.S.C. §3602(a). . . .

Historically, the function of the presentence report has been to provide information to assist the judge in making an informed sentencing decision. [A]t sentencing, information that may have been neither relevant nor admissible prior to conviction may be considered. The defendant's criminal record, biographical background, and financial condition must be researched. In the majority of cases entailing entry of a guilty plea where the court does not have the benefit of information presented at trial, the details of the offense and effect on the victim present critical factors for the court to weigh. . . .

Criminal procedures are adversarial in the pretrial and trial phases with the two sides guarding the interests of the client or the government by introducing information for the court's consideration and debating whether it is admissible. At sentencing, on the other hand, the primary source of information is the presentence investigation report, a document submitted from the vantage of a third party. The notion is that the investigation should be conducted by one who has not been a party to the case prior to conviction, is theoretically neutral, and is strictly responsible to the court. In this role, the probation officer acts as an "arm" of the court. . . .

Even if misdirected, why has the role of the probation officer received vituperative attention? . . .

In the past, an officer could collect facts from several sources and present various renditions of the facts of the offense (the prosecution version, the defendant's version, and the victim's version). Under the guidelines, however, the officer is required to sort out and analyze the facts with the goal of determining, on the best available information, what happened during the course of the offense. This investigation is necessary in order to apply the facts to the guideline provisions. Because a specific fact, such as the presence of a gun, or the dimension of a fact, such as the amount of drugs, may translate to a difference in exposure to a prison term, effective advocates will challenge the officer's guideline application in order to protect the interest of the defendant or government. This process may bring the officer into conflict with the attorneys. Although the officer does not have an adversarial role in the sentencing process, he may find himself in the gunsight of one attorney or be caught in the crossfire of both. . . .

If the officer's role is not the appropriate target for discontent, where should the concern be directed? . . . Fewer defendants are eligible for probation and community alternatives to incarceration than under the old sentencing law. Prison sentences are finite, without reconsideration or early release, and with less credit for good conduct. These features of the [Sentencing Reform Act] place a premium on the contents of the presentence report for the interested parties, and the probation officer is often the bearer of bad news. . . .

A Probation Officer's Perception of the Allocation of Discretion, Frank S. Gilbert
4 Fed. Sentencing Rep. 109 (1991)

[T]he probation officer has a statutory responsibility to present the court with a guideline computation based on the facts known to the officer. The officer is therefore thrust into the role of "guardian of the guidelines" in that he or she, contrary to any agreement by the parties, must apply the guidelines as intended by the Commission. Needless to say, this responsibility frequently results in a great deal of conflict and controversy. In applying the guidelines, particularly to cases in which the parties have agreed to certain facts or guideline applications which are at odds with the officer's perception of the matter at hand, does the officer strictly adhere to his guideline manual and cause a further independent and time-consuming investigation, provoke argument, create the need to prepare a presentence addendum in defense of his position, and ultimately find that no one will argue his view at the time of the sentencing hearing? Or, will the officer pursue the path of least resistance and prepare the computations based upon the parties' agreement? While one might hope that this never occurs, a perfunctory understanding of human behavior suggests otherwise.

At the time of the sentencing hearing, the court is frequently faced with an agreement between the parties which produces a much different guideline computation than the one presented by the probation officer. This situation poses the potential for lengthy fact-finding hearings. Not infrequently, the prosecutor may take the position that the government cannot prove those facts contained in the probation officer's report by a preponderance of evidence standard. How is an already overburdened court — inundated by increasing numbers of drug related crimes — to respond? Should the court challenge the prosecutor's professional judgement in this regard and engage in a complex fact-finding hearing for which neither party has any enthusiasm . . . , or should it simply accept the statement of the parties and make findings that may substantially reduce the sentencing guideline range? To what extent should the court intervene in the government's bargaining practices? . . .

> ## Looking at the Federal Sentencing Process One Judge at a Time, One Probation Officer at a Time, Leslie A. Cory
> ### 51 Emory L.J. 379 (2002)

Probation officers are employees of the court, hired and fired by the sentencing judges for whom they write presentence reports. While 18 U.S.C. §3603 sets out the duties of the probation officer in regard to the court, 28 U.S.C. §995(a) authorizes the Sentencing Commission to "monitor the performance of probation officers with regard to sentencing recommendations, including application of the Sentencing Commission guidelines and policy statements"; and to "issue instructions to probation officers concerning the application of Commission guidelines and policy statements. . . ." If the instructions of the Sentencing Commission and the judge for whom the probation officer works diverge, the officer will be forced to choose whose instructions take precedence.

[H]ow do probation officers view their role? One study found that probation officers' perceptions of their role varied from one district to another. Some officers viewed their role as enforcers of the sentencing guidelines. Others viewed themselves as employees of the court, gathering whatever information on sentencing factors, including offender characteristics, the judges will want to evaluate at sentencing. In that study, neither group of officers acknowledged that the particular officer writing the presentence report might have a significant impact on the sentencing outcome. The officers did comment upon an informal policy in each district, set by the judges, of either giving offender characteristics significant consideration in sentencing decisions or of disregarding offender characteristics as a sentencing consideration.

Because the probation officer stands between the sentencing judge and the other parties, the other parties may regard the officer as an obstacle to the achievement of their purposes. From some officers' perspective, the source of the conflict is that, unlike defense attorneys and prosecutors, the probation officer is required to make an "impartial" determination of the guidelines. And unlike the judge, the probation officer is not insulated from ex parte communications. The officer is required to meet with the parties and to develop relationships with them. The positive implication of the probation officer's availability is that the parties have far more of an opportunity to persuade the officer than they do the judge.

The parties involved in the sentencing process often consider the probation officer the sentencing expert. Probation officers ought to be sentencing experts. However, because they have so much discretion in interpreting and applying the guidelines, probation officer error can have a powerful impact upon sentences. A study conducted by the Federal Judicial Center . . . demonstrated the possible impact on sentencing of probation officer error in interpreting the guidelines.[78] In this study, forty-seven probation officers were given the same crime scenario, dealing with three defendants involved in a drug conspiracy. The officers' assignment was to determine the quantity of drugs attributable to each defendant. Based upon the same set of facts, the officers came up with widely varying offense levels, depending upon how the officers interpreted the provisions of the Relevant Conduct guideline. Over-reliance on probation officer expertise, by defense attorneys, prosecutors, or judges, can be disastrous for defendants.

How a judge uses a presentence report varies according to the judge's assessment of the Sentencing Commission and its sentencing guidelines, and according to how much control the judge chooses to exercise over the sentencing process. . . .

The use a judge makes of the presentence report will also vary according to the judge's attitude toward plea agreements. A judge who believes sentencing outcomes should be determined by the parties (defendant, defense attorney, and prosecutor) may forego inquiry into whether the plea agreement adequately reflects the statutory purposes of sentencing. . . .

When a probation officer presents to a judge the facts that the officer believes are relevant to sentencing, the officer exercises great informal discretion — it is the officer alone who decides which facts are relevant. Policy may guide, but the officer decides. When a judge disregards facts that are arguably relevant under the guidelines, to achieve a lower offense level, the judge is exercising her discretion. Whether that exercise is legitimate depends upon the judge's motivation. Whether it appears legitimate depends upon the care with which she frames her explanation. Each participant in the sentencing process exercises the discretion accorded to him or her in a unique manner. A passive prosecutor may defer to an aggressive defense attorney. A laissez-faire judge may defer to whatever compromises the prosecution and defense are prepared to accept. An inexperienced probation officer may rely heavily on the input of the prosecutor. . . .

The study suggests the following conclusions . . . :

3. Some probation officers are more inclined to recommend sentences that cover the entire spectrum of the guideline range. Others are more inclined to recommend sentences toward the bottom. Judges frequently rely on these recommendations, with the result that where within the guideline range a defendant's sentence is imposed will depend in part upon who the probation officer is. . . .

5. Although judges depart with far less frequency than probation officers suggest grounds for departure, judges do rely on the information supplied by probation officers for making the departure decision. Some probation officers are more inclined than others to suggest possible grounds for departure.

6. Defendants who object to the presentence report experience no adverse consequences, and have a relatively good record of success. . . .

---

78. Pamela B. Lawrence & Paul J. Hofer, An Empirical Study of the Application of the Relevant Conduct Guideline 1B1.3, 10 Fed. Sentencing Rep. 16 (1997).

NOTE

Probation officers: guardians of the guidelines? As these readings indicate, the role of the probation officer in the federal system, while long important to the administration of justice, has taken on a more central and contested role under the sentencing guidelines. Does the apparent frustration directed by some counsel (sometimes prosecution, but more frequently defense) at probation officers obscure frustration with judges for deferring to probation officers, or to the guidelines that the probation officers apply? Can prosecutors use probation officers to get around plea negotiations by identifying case agents and others who will identify aggravating facts to the probation officers? Have probation officers become an arm of the prosecution rather than of the court? Have probation officers become an arm of the sentencing commission rather than of the court?

3. *Sentencing Hearings*

After prosecutors and defense counsel strike a plea bargain (or after the jury returns a guilty verdict in those rare cases that go to trial), and after a probation officer has completed a presentencing investigation report, the sentencing drama moves to its most public setting, the courtroom for a sentencing hearing. Do sentencing hearings resemble trials? What is the standard for admission of evidence? What rules and procedures are used to test evidence? Should the sentencing hearing be a minitrial?

|| ***Federal Rule of Criminal Procedure 32(i)***
Sentencing and Judgment ||

(i) Sentencing.
    (1) *In General.* At sentencing, the court:
        (A) must verify that the defendant and the defendant's attorney have read and discussed the presentence report and any addendum to the report;
        (B) must give to the defendant and an attorney for the government a written summary of — or summarize in camera — any information excluded from the presentence report . . . on which the court will rely in sentencing, and give them a reasonable opportunity to comment on that information;
        (C) must allow the parties' attorneys to comment on the probation officer's determinations and other matters relating to an appropriate sentence; and
        (D) may, for good cause, allow a party to make a new objection at any time before sentence is imposed.
    (2) *Introducing Evidence; Producing a Statement.* The court may permit the parties to introduce evidence on the objections. . . .
    (3) *Court Determinations.* At sentencing, the court:
        (A) may accept any undisputed portion of the presentence report as a finding of fact;

(B) must — for any disputed portion of the presentence report or other controverted matter — rule on the dispute or determine that a ruling is unnecessary either because the matter will not affect sentencing, or because the court will not consider the matter in sentencing; . . .

(4) *Opportunity to Speak.*

(A) *By a Party.* Before imposing sentence, the court must:

(i) provide the defendant's attorney an opportunity to speak on the defendant's behalf;

(ii) address the defendant personally in order to permit the defendant to speak or present any information to mitigate the sentence; and

(iii) provide an attorney for the government an opportunity to speak equivalent to that of the defendant's attorney.

(B) *By a Victim.* Before imposing sentence, the court must address any victim of a crime of violence or sexual abuse who is present at sentencing and must permit the victim to speak or submit any information about the sentence. Whether or not the victim is present, a victim's right to address the court may be exercised by the following persons if present:

(i) a parent or legal guardian, if the victim is younger than 18 years or is incompetent; or

(ii) one or more family members or relatives the court designates, if the victim is deceased or incapacitated.

(C) *In Camera Proceedings.* Upon a party's motion and for good cause, the court may hear in camera any statement made under Rule 32(i)(4).

U.S. Sentencing Guidelines Manual §6A1.3 (Policy Statement)

§6A1.3 RESOLUTION OF DISPUTED FACTORS

(a) When any factor important to the sentencing determination is reasonably in dispute, the parties shall be given an adequate opportunity to present information to the court regarding that factor. In resolving any dispute concerning a factor important to the sentencing determination, the court may consider relevant information without regard to its admissibility under the rules of evidence applicable at trial, provided that the information has sufficient indicia of reliability to support its probable accuracy.

(b) The court shall resolve disputed sentencing factors at a sentencing hearing in accordance with Rule 32(c)(1), Fed. R. Crim. P.

COMMENTARY

In pre-guidelines practice, factors relevant to sentencing were often determined in an informal fashion. The informality was to some extent explained by the fact that particular offense and offender characteristics rarely had a highly specific or required sentencing consequence. This situation no longer exists under sentencing guidelines. The court's resolution of disputed sentencing factors usually has a measurable effect on the applicable punishment. More formality is therefore unavoidable if the sentencing process is to be accurate and fair.

Although lengthy sentencing hearings seldom should be necessary, disputes about sentencing factors must be resolved with care. When a dispute exists about any factor important to the sentencing determination, the court must ensure that the parties have an adequate opportunity to present relevant information. Written statements of counsel or affidavits of witnesses may be adequate under many circumstances. An evidentiary hearing may sometimes be the only reliable way to resolve disputed issues. The sentencing court must determine the appropriate procedure in light of the nature of the dispute, its relevance to the sentencing determination, and applicable case law.

In determining the relevant facts, sentencing judges are not restricted to information that would be admissible at trial. See 18 U.S.C. §3661; see also United States v. Watts, 117 S. Ct. 633, 635 (1997) (holding that lower evidentiary standard at sentencing permits sentencing court's consideration of acquitted conduct); Witte v. United States, 515 U.S. 389 (1995) (noting that sentencing courts have traditionally considered wide range of information without the procedural protections of a criminal trial, including information concerning criminal conduct that may be the subject of a subsequent prosecution); Nichols v. United States, 511 U.S. 738 (1994) (noting that district courts have traditionally considered defendant's prior criminal conduct even when the conduct did not result in a conviction). Any information may be considered, so long as it has sufficient indicia of reliability to support its probable accuracy. Out-of-court declarations by an unidentified informant may be considered where there is good cause for the non-disclosure of the informant's identity and there is sufficient corroboration by other means.

The Commission believes that use of a preponderance of the evidence standard is appropriate to meet due process requirements and policy concerns in resolving disputes regarding application of the guidelines to the facts of a case.

NOTES

1. *Sentencing hearings.* How much do the federal sentencing guidelines have to say about the procedures that should govern sentencing hearings? What are the key procedural questions that should be determined by statute or rule? For example, do the federal rules determine what proof and procedure will be allowed at sentencing hearings? Questions raised by the constitutional debate over *Apprendi* arise again in the context of sentencing hearings. What does it mean for a judge to accept testimony with "sufficient indicia of reliability"? How does that standard relate to the more familiar standards and evidentiary rules at trial? See Susan N. Herman, The Tail that Wagged the Dog: Bifurcated Fact-Finding and the Limits of Due Process Under the Federal Sentencing Guidelines, 66 S. Cal. L. Rev. 289 (1992); Deborah Young, Fact-Finding at Federal Sentencing: Why the Guidelines Should Meet the Rules, 79 Cornell L. Rev. 299 (1994); David Adair, House Built on Weak Foundation — Sentencing Guidelines and the Preponderance Standard of Proof, 10 Fed. Sentencing Rep. 41 (1997).

2. *Exclusionary rule at the sentencing hearing.*   Most jurisdictions allow sentencing judges to consider evidence obtained in violation of a defendant's constitutional rights, even when that evidence is suppressed at trial. See Elson v. State, 659 P.2d 1195 (Alaska 1983) (allowing evidence obtained illegally at sentencing unless violation was for purpose of obtaining facts to enhance sentencing); Smith v. State, 517 A.2d 1081 (Md. 1986). The federal courts are split on whether the exclusionary rule applies in sentencing proceedings. The U.S. Supreme Court held in Estelle v. Smith, 451 U.S. 454 (1981), that a sentencing judge in a capital case could not consider a statement obtained in violation of the Fifth Amendment, but the Court has never addressed whether the exclusionary rule applies in noncapital sentencing proceedings. Some state statutes and cases allow the introduction of illegally obtained evidence in capital cases, at least within the boundaries of Estelle v. Smith. See, e.g., Utah Code §76-3-207(2) ("Any evidence the court deems to have probative force may be received regardless of its admissibility under the exclusionary rules of evidence."); Stewart v. State, 549 So. 2d 171 (Fla. 1989). Most lower federal courts have decided that the exclusionary rule does not apply at sentencing in noncapital proceedings. See, e.g., United States v. Torres, 926 F.2d 321 (D.C. Cir. 1991). A smaller group applies the exclusionary rule at sentencing. See Pens v. Bail, 902 F.2d 1464 (9th Cir. 1991).

3. *The right of allocution.*   Federal Rule of Criminal Procedure 32 gives the defendant the right to speak at sentencing, which is often known as a right of allocution. As *Black's Law Dictionary* explains, an allocution is "an unsworn statement from a convicted defendant to the sentencing judge or jury in which the defendant can ask for mercy, explain his or her conduct, apologize for the crime, or say anything else in an effort to lessen the impending sentence. This statement is not subject to cross-examination." *Black's Law Dictionary* 75 (7th ed. 1999).

Perhaps in part because most states, like the federal system, expressly grant defendants the right to speak at sentencing, the Supreme Court has never squarely addressed whether the constitution protects the right of allocution. The Court has, however, spoken grandly of the history and importance of this right:

> [Rule 32's] legal provenance was the common-law right of allocution. As early as 1689, it was recognized that the court's failure to ask the defendant if he had anything to say before sentence was imposed required reversal. . . . Taken in the context of its history, there can be little doubt that the drafters of Rule 32 intended that the defendant be personally afforded the opportunity to speak before imposition of sentence. We are not unmindful of the relevant major changes that have evolved in criminal procedure since the seventeenth century — the sharp decrease in the number of crimes which were punishable by death, the right of the defendant to testify on his own behalf, and the right to counsel. But we see no reason why a procedural rule should be limited to the circumstances under which it arose if reasons for the right it protects remain. None of these modern innovations lessens the need for the defendant, personally, to have the opportunity to present to the court his plea in mitigation. The most persuasive counsel may not be able to speak for a defendant as the defendant might, with halting eloquence, speak for himself.

Green v. United States, 365 U.S. 301, 303 (1961). And yet, in Hill v. United States, 368 U.S. 424 (1962), the Court held that a trial judge's failure to expressly ask a defendant represented by counsel whether he wished to make a statement at sentencing was not an error of constitutional dimension and therefore provided no basis for a collateral attack.

Lower state and federal courts split over whether a right of allocution is constitutionally protected, although most of these cases turn on whether defendants were fully afforded their statutory right to speak at sentencing and what the appropriate remedy should be for statutory violations. See, e.g., Michigan v. Petit, 648 N.W.2d 193 (Mich. 2002); In re Personal Restraint of Echeverria, 6 P.3d 573 (Wash. 2000).

The practical importance of the right of allocution may be as debatable as its legal standing. Especially in sentencing systems with structured sentencing rules, it is far more likely for a defendant's statement to have symbolic value than to present information directly relevant to a judge's or jury's sentencing determination. Even if allocution is likely to be only symbolic most of the time, is there anything wrong with symbolic rights? Allocution can have tangible costs for a defendant: an admission made during an allocution might be used against the defendant at retrial or re-sentencing. If concerns about the possible future use of an allocution statement might chill the practice, should jurisdictions adopt rules limiting the later use of allocution statements against defendants?

4. *Victims' right to speak at sentencing.*   Is the right of victims or their representatives to speak also merely symbolic? The inclusion of victim statements is now widespread throughout the United States in response to the victims' rights movement that emerged in the 1980s. The Victim and Witness Protection Act of 1982 amended the Federal Rules of Criminal Procedure to require the inclusion of a victim impact statement as a part of the presentence report in federal court. Proposed federal legislation and constitutional amendments would increase victim participation at sentencing.

Over the past 20 years, nearly every state has decided to allow victim involvement at sentencing. See generally National Victim Center, The 1996 Victims' Rights Sourcebook: A Compilation and Comparison of Victims' Rights Laws (1996). It is difficult to capture the depth, range, and impact of this dramatic change in sentencing practice. Almost all states allow victim input through the presentence report. Many allow victims a separate opportunity to make a written or oral statement regarding sentencing, often specifying the kinds of information victims may offer. A few states have retained sharper limits: Several allow judges to choose whether to admit or refuse victim impact information; Texas allows victim to make a statement only after sentencing, Tex. Code Crim. Proc. art. 42.03.

The rich variety of statutes has not produced a substantial caselaw regarding victim impact statements in the noncapital context. Challenges to such statements often assert that the judge was biased or unduly influenced by the information. Should judges rely on their own sense of the unique nature of harm imposed in particular cases? Does victim impact information differ in kind from other types of new information, such as information about the offender?

=7=

Sentencing Outcomes: The Scale of Imprisonment

We have reviewed the typical "inputs" that influence the choice of sentences in a particular case and the procedural setting for the sentencing decision. Now we turn to the typical outcomes of the sentencing decision, beginning with imprisonment.

We start with prison, although it is not the most common sentencing outcome. Very few misdemeanors result in a prison term, and many of the least serious felonies (which account for the greatest number of felonies) also result in a nonprison punishment. Yet prison is the sentence that occupies a large place in public debates and the largest place in public budgets. In the United States, it is the expected sentence for the most serious felonies. Gustave du Beaumont and Alexis de Tocqueville, who toured prisons in the United States on behalf of the French government in 1831, noted the emphasis that Americans placed on the prison early in its history: "they have caught the monomania of the penitentiary system, which to them seems the remedy for all the evils of society." Gustave de Beaumont and Alexis de Tocqueville, On the Penitentiary System in the United States and Its Application in France 80 (Francis Lieber trans., 1833).

In this chapter we consider why criminal justice in the United States relies as much as it does on the prison sanction. What do governments hope to accomplish when they use prison rather than other punishments for crimes? Which of the limits on the use of prison are legal, and which are political or cultural?

A. INCARCERATION TRENDS

Prison began as a distinctly American contribution to criminal justice, and today the United States is unmatched in its use of prison as a criminal punishment. But our reliance on prison has changed in interesting ways over time. In

457

the following passage, Norval Morris briefly summarizes the history of prison as a sanction for crimes, emphasizing its American origins. He then evokes a moment that is now difficult to reconstruct: a time in the 1960s and 1970s when a serious debate occurred in the United States about whether to abolish or seriously limit the use of prison.

That moment has passed. Since the early 1980s, governments in the United States have embraced prison as never before. The tables following the Morris excerpt track the increases in the rate of imprisonment in the United States since 1971; of particular significance are the differences among various regions and states. The section concludes with a comparative discussion of imprisonment rates in other nations.

The Future of Imprisonment, Norval Morris
Pages 3-9 (1974)

[Until] quite recently the serious offender, other than the political criminal, was not imprisoned as a penal sanction. He may have been penned for other purposes but not imprisoned as a punishment. Felons were dealt with by exile, banishment, transportation, and a diversity of demeaning and painful corporal punishments — the "cat," the ear and nose cropper, the branding iron, and that reliable standby, capital punishment. Prisons for felons arose as a reaction to the excesses and barbarisms of earlier punishments; imprisonment was one of the early "diversions" from traditional criminal sanctions.

The jail, the workhouse, the almshouse, the reformatory, and the convict ship all antedate the prison. The castle keep for the political personage out of favor or office and the church's cell for retreat and penance were part of the genesis of the prison, but they were established for different social classes and different political purposes. What is sometimes forgotten . . . is that the prison is an American invention, an invention of the Pennsylvania Quakers of the last decade of the eighteenth century, though one might also note the confining "People Pen" put up by the Massachusetts Pilgrims nearly two centuries earlier. In their "penitentiary" the Quakers planned to substitute the correctional specifics of isolation, repentance, and the uplifting effects of scriptural injunctions and solitary Bible reading for the brutality and inutility of capital and corporal punishments. These three treatments — removal from corrupting peers, time for reflection and self-examination, the guidance of biblical precepts — would no doubt have been helpful to the reflective Quakers who devised the prison, but relatively few of them ever became prisoners. The suitability of these remedies for the great mass of those who subsequently found their way to the penitentiary is more questionable. . . .

At all events, in 1790 a cell block was opened in the Walnut Street Jail of Philadelphia as the "penitentiary" for the Commonwealth of Pennsylvania. In 1796, Newgate began service as the penitentiary for the State of New York, modeled on the Walnut Street Jail but taking its name from an earlier English institution serving a different clientele (civil and criminal debtors and those awaiting trial or punishment).

Prisons grew and flourished throughout America and later throughout the world; they are a pervasive American export, like tobacco in their international acceptance and perhaps also in their adverse consequences. The Pennsylvania

Quakers must be praised or blamed for the invention or reinvention of the prison. Their vision and initiative gave us our hulking penal institutions, our "edifice complex." It was a gift born of benevolence not malevolence, of philanthropy not punitiveness, so that the most important contemporary lesson of this historical sketch may well be a deeper appreciation of the truth that benevolent intentions do not necessarily produce beneficent results.

ABOLITION OR ABATEMENT OF IMPRISONMENT

Contemporary Quakers in the American Friends Service Committee's book, *Struggle for Justice,* recognize that "the horror that is the American prison system grew out of an eighteenth century reform" proposed by their ideological forebears. Their criticism is of a cruelty characteristic of intrafamilial disputes, but they are by no means alone in their castigation of imprisonment. . . . Both national crime commissions of the past decade recommended the swift abatement of imprisonment, and the 1973 commission urged a moratorium on the construction of all new institutions for adult or juvenile offenders, a position also adopted by the National Council on Crime and Delinquency. Judge James E. Doyle, a federal district judge of the Western District of Wisconsin, was formidably direct in the matter. In Morales v. Schmidt, 340 F. Supp. 544, 548-549 (W.D. Wis. 1972), a prison mail censorship case, he said: "I am persuaded that the institution of prison probably must end. In many respects it is as intolerable within the United States as was the institution of slavery, equally brutalizing to all involved, equally toxic to the social system, equally subversive of the brotherhood of man, even more costly by some standard, and probably less rational."

The 1973 national commission, the National Advisory Commission on Criminal Justice Standards and Goals, recommended that "the institution should be the last resort for correctional problems," gave their reasons — failure to reduce crime, success in punishing but not in deterring, providing only temporary protection to the community, changing the offender but mostly for the worse — and concluded that "the prison . . . has persisted, partly because a civilized nation could neither turn back to the barbarism of an earlier time nor find a satisfactory alternative.". . .

Imprisonment has been too much used, it has discriminated against races and classes, sentences imposed have been too long, and too many of them have been served in degrading and brutalizing circumstances. There is widespread advocacy of the swift abatement if not an abolition of imprisonment. How is this to be achieved?

THE PATHS TO ABATEMENT OF IMPRISONMENT

[Several] paths are believed to lead to the abatement of imprisonment. First, the "overreach" of the criminal law is to be reduced. . . . Regulatory systems, backed by the criminal sanctions if regulations are flouted, should be substituted for the mass of prohibitory propositions at present brought to bear on a wide swath of behavior. Though much of what now busies the criminal justice system may be immoral or troublesome or distasteful or unseemly or injurious to the actor and those who love him or depend on him, it does not represent a serious threat to the physical safety of others nor a major depredation to property nor a serious challenge to governmental authority. . . .

Just as there has been an overemphasis on the use of the prohibitory sanctions of the criminal law, so there has been an overemphasis on custody. It is widely recognized that we have locked up too many social nuisances who are not social threats, too many petty offenders and minor thieves, severing such few social ties as they have and pushing them further toward more serious criminal behavior. This excessive use of incarceration, the prison and the jail, the reformatory and the detention center, has been expensive, criminogenic, and unkind. Hence, increasingly we try to "divert" different categories of offenders from the criminal justice system and from penal institutions.

Diversions from the criminal justice system and from prisons grow apace at the police, prosecutorial, and judicial levels. Police diversions to mental health, social welfare, and addiction treatment units reduce the flow to prison as do judicial and prosecutorial diversions to probationary and similar supervisory and supportive services. There is also support for increased reliance on the fine and on restitution and compensation payments to the victims of crime as an alternative to imprisonment. . . .

Despite these movements, the prison population remains stable at about the 200,000 mark (I do not count the jails), though an increased proportion of convicted offenders are on probation, in "halfway" houses and probation hostels, and in other community-based treatments. . . .

> || *Sourcebook of Criminal Justice Statistics,* ||
> || *U.S. Department of Justice,* ||
> || *Bureau of Justice Statistics* ||

Rate (per 100,000 residents) of Sentenced Prisoners under Jurisdiction of State and Federal Correction Authorities

	U.S Total	% Change	Northeast	% Change	Midwest	% Change	West	% Change	South	% Change
1971	**96**	—	**56**	—	**73**	—	**82**	—	**124**	—
1972	95		57		66		79		125	
1973	98		60		63		89		128	
1974	104		63		69		94		135	
1975	113	+18%	70	+25%	84	+15%	84	+2%	150	+21%
1976	123		73		95		91		161	
1977	129		77		108		92		169	
1978	135		82		104		99		181	
1979	136		84		105		101		196	
1980	139	+45%	87	+55%	109	+49%	105	+28%	188	+52%
1981	153		103		121		119		201	
1982	170		115		130		139		224	
1983	179		127		135		152		225	
1984	188		136		144		166		231	
1985	200	+108%	145	+159%	161	+121%	176	+115%	236	+90%
1986	216		157		173		197		248	
1987	228		169		184		214		255	
1988	244		186		200		234		266	

	U.S Total	% Change	Northeast	% Change	Midwest	% Change	West	% Change	South	% Change
1989	271		215		225		256		292	
1990	292	+204%	232	+314%	239	+227%	277	+238%	316	+155%
1991	310		248		255		287		333	
1992	330		261		273		299		355	
1993	350		272		282		319		380	
1994	389		286		299		334		454	
1995	411	+328%	301	+438%	310	+325%	358	+337%	483	+290%
1996	427		308		327		384		490	
1997	445		317		346		405		506	
1998	461		328		360		417		520	
1999	476		330		367		421		543	
2000	**478**	**+398%**	**320**	**+471%**	**371**	**+408%**	**423**	**+416%**	**539**	**+335%**

Sources: Sourcebook 2000, table 6.28; Sourcebook 1991, table 6.72.

The 15 Highest and 15 Lowest Jurisdictions for Selected Characteristics of the Prison Population, Year End 2000

Prison Population	# of Inmates	Incarceration Rates, 2000	Rate per 100,000	Growth since 1990	Avg. Yearly % Change
California	163,001	Louisiana	801	Idaho	10.9
Texas	157,997	Texas	730	Texas	10.2
Federal	145,416	Mississippi	688	Federal	9.5
Florida	71,319	Oklahoma	685	West Virginia	9.3
New York	70,198	Georgia	550	Mississippi	9.1
Michigan	47,718	Alabama	549	North Dakota	8.6
Ohio	45,833	South Carolina	532	Washington	8.4
Illinois	45,281	Nevada	518	Colorado	8.2
Georgia	44,232	Arizona	515	Montana	8.1
Pennsylvania	36,847	Delaware	513	Tennessee	7.9
Louisiana	35,047	Missouri	494	Hawaii	7.6
North Carolina	31,266	Michigan	480	Georgia	7.4
Virginia	30,168	California	474	Iowa	7.2
New Jersey	29,784	Florida	462	Minnesota	7.0
Missouri	27,323	Arkansas	458	Vermont	6.8
Utah	5,630	Hawaii	302	Indiana	4.8
Idaho	5,526	New Mexico	279	Alabama	4.6
New Mexico	5,342	Iowa	276	North Carolina	4.3
Hawaii	5,053	Utah	254	Wyoming	4.2
Alaska	4,173	Massachusetts	252	Kansas	3.7
Nebraska	3,895	Washington	251	Ohio	3.7
West Virginia	3,856	Nebraska	228	New Jersey	3.5
Rhode Island	3,286	Vermont	218	Michigan	3.4
Montana	3,105	West Virginia	211	Maryland	3.0
South Dakota	2,616	Rhode Island	197	South Carolina	2.6
New Hampshire	2,257	New Hampshire	185	New York	2.5
Vermont	1,697	North Dakota	158	Rhode Island	2.2
Wyoming	1,680	Maine	129	Massachusetts	1.8
Maine	1,679	Minnesota	128	Alaska	1.4
North Dakota	1,076	Federal	45	Maine	1.0

Sources: NCJ 188207; Sourcebook 2000, tables 6.28, 6.29, 6.30.

Incarceration Rates Across the World, Andre Kuhn
10 Overcrowded Times, no. 2 (April 1999)

[The number of prison inmates per 100,000 inhabitants in different countries] varies today from about 20 in Indonesia to about 685 in the Russian Federation. In Western Europe it varies between 35 (Cyprus) and 145 (Portugal) and in the United States there were at midyear 1998 about 668 inmates per 100,000 population. [This] article tries to show national trends in prison population rather than to analyze differences between countries. A number of generalizations emerge from examination of penal patterns in the countries discussed. First, though crime rates increased substantially in most industrialized countries in the 1970s and 1980s, there is no standard of incarceration rate patterns. Finland and Japan have experienced declining rates for several decades, the U.S. has experienced unbroken increases since 1973, and other countries' patterns vary between those extremes. Second, . . . prison population trends are powerfully shaped by countries' cultures and histories and by contemporary politics and ideologies; whether imprisonment-use changes inevitably must follow or can themselves lead penal attitudes, remains to be seen.

The Netherlands illustrates the recent increase in incarceration rates in many European countries. Although the Netherlands is well known for its low incarceration rate, its prison population increased from 28 prisoners per 100,000 popular in 1983 to about 74 in 1997, an increase of 164 percent. The increase is attributable largely to longer sentences for sentenced offenders rather than to growth in the numbers of sentenced or pretrial inmates.

[The] Swiss incarceration rate fell by half between the 1930s and 1980s, suggesting that the contemporary criminal justice system is less severe than formerly. Between 1982 and 1997, however, the average length of sentences increased by 132 percent, from 74 to 172 days, while the median term increased by only 50 percent, from 28 to 42 days. This suggests that [most] sentences stayed short but that longer ones became substantially longer.

[In Italy between] 1991 and 1997, the total incarceration rate increased significantly, from 56 to 86 per 100,000. This seems to be an effect of illegal Albanian immigration, enlargement of the anti-Mafia fight after the assassination of judges, and anticorruption operations led by the magistrates. . . .

Between 1983 and 1991, the German incarceration rate fell significantly from 93.3 to 69.2 per 100,000. This phenomenon has not been fully explained by criminal policy specialists, although it may be attributable, in part, to change in judges' and prosecutors' attitudes. Nonetheless, . . . the German incarceration rate increased between 1990 and 1997 by 15.7 percent [to reach] ninety prisoners per 100,000 inhabitants. This remains, however, below the 1983 level. . . .

Finland, unlike any other European country discussed here, has long had a decreasing incarceration rate. . . . Twenty years ago, the Finnish incarceration rate was one of the highest in Europe. Today, with about 60 inmates per 100,000 population, Finland has one of the lowest. . . . Finland has moved gradually toward a criminal justice system based on general prevention, which holds that it is important that criminals are caught and punished, but that the severity of the sanction is, in comparison, a minor issue. The Finnish criminal justice system therefore emphasizes the *certainty* of the sanction rather than its *severity*. That philosophy, according to which it is not useful to sentence an offender to several months of deprivation of liberty if several weeks will equally effectively demonstrate society's condemnation, has affected incarceration rates.

[Japan] has experienced decreasing incarceration rates since 1950 and has one of the lowest incarceration rates (37 per 100,000 in 1995) among the industrialized countries. . . . Notions of a hierarchical social order remain important in Japan today: knowing one's place in the societal scheme, fulfilling the Confucian obligations that the ruler be benevolent and the ruled be obedient, and holding the respect of others by maintaining social harmony, even at the expense of self-interest, remain widely held norms. The law breaker is expected to be repentant and to undertake self correction. It is therefore understandable that the criminal justice system is "lenient" toward offenders who express repentance and show willingness and capacity for self correction. Legal standards and procedures permit diversion extensively of defendants from trials and suspended prison sentences. . . . Japan decreased its prison population principally by reducing the number of entries into prison from 64,112 in 1951 to 31,122 in 1989. The incarceration rate dropped despite growth in the mean length of sentence from 17.5 months in 1970 to 20.9 months in 1990 and despite a rising crime rate. . . .

The differences [in incarceration rates] between Europe and the United States are largely ideological. Americans tend to accept the proposition that human beings are possessed of free will and are capable of making rational choices. They are generally receptive to the idea that people succeed or fail as a result of their own initiative. That ideology views crimes as the moral failure of individuals who freely elect to commit crimes, and who can therefore be held to account for their behavior. In this light, punishment ought to be designed to increase the costs of crime to such an extent that rationally acting individuals will no longer have incentives to commit crimes. Europeans more often view human behavior as more than just a function of free will. Human behavior is influenced by social circumstances such as education, peer relationships, and many other variables. All are important factors in the progression of events that lead to crime. Viewing crime as the product of both social and individual circumstances inclines Europeans more readily to accept responses to crime that include rehabilitative measures. That reflects the moral understanding that if individuals cannot be held solely responsible for what they become and what they do, society has an obligation to try to correct the influences or the conditions which may have led an individual into crime.

NOTES

1. *Origins of the prison.*   The prison has especially strong historical ties to the rehabilitative ideal. As prisons became the predominant criminal punishment in the late eighteenth and early nineteenth centuries, the legal system relied heavily on the hope or assumption that the penitentiary would create genuine penitence and change for the offenders living within its walls. See Edgardo Rotman, The Failure of Reform, in The Oxford History of the Prison 169-197 (Norval Morris and David Rothman eds., 1995); David J. Rothman, The Discovery of the Asylum: Social Order and Disorder in the New Republic (1971).

Prison began as an alternative to the death penalty and to various types of corporal punishment such as the public stockade. Prison was also believed to be a humane alternative to banishment, which is still used on a limited (and often informal) basis in the United States. A sentencing judge "banishes" an offender by prohibiting him from entering the jurisdiction. See State v. Collett, 208 S.E.2d 472 (Ga. 1974) (banishment of the defendant from seven counties in Georgia, imposed as condition for suspension of 12-month sentence for drug offense, was not unconstitutional or violative of public policy); but see McCreary v. State, 582 So. 2d 425 (Miss. 1991) (banishment from state does not serve a rehabilitative function and dumps offenders on other states). In Germany, prison replaced exile as a sanction for serious crimes during the eighteenth century.

2. *Prison trends before 1970.*   Although our knowledge of crime rates before 1970 is a bit sketchy, we do have fairly complete information about imprisonment rates in the twentieth century. The rate stayed within a reasonably stable range between 1925 and 1975, and increased above those earlier levels during the last quarter of the century. Criminologist Alfred Blumstein, writing in 1979, proposed a "stability of punishment" thesis, suggesting that states tend to reduce their arrests, convictions, and prison terms whenever the prison population goes too high and increase the coverage of the criminal law when prison populations become too low. He found that about 20 states were trendless over the 50-year period of his study, while the states with long-term changes in rates of imprisonment showed relatively small changes, and most showed a small decrease in the rate of imprisonment over time. Alfred Blumstein and Soumyo Moitra, An Analysis of Time Series of the Imprisonment Rate in the States of the United States: A Further Test of the Stability of Punishment Hypothesis, 70 J. Crim. L. & Criminology 376-390 (1979). As the data above reveal, prison populations have been anything but stable since 1980.

3. *Types of prisons.*   Prisons are not interchangeable. States run prisons with different levels of security, meaning different types of restrictions on liberty and different levels of staffing. For instance, the Bureau of Prisons in the federal system gives the following description of security levels:

> The Bureau operates institutions at four security levels (minimum, low, medium, and high) to meet the various security needs of its diverse inmate population and has one maximum-security prison for the less than 1 percent of the inmates who require that level of security. It also has administrative facilities, such as pretrial detention centers and medical referral centers, that have specialized missions and confine offenders of all security levels. The characteristics that help to define the security level of an institution are perimeter security measures (such as fences, patrol officers, and towers), the level of staffing, the internal controls for inmate movement and accountability, and the type of inmate living quarters (such as cells or open dormitories). The Bureau's graduated security scheme allows staff to assign an inmate to an institution in accordance with the inmate's individual security needs. Inmates who are able to function with relatively little supervision, without disrupting institution operations or threatening the safety of staff, other inmates, or the public, can be housed in lower security level institutions.

U.S. Department of Justice, About the Federal Bureau of Prisons (July 2001). The maximum security prisons cost the most both to build and to operate. Keep in mind that prisons are not the only secure facilities that governments operate: other institutions serving similar functions include secure mental health facilities and immigration detention facilities.

Recent prison classifications include a "supermax" prison, in which the emphasis lies on incapacitation rather than rehabilitation. Supermax prisons have provoked international objections on human rights grounds, including critical reports from the United Nations Committee against Torture. See http://193.194.138.190/html/menu2/6/cat.htm.

4. *Prison capacity and overcrowding.* Prisons in the United States are routinely said to operate above capacity, but the concept of capacity has several layers. Rated capacity is the maximum number of beds assigned to a particular facility by corrections accrediting bodies. Operational capacity is set by state officials based on the facility's staff and programs. Design capacity represents the number of inmates that the designers of the facility intended for it to hold. Overcrowding is a perennial complaint recorded by those who survey criminal justice systems in the United States, dating back to when prison populations were much lower. See National Commission on Law Observance and Enforcement (Wickersham Commission), Report on Penal Institutions, Probation and Parole 211, 231-238 (1931); President's Commission on Criminal Justice and the Administration of Justice, The Challenge of Crime in a Free Society 45 (1967).

Federal courts have occasionally ruled in favor of prison inmates who allege that overcrowded prisons violate the Eighth Amendment's prohibition of cruel and unusual punishments. See Malcolm M. Feeley and Edward L. Rubin, Judicial Policy Making and the Modern State: How the Courts Reformed America's Prisons (1998). Thus, constitutional law doctrine also has some influence on the definition of a prison's capacity.

5. *Demographic impact of incarceration rates.* Many prisoners in the United States have committed nonviolent crimes, such as low-level drug trafficking. Over the long haul, their sentences affect the demographic makeup of the prison population. For instance, the prison population now includes more black inmates than it once did, because blacks are arrested and convicted more often for the drug crimes that receive the longest prison terms. Blacks account for about three-fourths of all those sentenced to prison for drug offenses, although about 13 percent of drug users in the United States are black. The prison population today also includes a larger number of older inmates—who require more expensive prison operations such as health care—because prison terms have been getting longer in the United States for several decades. While the male prison population substantially surpasses the number of female inmates, the latter grew dramatically faster during the 1990s. We explore further the distribution of sentencing outcomes across race, class, and gender in Chapter 9.

6. *Imprisonment rates abroad.* As the materials above indicate, imprisonment rates in the United States average much higher than those in most other industrialized countries. There is some question whether that difference derives from shorter prison terms or fewer prison terms or some combination of the two in other countries. Sheryl Van Horne and Graham Farrell, Drug Offenders in the Global Criminal Justice System (European Institute for Crime Prevention and Control affiliated with the United Nations, HEUNI Paper No. 13, 1999, available at www.heuni.fi/uploads/jh0bv0x.pdf) (larger number of drug

prosecutions rather than severity of drug sentences is the primary contributor to the difference between United States and Western Europe); Michael Tonry, Prisons and Imprisonment, in 18 International Encyclopedia of the Social and Behavioral Sciences 12,062 (2001). Do any of the differences in prison trends in industrialized nations surprise you? For instance, can you explain why imprisonment rates in Finland fell over time while rates in Italy increased? For more detailed accounts of the evolution of sentencing policies in other nations, see Michael Tonry and Richard Frase, Sentencing and Sanctions in Western Countries (2001); James Q. Whitman, Harsh Justice: Criminal Punishment and the Widening Divide Between America and Europe (2003).

7. *An imaginary future.*   Imagine a world without prison. Such a world did exist, and in historical perspective it was not so long ago, only a few hundred years. The Norval Morris passage reprinted above appears as part of a larger effort to consider whether modern society could get along without prisons. Could such a world exist again today? What would it look like? Cf. John Braithwaite, A Future Where Punishment Is Marginalized: Realistic or Utopian?, 46 UCLA L. Rev. 1727 (1999).

B.   COMPETING EXPLANATIONS FOR GROWTH

A massive change in practice, such as the enormous increase in American incarceration rates over the last 30 years, begs for some explanation. There is likely no single reason, but many criminologists, political scientists, and criminal law scholars have offered theories. The materials below begin with one of the more straightforward theories: prison rates go up as a rational governmental response to increases in crime (or increases in certain serious crimes). The later materials point out some difficulties in linking crime rates and imprisonment rates, and explain our increased use of prison as a product of our national politics and our social psyche.

|| *Sourcebook of Criminal Justice Statistics,*
 U.S. Department of Justice,
 Bureau of Justice Statistics ||

Rate of Prisoners in Custody per 1,000 Reported FBI Index Crimes and Violent Crimes

Year	Rate per 1000 Index Crimes	% Change from 1960	Rate per 1000 Violent Crimes	% Change from 1960	Year	Rate per 1000 Index Crimes	% Change from 1960	Rate per 1000 Violent Crimes	% Change from 1960
1960	63	—	738	—	1965	44	−30%	544	−26%
1961	63		761		1966	38		464	
1962	58		726		1967	33		390	
1963	53		686		1968	28		315	
1964	47		588		1969	27		298	

Year	Rate per 1000 Index Crimes	% Change from 1960	Rate per 1000 Violent Crimes	% Change from 1960	Year	Rate per 1000 Index Crimes	% Change from 1960	Rate per 1000 Violent Crimes	% Change from 1960
1970	24	−62%	266	−64%	1985	37	−41%	350	−53%
1971	23		243		1986	38		338	
1972	24		235		1987	40		364	
1973	23		233		1988	42		373	
1974	21		224		1989	46		397	
1975	21	−67%	231	−69%	1990	49	−22%	392	−47%
1976	23		262		1991	51		398	
1977	25		268		1992	57		423	
1978	25		262		1993	62		455	
1979	24	−62%	241	−67%	1994	68		513	
1980	23	−64%	227	−69%	1995	75	+19%	577	−22%
1981	26		253		1996	80		644	
1982	30		291		1997	86		691	
1983	33		322		1998	94		766	
1984	36		337		1999	106	+68%	862	+17%

Source: Sourcebook 2000, table 6.46. The FBI includes the following offenses in its survey of violent offenses: murder, nonnegligent manslaughter, forcible rape, robbery, and aggravated assault. The property offenses in the crime index include burglary, larceny-theft, motor vehicle theft, and arson.

The Social Benefits of Confining Habitual Criminals, Kent Scheidegger and Michael Rushford
11 Stan. L. & Poly. Rev. 59 (1999)

. . . The cycle of rising and dropping crime rates appears to correspond to the level of public and political resolve to aggressively capture and incapacitate criminal offenders. In periods when crime rates and public concern about crime have been relatively low, the premium on aggressive law enforcement appears to diminish, while programs attempting to socialize rather than punish offenders enjoy popularity in political and academic circles. Later, as crime rates and public concern about crime increase, such increases are accompanied by political pressure for a return to aggressive law enforcement and the incapacitation of criminals.

The simple truth is that imprisonment works. Locking up more criminals for longer periods reduces the level of crime. The benefits of doing so far offset the costs.

THE CURRENT CYCLE

The national reduction in crime over the past eight years (1990-1998) is rooted in a crime policy cycle that began in the mid-1970s, with the public's response to a doubling of the rate of serious crimes between 1965 and 1975. The initial indicators in California, which played a leading role in this cycle, included a ballot initiative to reinstate capital punishment in 1972, the Legislature's adoption of the "Use a Gun, Go to Prison" law in 1975, the override of the Governor's veto of another death penalty law in 1977, and the adoption of strict sentencing increases for habitual criminals as part of the "Victims' Bill of Rights" initiative in 1982.

The sentence increases in the 1982 initiative represented a major statewide policy shift toward lengthened incarceration of habitual felons. In accordance with the new law, a California judge could sentence a convicted felon to an additional five years in prison for each prior felony conviction. A 1995 study led by Berkeley law professor Franklin Zimring, a well-known opponent of tough sentencing, credited increased incarceration with a marked drop in burglary and larceny crimes between 1980 and 1991, but found the evidence more ambiguous for violent offenses. . . .

In the early 1990s, several states began to adopt sentence increases for habitual criminals. Washington State's adoption of Initiative 593 in November of 1993, which mandated life in prison without parole upon conviction of a third violent felony, set a standard duplicated in some form by several other states. California's "Three Strikes and You're Out" law modified this approach by providing increased sentences for all repeat felons and a top term of 25 years to life for those convicted of any felony if they had two prior convictions for violent or serious felonies. While California's earlier sentencing and procedural reforms corresponded with a 10 percent reduction in the crime rate between 1991 and 1994, after adoption of the Three Strikes in 1994 the crime rate plummeted over 21 percent during the next 3 years. . . .

During the 15-year period between 1982 and 1997, as the state more than tripled its prison commitment rate with a focus on incarcerating habitual felons, the number of California victims of serious crime dropped from 4,777.1 per 100,000 in 1982 to 2,381.4 per 100,000 in 1997, less than half the previous figure. . . . The increase of young males in the population may well have contributed to the growth in the rate of incarceration, especially over the past 7 years, but it appears that the correct criminal justice policies were in place to prevent the predicted rise in crime.

COMMON SENSE AND EMPIRICAL EVIDENCE

The idea that increased incarceration of criminals will reduce the rate of crime has two bases in common sense. First, incentives matter. When the incentives to engage in or refrain from a particular behavior change, the number of people who choose to engage in that behavior also changes. In criminology, this effect is called deterrence. Second, the crime rate is determined by the number of criminals, not by the availability of victims, and removing a criminal from the street to prison prevents him from committing crimes against the general public. Reducing crime by direct restraint is called incapacitation.

The anti-incarceration hypothesis that neither effect is significant, i.e., that prison neither deters nor incapacitates, is extremely difficult to swallow. There will always be some people who cannot be deterred because they act without thinking. There will always be some who do not need to be deterred because their character and conscience would prevent them from committing crimes even if they could do so with impunity. Between the wild beasts and the saints,

FIGURE 1
Crime and Incarceration Rates

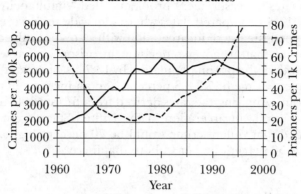

— Crimes   --- Prisoners

though, there will always be a large segment of the population that refrains from crime out of fear of the consequences, i.e., that is deterrable, and the size of that segment naturally depends on the severity of the consequences. For incapacitation, the often-heard notion that if we incarcerate one criminal another will take his place assumes that there are a fixed number of places. This assumption makes no sense. As high as the rates of burglary and robbery are, there are still far more targets than crimes each year.

The anti-incarceration hypothesis is so strongly contrary to common sense that it would take powerful empirical evidence to support it. In fact, there is substantial empirical reason to believe that imprisonment works.

For an initial, admittedly simplistic overview, Figure 1 plots incarceration versus crime. The solid line represents the FBI crime index per 100,000 population. The dotted line represents prisoners in custody per 1000 index crimes. As imprisonment fell sharply in the 1960s, the crime rate more than doubled. As imprisonment remained low in the 1970s, the crime rate continued its rise. As imprisonment rose in the 1980s, the crime rate fluctuated, dropping in the early part of the decade then rising during the crack epidemic of 1985-1990. Finally, as imprisonment rose sharply in the 1990s, the crime rate went steadily down, although the rate still remains far above where it was in 1960.

These time-line data provide an indication, but not proof. There is a possibility that other changes occurring in society could account for the crime rate changes. The claim is often made, for example, that the sharp increase in crime in the 1960s was due primarily, if not entirely, to the young males of the "baby boom" reaching their peak crime-prone years. There can be no doubt that punishment is only one of many factors affecting crime rates. The simple time-line data need to be confirmed by other methods that control, at least partially, for these other variables. . . .

A more sophisticated cross-jurisdictional comparison was done by University of Chicago economist Steven Levitt. See Steven D. Levitt, The Effect of Prison Population Size on Crime Rates: Evidence from Prison Overcrowding Litigation, 109 Q. J. Econ. 319 (1996). Levitt grappled with the problem of separating cause from effect in the connection between crime rates and incarceration rates.

"Increased incarceration is likely to reduce the amount of crime, but there is also little question that increases in crime will translate into larger prison populations." This creates a measurement problem called "simultaneity bias." To control this effect, Levitt compared states where statewide prison overcrowding litigation had capped the use of incarceration with states not subject to such caps.

Levitt found that an adverse decision in prison overcrowding litigation slowed the growth of the prison population by 13.7-19.7 percent. This caused an increase in violent crime of 7.9-8.3 percent, and an increase in property crime of 5.7-6.2 percent. Applying the rates derived from this study to the 272 percent increase in per capita incarceration in the United States from 1971 to 1993, Levitt concluded that violent crime would be 70 percent higher and property crime would be 50 percent higher without that increase. . . .

COSTS AND BENEFITS

Is the benefit of reducing crime through tough sentencing worth the cost? The answer, we believe, is quite clearly yes. In 1994, during the debate over Three Strikes, RAND Corporation produced a study predicting a 22-34 percent reduction in crime at a cost of $4.5-6.5 billion. The law appears to have a much lower cost than predicted.

RAND's cost figures were based on prison population projections showing, for example, about 250,000 prisoners by 1999 under Three Strikes, compared with about 120,000 under prior law. The actual prison population at present is 159,706, closer to RAND's "prior law" figure than its Three Strikes figure. In part, the lower cost is the result of court decisions implementing Three Strikes less severely than RAND anticipated. It is also likely, though, that tougher sentencing is simply more effective than anticipated at bringing down the crime rate and thus reducing the number of repeat felons who need to be imprisoned. RAND's projections were based on an assumption of a zero deterrent effect, a highly doubtful assumption. . . .

Tough sentencing is effective and economically efficient. We can and should investigate crime prevention and operate pilot programs to find out what works on the front end of criminal careers. We should not, however, turn career criminals loose on the streets to prey upon innocent people.

Why Are U.S. Incarceration Rates So High?, Michael Tonry
45 Crime & Delinq. 419 (1999)

American imprisonment rates, 668 per 100,000 residents behind bars in mid-1998, have reached unprecedented levels compared with other times in United States history or with current times in other Western democracies. . . . Only in the United States are prison sentences longer than 1 or 2 years common; in most countries, fewer than 5 percent of sentences are for a year or longer. In the United States, in 1994, the average sentence among people sent to state prisons for felonies was 71 months. Among those in prison, more than half were serving terms exceeding 10 years.

All of this is a drastic change from earlier times. In the 1930s, for example, the United States had incarceration rates comparable to or lower than European countries such as England, France, Switzerland, and Finland. More recently, in the 1960s, the United States was in the mainstream. The death penalty was withering away, the incarceration rate was dropping and comparable to those in other Western countries, the courts were establishing and refining defendants' procedural protections, and crime control was not generally viewed as a partisan or ideological issue.

Now, of course, the United States is unique. The aim of this article is to offer and assess alternate explanations for why American policies have diverged so far from our own past practices and from the practices of other Western countries. . . .

CRUDE EMPIRICISM

The first explanation for why so many Americans are in prison, that our crime rates are higher or faster rising than other countries', has virtually no validity. Crime rates in the United States in the 1990s are, for the most part, no higher than in other Western countries. . . . For property crimes, the United States is in the middle of the pack. Chances of being burglarized, having your pocket picked, or having your car stolen are considerably higher in England and several other European countries. For most violent crimes, American rates are among the highest, along with Australia, Canada, Spain, and France, but not the highest. Chances of being robbed, being assaulted, or being a victim of a stranger rape are higher in several other Western countries.

[Trends] in American imprisonment, homicide, and violent crime rates from 1960 to 1993 . . . suggest that violent crime and imprisonment at least initially rose together (more recently, however, imprisonment rates have continued their steep climb whereas violence rates have dropped sharply). However, . . . data for Finland and Germany during the same period indicate that there is no [necessary connection between crime rates and imprisonment rates]. Although the homicide and violent crime curves in Finland and Germany rose as steeply as the U.S. curves . . . the imprisonment rate in Germany fell throughout the 1960s and remained roughly level thereafter, and the incarceration rate in Finland fell sharply and steadily throughout the entire period. The reasons for those two countries' patterns are somewhat different, but the important point is that they reflect policy decisions that are based on the belief that increased incarceration is neither an appropriate nor an effective response to rising crime rates. American politicians decided otherwise. American imprisonment rates did not rise simply because crime rates rose. They rose because American politicians wanted them to rise.

Something was not working, and deterrence and incapacitation were chosen as strategies to lower crime rates. The only problem with this is that the most drastic such strategies were adopted long after crime rates began to fall. [Crime] rates for most crimes peaked around 1980, fell through the mid-1980s, rose for awhile for reasons largely associated with the crack cocaine epidemic, and have since fallen sharply. However, the first three-strikes law was enacted in 1993, and the federal truth-in-sentencing law, which authorized $8 billion for state prison construction, was passed in 1994. The meanings of these data are complex, but whatever else they show, they do not show any simple interaction between crime trends and imprisonment patterns.

PUBLIC OPINION

The second explanation for the high imprisonment rate is that public opinion survey results sometimes show that crime and drugs come in first as America's most pressing problem, that large majorities often express the view that sentencing is too lenient, and that people demand that criminal punishment be made tougher. On this account, elected officials have merely respected the public will, and imprisonment rates have risen as a result.

There are two serious deficiencies in this story. [First,] ordinary citizens base their opinions on what they know about crime from the mass media. Consequently, they regard heinous crimes and bizarre sentences as the norms, they believe sentences are much softer than they are, and they believe crime rates are rising when they are falling. As a result, majorities nearly always report that judges' sentences are too lenient; yet, when they are asked to propose sentences appropriate for individual cases, they generally propose sentences that are shorter than those actually imposed. . . .

The second point is more important. Public nomination of crime as the nation's most pressing problem and public support for harsh laws typically follow, not precede, media and political preoccupation with crime. Although politicians who attempt to win favor by demonstrating their toughness nearly always say that they are honoring citizens' wishes, the evidence is that harping by politicians and the media on crime issues is what causes citizens to become concerned. . . .

PARTISAN POLITICS

Crime and punishment have been high on American political agendas since the late 1960s. Before Republican presidential candidate Barry Goldwater raised crime in the streets as a partisan issue in his unsuccessful 1964 campaign, public safety was generally seen as one among several important, but unglamorous, core functions of government, like public health, public transit, and public education. Public officials were expected to do their work conscientiously and well. . . . Reasonable people differed over the best approaches for addressing particular problems, but the debates were seldom partisan or ideological. Criminal justice policy was a subject for practitioners and technocrats, and sentencing was the specialized case-by-case business of judges and corrections officials.

In recent decades, however, crime control has been at the center of partisan politics, and policies have been shaped more by symbols and rhetoric than by substance and knowledge. [During the 1960s, a fissure developed] within the Democratic Party between racial and social policy liberals and racial and social policy conservatives. This occurred initially in the South, and eventually nation wide. Republican strategists seized the opportunity to appeal to Nixon (later Reagan) Democrats by defining sharp differences between the parties on three wedge issues: crime control, welfare, and affirmative action. On crime control, conservatives blamed rising crime rates on lenient judges and soft punishments, and demanded toughness. . . .

Crime's role as a wedge issue has had important consequences. Issues that are debated on television and examined in 15- and 30-second commercials necessarily are presented in simplistic and emotional terms. Matters judges and prosecutors agonize over in individual cases are addressed in slogans and symbols, which often leads to the adoption of ham-fisted and poorly considered policies. Notable recent examples include widespread adoption of broadly defined three-strikes laws, mandatory minimum-sentence laws, sexual psychopath laws, and the federal sentencing guidelines. . . . When issues are defined in polar terms of morality and immorality, or responsibility and irresponsibility, few elected officials are prepared to be found at the wrong pole. . . .

What is needed is an explanation for why crime and punishment served so nicely as a wedge issue, and why so many elected officials were prepared, in recent decades, to behave in ways that their opponents and many observers often perceived as demagogic. [One such explanation] comes from the work of historian David Musto, which suggests that crime policies, political sensibilities, and the nature of public attitudes about crime are determined by cyclical trends in criminality and responses to it. David Musto, The American Disease: Origins of Narcotic Control (1987).

HISTORICAL CYCLES

Historians have long known that crime rates rise and fall over extended periods for reasons that have little to do with crime control policies. The three most influential scholars of the subject — historian Roger Lane and political scientists Ted Robert Gurr and James Q. Wilson — concur in the view that crime rates in the United States, England, Germany, France, and other Western countries have followed a U-shaped or a backwards J-shaped curve, falling from the second quarter of the nineteenth century through the middle of the twentieth century and rising until late in the twentieth century. . . .

More recently, there is evidence that crime rates in Western countries may be in another long-term decline. In the United States, for example, data from the National Crime Victimization Survey show that rates for many crimes fell steadily from 1973 to the 1980s, after which, they increased or stabilized for a few years and resumed a downward path. Police data from the Federal Bureau of Investigation's Uniform Crime Reports show a somewhat different (but reconcilable) pattern of crime rates that rose through 1981, fell through 1986, rose again through 1991, and have plummeted since then to levels that, for some crimes, have not been seen since the 1960s. English, Dutch, Swedish, and Norwegian data likewise show significant victimization-rate declines in the 1990s. . . .

Yale historian David Musto has shown that antidrug policies interact in predictable ways with patterns of drug use. Seemingly perverse but, on reflection understandable, the harshest policies are adopted and the most vigorous prosecutions are carried out after drug use has begun to decline. In our era, for example, self-reported use of marijuana, heroin, and amphetamines peaked for every age group in 1979 to 1980 (for cocaine, in 1984 to 1985) and fell steadily thereafter, but the harshest federal antidrug laws were not enacted until 1986 and 1988, and the first federal drug czar was not named until 1989. If reduced drug use was its aim, the war was being won a decade before it was declared.

The reason all this is understandable is that recreational drug use during prohibitionistic periods is widely seen as immoral and socially destructive. Such attitudes explain why an increasing number of people stop using and experimenting with drugs and why, after drug use begins falling, comparatively few voices are raised in opposition to harsh policies. Few people, especially elected public officials, are comfortable speaking out on behalf of immorality. . . . In more tolerant periods, by contrast, many more people celebrate Enlightenment ideals of moral autonomy and individuals' rights to make choices about their own lives, and comfortably oppose harsh laws and policies on those grounds.

I mention the recurrent interaction between drug-use patterns and drug abuse policy because similar patterns may characterize interactions between contemporary crime patterns and crime-control policies. [The] harshest crime control policies — three-strikes laws; lengthy mandatory minimum sentence laws; truth-in-sentencing laws; and increased use of the death penalty — date from the early and mid-1990s, long after crime rates began their steep decline.

[Enhancing] people's predisposition to believe that harsh measures work, harsh laws are often enacted when crime rates are already falling. People who want to make year-to-year comparisons can easily show that the new, tougher policies have worked, because crime rates have fallen in the years immediately after the change when compared with the year immediately before. This happened in relation to New York City's adoption in the early 1990s of zero-tolerance policing, California's adoption in 1994 of a broadly defined three-strikes law, and many states' passage in the mid-1990s of truth-in-sentencing laws. These may be plausible claims on the part of people who are unaware of long-term crime trends, but for people who are, they are disingenuous. The year-to-year crime-rate declines are at least as likely merely to be a continuation of long-term trends as they are to be effects of policy changes. . . .

As a hypothesis, Musto's paradigm provides a richer account of American exceptionalism in the past quarter century than do any of the other accounts that I have attempted. It explains why public attitudes are harsher when crime rates are falling than when they are rising and, consequently, why law-and-order appeals fell on fertile electoral ground. It explains why politicians feel comfortable appealing to base instincts and proposing policies that, in other times, would have seemed demagogic and cruel. It explains not only why so few voices were raised in opposition to those policies but also why few people felt a need to speak out in opposition. It explains why people were inclined to believe that declining crime and drug-use rates showed that harsh policies worked. . . .

America's unprecedented and unmatched taste for imprisonment and harsh criminal justice policies has little to do with them — the offenders who get dealt with one way or another — and everything to do with us. If we took the historical lessons to heart, we might be less quick to adopt harsh crime policies. In our private lives, we know these things, and our folk wisdom celebrates it — do not strike in anger; sit down and count to 10; do not take your frustrations out on your child, your spouse, or your employee; and write the angry letter, but put it aside until tomorrow and see if you still want to send it. Whether those private insights will soon shape our public policies remains to be seen. . . .

NOTES

1. *Crime control through deterrence.*   The most straightforward way to explain why U.S. legal systems rely so heavily on prison relates to crime control. Prison, the argument goes, both deters crimes and incapacitates criminals better than the alternatives, so the heavy use of prison in the United States is a rational effort to reduce crime. There are powerful theoretical reasons to believe that at least some use of prison can deter crime. For instance, one could analogize potential criminals to rational economic actors, who weigh the benefits of crime against the likelihood of conviction and the severity of the punishment. Longer prison terms, in this model, increase the cost of crime and encourage more people to avoid it. See Gary S. Becker, Crime and Punishment: An Economic Approach, 76 J. Pol. Econ. 169 (1968).

The difficulty arises in the gap between theory and experience. While many agree that at least some use of prison deters crime, there is strong debate over whether marginal increases in the use of prison translate into marginal increases in deterrence. See Cassia Spohn and David Holleran, The Effect of Imprisonment on Recidivism Rates of Felony Offenders: A Focus on Drug Offenders, 40 Criminology 329 (2002) (comparison of drug offenders in Missouri sentenced to prison and probation; prison increases rather than reduces likelihood of recidivism); Richard A. Wright, The Evidence in Favor of Prisons, in Crime and Criminals (Frank R. Scarpitti and Amiel Nelsen eds., 1999). What specific claims do Scheidegger and Rushford make about deterrence, and what specific evidence do they use? Does Tonry address their evidence?

2. *Crime control through incapacitation.*   There is no question that prison incapacitates some offenders from committing new crimes during their prison term. Given the number of career criminals and the short span of years that constitutes the criminal "career" for many offenders, it should be possible in theory to reduce crime through heavier use of prison. One practical difficulty is deciding how to target the offenders who are most likely to commit new crimes, a practice known as "selective incapacitation." See James Q. Wilson, Thinking About Crime 193-194 (1977); Shlomo Shinnar and Reuel Shinnar, The Effects of the Criminal Justice System on the Control of Crime: A Quantitative Approach, 9 Law & Socy. Rev. 581 (1975). Given the difficulty of predicting which offenders are the best targets, some argue for general incapacitation, claiming that higher levels of incapacitation will generally reduce crime even if we cannot know which offenders would have committed the extra crimes. Apart from the costs of this approach (both in human and economic terms), it is doubtful that it works across all categories of crimes. For some crimes (perhaps narcotics sales), new criminals may simply step forward to fill the positions vacated by those sentenced to prison.

3. *Economics and demographics.*   We could also explain imprisonment rates not as a product of deliberate policy but as a natural outcome of a slowdown in the economy and a corresponding increase in crime. Similarly, levels of imprisonment might be driven by demographics (such as the number of young males in the population at a given time). How would you go about testing these hypotheses? See Frank Zimring and Gordon Hawkins, The Scale of Imprisonment 119-136 (1991) (reviewing potential explanations for prison rates in the United

States, including crime rates, public opinion, demographics, economics, and drug use).

4. *Politics and public opinion.*　Michael Tonry and others have argued that U.S. politics is uniquely pathological when it comes to crime. The political rhetoric in the United States has remained partisan and "tough on crime" for several generations. The debate has marginalized rehabilitation as a purpose of criminal sanctions and has suggested that prison is the only "real" sanction. What in particular about the U.S. political system produces these results? Sara Sun Beale traces the influence to the news media's focus on crime for purposes of attracting high ratings: the coverage affects public perceptions of the level of serious crime, and it shapes the political agenda that gets a positive response from the public. Beale, What's Law Got to Do with It? The Political, Social, Psychological and Other Non-legal Factors Influencing the Development of (Federal) Criminal Law, 1 Buff. Crim. L. Rev. 23 (1997). See also Katherine Beckett, Making Crime Pay: Law and Order in Contemporary American Politics (1997); Bert Useem, Raymond V. Liedka, and Anne Morrison Piehl, Popular Support for the Prison Build-up, 5 Punishment and Socy. 5 (2003).

5. *Social control or social cohesion.*　Some accounts of prison look beyond the instrumental reasons such as deterrence or incapacitation and emphasize the prison's place in struggles among social groups or in creating social solidarity. Some of these "social control" arguments draw generally on Marxist theory. For instance, Georg Rusche and Otto Kirchheimer, in Punishment and Social Structure (1939), suggest that the demands of the labor market shape the penal system and determine its transformation over time. In years of high employment, prisons must shrink to provide more workers for society, while in years of lower employment, prisons expand to maintain control over the unemployed. Cf. Christian Parenti, Lockdown America: Police and Prisons in the Age of Crisis (1998). Social theorist Michel Foucault's famous work, Discipline and Punish: The Birth of the Prison (1977) (excerpted in Chapter 1), describes the prison as one among many tools used in modern societies to exert more minute control over the human body as a way of making the masses more useful and docile.

"Social cohesion" theories, in contrast, stress the role of prison in creating agreement and shared ideologies across social groups rather than in controlling unruly social orders. Sociologist Émile Durkheim pointed to criminal law and punishment as a method of expressing and creating social consensus. As traditional communities give way to complex economic arrangements and societies that celebrate individual freedom, criminal law becomes an especially important source of social solidarity. See Émile Durkheim, The Division of Labor (1933); cf. Joseph Kennedy, Monstrous Offenders and the Search for Solidarity Through Modern Punishment, 51 Hastings L.J. 829 (2000). For an overview of the different perspectives that social theory brings to questions of punishment, see Jonathan Simon, Sanctioning Government: Explaining America's Severity Revolution, 56 U. Miami L. Rev. 217 (2001).

Earlier we considered social and political forces that could explain the remarkable growth in U.S. prisons over the past quarter-century. Now we examine the other side of the coin: What political forces or institutions might operate to *check* the growth of prisons?

One of those limiting forces might be money. Prisons are more expensive to build and operate than any other criminal sanction. In difficult economic times, as Marc Miller explains, budgetary considerations become especially powerful at the state and local levels of government:

> Criminal justice expenditures, and spending on corrections in particular, increasingly occupy a noticeable chunk of total state budgets. The growth of corrections budgets is so great that they have come to threaten other major categories of government expenditure. In California, for example, the corrections budget equaled 85 percent of the higher education budget in 1994, and by 1995 corrections had surpassed higher education. (A few years earlier, in the late 1980s, corrections cost only one-half the total spent on higher education.) [State] governments spend almost all of their funds on a handful of areas — education, health and welfare, transportation, housing, and crime. When criminal justice expenditures go up, they compete with these other basic services, not with the purchase of aircraft carriers or with foreign aid.
>
> [Policy] and budget changes are much harder to hide at the local government level. [The] smaller size of the budgets and political playing fields makes the budget [effect] more likely to be noticed for all budget expenditures. It is more likely that a county hospital or city clinic or board of education (in states where local funds support primary education) will feel that dollars put into corrections are dollars out of their pockets than will health care or educational representatives at state and federal levels. At higher levels of government, with bigger budgets and more abstract debates, a decision about prisons will rarely seem like a choice about schools or hospitals. At local levels, even modest proposed expenditures will be seen to compete with the full range of social services provided by local government. . . .

Marc Miller, Cells vs. Cops vs. Classrooms, in The Crime Conundrum 127 (Lawrence M. Friedman and George Fisher eds., 1997).

The two statutes below build on the observation that prison growth can be slowed if the relevant decision makers are forced to consider long-term budgets when making choices that would expand the use of prisons. Note the differences between the budgetary mechanisms at work in these two statutes. Can you devise similar strategies that might apply to other sentencing actors, such as judges or prosecutors? The following statistical study by David Greenberg and Valerie West examines the larger political and social context to identify factors limiting prison growth.

‖ *North Carolina General Statutes §120-36.7(d)* ‖

Every bill and resolution introduced in the General Assembly proposing any change in the law that could cause a net increase in the length of time for which persons are incarcerated or the number of persons incarcerated, whether by increasing penalties for violating existing laws, by criminalizing behavior, or by any other means, shall have attached to it at the time of its consideration by the General Assembly a fiscal note prepared by the Fiscal Research Division. The fiscal note shall be prepared in consultation with the Sentencing Policy and Advisory Commission and shall identify and estimate, for the first five fiscal years the proposed change would be in effect, all costs of the proposed net increase in incarceration, including capital outlay costs if the legislation would require increased cell space. . . . No comment or opinion shall be included in the fiscal note with regard to the merits of the measure for which the note is prepared. . . .

The sponsor of each bill or resolution to which this subsection applies shall present a copy of the bill or resolution with the request for a fiscal note to the Fiscal Research Division. . . . The Fiscal Research Division shall prepare the fiscal note and transmit it to the sponsor within two weeks after the request is made, unless the sponsor agrees to an extension of time. . . .

‖ *Kansas Statutes §74-9101(b)* ‖

(1) . . . In developing its recommended sentencing guidelines, the [Kansas sentencing] commission shall take into substantial consideration current sentencing and release practices and correctional resources, including but not limited to the capacities of local and state correctional facilities. . . .

(6) [The commission shall] advise and consult with the secretary of corrections and members of the legislature in developing a mechanism to link guidelines sentence practices with correctional resources and policies, including but not limited to the capacities of local and state correctional facilities. Such linkage shall include a review and determination of the impact of the sentencing guidelines on the state's prison population. . . .

(15) [The commission shall] produce official inmate population projections annually on or before six weeks following the date of receipt of the data from the department of corrections. When the commission's projections indicate that the inmate population will exceed available prison capacity within two years of the date of the projection, the commission shall identify and analyze the impact of specific options for (A) reducing the number of prison admissions; or (B) adjusting sentence lengths for specific groups of offenders. . . .

‖ *State Prison Populations and Their Growth, 1971-1991, David F. Greenberg and Valerie West* ‖
39 Criminology 615 (2001)

. . . Between 1970 and midyear 2000, the federal and state imprisonment rate increased by a factor of almost five, from 98 per 100,000 to 476 per 100,000. These national figures disguise much variation among states in the rates of growth. In Oklahoma, for example, the imprisonment rate in 1981 was just 17% higher than it had been ten years earlier, whereas in Montana, it was 196% higher. . . .

Previous research on state differences in imprisonment rates . . . has focused on a small number of explanatory variables — state crime rates, racial composition, and economic conditions (unemployment or labor force participation, income level). . . . In so doing, this work slights the policy choices that structure a state's response to its circumstances. Our work extends the theoretical scope of this body of research by [examining] the importance of a state's culture and political arrangements to policy outcomes in a number of different domains, such as welfare. . . .

THEORIZING IMPRISONMENT RATES

[We expect] institutional responses to law violations to be determined at least in part by the volume of crime in that state, but only in part. We expect a state's responses to be conditioned by its ability to finance their cost, and by its political culture. The anxieties and fears that lead residents and politicians to support the expanded use of imprisonment can be heightened or moderated by factors other than crime. . . .

Crime Rates.   If imprisonment is a strategy for coping with crime, one would expect states with more crime to make more extensive use of imprisonment. We expect imprisonment to be more strongly related to violent crime than to property crime because violent crimes are considered more serious than are nonviolent crimes of acquisition. Defendants convicted of violent crimes are more likely to be sentenced to prison terms than are those convicted of stealing. Nevertheless, substantial numbers of prisoners are serving sentences for property offenses. . . . We thus consider the violent crime rate and the property crime rate as two measures of the "problem" to which the prison is supposedly a response. . . .

Drug law violations are expected to influence imprisonment rates because publicity about arrests contributes to public perceptions about the seriousness of crime as a social problem and thus influences public punitiveness. Drug arrestees also represent a caseload burden: if convicted, many drug arrestees will be sentenced to a term of imprisonment. . . .

Fiscal Constraint.   Prison construction and maintenance are expensive. Costs of prison construction have been estimated at $23,000 to $54,000 per bed, and operating costs from $9500 to $39,000 per prisoner each year. . . . Less affluent states may have to restrict spending on criminal justice in order to repair potholes, plant trees, pay teachers, and shelter the homeless. For this reason, we predict a positive relationship between imprisonment rates and the state's capacity to tax its citizens and business enterprises.

Perceived Threat.   Students of penality have argued that imprisonment can be a response to anxiety-provoking conditions other than crime. In particular, it may be targeted at "the dangerous classes"— populations perceived as threatening because of their economic circumstances, race, or ethnicity, independently of their involvement in crime. . . . We introduce the percentage of families below the poverty line as an alternative measure of the population that might be seen as having little to lose and who must, therefore, be dealt with through imprisonment.

The numerical overrepresentation of blacks in prison is high. Even though blacks make up about 12 percent of the population, slightly more than half of all new court commitments to prison are black, a rate that is approximately 6.5

times as high as that of whites. . . . By looking at the effect of a state's racial composition on the prison population controlling for crime rates, we should be able to clarify the relationship between race and imprisonment. . . .

Cultural Influences.   . . . Social structural theories of social control suggest that urbanized polities will make greater use of formal methods of control, such as courts and prisons, to make up for deficiencies in informal social control. The anonymity and heterogeneity of large urban populations linked by impersonal market transactions supposedly impair informal social control, leading to the compensatory strengthening of governmental control. Rural regions, on the other hand, are presumed to require less vigorous formal social control because they can rely on personal ties based on kinship and multiplex patterns of informal association. On this basis, one would expect imprisonment rates to be higher in states whose populations are highly urbanized. On the other hand, urban criminal courts may face especially heavy caseloads, necessitating more generous concessions in plea bargaining to induce guilty pleas. This should slow prison growth. Moreover, urban populations, exposed as they are to greater cultural diversity, should be more tolerant of rule breakers and, thus, less punitive. . . .

Historically, welfare benefits were instituted as alternatives to human institutions for poor and marginalized populations. . . . If imprisonment indeed reflects an exclusionary stance toward those who have broken the law, . . . it should be used with greater reluctance in those states that are relatively generous toward the poor by providing greater welfare benefits, [and] cuts in welfare should be accompanied by increases in imprisonment. . . .

Political Factors.   . . . We examine the influence of officeholders' party affiliation at the state level. We focus on the governor because it is the governor who prepares budgets, making decisions about prison construction that should ultimately impact on prison populations. It is also the governor who appoints parole board members. . . .

A number of policy analysts have attributed growth in prison populations to determinate sentencing legislation that severely restricts judicial discretion to impose a sentence and eliminates release on parole for prison inmates. [Ten] states adopted fixed sentencing legislation ending release on parole between the mid-1970s and mid-1980s. Because the adoption of determinate sentencing legislation was often accompanied by "get tough" rhetoric, one might expect that states with determinate sentencing legislation will have higher prison populations and experience more rapid growth in these rates. . . .

METHODS AND RESULTS

[We used a statistical technique known as regression analysis to measure the impact of each of these variables on a state's imprisonment rate between 1971 and 1991. We used a second model to estimate the impact of these variables on the *changes* in rates of imprisonment that each state experienced during these two decades.]

Consistent with public choice theory, states with high violent crime rates have higher levels of imprisonment. An increase in the violent crime rate of

1 per 100,000 is associated with an increase of .12 per 100,000 in the imprisonment rate, whereas the increase associated with the property crime rate is smaller and not statistically significant. An increase in the narcotics arrest rate of 1 per 100,000 increases the imprisonment rate by about .11 per 100,000.

As expected, states with higher revenues have higher prison populations. Although economic inequality and urbanization are unrelated to imprisonment, there are more people in prison in states with higher unemployment rates and where there is a higher percentage of blacks in the population. Other things being equal, an increase in the unemployment rate of 5% corresponds to an imprisonment rate that is higher by about 16.5 per 100,000. A state with a population that is 10% black will have an imprisonment rate higher than that of a state that has no blacks by . . . 91 per 100,000, a substantial amount. The presence of Latinos, however, does not raise imprisonment rates. . . .

Several measures of a state's political culture are related to its imprisonment rate. States that are more generous with welfare payments had lower prison populations. An increase of $30 per person in welfare spending is associated with an imprisonment rate that is smaller by about 19 per 100,000. . . .

In states where there were more conservatives, imprisonment rates were not only higher, but also grew more rapidly. . . . If cultural differences are associated with the South, they did not contribute to high rates of imprisonment growth; quite the contrary, growth rates were significantly slower in the South than elsewhere, so that by 1991, regional disparities in imprisonment rates were substantially smaller than in 1971. In other words, in recent years regions outside the South have been catching up to the South in imprisonment. . . .

Contrary to popular opinion, the adoption of determinate sentencing legislation did not increase imprisonment rates; it moderately reduced them. The adoption of these laws may have helped to placate a punitive public, reducing pressure on state officials to impose harsh sentences. [Perhaps] these laws were carefully crafted to be largely symbolic and, in many states, had little effect because prosecutors and judges took steps to minimize their impact.

Some of the most striking findings concern state economic and demographic characteristics. Unemployment was associated with higher rates of prison population growth, as was change in unemployment. Economic inequality was not. Growth in imprisonment rates was also related to the size of the black population and its increase. It cannot be stressed too strongly that the coefficients for unemployment and race are direct effects, with crime rates controlled, and so they cannot be explained away by claims that crime rates are higher where there is more unemployment or where more blacks live.

Consistent with much research showing that party control of state government has little or no impact on state policy and is unrelated to the liberalism or conservatism of the state's voters, the political party of a state's governor failed to make a significant contribution to prison populations or their growth. It appears that the political incentives for an expansive prison policy transcend party affiliations. States governed by Democrats responded to the crime issue no differently from states governed by Republicans. . . .

Our results are equally consistent with the presence and absence of racial discrimination. [A] positive relationship between percent black in a state and the state's imprisonment rate could occur in the absence of racial discrimination. [At the same time, our] results are consistent with the "racial threat" hypothesis. Blacks — black males in particular — appear to have become "symbolic assailants" whose presence in a city evokes fear of crime independently of the actual level of crime. . . . That the presence of Latinos is not associated with imprisonment rate growth indicates that it is not minorities in general, but blacks in particular, who are perceived as threatening. Our results also point to unemployment as a separate, distinct source of threat or anxiety. . . . We think that welfare is important to imprisonment not because it directly restrains legislators, prosecutors, and judges; rather, we see the comparative leniency in high-welfare states as reflecting a more general policy of avoiding excessively harsh treatment of the poor, who make up the bulk of criminal court defendants. . . .

NOTES

1. *Prisons and state budget cycles.*   From time to time, budgetary constraints restrict further prison expansions. For examples, see Robin Campbell, Dollars and Sentences: Legislators' Views on Prisons, Punishment, and the Budget Crisis (Vera Institute, July 2003, available at http://www.vera.org).

Traditional legislative debates do not make the connection between setting criminal penalties and funding adequate space in the prison. Some extraordinary debates, however, do underscore the connection, and yet legislators are still sometimes willing to change the penalties without funding the prisons that new sentencing laws will require. See Franklin Zimring, The New Politics of Criminal Justice: Of "Three Strikes," Truth-in-Sentencing, and Megan's Laws (The Earl Warren Legal Institute, University of California, Berkeley, Dec. 8, 1999).

Sentencing commissions are considered one of the most important institutions in state government to highlight the connection between corrections budgets and sentencing rules. According to a 2003 survey by the National Association of Sentencing Commissions, 12 of the 19 responding states gave their commissions responsibility to create impact statements for at least some criminal justice bills after their introduction in the state legislature. Note the distinction, however, between a commission advocating a smaller prison system and a commission advocating a fully funded prison system.

2. *More on costs and benefits of prison.*   The balance between the costs and benefits of longer prison terms could shift if one considers as a benefit the crimes prevented through detention. Economists have employed statistical techniques to estimate the number of crimes prevented and the monetary value of the harm that would have occurred if those crimes had happened. See Edwin W. Zedlewski, Making Confinement Decisions (National Institute of Justice, Research in Brief, 1987); Joanna Mehlhop Shepherd, Police, Prosecutors, Criminals, and Determinate Sentencing: The Truth About Truth-in-Sentencing Laws, 45 J.L. & Econ. 509 (2002) (estimating that sentencing laws requiring violent offenders to serve at least 85 percent of their prison sentences decrease murders by 16 percent, aggravated assaults by 12 percent, robberies by 24 percent, rapes by 12 percent, and larcenies by 3 percent; however, violent offenders shift to property crimes, meaning that burglaries increase by 20 percent and auto thefts by 15 percent). What types of data are used to make estimates of these sorts? What uncertainties are involved in constructing the estimates?

C.   THE HUMAN EXPERIENCE OF PRISON

Part of understanding the nature of prison is to see the size of the institution and its functions over the years. The statistics and trends we have discussed thus far address these questions, but they miss the profound human experience of prison. The offenders who fill prisons in large numbers, for long periods of time, are individuals who experience the daily routines and restrictions of life in prison. The victims of their crimes are individuals who remain aware of their stay in prison and (sometimes) the moment of their release. The officers who run the prisons work under extraordinarily tough conditions.

The law surrounding conditions in prison is complex and deserves far more attention than we can offer here. See Michael B. Mushlin, Rights of Prisoners (2d ed. 1993). Instead, we aim for a more personal glimpse into prison life as a way to place the law of sentencing in context. In the following excerpt, Norval Morris presents a rewritten version of a diary, recording the mundane events in the day of an inmate, Sam Gutierrez, incarcerated in Stateville Prison in Illinois.

> ### *The Contemporary Prison, 1965-Present,*
> ### *Norval Morris*
> ### The Oxford History of the Prison: The Practice of
> ### Punishment in Western Society 202, 203-211 (1998)

. . . It is not easy to describe a day of monotony and boredom other than as monotonous and boring. Before I start on the diary, let me say this: if you expect the usual prison tale of constant violence, brutal guards, gang rapes, daily escape efforts, turmoil, and fearsome adventures, you will be deeply disappointed. . . .

6:00 A.M.:
. . . As F House came to life, the noise began — radios, TVs, shouting from cell to cell — and so it would go on till night, with an occasional scream of rage or fear through the night. Tyrone and I did our best to keep out of each other's way in the space of nine feet by six in our cell while we used our toilet and washed and dressed and pulled up the blankets on our steel bunks. We change our outer clothes sometimes twice a week, sometimes once a week, and our socks and underwear every other day. If you have money, or influence, or a friend in the laundry, you can do better than this. Our dress in summer is blue jeans and a blue shirt or a white T-shirt; in winter we wear blue jeans, a blue shirt, and one of those heavy, lined, blue jackets. Our sartorial flourish is our sneakers, with Nike outranking Reebok and so on down the line; they cost a lot, but in this place they are worth it. . . .

6:30 A.M.:
F House began to be unlocked, with the loudspeaker from the tower guards bellowing, "Three and four galleries: in the tunnel for chow." I turned off the radio and flipped the light switch at the back of the cell, on and off, on and off, the flickering light being my request to the tower guard to open the door to this cell, which he does. . . .

Food is served cafeteria style. We pick up our trays and wait in line. The food is either waiting in bowls for us to pick up, as we file by, or is served onto our plates by the kitchen detail. Knives and forks and spoons are of plastic, not particularly useful for making weapons, though they are sometimes smuggled back to the cells and narrowed and sharpened for this purpose. . . .

They serve meals here, three times a day, to over two thousand prisoners each meal, 365 times a year, on a twelve-day repeating menu. I calculate that this comes to more than two million meals a year. I suppose I should expect it to be dull and lifeless food — and it is. But guys mostly tend to put on weight in prison; I know I do. The meals are not light on carbohydrates. The cartons of milk cannot be spoiled by our prison cooks, and I usually manage to collect two of them with whatever else is handed to me. I did this today.

After you get your food you walk back to the seating area, metal tables with six metal seats fixed to them. You have to be careful where you sit; there are "regulars" who sit together and expect this to be known. And, of course, the blacks and Hispanics don't welcome a white guy joining their tables. The prison is more than 90 percent black and Hispanic, but this causes no great problem — the whites tend to congregate with one another in the mess hall and in the yard. . . .

8:30 A.M.:

[I went to the yard to] get a workout, bench-pressing some weights. . . . The yard is of playing-field size and of rounded, triangular shape, with a rough baseball diamond, with other areas of grass and of packed earth, surrounded by a running track and a fence. Some sparse outdoor gym equipment is in one corner. There are two telephones, protected a little from the weather by steel surrounds; a small line formed. Guys ran around the track or walked around in twos or small groups. Five or six of us worked out on the equipment.

The telephones here and in F House are monitored, and every few minutes a voice interrupts telling you and whomever you are speaking to that this is a call from a "state correctional facility." And the time you are allowed for any one call is limited, depending on whatever the prison authorities have arranged with the telephone company. Of course, only collect calls can be made, so that no one outside has to talk to a prisoner on the telephone, and this makes the telephone expensive for the person you are calling, particularly long-distance calls.

10:30 A.M.:

[I showered after my workout]. The showers are dangerous places; gangs tend to shower together as a protective measure; only a very few prisoners shower alone and without security, as I do. I am known as a loner and dangerous to cross and tend therefore to be left alone. . . .

When you come to prison it is wise to leave all shyness behind. But I am not anxious for myself in the showers. Here in Stateville there aren't gang rapes or even rapes that I hear about, though they are reputed to take place occasionally, and they are certainly more frequent in the jails. . . . Prisoners taking showers need security from gang attacks, not from sexual attacks. Still, I suppose I am always a little anxious in the showers; I avoid being alone in the showers with any one or more who might have some particular reason to dislike me. Even if violence is not all that common, still there is often tension and anxiety and, I suppose, fear.

11:30 A.M.:

I looked for some semi-clean socks, got dressed, and started typing a letter. I was waiting for the call to lunch, though I hate the mess hall at lunchtime. It is chaos at lunch; the prisoners refuse to act "orderly," and the guards do not take the trouble to enforce order. The gang element is definitely in control. Nevertheless, to the sound of "Chow going out the door," I joined the mass of prisoners heading for the tunnel. . . .

1:00 P.M.:

I joined the "school" detail and with six others from F House went off to a course on computers run in the school area. Unlike all but a few prisoners in Stateville, I am a genuine high school graduate. [The] majority of my fellow prisoners in Stateville are functionally illiterate, and only a handful have any sort of a record of high school academic achievement. In earlier years in Stateville I worked in the furniture factory and in the tailor shop, earning more than I can earn at school; but the computer course interested me, and I applied for it and got it. I have now been in it for three months and am beginning to be able to write programs. The course is taught by an Indian who speaks strangely but knows what he is doing. It fills my afternoons, three days a week, two hours each day.

The better-educated have the pick of the jobs in Stateville. Though it is poorly paid, the library, particularly the law library, is probably the best job, passing prison time more swiftly than other prison jobs, having influence in the prison, and being left alone by the guards; but the computer class seems to me in some ways even better. In the distant years when I am free I may be able to use what I am learning about computer programming, but I doubt it; the point is that it helps to keep me alive here. . . .

3:30 P.M.:

Two guards escorted the school detail back to F House. I went back to my cell. Tyrone was showering, his work in the tailor shop finished. While he was away I turned on the TV. It is my set, but I cannot control what we watch, since his friends outside could afford to give him a set if he wanted it. So, if we are to share this cell, we have to strike some bargain about what we watch. I am fortunate; he mostly falls in with my preferences, and when he doesn't, I yield.

I've never watched so much TV as I do here. My set is a thirteen-inch RCA color TV. . . . The TV is on a little table we have rigged up beside the toilet; it is best watched by lying on one's bunk. Tyrone came in and lay down on his bunk without speaking. It's the best way; avoid useless chatter. I got sleepy and dozed. I was awakened by the mailman rapping on the bars of our cell and giving a small package of mail to Tyrone. Nothing for me; after a year or two in prison, incoming mail dries up to a trickle, even if you write regularly. . . .

7:00 P.M.:

[After dinner at 5:25, the evening count of inmates] went smoothly. Most everyone was by now back in the cell houses, and there were fewer places — schoolroom, gym, yard, industry, barbershop, kitchen, and so on — to be counted.

It was F House's turn for evening gym. Many, including Tyrone, went to throw basketballs around. I stayed in the cell and followed a batch of my favorite

TV programs — they passed the time well for me, and I had had my exercise for that day.

And so the evening went: TV, reading a little in my computer training manual, TV again, and by nine o'clock Tyrone was back in the cell, and I got out of my clothes, except my undershorts, and got into my bunk. The central lights in F House stay on through the night. I wondered if perhaps we should put up some sort of curtains, and with that thought the day ended for me.

[Let me comment a bit on my diary.] Yesterday was unusually uneventful. Often in prison something happens to disturb the dull flow of the day. . . . There are times to go to the library and to the law library for those of us still appealing our convictions or pursuing prisoners' rights litigation, which they tell me is a good way to "do time" but rarely produces any success in the courts. And then there are the hard-to-avoid confrontations with some of the guards — leading to tickets and segregation and loss of "good time." Even worse are the collective punishments of the "lockdown," when cells are locked for all twenty-four hours, sometimes for months, with only one shower a week out of the cell; time moves even slower then.

Neither Tyrone nor I use prison hooch [alcohol] or drugs to get through the days and nights, but many prisoners do, and the disorder of prison, the frequency of punishments and of lockdowns, is increased because of it. Drugs, all drugs, are readily available at about twice their street price, payable inside or outside the prison. . . .

There are regular and intermittent shakedowns of all the cells and other areas for shanks and other contraband. It is a violent place, but most prisoners do their time without being victimized physically unless they are looking to prove something to themselves or unless they get into trouble with betting, or hooch, or drugs, or with the gangs.

[This diary] fails to capture the constant unhappiness of prison life and the constant sense of danger. [It] misses the relentless, slow-moving routine, the dull repetitiveness, the tension mixed with occasional flashes of fear and rage; it misses the consuming stupidity of living this way. I am sorry; it is not easy. . . .

NOTES

1. *Prisoners and correctional officers.*   The officers who maintain order in a prison have a complex relationship with the inmates they monitor every day. The stereotype of the brutal prison guard is a staple of literature and movies such as *Cool Hand Luke* (1967) and *The Shawshank Redemption* (1994). The following passage from a prison memoir (written by a former middle manager at a telephone company, convicted in Nevada for manslaughter) summarizes the nature of this relationship from the vantage point of the inmate:

> The sergeant glared down at the benches till the dawgs hushed. "Rule number one," he continued, "y'all got *nothin'* coming! Rules number two to two thousand — see rule number one." The sergeant paused to let us bask in this bit of penological cleverness.
> "My name is Sergeant Grafter. I am a correctional officer — not a fucking prison guard and not a cop. You will address me as 'C.O.' or 'Sergeant.' . . . cause you're *convicts!* Your job here is to lie, cheat, steal, extort, get tattoos, take

drugs, sell drugs, shank, sock, fuck, and suck each other. Just don't let us catch you — that's *our* job." . . .

"The warden and prison medical director have asked me to pass along a . . . health advisory. This prison has a combined HIV and hepatitis C infection rate of 60 percent. If you choose to just say yes, and use drugs, and you will — that's your job — then snort them, smoke them, or swallow them, but don't shoot them." Grafter irritably perused the rest of the memo before crushing it into a ball and tossing it over the rail. . . .

"Finally, don't cross the red lines unless you like getting shot. Above all, *don't get caught!* We catch you, you got nothin' comin'."

Jimmy A. Lerner, You Got Nothing Coming: Notes from a Prison Fish 37-38 (2002).

The relationship looks different from the perspective of the correctional officer. Writer Ted Conover worked for a year as a correctional officer in New York's legendary Sing Sing prison; his account of that year emphasizes the combination of boredom and danger in the atmosphere: "I always thought of an assembly line in a poorly run explosives factory. Tedium, tedium, tedium, then — *bang*— you'd be missing your hands." Conover describes the tension between inmates and officers in these terms:

> A consequence of putting men in cells and controlling their movements is that they can do almost nothing for themselves. For their various needs they are dependent on one person, their gallery officer. Instead of feeling like a big, tough guard, the gallery officer at the end of the day often feels like a waiter serving a hundred tables or like the mother of a nightmarishly large brood of sullen, dangerous, and demanding children. When grown men are infantilized, most don't take to it nicely.
>
> That morning, I decided to count the number of times I said no before lunch. . . .
>
> — CO, can you find out when my disciplinary hearing is?
> — CO, can you call to see why my laundry bag didn't come back? . . .
> — CO, do all you guys get your hair cut in the same place? (a joke). . .
> — CO, do you got any more state soap?
> — CO, can I go on the W side and borrow a belt from my homey? I got a visit. . . .
>
> Not all of these were improper requests; but the others were mainly favors, to be done when I had spare time, which was seldom. You had to get good at saying no. . . .

Ted Conover, Newjack: Guarding Sing Sing 234-235, 250 (2000).

2. *Violence, gangs, and race in prison.* One constant in the fictional and nonfictional accounts of prison life is violence and — more commonly — the threat of violence. In 2003 Congress passed the Prison Rape Elimination Act, which funds a study of sexual assaults in male and female prisons and creates preventive programs.

Many inmates, including female inmates, join gangs in prison for a sense of security, and the gangs tend to break down along racial lines and to deepen racial tensions in prisons. See *American History X* (1998). Jimmy Lerner's prison memoirs chronicle the racial tension at the center of prison life, observing that the correctional officers assigned cell mates on the basis of race: "Following some unwritten rule, he scrupulously placed blacks with the blacks, the white dawgs with the white dawgs."

Racial injustice in society spills over into the views of inmates about the legitimacy of their own punishment. Consider this classic passage from Eldridge Cleaver:

> One thing that the judges, policemen, and administrators of prisons seem never to have understood, and for which they certainly do not make any allowances, is that Negro convicts, basically, rather than see themselves as criminals and perpetrators of misdeeds, look upon themselves as prisoners of war, the victims of a vicious, dog-eat-dog social system that is so heinous as to cancel out their own malefactions: in the jungle there is no right or wrong.
>
> Rather than owing and paying a debt to society, Negro prisoners feel that they are being abused, that their imprisonment is simply another form of the oppression which they have known all their lives. Negro inmates feel that they are being robbed, that it is "society" that owes them, that should be paying them, a debt. America's penology does not take this into account. . . .

Eldridge Cleaver, Soul on Ice 58-59 (1968).

3. *Women in prison.*   The female prison population differs from the male in several respects. Women tend to be incarcerated for nonviolent offenses, such as prostitution and theft, or for drug crimes. Women tend to be economically worse off than male offenders. Drug usage of women admitted into state prisons is substantially higher than that of men. More women than men test HIV-positive upon admission, usually because of intravenous drug use or work in the sex industry.

Female inmates often enter prison with a different background from that of male prisoners. Almost 60 percent of female state prisoners have a history of physical or sexual abuse or both.

> One late afternoon as we sit in [Delia's] room, she tells me that her stepfather had sexually molested her at the age of eleven. She hoped that by telling her mother the man would be thrown out of the house. Instead she was sent from her home to live with an aunt. At twelve, she had her first child. From that point on, her life revolved around a series of violent relationships with men.

Andi Rierden, The Farm: Life Inside a Women's Prison 81 (1997). Often the abuse continues in prison, as male correctional officers and other prison employees sexually assault female prisoners or coerce them into sexual relationships. See Human Rights Watch Women's Rights Project, Human Rights Watch, All Too Familiar: Sexual Abuse of Women in U.S. State Prisons (1996).

The most important differences between female and male inmates are related to reproduction and parenting. Five to 10 percent of women who enter prisons are pregnant, but only three prisons in the country permit women to spend time with their newborns.

Sixty-four percent of state inmates lived with their minor children prior to incarceration. In contrast to the children of male prisoners, the children of female inmates do not usually end up living with their other parent but with other close family members. Because of the smaller number of female prisons, women are often incarcerated far from their families. Not seeing their children during incarceration is difficult, but seeing them can be equally excruciating. The excerpt below is taken from the 1995 inmate handbook of the Edna Mahon Correctional Facility for Women:

> All visits will be conducted in a quiet, orderly and dignified manner. Handshaking, embracing and kissing by the immediate family members and close friends are permitted within the bounds of good taste at the beginning and at the end of the visit only. Hand holding, in full view, is the only body contact allowed between a visitor and their inmate during a visit. Visitors and inmates must sit facing each other. Visiting children must remain under the inmate's supervision. Failure to properly supervise visiting children will be cause to terminate the visit.

Kathryn Watterson, Women in Prison: Inside the Concrete Womb 215 (rev. ed. 1996). Visiting with children is particularly difficult:

> Two weeks in segregation, with no visitors, nothing but stone-cold walls, a window to a parking lot, a pot to pee in, and thoughts, thoughts, thoughts. . . . Two weeks later [BeBe] emerges from segregation, from the cell block of her mind, raw, humiliated, shamed. Her two children visit. They are very young, under ten. They still think they are visiting their mommy in the hospital. It is the lie a lot of inmates spin. BeBe prays they never learn the truth. "When will you be better, mommy?" they ask her. Soon babies, soon.

Rierden, The Farm at 125. For a fictionalized but realistic account of life in prison, see Olivia Goldsmith, Pen Pals (2002).

   4. *Release.*   Especially for inmates who have served long sentences, release is both joyful and stressful, according to an inmate:

> You just come out *bam.* . . . And you don't know how to deal with it. You don't have a family to go to, half the time. You don't have a home or a job. All this time you've been fantasizing about the way things are and the way things are going to be when you really have no way of knowing how they are. You can imagine the shock. A lot of times the only thing left for a person to do is commit a new crime.
>
>   Besides that, prisons really help produce crime. You take away any human being and put them out of contact and take away all their responsibility and you're denying them an opportunity to grow. So to expect a person to leave here being grown and responsible, you're making an impossible demand, because all her sense of responsibility and her ability to interact has been brutalized.
>
>   To deal with society you have to interact with society. We only know how to interact with one society — and that's prison society.

Watterson, Women in Prison at 311.

D.   LIMITING IMPRISONMENT UNDER THE EIGHTH AMENDMENT

   The Supreme Court and lower courts have spent much effort explicating the meaning of the Eighth Amendment to guide states when imposing the death penalty. To a lesser extent, courts interpreting the Eighth Amendment have also restricted the imposition of other sentences, especially imprisonment. A series of Supreme Court cases set out the type of proportionality review needed to assess the constitutionality of a prison sentence.

|| ***John Albert Ewing v. California*** ||
538 U.S. 11 (2003)

O'CONNOR, J.*

In this case, we decide whether the Eighth Amendment prohibits the State of California from sentencing a repeat felon to a prison term of 25 years to life under the State's "Three Strikes and You're Out" law.

I

California's three strikes law reflects a shift in the State's sentencing policies toward incapacitating and deterring repeat offenders who threaten the public safety. The law was designed "to ensure longer prison sentences and greater punishment for those who commit a felony and have been previously convicted of serious and/or violent felony offenses." Cal. Penal Code §667(b). . . .

California's current three strikes law consists of two virtually identical statutory schemes designed to increase the prison terms of repeat felons. When a defendant is convicted of a felony, and he has previously been convicted of one or more prior felonies defined as "serious" or "violent" in Cal. Penal Code Ann. §§667.5 and 1192.7, sentencing is conducted pursuant to the three strikes law. . . . If the defendant has one prior "serious" or "violent" felony conviction, he must be sentenced to twice the term otherwise provided as punishment for the current felony conviction. If the defendant has two or more prior "serious" or "violent" felony convictions, he must receive an indeterminate term of life imprisonment. Defendants sentenced to life under the three strikes law become eligible for parole on a date calculated by reference to a "minimum term," which is the greater of (a) three times the term otherwise provided for the current conviction, (b) 25 years, or (c) the term determined by the court pursuant to §1170 for the underlying conviction, including any enhancements.

Under California law, certain offenses may be classified as either felonies or misdemeanors. These crimes are known as "wobblers." Some crimes that would otherwise be misdemeanors become "wobblers" because of the defendant's prior record. For example, petty theft, a misdemeanor, becomes a "wobbler" when the defendant has previously served a prison term for committing specified theft-related crimes. Other crimes, such as grand theft, are "wobblers" regardless of the defendant's prior record. Both types of "wobblers" are triggering offenses under the three strikes law only when they are treated as felonies. Under California law, a "wobbler" is presumptively a felony and remains a felony

---

*Additional parts of the decision in *Ewing*, focusing on the rationale for recidivist statutes, appear in Chapter 1. The portions of the opinion appearing here address the federal "proportionality" test under the Eighth Amendment and the relevance of prosecutorial and judicial discretion under the California recidivist scheme.— EDS.

except when the discretion is actually exercised to make the crime a misdemeanor.

In California, prosecutors may exercise their discretion to charge a "wobbler" as either a felony or a misdemeanor. [Trial] courts may avoid imposing a three strikes sentence in two ways: first, by reducing "wobblers" to misdemeanors (which do not qualify as triggering offenses), and second, by vacating allegations of prior "serious" or "violent" felony convictions.

On parole from a 9-year prison term, petitioner Gary Ewing walked into the pro shop of the El Segundo Golf Course in Los Angeles County on March 12, 2000. He walked out with three golf clubs, priced at $399 apiece, concealed in his pants leg. A shop employee, whose suspicions were aroused when he observed Ewing limp out of the pro shop, telephoned the police. The police apprehended Ewing in the parking lot.

Ewing is no stranger to the criminal justice system. In 1984, at the age of 22, he pleaded guilty to theft. The court sentenced him to six months in jail (suspended), three years' probation, and a $300 fine. In 1988, he was convicted of felony grand theft auto and sentenced to one year in jail and three years' probation. After Ewing completed probation, however, the sentencing court reduced the crime to a misdemeanor, permitted Ewing to withdraw his guilty plea, and dismissed the case. In 1990, he was convicted of petty theft with a prior and sentenced to 60 days in the county jail and three years' probation. In 1992, Ewing was convicted of battery and sentenced to 30 days in the county jail and two years' summary probation. One month later, he was convicted of theft and sentenced to 10 days in the county jail and 12 months' probation. In January 1993, Ewing was convicted of burglary and sentenced to 60 days in the county jail and one year's summary probation. In February 1993, he was convicted of possessing drug paraphernalia and sentenced to six months in the county jail and three years' probation. In July 1993, he was convicted of appropriating lost property and sentenced to 10 days in the county jail and two years' summary probation. In September 1993, he was convicted of unlawfully possessing a firearm and trespassing and sentenced to 30 days in the county jail and one year's probation.

In October and November 1993, Ewing committed three burglaries and one robbery at a Long Beach, California, apartment complex over a 5-week period. [During the robbery], Ewing accosted a victim in the mailroom of the apartment complex. Ewing claimed to have a gun and ordered the victim to hand over his wallet. When the victim resisted, Ewing produced a knife and forced the victim back to the apartment itself. While Ewing rifled through the bedroom, the victim fled the apartment screaming for help. Ewing absconded with the victim's money and credit cards. . . . A jury convicted Ewing of first-degree robbery and three counts of residential burglary. Sentenced to nine years and eight months in prison, Ewing was paroled in 1999.

Only 10 months later, Ewing stole the golf clubs at issue in this case. He was charged with, and ultimately convicted of, one count of felony grand theft of personal property in excess of $400. As required by the three strikes law, the prosecutor formally alleged, and the trial court later found, that Ewing had been convicted previously of four serious or violent felonies for the three burglaries and the robbery in the Long Beach apartment complex. . . .

Before sentencing Ewing, the trial court took note of his entire criminal history, including the fact that he was on parole when he committed his latest offense. . . . In the end, the trial judge determined that the grand theft should remain a felony. The court also ruled that the four prior strikes for the three burglaries and the robbery in Long Beach should stand. As a newly convicted felon with two or more "serious" or "violent" felony convictions in his past, Ewing was sentenced under the three strikes law to 25 years to life. . . .

II

The Eighth Amendment, which forbids cruel and unusual punishments, contains a narrow proportionality principle that applies to noncapital sentences. We have most recently addressed the proportionality principle as applied to terms of years in a series of cases beginning with Rummel v. Estelle, 445 U.S. 263 (1980).

In *Rummel*, we held that it did not violate the Eighth Amendment for a State to sentence a three-time offender to life in prison with the possibility of parole. Like Ewing, Rummel was sentenced to a lengthy prison term under a recidivism statute. Rummel's two prior offenses were a 1964 felony for "fraudulent use of a credit card to obtain $80 worth of goods or services," and a 1969 felony conviction for "passing a forged check in the amount of $28.36." His triggering offense was a conviction for felony theft — "obtaining $120.75 by false pretenses."

This Court ruled that having twice imprisoned him for felonies, Texas was entitled to place upon Rummel the onus of one who is simply unable to bring his conduct within the social norms prescribed by the criminal law of the State. The recidivism statute is nothing more than a societal decision that when such a person commits yet another felony, he should be subjected to the admittedly serious penalty of incarceration for life, subject only to the State's judgment as to whether to grant him parole. We noted that this Court has on occasion stated that the Eighth Amendment prohibits imposition of a sentence that is grossly disproportionate to the severity of the crime. But outside the context of capital punishment, successful challenges to the proportionality of particular sentences have been exceedingly rare. Although we stated that the proportionality principle would "come into play in the extreme example . . . if a legislature made overtime parking a felony punishable by life imprisonment," we held that the mandatory life sentence imposed upon this petitioner does not constitute cruel and unusual punishment under the Eighth and Fourteenth Amendments. . . .

Three years after *Rummel*, in Solem v. Helm, 463 U.S. 277, 279 (1983), we held that the Eighth Amendment prohibited "a life sentence without possibility of parole for a seventh nonviolent felony." The triggering offense in *Solem* was uttering a "no account" check for $100. We . . . explained that three factors may be relevant to a determination of whether a sentence is so disproportionate that it violates the Eighth Amendment: "(i) the gravity of the offense and the harshness of the penalty; (ii) the sentences imposed on other criminals in the same jurisdiction; and (iii) the sentences imposed for commission of the same crime in other jurisdictions."

Applying these factors in *Solem*, we struck down the defendant's sentence of life without parole. We specifically noted the contrast between that sentence and the sentence in *Rummel*, pursuant to which the defendant was eligible for parole. Indeed, we explicitly declined to overrule *Rummel*. . . .

Eight years after *Solem,* we grappled with the proportionality issue again in Harmelin v. Michigan, 501 U.S. 957 (1991). *Harmelin* was not a recidivism case, but rather involved a first-time offender convicted of possessing 672 grams of cocaine. He was sentenced to life in prison without possibility of parole. A majority of the Court rejected Harmelin's claim that his sentence was so grossly disproportionate that it violated the Eighth Amendment. The Court, however, could not agree on why his proportionality argument failed. Justice Scalia, joined by the Chief Justice, wrote that the proportionality principle was "an aspect of our death penalty jurisprudence, rather than a generalizable aspect of Eighth Amendment law." He would thus have declined to apply gross disproportionality principles except in reviewing capital sentences.

Justice Kennedy, joined by two other Members of the Court, concurred in part and concurred in the judgment. Justice Kennedy specifically recognized that "the Eighth Amendment proportionality principle also applies to noncapital sentences." He then identified four principles of proportionality review — "the primacy of the legislature, the variety of legitimate penological schemes, the nature of our federal system, and the requirement that proportionality review be guided by objective factors"— that inform the final one: "The Eighth Amendment does not require strict proportionality between crime and sentence. Rather, it forbids only extreme sentences that are 'grossly disproportionate' to the crime." . . .

III

Against this backdrop, we consider Ewing's claim that his three strikes sentence of 25 years to life is unconstitutionally disproportionate to his offense of "shoplifting three golf clubs." We first address the gravity of the offense compared to the harshness of the penalty. At the threshold, we note that Ewing incorrectly frames the issue. The gravity of his offense was not merely "shoplifting three golf clubs." Rather, Ewing was convicted of felony grand theft for stealing nearly $1,200 worth of merchandise after previously having been convicted of at least two "violent" or "serious" felonies. Even standing alone, Ewing's theft should not be taken lightly. . . . Theft of $1,200 in property is a felony under federal law, 18 U.S.C. §641, and in the vast majority of States.

That grand theft is a "wobbler" under California law is of no moment. Though California courts have discretion to reduce a felony grand theft charge to a misdemeanor, it remains a felony for all purposes unless and until the trial court imposes a misdemeanor sentence [because] the rehabilitation of the convicted defendant either does not require or would be adversely affected by, incarceration in a state prison as a felon. . . .

In weighing the gravity of Ewing's offense, we must place on the scales not only his current felony, but also his long history of felony recidivism. Any other approach would fail to accord proper deference to the policy judgments that find expression in the legislature's choice of sanctions. . . .

To be sure, Ewing's sentence is a long one. But it reflects a rational legislative judgment, entitled to deference, that offenders who have committed serious or violent felonies and who continue to commit felonies must be incapacitated. . . . Ewing's is not the rare case in which a threshold comparison of the crime committed and the sentence imposed leads to an inference of gross disproportionality. We hold that Ewing's sentence of 25 years to life in prison, imposed for the offense of felony grand theft under the three strikes law, is not grossly disproportionate and therefore does not violate the Eighth Amendment's prohibition on cruel and unusual punishments. . . .

STEVENS, J., dissenting.
. . . The Eighth Amendment succinctly prohibits "excessive" sanctions. See U.S. Const., Amdt. 8 ("Excessive bail shall not be required, nor excessive fines imposed, nor cruel and unusual punishments inflicted"). Faithful to the Amendment's text, this Court has held that the Constitution directs judges to apply their best judgment in determining the proportionality of fines, bail, and other forms of punishment, including the imposition of a death sentence, see, e.g., Coker v. Georgia, 433 U.S. 584 (1977). It would be anomalous indeed to suggest that the Eighth Amendment makes proportionality review applicable in the context of bail and fines but not in the context of other forms of punishment, such as imprisonment. . . .

Throughout most of the Nation's history — before guideline sentencing became so prevalent — federal and state trial judges imposed specific sentences pursuant to grants of authority that gave them uncabined discretion within broad ranges. . . . In exercising their discretion, sentencing judges wisely employed a proportionality principle that took into account all of the justifications for punishment — namely, deterrence, incapacitation, retribution and rehabilitation. . . . Likewise, I think it clear that the Eighth Amendment's prohibition of "cruel and unusual punishments" expresses a broad and basic proportionality principle that takes into account all of the justifications for penal sanctions. It is this broad proportionality principle that would preclude reliance on any of the justifications for punishment to support, for example, a life sentence for overtime parking. Accordingly, I respectfully dissent.

BREYER, J., dissenting. . . .
[Courts] faced with a "gross disproportionality" claim must first make "a threshold comparison of the crime committed and the sentence imposed." *Harmelin*, 501 U.S., at 1005 (Kennedy, J., concurring). If a claim crosses that threshold — itself a *rare* occurrence — then the court should compare the sentence at issue to other sentences imposed on other criminals in the same, or in other, jurisdictions. The comparative analysis will validate or invalidate an initial judgment that a sentence is grossly disproportionate to a crime. . . . I believe that the case before us is a "rare" case — one in which a court can say with reasonable confidence that the punishment is "grossly disproportionate" to the crime.

Ewing's claim crosses the gross disproportionality "threshold." [Precedent] makes clear that Ewing's sentence raises a serious disproportionality question. Ewing is a recidivist. Hence the two cases most directly in point are those in which the Court considered the constitutionality of recidivist sentencing: *Rummel* and *Solem*. Ewing's claim falls between these two cases. It is stronger than the claim presented in *Rummel*, where the Court upheld a recidivist's sentence as constitutional. It is weaker than the claim presented in *Solem*, where the Court struck down a recidivist sentence as unconstitutional.

Three kinds of sentence-related characteristics define the relevant comparative spectrum: (a) the length of the prison term in real time, i.e., the time that the offender is likely actually to spend in prison; (b) the sentence-triggering criminal conduct, i.e., the offender's actual behavior or other offense-related circumstances; and (c) the offender's criminal history. . . .

In *Rummel,* the Court held constitutional (a) a sentence of life imprisonment *with parole available within 10 to 12 years,* (b) for the offense of obtaining $120 by false pretenses, (c) committed by an offender with two prior felony convictions (involving small amounts of money). . . . In *Solem,* the Court held unconstitutional (a) a sentence of life imprisonment *without parole,* (b) for the crime of writing a $100 check on a nonexistent bank account, (c) committed by an offender with six prior felony convictions (including three for burglary). . . . Which of the three pertinent comparative factors made the constitutional difference? . . .

The one critical factor that explains the difference in the outcome is the length of the likely prison term measured in real time. In *Rummel,* where the Court upheld the sentence, the state sentencing statute authorized parole for the offender, Rummel, after 10 or 12 years. In *Solem,* where the Court struck down the sentence, the sentence required the offender, Helm, to spend the rest of his life in prison.

Now consider the present case. The third factor, *offender characteristics*— i.e., prior record — does not differ significantly here from that in *Solem.* Ewing's prior record consists of four prior felony convictions (involving three burglaries, one with a knife) contrasted with Helm's six prior felony convictions (including three burglaries, though none with weapons). The second factor, *offense behavior,* is worse than that in *Solem,* but only to a degree. It would be difficult to say that the actual behavior itself here (shoplifting) differs significantly from that at issue in *Solem* (passing a bad check) or in *Rummel* (obtaining money through false pretenses). Rather the difference lies in the *value* of the goods obtained. That difference, measured in terms of the most relevant feature (loss to the victim, i.e., wholesale value) and adjusted for the irrelevant feature of inflation, comes down (in 1979 values) to about $379 here compared with $100 in *Solem,* or (in 1973 values) to $232 here compared with $120.75 in *Rummel.* . . .

The difference in *length* of the real prison term — the first, and critical, factor in *Solem* and *Rummel*— is considerably more important. Ewing's sentence here amounts, in real terms, to at least 25 years without parole or good-time credits. That sentence is considerably shorter than Helm's sentence in *Solem,* which amounted, in real terms, to life in prison. Nonetheless Ewing's real prison term is more than twice as long as the term at issue in *Rummel,* which amounted, in real terms, to at least 10 or 12 years. And, Ewing's sentence, unlike Rummel's (but like Helm's sentence in *Solem*), is long enough to consume the productive remainder of almost any offender's life. (It means that Ewing himself, seriously ill when sentenced at age 38, will likely die in prison.) The upshot is that the length of the real prison term — the factor that explains the *Solem/Rummel* difference in outcome — places Ewing closer to *Solem* than to *Rummel.* . . .

Believing Ewing's argument a strong one, sufficient to pass the threshold, I turn to the comparative analysis. A comparison of Ewing's sentence with other sentences requires answers to two questions. First, how would other jurisdictions (or California at other times, i.e., without the three strikes penalty) punish the *same offense conduct*? Second, upon what other conduct would other jurisdictions (or California) impose the *same prison term*? Moreover, since hypothetical punishment is beside the point, the relevant prison time, for comparative purposes, is *real* prison time, i.e., the time that an offender must *actually serve.* . . .

As to California itself, we know the following: First, between the end of World War II and 1994 (when California enacted the three strikes law, . . .), *no one* like Ewing could have served more than *10* years in prison. . . . Second, statistics suggest that recidivists *of all sorts* convicted during that same time period in California served a small fraction of Ewing's real-time sentence. On average, recidivists served three to four additional (recidivist-related) years in prison, with 90 percent serving less than an additional real seven to eight years. Third, we know that California has reserved, and still reserves, Ewing-type prison time, i.e., at least 25 real years in prison, for criminals convicted of crimes far worse than was Ewing's. Statistics for the years 1945 to 1981, for example, indicate that typical (nonrecidivist) male first-degree murderers served between 10 and 15 real years in prison, with 90 percent of all such murderers serving less than 20 real years. . . .

As to other jurisdictions, we know the following: The United States, bound by the federal Sentencing Guidelines, would impose upon a recidivist, such as Ewing, a sentence that, in any ordinary case, would not exceed 18 months in prison. USSG §2B1.1(a) (assuming a base offense level of 6, a criminal history of VI, and no mitigating or aggravating adjustments). The Guidelines, based in part upon a study of some 40,000 actual federal sentences . . . reserve a Ewing-type sentence for Ewing-type *recidivists* who currently commit such crimes as murder, §2A1.2; air piracy, §2A5.1; robbery (involving the discharge of a firearm, serious bodily injury, and about $1 million), §2B3.1; drug offenses involving more than, for example, 20 pounds of heroin, §2D1.1; aggravated theft of more than $100 million, §2B1.1; and other similar offenses. . . .

[We] do not have before us information about actual time served by Ewing-type offenders in other States. We do know, however, that the law would make it legally impossible for a Ewing-type offender to serve more than 10 years in prison in 33 jurisdictions, as well as the federal courts, . . . more than 15 years in 4 other States, . . . and more than 20 years in 4 additional States, . . . In nine other States, the law *might* make it legally possible to impose a sentence of 25 years or more, [but that] does not mean that judges have actually done so. . . .

The upshot is that comparison of other sentencing practices, both in other jurisdictions and in California at other times (or in respect to other crimes), validates what an initial threshold examination suggested. . . . Outside the California three strikes context, Ewing's recidivist sentence is virtually unique in its harshness for his offense of conviction, and by a considerable degree.

This is not the end of the matter. [It] is important to consider whether special criminal justice concerns related to California's three strikes policy might justify including Ewing's theft within the class of triggering criminal conduct (thereby imposing a severe punishment), even if Ewing's sentence would otherwise seem disproportionately harsh.

I can find no such special criminal justice concerns that might justify this sentence. The most obvious potential justification for bringing Ewing's theft within the ambit of the statute is administrative. California must draw some kind of workable line between conduct that will trigger, and conduct that will not trigger, a "three strikes" sentence. . . . The administrative line that the statute draws separates "felonies" from "misdemeanors." [However], California uses those words in a way unrelated to the seriousness of offense conduct in a set of criminal statutes called "wobblers,". . . , one of which is at issue in this case. . . .

"Wobbler" statutes cover a wide variety of criminal behavior, ranging from assault with a deadly weapon, §245, vehicular manslaughter, §193(c)(1), and money laundering, §186.10(a), to the defacement of property with graffiti, §594(b)(2)(A), or stealing more than $100 worth of chickens, nuts, or avocados, §487(b)(1)(A); §489. Some of this behavior is obviously less serious, even if engaged in twice, than other criminal conduct that California statutes classify as pure misdemeanors. . . .

There is no obvious reason why the statute could not enumerate, consistent with its purposes, the relevant triggering crimes. Given that possibility and given the anomalies that result from California's chosen approach, I do not see how California can justify on *administrative* grounds a sentence as seriously disproportionate as Ewing's.

. . . Given the omission of vast categories of property crimes — including grand theft (unarmed) — from the "strike" definition, one cannot argue, on *property-crime-related incapacitation grounds,* for inclusion of Ewing's crime among the triggers.

. . . No one argues for Ewing's inclusion within the ambit of the three strikes statute on grounds of "retribution." [I]n terms of "deterrence," Ewing's 25-year term amounts to overkill. And "rehabilitation" is obviously beside the point. The upshot is that, in my view, the State cannot find in its three strikes law a special criminal justice need sufficient to rescue a sentence that other relevant considerations indicate is unconstitutional. . . .

People v. Leon Miller
781 N.E.2d 300 (Ill. 2002)

FITZGERALD, J.

Defendant, Leon Miller, a 15-year-old juvenile, was charged with two counts of first degree murder based upon accountability. Defendant was transferred to the criminal division of the Cook County circuit court and prosecuted as an adult. Following a jury trial, defendant was convicted of both counts, and the State requested that the circuit court sentence defendant to natural life imprisonment under the multiple-murder provision of the Unified Code of Corrections. The circuit court declined to impose the statutorily mandated sentence, holding that application of the statute to defendant would offend the proportionate penalties clause of the Illinois Constitution (Ill. Const. 1970, art. I, §11) and the eighth amendment of the United States Constitution. Instead, the circuit court sentenced defendant to a term of 50 years in prison. The State appealed directly to this court. . . .

According to defendant, on the night of the murders, Arthur Beckom and Kentrell Stoutmire observed people walking through their neighborhood that they believed belonged to a rival gang. Beckom and Stoutmire approached defendant, who was standing outside on a corner in the neighborhood, and asked him to stand as a lookout. Defendant saw that both Beckom and Stoutmire had guns in their possession, and although defendant never handled or touched the guns, he agreed to stand as a lookout. One minute later, Beckom and Stoutmire fired gunshots in the direction of [Tommy Jones and Keith Alexander], who both died as a result of their injuries. Once the shooting began, defendant ran to his girlfriend's house.

Four individuals were charged for their participation in the shooting. The first degree murder indictment charged Stoutmire and Beckom as the alleged shooters and defendant and another 15-year-old male, Douglas Baskerville, for their participation as lookouts. At separate jury trials, Beckom and Baskerville were acquitted. Stoutmire, who was 17 years old at the time of the murders, was convicted and sentenced to natural life in prison. Defendant was also convicted of the murders. At sentencing, however, [Miller] argued that a sentence of natural life imprisonment, pursuant to the multiple-murder sentencing statute, violated the proportionate penalties clause of the Illinois Constitution, the prohibition against cruel and unusual punishment contained within the federal constitution, as well as international law, which prohibits the imposition of a natural life sentence on a juvenile. Conversely, the State argued that the circuit court was obligated by the statute to impose a sentence of natural life imprisonment.

At the conclusion of the sentencing hearing, the circuit court discussed its inability to sentence defendant pursuant to the terms of the multiple-murder sentencing statute:

> I have from the moment that the Jury came back with their findings been very concerned about what this meant [to this defendant] as a 15-year-old child, what this meant to society at large, to be part of a society where a 15-year-old child on a theory of accountability only, passive accountability, would suffer a sentence of life in the Penitentiary without the possibility of parole. . . . I feel that it is clear that in my mind this is blatantly unfair and highly unconscionable, and let me state that I do not believe for a second that Mr. Miller is innocent of these charges. . . . I am concerned that a person under the age of 18 under Illinois law can do everything that John Gacy did, can torture and abuse and murder over 30 people, and would be in the same boat as [defendant] right now looking at a sentence of a minimum and maximum of life without the possibility of parole. . . . I have a 15-year-old child who was passively acting as a look-out for other people, never picked up a gun, never had much more than — perhaps less than a minute — to contemplate what this entire incident is about, and he is in the same situation as a serial killer for sentencing purposes.

. . . Defendant was sentenced to a term of 50 years' imprisonment.

[Our] review begins with the presumption that the statute is constitutional. Because of this presumption, the party challenging the statute bears the burden of showing its invalidity. A circuit court's finding that a statute is unconstitutional is reviewed de novo.

The multiple-murder sentencing statute provides, in pertinent part:

> [For] first degree murder . . . the court shall sentence the defendant to a term of natural life imprisonment when the death penalty is not imposed if the defendant . . . is a person who, at the time of the commission of the murder, had attained the age of 17 or more and is found guilty of murdering an individual under 12 years of age; or, irrespective of the defendant's age at the time of the commission of the offense, is found guilty of murdering more than one victim.

730 ILCS 5/5-8-1(a)(1)(c)(ii).

We have repeatedly recognized that the legislature has discretion to pre-scribe penalties for defined offenses. The legislature's discretion necessarily includes the power to prescribe mandatory sentences, even if these mandatory sentences restrict the judiciary's discretion in imposing sentences. However, the power to impose sentences is not without limitation; the penalty must satisfy constitutional constrictions. . . .

The State . . . argues that Illinois courts have previously upheld the consti-tutionality of the multiple-murder sentencing statute as applied to juveniles against proportionate penalty challenges. See People v. Cooks, 648 N.E.2d 190 (Ill. App. Ct. 1995) (holding that the multiple-murder sentencing statute did not violate the United States or Illinois Constitutions as applied to a 14-year-old principal offender).

We reject the State's assertion that the question at issue in this appeal has been decided. Illinois courts have only upheld application of the statute to ju-venile principals and adult accomplices. The issue we address — the application of the statute to a *juvenile* convicted upon a theory of *accountability* — is an issue of first impression. We begin with a discussion of the proportionate penalties clause of the Illinois Constitution.

The proportionate penalties clause of the Illinois Constitution declares that "all penalties shall be determined . . . according to the seriousness of the of-fense." Ill. Const. 1970, art. I, §11. While courts of review are generally reluctant to override the judgment of the General Assembly with respect to criminal penalties, it is also true that when defining crimes and their penalties, the legis-lature must consider the constitutional goals of restoring an offender to useful citizenship and of providing a penalty according to the seriousness of the of-fense. With regard to the statute at issue, we have recognized that the legislature considered the possible rehabilitation of an offender who commits multiple murder, and the seriousness of that offense, in determining that a mandatory minimum sentence of natural life imprisonment is appropriate for the offense of multiple murders. People v. Taylor, 464 N.E.2d 1059 (Ill. 1984).

However, the instant matter concerns a different type of challenge under the proportionate penalties clause and a different set of circumstances not ad-dressed in *Taylor*. We have recognized three different forms of proportionality review. A statute may be deemed unconstitutionally disproportionate if (1) the punishment for the offense is cruel, degrading, or so wholly disproportionate to the offense as to shock the moral sense of the community; (2) similar offenses are compared and the conduct that creates a less serious threat to the public health and safety is punished more harshly; or (3) identical offenses are given different sentences. Here, the circuit court ruled that application of the mul-tiple-murder sentencing statute to defendant was "highly unconscionable," and, therefore, we first consider whether the statute as applied to defendant is shock-ing to the moral sense of the community. . . .

We have never defined what kind of punishment constitutes "cruel," "de-grading," or "so wholly disproportioned to the offense as to shock the moral sense of the community." This is so because, as our society evolves, so too do our concepts of elemental decency and fairness which shape the "moral sense" of the community. Similarly, our United States Supreme Court has stated in the context of the eighth amendment that "proportionality review under those evolving standards should be informed by objective factors to the maximum possible extent." Atkins v. Virginia, 536 U.S. 304 (2002). However, this objective evidence, though of great importance, does not wholly determine the controversy, for the Constitution contemplates that in the end our own judgment will be brought to bear on the question.

We review the gravity of the defendant's offense in connection with the severity of the statutorily mandated sentence within our community's evolving standard of decency. Here, a sentence of natural life imprisonment would be the result of three converging statutes. Section 5-4(6)(a) of the Juvenile Court Act of 1987 (705 ILCS 405/5-4(6)(a)) mandates that all 15- or 16-year-old offenders charged with murder be automatically transferred and prosecuted as adults in criminal court. The accountability statute (720 ILCS 5/5-2(c)) effectively bars courts from considering the offender's degree of participation in the crime by making all persons who participate in a common criminal design equally responsible. Finally, the multiple-murder sentencing statute (730 ILCS 5/5-8-1(a)(1)(c)(ii)) does not allow a court to consider the age of the offender or the offender's participation in the crime at the time of sentencing. . . . When these three statutes converge, a court never considers the actual facts of the crime, including the defendant's age at the time of the crime or his or her individual level of culpability.

Accordingly, we hold that the penalty mandated by the multiple-murder sentencing statute as applied to this defendant is particularly harsh and unconstitutionally disproportionate. We agree with defendant that a mandatory sentence of natural life in prison with no possibility of parole grossly distorts the factual realities of the case and does not accurately represent defendant's personal culpability such that it shocks the moral sense of the community. This moral sense is particularly true, as in the case before us, where a 15-year-old with one minute to contemplate his decision to participate in the [incident, who] stood as a lookout during the shooting, but never handled a gun, is subject to life imprisonment with no possibility of parole — the same sentence applicable to the actual shooter. Our decision does not imply that a sentence of life imprisonment for a juvenile offender convicted under a theory of accountability is never appropriate. It is certainly possible to contemplate a situation where a juvenile offender actively participated in the planning of a crime resulting in the death of two or more individuals, such that a sentence of natural life imprisonment without the possibility of parole is appropriate. . . .

Our decision is consistent with the longstanding distinction made in this state between adult and juvenile offenders, a distinction underscored by the reality that our state was the first to create a court system dedicated exclusively to juveniles. 1899 Ill. Laws 131. Illinois led the nation with our policy towards the treatment of juveniles in first forming the juvenile court, and, traditionally, as a society we have recognized that young defendants have greater rehabilitative potential. . . . Therefore, in many cases courts have discretion to grant leniency to a juvenile even if he or she is prosecuted as an adult. See, e.g., People v. Kolakowski, 745 N.E.2d 62 (Ill. App. Ct. 2001) (noting that defendant's sentence was less than her codefendant's because of her age and potential for rehabilitation). [As] with juvenile offenders, courts in some cases may grant leniency in sentencing to offenders guilty by accountability. Disparate sentences between an offender convicted by accountability and a principal offender reflect the different degrees of participation in the crime. See, e.g., People v. Godinez, 434

N.E.2d 1121 (Ill. 1982) (finding that a defendant who stood as a lookout deserved a lesser sentence than his codefendant who was convicted as the principal). . . . A life sentence without the possibility of parole implies that under any circumstances a juvenile defendant convicted solely by accountability is incorrigible and incapable of rehabilitation for the rest of his life. The trial judge in this case did not agree with such a blanket proposition. We also decline to find that the sentence mandated by the multiple-murder sentencing statute in this case satisfies the proportionate penalties clause of the Illinois Constitution. . . . We affirm the circuit court's imposition of a term of 50 years' imprisonment. . . .

PROBLEM 7-1. FAMILY BUSINESS

Angela Thompson was reared in Jamaica by her grandmother and then lived with a variety of family members in Jamaica and later in the United States. Her uncle, Norman Little, ran a major drug-selling operation in Harlem, and he employed Thompson in his illegal enterprise when she was 17 years old. One summer afternoon, an undercover police officer bought 200 vials of cocaine from her for $2,000 on the street outside Little's residence. The officer claimed that it was customary in a sale of this size for him to receive a bonus of 20 additional vials. Thompson, however, gave him only 14 extra vials and promised to "take care" of him personally the next time he made a purchase.

On that same day, officers also made five separate purchases from Little, and one purchase from another of Little's employees, a young woman known as "Shorty." Uniformed officers later arrested Thompson and Little. They decided, however, not to arrest Shorty because they were afraid that an arrest would reveal the identity of an undercover officer. Thompson had no previous encounters with law enforcement officials.

Thompson was indicted for the sale of 2.13 ounces of cocaine, a class A-I felony that carries a mandatory prison sentence. Under the New York statute, the judge must impose a minimum prison term of between 15 and 25 years and a maximum term of life. If Thompson had not awarded the bonus vials to the undercover officer, the government could have charged her only with an A-II sale (less than two ounces), whose mandatory minimum sentence is three years.

Little was indicted for five criminal sales of a controlled substance in the first degree. He had three prior felony and seven prior misdemeanor convictions; Little pleaded guilty to one illicit sale in exchange for dismissal of the remaining four counts and a sentence of 15 years to life imprisonment. The prosecutor offered Thompson a plea bargain carrying a sentence of three years to life, but she rejected the offer and went to trial. The jury convicted her of the A-I felony.

As defense counsel, how would you convince the sentencing judge that a minimum sentence of 15 years for Angela Thompson is cruel and unusual punishment, under either the federal or state constitutions? Compare People v. Thompson, 633 N.E.2d 1074 (N.Y. 1994).

NOTES

1. *Eighth Amendment limits on legislative choice of sanctions.* The language of Eighth Amendment and similar provisions in state constitutions goes back to the

English Bill of Rights of 1689, which prohibited "cruel and unusual punishments." This provision arose from concerns about the unwarranted infliction of pain through unlimited state power.

The Supreme Court's proportionality analysis in imprisonment situations has been limited. The truncated review of prison sentences may indicate the degree to which the death penalty drives the entire sentencing structure in the United States. After all, if death is available as the ultimate sanction, how can life without parole be disproportionate? The *Ewing* opinion summarizes the cases in this area, including the three-part test in Solem v. Helm, 463 U.S. 277 (1983), and the modified version of that test developed by Justice Kennedy in Harmelin v. Michigan, 501 U.S. 957 (1991). In a companion case to *Ewing*, Lockyer v. Andrade, 538 U.S. 63 (2003), the defendant stole videotapes worth $154 from two Kmart stores. Andrade also had a criminal record with several convictions for misdemeanor theft, residential burglary, and transportation of marijuana. Although Andrade was sentenced under California's three-strikes law to a life term lasting at least 50 years, the Court upheld the sentence. How can the Court assess the first prong of its test — the gravity of the offense and the harshness of the penalty — other than by relying on prongs two and three to provide an answer?

Does the decision in *Ewing* reflect merely the predilections of the majority of the Court rather than a principled assessment of the sentence? Would it have been more honest for the Court to decline proportionality review in imprisonment cases generally? Cf. Henderson v. Norris, 258 F.3d 706 (8th Cir. 2001) (life sentence for first offense of delivery of .238 grams of cocaine base held cruel and unusual punishment).

The Canadian Supreme Court's proportionality test requires an assessment of the circumstances of the particular conduct involved in an individual case and the defendant's personal characteristics. A sentence would have to fall if it either "outraged decency" or was grossly disproportionate in some reasonably imaginable hypothetical situation. R. v. Goltz, [1991] S.C.R. 485.

In the International Criminal Court (ICC), the maximum penalties under the Statute of Rome are a term of 30 years or a life sentence; the latter must be justified in light of the "extreme gravity of the crime" and the personal circumstances of the defendant. The ICC's governing statute explicitly grants prosecutors and the convicted person the right to appeal "on the ground of disproportion between the crime and the sentence." Statute of Rome, Art. 81(2)(a). Should the Appeals Chamber find the sentence disproportionate, it may vary the sentence. Art. 83(3). What test, if any, should the ICC adopt in determining whether a sentence is disproportionate?

2. *Deference to the legislature.*   In the Supreme Court proportionality opinions, the Justices have emphasized their deference to legislative decisions. In *Ewing* Justices Scalia and Thomas concluded that federal courts should never inquire into the proportionality of noncapital offenses because this concern is purely a legislative issue. Nevertheless, state and federal courts still insist that they can engage in an abbreviated proportionality review. Is it appropriate for courts to defer substantially to the legislature in defining the Eighth Amendment? Would such deference be more justified if a sentencing commission developed the sentence range?

The Judicial Committee of the Privy Council rejected a constitutional challenge to a statute from the former Southern Rhodesia, which imposed a mandatory death sentence for assisting in an arson attempt. The Judicial Committee noted that "[it] can hardly be for the courts, unless clearly so empowered or directed to rule as to the necessity or propriety of particular legislation. The provision [barring inhuman or degrading punishment] enables the court to adjudicate as to whether some form or type or description of punishment, . . . is inhuman or degrading, but it does not enable the Court to declare an enactment imposing a punishment to be ultra vires on the ground that the court considers that the punishment laid down by the enactment is inappropriate or excessive for the particular offence." Runyowa v. R. [1967] A.C. 26 (P.C.). In a recent decision, the Privy Council questioned the authority of *Runyowa*, noting that the international jurisprudence on human rights was rudimentary at the time of the decision. Reyes v. R. [2002] 2 A.C. 235 (P.Q.).

3. *Multiple charges and the Eighth Amendment.* In Close v. People, 48 P.3d 528 (Colo. 2002), the Colorado court upheld a 60-year term for a teenager charged with multiple offenses arising from a single incident. In its review of consecutive sentences, the Colorado court relied on O'Neil v. Vermont, 144 U.S. 323 (1892), in which the Supreme Court analyzed the severity of a defendant's sentence in light of the number of crimes he had committed. The *Close* court concluded that a proportionality review can be applied only to each conviction, not to the sum of the consecutive prison terms imposed. This approach gives prosecutors room to increase the maximum available sentence by adding counts to the indictment, without running into Eighth Amendment problems. Typically, judges counter this prosecutorial power by imposing concurrent rather than consecutive sentences. Is it possible to craft a constitutional rule here that would still ordinarily allow a defendant who commits more offenses to receive a more severe punishment?

4. *Life is different?* In *Solem* and *Harmelin*, the defendants received life-without-parole terms. In *Miller*, the trial court refused to impose this sanction. The *Solem* Court contrasted the sentence facing the defendant with the life sentence in *Rummel*, which allowed for parole after 12 years. Should a life-without-parole term change the parameters of the proportionality review employed? In proportionality decisions, the courts frequently refer to the more searching proportionality review used in death cases, under the notion that "death is different." Does the impact of a life-without-parole sanction also justify a different approach?

Many countries in Latin America and Europe, including Portugal and Mexico, prohibit the imposition of life-without-parole sentences. They view such a penalty as violating human dignity and as inherently inhumane because it denies an individual the opportunity to rehabilitate herself. What purpose does the life-without-parole sentence serve? For an in-depth discussion of life imprisonment around the world, see Dirk van Zyl Smit, Taking Life Imprisonment Seriously in National and International Law (2002).

5. *Juveniles and proportionality.* In *Miller* a juvenile was the defendant; the court emphasized his age but stated explicitly that the defendant's youth alone would not have rendered the sentence disproportionate. A 1998 study indicates

that most U.S. courts refuse to consider a defendant's age when engaging in a proportionality analysis under the Eighth Amendment. See Wayne A. Logan, Proportionality and Punishment: Imposing Life Without Parole on Juveniles, 33 Wake Forest L. Rev. 681 (1998).

In State v. Green, 502 S.E.2d 819, 833-834 (N.C. 1998), the Supreme Court of North Carolina upheld a life sentence imposed on a 13-year-old repeat offender convicted of first-degree sexual offense, attempted first-degree rape, and first-degree burglary. It considered the sentence to comport with "evolving standards of decency" in light of public and legislative concern about violent juvenile crime. In addition, it found the sentence not excessive in the constitutional sense in light of the violent nature of the crime, the defendant's culpability, his prior record, and the potential maximum sentence of four years that could have been imposed under the juvenile system. Finally, the court addressed the question whether the sentence was "unusual," as the defendant was the only 13-year-old offender who was convicted and sentenced under the legislative scheme that mandated a life term under similar circumstances:

> The fact that a particular punishment is "unusual," in the sense that few defendants fall within its purview, is largely irrelevant to our inquiry. . . . This Court and the United States Supreme Court traditionally have not afforded separate treatment to the words "cruel" and "unusual," but have looked only to whether a particular punishment involves basic inhuman treatment. . . . The suggestion that an equally applicable punishment is rendered unconstitutional by virtue of the fact that few choose to commit the crime underlying it, or that only one of many who commit such crime is the one caught and convicted, does not fall within the bounds of any reasonable constitutional discourse.

6. *The jurisprudence of state courts.*   State courts have applied the *Harmelin* test under the Eighth Amendment to bar some disproportionate sentences. See Crosby v. State, 824 A.2d 894 (Del. 2003) (life sentence of 45-year fixed term for second degree forgery was excessive, even for defendant with prior felony convictions). It is more common for state courts to uphold a legislative choice of sanctions in the case at hand, even if they recognize that a proportionality challenge might succeed in theory. State v. Moss-Dwyer, 686 N.E.2d 109 (Ind. 1997) (recognizing possible proportionality challenges under state constitution, but refusing to declare a sentence disproportionate where statute made misinformation on a handgun permit application a greater crime than carrying a handgun without a license).

A few state courts have been willing to insist, under various provisions of their state constitutions, that the legislature select a punishment that is proportionate to the crime. The *Miller* court, for example, rested its decision solely on the Illinois constitution, without reaching the federal constitutional question. Whose standards — those of a state, of the nation, of a local community — should apply in determining what shocks the conscience?

Nonconstitutional limitations on imprisonment provide more meaningful day-to-day controls than do constitutional limitations. Sentencing guidelines, for example, set out presumptive sentencing ranges for specific offenses. While guideline regimes allow for departures, they require detailed justifications and are open to appellate challenges. Another statutory limitation on imprisonment is the federal safety valve program, which allows for the sentencing of low-level, nonviolent drug offenders to prison terms below the mandatory minimum. Other limitations may be imposed by state statutes mandating that certain offenders not be sentenced to prison. Among such legislation is the 2002 California referendum requiring drug treatment rather than imprisonment for first-time, nonviolent drug offenders. For discussion of a similar statute, see State v. DePiano, 926 P.2d 494 (Ariz. 1996) (despondent mother's unsuccessful attempt to commit suicide and infanticide by asphyxiation was punished by 34-year prison term; court reduced sentence under statute allowing reduction if "the punishment imposed is greater than under the circumstances of the case ought to be inflicted").

7. *Internal consistency: similar statutes, similar safety threats.*   In People v. Walden, 769 N.E.2d 928 (Ill. 2002), the court struck down a 15-year sentencing enhancement for the carrying of a firearm during an armed robbery as violating the proportionate penalties clause of the Illinois constitution. David Walden was charged with one count of armed robbery while in possession of a firearm. He challenged his sentence as disproportionate under the state constitution, because it punished him more severely than a related crime in the state code, armed violence predicated upon aggravated robbery. The appellate court reviewed the legislative history of the two provisions and concluded that they share a statutory purpose — the more severe punishment of violent crimes when committed with firearms:

> Having concluded that the two offenses share an identical statutory purpose, we next must determine whether one offense is more serious than the other. This is not a difficult inquiry, as armed violence predicated upon aggravated robbery is clearly the more serious offense. [Armed] violence predicated upon aggravated robbery . . . requires that the offender, while using or threatening the imminent use of force, inform the victim that he or she is presently armed with a firearm. Thus, armed robbery while in possession of a firearm may be committed while carrying a concealed firearm that is neither revealed nor even mentioned to the victim. . . .
>
> Our final inquiry, then, is whether armed robbery while in possession of a firearm is punished more or less severely than armed violence predicated upon aggravated robbery. [Armed] robbery while in possession of a firearm is punishable by 21 to 45 years in prison. Armed violence predicated upon aggravated robbery is a Class X felony punishable by either 10 to 30 or 15 to 30 years in prison, depending upon the type of firearm used in the offense. Thus, it is the less serious offense — armed robbery while in possession of a firearm — that is punished more severely. The 15-year enhancement for armed robbery while in possession of a firearm therefore violates the proportionate penalties clause of the Illinois Constitution and is unenforceable.

769 N.E.2d at 931-932. *Walden* is reminiscent of People v. Stewart (reprinted in Chapter 2), in which the Colorado court addressed an equal protection challenge to Stewart's conviction of reckless second-degree assault rather than vehicular assault, which carried a lesser sentence. The court denied the claim since it found a sufficient rational basis for distinguishing the offenses so as to justify the different penalties attached to them.

Should courts engage in a proportionality review of the internal consistency of state sentencing laws? How would you expect a state legislator to react to the *Walden* decision?

8. *Expanding on the prohibition of cruel and unusual punishments.*   Human rights law has borrowed heavily from U.S. legal principles, but the Eighth Amendment analogues have been drawn more broadly in the international arena. The International Covenant for Civil and Political Rights, which the United States has ratified, prohibits "cruel, inhuman or degrading treatment or punishment." The United States has taken a reservation to Art. 7, interpreting this provision to reach no further than the Fifth, Eighth, and Fourteenth Amendments. Article 3 of the European Convention on Human Rights prohibits "inhuman or degrading treatment or punishment." On their face, do these provisions differ with regard to proportionality of prison terms? How important should the drafters' intent be in reviewing sentences under these provisions?

9. *Proportionality analysis in extraditions.*   National courts have employed proportionality analysis to assess the penalty threatening an individual upon extradition. In 2002 the German courts, for example, rejected a Turkish extradition request based on a 1996 conviction for trafficking of .05 grams of heroin. The alleged offender was threatened with a sentence of three years and four months, which could be reduced to one year and four months upon good behavior. The court considered the penalty inappropriate because the defendant was a first offender and the Turkish authorities had waited five years to request extradition. If required to assess the proportionality of the penalty in extradition cases, courts frequently attempt to determine possible justifications for a particular sentence under the laws of the country requesting the extradition and then compare the sentence with penalties for comparable offenses in their home countries.

In a potential death penalty case involving extradition to the United States, the European Court of Human Rights held that a Council of Europe member state has "an inherent obligation not to extradite [where] the fugitive would be faced in the receiving State by a real risk of exposure to inhuman or degrading treatment or punishment" in violation of Article 3 of the European Convention on Human Rights. Soering v. United Kingdom, 11 Eur. H.R. Rep. 439, para. 88 (Eur. Ct. H.R. 1989). The court held that conditions on Virginia's death row (the so-called death row phenomenon) amounted to "inhuman or degrading treatment" under the convention. In other cases, the court has also applied the phrase "inhuman or degrading treatment or punishment" to prison sentences, depending on their length and conditions.

In 2002 the Mexican Supreme Court rejected extradition to the United States in cases in which the alleged offenders faced life-without-parole terms. Such sentences are prohibited under the Mexican constitution and therefore constitute a total barrier to extradition. How can U.S. prosecutors make successful extradition requests in cases in which the indictment charges offenses that carry life-without-parole as a sentencing option or as a mandatory sentence? Is it appropriate for national courts to hold the potential sentences of foreign countries as disproportionate under their own laws and therefore grounds for refusing to extradite?

=8=

Sentencing Outcomes: Nonprison Punishments

In the United States, the dominant criminal sanction appears to be imprisonment (see Chapter 7), but appearances can be deceiving: In reality, more criminal defendants receive nonprison sentences than prison sentences. Nevertheless, policy makers think (and speak) as if prison were the only penalty worth discussing, and much of the criminal justice system operates in an imprisonment monotone. Other countries and some U.S. jurisdictions, however, seek different options or operate under different punishment presumptions.

The terms "nonprison sanctions" and "alternatives to imprisonment" are revealing. Since imprisonment is frequently viewed as a default option, such sanctions appear credible only if they resemble prison in some way. Excellent examples are boot camp, which mimics prison, and home confinement.

The United Nations' Global Report on Crime and Justice distinguishes countries by the primary form of punishment they use. Some countries focus on imprisonment, others on fines, and still others on a combination of deprivation of liberty and probation. In most of the countries that responded to the UN survey, the fine is the most common noncustodial sentence. For example, more than 95 percent of Japanese offenders are assessed a fine. Noncustodial sanctions are little used in Latin America, Africa, and Asia — with the exception of Japan and South Korea — but are popular in Europe and North America.

The prevalence of noncustodial sanctions does not necessarily indicate a systematically low use of imprisonment. It may reflect a shift away from custody or an increase in the proportion of the population being criminally sanctioned. It may also be a response to other developments in the criminal justice arena, such as a focus on the risk certain offenders pose, increased opportunities to combine criminal with administrative sanctions, the development of new sentencing options, and the prosecution of new criminal actors such as organizations.

Noncustodial sanctions can serve a variety of purposes. Some sanctions, such as probation and annulment of licenses, aim to provide some degree of control and supervision over offenders, if less than imprisonment. Other sanctions, such as fines and confiscation, aim to punish without individual corporal control.

This chapter outlines the use of noncustodial sanctions in the United States. The first part addresses the dominant nonprison sanctions of probation and fines. The second part discusses modern alternative sanctions which have received much public attention but still relatively little use. The third section considers a set of punishments labeled "collateral sanctions" that are applied in addition to other sanctions, including imprisonment.

A. TRADITIONAL ALTERNATIVES

The most common and well-established nonprison sanctions are fines and probation. Much of the public debate over punishment turns on the rare but severe and highly symbolic imposition of capital punishment and the dominant coin of the realm — imprisonment. Yet most criminal sentences are some combination of fines and probationary sentences. The use of fines, both alone but especially in conjunction with prison or other sanctions, is far greater than public debate and indeed much of the scholarly literature would suggest. Even among felons, straight probation (with no time in jail or prison) is used in about one-third of all cases.

Sanctions often have several parts, but the public only takes note of the most severe aspects to the punishment. Of all felons sentenced in 2000 to either incarceration or probation, 39 percent were also given nonprison sanctions, including payment of a fine or victim restitution, drug treatment, or community service. Some fine was imposed on at least 25 percent of all convicted felons. See Bureau of Justice Statistics, Felony Sentences in State Courts, 2000 (NCJ 198821, June 2003).

For all sanctions, one key but often implicit issue is the purpose of punishment that the sanction is intended to address. When can fines and probation serve purposes similar to prison — that is, when can they "replace" imprisonment? How do political considerations limit the use of nonprison sanctions?

1. Fines

Fines have been used extensively in some European countries, where the amount of the penalty is keyed to the type of offense and the offender's income. This approach has not caught on in the United States, but the use of fines here has been increasing generally, even though judges often express reluctance to levy them. Like many European countries, the United States has also seen a steady increase in statutory or guideline requirements for restitution by criminal offenders to their victims. Only in the United States are offenders being asked to pay for some or all of the costs of punishment, though it is not clear how often such fines are in fact imposed or paid.

Some of the recurring issues with fines are whether they are fair to the poor and whether they impose a proportional punishment on either the poor or the rich. In the following case, the Mississippi Supreme Court addresses one aspect of these issues.

Mary Ann Moody v. State
716 So. 2d 562 (Miss. 1998)

BANKS, J.

Here we consider the question of whether a standard practice of extracting a set fine from persons accused of writing bad checks on the pain of suffering a full criminal prosecution for failure to do so comports with the Equal Protection Clause of the Fourteenth Amendment to the Constitution of the United States. We answer that it does not. . . .

On or about October 12, 1991, Mary Ann Moody wrote a check to the order of City Salvage for $123.89. The check was written in exchange for two doors for Moody's mother's house. The check was returned to City Salvage for "non-sufficient funds." On February 24, 1993, she was indicted by a Jones County Grand Jury, for the crime of False Pretense. Moody was appointed counsel as an indigent defendant. After indictment the District Attorney's office assessed a levy of $500 plus restitution. Moody was given the option of paying a $500 fine plus restitution and having the case nolle prossed, or not paying the fine and being subjected to prosecution. Jeanne Jefcoat of the district attorney's office testified that this fine is imposed automatically once a defendant is indicted. . . . Moody testified that she could not pay all the fine, restitution and other costs at one time. Moody's motion to dismiss the action was denied and the case proceeded to trial.

. . . She was subsequently convicted of the crime of false pretense [and sentenced to three years in the Mississippi Department of Corrections and fined $1,000, which was ordered one year suspended and $500 suspended] and appeals, raising a violation of the Fourteenth Amendment to the Constitution of the United States as her sole ground on appeal.

Moody claims that the district attorney's office lacks statutory or constitutional authority to automatically impose a set fine of $500 on all defendants indicted under the Mississippi Bad Check Law. Furthermore, she claims that such a fine violates an indigent's right to equal protection under the Fourteenth Amendment. The State argues that the fine is merely a plea bargain, and as such is in the discretion of the district attorney. This is a case of first impression before this Court. We are unable to find any cases directly on point in any other jurisdiction. . . .

In Bearden v. Georgia, 461 U.S. 660 (1983), the United States Supreme Court considered whether a sentencing court can revoke a defendant's probation for failure to pay the imposed fine and restitution. The *Bearden* Court stated:

> This Court has long been sensitive to the treatment of indigents in our criminal justice system. Over a quarter-century ago, Justice Black declared that "[t]here can be no equal justice where the kind of trial a man gets depends on the amount of money he has."

Bearden, 461 U.S. at 664 (quoting Griffin v. Illinois, 351 U.S. 12 (1956) (plurality opinion)). The Court held that before revocation of an indigent's probation, the court must inquire into the reasons for failure to pay. In holding such, the Court opined:

> If the probationer willfully refused to pay or failed to make sufficient bona fide efforts legally to acquire the resources to pay, the court may revoke probation and sentence the defendant to imprisonment within the authorized range of its sentencing authority. If the probationer could not pay despite sufficient bona fide efforts to acquire the resources to do so, the court must consider alternative measures of punishment other than imprisonment. Only if alternative measures are not adequate to meet the State's interests in punishment and deterrence may the court imprison a probationer who has made sufficient bona fide efforts to pay. To do otherwise would deprive the probationer of his conditional freedom simply because, through no fault of his own, he cannot pay the fine. Such a deprivation would be contrary to the fundamental fairness required by the Fourteenth Amendment.

See also Tate v. Short, 401 U.S. 395 (1971) (holding that a State cannot convert a fine imposed under a fine-only statute into a jail term solely because the defendant is indigent and cannot immediately pay the fine in full).

Moody cites Cassibry v. State, 453 So. 2d 1298 (Miss. 1984), where this Court held that an indigent may not be incarcerated because he is financially unable to comply with an otherwise lawfully imposed sentence of a fine. *Cassibry* is distinguishable in that, the defendant had failed to pay a fine and was subsequently imprisoned for failure to pay the fine while in this case, Moody was sentenced to an appropriate statutory prison term for her crime. But see Lee v. State, 457 So. 2d 920 (Miss. 1984) (stating *Cassibry* requires consideration of statutory alternatives to imprisonment for indigents financially unable to pay a fine). . . .

In a case similar to this one, the Oklahoma Criminal Court of Appeals considered whether a defendant was deprived of equal protection in plea bargaining. Gray v. State, 650 P.2d 880 (Okla. Crim. App. 1982). In *Gray* the defendant claimed that he was denied an opportunity to plea bargain because he was unable to contribute to a special community relations fund. The *Gray* court opined:

> The recognition of plea bargaining as an essential component of the administration of justice, however, does not elevate it to a constitutional right. That is not to say, that a prosecutor can accept or refuse plea negotiations in a way that discriminates against defendants on account of their race, religion, economic status or other arbitrary classification.

The court found that there was no violation of the defendant's equal protection rights, because he did not attempt to seek a plea bargain.

The State argues that Moody is confusing this fine with a plea bargain. There is no constitutional right to a plea bargain. Allman v. State, 571 So. 2d 244, 254 (Miss. 1990). The State argues that since there is no constitutional right to a plea bargain there can be no violation in this case. Furthermore, the State claims that since the fine or plea offer is offered to everyone who is indicted, there can be no equal protection violation, because it is treating everyone the same.

The record clearly indicates that after a defendant is indicted under the Bad Check law, an automatic $500 plus restitution is charged to drop the prosecution. The amount is due immediately. The defendant then has the option of paying the $500 and have the indictment nolle prossed or proceeding to trial.

Thus, one who is unable to pay will always be in a position of facing a felony conviction and jail time, while those with adequate resources will not. The automatic nature of the fine is what makes it discriminating to the poor, in that only the poor will face jail time. We hold that an indigent's equal protection rights are violated when all potential defendants are offered one way to avoid prosecution and that one way is to pay a fine, and there is no determination as to an individual's ability to pay such a fine. Subjecting one to a jail term merely because he cannot afford to pay a fine, due to no fault of his own, is unconstitutional.

Additionally, we note that this procedure does not involve a plea bargain at all because the only charge is nolle prosequi. There is no plea at all. What and all that happens is that a $500 fee is extracted in order to avoid prosecution. Thus the scheme is both procedurally and constitutionally flawed.

[W]e conclude that the only way to put Moody on a footing roughly equivalent to those able to purchase a nolle prosequi is to remand for new sentencing in which the trial court can withhold adjudication and place her on probation requiring restitution plus reasonable efforts to pay a reasonable fine and costs. This remedy does not restrict the trial judges where one complains of indigency. There are methods in use today which allow for indigent status where the penalty to be imposed is a fine. These include working out a payment schedule which is appropriate to the means of the offender. It is a proper solution for this case, granting Moody relief from an improper and unconstitutional practice subjecting her to disparate treatment based upon her indigency. In the future, it is to be hoped that this unconstitutional scheme will be abandoned and the matter of plea bargains will be handled in a proper manner which comports with the right to equal protection of the laws.

For the foregoing reasons, this matter is reversed and remanded to the circuit court for re-sentencing.

McRae, J., concurring in part and dissenting in part.

The Jones County District Attorney's approach to enforcing the Mississippi Worthless Check Law by charging a fine to avoid prosecution and incarcerating those who cannot pay discriminates against the poor in violation of the equal protection provisions of the United States Constitution and the Mississippi Constitution and offends the prohibition against imprisonment for civil debt found in art. 3, §30 of the Mississippi Constitution. It further allows the District Attorney's office to exercise powers well in excess of those afforded it by statute pursuant to the directive of art. 6, §174 of the Mississippi Constitution. The root of the problem, however, lies in our statutory framework that subjects one who "bounces" a check to criminal penalties. To remand Mrs. Moody's case for re-sentencing and merely "hope" that the practices used in her situation will be abandoned does nothing to remedy the larger problem.

Miss. Code Ann. §97-19-67(1)(d)(1994) sets the penalty for writing a bad check in excess of $100, regardless of whether a first or second offense, *upon conviction,* at a fine of not less than $100 and not more than $1000, *or* imprisonment for not more than three years *or* both, *in the discretion of the court.* Jeanne Jefcoat, the Worthless Check Director for the Jones County District Attorney's Office, however, testified that once an individual has been indicted by the grand jury for writing a bad check, he must immediately pay a set $500 fine, the amount of the check and a variety of fees, or else face trial. She stated that Mrs. Moody was told that to avoid prosecution, she would have to pay more than $800: the $123.89 check, the $500 fine, $163.50 court costs, a $40 processing fee levied by the District Attorney's Office and a $10 returned check fee. Thus, Mrs. Moody was fined before she was convicted and in essence, promised that if she paid the fine and costs, she wouldn't be convicted. Contrary to the State's argument, this cannot be construed as a "standard" plea bargain in any sense merely because Mrs. Moody was offered the opportunity to pay. . . .

Imprisonment may be an appropriate remedy for a defendant who refuses or neglects to pay a fine he can afford, or even when collection is unsuccessful despite the defendant's reasonable efforts to make payment. However, the imprisonment of an indigent defendant who cannot pay a fine imposed to avoid conviction is a violation of the fourteenth amendment to the United States Constitution as well as to art. 3, §30 of the Mississippi Constitution. . . .

Debtor's prison was abolished long ago. Our statutory system, nevertheless, allows for imprisonment of one who cannot pay all of the fines that may arise from "bouncing" a check. Further, while they may pursue actions for false pretenses, District Attorneys do not have the authority under our State Constitution or . . . Code . . . either to collect civil debts or to use criminal statutes to coerce payment of those debts and any fees and penalties which also might accrue. Moreover, the power to render fines and judgments belongs with the courts and not the District Attorney's Office. Accordingly, I do not think that the majority has gone far enough by recognizing only the fourteenth amendment problems or "hoping" that problematic debt collection practices are abandoned.

NOTES

1. *The use of fines.*   Straight fines (fines in the absence of other sanctions) are used most often for misdemeanants and other more minor offenders. Some states prohibit the use of fines for certain types of offenses. While only .5 percent of all those who committed felonies received a fine-only sentence, 26.8 percent of all misdemeanants did — with more than half of all traffic offenders receiving such a sentence. Fines are often only a part of the sentence imposed: They are used in about 21 percent of state felony cases, and 80 percent of all lower-court sentences include fines. The average fines in state courts are lower than $100. Straight fines are relatively uncommon in the federal system. In federal court 4 percent of all offenders sentenced between October 1, 1999 and September 30, 2000, received a fine-only sentence. Fines are also a component of other sentences; 13 percent of all convicted federal offenders are fined. The federal sentencing guidelines mandate that the court impose a fine unless the offender shows that he is unable to pay a fine and it is unlikely that that situation will change.

2. *Who gets fined?*   Men are more likely to be fined than women; whites are more likely to be fined than blacks or Hispanics; employed offenders are significantly more likely to be fined than unemployed offenders; older offenders are more likely to be fined than younger offenders; nondrug offenders are more likely to be fined than drug offenders. In urban settings fines are imposed less

frequently than in rural or suburban communities. In sum, fines are more likely to be used for low-level offenses and low-risk offenders, with judges considering defendants' actual or perceived wealth and income.

3. *Fines in white collar and corporate cases.*   The largest fines imposed are generally in antitrust prosecutions. The largest fine ever obtained in a federal criminal case was $500 million in the prosecution of an international vitamin cartel. Such fines are paid into the federal Crime Victims Fund and available for disbursement to crime victims and training programs the following year.

4. *Restitution.*   In more than one-third of the states, courts are statutorily required to order restitution unless there are compelling or extraordinary circumstances to the contrary. Other states allow broad exceptions. More than a dozen states require courts to state on the record the reasons for failing to order restitution or for ordering only partial restitution. Some states have enacted specific directives to order restitution to victims of particular offenses.

Restitution is awarded for crime-related expenses incurred by the victim or, in homicide cases, the victim's family; it includes medical and counseling expenses, lost wages, and lost or damaged property. Some states permit the award of future damages. Nevertheless, victims only infrequently receive restitution. The reasons include failure to request restitution, inability to demonstrate or calculate loss, the court's opinion that restitution is inappropriate in light of other penalties, and the defendant's inability to pay. Most states require courts to consider the defendant's financial resources and obligations when awarding restitution. Some states are beginning to move away from this requirement, instead merely considering the defendant's ability to pay when setting the payment schedule.

In 1996 Congress enacted the Mandatory Victims Restitution Act (MVRA) which mandates restitution to be ordered in full in certain cases to each victim, regardless of the offender's economic situation. In contrast to fines, restitution is not meant to be punitive but rather to make the victim whole. Despite the MVRA's mandate, in fiscal year 1997 of 48,000 federal offenders only about 20 percent were ordered to pay restitution while about 19 percent were ordered to pay fines. Factors courts used in determining whether an offender was sentenced to restitution included the offense of conviction, length and type of sentence imposed, and offender characteristics such as sex, race, education, and citizenship. But the most important factor was the judicial district or circuit in which the offender was sentenced. General Accounting Office, Federal Courts: Differences Exist in Ordering Fines and Restitution (May 1999).

The use of fines as the sole or primary sanction for offenses, both violent and nonviolent, raises two central questions. First, when can fines satisfy a sufficient mix of purposes to substitute for or improve on the use of imprisonment, and second, can fines be made relatively similar in impact for offenders of widely varying wealth? A related concern is whether people with more access to legitimate funds through family and friends will just "pay their way" out of a sanction, while poorer offenders may be induced to commit further crimes to pay their fines. Consider whether these issues are addressed in the following materials.

Day Fines, Sally T. Hillsman
Intermediate Sanctions in Overcrowded Times
(Michael Tonry and Kate Hamilton eds., 1995)

Day fines — fine sentences in which the amount is set in proportion to both the seriousness of the offense and the financial resources of the offender — have long been the sentence of choice in northern Europe for most offenses. The name derives from the practice of using the offender's daily income as the base for setting the fine amount.

Systematic day-fine systems typically rely upon flexible, written guidelines. They are increasingly attractive to American judges, prosecutors, and other criminal justice policymakers who look for a wider range of intermediate penalties that can be scaled to provide appropriate punishment for offenses of varying gravity, while reserving imprisonment for violent and predatory offenses.

The fine has always been an attractive sentence in American courts, and it is used more widely than is generally recognized. The fine's advantages are well known. Fines are unmistakably punitive; they deprive offenders of ill-gotten gain; they are inexpensive to administer; and they provide revenue to cover such things as the cost of collection or compensation to victims. Recent research has supported their deterrent impact: fines are associated with lower rates of recidivism than probation or jail for offenders with equivalent criminal records and current offenses.

Fines have not been used in the United States, particularly as a sole penalty, as frequently or for as wide a range of offenses as in European countries, which share many of our sentencing principles. In Germany, for example, 81 percent of adult offenses and 73 percent of crimes of violence are punished solely by fines. In England, 38 percent of offenses equivalent to our felonies and 39 percent of violent offenses result in fines.

A major impediment in American courts has been the widespread view that poor offenders cannot pay fines and that affluent offenders who do so are buying their way out of more punitive sanctions. Whatever truth there is in this view, however, stems largely from American use of "tariff" systems to set fine amounts. Tariff systems use informal "going rates" to guide judges in setting amounts. Because tariff systems tend to equate equity with consistency, they generally result in fines keyed to the lowest common economic denominator. This tends to limit judges' ability to adjust fines to an individual offender's financial means and to restrict their use of fines to less serious crimes or first offenders.

In contrast, day fines provide courts with greater capacity to vary fine amounts in a systematic and principled way. Day-fine systems accomplish this by a two-step process. First, the judge sentences an offender to a given number of fine units (e.g., 10, 15, or 90), which reflects the appropriate degree of punishment. Courts that rely on day fines have developed informal guidelines or benchmarks that suggest what number (or range) of units is appropriate for crimes of differing gravity.

The second step is to determine the monetary value of these units. Courts typically develop a rough but standardized method for calculating the proportion of a defendant's daily income that they view to be a "fair share" for the purposes of fining.

Using information routinely available from the police, a pretrial agency, probation, or (most often) the defendant, the judge will estimate the defendant's daily income and calculate the day-fine unit value. Multiplication of the number of units by this unit value produces the fine amount.

Since 1988, a day-fine system has been operating successfully in the Criminal Court of Richmond County, Staten Island, New York. A day-fine program has also been running successfully for over a year in the Maricopa Superior Court in Phoenix, Arizona. In Milwaukee, the day fine was introduced with considerable success as a strategy to reduce high levels of default among low-income offenders. Day-fine projects are under way in Oregon, Iowa, and Connecticut as part of a national demonstration project on "structured fines" sponsored by the Bureau of Justice Assistance. Numerous other jurisdictions are beginning to experiment with the concept, sometimes with encouragement from their state legislatures. In California, for example, legislation authorizes implementation of day-fine pilots.

Fines Reduce Use of Prison Sentences in Germany, Thomas Weigend
Intermediate Sanctions in Overcrowded Times
(Michael Tonry and Kate Hamilton eds., 1995)

Between 1968 and 1989, the former West Germany greatly reduced the proportion of convicted offenders sentenced to prison. In 1968, roughly a quarter of convicted offenders were sentenced to imprisonment. Two years later, the size of that group had dropped from 136,000 to 42,000, and the percentage of convicted offenders who were imprisoned had fallen from 24 percent to 7 percent. In 1989 (the latest year for which data are available), only 33,000 persons, less than 6 percent of adults convicted in West Germany, were sent directly to prison. . . .

The remarkable decline in prison use is due to a determined assault on use of short-term imprisonment. At the [start of the twentieth century], more than 50 percent of offenders received prison sentences of three months' duration or less. Legislation passed in 1921 obliged the courts to impose fines instead of short prison terms whenever the purpose of punishment could as well be achieved by a fine. Even so, the portion of short prison sentences among all prison sentences remained high; 83 percent of offenders sentenced to imprisonment in 1968 received sentences of six months or less. By that time, the German legislature had embraced the idea that short-term imprisonment does more harm than good: it disrupts the offender's ties with his family, job, and friends, introduces him into the prison subculture, and stigmatizes him for the rest of his life, but does not allow sufficient time for promising rehabilitative measures. Moreover, the data on the deterrent effectiveness of short-term imprisonment were inconclusive at best.

As a consequence, the German legislature in 1970 enacted section 47, sub. 1 of the Penal Code: "The court shall impose imprisonment below six months only if special circumstances concerning the offense or the offender's personality make the imposition of a prison sentence indispensable for reforming the offender or for defending the legal order." That amendment meant, in effect, that prison sentences below six months could be imposed only under exceptional

FIGURE 1
Criminal Sanctions, 1968 and 1989

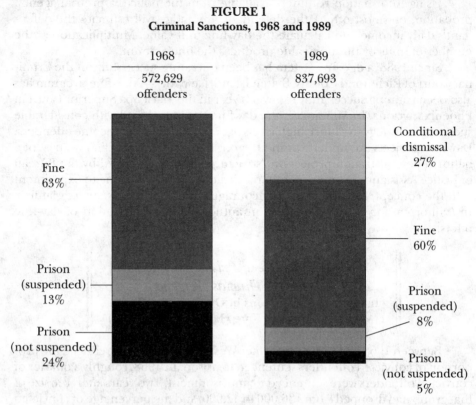

Sources: Statistisches Bundesamt, Fachserie A., Reihe 9: Rechtspflege 1968, p. 120; Statistisches Bundesamt, Fachserie 10, Reihe 3: Strafverfolgung 1989, p. 42; Statistisches Bundesamt Staatsanwaltschaften 1989, p. 14.

circumstances for purposes of rehabilitation or general prevention. The number of such sentences dropped dramatically from 184,000 (1968) to 56,000 (1970); after some ups and downs, that figure reached a low of 48,000 in 1989 (and many of these were suspended).

At the same time, the German legislature extended the possibility of suspending short-term prison sentences (suspension being the German equivalent of probation). . . .

The court can combine suspension with various conditions and restrictions, including the duty to make restitution to the victim or to pay a sum of money to the state or to a charitable organization. . . .

German courts have made use of the suspension option with consistently increasing frequency. In 1968, the year before the reform, only 36 percent of prison sentences were suspended. By 1979, that portion had climbed to 65 percent, and it has not significantly changed since then (1989 — 67 percent). Prison sentences of six months or less have been suspended even more liberally (1989 — 77 percent). Revocations of suspension have diminished despite the more generous use of suspension. Whereas 46 percent of suspensions were revoked in 1986, less than a third (29 percent) were revoked in 1989.

For minor offenses, German law since 1975 offers an additional option of informal sanctioning. According to section 153a of the Code of Criminal

FIGURE 2
Number of Persons Held in German Prisons, 1968–1989
(excluding pretrial detainees)

Sources: Statistisches Bundesamt, Fachserie A. Reihe 9: Rechtspflege 1968, 1971, 1973; Statistisches Bundesamt, Fachserie 10, Reihe 1: Ausgewählte Zahlen für die Rechtspflege 1984, 1988, 1989.

Procedure, either the public prosecutor or the court can "invite" a suspect to pay a sum of money to the state, the victim, or a charitable organization in exchange for dismissal of the criminal prosecution. The theory of this quasi-sanction is that the suspect, by making the payment, eliminates the public interest in prosecuting the minor offense. The payment neither requires a formal admission of guilt nor implies a criminal conviction, but the (presumed) offender must pay an amount of money roughly equivalent to the fine that might be imposed if he were convicted. The use of this procedural option has greatly increased since its inception; prosecutors and courts employ it not only in petty cases but also for sanctioning fairly serious, especially economic, offenses without trial. Taking the quasi-sanction of section 153a into account, the distribution of criminal sanctions in Germany before and after the reforms of 1970 and 1975 is shown in figure 1.

The de-emphasis of nonsuspended short prison sentences and the introduction of conditional dismissal produced a marked shift from custodial sentences (which, even in 1968, had a comparatively low incidence) to monetary sanctions. One might expect this shift to have led to a proportional depletion of German prisons. Curiously, that has failed to occur. Figure 2 shows the numbers of persons (excluding pretrial detainees) held in German prisons on March 31 of selected years.

[T]here are rational explanations for this development. First, the overall number of convicted offenders has increased, though not dramatically, from 573,000 (1968) to 609,000 (1989). More important, those who receive nonsuspended prison sentences tend to receive longer sentences than before: within fifteen years, the share of lengthy sentences (two to fifteen years) among all nonsuspended prison sentences increased from 9 percent (1974) to 15 percent. This change may be due to the increase in drug-related offenses, which tend to draw heavy sentences.

Moreover, the initial imposition of a noncustodial sentence does not necessarily mean that the offender can avoid prison, since about one third of suspended sentences are revoked (usually due to the commission of a new offense). Offenders who receive fines can be sent to prison for nonpayment. Under German law, nonpayment can transform a fine into a prison term; the state need not show that the offender willfully refused to pay although he had the means to do so (section 43, Penal Code). Although only 6-7 percent of fined offenders eventually serve a prison term because of nonpayment, this group, due to the large absolute numbers involved, imposes a heavy burden on the corrections system: each year approximately 30,000 such persons enter prison.

In recent years, the German states have increasingly attempted to reduce that number by offering destitute offenders an alternative to prison. They can enter community service programs and thereby work off the fine instead of "sitting it off." These programs, though reaching only a limited number of offenders, have been described as fairly successful, especially when they are adequately staffed and organized. . . .

NOTES

1. *Day fines.*   The underlying concept of day fines is that "punishment by a fine should be proportionate to the seriousness of the offense and should have roughly similar impact (in terms of economic sting) on persons with differing financial resources who are convicted of the same offense." Bureau of Justice Assistance, How to Use Structured Fines (Day Fines) as an Intermediate Sanction (NCJ 156242, 1996). The concept was first introduced in Sweden in the 1920s and then adopted in other Scandinavian and European countries. In Germany structured fines are used as the sole sanction for three-quarters of all offenders convicted of property crimes and two-thirds of offenders convicted of assaults. In the United States the first experiment with structured fines began on Staten Island, New York, in 1988. More than a half-dozen U.S. jurisdictions have tried structured fine systems experimentally in the meantime. Why has the concept not (yet) taken off nationally?

2. *Structuring day fines.*   Day fines present structural and policy challenges. First the court must determine the number of fine units for each offense, based on offense seriousness. Then the court sets the dollar amount by multiplying the number of fine units by a portion of the defendant's daily income, subject to adjustment for taxes, dependents, and special circumstances. Both determinations — the relative seriousness of offenses and calculations of relative ability to pay — involve multiple policy choices. How should courts treat unemployed offenders? How should they calculate day fines on offenders working in the shadow economy, engaged in legal but untaxed activity?

3. *Constitutional limitations on fines.*   The Eighth Amendment to the Constitution prohibits "excessive fines." The provision's history can be traced back to

the English Magna Carta, which gave judges the opportunity to overrule excessive penalties. In recent years the clause has been used most frequently to challenge punitive damage awards in civil cases as well as civil and criminal forfeitures, as discussed in more detail in Chapter 10. See, e.g., United States v. Bajakajian, 524 U.S. 321 (1998) (amount forfeited must be proportionate to the criminal offense); Austin v. United States, 509 U.S. 602 (1993). Might fines in criminal cases constitute less of an Eighth Amendment question of absolute proportionality than an equal protection issue, given their varying impact depending on a person's resources?

4. *Nonprison sanctions and crime rates.* Do countries adopt nonprison sanctions only at times of decreasing crime (or decreasing fear of crime)? Note that the emphasis on fines described by Weigend occurred during a time of increasing crime rates.

> [O]fficial sentencing policy in Germany has responded in an anticyclical fashion by discouraging the imposition of prison sentences in the face of a growing crime rate. . . . German policies, and the faithful implementation of their directives by prosecutors and courts, . . . led to a "cushioning" of the crime wave of the 1970s. A greater percentage of offenses than before were resolved without conviction, and potential overcrowding of prisons was avoided by increased use of fines and suspended sentences. The crime wave ebbed after 1983, independent of any action or inaction on the part of criminal justice policymakers.

To what extent have concerns about the negative impact of short-term prison sentences (less than six months) driven the introduction of day fines in Germany? Current social science research in Europe indicates that such short prison terms do not have the feared negative impact, and some countries are moving back toward the imposition of short prison sentences.

May fines be viewed as categorically insufficient for some types of offenders and offenses? The Department of Justice, for example, has indicated that for high-level corporate officials involved in white-collar crime, prison is the only appropriate sanction because of its deterrent value, stigmatizing effect, and ability to highlight the seriousness of the offense. See, e.g., James B. Comey Jr., The Genesis of the Sentencing Provisions of the Sarbanes-Oxley Act, "Are We Getting Really Tough on White-Collar Crime?" Hearing Before the Subcomm. on Crime and Drugs, S. Judiciary Comm. (June 19, 2002), pt. 1, 15 Fed. Sentencing Rep. 234 (2002).

2. Probation

Probation, an outgrowth of the belief in rehabilitation, emerged during the second half of the nineteenth century. Probationary sentences typically release the offender into the community after sentencing but restrict the offender's freedom and actions. Usually a probation officer is assigned to supervise the offender. Probationary sentences are by far the most common type of criminal sanction imposed. At the end of 2001, almost 4 million adults were on probation in the United States. Slightly more than half of them had been convicted of a felony, the others of misdemeanors and infractions. One-quarter of them were

drug offenders; 18 percent of them had been convicted of driving while intoxicated.

Probationary sentences involve two closely related issues: first, what are acceptable conditions of probation and second, what are the procedures and consequences for violation of those conditions?

a.   Probationary Conditions

The following case explores the foundations and limits of probationary
conditions. Consider whether each judge's gender might have affected his or her
view of the condition at issue.

|| ***State v. David Oakley*** ||
|| **629 N.W.2d 200 (Wis. 2001)** ||

WILCOX, J.
[W]e must decide whether as a condition of probation, a father of nine
children, who has intentionally refused to pay child support, can be required to
avoid having another child, unless he shows that he can support that child and
his current children. We conclude that in light of Oakley's ongoing victimization
of his nine children and extraordinarily troubling record manifesting his disregard for the law, this anomalous condition — imposed on a convicted felon facing the far more restrictive and punitive sanction of prison — is not overly broad
and is reasonably related to Oakley's rehabilitation. Simply put, because Oakley
was convicted of intentionally refusing to pay child support — a felony in Wisconsin — and could have been imprisoned for six years, which would have eliminated his right to procreate altogether during those six years, this probation
condition, which infringes on his right to procreate during his term of probation, is not invalid under these facts. Accordingly, we hold that the circuit court
did not erroneously exercise its discretion. . . .

David Oakley (Oakley), the petitioner, was initially charged with intentionally refusing to pay child support for his nine children he has fathered with
four different women. The State subsequently charged Oakley with seven counts
of intentionally refusing to provide child support as a repeat offender. His repeat offender status stemmed from intimidating two witnesses in a child abuse
case — where one of the victims was his own child. . . .

Oakley . . . entered into [a] plea agreement in which he agreed to enter a
no contest plea to three counts of intentionally refusing to support his children
and have the other four counts read-in for sentencing. . . . The State, in turn,
agreed that in exchange for his no contest plea, it would cap its sentencing recommendation to a total of six years on all counts. Oakley, however, was free to
argue for a different sentence.

Oakley had paid no child support and there were arrears in excess of
$25,000. Highlighting Oakley's consistent and willful disregard for the law and
his obligations to his children, the State argued that Oakley should be sentenced
to six years in prison. . . . Oakley, in turn, asked for the opportunity to maintain
full-time employment, provide for his children, and make serious payment
towards his arrears.

After taking into account Oakley's ability to work and his consistent disregard of the law and his obligations to his children, Judge Hazlewood observed that "if Mr. Oakley had paid something, had made an earnest effort to pay anything within his remote ability to pay, we wouldn't be sitting here," nor would the State argue for six years in prison. But Judge Hazlewood also recognized that "if Mr. Oakley goes to prison, he's not going to be in a position to pay any meaningful support for these children." Therefore, even though Judge Hazlewood acknowledged that Oakley's "defaults, are obvious, consistent, and inexcusable," he decided against sentencing Oakley to six years in prison . . . , as the State had advocated. Instead, Judge Hazlewood sentenced Oakley to three years in prison on the first count, imposed and stayed an eight-year term on the two other counts, and imposed a five-year term of probation consecutive to his incarceration. Judge Hazlewood then imposed the condition at issue here: while on probation, Oakley cannot have any more children unless he demonstrates that he has the ability to support them and that he is supporting the children he already has. After sentencing, Oakley filed for postconviction relief contesting this condition. . . .

Refusal to pay child support by so-called "deadbeat parents" has fostered a crisis with devastating implications for our children. Of those single parent households with established child support awards or orders, approximately one-third did not receive any payment while another one-third received only partial payment. For example, in 1997, out of $26,400,000,000 awarded by a court order to custodial mothers, only $15,800,000,000 was actually paid, amounting to a deficit of $10,600,000,000. These figures represent only a portion of the child support obligations that could be collected if every custodial parent had a support order established. Single mothers disproportionately bear the burden of nonpayment as the custodial parent. On top of the stress of being a single parent, the nonpayment of child support frequently presses single mothers below the poverty line. In fact, 32.1% of custodial mothers were below the poverty line in 1997, in comparison to only 10.7% of custodial fathers. . . .

The effects of the nonpayment of child support on our children are particularly troubling. In addition to engendering long-term consequences such as poor health, behavioral problems, delinquency and low educational attainment, inadequate child support is a direct contributor to childhood poverty. And childhood poverty is all too pervasive in our society. Over 12 million or about one out of every six children in our country lives in poverty. . . . Child support — when paid — on average amounts to over one-quarter of a poor child's family income. There is little doubt that the payment of child support benefits poverty-stricken children the most. Enforcing child support orders thus has surfaced as a major policy directive in our society.

In view of the suffering children must endure when their noncustodial parent intentionally refuses to pay child support, it is not surprising that the legislature has attached severe sanctions to this crime. . . . The legislature has amended this statute so that intentionally refusing to pay child support is now punishable by up to five years in prison.

But Wisconsin law is not so rigid as to mandate the severe sanction of incarceration as the only means of addressing a violation of §948.22(2). In sentencing, a Wisconsin judge can take into account a broad array of factors, including the gravity of the offense and need for protection of the public and potential victims. Other factors — concerning the convicted individual — that a judge can consider include:

> the past record of criminal offenses; any history of undesirable behavior patterns; the defendant's personality, character and social traits; the results of a presentence investigation; the vicious or aggravated nature of the crime; the degree of defendant's culpability; the defendant's demeanor at trial; the defendant's age, educational background and employment record; the defendant's remorse, repentance and cooperativeness; the defendant's need for close rehabilitative control; the rights of the public; and the length of pretrial detention.

After considering all these factors, a judge may decide to forgo the severe punitive sanction of incarceration and address the violation with the less restrictive alternative of probation coupled with specific conditions. Wisconsin Stat. §973.09(1)(a) provides:

> [I]f a person is convicted of a crime, the court, by order, may withhold sentence or impose sentence under s. 973.15 and stay its execution, and in either case place the person on probation to the department for a stated period, stating in the order the reasons therefor. The court may impose any conditions which appear to be reasonable and appropriate.

The statute, then, grants a circuit court judge broad discretion in fashioning a convicted individual's conditions of probation. As we have previously observed, "[t]he theory of the probation statute is to rehabilitate the defendant and protect society without placing the defendant in prison. To accomplish this theory, the circuit court is empowered by Wis. Stat. §973.09(1)(a) to fashion the terms of probation to meet the rehabilitative needs of the defendant." While rehabilitation is the goal of probation, judges must also concern themselves with the imperative of protecting society and potential victims. On this score, we have explained:

> [Probation] involves a prediction by the sentencing court society will not be endangered by the convicted person not being incarcerated. This is risk that the legislature has empowered the courts to take in the exercise of their discretion. . . .
> If the convicted criminal is thus to escape the more severe punishment of imprisonment for his wrongdoing, society and the potential victims of his antisocial tendencies must be protected.

State v. Evans, 252 N.W.2d 664, 666 (Wis. 1977). Thus, when a judge allows a convicted individual to escape a prison sentence and enjoy the relative freedom of probation, he or she must take reasonable judicial measures to protect society and potential victims from future wrongdoing. To that end — along with the goal of rehabilitation — the legislature has seen fit to grant circuit court judges broad discretion in setting the terms of probation.

[Judges] agree that judges should not abuse their discretion by imposing probation conditions on convicted individuals that reflect only their own idiosyncrasies. Instead, they should use their discretion in setting probation conditions to further the objective of rehabilitation and protect society and potential victims from future wrongdoing. . . .

In the present case, the record indicates that Judge Hazlewood was familiar with Oakley's abysmal history prior to sentencing. The record reveals that

Judge Hazlewood knew that Oakley had a number of support orders entered for his nine children, but he nevertheless continually refused to support them. He was aware that Oakley's probation for intimidating two witnesses in a child abuse case — where one of the witnesses was his own child and the victim — was in the process of being revoked. Judge Hazlewood was also apprised that Oakley had promised in the past to support his children, but those promises had failed to translate into the needed support. Moreover, he knew that Oakley had been employed and had no impediment preventing him from working. . . .

Judge Hazlewood asserted that some prison time coupled with conditional probation might convince Oakley to stop victimizing his children. With probation, Judge Hazlewood sought to rehabilitate Oakley while protecting society and potential victims — Oakley's own children — from future wrongdoing. The conditions were designed to assist Oakley in conforming his conduct to the law. . . . At the same time, Judge Hazlewood sought to protect the victims of Oakley's crimes — Oakley's nine children.

But Oakley argues that the condition imposed by Judge Hazlewood violates his constitutional right to procreate. This court, in accord with the United States Supreme Court, has previously recognized the fundamental liberty interest of a citizen to choose whether or not to procreate. Eberhardy v. Circuit Court for Wood County, 307 N.W.2d 881 (Wis. 1981); Skinner v. Oklahoma ex rel. Williamson, 316 U.S. 535 (1942) (recognizing the right to procreate as "one of the basic civil rights of man"). Accordingly, Oakley argues that the condition here warrants strict scrutiny. That is, it must be narrowly tailored to serve a compelling state interest. Although Oakley concedes, as he must, that the State's interest in requiring parents to support their children is compelling, he argues that the means employed here is not narrowly tailored to serve that compelling interest because Oakley's "right to procreate is not restricted but in fact eliminated." . . .

While Oakley's argument might well carry the day if he had not intentionally refused to pay child support, it is well-established that convicted individuals do not enjoy the same degree of liberty as citizens who have not violated the law. We emphatically reject the novel idea that Oakley, who was convicted of intentionally failing to pay child support, has an absolute right to refuse to support his current nine children and any future children that he procreates, thereby adding more child victims to the list. In an analogous case, Oregon upheld a similar probation condition to protect child victims from their father's abusive behavior in State v. Kline, 963 P.2d 697, 699 (Or. App. 1998). In *Kline,* the defendant physically and emotionally abused his wife and children, especially when high on methamphetamine, which caused him to become angry[, easily frustrated,] and hostile. [Upon fracturing his two-and-a-half-month-old baby girl's leg and bruising her head and chest, t]he defendant was convicted of criminal mistreatment and as a condition of his probation he was required to . . . obtain prior written approval of the court before fathering any future child. The defendant contested the condition as violating his fundamental right to procreate and asserted that strict scrutiny applied.

The court [responded] that "[t]he condition provides potential victims with protection from future injury and interferes with defendant's fundamental rights to a permissible degree." . . .

Oakley fails to note that incarceration, by its very nature, deprives a convicted individual of the fundamental right to be free from physical restraint, which in turn encompasses and restricts other fundamental rights, such as the right to procreate. Therefore, given that a convicted felon does not stand in the same position as someone who has not been convicted of a crime, we have previously stated that "conditions of probation may impinge upon constitutional rights as long as they are not overly broad and are reasonably related to the person's rehabilitation." Edwards v. State, 246 N.W.2d 109 (Wis. 1976). In Krebs v. State, 568 N.W.2d 26 (Wis. Ct. App. 1997), the court of appeals recently applied this established standard to uphold a condition of probation that required a defendant who sexually assaulted his own daughter to obtain his probation agent's approval before entering into an intimate or sexual relationship. The court found that although the condition infringed upon a constitutional right, it was reasonable and not overly broad.

Applying the relevant standard here, we find that the condition is not overly broad because it does not eliminate Oakley's ability to exercise his constitutional right to procreate. He can satisfy the condition of probation by making efforts to support his children as required by law. . . . If Oakley decides to continue his present course of conduct — intentionally refusing to pay child support — he will face eight years in prison regardless of how many children he has. Furthermore, this condition will expire at the end of his term of probation. He may then decide to have more children, but of course, if he continues to intentionally refuse to support his children, the State could charge him again under §948.22(2). Rather, because Oakley can satisfy this condition by not intentionally refusing to support his current nine children and any future children as required by the law, we find that the condition is narrowly tailored to serve the State's compelling interest of having parents support their children. It is also narrowly tailored to serve the State's compelling interest in rehabilitating Oakley through probation rather than prison. The alternative to probation with conditions — incarceration for eight years — would have further victimized his children. And it is undoubtedly much broader than this conditional impingement on his procreative freedom for it would deprive him of his fundamental right to be free from physical restraint. Simply stated, Judge Hazlewood preserved much of Oakley's liberty by imposing probation with conditions rather than the more punitive option of imprisonment.

Moreover, the condition is reasonably related to the goal of rehabilitation. A condition is reasonably related to the goal of rehabilitation if it assists the convicted individual in conforming his or her conduct to the law. See State v. Miller, 499 N.W.2d 215 (Wis. Ct. App. 1993) (ruling that condition on probationer convicted of making obscene telephone calls forbidding him to make calls to any woman other than a family member was reasonably related to his rehabilitation). Here, Oakley was convicted of intentionally refusing to support his children. The condition at bar . . . is narrowly tailored to serve the compelling state interest of requiring parents to support their children as well as rehabilitating those convicted of crimes. . . .

BABLITCH, J., concurring. . . .
The two dissents frame the issue in such a way that Oakley's intentional refusal to pay support evolves into an inability to pay support. This case is not at all about an inability to pay support; it is about the intentional refusal to pay support. . . .

The dissents conclude that the majority's means of advancing the state's interest is not narrowly tailored to advance the state's interest. The dissents fail to advance any realistic alternative solution to what they concede is a compelling state interest. As long as the defendant continues to intentionally refuse to pay support, the alternatives posed by the dissents will end up with incarceration — which of course accomplishes indirectly what the dissents say the state cannot do directly. . . .

I conclude that the harm to others who cannot protect themselves is so overwhelmingly apparent and egregious here that there is no room for question. Here is a man who has shown himself time and again to be totally and completely irresponsible. He lives only for himself and the moment, with no regard to the consequences of his actions and taking no responsibility for them. He intentionally refuses to pay support and has been convicted of that felony. The harm that he has done to his nine living children by failing to support them is patent and egregious. . . . Under certain conditions, it is overwhelmingly obvious that any child he fathers in the future is doomed to a future of neglect, abuse, or worse. That as yet unborn child is a victim from the day it is born.

I am not happy with this result, but can discern no other. And the dissents provide none. Accordingly, I join the majority opinion. . . .

BRADLEY, J., dissenting.

I begin by emphasizing the right that is at issue: the right to have children. The majority acknowledges this right, but certainly does not convey its significance and preeminence. The right to have children is a basic human right and an aspect of the fundamental liberty which the Constitution jealously guards for all Americans. See Skinner v. Oklahoma ex rel. Williamson, 316 U.S. 535 (1942).

Thus, the stakes are high in this case. The majority's decision allows, for the first time in our state's history, the birth of a child to carry criminal sanctions. Today's decision makes this court the only court in the country to declare constitutional a condition that limits a probationer's right to procreate based on his financial ability to support his children. Ultimately, the majority's decision may affect the rights of every citizen of this state, man or woman, rich or poor.

I wholeheartedly agree with the majority that the governmental interest at stake in this case is of great magnitude. . . . However, when fundamental rights are at issue, the end does not necessarily justify the means. The majority concludes that the means of effecting the state's interest are sufficiently narrow in light of this governmental interest. I disagree. . . .

The circuit court order forbids Oakley from fathering another child until he can first establish the financial ability to support his children. Oakley is not prohibited from having intercourse, either indiscriminately or irresponsibly. Rather, the condition of probation is not triggered until Oakley's next child is born. . . .

While on its face the order leaves room for the slight possibility that Oakley may establish the financial means to support his children, the order is essentially a prohibition on the right to have children. Oakley readily admits that unless he wins the lottery, he will likely never be able to establish that ability. The circuit court understood the impossibility of Oakley satisfying this financial requirement when it imposed the condition. . . . Stressing the realities of Oakley's situation, the circuit court explained:

> [Y]ou know and I know you're probably never going to make 75 or 100 thousand dollars a year. You're going to struggle to make 25 or 30. And by the time you take care of your taxes and your social security, there isn't a whole lot to go around, and then you've got to ship it out to various children.

In light of the circuit court's recognition of Oakley's inability to meet the condition of probation, the prohibition cannot be considered a narrowly drawn means of advancing the state's interest in ensuring support for Oakley's children. . . .

In addition to the obvious constitutional infirmities of the majority's decision, upholding a term of probation that prohibits a probationer from fathering a child without first establishing the financial wherewithal to support his children carries unacceptable collateral consequences and practical problems.

First, prohibiting a person from having children as a condition of probation has been described as "coercive of abortion.". . .

Because the condition is triggered only upon the birth of a child, the risk of imprisonment creates a strong incentive for a man in Oakley's position to demand from the woman the termination of her pregnancy. It places the woman in an untenable position: have an abortion or be responsible for Oakley going to prison for eight years. Creating an incentive to procure an abortion in order to comply with conditions of probation is a result that I am not prepared to foster.

Second, by allowing the right to procreate to be subjected to financial qualifications, the majority imbues a fundamental liberty interest with a sliding scale of wealth. Men and women in America are free to have children, as many as they desire. They may do so without the means to support the children and may later suffer legal consequences as a result of the inability to provide support. However, the right to have a child has never been rationed on the basis of wealth.

Nevertheless, the majority has essentially authorized a judicially-imposed "credit check" on the right to bear and beget children. Thus begins our descent down the proverbial slippery slope. While the majority describes this case as "anomalous" and comprised of "atypical facts," the cases in which such a principle might be applied are not uncommon. The majority's own statistical data regarding non-payment of support belies its contention that this case is truly exceptional.

Third, the condition of probation is unworkable. David Oakley is not restrained, and realistically cannot be stopped, from having intercourse — protected or otherwise. The condition of probation will not be violated until the woman with whom he has sexual relations carries her pregnancy to term. Then, Oakley will be imprisoned, and another child will go unsupported. . . .

In light of the constitutional problems and other dilemmas posed by a condition that limits a probationer's right to father a child without first establishing the financial ability to support his children, it is not surprising that the majority is the sole court in this country to conclude that the condition is constitutional. The majority fails to cite any case law in which a court has allowed the right to have children to be conditioned upon financial status. It does not because it cannot. There is no precedent to cite. . . .

Let there be no question that I agree with the majority that David Oakley's conduct cannot be condoned. It is irresponsible and criminal. However, we must keep in mind what is really at stake in this case. The fundamental right to have children, shared by us all, is damaged by today's decision. Because I will not join in the majority's disregard of that right, I dissent.

SYKES, J., dissenting.

Can the State criminalize the birth of a child to a convicted felon who is likely to be unwilling or unable to adequately support the child financially? That is essentially the crux of the circuit court order in this case, or at least its apparent practical effect. . . .

Oakley must seek the court's permission and obtain the court's approval before bringing another child into the world. He is subject to probation revocation and imprisonment if he fathers a child without prior court approval.

While I sympathize with the circuit court's understandable exasperation with this chronic "deadbeat dad," I cannot agree that this probation condition survives constitutional scrutiny. It is basically a compulsory, state-sponsored, court-enforced financial test for future parenthood. . . .

NOTES

1. *Probation: the most common U.S. sanction.*   At the end of 2001, almost four million adults were on probation in the United States. See Bureau of Justice Statistics, Probation and Parole in the United States, 2002 (NCJ 201135, August 2003). Of those sentenced to probation, the mean sentence length was 33.6 months, the median 36 months. The United States has the highest probation rate in the world with 536 per 100,000 population, followed by Canada (269) and England and Wales (217).

In federal court 18.2 percent of all offenders sentenced between October 1, 1999 and September 30, 2000, received a probation-only sentence. About half of the misdemeanants received such a sentence but only 13.3 percent of all felony offenders. Among those felons, however, a large disparity existed: Only 5 percent of those convicted of drug trafficking received straight probation but almost half of all larcenists and almost 90 percent of those convicted of gambling offenses received a probation sentence. Should certain types of offenders presumptively receive probationary sentences?

2. *Probationary conditions.*   While the specific condition in *Oakley* is unusual, the more general question it raises is pervasive: What conditions may or should be imposed as part of probationary sentences? Probationary sentences are inherently more varied than imprisonment, and idiosyncratic probation conditions, such as the one in *Oakley,* are often being challenged on appeal. For further examples and a critical review of such conditions, see Andrew Horwitz, Coercion, Pop-Psychology, and Judicial Moralizing: Some Proposals for Curbing Judicial Abuse of Probation Conditions, 57 Wash. & Lee L. Rev. 75 (2000). Is this flexibility always a virtue? Should lists of conditions be standardized? If so, by whom? See Demarce v. Willrich, 56 P.3d 76 (Ariz. Ct. App. 2002) (upholding lifetime probation for sex offender); People v. Kimbrell, 684 N.E.2d 443 (Ill. App. Ct. 1997) (upholding probation condition for theft offense forbidding contact with defendant's son's father).

3. *The nature and evolution of probationary sanctions.*   Probationary sanctions are beginning to focus on the idea of "responsibilization," shifting more responsibility to offenders to solve their own problems. Is probation a privilege? What obligations flow from it? Some newer probationary sanctions have tended to emphasize greater control than regular probation. Among them are intensive supervised probation and house arrest, which often includes electronic monitoring. Would it be more effective to move a smaller number of higher-risk offenders to increased supervision and decrease supervision for those considered a lesser or intermediate risk? Do the parallel trends of increasing "self-rescue" on the one hand and increasing intensive control on the other suggest differing conceptions of probation in general, or do they reflect the notion that probation may be structured to achieve different purposes for different offenders?

4. *The efficacy of probation.*   Research on the effectiveness of probation indicates that a high percentage of probationers either violate the conditions of probation or commit another offense while on probation. During 1990 17 percent of all persons arrested for felonies in large, urban counties were on probation. Nevertheless, risky behavior as well as criminal activity goes down during supervision. When the intensity of supervision increases, probation revocations also increase, largely because of technical violations.

b.   Probation Violations

Probation is violated when the offender acts contrary to the conditions of supervision established by the court or the probation department. The violation may be criminal, as in the commission of a new offense, or technical, as in the failure to meet a specific probation condition. Not all violations lead to automatic revocation of probation. While protection of the community is the guiding principle, after a violation other strategies to monitor and control offender behavior may be used.

Do the probation rules give probationers too many chances? Should all probation violations lead to immediate termination of probation?

Because probationary sentences involve substantially lower levels of social control than prison sentences and are served in the community, not only the specified conditions but also the processes for review and revocation reflect the essential qualities and purposes of such sentences. Consider the following policies and procedures in North Carolina.

> *Violations Policies — Procedures,*
> *North Carolina Department of Correction*
> *Division of Community Corrections*
> **March 1, 2002**

GENERAL PROVISIONS

A *violation* is any action by the offender that is contrary to the conditions of supervision established by the Court or Post-Release Supervision and Parole Commission. Violations may be criminal (involving the commission of a new offense) or technical (involving a failure to meet one or more specific conditions of the probation judgment or parole or post-release supervision agreement).

1.   *Violation Philosophy*

All responses to violation behavior will be considered in light of the Department's mission and objectives, as well as the goals of the supervision process. While protection of the community must always be the primary consideration, it does not follow that revocation is always, or even usually, the most effective or efficient way of achieving this goal. The goal of community supervision is to selectively and proactively intervene with offenders to reduce the likelihood of future criminal activity and promote compliance with the supervision strategy. Strategies involve holding offenders accountable for their actions, monitoring and controlling offender behavior, and referring to rehabilitation programs specific to offender needs. Another significant piece of the supervision strategy is ensuring an appropriate and proportionate response to all violations of the conditions of probation, taking into account offender risk, the nature of the violation, and the objective of offender accountability.

The purpose of this policy is to provide a framework to guide officer decision-making when a violation of probation has occurred. . . . Technical violations of the conditions of probation are inevitable. It is unrealistic to believe offenders, even if they sincerely desire to develop drug-free, pro-social lifestyles, will immediately have the skills or abilities to do so. The issues and forces that brought them into the system will most likely continue to impact their behavior to some extent until they learn new skills and methods of dealing with these forces.

The basic expectations underlying the Division's policy regarding probation violations are:

- There will be a response to every detected violation;
- Responses to violations will be proportional to the risk to the community posed by the particular offender, the severity of the violation, and the current situational risk;
- The least restrictive response necessary to respond to the behavior will be used;
- There will be consistency in handling similar violation behavior given similar risk factors;
- Responses to violations will hold some potential for long-term positive outcomes in the context of the supervision strategy;
- While response to violation behavior is determined by considering both risk and needs, risk to the community is the overriding consideration; *and*
- Probationers who demonstrate a habitual unwillingness to abide by supervision requirements or who pose undue risk to the community will be subject to revocation of probation.

2.   *Violation Response Procedures*

When a violation occurs the supervising officer will assess the type of violation (emergency or nonemergency) and take appropriate action.

A.   Emergency Violations

Emergency violations involve behavior that *requires the immediate arrest of the offender* in order to ensure public safety. Emergency violations include, but are not limited to, the following:

- An imminent threat by the offender of physical harm to self or others;
- Electronic House Arrest violations such as equipment tampering;
- For probation cases only, possession of contraband necessitating an arrest incidental to search and/or seizure;
- Willful violations of residential facility rules; and/or
- For sex offenders, violations of specific conditions directly related to the crime. . . .

B.   Non-emergency Violations

Non-emergency violations involve behavior that does not indicate the need for immediate arrest of the offender in order to ensure public safety. Non-emergency violations . . . include:

- A new conviction for any felony or a Class A1, 1 or 2 [or 3] misdemeanor;
- A new conviction for the same offense for which currently being supervised;
- Pending charges on a case about to expire;
- Being charged with a new offense in addition to [or without] one or more technical violations; Absconding;
- Financial arrearage of greater than six months for probation . . . cases . . . ;
- Lesser Electronic House Arrest violations that do not require immediate arrest;
- Possession of a weapon;
- Unwanted contact with the victim;
- Any violation related to substance abuse or any driving violation for DWI Level I or II cases;
- Pending technical violations at the expiration of the term of probation;
- Failure to comply with treatment;
- Notification of non-compliance with the rules of a Day Reporting Center, residential program, or the DART Program;
- Failure to report for jail time; . . .
- Non-compliance with community service requirement[;] . . .
- Verbal refusal to participate in substance abuse screening, not necessitating a Violation Report;
- Non-reporting for supervision; . . .
- Financial arrearage of less than six months for probation . . . cases . . . ; the Probation/Parole Officer may consider this violation an "A" violation for cases in which victim restitution is ordered;
- Curfew violation;

- Positive substance abuse screening;
- Unemployment, not seeking employment as ordered, or failure to notify the Probation [ ] Officer of employment loss;
- GED/school non-attendance;
- Leaving the jurisdiction or changing residence without permission;
- Going to restricted areas;
- Violating an order not to possess pagers or cellular phones;
- Failure to attend a prison tour; and
- Reporting in an unreasonable manner. . . .

Probation/Parole Officer will respond to non-emergency violations according to the Non-Emergency Violation Response Guidelines. The purpose for the Non-Emergency Violation Response Guidelines is to insure swift and certain response to every violation and to utilize the full continuum of sanctions prior to revocation. The Non-Emergency Response Guidelines apply to all technical violations except substance abuse testing violations. . . .

C.   Non-emergency Violation Response Guidelines

a. Level I Violation Response — Officer Response

Upon detection of the offender's first violation(s), the supervising officer will warn the offender either verbally or in writing or seek the assistance of the Chief Probation [ ] Officer in warning the offender either verbally or in writing. The Probation [ ] Officer may also require the offender to report more frequently. Subsequent violation(s) may be addressed at Level I or Level II Response.

b. Level II Violation Response — Officer/Chief Response

If the supervising Probation [ ] Officer determines a Level II Response is needed, the officer will staff the case with the Chief Probation [ ] Officer. Level II Response includes override of supervision level and use of delegated authority sanctions available within community or intermediate punishment. . . .

c. Level III Violation Response — Court/Hearing Response

A Level III Violation Response may be initiated only after options from Level I and Level II have been used. Level III options, which may be pursued after staffing the case with the Chief Probation [ ] Officer, include a recommendation for an Intermediate Punishment, extending/modifying probation or contempt of court. . . .

d. Level IV Violation Response — Revocation

Revocation may be recommended only after staffing the case with the Chief Probation [ ] Officer and a Level III response has been used.

3.   *Non-emergency Violation Response Charts*

The following [chart gives] non-emergency violation response guidelines for probation . . . cases.

Non-Emergency Violation Response Chart — Probation

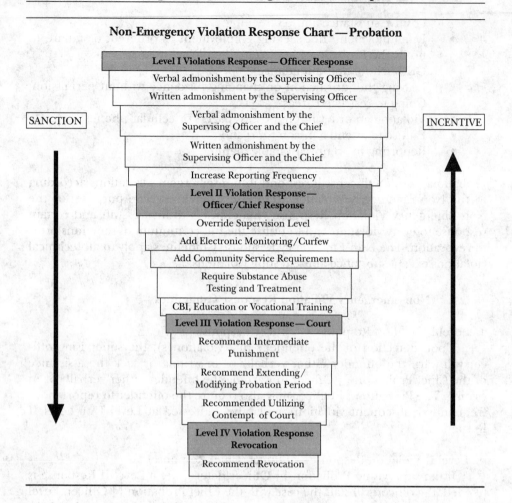

SANCTION · INCENTIVE

- Level I Violations Response—Officer Response
- Verbal admonishment by the Supervising Officer
- Written admonishment by the Supervising Officer
- Verbal admonishment by the Supervising Officer and the Chief
- Written admonishment by the Supervising Officer and the Chief
- Increase Reporting Frequency
- Level II Violation Response—Officer/Chief Response
- Override Supervision Level
- Add Electronic Monitoring/Curfew
- Add Community Service Requirement
- Require Substance Abuse Testing and Treatment
- CBI, Education or Vocational Training
- Level III Violation Response—Court
- Recommend Intermediate Punishment
- Recommend Extending/Modifying Probation Period
- Recommended Utilizing Contempt of Court
- Level IV Violation Response Revocation
- Recommend Revocation

4.   *Positive Substance Abuse Screening Guidelines*

Following confirmation of the first positive screen result, the Probation [] Officer will confront the offender with the positive screen result within ten (10) days:

A.   **Procedure for First Positive Drug Screen Result**

1. Offender Admits Illegal Drug Use
   a. If the offender agrees to seek treatment, make a referral to TASC where available for assessment and referral to treatment or to any licensed treatment program where TASC is unavailable.
   b. If the offender refuses to submit to assessment and/or treatment, the officer will staff the case with the Chief Probation [] Officer and will use delegated authority to have the offender submit to assessment and treatment. If delegated authority is not available issue a . . . Violation Report or . . . [a] Non-Compliance Report and

                 recommend a modification to the conditions of supervision requiring substance abuse assessment and compliance with the results.

  2.   Offender Denies Illegal Drug Use

      a.   If the offender refuses to submit to a treatment assessment, . . . obtain a confirmation test of the positive drug screen from the substance abuse screening lab and forward with a . . . Violation Report to the court of conviction or . . . to the Post-Release Supervision and Parole Commission; and,

      b.   During the violation hearing, recommend a modification to the conditions of supervision requiring substance abuse assessment and compliance with the results.

B. Procedure for Second or Subsequent Positive Result

Following receipt of the second or subsequent positive screen result, the Probation [ ] Officer will review the case with the Chief Probation [ ] Officer and treatment provider, if applicable, to evaluate the offender's treatment needs and determine an appropriate course of action, including but not limited to therapeutic sanctions. . . .

VIOLATION HEARINGS

     Violation hearings may be held in the District Court or Superior Court having original jurisdiction, the judicial district in which the offender resides, or the Judicial District in which he/she is alleged to have violated probation. . . .

NOTES

1. *Probation violations.* The structure, purpose, and efficacy of probationary sentences turn as much on the procedures and consequences of violations as on the terms of the sentence itself. One of the puzzles of probationary sentences is that more aggressive enforcement and more rigid responses to conditions such as drug screens can lead to very high rates of violation. Yet nonenforcement may undermine the purposes and goals of the particular sentences. Does the structured and graduated system in North Carolina respond to these concerns? How would you define success in the North Carolina system? Should other states adopt a similar system?

2. *Probation violators.* The most recent data on probation violators in state prisons are from 1991. They show a steady increase since the 1970s in the incarceration of probation violators. As of 1991, almost one-quarter of probationers were incarcerated for probation violations. One-quarter of them had probation revocation hearings because they had committed a new crime; 10 percent had failed a drug test; 36 percent did not report to their probation officer; 12 percent had failed to pay fines, restitution or comply with other financial commitments. See Robyn L. Cohen, Probation and Parole Violators in State Prison,

1991 (NCJ 149076, Aug. 1995). Is revocation of probation appropriate for any, or all, of these violations?

B.   MODERN ALTERNATIVE SANCTIONS

In the news much more often than probation and fines, but in reality much less frequent, is a range of new sentences — sometimes creations of the post-modern mind, and sometimes resurrections of sentences long dead (and perhaps justly so). The most significant of these are boot camp, home confinement, shaming sanctions, and community service.

While modern alternative sanctions are relatively rare, they appear to have captured the imagination of the public, politicians, and a fair number of legal scholars. They deserve attention here because of the public attention paid to them and because of the extent to which they reveal deeper symbolic aspects and needs of punishment (a point that may be made about capital sentences as well). Perhaps these unusual but dramatic sanctions highlight a demand for an "expressive" purpose distinct from (or perhaps a component of) the more traditional purposes of retribution and reinforcement of community norms. See Joel Feinberg, The Expressive Function of Punishment, reprinted in Joel Feinberg, Doing and Deserving 98 (1970).

These new sanctions also raise further concern about "netwidening." Will they be applied to offenders who otherwise would go to prison? Or instead will they be imposed on those who would receive probationary sanctions, or even those whose cases would be dismissed? In the latter cases, intermediate sanctions have become supplements rather than alternatives to more traditional criminal justice sanctions.

In thinking about these new kinds of sentences, a useful distinction can be drawn between those that include some degree of physical detention, and therefore either replace or mimic imprisonment, and those that do not.

1.   Nonprison Detention: Boot Camp and Home Confinement

In the mid-1990s, there were about 75 boot camps for adult offenders in more than 30 states and about 30 for juveniles, though since then the number of boot camps has declined. The adult state boot camps have a bed capacity of less than 7,000. The federal government has two so-called Intensive Confinement Centers (ICC), one for women and one for men.

The first boot camps — originally designed for adult men — were developed in 1983 in Georgia and Oklahoma to contain rising confinement costs and alleviate prison overcrowding. Over the next decade boot camps began to serve women and juvenile offenders as well. The average age of state boot camp inmates is between 19 and 20, while in the federal system it is 27.

Because boot camps are considered an intermediate sanction, only offenders convicted of less serious, nonviolent offenses are usually admitted, and for relatively short periods of time. While the first boot camps were modeled after military boot camps, they came to emphasize education, therapeutic and treatment services, and community aftercare, with the goal of reducing recidivism. Despite initially promising results and wide adoption, in recent years boot camps have fallen out of favor.

Based on the following study of boot camps, do you think they should be part of the array of available sanctions in your state? If so, for which offenders?

> ## Correctional Boot Camps: Lessons from a Decade of Research, Dale G. Parent
> ### (National Institute of Justice, NCJ 197018, July 2003)

In response to rising rates of serious crime, many correctional systems established boot camps as an alternative sanction that might reduce recidivism, prison populations, and operating costs. Despite a decade of popularity with policymakers and the public, boot camps have had difficulty meeting these objectives.

The National Institute of Justice (NIJ) sponsored an analysis of research conducted over a 10-year period beginning in the late 1980s. This analysis concluded that

- Boot camps generally had positive effects on the attitudes, perceptions, behavior, and skills of inmates during their confinement.
- With limited exceptions, these positive changes did not translate into reduced recidivism.
- Boot camps can achieve small relative reductions in prison populations and modest reductions in correctional costs under a narrow set of conditions (admitting offenders with a high likelihood of otherwise serving a conventional prison term and offering discounts in time served to those who complete boot camps).

The surveyed research identified three factors largely responsible for the failure of boot camps to reach goals related to prison population and recidivism:

- Mandates to reduce prison populations through early release made volunteering for boot camps unnecessary as a means of shortening sentences.
- Lack of a standard boot camp model.
- Insufficient focus on offenders' reentry into the community.

The camps' disciplined structure and therapeutic programs eliminated idleness and created a safer environment, which in turn improved inmate attitudes and behavior. Such structure, coupled with a therapeutic orientation, may apply to other correctional programs, especially those that target youthful offenders.

WHY BOOT CAMPS?

As the name implies, correctional boot camps are in-prison programs that resemble military basic training. They emphasize vigorous physical activity, drill and ceremony, manual labor, and other activities that ensure that participants have little, if any, free time. Strict rules govern all aspects of conduct and appearance. Correctional officers act as drill instructors, initially using intense verbal tactics designed to break down inmates' resistance and lead to constructive changes.

Three Generations of Camps. Boot camps proliferated in the late 1980s and early 1990s. By 1995, State correctional agencies operated 75 boot camps for adults, State and local agencies operated 30 juvenile boot camps, and larger counties operated 18 boot camps in local jails.

The camps evolved over time. . . . Although first-generation camps stressed military discipline, physical training, and hard work, second-generation camps emphasized rehabilitation by adding such components as alcohol and drug treatment and prosocial skills training. Some also added intensive postrelease supervision that may include electronic monitoring, home confinement, and random urine tests. A few camps admitted females, but this proved somewhat controversial. Recently, some boot camps, particularly those for juveniles, have substituted an emphasis on educational and vocational skills for the military components to provide comparable structure and discipline.

After the mid-1990s, the number of boot camps declined. By 2000, nearly one-third of State prison boot camps had closed — only 51 camps remained. The average daily population in State boot camps also dropped more than 30 percent.

Boot Camps' Goals. Boot camps had three main goals: reducing recidivism, reducing prison populations, and reducing costs.

Camps were expected to reduce recidivism by changing inmates' attitudes, values, and behaviors and by addressing factors that increase the likelihood of returning to prison (such as lack of job skills, addiction, and inability to control anger). Camps were expected to reduce prison populations by shortening time served. Reduced length of stay was expected to reduce costs.

Reducing Recidivism — An Unmet Goal. NIJ evaluation studies consistently showed that boot camps did not reduce recidivism regardless of whether the camps were for adults or juveniles or whether they were first-generation programs with a heavy military emphasis or later programs with more emphasis on treatment. Most of the research suggested that the limitations of boot camps prevented them from reducing recidivism or prison populations, even as they achieved other goals. These limitations mostly resulted from —

- Low "dosage" effects. The length of stay in boot camps — usually from 90 to 120 days — was too brief to realistically affect recidivism.
- Insufficient preparation of boot camp inmates for reentry into the community. Many boot camps provided little or no postrelease programming to prepare graduates to lead productive lives. In addition, the intensive supervision common to later generations of boot camps meant heightened surveillance levels for boot camp graduates. These factors combined to magnify the high rates of return for technical parole violations.
- Conflicting or unrealistic goals or mandates set by State legislatures. For example, most boot camp programs sought to reduce prison

populations. Shorter programs more effectively meet this goal, but they also lower dosage effects and reduce the likelihood that treatment programs will work, thereby potentially increasing recidivism.

- The absence of a strong underlying treatment model. Pragmatism and local politics often affected boot camp structure more than theory and research results. . . .

Improving Behavior — A Success Story.   Boot camps were almost universally successful in improving inmates' attitudes and behavior during the course of the program; they also produced safer environments for staff and residents, presumably due to their highly structured atmosphere and activities.

Several studies indicated that adult boot camp participants had better attitudes about their confinement experiences and had improved their prosocial attitudes more than comparison group members. One study concluded that inmates in adult boot camps had increased self-esteem, reduced antisocial attitudes, increased problem-solving skills, improved coping skills, and improved social support. In other studies, boot camp inmates improved their self-esteem and standardized education scores in reading and math more than comparison group members.

Anxiety and depression declined to a greater degree among juveniles in boot camps than among those in comparison facilities. Dysfunctional impulsivity (the inability to control one's impulses) increased among youths in comparison facilities but decreased among boot camp participants. Social attitudes improved among youths in boot camps, but worsened among those in comparison facilities.

Reducing Prison Population — Mixed Results.   NIJ-sponsored boot camp researchers agree that correctional boot camps might achieve small relative[14] reductions in prison populations. Boot camps could reduce the number of prison beds needed in a jurisdiction, which would lead to modest reductions in correctional costs. . . .

However, restrictive entry criteria for boot camp participants often made it impossible to reduce prison populations. For example, some jurisdictions required that boot camp inmates be nonviolent offenders convicted of their first felony. This small pool of eligible candidates typically serves short prison terms before parole. These inmates had little incentive to volunteer for boot camps that would not shorten their terms. When inmates sentenced to longer prison terms were recruited, however, a reduction in time served became a compelling incentive.

Efforts to meet the recidivism goal may work against meeting population and cost reduction goals. For example, lengthening a boot camp term to add more treatment programs in order to reduce the chances of recidivism would shorten the discount in time served and, thus, not reduce the population or prison bed costs.

---

14. Boot camps were unlikely to lower absolute prison population levels. The camps opened during a time when major changes in sentencing policies and practices caused prison populations to soar. Even at the height of their popularity, the total capacity of boot camps was minuscule compared to the total prison population.

Conclusions.   Correctional practitioners and planners might learn from boot camps' failure to reduce recidivism or prison populations by considering the following:

- Building reintegration into the community into an inmate's individual program and reentry plans may improve the likelihood he or she will not commit a new offense.
- Programs that offered substantial discounts in time served to those who completed boot camps and that chose candidates sentenced to serve longer terms were the most successful in reducing prison populations.
- Chances of reducing recidivism increased when boot camp programs lasted longer and offered more intensive treatment and postrelease supervision, activities that may conflict with the goal of reducing population.

Efforts to achieve multiple goals are likely the overall cause of boot camps' conflicting results. Program designers are urged to determine which options are best for their jurisdictions; for example, they may consider whether to implement more treatment programs or move inmates out of the system more rapidly. These decisions affect costs, as prison bed-space savings go up or down.

Other correctional programs are adopting some of the important elements of boot camps — for example, carefully structured programs that reduce idleness — to increase safety and improve conditions of confinement for younger offenders. However, in recent years, some jurisdictions facing rising costs have responded by cutting programs. One lesson for policymakers from 10 years of boot camp research is that curtailing programs may lead to increased violence, misconduct, and serious management problems.

Females in Boot Camps.   Some boot camp programs began accepting eligible female inmates in the early 1990s, but concerns soon emerged about whether the boot camp strategy is appropriate for women.

Findings from the limited research on female boot camp participants and their high dropout rate clearly indicate that this population faces unique problems. A 1992 study noted that the programs were designed for males and did not accommodate women's special needs or problems.

- Female inmates are more likely to have children and be the sole parent for those children. Boot camps often restricted, or even banned, visitation, creating difficult situations for mothers and their children. Also, the programs did not teach parenting skills.
- Female inmates are more likely to have a history of physical or sexual abuse. Although female inmates were four to five times more likely than male inmates to have been victims of physical or sexual abuse, most camps had no programs to help them cope with or avoid victimization. Derogatory boot camp tactics tended to retraumatize domestic violence victims.
- Female inmates are more likely to have a different history and pattern of drug use than males. Most substance abuse treatment used therapies designed for males.

- Female inmates are more likely to have been unemployed before imprisonment. Boot camps did little to prepare women for employment after release.

Female inmates at boot camps reported high stress levels, which may be why they tended to drop out of boot camp at a higher rate than male inmates. Stress stemmed from a physical training regimen designed for males; drill instructors' "in your face" tactics; lack of other female participants, often leading to isolation within the camp; and cross-gender supervision.

NOTES

1. *Boot camps.*   Has the 20-year experiment with boot camps failed? What lessons can be drawn about creative or modern sanctions more generally? Is the problem with boot camps in their conception? Their operation? Will there be any boot camps in operation in ten years? How could boot camps be reconfigured to fulfill their goals more effectively?

2. *Home confinement.*   While it is relatively rare, many jurisdictions make some use of home confinement as a sanction, especially for short periods of time. For example, in the federal system in 1999 about 16,000 defendants and offenders had home confinement orders. The majority of home confinements, however, occur before trial. Home confinement does not necessarily mean 24-hour confinement: It can allow for specific periods of work or other reasons to leave the home. What purpose does home confinement serve? Do its goals differ from those of imprisonment?

3. *Electronic monitoring.*   Electronic monitoring is often combined with home confinement, though the two concepts are distinct. Electronic monitoring adds a high-tech gloss by tracking the presence or absence of the offender at agreed locations (home, office, car). See People v. McNair, 642 N.Y.S.2d 597 (Ct. App. 1996) (sentence of one year of electronic monitoring for DUI defendant exceeded court's authority under general probation statutes). Is electronic monitoring efficient? Does it serve primarily an incapacitative function?

2.   *Nondetention Sanctions: Shaming and Community Service*

During the past two decades, shame has emerged as an explicit and independent sanction. Many criminal sentences may convey or carry some shame for the convicted offender. Indeed, the shame associated with the fact of conviction alone for some offenders may, from their perspective or the perspective of friends, family, or fellow workers, be a substantial punishment in itself.

Academics have led the call for officially shaming offenders. John Braithwaite, an Australian scholar, called for greater use of shame in criminal penalties in his 1989 book *Crime, Shame and Reintegration*. Braithwaite distinguished "reintegrative" shaming, which reaffirmed "the morality of the offender by expressing personal disappointment that the offender should do something so out of character" and invited the offender to rejoin the community, from "disintegrative" shaming, which further pushes the offender into outcast status. A leading academic proponent in the United States has been Professor Dan Kahan. A major critic of proposals to sanction through shame is Professor Toni Massaro, who questions the existence of the kind of societies and norms that would make social sanctions like shame fair, consistent, and effective. See generally Note, Shame, Stigma and Crime: Evaluating the Efficacy of Shaming Sanctions in Criminal Law, 116 Harv. L. Rev. 2186 (2003).

While rare, shaming sanctions are starting to appear in statutes and in individual cases. Consider the purposes and wisdom of the shaming sanctions in the following statute and case. Should shaming sanctions become more widely used? If so, for what offenses and offenders? And which institutions should design, implement, and test such sanctions?

Ohio Revised Code §4503.231
Special Plates for Vehicles Registered to Persons Whose Registration Certificates and License Plates Have Been Impounded

No motor vehicle registered in the name of a person whose certificate of registration and identification license plates have been impounded . . . shall be operated or driven on any highway in this state unless it displays identification license plates which are a different color from those regularly issued and carry a special serial number that may be readily identified by law enforcement officers. The registrar of motor vehicles shall designate the color and serial number to be used on such license plates, which shall remain the same from year to year and shall not be displayed on any other motor vehicles. . . .

People v. Glenn Meyer
680 N.E.2d 315 (Ill. 1997)

McMORROW, J.

The sole question presented for our review in the instant case is whether section 5-6-3(b) of the Unified Code of Corrections (Code) (730 ILCS 5/5-6-3(b) (West 1994)) authorizes a trial court to order, as a condition of probation, that the defendant post a large sign at all entrances to his family farm which reads "Warning! A Violent Felon lives here. Enter at your own risk!" The appellate court affirmed the trial court's imposition of this condition. . . . We reverse, and hold that the trial court exceeded the scope of its sentencing authority because posting a sign of this type is not a reasonable condition of probation under section 5-6-3(b) of the Code. Therefore, we vacate the order of the circuit court in part.

Following a jury trial, the defendant, Glenn Meyer, was convicted of the aggravated battery of Gary Mason. The trial testimony showed that on February 25, 1995, Gary Mason visited the defendant's farm in order to return some vehicle parts that he purchased from the defendant. Mason and the defendant began to quarrel over whether the parts were functioning properly. During the argument the defendant swung one of the parts at Mason, striking him in the nose and eye, causing several injuries.

At the defendant's sentencing hearing, evidence was presented in aggravation and mitigation. On behalf of the State, Tim Belford testified that in September 1986, he went to the defendant's farm in order to collect monies for two insufficient fund checks issued by defendant to Belford's employer, the First National Bank of Pittsfield. Belford stated that the defendant eventually gave him the money, but then kicked him and ordered him off the farm. Belford acknowledged that a jury acquitted the defendant of aggravated battery charges stemming from this incident.

Next, Harry Dyel testified that in May of 1990, he went to the defendant's farm on behalf of his employer, Shelter Insurance Company, in order to investigate a claim filed by the defendant. Dyel testified that the defendant became hostile because he was annoyed by the company's failure to process his claim promptly. Dyel stated that after he attempted to comply with the defendant's demands for payment, the defendant pushed him down and kicked him several times, causing injuries to his torso, arms, face and head. The defendant was convicted of the aggravated battery of Dyel. Finally, Gary Mason, the victim in the present case, testified regarding the defendant's actions on February 25, 1995.

Several witnesses testified in mitigation. Kenwood Foster testified that he is a licensed clinical social worker who operates a private counselling service. The defendant began seeing Foster in the fall of 1991. Foster testified that doctors at several different clinics have diagnosed the defendant as having "major depressive disorder" or clinical depression. Foster further stated that he believes that the defendant may also suffer from a condition similar to a type of post-traumatic stress disorder. He indicated that the defendant has been taking prescription medication known as Zoloft, to control his illness.

Foster further testified that certain stresses, such as a perceived threat to the defendant or his family, could trigger a change in the defendant's behavior. Foster acknowledged that the defendant may perceive certain behavior as threatening, even if the average individual would not feel threatened under similar circumstances.

Friends of the defendant, Gregg Smith, David Gratton and Bruce Lightle, also testified. All three described the defendant's good character and reputation within the community.

Mary Meyer, the defendant's wife of 36 years, testified that the defendant's elderly mother relies on the defendant, her only child, for care and assistance. Mrs. Meyer stated that she teaches high school, and has always relied on the defendant to manage the farm. She indicated that her family would suffer great hardship if the defendant were incarcerated. Mrs. Meyer also testified regarding the defendant's prolonged psychological illness and his efforts to control his sickness with medication.

In addition to the testimony of the witnesses, 20 letters were submitted by individuals from throughout the defendant's community. These letters chronicle examples of the defendant's generosity and willingness to assist friends and neighbors in need. The letters contain many descriptions of the defendant's good character and reputation.

Additionally, the presentence investigation report contains a detailed description of the defendant's mental health history. Several psychological evaluations of the defendant, dating from 1989, show that he suffers from major depressive disorder and possibly an additional psychological malady.

Upon evaluating all of the evidence in mitigation and aggravation, the trial court sentenced the defendant to 30 months' probation. The court considered the defendant's family members and the adverse impact that incarceration would have upon them. The court stated that it considered that the defendant was 62 years old, his mother's age and ill-health, and Mary Meyer's need to have the defendant care for the farm, in deciding to sentence the defendant to probation instead of prison.

The court conditioned defendant's probation on the following: (1) payment of $9,615.95 in restitution, (2) payment of a $7,500 fine, (3) payment of a $25 monthly probation services fee, (4) psychological psychiatric evaluation and treatment, (5) one-year home confinement and (6) the placement of a "violent felon" warning sign at each entrance to the defendant's property for the duration of the probation period. With respect to the sign requirement, the court stated that it believed that "maybe [the sign] will protect society." The court's supplemental order regarding the sign provides:

> As a condition of probation defendant shall erect and maintain at each entrance of his property a 4' × 8' sign with clearly readable lettering at least 8" in height reading: "Warning! A Violent Felon lives here. Enter at your own Risk!" To be erected by 8-11-95. . . .

The sole issue presented to us for review is whether the trial court was authorized to order the violent felon warning sign as a condition of probation. The defendant maintains that the trial court acted outside of the scope of its sentencing authority because the sign is not a reasonable condition of probation within the meaning of the Unified Code of Corrections. Section 5-6-3(b) of the Code lists 16 permissible probation conditions that the trial court may impose "in addition to other *reasonable conditions* relating to the nature of the offense or the rehabilitation of the defendant as determined for each defendant in the proper discretion of the Court." (Emphasis added.) The defendant maintains that the warning sign is not a reasonable condition of probation because it does not comport with traditional notions of punishment or probation in Illinois, and instead is an unauthorized "shaming penalty" or a scarlet letter type of punishment. The defendant argues that nothing in the Code supports the subjection of probationers to public ridicule as a goal of probation.

The State responds that while the sign may embarrass the defendant, it is not intended to subject him to public ridicule. Rather, the State and the amicus curiae, the American Alliance for Rights and Responsibilities, contend that this condition of probation furthers the goals of probation because it protects the public and serves to rehabilitate the defendant.

The State maintains that the sign protects the public by warning against provoking the defendant and by reducing the number of guests or business invitees who visit the farm. The State and the amicus argue that the goal of rehabilitation is fostered by the sign because it reminds the defendant that society disapproves of his criminal conduct. The amicus further argues that because the sign reminds the defendant of his offense, the defendant will modify his behavior and will be less likely to commit acts of violence in the future. Finally, both the State and the amicus argue that the trial court acted within its discretion by carefully fashioning the conditions of probation to correspond to the needs of the defendant and the public.

Generally, the trial court is afforded wide discretion in fashioning the conditions of probation for a particular defendant. However, while the trial court has discretion to impose probation conditions which will foster rehabilitation and protect the public, the exercise of this discretion is not without limitation.

Section 5-6-3(b) of the Code contains 16 permitted conditions of probation which may be imposed "in addition to other *reasonable* conditions." (Emphasis added.) Requiring the defendant to erect a sign on his property, proclaiming his status as a violent convicted felon, is not statutorily identified as one of the conditions of probation. The statute gives the trial court the discretion to impose additional conditions of probation provided that they are reasonable. In People v. Ferrell 659 N.E.2d 992 (Ill. App. 1995), the court determined that a probation condition not expressly enumerated in the statute may be imposed as long as it is (1) reasonable and (2) relates to (a) the nature of the offense or (b) the rehabilitation of the defendant as determined by the trial court. We must, therefore, determine whether compelling defendant to post a 4-foot by 8-foot sign in front of his residence which, in 8-inch-high letters, states that defendant is a violent felon is a reasonable condition under section 5-6-3 of the Code.

Section 1-1-2 of the Unified Code of Corrections provides:

> The purposes of this Code of Corrections are to:
>   (a) prescribe sanctions proportionate to the seriousness of the offenses and permit the recognition of differences in rehabilitation possibilities among individual offenders;
>   (b) forbid and prevent the commission of offenses;
>   (c) prevent arbitrary or oppressive treatment of persons adjudicated offenders or delinquents; and
>   (d) restore offenders to useful citizenship.
> 730 ILCS 5/1-1-2 (West 1994).

Consistent with this legislative intent, this court has recognized repeatedly that the purpose of probation is to benefit society by restoring a defendant to useful citizenship, rather than allowing a defendant to become a burden as an habitual offender. Probation simultaneously serves as a form of punishment and as a method for rehabilitating an offender. Protection of the public from the type of conduct that led to a defendant's conviction is one of the goals of probation....

Although the sign may foster the goals of probation to the extent that it punishes the defendant and protects the public, furtherance of these two goals alone does not render the condition reasonable. Indeed, we are persuaded by defendant's contention that the sign, in fact, may hamper the goal of rehabilitation, and that the erection of the sign is inconsistent with the conditions of probation listed in section 5-6-3(b). We recognize that the trial court labored arduously and sincerely to develop a sentence which would serve the needs of society and simultaneously avoid incarceration of the defendant. Nonetheless, we hold the sign condition of probation imposed in this case was unreasonable and did not serve the purposes of section 5-6-3(b).

The Tennessee Supreme Court in State v. Burdin, 924 S.W.2d 82 (Tenn. 1996), considered and rejected a comparable "shaming sign," finding that it was unreasonable. The Tennessee court held that the Tennessee statute at issue there did not authorize a condition of probation which required the defendant to erect a sign in the front yard of his residence which read, "Warning, all children. [Defendant] is an admitted and convicted child molester. Parents beware."

In *Burdin,* the defendant pleaded guilty to sexual battery of a 16-year-old victim. As a condition of probation, the court ordered the defendant to place the warning sign in front of his residence where he lived with his mother. . . .

The *Burdin* court stated:

> The consequences of imposing such a condition without the normal safeguards of legislative study and debate are uncertain. Posting a sign in the defendant's yard would dramatically affect persons other than the defendant and those charged with his supervision. . . . [C]ompliance with the condition would have consequences in the community perhaps beneficial, perhaps detrimental, but in any event unforeseen and unpredictable.

Similarly, in People v. Johnson, 528 N.E.2d 1360 (Ill. App. 1988), the court cautioned against allowing trial courts to impose unconventional conditions of supervision, which may have unknown consequences. The defendant in *Johnson* was convicted of driving under the influence of alcohol. As a condition of supervision, the trial court in *Johnson* ordered the defendant to place an advertisement in the local daily newspaper, which contained her booking picture and an apology. The appellate court vacated this condition, finding it to be inconsistent with the overall intent of section 5-3-6.1. . . .

We are mindful of the distinctions in the case sub judice and the *Burdin* and *Johnson* cases. However, we agree with the specially concurring opinion in *Johnson,* which observed:

> [T]o uphold the condition imposed here would encourage other courts to impose other unusual, dramatic conditions, and the proliferation of these types of conditions would cause problems of a greater magnitude than their propensity to rehabilitate.

See also People v. Harris, 606 N.E.2d 392 (Ill. App. 1992) (banishing the defendant from the state of Illinois as a condition of probation was unreasonable because no valid purpose would be served); People v. Letterlough, 655 N.E.2d 146 (N.Y. 1995) (condition of probation requiring the defendant to affix a fluorescent sign reading "convicted dwi" to the license plate of any vehicle he drove was not authorized); People v. Hackler, 16 Cal. Rptr. 2d 681 (Cal. App. 1993) (court not authorized to require probationer to wear a T-shirt bearing bold printed statement proclaiming his felony status); but see Lindsay v. State, 606 So. 2d 652 (Fla. App. 1992) (condition of probation requiring defendant to place a newspaper advertisement showing a mug shot, name and caption "DUI-convicted" upheld under Florida statute); Goldschmitt v. State, 490 So. 2d 123 (Fla. App. 1986) (bumper sticker reading "CONVICTED D.U.I.—RESTRICTED LICENSE" upheld); Ballenger v. State, 436 S.E.2d 793 (Ga. App. 1993) (court had the authority to require the defendant to wear a pink fluorescent bracelet reading "D.U.I. CONVICT").

We hold that section 5-6-3(b) of the Code did not authorize the trial court to require the sign as a condition of the defendant's probation. The sign contains a strong element of public humiliation or ridicule because it serves as a formal, public announcement of the defendant's crime. Thus, the sign is inconsistent with the conditions of probation listed in section 5-6-3(b), none of which identify public notification or humiliation as a permissible condition. Further, we determine that the sign may have unpredictable or unintended consequences which may be inconsistent with the rehabilitative purpose of probation.

Finally, the nature and location of the sign are likely to have an adverse effect on innocent individuals who may happen to reside with the defendant. At the time of sentencing in this case, the defendant's wife was living on the premises where the violent felon sign was to be displayed. The defendant's elderly mother also intended to live there. The record shows that the defendant has two adult children who visit the farm, as well as young grandchildren. We believe that the manner in which the sign affects others also renders it an impermissible condition of probation.

Conditions which label a defendant's person or property have a stigmatizing effect and are considered shaming penalties. D. Kahan, What Do Alternative Sanctions Mean? 63 U. Chi. L. Rev. 591 (1996). Although a probationer may experience a certain degree of shame from a statutorily identified condition of probation, shame is not the primary purpose of the enumerated conditions.

The judicially developed condition in the case at bar does not reflect present penological policies of this state as evidenced by our Unified Code of Corrections. The authority to define and fix punishment is a matter for the legislature. The drastic departure from traditional sentencing concepts utilized in this case is not contemplated by our Code. Therefore, we determine that the erection of the sign as a condition of probation was unreasonable, and may be counterproductive to defendant's rehabilitative potential. . . .

NOTES

1. *Shaming.* Shaming has been big news in academic circles since John Braithwaite's pioneering work in the late 1980s. Occasional shaming sanctions make news — sometimes national news — highly disproportionate to their modest character and infrequent use. Shaming sanctions raise many issues: As is so often the habit of lawyers and legal scholars, among the first questions to be addressed is whether shaming sanctions are "legal" or, in the more common and often distorting reaction, whether they are constitutional. The much more difficult and important questions, however, have received less attention. Are shaming sanctions moral? Effective? To what purpose? Which institutions should authorize, design, impose, and review them? See James Q. Whitman, What Is Wrong with Inflicting Shame Sanctions?, 107 Yale L.J. 1055 (1998). In People v. Letterlough, 631 N.Y.S.2d 105 (N.Y. 1995), the court rejected a condition of probation for a DUI offender that he affix to any car he drove a fluorescent sign stating "convicted DWI." In response to *Letterlough* and People v. McNair, 642 N.Y.S.2d 597 (N.Y. 1996) (rejecting a one-year electronic monitoring sentence as beyond statutory authority), the New York legislature amended the relevant statute in 1996 to expand the authorized purposes of probation:

> New York Penal Law §65.10. When imposing a sentence of probation the court may, in addition to any conditions imposed pursuant to [existing authority],

require that the defendant comply with any other reasonable condition as the
court shall determine to be necessary or appropriate to ameliorate the conduct
which gave rise to the offense or to prevent the incarceration of the defendant.

Based on this statutory mandate, what review powers, if any, do New York appellate courts have over probation conditions?

2. *Community service sanctions.*   A more common nondetention alternative
is the community service order, either as a stand-alone sentence or in conjunction with fines or shorter periods of incarceration. Community service sanctions
seem to be used most often for low-level offenders, perhaps as a more intensive
substitute for straight probation. New York instituted a community service sentence program designed both to broaden the base of offenders punished and
to reduce the number of offenders serving short jail terms. See Douglas Corry
McDonald, Punishment Without Walls: Community Service Sentences in New
York City (1986). Community service sentences are usually imposed under the
general authority of probationary sanctions. It is very hard to determine how
many community service sentences are imposed in the United States, whether
they are stand-alone sentences, and how many are successful.

3. Alternative Courts

Sometimes alternative sentences have different purposes than traditional sanctions and call for different adjudicative or sentencing institutions. One prominent example of an alternative court that appears to seek traditional goals is drug
court. The growth of drug courts has been dramatic. The first self-identified drug
court was created in 1989 at the urging of Judge Herbert Klein in Miami. See
Peter Finn and Andrew Newlyn, Miami's Drug Court: A Different Approach
(NCJ 142412, 1996). As of May 2003 there were more than 1,000 reported drug
courts in operation and more than 400 more in planning stages. See Summary of
Drug Court Activity by State and County (2003) (cited at http://www.ncjrs.org/
drug_courts/summary.html). Part of this growth may be attributed to the federal Drug Courts Program Office (created and funded by the Violent Crime
Control and Law Enforcement Act of 1994), which spent $56 million to support
the creation of drug courts between 1995 and 1997.

Judges and reformers created drug courts in response to both the limited
range of sentencing options in traditional criminal courts for drug users and
concerns about the effectiveness and cost of punishment instead of — or at least
in the absence of — drug treatment. Drug courts typically use a less adversarial
approach that tries to ensure public safety. In some states drug courts amount to
a diversionary program, where offenders must perform successfully to prevent a
criminal conviction. Increasingly, however, drug court programs form part of a
probationary sentence or follow a guilty plea while sentencing is being deferred.

Drug courts have not only spread like wildfire, they have offered a model for
breaking the heavily socialized punishment settings of traditional courts and the
erosion of rehabilitation. For drug offenders and others the rehabilitative ideal
remains, or is again vibrant, as a goal of "punishment" (though perhaps the goal
of rehabilitation is in some important way different from punishment). The
broader philosophical and practical labels used to describe this larger movement

are "restorative justice" and "therapeutic courts." We already saw one illustration of restorative purposes in the sentencing circle examined in Chapter 1.

> || *Therapeutic Justice in Alaska's Courts, Teresa* ||
> || *Carns, Michael Hotchkin, and Elaine Andrews* ||
> || 19 Alaska L. Rev. 1 (2002) ||

I.   THERAPEUTIC COURTS IN ALASKA: HISTORY, DEVELOPMENT AND PRESENT STRUCTURES

Wellness Court . . . Anchorage Felony Drug Court . . . Mental Health Court . . . Therapeutic Justice Courts. . . . Underlying these new projects is a growing change in the justice system's response to the difficult problems presented by defendants whose substance abuse or mental disabilities appear to be related inextricably to repeated criminal behavior. Justice professionals describe this approach as "therapeutic justice." . . .

Therapeutic justice emphasizes the need to address the root causes of a specific offender's criminality, to treat the offender to remove the problems and to return the offender to the community as a responsible citizen. Restorative justice emphasizes repair of the relationships between the victim, community and offender. Retributive justice, the model on which much of the United States' criminal justice system is based, emphasizes fairness and punishment as more important values than rehabilitation or other interests. Each model seeks to express community condemnation in order to protect public safety and deter or dissuade the specific offender and others from similar behavior in the future. . . .

C.   Therapeutic Courts: Assets and Liabilities

[P]olicymakers and justice system professionals have identified a wide range of benefits and concerns based on their experiences [with therapeutic courts].

1. The Views of Judges and Court Administrators.   Judges and court administrators differ strongly in their beliefs about the benefits of the therapeutic justice approach. Proponents of therapeutic justice courts believe that the therapeutic justice model has reduced recidivism and increased the chances that defendants can return to their communities as productive individuals. Judges are willing to see a defendant repeatedly in a structured setting for months if they believe that in the end they will not see that defendant back before them for sentencing on repeated offenses. . . . Some judges see the situation as particularly troublesome for misdemeanor offenders who receive at best minimal supervision and often little or no treatment. . . .

Some court administrators and other judges express concerns that the therapeutic courts will be of limited benefit to a few defendants while consuming scarce resources at a rapid rate. In the short term, the projects require extra time to (1) facilitate the frequent meetings among the professionals and court staff involved in each case, (2) hold regular hearings and (3) administer the network of services, sanctions and incentives required to make the therapeutic process work. Project funding often does not include resources to pay for the increased clerical burden on the courts or for the additional administrative time needed for judges to oversee the court's operations. Other justice system professionals are equally concerned about the lack of resources for the added work involved in each therapeutic justice project case.

Other concerns include worries that therapeutic courts may be coercive, may become more paternalistic and repressive than the existing system and may be "net-widening," i.e., they may impose harsher penalties or expectations on relatively less serious offenders rather than targeting more serious offenders. . . .

Perhaps the most serious concern is that courts will be unable to apply therapeutic justice concepts to more than a select few defendants. In a climate where all courts struggle for resources to address their caseloads' demands, resource-intensive therapeutic processes appear out of reach for most cases. Therapeutic courts typically serve only a fraction of potentially eligible defendants. . . . [Some o]bservers . . . believe that drug court procedures eventually may become abbreviated and perfunctory if they "go to scale" to serve a majority of the defendants with substance abuse problems. Under such a system, defendants will lose the benefits of individualized attention and therapeutic justice approaches will devolve into pro forma applications that would be no more effective than the court procedures they replaced.

2. The Views of Defendants.   One stated purpose of therapeutic justice projects is to provide defendants with the structure, resources and incentives to end their addictions or help them resolve the problems that prevent them from leading satisfying and productive lives. Some defendants in therapeutic projects participate because they share the belief that rehabilitation is possible. Other defendants may participate because they believe that the projects are a less onerous choice than incarceration.

Proponents of therapeutic justice cite substantial evidence that coercing treatment through structures such as drug courts may result in better outcomes. Evidence suggests that people in coerced or mandated treatment (as distinct from voluntary treatment) are more likely to complete the treatment. Completion of treatment is critical to significant reduction in the likelihood of relapse.

Conversely, defendants may assess the difficulties of therapeutic justice projects and decide that incarceration is preferable. They may believe that they would fail in any case and would prefer to serve time in custody and be done with it. Some do not believe that they have a problem that needs treatment or that is amenable to the treatment offered, and they may decline to participate on those grounds. Additionally, defense attorneys perceive incarceration as less damaging for some defendants than participation in programs in which the defendant can be repeatedly incarcerated for violations of program guidelines.

3. The Views of Prosecutors.   Prosecutors who favor drug courts tend to believe that their role is to "represent[ ] the community's interest in public order." Other prosecutors question that "broader vision" and suggest instead that the goal of the criminal justice system is for prosecutors to "put bad guys in jail" by winning individual cases. Supporters of the therapeutic approach suggest that prosecutors working in therapeutic courts are as zealous as those working in regular courts, but more accountable. . . .

Some prosecutors may object to specific ways of administering therapeutic justice programs. For example, many oppose pre-plea programs that preserve defendants' options for going back to trial. "As time passes I am in a weaker position as to my case and my expenditure of resources." For this reason, many prosecutors insist on a plea from the defendant as a condition of entry into a therapeutic justice project. Other prosecutors perceive therapeutic justice's collaborative, non-adversarial approach as incompatible with "the public safety-and punishment-oriented goals of the prosecution[.]" They may reserve use of this approach for specific types of defendants and consider it inappropriate for others.

4. Other Justice System Perspectives. Departments of Corrections and the public have responded favorably to therapeutic justice projects in their current form and scope. They favor the projects' potential for reducing incarceration costs and for successfully treating addictions. . . .

Many treatment providers also are supportive, although some individuals believe that the process may be too coercive and that coerced treatment does not work. Thorny confidentiality issues may arise with therapeutic justice projects because the projects require agencies to share and discuss information that is otherwise protected by complex confidentiality laws and regulations. Another concern is the change in the role of treatment providers from serving "exclusively as the gatekeepers to treatment, as they have been accustomed to doing," to having "courts . . . decide who will be sent to treatment and when treatment can be terminated for poor performance."

D. Effectiveness of Therapeutic Courts

. . . Although fewer than one hundred evaluations of therapeutic courts have been published in the last ten years, many are underway. A number of preliminary or partial evaluations have been completed and researchers have considered the effectiveness of many of the separate components of drug courts, particularly the use of monitoring and supervision, completion of treatment programs and use of coerced treatment.

1. Treatment of Addiction/Disease. Various researchers have demonstrated that treatment, if completed, reduces recidivism. Partial completion of treatment often appears to be better than no treatment in reducing recidivism, but length of time in treatment generally predicts the addict's post-treatment success. Other studies have shown that some types of treatment correlate more significantly with reduced recidivism than others. . . .

Other components of drug or therapeutic courts also have proven effective when used separately or outside the context of the therapeutic court. In a Washington, D.C. study, monitoring and closely supervising offenders on probation by itself reduced the incidence of positive drug tests. A Florida program uses intensive supervision of probationers for DWI offenders . . . and has shown significant reduction in recidivism.

The combination of these separate effective elements into therapeutic justice courts has proven successful in many, though not all, instances. Published research shows that many drug courts have reduced recidivism during their existence. However, a few projects have not been able to demonstrate that the drug court population fared any better in terms of post-program recidivism rates than the control or comparison groups.

2. Recidivism. Researchers have conducted very few follow-up evaluations analyzing re-arrest rates and experiences of participants and controls in drug court programs over the months or years after completion of the program. The difficulties posed by long-term evaluations include the added costs of more evaluations, the problem of finding former participants and control group subjects and the management of confidentiality issues. Since most drug court programs are relatively new, insufficient time has elapsed to make realistic follow-up evaluations possible. A similar situation exists for mental health courts and other therapeutic justice projects. . . .

E.   Costs of Therapeutic Justice

Therapeutic justice projects are resource intensive. Even the projects that have functioned for some period of time without outside funding have managed only by using substantial time volunteered by judges, attorneys and other persons and organizations in the community. . . . The resources needed for therapeutic justice projects include added time for judges, attorneys and clerical staff, increased treatment resources, increased monitoring and drug testing of defendants, and expenses (in most programs) for case managers and coordinators. . . .

A [ ] realistic analysis would compare the costs for a drug court to the costs of incarcerating the same defendant for at least a year (the typical length of many drug court programs) and the costs of releasing the defendant untreated (the typical situation for most defendants). In Alaska, the cost for an Anchorage Felony Drug Court participant is estimated at $16,950 annually, as compared to the cost of more than $40,000 per year for incarceration. One observer suggests that because many of the defendants are repeat offenders who face presumptive sentences of two years or more, the actual costs of incarceration usually would be double the $40,000. The cost of incarceration does not include any of the costs associated with investigating the crimes charged, the costs of court processing (clerical and judge time, prosecution and defense costs) or costs of pretrial incarceration or pre-sentence report preparation for felony defendants. The cost for the Anchorage Felony Drug Court does include some attorney time, but neither judge time nor clerical time for any of the participants.

Depending on the program, defendants bear some of the costs. . . .

These differences in practices highlight different philosophies underlying similar projects. Proponents of having defendants pay argue that even if some defendants cannot participate due to very limited resources, those defendants who can should participate. Others contend that requiring any payment unfairly limits the program to those who have the economic resources to participate. . . .

5. Anchorage DUI and Bethel Therapeutic Justice Courts.   [In the spring of 2001 the Alaska legislature] established pilot therapeutic court projects to handle repeat alcohol- and drug-related offenses.

The therapeutic court law established new superior court judgeships in [two] Judicial Districts to provide staff resources for therapeutic justice projects that would achieve "lasting sobriety of offenders, protection of society from alcohol-related and drug-related crime, prompt payment of restitution to victims of crimes, effective interaction and use of resources among criminal justice and community agencies, and long-term reduction of costs relating to arrest, trial, and incarceration." . . . The legislature [ ] intended that these therapeutic courts "focus on defendants charged with multiple driving while intoxicated offenses[,] . . . serve as working models for the development of other similar courts in other areas of the state . . . [and] be adapted to fit the available local resources and cultural traditions" of their locales. . . .

In addition to requiring that these courts possess the attributes typical of the drug court model for defendants (such as emphasis on personal responsibility, frequent appearances before a designated judge and timely recognition of progress and sanctions for relapses), the legislation requires these courts to serve offenders who live in areas of the state without judges, provide for prompt payment of restitution to victims and allow community work service as restoration to the community. The courts must develop a list of sanctions that the program will use if defendants violate program conditions and must give the list to all defendants who request referral to the court. The legislation also directs the courts to consider pharmaceutical treatment for physical alcohol or drug addiction . . . and allows the court to impose house arrest and electronic monitoring on participants. The prosecutor, defense or judge may refer a defendant to the court, but the State may not consent to a referral until the prosecutor has consulted the victim (if any) of the crime. Victims are entitled to periodic reports on the defendant's participation and progress in the program. [D]efendants must plead guilty or no contest or admit to a probation violation before starting the program. Defense and prosecution may join in a plea agreement regarding the charges, and imposition of a sentence is suspended pending completion of the program. . . .

6. Other Therapeutic Court Projects.   Several other groups in Alaska are considering the development of projects using a therapeutic model that includes consolidation of all related cases under one judge, judicial supervision of court-imposed conditions, a strong emphasis on treatment, monitoring to assure sobriety and a specific program of incentives and sanctions. One group is considering a family court that would use this model in Child in Need of Aid cases. The consolidation concept presents several difficult issues, including the possible combination of civil and criminal cases under one judge, which may raise due process and confidentiality problems. . . .

Some judges are considering specialty courts that resemble therapeutic courts in important ways but differ enough in other aspects that planners are not using the term "therapeutic." Several judges are developing projects that use restorative justice concepts, and the increasing number of unfamiliar terms being employed in these contexts results in confusion between these new projects and the therapeutic justice courts. . . .

II.   THERAPEUTIC JURISPRUDENCE: LEGAL ISSUES

[T]he therapeutic justice projects discussed in this Article describe a well-defined approach that differs significantly from that embodied in the traditional

American adversarial system. Most of the legal issues that therapeutic justice approaches raise have not been resolved by the courts, although a few courts have issued opinions addressing them. . . .

A. Constitutional Issues

Courts that have considered cases involving drug courts have dealt with a fairly limited range of the possible constitutional issues that could arise. . . .

1. Separation of Powers.   Many drug court-related cases deal with the defendant's rights in plea bargaining situations and the balance of powers between the executive and judicial branches in determining who is eligible for drug court programs and who makes the final decisions on admission to them. Most of the courts deciding cases related to plea bargains appear to treat drug court agreements as any other plea bargain.

For example, the Alabama Court of Criminal Appeals decided, based on existing case law, that the defendant had a binding agreement with the district attorney that the district attorney could not subsequently repudiate. In a Florida case, the District Court of Appeal ruled that because the defendant successfully completed a pretrial program, the State was bound by the fact that it had offered the defendant the chance to participate in the program and was obliged to dismiss the charges. . . .

The other major separation of powers issue focuses on the prosecutor's exclusive right to decide initial eligibility for drug court admission versus the judge's right to make the final decision about admission to the drug court. Several state courts, including those in Oklahoma and Florida, have held that separation of powers requires that prosecutors be permitted to make the first determination of admission to drug courts. Judges are not allowed to admit defendants to drug courts over the objections of prosecutors. On the other hand, Iowa and Louisiana courts have held that judges have the power to make the final decision about admission to drug court and are under no obligation to accept the prosecutor's recommendation.

2. Due Process.   A few cases address due process issues that have arisen in drug courts. For example, a Washington case held that the defendant must have a meaningful opportunity to respond to allegations of non-compliance before being terminated from the program. An Oklahoma case held that the court must give written reasons for termination of a defendant. This opinion also held that the court must state why the program sanctions were inadequate or inappropriate for the defendant.

3. Equal Access to Courts (Equal Protection).   Several courts have decided that defendants have no right to be admitted to drug courts and that they can be excluded on a variety of grounds. Prior felonies often are mentioned as grounds for ineligibility. A Florida case held that a defendant does not have a constitutional right to participate in a drug court if one had not been established in the circuit in which he was charged. . . . One author has warned that therapeutic justice projects "need to be sensitive to class and race bias, real or apparent. Unless care is taken, diversion courts may tend disproportionately to work with white and middle-class substance abusers."

Several authors have discussed the question of equal access to drug courts when programs do not have enough slots to serve all of the eligible defendants, as well as the question of whether the costs of programs where defendants pay all or part of the costs prohibit indigent defendants from using them. These problems have often been addressed in the context of "going to scale" or expanding the programs to serve the estimated seventy to eighty percent of defendants who have substance abuse problems. One court commentator noted: "We must address the fact that we are providing more resources for a misdemeanor drug offense than we are for a non-capital murder offense or a rape offense. Most states can't afford to continue to do this — politically and fiscally — if problem-solving courts go to scale." . . .

4. First Amendment.   Two New York cases do not directly relate to drug courts but address the question of whether defendants can be required to participate in AA programs as a condition of probation or eligibility for other programs while incarcerated. In 1999, the United States Court of Appeals for the Second Circuit held that the Orange County Department of Probation violated the First Amendment by recommending the plaintiff's participation in AA as a condition of a probationary sentence. Another case, decided in 1996 by the Court of Appeals of New York, held that because of the religious nature of AA, the prison could not impose a requirement that the defendant participate as a condition of eligibility for a Family Reunion program.

These cases are important because AA programs or similar programs often are recommended or required as one of the conditions of drug court participation in addition to any other requirements. . . .

5. Other Issues.   The non-adversarial approach used in therapeutic courts raises questions for many attorneys. Defense attorneys suggest that the drug court environment creates too much pressure to give up suppression motions, legal defenses to the charges and other defense tools before trial.

Some writers, however, suggest that problem-solving courts can protect individual rights prior to trial by using an adversarial approach at that point, saving the collaborative approach for the post-conviction therapeutic activities. They suggest that in the traditional plea system, the defense attorney's role is mostly limited to sentencing advocacy because few cases go to trial. Others note that the traditional plea system is coercive for most defendants, allowing relatively little time for defendants to consider plea offers, and argue that drug courts are no more coercive than the existing plea bargaining system. Not all are comfortable with the change in the defense attorney's approach from adversarial, focusing on minimizing "a client's exposure to criminal sanctions," to collaborative, focusing on aiding the defendant's "recovery from addiction and not [on] the exercise of the full panoply of the defendant's rights." . . .

NOTES

1. *Therapeutic courts and restorative justice.*   While the concepts of therapeutic courts and restorative justice have exploded in policy and scholarly debates

in the 1990s, these ideas, and the closely linked traditional purpose of rehabilitation, have deep historic roots.

The restorative justice movement has become very popular in developed countries in recent years, though African countries have used it for decades in the form of informal customary practices. The goal of the restorative justice movement is to restore the victim and the community that has been harmed. While it has become only recently popular for street offenses, it has been used for decades to address business regulatory challenges. Business regulatory practices focus on restitution, victim empowerment, and the restoration of trust and relationships. Restorative justice can be viewed as an extension of the victim–offender mediation and restorative justice conferences used in business disputes.

2. *Judicial and prosecutorial discretion and power sharing.*   Legislatures have limited judicial discretion in recent years through mandatory sentences and sentencing guidelines. As judicial discretion has narrowed, prosecutorial discretion has broadened. How has the tension between prosecutorial and judicial discretion been resolved in therapeutic courts? To what extent are legislative actions required to institute therapeutic courts? In what areas would legislative action be helpful to facilitate the work of therapeutic courts? See Daniel Van Ness and Pat Nolan, Legislating for Restorative Justice, 10 Regent U. L. Rev. 53 (1998).

3. *Drug courts.*   Drug courts have emerged as the most common illustration of therapeutic courts. They provide intensive, long-term treatment services to offenders with long histories of drug use and criminal justice contacts and high rates of health and social problems. Most drug court participants are men with poor employment and educational records, fairly extensive criminal histories, and prior failed treatment. Usually drug courts target offenders who constitute a medium risk to the community. Hallmarks of the program are access to treatment and rehabilitation services as well as frequent alcohol and drug testing, all under ongoing judicial supervision and interaction with each participant. Usually treatment programs run for one year and are outpatient. The drug court judge is assisted by a team of social workers and substance abuse counselors. Occasional lapses are assumed, and sanctions and rewards are built into the program. The penalty is designed to enforce the prescribed treatment rather than solely to punish.

Even though drug courts enjoy widespread popularity and substantial funding, their success in terms of long-term treatment and recidivism is less clear. See generally Richard Gebelein, The Promise and Perils of Drug Courts (U.S. Dept. of Justice, Office of Justice Programs, May 2000). Graduation rates of drug court enrollees are slightly less than 50 percent, with almost 75,000 having already graduated by the end of 2000. This result is better than for other community-based offender treatment programs. During drug court enrollment, criminal activity and drug use are reduced, but the duration of such success remains undetermined. Some program-specific studies have found beneficial longer-term results, especially a decrease in recidivism and a greater likelihood of employment. See, e.g., Denise C. Gottfredson and M. Lyn Exum, The Baltimore City Drug Treatment Court: One-Year Results from a Randomized Study, 39 J. Res. Crime & Delinq. 337 (2002); The National Center on Addiction and Substance Abuse at Columbia University, Crossing the Bridge: An Evaluation of the Drug Treatment Alternative-to-Prison (DTAP) Program, A CASA White Paper (Mar. 2003).

Some critics of drug courts believe the courts undermine the adversarial system, since offenders must waive some of their rights to be enrolled: Courts have a right of access to all treatment records and are permitted ex parte communications with the prosecution. Another concern, documented in some individual studies, is that drug court participants receive harsher sentences than other offenders, but a greater proportion of their sentences was suspended. This indicates that judges manipulate the severity of punishment so as to reimpose the suspended sentence when an offender recidivates.

The drug court model has been exported abroad. In 2001 Glasgow established the first drug court in Scotland. Canada and Ireland already have similar programs. While the U.S. programs are based on abstinence, this is not always true of drug courts in other countries.

An overview of the literature and research on existing drug courts can be found in Steven Belenko, Research on Drug Courts: A Critical Review — 2001 Update (June 2001; original study done in 1998).

4. *Drug courts and prosecutorial discretion.* Should imposition of a drug court probation sentence depend on the prosecutor's recommendation? In Louisiana v. Taylor, 769 So. 2d 535 (La. 2000), the Louisiana Supreme Court held that a trial court is not authorized to place a defendant in a drug court program absent the prosecutor's recommendation. How can such a limitation on judicial discretion be justified in this context?

5. *Confidentiality concerns.* Therapeutic justice courts raise difficult confidentiality concerns, as Carns, Hotchkin, and Andrews observe:

> Drug and alcohol courts require access to participants' drug and alcohol abuse treatment records. . . . The program's treatment assessor uses this information in determining whether the defendant is diagnostically appropriate for inclusion in the program and in designing an appropriate case plan. Once a program has accepted a defendant, the drug or alcohol court team uses reports of that person's ongoing treatment compliance and prognosis to assess the person's progress. The judge uses the reports to award incentives, impose sanctions and determine whether the participant should graduate, continue in the program or be terminated from the program. . . .
>
> Drug and alcohol courts face two significant issues created by [the] federal regulatory scheme [protecting information about an individual's participation in drug or alcohol abuse treatment programs]. First, . . . [p]articipants consent to release treatment information, both past and future, when they first apply for the programs. . . .
>
> The second issue facing drug and alcohol courts stems from the fact that the regulatory definition of "program" encompasses virtually all of these courts. This subjects them to the regulatory restrictions on disclosure of information that might identify a patient as an alcohol or drug abuser. A problem arises because the courts conduct public proceedings. Although most interactions among judges, attorneys and offenders in drug court do not go into significant detail about a participant's treatment, the mere fact that a person is participating in a drug or alcohol court program indicates that the person has abused alcohol or drugs. One author notes that part of drug court procedure is for the judge to "hold[ ] the offender publicly accountable for the results of the [drug use] test and the treatment progress." The regulations thus create a conflict between public access to court proceedings and the court's duty not to identify or discuss drug and alcohol court participants in a public setting. . . .
>
> . . . Drug court team members are permitted to use such information for their "official duties with regard to the patient's conditional release or other

action in connection with which the consent was given." One authority states that the federal regulations have been interpreted to allow team members to mention confidential information in court. . . . The authority goes on to say that drug court officials should be mindful that consent has not been given to disclose confidential information to unnamed third party bystanders in the courtroom (e.g., public, press and law enforcement). Therefore, courtroom discussions should avoid specific, confidential details of a person's treatment experience and, instead, focus on more general concerns such as the participant's progress.

The same authority notes that the question of whether confidentiality rules apply to drug courts has not been fully resolved. . . .

19 Alaska L. Rev. at 48-49. Should there be more concern about confidentiality in other areas of sentencing?

C. COLLATERAL SANCTIONS

Collateral sanctions, or "collateral consequences," as they have been called more traditionally, have been part of the U.S. criminal justice system for centuries, and in recent years they have won renewed support from legislatures and policy makers. The origin of collateral sanctions can be found in so-called civil death provisions, prevalent in the nineteenth century and earlier in the United States and Europe. Civil death made it impossible for convicted felons to enter into contracts, arranged for automatic divorce from their spouse, prevented them from making a will, and imposed a whole host of other sanctions on them that amounted to legal death. While many of the most offensive of these restrictions have been removed, many more remain, some of which are particularly restrictive in a regulatory welfare state. For some offenders, collateral sanctions may be more dramatic and have longer-term consequences than the sentence imposed in court.

The offenders released from U.S. prisons every year — 625,000 in 2003 — are not again "free" citizens. To the contrary, they often find such a large number of restrictions that some have called the postrelease period a time of "invisible punishment." Offenders are barred from a large number of jobs, from bartender to barber, from securities trader to bail bondsperson, from nurse to beautician. They may be automatically disqualified by their felony conviction, the specific offense they committed, or restrictions on necessary licenses or mobility. Ironically, in some prisons, inmates continue to be trained for jobs they cannot hold after release.

With the expansion of the welfare state, limitations or outright bans on public benefits have become a new form of collateral sanction. Drug and sex offenders are not eligible for public housing; drug offenders are barred from welfare benefits and student loans. Political rights are also restricted. In many states offenders remain barred from the voting booth, the jury box, and political office — sometimes forever.

For a general discussion of collateral consequences, see Nora V. Demleitner, Preventing Internal Exile: The Need for Restrictions on Collateral Sentencing Consequences, 11 Stanford L. & Poly. Rev. 153 (1999); Invisible Punishment: The

Collateral Consequences of Mass Incarceration (Marc Mauer and Meda Chesney-Lind eds., 2002). For a review of collateral sanctions imposed on drug offenders, see Nora V. Demleitner, "Collateral Damage": No Re-entry for Drug Offenders, 47 Villanova L. Rev. 1027 (2002).

There are so many collateral sanctions that judges, prosecutors, and criminal defense attorneys are unable to inform most defendants of all the sanctions that will apply to them. For that reason, the American Bar Association has demanded that such sanctions be cataloged and that defendants be informed of them before they plead guilty. American Bar Association, Criminal Justice Standards, ch. 19 (2003).

Courts have declared collateral sanctions civil rather than criminal sanctions. They are assumed to protect the public against risk rather than constitute further punishment of the offender. Because they are civil sanctions, they lack the procedural protections that apply in criminal cases.

1. Automatic Disabilities

a. Disenfranchisement

All but two states — Maine and Vermont — prohibit prison inmates from voting. Most states also prevent offenders while under a criminal justice sentence from voting: 32 states prohibit felons from voting while they are on parole, and 28 of those also exclude felony probationers. Some states prohibit voting only if the criminal has committed certain crimes; others do so for all felonies. Offenders automatically regain the right to vote in most states upon completion of their sentence. In a small number of states, a felon must apply for a pardon to be permitted to vote.

Currently almost 4 million U.S. citizens are denied the right to vote because of criminal convictions. More than 1 million of them have completed their sentences but live in states that deny voting rights to anyone who has been convicted of a felony and has not received a gubernatorial pardon. State rather than federal law governs voting rights, including the right to vote in presidential and congressional elections.

The Washington state constitution denies persons the right to vote unless their civil rights have been restored. Civil rights are restored when offenders complete all aspects of their sentence, including paying fines and restitution. In Washington State, 45,000 offenders have not had their civil rights restored because of unpaid legal obligations and thus are denied the right to vote. Does this arrangement reinstitute monetary payment as a requisite for voting?

In 1974 the Supreme Court confronted the question whether the denial of the right to vote for felons who had served their sentences violated the Equal Protection Clause. Richardson v. Ramirez, 418 U.S. 24 (1974). In its decision the Court stated that the drafting history, historic practice, and language of section 2 of the Fourteenth Amendment, the Apportionment Clause, justified state disenfranchisement of felons. The clause reads in part:

> [W]hen the right to vote at any election . . . is denied to any of the male inhabitants of such State, being twenty-one years of age, and citizens of the United

States, or in any way abridged, *except for participation in rebellion, or other crime,* the basis of representation therein shall be reduced in the proportion which the number of such male citizens shall bear to the whole number of male citizens twenty-one years of age in such State. [Emphasis added.]

In his dissent, Justice Marshall questioned the majority's analysis of section 2 and advocated addressing the disenfranchisement question under section 1 of the Fourteenth Amendment. He considered the state as having failed its burden of justifying felon disenfranchisement under the compelling interest standard. The state had advocated felon voting restrictions because it wished to prevent voting fraud and because the "likely voting pattern [of felons] might be subversive of the interests of an orderly society." Are these grounds valid?

About a decade later the Court revisited the issue of felon disenfranchisement in Hunter v. Underwood, 471 U.S. 222 (1985). There the Court struck down Alabama's constitutional provision barring felons convicted of "any crime [felony and misdemeanor] . . . involving moral turpitude" from voting. The Court found a violation of the Equal Protection Clause because the state constitutional provision had been passed with a racially discriminatory motive — the exclusion of blacks (and poor whites) from the ballot box.

State courts and lower federal courts have heard numerous challenges on constitutional and statutory grounds to felon disenfranchisement provisions. The most recent state case challenging the disenfranchisement of imprisoned offenders, Fischer v. Governor, 749 A.2d 321 (N.H. 2000), denied voting rights to them. The most frequently cited objections to inmate voting are practical difficulties in arranging for in-prison voting and philosophical objections to granting those who violated society's laws the right to participate in the making of laws. For a different perspective, more characteristic of other Western democracies, consider the following case.

Richard Sauvé v. Canada (Chief Electoral Officer)
[2002] S.C.R.—, 2002 SCC 68

McLACHLIN, C.J.

1. The right of every citizen to vote, guaranteed by s. 3 of the *Canadian Charter of Rights and Freedoms,* lies at the heart of Canadian democracy. The law at stake in this appeal denies the right to vote to a certain class of people — those serving sentences of two years or more in a correctional institution. The question is whether the government has established that this denial of the right to vote is allowed under s. 1 of the Charter as a "reasonable limit . . . demonstrably justified in a free and democratic society." I conclude that it is not. The right to vote, which lies at the heart of Canadian democracy, can only be trammeled for good reason. Here, the reasons offered do not suffice.

2. The predecessor to s. 51(e) of the Canada Elections Act, R.S.C. 1985, c. E-2, prohibited all prison inmates from voting in federal elections, regardless of the length of their sentences. This section was held unconstitutional as an unjustified denial of the right to vote guaranteed by s. 3 of the Charter. Parliament responded to this litigation by replacing this section with a new s. 51(e), which denies the right to vote to all inmates serving sentences of two years or more. . . .

7. To justify the infringement of a Charter right, the government must show that the infringement achieves a constitutionally valid purpose or objective, and that the chosen means are reasonable and demonstrably justified. This two-part inquiry—the legitimacy of the objective and the proportionality of the means — ensures that a reviewing court examine rigorously all aspects of justification. Throughout the justification process, the government bears the burden of proving a valid objective and showing that the rights violation is warranted — that is, that it is rationally connected, causes minimal impairment, and is proportionate to the benefit achieved. . . .

20. The objectives' analysis entails a two-step inquiry. First, we must ask what the objectives are of denying penitentiary inmates the right to vote. This involves interpretation and construction, and calls for a contextual approach. Second, we must evaluate whether the objectives as found are capable of justifying limitations on Charter rights. The objectives must not be "trivial," and they must not be "discordant with the principles integral to a free and democratic society." . . .

21. Section 51(e) denying penitentiary inmates the right to vote was not directed at a specific problem or concern. Prisoners have long voted, here and abroad, in a variety of situations without apparent adverse effects to the political process, the prison population, or society as a whole. In the absence of a specific problem, the government asserts two broad objectives as the reason for this denial of the right to vote: (1) to enhance civic responsibility and respect for the rule of law; and (2) to provide additional punishment, or "enhance the general purposes of the criminal sanction." . . .

22. This leaves the question of whether the objectives of enhancing respect for law and appropriate punishment are constitutionally valid and sufficiently significant to warrant a rights violation. . . . However, precisely because they leave so little room for argument, vague and symbolic objectives make the justification analysis more difficult. Their terms carry many meanings, yet tell us little about why the limitation on the right is necessary, and what it is expected to achieve in concrete terms. The broader and more abstract the objective, the more susceptible it is to different meanings in different contexts, and hence to distortion and manipulation. . . .

26. Quite simply, the government has failed to identify particular problems that require denying the right to vote, making it hard to say that the denial is directed at a pressing and substantial purpose. Nevertheless, despite the abstract nature of the government's objectives and the rather thin basis upon which they rest, prudence suggests that we proceed to the proportionality analysis, rather than dismissing the government's objectives outright. The proportionality inquiry allows us to determine whether the government's asserted objectives are in fact capable of justifying its denial of the right to vote. At that stage, as we shall see, the difficulties inherent in the government's stated objectives become manifest.

27. At this stage the government must show that the denial of the right to vote will promote the asserted objectives (the rational connection test); that the denial does not go further than reasonably necessary to achieve its objectives (the minimal impairment test); and that the overall benefits of the measure outweigh its negative impact (the proportionate effect test). . . .

28. Will denying the right to vote to penitentiary inmates enhance respect for the law and impose legitimate punishment? The government must show that this is likely, either by evidence or in reason and logic.

29. The government advances three theories to demonstrate rational connection between its limitation and the objective of enhancing respect for law. First, it submits that depriving penitentiary inmates of the vote sends an "educative message" about the importance of respect for the law to inmates and to the citizenry at large. Second, it asserts that allowing penitentiary inmates to vote "demeans" the political system. Finally, it takes the position that disenfranchisement is a legitimate form of punishment, regardless of the specific nature of the offence or the circumstances of the individual offender. . . .

30. The first asserted connector with enhancing respect for the law is the "educative message" or "moral statement" theory. The problem here, quite simply, is that denying penitentiary inmates the right to vote is bad pedagogy. . . .

31. Denying penitentiary inmates the right to vote misrepresents the nature of our rights and obligations under the law and consequently undermines them. In a democracy such as ours, . . . the legitimacy of the law and the obligation to obey the law flow directly from the right of every citizen to vote. As a practical matter, we require all within our country's boundaries to obey its laws, whether or not they vote. But this does not negate the vital symbolic, theoretical and practical connection between having a voice in making the law and being obliged to obey it. This connection, inherited from social contract theory and enshrined in the Charter, stands at the heart of our system of constitutional democracy.

32. The government gets this connection exactly backwards when it attempts to argue that depriving people of a voice in government teaches them to obey the law. The "educative message" that the government purports to send by disenfranchising inmates is both anti-democratic and internally self-contradictory. Denying a citizen the right to vote denies the basis of democratic legitimacy. It says that delegates elected by the citizens can then bar those very citizens, or a portion of them, from participating in future elections. But if we accept that governmental power in a democracy flows from the citizens, it is difficult to see how that power can legitimately be used to disenfranchise the very citizens from whom the government's power flows. . . .

38. The theoretical and constitutional links between the right to vote and respect for the rule of law are reflected in the practical realities of the prison population and the need to bolster, rather than to undermine, the feeling of connection between prisoners and society as a whole. The government argues that disenfranchisement will "educate" and rehabilitate inmates. However, disenfranchisement is more likely to become a self-fulfilling prophecy than a spur to reintegration. Depriving at-risk individuals of their sense of collective identity and membership in the community is unlikely to instill a sense of responsibility and community identity, while the right to participate in voting helps teach democratic values and social responsibility. . . .

To deny prisoners the right to vote is to lose an important means of teaching them democratic values and social responsibility.

39. Even if these difficulties could be overcome, it is not apparent that denying penitentiary inmates the right to vote actually sends the intended message to prisoners, or to the rest of society. People may be sentenced to imprisonment for two years or more for a wide variety of crimes, ranging from motor vehicle and regulatory offences to the most serious cases of murder. The variety of offences and offenders covered by the prohibition suggest that the educative message is, at best, a mixed and diffuse one.

40. It is a message sullied, moreover, by negative and unacceptable messages likely to undermine civic responsibility and respect for the rule of law. Denying citizen law-breakers the right to vote sends the message that those who commit serious breaches are no longer valued as members of the community, but instead are temporary outcasts from our system of rights and democracy. More profoundly, it sends the unacceptable message that democratic values are less important than punitive measures ostensibly designed to promote order. If modern democratic history has one lesson to teach it is this: enforced conformity to the law should not come at the cost of our core democratic values. . . .

42. The government also argues that denying penitentiary inmates the vote will enhance respect for law because allowing people who flaunt the law to vote demeans the political system. The same untenable premises we have been discussing resurface here — that voting is a privilege the government can suspend and that the commission of a serious crime signals that the offender has chosen to "opt out" of community membership. But beyond this, the argument that only those who respect the law should participate in the political process is a variant on the age-old unworthiness rationale for denying the vote.

43. . . . Until recently, large classes of people, prisoners among them, were excluded from the franchise. The assumption that they were not fit or "worthy" of voting — whether by reason of class, race, gender or conduct — played a large role in this exclusion. We should reject the retrograde notion that "worthiness" qualifications for voters may be logically viewed as enhancing the political process and respect for the rule of law. . . .

45. This brings us to the government's final argument for rational connection — that disenfranchisement is a legitimate weapon in the state's punitive arsenal against the individual lawbreaker. Again, the argument cannot succeed. The first reason is that using the denial of rights as punishment is suspect. The second reason is that denying the right to vote does not comply with the requirements for legitimate punishment established by our jurisprudence.

46. . . . I do not doubt that Parliament may limit constitutional rights in the name of punishment, provided that it can justify the limitation. But it is another thing to say that a particular class of people for a particular period of time will completely lose a particular constitutional right. This is tantamount to saying that the affected class is outside the full protection of the Charter. It is doubtful that such an unmodulated deprivation, particularly of a right as basic as the right to vote, is capable of justification under s. 1. Could Parliament justifiably pass a law removing the right of all penitentiary prisoners to be protected from cruel and unusual punishment? I think not. What of freedom of expression or religion? Why, one asks, is the right to vote different? The government offers no credible theory about why it should be allowed to deny this fundamental democratic right as a form of state punishment.

47. The social compact requires the citizen to obey the laws created by the democratic process. But it does not follow that failure to do so nullifies the citizen's continued membership in the self-governing polity. Indeed, the remedy of imprisonment for a term rather than permanent exile implies our acceptance of continued membership in the social order. Certain rights are justifiably limited for penal reasons, including aspects of the right to liberty, security of the person, mobility, and security against search and seizure. But whether a right is justifiably

limited cannot be determined by observing that an offender has, by his or her actions, withdrawn from the social compact. Indeed, the right of the state to punish and the obligation of the criminal to accept punishment is tied to society's acceptance of the criminal as a person with rights and responsibilities. . . .

48. The second flaw in the argument that s. 51(e) furthers legitimate punishment is that it does not meet the dual requirements that punishment must not be arbitrary and must serve a valid criminal law purpose. Absence of arbitrariness requires that punishment be tailored to the acts and circumstances of the individual offender. . . . Section 51(e) qua punishment bears little relation to the offender's particular crime. It makes no attempt to differentiate among inmates serving sentences of two years and those serving sentences of twenty. . . . For them the message is doubly invidious — not that they are cast out for their apparently voluntary rejection of society's norms, but that they are cast out arbitrarily, in ways that bear no necessary relation to their actual situation or attitude towards state authority.

49. Punishment must also fulfill a legitimate penal purpose. These include deterrence, rehabilitation, retribution, and denunciation. Neither the record nor common sense supports the claim that disenfranchisement deters crime or rehabilitates criminals. On the contrary, . . . participation in the political process offers a valuable means of teaching democratic values and civic responsibility.

50. This leaves retribution and denunciation. Parliament may denounce unlawful conduct. But it must do so in a way that closely reflects the moral culpability of the offender and his or her circumstances. . . .

Denunciation as a symbolic expression of community values must be individually tailored in order to fulfill the legitimate penal purpose of condemning a *particular* offender's conduct and to send an appropriate "educative message" about the importance of law-abiding behavior. . . .

52. When the facade of rhetoric is stripped away, little is left of the government's claim about punishment other than that criminals are people who have broken society's norms and may therefore be denounced and punished as the government sees fit, even to the point of removing fundamental constitutional rights. Yet, the right to punish and to denounce, however important, is constitutionally constrained. It cannot be used to write entire rights out of the Constitution, it cannot be arbitrary, and it must serve the constitutionally recognized goals of sentencing. On all counts, the case that s. 51(e) furthers lawful punishment objectives fails. . . .

60. The negative effects of s. 51(e) upon prisoners have a disproportionate impact on Canada's already disadvantaged Aboriginal population, whose over-representation in prisons reflects "a crisis in the Canadian criminal justice system." To the extent that the disproportionate number of Aboriginal people in penitentiaries reflects factors such as higher rates of poverty and institutionalized alienation from mainstream society, penitentiary imprisonment may not be a fair or appropriate marker of the degree of individual culpability. . . . Aboriginal people in prison have unique perspectives and needs. Yet, s. 51(e) denies them a voice at the ballot box and, by proxy, in Parliament. That these costs are confined to the term of imprisonment does not diminish their reality. The silenced messages cannot be retrieved, and the prospect of someday participating in the political system is cold comfort to those whose rights are denied in the present. . . .

62. . . . I leave for another day whether some political activities, like standing for office, could be justifiably denied to prisoners under s. 1. It may be that practical problems might serve to justify some limitations on the exercise of derivative democratic rights. Democratic participation is not only a matter of theory but also of practice, and legislatures retain the power to limit the modalities of its exercise where this can be justified. Suffice it to say that the wholesale disenfranchisement of all penitentiary inmates, even with a two-year minimum sentence requirement, is not demonstrably justified in our free and democratic society.

GONTHIER, J., dissenting.

67. . . . If the social or political philosophy advanced by Parliament reasonably justifies a limitation of the right in the context of a free and democratic society, then it ought to be upheld as constitutional. I conclude that this is so in the case at bar.

68. I am of the view that by enacting s. 51(e) of the Act, Parliament has chosen to assert and enhance the importance and value of the right to vote by temporarily disenfranchising serious criminal offenders for the duration of their incarceration. . . . The Chief Justice and I are in agreement that the right to vote is profoundly important, and ought not to be demeaned. Our differences lie principally in the fact that she subscribes to a philosophy whereby the temporary disenfranchising of criminals does injury to the rule of law, democracy and the right to vote, while I prefer deference to Parliament's reasonable view that it strengthens these same features of Canadian society. . . .

70. . . . While there is little logical correlation between maintaining a "decent and responsible citizenry" and any of the past discriminatory exclusions (such as land-ownership, religion, gender, ethnic background), there clearly is such a logical connection in the case of distinguishing persons who have committed serious criminal offences. "*Responsible* citizenship" does not relate to what gender, race, or religion a person belongs to, but is logically related to whether or not a person engages in serious criminal activity.

71. [S]erious criminal offenders are excluded from the vote for the reason that they are the *subjects of punishment.* The disenfranchisement only lasts as long as the period of incarceration. Thus, disenfranchisement, as a dimension of punishment, is attached to and mirrors the fact of incarceration. This fact makes the Canadian experience significantly different from the situation in some American states which disenfranchise ex-offenders for life.

72. It is important to look at prisoner disenfranchisement from the perspective of each serious criminal offender rather than perceive it as a form of targeted group treatment. Disenfranchised prisoners can be characterized loosely as a group, but what is important to realize is that each of these prisoners has been convicted of a serious criminal offence and is therefore serving a personalized sentence which is proportionate to the act or acts committed. Punishment is guided by the goals of denunciation, deterrence, rehabilitation and retribution and is intended to be morally educative for incarcerated serious criminal offenders. Each prisoner's sentence is a temporary measure aimed at meeting these goals, while also being aimed at the long-term objective of reintegration into the community. . . .

75. The argument that the temporary disenfranchisement of serious criminal offenders undermines the inherent "worth" or "dignity" of prisoners

presents a potentially problematic line of reasoning. Is it possible to "punish" serious criminals without undermining their "worth"? It must be so. This is inherently recognised in the Charter itself insofar that s. 12 only renders unconstitutional punishment that is "cruel and unusual." The *Criminal Code* and its provisions are declaratory of values, values on which Canadian society rests. Protecting and enhancing these values through the imposition of punishment for criminal activity is not an affront to dignity. On the contrary, the temporary disenfranchisement of serious criminal offenders reiterates society's commitment to the basic moral values which underpin the Criminal Code; in this way it is morally educative for both prisoners and society as a whole. . . .

116. Permitting the exercise of the franchise by offenders incarcerated for serious offences undermines the rule of law and civic responsibility because such persons have demonstrated a great disrespect for the community in their committing serious crimes: such persons have attacked the stability and order within our community. Society therefore may choose to curtail temporarily the availability of the vote to serious criminals both to punish those criminals and to insist that civic responsibility and respect for the rule of law, as goals worthy of pursuit, are prerequisites to democratic participation. . . .

119. . . . The disenfranchisement of serious criminal offenders serves to deliver a message to both the community and the offenders themselves that serious criminal activity will not be tolerated by the community. In making such a choice, Parliament is projecting a view of Canadian society which Canadian society has of itself. The commission of serious crimes gives rise to a temporary suspension of this nexus: on the physical level, this is reflected in incarceration and the deprivation of a range of liberties normally exercised by citizens and, at the symbolic level, this is reflected in temporary disenfranchisement. The symbolic dimension is thus a further manifestation of community disapproval of the serious criminal conduct.

120. From the perspective of the person whose criminal activity has resulted in their temporary disenfranchisement, their benefiting from society brought with it the responsibility to be subjected to the sanctions which the state decides will be attached to serious criminal activity such as they have chosen to undertake. This understanding is complemented by the rehabilitative view that those who are in jail will hope and expect to regain the exercise of the vote on their release from incarceration, just like they hope and expect to regain the exercise of the fullest expressions of their liberty. Once released from prison, they are on the road to reintegration into the community. Obtaining the vote once released or paroled is a recognition of regaining the nexus with the community that was temporarily suspended during the incarceration. . . .

159. [G]iven that, the objectives are largely symbolic, common sense dictates that social condemnation of criminal activity and a desire to promote civic responsibility are reflected in disenfranchisement of those who have committed serious crimes. This justification is rooted in a reasonable and rational social and political philosophy which has been adopted by Parliament. Further, it can hardly be seen as "novel." . . . The view of the courts below is that generally supported by democratic countries. Countries including the United States, the United Kingdom, Australia, New Zealand, and many European countries such as France and Germany, have, by virtue of choosing some form of prisoner disenfranchisement,

also identified a connection between objectives similar to those advanced in the case at bar and the means of prisoner disenfranchisement. . . .

NOTES

1. *Voting restrictions on felons in the United States.*   In the United States voting restrictions based on a prior criminal record go back to the beginning of the Republic. They did not begin to play a prominent role until after the Civil War, when Southern legislatures in particular used them to prevent blacks from voting. See Hunter v. Underwood, 471 U.S. 222 (1985) (striking down Alabama voting restriction because it was motivated by racial animus). Even though in recent years states have cut back on voting restrictions, currently 48 states prevent inmates from voting. Most states also bar felons from voting while they are on parole, and more than half deny the vote to probationers. Thirteen states deny offenders the right to vote even after they have been released from or fully satisfied a criminal justice sanction.

2. *Justifications for felon disenfranchisement.*   Felon disenfranchisement has been justified on a number of grounds. Some have claimed that felons violate the implicit social contract and should therefore be excluded from voting. Others have stated that civic virtues are needed to participate in political decision making; in their absence, individuals should be excluded from the polity. Among the more practical and frequently raised arguments are potential election fraud by convicted felons (the "purity of the ballot box" argument), potential problems of arranging for voting in prisons, and in the past, racial arguments defending felon disenfranchisement as a way of excluding blacks (and sometimes also poor whites) from voting. For a discussion of the political philosophies underlying criminal disenfranchisement, see Alec Ewald, "Civil Death": The Ideological Paradox of Criminal Disenfranchisement Law in the United States, 2002 Wis. L. Rev. 1045. Do you consider these defenses valid, especially in light of the Canadian high court's decision?

3. *Race and felon disenfranchisement.*   Despite challenges to disenfranchisement provisions on equal protection grounds, the Supreme Court has upheld state laws disenfranchising felons generally. See Richardson v. Ramirez, 418 U.S. 24 (1974). In a handful of subsequent cases, however, courts have struck down disenfranchisement provisions that were animated by racial bias, in violation of the Equal Protection Clause.

A 1998 study published by Human Rights Watch and the Sentencing Project illuminated the racially disproportionate impact of the exclusion of felons from voting. The Sentencing Project and Human Rights Watch, Losing the Vote: The Impact of Felony Disenfranchisement in the United States (Oct. 1998) (available at www.sentencingproject.org/pdfs/9080.pdf). Because of their overrepresentation among convicted felons and their large numbers in states that allow for disenfranchisement after an offender's sentence has been served, 1.8 million African Americans are excluded from the franchise. Should the disproportionate racial impact on a fundamental constitutional right — the franchise — be a reason for striking down such legislation on equal protection grounds? How could a legislator use the study to argue for or against the abolition or at least the restriction of felon disenfranchisement?

4. *The impact of felon disenfranchisement in elections.*   The 2000 presidential election, whose outcome hinged on the result in the state of Florida, focused national attention in part on felon disenfranchisement. The state, with its large inmate population, disenfranchises not only prison inmates but also ex-offenders released from any criminal justice sanction unless they have obtained a gubernatorial pardon — a difficult and protracted process. Many argued that felon disenfranchisement changed the outcome of the presidential election in Florida. For some empirical support for the possible impact of felon disenfranchisement on election outcomes, see Christopher Uggen and Jeff Manza, Democratic Contraction? The Political Consequences of Felon Disenfranchisement in the United States, 67 Am. Soc. Rev. 777 (2002).

5. *Restoration of voting rights.*   Most states automatically restore voting rights to all offenders after they have served their criminal justice sentence. Some, however, restrict automatic restoration provisions to first-time or nonviolent offenders. States that do not have automatic restoration provisions offer administrative, judicial, or legislative relief. The difficulty and cost of obtaining relief varies based on the procedure and the state:

> Alabama's voting rights restoration process is complex and potentially intimidating. Those seeking restoration must first obtain a pardon from the Board of Pardons and Paroles. Before applying for pardon, ex-felons must complete three years of permanent parole. Certain offenders must provide the Board with DNA samples before they are eligible for a pardon. Obtaining a pardon alone, however, is insufficient; the Board must next vote affirmatively to restore the applicant's voting rights. . . .
>
> Any ex-felon seeking restoration [in Florida] must apply to the Governor's Executive Clemency Board. This process has been criticized in the past several years, most recently when the Florida Department of Corrections reported granting only 927 restorations in the year 2000 — compared with an average of 11,800 between 1986 and 1991 — despite the state's large disenfranchised population. . . .
>
> In 2000, Virginia passed a measure that allows ex-felons not convicted of drug offenses to apply to circuit courts for restoration after a five-year waiting period; ex-felons convicted of drug offenses must wait seven years before they become eligible for restoration. The circuit court's decision is not final; the Governor must review and approve any favorable decision. Despite an active reform campaign in the state legislature and the press, felons remain subject to one of the nation's most cumbersome restoration regimes.

Developments in the Law — The Law of Prisons, Part VI. One Person, No Vote: The Laws of Felon Disenfranchisement, 115 Harv. L. Rev. 1939, 1944-1945, 1947-1948 (2002).

6. *Felon disenfranchisement — uniquely American?*   In most other Western democracies, voting restrictions on convicted felons are very limited. Germany, for example, allows disenfranchisement only upon conviction of a very small number of offenses, including treason and voting fraud, for a maximum period of five years, and if imposed by a judge at sentencing in open court. See Nora V. Demleitner, Continuing Payment on One's Debt to Society: The German Model of Felon Disenfranchisement as an Alternative, 84 Minn. L. Rev. 753 (2000). In

Sauvé, the Supreme Court of Canada surveyed the practices in other Western democracies:

> European countries demonstrate a broad range of practices. Eighteen European countries have no form of electoral ban for incarcerated offenders: Bosnia, Croatia, Cyprus, Denmark, Iceland, Ireland, Finland, Latvia, Lithuania, Macedonia, Netherlands, Poland, Slovenia, Spain, Sweden, Switzerland and the Ukraine. In Greece, prisoners serving life sentences or indefinite sentences are disqualified; otherwise the matter is left to the discretion of the court. In some other European countries, electoral disqualification depends on the crime committed or the length of the sentence: Austria, Malta and San Marino ban all prisoners serving more than one year from voting; Belgium disqualifies all offenders serving sentences of four months or more; Italy disenfranchises based on the crime committed and/or the sentence length; Norway removes the vote for prisoners sentenced for specific offences; and in France and Germany, the disqualification of a prisoner is dependent upon the sentence handed down by the court specifically providing for disenfranchisement (in France, certain crimes are identified which carry automatic forfeiture of political rights; in Germany, prisoners convicted of offences which target the integrity of the German state or its democratic order lose the vote). Armenia, Bulgaria, the Czech Republic, Estonia, Hungary, Luxembourg, Romania and Russia all have complete bans for sentenced offenders.
>
> Australia, New Zealand and the United Kingdom all disenfranchise at least some of the inmate population. In Australia, prisoners vote in two of seven states. In federal elections, inmates serving sentences of five years or more are disqualified from voting. In New Zealand, prisoners serving sentences for three years or more, preventative detention or life imprisonment are not qualified to vote. In the United Kingdom, prisoners are completely disenfranchised for Parliamentary elections, elections to the European Assembly, and local government elections. The only exceptions are for remand prisoners, persons imprisoned for contempt of court and persons detained for default in complying with their sentence. . . .
>
> Certain international instruments also address the issue of prisoner voting. Article 25 of the International Covenant on Civil and Political Rights ("ICCPR") states that every citizen shall have the "right and the opportunity" to vote "without unreasonable restrictions": ICCPR, 999 U.N.T.S. 171, entered into force March 23, 1976. The United Nations Human Rights Committee, in a comment on Art. 25 of the ICCPR, stated that restrictions on the right to vote should be "objective and reasonable" and that "[i]f conviction for an offence is a basis for suspending the right to vote, the period of such suspension should be proportionate to the offence and the sentence": "General Comment Adopted by the Human Rights Committee Under Article 40, Paragraph 4 of the International Comment on Civil and Political Rights," General Comment No. 25(57), Annex V(1), CCPR/C/21, Rev. 1, Add. 7, August 27, 1996. It is likely caveats, such as the one in Art. 25 of the ICCPR, which led the international non-governmental organization Penal Reform International, in their 1995 publication Making Standards Work—An International Handbook on Good Prison Practice, at pp. 13-14, to distinguish between "retained rights," which it advocated must be retained in a prison setting, and other rights which may be limited, amongst which was listed the right to vote.

Sauvé, 2002 SCC at ¶¶ 130, 131, and 133.

In a seminal opinion, the Constitutional Court of South Africa in August v. Electoral Commn., 1999 (3) SA 1 (CC), struck down the disenfranchisement of felons; the high court's rationale was followed most recently by the Supreme Court of Canada in *Sauvé.*

b. Notification and Registration

In recent years sanctions have increased dramatically against sex offenders as a class. States and federal legislatures and guideline commissions have lengthened prison sentences; numerous states have passed civil confinement statutes that allow judges to commit sex offenders civilly after their release from prison, a development sanctioned by the Supreme Court in Hendricks v. Kansas, 521 U.S. 346 (1996), and discussed in Chapter 11.

These harsher sanctions came in response to assessments that sentences for sex offenses were disproportionately low compared to other violent and nonviolent crimes and in light of beliefs about the future danger such offenders pose. Incapacitative goals animate sex offender civil commitment statutes, which are based on risk assessments derived from the offender's prior criminal record and assumptions about whether he is likely to reoffend. In addition to civil commitment laws, registration statutes enacted in the mid-1990s require that sex offenders register with local police upon release so that their names can be entered into a database. Notification statutes also require police to alert neighbors, schools, and certain other institutions when a sex offender moves into the area.

|| *Delbert Smith v. John Doe I* ||
|| 538 U.S. 84 (2003) ||

KENNEDY, J.

The Alaska Sex Offender Registration Act requires convicted sex offenders to register with law enforcement authorities, and much of the information is made public. We must decide whether the registration requirement is a retroactive punishment prohibited by the Ex Post Facto clause.

The State of Alaska enacted the Alaska Sex Offender Registration Act (Act) on May 12, 1994. Like its counterparts in other States, the Act is termed a "Megan's Law." Megan Kanka was a 7-year-old New Jersey girl who was sexually assaulted and murdered in 1994 by a neighbor who, unknown to the victim's family, had prior convictions for sex offenses against children. The crime gave impetus to laws for mandatory registration of sex offenders and corresponding community notification. In 1994, Congress passed the Jacob Wetterling Crimes Against Children and Sexually Violent Offender Registration Act, 42 U.S.C. §14071, which conditions certain federal law enforcement funding on the States' adoption of sex offender registration laws and sets minimum standards for state programs. By 1996, every State, the District of Columbia, and the Federal Government had enacted some variation of Megan's Law.

The Alaska law . . . contains two components: a registration requirement and a notification system. Both are retroactive. The Act requires any "sex offender or child kidnapper who is physically present in the state" to register, either with the Department of Corrections (if the individual is incarcerated) or with the local law enforcement authorities (if the individual is at liberty). Prompt registration is mandated. . . . The sex offender must provide his name, aliases, identifying features, address, place of employment, date of birth, conviction information, driver's license number, information about vehicles to which he has access, and postconviction treatment history. He must permit the authorities to photograph and fingerprint him.

If the offender was convicted of a single, nonaggravated sex crime, he must provide annual verification of the submitted information for 15 years. If he was convicted of an aggravated sex offense or of two or more sex offenses, he must register for life and verify the information quarterly. The offender must notify his local police department if he moves. A sex offender who knowingly fails to comply with the Act is subject to criminal prosecution.

The information is forwarded to the Alaska Department of Public Safety, which maintains a central registry of sex offenders. Some of the data . . . is kept confidential. The following information is made available to the public: "the sex offender's or child kidnapper's name, aliases, address, photograph, physical description, description[,] license [and] identification numbers of motor vehicles, place of employment, date of birth, crime for which convicted, date of conviction, place and court of conviction, length and conditions of sentence, and a statement as to whether the offender or kidnapper is in compliance with [the update] requirements . . . or cannot be located." . . . Alaska has chosen to make most of the nonconfidential information available on the Internet.

Respondents John Doe I and John Doe II were convicted of sexual abuse of a minor, an aggravated sex offense. . . . Both were released from prison in 1990 and completed rehabilitative programs for sex offenders. Although convicted before the passage of the Act, respondents are covered by it. After the initial registration, they are required to submit quarterly verifications and notify the authorities of any changes. Both respondents, along with respondent Jane Doe, wife of John Doe I, brought an action . . . seeking to declare the Act void as to them under the Ex Post Facto Clause of Article I, §10, cl. 1, of the Constitution and the Due Process Clause of §1 of the Fourteenth Amendment. . . .

This is the first time we have considered a claim that a sex offender registration and notification law constitutes retroactive punishment forbidden by the Ex Post Facto Clause. The framework for our inquiry, however, is well established. We must "ascertain whether the legislature meant the statute to establish 'civil' proceedings." Kansas v. Hendricks, 521 U.S. 346, 361 (1997). If the intention of the legislature was to impose punishment, that ends the inquiry. If, however, the intention was to enact a regulatory scheme that is civil and nonpunitive, we must further examine whether the statutory scheme is "'so punitive either in purpose or effect as to negate [the State's] intention' to deem it 'civil.'" Because we "ordinarily defer to the legislature's stated intent," "'only the clearest proof' will suffice to override legislative intent and transform what has been denominated a civil remedy into a criminal penalty," Hudson v. United States, 522 U.S. 93, 100 (1997); United States v. One Assortment of 89 Firearms, 465 U.S. 354 (1984). . . .

Whether a statutory scheme is civil or criminal "is first of all a question of statutory construction." We consider the statute's text and its structure to determine the legislative objective. Flemming v. Nestor, 363 U.S. 603 (1960). A conclusion that the legislature intended to punish would satisfy an ex post facto challenge without further inquiry into its effects, so considerable deference must be accorded to the intent as the legislature has stated it.

The courts "must first ask whether the legislature, in establishing the penalizing mechanism, indicated either expressly or impliedly a preference for one label or the other." Here, the Alaska Legislature expressed the objective of the law in the statutory text itself. The legislature found that "sex offenders pose a high risk of reoffending," and identified "protecting the public from sex offenders" as the "primary governmental interest" of the law. The legislature further determined that "release of certain information about sex offenders to public agencies and the general public will assist in protecting the public safety." As we observed in *Hendricks,* where we examined an ex post facto challenge to a post-incarceration confinement of sex offenders, an imposition of restrictive measures on sex offenders adjudged to be dangerous is "a legitimate nonpunitive governmental objective and has been historically so regarded." In this case, as in *Hendricks,* "nothing on the face of the statute suggests that the legislature sought to create anything other than a civil . . . scheme designed to protect the public from harm."

Respondents seek to cast doubt upon the nonpunitive nature of the law's declared objective by pointing out that the Alaska Constitution lists the need for protecting the public as one of the purposes of criminal administration. As the Court stated in Flemming v. Nestor, rejecting an ex post facto challenge to a law terminating benefits to deported aliens, where a legislative restriction "is an incident of the State's power to protect the health and safety of its citizens," it will be considered "as evidencing an intent to exercise that regulatory power, and not a purpose to add to the punishment." [P]recedents instruct us that even if the objective of the Act is consistent with the purposes of the Alaska criminal justice system, the State's pursuit of it in a regulatory scheme does not make the objective punitive.

Other formal attributes of a legislative enactment, such as the manner of its codification or the enforcement procedures it establishes, are probative of the legislature's intent. In this case these factors are open to debate. The notification provisions of the Act are codified in the State's "Health, Safety, and Housing Code," confirming our conclusion that the statute was intended as a nonpunitive regulatory measure. The Act's registration provisions, however, are codified in the State's criminal procedure code, and so might seem to point in the opposite direction. These factors, though, are not dispositive. The location and labels of a statutory provision do not by themselves transform a civil remedy into a criminal one. In *89 Firearms,* the Court held a forfeiture provision to be a civil sanction even though the authorizing statute was in the criminal code. The Court rejected the argument that the placement demonstrated Congress' "intention to create an additional criminal sanction," observing that "both criminal and civil sanctions may be labeled 'penalties.'"

The same rationale applies here. Title 12 of Alaska's Code of Criminal Procedure (where the Act's registration provisions are located) contains many provisions that do not involve criminal punishment. . . . Although some of these provisions relate to criminal administration, they are not in themselves punitive. The partial codification of the Act in the State's criminal procedure code is not sufficient to support a conclusion that the legislative intent was punitive.

The procedural mechanisms to implement the Act do not alter our conclusion. After the Act's adoption Alaska amended its Rules of Criminal Procedure concerning the acceptance of pleas and the entering of criminal judgments. The rule[s] on pleas [and written judgments for sex offenses and child kidnapping] now requires the court to "inform the defendant in writing of the requirements of [the Act] and, if it can be determined by the court, the period of registration required." . . .

The policy to alert convicted offenders to the civil consequences of their criminal conduct does not render the consequences themselves punitive. When a State sets up a regulatory scheme, it is logical to provide those persons subject to it with clear and unambiguous notice of the requirements and the penalties for noncompliance. . . . Although other methods of notification may be available, it is effective to make it part of the plea colloquy or the judgment of conviction. Invoking the criminal process in aid of a statutory regime does not render the statutory scheme itself punitive.

Our conclusion is strengthened by the fact that, aside from the duty to register, the statute itself mandates no procedures. Instead, it vests the authority to promulgate implementing regulations with the Alaska Department of Public Safety — an agency charged with enforcement of both criminal *and* civil regulatory laws. The Act itself does not require the procedures adopted to contain any safeguards associated with the criminal process. That leads us to infer that the legislature envisioned the Act's implementation to be civil and administrative. . . .

We conclude . . . that the intent of the Alaska Legislature was to create a civil, nonpunitive regime.

In analyzing the effects of the Act we refer to the seven factors noted in Kennedy v. Mendoza-Martinez, 372 U.S. 144 (1963), as a useful framework. These factors, which migrated into our ex post facto case law from double jeopardy jurisprudence, have their earlier origins in cases under the Sixth and Eight Amendments, as well as the Bill of Attainder and the Ex Post Facto Clauses. . . . The factors most relevant to our analysis are whether, in its necessary operation, the regulatory scheme: has been regarded in our history and traditions as a punishment; imposes an affirmative disability or restraint; promotes the traditional aims of punishment; has a rational connection to a nonpunitive purpose; or is excessive with respect to this purpose.

A historical survey can be useful because a State that decides to punish an individual is likely to select a means deemed punitive in our tradition, so that the public will recognize it as such. . . . Respondents argue [ ] that the Act — and, in particular, its notification provisions — resemble shaming punishments of the colonial period.

Some colonial punishments indeed were meant to inflict public disgrace. Humiliated offenders were required "to stand in public with signs cataloguing their offenses." Hirsh, From Pillory to Penitentiary: The Rise of Criminal Incarceration in Early Massachusetts, 80 Mich. L. Rev. 1179 (1982); see also L. Friedman, Crime and Punishment in American History 38 (1993). At times the labeling would be permanent: A murderer might be branded with an "M," and a thief with a "T." R. Semmes, Crime and Punishment in Early Maryland 35 (1938); see also Massaro, Shame, Culture, and American Criminal Law, 89 Mich. L. Rev. 1880 (1991). The aim was to make these offenders suffer "permanent stigmas, which in effect cast the person out of the community." The most serious offenders were banished, after which they could neither return to their original community nor, reputation tarnished, be admitted easily into a new one. . . .

Any initial resemblance to early punishments is, however, misleading. Punishments such as whipping, pillory, and branding inflicted physical pain and staged a direct confrontation between the offender and the public. Even punishments that lacked the corporal component, such as public shaming, humiliation, and banishment, . . . either held the person up before his fellow citizens for face-to-face shaming or expelled him from the community. By contrast, the stigma of Alaska's Megan's Law results not from public display for ridicule and shaming but from the dissemination of accurate information about a criminal record, most of which is already public. Our system does not treat dissemination of truthful information in furtherance of a legitimate governmental objective as punishment. . . . In contrast to the colonial shaming punishments, however, the State does not make the publicity and the resulting stigma an integral part of the objective of the regulatory scheme.

The fact that Alaska posts the information on the Internet does not alter our conclusion. . . . Widespread public access is necessary for the efficacy of the scheme, and the attendant humiliation is but a collateral consequence of a valid regulation.

The State's Web site does not provide the public with means to shame the offender by, say, posting comments underneath his record. An individual seeking the information must take the initial step of going to the Department of Public Safety's Web site, proceed to the sex offender registry, and then look up the desired information. The process is more analogous to a visit to an official archive of criminal records than it is to a scheme forcing an offender to appear in public with some visible badge of past criminality. The Internet makes the document search more efficient, cost effective, and convenient for Alaska's citizenry.

We next consider whether the Act subjects respondents to an "affirmative disability or restraint." Here, we inquire how the effects of the Act are felt by those subject to it. If the disability or restraint is minor and indirect, its effects are unlikely to be punitive.

The Act imposes no physical restraint, and so does not resemble the punishment of imprisonment, which is the paradigmatic affirmative disability or restraint. The Act's obligations are less harsh than the sanctions of occupational debarment, which we have held to be nonpunitive. See [*Hudson*] (forbidding further participation in the banking industry); De Veau v. Braisted, 363 U.S. 144 (1960) (forbidding work as a union official); Hawker v. New York, 170 U.S. 189 (1898) (revocation of a medical license). The Act does not restrain activities sex offenders may pursue but leaves them free to change jobs or residences.

The Court of Appeals sought to distinguish *Hawker* and cases which have followed it on the grounds that the disability at issue there was specific and "narrow," confined to particular professions, whereas "the procedures employed under the Alaska statute are likely to make [respondents] *completely unemployable*" because "employers will not want to risk loss of business when the public learns that they have hired sex offenders." This is conjecture. Landlords and employers could conduct background checks on the criminal records of prospective employees or tenants even with the Act not in force. The record in this case contains no evidence that the Act has led to substantial occupational or housing disadvantages for former sex offenders that would not have otherwise occurred through the use of routine background checks by employers and landlords. The Court of Appeals identified only one incident from the 7-year history of Alaska's law where a sex offender suffered community hostility and damage to his business after the information he submitted to the registry became public. This could have occurred in any event, because the information about the individual's conviction was already in the public domain.

Although the public availability of the information may have a lasting and painful impact on the convicted sex offender, these consequences flow not from the Act's registration and dissemination provisions, but from the fact of conviction, already a matter of public record. The State makes the facts underlying the offenses and the resulting convictions accessible so members of the public can take the precautions they deem necessary before dealing with the registrant.

. . . The Court of Appeals held that the registration system is parallel to probation or supervised release in terms of the restraint imposed. This argument has some force, but, after due consideration, we reject it. Probation and supervised release entail a series of mandatory conditions and allow the supervising officer to seek the revocation of probation or release in case of infraction. By contrast, offenders subject to the Alaska statute are free to move where they wish and to live and work as other citizens, with no supervision. Although registrants must inform the authorities after they change their facial features (such as growing a beard), borrow a car, or seek psychiatric treatment, they are not required to seek permission to do so. A sex offender who fails to comply with the reporting requirement may be subjected to a criminal prosecution for that failure, but any prosecution is a proceeding separate from the individual's original offense. [T]he registration requirements make a valid regulatory program effective and do not impose punitive restraints in violation of the Ex Post Facto Clause.

The State concedes that the statute might deter future crimes. Respondents seize on this proposition to argue that the law is punitive, because deterrence is one purpose of punishment. This proves too much. Any number of governmental programs might deter crime without imposing punishment. "To hold that the mere presence of a deterrent purpose renders such sanctions 'criminal' . . . would severely undermine the Government's ability to engage in effective regulation."

The Court of Appeals was incorrect to conclude that the Act's registration obligations were retributive because "the length of the reporting requirement appears to be measured by the extent of the wrongdoing, not by the extent of the risk posed." The Act, it is true, differentiates between individuals convicted of aggravated or multiple offenses and those convicted of a single nonaggravated offense. The broad categories, however, and the corresponding length of the reporting requirement, are reasonably related to the danger of recidivism, and this is consistent with the regulatory objective.

The Act's rational connection to a nonpunitive purpose is a "most significant" factor in our determination that the statute's effects are not punitive. . . . A statute is not deemed punitive simply because it lacks a close or perfect fit with the nonpunitive aims it seeks to advance. The imprecision respondents rely upon does not suggest that the Act's nonpunitive purpose is a "sham or mere pretext."

. . . Alaska could conclude that a conviction for a sex offense provides evidence of substantial risk of recidivism. The legislature's findings are consistent with grave concerns over the high rate of recidivism among convicted sex offenders and their dangerousness as a class. The risk of recidivism posed by sex offenders is "frightening and high." McKune v. Lile, 536 U.S. 24, 33 (2002) ("When convicted sex offenders reenter society, they are much more likely than any other type of offender to be rearrested for a new rape or sexual assault") (citing U.S. Dept. of Justice, Bureau of Justice Statistics, Sex Offenses and Offenders 27 (1997); U.S. Dept. of Justice, Bureau of Justice Statistics, Recidivism of Prisoners Released in 1983, p. 6 (1997)).

The Ex Post Facto Clause does not preclude a State from making reasonable categorical judgments that conviction of specified crimes should entail particular regulatory consequences. We have upheld against ex post facto challenges laws imposing regulatory burdens on individuals convicted of crimes without any corresponding risk assessment. . . . The State's determination to legislate with respect to convicted sex offenders as a class, rather than require individual determination of their dangerousness, does not make the statute a punishment under the Ex Post Facto Clause.

. . . The duration of the reporting requirements is not excessive. Empirical research on child molesters, for instance, has shown that, "contrary to conventional wisdom, most reoffenses do not occur within the first several years after release," but may occur "as late as 20 years following release." R. Prentky, R. Knight, and A. Lee, U.S. Dept. of Justice, National Institute of Justice, Child Sexual Molestation: Research Issues 14 (1997).

. . . Given the general mobility of our population, for Alaska to make its registry system available and easily accessible throughout the State was not so excessive a regulatory requirement as to become a punishment. See D. Schram & C. Milloy, Community Notification: A Study of Offender Characteristics and Recidivism 13 (1995) (38% of recidivist sex offenses in the State of Washington took place in jurisdictions other than where the previous offense was committed).

The excessiveness inquiry of our ex post facto jurisprudence is not an exercise in determining whether the legislature has made the best choice possible to address the problem it seeks to remedy. The question is whether the regulatory means chosen are reasonable in light of the nonpunitive objective. The Act meets this standard.

. . . Our examination of the Act's effects leads to the determination that respondents cannot show, much less by the clearest proof, that the effects of the law negate Alaska's intention to establish a civil regulatory scheme. The Act is nonpunitive, and its retroactive application does not violate the Ex Post Facto Clause. . . .

STEVENS, J., dissenting.
. . . The Court's opinion[ ] fail[s] to decide whether the statutes deprive the registrants of a constitutionally protected interest in liberty. . . .

The statutes impose significant affirmative obligations and a severe stigma on every person to whom they apply. . . .

The registration and reporting duties imposed on convicted sex offenders are comparable to the duties imposed on other convicted criminals during periods of supervised release or parole. And there can be no doubt that the "widespread public access," to this personal and constantly updated information has a severe stigmatizing effect. In my judgment, these statutes unquestionably affect a constitutionally protected interest in liberty.

It is also clear beyond peradventure that these unique consequences of conviction of a sex offense are punitive. They share three characteristics, which in the aggregate are not present in any civil sanction. The sanctions (1) constitute a severe deprivation of the offender's liberty, (2) are imposed on everyone who is convicted of a relevant criminal offense, and (3) are imposed only on those criminals. Unlike any of the cases that the Court has cited, a criminal conviction under these statutes provides both a *sufficient* and a *necessary* condition for the sanction.

[T]he Constitution prohibits the addition of these sanctions to the punishment of persons who were tried and convicted before the legislation was enacted. As the Court recognizes, "recidivism is the statutory concern" that provides the supposed justification for the imposition of such retroactive punishment. . . . Reliance on that rationale here highlights the conclusion that the retroactive application of these statutes constitutes a flagrant violation of the protections afforded by the Double Jeopardy and Ex Post Facto Clauses of the Constitution.

[T]he State may impose registration duties and may publish registration information as a part of its punishment of this category of defendants. Looking to the future, these aspects of their punishment are adequately justified by two of the traditional aims of punishment — retribution and deterrence. Moreover, as a matter of procedural fairness, Alaska requires its judges to include notice of the registration requirements in judgments imposing sentences on convicted sex offenders and in the colloquy preceding the acceptance of a plea of guilty to such an offense. Thus, I agree with the Court that these statutes are constitutional as applied to postenactment offenses. . . .

GINSBURG, J., dissenting.

[I]n resolving whether the Act ranks as penal for ex post facto purposes, I would not demand "the clearest proof" that the statute is in effect criminal rather than civil. Instead, guided by Kennedy v. Mendoza-Martinez, 372 U.S. 144 (1963), I would neutrally evaluate the Act's purpose and effects.

. . . What ultimately tips the balance for me is the Act's excessiveness in relation to its nonpunitive purpose. . . . The Act applies to all convicted sex offenders, without regard to their future dangerousness. And the duration of the reporting requirement is keyed not to any determination of a particular offender's risk of reoffending, but to whether the offense of conviction qualified as aggravated. The reporting requirements themselves are exorbitant: The Act requires aggravated offenders to engage in perpetual quarterly reporting, even if their personal information has not changed. And meriting heaviest weight in my judgment, the Act makes no provision whatever for the possibility of rehabilitation: Offenders cannot shorten their registration or notification period, even on the clearest demonstration of rehabilitation or conclusive proof of physical incapacitation. However plain it may be that a former sex offender currently poses no threat of recidivism, he will remain subject to long-term monitoring and inescapable humiliation.

John Doe I, for example, pleaded nolo contendere to a charge of sexual abuse of a minor nine years before the Alaska Act was enacted. He successfully completed a treatment program, and gained early release on supervised probation in part because of his compliance with the program's requirements and his apparent low risk of re-offense. He subsequently remarried, established a business, and was reunited with his family. He was also granted custody of a minor daughter, based on a court's determination that he had been successfully rehabilitated. The court's determination rested in part on psychiatric evaluations concluding that Doe had "a very low risk of re-offending" and is "not a pedophile." Notwithstanding this strong evidence of rehabilitation, the Alaska Act requires

Doe to report personal information to the State four times per year, and permits the State publicly to label him a "Registered Sex Offender" for the rest of his life.

Satisfied that the Act is ambiguous in intent and punitive in effect, I would hold its retroactive application incompatible with the Ex Post Facto Clause, and would therefore affirm the judgment of the Court of Appeals.

NOTES

1. *Risk assessment.*   The Supreme Court held that individual risk assessments were not needed for entry into sex offender databases. Therefore, states can continue to classify offenders based on the offense of conviction. Different states take different offenses as predicate crimes for entry into the database. Recent research has indicated that the prediction of whether an offender will commit another serious sex-based violent crime in the short term is most effective when it combines an actuarial risk assessment, based on prior record, type of sex offense, and similar factors, with a clinical prediction model. Eric S. Janus and Robert A. Prentky, Forensic Use of Actuarial Risk Assessment with Sex Offenders: Accuracy, Admissibility and Accountability, 39 Am. Crim. L. Rev. __ (2003).

2. *Recidivism and sex offenses.*   The *Doe* Court relies in part on the substantial risk that convicted sex offenders pose to the public. It cites a study indicating that sex offenders are much more likely than other offenders to commit a sex crime. But the same holds true for other types of criminals, such as drug and property offenders. Moreover, reconviction rates for sex offenders are the second lowest of all offenders. Does this indicate that the Court's analysis is incorrect? Or does it support a more limited sex offender registry?

3. *Civil and criminal sanctions.*   The Court confirmed that sex offender notification and registration statutes are collateral sanctions that lack the procedural protections available when criminal sanctions are imposed.

4. *Conduct-based ban.*   May sanctions or limits be imposed on offenders based on noncriminal conduct after sentencing? In Doe v. City of Lafayette, Ind., 334 F.3d 606, *vacated and reh'g granted,* 2003 U.S. App. LEXIS 16563 (7th Cir. 2003), a panel of the Seventh Circuit struck down the city's decision to ban a sex offender from all park property for life after he had visited a park and admitted to having had sexual urges while observing the children playing there. In this case the offender's prior criminal record combined with his later conduct (or thoughts?) caused the city to act. Administrative agencies and courts may also impose sanctions based on criminal conduct, even if no criminal conviction occurs. See Department of Housing and Urban Development v. Rucker, 535 U.S. 125 (2002) (eviction from public housing upheld when a member of the household or a guest engaged in drug-related criminal activity, regardless of whether the tenant knew, or should have known, of the drug-related activity).

c. Firearms

For convicted felons, the most common collateral sanction (sometimes called a disability), which may be imposed for a term or for life, is the state and federal prohibition of the possession of firearms. Some statutes single out certain types of felony offenses or classes of offenses as the ones that trigger a firearms ban. Typically drug offenses are included in this category. What rationale animates this collateral sanction?

Given the broad applicability of such prohibitions, the wide availability of firearms, and the strong legal, cultural, and social traditions of gun ownership, it is not surprising that the desire to own firearms is among the most frequent bases for requests for relief from collateral sanctions.

Ohio Revised Code §2923.13
Having Weapons While Under Disability

(A) [N]o person shall knowingly acquire, have, carry, or use any firearm or dangerous ordnance, if any of the following apply:

(1) The person is a fugitive from justice.

(2) The person is under indictment for or has been convicted of any felony offense of violence. . . .

(3) The person is under indictment for or has been convicted of any offense involving the illegal possession, use, sale, administration, distribution, or trafficking in any drug of abuse. . . .

(4) The person is drug dependent, in danger of drug dependence, or a chronic alcoholic.

(5) The person is under adjudication of mental incompetence.

(B) No person who has been convicted of a felony of the first or second degree shall violate division (A) of this section within five years of the date of the person's release from imprisonment or from post-release control that is imposed for the commission of a felony of the first or second degree.

(C) Whoever violates this section is guilty of having weapons while under disability. A violation of division (A) of this section is a felony of the fifth degree [punishable by six, seven, eight, nine, ten, eleven, or twelve months]. A violation of division (B) of this section is a felony of the third degree [punishable by one, two, three, four, or five years].

Ohio Revised Code §2923.14
Relief from Disability

(A) Any person who, solely by reason of the person's disability under division (A)(2) or (3) of section 2923.13 of the Revised Code, is prohibited from acquiring, having, carrying, or using firearms, may apply to the court of common pleas in the county in which the person resides for relief from such prohibition.

(B) The application shall recite the following:

(1) All indictments, convictions, or adjudications upon which the applicant's disability is based, the sentence imposed and served, and any release granted under a community control sanction, post-release control sanction, or parole, any partial or conditional pardon granted, or other disposition of each case;

(2) Facts showing the applicant to be a fit subject for relief under this section.

(C) A copy of the application shall be served on the county prosecutor. . . .

(D) Upon hearing, the court may grant the applicant relief pursuant to this section, if all of the following apply:

(1) The applicant has been fully discharged from imprisonment, community control, post-release control, and parole, or, if the applicant is under indictment, has been released on bail or recognizance.

(2) The applicant has led a law-abiding life since discharge or release, and appears likely to continue to do so.

(3) The applicant is not otherwise prohibited by law from acquiring, having, or using firearms. . . .

NOTES

1. *Felon-in-possession statutes.*   State and federal law prohibits some convicted felons from owning and using firearms. Federal law prohibits a convicted felon whose crime was "punishable by a term exceeding one year" from possessing firearms. Do you believe felon-in-possession statutes are effective as law-enforcement tools? Are statutes such as Ohio's over- or underinclusive? As a state legislator, would you support such legislation? Why?

2. *Removal of firearms disabilities.*   Most states provide judicial or administrative relief from firearms disabilities, but no equivalent procedure exists at the federal level. A part of the federal felon-in-possession statute grants the secretary of the treasury the right to reinstate a former felon's firearms privileges if past good conduct indicates that the disability should be removed. Since 1992, however, Congress has failed to fund this portion of the secretary's work. Courts have split on whether federal district courts may review such petitions. See Rice v. United States Dept. of Alcohol, Tobacco and Firearms, 68 F.3d 702 (3d Cir. 1995). But see United States v. McGill, 74 F.3d 64 (5th Cir. 1996).

PROBLEM 8-1.   FOREIGN CONVICTIONS

On February 16, 2001, Rohan Ingram was arrested in a Plattsburgh, New York, hotel upon suspicion that he had illegally entered the United States from Canada. Soon after his arrest, authorities discovered a large quantity of firearms stored in boxes in his hotel room. Ingram subsequently was charged in a superseding indictment with three counts: conspiracy to export defense articles designated on the United States Munitions List; conspiracy to travel with intent to engage in the illegal acquisition of firearms; and being a felon in possession of a firearm, in violation of 18 U.S.C. §§922(g)(1), 924(a)(2).

The predicate offense underlying the felon-in-possession count was Ingram's 1996 conviction in Canada for violating section 85(1)(a) of Canada's Criminal Code for use of a firearm in the commission of an indictable offense. Ingram moves to dismiss the felon-in-possession count, maintaining that because his prior felony conviction did not occur in the United States, Ingram was not a felon within the meaning of the statute. The government argues that Ingram's conviction in Canada constitutes a conviction "in any court" under the terms of section 922(g)(1).

Can Ingram's 1996 conviction in a Canadian court satisfy the element of the statute that requires a conviction "in any court"? The federal felon-in-possession statute was enacted as part of the Gun Control Act of 1968. That statute currently provides, in relevant part:

> (g) It shall be unlawful for any person — (1) who has been *convicted in any court* of a crime punishable by imprisonment for a term exceeding one year; . . . to ship or transport in interstate or foreign commerce, or possess in or affecting commerce, any firearm or ammunition; or to receive any firearm or ammunition which has been shipped or transported in interstate or foreign commerce.

18 U.S.C. §922 (emphasis added). In 1996 Ingram was convicted for violating section 85(1)(a) of Canada's Criminal Code, which criminalizes the use of a firearm in commission of an indictable offense and carries a maximum imprisonment term of 14 years. If this conviction were entered by an American court, it would qualify as a predicate offense under section 922(g)(1) because the crime was "punishable by imprisonment for a term exceeding one year."

The determinative issue therefore becomes whether the phrase "convicted in any court" refers solely to convictions by courts in the United States or includes foreign convictions as well.

In section 921, the Gun Control Act's general statutory definition section, Congress limited the sorts of crimes that constitute predicate offenses for a section 922(g)(1) conviction:

> The term "crime punishable by imprisonment for a term exceeding one year" does not include —
>
> (A) any *Federal* or *State* offenses pertaining to antitrust violations, unfair trade practices, restraints of trade, or other similar offenses relating to the regulation of business practices, or
>
> (B) any *State* offense classified by the laws of the State as a misdemeanor and punishable by a term of imprisonment of two years or less. [emphasis added]

Since the language of the statute does not provide an obvious answer, consider its legislative history:

> The Senate Judiciary Committee Report on the Gun Control Act strongly suggests that Congress did not intend foreign convictions to serve as predicate offenses under the felon-in-possession statute. The Senate Report explained the meaning of the term "felony" as follows: "The definition of the term 'felony,' as added by the committee is a new provision. It means a Federal crime punishable by a term of imprisonment exceeding 1 year and in the case of State law, an offense determined by the laws of the State to be a felony." S. Rep. No. 90-1501, at 31 (1968).
>
> Further evidence of Congress's intent to exclude foreign convictions comes from the conference Report. The Conference Report adopted the House version of the bill, which contained the statute's current language, "crime punishable by imprisonment for a term exceeding one year." Notably, however, the Conference Report voiced no disagreement with the Senate Report's explicit limitation of felonies to include only convictions attained in domestic courts. Rather, the Conference Report merely chose the phrase, "crime punishable by imprisonment for a term exceeding 1 year," over the word, "felony." Moreover, nowhere did the Conference Report mention foreign convictions serving as predicate offenses.

United States v. Gayle, 342 F.3d 89 (2d Cir. 2003).

How would you rule? Compare United States v. Gayle (reversing conviction under felon-in-possession statute that was predicated on earlier Canadian felony conviction) with United States v. Atkins, 872 F.2d 94 (4th Cir. 1989) (holding that the term "any court" includes foreign courts).

2. Administrative Sanctions

While many collateral sanctions befall the offender automatically upon conviction, others are imposed in regulatory hearings. One of the most important and pervasive illustrations of such a collateral sanction is deportation, which is declared by an immigration judge or the immigration agency rather than the criminal court. For a proposal to allow the criminal sanctioning and the deportation decisions to be made by the sentencing judge, see Margaret Taylor and Ronald Wright, The Sentencing Judge as Immigration Judge, 51 Emory L.J. 1131 (2002).

Since the 1996 immigration acts, deportation of criminal offenders has expanded dramatically. In 1986 not quite 2,000 noncitizens were removed for criminal violations; by 2002 the figure had risen to almost 71,000, with 41 percent of the convictions that form the basis for deportation involving drug offenses. Removal is now mandatory for all noncitizens convicted of "aggravated felonies," a large category of offenses that includes more than just the most heinous crimes that the term evokes. Moreover, deportation can occur upon conviction of "crimes of moral turpitude." The circuit courts disagree on the definition of some these terms. The Tenth and Eleventh Circuits, for example, have held felony drunk driving convictions to amount to aggravated felonies because they are crimes of violence carrying possible prison terms of more than one year, while the Second, Fifth, Seventh, and Ninth have come out differently.

Immediately upon the passage of the 1996 legislation, the Immigration and Naturalization Service enforced the deportation provisions retroactively. This means individuals who had pled guilty to offenses many years, and often decades, in the past were detained and deported without having available to them the more generous discretionary relief provisions they had relied on in earlier legislation. In its 2001 decision in INS v. St. Cyr, 533 U.S. 289 (2001), the Supreme Court held that such discretionary relief remained available to these individuals since they relied on them in working out plea bargains.

Whether criminal defendants need to be informed of the immigration consequences of a guilty plea by the court, the prosecutor, or their counsel has been an important question, with far-reaching consequences also for other, albeit less dramatic, collateral sanctions.

|| **United States v. Marino Amador-Leal** ||
276 F.3d 511 (9th Cir. 2002)

RYMER, J.

Marino Amador-Leal appeals his conviction and sentence pursuant to a guilty plea on one count of possession with intent to distribute cocaine base in violation of 21 U.S.C. §841(a)(1). The magistrate judge did not explain the potential immigration consequences of Amador-Leal's conviction when the plea was taken. The question presented here is whether immigration consequences are collateral, as we held in Fruchtman v. Kenton, 531 F.2d 946 (9th Cir.), *cert. denied,* 429 U.S. 895 (1976), or have become direct in light of the aggravated felony provisions of the Antiterrorism and Effective Death Penalty Act of 1996 (AEDPA), and the Illegal Immigration Reform and Immigrant Responsibility Act of 1996 (IIRIRA), such that a defendant must be advised of them in order for his plea to be voluntary. We . . . conclud[e] that *Fruchtman* is still good law, and that immigration consequences remain collateral. . . .

Amador-Leal is an illegal alien who was caught selling crack in February, 2000. . . .

Pursuant to a written plea agreement . . . , Amador-Leal entered a plea of guilty to [a] possession [with intent to distribute cocaine base] count on May 18, 2000. The magistrate judge reviewed the charges with Amador-Leal, explained his rights and the implications of his plea, and found that he knowingly and voluntarily agreed to the plea. Based on the plea agreement and Amador-Leal's cooperation, the district court accepted the government's recommendation for a two level downward departure and sentenced Amador-Leal to 87 months in custody. . . .

Amador-Leal submits that his plea neither conforms to Rule 11 nor comports with due process because, for a plea to be considered voluntary, district courts must inform defendants pleading guilty of the direct consequences of their plea and resulting conviction; immigration consequences are direct as they flow automatically from a statute; and United States v. Littlejohn, 224 F.3d 960 (9th Cir. 2000), requires advice about statutorily mandated ineligibility to apply for a benefit such as relief with respect to immigration status or removal. He distinguishes *Fruchtman* on the footing that he and Littlejohn are similarly situated in that both suffer statutorily mandated ineligibility to apply for certain federal benefits, and that *Fruchtman* faced only the potential of deportation whereas his own removal is "practically guaranteed" under immigration laws enacted since *Fruchtman* was decided in 1976. We should therefore, in his view, find *Fruchtman* no longer controlling.

To start with the obvious, guilty pleas must be knowing and voluntary. As we explained in Torrey v. Estelle, 842 F.2d 234 (9th Cir. 1988):

> A plea is voluntary only if it is entered by one fully aware of the direct consequences of his plea of guilty. . . . This court, in harmony with other circuits, has held that although a defendant is entitled to be informed of the direct consequences of the plea, the court need not advise him of all the possible collateral consequences.

District courts are obliged to advise a defendant of direct consequences even if the particular consequence is not listed among the issues that Rule 11(c) requires the court to cover. However, there is no obligation to advise of collateral consequences. "The distinction between a direct and collateral consequence of a plea turns on whether the result represents a definite, immediate and largely automatic effect on the range of the defendant's punishment."

As Amador-Leal recognizes, we decided in *Fruchtman* that immigration consequences are collateral. In *Fruchtman,* the defendant was an alien who also was not advised by the district court that his conviction would subject him to deportation proceedings. Fruchtman argued on appeal that his plea was not voluntary because deportation is a drastic measure of which he should have been advised before his plea was accepted. We recognized that administration of Rule 11 "requires the development of some limiting guide to define the nature of the consequences of which a defendant must be advised so that the requirements of the rule shall have been met," and that the "common distinction" drawn is between consequences that are direct and those that are collateral. Noting that other appellate courts had resolved the issue, we adopted the reasoning of the Court of Appeals for the Second Circuit that "when, as in the case of deportation, the consequence in issue 'was not the sentence of the court which accepted the plea but of another agency over which the trial judge has no control and for which he has no responsibility,' Rule 11 imposes no duty on the District Court to advise a defendant of such consequences."

We must, of course, follow *Fruchtman* unless it is distinguishable or undermined. First, relying on *Littlejohn*, Amador-Leal suggests that the proper inquiry for determining whether a statutorily created ineligibility to apply for some form of government benefit is a direct or collateral consequence is not whether the benefit is denied later by some agency other than the court, but whether the ineligibility is an automatic consequence of a statute. However, . . . we decline to embrace the test that Amador-Leal proposes. No court has, and it would be totally unworkable in practice.

In *Littlejohn*, the defendant pled guilty to a drug offense. His conviction automatically rendered him ineligible for certain food stamp and social security benefits pursuant to 21 U.S.C. §§862(a) and 862a, but the court did not say so during the Rule 11 colloquy. On appeal, Littlejohn argued that his plea was involuntary because he had not been warned that he would suffer ineligibility, and we agreed. We contrasted direct consequences . . . as consequences that have

> "a definite, immediate and largely automatic effect on the range of the defendant's punishment," [with collateral consequences that] have included the possibility of a felony prosecution for reentry following deportation; imposition of a consecutive rather than concurrent sentence where the district court has discretion to choose between the two; the possibility of being resentenced to a maximum term if a state agency determines that the defendant is not amenable to treatment; exposure to potential civil tax litigation; revocation of parole from a separate conviction where such revocation is within the power of a parole board; and the potential of deportation, where a separate agency has authority over such deportation. . . .

Littlejohn, 224 F.3d at 965. We then concluded that the benefit-stripping effect of both sections 862(a) and 862a was a direct consequence of conviction because "the ineligibility itself is not a result of other governmental agencies' actions, and it is not dependent upon Littlejohn's own future conduct. It is an automatic product of Littlejohn's conviction." For this reason, we held that district courts must advise defendants of §862a ineligibility, although we went on to say that the error was harmless given that Littlejohn would have pled guilty anyway. We treated §862(a) differently, holding that courts have no obligation to inform defendants of §862(a) ineligibility because applicability of this section depends upon the existence of prior convictions about which the judge would be unaware when taking the plea.[3]

Littlejohn itself puts the potential for deportation firmly within the category of collateral consequences. Indeed, our decision in *Littlejohn* turned on the rationale articulated by *Fruchtman* for determining whether a consequence is direct or collateral. As we summed up in *Littlejohn*, "where the consequence is contingent upon action taken by an individual or individuals other than the sentencing court — such as another governmental agency or the defendant himself — the consequence is generally 'collateral.'" Thus, the *Fruchtman* test remains intact.

Nevertheless, Amador-Leal maintains, *Fruchtman* can no longer control in the context of deportation because AEDPA and IIRIRA have changed the landscape for illegal aliens convicted of aggravated felonies. No doubt the landscape has changed, because it is now virtually certain that an aggravated felon will be removed. Yet whether an alien will be removed is still up to the INS. There is a process to go through, and it is wholly independent of the court imposing sentence. The Supreme Court has made this clear by describing deportation as a "purely civil action" separate and distinct from a criminal proceeding. INS v. Lopez-Mendoza, 468 U.S. 1032 (1984). Removal is not part of the sentence; future immigration consequences do not bear on the "range of the defendant's punishment" imposed by the court, and deportation is not punishment for the crime. By contrast, the statutes at issue in *Littlejohn* are part of the criminal code. Also unlike the removal statutes, §§862(a) and 862a are self-executing upon imposition of sentence. A defendant receiving government benefits is immediately and automatically ineligible for them once convicted; however, immigration consequences will not be felt until the court's sentence has been served, the INS assumes control of the defendant, and the process of removal has been initiated and executed. In short, no matter what changes have been wrought by AEDPA and IIRIRA, removal remains the result of another governmental agency's subsequent actions. . . .

Therefore, immigration consequences continue to be a collateral consequence of a plea and the resulting conviction. This means that district courts are not constitutionally required to warn defendants about potential removal in order to assure voluntariness of a plea; but it does not mean that they should not do so. Many district judges comment in their Rule 11 colloquy that a plea of guilty and resulting conviction may affect an alien's status in this country, and inquire whether the defendant understands the possible immigration consequences of his plea. Although not required by Rule 11 or due process, we commend this sort of dialogue for there is no question that immigration consequences of a conviction are important to aliens contemplating a plea. See [INS v.] St. Cyr, 121 S. Ct. at 2291; Magana Pizano v. INS, 200 F.3d 603, 612 (9th Cir. 1999).[4] However, because immigration consequences are collateral, neither Rule 11 nor Amador-Leal's right to due process was violated in this case. . . .

---

3. The same feasibility concerns that animated this different treatment in *Littlejohn* are also present here: district courts generally have no information about a defendant's immigration status at the Rule 11 proceeding.

4. Many states have enacted statutes that require courts to advise a defendant of the immigration consequences of a plea, see *St. Cyr*, 121 S. Ct. at 2291 n.48 (listing states with statutory requirement), but the general rule post-AEDPA and IIRIRA remains that there

PROBLEM 8-2.   WHAT'S WORSE?

Juan Nico, a permanent resident alien who entered the United States at age three and has lived here since then, got caught up in a bar brawl. He admits to having been drunk when his sister's ex-boyfriend, Bob Friendly, came into the bar. His sister had told him about the abuse Bob had inflicted on her, and he decided to show Bob what it would be like to be beaten up. Bob had not fully sat down when Juan attempted to throw a beer mug at him but missed. Juan and Bob got into a fight which ended when other patrons separated them. Both had minor injuries, largely scrapes and bruises.

The district attorney suggests that Nico plead guilty to assault with a one-year suspended sentence. It is the local district attorney's policy to offer such pleas to noncitizens. Had Nico been a citizen, the district attorney would have insisted on some jail time.

If he accepts the plea, Nico will become automatically deportable as an aggravated felon since he committed a crime of violence. As Nico's attorney, what options do you have at your disposal? Could you attack the district attorney's policy offering different pleas to citizens and noncitizens?

NOTES

1. *Deportation as a civil sanction.*   A long line of cases defines deportation as a civil rather than a criminal sanction. The distinction has traditionally been that collateral sanctions are indirect, and in the case of deportation they are imposed by an agency outside the criminal justice system. None of the procedural protections that attach in criminal cases, therefore, apply in deportation hearings. See INS v. Lopez-Mendoza, 468 U.S. 1032 (1984). This is the case even though deportation for a criminal offense includes a long-term ban on reentry and often requires the offender to uproot his entire life and be separated from his family.

2. *Notification.*   After the 1996 immigration laws substantially expanded the category of crimes making aliens deportable, some state legislatures mandated that courts inform noncitizen criminal defendants of potential immigration consequences. See, e.g., Cal. Penal Code §1016.5 (West 2001). In some other states, courts have ruled to that effect. Chapter 19 of the new ABA Standards on Collateral Sanctions (2003) recommends that judges inform criminal defendants before the guilty plea of the whole panoply of potential collateral sanctions. This would necessitate courts to compile a list of existing sanctions, many of which are currently unknown to judges, prosecutors, and defense counsel. In In re Resendiz, 19 P.3d 1171 (Cal. 2001), the California Supreme Court held that in certain cases affirmative misadvice regarding immigration consequences could constitute ineffective assistance of counsel in the criminal case.

is no due process requirement for defendants to be informed of immigration consequences because immigration consequences are collateral. See, e.g., State v. Ramirez, 636 N.W.2d 740, 2001 WL 1035928 at *1 (Iowa 2001); State v. Jamison, 105 Wn. App. 572, 20 P.3d 1010 (Wash. App. 2001); State v. Jimenez, 987 S.W.2d 886 (Tex. Crim. App. 1999); State v. Modi, 1998 Del. Super. LEXIS 331, 1998 WL 735881 (Del. Super. Sept. 25, 1998); People v. Agero, 234 A.D.2d 94, 651 N.Y.S.2d 430 (App. Div. 1996).

3. *Prosecutorial manipulation of collateral sanctions.* Prosecutors are able to influence the imposition of collateral consequences through charging decisions and plea offers. If a defendant refuses to accept an apparently generous plea offer because of a collateral consequence, and the judge both agrees with the defendant's decision and considers the collateral sanction too harsh, what options does the judge have?

4. *Welfare and financial aid benefits.* Federal law gives sentencing courts discretion to bar drug offenders temporarily from access to benefits. 21 U.S.C. §862(a). Studies have shown that neither state nor federal courts take advantage of this provision. See Robert Musser Jr., Denial of Federal Benefits to Drug Traffickers and Drug Possessors: A Broad-Reaching but Seldom Used Sanction, 12 Fed. Sentencing Rep. 252 (2000). Upon a third conviction for sale of illegal narcotics, the ban becomes mandatory. 21 U.S.C. §862a requires that states permanently deny certain welfare benefits and food stamps to people convicted of state or federal felony drug possession, use, or sale offenses, unless the state explicitly opts out of such a ban. Currently, 22 states retain the ban. The denial of welfare benefits has been found to have a particularly devastating impact on women released from prison, since they are more likely to suffer a relapse. See Amy E. Hirsch, Parents with Criminal Records and Public Benefits: "Welfare Helps Us Stay in Touch with Society," in Every Door Closed: Barriers Facing Parents with Criminal Records 27, 31 (Community Legal Services, Amy E. Hirsch et al., 2002). The first conviction for a drug possession or sale offense also carries with it a temporary denial of financial aid benefits for students applying to or enrolled in institutions of higher learning. The sponsor of the legislation wanted the provision to apply only when the conviction occurs while the student receives such benefits, but currently it is being implemented to apply to anyone with a drug offense conviction, however far in the past. The third possession or second sale offense results in indefinite suspension of financial aid. Students may restore their eligibility if they complete a drug rehabilitation program that complies with certain criteria. See 20 U.S.C. §1091(r).

5. *Administrative sanctions based on criminal conduct.* Collateral sanctions depend on a criminal conviction. Some administrative restrictions, however, are not based on a criminal conviction but rather on criminal conduct. For example, involvement in drug activity carries with it a ban from public housing, irrespective of whether the renter was convicted of a drug offense. While criminal conduct is most easily proven through a criminal record, such is not required.

6. *Extralegal collateral sanctions.* Employers such as schools, long-term care facilities, and security services are statutorily obligated to investigate the criminal record of job applicants. In addition to governmental disabilities imposed on offenders after they have served their criminal justice sentence, nongovernmental (private) disabilities apply as well. Many employers voluntarily check criminal records and refuse to hire ex-offenders. Licensing boards frequently deny ex-offenders licenses for employment ranging from attorney to beautician. Ex-offenders also find it increasingly difficult to rent apartments and homes. This is particularly problematic for sex offenders, but many others are also denied housing by rental agencies and home owners. Should the government protect the civil rights of ex-offenders who have served their sentences? Would an ex-offender nondiscrimination act have a chance of being enacted?

=9=

‖ *Race, Class, and Gender* ‖

Fundamental constitutional and philosophical principles of equal treatment suggest that people should not be punished more or less severely because of their race (or ethnicity), social or economic class, or gender. These abstract principles quickly confront a dramatic reality of American criminal justice: overwhelmingly, criminal defendants, as a group, are male and poor. Equally striking, African Americans and Native Americans are convicted of crimes at highly disproportionate levels. These unsettling facts of the American criminal justice system — disproportions shared in varying degrees by other countries — raise many questions: why are men, members of (some) racial minority groups, and the poor convicted more frequently than others? This chapter considers the charge that racism, classism, and sexism are an inherent part of the criminal justice process and that their end product is highly disproportionate rates and degrees of punishment.

For a good part of U.S. history, state laws explicitly justified differential treatment on the basis of race and gender. See, e.g., Commonwealth v. Butler, 328 A.2d 851 (Pa. 1974) (statute requiring mandatory minimum sentence for men but not women declared unconstitutional). But such laws have for some time been anathema to the U.S. legal system. Now, the issue of whether people are sentenced more severely on the basis of their race, ethnicity, wealth, or gender has become more subtle and difficult to answer.

Studies conducted in the United States find little difference between races in their formal treatment by the criminal justice system after controlling for other differences among cases. Some of the racial disproportionality in prison sentences appears to be largely contextual: African American defendants are more likely to go to prison in areas of high unemployment, in places where blacks constitute a larger percentage of the population, and in the South. Combined with geographic differences in arrests, these distinctions result in stark variations in the black–white imprisonment ratio across the country. For other racial groups the data are more ambiguous and more difficult to explain. Economic differences are largely anecdotal even though the few empirical studies done on inmate populations indicate that those sentenced to custodial terms are largely poorer than the rest of the population. The gender data are clear: despite rising imprisonment rates for women, they are dramatically underrepresented, and the offenses of which they are convicted tend to be less violent than those of male offenders.

Variations in outcome raise an array of questions: In what ways and at what points are people who commit similar acts treated differently, and why? What does it mean to say someone commits a "similar act"? Might there be positive justifications for differential treatment based on characteristics of the offender — such as gainful employment or single parenthood — and not the offense?

This chapter focuses on the question whether disproportionate treatment exists on the basis of race, ethnicity, class, and gender, and if so, whether some of these differences can be justified. The chapter also raises the question whether the criminal justice system in general, and sentencing law in particular, is an appropriate place to remedy bias that may stem from more pervasive societal and historical forces.

A.   AFRICAN AMERICANS IN THE CRIMINAL JUSTICE SYSTEM

> There is nothing more painful to me at this stage in my life than to walk
> down the street and hear footsteps and start thinking about robbery —
> then look around and see somebody white and feel relieved.
>
> *Jesse Jackson, 1993*

Race is an unavoidable part of modern American criminal procedure. Difficult questions arise at all stages of the criminal process: What is the role of race in stops and investigations? When are racial disparities sufficient to justify challenges to charging practices? What role should race play in jury selection? In arguments at trial? But perhaps the most common and visible questions about race arise at the end of the process, in the form of claims that black Americans and other minorities are punished more severely than whites. This section asks whether racism in some form produces these highly disproportionate rates and degrees of punishment. In some situations, the responsible decision makers may be identifiable; in other situations, the source of racial disparities may be hard to specify even when disparity clearly exists.

The first section sets the stage by identifying the aggregate racial disparities in sanctioning and by raising some preliminary arguments about the source of those disparities. The next part examines the 1987 decision of the U.S. Supreme Court in McCleskey v. Kemp, one of the most difficult and contentious racial cases of the past quarter-century. *McCleskey* addresses a claim that the state of Georgia discriminates on the basis of the *victim's* race when it imposes the death penalty. The last section considers the link between decisions made in investigations or charging and the pattern of sentencing outcomes. Sometimes early decisions by police and by prosecutors become de facto decisions about punishment, and the entire criminal justice process can be said to be racially skewed. In what circumstances — and in what legal institutions — should challenges to entire systems be allowed based on claims of racial bias?

These materials provoke recurring questions: Does the criminal justice system exacerbate or mediate larger social problems? Can criminal justice systems respond to intentional or unintentional racial bias in society? If so, what is the proper role for courts, police, prosecutors, and legislators in crafting such a response?

1.   An American Dilemma

It seems obvious to many that there is a relationship between race and punishment, but it is difficult to study or discuss. Problems with studying racial disparities include difficulties in defining race, the propriety and cost of collecting useful data, and the difficulties in knowing what conclusions to draw from the information. What exactly are the effects of criminal punishments on different racial groups? Does the very pervasiveness of racial tension, and the difficulty of frank discussion about race in the United States, make it impossible to explain the numbers satisfactorily?

Much of the race focus in the United States has been on the black–white disparity. In June 2002, 44.2 percent of the inmates in state and federal prisons and local jails were African American, although African Americans constitute only about 13 percent of the population. The rate of imprisonment for black men ages 25 to 29 is about 12.9 percent, while the rate for Hispanic men of the same age group is 4.3 percent, and the comparable rate for white men is 1.6 percent. Bureau of Justice Statistics, Prison and Jail Inmates at Midyear 2002 (NCJ 198877, 2003). After combining the number of young men on probation or parole and the number in prison or jail, almost one-third of young black men are under criminal justice supervision on any given day. In some states 10-15 percent of the black male population is in prison. As was the case throughout the 1990s, African American women remain the fastest growing group in prisons and jails, and female incarceration rates replicate the racial and ethnic differences discernible for men. In 15 states the rate of black incarcerated women is 10 to 35 times greater than that of white women.

Drug offenses have contributed more than any other crimes to the fast growth in the imprisonment rate for African Americans, as Marc Mauer and Tracy Huling note:

> While African American arrest rates for violent crime — 45% of arrests nationally — are disproportionate to their share of the population, this proportion has not changed significantly for twenty years. For drug offenses, though, the African American proportion of arrests increased from 24% in 1980 to 39% in 1993, well above the African American proportion of drug users nationally.

Marc Mauer and Tracy Huling, Young Black Americans and the Criminal Justice System 1 (1995).

Malign Neglect: Race, Crime and Punishment in America, Michael Tonry
Pages 4, 29-30, 49-52 (1995)

Crime by blacks is not getting worse. The proportions of serious violent crimes committed by blacks have been level for more than a decade. Since the mid-1970s, approximately 45 percent of those arrested for murder, rape, robbery, and aggravated assault have been black (the trend is slightly downward). Disproportionate punishment of blacks, however, [has] been getting worse, especially since Ronald Reagan became president. Since 1980, the number of blacks in prison has tripled. . . .

Black Americans are far more likely than whites to be in prison or jail. [In June 2002 4,810 black American men per 100,000 were in prison or jail; among white American men, 649 per 100,000 were in prison or jail. For women the comparable figures were 349 and 68.]

Another even more remarkable pattern of black–white disparities has been revealed by a series of studies attempting to determine the proportions of blacks under the control of the criminal justice system on a given day. Of all the people in prison or jail, on probation or parole, or released on bail or recognizance pending trial, what percentage are black? . . .

The Correctional Association of New York found that 23 percent of black males aged 20 to 29 were under justice system control in 1990. California's Center on Juvenile and Criminal Justice found in 1990 that 33 percent of black males aged 20 to 29 were under justice system control.

. . . In Washington, D.C., . . . 42 percent of black males aged 18 to 35 were under justice system control in 1991. In Baltimore in 1991, the corresponding figure for 18- to 35-year-old black males was 56 percent. . . .

Three findings about race, crime, and punishment stand out concerning blacks. First, at every criminal justice stage from arrest through incarceration, blacks are present in numbers greatly out of proportion to their presence in the general population. . . . Second, although black disproportions in the front of the system — as offenders and arrestees — are essentially stable, since the early 1980s they have steadily grown worse at the back [in sentencing and in prison populations]. Third, perhaps surprisingly, for nearly a decade there has been a near consensus among scholars and policy analysts that most of the black disproportions result not from racial bias or discrimination within the system but from patterns of black offending and of blacks' criminal records. Drug law enforcement is the conspicuous exception. . . .

Do not misunderstand. A conclusion that black overrepresentation among prisoners is not primarily the result of racial bias does not mean that there is no racism in the system. Virtually no one believes that racial bias and enmity are absent, that no police, prosecutors, or judges are bigots, or that some local courts or bureaucracies are not systematically discriminatory. The overwhelming weight of evidence, however, is that invidious bias explains much less of racial disparities than does offending by black offenders. Much offending is intraracial, which means that a failure by the state to take crimes by blacks seriously depreciates the importance of victimization of blacks — discrimination little less objectionable than bias against black offenders. Virtually every sophisticated review of social science evidence on criminal justice decision making has concluded, overall, that the apparent influence of the offender's race on official decisions concerning individual defendants is slight. . . .

How is it possible that black participation in serious crime has not increased while rising numbers and proportions of blacks are in prison or jail, and yet racial bias does not pervade the system? . . . There is an answer, and it lies not in the criminal justice system but in the . . . aggressive promotion of punitive crime control policies and a "War on Drugs." [These policies have] caused the ever harsher treatment of blacks by the criminal justice system, and it was foreseeable that they would do so. Just as the tripling of the American prison population between 1980 and 1993 was the result of conscious policy decisions, so also was the greater burden of punishment borne by blacks. Crime control politicians wanted more people in prison and knew that a larger proportion of them would be black.

NOTES

1. *Data and knowledge.*   Surprisingly little race data is available in the criminal justice system. In most states, "race data are virtually nonexistent with regard to victims; information on the race of the offender is limited. Race data on offenders are collected by law enforcement at arrest and maintained in the criminal history record for felons and gross misdemeanants. Race data on offenders are also collected by probation officers on sentencing worksheets. . . . There are no race data anywhere on misdemeanants." Debra Dailey, Minnesota's Continuing Efforts to Address Racial Disparities in Sentencing, 8 Fed. Sentencing Rep. 89, 89 (1995) (describing the situation in Minnesota as typical for most states). Is the basic problem with race and punishment a lack of data on the treatment of racial groups in the justice system? If so, are the social and financial costs of collecting additional data likely to be worth the benefits? Should the United States follow the model of many European states that do not collect racial data on offenders, or does its history make this impossible? What dangers are inherent in the collection of race data? Dailey provides this cautionary note:

> One reason for the paucity of data is ambivalence as to whether the race of individuals ought to be recorded at all. In 1993, for instance, the mayor of Minneapolis declared that "the use of race in crime statistics is an abomination and an outrage." The mayor questioned the purpose of reporting arrest data by race and expressed concern that such data can lead to improper inferences about the relationship between crime and race. He convinced the public safety department to include a footnote with any statistics displayed by race. . . .
>
> Racial or ethnic data must be treated with caution because of the varying circumstances under which such information is recorded or reported. For example, under the protocol governing birth records, the race or ethnicity of the mother controls the description on the birth certificate of the child regardless of the race or ethnicity of the father. Race and ethnicity may be recorded from observation or from self-identification. The use of racial or ethnic descriptions may reflect social custom rather than genetic or hereditary origins. Moreover, existing research on crime has generally shown that racial or ethnic identity is not predictive of crime behavior within data which has been controlled for social or economic factors such as education levels, family status, income, housing density, and residential mobility.

Id. at 89. Is race merely a proxy for other factors? With increasing rates of inter-marriage and offspring with multiple racial identities, will collections of racial data become misleading or even irrelevant? How can existing data explain the racially disparate outcomes? Are such explanations the ultimate goal, or are they merely the starting point for a discussion about how society functions?

2. *Who takes action?*   Even if we do understand the sources of some racial disparities in the criminal justice system, how can we best implement changes? In 1993 the Minnesota legislature created the Criminal and Juvenile Justice Information Policy Group to provide leadership and support for improving criminal justice. Made up of representatives from the state's sentencing commission, the judiciary, and other governmental bodies, the group is expected to recommend a framework for integrating criminal justice information, including information about race and ethnicity. Is the Minnesota legislature likely to defer to the group's recommendations? What institutions are most likely to make changes in law that will reduce disparate racial effects throughout the criminal justice system? Are courts the best avenue to bring about such changes? Sentencing commissions? If there are none, then what should we do? Wait for society to improve?

2.   *Whose Race?*

Our exploration of the influence of race on punishment begins where the issue has received the most sustained attention: in the context of capital punishment. On the morning of May 13, 1978, Warren McCleskey and three other men planned to rob a furniture store. McCleskey had a .38 caliber Rossi nickel-plated revolver, which he had stolen in an armed robbery of a grocery store a month earlier. The others carried a sawed-off shotgun and pistols. McCleskey, who was black, entered the front of the store, and the other three came through the rear. While the robbers tied up all the employees, Officer Frank Schlatt, who was white, answered a silent alarm and entered the store, where he was fatally shot. The robbers fled but, some time later, McCleskey was arrested in Cobb County in connection with another armed robbery. He confessed to the furniture store robbery but denied the shooting. Ballistics showed that Schlatt had been shot by a .38 caliber Rossi revolver. The weapon was never recovered.

McCleskey was convicted in 1978. The jury found two aggravating circumstances that authorized the use of the death penalty: (1) the murder was committed while the offender was committing another capital felony (armed robbery), and (2) the murder was committed against a police officer engaged in the performance of his official duties. The jury sentenced McCleskey to death for murder. One co-defendant was sentenced to life imprisonment, while another received a 20-year sentence.

On direct appeal in the Georgia courts, McCleskey first raised the claim that the death penalty violates the due process and equal protection provisions of the federal and state constitutions because prosecutorial discretion permits the government to apply the penalty in a racially discriminatory way. The Georgia Supreme Court rejected this claim as follows: "Appellant's argument is without merit. Gregg v. Georgia, 428 U.S. 153 (1976); Moore v. State, 243 S.E.2d 1 (Ga. 1978)." McCleskey v. State, 263 S.E.2d 146, 148 (Ga. 1980). After his direct appeals were exhausted, McCleskey began to file a series of state and federal habeas challenges to his conviction and sentence, which culminated in a decision by the U.S. Supreme Court.

Warren McCleskey v. Ralph Kemp
481 U.S. 279 (1987)

POWELL, J.

This case presents the question whether a complex statistical study that indicates a risk that racial considerations enter into capital sentencing determinations proves that petitioner McCleskey's capital sentence is unconstitutional under the Eighth or Fourteenth Amendment.

THE BALDUS STUDY

[In support of his habeas claim], McCleskey proffered a statistical study performed by Professors David Baldus, Charles Pulaski, and George Woodworth (the Baldus study) that purports to show a disparity in the imposition of the death sentence in Georgia based on the race of the murder victim and, to a lesser extent, the race of the defendant. The Baldus study is actually two sophisticated statistical studies that examine over 2,000 murder cases that occurred in Georgia during the 1970's. The raw numbers collected by Professor Baldus indicate that defendants charged with killing white persons received the death penalty in 11% of the cases, but defendants charged with killing blacks received the death penalty in only 1% of the cases. . . . Baldus also divided the cases according to the combination of the race of the defendant and the race of the victim. He found that the death penalty was assessed in 22% of the cases involving black defendants and white victims; 8% of the cases involving white defendants and white victims; 1% of the cases involving black defendants and black victims; and 3% of the cases involving white defendants and black victims. . . .

Baldus subjected his data to an extensive analysis, taking account of 230 variables that could have explained the disparities on nonracial grounds. One of his models concludes that, even after taking account of 39 nonracial variables, defendants charged with killing white victims were 4.3 times as likely to receive a death sentence as defendants charged with killing blacks. According to this model, black defendants were 1.1 times as likely to receive a death sentence as other defendants. Thus, the Baldus study indicates that black defendants, such as McCleskey, who kill white victims have the greatest likelihood of receiving the death penalty. . . .

DISCRIMINATORY INTENT AND STATISTICS

McCleskey's first claim is that the Georgia capital punishment statute violates the Equal Protection Clause of the Fourteenth Amendment. He argues that race has infected the administration of Georgia's statute. . . . McCleskey's claim of discrimination extends to every actor in the Georgia capital sentencing process, from the prosecutor who sought the death penalty and the jury that imposed the sentence, to the State itself that enacted the capital punishment statute and allows it to remain in effect despite its allegedly discriminatory application. [T]his claim must fail.

[T]o prevail under the Equal Protection Clause, McCleskey must prove that the decisionmakers in his case acted with discriminatory purpose. He offers no evidence specific to his own case that would support an inference that racial considerations played a part in his sentence. Instead, he . . . argues that the Baldus study compels an inference that his sentence rests on purposeful discrimination. McCleskey's claim that these statistics are sufficient proof of discrimination, without regard to the facts of a particular case, would extend to all capital cases in Georgia, at least where the victim was white and the defendant is black.

The Court has accepted statistics as proof of intent to discriminate in certain limited contexts. First, this Court has accepted statistical disparities as proof of an equal protection violation in the selection of the jury venire in a particular district. Although statistical proof normally must present a "stark" pattern to be accepted as the sole proof of discriminatory intent under the Constitution, because of the nature of the jury-selection task, we have permitted a finding of constitutional violation even when the statistical pattern does not approach such extremes. Second, this Court has accepted statistics in the form of multiple-regression analysis to prove statutory violations under Title VII of the Civil Rights Act of 1964.

But the nature of the capital sentencing decision, and the relationship of the statistics to that decision, are fundamentally different from the corresponding elements in the venire-selection or Title VII cases. Most importantly, each particular decision to impose the death penalty is made by a petit jury selected from a properly constituted venire. Each jury is unique in its composition, and the Constitution requires that its decision rest on consideration of innumerable factors that vary according to the characteristics of the individual defendant and the facts of the particular capital offense. Thus, the application of an inference drawn from the general statistics to a specific decision in a trial and sentencing simply is not comparable to the application of an inference drawn from general statistics to a specific venire-selection or Title VII case. In those cases, the statistics relate to fewer entities, and fewer variables are relevant to the challenged decisions.

Another important difference between the cases in which we have accepted statistics as proof of discriminatory intent and this case is that, in the venire-selection and Title VII contexts, the decisionmaker has an opportunity to explain the statistical disparity. Here, the State has no practical opportunity to rebut the Baldus study. Controlling considerations of public policy dictate that jurors cannot be called to testify to the motives and influences that led to their verdict. Similarly, the policy considerations behind a prosecutor's traditionally wide discretion suggest the impropriety of our requiring prosecutors to defend their decisions to seek death penalties, often years after they were made. Moreover, absent far stronger proof, it is unnecessary to seek such a rebuttal, because a legitimate and unchallenged explanation for the decision is apparent from the record: McCleskey committed an act for which the United States Constitution and Georgia laws permit imposition of the death penalty.

Finally, McCleskey's statistical proffer must be viewed in the context of his challenge. McCleskey challenges decisions at the heart of the State's criminal justice system. "[O]ne of society's most basic tasks is that of protecting the lives of its citizens and one of the most basic ways in which it achieves the task is through criminal laws against murder." Gregg v. Georgia, 428 U.S. 153, 226 (1976) (White, J., concurring). Implementation of these laws necessarily requires discretionary judgments. Because discretion is essential to the criminal justice process, we would demand exceptionally clear proof before we would infer that the discretion has been abused. . . . Accordingly, we hold that the Baldus study is clearly insufficient to support an inference that any of the decision-makers in McCleskey's case acted with discriminatory purpose. . . .

ARBITRARY AND CAPRICIOUS

[McCleskey also] contends that the Georgia capital punishment system is arbitrary and capricious in application, and therefore his sentence is excessive [and contrary to the Eighth Amendment], because racial considerations may influence capital sentencing decisions in Georgia. . . .

To evaluate McCleskey's challenge, we must examine exactly what the Baldus study may show. Even Professor Baldus does not contend that his statistics prove that race enters into any capital sentencing decisions or that race was a factor in McCleskey's particular case. Statistics at most may show only a likelihood that a particular factor entered into some decisions. There is, of course, some risk of racial prejudice influencing a jury's decision in a criminal case. There are similar risks that other kinds of prejudice will influence other criminal trials. The question is at what point that risk becomes constitutionally unacceptable. McCleskey asks us to accept the likelihood allegedly shown by the Baldus study as the constitutional measure of an unacceptable risk of racial prejudice influencing capital sentencing decisions. This we decline to do.

Because of the risk that the factor of race may enter the criminal justice process, we have engaged in "unceasing efforts" to eradicate racial prejudice from our criminal justice system. Our efforts have been guided by our recognition that "the inestimable privilege of trial by jury . . . is a vital principle, underlying the whole administration of criminal justice," Ex parte Milligan, 4 Wall. 2, 123 (1866). . . .

Individual jurors bring to their deliberations qualities of human nature and varieties of human experience, the range of which is unknown and perhaps unknowable. The capital sentencing decision requires the individual jurors to focus their collective judgment on the unique characteristics of a particular criminal defendant. It is not surprising that such collective judgments often are difficult to explain. But the inherent lack of predictability of jury decisions does not justify their condemnation. On the contrary, it is the jury's function to make the difficult and uniquely human judgments that defy codification and that build discretion, equity, and flexibility into a legal system.

McCleskey's argument that the Constitution condemns the discretion allowed decisionmakers in the Georgia capital sentencing system is antithetical to the fundamental role of discretion in our criminal justice system. Discretion in the criminal justice system offers substantial benefits to the criminal defendant. Not only can a jury decline to impose the death sentence, it can decline to convict or choose to convict of a lesser offense. Whereas decisions against a defendant's interest may be reversed by the trial judge or on appeal, these discretionary exercises of leniency are final and unreviewable. Similarly, the capacity of prosecutorial discretion to provide individualized justice is firmly entrenched in American law. As we have noted, a prosecutor can decline to charge, offer a plea bargain, or decline to seek a death sentence in any particular case. Of course, the power to be lenient also is the power to discriminate, but a capital punishment system that did not allow for discretionary acts of leniency would be totally alien to our notions of criminal justice. . . .

At most, the Baldus study indicates a discrepancy that appears to correlate with race. Apparent disparities in sentencing are an inevitable part of our criminal justice system. The discrepancy indicated by the Baldus study is a far cry from the major systemic defects identified in Furman v. Georgia, 408 U.S. 238 (1972), [which struck down existing capital punishment statutes because they imposed the punishment arbitrarily and capriciously. There] can be no perfect procedure for deciding in which cases governmental authority should be used to impose death. Despite these imperfections, our consistent rule has been that constitutional guarantees are met when the mode for determining guilt or punishment itself has been surrounded with safeguards to make it as fair as possible. Where the discretion that is fundamental to our criminal process is involved, we decline to assume that what is unexplained is invidious. In light of the safeguards designed to minimize racial bias in the process, the fundamental value of jury trial in our criminal justice system, and the benefits that discretion provides to criminal defendants, we hold that the Baldus study does not demonstrate a constitutionally significant risk of racial bias affecting the Georgia capital sentencing process.

Two additional concerns inform our decision in this case. First, McCleskey's claim, taken to its logical conclusion, throws into serious question the principles that underlie our entire criminal justice system. The Eighth Amendment is not limited in application to capital punishment, but applies to all penalties. Thus, if we accepted McCleskey's claim that racial bias has impermissibly tainted the capital sentencing decision, we could soon be faced with similar claims as to other types of penalty. Moreover, the claim that his sentence rests on the irrelevant factor of race easily could be extended to apply to claims based on unexplained discrepancies that correlate to membership in other minority groups, and even to gender. Similarly, since McCleskey's claim relates to the race of his victim, other claims could apply with equally logical force to statistical disparities that correlate with the race or sex of other actors in the criminal justice system, such as defense attorneys or judges. Also, there is no logical reason that such a claim need be limited to racial or sexual bias. If arbitrary and capricious punishment is the touchstone under the Eighth Amendment, such a claim could — at least in theory — be based upon any arbitrary variable, such as the defendant's facial characteristics, or the physical attractiveness of the defendant or the victim, that some statistical study indicates may be influential in jury decisionmaking. As these examples illustrate, there is no limiting principle to the type of challenge brought by McCleskey. The Constitution does not require that a State eliminate any demonstrable disparity that correlates with a potentially irrelevant factor in order to operate a criminal justice system that includes capital punishment. . . .

Second, McCleskey's arguments are best presented to the legislative bodies. It is not the responsibility — or indeed even the right — of this Court to

determine the appropriate punishment for particular crimes. It is the legislatures, the elected representatives of the people, that are constituted to respond
to the will and consequently the moral values of the people. Legislatures also are
better qualified to weigh and evaluate the results of statistical studies in terms of
their own local conditions and with a flexibility of approach that is not available
to the courts. Capital punishment is now the law in more than two-thirds of our
States. It is the ultimate duty of courts to determine on a case-by-case basis
whether these laws are applied consistently with the Constitution. Despite
McCleskey's wide-ranging arguments that basically challenge the validity of capital punishment in our multiracial society, the only question before us is whether
in his case the law of Georgia was properly applied. [T]his was carefully and correctly done in this case. . . .

BRENNAN, J., dissenting.

At some point in this case, Warren McCleskey doubtless asked his lawyer
whether a jury was likely to sentence him to die. A candid reply to this question
would have been disturbing. First, counsel would have to tell McCleskey that few
of the details of the crime or of McCleskey's past criminal conduct were more
important than the fact that his victim was white. Furthermore, counsel would
feel bound to tell McCleskey that defendants charged with killing white victims
in Georgia are 4.3 times as likely to be sentenced to death as defendants charged
with killing blacks. In addition, frankness would compel the disclosure that it
was more likely than not that the race of McCleskey's victim would determine
whether he received a death sentence: 6 of every 11 defendants convicted of
killing a white person would not have received the death penalty if their victims
had been black, while, among defendants with aggravating and mitigating factors comparable to McCleskey's, 20 of every 34 would not have been sentenced
to die if their victims had been black. Finally, the assessment would not be complete without the information that cases involving black defendants and white
victims are more likely to result in a death sentence than cases featuring any
other racial combination of defendant and victim. The story could be told in a
variety of ways, but McCleskey could not fail to grasp its essential narrative line:
there was a significant chance that race would play a prominent role in determining if he lived or died. . . .

Georgia's legacy of a race-conscious criminal justice system, as well as this
Court's own recognition of the persistent danger that racial attitudes may affect
criminal proceedings, indicates that McCleskey's claim is not a fanciful product
of mere statistical artifice.

For many years, Georgia operated openly and formally precisely the type
of dual system the evidence shows is still effectively in place. The criminal law expressly differentiated between crimes committed by and against blacks and
whites, distinctions whose lineage traced back to the time of slavery. During the
colonial period, black slaves who killed whites in Georgia, regardless of whether
in self-defense or in defense of another, were automatically executed.
A. Higginbotham, In the Matter of Color: Race in the American Legal Process
256 (1978).

By the time of the Civil War, a dual system of crime and punishment was
well established in Georgia. See Ga. Penal Code (1861). The state criminal code
contained separate sections for "Slaves and Free Persons of Color," and for all

other persons. The code provided, for instance, for an automatic death sentence for murder committed by blacks, but declared that anyone else convicted of murder might receive life imprisonment if the conviction were founded solely on circumstantial testimony or simply if the jury so recommended. The code established that the rape of a free white female by a black "shall be" punishable by death. However, rape by anyone else of a free white female was punishable by a prison term not less than 2 nor more than 20 years. The rape of blacks was punishable "by fine and imprisonment, at the discretion of the court.". . .

Citation of past practices does not justify the automatic condemnation of current ones. But it would be unrealistic to ignore the influence of history in assessing the plausible implications of McCleskey's evidence. . . .

The Court . . . states that its unwillingness to regard petitioner's evidence as sufficient is based in part on the fear that recognition of McCleskey's claim would open the door to widespread challenges to all aspects of criminal sentencing. Taken on its face, such a statement seems to suggest a fear of too much justice. Yet surely the majority would acknowledge that if striking evidence indicated that other minority groups, or women, or even persons with blond hair, were disproportionately sentenced to death, such a state of affairs would be repugnant to deeply rooted conceptions of fairness. The prospect that there may be more widespread abuse than McCleskey documents may be dismaying, but it does not justify complete abdication of our judicial role.

[T]o reject McCleskey's powerful evidence . . . is to ignore both the qualitatively different character of the death penalty and the particular repugnance of racial discrimination, considerations which may properly be taken into account in determining whether various punishments are "cruel and unusual." Furthermore, it fails to take account of the unprecedented refinement and strength of the Baldus study.

. . . . Warren McCleskey's evidence confronts us with the subtle and persistent influence of the past. His message is a disturbing one to a society that has formally repudiated racism, and a frustrating one to a Nation accustomed to regarding its destiny as the product of its own will. Nonetheless, we ignore him at our peril, for we remain imprisoned by the past as long as we deny its influence in the present.

. . . The destinies of the two races in this country are indissolubly linked together, and the way in which we choose those who will die reveals the depth of moral commitment among the living. . . .

PROBLEM 9-1. OFFENDER'S RACE AND RECORD

You represent Gerald Lane, a black man who is accused of murder. Lane claims that the Washoe County, Nevada, district attorney's office seeks the death penalty much more frequently when the defendant in a murder case is black. "If a person is accused of murder in Washoe County," Lane asserts, "it is better to be a white felon than a black with no prior felony convictions."

In support of this charge, you evaluate the 86 murder cases prosecuted by the Washoe County district attorney's office since Nevada's death penalty law took effect. In approximately 80 percent of cases involving a white defendant with at least one prior felony conviction, the district attorney did not seek the death penalty. By contrast, in approximately 80 percent of cases involving a black defendant without prior felony convictions, the district attorney did seek the death penalty. In other words, Lane argues that the Washoe County district attorney's office seeks the death penalty for only one out of five white murderers with past felonies and seeks the death penalty for four out of five black murderers without prior felonies.

In what legal terms will you frame the claim that might bar the use of the death penalty against Lane? How would you distinguish *McCleskey*? How would you use it? Compare Lane v. State, 881 P.2d 1358 (Nev. 1994).

NOTES

1. *Compelling evidence of intent.*   What sort of statistical study might provide the circumstantial evidence necessary to convince a court that arbitrary racial discrimination plays enough of a role in a sentencing system to invalidate the outcome in one case? Is such a statistical study possible? If racial discrimination does influence some decision makers in some cases, how might one demonstrate that fact in a court of law? In *McCleskey* both the court of appeals and the Supreme Court concluded that a stronger statistical showing would be necessary before racial influences in sentencing would amount to a constitutional problem. What sort of evidence did the courts have in mind?

2. *Whose race, victim's or defendant's?*   Note that the Baldus study found that the race of the *defendant* had no statistically significant effect on the use of capital punishment. In Furman v. Georgia, 408 U.S. 238 (1972), the Supreme Court struck down several capital punishment statutes, declaring that the death penalty (as administered at that time) was a "cruel and unusual punishment" in violation of the Eighth Amendment. Among the many reasons for this decision discussed in the various concurring opinions excerpted in Chapter 3, several of the Justices argued that capital punishment could not stand because it was imposed disproportionately against the poor and racial minorities. Would the Supreme Court have reached a different outcome in *McCleskey* if the Baldus study had pointed to racial discrimination based on the defendant's race rather than the victim's race? Can a punishment be racially discriminatory if the government imposes it equally on defendants of all races?

3. *Other venues.*   Suppose that on the day after the district court issued its order, the NAACP sends a copy of the Baldus study to a member of the Georgia legislature, and that member distributes copies. As the chair of the senate's committee on criminal justice matters, would you hold hearings? If so, what would be the topic of the hearings: the validity of the study or the most appropriate response to the study? If the Supreme Court had concluded instead that the influence of race in Georgia's capital punishment system rendered McCleskey's sentence unconstitutional, how would you advise Georgia legislators and prosecutors to respond? Would a victory for McCleskey mean abolition of the death penalty in Georgia? Would it necessitate any other changes or inquiries into Georgia's sentencing system?

4. *Statistical studies of capital punishment after* McCleskey.   The "race of the victim" effect that appeared in the Baldus study in Georgia has also appeared in statistical studies of other states. See, e.g., Glenn L. Pierce and Michael L. Radelet, Race, Region, and Death Sentencing in Illinois, 1988-1997, 81 Or. L. Rev. 39 (2002). These claims have received little serious attention from courts; many simply cite *McCleskey* and refuse to consider the studies as relevant evidence of racial discrimination in the use of capital punishment. See People v. Davis, 518 N.E.2d 78 (Ill. 1987). The Supreme Court of New Jersey has indicated that evidence along the lines of that presented in *McCleskey* could be sufficient to establish a prima facie case of a violation of the state constitution. The court has also indicated, however, that New Jersey has not yet executed enough people to form the basis for a convincing statistical study. See State v. Bey, 645 A.2d 685, 712 (N.J. 1994) ("Our abiding problem with analyzing the effect of race is that the case universe still contains too few cases to prove that the race of a defendant improperly influences death sentencing").

5. *The Kentucky Racial Justice Act.*   On April 2, 1998, Kentucky's governor signed into law "An Act relating to the fair and reliable imposition of capital sentences":

Section 1. . . .

(1) No person shall be subject to or given a sentence of death that was sought on the basis of race.

(2) A finding that race was the basis of the decision to seek a death sentence may be established if the court finds that race was a significant factor in decisions to seek the sentence of death in the Commonwealth at the time the death sentence was sought.

(3) Evidence relevant to establish a finding that race was the basis of the decision to seek a death sentence may include statistical evidence or other evidence, or both, that death sentences were sought significantly more frequently:

(a) Upon persons of one race than upon persons of another race; or

(b) As punishment for capital offenses against persons of one race than as punishment for capital offenses against persons of another race.

(4) The defendant shall state with particularity how the evidence supports a claim that racial considerations played a significant part in the decision to seek a death sentence in his/her case. The claim shall be raised by the defendant at the pre-trial conference. The court shall schedule a hearing on the claim and shall prescribe a time for the submission of evidence by both parties. If the court finds that race was the basis of the decision to seek the death sentence, the court shall order that a death sentence shall not be sought.

(5) The defendant has the burden of proving by clear and convincing evidence that race was the basis of the decision to seek the death penalty. The Commonwealth may offer evidence in rebuttal of the claims or evidence of the defendant.

Section 2. . . .

Section 1 of this Act shall not apply to sentences imposed prior to the effective date of this Act.

Is this law an appropriate response to the Baldus study and other evidence concerning the impact of race on the application of the death penalty? Would a capital defendant in Kentucky armed with a Kentucky version of the Baldus study be able to prevail on a claim based on this Act?

As a legislator in a death penalty state, would you advocate the adoption of such a law? Does this legislation go far enough to address racial disparities in the application of the death penalty? Or does it go too far by providing all capital defendants with an additional set of arguments to delay appropriate and otherwise lawful executions?

6. *The federal death penalty.*   The federal death penalty, which had been defunct for many decades until the early 1990s, has been the focus of much recent race-based debate. More than 80 percent of the federal death row inmates are nonwhite. The first individual executed since the reinstitution of the federal death penalty — Timothy McVeigh — was white, however. See, e.g., U.S. Department of Justice, The Federal Death Penalty System: A Statistical Survey (1988-2000), 14 Fed. Sentencing Rep. 35 (2002); U.S. Department of Justice, The Federal Death Penalty System: Supplementary Data, Analysis and Revised Protocols for Capital Case Review, 14 Fed. Sentencing Rep. 40 (2002). Nevertheless, criticism of the racial makeup on federal death row continues. How should this debate affect prosecutorial discretion? As a federal prosecutor, would you be more inclined to ask for capital punishment in the case of a white defendant since you know about the existing disparity? Federal death penalty decisions appear to be centralized in the hands of the Attorney General. Will a centralized decision-making structure protect better against racial disparity across the country? *See, e.g.,* Robin Campbell, Issues of Consistency in the Federal Death Penalty: A Roundtable Discussion on the Role of the U.S. Attorney, 14 Fed. Sentencing Rep. 52 (2002).

3. Discretionary Decisions and Race

Racial disparities at sentencing can also result from decisions made at various earlier stages of the criminal justice process. If prosecutors discriminate on the basis of race (or gender or on other objectionable grounds), the U.S. Supreme Court has stated that it is possible, at least in theory, to overturn a prosecutor's charging decision. A defendant who makes such a claim must establish that the prosecutor (1) made different charging decisions for similarly situated suspects (a discriminatory effect) and (2) intentionally made the decision on the basis of an "arbitrary" classification (a discriminatory intent). Arbitrary classifications would include "suspect classes" under equal protection doctrine or those defendants exercising their constitutional liberties such as freedom of speech or religion. See Oyler v. Boles, 368 U.S. 448 (1962); Wayte v. United States, 470 U.S. 598 (1985).

The *Wayte* decision made it clear that the government must choose the defendant for prosecution "because of" and not "despite" the protected conduct or status of the defendant. This basic federal framework for analyzing constitutional challenges to discriminatory charging policies has also been influential in state courts. See, e.g., State v. Muetze, 534 N.W.2d 55 (S.D. 1995) (no proof that non–Native Americans who were not charged were similarly situated).

In 1996 the U.S. Supreme Court considered the claim of Christopher Armstrong, who was indicted in 1992 for crack distribution and who, along with other defendants, responded by filing a motion for discovery or for dismissal of the indictment, alleging that he had been selected for federal prosecution because he is black. The issue in the case was not whether Armstrong had shown selective prosecution but what burden he had to carry to obtain discovery on a selective prosecution claim. Armstrong based his initial motion on evidence that the defendant was black in all 24 narcotics cases closed in 1991 by the U.S. Attorney's office that had prosecuted him.

The Supreme Court rejected Armstrong's claim, holding that a court hearing a claim of selective prosecution may grant discovery to the defendant if there is "some evidence" to support each of the elements of the claim, but finding that in this case, the "study" presented by Armstrong "failed to identify individuals who were not black, could have been prosecuted for the offenses for which respondents were charged, but were not so prosecuted." The Court did not explain how Armstrong or other claimants should obtain information about the pool of nonprosecuted suspects. Armstrong v. United States, 517 U.S. 456 (1996). Very few courts have reversed convictions on selective prosecution grounds, and no U.S. Supreme Court decisions have done so on racial grounds except for Yick Wo v. Hopkins, 118 U.S. 356 (1886). In United States v. Bass, 536 U.S. 862 (2002), the Supreme Court held that national charging and plea bargaining statistics on the race of offenders in federal death penalty cases were insufficient under *Armstrong*'s credible evidence requirement to trigger a discovery order.

Claims of selective prosecution are difficult to pursue successfully, not only because of the difficult proof requirements under federal law, but also because prosecutorial decision making may not be the only or even the principal cause of racially disproportionate outcomes in the criminal justice system. A strong bias in investigations or arrests may be concealed and perhaps even validated by studies showing unbiased decision making at a later stage of the process. For example, if whites and blacks who are convicted of a particular offense are punished identically, but members of one race are disproportionately investigated, then the sanction will appear neutral but will in fact be highly disparate, at least to the extent the investigatory practices do not accurately reflect underlying behavior. It is not only police decisions that can generate sharp but undetected disparities: Prosecutors may disproportionately direct cases involving members of one race to state court and identical cases by another race to federal court, where very different punishments attach to analogous state and federal charges. Or prosecutors may offer pleas in a racially disproportionate fashion.

Racial disparity may stem from decisions made by a variety of actors in one case — including prosecutors, police, judges, probation officers, and decision makers in a variety of other institutions, such as schools — or from decisions made by actors at different points in time. Much of the racial disparity in the criminal justice system can be explained through the offender's criminal record. As detailed in Chapter 5, offenders with prior convictions are typically punished more harshly; many minority offenders have such records. Studies indicate that one of the most discriminatory elements of the criminal justice system is the juvenile system. African American boys, in particular, are more likely to come under its supervision than white youngsters who commit similar offenses. Barry C. Feld, Juvenile and Criminal Justice Systems' Responses to Juvenile Violence, 24 Crime & Just. 189, 231-232 (1998). The juvenile case becomes the stepping stone into the adult criminal justice system.

This section highlights the difficulty of proving the source of discrimination in large, complicated systems with many participants. Discrimination may be especially hard to unearth when it is the product of repeated, low-level behavior of a large group of criminal justice officials and, perhaps, the result of unconscious influences on decision making. This section also raises questions about the law's capacity to change group behavior.

|| *Freddie Stephens v. State* ||
|| 456 S.E.2d 560 (Ga. 1995) ||

FLETCHER, J.

Freddie Stephens challenges the constitutionality of OCGA §16-13-30(d), which provides for life imprisonment on the second conviction of the sale or possession with intent to distribute a controlled substance. He contends that the provision as applied is irrational and racially discriminatory in violation of the United States and Georgia Constitutions. . . . The challenged statute states:

> [A]ny person who violates subsection (b) of this Code section with respect to a controlled substance in Schedule I or a narcotic drug in Schedule II shall be guilty of a felony and, upon conviction thereof, shall be punished by imprisonment for not less than five years nor more than 30 years. Upon conviction of a second or subsequent offense, he shall be imprisoned for life.

Subsection (b) makes it unlawful to "manufacture, deliver, distribute, dispense, administer, sell, or possess with intent to distribute any controlled substance." For a defendant to receive a life sentence for a second conviction, the state must notify the defendant prior to trial that it intends to seek the enhanced punishment based on past convictions.

Stephens contends that the statute as applied discriminates on the basis of race. He argues that this court should infer discriminatory intent from statewide and county-wide statistical data on sentences for drug offenders. In Hall County, where Stephens was convicted, the trial court found that one hundred percent (14 of 14) of the persons serving a life sentence under OCGA §16-13-30(d) are African-American, although African-Americans make up less than ten percent of the county population and approximately fifty to sixty percent of the persons arrested in drug investigations. Relying on evidence provided by the State Board of Pardons and Paroles, the trial court also found that 98.4 percent (369 of 375) of the persons serving life sentences for drug offenses as of May 1, 1994 were African-American, although African-Americans comprise only 27 percent of the state's population. Finally, a 1994 Georgia Department of Corrections study on the persons eligible for a life sentence under subsection (d) shows that less than one percent (1 of 168) of the whites sentenced for two or more convictions for drug sales are serving a life sentence, compared to 16.6 percent (202 of 1219) of the blacks.

In an earlier challenge to death penalty sentencing in Georgia based on statistics showing that persons who murder whites are more likely to be sentenced to death than persons who murder blacks, the United States Supreme Court held that the defendant had the burden of proving the existence of purposeful discrimination and that the purposeful discrimination had a discriminatory effect on him. McCleskey v. Kemp, 481 U.S. 279 (1987). . . .

Stephens concedes that he cannot prove any discriminatory intent by the Georgia General Assembly in enacting the law or by the Hall County district attorney in choosing to seek life imprisonment in this case. . . . These concessions preclude this court from finding an equal protection violation under the United States Constitution.

We also conclude that the statistical evidence Stephens presents is insufficient evidence to support his claim of an equal protection violation under the Georgia Constitution. Stephens fails to present the critical evidence by race concerning the number of persons eligible for life sentences under OCGA §16-13-30(d) in Hall County, but against whom the district attorney has failed to seek the aggravated sentence. Because the district attorney in each judicial circuit exercises discretion in determining when to seek a sentence of life imprisonment, a defendant must present some evidence addressing whether the prosecutor handling a particular case engaged in selective prosecution to prove a state equal protection violation. . . .

Stephens's argument about inferring intent from the statistical evidence also ignores that other factors besides race may explain the sentencing disparity. Absent from the statistical analysis is a consideration of relevant factors such as the charges brought, concurrent offenses, prior offenses and sentences, representation by retained or appointed counsel, existence of a guilty plea, circuit where convicted, and the defendant's legal status on probation, in prison, or on parole. Without more adequate information about what is happening both statewide and in Hall County, we defer deciding whether statistical evidence alone can ever be sufficient to prove an allegation of discriminatory intent in sentencing under the Georgia Constitution.

The dissent argues that McCleskey v. Kemp is not the controlling precedent, instead relying on the United States Supreme Court decision on peremptory challenges in jury selections in Batson v. Kentucky, 476 U.S. 79 (1986). We must look to *McCleskey* for a proper analysis of the substantive issue before us, rather than *Batson,* because *McCleskey* dealt with the use of statistical evidence to challenge racial disparity in sentencing, as does this case.

The Supreme Court in *McCleskey* pointed out several problems in requiring a prosecutor to explain the reasons for the statistical disparity in capital sentencing decisions. Many of these same problems exist in requiring district attorneys to justify their decisions in seeking a life sentence for drug offenses based on statewide, and even county-wide, statistics of persons serving life sentences in state prisons for drug offenses.

First, "requiring a prosecutor to rebut a study that analyzes the past conduct of scores of prosecutors is quite different from requiring a prosecutor to rebut a contemporaneous challenge to his own acts. See Batson v. Kentucky, 476 U.S. 79 (1986)." *McCleskey,* 481 U.S. at 296. Second, statewide statistics are not reliable in determining the policy of a particular district attorney. Finally, the Court stated that the policy considerations behind a prosecutor's discretion argue against requiring district attorneys to defend their decisions to seek the death penalty. Since district attorneys are elected to represent the state in all criminal cases, it is important that they be able to exercise their discretion in determining who to prosecute, what charges to bring, which sentence to seek, and when to appeal without having to account for each decision in every case.

. . . Stephens also argues that the statute violates due process and equal protection by creating an irrational sentencing scheme. Seeking to deter repeated drug sales by the same person is not irrational. Therefore, we adhere to our previous decision that there is a rational basis for the sentencing scheme in OCGA §16-13-30(d) and that it does not deprive persons of due process or equal protection under the law. . . .

THOMPSON, J., concurring.

[W]e are presented once again with the claim that OGCA §16-13-30(d) is being used in a discriminatory fashion. This time, we are introduced to statewide statistical information which must give us pause: From 1990 to 1994, OCGA §16-13-30(d) was used to put 202 out of 1,107 eligible African-Americans in prison for life. During that same period, the statute was used to put 1 out of 167 eligible whites in prison for life. A life eligible African-American had a 1 in 6 chance of receiving a life sentence. A life eligible white had a 1 in 167 chance of receiving a life sentence. An African-American was 2,700 percent more likely to receive a life sentence than a white. . . . These statistics are no doubt as much a surprise to those who work and practice within the judicial system as to those who do not.

Statistical information can inform, not explain. It can tell what has happened, not why. However, only a true cynic can look at these statistics and not be impressed that something is amiss. That something lies in the fact that OCGA §16-13-30(d) has been converted from a mandatory life sentence statute into a statute which imposes a life sentence only in those cases in which a district attorney, in the exercise of his or her discretion, informs a defendant that the State is seeking enhanced punishment. . . .

McCleskey v. Kemp, 481 U.S. 279 (1987), should continue to be applied in death penalty cases where there is a system of checks and balances to ensure that death sentences are not sought and imposed autocratically. Likewise *McCleskey* should be applied in other cases where the courts have discretion to determine the length of time to be served. However, *McCleskey* probably should not be applied where a district attorney has the power to decide whether a defendant is sentenced to life, or a term of years. . . .

I am persuaded that Batson v. Kentucky, 476 U.S. 79 (1986), could be used to supply a general framework in analyzing cases of this kind. . . . Nevertheless, it is my considered view that the judgment in this case must be affirmed because the defendant has failed to meet his burden even under a *Batson*-type analysis.

In order to establish a prima facie case under *Batson,* a defendant must prove systematic discrimination in his particular jurisdiction. Although the statistics presented by defendant are indicative of a statewide pattern of discrimination in the use of OCGA §16-13-30(d), the Hall County statistics are insufficient to make such a case. They simply show that all the persons in Hall County serving a life sentence under OCGA §16-13-30(d) are African-Americans. They do not show how many African-Americans were eligible to receive a life sentence under the statute; nor do they show how many whites were eligible. Moreover, they offer no information concerning the record of the district attorney in this case. Thus, upon careful review, I must conclude that this defendant, in this case and on this record, failed to prove a pattern of systematic discrimination in his jurisdiction. . . .

Statewide, approximately 15 percent of eligible offenders receive a life sentence under OCGA §16-13-30(d). The statistical evidence presented in this case serves as notice to the General Assembly of Georgia that the mandatory life sentence provision of OCGA §16-13-30(d) has been repealed de facto. With such notice, there are at least three courses of action the legislature might now choose to pursue.

One. The General Assembly could choose to leave the mandatory life sentence on the books realizing that it is being used in a small percentage of the eligible cases. Militating against this course of action is the fact that all laws passed by the legislature should be followed. Contempt for and failure to follow any law breeds contempt for and failure to follow other laws.

Two. The General Assembly could reaffirm its commitment to a mandatory life sentence by requiring district attorneys to inform all defendants of prior convictions and thus enforce OCGA §16-13-30(d) with respect to all life eligible offenders. Militating against this course of action is the fact that mandatory life sentences are not favored by the prosecuting bar or by the defense bar. That is evidenced by the fact that from 1990 to 1994 only 203 out of 1,274 life eligible defendants actually received a life sentence under OCGA §16-13-30(d). . . .

Three. The General Assembly could choose to change the mandatory life sentence penalty to one of several sentencing options which the court could impose. For example, the penalty for a second or subsequent sale could be imprisonment for not less than 5 nor more than 30 years, or life. . . .

It is my concern that these problems be resolved in whatever way the General Assembly deems best and that, thereafter, the prosecutors and the courts carry out that legislative will.

BENHAM, P.J., dissenting.

Of those persons from Hall County serving life sentences pursuant to OCGA §16-13-30(d), which mandates a life sentence for the second conviction for sale of or possession with intent to distribute certain narcotics, 100 percent are African-American, although African-Americans comprise only approximately 10 percent of Hall County's population. In our state prison system, African-Americans represent 98.4 percent of the 375 persons serving life sentences for violating OCGA §16-13-30(d). These statistics were part of the finding of the trial court in this case. In the face of such numbing and paralyzing statistics, the majority say there is no need for inquiry. It is with this determination that I take issue and from which I respectfully dissent. . . .

[In Batson v. Kentucky, 476 U.S. 79 (1986), the Supreme Court] installed a system that shifted the burden to the prosecutor to give race-neutral reasons for the peremptory challenges once the defendant established facts supporting an inference that the prosecutor's use of peremptory challenges was racially motivated. [T]he court in *Batson* stated that an inference of discriminatory intent could be drawn from certain conduct or statistical data. Beyond its effect on peremptory challenges, the importance of *Batson* was that it significantly reduced the burden on one claiming discrimination, recognizing that under certain circumstances, the crucial information about an allegedly discriminatory decision could only come from the one who made the decision.

This is the course of reasoning we need to follow in analyzing the issue in this case rather than the more restrictive course taken in McCleskey v. Kemp and applied by the majority. . . .

I am not unmindful or unappreciative of the vital and taxing role district attorneys are called upon to undertake in the ongoing battle against the blight of illicit drug trafficking. Throughout this state, they shoulder an enormous burden of responsibility for advancing the fight against drugs, and to do so successfully, they must be invested with considerable discretion in making decisions about ongoing prosecutions. However, it is the very breadth of that discretion, concentrated in a single decision-maker, which makes it necessary that the one exercising the discretion be the one, when confronted with facts supporting an inference of discriminatory application, to bear the burden of establishing that the discretion was exercised without racial influence. This case is more like *Batson* than *McCleskey* because all the discretion in the sentencing scheme involved in this case resides in the district attorney, to the exclusion of the trial court, whereas in death penalty cases such as *McCleskey,* the spread of discretion among the prosecutor, the trial court, and the jurors introduces variables which call for more rigorous statistical analysis. In addition, the complexity of the death penalty procedure, with its many safeguards and the recurring necessity of specific findings at every stage from the grand jury to the sentencing jury, differentiates it from the relative simplicity of the sentencing scheme applicable to this case.

[T]he U.S. Supreme Court recognized in *McCleskey* itself that statistical proof which presents a "stark pattern" may be accepted as the sole proof of discriminatory intent. In distinguishing *McCleskey* from such a case, the Supreme Court mentioned in a footnote two cases in which "a statistical pattern of discriminatory impact demonstrated a constitutional violation." . . . The statistics in those cases presented a "stark pattern," but no more stark than the pattern presented in this case. In the present case, based on evidence from law enforcement officers who testified as to arrest rates and other relevant statistics, the trial court found that 100% of the people from that county who were serving life sentences pursuant to OCGA §16-13-30(d) were African-Americans and that statewide, 98.4% of all the persons serving life sentences pursuant to OCGA §16-13-30(d) were African-Americans. . . .

I believe it is necessary that we adopt a procedure which will make it possible to address the issue openly and honestly in the trial courts. . . . I would hold, therefore, as a matter purely of state constitutional law, that equal protection of the law in the context of OCGA §16-13-30(d) requires that the prosecution be required, when a defendant has made a prima facie showing sufficient to raise an inference of unequal application of the statute, to "demonstrate that permissible racially neutral selection criteria and procedures have produced the monochromatic result." *Batson,* 476 U.S. at 94. . . .

Because appellant has made a sufficient showing of discriminatory application of OCGA §16-13-30(d) that the State should be required to give race-neutral reasons for the "monochromatic" application of that statute in Hall County, this court should vacate the life sentences and remand this case to the trial court for a hearing. At such a hearing, should the trial court find that the prosecution could not provide race-neutral reasons for the "monochromatic result" of the application of OCGA §16-13-30(d) in Hall County, sentencing for the offenses involved would still be permissible, but not with the aggravation of punishment authorized by OCGA §16-13-30(d). On the other hand, should the trial court find that the State has provided appropriate race-neutral reasons, the life sentences would be reimposed, whereupon appellant would be entitled to a new appeal.

Just as the prosecution was reined in by *Batson,* it must also be reined in here and called upon to give an account of itself. The statistics offered in this case show an enormous potential for injustice, and those statistics are just like the tip of an iceberg, with the bulk lying below the surface, yet to be realized. . . .

PROBLEM 9-2.   TOWN AND COUNTRY

Darryl Pierre Wooden, an African American man sentenced to ten years in prison for selling illegal narcotics, believes that a new Alabama law is racially discriminatory and asks for your help. His sentence was the product of the following two statutes, each of which mandates a five-year term:

- §13A-12-250. In addition to any penalties . . . provided by law for any person convicted of an unlawful sale of a controlled substance, there is hereby imposed a penalty of five years' incarceration in a state corrections facility with no provision for probation if the situs of such unlawful sale was on the campus or within a three-mile radius of the campus boundaries of any public or private school . . . or other educational institution in this state.
- §13A-12-270. In addition to any penalties . . . provided by law for any person convicted of an unlawful sale of a controlled substance, there is hereby imposed a penalty of five years' incarceration in a state corrections facility with no provision for probation if the situs of such unlawful sale was within a three-mile radius of a public housing project owned by a housing authority.

Wooden's conviction and ten-year mandatory sentence resulted from his sale to an undercover police officer of one tablet of "hydromorphone." Indisputably, this $50 transaction, which occurred on the 100 block of Fourth Avenue North in Birmingham, occurred within a three-mile radius both of a school and of a housing project. Wooden claims these statutes disproportionately impose a heavier sentence on black defendants in Jefferson County than on similar defendants in other Alabama counties because the conditions described in the statute ordinarily are present in an urban setting rather than a rural setting, and the overwhelming majority of citizens living in the city of Birmingham are black.

You gather the following evidence: Birmingham Police Officer B. H. Butler reports that of 150 persons he arrested for the "unlawful sale of a controlled substance," 145 were black and were subject to the enhanced sentence provisions of §§13A-12-250 and 13A-12-270. Officer Eric Benson asserts that of approximately 100 persons he arrested for the "unlawful sale of a controlled substance" in the preceding year, 70 were black. He also states that "any sale of a controlled substance within the city limits of Birmingham would be within three miles of both a school and a housing project, and that 98 percent to 99 percent of those living in these housing projects are black."

Alabama Administrative Office of Courts official Larry Forston provides computer data gleaned from circuit court clerks' offices throughout the state. He tells you that from 1989, when the three-mile-radius provisions were adopted, through 1994, only three black defendants and one white defendant were sentenced in Jefferson County under either statute, compared with 267 black defendants and 90 white defendants sentenced elsewhere in the state.

Is Wooden right to focus on the application of the law to his county? How would you frame that claim? What other information would you try to obtain? Whose actions are suspect? Compare Ex parte Wooden, 670 So. 2d 892 (Ala. 1995).

NOTES

1. *Who discriminates against whom?* What discrimination does Freddie Stephens claim? Other than the fact that both McCleskey and Stephens asserted that race was the basis for discrimination, were these similar claims? A controversial case at all stages, *Stephens* garnered additional attention when, 13 days before issuing the above opinion, the Georgia justices issued a slip opinion with a majority written by Justice Hugh Thompson announcing the "watershed" conclusion that under the equal protection clauses of both the federal and state constitutions these statistics required a prosecutor to provide a race-neutral explanation for the decision to apply the statute to Stephens. The slip opinion was bitterly attacked by the Georgia attorney general and the 46 state district attorneys, who together filed a brief asking that it be reversed. Attorney General Michael Bowers asserted that it was the worst decision from the Georgia Supreme Court in more than 20 years and that it "sets up sentencing quotas."

2. *Competing analogies.* Did the majority in Stephens v. State think that Stephens's claim was the same as McCleskey's? Did the concurrence think so? The dissent? Were you convinced by the competing analogy to discriminatory jury selection in Batson v. Kentucky? Did you find convincing Justice Thompson's application of *Batson* in the concurring opinion? Justice Robert Benham, dissenting in *Stephens*, argued that sentencing under the Georgia drug statute was different from capital punishment because it concentrates the decision in the hands of the district attorney. Do you agree? Are there ways a police officer might influence who receives a life sentence under the statute? Does the judge have some control over this question? The defense counsel? The state attorney general? Voters in the county or in the state?

3. *The federalization of drug law enforcement.* In many criminal cases, state and federal prosecutors both have jurisdiction. Sometimes they investigate cases together and then allocate prosecutorial responsibilities; sometimes state prosecutors call in federal investigatory assistance; and sometimes federal prosecutors refer cases, especially those of a minor nature, to the state for trial. The different penalty structures in state and federal courts, together with procedural differences, may provide an incentive for state and federal prosecutors to send cases to federal court. This is true particularly when higher penalties exist under the federal sentencing guidelines or congressional mandatory sentences. While the so-called federalization of crime has been thoroughly criticized, it provides prosecutors with substantial additional discretion. See American Bar Association, Criminal Justice Section, Task Force on the Federalization of Criminal Law, Report on the Federalization of Criminal Law (1998). Results may also

be startling. Hispanics, for example, make up 17 percent of the inmates in state prisons but 27 percent of the inmates in federal prisons. The substantial difference likely reflects Hispanics' higher rate of federal drug and especially immigration convictions. In FY 2001, 40 percent of those sentenced under the federal guidelines were Hispanic; almost 45 percent of all drug trafficking offenders and almost 90 percent of all immigration offenders were Hispanic.

In a study of charging for crack cocaine offenses in Los Angeles, Richard Berk and Alex Campbell found that black defendants are more likely than white or Latino defendants to be charged in federal court with sale of crack cocaine (which translates into more severe punishments than for comparable charges in state court). While black defendants represented 58 percent of those arrested by the Los Angeles Sheriff's Department for sale of crack cocaine between 1990 and 1992, they made up 83 percent of the defendants charged with that crime in federal court. White and Latino defendants arrested for this crime were more likely to be prosecuted in state court. Richard Berk and Alex Campbell, Preliminary Data on Race and Crack Charging Practices in Los Angeles, 6 Fed. Sentencing Rep. 36 (1993). What might explain the racially disparate federal crack prosecutions reported by Berk and Campbell?

4. *Racial patterns in charging.* Racial minorities are charged with crimes in a number disproportionate to their percentage in the population. But are minorities charged with crimes at a higher rate, once one accounts for different levels of participation in crime? Criminologists addressing this question have studied records of large numbers of cases, using statistical techniques (especially regression analysis) to compare similar cases and to sort out racial and nonracial influences over charging decisions. See, e.g., Cassia Spohn, John Gruhl, and Susan Welch, The Impact of the Ethnicity and Gender of Defendants on the Decision to Reject or Dismiss Felony Charges, 25 Criminology 175 (1987) (study of 33,000 felony cases between 1977 and 1980 to determine whether racial bias influenced prosecutors' decisions to decline felony charges; declinations occur more frequently for white suspects after controlling for age, criminal record, and seriousness of offense); Developments in the Law — Race and the Criminal Process, 101 Harv. L. Rev. 1520, 1525-1530 (1988) (summarizing other studies). Does any of this analysis support the conclusion that selective prosecution doctrine is a failure? If racial discrimination in charging is indeed widespread, is it unrealistic to ask a defendant to make a prediscovery showing? Or is it necessary to limit litigation to the most egregious cases of racial discrimination in prosecutorial decision making? How egregious must the disparity be?

5. *Drug offenses on Native American reservations.* Enhancement provisions for the selling of illegal drugs on or near school grounds and public housing projects exist in the states and the federal system. On Native American reservations most of the housing is "public" in the sense that it is constructed and owned by the federal government. In contrast to urban housing projects, however, reservation public housing consists of single-family dwellings. If a Native American drug offender is charged with dealing drugs near a public housing project, as the law clerk to a federal judge, how would you assess the applicability of the enhancement? See Charles B. Kornmann, Injustices: Applying the Sentencing Guidelines and Other Federal Mandates in Indian Country, 13 Fed. Sentencing Rep. 71 (2000).

6. *Influence of race on sentencing in the United Kingdom.* The United States is not the only nation in which the influence of race on sentencing has ignited controversy. In a study of the English crown courts of Birmingham, Wolverhampton, Coventry, Warwick, and Stafford in 1989, Roger Hood noted that blacks were given prison sentences rather than a nonprison alternative more often than whites (56.6 percent of blacks sentenced, and 48.4 percent of whites). After attempting to account statistically for any difference in cases based on arguably nonracial factors such as the seriousness of the offense or past criminal record, Hood concluded that race still had a small influence on the custody decision: There was a "5 percent greater probability of a male black defendant being sentenced to custody than a white male." Race seemed to have more influence in cases of "medium seriousness": Black defendants had a 13 percent higher probability of receiving custody in these cases. Roger Hood, Race and Sentencing: A Study in the Crown Court 198 (1992). Why is this specific racial difference of particular concern?

PROBLEM 9-3. THE CRACK–POWDER DIFFERENTIAL

In 1986 Congress passed the Anti-Drug Abuse Act to increase the penalties for various drug crimes. The new law imposed heavier penalties on cocaine base (crack) than on cocaine powder, a relationship later known as the "100-to-1 ratio." An offense involving mixtures weighing 5 grams or more containing cocaine base was subject to the same punishment as an offense involving mixtures weighing 500 grams or more containing cocaine powder. Congress considered crack cocaine to be more dangerous than cocaine powder because of crack's potency, its more highly addictive nature, and its greater accessibility because of its relatively low cost.

Some of the impetus for the federal law came from the news media. Stories associated the use of crack cocaine with social maladies such as gang violence and parental neglect among user groups. Critics of the federal law, however, argued that these social problems resulted not from the drug itself but from the disadvantaged social and economic environment in places where the drug is often used.

In practice, the increased penalties for crack meant that African-American defendants received heavier penalties than whites for possession and sale of cocaine. More than 90 percent of all people arrested for sale or possession of crack were African American; roughly 80 percent of all people arrested for sale or possession of powder cocaine were white.

By 1989, the Minnesota legislature was debating the sentencing of crack offenses. The legislators considered a bill that would make a person who possessed three or more grams of crack cocaine guilty of a third-degree offense. Under the same statute, a person who possessed ten or more grams of cocaine powder would be guilty of the same offense; someone who possessed fewer than ten grams of cocaine powder would be guilty of a fifth-degree offense. The bill became known as the "10-to-3 ratio" law.

The sponsors of the bill argued that this structure facilitated prosecution of street-level drug dealers. Law enforcement officers who testified at legislative hearings suggested that three grams of crack and ten grams of powder indicated a level at which dealing, not merely using, took place. A person convicted of selling 100 grams of crack may often be characterized as a midlevel dealer (someone who provides the drug to street-level retailers). By comparison, 100 grams of powder usually typifies a low-level retailer; 500 grams is more indicative of a midlevel dealer. But witnesses from the Department of Public Safety Office of Drug Policy contradicted these estimates for the typical amount of drugs carried by dealers, suggesting that most cocaine powder users are dealers as well.

The customary unit of sales for the two drugs are also different. The typical unit of crack is a rock weighing .1 gram, which at the time sold for $20 to $25. The customary unit of powder is the 8-ball, one-eighth of an ounce or about 3.5 grams, which sold for about $350. Ten grams of powder cocaine could be easily converted into more than three grams of crack.

Sponsors of the bill echoed Congress's argument that crack is more addictive and dangerous than cocaine powder, and witnesses at the hearings supported this contention. But other witnesses pointed out that crack and powder cocaine have the same active ingredient and produce the same type of pharmacological effects. The difference in effect between the two drugs stems from the fact that cocaine powder is sniffed through the nostrils while crack cocaine is smoked. If powder cocaine is dissolved and injected, it is just as addictive as crack.

As a member of the Minnesota legislature, would you support the 10-to-3 ratio bill? What else would you like to know before you vote? Compare State v. Russell, 477 N.W.2d 886 (Minn. 1991).

NOTES

1. *Constitutional challenges to punishment differentials: majority position.* Racial disparities in the application of death penalty laws highlight several distinct forms of discrimination. A law can be discriminatory in intent, either at the point of creation or when it is applied. Some laws have racially discriminatory effects, even though the people who create and enforce the law do not intend to burden one racial group more than another and even though they apply the law with complete evenhandedness. These effects occur when the criminal sanctions apply to behavior that people of one race engage in more often than people of other races. Would it ever be unconstitutional for a legislature to criminalize conduct when one racial group is more likely to engage in it?

A number of defendants convicted of trafficking in crack cocaine have argued for a downward departure from the guideline sentence (or an invalidation of the relevant guidelines and statutes) based on an equal protection claim. Federal courts have uniformly rejected this assertion, reasoning that any racial impact of the crack cocaine statutes and guidelines was unintentional. See, e.g., United States v. Reece, 994 F.2d 277 (6th Cir. 1993) (per curiam); United States v. Thomas, 900 F.2d 37 (4th Cir. 1990). While not often addressing such claims, high state courts have also usually rejected the constitutional challenges.

2. *Legislative response.* The Minnesota Supreme Court struck down the legislation described in Problem 9-3 based on the state's equal protection clause in State v. Russell, 477 N.W.2d 886 (Minn. 1991). The legislature responded by

increasing the penalties for powder to equal the former penalties for crack. Minn. Stat. §152.021-023. Minnesota's cocaine penalties are now among the toughest in the country — stiffer in some ways than in the federal system.

3. *Crack and cocaine sentences in the federal system.*   The federal penalty structure punishes cocaine powder and cocaine crack offenders equally for amounts that differ 100 times — the so-called 100-to-1 ratio. Note that this is not a ratio of penalties but of the amounts of drugs that spur similar penalties. In 1994 Congress ordered the U.S. Sentencing Commission to report on cocaine punishment policies in the federal system. The following year the commission issued a report attacking the 100-to-1 quantity ratio and recommending instead a 1-to-1 crack–powder quantity ratio to be achieved by lowering the penalties for crack along with other changes in the federal system that would more severely punish behavior associated with crack offenses.

The commission's proposed ratio came under attack from legislators across the political spectrum. Congress passed legislation to overturn the commission's proposal on October 18, 1995, by a vote of 332 to 83, and President Clinton signed the measure. This was the first time in the history of the commission that Congress voted to override a proposed amendment to the sentencing guidelines. The 100-to-1 quantity ratio remains in effect in the federal system.

As a matter of political reality, how could the U.S. Sentencing Commission unanimously recommend the rejection of a policy (the 100-to-1 quantity ratio) that had already received the overwhelming endorsement of the legislative branch when the cocaine penalties were originally enacted? Would Congress have reacted differently to a proposal to reduce, but not eliminate, the penalty differences between crack and powder? Is this equivalent to arguing that a small amount of racial discrimination is acceptable?

In May 2002, the U.S. Sentencing Commission, consisting of an entirely different group of commissioners than in 1995, recommended to Congress that the amount required to trigger a five-year mandatory minimum sentence be increased from five to at least 25 grams of crack and that the amount of crack required to trigger a ten-year mandatory sentence be increased from 50 to at least 250 grams, producing a quantity ratio of at least 20 to 1. In explaining its recommendation, the commission determined that the current penalties were flawed in a number of ways: they exaggerate the relative harmfulness of crack cocaine; they sweep too broadly and apply most often to lower-level offenders; they overstate the seriousness of most crack offenses and fail to provide adequate proportionality; and their severity mostly affects minorities. The commission's recommendation accords with the majority of state systems, whose sentencing structures generally do not distinguish between crack and powder cocaine. So far, Congress has not responded to the commission's recommendation.

4. *Race and crack.*   Are racial differentials the central issue in the crack–powder punishment debate, or are they rather a by-product of social structure? Do different parts of the criminal world just happen to be controlled by groups of a particular race or ethnicity, as the analogy to the use of racketeering laws against the Mafia suggests? Or do you find convincing the position that, in effect, racially disproportionate effects (but not intent) justify reworking the system to start with a 1-to-1 quantity ratio?

In an excerpt reprinted in the first part of this section, Michael Tonry asserted that politicians pursued the war on drugs with full knowledge that "the greater burden of punishment [would be] borne by blacks. Crime control politicians wanted more people in prison and knew that a larger proportion of them would be black." Is this the sort of discriminatory intent that could form the basis for an equal protection challenge? Does this argument create a politically viable basis for revising penalties for drug offenses?

B.   NATIVE PEOPLES

The concept of race, and especially the distinction between black and white, has dominated U.S. history. In recent years other racial groups have been governmentally recognized in the United States, among them Asians. But some groups, such as Arabs, remain statistically uncounted. Increasingly, the concept of race has been discredited and undermined by the growing diversity of racialized identities. The most prominent example is professional golfer Tiger Woods.

Nevertheless, race remains a powerful concept in U.S. legal discourse. Equality is constitutionally guaranteed, and limits on unequal treatment are reinforced in statutes and rules. Congress required the U.S. Sentencing Commission to "assure that the guidelines and policy statements are entirely neutral as to the race, sex, national origin, creed, and socioeconomic status of offenders." 28 U.S.C. §994(d). In accordance with this mandate, the guidelines state unequivocally that race, sex, national origin, creed, religion, and socioeconomic status "are not relevant in the determination of a sentence." U.S. Sentencing Guidelines Manual §5H1.10. Should national origin never be relevant in a sentence determination?

The strong statements of equal treatment, grounded in constitutional principle, contrast sharply with the social realities of Native Americans. This contrast generates puzzles for courts trying to balance the defendants they see with the constitutional, statutory, and guideline nondiscrimination provisions that seem to prohibit the recognition of racial and ethnic differences. In *Big Crow*, excerpted below, does the court find a legitimate and harmonious solution to the problem?

Native Americans in South Dakota: An Erosion of Confidence in the Justice System
South Dakota Advisory Committee to the United States Civil Rights Commission, Mar. 2000

South Dakota Demographics.   . . . The estimated white population in South Dakota is 669,007, or 90.6 percent. American Indians are by far the largest minority group, making up 8 percent (59,292) of the population. Only Alaska and New Mexico have larger percentages of American Indian residents. . . .

Native Americans in South Dakota.   Nationwide, American Indians number approximately 1.2 million, with 900,000 living on or near Indian reservations. . . .

South Dakota's nine reservations vary in size from Lower Brule, with about 1,200 residents to Pine Ridge, with more than 30,000, making it the second largest reservation in the United States.

Economic Conditions.   Despite a booming economy, nationwide half of the potential work force in Indian Country is unemployed. For American Indians in South Dakota the statistics are even worse. [More than 50 percent of the labor force was unemployed in 1997 on 8 of the 9 reservations in the state, with unemployment reaching as high as 85 percent at Yankton and 80 percent at Cheyenne River.]

Of the 10 poorest counties in the United States in 1990, 4 were on Indian reservations in South Dakota. The poorest county in the Nation is Shannon County, which includes much of Pine Ridge Reservation: 63.1 percent of county residents have incomes that fall below the poverty line. The average annual income for families living on Pine Ridge is just $3,700.

The effects of poverty are far reaching. According to the director of [the Bureau of Indian Affairs' (BIA's)] Great Plains Regional Office, on South Dakota's reservations "economic depression has manifested itself in the form of suicides, alcohol and drug abuse, juvenile gangs, and dropping out of school, to physical abuse, sexual abuse, and child abuse."

Health.   On average, men in Bangladesh can expect to live longer than Native American men in South Dakota. A study by the Harvard School of Health in conjunction with health statisticians from the Centers for Disease Control found that Native American men living in six South Dakota counties had the shortest life expectancy in the Nation. . . . Indian men in South Dakota . . . usually live only into their mid-50s. . . .

In 1993, age-adjusted death rates for the following causes were considerably higher for American Indians [than for the general population]: alcoholism, 579 percent greater; tuberculosis, 475 percent; diabetes mellitus, 231 percent; accidents, 212 percent; suicide, 70 percent; pneumonia and influenza, 61 percent; and homicide, 41 percent. Further, infant mortality in Indian Country is double the national average, and Pine Ridge Reservation has the highest infant mortality rate in the Nation.

Crime.   In an October 1997 report, the Justice Department's Criminal Division concluded "there is a public safety crisis in Indian Country." While most of the Nation has witnessed a drastic reduction in serious crime over the past 7 years, on Indian reservations crime is spiraling upwards. Between 1992 and 1996, the overall crime rate dropped about 17 percent, and homicides were down 22 percent. For the same period, however, the Bureau of Indian Affairs reported that murders on America's Indian reservations rose sharply. Some tribes, the Justice Department report says, "have murder rates that far exceed those of urban areas known for their struggles against violent crime." And other violent crimes parallel the rise in homicide.

Tribal law enforcement agencies do not have the resources to meet their growing caseloads. The Criminal Division's report concluded, "The single most glaring problem is a lack of adequate resources in Indian Country. Any solution requires a substantial infusion of new money in addition to existing funds." A chronic shortage of personnel plagues most agencies. For example, in 1996

Indian Country residents were served by less than one-half the number of officers provided to small non-Indian communities. Tribal officers are also in dire need of training. According to the BIA, no reservation in South Dakota has a fully staffed, adequately trained law enforcement program.

[A 1999 study by the Bureau of Justice Statistics found] that American Indians experience per capita rates of violence which are more than twice those of the U.S. population. From 1992 through 1996 the average annual rate of violent victimizations among Indians 12 years and older was 124 per 1,000 residents, compared with 61 for blacks, 49 for whites, and 29 for Asians. The rate of violent crime experienced by American Indian women is nearly 50 percent higher than that reported by black males.

Annual Average Rate of Violent Victimization by Race of Victim, 1992-96

Number of victimizations per 1,000 persons age 12 or older in each racial group

	All Races	American Indian	White	Black	Asian
Violent victimizations	50	124	49	61	29
Rape/sexual assault	2	7	2	3	1
Robbery	6	12	5	13	7
Aggravated assault	11	35	10	16	6
Simple assault	31	70	32	30	15

The report also found that in 7 out of 10 violent victimizations of American Indians the assailant was someone of a different race, a substantially higher incidence of interracial violence than experienced by white or black victims. Among white victims, 69 percent of the offenders were white; similarly, black victims are most likely to be victimized by a black assailant (81 percent). For American Indian victims of rape/sexual assault, the offender is described as white in 82 percent of the cases.

Alcohol is more often a factor in crimes committed by and against American Indians than for other races. Seventy percent of Indians in local jails for violent crimes had been drinking when they committed the offense, nearly double the rate for the general population. In 55 percent of violent crimes against American Indians, the victim said the offender was under the influence of alcohol and/or drugs. The offender's use of alcohol is less likely for white and black victims (44 and 35 percent, respectively).

Other important findings of the study are as follows:

- The arrest rate for alcohol-related offenses among American Indians (drunken driving, liquor law violations and public drunkenness) was more than double that for the total population during 1996. However the drug arrest rate was lower than for other races.
- Almost four in 10 American Indians held in local jails had been charged with a public order offense — most commonly driving while intoxicated.
- During 1996 the American Indian arrest rate for youth violence was about the same as that for white youths.
- On any given day an estimated one in 25 American Indians 18 years old and older is under the jurisdiction of the nation's criminal justice

system. This is 2.4 times the rate for whites and 9.3 times the per capita rate for Asians but about half the rate for blacks.

- The number of American Indians per capita confined in the state and federal prisons is about 38 percent above the national average. However, the rate of confinement in local jails is estimated to be nearly 4 times the national average.

MAJOR CONCERNS AND CONCLUSIONS

1. Many Native Americans in South Dakota have little or no confidence in the criminal justice system and believe that the administration of justice at the Federal and State levels is permeated by racism. There is a strongly held perception among Native Americans that there is a dual system of justice and that race is a critical factor in determining how law enforcement and justice functions are carried out. This perception includes a belief that violent crimes involving Native Americans are dealt with differently from those involving whites. It is believed that crimes perpetrated by whites against Indians are investigated and prosecuted with less vigor than those committed by Indians against whites. . . . Information was received by the Advisory Committee suggesting disparities in many aspects of the criminal justice system, including law enforcement stops and racial profiling, arrests, prosecutions, legal representation, and sentencing. . . .

6. The Advisory Committee heard many complaints concerning Federal sentencing guidelines. It was alleged that crimes prosecuted in the Federal system require harsher sentences than similar offenses prosecuted in State courts. Because of the much broader Federal jurisdiction applicable to crimes committed by Native Americans in Indian Country, disparate sentencing — with more severe punishment for Native Americans — may result. This serves to reinforce and strengthen the perception of unequal justice for American Indians. . . .

8. Native Americans are underrepresented in the employment of all institutions involved in the administration of justice, at the Federal, State, and local levels. They are also largely excluded from elected positions and other decisionmaking positions that govern the administration of justice. . . .

13. There appear to be limited legal resources available for Native Americans in South Dakota. Victims of discrimination often find it difficult to secure legal representation. Court-appointed defense attorney systems and local public defender programs have been described as inadequate, due to inexperience, lack of funding, and potential conflicts of interest. There are also few Native Americans in the legal professions. National civil rights legal organizations are not easily accessible, and there are few such programs at the State level. . . .

While some have overcome the obstacles and achieved great success, most American Indians have been left behind. For the most part, Native Americans are very much separate and unequal members of society. Thus, it is not surprising that they are underrepresented in terms of economic status and overrepresented in the population of the State's jails, juvenile facilities, and prisons. Systemic, institutionalized, and historic discrimination disadvantage Native Americans in many ways, and therefore the problems they encounter when caught up in the criminal justice system are wholly consistent with other forms of discrimination.

Despair is not too strong a word to characterize the emotional feelings of many Native Americans who believe they live in a hostile environment. . . .

|| *United States v. David Big Crow* ||
|| 898 F.2d 1326 (8th Cir. 1990) ||

HEANEY, J.

. . . In the early morning of October 9, 1988, following an evening of heavy drinking, Big Crow and his wife, Margaret, returned from a dance to their trailer home near Porcupine, South Dakota, on the Pine Ridge Indian Reservation. They were met there by Cheryl Ferguson, Donald Twiss, and James Twiss, friends of the Big Crows who had attended the same dance and who also had been drinking. On entering the Big Crow residence, James Twiss went to sleep on a couch. The others, accompanied by Tanya Kills Warrior, who had attended the dance with the Big Crows, and Cathy Iron Cloud, who had been babysitting the Big Crow children, began to play a drinking game called quarter pitch. A half hour later, Donald Twiss left the game and went to sleep on the floor next to the couch his brother occupied. . . .

Some time later, Big Crow also got up and left the kitchen, where the game took place. When he returned, Margaret Big Crow was making a telephone call. Big Crow tackled her and the two fell into the living room. Margaret Big Crow testified that they fell on Donald Twiss, who had been asleep on the floor, and that Twiss then moved across the room. Donald Twiss testified that he awoke feeling a sharp pain above his eye and bleeding from his forehead. Twiss also stated that Big Crow was standing next to him with a piece of firewood in his hand, making derogatory remarks about the Twiss family. . . . James Twiss then got up from the couch. Big Crow challenged James Twiss with the piece of firewood. . . . James Twiss then knocked Big Crow to the floor. James Twiss testified that Big Crow hit him in the ribs with the firewood, after which he hit Big Crow, who then ran outside. . . .

Iron Cloud and James Twiss then took Donald Twiss into the bathroom to try to stop the bleeding from his head. Five minutes later they heard yelling in the kitchen and emerged from the bathroom to see Big Crow holding a folding chair and Margaret Big Crow falling to the floor, unconscious. Donald Twiss testified that he saw Big Crow hit Margaret Big Crow with the chair. Neither James Twiss nor Iron Cloud actually witnessed Margaret Big Crow being struck.

Big Crow then left the trailer. Donald Twiss called the police and requested an ambulance for Margaret Big Crow. Approximately thirty minutes later, police arrived and Donald Twiss and Margaret Big Crow were taken to a hospital in Pine Ridge. Twiss had a severe forehead laceration with an underlying bone fracture. Margaret Big Crow remained unconscious until noon on October 9. . . .

Big Crow was charged with assault with a dangerous weapon and assault resulting in serious bodily injury for the attack on Donald Twiss. He pleaded not guilty and a jury convicted him of both counts. . . .

Under the Guidelines, aggravated assault has a base offense level of 15. Use of a dangerous weapon and the infliction of serious bodily injury increase the offense level by 8 levels for a total of 23. U.S.S.G. §§2A2.2(b)(2)(B), 2A2.2(b)(3)(B). Big Crow had no criminal record, giving him a criminal history category of I. The United States Probation Officer's presentence investigation report recommended that Big Crow receive two points for acceptance of responsibility, and suggested that a departure from the Guideline range might be warranted because Big Crow's offense was out of character and he had been a decent citizen living in a difficult environment. An offense level of . . . 21 has a range of 37-46 months.

[The district court] departed downward from the Guideline range, sentencing Big Crow to 24 months imprisonment and two years of supervised release to include treatment for alcohol abuse. The court's reasons for the departure were Big Crow's intoxication at the time of the offense, his lack of a prior criminal record, his excellent employment history, and his consistent efforts to overcome the adverse living conditions on the Pine Ridge reservation. The court also noted that it had received and considered letters written on Big Crow's behalf by community leaders and a Bureau of Indian Affairs official. . . . The Government claims that the district court misapplied the Sentencing Guidelines in . . . departing below the Guideline range in sentencing Big Crow. . . .

Our procedure for review of a sentence outside the Guideline range is set forth at 18 U.S.C. §3742(e)(3). We are to consider the factors established under the Guidelines for imposing sentences and the reasons the district court gave for imposing the sentence in question to determine whether the departure from the Guideline range is unreasonable.

The district court's stated reasons for departing from the Guidelines were as follows:

> This is not a case that is different from any of those cases that the court sees involving perhaps more in the Indian country than non-Indian country, but in any event, offenses which are committed in conditions of extreme intoxication or at least some extent of intoxication. . . . In this particular case, you never had a criminal record. . . . You have been a hard worker in your job, and not too pleasant of a job. You at least tried in your young life to overcome many of the difficult conditions, which the court knows exists [*sic*] in Indian country. . . . By reason of the fact that this was a one-time matter, by reason of the fact that you have been trying to lead a good and decent life, I am going to deviate further from the guidelines. . . . I think this is a legitimate argument that your conduct was not entirely intentional.

Our task is to determine whether the mitigating circumstances the district court relied on are of a kind or degree appropriate to justify departure, whether these circumstances actually exist in this case, and whether the degree of departure is reasonable.

Big Crow concedes that two of the district court's stated reasons for departure, his intoxication at the time of the offense and his lack of a prior criminal record, are not appropriate reasons for deviating from the Guideline range. The specific offender characteristic of alcohol abuse "is not a reason for imposing a sentence below the guidelines." U.S.S.G. §5H1.4 (policy statement). Similarly, although a defendant's prior criminal record has relevance in determining his sentence, U.S.S.G. §5H1.8 (policy statement), we believe that the Sentencing Commission adequately accounted for criminal history in formulating the Sentencing Table.

The district court's additional reasons for sentencing Big Crow to a term of imprisonment less than the Guideline range, however, are appropriate and are supported by the record. Specifically, the district court noted Big Crow's excellent employment record and his consistent efforts to overcome the adverse environment of the Pine Ridge reservation. Guideline policy statements indicate that previous employment record and family ties and responsibilities and community ties are "not *ordinarily* relevant in determining whether a sentence should be outside the guidelines." U.S.S.G. §§5H1.5, 5H1.6 (policy statements) (emphasis added). We believe that Big Crow's case presents mitigating circumstances in these areas of a magnitude "not adequately taken into consideration by the Sentencing Commission in formulating the guidelines." See 18 U.S.C. §3553(b).

The unemployment rate on the Pine Ridge Indian Reservation is 72 percent. Per capita annual income on the reservation is estimated at $1,042.[3] Big Crow, who was twenty-three at the time of his offense, has worked steadily since the age of seventeen. With his wife's help, he provides more than adequately for the needs of their family, which includes two children. Since 1985, Big Crow has worked as a forestry aid and firefighter for the Bureau of Indian Affairs. His employer indicated that Big Crow is a valued employee with an excellent record and expressed willingness to hold Big Crow's job for him until he is released from custody.

Five members of Big Crow's community sent unsolicited letters on his behalf to the sentencing court. The writers included a local school principal, the president of the Oglala Sioux Tribe, and the agency safety officer of the Bureau of Indian Affairs. The presentence investigation report also noted that Big Crow has a positive reputation in his community and is well-liked by his employers and area law enforcement personnel.

We believe that the district court acted within its discretion in sentencing Big Crow below the Guideline range, and that Big Crow's excellent employment history, solid community ties, and consistent efforts to lead a decent life in a difficult environment are sufficiently unusual to constitute grounds for a departure from the Guidelines in this case. We also find that the sentence the district court imposed is reasonable and adequate to serve the ends which sentencing under the Guidelines should promote. See 18 U.S.C. §3553(a). . . . Accordingly, we affirm the decision of the district court.

WOLLMAN, J., concurring in part; dissenting in part.

. . . Although as an abstract matter I have no disagreement with the sentence imposed by the district court, I do not believe that the Guidelines authorize the downward departure. Guideline §5H1.10 unequivocally prohibits courts

---

3. A policy statement in the Guidelines states that race, national origin, and socioeconomic status are not relevant in the determination of a sentence. U.S.S.G. §5H1.10 (policy statement). Commentators note, however, that the "legislative history suggests that the use of the phrase 'are not relevant' may be too sweeping because the Senate Judiciary Committee's report states that 'the requirement of neutrality . . . is not a requirement of blindness.'" T. Hutchison & D. Yellen, Federal Sentencing Law and Practice §5H1.10, at 376 annot. 2 (1989) (quoting S. Rep. No. 225, 98th Cong., 1st Sess. 171 n.409 (1983)).

from conferring any relevance to race, national origin, and socio-economic status when sentencing. Nevertheless, the majority opinion finds Big Crow's residence on the Pine Ridge Indian Reservation, as well as the Reservation's unemployment rate and per capita income, to be appropriate mitigating circumstances for departure. The opinion explains this away in a footnote by pointing to a Senate Judiciary Committee report that says that the section 5H1.10 requirement of neutrality is not a requirement of blindness. The little that this statement tells us, however, is also irrelevant to our review of Guidelines application because 18 U.S.C. §3553(b) excludes consideration of legislative history. That statute permits courts to consider only the sentencing guidelines, policy statements, and official commentary in determining whether the Sentencing Commission adequately took a circumstance into consideration. Section 5H1.10 shows that the Sentencing Commission considered race, national origin and socio-economic status, but then chose to foreclose these factors as a basis for sentencing.

Likewise, as recognized in the majority opinion, sections 5H1.5 and 5H1.6 provide that employment record, family ties and responsibilities, and community ties are not ordinarily relevant in determining whether a sentence should be outside the Guidelines. Granted that Big Crow has apparently established an excellent reputation for maintaining steady employment, maintaining close community ties, and meeting his family obligations, what is there that distinguishes his situation from that of other defendants who can make the same showing? To ask this question is not to depreciate that what Big Crow has accomplished. Under the pre-Guidelines regime, the sentence imposed would not be subject to attack. As a practical matter, one wonders why the government attacks it here. There are some things that are better left alone, and Big Crow's sentence is one of them.

Congress made a policy decision — perhaps ill considered, perhaps not — when it created the Sentencing Commission and adopted as one of the goals of guidelines sentencing the elimination of what it perceived to be unwarranted disparity in sentencing. We should not approve departures that, however appealing they may be in their result, subvert both that goal and the spirit of the Guidelines.

NOTES

1. *Principles of equality.*   U.S. law is based on principles of equality. All individuals, independent of their race, ethnicity, or national origin, should be treated the same. The federal sentencing guidelines as well as state sentencing regimes reflect this mantra. Such neutrality can lead to injustice, however, when the situations of individuals are so different that equal treatment in the criminal justice system merely magnifies the unequal treatment in other aspects of life.

As the above materials indicate, Native Americans who commit offenses on reservations are tried in federal court and sentenced under the federal guidelines. Historically, the guarantee of criminal trials in federal courts was designed to protect Native Americans from discriminatory state courts. Today, however, when federal sentences are perceived as harsher than those in many states, many Native Americans consider themselves treated unfairly. While the guidelines appear to have decreased racial disparity within the federal system, federal courts have refused to engage in state–federal comparisons to determine whether a sentence is too harsh.

2. *Inequality and the State.*   In contrast to the current approach to race equality, an alternative sentencing system might deliberately take group differences into account. But considering group status at sentencing could undermine the concept of one nation and the equal value of the victims of crime. It could also excuse the state's inability or unwillingness to equalize the social and economic starting points of all members of society.

Perhaps it is the principle of equality itself that should be moderated to take account of racial, ethnic, biological, social, or historical circumstances. The Canadian Charter, for example, mandates consideration of the disadvantaged circumstances in which Native Americans find themselves at sentencing. Does this make for fairer sentences in light of the extreme economic disadvantage of aborigines? Should all those who are defined as aborigines benefit from such special consideration, or is it designed only for those on reservations? Is the differentiating characteristic race or race "plus" some other features? Consider the solution offered by the legislature and high court in Canada.

|| *Jamie Tanis Gladue v. R.* ||
|| [1999] S.C.R. 688 ||

CORY AND IACOBUCCI, JJ.

[Criminal Code §718.2(e)] provides that all available sanctions other than imprisonment that are reasonable in the circumstances should be considered for all offenders, with particular attention to the circumstances of aboriginal offenders. This appeal must consider how this provision should be interpreted and applied.

FACTUAL AND PROCEDURAL BACKGROUND

. . . The appellant and the victim Reuben Beaver started to live together in 1993, when the appellant was 17 years old. Thereafter they had a daughter, Tanita. . . . By September 1995, the appellant and Beaver were engaged to be married, and the appellant was five months pregnant with their second child. . . .

In the early evening of September 16, 1995, the appellant was celebrating her 19th birthday. She and Reuben Beaver, who was then 20, were drinking beer with some friends and family members in the townhouse complex. The appellant suspected that Beaver was having an affair with her older sister, Tara. During the course of the evening she voiced those suspicions to her friends. The appellant was obviously angry with Beaver. She said, "the next time he fools around on me, I'll kill him." . . .

The appellant and Beaver returned separately to their townhouse and they started to quarrel. During the argument, the appellant confronted him with his infidelity and he told her that she was fat and ugly and not as good as the others. . . .

Mr. Gretchin[, a neighbor,] saw the appellant run toward Beaver with a large knife in her hand and, as she approached him, she told him that he had better run. Mr. Gretchin heard Beaver shriek in pain and saw him collapse in a pool of blood. The appellant had stabbed Beaver once in the left chest, and the knife had penetrated his heart. As the appellant went by on her return to her apartment, Mr. Gretchin heard her say, "I got you, you fucking bastard." The appellant was described as jumping up and down as if she had tagged someone. Mr. Gretchin said she did not appear to realize what she had done. At the time of the stabbing, the appellant had a blood-alcohol content of between 155 and 165 milligrams of alcohol in 100 millilitres of blood.

[A]fter a jury had been selected, the appellant entered a plea of guilty to manslaughter. [The government had evidence] that Beaver had subjected the appellant to some physical abuse in June 1994, while the appellant was pregnant with their daughter Tanita. Beaver was convicted of assault, and was given a 15-day intermittent sentence with one year's probation. The neighbour, Mr. Gretchin, told police that the noises emanating from the appellant's and Beaver's apartment suggested a fight. . . . Bruises later observed on the appellant's arm and in the collarbone area were consistent with her having been in a physical altercation on the night of the stabbing. However, the trial judge found that the facts as presented before him did not warrant a finding that the appellant was a "battered or fearful wife."

The appellant's sentencing took place 17 months after the stabbing. Pending her trial [s]he took counselling for alcohol and drug abuse at Tillicum Haus Native Friendship Centre in Nanaimo, and completed Grade 10 and was about to start Grade 11. After the stabbing, the appellant was diagnosed as suffering from a hyperthyroid condition, which was said to produce an exaggerated reaction to any emotional situation. . . .

In his submissions on sentence at trial, the appellant's counsel did not raise the fact that the appellant was an aboriginal offender but, when asked by the trial judge whether in fact the appellant was an aboriginal person, replied that she was Cree. When asked by the trial judge whether the town of McLennan, Alberta, where the appellant grew up, was an aboriginal community, defence counsel responded: "it's just a regular community." No other submissions were made at the sentencing hearing on the issue of the appellant's aboriginal heritage. Defence counsel requested a suspended sentence or a conditional sentence of imprisonment. Crown counsel argued in favour of a sentence of between three and five years' imprisonment. The appellant was sentenced to three years' imprisonment and to a ten-year weapons prohibition. . . .

The trial judge noted that both the appellant and the deceased were aboriginal, but stated that they were living in an urban area off-reserve and not "within the aboriginal community as such." He found that there were not any special circumstances arising from their aboriginal status that he should take into consideration. He stated that the offence was a very serious one, for which the appropriate sentence was three years' imprisonment with a ten-year weapons prohibition.

The appellant appealed her sentence of three years' imprisonment [on the ground that] the trial judge failed to give appropriate consideration to the appellant's circumstances as an aboriginal offender. The appellant also sought to adduce fresh evidence at her appeal regarding her efforts since the killing to maintain links with her aboriginal heritage. . . .

INTERPRETATION OF SENTENCING PROVISION

The issue in this appeal is the proper interpretation and application to be given to §718.2(e) of the Criminal Code. The provision reads as follows:

> A court that imposes a sentence shall also take into consideration the following principles: . . . (e) available sanctions other than imprisonment that are reasonable in the circumstances should be considered for all offenders, with particular attention to the circumstances of aboriginal offenders.

. . . As a general principle, §718.2(e) applies to all offenders, and states that imprisonment should be the penal sanction of last resort. Prison is to be used only where no other sanction or combination of sanctions is appropriate to the offence and the offender.

The next question is the meaning to be attributed to the words "with particular attention to the circumstances of aboriginal offenders." The phrase cannot be an instruction for judges to pay "more" attention when sentencing aboriginal offenders. It would be unreasonable to assume that Parliament intended sentencing judges to prefer certain categories of offenders over others. Neither can the phrase be merely an instruction to a sentencing judge to consider the circumstances of aboriginal offenders just as she or he would consider the circumstances of any other offender. There would be no point in adding a special reference to aboriginal offenders if this was the case. Rather, the logical meaning to be derived from the special reference to the circumstances of aboriginal offenders, juxtaposed as it is against a general direction to consider "the circumstances" for all offenders, is that sentencing judges should pay particular attention to the circumstances of aboriginal offenders *because those circumstances are unique*, and different from those of non-aboriginal offenders. The fact that the reference to aboriginal offenders is contained in §718.2(e) . . . dealing with restraint in the use of imprisonment, suggests that there is something different about aboriginal offenders which may specifically make imprisonment a less appropriate or less useful sanction. . . .

Section 718 now sets out the purpose of sentencing in the following terms:

> The fundamental purpose of sentencing is to contribute, along with crime prevention initiatives, to respect for the law and the maintenance of a just, peaceful and safe society by imposing just sanctions that have one or more of the following objectives:
> (a) to denounce unlawful conduct;
> (b) to deter the offender and other persons from committing offences;
> (c) to separate offenders from society, where necessary;
> (d) to assist in rehabilitating offenders;
> (e) *to provide reparations for harm done to victims or to the community;* and
> (f) *to promote a sense of responsibility in offenders, and acknowledgment of the harm done to victims and to the community.* [Emphasis added.]

Clearly, §718 is, in part, a restatement of the basic sentencing aims, which are listed in paras. (a) through (d). What are new, though, are paras. (e) and (f), which along with para. (d) focus upon the restorative goals of repairing the harms suffered by individual victims and by the community as a whole, promoting a sense of responsibility and an acknowledgment of the harm caused on the part of the offender, and attempting to rehabilitate or heal the offender. [A]s a general matter restorative justice involves some form of restitution and reintegration into the community. The need for offenders to take responsibility for their actions is central to the sentencing process. Restorative sentencing goals do not usually correlate with the use of prison as a sanction. In our view, Parliament's choice to include (e) and (f) alongside the traditional sentencing goals must be understood as evidencing an intention to expand the parameters of the sentencing analysis for all offenders. . . .

The parties and interveners agree that the purpose of §718.2(e) is to respond to the problem of overincarceration in Canada, and to respond, in particular, to the more acute problem of the disproportionate incarceration of aboriginal peoples. They also agree that one of the roles of §718.2(e) . . . is to encourage sentencing judges to apply principles of restorative justice alongside or in the place of other, more traditional sentencing principles when making sentencing determinations. . . .

Although the United States has by far the highest rate of incarceration among industrialized democracies, at over 600 inmates per 100,000 population, Canada's rate of approximately 130 inmates per 100,000 population places it second or third highest. Moreover, the rate at which Canadian courts have been imprisoning offenders has risen sharply in recent years, although there has been a slight decline of late. This record of incarceration rates obviously cannot instil a sense of pride. . . .

If overreliance upon incarceration is a problem with the general population, it is of much greater concern in the sentencing of aboriginal Canadians. In the mid-1980s, aboriginal people were about 2 percent of the population of Canada, yet they made up 10 percent of the penitentiary population. In Manitoba and Saskatchewan, aboriginal people constituted something between 6 and 7 percent of the population, yet in Manitoba they represented 46 percent of the provincial admissions and in Saskatchewan 60 percent. The situation has not improved in recent years. By 1997, aboriginal peoples constituted closer to 3 percent of the population of Canada and amounted to 12 percent of all federal inmates. The situation continues to be particularly worrisome in Manitoba, where in 1995-96 they made up 55 percent of admissions to provincial correctional facilities, and in Saskatchewan, where they made up 72 percent of admissions. A similar, albeit less drastic situation prevails in Alberta and British Columbia. . . .

Not surprisingly, the excessive imprisonment of aboriginal people is only the tip of the iceberg insofar as the estrangement of the aboriginal peoples from the Canadian criminal justice system is concerned. Aboriginal people are overrepresented in virtually all aspects of the system. As this Court recently noted in R. v. Williams, [1998] 1 S.C.R. 1128, at para. 58, there is widespread bias against aboriginal people within Canada, and "[t]here is evidence that this widespread racism has translated into systemic discrimination in the criminal justice system." . . . The figures are stark and reflect what may fairly be termed a crisis in the Canadian criminal justice system. [Section 718.2(e)] may properly be seen as Parliament's direction to members of the judiciary to inquire into the causes of the problem and to endeavour to remedy it, to the extent that a remedy is possible through the sentencing process.

It is clear that sentencing innovation by itself cannot remove the causes of aboriginal offending and the greater problem of aboriginal alienation from the criminal justice system. The unbalanced ratio of imprisonment for aboriginal offenders flows from a number of sources, including poverty, substance abuse, lack of education, and the lack of employment opportunities for aboriginal people. It arises also from bias against aboriginal people and from an unfortunate institutional approach that is more inclined to refuse bail and to impose more and longer prison terms for aboriginal offenders. There are many aspects of this sad situation which cannot be addressed in these reasons. What can and must be addressed, though, is the limited role that sentencing judges will play in remedying injustice against aboriginal peoples in Canada. Sentencing judges are among those decision-makers who have the power to influence the treatment of aboriginal offenders in the justice system. They determine most directly whether an aboriginal offender will go to jail, or whether other sentencing options may be employed which will play perhaps a stronger role in restoring a sense of balance to the offender, victim, and community, and in preventing future crime.

How are sentencing judges to play their remedial role? The words of §718.2(e) instruct the sentencing judge to pay particular attention to the circumstances of aboriginal offenders, with the implication that those circumstances are significantly different from those of non-aboriginal offenders. . . . The background factors which figure prominently in the causation of crime by aboriginal offenders are by now well known. Years of dislocation and economic development have translated, for many aboriginal peoples, into low incomes, high unemployment, lack of opportunities and options, lack or irrelevance of education, substance abuse, loneliness, and community fragmentation. These and other factors contribute to a higher incidence of crime and incarceration.

[T]he circumstances of aboriginal offenders differ from those of the majority because many aboriginal people are victims of systemic and direct discrimination, many suffer the legacy of dislocation, and many are substantially affected by poor social and economic conditions. Moreover, as has been emphasized repeatedly in studies and commission reports, aboriginal offenders are, as a result of these unique systemic and background factors, more adversely affected by incarceration and less likely to be "rehabilitated" thereby, because the internment milieu is often culturally inappropriate and regrettably discrimination towards them is so often rampant in penal institutions.

. . . In cases where [unique background and systemic] factors have played a significant role [in bringing the particular offender before the courts], it is incumbent upon the sentencing judge to consider these factors in evaluating whether imprisonment would actually serve to deter, or to denounce crime in a sense that would be meaningful to the community of which the offender is a member. In many instances, more restorative sentencing principles will gain primary relevance precisely because the prevention of crime as well as individual and social healing cannot occur through other means.

Closely related to the background and systemic factors which have contributed to an excessive aboriginal incarceration rate are the different conceptions of appropriate sentencing procedures and sanctions held by aboriginal people. A significant problem experienced by aboriginal people who come into contact with the criminal justice system is that the traditional sentencing ideals of deterrence, separation, and denunciation are often far removed from the understanding of sentencing held by these offenders and their community. [M]ost traditional aboriginal conceptions of sentencing place a *primary* emphasis upon the ideals of restorative justice. This tradition is extremely important to the analysis under §718.2(e).

[R]estorative justice may be described as an approach to remedying crime in which it is understood that all things are interrelated and that crime disrupts the harmony which existed prior to its occurrence, or at least which it is felt should exist. The appropriateness of a particular sanction is largely determined by the needs of the victims, and the community, as well as the offender. The focus is on the human beings closely affected by the crime.

The existing overemphasis on incarceration in Canada may be partly due to the perception that a restorative approach is a more lenient approach to crime and that imprisonment constitutes the ultimate punishment. Yet in our view a sentence focussed on restorative justice is not necessarily a "lighter" punishment. . . .

In describing the effect of §718.2(e) in this way, we do not mean to suggest that, as a general practice, aboriginal offenders must always be sentenced in a manner which gives greatest weight to the principles of restorative justice, and less weight to goals such as deterrence, denunciation, and separation. It is unreasonable to assume that aboriginal peoples themselves do not believe in the importance of these latter goals, and even if they do not, that such goals must not predominate in appropriate cases. Clearly there are some serious offences and some offenders for which and for whom separation, denunciation, and deterrence are fundamentally relevant.

Yet, even where an offence is considered serious, the length of the term of imprisonment must be considered. In some circumstances the length of the sentence of an aboriginal offender may be less and in others the same as that of any other offender. Generally, the more violent and serious the offence the more likely it is as a practical reality that the terms of imprisonment for aboriginals and non-aboriginals will be close to each other or the same, even taking into account their different concepts of sentencing. . . .

How then is the consideration of §718.2(e) to proceed in the daily functioning of the courts? The manner in which the sentencing judge will carry out his or her statutory duty may vary from case to case. In all instances it will be necessary for the judge to take judicial notice of the systemic or background factors and the approach to sentencing which is relevant to aboriginal offenders. However, for each particular offence and offender it may be that some evidence will be required in order to assist the sentencing judge in arriving at a fit sentence. Where a particular offender does not wish such evidence to be adduced, the right to have particular attention paid to his or her circumstances as an aboriginal offender may be waived. Where there is no such waiver, it will be extremely helpful to the sentencing judge for counsel on both sides to adduce relevant evidence. . . .

However, even where counsel do not adduce this evidence, where for example the offender is unrepresented, it is incumbent upon the sentencing judge to attempt to acquire information regarding the circumstances of the offender as an aboriginal person. Whether the offender resides in a rural area, on a reserve or in an urban centre the sentencing judge must be made aware of alternatives to incarceration that exist whether inside or outside the aboriginal community of the particular offender. The alternatives existing in metropolitan areas must, as a matter of course, also be explored. Clearly the presence of an aboriginal offender will require special attention in pre-sentence reports. Beyond the use of the pre-sentence report, the sentencing judge may and should in appropriate circumstances and where practicable request that witnesses be called who may testify as to reasonable alternatives.

Similarly, where a sentencing judge at the trial level has not engaged in the duty imposed by §718.2(e) as fully as required, it is incumbent upon a court of appeal in considering an appeal against sentence on this basis to consider any fresh evidence which is relevant and admissible on sentencing. [A]lthough §718.2(e) does not impose a statutory duty upon the sentencing judge to provide reasons, it will be much easier for a reviewing court to determine whether and how attention was paid to the circumstances of the offender as an aboriginal person if at least brief reasons are given. . . .

The fact that a court is called upon to take into consideration the unique circumstances surrounding these different parties is not unfair to non-aboriginal people. Rather, the fundamental purpose of §718.2(e) is to treat aboriginal offenders fairly by taking into account their difference. . . .

The class of aboriginal people who come within the purview of the specific reference to the circumstances of aboriginal offenders in §718.2(e) must be, at least, . . . an estimated 799,010 people [who] were identified as aboriginal in [the] 1996 [census]. Of this number, 529,040 were Indians (registered or non-registered), 204,115 Metis and 40,220 Inuit.

Section 718.2(e) applies to all aboriginal offenders wherever they reside, whether on- or off-reserve, in a large city or a rural area. Indeed it has been observed that many aboriginals living in urban areas are closely attached to their culture. . . .

Based on the foregoing, the jail term for an aboriginal offender may in some circumstances be less than the term imposed on a non-aboriginal offender for the same offence. . . .

APPLICATION OF PRINCIPLES

In most cases, errors such as those in the courts below would be sufficient to justify sending the matter back for a new sentencing hearing. It is difficult for this Court to determine a fit sentence for the appellant according to the suggested guidelines set out herein on the basis of the very limited evidence before us regarding the appellant's aboriginal background. However, as both the trial judge and all members of the Court of Appeal acknowledged, the offence in question is a most serious one, properly described . . . as a "near murder." Moreover, the offence involved domestic violence and a breach of the trust inherent in a spousal relationship. That aggravating factor must be taken into account in the sentencing of the aboriginal appellant as it would be for any offender. For that offence by this offender a sentence of three years' imprisonment was not unreasonable.

More importantly, the appellant was granted day parole on August 13, 1997, after she had served six months in the Burnaby Correctional Centre for Women. She was directed to reside with her father, to take alcohol and substance abuse counselling and to comply with the requirements of the Electronic Monitoring Program. On February 25, 1998, the appellant was granted full parole with the same conditions as the ones applicable to her original release on day parole.

In this case, the results of the sentence with incarceration for six months and the subsequent controlled release were in the interests of both the appellant and society. In these circumstances, we do not consider that it would be in the interests of justice to order a new sentencing hearing in order to canvass the appellant's circumstances as an aboriginal offender. . . .

NOTES

1. *Aboriginal offenders in prison.* The *Gladue* court recognized the disproportionate imprisonment of aboriginal offenders in Canada. In response to the problem, Parliament had added Criminal Code §718.2(e). In Australia aborigines are also overrepresented in prisons. In fact, the racial disparities in Canada and Australia between aborigines and nonaborigines are worse than those between blacks and whites in the United States. What factors account for the high imprisonment rates of natives? Much of Australia's high aboriginal imprisonment rate has been blamed on mandatory sentencing laws for relatively minor property offenses. Why would mandatory sentences not lead to *greater* ethnic equality? Should the disparate impact on minority groups be a reason for abolishing such legislation?

2. *Aboriginal sentencing practices.* In a later decision, Canada's highest court emphasized that in cases of aboriginal offenders sentencing judges must consider "the types of sentencing procedures and sanctions which may be appropriate in the circumstances for the offender because of his or her particular Aboriginal heritage or connection. In particular, given that most traditional Aboriginal approaches place a primary emphasis on the goal of restorative justice, the alternative of community-based sanctions must be explored." R. v. Wells, [2000] S.C.R. 207, para. 53. To what extent can and should U.S. courts consider the punishment practices of native courts? While some aboriginal groups have focused on restorative justice, others have used punishment practices that many today would consider torture. How should the courts accommodate considerations of traditional practice and modern human rights concerns? See Rick Sarre, Sentencing in Customary or Tribal Settings: An Australian Perspective, 13 Fed. Sentencing Rep. 74 (2000).

3. *Native Americans, blacks, and other minority offenders.* In many countries with native populations, natives are not the only ones overrepresented in prison. Should the situation of native offenders be any more disconcerting than the situation of offenders from other racial groups? Why? To what extent can sentencing judges be expected to "fix" racial disparity at individualized sentencing hearings? Will such attempts not merely lead to other forms of injustice?

4. *Ethnicity.*   Ethnicity has become an alternative to race in describing human diversity, but the term also carries deep ambiguities. Ethnicity focuses on the cultural distinctiveness of a group: Country of origin, language, religion, food, and values all create a particular ethnic identity. Which of these characteristics are relevant and the extent to which one should be allowed to self-classify as a member of a particular ethnic group remain ambiguous. Ethnicity allows for distinctions within racial groups (blacks emigrating from the Caribbean, for example, differ from those hailing from the African continent), but it also encompasses racial differences (blacks and whites from Brazil are both considered Hispanics). Often ethnicity appears to be a substitute for national origin, but in fact the latter is usually limited to first- and possibly second-generation immigrant populations.

5. *Immigrants and crime.*   With growing immigration, new groups add to the existing racial and ethnic diversity in the United States. In Western Europe and North America crime and incarceration rates for members of some minority groups greatly exceed those for the majority population. The same minority groups are also socially and economically disadvantaged (but not all disadvantaged groups are also high crime groups). While some discrimination may be present, the principal cause for the disparities appears to be differences in offending rather than official bias. How should the criminal justice system react to such increasing diversity and disparity?

One approach would be to exempt certain immigrant groups from the coverage of select substantive criminal law provisions that are legally and culturally foreign to them. So far, no one has seriously considered this idea. Another notion would be to consider an offender's ethnicity at the sentencing stage. For example, when a recent immigrant from a country that allows the marriage of adult men to teen girls gets convicted of statutory rape, the sentencing court may consider as a mitigating circumstance that the immigrant and his teen "wife" viewed the marriage as legitimate. Feminists, however, have objected that such exemptions generally come at the expense of women's rights as in many societies around the world women and girls have fewer legal rights than in the United States. Can a color-blind society permit courts and prosecutors to consider ethnicity when it prohibits them from basing their sentences on race or national origin? Should the court be allowed to consider the laws prevalent in the defendants' home country and their cultural immersion in such values? How should home and host country values and laws be reconciled? Should such special treatment exist for all first-generation immigrants? For all members of an ethnic group? For all members of an ethnic group growing up in a distinctly ethnic environment?

6. *Culture and sentencing.*   Offenders from some ethnic groups may be culturally conditioned or socialized not to enter guilty pleas. Since guilty pleas often result in a sentence reduction, offenders who insist on their right to trial may receive longer sentences. In imposing a sentence, should a court consider whether the choice of trial may be characteristic of the offender's ethnic group? If not, is the offender not being punished for a cultural value that differs from that of mainstream society rather than for offense-relevant conduct? Australia's Crimes Act requires courts to consider the "cultural background" of an offender, including "ethnic, environmental and cultural matters." Would the insistence on going to trial be a cultural factor?

7. *Culture and victims.*   Most crime is committed *within* the same racial and ethnic groups. Different sentences based on the offender's culture, therefore, often parallel the victim's ethnicity and culture. Do lower sentences based on the offenders' cultural background devalue the suffering of their victims or indicate that the victims deserve less state protection?

PROBLEM 9-4.   ALIEN STATUS

Peter Onwuemene, a Nigerian citizen, and other Nigerians participated in a nationwide automobile insurance fraud scheme that caused losses of about $1 million to several insurance companies. A member of the group would obtain liability insurance on an old car from ten to fifteen insurance companies. Thereafter, the policy owner would report a collision with an expensive, late-model car owned by another member of the group, who would claim damage to his car.

Onwuemene was charged with four counts of mail fraud. He pleaded guilty to one of the counts in return for the government's agreement to recommend dismissal of the others. Onwuemene faced a sentencing range under the federal sentencing guidelines of six to 12 months. The presentence investigation report recommended six months' incarceration and a work release program. At sentencing, Onwuemene agreed to pay restitution of $3,723.

The district court sentenced him to twelve months' imprisonment, the top of the sentencing range, because the crime was serious and could have resulted in a much greater loss if the victims had failed to discover it and because Onwuemene "failed or refused" to identify the other participants in the fraud. The court then added:

> The other thing that I feel that warrants imposition at the high end of the guideline range: You are not a citizen of this country. This country was good enough to allow you to come in here and to confer upon you . . . a number of the benefits of this society, form of government, and its opportunities, and you repay that kindness by committing a crime like this. We have got enough criminals in the United States without importing any.

Onwuemene appeals. A federal sentence imposed within the applicable guidelines range is reviewable only if it is imposed in violation of the law or as a result of an incorrect application of the guidelines. How should the appellate court rule? See United States v. Onwuemene, 933 F.2d 650 (8th Cir. 1991).

NOTES

1. *Immigration status and sentencing.*   Large-scale immigration into North America and Western Europe has caused ever more immigrants to be involved in the criminal justice system. May a court consider an offender's immigration status at sentencing? Because of the possibility or even likelihood of deportation, a court could impose a lesser sentence than it would on a citizen offender. Federal courts, however, have generally rejected downward departures based on a noncitizen's deportability. See, e.g., United States v. Restrepo, 999 F.2d 640

(2nd Cir. 1993); United States v. Lopez-Salas, 266 F.3d 842 (8th Cir. 2001). But see United States v. Gallo-Vasquez, 284 F.3d 780, 784 (7th Cir. 2002) (district court may depart downward when "defendant's status as a deportable alien . . . may lead to conditions of confinement, or other incidents of punishment, that are substantially more onerous than the framers of the guidelines contemplated in fixing the punishment range for the defendant's offense").

Alternatively, a court may view an immigrant's offense as more heinous because he abused his guest status, as did the trial court in Problem 9-4. When judges explicitly refer to alien status, some federal courts have held that sentencing an offender on the basis of factors such as race, national origin, or alienage violates the Constitution. See United States v. Onwuemene, 933 F.2d 650 (8th Cir. 1991) (consideration of defendant's alien status violates his constitutional rights); United States v. Borrero-Isaza, 887 F.2d 1349, 1352 (9th Cir. 1989) (imposing stricter sentence on defendant because of his national origin and alienage violated right to due process). One state court tried to impose a higher sentence on a member of an ethnic community: "sometimes it is necessary in sentencing to send a message to the community, and I am sending a message by this sentence to a small segment of the Albanian community that they now live in the United States and they are governed by our laws, and we are not going to tolerate whatever the customs may be in Albania, and that includes the customs of dealing with family members as well as the use of guns." The appellate court considered this justification an impermissible consideration of defendant's national origin. People v. Gjidoda, 364 N.W.2d 698 (Mich. 1985).

2. *Noncitizen offenses.*   A number of immigration offenses, such as reentry of a convicted felon, can be committed only by noncitizens. Do such statutes not discriminate based on national origin? Because of increases in congressional funding and changes in law enforcement priorities and federal sentencing, between the mid-1980s and 2000, the number of noncitizens sentenced for immigration offenses — primarily unlawful entry and reentry upon deportation — more than doubled, the rate of incarceration increased eightfold, and the length of incarceration rose from an average of four months to 21 months. Currently about 80 percent of the offenders prosecuted for reentry offenses are Mexican nationals, and more than half of all immigration offenders hail from Mexico. 2002 Yearbook of Immigration Statistics, Enforcement, Fiscal Year 2002.

3. *What sentencing practices and values?*   Some have argued that immigrant offenders should be punished based on the sentence that would be appropriate in their home country. The reason given is that the sentencing regime in the United States is too lenient to deter offenders from countries where the death penalty is available for more offenses, where physical punishments such as flogging are available, and where longer prison terms may be imposed for select offenses.

In a number of federal cases, courts have departed from the applicable guideline range because of the offender's adoption of American values. See, e.g., United States v. Rodriguez-Montelongo, 263 F.3d 429, 432-434 (5th Cir. 2001) (cultural assimilation considered a mitigating factor). Is that an appropriate ground for departure?

C. CLASS

Legal scholars, sociologists, political scientists and public commentators all tend to pay less attention to class in the United States than do people in other Western countries. Race-based analysis has replaced much of the class argument. While race and poverty are not co-equal, they do overlap.

It is relatively difficult to define class. If measured in terms of annual income, some members of the Rockefeller family may be poor. If measured in educational attainment or status of employment, to what economic class do the stay-at-home spouses of executives of major corporations belong? Because of intellectual habits in the United States combined with these definitional difficulties and related challenges in data collection, it is difficult to find empirical studies on class.

Courts are also reluctant to name "class." Often white-collar offenses are associated with high-class defendants, while blue-collar defendants are generally viewed as lower class. This may not always be true, especially since many embezzlers are members of the middle class. Even though the concept of class is commonly associated with lower classes in occasional scholarly and public discourse, in-court arguments often focus on high-status offenders. A prosecutor may ask for a higher sentence "from someone who had choices," or a defense lawyer may argue that "family" or "community" contributions and good works should justify a lower sentence. Consider the relevance of class in the following case.

|| **United States v. Frank Serafini** ||
|| 233 F.3d 758 (3d Cir. 2000) ||

RENDELL, J.

In this appeal, Frank Serafini challenges his conviction and sentence for one count of perjury in violation of 18 U.S.C. §1623. Serafini, a popular state legislator in northeastern Pennsylvania, was convicted based on his false testimony before a federal grand jury; the grand jury was investigating a scheme wherein corporate political contributions were funneled through third-party conduits in violation of federal election laws. In his grand jury testimony, Serafini had denied that he was reimbursed for a contribution he had made to Senator Bob Dole's presidential campaign. [The government appeals] Serafini's sentence, contesting . . . the District Court's three-level downward departure for exceptional civic or charitable contributions pursuant to U.S.S.G. §5H1.11. [We conclude that the District Court's downward departure was] not an abuse of its discretion. . . .

Serafini was subpoenaed to testify before a grand jury that was investigating possible violations of the Federal Election Campaign Act (FECA).[5] The

---

5. FECA prohibits corporations from making contributions in connection with any federal election. FECA also makes it unlawful for any person to make a contribution in the name of another person (referred to in this opinion as a "conduit"), or for any person to permit his or her name to be used as a conduit. FECA limits individual contributions to federal candidates to $1,000 per election per candidate.

principal targets of the probe were Renato Mariani, president of Empire Sanitary Landfill, Inc. (Empire), and Serafini's nephew, Michael Serafini. The apparent violations were that Michael Serafini and his secretary had solicited numerous employees, business associates, and family members to make $1,000 contributions to Senator Bob Dole's presidential campaign, and that Michael reimbursed them for these contributions; the resulting transactions between Michael and these "conduits" therefore allegedly violated FECA. . . .

Serafini was called before the grand jury to answer questions about Michael's having solicited Serafini for a $1,000 contribution and allegedly having reimbursed him for that contribution. . . . The [government] sought and received an order immunizing Serafini so that the government could compel his testimony before the grand jury; the resulting subpoena ordered him to produce "[all] documents relative to political contributions you were reimbursed for." During Serafini's appearance before the grand jury, the Assistant U.S. Attorney informed him that he could be prosecuted if he provided false testimony. Although Serafini did acknowledge that Michael had solicited and obtained from him a $1,000 contribution to Dole, he denied that a $2,000 check given to him by Michael that same week was in part a reimbursement for that contribution. Instead, Serafini maintained that the $2,000 probably represented Michael's reimbursing Serafini for payments that Serafini made to a mechanic who had fixed Michael's Porsche. [Serafini repeatedly asserted that he was not reimbursed for any contributions.

The jury convicted Serafini of perjury.] After ascertaining that the base offense level for perjury before a grand jury was 12, see U.S.S.G. §2J1.3(a), the District Court applied a three-level enhancement for "substantial interference with the administration of justice," *id.* §2J1.3(b)(2). [We] conclude that the enhancement for "substantial interference" was permissible. . . . When combined with Serafini's criminal history category of I, this adjusted offense level resulted in a guideline range of 18 to 24 months' imprisonment. However, the District Court granted a three-level downward departure for Serafini's community and charitable activities. The government argues that the District Court's departure is an abuse of discretion.

In Koon v. United States, 518 U.S. 81 (1996), the Supreme Court outlined the methodology for a district court to use when considering a departure from the applicable guideline range. [First, a court should] identify the factor or factors that potentially take the case outside the Guidelines' "heartland" and make it special or unusual. [If the Guidelines discourage reliance on a factor as a departure ground], the court should depart only if the factor is present to an exceptional degree, or in some other way makes the case different from the ordinary case in which the factor is present. [A] reviewing court must give substantial deference to the district court's discretionary decision to depart from the guideline range.

The District Court described the appropriate analytical steps and correctly determined that departing on the basis of civic and charitable good works was discouraged, but not forbidden, by the Guidelines. U.S.S.G. §5H1.11 ("Military, civic, charitable, or public service; employment-related contributions; and similar prior good works are not ordinarily relevant in determining whether a sentence should be outside the applicable guideline range"). The District Court recognized that, in order to depart downward on this basis, it must find that this factor existed "to an exceptional degree or, in some way, that makes the case different from the ordinary case in which the factor is present." The District Court made a finding that Serafini's civic and charitable contributions did exist to such an exceptional degree, or in an extraordinary manner. . . .

At the sentencing hearing, the District Court was presented with several character witnesses, and more than 150 letters. The letters submitted to the Court fall into three categories: (i) the first category presents Serafini as a good person; (ii) the second category refers to his activities as a state legislator; and (iii) the third category refers to his assistance, in time and money, to individuals and local organizations.

As to the first category, these can be quickly dismissed with the observation that being a "good person," a quality indeed to be admired, does not qualify as extraordinary or exceptional civic or charitable conduct.

As to Serafini's activities as a state legislator, they are work-related and political in character. For example, a letter from the Fire Chief of Greenfield Township Volunteer Fire Company stated that he "had worked tirelessly to obtain grant monies to help the community afford the lifesaving equipment they need." . . . Conceptually, if a public servant performs civic and charitable work as part of his daily functions, these should not be considered in his sentencing because we expect such work from our public servants. [To] the extent this second group of letters does not evidence extraordinary community service under Guideline §5H1.11, but instead, reflects merely the political duties ordinarily performed by public servants, we are of the view that they cannot form the basis of a departure.

However, unlike the first and second categories of letters the Court received, the third category of letters provided an adequate basis for the District Court's conclusion that Serafini's community service warranted a downward departure. Many of the letters that fall within this last group contain substantive descriptions of Serafini's generosity with his time as well as his money. Several constituents and friends described situations in which Serafini extended himself to them in unique and meaningful ways during times of serious need. In particular, three letters are especially noteworthy.

William Drazdowski, an accountant and "a close personal friend" of the defendant, explains Serafini's role in providing a $300,000 guarantee to Dr. Edward Zaloga so that he could secure new cutting edge data from certain Tokyo physicians for the treatment of his brother's brain tumor. Dr. Zaloga testified at the sentencing hearing that he telephoned Serafini at 1:00 A.M. seeking his assistance in raising the money. Just thirty minutes later, Serafini called back and informed Dr. Zaloga "that everything was in place." . . . In reading the Zaloga letter, both Serafini's readiness to help and his reluctance to seek gratitude make a strong impression. Such behavior is hardly part of the normal duties of a local politician.

Another letter came from George E. Seig, who also testified at the sentencing hearing. He sustained a serious injury as a result of an accident while he was a college student. The physicians' prognosis was that he would never be able to carry on any form of normal social functioning. After a year of frustrating physical therapy, Seig lost all ambition to return to school. Then, he was contacted by Serafini's office who told him that Serafini had heard of the tragic incident and wanted Seig to come work for him. The record reflects that Serafini's offer of employment went far beyond just hiring a young person on his staff. Serafini took Seig under his wing, mentored him, and strongly encouraged him to attend college. He even loaned him money until Seig could repay it. The letter from Seig — now an attorney — reflects his immense gratitude and his feeling that Serafini is responsible for turning his life around.

A third letter came from a widow who approached Serafini in tears because she was about to lose her house. He wrote her a personal check for $750 to forestall foreclosure. She expressed doubt about her future ability to repay him, but Serafini insisted that she need not do so unless she could afford it.

The remaining letters, taken as a whole, depict Serafini as an exceptionally giving person. . . . For example, the letters describe Serafini's volunteer work as an usher at St. Mary's Church; at the Abington Heights School District; and at Lackawanna Trail High School. In addition, he helped to establish a fund to defray the cost of a bone marrow transplant for a man suffering from leukemia. Several letters note that Serafini was generous with his time even with people who lived outside his district. The letters also describe Serafini's financial contributions to organizations such as The Arc (a nonprofit agency serving people with mental retardation and their families); the Rotary Run Against Drugs; the Scranton Lackawanna Human Development Agency; the Little League; the Boy Scouts; St. Francis of Assisi Kitchen; the Abington Heights School District; and the leukemia sufferer's fund mentioned above. A letter from an official at the University of Scranton refers to Serafini's financial assistance to college students, and a letter from a high school social studies teacher describes Serafini's contributions to a scholarship for graduating seniors. . . .

The District Court concluded that the letters and testimony demonstrated that Serafini had distinguished himself, "not by the amount of money [he has] given, but by the amount of time that [he has] devoted." The District Court found that these efforts made Serafini's community and charitable activities "exceptional" when compared to what an average person in Serafini's circumstances would have done:

> Those weren't acts of just giving money, they were acts of giving time, of giving one's self. That distinguishes Mr. Serafini, I think, from the ordinary public servant, from the ordinary elected official, and I had ample testimony, today, that says that Mr. Serafini distinguishes himself, that these are acts not just undertaken to assure his re-election, but are taken because of the type of person he is. . . .

We realize, as did the District Court, that Serafini's largesse was in part financial, and in part, devotion of himself and his time. Since he is a wealthy individual, we must ensure that a district court does not run afoul of the prohibition against considering socioeconomic differences in relying on financial contributions as a basis for a departure. See U.S.S.G. §5H1.11. However, the District Court here recognized this particular aspect of Serafini's situation, but nonetheless found *all* his contributions, not merely monetary ones, exceptional.

It is not our role to decide in the first instance whether Serafini's civic and charitable contributions were exceptional given Serafini's role as a public servant and his apparent wealth. Our review is far more deferential. We conclude that the District Court had an adequate basis for its factual finding, and that the District Court's decision was not clearly out of line with other reported cases.

See, e.g., United States v. Woods, 159 F.3d 1132, 1136 (8th Cir. 1998) (upholding defendant's downward departure for charitable activities, which included bringing two troubled young women into her home and paying for them to attend a private high school, as well as helping to care for an elderly friend, where the court found no basis to overturn the district court's finding that these efforts were exceptional).

In reaching this conclusion, we have not overlooked the decision of the Court of Appeals for the Eighth Circuit in United States v. Morken, 133 F.3d 628 (8th Cir. 1998). There, the court concluded that the defendant's activities, which consisted of advising local business owners, hiring young people, serving on a church council, and raising money for charity, were "laudable, [but] neither exceptional nor out of the ordinary for someone of his income and preeminence in a small Minnesota town with a population barely over a thousand." Accordingly, the court of appeals reversed the district court's downward departure.

However, in *Morken,* the court essentially found that, given Morken's station in life, his contributions were not extraordinary. Here, the District Court was careful to view Mr. Serafini's activities in light of his career and resources, and taking that into account, found that his charitable activities were in fact sufficiently beyond the norm for a wealthy politician, and were sufficiently exceptional so as to warrant a departure under the Guidelines. [The District Court found] that Serafini's acts of personal kindness and good works were above and beyond customary political or charitable giving. We also note that while many of Serafini's acts involved the giving of money, the monetary aid was only one aspect of otherwise charitable conduct on his part, distinguishing his acts from the impersonal writing of checks that is the norm for many wealthy individuals. By taking such giving into account, the District Court did not grant the departure based on socioeconomic conditions. We conclude that the District Court did not abuse its discretion by finding that Serafini's civic and charitable contributions were exceptional and thus warranted a downward departure. . . .

ROSENN, J., dissenting.
. . . I believe that when it came to sentencing, the voluminous letters from the defendant's political constituents, colleagues, and other friends misled the Court to depart downward from the Guidelines. . . .

The Sentencing Guidelines are clear that a defendant's record of charitable work and community service are a discouraged justification for a sentencing departure. The historical note to the Civic and Charitable Amendment to the Guidelines (§5H1.11) "expresses the Commission's intent that the factors set forth in this part are not ordinarily relevant in determining whether a sentence should be outside the applicable guideline range. . . ." This appears to be a recognition that in our culture and society, every person is expected reasonably to contribute charity to the poor and to non-profit organizations dedicated to educational, health, and religious purposes.[1]

---

1. According to a national survey by Independent Sector on "Giving and Volunteering in the United States," approximately 69% of all households in the United States made voluntary contributions to charity in 1995. See Statistical Abstract of the United States 404 (1999).

Thus, the critical question is whether the discouraged factor is present in this case to "an exceptional degree or in some other way that makes this case different from the ordinary case where the factor is present." [We] have a substantial record here from which to assess. It shows that Serafini's charitable works were not exceptional or extraordinary by any reasonable standard.

In the ordinary course of events, a taxpayer, especially one with substantial annual income, will specifically list every available charitable contribution as a tax deduction in his federal income tax return. Serafini filed such returns and specifically claimed charitable deductions. These returns are the best evidence of his charitable contributions; they are not vague, indefinite opinions of friends and political constituents tendered to a sentencing judge in an effort to obtain a reduced sentence. . . .

The defendant is not only a wealthy individual, but his federal income tax returns show substantial income from sources other than his salary as a state official. Included are substantial royalties from the Empire Landfill. A financial analysis of his pertinent income returns for the period 1991 through 1996 reveals the following undisputed evidence.

Year	$ Total Income	$ Charitable Deductions	Charity as % of Income
1991	724,019	13,407	1.8
1993	857,000	22,604	2.6
1994	855,000	16,620	1.9
1995	908,172	17,385	1.9
1996	1,101,276	20,310	1.8

Except for 1993, in which his contributions exceeded 2%, all of his contributions are less than 2% per annum. Donating less than 2% of one's income to charity — even 2.6% — is lackluster and pedestrian by any measure; it is not exceptional. It is far below the average measure of giving in the United States by people in the defendant's socioeconomic status.[2]

Serafini's charitable contributions of his annual income is ordinary at best when compared to national figures. It pales in comparison to tithing, the practice in many religious organizations of giving ten percent of one's income to one's religious institution. . . .

As noted, the majority and the District Court were persuaded by Serafini's non-financial charitable acts. But much of Serafini's civic participation was either honorary or obligatory because of his job as a Representative. Numerous letters submitted on his behalf were written by constituents or other beneficiaries of his public position. The majority finds three letters noteworthy. One comes from William Drazdowski, "a close personal friend," which explains defendant's role in providing a $300,000 guarantee to Dr. Edward Zaloga. . . . Neither Drazdowski, an accountant, nor Dr. Zaloga claim that Serafini personally made the guarantee; nor does the defendant. There is no information how the guarantee was accomplished, to whom it was made, who made it, and the

2. According to the Statistical Abstract of the United States, the average American household contributed 2.2% of its income to charity in 1991. . . . In 1995, households with greater than $100,000 income contributed 3.4% of their household income to charity. . . .

substance of the guarantee, or the relationship between Dr. Zaloga and the defendant. The majority believes this assistance "is hardly part of the normal duties of a local politician." On the other hand, the entirely obscure and mysterious incident may very well have its genesis in defendant's political agenda. In any event, it hardly rises to the level of significant community service.

The Seig letter attests to Serafini's offer to employ Seig, a young friend of the family, on the defendant's legislative staff, a loan to him of an unstated sum of money, and encouragement to Seig to attend college. The third letter reports a personal check of $750 from the defendant to a widow who was about to lose her home through foreclosure. The widow expressed doubt about her ability to repay and defendant insisted she need not do so unless able.

These three "noteworthy" letters do reflect commendable action by the defendant, but neither they, nor the other letters, show community service to an exceptional or extraordinary degree. A few acts of personal kindness to individual friends do not add up to community service; they do not fulfill the purpose of the Guidelines. The District Court relied considerably on the defendant's gift "of time." I can find no evidence of the amount of time given to community service, as distinguished from some personal favors to friends and political constituents.

The Guidelines do not suggest a sentence departure for time spent aiding friends or family, or time in performing acts of kindness — even unusual acts of kindness to individuals. Construing such personal acts to individuals as exceptional community service under the Guidelines opens up an area as vast and deep as the Seven Seas. The Guidelines speak in terms of community service and there is nothing in the record of this case that definitively shows Serafini gave community service, independent of his political activities. The 1999 Statistical Abstract of the United States reveals that in the year 1995, persons in the United States with income of $100,000 or more contributed an average of 4.4 hours per week to volunteer work without monetary pay. In this case, although Serafini earned many times more than $100,000 in 1994 and 1995, we have no record that he gave any amount of time to volunteer work, whether it was for one or more weeks during the year, or for fifty-two weeks.

The cases support the foregoing analysis. Courts may not leniently interpret the requirement of extraordinary circumstances to grant a downward departure. See, e.g., United States v. Rybicki, 96 F.3d 754, 758 (4th Cir. 1996) (defendant was a highly-decorated Vietnam veteran, had saved an innocent civilian during the My Lai massacre, and had served with the Secret Service; these deeds did not warrant a departure); United States v. McHan, 920 F.2d 244, 247 (4th Cir. 1990) (defendant's work history, family ties and responsibilities, and extensive contribution to the town's economic well-being could not justify downward departure.). . . .

Measured by any reasonable standard, whether it be tithing to his church and community, or other charitable contributions of money or community time, Serafini's charitable and community service was far from exceptional or extraordinary. It was quite ordinary for a man in his preeminent position and financial circumstances. Nor were his charitable contributions or community services of the level or character exacting personal sacrifice, a deprivation of something of substance because of his contributions.

I therefore conclude that it was impermissible under the Guidelines for the District Court to depart from the Sentencing Guidelines.

NOTES

1. *Higher class status and sentencing advantage.* Is membership in a privileged class a basis for increased or decreased sentencing, or should it be irrelevant? Should monetary charity ever be considered a basis for adjusting a sentence downward? If money is a poor indicator of anything other than class, are there aspects of social or community behavior not tied to class that should nonetheless be relevant to sentencing?

For a different perspective on a downward departure in the case of a wealthy white-collar defendant based on charitable giving and good deeds, see United States v. Thurston, 338 F.3d 50 (1st Cir. 2003) (review of downward departure de novo, following 2003 congressional change to the appellate review standard established in Koon v. United States, 518 U.S. 81 (1996)).

2. *Lower class status and sentencing disadvantage.* The striking reality of U.S. criminal justice systems is the disproportionate presence of members of the lower class. Should the disproportionate presence of the poor in U.S. courts, prisons, and jails bring about changes in our sentencing systems or our social systems? In a survey of federal judges conducted in 2002, only 54-60 percent of them believed that there was "almost always" neutrality with regard to the offender's socioeconomic status, in contrast to 62-68 percent who believed the same with regard to race and almost 90 percent who shared that belief with regard to religion or creed.

D. GENDER

Criminal laws used to distinguish explicitly between men and women. Some, such as rape laws, made it impossible for women to commit the crime; others relegated them automatically to victimhood. See, e.g., M. v. Superior Court of Sonoma County, 450 U.S. 464 (1981) (state statute criminalizing only the male's conduct in having sexual intercourse with an underage woman did not violate the Equal Protection Clause); People v. Liberta, 474 N.E.2d 567 (N.Y. 1984) (statute that prohibited only forcible rape of women by men violated the Equal Protection Clause; conviction could stand as court extended coverage to rape of men by women). Because such legislation treated women differently, often in a childlike manner, feminists urged their abolition. Ultimately these arguments succeeded; the few gender-based distinctions that remain usually revolve around the childbearing functions of women. For example, until recently Ohio mandated the imposition of nonprison sentences involving prenatal care and drug rehabilitation for pregnant drug abusers who were willing to enter treatment.

Although gender equality has become the nominal hallmark of our criminal justice system, issues of different treatment continue to rear their head in substantive criminal law and sentencing. Most frequent are charges of preferential sentencing. Traditionally, women have benefited from the paternalism and chivalry of a largely male judiciary. Women often receive lesser sentences because men believe they need protection and help.

While some of this discrimination may be due to gender stereotypes, some judges may implicitly recognize the reality of the lives of many female offenders. They are dominated or abused by fathers, husbands, or boyfriends who involve them in criminal activities; their offenses are designed to benefit their families; and, perhaps most significant, their incarceration sends children into foster homes.

But prosecutors and judges do not favor all women. Rather they distinguish between "good" and "bad" women. As crime victims the former — or their male representatives — are taken seriously; as offenders they appear to receive substantially lower sentences than men convicted of the same offenses. The criminal justice system, however, is often not so generous to women who violate social norms — prostitutes, for example, or women who assault and kill their children or mates — by engaging in behavior that is considered "unnatural." Minority and poor women also tend to be among those who receive harsher sentences.

Whether anecdotal evidence of differential treatment amounts to gender-based discrimination is more difficult to determine. The number of women committing crimes (especially violent crimes) is small. Possible sentencing discrimination remains hidden behind a process that makes it difficult to decide whether similar offenders receive similar sentences.

One set of challenges to unequal treatment, familiar from other areas of discrimination, focuses on discriminatory patterns and practices of charging, plea-bargaining, sentencing, and in-prison treatment. The necessary data, however, are often difficult or impossible to unearth. Even if policies are facially discriminatory, courts do not strike them down as violating the federal and state equal protection clauses. Consider the following case, in which the defendant challenged a blatantly gender-based policy.

Virginia Salaiscooper v. Eighth Judicial District
34 P.3d 509 (Nev. 2001)

PER CURIAM

Petitioner Virginia Anchond Salaiscooper contends that, in prosecuting her for solicitation of prostitution, Clark County District Attorney Stewart Bell is engaging in impermissible unconstitutional selective prosecution that violates her right to equal protection under the law. More specifically, Salaiscooper contends that the district attorney intended to discriminate against females by implementing a policy that prohibited his deputies from entering into plea negotiations with female defendants charged with solicitation of prostitution, thereby foreclosing any possibility that they could attend a diversion class in order to avoid solicitation convictions. . . .

The policy at issue was summarized in a December 1999 memo from Clark County District Attorney Stewart Bell to his deputies. The memo provided:

In light of some changes in policy at the Las Vegas Metropolitan Police Department with regard to work card licensing for exotic dancers charged with prostitution, it has been agreed . . . that (*except in cases of first time male offenders who opt for the diversion program*) we will not negotiate the nature of cases of soliciting prostitution, nor will we agree that they may be in the future dismissed for any reason.

The policy was implemented due to the American Civil Liberties Union's (ACLU) objection to the fact that the Las Vegas Metropolitan Police Department (Metro) was revoking adult entertainment industry employees' work cards based merely on an arrest for solicitation of prostitution. The ACLU contended that revoking a work card needed to work in the entertainment industry without an underlying conviction violated due process. In response to the ACLU's objection, the district attorney implemented a no-plea-bargain policy that prohibited his deputies from entering into a plea agreement with a defendant charged with solicitation of prostitution allowing a plea to a lesser charge. The plain language of the policy prohibiting plea bargains excepted first time male defendants.

Because the justice court was concerned with the gender-specific language used in the policy, it ordered an evidentiary hearing where both sides could present evidence to support or refute a specific finding of discriminatory purpose. . . .

The State called . . . Dr. Roxanne Clark Murphy, a clinical psychologist and the Program Coordinator for the First Offender Program for Men in Las Vegas. Murphy testified that she developed the First Offender Program in collaboration with Metro and that it boasted an extremely low recidivism rate of less than one percent. Murphy explained that the diversionary program was designed for buyers of sex that are statistically almost always male. Murphy also described the requisite for entrance into the program was that a defendant must be a first-time offender charged with soliciting a prostitute.

Murphy testified that the vast majority of sellers of sex are females. Murphy also stated that it would take a minimum of a year to successfully rehabilitate a seller of sex. Murphy explained that, in order for a diversion program to be an effective deterrent, it would need to be a residential program that would protect women from their pimps, teach them job skills, and provide substance abuse and psychological counseling. Murphy further explained that more effort is required to rehabilitate and deter sex sellers than buyers because many prostitutes have been sexually abused, selling sex since the age of 13 to 14, disassociated from their actions through the use of drugs and alcohol, and/or controlled by a violent pimp or procurer. . . .

Judge Togliatti issued a lengthy order stating that the Las Vegas Justice Court had unanimously found that the policy did not discriminate on the basis of gender and that its distinction based on buyers of sex and sellers of sex was constitutionally permissible. In so finding, Judge Togliatti qualified this conclusion by stating that the judges were relying on the district attorney's representations that his policy applied to all sellers of sex regardless of gender, and consequently ordered Mr. Bell to clarify this fact in writing to his deputies within ten days.

In response to the court's order, Mr. Bell filed a clarification of policy in the justice court, affirming that he had distributed a memo clarifying that the First Offender Program for Men was available only to buyers of sex regardless of whether they were male or female. Accordingly, under the clarified policy, if a female buyer of sex was charged with solicitation of prostitution, she, like a male buyer of sex, would have the option of attending the First Offender Program, thereby avoiding a solicitation conviction. . . .

Salaiscooper argues that, in enacting the policy, the district attorney engaged in impermissible and unconstitutional selective prosecution that violated her right to equal protection under the law. Specifically, Salaiscooper argues that the policy's distinction between buyers and sellers of sex is "nothing more than a facade" concealing "conscious, intentional discrimination" against women, and thereby violates the Equal Protection Clauses of the United States and Nevada Constitutions. We conclude that Salaiscooper's argument lacks merit.

The government's decision to deny an arrestee admission into a diversion program is a decision to prosecute and [on review is treated] as a claim of selective prosecution. A defendant alleging unconstitutional selective prosecution has an onerous burden. Indeed, a district attorney is vested with immense discretion in deciding whether to prosecute a particular defendant that "necessarily involves a degree of selectivity." In exercising this discretion, the district attorney is clothed with the presumption that he acted in good faith and properly discharged his duty to enforce the laws. Although the district attorney's prosecutorial discretion is broad, it is not without limitation. The Equal Protection Clause constrains the district attorney from basing a decision to prosecute upon an unjustifiable classification, such as race, religion or gender.

The requisite analysis for a claim of unconstitutional selective prosecution is two-fold. First, the defendant has the burden to prove a prima facie case of discriminatory prosecution. To establish a prima facie case, the defendant must show that a public officer enforced a law or policy in a manner that had a discriminatory effect, and that such enforcement was motivated by a discriminatory purpose. A discriminatory effect is proven where a defendant shows that other persons similarly situated "are generally not prosecuted for the same conduct." A discriminatory purpose or "evil eye" is established where a defendant shows that a public administrator chose a particular course of action, at least in part, because of its adverse effects upon a particular group. If a defendant proves a prima facie case, the burden then shifts to the State to establish that there was a reasonable basis to justify the unequal classification. Where the classification is based on gender, the court applies an intermediate standard of scrutiny; in other words, the court must conclude the unequal classification in the policy is "reasonable, not arbitrary, and [rests] upon some ground of difference having a fair and substantial relation to the object of the legislation."

In the instant case, the justice court found that the district attorney had a valid, gender-neutral motivation for creating the policy classification — to draw a distinction between buyers and sellers of sex in order to deter acts of prostitution. More specifically, the justice court found that it was reasonable for the district attorney to prohibit sellers of sex from attending the one-day diversion program because it would have no deterrent effect. The justice court opined that the classification was therefore necessary because buyers of sex should not be precluded from participating in a successful diversion program merely because such treatment would be ineffective in rehabilitating the sellers. Finally, the justice court found that there was "nothing sinister" about the district attorney's primary goal of obtaining solicitation of prostitution convictions against sellers of sex so that he could revoke their work cards and, ultimately, stop prostitutes from working in the adult entertainment industry.

The lower court's findings with respect to the district attorney's motivation and intent underlying the policy are findings of fact to be given deference, and they should not be reversed if supported by substantial evidence. The district court correctly concluded that there is substantial evidence in support of the justice court's factual findings. In particular, Dr. Murphy testified that the diversion class would not be an effective deterrent for sex sellers because they would need a one-year rehabilitation program in light of the deeply-entrenched culture of drug abuse, psychological abuse, and violence associated with prostitution. Moreover, [there was testimony] that the district attorney needed solicitation convictions against sellers of sex so that Metro could revoke their work cards and eradicate prostitution from the strip clubs. Because the State presented evidence that the purpose of the policy's buyer/seller distinction was to deter acts of prostitution, the justice court's findings that the policy did not run afoul of the Equal Protection Clause is supported by substantial evidence.

Other jurisdictions have reached an analogous conclusion, holding that it is constitutionally permissible to treat prostitutes differently than the customers who patronize them. In People v. Superior Court of Alameda County, 562 P.2d 1315, 1320 (Cal. 1977), the Supreme Court of California, sitting en banc, held that it was permissible for law enforcement officials to target sellers of sex, because the "sexually unbiased policy of concentrating its enforcement effort on the profiteer" was not initiated by an intent to discriminate. The court reasoned that the policy was created because of the belief that focusing criminal prosecution on the sellers of sex had the most deterrent effect: "Prostitutes, the municipal court found, average five customers per night; the average customer does not patronize prostitutes five times a year. Because of an effective grapevine, arrest of one prostitute by an undercover officer will deter others, at least for a time."

Like the law enforcement officials in *Alameda*, [t]he State presented evidence in support of its belief that a one-day class would not stop a prostitute from selling sex. . . . In light of our conclusion that the policy does not violate the Equal Protection Clauses of the United States and Nevada Constitutions, we conclude that extraordinary relief is not warranted in this matter. The legislature has vested the district attorney with prosecutorial discretion, and we conclude it is within the purview of the district attorney's prosecution powers to treat buyers of sex differently than sellers of sex. After all, the decision to prosecute, including the offer of a plea bargain, is a complex decision involving multiple considerations, including prior criminal history, the gravity of the offense, the need to punish, the possibility of rehabilitation, and the goal to deter future crime. Unless a defendant can prove that a district attorney's decision to prosecute arose from an impermissible desire to discriminate on the basis of race, gender or other protected class, our federal and state constitutions do not compel our intervention. Because there is no evidence of a discriminatory motive in the case before us, we deny Salaiscooper's petition.

PROBLEM 9-5.   SENTENCING AND MOTHERHOOD

Amrhu Dyce, an immigrant in her twenties, pled guilty in federal court to conspiracy to commit possession with intent to distribute crack cocaine. She had carried drugs from New York City to North Carolina, largely to increase her limited household budget. Under the federal sentencing guidelines, Dyce faced an imprisonment range of 121 to 151 months. At sentencing she argued for a substantial downward departure based on her "extraordinary" family responsibilities, claiming that her case fell outside the heartland of cases for which the U.S. Sentencing Commission had declared family responsibilities "not ordinarily relevant." At the time of the sentencing hearing, Dyce had three small children. She breastfed the youngest, a newborn (a practice the U.S. government recommends at least for the first year of a baby's life while the World Health Organization suggests two years). The other two children were one and three years old. Dyce's boyfriend, the father of her children, was not involved in her criminal activities but seemed incapable of raising one, let alone all three, of his children. Dyce's mother and sister, who live in England, were willing and able to take in only the middle child.

Because of the father's inability to bring up two children, the youngest and the eldest may have to be placed in foster care should Dyce be sentenced to prison. Should the court consider her family circumstances extraordinary so as to allow for a nonprison sentence? Should it matter whether residential treatment facilities are available that would allow Dyce to live in a restrictive environment but keep at least the infant, and possibly even the other two children with her? May the court consider the separation of the family and the impossibility of visitation should one of the children be removed from the United States? See United States v. Amrhu Dyce, 91 F.3d 1462 (D.C. Cir. 1996).

NOTES

1. *Backfiring.* Much feminist criticism of law enforcement has centered on gender-specific offenses such as prostitution, domestic violence, and rape. Substantive law and enforcement practices have changed in all three, but the impact of the changes is often imperceptible or ambiguous.

Consider prostitution. As *Salaiscooper* indicates, much of the enforcement of gender-neutral statutes still centers on the provider of the service — largely women. What justifies this enforcement focus? Who is in the best position to ascertain the information to make this decision?

Imagine a reverse world in which legislation criminalizes only the purchasing of sexual services. What could justify the sole prosecution and sentencing of the largely male customer? Prostitution is frequently deemed particularly harmful to the female providers, many of whom were abused as children, are drug addicted, suffer from low self-esteem, and do not view themselves as having other employment options. Would such legislation if adopted in a U.S. jurisdiction run afoul of the Equal Protection Clause? See Vermont v. George, 602 A.2d 953 (Vt. 1991). What effect do you expect such a changed enforcement practice to have on the supply and demand for prostitution services? Sweden has adopted this model, but there have been few prosecutions of male customers. Is this a function of enforcement effort or of the particular offense involved?

2. *Criminal law defenses and sentencing.* Feminists have charged that substantive criminal law, and especially the area of criminal defenses, focuses on men. This issue has been publicized most frequently with regard to abused

women who kill their batterers. The women often argue that they acted in self-defense, and they frequently introduce the battered spouse syndrome to bolster their claim. Juries usually either reject the defense outright or find liability for a lesser included offense. Once the defense has been fully or partially rejected, the lesser culpability of the defendant can be recognized merely through the sentence. See United States v. Whitetail, 956 F.2d 857 (8th Cir. 1992) (federal sentencing guidelines allow for consideration of battered spouse syndrome through downward departures).

The same situation occurs when a female defendant raises a duress defense. While the defense may fail in the guilt phase, circumstances, such as emotional, psychological, or sexual dependence on a male partner who abused the defendant, may justify distinguishing her conduct from that normally present and may allow the court to impose a lesser sentence. See United States v. Gaviria, 804 F. Supp. 476 (E.D.N.Y. 1992).

3. *More female offenders?* The number of women in state and federal prison rose by 573 percent between 1980 and 1997. During this period the number of women imprisoned has increased at almost twice the male rate. Drug offenses accounted for almost half of the rise in women's incarceration, and federal prisons outpaced state facilities in female admissions. African American and, to a lesser extent, Hispanic women bore the brunt of this development.

What explains the explosion in female imprisonment? Some blame a change in enforcement strategies; some point to enforcement and sentencing practices stemming largely from the war on drugs that no longer discriminate in favor of women; some see women rise in the drug underworld, paralleling their rise in the legitimate business world; some blame the feminization of poverty. See Phyllis Goldfarb, Counting the Drug War's Female Casualties, 6 J. Gender, Race & Just. 277 (2002).

Despite the increase in female convicts, the gender differences in incarceration rates remain striking. At year-end 2001, about 1,313,000 men (1 in 112) were incarcerated in state and federal prisons, but only about 93,000 women (1 in 1,724) were incarcerated. Why are so few women imprisoned, comparatively speaking? Victimization studies indicate that men commit more offenses, especially more violent crimes. In 1996 women accounted for 16 percent of all felons convicted in state courts: They made up almost one-quarter of property offenders but less than one-tenth of violent criminals. However, the number of women who commit violent crimes has been rising steadily, especially among adolescents. Of female offenders about one-third are serving time for a drug offense. Even if these numbers were to underestimate female offending somewhat, they still raise the issue whether biological differences or socialization or both explain why men are more violent and more likely to engage in crime generally.

4. *Women are different.*   In contrast to racial differences, men and women truly differ. Some of these differences are clearly biological, others may or may not be. To what extent should the criminal justice system consider a woman's ability to bear children? There is an international consensus that pregnant women should not be executed, but beyond that, criminal justice systems differ on whether and to what extent biological differences should be considered.

In imposing a 20-year prison sentence on a 25-year-old woman and a 25-year-old man, should a court consider that this makes it virtually impossible for the woman to bear a child (putting aside expensive and often unsuccessful modern reproductive technologies) but not for the man to father a child? Cf. Gerber v. Hickman, 291 F.3d 617, 623 (9th Cir. 2002) ("[T]he right to procreate while in prison is fundamentally inconsistent with incarceration."); Goodwin v. Turner, 908 F.2d 1395, 1396 (8th Cir. 1990) (Bureau of Prisons' restriction on allowing inmate to ejaculate into a clean container so that his semen could be used to artificially inseminate his wife "is reasonably related to legitimate penological interest of treating all prisoners equally"). As of December 2002, the British Home Office had granted six inmates the right to father a child through artificial insemination. The prisoners most likely to benefit are those with long prison sentences whose spouses would likely be too old to conceive a child upon their release. The policy extends also to female inmates, but none have requested artificial insemination yet.

Concerned that women will become pregnant to avoid incarcerative sentences, courts have declined to consider pregnancy, childbirth, and having a young child as mitigating sentencing factors. If courts should not and cannot consider such biological differences in their sentencing, is there a societal responsibility to create institutional facilities that allow female offenders to keep their children with them?

5. *Pregnancy and drugs.* In 19 states and the District of Columbia, pregnant women have been prosecuted for substance abuse. Some prosecutors have argued that the small amount of drugs that travels from the mother to the child either during the pregnancy or through the umbilical cord at birth constitutes drug trafficking — and a more severe form since the drugs are delivered to a minor. In South Carolina, Charleston prosecutors filed child neglect charges against women who had just given birth in a state hospital. The U.S. Supreme Court struck down this policy because the hospital's practice of collecting urine samples, without the patient's consent, to obtain evidence of the patient's criminal conduct constituted an unreasonable search. It reached this result even though the state's interest in deterring pregnant women from using cocaine is high. See Ferguson v. City of Charleston, 532 U.S. 67 (2001). Particularly disturbing is the fact that the vast majority of such drug prosecutions are aimed at poor African American women, generally because they frequent public hospitals and because of the allegedly more destructive impact of crack on a fetus.

6. *Gender equality redux.* Gender equality has been writ large in the legal system. Does it make sense if there is no equality in the larger society? While many male inmates are also fathers, data on state prisoners indicate that 90 percent of fathers who were incarcerated had wives who cared for their children. For female offenders, less than one-quarter had husbands who cared for their children. Because of changes in foster care and adoption laws, a likely consequence of long-term imprisonment for single parents who cannot find another caregiver for their children is loss of parental rights. While differences in caregiving may not be solely biological, should a court consider them? Such consideration would also benefit men who are not able to find stable caregiving arrangements for their minor children during imprisonment. Alternatively, should large numbers of single parents in the criminal justice system (and society at large) counsel against consideration of single-parent status at sentencing?

Federal courts that consider family circumstance in their departure jurisprudence frequently note the defendants' financial contribution to the family. Women who do not appear to be gainfully employed, even if they are the sole caregiver for minor children, are thus at a disadvantage. Does such an approach not privilege one type of parenting over another? May it not also discriminate against minority groups in which the mother is expected to stay at home with her children?

7. *The numbers disadvantage in imprisonment.* Because there are substantially fewer prisons for women than men, often their conditions of incarceration differ. In the federal system especially, the small number of female offenders and the location of women's prisons often necessitate incarceration far from family and friends. This is particularly difficult for women with young children and women whose families cannot afford lengthy trips, either financially or for other reasons. Should courts consider such well-known facts in deciding whether to impose a prison sentence?

Female prisons also offer different conditions than all-male institutions. Many have fewer or different educational programs, and most have only limited employment options. This may further disadvantage women who entered the system with educational and vocational deficits. Nevertheless, courts have not found equal protection violations based on different prison conditions. See Klinger v. Department of Corrections, 31 F.3d 727, 731 (8th Cir. 1994) (substantial differences between men's and women's prisons did not constitute an equal protection violation because male and female prisoners "were not similarly situated for purposes of prison programs and services"). At the same time, women often enjoy better prison facilities and more privacy than men. In those cases, courts, relying on *Klinger,* have also found no constitutional violations. See Oliver v. Scott, 276 F.3d 736 (5th Cir. 2002).

8. *Female recidivism and risk-based sentencing.* Women commit fewer violent offenses and have lower recidivism rates than men. If the risk of future offending were the focus of sentencing, most women would receive lesser sentences than most men for a similar offense. Does risk-based sentencing violate the equal protection clause? Without risk-based sentencing, doesn't equal treatment put women at a disadvantage?

9. *Women as crime victims.* Men are disproportionately the victims of crime. While this finding may contradict public perception, it holds true for most offenses. Women make up the majority of domestic violence and rape victims, however — both destructive, usually violent offenses that are vastly underreported. Normatively, the victimization of women is considered substantially more heinous than that of men. Why?

Women are often the targets of crime because offenders consider them more vulnerable. Imagine, for example, a young man choosing a robbery victim: The 5'2", 90-pound woman is a more attractive target than most men, possibly barring Woody Allen. Should offenders who pick vulnerable female targets be subject to sentence enhancements? Or is a new substantive criminal law provision more appropriate? Consider one proposed definition for hate crimes: "a crime in which the defendant intentionally selects a victim, or in the case of a property crime, the property that is the object of the crime, because of the actual or perceived . . . gender . . . of any person."

PROBLEM 9-6. SAUCE FOR THE GANDER

Gilberto Redondo-Lemos was charged in Arizona federal court for acting as a drug courier. He alleged that prosecutors in the U.S. Attorney's office violated his right to equal protection by offering more favorable plea bargains to female couriers.

The district court held an evidentiary hearing. At the hearing, the assistant U.S. Attorney (AUSA) handling the Redondo-Lemos prosecution said that she offered, in exchange for a guilty plea, to recommend the lowest sentence allowed by the federal sentencing guidelines and the mandatory minimum. She testified that she assessed the strength of her case, followed the factors set out in departmental memos dealing with plea bargains generally, was not motivated by defendant's gender, and knew of no office policy of plea bargaining on the basis of gender.

Another AUSA's testimony concerned a case against a couple where the evidence was actually stronger against the woman. The AUSA nonetheless agreed to let the husband plead guilty to a lesser charge in exchange for allowing the wife to go free and take care of their three children. The AUSA noted that, after 25 years of experience, he'd observed that it was "usually the Mexican men that will stand up and take responsibility," and he'd come to expect it. The AUSA noted that when couples are faced with a choice, they usually select the woman to care for the children and that allowing this choice reflects no government policy of gender discrimination. The government argued that it was the private party, not the government, who made the decision and "discriminated." The government simply practiced compassion when it allowed parents to decide which parent would be the better caregiver for children who otherwise would be effectively orphaned.

In ten additional cases that concerned the district judge, the responsible AUSAs testified that they based their plea bargaining decisions on the strength of the evidence, the legality of the stops and searches, the defendant's cooperation, the level of the defendant's involvement, and special circumstances of particular defendants. In one case, the AUSA allowed a woman who was overdue in her pregnancy to plead guilty to a misdemeanor. Because the Marshal's Service indicated it couldn't give her proper medical care, she was sentenced to time served, while her male partner, who had a record, pleaded guilty and was sentenced to 90 months in prison. The AUSA explained that she would have responded the same way had the Marshal's Service expressed concern about medical care for a male defendant.

The court considered two sets of statistics to show intentional discrimination in plea bargaining with male "mules" in the District of Arizona. Statistics from the local probation office showed that male drug offenders in the District of Arizona were sentenced to an average of 36 months compared to 32 months for females and that only 11 percent of all males received probation compared to 35 percent of females. A U.S. Sentencing Commission report showed that nationwide, 61.5 percent of men who committed crimes subject to mandatory minimum sentences received them while only 50 percent of women did.

The district court rejected the explanations by the AUSAs as "mere general assertions that the AUSAs did not discriminate." In the case of the couple, the court found the discriminatory plea to be unjustified. Based on that case and the two sets of statistics, the district court found intentional invidious discrimination and sentenced Redondo-Lemos below the statutory minimums for the offenses of which he was convicted.

Suppose the government appeals the finding of invidious discrimination and the remedy of ordering sentences below the statutory minimum. How should the appellate court rule? See United States v. Redondo-Lemos, 27 F.3d 439 (9th Cir. 1994).

NOTES

1. *Male claims of bias.*   A striking feature of gender bias claims is that they are often raised by men rather than women. Why? Claims of gender bias face the problems of definition and proof confronted by Warren McCleskey and others making claims of bias based on race and other factors.

2. *The centrality of plea bargaining.*   Defendants who plea bargain face two obstacles in challenging bias in their prosecution and sentence. First, by plea bargaining they may have waived some right to challenge any bias in treatment and sentence; second, bias challenges to charges and pleas are almost always based on claims of systematic rather than individual bias. Are the doctrines of equality able to make the leap from individual to collective treatment, from individual bias to disparate outcome, which may or may not be based on biased judgments and rules by the decision maker whose actions are challenged?

3. *Information on sentencing disparities.*   Does the focus on legally compelling claims of bias obscure important policy issues with respect to equal treatment? How should policy makers, scholars, or judges concerned with issues of bias in sentencing or the criminal justice system address or illuminate those issues?

=10=

Alternatives to Criminal Sentences

Criminal punishments presuppose a criminal conviction, and the collateral consequences discussed in Chapter 8 occur only after a criminal conviction. But there are alternatives to criminal punishment that create many of the effects of a criminal sanction without first obtaining a criminal conviction. As you read about the alternative sanctions surveyed in this chapter, ask whether they differ in meaningful ways from true criminal sanctions. When might the lack of a criminal conviction make it improper or difficult to impose some of these alternatives?

A. DIVERSION PROGRAMS

Diversion threatens but does not use the criminal process. Its goal is to protect the offender from the sanctions and stigma arising from a criminal conviction while saving criminal justice resources. Precharge diversion has always been part of prosecutorial discretion. Diversion programs started with juvenile cases and expanded to include adult drug offenses in the 1960s; more formalized programs exist today in the state and federal systems.

Diversion programs can take several forms, each attaching at a different point in the criminal process. Pre-arrest diversion allows the police or the prosecutors to divert offenders at the earliest stage, without ever starting the criminal process. Its informality may open the process to possible abuse and prevent structured oversight of the offender's subsequent actions. But it protects the offender from having an arrest record.

Pre-arraignment diversion directs individual offenders out of the system after their arrest but prior to the formal filing of charges. This process ensures prosecutorial control over the diversion process and enables more screening to remove unsuitable offenders from the program. It does so while saving the criminal justice system the costs of prosecution, without saddling the offender with a criminal record.

Diversion may occur at later stages in the process, after formal charges have been filed but before a judgment has been rendered. Pretrial diversion, for example, allows charges to be dismissed after a defendant has successfully fulfilled the conditions the prosecutor imposed. In some cases defendants may plead guilty conditionally with the understanding that the judge will vacate the plea after the offender completes all the required conditions.

Prosecutors and judges use diversion programs especially often in drug cases. Minor, nonviolent drug users in particular benefit from programs that move them into drug treatment. Diversion can be used for defendants ranging from juveniles to corporations. A corporation might escape potentially damaging publicity in exchange for monetary payment. The juvenile might perform community service or pay a fine. Among the more imaginative diversion programs are those using offender-victim mediation.

The prosecutor typically controls access to these diversion programs (also known as "deferred prosecution" programs). But given their functional similarity to criminal sentences, should judges also have a role in selecting who gets diverted and what conditions the defendant must meet?

State v. Carolyn Curry
988 S.W.2d 153 (Tenn. 1999)

ANDERSON, C.J.

. . . The defendant, Carolyn C. Curry, worked as an assistant clerk for the City of McKenzie, Tennessee, from 1985 to 1995. Over a two-year period from July of 1993 to July of 1995, Curry embezzled over $27,000 from the City. She later was indicted for theft of property valued between $10,000 and $60,000.

Curry applied for pretrial diversion. According to her application, she was a divorced, 34-year-old mother of three children, ages 19, 13, and 8. Curry had graduated from college with honors in 1983, and she served in the Tennessee National Guard from 1983 to 1990, when she was honorably discharged. She was an active member of her church and numerous charitable and community organizations including the United Way, United Neighbors, Concerned Citizens, and youth softball. Numerous letters included with her application attested to her charitable and community involvement. Curry had no prior arrests or convictions. She cooperated with authorities in this case when her actions were discovered, admitting that she took money for family and living expenses and proposing a restitution program. She stated that: "I sincerely regret my actions and regret the shame that my actions have brought to bear on myself and my family."

In denying the application for pretrial diversion, the prosecutor, in a written response, gave the following reasons:

> . . . We have carefully reviewed the application and the attached letters. . . . We have considered the defendant's past history and her conduct for two years in defrauding the City of McKenzie. This was a calculated criminal scheme that took planning and thought. It manifests a criminal intent for a long period of time and not something that happened at once. We cannot believe that it would

be in the best interests of the public, the defendant, and justice to overlook a criminal scheme of this proportion and grant pre-trial diversion. . . .

Curry sought review of the prosecutor's decision by filing a petition for writ of certiorari in the trial court. After hearing argument of counsel, the trial court found that diversion had been denied solely based upon the circumstances of the offense, specifically, the two-year duration, and ruled [that the district attorney's office had "abused its discretion in denying pretrial diversion" and that Curry should be placed on pretrial diversion].

The pretrial diversion program, drafted and enacted by the Legislature, allows the District Attorney General to suspend a prosecution against a qualified defendant for a period of up to two years. Tenn. Code Ann. §40-15-105(a)(1)(A). A qualified defendant pursuant to the statute is one who has not previously been granted diversion and does not have a prior misdemeanor conviction for which confinement was served or a prior felony conviction within a five year period after completing the sentence or probationary period for the conviction. The offense for which diversion is sought may *not* be a class A felony, a class B felony, a sexual offense, driving under the influence, or vehicular assault. Tenn. Code Ann. §40-15-105(a)(1)(B)(i)(c).

Any grant of diversion must be conditioned on one or more of the following conditions: that the defendant not commit any criminal offense; that the defendant refrain from activities, conduct, or associations related to the charge; that the defendant receive rehabilitative treatment, counseling and education; that the defendant make restitution to the victim; that the defendant pay court costs and the costs of the diversion; and that the defendant abide by any other terms or conditions as may be agreed upon. Tenn. Code Ann. §40-15-105(a)(2)(A)-(H). If the defendant violates a term or condition, the prosecution may terminate diversion and resume the criminal prosecution.

One who is statutorily eligible is not presumptively entitled to diversion. Instead, whether to grant pretrial diversion to a qualified defendant who is statutorily eligible is a determination that lies in the discretion of the district attorney general. The relevant considerations for the prosecutor are as follows:

> When deciding whether to enter into a memorandum of understanding under the pretrial diversion statute a prosecutor should focus on the defendant's amenability to correction. Any factors which tend to accurately reflect whether a particular defendant will or will not become a repeat offender should be considered. . . . Among the factors to be considered in addition to the circumstances of the offense are the defendant's criminal record, social history, the physical and mental condition of a defendant where appropriate, and the likelihood that pretrial diversion will serve the ends of justice and the best interest of both the public and the defendant.

State v. Pinkham, 955 S.W.2d 956, 959-960 (Tenn. 1997).

If the district attorney general denies pretrial diversion, the denial must be in writing and must include an enumeration of the evidence that was considered and a discussion of the factors considered and weight accorded each. This requirement entails more than an abstract statement in the record that the district attorney general has considered these factors. Instead, the factors considered must be clearly articulable and stated in the record. . . .

The prosecutor's response must be in writing. [The written statement compels] the prosecutor to think about and justify his denial in terms of the applicable standards. [The] statement of reasons [also restricts] the prosecutor to a particular rationale and insure[s] that the prosecutor would offer no new reasons at the evidentiary hearing. The prosecutor's written response must also identify any factual disputes between the evidence relied upon and the application filed by the defendant.

If the application for pretrial diversion is denied, the defendant may appeal by petitioning the trial court for a writ of certiorari. Tenn. Code Ann. §40-15-105(b)(3). The only evidence that may be considered by the trial court is the evidence that was considered by the district attorney general. The trial court may conduct a hearing only to resolve any factual disputes raised by the prosecutor or the defendant concerning the application, but not to hear additional evidence that was not considered by the prosecutor. The action of the prosecutor is presumptively correct, and it is subject to review by the trial court only for an abuse of discretion.

[In this case,] the prosecutor's primary consideration in the written denial of diversion was the circumstances of the offense, specifically, the amount of money taken and the duration of the criminal activity. The denial letter stated that diversion was not "in the best interest of the public," which, although imprecise, arguably includes deterrence. Although the prosecutor asserts that he had "carefully reviewed the application and the attached letters," the denial does not discuss the defendant's favorable social history, lack of a criminal record, and potential for rehabilitation. Moreover, assuming these essential factors were, in fact, considered, there is no explanation as to how much weight they were afforded and no rationale as to why they were outweighed by the other factors in denying diversion.

The State argues, and the dissent writes, that the seriousness of the offense itself may justify a denial of diversion. A review of the case law reveals, however, that the circumstances of the offense and the need for deterrence may alone justify a denial of diversion, *but only if all of the relevant factors have been considered as well.* See State v. Washington, 866 S.W.2d 950, 951 (Tenn. 1993) ("circumstances of the case and the need for deterrence may be considered as two of the many factors, [but] they cannot be given controlling weight unless they are of such overwhelming significance that they . . . outweigh all other factors"). The facts and circumstances of nearly all criminal offenses are by definition serious; only by analyzing all of the relevant factors, including those favorable to the defendant, can appropriate candidates for this legislative largess be identified in a manner consistent with the purpose of the pretrial diversion act.

In *Pinkham,* for instance, the defendant was charged with falsely representing himself as a lawyer, impersonating a licensed professional, and aggravated perjury. The denial of diversion emphasized the circumstances of the offense, the losses sustained by the victim, and the "systematic and continuing criminal activity," but also gave extensive consideration to the other relevant factors:

> In making this decision to reject the defendant's diversion application, I have considered that [the defendant] is a 50 year old man with no criminal record. I have considered his exemplary social history. I have considered that [the defendant] appears to be a leader in his community, as evidenced by the character and reference letters from lawyers, teachers, professors, ministers,

doctors, et al. I have considered all of the parameters of [the defendant's] social, family, personal, educational and professional background. . . . Since [the defendant] is a highly educated person who holds a law degree, [the defendant] knew that his conduct was unlawful and unethical. . . .

955 S.W.2d at 959.

In contrast, the defendant in State v. Herron, 767 S.W.2d 151, 155 (Tenn. 1989), a 24-year-old woman with no prior criminal record, was charged with two counts of larceny by trick, one offense involving $5000 and the other involving $6000. The prosecutor's denial of pretrial diversion was based primarily on the circumstances of the "contrived, deliberate" offenses and the need to deter such offenses. Although the trial court denied the defendant's petition for certiorari, [this court held that] both the prosecutor and the trial court failed to consider "that defendant did not have any criminal record, her social history, her physical and mental condition, including her educational background, her employment history as well as the stability and continued support of her family."

[The] dissent strains to conclude that the evidence regarding the defendant's background was unfavorable and that her potential for rehabilitation was minimal simply by looking only to the circumstances and time span of the offense. Under such an analysis, in which the facts and circumstances are given conclusive weight against a defendant's potential for correction, rare is the defendant who would qualify for pretrial diversion. . . .

HOLDER, J., dissenting.

. . . Pretrial diversion is a legislative largess as well as extraordinary relief. Pretrial diversion relieves criminal defendants of the burden of being tried for or convicted of a crime for which they are guilty. Once defendants have completed a diversion program, they are under no legal obligation to disclose their offenses to prospective employers, and their public records are expunged. Mere eligibility for diversion should not provide a presumption for program suitability.[1] Defendants, therefore, should at all times carry the burden of establishing suitability given the extraordinary nature of diversionary relief. . . .

The pretrial diversion statute does not enumerate specific criteria that a prosecuting attorney should use when making pretrial diversion determinations. The legislature apparently recognized the extraordinary relief provided by the pretrial diversion statute and intended to provide prosecuting attorneys substantial discretion in making pretrial diversion decisions. This grant of discretion would presumptively include the broad discretion to determine not only the relevant criteria and considerations of each case but also the weight to be afforded the relevant considerations of each diversionary decision. Courts, however, have judicially imposed general considerations to guide a prosecuting attorney's decision.

. . . In the case now before us, the prosecuting attorney set out the following reasons in support of the pretrial diversion denial: (1) the long-term and

---

1. Pursuant to Tenn. Code Ann. §40-15-105, defendants committing extremely serious offenses such as aggravated assault, voluntary manslaughter, vehicular homicide (not involving intoxication), kidnapping, robbery, arson, and aggravated burglary may be eligible for pretrial diversion.

continuing nature of the offense; (2) the fact that the circumstances of the offense reveal a systematic scheme to commit crimes which "manifest a criminal intent for a long period of time" and not a crime of impulse; (3) the magnitude of the offense, noting the amount of money ($27,368.73) embezzled during a period from July 1, 1993 to July 11, 1995; (4) the deceitful nature of the criminal violations; and (5) the deterrent effect of crimes to defraud city or municipal organizations ("[w]e cannot believe that it would be in the best interests of the public, the defendant and justice to overlook a criminal scheme of this proportion and grant pre-trial diversion to the defendant").

The reasons cited by the prosecutor are well-supported by the record and have been held sufficient for denials of pretrial diversion in numerous published opinions involving similar crimes and crimes of a less serious nature. . . . In State v. Carr, 861 S.W.2d 850, 854 (Tenn. App. 1993), the defendant's crimes were very similar to the crimes in the case now before us. Pretrial diversion was denied based on the following factors:

(1) The circumstances show "a systematic scheme to defraud . . . not a crime of impulse," involving considerable planning which would have continued absent discovery.
(2) The magnitude of the offense, noting the amount of money ($23,370.85). . . .
(3) The number of individual claims and continuing nature of the offense.
(4) The particular need for deterrence because of the considerable opportunity for Medicaid fraud, which is serious and prevalent.
(5) The defendant's statements indicate little remorse and failure to accept responsibility.

The appellate court stated that . . . in a close case, the courts should defer to the prosecutor's decision. The appellate court held that substantial evidence in the record supported the denial based on the circumstances of the crime and the need for deterrence. . . .

In the case now before us, I believe that the record is replete with substantial evidence supporting the district attorney's reasons for denying pretrial diversion. . . . I would hold that the district attorney's letter denying diversion more than adequately addressed the criteria set forth in *Pinkham,* even though the letter could have been more detailed. . . . The circumstances of the defendant's offense and the need to deter fraud as well as thefts of large sums of money are sufficiently overwhelming to justify denial of pretrial diversion in this case. . . .

I disagree with the majority's finding that the defendant has a "favorable" social history and background. I believe that someone who continually commits serious crimes involving deception, planning, and fraud over a two-year period of time has a less than favorable social history, has an extensive criminal background, and is a poor candidate for rehabilitation. Moreover, the defendant ceased her criminal activity only when she was caught, and her criminal activity would likely have continued had she not been caught.

I disagree with the majority's decision that an abuse of discretion occurred merely due to a district attorney's failure to specifically or explicitly address non-statutory criteria. . . . The majority's holding could effectively allow defendants committing serious offenses such as manslaughter, kidnapping, and vehicular homicide to avoid prosecution merely because a district attorney commits a non-prejudicial omission affecting neither a constitutional nor a statutory right.

> ## *U.S. Attorneys' Manual*
> ## *Pretrial Diversion Program*
> ### U.S. Department of Justice

9-22.100   ELIGIBILITY CRITERIA

The U.S. Attorney, in his/her discretion, may divert any individual against whom a prosecutable case exists and who is not:

1. Accused of an offense which, under existing Department guidelines, should be diverted to the State for prosecution;
2. A person with two or more prior felony convictions;
3. An addict;
4. A public official or former public official accused of an offense arising out of an alleged violation of a public trust; or
5. Accused of an offense related to national security or foreign affairs.

> ## *Criminal Resource Manual*
> ## *715 USA Form 186 — Pretrial Diversion*
> ## *Agreement*
> ### U.S. Department of Justice

. . . Upon accepting responsibility for your behavior and by your signature on this Agreement, it appearing, after an investigation of the offense, and your background, that the interest of the United States and your own interest and the interest of justice will be served by the following procedure; therefore

On the authority of the Attorney General of the United States, by _____, United States Attorney for the _____ District of _____, prosecution in this District for this offense shall be deferred for the period of ____ months from this date, provided you abide by the following conditions and the requirements of this Agreement set out below.

Should you violate the conditions of this Agreement, the United States Attorney may revoke or modify any conditions of this pretrial diversion program or change the period of supervision, which shall in no case exceed eighteen months. The United States Attorney may release you from supervision at any time. The United States Attorney may at any time within the period of your supervision initiate prosecution for this offense should you violate the conditions of this Agreement. In this case [he/she] will furnish you with notice specifying the conditions of the Agreement which you have violated.

After successfully completing your diversion program and fulfilling all the terms and conditions of the Agreement, no prosecution for the offense . . . will be instituted in this District, and the charges against you, if any, will be dismissed.

Neither this Agreement nor any other document filed with the United States Attorney as a result of your participation in the Pretrial Diversion Program will be used against you, except for impeachment purposes, in connection with any prosecution for the above-described offense.

GENERAL CONDITIONS OF PRETRIAL DIVERSION

1. You shall not violate any law (Federal/State/Local). You shall immediately contact your pretrial diversion supervisor if arrested and/or questioned by any law enforcement officer.
2. You shall attend school or work regularly at a lawful occupation or otherwise comply with the terms of the special program described below. If you lose your job or are unable to attend school, you shall notify your pretrial diversion supervisor at once. You shall consult him/her prior to job or school changes.
3. You shall report to your supervisor as directed and keep him/her informed of your whereabouts.
4. You shall follow the program and such special conditions as may be described below. . . .

I hereby state that the above has been read and explained to me. I understand the conditions of my pretrial diversion program and agree that I will comply with them.

[Defendant] _____
Defense Attorney _____
United States Attorney _____
Chief Pretrial Services Officer (or Chief Probation Officer) _____

PROBLEM 10-1.   IN NEED OF TREATMENT?

Melissa has abused legal and illegal narcotics for years. One day she asks her best friend, Claire, to pick up a package for her in a neighborhood with a reputation for drug trafficking. Melissa's husband no longer allows her to leave the house without their driver, so she has no other way of getting drugs. Claire feels uncomfortable about this errand, but she owes Melissa a major favor, and agrees.

Claire picks up the package and is arrested shortly after leaving the drug house. A police officer arrests Claire with about three ounces of cocaine in her pocket and informs her of her *Miranda* rights. On her way to the station house, she overhears two police officers discuss the high sentences that apply to drug crimes. Upon arrival there, the police begin to interrogate Claire. They tell her that she has the right to an attorney but that if she cooperates with them and admits her guilt, they might be able to keep her from "going to court." Her interrogator suggests that with a quick admission of guilt, the case would basically be over for her. Surely, he intimates, she would prefer that over seeing her name and picture in the newspaper and having a criminal record. When she mentions her children, he tells her that only her agreement to go through a diversion program would guarantee that she could keep her children. Claire also speaks quickly to a harried assistant district attorney. She then agrees to enroll in a drug treatment program and to complete it successfully in exchange for the prosecutor's agreement not to file charges against her. Is Claire an appropriate candidate for diversion? What purpose(s) would the prosecutor serve by diverting her case?

NOTES

1. *Purposes of diversion.* According to the *U.S. Attorneys' Manual,* the purposes of diversion are to prevent future criminal activity, to save prosecutorial and judicial resources for major cases, and to provide restitution to communities and victims. Section 712 of the *Criminal Resource Manual for U.S. Attorneys* states that a pretrial diversion program "should be tailored to the offender's needs and may include employment, counseling, education, job training, psychiatric care," and so forth. The provision also endorses restitution and community service and strongly encourages "innovative approaches." Which of the traditional purposes of the criminal law does this provision emphasize? How successfully were any of these accomplished in Claire's case (Problem 10-1)?

2. *Prevalence of diversion.* Diversion of arrestees is less common than the outright rejection of criminal charges. Prosecutors are most likely to offer diversion to suspects who face misdemeanor charges. Less than 5 percent of all felony arrestees in the largest urban counties in 1998 took part in diversion or "deferred adjudication" programs. Bureau of Justice Statistics, Felony Defendants in Large Urban Counties, 1998 (NCJ 187232, Nov. 2001). Federal diversion programs are even smaller: just over 1,000 suspects were handled through pretrial diversion in 2000 (compared to more than 70,000 cases prosecuted and 30,000 cases declined). Why do diversion programs remain relatively rare? What resource limitations might restrict their availability? See Steven Belenko, The Challenges of Integrating Drug Treatment into the Criminal Justice Process, 63 Alb. L. Rev. 833 (2000).

3. *Prosecutors and judges as gatekeepers.* Prosecutors retain complete control over precharge diversion programs but often share authority with judges over diversion programs that begin after charges are filed. State statutes dealing with postcharge diversion programs ordinarily empower the judge to approve the prosecutor's recommendations for offenders to enter the program. See Mont. Code Ann. §46-16-130(2) ("After a charge has been filed, a deferral of prosecution may be entered into only with the approval of the court"). Yet as the Tennessee court in *Curry* recognized, it is usually the prosecutor who decides which defendants or suspects enter a pretrial diversion program, and the court is loath to interfere with the prosecutor's decision. Indeed, courts in many states refuse to review the prosecutor's decision whether to offer diversion to a suspect unless the prosecutor relies on unconstitutional grounds such as racial discrimination. See Cleveland v. State, 417 So. 2d 653 (Fla. 1982) (decision on pretrial intervention is prosecutorial, rather than judicial, in nature and is not subject

to judicial review; review of arbitrary decisions allowed in other jurisdictions because statutes explicitly authorize review). Statutes in about a dozen states give prosecutors complete control over who may enter pretrial diversion programs.

Prosecutors' offices sometimes create uniform policies to govern eligibility for diversion, at least for some types of cases. Are the guidelines provided in the *U.S. Attorneys' Manual* sufficiently precise to limit prosecutorial discretion? Why does the manual exclude drug addicts from access to the diversion program?

In many Continental European countries, such as Germany, where prosecutors have traditionally not been assumed to have any discretion, diversion programs may indicate an increase in prosecutorial power. Is that also true for the United States, or do diversion programs tend to circumscribe prosecutorial discretion by creating judicial supervision over the prosecutor's choices?

4. *Other gatekeepers.*   Pre-arrest diversion programs tend to shift the police function from law enforcement to social work without providing guidance as to which offenders are well suited for a diversion program. What role should experts such as probation officers play in the initial recommendation process? In the federal system, prosecutors are instructed to refer potential candidates for pretrial diversion to the chief pretrial services officer or the chief probation officer for the district. See *Criminal Resources Manual* 712 B 2. What can the probation officer add that the prosecutor does not know or see?

Should the victim have any input in deciding whether an offender may enter a diversion program? The German Juvenile Justice Act permits prosecutors to dismiss cases after the juvenile offender has tried to reach a settlement with the victim.

Legislatures also create some preconditions for defendants or suspects to participate in pretrial diversion programs. See, e.g., Ind. Code §33-14-1-7 (prosecutor "may" withhold prosecution against a person charged with a misdemeanor if the person agrees to the conditions of the pretrial diversion program); S.C. Code §17-22-50 (no pretrial intervention for repeat offenders); Utah Code §77-36-2.7 (court may not approve diversion for domestic violence defendants but may hold guilty plea in abeyance during treatment program). If the prosecutor and the suspect disagree about the statutory eligibility requirements, should a court be able to review the prosecutor's decision based on its independent interpretation of the statute?

5. *Who decides if the defendant has completed the program?*   Suppose a defendant believes that she has fulfilled all the conditions of the diversion program but the prosecutor disagrees and files criminal charges. Will a court review the prosecutor's conclusion that the defendant failed to complete the program? Is there any reason to treat this question differently from the question of who will enter a diversion program? Among states with statutes addressing judicial review, the majority require some sort of court approval for a decision to remove an offender from a diversion program; some (fewer than ten) grant this decision exclusively to the prosecutor. See Fla. Stat. §948.08; State v. Hancich, 513 A.2d 638 (Conn. 1986) (once defendant was admitted to pretrial alcohol education program following her first arrest for driving under the influence, she could not be removed unless court independently determined that she had lost her eligibility or that she had not completed the program successfully). What

circumstances might make a court more willing to judge the defendant's success or failure in the program?

6. *Admission of guilt and involvement of counsel.*   The existence of a diversion program may be used to pressure individuals to waive their rights and admit guilt to gain entrance. How could a precharge diversion program be structured to avoid such problems? The federal system requires the involvement of a defense attorney. If a suspect or defendant cannot afford counsel, one is appointed. The Canadian statute governing diversion involving juveniles requires that the juvenile, before consenting to participate in a diversion program, be "advised of his right to be represented by counsel and [be] given a reasonable opportunity to consult with counsel." Young Offenders Act, R.S.C., ch. 110 (1984) (Can.). Why does the *U.S. Attorneys' Manual* mandate that counsel be involved rather than simply require that defendants be informed of their right to counsel?

7. *Widening the net.*   The beginning of formal diversion programs can be traced back to juvenile courts in the early twentieth century. Diversion was formally extended to narcotics cases in the 1960s. Since then concerns have existed about "widening the net" of such programs. The fear is that individuals who would have previously been released without any action are now being diverted into programs while the cases of more serious offenders, who would not be eligible for diversion, are dismissed. Does diversion amount to decriminalization of certain offenses or offender groups? Or does it instead increase the level of social control over offenders, as community service and drug treatment complement the traditional prison sanctions?

8. *Female offenders and diversion.*   Might diversion programs be particularly suitable for and attractive to female defendants? Many of these offenders commit nonviolent crimes and have dependent children. Long pretrial detention or incarceration forcibly separate the mothers from their children whereas diversion programs allow them to remain together. Should such family considerations help determine which offenders qualify for admission into diversion programs? If not, should offense type be the sole determining factor?

B.   DOMESTIC VIOLENCE PROTECTION ORDERS

Crime victimization surveys show that, in 2001, almost 700,000 non-fatal violent incidents occurred between intimate partners in the United States. These included rapes and sexual assaults, robberies, aggravated assaults, and (most common) simple assaults. Eighty-five percent of that violence was directed at women.

In domestic violence cases, the state may file criminal charges against the perpetrator. But other avenues are available: In all states, a family member who is the victim of domestic violence can get a so-called civil protection or restraining order. Survey data indicate that about 17 percent of the women and 3.5 percent of the men physically assaulted by an intimate obtain such an order. Over 1.1 million victims of intimate violence obtain a protective or restraining order annually. Currently, there appear to be two million active restraining orders. Patricia Tjaden and Nancy Thoennes, Extent, Nature and Consequences of Intimate Partner Violence: Findings From the National Violence Against Women Survey 52-54 (National Institute of Justice, 2000); U.S. Department of Justice, Office for Victims of Crime, Enforcement of Protective Orders 4 (2002).

Protection orders are designed to empower the victim, allowing her to act when the state is unwilling to file a criminal complaint against the batterer. In this sense, civil protection orders create an alternative to the criminal justice process. The goal of such an order is to break the cycle of violence by removing the perpetrator from the battering relationship without subjecting the offender immediately to the criminal justice system. A civil protection order prohibits a named person from harassing, stalking, or threatening an intimate partner. In addition, protection orders may restrict the person from contacting the victim, require the person to vacate a joint household, or set conditions for child visitation and financial support.

Protection orders are relatively easy to obtain, allowing victims to proceed without an attorney. Frequently, victims get help from nonattorney domestic violence advocates. A judge issues a preliminary order after an ex parte hearing, and a final protection order follows a hearing at which both sides appear and present evidence.

Protection orders, while technically the product of a civil process, sit between the civil and criminal arena. Those who violate a protection order can be sanctioned for disobeying the court, through misdemeanor charges or contempt charges or both. This civil process, therefore, carries a criminal sanction if its target fails to comply with the civil order. Of course, the state may file a criminal complaint if the violation of the protection order also amounts to a substantive offense, such as assault or attempted murder. Nevertheless, about 60 percent of restraining orders are violated.

PROBLEM 10-2.   RESTRAINT

John and Miriam lived in Louisville, Kentucky and they were having marital difficulties. Even though they hoped to reconcile, they agreed that it would be best if John moved out. One night, John came over to pick up their son for a walk. When John asked his son to get ready, five-year-old Ben said, "get out of my face." John then began to shout at Miriam for failing to teach Ben to respect his father. She responded, also in a raised voice, that Ben's attitude might be John's fault because he was not a good father or husband. John lost his temper and slapped Miriam. She then yelled, "I'll divorce you." John yelled back that he would "bury" her if she filed for divorce, and stormed off.

Based on this exchange, Miriam filed for an emergency protective order requiring John to keep his distance from her and Ben. The court granted the protective order and sent notice to John immediately after granting the order.

A week later, Miriam's car broke down on the highway. She called John at work and asked him whether he could pick her up and fix the car. John arrived immediately. While he was driving Miriam home, they began to quarrel again. When they arrived at home, both got out of the car. John then screamed at Miriam so loudly that her neighbor came out of the house to see what was going on. At that point, John raised his hand as if he were about to hit Miriam, but then thought better of it and instead continued berating her. Miriam asked the neighbor to call the police. Within minutes the police arrived and arrested John for violating the protective order.

At his trial for violation of the protective order and attempted assault, John challenges the validity of the initial protective order. He argues that the court violated the constitution when it issued the protective order without hearing from him, and he contends that the government has not established the statutory requirements to convict him of violating the restraining order and attempted assault.

As prosecuting counsel, how do you respond? As you answer this question, consult the Kentucky statutes below that describe the relevant procedures for protective orders.

|| *Kentucky Statutes §§403.720 to 403.760* ||

§403.720

As used in [this chapter], (1) "Domestic violence and abuse" means physical injury, serious physical injury, sexual abuse, assault, or the infliction of fear of imminent physical injury, serious physical injury, sexual abuse, or assault between family members or members of an unmarried couple; (2) "Family member" means a spouse, including a former spouse, a parent, a child, a stepchild, or any other person related by consanguinity or affinity within the second degree; and (3) "Member of an unmarried couple" means each member of an unmarried couple which allegedly has a child in common, any children of that couple, or a member of an unmarried couple who are living together or have formerly lived together.

§403.740

(1) If, upon review of the petition, . . . the court determines that the allegations contained therein indicate the presence of an immediate and present danger of domestic violence and abuse, the court shall issue, upon proper motion, ex parte, an emergency protective order:

(a) Restraining the adverse party from any contact or communication with the petitioner except as directed by the court;

(b) Restraining the adverse party from committing further acts of domestic violence and abuse;

(c) Restraining the adverse party from disposing of or damaging any of the property of the parties;

(d) Directing the adverse party to vacate the residence shared by the parties to the action;

(e) [Granting] temporary custody; or

(f) [Entering] other orders the court believes will be of assistance in eliminating future acts of domestic violence and abuse; or any combination thereof.

(2) [If] the court issues an emergency protective order pursuant to subsection (1) of this section, the court shall not order or refer the parties to mediation for resolution of the issues alleged in the petition [unless the victim of the alleged domestic abuse voluntarily requests it and mediation is a realistic and viable alternative to or adjunct to a protective order].

(3) An emergency protective order issued in accordance with this section shall be issued without bond being required of the petitioner.

(4) An emergency protective order issued in accordance with this section shall be effective for a period of time fixed in the order, but not to exceed fourteen days. Upon the issuance of an emergency protective order, a date for a full hearing . . . shall be fixed not later than the expiration date of the emergency protective order. An emergency protective order shall be reissued for a period not to exceed fourteen days if service has not been made on the adverse party by the fixed court date and time or as the court determines is necessary for the protection of the petitioner. . . .

§403.745

If, upon review of the petition . . . , the court determines that the allegations contained therein do not indicate the presence of an immediate and present danger of domestic violence and abuse, the court shall fix a date, time, and place for a hearing and shall cause a summons to be issued for the adverse party. . . . The hearing shall be fixed not later than fourteen days following the issuance of the summons.

§403.750

(1) Following the hearing provided for under §§403.740 and 403.745, the court, if it finds from a preponderance of the evidence that an act or acts of domestic violence and abuse have occurred and may again occur, may [take any actions described in §403.740(1), or it may] award temporary support [or direct] that either or both parties receive counseling services available in the community. [The court] shall not order or refer the parties to participate in mediation for resolution of the issues alleged in the petition [unless the victim of the alleged domestic abuse voluntarily requests it and mediation is a realistic and viable alternative to or adjunct to a protective order].

(2) Any order entered pursuant to this section shall be effective for a period of time, fixed by the court, not to exceed three years and may be reissued upon expiration for an additional period of up to three years. The number of times an order may be reissued shall not be limited. With respect to whether an order should be reissued, any party may present to the court testimony relating to the importance of the fact that acts of domestic violence or abuse have not occurred during the pendency of the order. . . .

§403.760

(1) Violation of the terms or conditions of an order issued under the provisions of §§403.740 or 403.750, whether an emergency protective order,

or an order following hearing, after service of the order on the respondent, or notice of the order to the respondent, shall constitute contempt of court.

(2) Any peace officer having probable cause to believe a violation has occurred of an order issued under the provisions of §§403.740 or 403.750 . . . shall arrest the respondent without a warrant for violation of a protective order. . . . Following a hearing the District Court in the county in which the peace officer made the arrest for the violation may punish the violation of a protective order. . . .

(4) Nothing in this section shall preclude the Commonwealth from prosecuting and convicting the respondent of criminal offenses other than violation of a protective order.

(5) Civil proceedings and criminal proceedings for . . . violation of a protective order shall be mutually exclusive. Once either proceeding has been initiated the other shall not be undertaken regardless of the outcome of the original proceeding.

NOTES

1. *Goals of civil protection orders.* What goals are civil protection orders intended to achieve? Why can these not be accomplished with criminal actions? Civil protection orders appear to be a valuable alternative to the criminal justice process when the criminal justice system either does not act or does not act quickly enough. Such orders also serve important symbolic ends by allowing the victim to demonstrate her ability to act, her strength, and her independent decision making skills. They constitute a direct action by the victim against the abuser.

Despite the support of the justice system, however, restraining orders may not reduce domestic violence. See Elaine Chiu, Confronting the Agency in Battered Mothers, 74 S. Cal. L. Rev. 1223 (2001). Is a civil process insufficiently stigmatizing to keep the offender from battering again? Many abusers in domestic violence situations have criminal records that resemble those of other violent criminals. Should restraining orders be utilized only for first-time domestic violence offenders or for individuals without a criminal record?

Some have argued that restraining orders may be unsuccessful because batterers do not perceive the process as fair. Often they do not understand the difference between the civil and criminal systems and are left alone to navigate the judicial system. Should batterers be provided with more process, such as information about the system or even the right to counsel? May such services be advisable only if it is shown that they increase compliance? See Deborah Epstein, Procedural Justice: Tempering the State's Response to Domestic Violence, 43 Wm. & Mary L. Rev. 1843 (2002).

In some counties in Kentucky, domestic violence orders have earned the nickname "the poor man's [and woman's] divorce." Domestic violence orders may accomplish some of the goals of divorce, but much more quickly. How could such abuses of the system be prevented without limiting access for abused persons?

2. *Ex parte civil proceedings.* Emergency protection orders are granted without a hearing and without notice being provided to the respondent. They

often stay in place for about two weeks. Many states provide extensive self-help manuals for battered spouses, explaining how to obtain a restraining order. Shortly before the emergency protection order runs out, the court holds a hearing in which both sides are present. Because the grant of civil protection orders takes place in a civil proceeding, the petitioner (note the civil terminology) has to show the occurrence of domestic violence merely by a preponderance of the evidence.

There is no right to publicly funded counsel in civil proceedings, including hearings on civil protection orders. Petitioners, however, are frequently represented by women's advocates or law school clinics in their request for emergency protection orders. These advocates become regular players in the process while the respondents remain largely unrepresented until they violate a protection order. Once criminal proceedings are under way, the alleged batterer has the right to an attorney.

3. *Specialized judges.*   In some states, specially designated domestic violence judges grant civil protection orders, sit on domestic violence cases, and deal with violations of civil protection orders. What reasons are there for the creation of such one-stop shopping? What advantages and disadvantages flow from subject-matter-focused judging? See Randal B. Fritzler and Leonore M.J. Simon, The Development of a Specialized Domestic Violence Court in Vancouver, Washington: Utilizing Innovative Judicial Paradigms, 69 UMKC L. Rev. 139 (2000).

4. *Double jeopardy and domestic violence orders.*   The violation of a civil protection order may lead to a panoply of actions against the batterer. The breach of the court's order could lead to a contempt citation or a criminal prosecution for the violation; an assault and battery could also lead to a separate criminal action. In United States v. Dixon, 509 U.S. 688 (1993), the Supreme Court addressed whether charges of assault and threats were barred by the Double Jeopardy Clause because the charges were filed after a misdemeanor contempt conviction based on the same conduct. The Court, in a splintered opinion, held that the misdemeanor assault prosecution was barred, but the prosecutions for assault with intent to kill and felony threats could go forward because misdemeanor contempt and each of the latter crimes required proof of an element that the other did not. See Blockburger v. United States, 284 U.S. 299 (1932) (describing traditional "same elements" test to determine which crimes qualify as the same offense and thus are barred by double jeopardy). Does this decision deter prosecutors from filing criminal assault charges after the courts have issued contempt citations? See David M. Zlotnick, Battered Women and Justice Scalia, 41 Ariz. L. Rev. 847 (1999).

5. *Weapon possession and protection orders.*   The federal Violence Against Women Act, enacted in 1994, prohibits anyone under a civil protection order from possessing firearms or ammunition. See 18 U.S.C. §922(g)(8). Federal law and most state statutes, however, prohibit possession of weapons only upon a finding of abuse after an evidentiary hearing that gives the defendant an opportunity to be heard. This means that in many states an emergency protective order will not bring the respondent within the gun ban. Some commentators argue that without an immediate confiscation of weapons when the court issues

the emergency order, the threat to the victim continues until the hearing. See Maria Kelly, Domestic Violence and Guns: Seizing Weapons Before the Court Has Made a Finding of Abuse, 23 Vt. L. Rev. 349 (1998).

6. *Control of litigation.*   In situations in which physical harm is inflicted or threatened, the state asserts its interest as a representative of the people, not merely of the victim of the alleged crime. This means that the decision whether to prosecute is made by a state agent rather than the victim. In many jurisdictions, mandatory prosecution in domestic violence cases (sometimes required by statute, more often by prosecutorial office policy) does not leave the victim any option. Should she refuse to testify or choose to testify falsely, the criminal justice system can sanction her. Because the victim and the offender in a domestic violence situation have a relationship — and sometimes try to preserve that relationship — the traditional adversarial criminal justice model may break down.

In what other situations may civil actions be preferable over criminal actions? Are there other types of criminal offenses in which the victim's interests may not be adequately represented by the state? In corporate embezzlement and similar types of business crimes, businesses often choose to settle with the offenders, under the threat of reporting them to the criminal justice system, without ever involving the official system. This is possible because the victimized business is in a more advantageous bargaining position than the offender — and its sole interest is recouping financial loss rather than vindicating a greater goal. In fraud crimes committed against the government, prosecutors often threaten to file criminal suits while also proceeding civilly. The threat of criminal litigation can lead to more advantageous civil settlements for the government. Should there be constitutional or statutory limits on the use of such dual threats?

C. ASSET FORFEITURE

While the alternatives to criminal sentences we have considered so far all emphasize restrictions on liberty, other alternative remedies depend on taking the property of a suspected wrongdoer. Asset forfeiture is among the most important of these techniques. Technically, most asset forfeiture occurs through civil proceedings, with no necessary connection to criminal charges. In practice, asset forfeiture is tightly integrated with criminal enforcement. Asset forfeiture has become an important part of prosecution and punishment, especially for crimes with an economic motive such as drug offenses, money laundering, and racketeering. Forfeiture is said to "take the profit out of crime."

The effectiveness of asset forfeiture lies partly in the procedural edge it gives the prosecution. Civil asset forfeiture gives the prosecution a more favorable standard of proof, extensive discovery, and summary judgment, among other advantages. Forfeiture can also take place during proceedings following on the heels of a criminal conviction, essentially as part of the criminal sentencing. Such "criminal forfeitures" are less common than civil forfeitures, however, because of the relative procedural difficulties they present to the government.

The destination of forfeited property also makes it an attractive device for law enforcement. Federal statutes and executive policies, along with most state statutes, assign forfeited property directly to the budgets of law enforcement agencies. Forfeitures carried out under state law generally go to local police and sheriff's offices, after reimbursing prosecutors for the costs of processing the forfeiture. When federal agents complete a forfeiture, the proceeds go to the participating federal agencies. Moreover, the federal government can "adopt" the forfeitures of state or local authorities. If state or local police seize property that is forfeitable under federal law, and federal prosecutors obtain the final forfeiture order in federal court, they split the proceeds.

Because the police and prosecutors who select property for forfeiture directly benefit from the forfeitures, property owners have argued that the police have an incentive to abuse the practice. Alleged abuses in spending forfeited funds make big headlines. For instance, news reports widely noted a small-town sheriff who seized a Rolls-Royce from a drug dealer and used it as his personal car.

In this section, we examine the asset forfeiture procedures that operate in tandem with the criminal justice system. Consider the ways in which civil forfeiture proceedings differ from criminal proceedings, and ask whether those differences are justified by the different purposes of these systems or by the different consequences flowing from them.

1. Property Subject to Forfeiture

The forfeiture laws aim only at property with some defined connection to a crime. It is ordinarily not enough for an accused felon to own property; the suspect must use it to commit a crime or acquire it as a result of the crime. The materials below describe the property that the law targets for forfeiture and the property it exempts from forfeiture. Consider what these categories reveal about the objectives of the forfeiture laws and their imperfect overlap with the objectives of criminal law enforcement.

In the federal system, roughly 200 criminal statutes provide for forfeiture. Many of these statutes deal with violations of customs laws or food and drug laws. Most federal forfeitures, however, take place under the laws against money laundering, racketeering, and illicit drugs. The same pattern holds true for most state forfeiture laws: They apply primarily to violations of drug, gambling, liquor, and racketeering laws. In a few states, any felony can serve as the basis for a forfeiture. See Fla. Stat. §932.701(2)(a); Nev. Rev. Stat. §179.121. The following case discusses the necessary connection between the crime and the forfeited property under an early federal statute.

United States v. Cargo of the Brig Malek Adhel
43 U.S. 210 (1844)

STORY, J.

[The information in this case alleged that the brig *Malek Adhel* was used to commit "piratical aggression and restraint upon the high seas" against five vessels. The government pursued forfeiture proceedings against the ship and its cargo after it arrived in Maryland. The firm of Peter Harmony and Co. of New York claimed the ship and cargo as its property and attempted to prevent the forfeiture. At the hearing in district court, the vessel was condemned and the cargo acquitted. Peter Harmony and Co. brought this appeal.]

It was fully admitted in the court below, that the owners of the brig and cargo never contemplated or authorized the acts complained of; that the brig was bound on an innocent commercial voyage from New York to Guayamas, in California; and that the equipments on board were the usual equipments for such a voyage. It appears from the evidence that the brig sailed from the port of New York on the 30th of June, 1840, under the command of one Joseph Nunez, armed with a cannon and ammunition, and with pistols and daggers on board. The acts of aggression complained of, were committed at different times under false pretences, and wantonly and wilfully without provocation or justification, between the 6th of July, 1840, and the 20th of August, 1840, when the brig arrived at Bahia; where, in consequence of the information given to the American consul by the crew, the brig was seized by the United States ship *Enterprize,* then at that port, and carried to Rio Janeiro, and from thence brought to the United States. . . . Now upon this posture of the case, it has been contended [that] neither the brig nor the cargo are liable to condemnation, because the owners neither participated in nor authorized the piratical acts, but are entirely innocent thereof. . . .

The [first] question is, whether the innocence of the owners can withdraw the ship from the penalty of confiscation under the act of Congress. Here, . . . it may be remarked that the act makes no exception whatsoever, whether the aggression be with or without the co-operation of the owners. The vessel which commits the aggression is treated as the offender, as the guilty instrument or thing to which the forfeiture attaches, without any reference whatsoever to the character or conduct of the owner. The vessel or boat (says the act of Congress) from which such piratical aggression, &c., shall have been first attempted or made shall be condemned. . . . And this is done from the necessity of the case, as the only adequate means of suppressing the offence or wrong, or insuring an indemnity to the injured party. The doctrine also is familiarly applied to cases of smuggling and other misconduct under our revenue laws. . . . In short, the acts of the master and crew, in cases of this sort, bind the interest of the owner of the ship, whether he be innocent or guilty; and he impliedly submits to whatever the law denounces as a forfeiture attached to the ship by reason of their unlawful or wanton wrongs. . . .

The ship is also by the general maritime law held responsible for the torts and misconduct of the master and crew thereof, whether arising from negligence or a wilful disregard of duty; as, for example, in cases of collision and other wrongs done upon the high seas or elsewhere within the admiralty and maritime jurisdiction, upon the general policy of that law, which looks to the instrument itself, used as the means of the mischief, as the best and surest pledge for the compensation and indemnity to the injured party. The act of Congress has therefore done nothing more on this point than to affirm and enforce the general principles of the maritime law and of the law of nations.

The remaining question is, whether the cargo is involved in the same fate as the ship. In respect to the forfeiture under the act of 1819,* it is plain that the cargo stands upon a very different ground from that of the ship. Nothing is said in relation to the condemnation of the cargo in the fourth section of the act; and in the silence of any expression of the legislature, in the case of provisions confessedly penal, it ought not to be presumed that their intention exceeded their language. . . .

So far as the general maritime law applies to torts or injuries committed on the high seas and within the admiralty jurisdiction, the general rule is, not forfeiture of the offending property; but compensation to the full extent of all damages sustained or reasonably allowable, to be enforced by a proceeding therefor in rem or in personam. It is true that the law of nations goes in many cases much farther, and inflicts the penalty of confiscation for very gross and wanton violations of duty. But, then, it limits the penalty to cases of extraordinary turpitude or violence. For petty misconduct, or petty plunderage, or petty neglect of duty, it contents itself with the mitigated rule of compensation in damages. . . .

The present case seems to us fairly to fall within the general principle of exempting the cargo. The owners are confessedly innocent of all intentional or meditated wrong. They are free from any imputation of guilt, and every suspicion of connivance with the master in his hostile acts and wanton misconduct. [The act of Congress limits] the penalty of confiscation to the vessel alone, [showing] that the public policy of our government in cases of this nature is not intended to embrace the cargo. It is satisfied by attaching the penalty to the offending vessel, as all that public justice and a just regard to private rights require. For these reasons, we are of opinion that the decrees condemning the vessel and restoring the cargo, rendered in both the courts below, ought to be affirmed. . . .

NOTES

1. *Objectives of forfeiture.*   Why did the government seek forfeiture of the ship and its cargo? The statute in question called for the forfeiture proceeds to become government property and did not mention use of the property to compensate victims of wrongdoing. Was the forfeiture done to prevent future criminal uses of the property? Won't future pirates be able to use some other ordinary vessel just as readily? Did Peter Harmony do anything wrong? Does it matter in forfeiture proceedings whether he was responsible for the piracy?

2. *Statutory connection to vessel and cargo.*   Why did the Court in *Malek Adhel* interpret the statute to allow forfeiture of the vessel but not the cargo? Would the Court have enforced a statute that clearly provided for the forfeiture of the cargo, or could the law of admiralty and the law of nations actually trump the

---

* The act of 1819 provides as follows: "[W]henever any vessel or boat from which any piratical aggression . . . shall have been first attempted or made, shall be captured and brought into any port of the United States, the same shall and may be adjudged and condemned to their use and that of the captors, after due process and trial in any court have admiralty jurisdiction, . . . and the same court shall thereupon order a sale and distribution thereof accordingly, and at their discretion."—EDS.

statute? Why does the law of admiralty and the law of nations require gross and wanton acts before allowing forfeiture of cargo? Consider whether this is an early indication of a need for proportionality between the crime committed and the assets forfeited.

3. *The expanding statutory connection.* Legislatures have steadily increased the categories of property subject to forfeiture. Take, for instance, the evolution of one of the primary federal forfeiture statutes, 21 U.S.C. §881. The original 1970 version of the statute applied to (1) all controlled substances; (2) all raw materials, products, and equipment used or intended to be used to manufacture or deliver controlled substances; (3) all containers for property described in the first two categories; (4) all conveyances (including aircraft, vehicles, and vessels) used or intended to be used to facilitate the transportation, sale, receipt, possession, or concealment of property described in the first two categories; and (5) all books, records, and research used in violation of controlled substances laws. Law enforcement officers were not able to forfeit much property meeting these criteria — only $30 million during the first nine years following passage of the law. A 1978 amendment expanded forfeiture to reach (1) all money, securities, and other "things of value furnished or intended to be furnished" in exchange for a controlled substance; (2) all proceeds traceable to such an exchange; and (3) all money, negotiable instruments, and securities used or intended to facilitate a violation of the drug laws. In 1984 the statute was expanded further to allow forfeiture of all real property used or intended "to commit, or to facilitate" a violation of drug laws. For a discussion of the "widening net" of property subject to forfeiture under federal forfeiture laws, see Jimmy Gurulé and Sandra Guerra, The Law of Asset Forfeiture ch. 5 (1999). Asset forfeiture has also become an important tool in punishing and preventing financial crimes in many European nations. See Peter Alldridge, The Moral Limits of the Crime of Money Laundering, 5 Buff. Crim. L. Rev. 279 (2001) (surveying forfeiture practices in United Kingdom).

4. *Forfeiture of estate.* None of the major forfeiture statutes attempts to forfeit *all* of the property of a person suspected, accused, or convicted of a crime. Is there anything stopping Congress and the state legislatures from adopting a statute along these lines? In eighteenth-century English practice, felons and traitors forfeited all their property. As William Blackstone explained it, allowing forfeitures of an entire estate "will help to restrain a man, not only by the sense of his duty, and dread of personal punishment, but also by his passions and natural affections; and will interest every dependent and relation he has, to keep him from offending." 4 William Blackstone, Commentaries on the Laws of England *375. The U.S. Constitution forbids forfeiture of estate as a punishment for treason, although it is allowed "during the Life of the Person attainted." U.S. Const. art. III, §3, cl. 2. The First Congress passed a law prohibiting federal forfeiture of estate as a punishment for other felonies. Could a state pass a statute providing for forfeiture of estate? What abuses might have occurred under English law to create such a reaction among early American lawmakers?

PROBLEM 10-3. WEAPONS ON WHEELS

In 1999, New York City began a "Zero Tolerance Drinking and Driving Initiative." Under this policy, police officers who arrest someone for driving while intoxicated (registering .10 or higher on a breathalyzer test) may seize the automobile. The policy prevents the police from seizing a vehicle in cases where drivers are arrested for the lesser offense of "driving while impaired" (registering between .06 and .10 on a breathalyzer test). The seized car is searched and stored in a city facility. If the driver is either the owner or principal user of the car, the city will begin a civil forfeiture proceeding to take the car away. If the owner of the car knows that someone else will use it to commit a crime (including driving while intoxicated) the car is also subject to forfeiture. Before the city adopted this new policy, the police held the cars of people arrested for drunken driving until some other person arrived at the station to pick up the car. The city sometimes asked for forfeiture of the car, but only after a criminal conviction.

The change in policy was based on an existing provision of the Administrative Code of the City of New York. Section 14-140 provides that the Police Property Clerk may take possession of all property "suspected of having been used as a means of committing crime." A person who uses property in furtherance of a crime "or suffers the same to be used . . . shall not be deemed to be the lawful claimant."

The mayor explained the new policy as follows: "It isn't punishment. It's remedial. The car is seized to protect society against this car being driven around in the communities of New York City because it's been demonstrated that this car will be operated unsafely." The forfeiture action is "a way of preventing the use of what, in fact, is a weapon when driven while intoxicated against the public." There were 6,368 arrests of drunken drivers in New York City in 1998, and 31 fatalities attributed to driving while intoxicated.

Francisco Almote, one of the first motorists whose vehicle was seized under the new policy, had been convicted five times previously on charges that he drove while intoxicated. Police seized his 1987 Toyota when they arrested him. A second driver whose car was seized was Pavel Grinberg, who was driving with his wife in Brooklyn one night when he was pulled over for not wearing a seat belt. Police officers said that a breathalyzer test showed a blood alcohol level of 0.11 percent, so the officers arrested Grinberg and seized his 1988 Acura Integra (with a book value of about $1,650). "I was at my good friend's daughter's first birthday party and I had one beer — that was it," Grinberg said.

You are an attorney in the office of the Corporation Counsel for New York City. What difficulties (if any) do you foresee in enforcing this policy? How should the city respond in cases where the defendant charged with driving while intoxicated is willing to plead guilty to the lesser charge of driving while impaired (a charge that is not a basis for seizing the car under the city's policy)? What if the defendant is willing to "settle" the forfeiture proceeding by paying one-quarter of the car's value?

|| ***Richard Austin v. United States*** ||
|| **509 U.S. 602 (1993)** ||

BLACKMUN, J.

In this case, we are asked to decide whether the Excessive Fines Clause of the Eighth Amendment applies to forfeitures of property under 21 U.S.C.

§§881(a)(4) and (a)(7). We hold that it does and therefore remand the case for consideration of the question whether the forfeiture at issue here was excessive.

On August 2, 1990, petitioner Richard Lyle Austin was indicted on four counts of violating South Dakota's drug laws. Austin ultimately pleaded guilty to one count of possessing cocaine with intent to distribute and was sentenced by the state court to seven years' imprisonment. On September 7, the United States filed an in rem action in the United States District Court for the District of South Dakota seeking forfeiture of Austin's mobile home and auto body shop under 21 U.S.C. §§881(a)(4) and (a)(7). Austin filed a claim and an answer to the complaint.

[According to affidavits supporting a government motion for summary judgment], Austin met Keith Engebretson at Austin's body shop on June 13, 1990, and agreed to sell cocaine to Engebretson. Austin left the shop, went to his mobile home, and returned to the shop with two grams of cocaine which he sold to Engebretson. State authorities executed a search warrant on the body shop and mobile home the following day. They discovered small amounts of marijuana and cocaine, a .22 caliber revolver, drug paraphernalia, and approximately $4,700 in cash. [The district court granted summary judgment to the government, and the Eighth Circuit affirmed.]

Austin contends that the Eighth Amendment's Excessive Fines Clause applies to in rem civil forfeiture proceedings. . . . The United States now argues that "any claim that the government's conduct in a civil proceeding is limited by the Eighth Amendment generally, or by the Excessive Fines Clause in particular, must fail unless the challenged governmental action, despite its label, would have been recognized as a criminal punishment at the time the Eighth Amendment was adopted." It further suggests that the Eighth Amendment cannot apply to a civil proceeding unless that proceeding is so punitive that it must be considered criminal under [our prior cases]. We disagree. . . .

The purpose of the Eighth Amendment, putting the Bail Clause to one side, was to limit the government's power to punish. The Cruel and Unusual Punishments Clause is self-evidently concerned with punishment. The Excessive Fines Clause limits the Government's power to extract payments, whether in cash or in kind, as punishment for some offense. The notion of punishment, as we commonly understand it, cuts across the division between the civil and the criminal law. It is commonly understood that civil proceedings may advance punitive and remedial goals, and, conversely, that both punitive and remedial goals may be served by criminal penalties. Thus, the question is not, as the United States would have it, whether forfeiture under §§881(a)(4) and (a)(7) is civil or criminal, but rather whether it is punishment. . . . We turn, then, to consider whether, at the time the Eighth Amendment was ratified, forfeiture was understood at least in part as punishment and whether forfeiture under §§881(a)(4) and (a)(7) should be so understood today.

Three kinds of forfeiture were established in England at the time the Eighth Amendment was ratified in the United States: deodand, forfeiture upon conviction for a felony or treason, and statutory forfeiture [for violations of the customs and revenue laws]. Each was understood, at least in part, as imposing punishment. At common law the value of an inanimate object directly or indirectly causing the accidental death of a King's subject was forfeited to the Crown as a deodand. . . . The value of the instrument was forfeited to the King, in the belief that the King would provide the money for Masses to be said for the good of the dead man's soul, or insure that the deodand was put to charitable uses. When application of the deodand to religious or eleemosynary purposes ceased, and the deodand became a source of Crown revenue, the institution was justified as a penalty for carelessness. . . .

Of England's three kinds of forfeiture, only the third took hold in the United States. [The] common law courts in the Colonies — and later in the states during the period of Confederation — were exercising jurisdiction in rem in the enforcement of English and local forfeiture statutes. The First Congress passed laws subjecting ships and cargos involved in customs offenses to forfeiture. . . .

Our cases also have recognized that statutory in rem forfeiture imposes punishment. [This] understanding of forfeiture as punishment runs through our cases rejecting the "innocence" of the owner as a common-law defense to forfeiture. In these cases, forfeiture has been justified on two theories — that the property itself is "guilty" of the offense, and that the owner may be held accountable for the wrongs of others to whom he entrusts his property. . . . In *Brig Malek Adhel,* it reasoned that "the acts of the master and crew, in cases of this sort, bind the interest of the owner of the ship, whether he be innocent or guilty; and he impliedly submits to whatever the law denounces as a forfeiture attached to the ship by reason of their unlawful or wanton wrongs." . . . Like the guilty-property fiction, this theory of vicarious liability is premised on the idea that the owner has been negligent. . . . We conclude, therefore, that forfeiture generally and statutory in rem forfeiture in particular historically have been understood, at least in part, as punishment.

We turn next to consider whether forfeitures under 21 U.S.C. §§881(a)(4) and (a)(7) are properly considered punishment today. We find nothing in these provisions or their legislative history to contradict the historical understanding of forfeiture as punishment. Unlike traditional forfeiture statutes, §§881(a)(4) and (a)(7) expressly provide an "innocent owner" defense. . . . These exemptions serve to focus the provisions on the culpability of the owner in a way that makes them look more like punishment, not less. . . .

The legislative history of §881 confirms the punitive nature of these provisions. When it added subsection (a)(7) to §881 in 1984, Congress recognized "that the traditional criminal sanctions of fine and imprisonment are inadequate to deter or punish the enormously profitable trade in dangerous drugs." It characterized the forfeiture of real property as "a powerful deterrent." . . .

The Government argues that §§881(a)(4) and (a)(7) are not punitive but, rather, should be considered remedial in two respects. First, they remove the "instruments" of the drug trade "thereby protecting the community from the threat of continued drug dealing." Second, the forfeited assets serve to compensate the Government for the expense of law enforcement activity and for its expenditure on societal problems such as urban blight, drug addiction, and other health concerns resulting from the drug trade.

In our view, neither argument withstands scrutiny. Concededly, we have recognized that the forfeiture of contraband itself may be characterized as remedial because it removes dangerous or illegal items from society. The Court, however, previously has rejected government's attempt to extend that reasoning to conveyances used to transport illegal liquor, [because there] is nothing even remotely criminal in possessing an automobile. The same, without question, is true of the properties involved here, and the Government's attempt to characterize these properties as "instruments" of the drug trade must meet the same fate.

The Government's second argument about the remedial nature of this forfeiture is no more persuasive. We previously have upheld the forfeiture of goods involved in customs violations as a reasonable form of liquidated damages. But the dramatic variations in the value of conveyances and real property forfeitable under §§881(a)(4) and (a)(7) undercut any similar argument with respect to those provisions. . . .

Fundamentally, even assuming that §§881(a)(4) and (a)(7) serve some remedial purpose, the Government's argument must fail. A civil sanction that cannot fairly be said solely to serve a remedial purpose, but rather can only be explained as also serving either retributive or deterrent purposes, is punishment, as we have come to understand the term. In light of the historical understanding of forfeiture as punishment, the clear focus of §§881(a)(4) and (a)(7) on the culpability of the owner, and the evidence that Congress understood those provisions as serving to deter and to punish, we cannot conclude that forfeiture under §§881(a)(4) and (a)(7) serves solely a remedial purpose. We therefore conclude that forfeiture under these provisions constitutes payment to a sovereign as punishment for some offense, and, as such, is subject to the limitations of the Eighth Amendment's Excessive Fines Clause.

Austin asks that we establish a multifactor test for determining whether a forfeiture is constitutionally "excessive." We decline that invitation. . . . Prudence dictates that we allow the lower courts to consider that question in the first instance. . . . The judgment of the Court of Appeals is reversed and the case is remanded to that court for further proceedings consistent with this opinion. It is so ordered.

SCALIA, J., concurring.

. . . However the theory may be expressed, it seems to me that this taking of lawful property must be considered, in whole or in part, punitive. Its purpose is not compensatory, to make someone whole for injury caused by unlawful use of the property. Punishment is being imposed, whether one quaintly considers its object to be the property itself, or more realistically regards its object to be the property's owner. . . . The Court apparently believes, however, that only actual culpability of the affected property owner can establish that a forfeiture provision is punitive, and sets out to establish that such culpability exists in the case of in rem forfeitures. [But we] have never held that the Constitution requires negligence, or any other degree of culpability, to support such forfeitures. . . .

That this forfeiture works as a fine raises the excessiveness issue, on which the Court remands. I agree that a remand is in order, but think it worth pointing out that on remand the excessiveness analysis must be different from that applicable to monetary fines and, perhaps, to in personam forfeitures. In the case of a monetary fine, the Eighth Amendment's origins in the English Bill of Rights, intended to limit the abusive penalties assessed against the king's opponents, demonstrate that the touchstone is value of the fine in relation to the offense. [T]he same is true for in personam forfeiture. . . .

Unlike monetary fines, statutory in rem forfeitures have traditionally been fixed, not by determining the appropriate value of the penalty in relation to the committed offense, but by determining what property has been "tainted" by unlawful use, to which issue the value of the property is irrelevant. Scales used to measure out unlawful drug sales, for example, are confiscable whether made of the purest gold or the basest metal. But an in rem forfeiture goes beyond the traditional limits that the Eighth Amendment permits if it applies to property that cannot properly be regarded as an instrumentality of the offense — the building, for example, in which an isolated drug sale happens to occur. Such a confiscation would be an excessive fine. The question is not how much the confiscated property is worth, but whether the confiscated property has a close enough relationship to the offense. . . .

‖ *Kansas Constitution Art. 15, §9* ‖

A homestead to the extent of . . . one acre within the limits of an incorporated town or city, occupied as a residence by the family of the owner, together with all improvements on the same, shall be exempted from forced sale under any process of law, and shall not be alienated without the joint consent of husband and wife. . . .

‖ *Philadelphia Police Department Directive 102* ‖

. . . The Police Department has established the following minimal value guidelines for seizure under Drug Forfeiture Laws:

Currency	$1,000	Vehicles	$2,500
Jewelry	$5,000	Aircraft, Vessels	$5,000
Real Estate	$10,000	Other Property	$1,000

PROBLEM 10-4.   HIGH ROLLERS

The government seeks forfeiture of the $150,000 Miami residence of Emilio and Yolanda Delio because it was used in an illegal gambling operation. Emilio Delio is an 80-year-old wheelchair-bound man residing at the property with his 66-year-old wife, Yolanda. Emilio and Yolanda own the property jointly. Their adult children also reside at the house.

Mr. Delio conducted a poker game at his home, involving some of his relatives and associates, on Wednesday nights. Government agents observed poker games at the house on five occasions between September 12 and October 10. Witnesses later said that the poker games were held at the house on a regular basis. The government charged Delio and other members of the family with directing a gambling operation and obtained criminal convictions against Emilio and three other participants (including one of Emilio's sons). The statute applied only to gambling businesses (1) owned or directed by five or more persons, (2) remaining in "substantially continuous operation" for more than 30 days, (3) with a gross revenue of $2,000 in any single day. In the separate civil forfeiture proceedings, the government seeks summary judgment.

Will the government obtain forfeiture of this property? How should the "excessiveness" of this fine be measured? Compare United States v. One Single Family Residence at 18755 North Bay Road, Miami, 13 F.3d 1493 (11th Cir. 1994).

NOTES

1. *Excessive fines and forfeitures: majority position.* The *Austin* opinion left for other courts the task of deciding how to measure the excessiveness of a forfeiture under the Eighth Amendment. The lower federal courts developed a proportionality test that weighs the severity of the offense, the harshness of the sanction, and the culpability of the claimant. Then the Supreme Court returned to the question of what standard to use in measuring the excessiveness of a forfeiture in United States v. Bajakajian, 524 U.S. 321 (1998).

Bajakajian was waiting in the Los Angeles airport to board an international flight when a customs inspector approached him and told him that he was required to report all cash in excess of $10,000 in his possession or baggage. Bajakajian lied about the amount of cash he was holding; cash-sniffing dogs indicated the presence of currency in his luggage, and customs inspectors found $357,144. Bajakajian pleaded guilty to the currency reporting offense and elected to have a bench trial on the forfeiture. The trial judge found that the funds were not connected to any other crime and that Bajakajian was transporting the money to repay a lawful debt; he held that forfeiture of the entire amount was constitutionally excessive and reduced the forfeiture to $15,000.

The Supreme Court held that the forfeiture was a punishment for purposes of the Excessive Fines Clause because the statute authorized an in personam forfeiture that applied only to the property of a person who willfully fails to report the cash. The Court then described the proper method for a court to use in determining whether a forfeiture is excessive:

> [There are two considerations] that we find particularly relevant. The first . . . is that judgments about the appropriate punishment for an offense belong in the first instance to the legislature. The second is that any judicial determination regarding the gravity of a particular criminal offense will be inherently imprecise. Both of these principles counsel against requiring strict proportionality between the amount of a punitive forfeiture and the gravity of a criminal offense, and we therefore adopt the standard of gross disproportionality articulated in our Cruel and Unusual Punishments Clause precedents. See Solem v. Helm, 463 U.S. 277 (1983); Rummel v. Estelle, 445 U.S. 263 (1980).
>
> In applying this standard, the district courts in the first instance, and the courts of appeals, reviewing the proportionality determination de novo, must compare the amount of the forfeiture to the gravity of the defendant's offense. If the amount of the forfeiture is grossly disproportional to the gravity of the defendant's offense, it is unconstitutional.
>
> Under this standard, the forfeiture of respondent's entire $357,144 would violate the Excessive Fines Clause. Respondent's crime was solely a reporting offense. It was permissible to transport the currency out of the country so long as he reported it. . . . Furthermore, as the District Court found, respondent's violation was unrelated to any other illegal activities. The money was the proceeds of legal activity and was to be used to repay a lawful debt. Whatever his other vices, respondent does not fit into the class of persons for whom the statute was principally designed: He is not a money launderer, a drug trafficker, or a tax evader. And under the Sentencing Guidelines, the maximum sentence that

could have been imposed on respondent was six months, while the maximum fine was $5,000. . . .

The harm that respondent caused was also minimal. Failure to report his currency affected only one party, the Government, and in a relatively minor way. There was no fraud on the United States, and respondent caused no loss to the public fisc. Had his crime gone undetected, the Government would have been deprived only of the information that $357,144 had left the country. . . . Comparing the gravity of respondent's crime with the $357,144 forfeiture the Government seeks, we conclude that such a forfeiture would be grossly disproportional to the gravity of his offense.

The states have assumed that the Excessive Fines Clause of the Eighth Amendment applies to them. Like the lower federal courts, many high state courts seem content for now to ask trial judges to consider a range of factors in judging the excessiveness of fines, including the value of the property, the amount of the illicit transaction, and the physical and temporal extent of involvement between the property and the crime. Commonwealth v. Fint, 940 S.W.2d 896 (Ky. 1997); State v. Hill, 635 N.E.2d 1248 (Ohio 1994).

2. *Instrumentalities versus proceeds.*   Should the proceeds of crimes be subject to a proportionality test at all? What about the property offered in exchange for illicit drugs? See United States v. 15,538 Panulirus Argus Lobster Tails, 834 F. Supp. 385 (S.D. Fla. 1993) (contraband forfeited will always be proportional to crime committed). Suppose that a government agent posing as a buyer had first approached Austin in a public park and had proposed that they complete their transaction in the privacy of Austin's shop? If the government influences the choice of property that will facilitate a crime, should the property still be forfeited?

3. *Punitive versus remedial label.*   Why was Justice Blackmun so intent on demonstrating that the forfeiture in *Austin* was individual punishment? Justice Scalia and three other justices did not agree that all forfeitures involve some type of punishment. What is at stake in this argument over the label "punishment"? Will the holding in this case apply also to statutes containing no innocent owner defense?

4. *Forfeiture and criminal sentencing.*   Civil forfeiture sometimes takes place after the owner has been convicted and sentenced for a crime in a separate proceeding. If the offender was fined or otherwise suffered a loss of property during the criminal process, should this reduce the amount of property subject to civil forfeiture? In other words, should proportionality analysis account for related criminal sanctions? See Sandra Guerra, Reconciling Federal Asset Forfeitures and Drug Offense Sentencing, 78 Minn. L. Rev. 805 (1994) (urging Congress and courts to factor amount of forfeited property into criminal sentence).

5. *Exempt property.*   Residences seem to create the most difficult forfeiture cases for the government. Homestead property is exempt from forfeiture under some state constitutions and statutes, even though it has a clear connection to the commission of a crime and even though its forfeiture would be proportionate to the crime. State courts have vigorously enforced exceptions for homestead property.

The purpose of the homestead exemption has been described broadly as being to protect the family, and to provide for it a refuge from misfortune, without any requirement that the misfortune arise from a financial debt. [The homestead protections] create no personal qualifications touching the moral character of the resident nor do they undertake to exclude the vicious, the criminal, or the immoral from the benefits so provided.

Butterworth v. Caggiano, 605 So. 2d 56, 60 (Fla. 1992). Does the exemption of a home used to commit a crime further the family security that the drafters of the homestead exemptions hoped to achieve? Cf. Unif. Controlled Substances Act §§505(c)(3), (d) (1994) (homestead exemptions). Should a homestead exemption apply to any home, regardless of size and value? Would the same logic apply to a residence purchased with assets obtained through criminal activity? The federal government is not bound by such limitations in state law, even when seeking forfeiture of property within the state. Furthermore, the federal government offers to adopt the forfeiture of property seized during investigations by state law enforcers. In light of the federal adoption alternative, are the homestead exemptions under state law now dead letters?

The Philadelphia Police Department directive indicates that there is some forfeitable property that police and prosecutors will not bother to obtain. Although covered by the statute, as a practical matter such property is immune from forfeiture. Why would law enforcement agencies decline to pursue a small amount of property even when it is clearly within the coverage of the forfeiture statute? Some state statutes also exempt certain property from forfeiture if the criminal activity is relatively insignificant. For instance, a South Carolina statute exempts vehicles from forfeiture if they transport less than ten grams of cocaine or one pound of marijuana. S.C. Code §44-53-520(a)(6). Some police department rules require officers to have higher levels of certainty about the forfeitability of property when the property value is small.

2.   *Procedures for Resolving Forfeitures*

The government may begin forfeiture proceedings in several ways. It might simply file a civil complaint against either the property (in rem) or the owner (in personam). The government might also choose criminal forfeiture proceedings, which begin as part of the criminal action, with the final forfeiture hearing occurring after conviction. In criminal forfeiture cases the government must prove beyond a reasonable doubt that the defendant committed the crime (or it must obtain a guilty plea reflecting such a conclusion). Further findings are also necessary to show the relationship between the property at issue and the crime of conviction. In most states, civil forfeiture is far more common than criminal forfeiture.

Judges and juries do not often resolve civil forfeitures; instead, most forfeitures are handled administratively. After a government attorney sends notice to all interested parties, the property owners might choose not to contest the forfeiture. For forfeitures below a designated dollar amount, the government can then take possession of the property through an uncontested administrative forfeiture without any judicial proceedings at all.

Because the property owner might attempt to dispose of the disputed property before the government can take possession, the government often seizes or arrests the property at the beginning of the civil proceedings. The government may take physical possession of a movable asset such as a vehicle; it may ask a financial institution to freeze an account. For real property, the government often files a notice of lis pendens against the property; in a few cases, it takes actual possession of the property and renegotiates the rental arrangements with residents on the property. For some ongoing businesses seized, the government continues to operate the business and collect the revenue pending the final forfeiture determination.

No property may be seized or arrested for purposes of forfeiture unless the government has probable cause to believe it is subject to forfeiture. Probable cause can be demonstrated in different ways. Most often, the government arrests the property after obtaining a warrant in an ex parte hearing. An adversarial probable cause hearing takes place after the seizure. Before real property can be seized, however, the person with a claim to the property must be given notice and an opportunity to be heard. United States v. James Daniel Good Real Property, 510 U.S. 43, 44, 58, 62 (1993) ("Because real property cannot abscond, the court's jurisdiction can be preserved without prior seizure. . . . Sale of the property can be prevented by filing a notice of lis pendens. [B]ased upon the importance of the private interests at risk and the absence of countervailing Government needs, we hold that the seizure of real property . . . is not one of those extraordinary instances that justify the postponement of notice and hearing.").

Once the government has frozen the property it hopes to obtain through forfeiture, any claimant may file a bond, hire an attorney, and contest the validity of the forfeiture. If the claimant loses the judicial challenge, she forfeits the value of the bond along with the property in dispute. The stated purpose of the bond is to reimburse the government for expenses incurred in litigating a "frivolous" forfeiture action. Does the bond requirement explain why the great majority of forfeiture cases are never challenged in court? Or do most forfeitures go unchallenged because the owners have no realistic prospect of prevailing in court? One of the most important features of the Civil Asset Forfeiture Reform Act of 2000, P.L. 106-185 (codified at 18 U.S.C. §983(a)(2)(E)), was its elimination of the bond requirement for parties challenging a forfeiture in federal court. The Act does not change the procedure in state court.

Forfeiture statutes take various positions on the relevant burden of proof and standard of proof. Consider the following constitutional decision on the subject.

	Department of Law Enforcement v.	
	Real Property	
	588 So. 2d 957 (Fla. 1991)	

BARKETT, J.

[We hold today that the Florida Contraband Forfeiture Act] is facially constitutional provided that it is applied consistent with the minimal due process requirements of the Florida Constitution as set forth in this opinion. Charles De-Carlo was arrested on drug trafficking charges on May 15, 1990, stemming from a reverse sting operation conducted by [the] Florida Department of Law Enforcement (FDLE) and the Levy County Sheriff's Department. On May 16, the state initiated forfeiture proceedings in circuit court against [a 60-acre tract of land, part of which includes an extension of an airstrip; 420 acres subdivided for mobile home sites and 300 permanent residences; and a personal residence and property, including garages and sheds].

Based solely on an affidavit executed by an FDLE special agent, the circuit court on May 16 issued warrants to seize the aforementioned properties. The state that day also filed a notice of lis pendens against those properties and petitioned for a rule to show cause why the properties should not be forfeited. . . . The claimants moved to dismiss the petitions on constitutional grounds. . . .

The basic due process guarantee of the Florida Constitution provides that "[n]o person shall be deprived of life, liberty or property without due process of law." Art. I, §9, Fla. Const. . . . Procedural due process serves as a vehicle to ensure fair treatment through the proper administration of justice where substantive rights are at issue. Procedural due process under the Florida Constitution guarantees to every citizen the right to have that course of legal procedure which has been established in our judicial system for the protection and enforcement of private rights. It contemplates that the defendant shall be given fair notice and afforded a real opportunity to be heard and defend in an orderly procedure, before judgment is rendered against him. . . .

The process provided in the Act [as amended in 1989] enables the state to seize property — whether real or personal — "which has been or is being used" to commit one of the enumerated offenses, or "in, upon or by means of which" any enumerated violation "has taken or is taking place." . . . After seizure, the state must "promptly proceed" against the property "by rule to show cause in the circuit court," and may have the property forfeited "upon producing due proof" that the property was being used in violation of the Act. If the state does not initiate proceedings within 90 days after the seizure, the claimant may maintain an action to recover the property. . . . Owners may raise a defense only after the property has been seized, and they must bear the burden in forfeiture proceedings of proving that they neither knew, nor should have known after a reasonable inquiry, that the property was being used or was likely to be used to commit an enumerated crime. Lienholders who can establish their perfected interests also may raise a defense only after seizure, and they bear the same burden as property owners plus an additional burden of proving that they did not consent to having the property used to commit a crime. At some point, the court is to issue a "final order of forfeiture" perfecting title in the seizing agency relating back to the date of seizure. Legal title to the property, or proceeds derived from the property after satisfaction of bona fide liens, are then transferred to [a specified agency or fund].

The Act raises numerous constitutional concerns that touch upon many substantive and procedural rights protected by the Florida Constitution. In construing the Act, we note that forfeitures are considered harsh exactions, and as a general rule they are not favored either in law or equity. Therefore, this Court has long followed a policy that it must strictly construe forfeiture statutes. Strict construction, however, may clash with the traditional judicial policy that all doubts as to the validity of a statute are to be resolved in favor of constitutionality where reasonably possible. . . .

The Act provides that after the property is first seized, the state must file a petition for a rule to show cause in the circuit court, and upon producing due proof that the property was used in violation of the Act, the court shall issue a final order of forfeiture vesting legal title in the appropriate agency under the Act. However, that is the sum total of direction given by the Act. The Act does not set out any procedures for filing the petition or issuing the rule to show cause, except that a rule shall issue upon the showing of "due proof." The Act does not address any requirements for filing the petition; which procedural rules should apply to control the litigation; what standard and burden of proof is "due" for issuance of the rule; whether a trial — with or without a jury — is required to decide the merits of the action once the rule has been issued; what standard and burden of proof apply in deciding the ultimate issue, including defenses; and whether and how property is to be divided or partitioned to ensure that only the "guilty" property is forfeited. . . .

It is now well settled that the ultimate issue of forfeiture must be decided by jury trial unless claimants waive that right. That substantive right is also subsumed within article I, section 9 of the Florida Constitution. However, the issue of standard and burden of proof has not been previously addressed by this Court. The state argues that the agency seeking forfeiture need establish its case by at most a preponderance of the evidence, whereas the claimants argue that the constitution requires proof beyond a reasonable doubt, or alternatively, by clear and convincing evidence. Case law reflects no uniformity in this state as to the appropriate burden and standard of proof.

We conclude that the state has the burden of proof at trial, which should be by no less than clear and convincing evidence. The state and the decisions on which it relies fail to recognize the significance of the constitutionally protected rights at issue and the impact forfeiture has on those rights. In forfeiture proceedings the state impinges on basic constitutional rights of individuals who may never have been formally charged with any civil or criminal wrongdoing. This Court has consistently held that the constitution requires substantial burdens of proof where state action may deprive individuals of basic rights. For example, when an individual is charged with a crime, the government cannot deprive that person of life, liberty, or property unless it carries the burden of proof beyond every reasonable doubt as to each essential element. In noncriminal contexts [such as termination of parental rights, termination of an incompetent patient's life support, defamation suits brought by public figures, or establishment of land ownership through adverse possession], this Court has held that constitutionally protected individual rights may not be impinged with a showing of less than clear and convincing evidence.

Accordingly, "due proof" under the Act constitutionally means that the government may not take an individual's property in forfeiture proceedings unless it proves, by no less than clear and convincing evidence, that the property being forfeited was used in the commission of a crime. Lack of knowledge of the holder of an interest in the property that the property was being employed in criminal activity is a defense to forfeiture, which, if established by a preponderance of the evidence, defeats the forfeiture action as to that property interest. . . .

This Court is obliged and authorized to establish rules to enforce the Florida Constitution and to administer the courts of this state. Although we are concerned with the multitude of procedural deficiencies in the Act, the procedures described above are required to satisfy due process and are not inconsistent with the language and intent of the Act. We conclude that the Act can be reasonably construed as constitutional provided that it is applied consistent with the due process requirements summarized in this opinion.

Turning to the facts of this case, it is clear that the state did not comply with due process: It seized real property, including residential property, prior to giving the claimants any notice or opportunity to be heard. Accordingly, we affirm the result reached by the [lower] court in dismissing the forfeiture action. . . .

NOTES

1. *Burden of proof: majority position.*   It is most common for civil forfeiture statutes to place the burden of proof on the state to demonstrate that the property is forfeitable; the claimant then has the burden of proof to demonstrate that any exemptions or exceptions apply. The federal government and more than 30 states allocate the burden in this way. Roughly a dozen other states follow a different approach to the burden of proof: After the prosecution establishes probable cause to believe that property is forfeitable, the claimant carries the burden of persuasion and must show that the property is not forfeitable. Court challenges to the constitutionality of this burden of proof have mostly failed.

In the federal system, the Civil Asset Forfeiture Reform Act of 2000 changed the burden of proof in civil forfeiture. Before this amendment to the federal statutes, the burden of proof on the question of forfeitability shifted to a claimant after the government showed probable cause to believe that the property was forfeitable. Would you expect this statutory amendment to lead to a different outcome in many cases? Will this amendment change more outcomes than the elimination of the bond requirement (also a part of the Civil Asset Forfeiture Reform Act)?

Civil forfeiture statutes commonly include a provision creating a "presumption of forfeitability" for certain property, such as large amounts of currency found near narcotics. This presumption effectively shifts the burden of proof back to the claimant. Is this feature of the asset forfeiture laws likely to survive a court ruling that requires the government to carry the burden of proof in forfeiture proceedings?

2. *Standard of proof: majority position.*   In more than 30 states, civil forfeiture statutes require a party to establish facts by a preponderance of the evidence. For *criminal* forfeiture actions, which are resolved after a criminal conviction for the underlying crime, the government must prove the elements of the crime beyond a reasonable doubt. But after conviction, in the sentencing phase, the government usually must establish the forfeitability of the property only by a preponderance of the evidence rather than beyond a reasonable doubt. See 21 U.S.C. §853(d). Clear and convincing evidence is the government's standard of proof in the civil forfeiture statutes of about a half-dozen states. See Minn. Stat. §609.531(6a)(a). A handful require proof beyond a reasonable doubt for some civil forfeitures, e.g., Neb. Rev. Stat. §28-431(4). Why would a prosecutor ever use a civil forfeiture statute that requires proof beyond a reasonable doubt?

The Florida decision in the *Real Property* case was unusual in requiring a particular burden of proof and standard of proof as a matter of constitutional law. The Florida constitution forbids one of the branches of government from invading the province of another. Did the court invade the province of the legislature with its decision in *Real Property*? Or did it instead create law within its area of special expertise — procedural fairness — at the implicit invitation of the legislature? The Florida legislature later amended the statute dealing with civil forfeiture actions, without changing the "due proof" language relating to the procedure at trial.

3. *Juries.* Most state courts have concluded that their state statutes or constitutions require a jury trial for civil asset forfeiture proceedings. The relevant constitutional provision often protects the right to jury trial in any action recognized at common law at the time the state first adopted a constitution. Since civil in rem forfeitures were common law actions available during the relevant time period, jury trial is still available. See, e.g., Idaho Department of Law Enforcement v. Real Property, 885 P.2d 381 (Idaho 1994). About a dozen states, however, have reached the opposite conclusion. Federal courts have concluded that the Seventh Amendment requires jury trial for in rem forfeitures on the question of forfeitability. In practice, juries do not hear many civil asset forfeiture cases, in part because claimants rarely exercise their right to a jury trial and because the rules of civil procedure allow the government to move for summary judgment. When these motions succeed, as they often do, the court disposes of the case before it reaches a jury.

4. *Counsel fees from frozen assets.* In civil forfeiture proceedings, there is no federal constitutional right to appointed counsel. The U.S. Supreme Court in Caplin and Drysdale, Chartered v. United States, 491 U.S. 617 (1989), concluded that the right to counsel does not prevent the government from freezing assets necessary to hire criminal defense counsel so long as the assets are potentially subject to forfeiture. Most state courts agree. See State v. Nine Thousand One Hundred Ninety-Nine Dollars, 791 P.2d 213 (Utah 1990).

Constitutions are not the only source of law that determines whether forfeitable funds may be used for attorneys' fees. Some state forfeiture statutes explicitly allow a court to order the release of some frozen assets to permit a defendant to hire an attorney. New York statutes allow the release of such funds to hire an attorney for representation during civil forfeiture proceedings, criminal forfeiture proceedings, or related criminal proceedings. See N.Y. C.P.L.R. 1312(4); N.Y. Crim. Proc. Law §480.05(3) (allows payment for "bona fide fees" for legal services).

The Civil Asset Forfeiture Reform Act of 2000 expands access to attorneys for claimants of property being subject to civil asset forfeiture proceedings in federal court. The federal government now provides legal counsel for indigent claimants of property that the government is attempting to seize, along with attorneys' fees for winning claimants. Would expanded access to fees in civil proceedings be enough to convince private defense counsel to accept a forfeiture case?

PROBLEM 10-5. JOINT OWNERS

Tina and John Bennis jointly owned an 11-year-old Pontiac. Detroit police arrested John after observing him engaged in a sexual act with a prostitute in the automobile while it was parked on a Detroit city street. He was convicted of gross indecency. The state then filed a civil action to have the car declared a public nuisance (and therefore forfeited) under Michigan statutes.

Tina defended against the forfeiture of her interest in the car on the ground that she did not know her husband would use the car to violate Michigan's indecency law. The circuit court rejected this argument and declared the car a public nuisance. Even though the statute gave the judge the authority to award half of the sale proceeds to Tina (as an innocent titleholder) and the other half to the state, the judge refused to divide the proceeds. The judge noted that the couple owned another automobile and that the Pontiac was worth only $600. Is there any constitutional bar to the forfeiture of the car under these circumstances? Compare Bennis v. Michigan, 516 U.S. 442 (1996).

NOTES

1. *Innocent owners under federal statutes.*   Under 18 U.S.C. §983(d)(2)(A), an innocent property owner can reclaim property that might otherwise be forfeited if the owner can show that he "did not know of the conduct giving rise to forfeiture [or] upon learning of the conduct giving rise to the forfeiture, did all that reasonably could be expected under the circumstances to terminate such use of the property." The property owner may establish his "innocence" even if he obtains the property after the previous owner commits a crime that makes the property forfeitable. The U.S. Supreme Court, in United States v. 92 Buena Vista Avenue, Rumson, New Jersey, 507 U.S. 111 (1993), decided that the unqualified language of the innocent owner provision (it applies to any "owner") precludes any per se bar against using the defense, even for persons who obtain the property after it becomes forfeitable. Under what circumstances can persons who were paid with illegal proceeds for providing goods or services to drug traffickers claim to be innocent owners?

2. *Innocent owners under state statutes.*   While most state forfeiture statutes do provide innocent owner defenses, a few statutes without such a defense remain in place. The elements of the defense vary from state to state. Compare the two major model statutes, the Forfeiture Reform Act (FRA), of the President's Commission on Model State Drug Laws, and the Uniform Controlled Substances Act (UCSA), of the National Conference of Commissioners on Uniform State Laws. When it comes to an owner who acquires property interests before the property becomes forfeitable, the FRA requires that the owner either "did not and could not reasonably have known" about the likelihood of conduct making the property forfeitable or "acted reasonably to prevent the conduct." Section 8(a). The UCSA requires that the owner either "did not know the conduct would occur" or acted "in a manner the owner reasonably believed appropriate to prevent" the wrongful conduct. Sections 505(b), (c). On which drafting commission do you think prosecutors had more influence? Would Tina Bennis have been able to meet either test?

3. *Constitutions and innocent owners.*   There is no federal constitutional bar to the forfeiture of an innocent owner's property when the forfeiture is allowed by state or federal statute. In Bennis v. Michigan, 516 U.S. 442 (1996), the basis

for Problem 10-5, the Supreme Court decided that due process was not violated by the forfeiture of an innocent owner's property without compensation: A "long and unbroken line of cases holds that an owner's interest in property may be forfeited by reason of the use to which the property is put even though the owner did not know that it was to be put to such use." The Court said that forfeiture of property — even an innocent owner's property — serves a deterrent purpose by preventing further illicit use of the property and by making illegal behavior unprofitable.

In an oft-cited case, State v. Richards, 301 S.W.2d 597 (Tex. 1957), the Texas Supreme Court upheld the forfeiture of a pickup truck when the owner lent it to an acquaintance who (unbeknownst to the truck's owner) was carrying two Dolophine pills in his shirt pocket. A dissenting justice declared that the "right to acquire and own property" is a "natural right" and that forfeiture interferes with this right. Many critics of forfeiture argue that the practice should remain limited because forfeiture is based on the "legal fiction" that the property reverts to the government as soon as the crime is committed. What is a legal fiction? Aren't all property rights recognized and enforced through a fiction of sorts? Is there a difference between a government declaration that a private party owns certain property and a government declaration that property used to commit a crime automatically belongs to the government? Does your answer to these questions depend on your views of the source of individual rights?

4. *Multiple owners.*   Often the criminal offender's interest in the property is less valuable than the innocent owner's interest, as when the offender borrows or leases the property. In other cases, the innocent owner and the offender are equal co-owners of the property in question. In that situation, should the property become forfeitable even if the innocent owner qualifies in every respect for the statutory defense? If so, what is the proper remedy? Forced sale of the property followed by an equal split of the proceeds? Should the innocent owner have to pay her share of the litigation costs? A number of statutes provide special protection to spouses who own forfeitable property jointly with wrongdoers. See Wash. Rev. Code §69.50.505(d) (innocent spouse with community property interest can block forfeiture). Should a formal property interest be necessary before this protection applies? See Sandra Guerra, Family Values? The Family as an Innocent Victim of Civil Drug Asset Forfeiture, 81 Cornell L. Rev. 343 (1996).

5. *The innocent tenant.*   Under section 715 of New York's Real Property Actions and Proceedings Law, the owner of any real property "used or occupied in whole or in part . . . for any illegal trade, business or manufacture" may bring expedited civil proceedings to evict the tenant. If the landlord refuses to evict the tenant, the district attorney may bring a civil action against the tenant and recover litigation expenses from the landlord. See Peter Finn, The Manhattan District Attorney's Narcotics Eviction Program (National Institute of Justice, NCJ 153146, May 1995). If the statute itself contains no provision for an innocent co-tenant, what charging limitations (if any) should the district attorney employ? Should the D.A. evict any tenant (say, a grandmother) who "knew or should have known" about illegal activity of another tenant (say, a grandson)? If "reasonable efforts" to stop the illegal activity are enough to avoid eviction, how much effort is considered reasonable? Pleading with the grandson to stop the illegal activity? Reporting it to the police? Cf. Department of Housing and Urban

Development v. Rucker, 535 U.S. 125 (2002) (Anti-Drug Abuse Act required lease terms that gave local public housing authorities discretion to terminate lease when any member of household or guest engaged in drug-related activity).

6. *Bypassing the criminal process.* One of the virtues of asset forfeiture from the perspective of law enforcement is its efficiency. It allows the government to remove dangerous or illicit goods from circulation quickly, and as a practical matter it allows for some punishment of guilty property owners without having to clear the hurdles of the criminal process. Elsewhere in this chapter we have considered other legal procedures that accomplish some of the objectives of criminal sentences without going through the criminal process. Do these procedures differ from one another in important ways? Do some present greater potential for abuse by prosecutors or other law enforcement officials?

D. CIVIL AND ADMINISTRATIVE REMEDIES

Rather than pursuing criminal charges against wrongdoers, government enforcers sometimes go to court to obtain civil sanctions such as fines or injunctions. Or they make their claims against the wrongdoer in administrative proceedings, without involving the judicial branch at all. Under what circumstances do government enforcers tend to ask for civil or administrative remedies rather than filing criminal charges? What are the risks for potential targets who face criminal and civil proceedings simultaneously?

|| *John Hudson v. United States* ||
522 U.S. 93 (1997)

REHNQUIST, C.J.

The Government administratively imposed monetary penalties and occupational debarment on petitioners for violation of federal banking statutes, and later criminally indicted them for essentially the same conduct. We hold that the Double Jeopardy Clause of the Fifth Amendment is not a bar to the later criminal prosecution because the administrative proceedings were civil, not criminal. . . .

During the early and mid-1980's, petitioner John Hudson was the chairman and controlling shareholder of the First National Bank of Tipton and the First National Bank of Hammon. During the same period, petitioner Jack Rackley was president of Tipton and a member of the board of directors of Hammon, and petitioner Larry Baresel was a member of the board of directors of both Tipton and Hammon. An examination of Tipton and Hammon led the Office of the Comptroller of the Currency to conclude that petitioners had used their bank positions to arrange a series of loans to third parties in violation of various federal banking statutes and regulations. According to the OCC, those loans, while nominally made to third parties, were in reality made to Hudson in order to enable him to redeem bank stock that he had pledged as collateral on defaulted loans.

On February 13, 1989, OCC issued a "Notice of Assessment of Civil Money Penalty." The notice alleged that petitioners had violated 12 U.S.C. §§84(a)(1) and 375b and 12 CFR §§31.2(b) and 215.4(b) by causing the banks with which they were associated to make loans to nominee borrowers in a manner that unlawfully allowed Hudson to receive the benefit of the loans. The notice also alleged that the illegal loans resulted in losses to Tipton and Hammon of almost $900,000 and contributed to the failure of those banks. However, the notice contained no allegation of any harm to the Government as a result of petitioners' conduct. After taking into account the size of the financial resources and the good faith of petitioners, the gravity of the violations, the history of previous violations and other matters . . . OCC assessed penalties of $100,000 against Hudson and $50,000 each against Rackley and Baresel. On August 31, 1989, OCC also issued a "Notice of Intention to Prohibit Further Participation" against each petitioner. These notices, which were premised on the identical allegations that formed the basis for the previous notices, informed petitioners that OCC intended to bar them from further participation in the conduct of any insured depository institution.

In October 1989, petitioners resolved the OCC proceedings against them by each entering into a "Stipulation and Consent Order." These consent orders provided that Hudson, Baresel, and Rackley would pay assessments of $16,500, $15,000, and $12,500 respectively. In addition, each petitioner agreed not to participate in any manner in the affairs of any banking institution without the written authorization of the OCC and all other relevant regulatory agencies.

In August 1992, petitioners were indicted in the Western District of Oklahoma in a 22-count indictment on charges of conspiracy, misapplication of bank funds, and making false bank entries. The violations charged in the indictment rested on the same lending transactions that formed the basis for the prior administrative actions brought by OCC. Petitioners moved to dismiss the indictment on double jeopardy grounds [and the trial court granted the motion].

The Double Jeopardy Clause provides that no "person [shall] be subject for the same offence to be twice put in jeopardy of life or limb." We have long recognized that the Double Jeopardy Clause does not prohibit the imposition of all additional sanctions that could, in common parlance, be described as punishment. The Clause protects only against the imposition of multiple *criminal* punishments for the same offense, and then only when such occurs in successive proceedings.

Whether a particular punishment is criminal or civil is, at least initially, a matter of statutory construction. A court must first ask whether the legislature, in establishing the penalizing mechanism, indicated either expressly or impliedly a preference for one label or the other. Even in those cases where the legislature has indicated an intention to establish a civil penalty, we have inquired further whether the statutory scheme was so punitive either in purpose or effect as to transform what was clearly intended as a civil remedy into a criminal penalty.

In making this latter determination, the factors listed in Kennedy v. Mendoza-Martinez, 372 U.S. 144, 168-169 (1963), provide useful guideposts, including: (1) whether the sanction involves an affirmative disability or restraint; (2) whether it has historically been regarded as a punishment; (3) whether it comes into play only on a finding of scienter; (4) whether its operation will promote the traditional aims of punishment—retribution and deterrence; (5) whether the behavior to which it applies is already a crime; (6) whether an alternative purpose to which it may rationally be connected is assignable for it; and (7) whether it appears excessive in relation to the alternative purpose assigned. It is important to note, however, that these factors must be considered in relation to the statute on its face, and "only the clearest proof" will suffice to override legislative intent and transform what has been denominated a civil remedy into a criminal penalty.

Our opinion in United States v. Halper, 490 U.S. 435 (1989), marked the first time we applied the Double Jeopardy Clause to a sanction without first determining that it was criminal in nature. In that case, Irwin Halper was convicted of violating the criminal false claims statute based on his submission of 65 inflated Medicare claims each of which overcharged the Government by $9. He was sentenced to two years' imprisonment and fined $5,000. The Government then brought an action against Halper under the civil False Claims Act, 31 U.S.C. §§3729-3731. The remedial provisions of the False Claims Act provided that a violation of the Act rendered one "liable to the United States Government for a civil penalty of $2,000, an amount equal to 2 times the amount of damages the Government sustains because of the act of that person, and costs of the civil action." Given Halper's 65 separate violations of the Act, he appeared to be liable for a penalty of $130,000, despite the fact he actually defrauded the Government of less than $600.

[This Court held that a penalty of this magnitude would violate the Double Jeopardy Clause in light of Halper's previous criminal conviction. As the *Halper* Court saw it, any] sanction that was so overwhelmingly disproportionate to the injury caused that it could not "fairly be said *solely* to serve the remedial purpose" of compensating the Government for its loss, was thought to be explainable only as "serving either retributive or deterrent purposes."

The analysis applied by the *Halper* Court deviated from our traditional double jeopardy doctrine in two key respects. First, the *Halper* Court bypassed the threshold question: whether the successive punishment at issue is a "criminal" punishment. Instead, it focused on whether the sanction, regardless of whether it was civil or criminal, was so grossly disproportionate to the harm caused as to constitute "punishment." In so doing, the Court elevated a single *Kennedy* factor — whether the sanction appeared excessive in relation to its nonpunitive purposes — to dispositive status. But as we emphasized in *Kennedy* itself, no one factor should be considered controlling as they may often point in differing directions. The second significant departure in *Halper* was the Court's decision to assess the "character of the actual sanctions imposed," rather than, as *Kennedy* demanded, evaluating the "statute on its face" to determine whether it provided for what amounted to a criminal sanction. . . .

As subsequent cases have demonstrated, *Halper*'s test for determining whether a particular sanction is "punitive," and thus subject to the strictures of the Double Jeopardy Clause, has proved unworkable. We have since recognized that all civil penalties have some deterrent effect. See Department of Revenue of Montana v. Kurth Ranch, 511 U.S. 767, 777 n.14 (1994) [applying a *Kennedy*-like test before concluding that Montana's dangerous drug tax was "the functional equivalent of a successive criminal prosecution"]; United States v. Ursery, 518 U.S. 267, 284-285 (1996) [civil in rem forfeitures do not violate the Double

Jeopardy Clause]. If a sanction must be "solely" remedial (i.e., entirely nondeterrent) to avoid implicating the Double Jeopardy Clause, then no civil penalties are beyond the scope of the Clause.

[It] should be noted that some of the ills at which *Halper* was directed are addressed by other constitutional provisions. The Due Process and Equal Protection Clauses already protect individuals from sanctions which are downright irrational. The Eighth Amendment protects against excessive civil fines, including forfeitures. The additional protection afforded by extending double jeopardy protections to proceedings heretofore thought to be civil is more than offset by the confusion created by attempting to distinguish between "punitive" and "nonpunitive" penalties.

Applying traditional double jeopardy principles to the facts of this case, it is clear that the criminal prosecution of these petitioners would not violate the Double Jeopardy Clause. It is evident that Congress intended the OCC money penalties and debarment sanctions imposed for violations of 12 U.S.C. §§84 and 375b to be civil in nature. As for the money penalties, both §§93(b)(1) and 504(a), which authorize the imposition of monetary penalties for violations of §§84 and 375b respectively, expressly provide that such penalties are "civil." While the provision authorizing debarment contains no language explicitly denominating the sanction as civil, we think it significant that the authority to issue debarment orders is conferred upon the appropriate Federal banking agencies. That such authority was conferred upon administrative agencies is prima facie evidence that Congress intended to provide for a civil sanction.

[There] is little evidence, much less the clearest proof that we require, suggesting that either OCC money penalties or debarment sanctions are so punitive in form and effect as to render them criminal despite Congress' intent to the contrary. First, neither money penalties nor debarment has historically been viewed as punishment. We have long recognized that revocation of a privilege voluntarily granted, such as a debarment, "is characteristically free of the punitive criminal element." Helvering v. Mitchell, 303 U.S. 391, 399 (1938). . . .

Second, the sanctions imposed do not involve an "affirmative disability or restraint," as that term is normally understood. While petitioners have been prohibited from further participating in the banking industry, this is certainly nothing approaching the "infamous" punishment of imprisonment. Third, neither sanction comes into play "only" on a finding of scienter. The provisions under which the money penalties were imposed, 12 U.S.C. §§93(b) and 504, allow for the assessment of a penalty against any person "who violates" any of the underlying banking statutes, without regard to the violator's state of mind. "Good faith" is considered by OCC in determining the amount of the penalty to be imposed, but a penalty can be imposed even in the absence of bad faith. The fact that petitioners' "good faith" was considered in determining the amount of the penalty to be imposed in this case is irrelevant, as we look only to "the statute on its face" to determine whether a penalty is criminal in nature. Similarly, while debarment may be imposed for a "willful" disregard for the safety or soundness of an insured depository institution, willfulness is not a prerequisite to debarment; it is sufficient that the disregard for the safety and soundness of the institution was "continuing." §1818(e)(1)(C)(ii).

Fourth, the conduct for which OCC sanctions are imposed may also be criminal (and in this case formed the basis for petitioners' indictments). This fact is insufficient to render the money penalties and debarment sanctions criminally punitive, particularly in the double jeopardy context. See United States v. Dixon, 509 U.S. 688 (1993) (rejecting "same-conduct" test for double jeopardy purposes).

Finally, we recognize that the imposition of both money penalties and debarment sanctions will deter others from emulating petitioners' conduct, a traditional goal of criminal punishment. But the mere presence of this purpose is insufficient to render a sanction criminal, as deterrence may serve civil as well as criminal goals. For example, the sanctions at issue here, while intended to deter future wrongdoing, also serve to promote the stability of the banking industry. To hold that the mere presence of a deterrent purpose renders such sanctions "criminal" for double jeopardy purposes would severely undermine the Government's ability to engage in effective regulation of institutions such as banks.

In sum, there simply is very little showing . . . that OCC money penalties and debarment sanctions are criminal. The Double Jeopardy Clause is therefore no obstacle to their trial on the pending indictments, and it may proceed. . . .

STEVENS, J., concurring.

. . . As is evident from the first sentence of the Court's opinion, this is an extremely easy case. It has been settled since the decision in Blockburger v. United States, 284 U.S. 299 (1932), that the Double Jeopardy Clause is not implicated simply because a criminal charge involves "essentially the same conduct" for which a defendant has previously been punished. Unless a second proceeding involves the "same offense" as the first, there is no double jeopardy. The two proceedings at issue here involved different offenses that were not even arguably the same under *Blockburger*.

Under *Blockburger*'s "same-elements" test, two provisions are not the "same offense" if each contains an element not included in the other. The penalties imposed on the petitioners in 1989 were based on violations of 12 U.S.C. §§84(a)(1) and 375b and 12 CFR §§31.2(b) and 215.4(b). Each of these provisions required proof that extensions of credit exceeding certain limits were made, but did not require proof of an intent to defraud or the making of any false entries in bank records. The 1992 indictment charged violations of 18 U.S.C. §§371, 656, and 1005 and alleged a conspiracy to willfully misapply bank funds and to make false banking entries, as well as the making of such entries; none of those charges required proof that any lending limit had been exceeded. Thus, I think it would be difficult to find a case raising a double jeopardy claim that would be any easier to decide than this one. . . .

Despite my disagreement with the Court's decision to use this case as a rather lame excuse for writing a gratuitous essay about punishment, I do agree with its reaffirmation of the central holding of *Halper*, [which held] that sanctions imposed in civil proceedings constituted "punishment" barred by the Double Jeopardy Clause. Those holdings reconfirmed the settled proposition that the Government cannot use the "civil" label to escape entirely the Double Jeopardy Clause's command, as we have recognized for at least six decades. That proposition is extremely important because the States and the Federal Government have an enormous array of civil administrative sanctions at their disposal that are capable of being used to punish persons repeatedly for the same offense, violating the bedrock double jeopardy principle of finality. . . .

BREYER, J. concurring.

. . . I would not decide now that a court should evaluate a statute only "on its face," rather than assessing the character of the actual sanctions imposed. *Halper* involved an ordinary civil-fine statute that as normally applied would not have created any "double jeopardy" problem. It was not the statute itself, but rather the disproportionate relation between fine and conduct as the statute was applied in the individual case that led this Court, unanimously, to find that the "civil penalty" was, in those circumstances, a second "punishment" that consti-tuted double jeopardy. . . . It seems to me quite possible that a statute that pro-vides for a punishment that normally is civil in nature could nonetheless amount to a criminal punishment as applied in special circumstances. And I would not now hold to the contrary. . . .

NOTES

1. *Double jeopardy and civil sanctions: majority position.* If the government seeks a penalty in a civil proceeding, it can occur after a criminal conviction, be-fore a criminal conviction, or indeed in the absence of any criminal conviction or criminal charges. The possibility of facing two separate proceedings raises the concern that the government will pursue a second "punishment" for a crime if it is dissatisfied with the punishment after the first set of proceedings. Never-theless, in *Hudson* the U.S. Supreme Court decided that civil penalties usually do not constitute "punishment" for purposes of the Double Jeopardy Clause of the Eighth Amendment. As a result, there is no double jeopardy bar to the govern-ment's bringing both criminal charges and civil forfeiture proceedings based on the same conduct or transaction. See also United States v. Ursery, 518 U.S. 267 (1996) (civil in rem forfeiture proceedings are not punishment for double jeop-ardy purposes).

2. *Choice of proceedings.* While the government's ability to pursue both criminal and civil sanctions (or criminal fines and civil money penalties) is now clearly accepted, it was not always so. For an early survey of the issues, see Wal-ter Gellhorn, Administrative Prescription and Imposition of Penalties, 1970 Wash. L.Q. 265. Defendants might worry that the government will use civil pro-ceedings as an insurance policy against an unfavorable outcome in the criminal process. For instance, if the government fails to obtain a conviction or the court imposes a sentence unsatisfactory to the prosecutor, the government could try to obtain a more favorable outcome by pursuing civil charges. Can courts pre-vent this sort of manipulation by insisting that the civil proceedings commence before the verdict or sentence in the criminal case? See Mary M. Cheh, Consti-tutional Limits on Using Civil Remedies to Achieve Criminal Law Objectives: Understanding and Transcending the Criminal-Civil Law Distinction, 42 Hast-ings L.J. 1325 (1991); Kenneth Mann, Punitive Civil Sanctions: The Middle-ground Between Criminal and Civil Law, 101 Yale L.J. 1795 (1992). The govern-ment also might use the relatively broad discovery devices of civil litigation to get around the barriers built into discovery for criminal proceedings.

3. *The publicity alternative.* Consider this alternative to criminal proceed-ings: After the end of apartheid in South Africa, the government established the

Truth and Reconciliation Commission to create some accountability and public disclosure for many acts of public wrongdoing during the earlier era. The commission did not impose criminal sanctions, but its proceedings and findings received intense public attention. Perpetrators of apartheid crimes who did not appear before the commission could end up in front of a criminal court — and all perpetrators could still face criminal charges before an international or non-national tribunal. In what situations is intense public scrutiny and debate an acceptable alternative to criminal punishments? To what extent should a country be allowed to opt for forgiveness instead of criminal sanctions for serious offenses, such as apartheid, torture, or crimes against humanity?

   4. *Drug taxes.* A majority of states impose taxes on illegal drugs or on those who distribute them. The statutes typically require any possessor of a controlled substance to purchase "tax stamps" for each ounce of the controlled substance. Some of the drug tax statutes apply regardless of whether the owner of the controlled substance was ever arrested or convicted. In Department of Revenue of Montana v. Kurth Ranch, 511 U.S. 767 (1994), the Supreme Court held that such a drug tax might qualify as an additional "punishment" for conduct; the double jeopardy bar means that the tax cannot be used in conjunction with a criminal prosecution. The Court described the statute and its reasons as follows:

> Montana's Dangerous Drug Tax Act . . . imposes a tax "on the possession and storage of dangerous drugs," and expressly provides that the tax is to be "collected only after any state or federal fines or forfeitures have been satisfied." The tax is either 10 percent of the assessed market value of the drugs . . . or a specified amount depending on the drug ($100 per ounce for marijuana, for example, and $250 per ounce for hashish), whichever is greater. [At] the time of arrest law enforcement personnel shall complete the dangerous drug information report as required by the department and afford the taxpayer an opportunity to sign it. If the taxpayer refuses to do so, the law enforcement officer is required to file the form within 72 hours of the arrest. . . . The taxpayer has no obligation to file a return or to pay any tax unless and until he is arrested. . . .
>
> Whereas fines, penalties, and forfeitures are readily characterized as sanctions, taxes are typically different because they are usually motivated by revenue-raising rather than punitive purposes. Yet at some point, an exaction labeled as a tax approaches punishment, and our task is to determine whether Montana's drug tax crosses that line.
>
> We begin by noting that neither a high rate of taxation nor an obvious deterrent purpose automatically marks this tax a form of punishment. . . . A significant part of the assessment was more than eight times the drug's market value — a remarkably high tax. That the Montana legislature intended the tax to deter people from possessing marijuana is beyond question. . . .
>
> Other unusual features . . . set the Montana statute apart from most taxes. First, this so-called tax is conditioned on the commission of a crime. [The] assessment not only hinges on the commission of a crime, it also is exacted only after the taxpayer has been arrested for the precise conduct that gives rise to the tax obligation in the first place. . . . The Montana tax is exceptional for an additional reason. Although it purports to be a species of property tax — that is, a "tax on the possession and storage of dangerous drugs," — it is levied on goods that the taxpayer neither owns nor possesses when the tax is imposed. Indeed, the State presumably destroyed the contraband goods in this case before the tax on them was assessed.

Id. at 770, 778-783. The Court concluded that the imposition of the drug tax in Montana constituted "punishment" and therefore created a double jeopardy bar that prevented the state from bringing criminal charges for possession of drugs.

State tax provisions have withstood some, but not all, challenges under various provisions of state constitutions. The state courts have split when deciding whether their statutes violated the state or federal rules against double jeopardy. The statutes surviving a double jeopardy challenge are usually different from the Montana statute in *Kurth Ranch* because they provide for collection of the tax and punishment of violators even when there is no prosecution or conviction for other narcotics violations. See Covelli v. Commissioner of Revenue Services, 668 A.2d 699 (Conn. 1995).

5. *Driver's license.*   Persons who are arrested for driving while intoxicated often lose their driver's license in an administrative hearing and are convicted of a crime in separate criminal proceedings. The defendants sometimes claim that the two proceedings amount to double jeopardy. Such arguments have failed in about 30 states and have succeeded in almost 20 (mostly in the intermediate appellate courts). Compare State v. Young, 544 N.W.2d 808 (Neb. 1996) (no double jeopardy violation) with State v. Gustafson, 668 N.E.2d 435 (Ohio 1996) (double jeopardy violation). How might you argue that the loss of a driver's license is different from civil in rem forfeiture of assets? Should the legal analysis change if the government is threatening to remove some other form of license, such as a license to practice medicine or law?

= 11 =
‖ *Sentences Reconsidered* ‖

As discussed in detail in Chapter 2, many institutions and individuals have input into the sentences imposed on convicted offenders. We often think of this input as culminating in the decision of a sentencing judge. The realities of sentencing decision making, however, are far more dynamic, and many different players have the opportunity to reconsider sentencing choices made by other sentencing decision makers.

Some of the legal structures through which sentences are reconsidered involve the judiciary, as detailed in the first half of this chapter; others involve executive branch officials, as discussed in the second half. In all settings, the officials may reconsider not only specific sentencing outcomes but also some or all of the theoretical, policy-based, and legal arguments that influenced initial sentencing decisions. As you read this chapter, examine and question what are appropriate grounds for a court or an executive official to reconsider and potentially modify sentencing decisions. Also note the development of unique doctrines to reconsider death sentences.

A. JUDICIAL RECONSIDERATION OF SENTENCES

Judges are commonly viewed as central figures in making initial sentencing determinations. Yet, as we have seen throughout the book, many other institutions and individuals — legislatures, sentencing commissions, prosecutors, and probation officers — play a key role in determining what types of sentences judges are able to impose. Indeed, when a legislature enacts a mandatory sentencing provision, or when a sentencing commission establishes strict sentencing guidelines, the judiciary's role in determining initial sentences can seem more administrative than substantive.

While many structured sentencing reforms have led to institutions other than courts playing an increasingly larger part in initial sentencing decisions, other legal developments have increased the judiciary's role in the reconsideration of initial sentencing decisions. The judicial role in sentence reconsideration, especially through appeals and collateral review, is relatively new: Review of convictions and sentences were historically part of an appeal made to the sovereign — the governor or president. But no longer is such an appeal to the sovereign an offender's only avenue for relief. There are now elaborate legal structures and rules that establish means and mechanisms for offenders to obtain judicial review of their convictions and sentences.

1.   *Sentencing Judge*

Though sentencing judges are typically thought to make initial sentencing decisions, in many ways they always reconsider sentencing choices made by others. Whatever sentencing choices are initially made by legislatures, sentencing commissions, and prosecutors are inevitably reexamined and reassessed by a sentencing judge when she decides what specific sentence she can and should impose on a particular offender.

As the following case highlights, modern systems with defined sentencing rules present sentencing judges with opportunities to reconsider the appropriateness and the application of general sentencing rules in individual cases.

California v. Superior Court of San Diego County (Jesus Romero, Real Party in Interest)
917 P.2d 628 (Cal. 1996)

Werdegar, J.

Penal Code section 1385, subdivision (a), authorizes a trial court to dismiss a criminal action "in furtherance of justice" on its own motion. . . . This case raises the question whether a court may, on its own motion, strike prior felony conviction allegations in cases arising under the law known as "Three Strikes and You're Out." . . .

I.   Background

A.   *The Three Strikes Law*

The Three Strikes law consists of two, nearly identical statutory schemes designed to increase the prison terms of repeat felons. . . . In summary, both statutes have this effect: When a defendant is convicted of a felony, and it is pleaded and proved that he has committed one or more prior felonies defined as "violent" or "serious," sentencing proceeds under the Three Strikes law. Prior felonies qualifying as "serious" or "violent" are taken into account regardless of their age. The current felony need not be "violent" or "serious." If the defendant has only one qualifying prior felony conviction, the prescribed term of imprisonment . . . is twice the term otherwise provided as punishment for the current felony conviction. If the defendant has two or more prior qualifying felonies, the prescribed sentence is an indeterminate term of life imprisonment [with a minimum term before parole eligibility of] the greater of: (a) three times the term otherwise provided for the current conviction; (b) twenty-five years; or (c) the term required [under other statutes]. In sentencing, the court may not grant probation, suspend execution or imposition of sentence, divert the defendant, or commit the defendant to any facility other than state prison.

B. Facts

On June 3, 1994, the District Attorney of San Diego County filed an information in the superior court charging defendant Jesus Romero with possession of a controlled substance, namely 0.13 grams of cocaine base. The information also alleged defendant had previously been convicted of the following felonies on the dates indicated: second degree burglary on June 25, 1980; attempted burglary of an inhabited dwelling on November 16, 1984; first degree burglary of an inhabited dwelling on September 2, 1986; and possession of a controlled substance on April 6, 1992, and June 8, 1993.

Defendant's two prior serious felonies, namely burglary and attempted burglary of inhabited dwellings, made him eligible for a life sentence under the Three Strikes law. Without the prior felony conviction allegations, defendant's sentence would fall between one and six years. . . . Defendant pled not guilty. At a subsequent hearing, the court indicated its willingness to consider striking the prior felony conviction allegations if defendant changed his plea to guilty as charged on all counts. The prosecutor objected to that procedure, arguing the court had no power to dismiss prior felony allegations in a Three Strikes case unless the prosecutor asked the court to do so. The court disagreed [and] permitted defendant to change his plea and struck the prior felony conviction allegations. [The court] imposed a sentence of six years in state prison. . . .

II. DISCUSSION

The ultimate question before us is whether a trial court may dismiss prior felony conviction allegations in furtherance of justice on its own motion in a case brought under the Three Strikes law. In answering this question, two statutes are of central importance. The first is section 1385. It provides as follows:

> (a) The judge or magistrate may, either of his or her own motion or upon the application of the prosecuting attorney, and in the furtherance of justice, order an action to be dismissed. The reasons for the dismissal must be set forth in an order entered upon the minutes. . . .
> (b) This section does not authorize a judge to strike any prior conviction of a serious felony for purposes of enhancement of a sentence under Section 667.

[W]e have construed section 1385(a) as permitting a judge to dismiss not only an entire case, but also a part thereof, including the allegation that a defendant has previously been convicted of a felony. When a court strikes prior felony conviction allegations in this way, it does not wipe out such prior convictions or prevent them from being considered in connection with later convictions. Instead, the order striking such allegations simply embodies the court's determination that, in the interest of justice, defendant should not be required to undergo a statutorily increased penalty which would follow from judicial determination of the alleged fact.

The other statute of central importance to this case is section 667, subdivision (f). A part of the Three Strikes law, the statute provides as follows:

> (f) (1) Notwithstanding any other law, subdivisions (b) to (i), inclusive, shall be applied in every case in which a defendant has a prior felony conviction as defined in subdivision (d). The prosecuting attorney shall plead and prove each prior felony conviction except as provided in paragraph (2).
>
> (2) The prosecuting attorney may move to dismiss or strike a prior felony conviction allegation in the furtherance of justice pursuant to Section 1385, or if there is insufficient evidence to prove the prior conviction. If upon the satisfaction of the court that there is insufficient evidence to prove the prior felony conviction, the court may dismiss or strike the allegation.

Defendant argues that the Three Strikes law, if interpreted to permit a court to strike a prior felony conviction allegation *only* on the prosecutor's motion, violates the doctrine of separation of powers. [I]n People v. Tenorio, [we held] unconstitutional a statute purporting to empower a prosecutor to veto a court's decision to dismiss a prior conviction allegation. . . . One may fairly summarize the court's reasoning in this way: [C]onceding the Legislature's power to bar a court from dismissing certain charges altogether, when the Legislature does permit a charge to be dismissed the ultimate decision whether to dismiss is a judicial, rather than a prosecutorial or executive, function; to require the prosecutor's consent to the disposition of a criminal charge pending before the court unacceptably compromises judicial independence. In subsequent cases, the court relied on People v. Tenorio, to hold unconstitutional other statutes purporting to give prosecutors the power to veto similar judicial decisions related to the sentencing or other disposition of criminal charges. . . .

The Attorney General suggests the Three Strikes law serves the purpose of the separation of powers doctrine by making the decision to dismiss under section 1385 a "joint" decision, in the sense that the court and the prosecutor each may veto the other's preferred disposition. [But] interference with the traditional prerogatives of the executive cannot justify interference with the independence of the judiciary. . . . That the Legislature and the electorate may eliminate the courts' power to make certain sentencing choices may be conceded. Subject to the constitutional prohibition against cruel and unusual punishment, the power to define crimes and fix penalties is vested exclusively in the legislative branch. It does not follow, however, that having given the court the power to dismiss, the Legislature may therefore condition its exercise upon the approval of the district attorney. This court has not upheld any law purporting to subject to prosecutorial approval the court's discretion to dispose of a criminal charge. Instead, we have consistently held such laws unconstitutional. . . .

We thus arrive at this question: Does the Three Strikes law contain a "clear legislative direction" that courts may not strike sentencing allegations in furtherance of justice under section 1385 without the prosecutor's approval? [It is] self-evident that the Legislature assumed a court would at least have the power to grant the prosecutor's motion to strike a prior felony allegation in the furtherance of justice. The question then becomes: Does the court also have the power to strike such an allegation on its own motion?

[D]efendant contends, the Three Strikes law confirms that the court retains its powers under section 1385: Because section 667(f)(2) permits the prosecuting attorney to "move to dismiss or strike a prior felony conviction allegation in the furtherance of justice *pursuant to Section 1385*" (italics added), a fortiori the court must have power to grant the motion *pursuant to section 1385*. . . .

[T]here is a long history of dispute among the various branches of state government over the application of section 1385 to sentencing allegations[, and] the lesson of section 1385's controversial history is that references to the section in sentencing statutes are not lightly or thoughtlessly made. The drafter's express invocation of section 1385 in the Three Strikes law, together with the absence of any language purporting to bar courts from acting pursuant to it, virtually compels the conclusion no such prohibition was intended. . . .

The district attorney [ ] argues that section 1385(b) independently bars a court from striking prior felony allegations in Three Strikes cases [because it] qualifies the general power to dismiss granted to courts in section 1385(a), in these words: "This section does not authorize a judge to strike any prior conviction of a serious felony for purposes of enhancement of a sentence under Section 667." The Three Strikes law, the district attorney contends, was codified as part of section 667 and articulates a sentence "enhancement" within the meaning of section 1385(b). . . . Defendant's [main response is] that section 1385(b) cannot fairly be read as referring to the Three Strikes law [because it was enacted first and because it is not an "enhancement" under the terms of section 1385(b)]. [L]egislative intent is the governing consideration. [T]he Legislature's decision to place the Three Strikes law within section 667 falls short of a "clear legislative direction" to eliminate courts' power to strike prior felony allegations sua sponte. . . .

The district attorney [further argues that the] Three Strikes initiative was motivated by the voters' desire for longer sentences and by a mistrust of judges. The proponents of the initiative argued in its favor that "soft-on-crime judges, politicians, defense lawyers and probation officers care more about violent felons than they do victims. They spend all of their time looking for loopholes to get rapists, child molesters and murderers out on probation, early parole, or off the hook altogether."

Plainly the Three Strikes initiative, as well as the legislative act embodying its terms, was intended to restrict courts' discretion in sentencing repeat offenders. . . . Both versions of the Three Strikes law expressly declare that a court, in sentencing, may not grant probation, suspend execution or imposition of sentence, divert the defendant, or commit the defendant to any facility other than state prison. But to say the intent of a law was to restrict judicial discretion begs the question of *how* judicial discretion was to be restricted. The answer to that question can be found only by examining the language of the act. In it, one finds the express restrictions on the courts' power mentioned above, but no others. . . .

For these reasons, we conclude that section 1385(a) does permit a court acting on its own motion to strike prior felony conviction allegations in cases brought under the Three Strikes law. Our holding respects the principle that legislative acts are construed, if at all possible, to be constitutional. Our holding also avoids conflict with the principle that ambiguous penal statutes are construed to favor the defendant.

To guide the lower courts in the exercise of their discretion under section 1385(a), whether acting on their own motion or on motion of the prosecuting attorney, we emphasize the following: A court's discretion to strike prior felony conviction allegations in furtherance of justice is limited . . . and is subject to review for abuse. We reviewed the applicable principles in People v. Orin [13 Cal.3d 937, 945 (Cal. 1975)]:

> The trial court's power to dismiss an action under section 1385 . . . is limited by the amorphous concept which requires that the dismissal be "in furtherance of justice." . . . From the case law, several general principles emerge. Paramount among them is the rule "that the language of [section 1385], 'in furtherance of justice,' requires consideration both of the constitutional rights of the defendant, and *the interests of society represented by the People,* in determining whether there should be a dismissal." At the very least, the reason for dismissal must be "that which would motivate a reasonable judge." . . .

From these general principles it follows that a court abuses its discretion if it dismisses a case, or strikes a sentencing allegation, solely to accommodate judicial convenience or because of court congestion. A court also abuses its discretion by dismissing a case, or a sentencing allegation, simply because a defendant pleads guilty. Nor would a court act properly if guided solely by a personal antipathy for the effect that the Three Strikes law would have on a defendant, while ignoring defendant's background, the nature of his present offenses, and other individualized considerations.

. . . Section 1385 anticipates, and facilitates, appellate review with the requirement that "[t]he reasons for the dismissal must be set forth in an order entered upon the minutes." The statement of reasons is not merely directory, and neither trial nor appellate courts have authority to disregard the requirement. It is not enough that on review the reporter's transcript may show the trial court's motivation; the *minutes* must reflect the reason so that all may know why this great power was exercised.

Having decided that section 1385(a) applies to this case, we must determine the appropriate disposition. [Here] the record does not contain all of the material a reviewing court should consider . . . because the trial court did not set forth its reasons for striking the prior felony conviction allegations in the relevant minute order, as required by section 1385(a). . . . Under these circumstances, the appropriate remedy is to vacate the judgment, to permit defendant to withdraw his plea, and otherwise to proceed in conformity with this opinion. . . .

NOTES

1. *Means for judicial sentencing reconsideration: constitutional review.* Though the decision in *Romero* is based ultimately on an interpretation of a California statute, the court's discussion reveals that judges always have an opportunity — indeed, an obligation — to reexamine sentencing decisions made by legislatures and others in light of prevailing state and federal constitutional rules. The federal Constitution's mandates of due process and separation of powers and its prohibition of cruel and unusual punishments create procedural and substantive limits on sentencing structures and outcomes that judges can and do enforce.

Many states also have additional constitutional provisions and precedents that enable judges to reconsider — and sometimes refuse to give effect to — sentencing decisions made by legislatures, sentencing commissions, and others.

Because constitutional provisions are usually vague and subject to interpretation, there has been a robust debate concerning how judges should review sentencing determinations in light of constitutional norms. See Ewing v. California, 538 U.S. 11 (2003) (explaining that the Supreme Court has a long-standing tradition of deferring to state legislatures in making and implementing important policy decisions regarding sentencing); Harmelin v. Michigan, 501 U.S. 957 (1991) (developing arguments for why the Supreme Court should not rigorously review state sentencing choices on constitutional grounds). Should broad constitutional provisions such as due process and separation of powers justify more searching analysis in the review of sentences? Do you think the standards for constitutional review ought to differ depending on the nature and severity of the sentence at issue — that is, should constitutional review of death sentences or lengthy prison terms be more exhaustive than review of shorter terms of imprisonment or alternative sanctions?

2. *Means for judicial sentencing reconsideration: statutory authority.* Though influenced by constitutional concerns, the decision in *Romero* makes clear that sentencing judges in California derive their power to strike prior felony allegations (and thereby avoid application of the three-strikes law) from a statutory grant of authority. In this way, the *Romero* case highlights another means judges may be able to reconsider general sentencing rules in particular cases. The decision details inappropriate grounds for striking prior felony allegations, but it does not indicate what grounds may be appropriate. What types of reasons for striking prior felony allegations would be "in the furtherance of justice"?

Though relatively few jurisdictions give sentencing judges direct means to avoid the application of mandatory sentencing statutes, nearly all jurisdictions that employ guideline sentencing systems have granted sentencing judges some express statutory authority to depart from these guidelines. In the federal system, under 18 U.S.C. §3553(b), a sentencing court may impose a sentence outside the presumptive guideline range if it finds "that there exists an aggravating or mitigating circumstance of a kind, or to a degree, not adequately taken into consideration by the Sentencing Commission in formulating the guidelines that should result in a sentence different from that described." In most state systems, departures from the presumptive sentences established in the guidelines are authorized when the sentencing judges find "substantial and compelling circumstances." Like the provisions at issue in *Romero*, departure statutes generally require judges to explain the basis for any departure, and an inadequate explanation can lead to reversal on appeal.

3. *Means for judicial sentencing reconsideration: circumvention.* In any taxonomy of the ways sentences get reconsidered, one should not overlook the extralegal "authority" judges possess to circumvent the application of sentencing rules established by legislatures and sentencing commissions. Especially when a sentencing judge is disconcerted by the application of a mandatory sentencing provision in a particular case, he might condone (and even encourage) a plea bargain in which the offender pleads to a lesser offense. See U.S. Sentencing

Commission, Special Report to Congress: Mandatory Minimum Penalties in the Federal Criminal Justice System 56-58 (Aug. 1991). In a series of articles based on empirical research of the operation of the federal sentencing guidelines, Professors Stephen Schulhofer and Ilene Nagel concluded that the guidelines were circumvented in up to one-third of all federal cases during the period studied. See Schulhofer and Nagel, Plea Negotiations Under the Federal Sentencing Guidelines: Guideline Circumvention and Its Dynamics in the Post-*Mistretta* Period, 91 Nw. U. L. Rev. 1284, 1305 (1997); Schulhofer and Nagel, Negotiated Pleas Under the Federal Sentencing Guidelines: The First Fifteen Months, 27 Am. Crim. L. Rev. 232, 272-278 (1989).

   4. *Judicial override in death sentencing systems.*   Most of the 38 states that authorize capital punishment rely on juries to decide whether an offender should be sentenced to die and give the trial judge authority to reconsider a jury's capital sentencing decision. In many states, a judge has the authority to override a jury's recommendation only by imposing a life sentence after the jury has recommended death. See, e.g., Ohio Rev. Code §2727.16. But four states — Alabama, Delaware, Florida, and Indiana — use "advisory" juries in their capital-sentencing process, which means that the trial judge has authority to override a jury's recommendation in either direction: The judge might impose a life sentence when the jury voted for death or might impose a death sentence even when a jury has recommended life. See Ala. Stat. §13A-5-46; Del. Code tit. 11, §4209; Fla. Stat. §921.141; Ind. Code Ann. §35-50-2-9. The constitutionality of permitting judges to impose a death sentence has been thrown into question by the Supreme Court's decision in Ring v. Arizona, 536 U.S. 584 (2002), which held that a jury must make any factual findings that allows a sentence of death under the applicable state statute. Most courts, however, have upheld the review of jury capital decision making by trial judges after *Ring* so long as juries play a central role in finding the facts on which a death sentence is based. See Stephanos Bibas, *Apprendi* in the States, 94 J. Crim. L. & Criminology 1 (2003).

2.   Direct Appeal of Sentences

As mentioned earlier, a defendant's right to file an appeal or seek review of a conviction or sentence is relatively new; at one time the only means for appeal and review of a criminal case was through a request for reconsideration made to the sovereign. Indeed, the Supreme Court held in McKane v. Durston, 153 U.S. 684 (1894), that there is no federal constitutional right to appeal, and most state constitutions lack express provisions guaranteeing appeals in criminal cases.

   Nevertheless, all American jurisdictions have long provided for appellate review of convictions, and statutes and rules of appellate procedure establish who can file an appeal and what issues the parties can raise. The modern history of appellate review of criminal *convictions* extends nearly a century, with a rich set of doctrines governing when and how trial error can be corrected; the modern history of appellate review of criminal *sentences* is far more abbreviated and much less evolved. Frequent appellate review of the outcome of capital cases did not begin until the 1970s, following the Supreme Court's decision in Furman v. Georgia, 408 U.S. 238 (1972), which struck down existing capital sentencing schemes. And, as Professor Kevin Reitz notes, serious appellate review of noncapital sentencing did not begin until a decade later, when jurisdictions started adopting guideline systems and other structured sentencing reforms:

> Prior to the guideline innovations of the 1980s, little meaningful appellate review of sentencing decisions had ever occurred in the United States, in federal or state courts. Those few appellate decisions that existed did not, for the most part, focus on substantive issues of the appropriate principles for punishment decisions, or the application of those principles to particular factual scenarios. Instead, the cases dealt primarily with constitutional issues: Did the penalty below exceed the cruel and unusual punishment standard of the Eighth Amendment? (Not often.) Did the procedures followed by the sentencing court violate the Due Process Clause? (Almost never.) Did the sentencing judge rely upon a constitutionally impermissible factor, such as race or religious belief, when imposing judgment? (If so, few trial judges ever made this explicit.) Only a minority of U.S. jurisdictions before the 1980s granted authority to their appellate courts to review sentences for substantive propriety. In the federal system, a "doctrine of non-reviewability" prevailed from 1891 until 1987, when the Federal Sentencing Guidelines became effective. Even in those states where a power of sentence review existed, it was used sparingly. Appellate courts refrained from interference with a sentence below unless it could be characterized as clearly excessive or as a clear abuse of discretion. . . .
>
> The absence, or near absence, of appellate input into the law of criminal punishment was due in part to the embarrassment that there was no substantive law of sentencing to be applied at the trial level. Under indeterminate sentencing schemes, trial judges were given discretion to fix any penalty within the ceiling provided by the statutory maximum. In so doing, judges were instructed to consult any and all factors having to do with the crime itself or the offender — including the offender's whole life, character, and background. With such a free-form thought process in gear, there were effectively no legal principles against which a sentence could be tested on review. Another disablement of appellate review was the widespread rule that trial courts were not obliged to explain the reasons for their sentencing decisions on the record[, which provided] little practical way for an appeals court to discover what thought process a trial judge had followed in a given case.

Kevin R. Reitz, Sentencing Guideline Systems and Sentence Appeals: A Comparison of Federal and State Experiences, 91 Nw. U. L. Rev. 1441, 1443-1446 (1997).

As this excerpt suggests, modern sentencing reforms radically changed the dynamics surrounding appellate review of noncapital sentencing. By creating defined sentencing law through mandatory sentencing provisions and guideline sentencing rules, structured sentencing reforms established a corpus of legal rules that sentencing judges had to apply and appellate judges could review. The following statute establishes the authority and the role of federal circuit courts in appellate review of decisions under the federal sentencing guidelines.

‖ *18 United States Code §3742* ‖

REVIEW OF A SENTENCE

(a) Appeal by a defendant. — A defendant may file a notice of appeal in the district court for review of an otherwise final sentence if the sentence —

(1) was imposed in violation of law;

(2) was imposed as a result of an incorrect application of the sentencing guidelines; or

(3) is greater than the sentence specified in the applicable guideline range to the extent that the sentence includes a greater fine or term of imprisonment, probation, or supervised release than the maximum established in the guideline range, or . . .

(4) was imposed for an offense for which there is no sentencing guideline and is plainly unreasonable.

(b) Appeal by the Government.— The Government may file a notice of appeal in the district court for review of an otherwise final sentence if the sentence —

(1) was imposed in violation of law;

(2) was imposed as a result of an incorrect application of the sentencing guidelines;

(3) is less than the sentence specified in the applicable guideline range to the extent that the sentence includes a lesser fine or term of imprisonment, probation, or . . .

(4) was imposed for an offense for which there is no sentencing guideline and is plainly unreasonable.

The Government may not further prosecute such appeal without the personal approval of the Attorney General, the Solicitor General, or a deputy solicitor general designated by the Solicitor General. . . .

(e) Consideration.— Upon review of the record, the court of appeals shall determine whether the sentence —

(1) was imposed in violation of law;

(2) was imposed as a result of an incorrect application of the sentencing guidelines;

(3) is outside of the applicable guideline range, and

(A) the district court failed to provide the written statement of reasons required by section 3553(c);

(B) the sentence departs from the applicable guideline range based on a factor that

(i) does not advance the objectives set forth in section 3553(a)(2); or

(ii) is not authorized under section 3553(b); or

(iii) is not justified by the facts of the case; or

(C) the sentence departs to an unreasonable degree from the applicable guidelines range, having regard for the factors to be considered in imposing a sentence, as set forth in section 3553(a) of this title and the reasons for the imposition of the particular sentence, as stated by the district court pursuant to the provisions of section 3553(c); or

(4) was imposed for an offense for which there is no applicable sentencing guideline and is plainly unreasonable.

The court of appeals shall give due regard to the opportunity of the district court to judge the credibility of the witnesses, and shall accept the findings of fact of the district court unless they are clearly erroneous and, except with respect to determinations under subsection (3)(A) or 3(B), shall give due deference to the district court's application of the guidelines to the facts. With respect to determinations under subsection (3)(A) or (3)(B), the court of appeals shall review de novo the district court's application of the guidelines to the facts.

PROBLEM 11-1.   HOW APPEALING?

Corrine Marie Denardi was convicted on a federal indictment charging conspiracy to distribute cocaine. At the time of sentencing, her attorney argued for a departure from the federal sentencing guidelines, citing mitigating factors such as the defendant's cooperation with the government, the absence of a prior criminal record, an exemplary work history, and a lifetime of love and devotion to friends and family. Ms. Denardi's attorney stressed that the imposition of a sentence within the recommended guideline range would cause extreme hardship on Ms. Denardi's family because she was the sole caretaker of three young children, one of whom was developmentally disabled. The relevant provision of the Sentencing Reform Act authorizing a departure from the guidelines, 18 U.S.C. §3553(b), states that a court may depart if there exists a "mitigating circumstance of a kind, or to a degree, not adequately taken into consideration by the Sentencing Commission in formulating the guidelines that should result in a sentence different from that described."

The district court refused to depart from the guidelines, and sentenced Ms. Denardi to 24 months' imprisonment. In so doing, the judge stated:

> I find nothing here that permits me to depart from the guidelines, and I am very much guided by them. I recognize all of the favorable points that the defendant has produced, and the best that I can do with those is to apply them to my choice of where within the guidelines the sentence would fall. . . . I have been asking and trying to get some factor that would justify a deviation, and . . . I haven't found any.

Based on the appellate review provisions of 18 U.S.C. §3742(a), does Ms. Denardi have a right to appeal the district court's decision not to depart from the sentencing guidelines? Does the answer to this question depend on whether the district court believed it lacked the legal authority to depart or instead simply made a discretionary decision not to exercise its departure authority? See United States v. Denardi, 892 F.2d 269 (3d Cir. 1989); see also David Yellen, Appellate Review of Refusals to Depart, 1 Fed. Sentencing Rep. 264 (1988).

PROBLEM 11-2.   WAIVING GOOD-BYE TO AN APPEAL?

In December 2001, Walter Grange's house was burglarized. During the course of the investigation, police seized from Grange's home a microwave oven, which contained 6.44 grams of crack cocaine residue coated on the inside, and a bag containing nearly $12,000 in cash. Pursuant to a plea agreement, Grange pleaded guilty to possessing crack cocaine in violation of 21 U.S.C. §844(a). The plea agreement stated that the government and the defendant agree that the total amount of drugs possessed was just over six grams of crack cocaine. The agreement also included the following statement:

> Defendant knowingly waives the right to appeal any sentence within the guideline range applicable to the statute of conviction as determined by the Court after resolution of any objections by either party to the presentence report to be prepared in this case, and defendant specifically agrees not to appeal the

determination of the Court in resolving any contested sentencing factor. In other words, Defendant waives the right to appeal the sentence imposed in this case except to the extent, if any, that the Court may depart upwards from the applicable sentencing guideline range as determined by the Court. The defendant also waives his right to challenge his sentence or the manner in which it was determined in any collateral attack. . . .

The probation officer investigating the offense and writing the presentence report for the sentencing court concluded that the $12,000 in cash should be converted into crack cocaine when computing the base offense level under the federal sentencing guidelines. At the sentencing hearing the prosecutor, when asked about the probation officer's computation, stated:

> On the $12,000, your Honor, I have nothing to add. I think the Probation Department set out the facts. That's all I know is the facts. . . . Also, I'm in a little bit of a difficult position because I signed a plea agreement agreeing to the 6.44 grams. . . . To be honest with the Court, it doesn't take a genius to know if you have that much residue in the facility that was cooking it, there's a little bit more involved there; but on the other hand, that was the extent of our evidence at that point.

The trial judge accepted the probation office's determination and sentenced Grange to 78 months in prison.

Under the terms of the plea agreement, can Grange appeal directly or file for a writ of habeas corpus? Can he attack the validity of the plea agreement, arguing that the government failed to live up to its promise? Can Grange assert that he received ineffective assistance of counsel as a means to try to void the plea agreement? If Grange filed a direct appeal of his sentence, how should an appellate court respond to these questions? See United States v. Brown, 328 F.3d 767 (5th Cir. 2003).

NOTES

1. *Whose right to appeal?*   Under U.S. law in every jurisdiction, the prosecution cannot appeal from an acquittal, while in civil law countries such an appeal is possible. In the United States, such appeals are considered a violation of double jeopardy prohibitions; civil law countries consider the trial and appeal to be part of one proceeding and therefore a direct appeal does not constitute double jeopardy.

As revealed by the federal appeals provision reprinted above, this American imbalance in appellate rights has generally not been carried over to sentencing; in nearly all jurisdictions, prosecutors as well as defendants may appeal from a guilty verdict and the sentence. Why should the prosecution have the right to appeal from a sentence, especially since it controls charging and has unique power during plea negotiations? Should it matter whether the case is in a guideline or a nonguideline jurisdiction?

2. *Dual functions of error correction and lawmaking.*   Appellate courts are often said to have the dual functions of correcting trial errors and expounding legal rules that control future cases through the force of precedent. Is one role more important than the other? Do you think appellate courts should be

primarily concerned with enforcing sentencing rules established by legislatures and sentencing commissions, or should they assume a more dynamic role by elucidating sentencing principles to be followed in future cases?

Many early advocates of modern sentencing reforms urged the more active role for appellate courts, hoping that appellate review would foster an "evolutionary and principled development of a common law of sentencing." Norval Morris, Towards Principled Sentencing, 37 Md. L. Rev. 267, 284 (1977); see also Marvin E. Frankel, Sentencing Guidelines: A Need for Creative Collaboration, 101 Yale L.J. 2043, 2050 (1992). But in a thorough assessment of appellate review in three guideline jurisdictions, Professor Kevin Reitz has documented that in practice, reviewing courts have favored the task of error correction over substantive lawmaking. In "hundreds of appellate decisions across different guideline jurisdictions," he notes, "one seldom encounters thoughtful opinions that advance our understanding of the substantive problems of punishment. Instead, guideline appeals lean toward technical, even technocratic, analyses." Reitz, 91 Nw. U. L. Rev. at 1450. Can you imagine why the reformist vision of developing a "common law of sentencing" has proven hard to achieve in practice?

3. *Standards for review.* The influence and impact of appellate review will often hinge on the standard of review employed by the court. In most appellate review settings, factual findings are reviewed for clear error, legal rulings are reviewed de novo, and discretionary judgments are reviewed for an abuse of discretion. Would you describe sentencing decisions made under guideline systems as factual findings, legal rulings, or discretionary judgments? Can you develop arguments to support a rigorous de novo standard of review for such sentencing decisions? Can you develop arguments to support a more deferential abuse of discretion standard?

The original version of the appellate review portion of the federal Sentencing Reform Act stated simply in 18 U.S.C. §3742(e) that circuit courts should "give due deference to the district court's application of the guidelines to the facts." This somewhat oblique instruction led the circuit courts to develop a range of approaches to reviewing certain guideline determinations, particularly decisions to depart from the guidelines. In Koon v. United States, 518 U.S. 81, 97 (1996), the U.S. Supreme Court, interpreting section 3742(e), stated that the deference to be given on appeal depends on the nature of the guideline question presented, and that a departure decision will in most cases be "due substantial deference" because "it embodies the sentencing court's traditional exercise of discretion." The Court thus concluded that circuit courts should apply an abuse of discretion standard when reviewing departures. The *Koon* decision generated considerable scholarly debate over the soundness and significance of the Supreme Court's effort to recast appellate review of departure authority. See Douglas A. Berman, Balanced and Purposeful Departures: Fixing a Jurisprudence that Undermines the Federal Sentencing Guidelines, 76 Notre Dame L. Rev. 21 (2000); Ian Weinstein, The Discontinuous Tradition of Sentencing Discretion: *Koon*'s Failure to Recognize the Reshaping of Judicial Discretion Under the Guidelines, 79 B.U. L. Rev. 493 (1999); Barry L. Johnson, Discretion and the Rule of Law in Federal Guidelines Sentencing: Developing Departure Jurisprudence in the Wake of Koon v. United States, 58 Ohio St. L.J. 1697 (1998).

Though the precise meaning of *Koon* was widely debated, data from the U.S. Sentencing Commission made clear that the number of downward departures granted by district courts began to increase steadily following the decision. The total number of downward departures granted for reasons other than a defendant's assistance to prosecutors nearly doubled in the six years following *Koon*. Concerns about the number of departures ultimately led Congress in 2003, as part of a package of reforms designed to decrease the number of downward departures, to modify the language of 18 U.S.C. §3742(e) to provide that when considering "determinations [to depart from the guidelines], the court of appeals shall review de novo the district court's application of the guidelines to the facts." Through this alteration of the appellate review standard from "abuse of discretion" to "de novo," Congress apparently intended not only that circuit judges more rigorously review questionable downward departures on appeal, but also that district judges feel more restrained in granting departures in the first instance. The exact impact of the heightened level of review of departures has already been the basis of varied rulings. Compare United States v. VanLeer, 270 F. Supp. 2d 1318 (D. Utah 2003), with United States v. Thurston, 338 F.3d 50 (1st Cir. 2003).

4. *Waivers of the right to appeal.*   Prosecutors in some federal districts routinely seek waivers of defendants' appeal rights in plea agreements. In 1995 the Department of Justice issued a memorandum to all U.S. Attorney's offices (reprinted in Chapter 6), providing guidance on the drafting and use of appeal waivers. That memo recognized that the use of appeal waivers is "helpful in reducing the burden of appellate and collateral litigation involving sentencing issues" but also cautioned that it "could result in guideline-free sentencing of defendants in guilty plea cases, and it could encourage a lawless district court to impose sentences in violation of the guidelines." In July 1996 the Committee on Criminal Law of the Judicial Conference of the United States, in a memorandum to aid district judges and probation officers in their consideration of appeal waiver provisions, noted "that waivers have been consistently upheld as legal, primarily because it is well established that a defendant can waive any right, even a constitutional right, as long as the waiver is knowing and voluntary." It also suggested that courts provide all defendants with a "qualified, yet informative, advisement of the right to appeal at sentencing," followed by a specific oral colloquy about the terms of any appeal waiver provision to which a defendant has agreed.

A number of circuit courts have expressed concerns about broad appeal waivers that eliminate all appellate rights concerning any guideline sentence that is imposed and have indicated that they would look closely at the particular facts of each case to ensure that the defendant fully understood and voluntarily accepted such a waiver. See United States v. Rosa, 123 F.3d 94 (2d Cir. 1997); see also United States v. Teeter, 257 F.3d 14, 18-25 (1st Cir. 2001) (holding that "presentence waivers of appellate rights are valid in theory" but their terms must be narrowly construed, and in extreme cases appellate courts must remain free to grant relief from such waivers). Some federal district judges have refused to accept pleas that include broad appeal waivers or have stricken the waivers from otherwise acceptable pleas. See United States v. Perez, 46 F. Supp. 2d 59 (D. Mass. 1999); United States v. Raynor, 989 F. Supp. 43 (D.D.C. 1997); see also Jack W. Campbell IV and Gregory A. Castanias, Sentencing-Appeal Waivers: Recent

Decisions Open the Door to Reinvigorated Challenges, The Champion, May 2000, at 34.

5. *Appeal rights under international law.* Article 14(5) of the International Covenant on Civil and Political Rights, which the United States has ratified, grants every defendant the right to have the conviction and sentence reviewed by a higher tribunal. Similar rights are granted in the American and European Human Rights Conventions. Exceptions apply to minor offenses and cases tried in front of the nations' highest tribunals. Notably, there was no appeal from the decisions of the two post–World War II tribunals in Nuremberg and Tokyo. Because of the evolution of international human rights law as a part of the due process norm, however, appeals are explicitly mentioned in the procedural rules for the ad hoc tribunals trying offenders for atrocities committed in the former Yugoslavia and in Rwanda as well as for the International Criminal Court. The ad hoc tribunals have allowed for sentence appeals, even in the case of guilty pleas.

In contrast to noncapital sentencing, in which appellate review is relatively new and still somewhat novel, death sentences have been subject to appellate scrutiny since the early 1900s. The severity and finality of the penalty not only have prompted capital defendants to appeal in greater numbers and with greater rigor but also have led appellate courts to examine more closely the legality and appropriateness of death sentences in individual cases. As the case below highlights, when states enacted new death penalty statutes after the Supreme Court struck down existing capital sentencing schemes in Furman v. Georgia, 408 U.S. 238 (1972), appellate review became a central tool in efforts to ensure that the death penalty was administered in a more consistent and reasoned way.

R. Pulley v. Robert Alton Harris
465 U.S. 37 (1984)

WHITE, J.

[Robert Alton] Harris was convicted of a capital crime in a California court and was sentenced to death. Along with many other challenges to the conviction and sentence, Harris claimed on appeal that the California capital punishment statute was invalid under the United States Constitution because it failed to require the California Supreme Court to compare Harris' sentence with the sentences imposed in similar capital cases and thereby to determine whether they were proportionate. . . .

The proportionality review sought by Harris . . . and provided for in numerous state statutes[1] . . . presumes that the death sentence is not dispropor-

---

1. Under the much-copied Georgia scheme, for example, the Supreme Court is required in every case to determine "[whether] the sentence of death is excessive or disproportionate to the penalty imposed in similar cases, considering both the crime and the defendant." Ga. Code Ann. §17-10-35(c)(3)(1982). If the court affirms the death sentence, it is to include in its decision reference to similar cases that it has taken into consideration. The court is required to maintain records of all capital felony cases in which the death penalty was imposed since 1970.

tionate to the crime in the traditional sense. It purports to inquire instead whether the penalty is nonetheless unacceptable in a particular case because disproportionate to the punishment imposed on others convicted of the same crime. The issue in this case, therefore, is whether the Eighth Amendment, applicable to the States through the Fourteenth Amendment, requires a state appellate court, before it affirms a death sentence, to compare the sentence in the case before it with the penalties imposed in similar cases if requested to do so by the prisoner. Harris insists that it does and that this is the invariable rule in every case. . . . We do not agree.

Harris' submission is rooted in Furman v. Georgia, 408 U.S. 238 (1972). In *Furman*, the Court concluded that capital punishment, as then administered under statutes vesting unguided sentencing discretion in juries and trial judges, had become unconstitutionally cruel and unusual punishment. The death penalty was being imposed so discriminatorily, so wantonly and freakishly, and so infrequently that any given death sentence was cruel and unusual. In response to that decision, roughly two-thirds of the States promptly redrafted their capital sentencing statutes in an effort to limit jury discretion and avoid arbitrary and inconsistent results. All of the new statutes provide for automatic appeal of death sentences. Most, such as Georgia's, require the reviewing court, to some extent at least, to determine whether, considering both the crime and the defendant, the sentence is disproportionate to that imposed in similar cases. Not every State has adopted such a procedure. In some States, such as Florida, the appellate court performs proportionality review despite the absence of a statutory requirement; in others, such as California and Texas, it does not.

Four years after *Furman*, this Court examined several of the new state statutes. We upheld one of each of the three sorts mentioned above. See Gregg v. Georgia, [428 U.S. 153 (1976)]; Proffitt v. Florida, 428 U.S. 242 (1976); Jurek v. Texas, 428 U.S. 262 (1976). Needless to say, that some schemes providing proportionality review are constitutional does not mean that such review is indispensable. . . . There is no basis in our cases for holding that comparative proportionality review by an appellate court is required in every case in which the death penalty is imposed and the defendant requests it.

Assuming that there could be a capital sentencing system so lacking in other checks on arbitrariness that it would not pass constitutional muster without comparative proportionality review, the 1977 California statute is not of that sort. Under this scheme, a person convicted of first-degree murder is sentenced to life imprisonment unless one or more "special circumstances" are found, in which case the punishment is either death or life imprisonment without parole. Special circumstances are alleged in the charging paper and tried with the issue of guilt at the initial phase of the trial [and] must be proved beyond a reasonable doubt. If the jury finds the defendant guilty of first-degree murder and finds at least one special circumstance, the trial proceeds to a second phase to determine the appropriate penalty. Additional evidence may be offered and the jury is given a list of relevant factors [and,] guided by the aggravating and mitigating circumstances referred to in this section, [ ] determine[s] whether the penalty shall be death or life imprisonment without the possibility of parole. If the jury returns a verdict of death, the . . . trial judge then reviews the evidence and, in light of the statutory factors, makes an independent determination as to whether the weight of the evidence supports the jury's findings and verdicts. The judge is required to state on the record the reasons for his findings. If the trial judge denies the motion for modification, there is an automatic appeal. The statute does not require comparative proportionality review or otherwise describe the nature of the appeal. It does state that the trial judge's refusal to modify the sentence "shall be reviewed.". . . As the California Supreme Court has said, "the statutory requirements that the jury specify the special circumstances which permit imposition of the death penalty, and that the trial judge specify his reasons for denying r̄ ɔdification of the death penalty, serve to assure thoughtful and effective appellate review, focusing upon the circumstances present in each particular case."

By requiring the jury to find at least one special circumstance beyond a reasonable doubt, the statute limits the death sentence to a small subclass of capital-eligible cases. The statutory list of relevant factors, applied to defendants within this subclass, provides jury guidance and lessens the chance of arbitrary application of the death penalty, guaranteeing that the jury's discretion will be guided and its consideration deliberate. The jury's "discretion must be suitably directed and limited so as to minimize the risk of wholly arbitrary and capricious action." *Gregg*, 428 U.S., at 189. Its decision is reviewed by the trial judge and the State Supreme Court. On its face, this system, without any requirement or practice of comparative proportionality review, cannot be successfully challenged under *Furman* and our subsequent cases. . . .

STEVENS, J., concurring in part and concurring in the judgment.
. . . While the cases relied upon by respondent do not establish that comparative proportionality review is a constitutionally required element of a capital sentencing system, I believe the case law does establish that appellate review plays an essential role in eliminating the systemic arbitrariness and capriciousness which infected death penalty schemes invalidated by Furman v. Georgia, 408 U.S. 238 (1972), and hence that some form of meaningful appellate review is constitutionally required.

The systemic arbitrariness and capriciousness in the imposition of capital punishment under statutory schemes invalidated by *Furman* resulted from two basic defects in those schemes. First, the systems were permitting the imposition of capital punishment in broad classes of offenses for which the penalty would always constitute cruel and unusual punishment. Second, even among those types of homicides for which the death penalty could be constitutionally imposed as punishment, the schemes vested essentially unfettered discretion in juries and trial judges to impose the death sentence. Given these defects, arbitrariness and capriciousness in the imposition of the punishment were inevitable, and given the extreme nature of the punishment, constitutionally intolerable. The statutes we have approved in *Gregg, Proffitt,* and *Jurek* were designed to eliminate each of these defects. Each scheme provided an effective mechanism for categorically narrowing the class of offenses for which the death penalty could be imposed and provided special procedural safeguards including appellate review of the sentencing authority's decision to impose the death penalty.

In *Gregg,* the opinion of Justices Stewart, Powell, and Stevens indicated that some form of meaningful appellate review is required, and . . . focused on the proportionality review component of the Georgia statute because it was a prominent, innovative, and noteworthy feature that had been specifically designed to combat effectively the systemic problems in capital sentencing which had invalidated the prior Georgia capital sentencing scheme. But observations that this innovation is an effective safeguard do not mean that it is the only method of ensuring that death sentences are not imposed capriciously or that it is the only acceptable form of appellate review. [I]n each of the statutory schemes approved in our prior cases, as in the scheme we review today, meaningful appellate review is an indispensable component of the Court's determination that the State's capital sentencing procedure is valid. Like the Court, however, I am not persuaded that the particular form of review prescribed by statute in Georgia — comparative proportionality review — is the only method by which an appellate court can avoid the danger that the imposition of the death sentence in a particular case, or a particular class of cases, will be so extraordinary as to violate the Eighth Amendment.

BRENNAN, J., with whom MARSHALL, J., joins, dissenting.

Almost 12 years ago, in Furman v. Georgia, 408 U.S. 238 (1972), the Court concluded that the death penalty, as then administered under various state and federal statutes, constituted a cruel and unusual punishment prohibited by the Eighth and Fourteenth Amendments. At that time, the Court was convinced that death sentences were being imposed in a manner that was so arbitrary and capricious that no individual death sentence could be constitutionally justified. Four years later, faced with new death penalty statutes enacted by the States of Georgia, Florida, and Texas, a majority of the Court concluded that the procedural mechanisms included in those statutes provided sufficient protection to ensure their constitutional application. Thus began a series of decisions from this Court in which, with some exceptions, it has been assumed that the death penalty is being imposed by the various States in a rational and non-discriminatory way. Upon the available evidence, however, I am convinced that the Court is simply deluding itself, and also the American public, when it insists that those defendants who have already been executed or are today condemned to death have been selected on a basis that is neither arbitrary nor capricious, under any meaningful definition of those terms. . . .

Disproportionality among sentences given different defendants can only be eliminated after sentencing disparities are identified. And the most logical way to identify such sentencing disparities is for a court of statewide jurisdiction to conduct comparisons between death sentences imposed by different judges or juries within the State. This is what the Court labels comparative proportionality review. Although clearly no panacea, such review often serves to identify the most extreme examples of disproportionality among similarly situated defendants. At least to this extent, this form of appellate review serves to eliminate some of the irrationality that currently surrounds imposition of a death sentence. If only to further this limited purpose, therefore, I believe that the Constitution's prohibition on the irrational imposition of the death penalty requires that this procedural safeguard be provided.

Indeed, despite the Court's insistence that such review is not compelled by the Federal Constitution, over 30 States now require, either by statute or judicial decision, some form of comparative proportionality review before any death sentence may be carried out. By itself, this should weigh heavily on the side of requiring such appellate review. In addition, these current practices establish beyond dispute that such review can be administered without much difficulty by a court of statewide jurisdiction in each State.

Perhaps the best evidence of the value of proportionality review can be gathered by examining the actual results obtained in those States which now require such review. For example, since 1973, . . . the Georgia Supreme Court has vacated at least seven death sentences because it was convinced that they were comparatively disproportionate. . . . Similarly, other States that require comparative proportionality review also have vacated death sentences for defendants whose crime or personal history did not justify such an extreme penalty.

What these cases clearly demonstrate, in my view, is that comparative proportionality review serves to eliminate some, if only a small part, of the irrationality that currently infects imposition of the death penalty by the various States. Before any execution is carried out, therefore, a State should be required under the Eighth and Fourteenth Amendments to conduct such appellate review.

NOTES

1. *Proportionality review of death sentences.* As suggested in Pulley v. Harris, most states with the death penalty require their appellate courts to review the proportionality of any death sentence. In a few states, notably Florida, many death sentences have been reversed on the basis of a finding of disproportionality. See Cooper v. State, 739 So. 2d 82 (Fla. 1999). Commentators have noticed, however, that the rigor and significance of proportionality review of death sentences seems to have waned after the Supreme Court held in *Pulley* that such review was not constitutionally mandated. Professor Penny White explains the trend:

> Through the process known as "proportionality review," which was created in post-*Furman* statutes, most state appellate courts began to assess proportionality before affirming death sentences. More recently, however, largely because of the Supreme Court decision in Pulley v. Harris, which held that proportionality review is not constitutionally mandated, meaningful proportionality review has become increasingly rare. Rather than conducting a meaningful comparison between similar cases, courts all too often simply state that a particular death sentence is proportionate and cite previous decisions without analyzing their similarities and differences, or the appropriateness of the death sentence. . . .
> . . . Examples of cases in which codefendants are treated disproportionately with the least culpable receiving the death sentence are not rare. Similarly, there are many cases in which almost identical defendants commit almost identical crimes, but are sentenced differently. . . . On occasion before *Pulley*, the appellate courts in most states (when their statutes mandated) would step in and correct what would otherwise have been a tragic injustice by reducing a disproportionate death sentence to life imprisonment. However, *Pulley*'s removal of what was believed to be proportionality's constitutional underpinning, coupled with the politically charged climate that surrounds most capital cases are undermining *Furman*'s mandate for nonarbitrary, nondiscriminatory death penalty schemes.

Penny J. White, Can Lightning Strike Twice? Obligations of State Courts after Pulley v. Harris, 70 U. Colo. L. Rev. 813, 816-817, 841-842 (1999). Since the decision in *Pulley,* eight states have repealed statutory provisions calling for proportionality review while three other states have established proportionality review. (Tennessee repealed and then reenacted its proportionality requirement after *Pulley.*) See Barry Latzer, The Failure of Comparative Proportionality Review of Capital Cases (with Lessons from New Jersey), 64 Alb. L. Rev. 1161, 1168 n.31 (2001).

What is it about death penalty cases that justifies proportionality review, a procedure that seems to entitle a defendant to a reduced sentence because of a failure to impose the same harsh sentence on other similarly situated defendants? Should all sentences, or at least all serious sentences (such as sentences of 25 or more years of imprisonment), be subject to proportionality review, or is this entire concept of substantive sentencing review unsound? Compare Latzer, 64 Alb. L. Rev. 1161 (suggesting that proportionality review in death penalty cases has been largely a waste of time and money) with Evan J. Mandery, In Defense of Specific Proportionality Review, 65 Alb. L. Rev. 883 (2002) (arguing that proportionality review with the right focus could be valuable).

2. *Automatic appellate review of death sentences.* Another unique feature of appellate review in capital cases is its automatic nature. Most states with the death penalty provide for automatic review of every death sentence, and some jurisdictions provide for expedited review by the state's highest court. See, e.g., Ala. Code §12-22-150; Del. Code tit. 11, §4209(g); Neb. Const. art. 1, §23 ("In all capital cases, appeal directly to the Supreme Court shall be as a matter of right.").

Suggesting that automatic appellate review provisions are in some ways akin to trial courts' review of negotiated plea agreements, Professor Richard Bonnie has explained that such procedures are fundamentally based in society's interest "in the integrity of its institutions of criminal punishment and in the dignity of the processes through which these punishments are carried out." Richard J. Bonnie, The Dignity of the Condemned, 74 Va. L. Rev. 1363, 1369 (1988). But Professor Bonnie has also noted that these interests have been given particularly broad application in the appellate review of death sentences:

> The practice of requiring automatic appeal of death sentences . . . would not represent a significant expansion of integrity-protecting procedures if it were limited to a review of the sufficiency of the substantive predicates for the sentence under state and federal law. The actual scope of appellate review, however, appears to be seldom so restricted. The prevailing practice appears to be to review all claims of error in automatic appeals in the same manner as they would have been reviewed had the appeal been brought at the defendant's own request. Thus, the interest being protected by current judicial practice in capital cases goes well beyond that suggested by the analogy to guilty pleas or to the ban on punishments not authorized by law. In death cases — and only in death cases — state appellate courts have assumed the responsibility of assuring that the death sentence is not tainted by any legal error. . . . Such an aggressive judicial posture must rest on the intuition that death sentences should be carried out only if the highest state court has determined that the process by which they were imposed adhered carefully and fully to all applicable norms.

Id. at 1372-1373.

PROBLEM 11-3.   VOLUNTEERING TO DIE

On October 7, 1976, Gary Mark Gilmore was convicted of murder and sentenced to death in a Utah court for killing a motel clerk and a gas station attendant. Gilmore's death sentence was imposed only months after the Supreme Court's 1976 decision in Gregg v. Georgia, holding that the death penalty could be constitutionally administered if certain sentencing procedures were carefully followed, and it came before any court had conclusively ruled on the constitutionality of Utah's capital sentencing procedures. Gilmore admitted to the murders throughout his trial, even telling the Utah supreme court that he was prepared to die on the day he was sentenced to die. Gilmore demanded that his attorneys not file an appeal or seek a stay of execution on his behalf, even though he was continually advised of his rights and of the fact that the constitutionality of Utah's death penalty statute had not been established.

Gilmore's efforts to accelerate his execution troubled his family as well as prosecutors, though Gilmore seemed to enjoy the frenzy and attention he had created. Gilmore's mother petitioned the U.S. Supreme Court for "next friend" standing to claim that her son was incompetent to waive his right to state appellate review. Her petition also raised the claim that given the importance and seriousness of establishing the constitutional validity of Gilmore's sentence, her son should be unable as a matter of law to waive the right to state appellate review. (The state court in Utah, relying on psychiatric reports and other evidence, had held that Gilmore was competent and legally entitled to waive his rights of appeal and that he was making a knowing and intelligent waiver.)

Should the U.S. Supreme Court, given the stakes involved, assume jurisdiction to consider the merits of the claims raised by Gilmore's mother? Should the Court examine the state court's conclusion that Gilmore was competent to waive his appeals? Do the principles underlying automatic appellate review of all death sentences also support a claim that such review cannot be waived by the defendant? Would your answer to these questions change if the procedures through which Utah sentenced Gilmore to death were clearly constitutionally flawed? See Gilmore v. Utah, 429 U.S. 1012 (1978); see also Franklin ex rel. Berry v. Francis, 144 F.3d 429 (6th Cir. 1998) (considering efforts by family members to intervene on behalf of a death row defendant with a history of mental illness who sought to waive appeal rights).

3. *Collateral Review of Sentences*

A conviction and appeal are not the end of the line for the criminal defendant. Even after the direct appeal is complete, the offender can still challenge the validity of the conviction and sentence in court. These postconviction review procedures take a variety of names and have somewhat different historical roots: the best-known form, mentioned in both federal and state constitutions, is the writ of habeas corpus, though some states structure postconviction processes around the writ of error coram nobis. Others have supplanted the traditional (and often quite limited) postconviction remedies with broader statutes, typically labeled postconviction review acts. These various postconviction review procedures are referred to under the general heading of collateral review. They are nominally civil proceedings in which aggrieved defendants file a complaint in trial court against a state official, alleging that their convictions or sentences are illegal or unconstitutional in some way. A judge who is convinced that the government obtained a conviction or imposed a sentence illegally often has the power to grant relief by overturning the conviction or sentence.

In this section, we briefly review the doctrines and dynamics surrounding collateral review of sentences. The following case involves a direct appeal, but it provides considerable background about the nature of collateral review and its relationship to direct review of convictions and sentences. In so doing, the case provides some preliminary insights into the two central questions that arise in this arena: What distinguishes collateral review procedures from direct appeals, and to what extent are such procedures necessary at all?

|| **_Commonwealth v. Robert Freeman_** ||
827 A.2d 385 (Pa. 2003)

CASTILLE, J.

On June 18, 1998, a jury sitting in the Court of Common Pleas of Philadelphia County convicted appellant of two counts of first-degree murder. . . . At the penalty hearing, the jury found one aggravating circumstance — that appellant had been convicted of another murder at the time of the current offense — and no mitigating circumstances; accordingly, the jury imposed a sentence of death. Trial counsel subsequently withdrew from the matter and present counsel entered the case. This direct appeal followed.

Before turning to . . . substantive issues . . . , we note this Court's recent decision in Commonwealth v. Grant, 813 A.2d 726 (Pa. 2002). _Grant_ overruled the procedural rule announced in Commonwealth v. Hubbard, 372 A.2d 687 (Pa. 1977), which required new counsel to raise claims of previous counsel's ineffectiveness at the first opportunity, even if that first opportunity is on direct appeal and the claims of ineffectiveness were not raised in the trial court. The new general rule announced in _Grant_ is that a defendant "should wait to raise claims of ineffective assistance of trial counsel until collateral review." 813 A.2d at 738. . . .

Grant affects the appeal sub judice in two ways. First, it affects the case directly because appellant is represented by new counsel on appeal and appellant raises numerous claims sounding in the ineffective assistance of trial counsel which were not raised below. Second, _Grant_ affects this case indirectly because there are a number of additional claims raised in this appeal which, though they do not sound in the alleged ineffective assistance of trial counsel, nevertheless were not raised below. These waived claims of trial court error are reviewable here, if at all, only under this Court's direct capital appeal relaxed waiver doctrine. For reasons explicated below, we believe that many of the same considerations powering our decision in _Grant_ require a similar reevaluation of the viability of the capital case relaxed waiver doctrine. Although we will still employ the doctrine to reach many of appellant's waived claims in this case, we abrogate and reshape that doctrine prospectively, so as to better ensure the fair and efficient administration of criminal justice in Pennsylvania.

I. Ineffective Assistance of Trial Counsel

Appellant raises eight primary claims of ineffective assistance of trial counsel involving both the guilt and penalty phases of trial. None of these claims were raised below. Consistently with *Grant,* we dismiss the claims without prejudice to appellant's right to pursue these claims, and any other available claims, via a petition for relief under the Post Conviction Relief Act (PCRA), 42 Pa. C.S. §9541 et seq.

II. Relaxed Waiver

Appellant also raises nine claims of trial court error. Many of these claims are waived because appellant failed to raise them in the trial court. Pa. R. A. P. 302 ("Issues not raised in the lower court are waived and cannot be raised for the first time on appeal."). However, since this is a direct appeal in a capital case, consistently with this Court's long-standing precedent, we have the discretion to reach claims of trial court error which, though waived, are resolvable from the record. . . . Nevertheless, [we find in this case] many of the same difficulties that prompted this Court . . . in *Grant* [to hold] that new claims of trial counsel ineffectiveness are generally better suited for review on collateral attack. We think a similar general rule should govern consideration of claims of trial court error in capital cases that were not raised before the trial court.

Grant noted that, as reflected in Appellate Rule 302(a), appellate courts generally will not entertain claims raised for the first time on appeal. We explained that:

> [S]uch a prohibition is preferred because the absence of a trial court opinion can pose a substantial impediment to meaningful and effective appellate review. Further, appellate courts normally do not consider matters outside the record or matters that involve a consideration of facts not in evidence. Most importantly, appellate courts do not act as fact finders, since to do so would require an assessment of the credibility of the testimony and that is clearly not our function.

Grant, 813 A.2d at 733-734. The *Grant* Court further noted, however, that in the area of ineffectiveness claims, and under *Hubbard,* appellate courts are routinely called upon to perform each of these disfavored tasks:

> In ruling on an ineffectiveness claim, it is rare that a trial court opinion exists which will aid the appellate court in examining the claim. Appellate courts are frequently called upon to consider matters outside the record. Moreover, appellate courts often engage in some fact finding by being required to speculate as to the trial strategy of trial counsel in order to rule upon these claims.

Id. [Also in *Grant,*] we noted that the general preference in the overwhelming majority of jurisdictions was to defer review of counsel ineffectiveness claims until collateral review. We also noted the difficult task facing appellate counsel . . . in attempting to uncover and develop extra-record claims of counsel ineffectiveness in the truncated time frame available on direct appeal review, a task further complicated by the fact that counsel's duty in this regard is not entirely clear, at least as a constitutional matter. . . .

Some of the same difficulties which led to [our decision in *Grant* to defer claims of ineffective assistance to collateral review procedures] also arise when this Court employs relaxed waiver in capital cases to address issues of trial error not raised below. This Court often is required to decide such issues without the benefit of a trial court opinion or other indication of the trial judge's view. We observed in *Grant* that "the trial court is in the best position to review claims related to trial counsel's error in the first instance as that is the court that observed first hand counsel's allegedly deficient performance." 813 A.2d at 737. This is no less true for claims of alleged trial court error — and particularly where discretionary decisions, such as the admission or exclusion of evidence, which often depend upon trial context, are involved. . . .

Similarly, the uncabined availability of relaxed waiver to resurrect unpreserved claims degrades the importance of the trial itself by providing an incentive not to raise contemporaneous objections so as to build in claims for appeal. [T]here are multiple, salutary reasons for this Court to encourage practices by which trial judges are given the initial opportunity to timely address claims of error, thereby ensuring prompt resolution at the most important stage of a case, and forestalling the necessity for appellate review and after-the-fact relief. . . . In light of these difficulties with the relaxed waiver doctrine, it is worth reexamining its history, purpose, and contours to see whether there is a compelling reason to retain this broad and unique exception to the basic requirement of contemporaneous objection and issue preservation.

As this Court noted in Commonwealth v. Albrecht, 720 A.2d 693 (Pa. 1998), the operating principle behind the relaxed waiver doctrine, as originally formulated, was to prevent this court from being instrumental in an unconstitutional execution. The doctrine has its genesis in [a set of decisions from this Court at a time of uncertainty about the structure of appellate review in death penalty cases] after the United States Supreme Court issued its landmark decision in Furman v. Georgia, 408 U.S. 238 (1972). [In a] footnote [in one case, this Court] provided the following rationale for the Court's determination not to adhere strictly to its normal rules of waiver in capital appeals:

> [B]ecause this Court has an independent, statutory obligation to determine whether a sentence of death was the product of passion, prejudice or some other arbitrary factor, whether the sentence is excessive or disproportionate to that imposed in similar cases, and to review the record for sufficiency of the evidence to support aggravating circumstances, we will not adhere strictly to our normal rules of waiver. The primary reason for this limited relaxation of waiver rules is that, due to the final and irrevocable nature of the death penalty, the appellant will have no opportunity for post-conviction relief wherein he could raise, say, an assertion of ineffectiveness of counsel for failure to preserve an issue or some other reason that might qualify as an extraordinary circumstance for failure to raise an issue. 19 P.S. §1180-4(2). Accordingly, significant issues perceived sua sponte by this Court, or raised by the parties, will be addressed and, if possible from the record, resolved. . . .

Commonwealth v. Zettlemoyer, 454 A.2d 937, 955 n.19 (Pa. 1982).

In the very next opinion from this Court discussing the relaxed waiver rationale, however, the Court concluded that the "primary reason" for [the] expanded version of relaxed waiver — the perceived unavailability of collateral review for death-sentenced prisoners — was "faulty." [But d]espite the fact that the primary rationale for [an] expansive view of relaxed waiver was so quickly deemed to be faulty . . . , the relaxed waiver rule became common in direct capital appeals and has been employed to reach a wide variety of claims.

Since [these early cases], this Court has had extensive experience with state post-conviction review in capital cases. This experience has proven with absolute certainty that [a] fear of an absence of collateral review, the primary basis for the [expanded] relaxed waiver doctrine, is erroneous. Death-sentenced prisoners in Pennsylvania have an opportunity for full post-conviction review, via the PCRA, where they can, and do, pursue waived claims through assertions of ineffective assistance of trial counsel. . . .

In addition to deriving from a faulty "primary" rationale, the [expanded] relaxed waiver rule has evolved in a way [that sets it] adrift from its unconstitutional execution moorings[, which] envisioned only a "limited" relaxation of waiver rules to address "significant issues." In practice, the rule has become such a matter of routine that it is invoked to capture a myriad of claims, no matter how comparatively minor or routine[, and has] been routinely employed to reach claims that were not merely "technically" waived, but which in fact were not raised at all in the trial court.

It is notable that, even when applying the rule, this Court in recent years has expressed its increasing unease and concern that the doctrine . . . be employed by counsel as a litigation tool:

> This Court does not countenance trial counsel intentionally sitting by silently at trial only later to complain of trial errors on appeal after an unfavorable verdict. That a matter is a death penalty case in no way relieves trial counsel of the duty to raise appropriate contemporaneous objections at trial to allow the trial court to cure any alleged error as well as preserve issues for appellate review.

Commonwealth v. Williams, 660 A.2d 1316, 1320 (Pa. 1995). In addition to warning that the doctrine was not an excuse for intentionally failing to raise trial objections, we have also warned against its abuse on appeal:

> Th[e] relaxed waiver doctrine . . . was never meant to serve as an invitation to appellate counsel to appear before this Court carte blanche and expect that we will resolve a litany of newly developed challenges not raised or objected to before the lower court. Clearly, such a practice would undermine the process of meaningful appellate review, which is fundamentally based on the official record of what happened at trial.

Commonwealth v. O'Donnell, 740 A.2d 198, 204 (Pa. 1999). In Commonwealth v. Brown, 711 A.2d 444, 455 (Pa. 1998), we further noted that we shared the concerns advanced by the Commonwealth in that case that the doctrine "'sabotages' the trial court's efforts to correct errors" and "encourages defense attorneys to withhold objections during trial for tactical reasons, and by that create an error upon which this Court may later grant relief."

We are also troubled by the potential equal protection implications arising from the near-indiscriminate availability of relaxed waiver to invigorate claims never pursued below. Assume a joint capital trial of two defendants, each

convicted of first-degree murder, but one receives a sentence of life imprisonment while the other receives the death penalty. Upon their appeals, these appellants perceive an identical claim, which both failed to raise below. If it is a
claim premised upon a new constitutional rule that came into existence after the
trial, the life-sentenced appellant will not be able to pursue it at all in the Superior Court, while the capital appellant will receive review in this Court and, possibly, relief. Even if it is not a claim based upon a new rule, the capital appellant
will have the much easier road of having his claim reviewed as if it were a preserved claim of trial error (even though it was not), subject to a mere showing of
error and harmfulness, while the otherwise identically-situated life-sentenced
appellant will be required to make the more difficult showing required under
the three-part standard applicable to ineffective assistance of counsel. Commonwealth v. Howard, 645 A.2d 1300, 1307 (Pa. 1994). Since the claims subject
to capital case relaxed waiver are not limited to the penalty phase, the fact of the
death sentence cannot rationally justify such a preferential, substantive treatment of a claim available to otherwise identically-situated defendants.

In light of these multiple concerns, and the unquestionable availability of
the PCRA as a vehicle to consider waived claims of trial court error through the
guise of claims of trial counsel ineffectiveness, we are convinced that the time
has come to return the relaxed waiver doctrine to its roots. . . . Having created
the rule, this Court is certainly empowered to modify or eliminate the doctrine
if jurisprudential concerns warrant a change from our current practice.

We hold that, as a general rule on capital direct appeals, claims that were
not properly raised and preserved in the trial court are waived and unreviewable.
Such claims may be pursued under the PCRA, as claims sounding in trial counsel's ineffectiveness or, if applicable, a statutory exception to the PCRA's waiver
provision. This general rule, like the rule announced in Commonwealth v.
Grant, reaffirms this Court's general approach to the requirements of issue
preservation. Since [our early cases] an assumption has arisen that all waived
claims are available for review in the first instance on direct appeal. The general
rule shall now be that they are not. In adopting the new rule, we do not foreclose
the possibility that a capital appellant may be able to describe why a particular
waived claim is of such primary constitutional magnitude that it should be
reached on appeal. Indeed, nothing we say today shall be construed as calling
into question the bedrock principles . . . concerning the necessity of reaching
fundamental and plainly meritorious constitutional issues irrespective, even, of
the litigation preferences of the parties. . . .

In reformulating this Court's approach to claims not raised below, we have
not lost sight of the undeniable fact that a death penalty appeal is different in
quality and kind because of the final and irrevocable nature of the penalty. But
our abrogation of relaxed waiver does not eliminate or diminish other substantial safeguards . . . which already serve to prevent this Court from being instrumental in an unconstitutional execution. These protections, not available in
other criminal matters, serve a function similar to the relaxed waiver rule. First,
this Court performs a self-imposed duty to review the sufficiency of the evidence
underlying the first-degree murder conviction in all capital direct appeals, regardless of whether the appellant has raised the issue. The Court is also required
to conduct a statutory review of the death sentence itself to determine whether
it was the product of passion, prejudice or any other arbitrary factor, and to

determine whether the evidence adduced at trial was sufficient to support the aggravating circumstance(s) found by the jury. . . . In addition to these special protections afforded capital appellants, the PCRA exists for them, as for other criminal defendants, as a vehicle for a full and fair, counseled proceeding through which they may challenge the stewardship of trial counsel and pursue other appropriate collateral claims.

This new general rule will be applied prospectively, beginning with those capital direct appeals in which the appellant's brief has not yet been filed in this Court, and is not due for thirty days or more after today's decision. It will then apply to all future capital appeals. . . . Prospective application of our new approach will avoid upsetting the expectations of capital appellants and their direct appeal counsel who have already briefed, or are in the process of briefing, their appeals in reliance upon the prospect that this Court, in its discretion, might reach the merits of some of their otherwise waived claims of trial error. . . . Since this Court has long emphasized that the relaxed waiver rule did not exist to permit capital defendants and their counsel to deliberately avoid raising contemporaneous objections, there is no ground upon which to further defer application of the new rule.

NOTES

1. *Means and methods of collateral review.* As the *Freeman* decision highlights, in addition to providing criminal defendants opportunities for "direct review" of convictions and sentences through traditional appellate mechanisms, jurisdictions also provide defendants with opportunities for "collateral review" through various procedural systems. The most common, and most commonly discussed, method of collateral review is the writ of habeas corpus, and defendants in some cases will have access to both state and federal habeas corpus review. Indeed, particularly in state death penalty cases (where defendants have the greatest interest and opportunity to seek every possible appellate review), it is not uncommon for a conviction and sentence to be reviewed in seven distinct stages: (1) direct review by a state intermediate court, (2) direct review by the state supreme court, (3) collateral state habeas corpus review by a state trial court, (4) appellate review of the state habeas corpus decision by a state appellate court, (5) collateral federal habeas corpus review by a federal district court, (6) appellate review of the federal habeas corpus decision by a federal circuit court, and (7) final appellate review by the U.S. Supreme Court.

Though many of these layers of review are available in all criminal cases, they are often uniquely structured and disproportionately invoked in death penalty cases. In capital cases, where the stakes are high and the consequences of an unlawful execution cannot be reversed, do you think these multiple layers of review are justified, or are capital defendants given too many "bites at the apple" of appellate review?

2. *Relationship between direct and collateral review.* As the *Freeman* decision reveals, appellate courts reviewing convictions and sentences are often aware of the various other opportunities for review that a defendant might invoke, and there is an unavoidable (though not often expressly discussed) tendency for

reviewing courts to alter their decision making in light of these realities. *Freeman* provides an interesting, but somewhat rare, example of a court limiting its approach to direct review because of the availability (and perceived appropriateness) of collateral review for certain claims. It is far more common to see courts that conduct collateral review limiting their examination of certain issues or claims because such matters were already decided (or preclusively waived) during a defendant's pursuit of direct review. (Indeed, the state and federal statutes that authorize various forms of collateral review typically restrict when and how certain claims can be considered.) See, e.g., 28 U.S.C. §2254(b)-(e), (i) (setting forth various limits on when a federal court can grant a writ of habeas corpus on behalf of a person in custody following a state conviction). Is it a sound practice to have the various fora for appellate review seek to coordinate when and how certain legal claims will be examined? Or is the whole point of collateral review to give defendants a chance to have decisions made on direct review double-checked?

3. *The British Criminal Cases Review Commission.*   The United Kingdom has a very limited appellate review system in criminal cases, and many defendants forgo the right to appeal. In the wake of a number of high-profile miscarriages of justice in the mid-1990s, however, the British government created the Criminal Cases Review Commission to review the applications of criminal defendants who claim to be wrongfully convicted. If the commission considers it "a real possibility that the conviction, verdict, finding or sentence would not be upheld," it refers the case to the court of appeal. As of October 2000, the Commission had referred 4.3 percent of the cases reviewed to the court that had heard 49 of them, and overturned more than three-quarters of these convictions.

Especially in light of recent evidence that many innocent persons were wrongly convicted and were able to establish their innocence only with the help of public interest organizations that donated time and money to conduct DNA testing and other forms of investigation, do you think such a commission should be created in the United States? What might be some of the benefits of using a commission, rather than a traditional court, to review the lawfulness and appropriateness of criminal convictions and sentences? If you think such a commission would be worthwhile, should it provide an additional means of review in criminal cases, or should it operate in place of certain levels of direct or collateral review? How would you try to structure its membership and operation to protect it from undue political influence?

4. *Political debates over federal habeas corpus review.*   A highly political debate about federalism arises when federal courts review and invalidate convictions obtained in state court through collateral review. Although the federal writ of habeas corpus has a constitutional foundation and a long history, debates over postconviction judicial review began to heat up following modern expansions of habeas corpus review of state court convictions in federal court. Expanded federal habeas review began in the mid-1960s after a few groundbreaking U.S. Supreme Court decisions, although there was some significant retrenchment in the opportunities and methods of review in the 1980s and 1990s. See generally Jordan Steiker, Restructuring Post-conviction Review of Federal Constitutional Claims Raised by State Prisoners: Confronting the New Face of Excessive Proceduralism, 1998 U. Chi. Legal F. 315 (discussing history and controversies over

federal habeas review and suggesting ways to redesign federal habeas review of state convictions in capital cases).

The impact of politics on federal habeas corpus review was reflected in Congress's passage of the Antiterrorism and Effective Death Penalty Act (AEDPA) in 1996 after the Oklahoma City bombing of the Murrah Federal Building by Timothy McVeigh. The enactment of the AEDPA has dramatically altered federal habeas corpus practice in many ways, establishing restrictions on the filing of federal habeas corpus petitions, new procedures for treating unexhausted claims and for appealing the denial or dismissal of a petition, and new standards for reviewing state court rulings. See generally Bryan A. Stevenson, The Politics of Fear and Death: Successive Problems in Capital Federal Habeas Corpus Cases, 77 N.Y.U. L. Rev. 699 (2002).

|| *A Broken System: Error Rates in Capital Cases,* ||
|| *1973-1995, James S. Liebman et al. (2000)* ||

SUMMARY OF CENTRAL FINDINGS

In Furman v. Georgia in 1972, the Supreme Court reversed all existing capital statutes and death sentences. The modern death-sentencing era began the next year with the implementation of new capital statutes designed to satisfy *Furman.* Unfortunately, no central repository of detailed information on post-*Furman* death sentences exists. In order to collect that information, we undertook a painstaking search, beginning in 1991 and accelerating in 1995, of all published state and federal judicial opinions in the U.S. conducting direct and habeas review of state capital judgments, and many of the available opinions conducting state post-conviction review of those judgments. We then (1) checked and catalogued all the cases the opinions revealed, and (2) collected hundreds of items of information about each case from the published decisions and the NAACP Legal Defense Fund's quarterly death row census, and (3) tabulated the results. Nine years in the making, our central findings thus far are these:

- Between 1973 and 1995, approximately 5,760 death sentences were imposed in the U.S. Only 313 (5.4%; one in 19) of those resulted in an execution during the period.
- Of the 5,760 death sentences imposed in the study period, 4,578 (79%) were finally reviewed on "direct appeal" by a state high court. Of those, 1,885 (41%; over two out of five) were thrown out because of "serious error," i.e., error that the reviewing court concludes has seriously undermined the reliability of the outcome or otherwise "harmed" the defendant.
- Nearly all of the remaining death sentences were then inspected by state post-conviction courts. Our data reveal that state post-conviction review is an important source of review in states such as Florida, Georgia, Indiana, Maryland, Mississippi, North Carolina, and Tennessee. In Maryland, at least 52 percent of capital judgments reviewed

on state post-conviction during the study period were overturned due to serious error; the same was true of at least 25 percent of the capital judgments that were similarly reviewed in Indiana, and at least 20 percent of those reviewed in Mississippi.

- Of the death sentences that survived state direct and post-conviction review, 599 were finally reviewed in a first habeas corpus petition during the 23-year study period. Of those 599, 237 (40%; two out of five) were overturned due to serious error.

- The "overall success rate" of capital judgments undergoing judicial inspection, and its converse, the "overall error-rate," are crucial factors in assessing the effectiveness of the capital punishment system. The "overall success rate" is the proportion of capital judgments that underwent, and passed, the three-stage judicial inspection process during the study period. The "overall error-rate" is the reverse: the proportion of fully reviewed capital judgments that were overturned at one of the three stages due to serious error. Nationally, over the entire 1973-1995 period, the overall error-rate in our capital punishment system was 68 percent.

- "Serious error" is error that substantially undermines the reliability of the guilt finding or death sentence imposed at trial. Each instance of that error warrants public concern. The most common errors are (1) egregiously incompetent defense lawyering (accounting for 37 percent of the state post-conviction reversals), and (2) prosecutorial suppression of evidence that the defendant is innocent or does not deserve the death penalty (accounting for another 16%-19%, when all forms of law enforcement misconduct are considered). As is true of other violations, these two count as "serious" and warrant reversal only when there is a reasonable probability that, but for the responsible actor's miscues, the outcome of the trial would have been different.

- The seriousness of these errors is also revealed by what happens on retrial, when the errors are cured. In our state post-conviction study, an astonishing 82 percent (247 out of 301) of the capital judgments that were reversed were replaced on retrial with a sentence less than death, or no sentence at all. In the latter regard, 7 percent (22/301) of the reversals for serious error resulted in a determination on retrial that the defendant was not guilty of the capital offense.

- The result of very high rates of serious, reversible error among capital convictions and sentences, and very low rates of capital reconviction and resentencing, is the severe attrition of capital judgments. As is illustrated by the flow chart below:

1. For every 100 death sentences imposed and reviewed during the study period, 41 were turned back at the state direct appeal phase because of serious error. Of the 59 that got through that phase to the second, state post-conviction stage, at least 10 percent — meaning 6 more of the original 100 — were turned back due to serious flaws. And, of the 53 that got through that stage to the third, federal habeas checkpoint, 40 percent — an additional 21

The Attrition of Capital Judgments

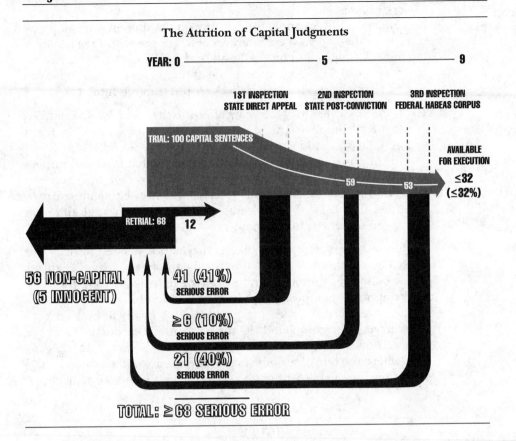

YEAR: 0 ———————————— 5 ———————————— 9

1ST INSPECTION   2ND INSPECTION   3RD INSPECTION
STATE DIRECT APPEAL   STATE POST-CONVICTION   FEDERAL HABEAS CORPUS

TRIAL: 100 CAPITAL SENTENCES

AVAILABLE FOR EXECUTION
≤32 (≤32%)

59 ——— 53

RETRIAL: 68   12

56 NON-CAPITAL (5 INNOCENT)

41 (41%) SERIOUS ERROR

≥6 (10%) SERIOUS ERROR

21 (40%) SERIOUS ERROR

TOTAL: ≥ 68 SERIOUS ERROR

of the original 100 — were turned back because of serious error. All told, at least 68 of the original 100 were thrown out because of serious flaws, compared to only 32 (or less) that were found to have passed muster — after an average of 9-10 years had passed.

2. And among the individuals whose death sentences were overturned for serious error, 82 percent (56 in our example) were found on retrial not to have deserved the death penalty, including 7 percent (5) who were found innocent of the offense.

- The 68 percent rate of capital error found by the three stage inspection process is much higher than the error rate of less than 15 percent found by those same three inspections in noncapital criminal cases.
- Appointed federal judges are sometimes thought to be more likely to overturn capital sentences than state judges, who almost always are elected in capital-sentencing states. In fact, state judges are the first and most important line of defense against erroneous death sentences. They found serious error in and reversed 90 percent of the capital sentences that were overturned during the study period. . . .
- Finding all this error takes time. Calculating the amount of time using information in published decisions is difficult. Only a small

percentage of direct appeals decisions report the sentence date. By the end of the habeas stage, however, a larger proportion of sentencing dates is reported in one or another decision in the case. Accordingly, it is possible to get a good sense of timing for only the 599 cases that were finally reviewed on habeas corpus. Among those cases:

1. It took an average of 7.6 years after the defendant was sentenced to die to complete federal habeas consideration in the 40 percent of habeas cases in which reversible error was found.
2. In the cases in which no error was detected at the third inspection stage and an execution occurred, the average time between sentence and execution was 9 years. Matters did not improve over time. In the last 7 study years (1989-95), the average time between sentence and execution rose to 10.6 years.

-   High rates of error, and the time consequently needed to filter out all that error, frustrate the goals of the death penalty system. Figure 1 below compares the overall rate of error detected during the state direct appeal, state post-conviction, and federal inspection process in the 28 states with at least one capital case in which both inspections have been completed, to the percentage of death sentences imposed by each state that it has carried out by execution. In general, where the rate of serious reversible error in a state's capital judgments reaches 55 percent or above (as is true for the vast majority of

FIGURE 1
Overall Error Rate and Percent of Death Sentences Carried Out, 1973-95

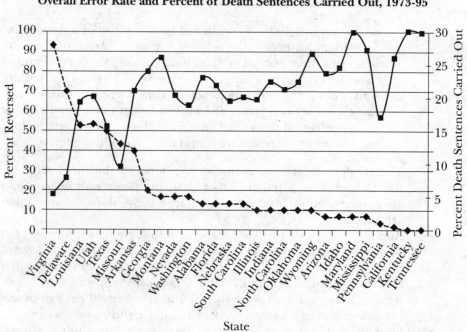

states), the state's capital punishment system is effectively stymied — with its proportion of death sentences carried out falling below 7 percent.

The recent rise in the number of executions is not inconsistent with these findings. Instead of reflecting improvement in the quality of death sentences under review, the rising number of executions may simply reflect how many more sentences have piled up for review. If the error-induced pile-up of cases is the cause of rising executions, their rise provides no proof that a cure has been found for disturbingly high error rates. To see why, consider a factory that produces 100 toasters, only 32 of which work. The factory's problem would not be solved if the next year it made 200 toasters (or added 100 new toasters to 100 old ones previously backlogged at the inspection stage), thus doubling its output of working products to 64. With, now, 136 duds to go with the 64 keepers, the increase in the latter would simply mask the persistence of crushing error rates.

FIGURE 2
Persons on Death Row and Percent and Number Executed, 1974-99

The decisive question, therefore, is not the number of death sentences carried out each year, but the proportion. And as Figure 2 below shows:

- In contrast to the annual number of executions (the middle line in the chart), the proportion of death row inmates executed each year (the bottom line) has remained remarkably stable — and extremely low. Since post-*Furman* executions began in earnest in 1984, the nation has executed an average of about 1.3 percent of its death row inmates each year; in no year has it ever carried out more than 2.6 percent — or 1 in 39 — of those on death row.

- Figure 1 thus suggests that executions are increasing, not because of improvements in the quality of capital judgments, but instead because so many more people have piled up on death row that, even consistently tiny proportions of people being executed — because of consistently prodigious error and reversal rates — are prompting the number of executions to rise. As in our factory example, rising output does not indicate better products, and instead seems to mask the opposite.

NOTES

1. *Success or failure?*   Though the title of the groundbreaking report by Professor James Liebman and his colleagues reveals that they think their data document "a broken system," can one rely on some of these data to claim the system works? Could the finding that from 1973 to 1995, two of every three death sentences were reversed at some point in the many layers of capital case reviews indicate that appellate courts have appropriately invested considerable time and energy to ensure greater confidence in the lawfulness and appropriateness of the death sentences that have been carried out? For an illuminating debate over the meaning and significance of the data in the Liebman study, see Joseph L. Hoffmann, Violence and the Truth, 76 Ind L.J. 939 (2001); Valerie West, Jeffrey Fagan, and James S. Liebman, Look Who's Extrapolating: A Reply to Hoffmann, 76 Ind. L.J. 951 (2001); Joseph L. Hoffmann, A Brief Response to Liebman, Fagan, and West, 76 Ind. L.J. 957 (2001).

One way we might consider what conclusions to draw from the Liebman data is to reflect on the finding that the "68 percent rate of capital error found by the three stage inspection process is much higher than the error rate of less than 15 percent found by those same three inspections in noncapital criminal cases." Why do you think the "error rate" is so much higher in capital than noncapital cases? Does this finding suggest that more fundamental mistakes are made in capital cases, or does it instead reveal that there are more legal regulations that apply in death penalty cases and thus many more possible bases for committing error? More provocatively, does this finding suggest that courts in capital cases review verdicts and sentences more seriously and therefore the only major difference between capital and noncapital cases is the rate at which error is detected?

2. *The time and costs of review.*   The Liebman study details not only the results of appellate review in death penalty cases, but also the considerable time it

takes to conduct this review. Specifically, the study reports that "in the cases in which no error was detected at the third inspection stage and an execution occurred, the average time between sentence and execution was 9 years," and that the time needed for all the layers of appellate review has grown longer, not shorter, over time. This timeline of appellate review is significant not only for the defendant sitting on death row and his family but also for the family members of the victim, who may (or may not) be eager for the defendant's execution to take place. In addition, though not specifically calculated in the Liebman study, the economic costs of all this review of capital verdicts is considerable (some rough estimates suggest that just the appellate review stages of a fully appealed capital case may cost up to $1 million). Not to be overlooked is the time that courts, state lawyers, defense attorneys, and other judicial personnel spend on death penalty appeals rather than on other important aspects of administering the criminal justice system or the legal system more generally.

In short, although it would be impossible to calculate precisely the economic and noneconomic costs of appellate review of capital cases, no one could reasonably question the conclusion that the costs are enormous in many respects. But like the data in the Liebman study, that determination does not suggest an obvious legal response. Should the enormity of the time and resources spent on appellate review in capital cases lead us to conclude that opportunities for review should be more sharply limited or that more money needs to be invested in ensuring that errors are not committed in capital cases in the first place? Or do the data suggest that we ought to abolish the death penalty altogether? See generally James Liebman, The Overproduction of Death, 100 Colum. L. Rev. 2030 (2000).

3. *Geographic and court variations in "error" data.* What conclusions can and should we draw from the fact that Professor Liebman's data reveal many variations in reversal rates based on geography and reviewing courts? This variation is most apparent in Figure 1 above, which shows, for example, that less than 20 percent of all capital cases in Virginia are reversed on appeal whereas nearly 100 percent of all capital cases in Tennessee are reversed on appeal. Do these numbers indicate that Tennessee is more "error-prone" in operating its capital sentencing system, or rather that the courts reviewing Tennessee death sentences detect more errors on appeal? More generally, do you need to know the reasons for reversals rather than the cumulative numbers in order to assess what the Liebman study establishes?

4. *Appellate review and punishment purposes.* The authors of the Liebman study assert that "[h]igh rates of error, and the time consequently needed to filter out all that error, frustrate the goals of the death penalty system." Is that conclusion indisputable? Does a "successful" death penalty system really depend on executing offenders efficiently and at a low cost, or should success be measured more in terms of whether defendants who deserve to die, and only those who deserve to die, are executed? More generally, can one effectively assess the success of appellate review in capital cases or of other sentencing outcomes without first reaching some conclusions about the purposes of punishment canvassed in Chapter 1?

5. *"Error" in nondeath cases.*   With some notable exceptions, the focus on errors in criminal convictions and sentences has been almost exclusively on death penalty cases. This is understandable because of the irreversibility of the sentence and also because many researchers have an anti–capital punishment agenda. But, is a system that is error-prone in death cases likely to function more accurately in other cases? How may the pressures vary between death and nondeath cases? Would a comprehensive, Liebman-type study be advisable for nondeath cases? What would you expect it to show? In countries without the death penalty, such as the United Kingdom, concern about error in criminal cases has focused almost exclusively on cases involving imprisonment.

4.   Supranational Review of Sentences

While the U.S. Supreme Court is the highest binding authority in direct appeals and collateral review in the United States, U.S. citizens and residents may bring complaints about their sentences before the Inter-American Human Rights Commission and the United Nations Human Rights Committee. Both of these institutions can issue recommendations to the U.S. government, though their decisions are not binding on any U.S. official.

In other countries, however, supranational courts may review sentences and issue decisions binding on national governments and courts. Among such institutions are the European Court of Human Rights (ECHR) and the Judicial Committee of the Privy Council, the highest court for former Commonwealth countries that continue to accept its jurisdiction. In recent years the Judicial Committee has heard a large number of death penalty appeals. The most famous may be the one set out below.

	Earl Pratt and Ivan Morgan v. The Attorney	
	General for Jamaica	
	(Appeal No. 10 of 1993)	

JUDGMENT OF THE LORDS OF THE JUDICIAL
COMMITTEE OF THE PRIVY COUNCIL

Lord GRIFFITHS.

The appellants, Earl Pratt and Ivan Morgan, were arrested 16 years ago for a murder committed on 6th October 1977 and have been held in custody ever since. On 15th January 1979 they were convicted of murder and sentenced to death. Since that date they have been in prison in that part of Saint Catherine's prison set aside to hold prisoners under sentence of death and commonly known as death row. On three occasions the death warrant has been read to them and they have been removed to the condemned cells immediately adjacent to the gallows. . . . The statement of these bare facts is sufficient to bring home to the mind of any person of normal sensitivity and compassion the agony of mind that these men must have suffered as they have alternated between hope and despair in the 14 years that they have been in prison facing the gallows. It is unnecessary to refer to the evidence describing the restrictive conditions of imprisonment and the emotional and psychological impact of this experience, for it only reveals that which it is to be expected. These men are not alone in their suffering for there are now 23 prisoners in death row who have been awaiting execution for more than ten years and 82 prisoners who have been awaiting execution for more than five years. It is against this disturbing background that their Lordships must now determine this constitutional appeal. . . .

The death penalty in the United Kingdom has always been carried out expeditiously after sentence, within a matter of weeks or in the event of an appeal even to the House of Lords within a matter of months. Delays in terms of years are unheard of. . . . The Report of the Royal Commission on Capital Punishment 1949-53 (Cmd. 8932) gave the average delay in 1950 as six weeks if there was an appeal and three weeks if there was not. In 1947 there was great public disquiet that men convicted of a murder on the Gold Coast had been under sentence of death for two years. . . . The concern expressed by members of Parliament in the course of the debate reflected the expectation that the Colonies would follow the long established practice in this country that execution would not be long delayed after sentence. . . .

The murder was committed on 6th October 1977 and the appellants were sentenced to death on 15th January 1979. Their application for leave to appeal was dismissed by the Court of Appeal on 5th December 1980 who said that they would hand down their reasons later. Although notice of application for leave to appeal was given within three days of the conviction on 18th January 1979, it took almost two years to arrange a hearing by the Court of Appeal. Making every allowance for the pressure of work on the Jamaican courts this does seem a long time to arrange a hearing in a capital case which one would have expected to have been expedited. . . .

[A]fter the dismissal of their application by the Court of Appeal [ ] their Lordships would have expected the Governor-General to refer the case to the Jamaican Privy Council (JPC) to advise him whether or not the men should be executed in accordance with sections 90 and 91 of the Constitution. . . . Their Lordships can perceive no reason why the appellants' case should not have been referred to the JPC for a decision early in 1981. . . .

Pratt [ ] on 16th August [1984] wrote to the Registrar of the Court of Appeal asking for the reasons why his application for leave to appeal was dismissed. It then transpired that no reasons had yet been prepared by the judge to whom the writing of the judgment had been assigned. The papers had apparently been put in the wrong bundle and forgotten. This was a serious oversight by the judge and by those in the office of the Court of Appeal who should have reminded him that reasons had not been provided in accordance with the practice of the Court of Appeal, which is to provide a reserved judgment or reasons within three months of a hearing. Prompted by Pratt's request reasons were quickly prepared and handed down on 24th September 1984. No immediate steps were, however, taken to petition the Judicial Committee of the Privy Council.

On 3rd October the [Inter-American Committee of Human Rights (IACHR), which Pratt had petitioned] rejected [his] submission that his trial was unfair; but recommended that his sentence be commuted for humanitarian reasons. . . . On 28th January 1986 Pratt petitioned the United Nations Human Rights Committee [UNHRC] under the International Covenant on Civil and Political Rights.

On 13th March 1986 the appellants lodged notice of intention to petition for special leave to appeal to the Judicial Committee of the Privy Council. The application for special leave was heard with reasonable dispatch and special leave to appeal was refused by the Judicial Committee of the Privy Council on 17th July 1986. . . . In dismissing the application Lord Templeman expressed the concern of the Judicial Committee that three years and nine months had elapsed between the dismissal of the appeal and the delivery of the reasons. . . .

On 21st July 1986 the UNHRC requested Jamaica not to carry out the death sentence on Pratt and Morgan before it had an opportunity to consider the admissibility of the complaint. On 18th November 1986 the [Jamaican Privy Council (JPC)], apparently for the first time, considered the appellants' case. They did not accede to the request of the UNHRC to stay the execution and the first warrant of execution was issued on 12th February 1987 for execution on 24th February.

On 23rd February the Governor-General issued a stay of execution. The reasons for the stay are not entirely clear but may have been the result of a telegram from the UNHRC urging a stay of execution and a letter from Mr. Noel Edwards Q.C., to the Governor-General informing him that the case of the appellants was due to be considered by the UNHRC on 23rd March 1987 and the IACHR on 26th March 1987. . . .

On 9th July 1987 the IACHR pursuant to further representations of Pratt and Morgan informed the Jamaican government of the following findings:

> Pratt and Morgan suffered a denial of justice during the period 1980-1984 violative of Article 5(2) of the American Convention on Human Rights. The Commission found that the fact that the Jamaican Court of Appeal issued its decision on December 5, 1980 but did not issue the reasons for that decision until four years later, September 24, 1984, was tantamount to cruel, inhuman and degrading treatment because during that four year delay the petitioners could not appeal to the Privy Council and had to suffer four years on death row awaiting execution. The Inter-American Commission on Human Rights . . . requests that the execution of Messrs. Pratt and Morgan be commuted for humanitarian reasons.

. . . On 13th October 1987 the JPC reconsidered the appellants' case. They did not accede to the request of the IACHR and on their advice the second warrant of execution was issued on 18th February 1988 for execution on 1st March.

On 29th February 1988 the second stay of execution was issued by the Governor-General. This time it appears to have been as a result of a further request from the UNHRC not to execute the men until the Committee had completed their review of the case. . . .

On 6th April 1989 the UNHRC gave their decision on the merits. They held that the failure of the Court of Appeal to deliver reasons for 45 months was a violation of Article 14 para. 3(c) and Article 14 para. 5 of the International Covenant on Civil and Political Rights and Optional Protocol which [states that everyone "shall be entitled to . . . be tried without undue delay" and "shall have the right to his conviction and sentence being reviewed by a higher tribunal according to law."].

The Committee gave the following reasons for their decision [and made the following recommendation]:

> 13.4 The State party has contended that the time span of three years and nine months between the dismissal of the authors' appeal and the delivery of the Court of Appeal's written judgement was attributable to an oversight and that the authors should have asserted their right to receive earlier the written judgement. The Committee considers that the responsibility for the delay of 45 months lies with the judicial authorities of Jamaica. This responsibility is neither dependent on a request for production by the accused in a trial nor is non-fulfilment of this responsibility excused by the absence of a request from the accused. The Committee further observes that the Privy Council itself described the delay as inexcusable. . . .
>
> 13.5 In the absence of a written judgement of the Court of Appeal, the authors were not able to proceed to appeal before the Privy Council, thus entailing a violation of article 14, paragraph 3(c) and article 14, paragraph 5. In reaching this conclusion it matters not that in the event the Privy Council affirmed the conviction of the authors. The Committee notes that in all cases, and especially in capital cases, accused persons are entitled to trial and appeal without undue delay, whatever the outcome of those judicial proceedings turns out to be.
>
> It is the view of the Committee that, in capital punishment cases, States parties have an imperative duty to observe rigorously all the guarantees for a fair trial set out in article 14 of the Covenant. Although in this case article 6 is not directly at issue, in that capital punishment is not per se unlawful under the Covenant, it should not be imposed in circumstances where there have been violations by the State party of any of its obligations under the Covenant. The Committee is of the view that the victims of the violations of articles 14, paragraph 3(c) . . . are entitled to a remedy; the necessary prerequisite in the particular circumstances is the commutation of the sentence.

Eighteen months then passed before a decision was taken by the JPC on this recommendation of the UNHRC. Press reports of parliamentary proceedings show that in June 1990 the question of the death penalty was under review by the Cabinet but that no conclusions had yet been reached on commuting sentences.

On 17th September 1990 the JPC again reconsidered the appellants' case. They rejected the recommendations made eighteen months earlier by the UNHRC. On 18th February 1991 the warrant of execution was issued for execution on 7th March 1991, the delay in issuing the warrant of execution from 17th September 1990 to 18th February 1991 apparently being accounted for by the wish of the Governor-General to obtain the Attorney-General's advice on the legal status of decisions of human rights bodies. This is advice which it would have been appropriate to place before the members of the JPC at a much earlier date, and before they considered any recommendations of such bodies. Their Lordships have not seen the Attorney-General's advice but do not doubt that it correctly advised that, Jamaica being a signatory to the International Covenant on Civil and Political Rights and to the Optional Protocol, the views of the UNHRC should be afforded weight and respect but were not of legally binding effect; and that the like considerations applied to the IACHR.

On 28th February 1991 the appellants commenced these proceedings. . . .

The primary submission of the appellants is that to hang them after they have been held in prison under sentence of death for so many years would be inhuman punishment or other treatment and thus in breach of section 17(1) of the Constitution. Section 17 of the Constitution provides [that] "No person shall be subjected to torture or to inhuman or degrading punishment or other treatment." . . .

There is an instinctive revulsion against the prospect of hanging a man after he has been held under sentence of death for many years. What gives rise to this instinctive revulsion? The answer can only be our humanity; we regard it as an inhuman act to keep a man facing the agony of execution over a long extended period of time. But before their Lordships condemn the act of execution as "inhuman or degrading punishment or other treatment" within the meaning of section 17(1) there are a number of factors that have to be balanced in weighing the delay. If delay is due entirely to the fault of the accused such as an escape from custody or frivolous and time wasting resort to legal procedures which amount to an abuse of process the accused cannot be allowed to take advantage of that delay for to do so would be to permit the accused to use illegitimate means to escape the punishment inflicted upon him in the interest of protecting society against crime.

A much more difficult question is whether the delay occasioned by the legitimate resort of the accused to all available appellate procedures should be taken into account, or whether it is only delay that can be attributed to the shortcomings of the State that should be taken into account.

There is a powerful argument that it cannot be inhuman or degrading to allow an accused every opportunity to prolong his life by resort to appellate procedures however extended may be the eventual time between sentence and execution. This is the view that currently prevails in some States in the United States of America and has resulted in what has become known as the death row phenomenon where men are held under sentence of death for many years while their lawyers pursue a multiplicity of appellate procedures. . . . Support for this view is also to be found in previous decisions of the Privy Council. . . .

There are other authorities which do not accept that delay occasioned by use of appeal procedures is to be disregarded. In Catholic Commission for Justice and Peace in Zimbabwe v. Attorney-General [Judgment No. S.C. 73/93, unreported, delivered on June 24, 1993] Gubbay C.J. said:

> It seems to me highly artificial and unrealistic to discount the mental agony and torment experienced on death row on the basis that by not making the maximum use of the judicial process available the condemned prisoner would have shortened and not lengthened his suffering. The situation could be otherwise if he had resorted to a series of untenable and vexatious proceedings which, in consequence, had the effect of delaying the ends of justice. . . .

In Soering v. United Kingdom (1989) 11 E.H.R.R. 439 the applicant, a West German national, alleged that the decision by the Secretary of State for the Home Department to extradite him to the United States of America to face trial in Virginia on a charge of capital murder would, if implemented, give rise to a breach by the United Kingdom of Article 3 of the European Convention for the Protection of Human Rights and Fundamental Freedoms (Cmd. 8969) which provides that no one should be subjected to torture or to inhuman or degrading treatment or punishment. . . . The European Court of Human Rights recognised that the death row phenomenon in Virginia where prisoners were held for a period of six to eight years before execution arose from repeated applications by the prisoner for a stay of execution but nevertheless held that such a long period of delay might go beyond the threshold set by Article 3. . . .

In their Lordships' view a State that wishes to retain capital punishment must accept the responsibility of ensuring that execution follows as swiftly as practicable after sentence, allowing a reasonable time for appeal and consideration of reprieve. It is part of the human condition that a condemned man will take every opportunity to save his life through use of the appellate procedure. If the appellate procedure enables the prisoner to prolong the appellate hearings over a period of years, the fault is to be attributed to the appellate system that permits such delay and not to the prisoner who takes advantage of it. Appellate procedures that echo down the years are not compatible with capital punishment. The death row phenomenon must not become established as a part of our jurisprudence.

The application of the appellants to appeal to the Judicial Committee of the Privy Council and their petitions to the two human rights bodies do not fall within the category of frivolous procedures disentitling them to ask the Board to look at the whole period of delay in this case. The total period of delay is shocking and now amounts to almost fourteen years. It is double the time that the European Court of Human Rights considered would be an infringement of Article 3 of the European Convention and their Lordships can have no doubt that an execution would now be an infringement of section 17(1) of the Jamaican Constitution.

To execute these men now after holding them in custody in an agony of suspense for so many years would be inhuman punishment within the meaning of section 17(1). In the last resort the courts have to accept the responsibility of saying whether the threshold has been passed in any given case and there may be difficult borderline decisions to be made. This, however, is not a borderline case. The delay in this case is wholly unacceptable and this appeal must be allowed. . . .

Section 25(2) of the Constitution provides [broad authority that] enables the court to substitute for the sentence of death such order as it considers appropriate. The appropriate order in the present case is that the sentence of death of each appellant should be commuted to life imprisonment.

Their Lordships are very conscious that many other prisoners under sentence of death are awaiting the outcome of this appeal. In an attempt to assist the Jamaican authorities who may be faced with a large number of appeals their Lordships wish to make some general observations. . . .

There may of course be circumstances which will lead the JPC to recommend a respite in the carrying out of a death sentence, such as a political moratorium on the death sentence, or a petition on behalf of the appellants to IACHR or UNHRC or a constitutional appeal to the Supreme Court. But if these respites cumulatively result in delay running into several years an execution will be likely to infringe section 17(1) and call for commutation of the death sentence to life imprisonment.

Their Lordships are very conscious that the Jamaican government faces great difficulties with a disturbing murder rate and limited financial resources at their disposal to administer the legal system. Nevertheless, if capital punishment is to be retained it must be carried out with all possible expedition. Capital appeals must be expedited and legal aid allocated to an appellant at an early stage. The aim should be to hear a capital appeal within twelve months of conviction. [I]t should be possible to complete the entire domestic appeal process within approximately two years. Their Lordships do not purport to set down any rigid timetable but to indicate what appear to them to be realistic targets which, if achieved, would entail very much shorter delay than has occurred in recent cases and could not be considered to involve inhuman or degrading punishment or other treatment.

The final question concerns applications by prisoners to IACHR and UNHRC. Their Lordships wish to say nothing to discourage Jamaica from continuing its membership of these bodies and from benefiting from the wisdom of their deliberations. It is reasonable to allow some period of delay for the decisions of these bodies in individual cases but it should not be very prolonged. The UNHRC does not accept the complaint unless the author "has exhausted all available domestic remedies." . . . A complainant [can] lodge a complaint immediately after his case has been disposed of by the Judicial Committee of the Privy Council. If, however, Jamaica is able to revise its domestic procedures so that they are carried out with reasonable expedition no grounds will exist to make a complaint based upon delay. And it is to be remembered that the UNHRC does not consider its role to be that of a further appellate court.

It therefore appears to their Lordships that provided there is in future no unacceptable delay in the domestic proceedings complaints to the UNHRC from Jamaica should be infrequent and when they do occur it should be possible for the Committee to dispose of them with reasonable dispatch and at most within eighteen months.

These considerations lead their Lordships to the conclusion that in any case in which execution is to take place more than five years after sentence there will be strong grounds for believing that the delay is such as to constitute "inhuman or degrading punishment or other treatment." If, therefore, rather than waiting for all those prisoners who have been in death row under sentence of death for five years or more to commence proceedings pursuant to section 25 of the Constitution, the Governor-General now refers all such cases to the JPC who, in accordance with the guidance contained in this advice, recommend commutation to life imprisonment, substantial justice will be achieved swiftly and without provoking a flood of applications to the Supreme Court for constitutional relief pursuant to section 17(1). . . .

Their Lordships will accordingly humbly advise Her Majesty that this appeal ought to be allowed, and the sentences of the appellants be commuted to life imprisonment.

NOTES

1. *The Privy Council and its death penalty jurisprudence.*   With the expansion of the British Empire during the nineteenth century, courts in the colonies increasingly gained the right to appeal to the Privy Council and, later, its Judicial Committee. The Judicial Committee is an independent court composed of

members of the high English judiciary and that of Commonwealth countries. Today it continues to hear appeals from British territories and the former English colonies that recognize it as their highest court.

The modern line of death penalty jurisprudence in the Judicial Committee began with *Pratt*, which found that unconscionable delay after the imposition of a death sentence violates the prohibition of cruel and inhuman punishment so long as the delay is not the defendant's fault. The Judicial Committee did not consider delay caused by the defendant's exhaustion of appeals to be his fault. The more significant outcome of the case was the Judicial Committee's new timetable for death penalty cases: Any execution occurring more than five years after the sentence was imposed would create a strong presumption of inhuman punishment. In later cases, the Judicial Committee held a less-than-five-year delay unconstitutional. Moreover, the Judicial Committee found that not only delay but also unreasonable speed could lead to sentence commutation, since a defendant deserved reasonable notice of his execution.

As a consequence of these decisions, in the Caribbean countries scores of death sentences were commuted to life, and new appellate procedures were instituted to shorten the delay. What problems do such changes entail? For the U.S. Supreme Court's view of delay in capital cases (as well as a discussion of the value of foreign opinions on such issues), see Knight v. Florida, 528 U.S. 990 (1999) (concurrence and dissent from denial of certiorari).

2. *The Inter-American Human Rights Commission, the Inter-American Court of Human Rights, and the European Court of Human Rights.* The Inter-American Human Rights system consists of two organs, a commission and a court. While not all countries have accepted the court's jurisdiction, their citizens and residents have the right to petition the commission unless expressly excluded. For signatories of the American Declaration of Human Rights only, such as the United States, the commission may issue a recommendation at the end of a factual investigation; if a country signed the American Convention on Human Rights, the commission can refer a complaint to the court.

In past cases, the commission has held the United States in violation of the international prohibition of the execution of juveniles and has chastised it for the disparate application of the death penalty. The Inter-American court, while not outlawing the death penalty, has applied strict scrutiny in capital cases.

In *Pratt* the Judicial Committee of the Privy Council noted the additional delay stemming from Pratt's petition to the commission and the U.N. Human Rights Committee. How do you explain delays by institutions committed to protecting human rights? Consider the staffing and meeting times of such institutions.

The European Human Rights system, with the European Court of Human Rights, has only rarely had the opportunity to consider the death penalty. In a seminal decision, the court ruled that Great Britain could not extradite a German national to Virginia because of the so-called death row phenomenon — the delay between sentence imposition and execution and the conditions on death row — unless it received guarantees that the German would not be sentenced to death. Soering v. United Kingdom, 11 Eur. H.R. Rep. 439 (Eur. Ct. H.R. 1989). This opinion has had lasting impact on other national and supranational tribunals around the world. For details on the recent European reaction to the death penalty in the United States, see Nora V. Demleitner,

The Death Penalty in the United States: Following the European Lead?, 81 Or. L. Rev. 131 (2002).

3. *The U.N. Human Rights Committee.*   The U.N. Human Rights Committee is a treaty body under the International Covenant on Civil and Political Rights and under the Convention against Torture and Other Cruel, Inhuman or Degrading Treatment or Punishment. In that capacity it can hear a complaint once an individual has exhausted domestic remedies. In 1994 the Human Rights Committee found the use of gas chambers in select U.S. states a violation of the International Covenant on Civil and Political Rights. Other subcommittees and U.N. rapporteurs have focused on the question of juvenile executions. Should a governor be influenced by pronouncements of the U.N. Human Rights Committee or other U.N. institutions in individual petitions or on larger questions pertaining to the application of the death penalty?

4. *The International Court of Justice (ICJ).*   The ICJ can hear only state-to-state complaints, some of them lodged by countries on behalf of individual citizens. In 1999 Germany asked the ICJ to issue a stay of execution in the case of a German citizen sentenced to death in Arizona. It alleged that the United States had violated the Vienna Convention on Consular Rights by failing to inform him and his brother, who had already been executed, that they had the right to contact the German embassy, which would have provided them with paid-for counsel. The state of Arizona proceeded to execute the German, in violation of the ICJ's stay order. The ICJ held that it had the power to issue such provisional measures and stated that in future cases in which the United States failed to live up to its treaty obligations and sentenced someone severely, a sentence commutation and monetary compensation to the German government were in order. LaGrand Case (Germany v. United States of America), 40 I.L.M. 1069 (I.C.J. 2001). The case was styled not as a death penalty case but rather as a case involving the violation of an important treaty. Currently, the Mexican government has a similar case against the United States pending before the ICJ. Avena and Other Mexican Nationals (Mexico v. United States of America). Are Germany and Mexico merely trying to protect the right to consular notification, or are they attempting to change U.S. law on the death penalty? If the latter, is such action legitimate?

B.   EXECUTIVE RECONSIDERATION OF SENTENCES

Even after trial, sentencing, appeals, and judicial postconviction challenges have ended and a convict begins to serve a sentence, the criminal justice process is not yet complete. A variety of rules and mechanisms under the control of executive branch agencies determine whether at some point before the sentence expires an offender should be released from prison and what continuing limits and controls can be placed on an offender once released.

The most common mechanism for early prison release decisions and for supervising offenders after release is parole, a period of conditional supervised release following a prison term. Parole was once a fundamental component of nearly every American sentencing system, but the past quarter-century has seen dramatic reforms. The purpose, structure, and operation of parole (and parole boards) have changed in significant ways over the past several decades, and in some jurisdictions, including the federal system, parole has been technically eliminated. Nevertheless, parole remains a key aspect of most state sentencing systems, and as of year-end 2002 more than 750,000 people were on parole.

Another form of executive review takes place when a governor or president issues a pardon or commutation. The pardon power typically has a constitutional foundation; like the role of parole, however, the role of pardons in modern sentencing systems has evolved considerably. In recent times, an executive decision to grant a pardon or commutation has become both rare and often controversial. These two fundamental forms of executive sentence review will occupy the second part of this chapter.

1.   Parole

At the start of the twentieth century, reformers introduced parole as a cornerstone of a new approach to sentencing and corrections, and by 1950, all of the states, the federal system, and the District of Columbia relied heavily on the parole function as part of an indeterminate sentence system. In indeterminate sentencing, judges could impose an initial sentence as broad as "zero to life" (though most sentences were imposed in a narrower range), and parole boards were authorized to consider offenders for release starting at a certain point within the broad sentencing ranges. Inherent in this system, and in the function of parole boards, was the belief that the primary purpose of imprisonment was to rehabilitate offenders. More specifically, the institution of parole assumed that offenders could be rehabilitated and that prisons could accomplish that job. The prevailing belief was that experts in the social and psychological sciences would be able to determine when an individual was rehabilitated and thereby ready for release. Parole boards were invested with broad discretion to assess whether rehabilitation had taken place.

Indeterminate sentencing came under heightened scrutiny in the 1970s as many began to doubt the ability and the appropriateness of achieving offender rehabilitation through the criminal justice system, and as concerns grew concerning the frequent lack of correspondence between the crime committed and the length of time served. The discretion exercised by both judges and parole boards in indeterminate sentencing systems was criticized on various grounds, and an array of reforms led to a movement in many jurisdictions away from indeterminate sentencing toward more determinate sentencing, in which offenders know their release date (subject to a slight decrease for good institutional behavior, so-called good time) on the day they are sentenced. Nevertheless, the model of indeterminate sentencing that dominated American sentencing systems for most of the twentieth century can still be found in more than half of the states, and thus parole continues to be critical in many jurisdictions.

As researchers Jeremy Travis and Sarah Lawrence have explained, parole and parole boards play three critical roles:

> First, parole boards determine the actual length of a prison sentence. With indeterminate sentencing, judges sentence an offender to a prison term,

specifying a minimum and a maximum length of prison stay. The parole board, an executive branch agency, then decides on a case-by-case basis whether a prisoner is ready to be released to the community.

Second, parole agencies supervise recently released individuals in the community for the remainder of their sentence. In the classic indeterminate sentencing model, a prisoner released on parole is not free. Rather, he or she is still serving a criminal sentence, in the community rather than in prison, and must abide by a number of conditions established by the parole board at the time of release. Thus, parole agencies are expected to play a critical role in overseeing the reintegration of returning prisoners.

Third, parole officers and parole boards are authorized to revoke a parolee's conditional liberty and return him or her to prison. If a parole officer (also referred to as a parole agent) determines that the parolee has failed to observe a condition of his release — for example, has committed a new crime, failed to maintain employment, or failed a drug test — the officer can recommend that parole be revoked. The parole board, or in some states a judicial officer, then decides whether to send the parolee back to prison for some or all of the remainder of the prison sentence. Thus, parole officers and parole boards play an important role in removing parolees from the community when infractions occur.

Jeremy Travis and Sarah Lawrence, Beyond the Prison Gates: The State of Parole in America 2 (Urban Institute, Nov. 2002)

In the sections that follow, we first examine the composition and authority of parole commissions, the key decision makers in parole systems. We then turn to an examination of the three major functions of parole commissions and boards: (1) determining when inmates will be released from prison, (2) supervising offenders on parole, and (3) creating rules for parole revocation. As you read these materials, it is worthwhile to review some of the doctrines and issues concerning probation covered in Chapter 8, since probation and parole both involve conditional releases into the community. They differ, however, in that probation is imposed at sentencing by a judge whereas parole is imposed by a parole board after an offender has already served a prison term.

a.   Parole Boards and Commissions

‖ *Iowa Code §§904A.1, 904A.2* ‖

The board of parole is created to consist of five members. Each member, except the chairperson, shall be compensated on a day-to-day basis. Each member shall serve a term of four years. . . . The terms shall be staggered. The chairperson of the board shall be a full-time, salaried member of the board. A majority of the members of the board constitutes a quorum to transact business.

The membership of the board shall be of good character and judicious background, shall include a member of a minority group, may include a person ordained or designated as a regular leader of a religious community and who is knowledgeable in correctional procedures and issues, and shall meet at least two of the following three requirements:

1. Contain one member who is a disinterested layperson.

2. Contain one member who is an attorney licensed to practice law in this state and who is knowledgeable in correctional procedures and issues.

3. Contain one member who is a person holding at least a master's degree in social work or counseling and guidance and who is knowledgeable in correctional procedures and issues.

‖ *Colorado Revised Statutes §17-22.5-404(7)* ‖

(a) There is hereby established in the department of public safety the Colorado commission on parole guidelines. The commission shall con-sist of the attorney general who shall serve as chairperson, the executive director of the department of public safety, the executive director of the department of corrections, the chairperson of the state board of parole, the chairperson of a community corrections board, a parole officer, a law enforcement officer, and a private citizen. The latter four members shall be appointed by the governor and confirmed by the senate. The director of the division of criminal justice of the department of public safety shall serve as an ex officio member of the commission.

(b) The commission . . . shall have the power to approve objective parole criteria . . . which are developed by the division of criminal justice.

NOTES

1. *Representation requirements: expertise and insulations.*   Parole board members are usually appointed by the governor for fixed terms. Traditional membership requirements have often included backgrounds in psychology and social work to assess the likely behavior and rehabilitation of inmates. More modern membership requirements focus on diverse representation, sometimes including specific allocation of spots to members of different political parties. The assumptions underlying the representation requirements on parole boards have changed over time. Why do statutes like the Iowa provisions now require membership of community members, religious leaders, and members of minority groups? Will such requirements increase diverse viewpoints of parole boards? What is the virtue of having a "disinterested layperson"? What influence can a layperson have if the other members of the parole board appear to be more knowledgeable in criminal justice matters?

2. *Political insulation.*   The structure and composition of parole boards can determine to what extent politics influences parole decision making. Colorado has two separate institutions to address parole issues: the parole board, which makes individual parole decisions, and the commission to review and approve parole guidelines. Why would Colorado create a separate body to set parole policy? Should a jurisdiction seek to maximize the political insulation of parole decision makers or instead create structures that ensure political accountability in parole decisions?

b.   Parole Guidelines and Release Decisions

Early in their history, parole boards typically had broad and almost unfettered discretion in making parole release decisions. One distinct feature of modern parole decision making is that boards are now typically governed by guidelines of varying detail. Usually those guidelines have been issued by the parole board itself, although they are sometimes produced under legislative direction. Some guidelines state principles to guide the parole board's release decisions; others specify particular parole terms for a given offender committing a specific offense. Some guidelines are based on rough assessments of a mix of factors related to the underlying offense, the offender's threat to the community or to individuals, or the inmate's likelihood of reoffending. Other guidelines are based on social science data reflecting risk factors and favor release of individuals who, based on their similarity to prior offenders, are predicted to be least likely to commit serious offenses in the near future.

‖ *Colorado Revised Statutes* ‖
‖ *§17-22.5-404(1),(2)* ‖

(1) As to any person . . . who is eligible for parole . . . , the board may consider all applications for parole, . . . and may parole any person who is sentenced or committed to a correctional facility when the board determines, by using the guidelines established by this section, that there is a strong and reasonable probability that the person will not thereafter violate the law and that his release from institutional custody is compatible with the welfare of society. The board shall first consider the risk of violence to the public in every release decision it makes.

(2) (a) In considering offenders for parole, the board shall consider, but need not be limited to, the following factors:

(I) The testimony of the victim of the crime or a relative of the victim, if the victim has died . . . ;

(II) The offender's conduct which would indicate whether he has substantially observed all of the rules and regulations of the institution or facility in which he has been confined and has faithfully performed the duties assigned to him;

(III) The offender's demonstration of good faith efforts to make restitution to the victim of his conduct for the actual damages that were sustained . . . ;

(IV) The offender's demonstration of good faith efforts to pay reasonable costs of parole supervision . . . ;

(V) The offender's demonstration of good faith efforts to devote time to a specific employment or occupation;

(VI) The offender's good faith efforts to enroll in a school, college, university, or course of vocational or technical training designed to fit the student for gainful employment;

(VII) Whether the offender has diligently attempted but has been unable to obtain employment that provides the offender sufficient income, whether the offender has an employment disability, or whether the offender's age prevents him or her from obtaining employment;

(VIII) The offender's demonstration of good faith efforts to remain within prescribed geographical boundaries and notify the court or the parole officer of any change in the offender's address or employment;

(IX) The offender's demonstration of good faith efforts to report as directed to the parole officer;

(X) The offender's demonstration of good faith efforts to participate in some type of community service work;

(XI) The offender has not harassed the victim either verbally or in writing;

(XII) The offender's demonstration of good faith efforts to provide support, including any court-ordered child support, for any minor children;

(XIII) The offender's participation in the literacy corrections programs.

(b) Nothing in this subsection . . . shall preclude the board from considering factors other than those stated in paragraph (a) . . . when considering applicants for parole.

Michael McDermott v. James McDonald
24 P.3d 200 (Mont. 2001)

Petitioner Michael McDermott (McDermott) is serving a thirty-year sentence for assault and felony bail jumping in the Crossroads Correctional Center. The Board of Pardons and Parole (Board) has denied his application for parole, based in part on his failure to participate in a sexual offender program (SOP). He petitions this Court for a writ of habeas corpus, alleging that the Board has illegally denied him parole. We deny his petition.

BACKGROUND

In May 1989, McDermott was charged by information with four counts of assault and four counts of incest against his two stepsons, then aged five and six. The information alleged that, between June 1985 and January 1986, McDermott assaulted his stepsons physically and sexually by burning their arms on the stove, knocking out their teeth, beating them on their legs, buttocks and penis with a wooden spoon and forcing them to engage in anal and oral intercourse. After being charged and released on bond, McDermott fled the jurisdiction. Eventually recaptured, he was extradited back to Montana and charged with an additional count of felony bail jumping.

McDermott pled guilty to the assault and bail jumping charges in exchange for dismissal of the four incest counts. The District Court sentenced him to five years on each assault charge and ten years on the bail jumping charge, for a total sentence of thirty years. Because of the violent nature of the assaults, because he committed them against young victims and because the court found that he represents a substantial danger to society, McDermott was designated a dangerous offender for purposes of parole.

McDermott began serving his sentence in May 1992. At that time, an initial needs assessment concluded that he suffers from "severe sexual problems" and recommended that he participate in the prison's treatment program for sexual offenders. McDermott elected not to participate in the SOP, and the Board later considered this fact during evaluations for placement in a prerelease center, for parole and for inmate classification purposes.

McDermott first applied for parole in September 1998. After notice and a hearing, the Board denied his application, citing McDermott's multiple offenses as well as their nature and severity. It noted that participation in the SOP would "enhance success on parole and further ensure that the applicant is willing and able to fulfill the obligations of a law-abiding citizen." McDermott again chose not to participate. As a result, he had four points added to his classification status for noncompliance with the Board's SOP recommendation. In September 1999, the Board again denied McDermott's parole application, citing the nature and severity of his offenses as well as his failure to comply with the Board's previous SOP recommendation.

McDermott contends that by requiring him to complete an SOP as a condition to early release on parole, the Board infringed upon his liberty interest in parole without due process of law. He petitions this Court for a writ of habeas corpus ordering his immediate release and rescinding the four points added to his classification status.

DISCUSSION

Our due process analysis requires us to determine whether McDermott has a protected liberty interest in parole, and, if so, what process he is due and whether he received that process.

A.   McDermott's Liberty Interest in Parole

As a general rule, inmates have no liberty interest in parole. Greenholtz v. Inmates of the Nebraska Penal and Correctional Complex, 442 U.S. 1, 7 (1979). We have, however, recognized an exception to this general rule for inmates who committed their offenses prior to 1989. Before that year, Montana's parole eligibility statute stated:

> the board *shall* release on parole . . . any person confined in the Montana state prison . . . when in its opinion there is reasonable probability that the prisoner can be released without detriment to the prisoner or to the community. [Emphasis added.]

Section 46-23-201, MCA (1985). The United States Supreme Court held that the mandatory language of this provision created a liberty interest in parole that is protected by the due process clause of the federal constitution. Board of Pardons v. Allen, 482 U.S. 369, 377 (1987). Although the Montana Legislature removed the mandatory language in 1989, we determined that inmates who committed offenses prior to the amendment continued to enjoy a federally-protected liberty interest in parole. Worden v. Montana Bd. of Pardons and Parole, 962 P.2d 1157 (Mont. 1998). McDermott committed his offenses in 1985 and 1986. Therefore, he has a protected liberty interest in parole under *Allen* and *Worden*.

Having determined that McDermott has a protected liberty interest in parole, the Fourteenth Amendment to the United States Constitution and Article

II, Section 17, of the Montana Constitution guarantee that it cannot be denied without due process.

B.   *The Process Due McDermott*

There is no absolute standard for what constitutes due process. Rather, the requirements of due process are flexible, so that they may be adapted to meet the procedural protections demanded by a particular situation. *Greenholtz,* 442 U.S. at 12. Thus, the process due in any given case varies according to the factual circumstances of the case, the nature of the interests at stake, and the risk of making an erroneous decision.

It is well established that a parole release determination is not subject to all the due process protections required to convict or confine. Nor must a parole release determination provide the same due process protections as are required in a parole revocation hearing. These situations present a much greater risk of error than a parole release determination because incarceration, whether as a result of conviction or parole revocation, involves a loss of liberty. Denial of parole, on the other hand, involves the loss of the mere anticipation of freedom — freedom to which the lawfully-convicted inmate is otherwise not entitled. As a consequence, the United States Supreme Court has held that due process is satisfied when the prisoner seeking parole is, at a minimum, provided with an opportunity to be heard and a written statement explaining why he was denied parole. *Greenholtz,* 442 U.S. at 16.

C.   *The Board's Authority to Consider McDermott's Participation in the SOP*

McDermott does not contend that he was denied an opportunity to come before the Board or that he did not receive a statement of the reasons his parole was denied. Rather, he argues that the Board does not have authority to consider his lack of participation in an SOP as a basis for denying him early release on parole. For support, he relies on two of this Court's recent decisions: State v. Ommundson, 974 P.2d 620 (Mont. 1999), in which we held that a district court could not force an offender to complete a sexual offender program that had no correlation or connection to the underlying offense, and State v. Field, 11 P.3d 1203 (Mont. 2000), in which we held that the Board had no authority to impose conditions on a probationer that were not a part of his original sentence. We conclude, however, that neither of these cases limit the Board's authority to consider McDermott's failure to participate in the recommended SOP.

In *Ommundson,* the defendant pled guilty to driving under the influence of alcohol (DUI). After a presentence investigation revealed that he had more than ten previous convictions for indecent exposure, the district court conditioned suspension of the defendant's DUI sentence on his participation in an SOP. On appeal, we struck down the SOP condition, holding that "a sentencing limitation or condition must have . . . some correlation or connection to the underlying offense for which the defendant is being sentenced." We based our decision on the requirement of MCA §46-18-202(1)(e), that a sentence be "reasonably related to the objectives of rehabilitation and protection of the victim and society."

McDermott characterizes the Board's consideration of his failure to participate in the SOP as a precondition to parole. He contends that the Board's authority to set such conditions can be no greater than a sentencing court's authority to set conditions on a sentence and, therefore, under *Ommundson,* the Board can only place conditions on parole that have some correlation or connection to the underlying offense. Since he was not convicted of a sex offense, McDermott contends that the Board has no authority to condition his parole on his participation in an SOP.

We find this argument without merit. . . . First, McDermott presents no evidence that the Board conditioned his release on his participation in the SOP. His initial parole review indicated that parole was denied because of the nature, number and severity of his offenses. . . .

Second, even if consideration of McDermott's failure to participate in the SOP can be viewed as a precondition to parole, our holding in *Ommundson* does not limit the Board's authority to set such conditions. McDermott's argument fails to recognize the fundamental difference between imposition of a sentence — as in *Ommundson*— and release on parole. A sentence, or condition included in that sentence, is a *limitation on liberty.* A condition on parole is not. The district court's authority is properly restrained when it acts to limit an individual's freedom. Once lawfully sentenced, however, a prisoner is not entitled to release prior to the completion of his full sentence. Parole, therefore, is a *grant of liberty.* A condition on parole only limits freedom to which the inmate is otherwise not entitled. As a general proposition, then, it is invalid to assume, as McDermott does, that the Board's authority to set conditions precedent to parole is necessarily limited by a court's sentencing authority.

More specifically, the statutory basis for the court's sentencing authority is not applicable to the Board. In *Ommundson,* this Court held that the statutory requirement that a sentence be "reasonably related to the objectives of rehabilitation and protection of the victim and society," requires that any sentencing limitation or condition have some "correlation or connection to the underlying offense for which the defendant is being sentenced." The "correlation or connection" standard, therefore, was based on a specific statutory limitation on the district court's sentencing authority. While the standard for release on parole is also limited by statute, the Board has considerably more discretion to impose conditions than does a sentencing court.

Under both Montana and federal precedent, parole is a privilege and not a right. Since parole is granted as a matter of grace, rather than right, the state may offer such grace under and subject to such conditions as it considers most conducive to accomplish the desired purpose. In Montana, that grace is offered only when, in the Board's opinion, three conditions have been satisfied: "there is a reasonable probability that the prisoner can be released without detriment to the prisoner or to the community," MCA §46-23-201(1) (1985); when it is in "the best interests of society"; and when the prisoner "is able and willing to fulfill the obligations of a law-abiding citizen." MCA §46-23-201(2). Rather than restricting the authority of the Board to set conditions precedent to parole, these provisions obligate the Board to ensure that no prisoner is released on parole who cannot meet these three criteria.

As a complement to its broad discretion to grant, deny, or condition parole, the Board is authorized to consider factors that may not be considered by the district court at trial and sentencing. For instance, parole authorities are not limited to consideration of formally adjudicated cases when determining the likelihood of a prisoner's success on parole. Christopher v. U.S. Board of Parole, 589 F.2d 924 (7th Cir. 1978). Moreover, they may consider evidence of offenses which were charged in dismissed counts. Robinson v. Hadden, 723 F.2d 59 (10th Cir. 1983). A parole board may even hear and consider evidence excluded at trial under the exclusionary rule. In re Martinez, 463 P.2d 734 (Cal. 1970). In Montana, the Board is specifically required to "consider all pertinent information regarding each prisoner, including the circumstances of his offense, his previous social history and criminal record, his conduct, employment and attitude in prison, and the reports of any physical and mental examinations which have been made." MCA §46-23-202 (1985).

We conclude that the Board's authority to condition parole is not limited by our holding in *Ommundson*. Furthermore, the Board's statutory authority is broad enough to permit its consideration of McDermott's dismissed incest counts, the results of his initial needs assessment showing severe sexual problems and his refusal to participate in an SOP when determining whether to grant him an early release on parole.

McDermott's second argument is based on this Court's recent holding in *Field*. In that case, we held that the Board could not impose a condition on a probationer's postrelease conduct that was not specifically authorized by his sentence. *Field* dealt with a prisoner who had served the full term of his unsuspended sentence and was released on probation. Prior to release, the Board imposed the condition that he have no unsupervised contact with minors. Violation of this condition was later used to rescind the probation and return Field to prison. On appeal, this Court applied MCA §46-18-801, which provides that no "offender may be *deprived of a civil or constitutional right* except as provided in the Montana Constitution or as specifically enumerated by the sentencing judge as a necessary condition of the sentence. . . ." We reversed recision of the suspended sentence after determining that the condition that Field have no unsupervised contact with minors was a violation of his constitutional right to freedom of association and that it was not specifically included as a condition of his sentence.

McDermott argues that the Board's authority to impose conditions on his *parole* can be no greater than its authority to impose postsentence conditions on Field. He contends that, even if the District Court had the authority to impose a condition that he participate in an SOP as part of his sentence, no such condition was included. Therefore, he asserts, as in *Field*, the Board cannot now impose it as a condition of his release. We disagree.

In applying this Court's holding in *Field*, it is important to distinguish release on *parole* and release on *probation*. Parole, as stated above, is a discretionary grant of freedom from incarceration. Probation is an original condition of sentence that, for some period of time, the offender will not be incarcerated. . . . Under *Field*, the Board has no authority to impose conditions on *probation* that were not part of the original sentence because, under the terms of the sentence, Field was entitled to be released at the time and under the conditions set by the court. But *Field* does not limit the Board's authority to place conditions on *parole*. The Board's placement of a condition on *probation* is a restriction on someone who would otherwise be free. A condition on *parole* is a limited grant of freedom to someone who would otherwise be incarcerated. We conclude that our holding in *Field* does not limit the Board's authority to impose conditions on parole and is not relevant to McDermott's case.

CONCLUSION

Under MCA §46-23-201 (1985), McDermott must be released on parole when, in the Board's opinion, he "can be released without detriment to [himself] or to the community," when release is in "the best interests of society," and when he is "able and willing to fulfill the obligations of a law-abiding citizen." . . . In making this determination, the Board must consider "all pertinent information regarding the prisoner." McDermott, while not a convicted sex offender, had four counts of incest dismissed pursuant to a plea bargain. He has been identified as having severe sexual problems. His completion — or lack of completion — of the SOP is pertinent to his ability to be released without "detriment to the . . . community" and "to fulfill the obligations of a law-abiding citizen." Therefore, the Board was well within its authority to consider McDermott's refusal to enroll in the recommended SOP when it denied his application for an early release.

PROBLEM 11-4.   BEING UNDER THE WEATHER

On October 20, 1981, Kathy Boudin was arrested in conjunction with the robbery of an armored car during which the driver, Peter Paige, had been killed. Boudin had not participated in the planning of the robbery of $1.6 million, and was unarmed at the time of her arrest. She belonged to a radical group, the Weather Underground, that was not averse to using violence to support its goals. After the robbery Boudin was riding in a U-Haul truck with those who had participated in the robbery. When the U-Haul was stopped at a roadblock, Boudin immediately surrendered to the police. Shortly thereafter, as police attempted to open the back of the truck, shooting erupted, and two police officers were killed.

Boudin pled guilty under New York's felony murder statute. She was sentenced to twenty years to life in prison for her role in the robbery. No charges were filed against her in connection with the death of the officers since she had already surrendered at the time they were killed. At sentencing, Judge Ritter imposed what he characterized as a "minimal" but "just" sentence. He explained his reasons for doing so: "In my judgment there is evidence of honest contrition and remorse, and abhorrence of violence as a technique to further goals, however noble." He concluded that Boudin's role in the tragedy was a "secondary one," and stated that "there is no evidence . . . to believe she is guilty of . . . any form of terrorist activity." Finally, Judge Ritter stated, "I see no reason in the world why Miss Boudin should not be paroled at the expiration of the twenty years."

In prison Boudin was a model inmate. While at Bedford Hills, New York's prison for women, she established a program for women inmates with HIV that served as the model for such programs nationwide. In addition, she set up programs in adult literacy and for incarcerated women with children. In that capacity she organized workshops and developed curricula. She also completed a master's degree in adult education while in prison and published widely on HIV, literacy, mother–child relationships, and higher education.

At her first parole hearing in August 2001, Boudin was denied parole; the parole board stated that "due to the violent nature and circumstances of the instant offenses, [Boudin's] release at this time would be incompatible with the welfare of society and would serve to deprecate the seriousness of the criminal behavior herein so as to undermine respect for the law." At her second parole hearing in May 2003, parole was again denied with reference to the seriousness of the nature of the crimes, and the fact that three individuals died in the crime spree.

Subsequent to the second parole hearing, a New York judge ordered a new hearing because the parole board had failed to consider adequately Judge Ritter's remarks at sentencing and Boudin's remarkable record while in prison. At her third hearing in the summer of 2003, Boudin was granted parole, effective October 1, 2003.

To what extent should the parole board be influenced by Judge Ritter's remarks? Should it have mattered to the parole board that some but not all of the victims' family members opposed the grant of parole? Would the parole decision for Boudin have been different under Colorado's parole guidelines (reprinted above)? Under Montana's parole rules (discussed in the *McDermott* case above)?

NOTES

1. *Right to parole.*   As noted in *McDermott,* in Greenholtz v. Inmates of the Nebraska Penal and Correctional Complex, 442 U.S. 1 (1979), the Supreme Court held that state prisoners do not have a constitutional right to parole and that there is no constitutionally protected interest in receiving parole unless a state's parole statute contains mandatory language restricting the parole board's discretion in making its decision. In such a case, the prisoner gains a legitimate expectation of parole that cannot be denied without due process. In *Greenholtz,* the Supreme Court held that the due process requirement was satisfied through an informal hearing in which the inmate had an opportunity to present letters and statements on his behalf.

2. *Parole procedures.*   Parole hearings are typically open to the public, and the offender as well as the victim or the victim's family are allowed to make statements. The members of the parole board are furnished information about the offense committed, the offender's behavior while incarcerated, and reports from prison psychiatrists, if applicable. Although the precise contours of prisoners' due process rights in parole proceedings have not been definitively established, most jurisdictions tend to provide a hearing (with prior notice provided), a defined opportunity for the presentation of information by the inmate, some form of notice of the criteria used to make the parole decision, and some form of notice of the decision together with reasons for denial. See Victoria J. Palacios, Go and Sin No More: Rationality and Release Decisions by Parole Boards, 45 S.C. L. Rev. 567 (1994).

Parole boards cannot act arbitrarily. A number of recent decisions in New York have held that the parole board must sincerely evaluate the inmate's prison record and rehabilitative efforts and that it must consider the sentencing judge's recommendation.

3. *Discretionary and mandatory parole releases and good time.*   Parole release schemes in which parole boards have broad, largely unfettered discretion to determine a release date have fallen out of favor over the past few years. Parole decision making has become increasingly more structured, and mandatory releases to parole supervision are much more common now than in the past. In 2002, 52 percent of all adults entering parole did so upon mandatory release. Mandatory release occurs largely in determinate sentencing systems, in which inmates are conditionally released from prison after serving a portion of their original sentence minus any good time earned.

Inmates earn so-called good-time credit for institutional behavior that shows adherence to prison rules and no major infractions. The ceiling on good-time credits varies by jurisdiction. In the past, in some systems, inmates earned a day (or more) of good time for every day served. This led to heavy criticism, as inmates were released substantially earlier than the community and the victims expected.

Many systems now cap good time at 15 percent of the total sentence imposed, and they have been encouraged to do so by federal funding criteria for prison construction grants. Under the federal prison-building "truth-in-sentencing" grants, states are strongly encouraged to keep violent offenders incarcerated for 85 percent of the prison time imposed. See generally Paula Ditton and Doris James Wilson, Truth in Sentencing in State Prisons (Bureau of Justice Statistics, NCJ 170032, 1999). The Minnesota system began with a good-time provision allowing credits of up to 33 percent of the pronounced term, but recent legislation has cut back on that authorization. See Minn. Stat. ch. 244 (West 2002). Why would a legislature decrease good-time credits inmates can earn? What advantages are there in the increase of good-time credits? Consider these questions from the perspective of a warden, a state legislator, and a member of a crime-ridden community.

4. *Elimination of parole and other changes in parole rules.*   Spurred in part by broad criticisms about the efficacy of parole systems as well as by federal funds tied to truth-in-sentencing requirements, more than a dozen states have abolished early releases by a parole board for all offenders, and several others have significantly restricted parole either through formal legal limits on eligibility or through the evolving decision making by parole boards. Even in states that have retained parole, parole boards have become more hesitant to grant it. In Texas, for example, 57 percent of all cases considered for parole release in 1988 were approved; by 1998, that figure had dropped to 20 percent. See Joan Petersilia, Parole and Prisoner Reentry in the United States, 26 Crime & Just. 479 (1999).

Defendants sometimes claim that formal changes in the rules governing parole eligibility can transgress the U.S. Constitution's Ex Post Facto Clause. In Johnson v. Commissioner of Corrections, 786 A.2d 1091 (Conn. 2002), the Connecticut Supreme Court cited such constitutional concerns when interpreting a state change in release rules that would have made violent offenders eligible for parole release only after serving 85 percent rather than 50 percent of their sentences to apply only prospectively. In a similar vein but reaching a different sort of result, the Supreme Court examined in Garner v. Jones, 529 U.S. 244 (2000), whether the retroactive application of a Georgia law permitting the extension of intervals between parole considerations violated the Ex Post Facto Clause. Defining the inquiry in terms of whether Georgia's change in parole rules created "a sufficient risk of increasing the measure of punishment attached to the covered crimes," the Court sent the case back to the Eleventh Circuit Court of Appeals to determine whether the change in Georgia's parole board rules did create a significant risk of increased punishment for inmate Jones.

5. *Supervised release under the federal sentencing guidelines.* As part of the Sentencing Reform Act of 1984, federal law formally eliminated parole and recast efforts at postincarceration supervision in terms of "supervised release." Federal judges must impose a term of supervised release if the offender is sentenced to at least one year in prison. The length of supervised release depends on the seriousness of the felony committed, ranging from a minimum of one year for minor felonies and the most serious misdemeanors to five years for the most serious felonies. Select offenses allow for the imposition of a life term of supervised release.

In addition, the district court may impose a specific condition of supervision so long as the condition meets four criteria: (1) it must be reasonably related to specified sentencing factors, namely the nature and circumstances of the offense and the history and characteristics of the defendant; (2) it must be reasonably related to the need to afford adequate deterrence, to protect the public from further crimes of the defendant, and to provide the defendant with necessary educational or vocational training, medical care, or other correctional treatment in the most effective manner; (3) it must involve no greater deprivation of liberty than is reasonably necessary to achieve these goals; and (4) it must be consistent with any pertinent policy statements issued by the U.S. Sentencing Commission. See 18 U.S.C. §§3583(d), 3563(d), 3553.

To what extent do parole and supervised release differ? How are they similar? Suppose a person who runs a credit repair business is convicted of conspiracy to distribute methamphetamine and has a prior conviction for passing counterfeit notes. In light of the provisions for supervised release, would it be appropriate for a court to impose on the defendant an occupational restriction demanding that he inform his clients of the conviction? See United States v. Britt, 332 F.3d 1229 (9th Cir. 2003).

6. *International tribunals.* Under the Statute of the International Criminal Court, the court reviews a sentence after the offender has served two-thirds, or in case of a life term 25 years, of the sentence imposed. At that point the sentence may be reduced and the individual may qualify for early release. The statute contemplates that early release be granted only to individuals who have cooperated with prosecutors, made attempts at reparation, and appear to be able to benefit from early release. The gravity of the offense also matters. How parole is to work in practice, however, remains unresolved. It is unclear, for example, in what country the offender should be released on parole — the country of imprisonment, the home state, or possibly a third country close to the home state.

c. Parole Conditions

Like sentencing courts, which establish conditions of probation (see Chapter 8), parole boards often establish conditions of parole. Some parole conditions are mandated by statute, but others are imposed as additional requirements or conditions. As you review the following materials and problems, consider whether and what sorts of parole conditions should be mandated in all cases, be subject to discretionary application, or be completely unavailable.

|| *Alaska Statutes §33.16.150* ||

(a) As a condition of parole, a prisoner released on special medical, discretionary, or mandatory parole

(1) shall obey all state, federal, or local laws or ordinances, and any court orders applicable to the parolee;

(2) shall make diligent efforts to maintain steady employment or meet family obligations;

(3) shall, if involved in education, counseling, training, or treatment, continue in the program unless granted permission from the parole officer assigned to the parolee to discontinue the program;

(4) shall report (A) upon release to the parole officer assigned to the parolee; (B) at other times, and in the manner, prescribed by the board or the parole officer assigned to the parolee;

(5) shall reside at a stated place and not change that residence without notifying, and receiving permission from, the parole officer assigned to the parolee;

(6) shall remain within stated geographic limits unless written permission to depart from the stated limits is granted the parolee;

(7) may not use, possess, handle, purchase, give, distribute, or administer a controlled substance . . . or a drug for which a prescription is required under state or federal law without a prescription from a licensed medical professional to the parolee;

(8) may not possess or control a firearm . . . ;

(9) may not enter into an agreement or other arrangement with a law enforcement agency or officer that will place the parolee in the position of violating a law or parole condition without the prior approval of the board;

(10) may not contact or correspond with anyone confined in a correctional facility of any type serving any term of imprisonment or a felon without the permission of the parole officer assigned to a parolee;

(11) shall agree to waive extradition from any state or territory of the United States and to not contest efforts to return the parolee to the state;

(12) shall provide a blood sample, an oral sample, or both, when requested by a health care professional acting on behalf of the state to provide the sample or samples, or an oral sample when requested by a juvenile or adult correctional, probation, or parole officer, or a peace officer, if the prisoner is being released after a conviction of an offense requiring the state to collect the sample or samples for the deoxyribonucleic acid identification system under AS 44.41.035.

(b) The board may require as a condition of special medical, discretionary, or mandatory parole, or a member of the board acting for the board under (e) of this section may require as a condition of mandatory parole, that a prisoner released on parole

(1) not possess or control a defensive weapon, a deadly weapon other than an ordinary pocket knife with a blade three inches or less in length, or ammunition for a firearm, or reside in a residence where there is a firearm capable of being concealed on one's person or a prohibited weapon . . . ;

(2) refrain from possessing or consuming alcoholic beverages;

(3) submit to reasonable searches and seizures by a parole officer, or a peace officer acting under the direction of a parole officer;

(4) submit to appropriate medical, mental health, or controlled substance or alcohol examination, treatment, or counseling;

(5) submit to periodic examinations designed to detect the use of alcohol or controlled substances;

(6) make restitution ordered by the court according to a schedule established by the board;

(7) refrain from opening, maintaining, or using a checking account or charge account;

(8) refrain from entering into a contract other than a prenuptial contract or a marriage contract;

(9) refrain from operating a motor vehicle;

(10) refrain from entering an establishment where alcoholic beverages are served, sold, or otherwise dispensed;

(11) refrain from participating in any other activity or conduct reasonably related to the parolee's offense, prior record, behavior or prior behavior, current circumstances, or perceived risk to the community, or from associating with any other person that the board determines is reasonably likely to diminish the rehabilitative goals of parole, or that may endanger the public; in the case of special medical parole, for a prisoner diagnosed with a communicable disease, comply with conditions set by the board designed to prevent the transmission of the disease. . . .

(f) In addition to other conditions of parole imposed under this section, the board may impose as a condition of special medical, discretionary, or mandatory parole for a prisoner serving a term for a crime involving domestic violence (1) any of the terms of protective orders under AS 18.66.100(c)(1)-(7); (2) a requirement that, at the prisoner's expense, the prisoner participate in and complete, to the satisfaction of the board, a program for the rehabilitation of perpetrators of domestic violence that meets the standards set by, and that is approved by, the department under AS 44.28.020(b); and (3) any other condition necessary to rehabilitate the prisoner. . . .

‖ *Colorado Revised Statutes §16-11.7-105(2)* ‖

Each sex offender placed on parole by the state board of parole on or after January 1, 1994, shall be required, as a condition of such parole, to undergo treatment to the extent appropriate to such offender. . . . Any such treatment shall be at a facility or with a person certified or approved by the board and at such offender's expense, based upon such offender's ability to pay for such treatment.

PROBLEM 11-5. BANISHMENT

John Beavers was paroled from prison after serving seven years of a 30-year sentence. As one of the special conditions of his parole, he was barred from Houston County, Alabama, where he and his family had lived prior to his incarceration. When he returned to Houston County without permission to see his two young daughters, he was arrested, and subsequently his parole was revoked. On appeal, what arguments should Beavers's counsel make to attack the revocation? Is the underlying parole condition constitutional? What purpose does the condition serve? See Beavers v. State, 666 So. 2d 868 (Ala. Crim. App. 1995).

NOTES

1. *Parole conditions.*   Paroled inmates are released before their maximum sentence has expired, but usually they must report regularly to a parole officer and comply with a host of conditions, such as gaining employment, abstaining from alcohol and illegal drugs, and not associating with convicted felons. How onerous are such conditions? Consider the predicament of a parolee who, having returned from prison to live with his parents, is visited one afternoon by his elder brother, a convicted felon.

At year-end 2002, about 80 percent of all parolees were under active parole supervision, which meant they were required to maintain regular contact with their parole officer. About 8 percent of parolees could not be located.

2. *Evolving nature of parole supervision and services.*   The rise of determinate sentences and the corresponding reduced reliance on parole mechanisms have significantly changed the nature of postrelease supervision. Professor Joan Petersilia has observed an evolution in parole supervision toward controlling the offender at the expense of providing social services necessary for reentry into society:

> Historically, parole agents were viewed as paternalistic figures who mixed authority with help. Officers provided direct services (e.g., counseling) and also knew the community and brokered services (e.g., job training) to needy offenders. Parole was originally designed to make the transition from prison to the community more gradual, and, during this time, parole officers were to assist the offender in addressing personal problems and searching for employment and a place to live. Many parole agencies still do assist in these "service" activities. Increasingly, however, parole supervision has shifted away from providing services to parolees and more toward monitoring and surveillance (e.g., drug testing, monitoring curfews, and collecting restitution). . . .
>
> There are a number of reasons for this. For one, a greater number of parole conditions are being assigned to released prisoners. In the federal system, for example, between 1987 and 1996 the proportion of offenders required to comply with at least one special supervision condition increased from

67 percent of entrants to 91 percent. Parolees in state systems are also more frequently being required to submit to drug testing, complete community service, and make restitution payments.

   Parole officers work for the corrections system, and if paroling authorities are imposing a greater number of conditions on parolees, then field agents must monitor those conditions. As a result, modern-day parole officers have less time to provide other services, such as counseling, even if they were inclined to do so. It is also true that the fiscal crises experienced in most states in recent years reduced the number of treatment and job-training programs in the community at large, and given the fear and suspicion surrounding ex-convicts, these persons are usually placed at the end of the waiting lists. . . . If there is one common complaint among parole officers in the United States, it is the lack of available treatment and job programs for parolees. . . .

   The main reason, however, that "services" are not delivered to most parolees is that parole supervision has been transformed ideologically from a social service to a law enforcement system.

Joan Petersilia, Parole and Prisoner Reentry in the United States, 26 Crime & Just. 479, 506-508 (1999).

PROBLEM 11-6.   COMPUTER CONDITION

   Gregory Sofsky received on his home computer via the Internet more than 1,000 images of child pornography in the form of both still and moving pictures. He did not produce any of the images but transferred some of them to CD-ROM disks. In addition, he used the Internet to exchange images of child pornography with other (apparently like-minded) individuals. He is prosecuted for receiving child pornography, a federal offense.

   The presentence report recommended that the judge impose a three-year period of supervised release. In addition to the standard conditions of supervised release, the report suggested that the court impose three special conditions: (1) the defendant must participate in mental health treatment, including a program for sexual disorders, (2) the defendant must permit a search of his premises at any time on reasonable suspicion that contraband or evidence of a violation of a condition of supervision may be found, and (3) the defendant must not view, purchase, or possess child pornography. The court followed the report's recommendations and added a fourth condition: the defendant must not "access a computer, the Internet, or bulletin board systems at any time, unless approved by the probation officer."

   On appeal Sofsky challenges the conditions of his supervised release. What standard of review should the appellate court apply? How should it assess the validity of the four conditions? For different answers, see United States v. Sofsky, 287 F.3d 122 (2d Cir. 2002); United States v. Paul, 274 F.3d 155 (5th Cir. 2002); United States v. White, 244 F.3d 1199 (10th Cir. 2001); United States v. Crandon, 173 F.3d 122 (3d Cir. 1999).

d.   Parole Revocation

   Should parolees be returned to prison for committing *any* infraction of the terms of parole? What procedures should be used to determine whether an offender has violated parole?

Consider the statistics described in the following study of prisoners. What accounts for the dramatic increase in reincarcerated parole violators? What is the relationship between the rigor of the parole condition and the consequences of violation? What process should be used to determine violations? In particular, should violation of a reporting condition, a geographic restriction, a work requirement, or a drug screen be cause for automatic parole revocation? If not, when should they?

> *Trends in Parole Supervision, 1990-2000,*
> *Timothy A. Hughes, Doris James Wilson, and*
> *Allen J. Beck*
> **Bureau of Justice Statistics (Sept. 2001)**

RE-RELEASES AN INCREASING PORTION OF STATE PAROLE ENTRIES

Among parole entries, the percentage who had been re-released rose between 1990 and 1999. Re-releases are persons leaving prison after having served time either for a violation of parole or other conditional release or for a new offense committed while under parole supervision. In 1990, 27% of entries to parole were re-releases; in 1999, 45% were re-releases. During 1999 an estimated 192,400 re-releases entered parole, an increase of 103% over the 94,900 re-releases in 1990.

After having been returned to prison for a parole or conditional release violation, re-releases served on average 13 months in prison in 1999. From 1990 to 1999 their average time served in prison following re-admission increased by 2 months. In both years about 7 in 10 re-releases had served less than 12 months in prison. . . .

PAROLE SUCCESS RATES UNCHANGED SINCE 1990

Of the 410,613 discharges from State parole in 1999, 42% successfully completed their term of supervision, 43% were returned to prison or jail, and 10% absconded. In 1990, 45% of State parole discharges were successful. Between 1990 and 1999 the percent successful among State parole discharges has ranged from 42% to 49%, without any distinct trend.

States differed in their rate of success among parole discharges. States with the highest rates of success in 1999 were Massachusetts and Mississippi (at 83% each), followed by North Carolina (80%) and North Dakota (79%). Utah (18%) and California (21%) had the lowest rates of success in 1999.

When comparing State success rates for parole discharges, differences may be due to variations in parole populations, such as age at prison release, criminal history, and most serious offense. Success rates may also differ based on the intensity of supervision and the parole agency policies related to revocation of technical violators.

SUCCESS RATES HIGHEST AMONG FIRST RELEASES AND DISCRETIONARY PAROLE RELEASES

In every year during the 1990's, first releases to State parole were more likely to have been successful than re-releases. Among State parole discharges in 1990, 56% of first releases successfully completed their supervision, compared to 15% of re-releases. Of all those exiting parole in 1999, 63% of first releases were successful, compared to 21% of re-releases.

Success rates also varied by method of release. In every year between 1990 and 1999, State prisoners released by a parole board had higher success rates than those released through mandatory parole. Among parole discharges in 1999, 54% of discretionary parolees were successful compared to 33% of those who had received mandatory parole. . . .

AMONG PAROLE DISCHARGES, SUCCESS RATES ROSE FOR BLACKS AND HISPANICS; DROPPED FOR WHITES

Between 1990 and 1999 the success rates among State parole discharges increased from 33% to 39% among blacks and increased from 31% to 51% among Hispanics, but dropped from 44% to 41% among whites. The 11 percentage-point difference in success rates between white and black parole discharges in 1990 narrowed to less than 2 percentage points in 1999. . . .

For female parole discharges, the rate of success rose over 10 percentage points (from 37% in 1990 to 48% in 1999). The success rate among male parole discharges increased from 36% to 39%.

Older parole discharges had the highest rates of success in both years. Accounting for 2.1% of discharges in 1999, parolees age 55 or older had the highest rate of successful completion (55%). Among parole discharges in other age groups, success rates fluctuated between 36% and 43%.

SUCCESS RATES HIGHEST AMONG FIRST RELEASES SERVING LESS THAN 12 MONTHS IN PRISON

Among parole discharges, 74% of first releases who had served less than 12 months in prison successfully completed parole, the highest success rate among paroled first releases. As the length of time served in prison increased for first releases, the success rate declined, with offenders with the longest time served (5 years or more) having the lowest success rate (62%). The rate of success for this group still exceeded the overall success rate of 42% for all parolees. . . .

RATES OF SUCCESSFUL TERMINATION HIGHER WHEN CALIFORNIA IS EXCLUDED

The size and make-up of California's parole population, combined with the low percent of successful terminations (25% in 1999), affect the national rate of success for parole discharges. . . .

Overall, California accounted for nearly 30% of all State parole discharges during 1999. Discretionary parole, though available as a method of release, is rarely used in California. In 1999 more than 99% of California's parole discharges had received mandatory parole. When California data are excluded, the success rate for all parole discharges rises to 53% (from 42%), and the rate for mandatory parolees increases to 64% (from 33%) in 1999.

NUMBER OF PAROLE VIOLATORS RETURNED TO PRISON CONTINUED TO RISE DURING THE 1990'S

In 1999, 197,606 parole violators were returned to State prison, up from 27,177 in 1980 and 131,502 in 1990. As a percentage of all admissions to State prison, parole violators more than doubled from 17% in 1980 to 35% in 1999.

Between 1990 and 1999 the number of parole violators rose 50%, while the number of new court commitments rose 7%. . . .

In 1999 parole violators accounted for more than 50% of State prison admission in California (67%), Utah (55%), Montana (53%), and Louisiana (53%). In five States — Florida (7%), Alabama (9%), Indiana (10%), Mississippi (10%) and West Virginia (10%) — parole violators comprised 10% or less of all admissions. . . .

NEARLY A QUARTER OF STATE PRISONERS IN 1997 WERE PAROLE VIOLATORS

Based on personal interviews of State inmates, an estimated 24% of prisoners in 1997 said they were on parole at the time of the offense for which they were serving time in prison (up from 22% in 1991). Of the 1,129,180 inmates under the jurisdiction of State prison authorities at yearend 1997, approximately 271,000 were parole violators.

Parole violators in prison in 1997 were older and more likely to have committed a public order or drug offense than parole violators in 1991. In 1997 about 25% of parole violators in prison were age 40 or older, compared to 17% in 1991. In 1997 an estimated 34% were serving time for a violent offense and 23% for a drug offense. In 1991, 36% of parole violators were in prison for a violent offense; 19% for a drug offense. In both years, more than 42% of parole violators reported having been incarcerated 3 or more times in the past.

70% OF PAROLE VIOLATORS IN PRISON IN 1997 RETURNED FOR A NEW OFFENSE

Among parole violators in State prison in 1997, 215,964 (85%) reported that their parole had been revoked or taken away for violating the conditions of their release. Of that number, 70% said that their parole had been revoked because of an arrest or conviction for a new offense; 22% said they had absconded or otherwise failed to report to a parole officer; 16% said they had a drug-related violation; and 18% reported other reasons such as possession of a gun, maintaining contact with known felons, or failure to maintain employment.

HALF OF PAROLE VIOLATORS INCARCERATED IN 3 STATES

The three largest State prison systems (California, Texas, and New York) held over half of all parole violators in prison in 1997. California held 22% of all parole violators in prison, Texas, 21%, and New York, 8%. Within each of these States, the percentage of prisoners who were parole violators was higher than the national level: 39% in Texas, 38% in California, and 28% in New York, compared to 24% nationally.

Among parole violators returned to prison, those held in California (60%) were the least likely to have been arrested or convicted for a new offense and the most likely to have been returned for a drug violation (23%). About 11% of parole violators in New York and Texas reported a drug violation as a reason for their return to prison.

CHARACTERISTICS OF PAROLE VIOLATORS VARIED AMONG THE 3 LARGEST STATES

A higher percentage of parole violators in California (7.1%) were women than in Texas (5.4%) and New York (3.3%). Nationally, 4.7% of parole violators in State prison in 1997 were women.

New York had the highest percentage of parole violators in prison who were black (54%), followed by Texas (50%) and California (33%). In New York, 11% of parole violators were white; in Texas, 23%; in California, 31%. The percent Hispanic among parole violators ranged from 26% to 33% in the three States.

New York had the highest percentage of parole violators convicted of a violent offense (41%), compared to 33% in Texas and 24% in California. New York also had the highest percentage of parole violators returned for a drug offense (34%), compared to 27% in California and 21% in Texas.

Among the three largest States, parole violators in California had the longest criminal histories. More than 58% of parole violators in California had been incarcerated at least 3 times in the past, compared to 42% in Texas and 35% in New York. Nationwide, 44% of parole violators reported three or more prior incarcerations.

NOTES

1. *The purposes of parole.* Traditionally, parole was supposed to help an offender reenter society successfully. Parole officers often had a background in social work. In recent years, the function of parole and background of parole officers have changed dramatically. Parole is increasingly viewed as a way to control offenders once they are back in the community. Parole officers more often have a criminal justice background and see themselves as enforcers of rules

rather than as assistants in the reintegration project. Parole violators thus tend to be returned to prison. In some jurisdictions, however, parole may be revoked but then immediately reinstated, often with new conditions added or following a warning that continued infractions will result in imprisonment. Do such differences account for the nationally disparate numbers of parole violators who return to prison?

2. *Types of violations.*   Data on parole violations tend to distinguish technical violations from new offenses, but sometimes a technical violation may amount to a new offense. Technical violations may include failing to meet with the parole officer, testing positive for drugs, or leaving the jurisdiction without informing the parole officer. Why should technical violations lead to reincarceration? What other sanctions are available? A recent study of juvenile parolees has indicated that young parolees who test positive for drugs during their first three months on parole are more likely to commit offenses while on parole than the other parolees. Can such findings be used to prevent later parole violations? How?

3. *Revocation procedures.*   The rights of parolees at revocation proceedings are limited since such proceedings are not part of a criminal prosecution and the liberty of parolees is considered only conditional. In Pennsylvania Board of Probation and Parole v. Scott, 524 U.S. 357 (1998), for example, the Supreme Court held that the exclusionary rule does not apply to parole revocation hearings. In Morrissey v. Brewer, 408 U.S. 470 (1972), however, the Supreme Court set out the necessary due process protections in parole revocation hearings, including written notice of the claimed violations of parole, disclosure to the parolee of the evidence against him, opportunity to be heard in person and to present witnesses and documentary evidence, generally the right to confront and cross-examine adverse witnesses, the right to be heard by a "neutral and detached" body whose members need not be judicial officers, and a written statement by the factfinders as to the evidence relied on and reasons for revoking parole. In some states the proceeding is heard by the parole board, in others by an administrative law judge. Many states allow for appeals from an adverse decision.

4. *Reentry courts.*   Because of the large number of parole violators who return to prison and the concomitant expense, criminal justice professionals and politicians have renewed their focus on the reentry of prisoners into the community. Some federally funded reentry projects have established reentry courts that follow the model of drug courts (discussed in Chapter 8). A judge regularly sees a parolee and monitors her progress. Successive violations carry sanctions of increasing magnitude, and successful program participation carries small rewards. The goal is to allow for occasional violations of parole rules but prevent future crime while assisting the offender in her reintegration.

2.   Civil Commitment

Parole provides a certain check on released offenders, largely by requiring that they report regularly to their parole officer, but it does not prevent all crime. Some offenders who are considered very dangerous may be released from prison at their mandatory release date. What should society do in that situation? One possibility is an enhanced level of parole in which released offenders are monitored through electronic bracelets or are subject to unannounced visits by parole officers.

In highly charged cases of sexual offenders, however, state legislators may not be willing to risk another offense. Therefore, a number of states have adopted special civil commitment statutes for sexual offenders. While civil commitment statutes have always existed for mentally ill individuals, they are of a different nature in the case of sex offenders. In most such cases, civil commitment appears to equal life imprisonment. Is civil commitment for sex offenders constitutional? What types of safeguards have to be in place?

Kansas v. Leroy Hendricks
521 U.S. 346 (1997)

THOMAS, J.

In 1994, Kansas enacted the Sexually Violent Predator Act, which establishes procedures for the civil commitment of persons who, due to a "mental abnormality" or a "personality disorder," are likely to engage in "predatory acts of sexual violence." Kan. Stat. Ann. §59-29a01 et seq. (1994). The State invoked the Act for the first time to commit Leroy Hendricks, an inmate who had a long history of sexually molesting children, and who was scheduled for release from prison shortly after the Act became law. Hendricks challenged his commitment on, inter alia, "substantive" due process, double jeopardy, and ex post facto grounds. . . .

I.   BACKGROUND

A.   Sexually Violent Predator Act

The Kansas Legislature enacted the Sexually Violent Predator Act (Act) in 1994 to grapple with the problem of managing repeat sexual offenders. [T]he legislature determined that existing civil commitment procedures were inadequate to confront the risks presented by "sexually violent predators." In the Act's preamble, the legislature explained:

> [S]exually violent predators generally have anti-social personality features which are unamenable to existing mental illness treatment modalities and those features render them likely to engage in sexually violent behavior. The legislature further finds that sexually violent predators' likelihood of engaging in repeat acts of predatory sexual violence is high. The existing involuntary commitment procedure . . . is inadequate to address the risk these sexually violent predators pose to society. The legislature further finds that the prognosis for rehabilitating sexually violent predators in a prison setting is poor, the treatment needs of this population are very long term and the treatment modalities for this population are very different than the traditional treatment modalities for people appropriate for commitment under the [general involuntary civil commitment statute].

Kan. Stat. Ann. §59-29a01 (1994).

As a result, the Legislature found it necessary to establish "a civil commitment procedure for the long-term care and treatment of the sexually violent predator." The Act defined a "sexually violent predator" as: "any person who has been convicted of or charged with a sexually violent offense and who suffers from a mental abnormality or personality disorder which makes the person likely to engage in the predatory acts of sexual violence." §59-29a02(a). A "mental abnormality" was defined, in turn, as a "congenital or acquired condition affecting the emotional or volitional capacity which predisposes the person to commit sexually violent offenses in a degree constituting such person a menace to the health and safety of others."

As originally structured, the Act's civil commitment procedures pertained to: (1) a presently confined person who, like Hendricks, "has been convicted of a sexually violent offense" and is scheduled for release; (2) a person who has been "charged with a sexually violent offense" but has been found incompetent to stand trial; (3) a person who has been found "not guilty by reason of insanity of a sexually violent offense"; and (4) a person found "not guilty" of a sexually violent offense because of a mental disease or defect.

The initial version of the Act, as applied to a currently confined person such as Hendricks, was designed to initiate a specific series of procedures. The custodial agency was required to notify the local prosecutor 60 days before the anticipated release of a person who might have met the Act's criteria. The prosecutor was then obligated, within 45 days, to decide whether to file a petition in state court seeking the person's involuntary commitment. If such a petition were filed, the court was to determine whether "probable cause" existed to support a finding that the person was a "sexually violent predator" and thus eligible for civil commitment. Upon such a determination, transfer of the individual to a secure facility for professional evaluation would occur. After that evaluation, a trial would be held to determine beyond a reasonable doubt whether the individual was a sexually violent predator. If that determination were made, the person would then be transferred to the custody of the Secretary of Social and Rehabilitation Services (Secretary) for "control, care and treatment until such time as the person's mental abnormality or personality disorder has so changed that the person is safe to be at large."

In addition to placing the burden of proof upon the State, the Act afforded the individual a number of other procedural safeguards. In the case of an indigent person, the State was required to provide, at public expense, the assistance of counsel and an examination by mental health care professionals. The individual also received the right to present and cross-examine witnesses, and the opportunity to review documentary evidence presented by the State.

Once an individual was confined, the Act required that "the involuntary detention or commitment . . . shall conform to constitutional requirements for care and treatment." Confined persons were afforded three different avenues of review: First, the committing court was obligated to conduct an annual review to determine whether continued detention was warranted. Second, the Secretary was permitted, at any time, to decide that the confined individual's condition had so changed that release was appropriate, and could then authorize the person to petition for release. Finally, even without the Secretary's permission, the confined person could at any time file a release petition. If the court found that the State could no longer satisfy its burden under the initial commitment standard, the individual would be freed from confinement.

B.   Leroy Hendricks

In 1984, Hendricks was convicted of taking "indecent liberties" with two 13-year-old boys. After serving nearly 10 years of his sentence, he was slated for release to a halfway house. Shortly before his scheduled release, however, the State filed a petition in state court seeking Hendricks' civil confinement as a sexually violent predator. . . .

Hendricks . . . requested a jury trial to determine whether he qualified as a sexually violent predator. During that trial, Hendricks' own testimony revealed a chilling history of repeated child sexual molestation and abuse, beginning in 1955. . . . He testified that despite having received professional help for his pedophilia, he continued to harbor sexual desires for children. . . .

Hendricks admitted that he had repeatedly abused children whenever he was not confined. He explained that when he "gets stressed out," he "can't control the urge" to molest children. Although Hendricks recognized that his behavior harms children, and he hoped he would not sexually molest children again, he stated that the only sure way he could keep from sexually abusing children in the future was "to die." Hendricks readily agreed with the state physician's diagnosis that he suffers from pedophilia and that he is not cured of the condition; indeed, he told the physician that "treatment is bull—." The jury unanimously found beyond a reasonable doubt that Hendricks was a sexually violent predator. The trial court subsequently determined, as a matter of state law, that pedophilia qualifies as a "mental abnormality" as defined by the Act, and thus ordered Hendricks committed to the Secretary's custody. . . .

II.   DISCUSSION

A.   Prerequisites of Civil Confinement: Dangerousness and Mental Abnormality

Kansas argues that the Act's definition of "mental abnormality" satisfies "substantive" due process requirements. We agree. Although freedom from physical restraint "has always been at the core of the liberty protected by the Due Process Clause from arbitrary governmental action," Foucha v. Louisiana, 504 U.S. 71, 80 (1992), that liberty interest is not absolute. The Court has recognized that an individual's constitutionally protected interest in avoiding physical restraint may be overridden even in the civil context.

Accordingly, States have in certain narrow circumstances provided for the forcible civil detainment of people who are unable to control their behavior and who thereby pose a danger to the public health and safety. We have consistently upheld such involuntary commitment statutes provided the confinement takes place pursuant to proper procedures and evidentiary standards. It thus cannot be said that the involuntary civil confinement of a limited subclass of dangerous persons is contrary to our understanding of ordered liberty.

The challenged Act unambiguously requires a finding of dangerousness either to one's self or to others as a prerequisite to involuntary confinement. Commitment proceedings can be initiated only when a person "has been convicted of or charged with a sexually violent offense," and "suffers from a mental abnormality or personality disorder which makes the person likely to engage in the predatory acts of sexual violence." The statute thus requires proof of more than a mere predisposition to violence; rather, it requires evidence of past sexually violent behavior and a present mental condition that creates a likelihood of such conduct in the future if the person is not incapacitated. As we have recognized, "previous instances of violent behavior are an important indicator of future violent tendencies." Heller v. Doe, 509 U.S. 312, 323 (1993). A finding of dangerousness, standing alone, is ordinarily not a sufficient ground upon which to justify indefinite involuntary commitment. We have sustained civil commitment statutes when they have coupled proof of dangerousness with the proof of some additional factor, such as a "mental illness" or "mental abnormality." These added statutory requirements serve to limit involuntary civil confinement to those who suffer from a volitional impairment rendering them dangerous beyond their control. The Kansas Act is plainly of a kind with these other civil commitment statutes: It requires a finding of future dangerousness, and then links that finding to the existence of a "mental abnormality" or "personality disorder" that makes it difficult, if not impossible, for the person to control his dangerous behavior. . . .

[T]he term "mental illness" is devoid of any talismanic significance. Not only do psychiatrists disagree widely and frequently on what constitutes mental illness, but the Court itself has used a variety of expressions to describe the mental condition of those properly subject to civil confinement. . . . Indeed, we have never required State legislatures to adopt any particular nomenclature in drafting civil commitment statutes. Rather, we have traditionally left to legislators the task of defining terms of a medical nature that have legal significance. . . .

. . . The mental health professionals who evaluated Hendricks diagnosed him as suffering from pedophilia, a condition the psychiatric profession itself classifies as a serious mental disorder. Hendricks even conceded that, when he becomes "stressed out," he cannot "control the urge" to molest children. This admitted lack of volitional control, coupled with a prediction of future dangerousness, adequately distinguishes Hendricks from other dangerous persons who are perhaps more properly dealt with exclusively through criminal proceedings. Hendricks' diagnosis as a pedophile, which qualifies as a "mental abnormality" under the Act, thus plainly suffices for due process purposes.

B. Civil v. Criminal Proceedings

. . . Hendricks [argues] that the Act establishes criminal proceedings; hence confinement under it necessarily constitutes punishment. He contends that where, as here, newly enacted "punishment" is predicated upon past conduct for which he has already been convicted and forced to serve a prison sentence, the Constitution's Double Jeopardy and Ex Post Facto Clauses are violated. We are unpersuaded by Hendricks' argument that Kansas has established criminal proceedings.

The categorization of a particular proceeding as civil or criminal is first of all a question of statutory construction. We must initially ascertain whether the legislature meant the statute to establish "civil" proceedings. If so, we ordinarily defer to the legislature's stated intent. Here, Kansas' objective to create a civil proceeding is evidenced by its placement of the Sexually Violent Predator Act within the Kansas probate code, instead of the criminal code, as well as its description of the Act as creating a "civil commitment procedure." Nothing on the face of the statute suggests that the legislature sought to create anything other than a civil commitment scheme designed to protect the public from harm.

Although we recognize that a civil label is not always dispositive, we will reject the legislature's manifest intent only where a party challenging the statute provides the clearest proof that the statutory scheme [is] so punitive either in purpose or effect as to negate [the State's] intention to deem it civil. In those limited circumstances, we will consider the statute to have established criminal proceedings for constitutional purposes. Hendricks, however, has failed to satisfy this heavy burden.

As a threshold matter, commitment under the Act does not implicate either of the two primary objectives of criminal punishment: retribution or deterrence. The Act's purpose is not retributive because it does not affix culpability for prior criminal conduct. Instead, such conduct is used solely for evidentiary purposes, either to demonstrate that a "mental abnormality" exists or to support a finding of future dangerousness. . . . In addition, the Kansas Act does not make a criminal conviction a prerequisite for commitment — persons absolved of criminal responsibility may nonetheless be subject to confinement under the Act. An absence of the necessary criminal responsibility suggests that the State is not seeking retribution for a past misdeed. Thus, the fact that the Act may be "tied to criminal activity" is "insufficient to render the statute punitive."

Moreover, unlike a criminal statute, no finding of scienter is required to commit an individual who is found to be a sexually violent predator; instead, the commitment determination is made based on a "mental abnormality" or "personality disorder" rather than on one's criminal intent. The existence of a scienter requirement is customarily an important element in distinguishing criminal from civil statutes. The absence of such a requirement here is evidence that confinement under the statute is not intended to be retributive.

Nor can it be said that the legislature intended the Act to function as a deterrent. Those persons committed under the Act are, by definition, suffering from a "mental abnormality" or a "personality disorder" that prevents them from exercising adequate control over their behavior. Such persons are therefore unlikely to be deterred by the threat of confinement. . . . The State has represented that an individual confined under the Act is not subject to the more restrictive conditions placed on state prisoners, but instead experiences essentially the same conditions as any involuntarily committed patient in the state mental institution. Because none of the parties argues that people institutionalized under the Kansas general civil commitment statute are subject to punitive conditions, even though they may be involuntarily confined, it is difficult to conclude that persons confined under this Act are being "punished."

Although the civil commitment scheme at issue here does involve an affirmative restraint, "the mere fact that a person is detained does not inexorably lead to the conclusion that the government has imposed punishment." United States v. Salerno, 481 U.S. 739, 746 (1987). The State may take measures to restrict the freedom of the dangerously mentally ill. This is a legitimate non-punitive governmental objective and has been historically so regarded. The Court has, in fact, cited the confinement of "mentally unstable individuals who present a danger to the public" as one classic example of nonpunitive detention. If detention for the purpose of protecting the community from harm *necessarily* constituted punishment, then all involuntary civil commitments would have to be considered punishment. But we have never so held.

Hendricks focuses on his confinement's potentially indefinite duration as evidence of the State's punitive intent. That focus, however, is misplaced. Far from any punitive objective, the confinement's duration is instead linked to the stated purposes of the commitment, namely, to hold the person until his mental abnormality no longer causes him to be a threat to others. If, at any time, the confined person is adjudged "safe to be at large," he is statutorily entitled to immediate release.

Furthermore, commitment under the Act is only *potentially* indefinite. The maximum amount of time an individual can be incapacitated pursuant to a single judicial proceeding is one year. If Kansas seeks to continue the detention beyond that year, a court must once again determine beyond a reasonable doubt that the detainee satisfies the same standards as required for the initial confinement. This requirement again demonstrates that Kansas does not intend an individual committed pursuant to the Act to remain confined any longer than he suffers from a mental abnormality rendering him unable to control his dangerousness.

Hendricks next contends that the State's use of procedural safeguards traditionally found in criminal trials makes the proceedings here criminal rather than civil. In [a prior case we explained] that the State's decision to provide some of the safeguards applicable in criminal trials cannot itself turn these proceedings into criminal prosecutions. The numerous procedural and evidentiary protections afforded here demonstrate that the Kansas Legislature has taken great care to confine only a narrow class of particularly dangerous individuals, and then only after meeting the strictest procedural standards. That Kansas chose to afford such procedural protections does not transform a civil commitment proceeding into a criminal prosecution.

Finally, Hendricks argues that the Act is necessarily punitive because it fails to offer any legitimate "treatment." Without such treatment, Hendricks asserts, confinement under the Act amounts to little more than disguised punishment. Hendricks' argument assumes that treatment for his condition is available, but that the State has failed (or refused) to provide it. . . .

[U]nder the appropriate circumstances and when accompanied by proper procedures, incapacitation may be a legitimate end of the civil law. Accordingly, the Kansas court's determination that the Act's "overriding concern" was the continued "segregation of sexually violent offenders" is consistent with our conclusion that the Act establishes civil proceedings, especially when that concern is coupled with the State's ancillary goal of providing treatment to those offenders, if such is possible. While we have upheld state civil commitment statutes that aim both to incapacitate and to treat, we have never held that the Constitution prevents a State from civilly detaining those for whom no treatment is available, but who nevertheless pose a danger to others. A State could hardly be seen as furthering a "punitive" purpose by involuntarily confining persons afflicted with an untreatable, highly contagious disease. Similarly, it would be of little value to require treatment as a precondition for civil confinement of the dangerously insane when no acceptable treatment existed. To conclude otherwise would obligate a State to release certain confined individuals who were both mentally ill and dangerous simply because they could not be successfully treated for their afflictions. . . .

. . . Although the treatment program initially offered Hendricks may have seemed somewhat meager, it must be remembered that he was the first person committed under the Act. That the State did not have all of its treatment procedures in place is thus not surprising. What is significant, however, is that Hendricks was placed under the supervision of the Kansas Department of Health and Social and Rehabilitative Services, housed in a unit segregated from the general prison population and operated not by employees of the Department of Corrections, but by other trained individuals. And, before this Court, Kansas declared "absolutely" that persons committed under the Act are now receiving in the neighborhood of 31.5 hours of treatment per week.

Where the State has "disavowed any punitive intent"; limited confinement to a small segment of particularly dangerous individuals; provided strict procedural safeguards; directed that confined persons be segregated from the general prison population and afforded the same status as others who have been civilly committed; recommended treatment if such is possible; and permitted immediate release upon a showing that the individual is no longer dangerous or mentally impaired, we cannot say that it acted with punitive intent. We therefore hold that the Act does not establish criminal proceedings and that involuntary confinement pursuant to the Act is not punitive. Our conclusion that the Act is nonpunitive thus removes an essential prerequisite for both Hendricks' double jeopardy and ex post facto claims. . . .

Hendricks argues that, as applied to him, the Act violates double jeopardy principles because his confinement under the Act, imposed after a conviction and a term of incarceration, amounted to both a second prosecution and a second punishment for the same offense. We disagree.

Because we have determined that the Kansas Act is civil in nature, initiation of its commitment proceedings does not constitute a second prosecution. Moreover, as commitment under the Act is not tantamount to "punishment," Hendricks' involuntary detention does not violate the Double Jeopardy Clause, even though that confinement may follow a prison term. Indeed, in Baxstrom v. Herold, 383 U.S. 107 (1966), we expressly recognized that civil commitment could follow the expiration of a prison term without offending double jeopardy principles. . . .

Hendricks' ex post facto claim is similarly flawed. The Ex Post Facto Clause, which forbids the application of any new punitive measure to a crime already consummated, has been interpreted to pertain exclusively to penal statutes. As we have previously determined, the Act does not impose punishment; thus, its application does not raise ex post facto concerns. Moreover, the Act clearly does not have retroactive effect. Rather, the Act permits involuntary confinement based upon a determination that the person *currently* both suffers from a "mental abnormality" or "personality disorder" and is likely to pose a future danger to the public. To the extent that past behavior is taken into account, it is used, as noted above, solely for evidentiary purposes. Because the Act does not criminalize conduct legal before its enactment, nor deprive Hendricks of any defense that was available to him at the time of his crimes, the Act does not violate the Ex Post Facto Clause.

III.   CONCLUSION

We hold that the Kansas Sexually Violent Predator Act comports with due process requirements and neither runs afoul of double jeopardy principles nor constitutes an exercise in impermissible ex post facto lawmaking.

KENNEDY, J., concurring.

[I write] to caution against dangers inherent when a civil confinement law is used in conjunction with the criminal process, whether or not the law is given retroactive application. [T]he power of the state to confine persons who, by reason of a mental disease or mental abnormality, constitute a real, continuing, and serious danger to society is well established. . . . The Kansas law, with its attendant protections, including yearly review and review at any time at the instance of the person confined, is within this pattern and tradition of civil confinement.

Notwithstanding its civil attributes, the practical effect of the Kansas law may be to impose confinement for life. At this stage of medical knowledge, although future treatments cannot be predicted, psychiatrists or other professionals engaged in treating pedophilia may be reluctant to find measurable success in treatment even after a long period and may be unable to predict that no serious danger will come from release of the detainee.

A common response to this may be, "A life term is exactly what the sentence should have been anyway," or, in the words of a Kansas task force member, "So be it." The point, however, is not how long Hendricks and others like him should serve a criminal sentence. With his criminal record, after all, a life term may well have been the only sentence appropriate to protect society and vindicate the wrong. The concern instead is whether it is the criminal system or the civil system which should make the decision in the first place. If the civil system is used simply to impose punishment after the State makes an improvident plea bargain on the criminal side, then it is not performing its proper function. These concerns persist whether the civil confinement statute is put on the books before or after the offense. We should bear in mind that while incapacitation is a goal common to both the criminal and civil systems of confinement, retribution and general deterrence are reserved for the criminal system alone.

On the record before us, the Kansas civil statute conforms to our precedents. If, however, civil confinement were to become a mechanism for retribution or general deterrence, or if it were shown that mental abnormality is too imprecise a category to offer a solid basis for concluding that civil detention is justified, our precedents would not suffice to validate it.

BREYER, J., dissenting.

I agree with the majority that the Kansas Act's definition of mental abnormality satisfies the "substantive" requirements of the Due Process Clause. Kansas, however, concedes that Hendricks' condition is treatable; yet the Act did not provide Hendricks (or others like him) with any treatment until after his release date from prison and only inadequate treatment thereafter. These, and certain other, special features of the Act convince me that it was not simply an effort to commit Hendricks civilly, but rather an effort to inflict further punishment upon him. The Ex Post Facto Clause therefore prohibits the Act's application to Hendricks, who committed his crimes prior to its enactment. . . .

Certain resemblances between the Act's "civil commitment" and traditional criminal punishments are obvious. . . . These obvious resemblances by themselves, however, are not legally sufficient to transform what the Act calls "civil commitment" into a criminal punishment. [W]ith important features of the Act pointing in opposite directions, I would place particular importance upon those features that would likely distinguish between a basically punitive and a basically nonpunitive purpose. And I note that the Court, in an earlier civil commitment case, looked primarily to the law's concern for treatment as an important distinguishing feature. [W]hen a State believes that treatment does exist, and then couples that admission with a legislatively required delay of such treatment until a person is at the end of his jail term (so that further incapacitation is therefore necessary), such a legislative scheme begins to look punitive. . . .

[O]ne would expect a nonpunitive statutory scheme to confine, not simply in order to protect, but also in order to cure. That is to say, one would expect a nonpunitively motivated legislature that confines *because of* a dangerous mental abnormality to seek to help the individual himself overcome that abnormality (at least insofar as professional treatment for the abnormality exists and is potentially helpful, as Kansas, supported by some groups of mental health professionals, argues is the case here). Conversely, a statutory scheme that provides confinement that does not reasonably fit a practically available, medically oriented treatment objective, more likely reflects a primarily punitive legislative purpose. . . .

[T]he laws of other States confirm, through comparison, that Kansas' "civil commitment" objectives do not require the statutory features that indicate a punitive purpose. I have found 17 States with laws that seek to protect the public from mentally abnormal, sexually dangerous individuals through civil commitment or other mandatory treatment programs. Ten of those statutes, unlike the Kansas statute, begin treatment of an offender soon after he has been apprehended and charged with a serious sex offense. Only seven, like Kansas, delay "civil" commitment (and treatment) until the offender has served his criminal sentence (and this figure includes the Acts of Minnesota and New Jersey, both of which generally do not delay treatment). Of these seven, however, six (unlike Kansas) require consideration of less restrictive alternatives. Only one State other than Kansas, namely Iowa, both delays civil commitment (and consequent treatment) and does not explicitly consider less restrictive alternatives. But the law of that State applies prospectively only, thereby avoiding ex post facto problems. Thus the practical experience of other States, as revealed by their statutes, confirms what the Kansas Supreme Court's finding, the timing of the civil commitment proceeding, and the failure to consider less restrictive alternatives, themselves suggest, namely, that for Ex Post Facto Clause purposes, the purpose of the Kansas Act (as applied to previously convicted offenders) has a punitive, rather than a purely civil, purpose. . . .

To find that the confinement the Act imposes upon Hendricks is "punishment" is to find a violation of the Ex Post Facto Clause. . . . To find a violation of that Clause here, however, is not to hold that the Clause prevents Kansas, or other States, from enacting dangerous sexual offender statutes. A statute that operates prospectively, for example, does not offend the Ex Post Facto Clause. Neither does it offend the Ex Post Facto Clause for a State to sentence offenders to the fully authorized sentence, to seek consecutive, rather than concurrent, sentences, or to invoke recidivism statutes to lengthen imprisonment. Moreover, a statute that operates retroactively, like Kansas' statute, nonetheless does not offend the Clause *if the confinement that it imposes is not punishment*— if, that is to say, the legislature does not simply add a later criminal punishment to an earlier one.

The statutory provisions before us do amount to punishment primarily because, as I have said, the legislature did not tailor the statute to fit the nonpunitive civil aim of treatment, which it concedes exists in Hendricks' case. The Clause in these circumstances does not stand as an obstacle to achieving important protections for the public's safety; rather it provides an assurance that, where so significant a restriction of an individual's basic freedoms is at issue, a State cannot cut corners. Rather, the legislature must hew to the Constitution's liberty-protecting line. See The Federalist, No. 78, p. 466 (C. Rossiter ed. 1961) (A. Hamilton).

NOTES

1. *Civil commitment for sex offenders.* The Supreme Court's decision in *Hendricks* clearly labeled commitment for sex offenders a civil sanction that can follow a criminal conviction or be imposed instead of one. In Seling v. Young, 531 U.S. 250 (2001), the Court rejected the claim that Washington state's sex offender commitment statute could be found punitive as applied to a particular sex offender. It found the "as applied" determination unworkable and rejected the notion that an "as applied" challenge could lead to release on ex post facto or substantive due process grounds.

2. *Prerequisites for sex offender commitment.* In *Hendricks,* the Supreme Court held that the statutory requirement of a "mental abnormality or personality disorder" satisfied due process requirements. In Kansas v. Crane, 534 U.S. 407 (2002), it held that requirement to imply that a sex offender have difficulty controlling his sexual urges before he can be committed civilly. There is no constitutional requirement, however, that the individual be unable to control his urges before commitment. Why does the Court require existence of a mental abnormality for civil commitment? Why does continued dangerousness of the offender not suffice?

3. *Treatment during confinement.* While the *Hendricks* Court showed some concerns about the minimal treatment Hendricks had received, Justice Breyer appeared the most concerned about the absence of treatment during imprisonment, which in turn seemed to imply the state's lack of interest in curing Hendricks. Justice Kennedy, in his concurrence, noted that treatment, as it is currently available, may never be useful to offenders such as Hendricks, leaving them in preventive detention for the rest of their lives. For a discussion of substantive due process considerations during civil commitment, see Eric S. Janus and Wayne A. Logan, Substantive Due Process and the Involuntary Confinement of Sexually Violent Predators, 35 Conn. L. Rev. 319 (2003). Should society's inability to develop successful treatment options be sufficient reason for virtual life imprisonment of offenders after they have served their criminal justice sanctions?

4. *Alternatives to civil commitment.*   Civil commitment statutes for sex offenders have generated much discussion in legal circles, but their practical impact has remained small as other risk control mechanisms have replaced or substituted for them. All states have enacted sex offender notification and registration laws (see Chapter 8), and many have lengthened criminal penalties for sex crimes. Are longer sentences for sex offenders generally desirable, based on a risk analysis? Consider that predictions of recurrent acts of sexual violence have gotten more accurate in the short term, but psychiatrists and psychologists are loath to make long-term predictions. See Eric S. Janus and Robert A. Prentky, Forensic Use of Actuarial Risk Assessment with Sex Offenders: Accuracy, Admissibility and Accountability 39 Am. Crim. L. Rev. ___ (forthcoming 2003).

3.   Sealed Records and Expungements

Many convicted individuals carry their criminal record with them until they die. In some states, however, administrative procedures are available to seal or expunge criminal records. Sealed records, which are common for juveniles, are inaccessible to anyone other than law enforcement agencies and courts, in case of a later conviction. Expunged records are no longer available to anyone. Some states allow expungement of criminal records only for certain first offenses, others for offenses in which the sentence was suspended or when the offender successfully completed probation. In a few jurisdictions courts expunge records, in others administrative agencies fulfill this function.

|| *Christopher John Dillingham v. INS* ||
267 F.3d 996 (9th Cir. 2001)

B. FLETCHER, J.
    In this case, we consider whether an alien's right to equal protection is violated if, in the course of removal proceedings, the Immigration and Naturalization Service ("INS") refuses to recognize the effects of a British expungement[1] statute on a simple drug possession offense that would have qualified for federal first offender treatment had it occurred in the United States. . . .

I

Dillingham pled guilty in April 1984 to criminal charges in Great Britain for possessing marijuana and cocaine, paying a £50 fine. As a first-time offender convicted of a minor controlled substance offense, Dillingham's conviction was later expunged pursuant to Great Britain's Rehabilitation of Offenders Act of

---

1. Throughout this opinion, we use the term "expungement" to refer generally to the effect of a rehabilitative statute on a prior conviction — regardless of whether, as a procedural matter, the statute allows for a deferral of the conviction itself, such that no judgment is ever entered (as under the [Federal First Offender Act]), or a judgment of conviction is entered but later removed from the books (as under various state rehabilitative statutes, as well as the British statute at issue in this case).

1974. Under the terms of the Act, a conviction is treated as "spent" if an offender complies with his sentence and is not convicted of a subsequent offense within five years. In such cases, the statute requires that the offender be treated "for all purposes in law as a person who has not committed or been charged with or prosecuted for or convicted of or sentenced for the offense," except that any penalty resulting from the conviction that extends beyond the five-year period is unaffected, and evidence of the conviction may be introduced in a subsequent criminal proceeding.

In September 1991, seven years after his drug conviction (and two years after his rehabilitation), Dillingham married his U.S.-citizen wife. Although his conviction rendered him inadmissible to the United States under [the Immigration and Naturalization Act], he was permitted to enter the country in July 1992 on a six-month nonimmigrant visitor visa, pursuant to the waiver provisions of 8 U.S.C. §1182(d)(3)(A). After his authorized period of stay had expired, Dillingham applied for adjustment of status to legal permanent resident on May 13, 1993, pursuant to an immediate relative visa petition filed by his wife. The INS district director in Portland, Oregon, denied his application on September 14, 1993, on the grounds that the British Rehabilitation of Offenders Act was not a counterpart to the Federal First Offender Act ("FFOA"), and that his prior drug conviction therefore rendered him inadmissible.

. . . At his hearing before an Immigration Judge ("IJ") . . . Dillingham cited the [Board of Immigration Appeals' (BIA's) decision in In re Manrique, Interim Decision] 3250 (BIA 1995), in which the Board established a policy of treating aliens who had been convicted of simple possession and rehabilitated under any state's expungement statute equivalently to those who had been convicted and rehabilitated under the FFOA.[5]

On June 13, 1996, the IJ ruled that *Manrique* did not extend to foreign rehabilitation statutes and denied the application for adjustment of status. . . .

On appeal, the BIA (sitting en banc) . . . affirmed the IJ's decision. . . . Specifically, the Board analogized the expungement of Dillingham's prior drug offense to a foreign pardon and declined to recognize it for U.S. immigration purposes. . . .

IV . . .

A

As a general rule, the BIA does not recognize expungements of controlled substance offenses for federal immigration purposes. However, in 1970,

---

5. The BIA's decision in *Manrique* followed our holding in [Garberding v. INS, 30 F.3d 1187 (9th Cir. 1994)] and constituted a reversal of its former policy of not recognizing, for immigration purposes, the effects of state rehabilitation laws that were not the exact counterparts of the FFOA. Under *Manrique,* the BIA created a four-part test for determining when an expungement pursuant to a state rehabilitative statute should be recognized: (1) the alien is a first offender; (2) the alien has pled to or been found guilty of a simple possession offense; (3) the alien has not been accorded first offender treatment under any law; (4) the court has entered an order pursuant to a state rehabilitative statute either deferring or dismissing the criminal proceedings.

Congress carved out a narrow exception for simple possession offenses when it enacted the Federal First Offender Act ("FFOA"). The FFOA, which applies exclusively to first-time drug offenders who are guilty only of simple possession, serves to expunge such convictions (after the successful completion of a probationary period) and was intended to lessen the harsh consequences of certain drug convictions, including their effects on deportation proceedings. Under the FFOA, no legal consequences may be imposed following expungement as a result of the defendant's former conviction. 18 U.S.C. §3607.

In Garberding v. INS, 30 F.3d 1187 (9th Cir. 1994), we rejected on equal protection grounds the BIA's policy that only expungements under exact state counterparts to the FFOA could be recognized in deportation proceedings. We held that this policy was inconsistent with the Constitution's equal protection guarantee, because there was no rational basis for treating two persons found guilty of the identical conduct differently based on the breadth of the rehabilitation statutes in their respective states, when both persons were eligible for relief under their own state's law and both would have been had the state law been an exact counterpart of the federal Act. . . . The Constitution is concerned with the differential treatment of persons not statutes; the government's rationale that it was justified in refusing to give effect to state statutes reflecting different purposes than those of the FFOA did not provide a rational basis for the differential treatment of persons. . . .

In [subsequent cases], we clarified that [our precedents] stand for the principle that equal protection requires that the INS treat federal and state expungement statutes similarly. Most significantly, we reached this conclusion in spite of the factual distinction that *Garberding* involved disparate treatment under parallel state statutes, rather than federal and state statutes, because "it is evident that our reasoning in [those] cases applies equally in both contexts."

We conclude that the petitioner's case is controlled by our decisions [, which] stand for the broad proposition that absent a rational basis (and as long as the FFOA remains extant), the INS may not discriminate against aliens convicted of simple possession offenses whose subsequent conduct would have qualified them for FFOA rehabilitation, but for the fact that they were convicted and rehabilitated under the laws of another sovereign. . . .

B

We evaluate Dillingham's constitutional challenge according to the requirements of equal protection law. In order to succeed on his challenge, the petitioner must establish that his treatment differed from that of similarly situated persons. Our prior cases dictate that persons similarly situated to petitioner for equal protection purposes are persons convicted of drug offenses based upon conduct for which they would have been eligible for relief under the FFOA, and whose convictions were ultimately expunged by the sovereign that imposed them.

For this reason, we find that the Board's categorical decision not to recognize foreign expungements for simple drug possession offenses did indeed result in differential treatment between the petitioner and persons whose federal and state expungements of identical crimes were honored by the INS. The BIA erred when it found that "the expungement of [Dillingham]'s conviction is akin to a foreign pardon and is therefore ineffective for immigration purposes.". . . By likening foreign expungements of simple drug possession offenses to foreign pardons of crimes of moral turpitude — a category of crimes for which Congress has not enacted a domestic rehabilitation statute analogous to the FFOA — the Board improperly skirted the constitutional issue of differential treatment in this case.

Unfortunately, as a result of the Board's false comparison, we can glean little of use from its opinion. . . . Had the Board restricted itself to a discussion of the propriety of recognizing foreign expungements for first offender minor drug convictions, it would have been forced to acknowledge that such recognition in fact furthers the desired objective of achieving greater uniformity in the administration of the immigration laws. In other words, such a policy arguably would aid the government to achieve its own expressed purpose of insulating aliens from the severely disproportionate punishment of deportation for simple possession drug offenses without requiring that it honor any grant of rehabilitation showing greater leniency than would have been available under federal law. Cf. Rehman v. INS, 544 F.2d 71, 75 (2d Cir. 1976) (reasoning that the INS ought to recognize a state expungement of marijuana possession because no "fear of undermining enforcement of federal deportation laws" can exist where such recognition "would extend no further than where Congress itself has gone for federal criminals"). . . .

Thus, having found differential treatment, we turn to the question of whether the Board's decision is supported by a rational basis. The government's chief contention is that its policy of not recognizing foreign expungements is justified because of the added administrative difficulty in verifying that an alien's conviction has indeed been validly expunged, and that he or she in fact complied with the requirements of the foreign expungement statute such that the alien also would have qualified for relief under the FFOA. The Supreme Court has held, however, that in cases where the petitioner's interest is substantial and the government's interest in putting forth the policy in question is unquantifiable or de minimis, such a policy cannot withstand even rational basis review. . . .

The private liberty interests involved in deportation proceedings are indisputably substantial. [Yet] the BIA would [] establish, by way of its decision in this case, an irrebuttable presumption against the validity of all foreign expungements — irrespective of where the offense in question occurred; how comparable to ours the system of criminal justice (including the operation of the expungement law) may be; and what degree of evidence verifying the expungement the alien may present. . . .

[A]lthough procedure by presumption is always cheaper and easier than individualized determination, we find that the government's interest in administrative convenience is insufficient to establish a rational basis for its categorical dismissal of foreign expungements. Indeed, we fail to see how the administrative burden of identifying and verifying foreign convictions (which the government already undertakes as a matter of course to determine whether an alien is admissible into the United States) is any different from the incremental burden of verifying foreign expungements — especially in light of the government's failure to provide any evidence in support of this claim in regard to the present case. We accordingly find the government's decision establishing an irrebuttable presumption against the validity of foreign expungements to be unacceptably overbroad, in light of an alien's substantial interest in avoiding deportation, as well as the government's minimal (or nonexistent) incremental burden in verifying that his or her conviction was expunged. Thus, we hold that the government's purported interest in administrative convenience does not constitute a legitimate basis for distinguishing aliens like Dillingham, whose illicit conduct and subsequent rehabilitation occurred on British soil (but who would otherwise have qualified for relief under the FFOA), from aliens whose convictions and expungements took place domestically under state procedures.

. . . Simply stated, under the facts of this case, there is no rational basis for precluding Dillingham from eligibility for adjustment of status, while permitting aliens convicted domestically of identical offenses (and rehabilitated under similar state and federal rehabilitative statutes) to seek such relief. . . .

FERNANDEZ, J., dissenting.

Dillingham argues that as a matter of constitutional law expungements in all of the countries of the world must be treated in the same manner as expungements within the United States because anything less would violate the principle of equal protection. I disagree.

While Congress could, no doubt, so decree, it is not compelled to do so by the Constitution. As in other equal protection claims, what we must ask is whether there was a rational basis for the choice made here. And in the immigration area [w]e will only overturn a classification if it is "wholly irrational."

I see nothing irrational in a determination that we will not treat aliens who obtain expungement of drug offenses in other countries in the same way that we treat those who obtain expungement of offenses in this country. Of course, under the Federal First Offender Act, 18 U.S.C. §3607, some simple drug possession convictions can be expunged. When they are, they are not used as a predicate for deportation; the Attorney General has so decided. On equal protection grounds, we have extended that to expungements under state laws.

As I see it, that is a far cry from stating that the Attorney General is equally required to treat the expungement statutes from all of the countries of the world in the same manner that he treats the FFOA and, by extension, state expungement statutes. It is no "mere fortuity" that foreign offenders are prosecuted in their own countries and not here. See [Paredes-Urrestarazu v. INS, 36 F.3d 801, 812 (9th Cir. 1994)]. Nor do foreign expungement laws have anything to do with "'uniform nationwide application of [our] immigration laws.'" In fact, foreign countries and their ways are not necessarily, or even particularly, the same as this country and its ways. A much more complex task is placed upon the shoulders of an administrative agency when it is told that it must not only review the varying ways and means of expungements all over the world, but also the full records of aliens who have admittedly committed foreign offenses, not to mention the difficulties that can be encountered in authenticating the accuracy of those records.

. . . That is not to say that it will be impossible to administer a system which requires ranging all over the world in that manner — we know that . . . [people can live] with and administer just about any kind of system, no matter how difficult. But it is to say that it is perfectly rational to decline to undertake that process. The Attorney General does not have to take on the burden of dealing with the rules and records of every country in the world simply because, at root, he decided to ignore convictions expunged under the FFOA.

In fine, equal protection does not require the progression we have here: recognition of FFOA expungements, to recognition of similar state statutes, to recognition of all state statutes and, finally, to recognition of enactments all over the world. To say that, does not enisle this country, although it does recognize that we are a separate nation. One world is a fine concept, but it is not a constitutional imperative. Not yet anyway.

Thus, I respectfully dissent.

PROBLEM 11-7. FIRE WHEN READY

In 1970 a Pennsylvania state court sentenced Philip Rice to probation for a number of felonies involving stolen auto parts. Federal law prohibits a convicted felon whose crime was "punishable by a term exceeding one year" from possessing firearms. Rice never violated the statute but would like to get a gun dealer's license.

Another part of the federal felon-in-possession statute grants the secretary of the treasury the right to reinstate a former felon's firearms privileges if past good conduct indicates that his disability should be removed. Rice applied for restoration of his firearms privileges, but the Bureau of Alcohol, Tobacco and Firearms refused to consider his application because Congress had not funded that part of its operation since 1992.

Rice decided to petition a federal district court for review since the statute allows him to seek judicial review of the denial of his petition and it empowers the court to hear additional evidence to prevent a miscarriage of justice. What should the court do?

See Rice v. United States Dept. of Alcohol, Tobacco and Firearms, 68 F.3d 702 (3d Cir. 1995). But see United States v. McGill, 74 F.3d 64 (5th Cir. 1996).

NOTES

1. *Expungement and sealing of records.* While the term "expungement" carries no universally agreed-upon meaning, an expunged criminal record is generally considered to be one that is no longer available to the public. The files documenting the conviction may be physically destroyed or sealed. In the latter case they are frequently available to law enforcement personnel but not to others such as private employers.

Once a criminal record is expunged, it has limited or no impact on the offender's future prospects. The types of conviction that can be expunged and the ramifications of expungement, however, vary widely by statute. Juvenile records, for example, are automatically expunged in almost all states once the juvenile reaches a particular age. In some states, the ex-offender does not have to reveal expunged convictions on employment applications; in other states, even expunged convictions may limit employment opportunities.

Criminal records may be expunged by administrative or judicial action. Some courts have recognized an inherent judicial power to expunge records, weighing privacy rights against the public's right of access to criminal records.

What purposes do expungement statutes serve? Some argue that ex-offenders should not continually pay for past crimes; others view expungement as a positive reward for a crime-free period. Expungement also restores the offender to the community. Without such statutes, an ever larger number of Americans would have criminal records (according to 1992 data, 50 million already do). See Julian V. Roberts, The Role of Criminal Record in the Sentencing Process, 22 Crime & Just. 303, 356 (1997). Should expungement be available for all offenses? Should some types of crimes — such as drug offenses, sex crimes, and murder — be categorically excluded from expungement? What drawbacks, if any, do you see to expungement of criminal records? Why would Congress create but not fund a provision that would allow for the expungement of a record for a limited purpose, the ability to acquire a gun license?

2. *Prior expunged convictions at sentencing.* The availability of expungement differs dramatically between the states. As we learned in Chapter 5, an offender's criminal record influences sentencing decisions in both guideline and nonguideline states. Why should a sentencing court not be able to consider the prior conviction of an offender who benefited from a generous expungement statute? Does this scheme provide an inappropriate advantage to this offender? Or does it place at an unfair disadvantage the offender whose prior record could not have been expunged because of a less generous statutory regime?

3. *Foreign convictions and expungement.* As the *Dillingham* court indicates, foreign countries often have more generous expungement provisions than the United States. Should U.S. courts consider such expungements? Do you see practical problems to such determinations, or are you more concerned about inequities between U.S. and foreign offenders? Should a court be able to consider a foreign expunged conviction at sentencing? Are you more or less concerned about that scenario than about the impact of collateral sanctions (see Chapter 8), as in *Dillingham*?

4. Pardons, Commutations, Clemencies, and Amnesties

A form of executive review distinct from the parole system takes place when a governor or president considers granting a pardon or commutation. The history and foundation of the pardon power run quite deep and typically have constitutional underpinnings. But the austere role of pardons has not insulated them from the same sorts of evolutionary developments that have occurred with the parole authority. Indeed, because pardons tend to be more visible, even though they are far less common than grants of parole, they also tend to be far more controversial. Most states give the governor unrestricted clemency power, although a substantial minority give clemency power to special pardoning boards. Some states require that a pardons board recommend pardons to the governor, who then can decide whether to implement those recommendations.

The differences among pardons, commutations, clemencies, and amnesties are slight and more a matter of semantics than substance. *Clemency* is an umbrella term encompassing pardons, commutations, and amnesties. A *pardon* typically removes all consequences of criminal conviction and may come with conditions precedent or subsequent. A *commutation* is a partial pardon, usually reducing a sentence but not erasing such consequences of conviction as voting bars, prohibitions from holding office, and restrictions on future gun ownership. In the United States, *amnesty* is a term often used in the context of war to connote a pardon for a war-related crime.

The number of pardons in states and the federal system has declined dramatically over the past century. Interestingly enough, in death cases more pardons were granted prior to the Supreme Court's decision in *Furman* than after it. In the early to mid-1940s governors pardoned those condemned to death in between one-fifth and one-fourth of all capital cases. In recent years, the federal system, in particular, has granted fewer pardons and commutations. President George H. W. Bush granted 38 pardons and one commutation during his four-year administration. In contrast, President Ronald Reagan granted 393 pardons and 13 commutations during his eight years in office. Looking back to the 1960s, President Lyndon Johnson granted 960 pardons and 227 commutations in his five years in office. No federal pardons or commutations were granted in 1992 or 1994.

Use of pardons and commutations varies substantially among the states. Pardons are granted for a variety of reasons. They may be granted in cases of miscarriage of justice, including a violation of substantive rules, or in cases in which the accused is proven to be innocent or is highly likely not to have committed the offense. In addition, individuals may be pardoned when the goals of their sentence appear accomplished, such as when they appear fully rehabilitated. Pardons are often requested to remove certain disabilities that go with a felony conviction, such as loss of voting rights. Occasionally a death sentence is commuted to a life sentence without possibility of parole, but such commutations have been rare in recent years.

The use of pardons and commutations also reflects changing social perspectives on the seriousness or justification for various kinds of crimes. Some governors, for example, have pardoned women who killed battering spouses or boyfriends after many years of abuse. At the time the women were convicted, the battered spouse syndrome was not used in their defense, and the governors believed that the women had served enough time for their offense.

‖ *U.S. Constitution Art. II, §2, Cl. 1* ‖

The President shall . . . have Power to grant Reprieves and Pardons for Offences against the United States, except in Cases of Impeachment.

‖ *Alabama Constitution Art. V, §124* ‖

GOVERNOR; PARDONS AND COMMUTATION OF SENTENCES

The governor shall have power to remit fines and forfeitures, under such rules and regulations as may be prescribed by law; and, after conviction, to grant reprieves, paroles, commutations of sentence, and pardons, except in cases of impeachment. The attorney-general, secretary of state, and state auditor shall constitute a board of pardons, who shall meet on the call of the governor, and before whom shall be laid all recommendations or petitions, for pardon, commutation, or parole, in cases of felony; and the board shall hear them in open session, and give their opinion thereon in writing to the governor, after which or on the failure of the board to advise for more than sixty days, the governor may grant or refuse the commutation, parole, or pardon, as to him seems best for the public interest. He shall communicate to the legislature at each session every remission of fines and forfeitures, and every reprieve, commutation, parole, or pardon, with his reasons therefor, and the opinion of the board of pardons in each case required to be referred, stating the name and crime of the convict, the sentence, its date, and the date of reprieve, commutation, parole, or pardon. Pardons in cases of felony and other offenses involving moral turpitude shall not relieve from civil and political disabilities, unless approved by the board of pardons and specifically expressed in the pardon.

‖ *Washington Revised Code §9.94A.150* ‖

(4) The governor, upon recommendation from the clemency and pardons board, may grant an extraordinary release for reasons of serious health problems, senility, advanced age, extraordinary meritorious acts, or other extraordinary circumstances; . . .

(6) The governor may pardon any offender; . . .

‖ *Ohio Adult Parole Authority v. Eugene Woodard* ‖
523 U.S. 272 (1998)

REHNQUIST, C.J.

The Ohio Constitution gives the Governor the power to grant clemency upon such conditions as he thinks proper. The Ohio General Assembly cannot curtail this discretionary decision-making power, but it may regulate the application and investigation process. The General Assembly has delegated in large part the conduct of clemency review to petitioner Ohio Adult Parole Authority.

In the case of an inmate under death sentence, the Authority must conduct a clemency hearing within 45 days of the scheduled date of execution. Prior to the hearing, the inmate may request an interview with one or more parole board members. Counsel is not allowed at that interview. The Authority must hold the hearing, complete its clemency review, and make a recommendation to the Governor, even if the inmate subsequently obtains a stay of execution. If additional information later becomes available, the Authority may in its discretion hold another hearing or alter its recommendation.

Respondent Eugene Woodard was sentenced to death for aggravated murder committed in the course of a carjacking. His conviction and sentence were affirmed on appeal. When respondent failed to obtain a stay of execution more than 45 days before his scheduled execution date, the Authority commenced its clemency investigation. It informed respondent that he could have a clemency interview on Sept. 9, 1994, if he wished, and that his clemency hearing would be on Sept. 16, 1994.

Respondent did not request an interview. Instead, he objected to the short notice of the interview and requested assurances that counsel could attend and participate in the interview and hearing. When the Authority failed to respond to these requests, respondent filed suit in United States District Court on September 14, alleging that Ohio's clemency process violated his Fourteenth Amendment right to due process and his Fifth Amendment right to remain silent. . . .

Respondent argues first . . . that there is a life interest in clemency broader in scope than the "original" life interest adjudicated at trial and sentencing. This continuing life interest, it is argued, requires due process protection until respondent is executed. . . .

In [Connecticut Bd. of Pardons v. Dumschat, 452 U.S. 458 (1981)], an inmate claimed Connecticut's clemency procedure violated due process because the Connecticut Board of Pardons failed to provide an explanation for its denial of his commutation application. The Court held that "an inmate has 'no constitutional or inherent right' to commutation of his sentence." 452 U.S. at 464. It noted that, unlike probation decisions, "pardon and commutation decisions have not traditionally been the business of courts; as such, they are rarely, if ever, appropriate subjects for judicial review." *Ibid.* The Court relied on its prior decision in Greenholtz v. Inmates of Neb. Penal and Correctional Complex, 442 U.S. 1 (1979), where it rejected the claim "that a constitutional entitlement to release [on parole] exists independently of a right explicitly conferred by the State." *Dumschat,* 452 U.S. at 463-464. The individual's interest in release or commutation "is indistinguishable from the initial resistance to being confined," and that interest has already been extinguished by the conviction and sentence. The Court therefore concluded that a petition for commutation, like an appeal for clemency, "is simply a unilateral hope." 452 U.S. at 465.

Respondent's claim of a broader due process interest in Ohio's clemency proceedings is barred by *Dumschat.* The process respondent seeks would be inconsistent with the heart of executive clemency, which is to grant clemency as a matter of grace, thus allowing the executive to consider a wide range of factors not comprehended by earlier judicial proceedings and sentencing determinations. [R]espondent maintains a residual life interest, e.g., in not being summarily executed by prison guards. However, as *Greenholtz* helps to make clear, respondent cannot use his interest in not being executed in accord with his sentence to challenge the clemency determination by requiring the procedural protections he seeks.

The reasoning of *Dumschat* did not depend on the fact that it was not a capital case. The distinctions accorded a life interest to which respondent and the dissent point are primarily relevant to trial. And this Court has generally rejected attempts to expand any distinctions further. . . . The Court's analysis in *Dumschat,* moreover, turned, not on the fact that it was a non-capital case, but on the nature of the benefit sought: "In terms of the Due Process Clause, a Connecticut felon's expectation that a lawfully imposed sentence will be commuted or that he will be pardoned is no more substantial than an inmate's expectation, for example, that he will not be transferred to another prison; it is simply a unilateral hope." A death row inmate's petition for clemency is also a "unilateral hope." The defendant in effect accepts the finality of the death sentence for purposes of adjudication, and appeals for clemency as a matter of grace.

Respondent also asserts that as in *Greenholtz,* Ohio has created protected interests by establishing mandatory clemency application and review procedures. . . .

Ohio's clemency procedures do not violate due process. Despite the Authority's mandatory procedures, the ultimate decisionmaker, the Governor, retains broad discretion. Under any analysis, the Governor's executive discretion need not be fettered by the types of procedural protections sought by respondent. There is thus no substantive expectation of clemency. Moreover, the availability of clemency, or the manner in which the State conducts clemency proceedings, does not impose atypical and significant hardship on the inmate in relation to the ordinary incidents of prison life. A denial of clemency merely means that the inmate must serve the sentence originally imposed.

Respondent also . . . claims that under the rationale of Evitts v. Lucey, 469 U.S. 387 (1985), clemency is an integral part of Ohio's system of adjudicating the guilt or innocence of the defendant and is therefore entitled to due process protection. Clemency, he says, is an integral part of the judicial system because it has historically been available as a significant remedy, its availability impacts earlier stages of the criminal justice system, and it enhances the reliability of convictions and sentences. Respondent further suggests that *Evitts* established a due process continuum across all phases of the judicial process.

In *Evitts,* the Court held that there is a constitutional right to effective assistance of counsel on a first appeal as of right. This holding, however, was expressly based on the combination of two lines of prior decisions [that] justified [a] conclusion that a criminal defendant has a right to effective assistance of counsel on a first appeal as of right.

The Court did not thereby purport to create a new "strand" of due process analysis. And it did not rely on the notion of a continuum of due process rights. Instead, the Court evaluated the function and significance of first appeal as of right, in light of prior cases. Related decisions similarly make clear there is no continuum requiring varying levels of process at every conceivable phase of the criminal system. [Murray v. Giarratano, 492 U.S. 1, 9-10 (1989)] (no right to counsel for capital inmates in state postconviction proceedings).

An examination of the function and significance of the discretionary clemency decision at issue here readily shows it is far different from the first appeal of right at issue in *Evitts*. Clemency proceedings are not part of trial — or even the adjudicatory process. They do not determine the guilt or innocence of the defendant, and are not intended primarily to enhance the reliability of the trial process. They are conducted by the Executive Branch, independent of direct appeal and collateral relief proceedings. . . . And they are usually discretionary, unlike the more structured and limited scope of judicial proceedings. While traditionally available to capital defendants as a final and alternative avenue of relief, clemency has not traditionally been the business of courts. Cf. Herrera v. Collins, 506 U.S. 390 (1993) (recognizing the traditional availability and significance of clemency as part of executive authority, without suggesting clemency proceedings are subject to judicial review). . . .

Thus, clemency proceedings are not "an integral part of the . . . system for finally adjudicating the guilt or innocence of a defendant," *Evitts, supra,* 469 U.S. at 393. Procedures mandated under the Due Process Clause should be consistent with the nature of the governmental power being invoked. Here, the executive's clemency authority would cease to be a matter of grace committed to the executive authority if it were constrained by the sort of procedural requirements that respondent urges. Respondent is already under a sentence of death, determined to have been lawfully imposed. If clemency is granted, he obtains a benefit; if it is denied, he is no worse off than he was before. . . .

Respondent also presses on us the Court of Appeals' conclusion that the provision of a voluntary inmate interview, without the benefit of counsel or a grant of immunity for any statements made by the inmate, implicates the inmate's Fifth and Fourteenth Amendment right not to incriminate himself. . . .

The Fifth Amendment protects against compelled self-incrimination. [W]e do not think that respondent's testimony at a clemency interview would be "compelled" within the meaning of the Fifth Amendment. It is difficult to see how a voluntary interview could "compel" respondent to speak. He merely faces a choice quite similar to the sorts of choices that a criminal defendant must make in the course of criminal proceedings, none of which has ever been held to violate the Fifth Amendment.

Long ago we held that a defendant who took the stand in his own defense could not claim the privilege against self-incrimination when the prosecution sought to cross-examine him. A defendant who takes the stand in his own behalf may be impeached by proof of prior convictions without violation of the Fifth Amendment privilege. A defendant whose motion for acquittal at the close of the Government's case is denied must then elect whether to stand on his motion or to put on a defense, with the accompanying risk that in doing so he will augment the Government's case against him. In each of these situations, there are undoubted pressures — generated by the strength of the Government's case against him — pushing the criminal defendant to testify. But it has never been suggested that such pressures constitute "compulsion" for Fifth Amendment purposes. . . .

Here, respondent has the same choice of providing information to the Authority — at the risk of damaging his case for clemency or for postconviction relief — or of remaining silent. But this pressure to speak in the hope of improving his chance of being granted clemency does not make the interview compelled. We therefore hold that the Ohio clemency interview, even on assumptions most favorable to respondent's claim, does not violate the Fifth Amendment privilege against compelled self-incrimination.

O'CONNOR, J., concurring in part and concurring in the judgment.

A prisoner under a death sentence remains a living person and consequently has an interest in his life. The question this case raises is the issue of what process is constitutionally necessary to protect that interest in the context of Ohio's clemency procedures. It is clear that once society has validly convicted an individual of a crime and therefore established its right to punish, the demands of due process are reduced accordingly. I do not, however, agree with the suggestion in the principal opinion that, because clemency is committed to the discretion of the executive, the Due Process Clause provides no constitutional safeguards. The Chief Justice's reasoning rests on our decisions [holding] that an inmate seeking commutation of a life sentence or discretionary parole had no protected liberty interest in release from lawful confinement. When a person has been fairly convicted and sentenced, his liberty interest, in being free from such confinement, has been extinguished. But it is incorrect, as Justice Stevens' dissent notes, to say that a prisoner has been deprived of all interest in his life before his execution. Thus, although it is true that pardon and commutation decisions have not traditionally been the business of courts, and that the decision whether to grant clemency is entrusted to the Governor under Ohio law, I believe that the Court of Appeals correctly concluded that some minimal procedural safeguards apply to clemency proceedings. Judicial intervention might, for example, be warranted in the face of a scheme whereby a state official flipped a coin to determine whether to grant clemency, or in a case where the State arbitrarily denied a prisoner any access to its clemency process.

In my view, however, a remand to permit the District Court to address respondent's specific allegations of due process violations is not required. The Ohio Death Penalty Clemency Procedure provides that, if a stay has not yet issued, the parole board must schedule a clemency hearing 45 days before an execution for a date approximately 21 days in advance of the execution. The board must also advise the prisoner that he is entitled to a pre-hearing interview with one or more parole board members. Although the Parole Authority complied with those instructions here, respondent raises several objections to the process afforded him. He contends that 3 days' notice of his interview and 10 days' notice of the hearing were inadequate; that he did not have a meaningful opportunity to prepare his clemency application because postconviction proceedings were pending; that his counsel was improperly excluded from the interview and permitted to participate in the hearing only at the discretion of the parole board chair; and that he was precluded from testifying or submitting documentary evidence at the hearing. I do not believe that any of these allegations amounts to a due process violation. The process respondent received, including notice of the hearing and an opportunity to participate in an interview, comports with Ohio's regulations and observes whatever limitations the Due Process Clause may impose on clemency proceedings. . . .

STEVENS, J., concurring in part and dissenting in part.

When a parole board conducts a hearing to determine whether the State shall actually execute one of its death row inmates — in other words, whether the State shall deprive that person of life — does it have an obligation to comply with the Due Process Clause of the Fourteenth Amendment? In my judgment, the text of the Clause provides the answer to that question. It expressly provides that no State has the power to "deprive any person of life, liberty, or property without due process of law." . . .

The text of the Due Process Clause properly directs our attention to state action that may "deprive" a person of life, liberty, or property. When we are evaluating claims that the State has unfairly deprived someone of liberty or property, it is appropriate first to ask whether the state action adversely affected any constitutionally protected interest. . . . There is [] no room for legitimate debate about whether a living person has a constitutionally protected interest in life. He obviously does. . . .

There are valid reasons for concluding that even if due process is required in clemency proceedings, only the most basic elements of fair procedure are required. Presumably a State might eliminate this aspect of capital sentencing entirely, and it unquestionably may allow the executive virtually unfettered discretion in determining the merits of appeals for mercy. Nevertheless, there are equally valid reasons for concluding that these proceedings are not entirely exempt from judicial review. I think, for example, that no one would contend that a governor could ignore the commands of the Equal Protection Clause and use race, religion, or political affiliation as a standard for granting or denying clemency. Our cases also support the conclusion that if a State adopts a clemency procedure as an integral part of its system for finally determining whether to deprive a person of life, that procedure must comport with the Due Process Clause.

Even if a State has no constitutional obligation to grant criminal defendants a right to appeal, when it does establish appellate courts, the procedures employed by those courts must satisfy the Due Process Clause. Likewise, even if a State has no duty to authorize parole or probation, if it does exercise its discretion to grant conditional liberty to convicted felons, any decision to deprive a parolee or a probationer of such conditional liberty must accord that person due process. Similarly, if a State establishes postconviction proceedings, these proceedings must comport with due process.

The interest in life that is at stake in this case warrants even greater protection than the interests in liberty at stake in those cases. For "death is a different kind of punishment from any other which may be imposed in this country. . . . It is of vital importance to the defendant and to the community that any decision to impose the death sentence be, and appear to be, based on reason rather than caprice or emotion." Gardner v. Florida, 430 U.S. 349, 357-358 (1977). Those considerations apply with special force to the final stage of the decisional process that precedes an official deprivation of life. . . .

NOTES

1. *Due process in clemency procedures?* Though Woodard's claims were rejected, five justices appear to have held that at least some modicum of process is constitutionally required in clemency proceedings. What sorts of "minimum procedural safeguards" do you think are now required? What if a state denies a death row prisoner any hearing and allows its parole board members to vote individually on clemency petitions by fax or phone without providing any reason for their votes and without even having a meeting to discuss the petition? Faulder v. Texas Bd. of Pardons and Paroles, 178 F.3d 343, 345 (5th Cir. 1999). What if a lawyer for the state screens information before it reaches the governor so that the ultimate decision maker does not know all the mitigating facts that might justify clemency? See Alan Berlow, The Texas Clemency Memos, The Atlantic Monthly, July/August 2003, at 91.

2. *The historical place for clemency.* In Herrera v. Collins, 506 U.S. 390 (1993), a defendant sentenced to death claimed that habeas corpus had to be available as a means of establishing his innocence and thus of obtaining further

review of his conviction and sentence after his initial appeals had been exhausted. In the course of rejecting this claim, Chief Justice William Rehnquist discussed the role of clemency in the criminal justice system, particularly as a means to redress wrongful convictions:

> Clemency is deeply rooted in our Anglo-American tradition of law, and is the historic remedy for preventing miscarriages of justice where judicial process has been exhausted.
>
> In England, the clemency power was vested in the Crown and can be traced back to the 700's. Blackstone thought this "one of the great advantages of monarchy in general, above any other form of government; that there is a magistrate, who has it in his power to extend mercy, wherever he thinks it is deserved: holding a court of equity in his own breast, to soften the rigour of the general law, in such criminal cases as merit an exemption from punishment." 4 W. Blackstone, Commentaries *397. Clemency provided the principal avenue of relief for individuals convicted of criminal offenses — most of which were capital — because there was no right of appeal until 1907. It was the only means by which one could challenge his conviction on the ground of innocence.
>
> Our Constitution adopts the British model and gives to the President the "Power to grant Reprieves and Pardons for Offences against the United States." Art. II, §2, cl. 1. . . .
>
> Of course, although the Constitution vests in the President a pardon power, it does not require the States to enact a clemency mechanism. Yet since the British Colonies were founded, clemency has been available in America. The original States were reluctant to vest the clemency power in the executive. And although this power has gravitated toward the executive over time, several States have split the clemency power between the Governor and an advisory board selected by the legislature. Today, all 36 States that authorize capital punishment have constitutional or statutory provisions for clemency.
>
> Executive clemency has provided the "fail safe" in our criminal justice system. It is an unalterable fact that our judicial system, like the human beings who administer it, is fallible. But history is replete with examples of wrongfully convicted persons who have been pardoned in the wake of after-discovered evidence establishing their innocence. In his classic work, Professor Edwin Borchard compiled 65 cases in which it was later determined that individuals had been wrongfully convicted of crimes. Clemency provided the relief mechanism in 47 of these cases; the remaining cases ended in judgments of acquittals after new trials. Borchard, Convicting the Innocent (1932). Recent authority confirms that over the past century clemency has been exercised frequently in capital cases in which demonstrations of "actual innocence" have been made. See M. Radelet, H. Bedau, and C. Putnam, In Spite of Innocence 282-356 (1992).

In recent years, however, clemency has been granted in substantially fewer cases than it was prior to the U.S. Supreme Court's 1972 decision declaring the form then used for administering the death penalty unconstitutional. Michael A.G. Korengold et al., And Justice for Few: The Collapse of the Capital Clemency System in the United States, 20 Hamline L. Rev. 349 (1996) (noting that in the United States from 1960 to 1970, 261 people were executed and clemency was granted to 204 death row inmates, whereas from 1985 to 1995, 281 people were executed and only twenty death row inmates were granted clemency). Among the factors accounting for this decline may be a changing political climate that encourages tougher criminal penalties and the erroneous belief that clemency is unnecessary today because death row inmates receive "super due process" in the courts.

3. *Pardon patterns.* Although many state legislatures require the governor or pardon board to issue reports on pardons every year, there is no readily available information on the number of pardons granted in the states, the basis for particular decisions, or pardon patterns over time. Consider Professor Daniel Kobil's summary of pardons in Ohio:

> At the close of his second term, former Ohio Governor Richard Celeste granted clemency to sixty-eight individuals. Many of the cases were controversial, with Celeste being alternately praised and vilified for reducing the punishments of, among others, twenty-five battered women who had killed or assaulted their purported abusers, eight condemned murderers, a famous country-western singer, and an embezzler of hundreds of thousands of dollars.

Daniel Kobil, Do the Paperwork or Die: Clemency, Ohio Style?, 52 Ohio St. L.J. 655 (1991). The country music star, for fans of such music, was Johnny Paycheck, the creator of the unforgettable song "Take This Job and Shove It." According to a newspaper article, Governor Celeste found the 7½-to-9-year sentence for the 1985 shooting of a man in a bar "unbelievably harsh." See Celeste Orders Paycheck Freed, Columbus Dispatch, Jan. 11, 1991, at 5B, col. 1.

4. *Clemency procedures.* Clemency and pardon power are traditionally exercised by the executive, with little judicial interference. The offender has only limited due process rights, such as the right to notice of the clemency proceeding and the right to be heard at the proceeding.

Nine states require that the governor have a recommendation of clemency from a board or advisory group before granting clemency. In three states the board makes the ultimate decision, and in another three states the governor sits on this board. In the remaining states, the governor is largely responsible for the decisions herself. See generally Death Penalty Information Center, Clemency Process by State (available at www.deathpenaltyinfo.org/article.php?did=126&scid=13#process). The setup of clemency procedures influences the number of clemencies granted. They are more likely to occur when an administrative board rather than the governor holds clemency authority. Why do you suppose this is the case?

5. *The effect of a pardon.* Many, and possibly all, national jurisdictions recognize some possibility of obtaining a pardon, but the effects of pardons vary. In England, for example, pardons do not exonerate the accused but merely amount to nonenforcement of the sentence. England also recognizes sentence remissions to reward prisoners who cooperate with authorities or to release those who are terminally ill. In the United States a pardon allows a person to hold himself out as innocent. However, disciplinary boards and professional licensing bodies may deny professional licenses based on the underlying criminal conduct even after the offender received a pardon. See In re William A. Borders, Jr., 797 A.2d 716 (D.C. Ct. App. 2002).

6. *Pardons and politics.* Critics have charged that the number of pardons and the types of cases in which they are granted depend on the political situation. While governors at the end of their term seem more inclined to take political gambles in granting pardons, other charges of influence peddling amount to corruption in the entire process. As Helen Prejean recounts in her book *Dead*

Man Walking, the former chair of the Louisiana Board of Pardons described some of the political maneuvering that went on:

> [The governor's chief legal counsel] told me that I knew the governor did not like to be confronted with these cases and wanted us to handle it. [This implied that the board, out of loyalty to the governor, had to follow the governor's decision, independent of their own opinion. Otherwise they would be replaced.]
>   [B]efore our Board hearings, I'd get the word from the governor's office about which deals would go down when the Board met. "The governor wants this one or that one," that's what they'd say. [T]here would be cases sometimes, where . . . some of the Board members would balk at giving the pardon, and [I]'d have to pull them aside and tell them the governor had already committed to the pardon and their task was to put it through.

Helen Prejean, Dead Man Walking 171, 173 (1993). Here the pardon board functioned less to insulate the governor from a difficult decision-making process than to camouflage the decision already made.

Female governors seem even less inclined than their male counterparts to issue pardons and commute sentences. How do you account for this disparity? Are female politicians less compassionate? Or may they face different challenges when exercising executive clemency?

7. *Women and clemency.*   Women receive executive clemency substantially more often than men. Even though their numbers on death row are already very small, they benefit disproportionately from gubernatorial commutations of death sentences. See Michael Heise, Mercy by the Numbers: An Empirical Analysis of Clemency and Its Structure, 89 Va. L. Rev. 239, 275-278 (2003). No longer is it the case, however, that governors can pardon women or commute their sentences merely because they are women. Frequently, pardons are granted to women who killed spouses or boyfriends who allegedly abused them and to women whose criminal activity stemmed from duress caused by a male figure in their lives. Nevertheless, governors frequently reserve such pardons and commutations until the very end of their terms in office.

8. *Clemency abroad.*   In some western European countries amnesties for entire groups of incarcerated offenders occur regularly. Often they are announced around Christmas. Why do you think such types of amnesties are not used in the United States?

9. *Compensation after release from wrongful conviction.*   In some cases governors have issued pardons when it became clear that an incarcerated offender was innocent of the offense but no judicial recourse remained to overturn his conviction. In such situations most European countries would allow for compensation after release from imprisonment following a wrongful conviction. The same does not hold true in all U.S. states. Moreover, even states that provide for such compensation often strictly limit it. Under New York's Unjust Conviction and Imprisonment Act, for example, the claimant must show by clear and convincing evidence that his conviction was reversed, that he did not commit any of the acts charged and that he did not by his own conduct cause or bring about his conviction. N.Y. Ct. Cl. Act §8-b (1984). Of the 12 successful claimants in New York — out of 200 claims filed between 1984 and 2002 — the awards ranged from $40,000 to $1.9 million, the latter for almost 20 years in

prison. The court of claims, however, appears not to use a clear standard in assessing the value of these claims.

> ## Pardon Us: Systematic Presidential Pardons, Charles Shanor and Marc Miller
> ### 13 Fed. Sentencing Rep. 139 (2001)

Scholars, judges and commentators often emphasize the individualized and mercy-driven nature of the pardon power. . . . We consider whether it is constitutional and appropriate to use the pardon power in a systematic way, applied to a group of offenders selected through consistent criteria and processes, and for reasons that may reflect concerns of justice, equality, and wise policy, rather than mercy.

1.   THE CONSTITUTIONALITY OF SYSTEMATIC PARDONS

One constitutional objection might be made to systematic use of the pardon power by a president to further a policy goal. If Congress passes a statute that directs differential penalties for two crimes, and the judiciary implements this law, even upholding its constitutionality in the process, does it violate the separation of powers to allow the president to undo what Congress and the courts have approved?

Of course, the president has an obligation to "take Care that the Laws be faithfully executed." Art. II, §3. However, we do not believe this obligation overrides, much less obliterates, the distinct constitutional power stating that the President "shall have Power to grant Reprieves and Pardons for Offences against the United States, except in Cases of Impeachment." Art II, §2, cl. 1.

Were the "faithful execution" duty extended so far, it would effectively remove the pardon power from the Constitution altogether. This power, explicitly given to the Executive responsible for enforcing the law rather than sharing with Congress, should be viewed as a limited exception to the general duty of the president to faithfully execute the laws. The pardon power qualifies the duty only in connection with enforcement of criminal statutes. It has no bearing on enforcement of regulatory statutes or on private civil actions established by Congress.

Moreover, even as to criminal law statutes, the pardon power operates only as a check on prosecutions or sentences; it in no way alters congressional criminalization of particular behavior. Indeed, because the pardon power is explicit in the Constitution's text, it seems less vulnerable to criticism on separation of powers grounds than the authority of the executive branch, regularly exercised, to decline to prosecute particular cases or to plea bargain for lesser offenses than those recognized by Congress as applicable to particular behaviors. . . .

At least a third of all United States presidents, including many of our greatest presidents, and from the earliest administrations, have used systematic pardons. This long history convinces us that even class-wide pardons, with the potential to dramatically limit the impact of federal criminal laws, are constitutional. [T]he following chart gives a [selective but] striking demonstration of "a systematic, unbroken, executive practice, long pursued to the knowledge of

Congress and never before questioned, engaged in by Presidents who have sworn to uphold the Constitution, making as it were such exercise of power a part of the structure of our government. . . ."

1795	Washington	Pardoned participants in the Pennsylvania Whiskey Rebellion. . . .
1801	Jefferson	Pardoned all persons convicted under the Alien and Sedition Acts. . . .
1862-1864	Lincoln	Granted amnesty to Confederate sympathizers.
1865-1868	Johnson	Granted amnesty to Confederate soldiers, officials, and sympathizers. . . .
1945	Truman	Pardoned pre-war convicts who served in the U.S. armed forces during World War II subject to review by presidential board.
1961-1963	Kennedy	Pardoned offenders sentenced under mandatory minimum penalties of Narcotics Act of 1956.
1974-1975	Ford	Pardoned Vietnam-era violators of Service Act subject to review by presidential board.
1977	Carter	Pardoned Vietnam-era violators of the Selective Service Act.

While a quick review of the historical record makes it difficult to determine the extent to which these were systematic pardons, this review does suggest a history of using the pardon power, not simply as an act of individualized mercy, or as a political tool to reward supporters, but as a tool to reconcile national divisions. . . .

2.   UNPARDONABLE AND IRREGULAR PARDONS

. . . The recent focus on pardon abuse may arise in part from the fact that the federal pardon power has fallen into desuetude. There have been over 20,000 presidential pardons and commutations granted during the twentieth century, and many thousands of additional war-related amnesties falling within the pardon power. However, the vast majority of those pardons occurred before 1980, and the percentage of pardons granted to those sought has been declining steadily for the past 40 years. . . .

President	Pardons Sought	Pardons Granted	Percent Granted
Nixon	2,591	923	35.6%
Ford	1,527	404	26.5%
Carter	2,627	563	21.4%
Reagan	3,404	406	11.9%
Bush	1,466	77	5.3%
Clinton	6,622	456	6.9%

Looking back even further, around 1300 pardons and commutations were granted in Lyndon Johnson's five years in office (around 31% of requests), and around 600 pardons were granted during John Kennedy's three years (around 36% of requests). . . .

The combination of the recent controversial pardons [at the end of President Clinton's second term] and the highly sporadic use of non-controversial pardons has obscured two important dimensions of the pardon power.

First, when the numbers of pardons are insubstantial, the pardon power offers little possibility for more consistent and substantial executive assessments of sentences. The low and decreasing number of pardons is even more striking in light of [large] size of the federal prison population. . . .

The significance of the small numbers and percentages of pardons in recent years is magnified even further by the fact that, prior to the implementation of the [federal sentencing] guidelines in 1987, all sentences were subject to standardized executive review of the U.S. Parole Commission. It seems that the elimination of the Parole Commission should have led to an increase in the use of presidential pardons, since one of the two major forms of traditional executive post-conviction review and adjustment is no longer available.

Second, the irregular and seemingly random Clinton pardons obscure the possibility of presidents using the pardon power as a principled, systematic policy tool.

3.   SOME MODERN SYSTEMATIC PARDONS

Presidents have sometimes issued multiple pardons on the same or different dates, and given the same reason for those pardons. Such pardons are not necessarily systematic, unless they are the product of articulated principles applied consistently to an identified group, so that all members of the group who satisfy the principles are pardoned or subject to a standard and reasonably structured process of review.

Wars.   The most common form of systematic pardons in the twentieth century appear to be amnesty or clemency for those who avoided military service or even opposed the U.S. during a conflict. The most recent illustration of this type of systematic pardon was President Carter's decision to pardon Vietnam-era violators of the Selective Service Act. . . .

Drugs.   An example of what may have been systematic, non-wartime, drug offense pardons appears, in brief form, in the Annual Reports of the Attorney General issued during the Kennedy administration. Those reports suggest that there was a large number of pardons or commutations reducing sentences under the Narcotic Control Act of 1956 [which included mandatory minimum sentences of five to thirty years for various drug offenses]. . . .

The 1964 report confirmed that "[as] in the years preceding, the commutations of sentence granted included some long-term narcotics offenders who, by statute, were not eligible for parole but whose sentences were considerably longer than average." The 1964 report also explicitly refers to efforts to make review of pardons and commutations more systematic:

"During the year, the Director of the Bureau of Prisons was called upon to encourage the wardens of the federal prisons to review cases in their institutions and present to the Attorney General selected cases which they considered to be worthy of clemency and whose sentences could be considered disparate. For the first time there is a policy of attempting to systematically review cases which may be deserving of commutation. As a result, a very sizeable increase in commutations has resulted."

While it is not clear whether the Narcotics Act commutations were fully systematic in the sense we suggest, they do combine a statement of principle (disparity) and a suggestion of regularized review to identify similarly situated offenders. . . .

4.   Wise Use of Systematic Pardons

Even if systematic pardons are constitutional, are they a desirable tool for the president compared to other possible strategies available to the executive branch, such as advocating changes in the laws, or changing executive charging, plea, or sentencing policies?

A president might believe that a distinction made by a federal criminal law is unconstitutional. This was the basis for President Jefferson's pardons of those convicted of violating the Alien and Sedition Acts, which Jefferson believed to be unconstitutional. . . . Under the oath of office, the president not only has the power but the duty to apply the commands of the constitution in the exercise of his office.

A president also might use systematic pardons when the constitutionality of the conviction and sentence is abundantly clear. . . . Presidents Truman, Ford, and Carter all believed that a process of amnesty would help to heal the many wounds of war at home. President Kennedy did not suggest that convictions under the mandatory minimum penalties of the Narcotics Act of 1956 were unconstitutional, but he did point to the excessive and unequal sentences imposed under those laws.

As a political matter, a president might hesitate to issue a series of class-wide pardons in the face of Congressional or public criticism. When Lincoln used the pardon power in 1865, he referenced not only his constitutional authority, but also Congressional support for pardoning a large class of southerners "guilty of treason." When Congress had passed laws calling for forfeiture of property by those in rebellion against the Union, it granted the President the authority to grant pardons or amnesty "on such conditions as he may deem expedient for the public welfare." The legislation was perhaps helpful to Lincoln, but it was also unnecessary, for Lincoln could have granted the pardons without it.

Systematic pardons would likely initiate reconsideration of punishment and incarceration policies by Congress. Given the political difficulty of generating rich discussions of criminal justice policy, confident and wise chief executives may be in the best position to generate such debate. Systematic pardons thus offer the chance for a visible and public dialogue about important legal issues. On the other hand, pardons cannot and should not supplant the legislative role on a continuing basis.

NOTES

1. *Systematic clemencies.*   Perhaps one of the most noteworthy and dramatic examples of systematic use of the clemency and pardon power occurred in

January 2003 when outgoing Illinois governor George Ryan granted clemency to all of the 156 death row inmates in Illinois (as well as 11 inmates who were awaiting sentencing or resentencing) in response to the flawed process in Illinois that led to these sentences. (A portion of Governor Ryan's speech announcing his decision is reprinted in Chapter 3.) Note that these grants of clemency did not result in the release of the inmates, since many still faced sentences of life in prison. Governor Ryan also completely pardoned four wrongly convicted death row inmates.

Do you think it is appropriate for governors or presidents to use their pardon and clemency powers systematically? Are such actions an effective way to influence criminal justice or sentencing policy? Should a change in administration and in criminal justice priorities provide a sound basis for considering the systematic use of the pardon power?

2. *Unsystematic pardons.*   Perhaps equally noteworthy and even more controversial than systematic pardons or clemencies are instances in which the pardon power is used in ways that seem particularly unsystematic. Only two hours before surrendering the White House, President Bill Clinton pardoned some persons involved in various scandals that touched the Clinton presidency, along with former Cabinet members, onetime fugitive heiress Patricia Hearst Shaw, and his own brother, Roger Clinton. The list and nature of these pardons not only superceded the magnitude and scope of last-minute pardons granted by previous presidents but also generated widespread public outrage. Both the Senate Judiciary Committee and the House Government Reform Committee scheduled hearings to investigate particularly whether Clinton's pardon of financier Marc Rich was motivated by campaign contributions made by Rich's former wife. For an insightful discussion of these pardons and the lessons to be learned from them, see Margaret Colgate Love, Fear of Forgiving: Rule and Discretion in the Practice of Pardoning, 13 Fed. Sentencing Rep. 125 (2001). See also Harold Krent, Conditioning the President's Conditional Pardon Power, 89 Cal. L. Rev. 1665 (2001).

3. *The decline in clemency.*   The drop in presidential pardons over the past few decades is startling, particularly in view of the dramatic rise in imprisonment rates during the same period (see Chapter 7). How do you explain the decrease in individual pardons? Is the current pardon process fatally flawed, as some have argued? In light of more systematic guideline sentencing, should we increasingly object to unsystematic executive clemency? Have presidents become less courageous?

Table of Cases

Table of Statutes, Rules, and Guidelines

Index